BIT-SLICE MICROPROCESSOR DESIGN

BIT-SLICE MICROPROCESSOR DESIGN

John Mick
Engineering Manager
Systems and Applications
Digital Bipolar Products
Advanced Micro Devices

James Brick
Manager of Systems and Applications
AM2900 Family
Advanced Micro Devices

McGraw-Hill Book Company

New York St. Louis San Francisco Auckland Bogotá
Hamburg Johannesburg London Madrid Mexico
Montreal New Delhi Panama Paris São Paulo
Singapore Sydney Tokyo Toronto

Advanced Micro-Devices reserves the right to make changes in its products without notice in order to improve design or performance characteristics. The authors and the company assume no responsibility for the use of any circuits described herein.

Library of Congress Cataloging in Publication Data

Mick, John.
Bit-slice microprocessor design.

Includes index.
1. Bit slice microprocessors—Design and construction. I. Brick, James, joint author. II. Title.
TK7895.M5M44 621.3819'535 80-10610
ISBN 0-07-041781-4

4567890 KPKP 8987654321

Note to the Reader: Advanced Micro Devices cannot assume responsibility for use of any circuitry described other than circuitry entirely embodied in an Advanced Micro Devices product.

CONTENTS

PREFACE

New integrated circuits are usually accompanied by a wealth of theory and data sheets. Shortly thereafter follow the application notes. The introduction of microprogrammable LSI parts, such as the Am2901 and subsequent ICs in the family, adhered to this pattern. We thought this was adequate in light of the previously successful introduction of fixed-instruction-set MOS microprocessors, which were more complex.

However, bit-slice microprocessor design proved more formidable than first realized. One reason was the intimate relationship between parts. These designs required the designer to pick and choose parts: How many slices are needed to do the job? Which microprogram sequencer and/or controller to select? Is a carry lookahead generator needed? And on, and on and. . . . All these devices had to play together; no single device was complete by itself.

For this added up-front design effort, the user got blazing speed and the utmost flexibility. The latter proved the second hinderance to easy designing. Users now had to design the instruction set as well as the hardware and applications programs. They no longer had the luxury of a fixed-instruction set. On the other hand, they could eliminate unnecessary instructions, easily modify or add instructions at a later date or emulate the existing instruction set of a slower CPU.

Complicating matters was the fact that the 2900 family did not spring whole into the world. Parts were introduced and redesigned over a period of years as engineering and processing resources could be brought to bear. This evolutionary process still goes on.

To alleviate matters, Advanced Micro Devices announced a nine-part course in microprogrammable microprocessing, each part to stand alone but to build logically upon the preceding part. And, because engineering talent is our most important resource, this course was to unfold over a 22-month period.

Since completion of the course, there has been no diminishing in demand for information on the material covered. In fact, the market for bipolar microprogrammable LSI parts doubled in each of the previous two years and showed no signs of slowing. So, as our copies of individual course materials dwindled, we thought it only natural to bring them all together under one cover. This book is the result.

We think the extraordinary time and effort was well worth it.

Acknowledgments

The authors wish to thank members of Advanced Micro Devices' bipolar applications department for their contributions to various chapters in this book. In particular we would like to thank Steve Cheng, Vernon Coleman, Mike Economidis, Jerry Gray, Jack Hong, Mike Miller, Warren Miller, Bob Schopmeyer, and Moshe Shavit.

We would also like to thank Mike Simmons and Lee McDonald of Monterey, CA, for allowing us to use their HEX-29 microprogrammable microcomputer in Chapter VIII.

BIT-SLICE MICROPROCESSOR DESIGN

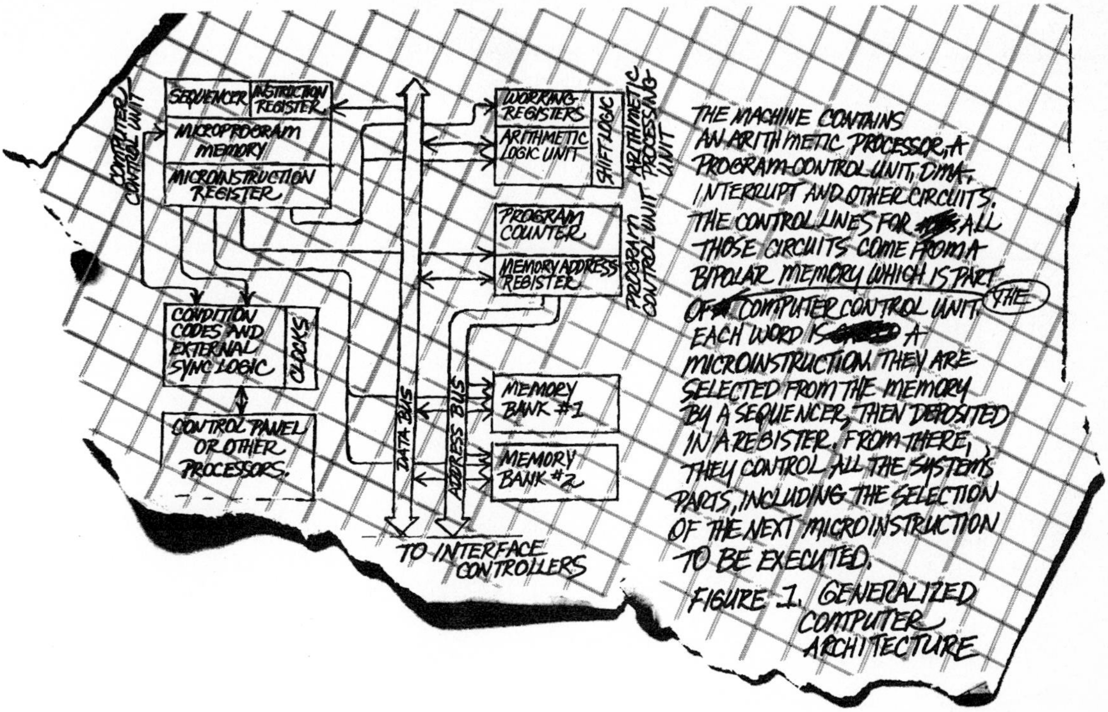

SEQUENCER
INSTRUCTION REGISTER
MICROPROGRAM MEMORY
MICROINSTRUCTION REGISTER
COMPUTER CONTROL UNIT
WORKING REGISTERS
ARITHMETIC LOGIC UNIT
SHIFT LOGIC
ARITHMETIC PROCESSING UNIT
PROGRAM COUNTER
MEMORY ADDRESS REGISTER
PROGRAM CONTROL UNIT
CONDITION CODES AND EXTERNAL SYNC LOGIC
CLOCKS
CONTROL PANEL OR OTHER PROCESSORS.
DATA BUS
ADDRESS BUS
MEMORY BANK #1
MEMORY BANK #2
TO INTERFACE CONTROLLERS
THE MACHINE CONTAINS AN ARITHMETIC PROCESSOR, A PROGRAM-CONTROL UNIT, DMA, INTERRUPT AND OTHER CIRCUITS. THE CONTROL LINES FOR ALL THOSE CIRCUITS COME FROM A BIPOLAR MEMORY WHICH IS PART OF THE COMPUTER CONTROL UNIT. EACH WORD IS A MICROINSTRUCTION. THEY ARE SELECTED FROM THE MEMORY BY A SEQUENCER, THEN DEPOSITED IN A REGISTER. FROM THERE, THEY CONTROL ALL THE SYSTEM'S PARTS, INCLUDING THE SELECTION OF THE NEXT MICROINSTRUCTION TO BE EXECUTED.
FIGURE 1. GENERALIZED COMPUTER ARCHITECTURE

Chapter I
Computer Architecture

PREFACE

In this introductory Chapter we intend to:

1). develop a common terminology for future chapters.
2). introduce several stored-program-computer design topics.
3). define some of the computer architect's problems (which will be solved in the subsequent chapters).

In order to achieve these goals, we will start with computer basics. It should be stressed that approaches and solutions can be chosen which are different from the ones described in this and the subsequent chapters. However, the general ideas described will be appropriate to gain familiarity with the microprogrammable bit-slice devices in order to use them in any design configuration.

BACK TO THE BASICS. . .

A STORED-PROGRAM-COMPUTER is defined as a machine capable of manipulating data according to predefined rules (instructions), where the program (collection of instructions) and data are stored in its memory (Fig. 1). Without some means of communication with the external world, the program and the data cannot be loaded into the memory nor can the results be read out. Therefore, an input/output device is required as shown in Fig. 2.

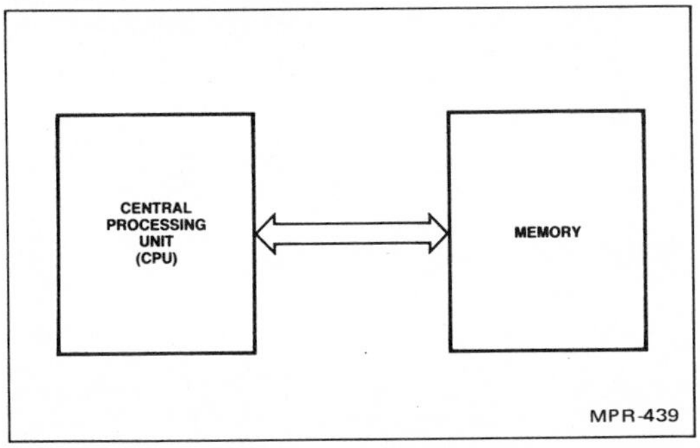

Figure 1. Basic Definition of a Stored-Program-Computer.

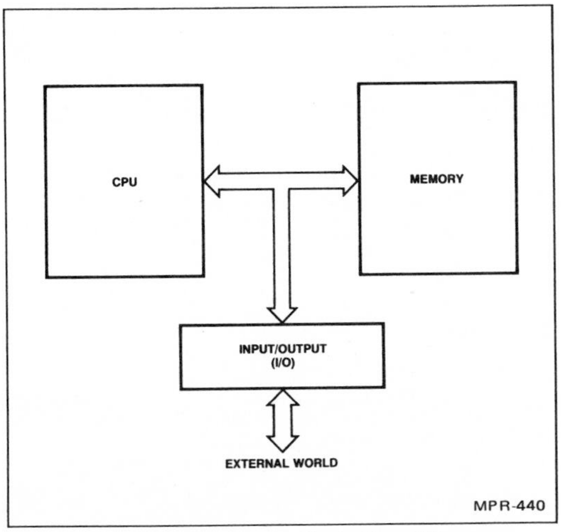

Figure 2. I/O Added to the Basic Stored-Program Computer.

The memory is usually organized in words, each containing N bits of information. A unique address is allocated for each word which defines its position relative to other words. The Central Processor Unit (CPU) usually reads or writes one word at a time by addressing the memory and then when the memory is ready, reading the contents of the word or writing new contents into that word. To perform this operation, two registers are usually used: The Memory Address Register (MAR), which contains the address and the Memory Data Register (MDR) which contains the data (Fig. 3).

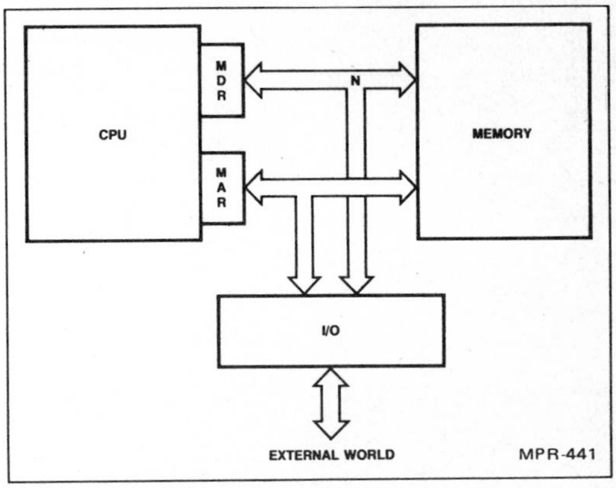

Figure 3. MAR and MDR Depicted for a Stored-Program Computer.

Since accessing a memory (reading from it or writing into it) is usually a relatively slow procedure, it is advantageous to have a few memory locations inside the CPU which can be read from or written into very fast. These locations are usually called Accumulators or Working Registers. Having these fast access registers inside the CPU (Fig. 4) enables many operations to be carried out without referring to the memory (through the MAR and the MDR) and therefore these operations are executed faster.

The unit which actually performs the data manipulation is called the Arithmetic & Logic Unit (ALU). It has two inputs for operands and one output for the result. It usually operates on all the bits of a word in parallel. The ALU can perform all or part of the following operations:

Arithmetic	**Logical**
Add	OR
Complement	AND
Subtract	XOR
Increment	NAND
Decrement	NOR
	XNOR
	Complement

In some architectures, one of the operands must always be in a special register (accumulator) and the result of the ALU operation is always transferred to this register. In a more general CPU, any two of the internal registers can contain the operands and the result of the ALU operation can be transferred to any one of them.

Another very useful feature of a CPU is the ability to shift the contents of a register or the output of the ALU one or more bits in either direction as shown in Fig. 5.

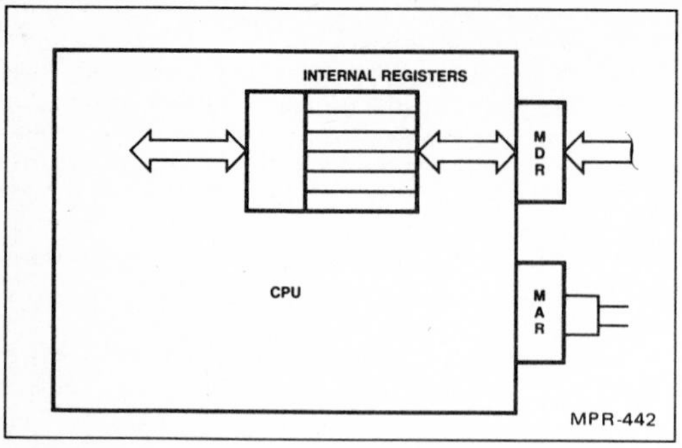

Figure 4. CPU with Internal High Speed Registers.

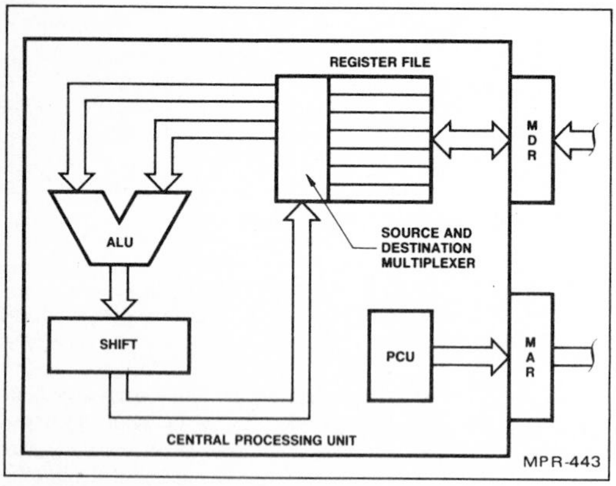

Figure 5. ALU and Shifter Added to the CPU Design.

We now have the elements to do any data manipulation required but we still need a unit which can properly set the MAR in order to find the next instruction of the program in the memory and to find its associated data. This unit is called the Program Control Unit (PCU) and its role is to load the MAR with the correct address in order to find the next instruction or data item or to point to a memory location where a data word should be written.

Often, the program steps (instructions, data) are written in the memory in consecutive locations, starting at address zero or at any other predefined address. The PCU can simply be incremented after each memory access thereby pointing to the address of the next instruction or data item. This counter-type PCU has very little flexibility. Sometimes we wish to change the "normal" flow of the instructions, particularly if we want to enable our computer to "make decisions" according to conditions prevailing at the current execution point. For example, we may want to execute one of two different sequences of instructions depending upon the result of the last operation performed. This is accomplished by loading the MAR with a new value (the address of the next instruction to be executed) rather than incrementing it. This operation is called a BRANCH or JUMP and can be unconditional (which allows execution of a non-contiguous string of instructions) or conditional (depending, for example, on whether the last operation's result was zero or not, was negative or positive, true or false, etc.).

Even more flexibility can be achieved by using a stack (a group of temporary internal or external memory locations) to store vital data. A stack pointer is used to address the memory location currently at the top of the stack. Indirect and relative addressing and other sophisticated addressing modes (all of which can be handled by the PCU) will be discussed later. Meanwhile, Fig. 5 shows the PCU as a part of the CPU.

Executing an instruction in our computer now requires the following steps:

a). The PCU loads the address of the next instruction to the MAR and signals to the memory that a Read is requested. Incidentally, the PCU may be as simple as a Program Counter equal to the address width. The memory loads the MDR with the contents of the location addressed.
b). The CPU decodes the instruction: i.e., (assuming operands are in internal registers) selects the proper registers to feed the ALU, selects the proper function to be performed by the ALU, sets up the shifter to displace the result, if required, and selects the register in which the result should be stored.
c). The ALU performs the function desired.
d). The result is loaded into the destination register.
e). The result is also examined to determine whether a BRANCH is to be performed.
f). The PCU calculates the address of the next instruction, (usually called a "FETCH").

This procedure becomes more complicated if the operands are not stored in the internal registers or if the result is not to be stored in one of them. Let's take an example instruction using relative addressing:

> "Take the first operand from the location specified by the sum of the word after this instruction (immediate) and the contents of register R1; take the second operand from the location specified by the sum of the second word after this instruction and the contents of R2; add the two operands and place the result in the location specified by the sum of the third word after this instruction and the contents of register R3. Then execute the instruction located at the address, which is the sum of the fourth word after this instruction and the contents of register R4 if there is a carry resulting from the addition. Otherwise continue sequentially".

The steps required to execute this instruction are as follows:

a). The PCU loads the address of the next instruction to the MAR, signalling to the memory that a Read is requested. The memory loads the MDR with the contents of the location addressed.
b). The CPU decodes the instruction, i.e., initiates the following steps.
c). The PCU is incremented and the next word is read from the memory.
d). Register R1 and the MDR are selected as source registers, MAR is the destination register.
e). The ALU performs "ADD" and the result is placed in the MAR.
f). The first operand is fetched from the memory and placed, for example, in R5.
g). The PCU is incremented and the next word is read from the memory.
h). Register R2 and the MDR are selected again as source registers and MAR as the destination.

i). The ALU performs "ADD" and the result is placed in MAR.
j). The second operand is fetched from the memory and is placed, for example, in R6.
k). The PCU is incremented, the next word is read from the memory.
l). Register R3 and the MDR are selected as source registers, the MAR as destination.
m). The ALU performs "ADD" and the result is placed in the MAR, which now points to the location where the sum of the operands should be stored.
n). Registers R5 and R6 are selected as sources (they contain the operands), MDR is now the destination.
o.) The ALU performs "ADD" and the result is placed in MDR.
p). A memory write cycle takes place and the contents of the MDR is stored at the desired address.
q). The carry is examined to determine the next step to be performed. Assume there is no carry.
r). The PCU is incremented twice (in order to skip the fifth word of the present instruction). It now points to the address of the next instruction.

As can be seen, 18 steps were used to perform a single addition using this complex relative addressing scheme. Obviously, our CPU needs some kind of "coordinator" which can:

1). Decode an instruction fetched from the memory.
2). Initiate the proper cycle of steps to be performed.
3). Set up the various controls for each step.
4). Execute the steps in an orderly sequence.
5). Make decisions according to the state of various signals (conditions).

We will call this coordinator the Computer Control Unit (CCU) and it is depicted in Fig. 6. Our CPU is now complete (more or less) and we will go into more detail later.

THE MEMORY

Let's now discuss the memory. The information stored in the memory is organized in words, where each word consists of N bits. N may be as small as 8 for very simple processors or as large as 64 in more powerful machines. The most common memory width for minicomputers is 16 bits. The number N is called the width of the memory and the number of bits in the MDR is obviously also N; equal to the width of the memory.

The depth of a memory is the number of words it contains. With a MAR having k bits, 2^k consecutive memory locations can be addressed. The addresses start from zero and range through 2^k-1.

The read access time of a memory directly accessible by the CPU is the time needed from stable address at the memory until the data is properly stored in the MDR. This access time depends on the type of memory used and can be as low as a few tens of nanoseconds and as large as several microseconds. Using high speed memory improves the performance of the computer as less time is wasted waiting for the memory to respond. In general, faster memories are costly, take more PC board area and use more power which results in more heat. A 32 bit wide, 2K (2048) word memory with 50 nanosecond access time may need 10 amps from the +5V power supply and may require a board area of 10" x 6". Yet this is a very small memory space.

It is usually not justified to have very large high-speed memories. Not all the programs and associated data need to reside in this memory at once. We may have the current program (or only a part of it) in the memory while other programs or data files can reside elsewhere and be brought into memory during the appropriate part of the program when needed.

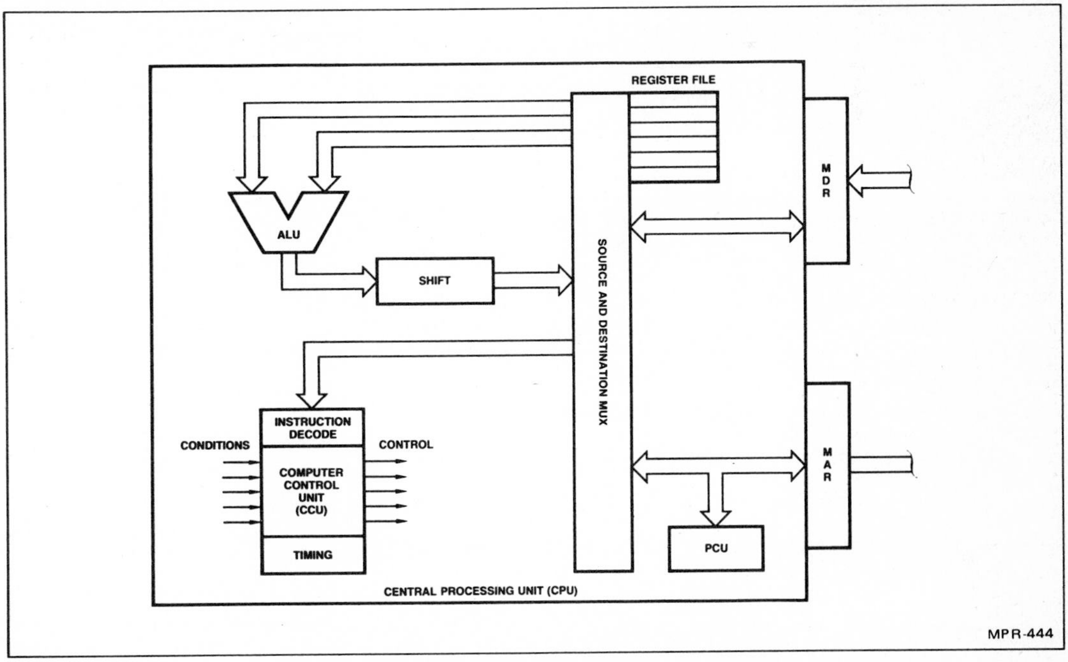

Figure 6. A Computer Control Unit (CCU) Included in a CPU.

This "elsewhere" may be a magnetic tape, cassette, disk, diskette, etc. and we will call it Bulk Memory. The distinctive characteristics of Bulk Memory are:

1). very large capacity
2). non-volatile (retains the information when not in use)
3). not randomly accessible
4). long access time
5). inexpensive (per bit)

Usually, Bulk Memory devices are serially accessible, i.e., the access time for the first word is large, but then consecutive words can be accessed relatively fast.

In a later chapter the most efficient process of communication between the main and the bulk memory, called the Direct Memory Access (DMA), will be discussed in detail.

THE EXTERNAL WORLD

In any useful machine, some means of communicating with the external word is needed. It may be a keyboard, a CRT, a card reader, a paper tape punch or, in a process controller, reading sensors or positioning actuators. The common denominator of almost all of the input/output devices is that they are much slower than the CPU and therefore a timing problem arises; the CPU must know when the I/O device is ready for data transfer. Usually, a signal is sent by the device to the CPU in order to draw its attention. The CPU now can do one of two things:

1). Test this signal periodically and when it is present, jump to a program which handles the data transfer. This type of operation is called "Polling". This technique has two major drawbacks: First, appreciable computer time is spent performing these periodic tests where most of them will fail (no "Ready" signal present). Second, the recognition by the computer CPU of the appearance of a signal is delayed until the CPU arrives at this device in its polling sequence.

   Imagine what will happen if there are a large number of I/O devices. Long latency times (delays) will occur if many I/O devices are busy simultaneously.

2). Include some hardware in the CPU which can sense the presence of a "Ready" signal and interrupt the normal flow of the instructions and force the computer to "Jump" to the I/O service program whenever there is a request. It can even send the CPU to different programs according to the I/O device whose "Ready" flag was detected and even establish priority among the different devices if more than one device would like to have the CPU's attention at the same time. Moreover, under program control, this circuitry can ignore some or all of the signals if the computer CPU must not be interrupted at that time. Obviously by paying the price of very little hardware, we gain enormously in computer performance. We will call this hardware the "Interrupt Controller" and will discuss it thoroughly later.

Our computer is now depicted in Fig. 7. We have included the ALU, the internal register file and the shift circuit in one block, which we call the "Arithmetic Processor Unit."

In the following pages and in the subsequent chapters, we will deal in more detail with each area of the machine.

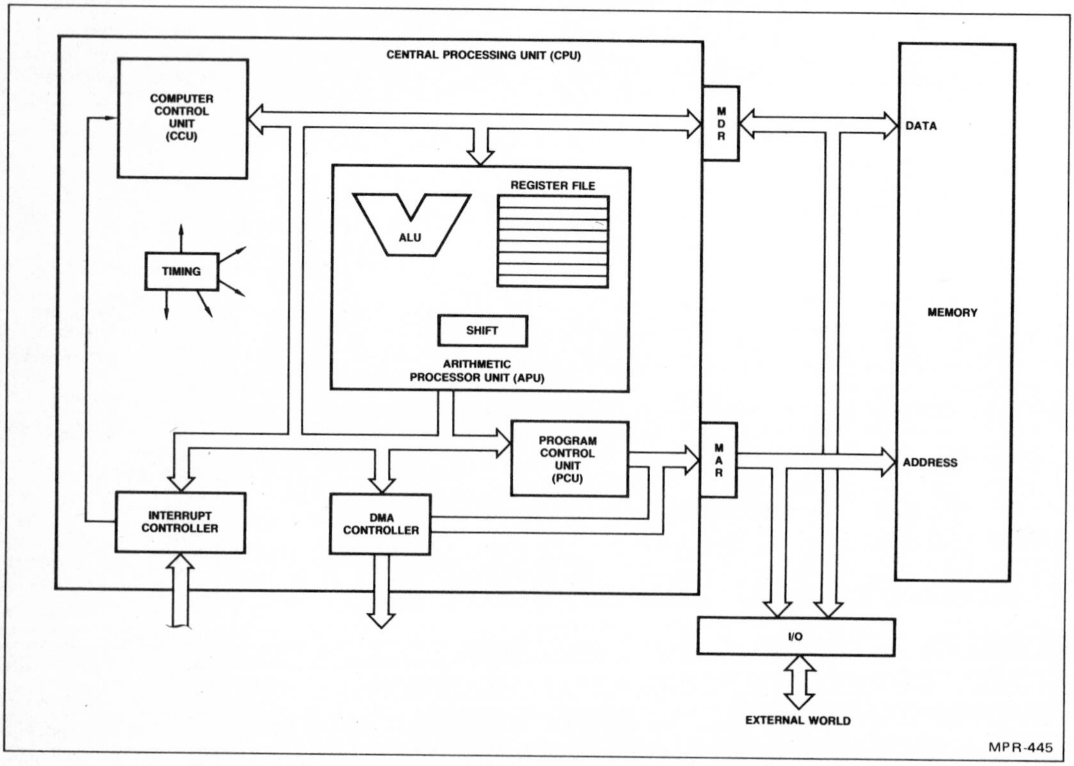

Figure 7. The Stored-Program-Computer with DMA and Interrupt Control Added.

A WORD ABOUT THE INSTRUCTION SET

The internal architecture of the CPU depends to some extent on the instruction set the computer is to execute. If the instruction set is large, some of the instructions usually are more complicated and the computer is more powerful, faster and more efficient. On the other hand, the internal circuitry is also more complicated. Some examples of these tradeoffs are as follows.

ALU Processing Capability:

Although with three basic functions (add, complement, and OR/AND) all the arithmetic and logic operations can be performed, most processors are built to perform subtract, NAND, XOR, etc. This is perhaps the most outstanding example of how performance and speed can be gained with little penalty on the complexity of the machine. With the added features an XOR operation can be performed in one instruction instead of 5.

Data Movement:

Let us assume 4 different computers whose data movement capabilities are described below:

Machine A). A word can be read from the memory and loaded into Register A only. The contents of Register A can be written into the memory, or can be moved into any other register. The contents of any register can be copied into Register A.

Machine B). The contents of any register can be copied into any other register or it can be written into the memory. A word read from the memory can be loaded into any register.

Machine C). As B above but with the added capability to read from one location in memory, to write that word into another location in memory.

Machine D). As C above and also the memory-to-memory operation can be performed on consecutive addresses repetitively. The number of word transfers (or upper and lower address limits) are specified by the instruction.

Machine A has very limited data movement capability. In order to perform an operation on two operands residing in the memory, we have to:

1). Bring the first operand from the memory into Register A.
2). Copy it into another register.
3). Bring the second operand into Register A.
4). Perform the operation required (result in A).
5). Store the contents of Register A into the memory.

If consecutive operations are required with several partial results, the drawbacks of machine A become more annoying, especially if the number of internal registers is small.

Moving a data block from one location in the memory to another location can be performed by one instruction in computer D, but requires the transfer of each word first to an internal register then to the new memory location in machines A, B (two instructions for each word transferred).

Obviously the decoding, multiplexing and sequencing of the computers grow in complexity as we proceed from machine A to machine D. We trade the complexity of hardware versus the software (programming), speed and performance.

Addressing:

The operands for an operation can be found in several ways:

- The operand is an explicit part of the instruction (Immediate)
- The address of the operand is an explicit part of the instruction. (Direct)
- The address of the operand is in an internal register; the register itself is specified by the instruction. (RR)
- The address of the operand is the sum of the contents of an internal register (specified by the instruction) and a number (called the displacement) which is an explicit part of the instruction. (RX)
- The contents of an internal register are added to a number found in an address specified by the instruction. The sum is the address of the operand. (Indirect)
- The contents of an internal register are added to a number which is an explicit part of the instruction. The sum points to the location where the address of the operand is written. (Indirect)
- The contents of an internal register are added to a number which can be found at the location explicitly specified by the instruction. The sum thus formed points to a location where the address of the operand is written.
- Etc.

Many other schemes can be formed by combining the above operations or by chaining them. In every case an "Effective Address" must be found by calculations and/or memory references. Again, we can gain performance by using more sophisticated addressing schemes but we will pay for it by adding complexity to our machine, especially in its control portion.

TIMING, SEQUENCING, CONTROLLING

In the previous paragraphs we have shown that we can gain performance in our computer by having a more complicated instruction set but more complex hardware is required, usually in the CCU. We have also shown an example for an "Add" operation which required 18 precisely controlled steps. Even if we assume that some of them can be performed simultaneously, we will need a multiphase clock to control these steps – something like that shown in Fig. 8. We can now load an instruction register at the beginning of an instruction with the first word of the instruction (the OP CODE) as is shown in Fig. 9. Using the outputs of the Instruction Register (IR_0 to IR_{n-1}), the different phases of the clock and the various condition inputs to the CCU, we can now try to write the logical equations which should satisfy all of the steps of all the instructions of our instruction set. Then use Karnough maps or other techniques to reduce these equations and finally realize them using AND, OR, INVERT gates and Flip Flops. Simple, isn't it? Imagine the complexity of a sophisticated computer and the debugging process it needs!

The question posed immediately is: Isn't there a more organized and more easily understandable way to do that? Or, perhaps, can we have some processor do the job for us? Can't we have some kind of "micro-machine" which can take care of all the timing, sequencing and controlling jobs of our computer – a computer inside the computer? With the advent of the Am2900 family – new Bipolar LSI devices – the answer is: Yes, we can!

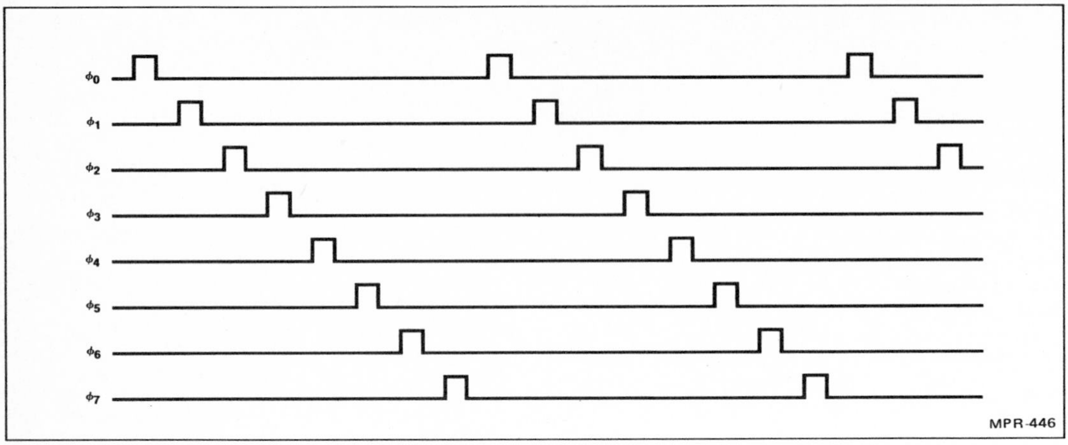

Figure 8. An 8-Phase Clock.

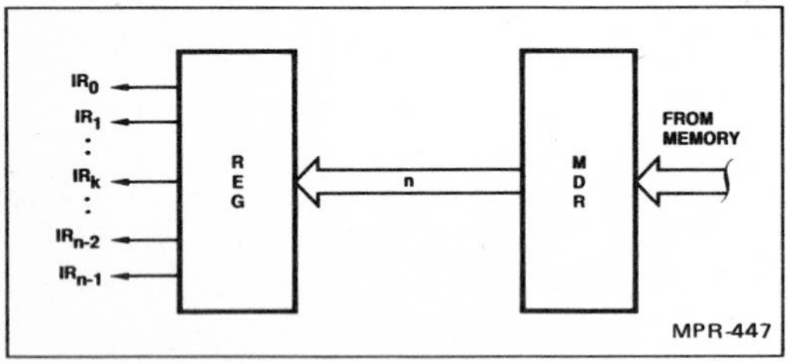

Figure 9. The Instruction Register Bits.

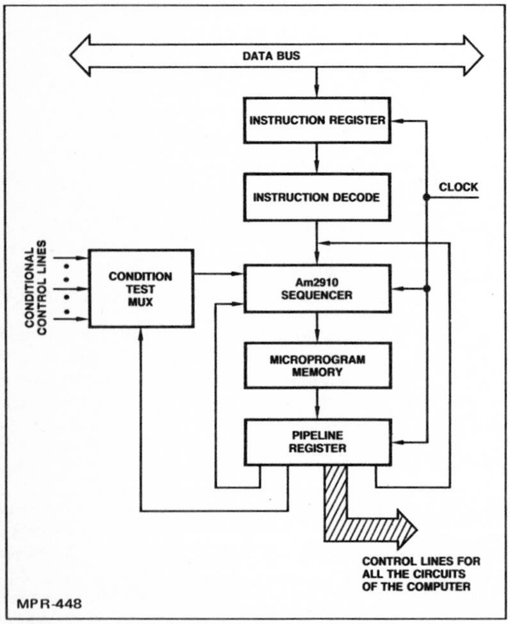

Figure 10. The Micromachine.

THE MICRO-MACHINE

What we need is essentially a machine which can execute a number of well defined sequences. But, remember that this is exactly the purpose of a stored program computer. The only difference between our micro-machine and a general purpose computer is that in the general purpose computer the program to be executed is changed from task to task, while in our micro-machine it is fixed. This allows the use of PROM for its memory instead of the RAM needed in the general purpose (GP) computer. Our Computer Control Unit (CCU) using this micro-machine may now look like Figure 10.

Basically, a microprogrammed machine is one in which a coherent sequence of microinstructions is used to execute various commands required by the machine. If the machine is a computer, each sequence of microinstructions can be made to execute a machine instruction. All of the little elemental tasks performed by the machine in executing the machine instruction are called microinstructions. The storage area for these microinstructions is usually called the microprogram memory.

A microinstruction usually has two primary parts. These are: (1) the definition and control of all elemental micro-operations to be carried out and (2) the definition and control of the address of the next microinstruction to be executed.

The definition of the various micro-operations to be carried out usually includes such things as ALU source operand selection, ALU function, ALU destination, carry control, shift control, interrupt control, data-in and data-out control, and so forth. The definition of the next microinstruction function usually includes identifying the source selection of the next microinstruction address and, in some cases, supplying the actual value of that microinstruction address.

Microprogrammed machines are usually distinguished from non-microprogrammed machines in the following manner. Older, non-microprogrammed machines implemented the control function by using combinations of gates and flip-flops connected in a somewhat random fashion in order to generate the required timing and control signals for the machine. Microprogrammed machines, on the other hand, are normally considered highly ordered and more organized with regard to the control function field. In its simplest definition, a microprogram control unit consists of the microprogram memory and the structure required to determine the address of the next microinstruction.

The OP-CODE (type of instruction to be executed by the computer) is loaded into the Instruction Register and the Instruction Decoder decodes it. Actually, it generates the microaddress where the first step of the execution sequence for that instruction resides in the microprogram memory. The Am2910 sequencer then generates the microaddress of the next microinstruction. The microprogram data supplies the control signals we need to control all the parts of the computer (and there are a lot of them), including the sequencer itself. When all the steps of a machine instruction are executed, the microprogram will cause the reading (fetch) of the next machine instruction from the computer main memory. Typically, the Computer Control Unit is used to fetch instructions and decode them using a PROM for mapping the op code to the initial address of the sequence of microinstructions used to execute this particular instruction. It will also fetch all of the operands needed by the machine instruction and deliver them to the ALU for processing. An example of the flow of a typical Computer Control Unit is shown in Figure 11.

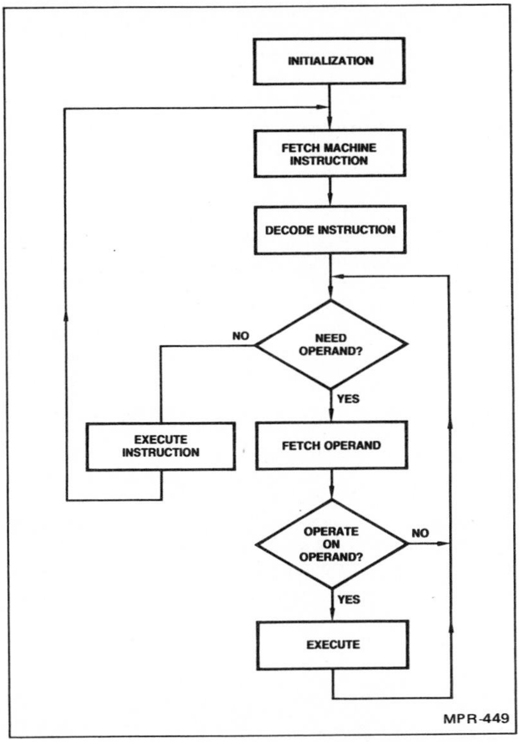

Figure 11. Computer Control Function Flow Diagram.

Assume the OP-CODE of the machine instruction that we fetch is 8 bits wide. This allows us to execute a minimum of 256 different instructions. Assume also that an average of 6 steps are needed to execute these instructions. Even if separate microprogram memory locations are used, a depth of this microprogram memory is only 1-1/2K (K = 1024). But in that case, the sequencer can almost be replaced by a simple counter. Usually we would like to share some micro-routines among different instructions. With very little effort, we can shrink the depth of the microprogram memory of Figure 10 to less than 1/2K. Of course the sequencer will be a little more sophisticated; it will perform conditional Branch and micro-subroutine CALL's; but we still don't need the complicated addressing schemes for microprogram control as were described earlier as a part of the machine instruction set.

On the other hand, the width of our microprogram memory may be large – maybe 60 to 100 bits. This will depend on the number of control lines needed in our computer. This is of no great disadvantage since the price of PROM devices is dropping constantly. In a future chapter we will discuss techniques to reduce the depth and width of the microprogram memory to save cost.

It is important to understand the distinction between machine level instructions and microprogram instructions. Figure 12 shows a typical machine instruction for a 16 bit minicomputer that has an 8-bit opcode to identify one of 256 instructions; a 4-bit source register specification to identify one of 16 source registers and a 4-bit destination register specification to identify one of 16 destination registers. The microprogram instruction of Figure 12 may contain from 32 to 128 bits in a typical design; or even more bits in a very fast, highly parallel microcoded machine. This microinstruction word usually will contain fields for the ALU source operand, ALU function, ALU destination, status load enable, shift multiplexer control, bus

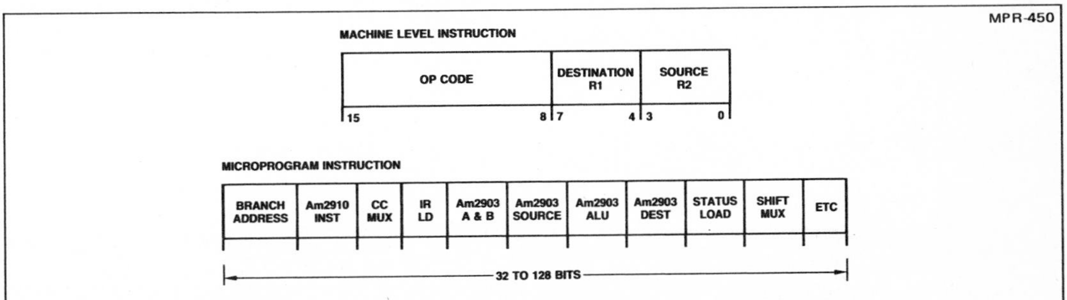

The machine instruction is 16-bits and consists of an op code, source register and destination register specification. The microprogram instruction defines all the elemental signals to control the various pieces of the machine.

Figure 12.

cycle control, etc. These fields are used to control the various devices within the machine so that its execution is as desired on each clock cycle. This is more straightforward than using combinatorial logic and yields a more organized design.

Let us now compare the depth-over-width (d/w) ratio of the computer's main memory to that of our microprogram memory.

In the Am9080A type microprocessor, the data field is 8 bits and the address field is 16 bits, allowing direct addressing of 64K locations. The ratio d/w is 8K. In some minicomputers, the data width is 16-32 bits and the addressing capability is 64-128K. The d/w ratio is about the same. In larger computers with 32-64 bit data width, we find 256-512K deep memories or even deeper ones. The d/w ratio again is 8K at least.

On the other hand, the d/w ratio in microprogram memories is seldom greater than a few tens. Even if we assume that it is 2K deep and only 64 bits wide, we arrive at a d/w ratio of only 32; usually it will be around 10. It is much easier to control a machine with a d/w ratio of 10 to 20 than to control one with d/w = 8K.

ONE MORE WORD

We have suggested a replacement of the "random logic" realization of the CCU by a micro-machine. We call this a "Microprogrammed Architecture". Perhaps the biggest advantage of this type of architecture is the ease of structuring the control sequence. We allocate a bit or a group of bits in the microprogram memory to control a certain function (e.g.: ALU source register selection, ALU function, ALU destination selection, condition selection, next address calculation selection, MDR destination selection, MAR source selection, etc., etc.) and for each microstep we write the appropriate state for these bits (LOW-HIGH) into this memory field. Later we will see that automated and sophisticated tools are available to perform this microprogram writing. One such tool is AMDASM™ as available on System 29. But, this is not the only advantage of the microprogrammed architecture.

As nobody is perfect, some "bugs" may inadvertently slip into the design. In a random logic architecture, we will have to redesign and usually rebuild the whole computer. On the other hand, in a microprogrammed machine it is usually sufficient to change a couple of bits in the microprogram to rectify the problem. This is even easier if a RAM instead of a PROM is used during the development and debugging phases. Of course, we must be able to load this memory with the microprogram by some external means. Again, a powerful tool is available: AMD's System/29™.

Finally, let's face the reality: The marketing guys usually change their requirements (i.e., the instruction set) when you are 80% through your logic design. Now you have to start over from scratch. Not so! Change some microcode, perhaps very little hardware too and here you are! It is even more convenient when only additions to the existing instruction set are considered. Just add a few lines to your microprogram to comply with those new ideas! A mere few minutes using System 29 – That's flexibility! Incidentally, don't tell the marketing guys how easy it is or you will NEVER get the product out!!

SUMMARY

The block diagram of Figure 13 shows a typical 16-bit minicomputer architecture. Also identified on this block diagram are various Am2900 family elements that might be used in each of these blocks. Such a design might use either 4-Am2901A's or 4-Am2903's for the data path ALU. An Am2910 could be used as the microprogram sequencer for control of up to 4K words of microprogram memory. Also shown on the block diagram are the Am9130 and Am9140 MOS Static RAM's which are potential candidates for use in the computer's main memory.

The following chapters will discuss various blocks of Figure 13 in detail and give design examples for each section. Needless to say, the design engineer can appropriately tailor any design to meet his throughput requirements. Also, special algorithms can be executed by adding the appropriate hardware and microcode to the blocks described.

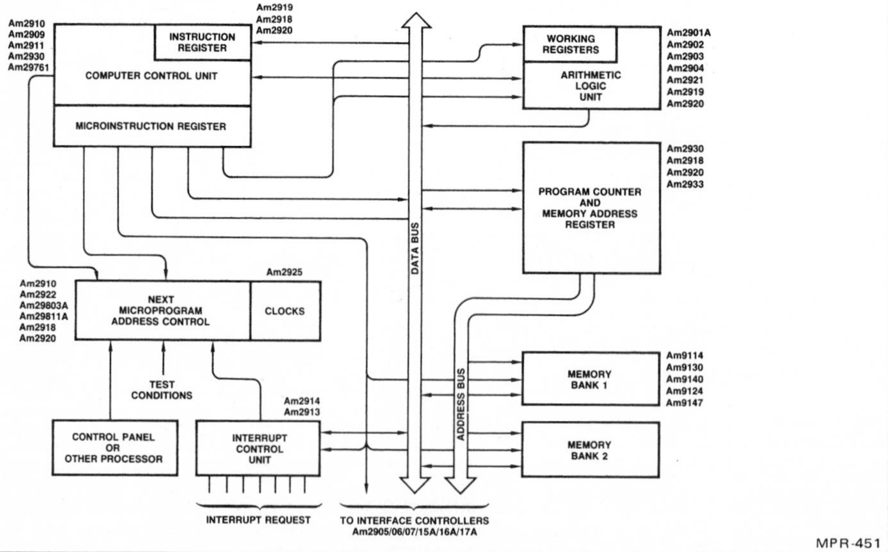

Figure 13. A Generalized Computer Architecture.

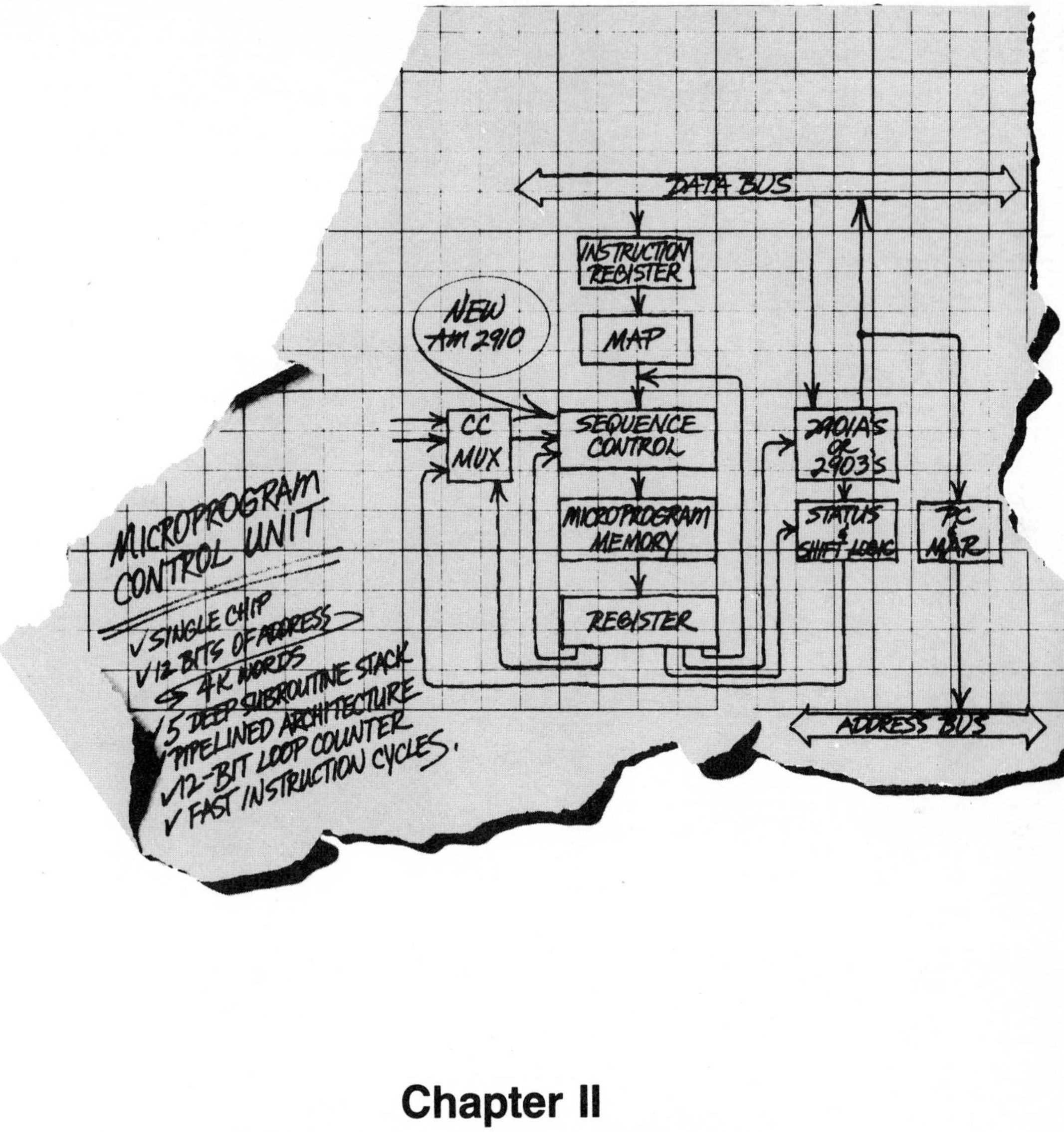

Chapter II
Microprogrammed Design

CHAPTER II
MICROPROGRAMMED DESIGN

INTRODUCTION

A microprogrammed machine is one in which a coherent sequence of microinstructions is used to execute various commands required by the machine. If the machine is a computer, each sequence of microinstructions can be made to execute a machine instruction. All of the little elemental tasks performed by the machine in executing the machine instruction are called microinstructions. The storage area for these microinstructions is usually called the microprogram memory. This technique was identified by Wilkes in the 1950's as a structured approach to the random control logic in a computer.

A microinstruction usually has two primary parts. These are: (1) the definition and control of all elemental micro-operations to be carried out and (2) the definition and control of the address of the next microinstruction to be executed.

The definition of the various micro-operations to be carried out usually includes such things as ALU source operand selection, ALU function, ALU destination, carry control, shift control, interrupt control, data-in and data-out control and so forth. The definition of the next microinstruction function usually includes identifying the source selection of the next microinstruction address, and in some cases, supplying the actual value of that microinstruction address.

Microprogrammed machines are usually distinguished from non-microprogrammed machines in the following manner. Older, non-microprogrammed machines implemented the control function by using combinations of gates and flip-flops connected in a somewhat random fashion in order to generate the required timing and control signals for the machine. Microprogrammed machines, on the other hand, are normally considered highly ordered and more organized with regard to the control function field. In its simplest definition, a microprogram control unit consists of the microprogram memory and the structure required to determine the address of the next microinstruction.

Microprogramming is normally selected by the design engineer as a control technique for finite state machines because it improves flexibility, performance, and LSI utilization. Several additional key features of microprogrammed designs are listed below:

- More structured organization
- Diagnostics can be implemented easily
- Design changes are simple
- Field updates are easy
- Adaptations are straightforward
- System definition can be expanded to include new features
- Documentation and Service are easier
- Design aids are available
- Cost and design time are reduced

THE MICROPROGRAM MEMORY

The microprogram memory is simply an N word by M bit memory used to hold the various microinstructions. For an N word memory, the address locations are usually defined as location 0 through N−1. For example, a 256-word microprogram memory will have address locations 0 through 255. Each word of the microprogram memory consists of M bits. These M bits are usually broken into various field definitions and the fields can consist of various numbers of bits. It is the definition of the various fields of a microprogram word that is usually referred to as FORMATTING.

An example of how microinstruction fields are defined in a typical machine microprogram memory word is as follows:

Field 1 – General purpose
Field 2 – Branch address
Field 3 – Next microinstruction address control
Field 4 – Condition code multiplexer control
Field 5 – Interrupt control
Field 6 – Fast clock/slow clock select
Field 7 – Carry control
Field 8 – ALU source operand control
Field 9 – ALU function control
Field 10 – ALU destination control
Field 11 – Shift multiplexer control
Field 12 – etc.

EXECUTING MICROINSTRUCTONS

Once the microprogram format has been defined, it is necessary to execute sequences of these microinstructions if the machine is to perform any real function. In its simplest form, all that is required to sequence through a series of microinstructions is a microprogram address counter. The microprogram address counter simply increments by one on each clock cycle to select the address of the next microinstruction. For example, if the microprogram address counter contains address 23, the next clock cycle will increment the counter and it will select address 24. The counter will continue to increment on each clock cycle thereby selecting address 25, address 26, address 27, and so forth. If this were the only control available, the machine would not be very flexible and it would be able to execute only a fixed pattern of microinstructions.

The technique of continuing from one microinstruction to the next sequential microinstruction is usually referred to as CONTINUE. Thus, in microprogram control definition, we will use the CONTINUE (CONT) statement to mean simply incrementing to the next microinstruction.

MICROPROGRAM JUMPING

If the microprogram control unit is to have the ability to select other than the next microinstruction, the control unit must be able to load a JUMP address. The load control of a counter can be a single bit field within the microprogram word format. Let us call this one-bit field the microprogram address counter load enable bit. When this bit is at logic 0, a load will be inhibited and when this bit is a logic 1, a load will be enabled. If the load is enabled, the JUMP address contained within the microprogram memory will be parallel loaded into the microprogram address counter. This results in the ability to perform an N-way branch. For example, if the branch address field is eight bits wide, a JUMP to any address in the memory space from word 0 through word 255 can be performed.

This simple branching control feature allows a microprogram memory controller to execute sequential microinstructions or perform a JUMP (JMP) to any address either before or after the address currently contained in the microprogram address counter.

CONDITIONAL JUMPING

While the JUMP instruction has added some flexibility to the sequencing of microprogram instructions, the controller still lacks any decision-making capability. This decision-making capability is provided by the CONDITIONAL JUMP (COND JMP) instruction. Figure 1 shows a functional block diagram of a microprogram memory/address controller providing the capability to jump on either of two different conditions. In this example, the load select control is a two-bit field used to control a

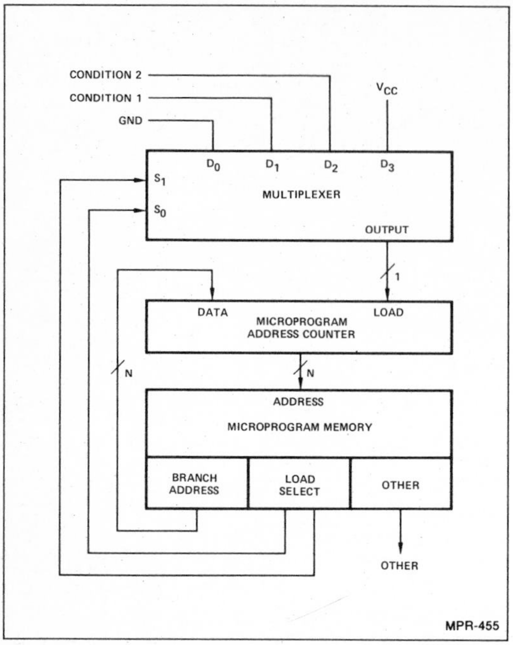

Figure 1. A Two-Bit Control Field Can be Used to Select CONTINUE, BRANCH, or CONDITIONAL BRANCH.

four-input multiplexer. When the two-bit field is equivalent to binary zero, the multiplexer selects the zero input which forces the load control inactive. Thus, the CONTINUE microprogram control instruction is executed. When the two-bit load select field contains binary one, the D_1 input of the multiplexer is selected. Now, the load control is a function of the Condition 1 input. If Condition 1 is logic 0, the microprogram address counter increments and if Condition 1 is logic 1, the jump address will be parallel loaded in the next clock cycle. This operation is defined as a CONDITIONAL JUMP. If the load select input contains binary 2, the D_2 input is selected and the same conditional function is performed with respect to the Condition 2 input. If the load select field contains binary 3, the D_3 input of the multiplexer is selected. Since the D_3 input is tied to logic HIGH, this forces the microprogram address counter to the load mode independent of anything else. Thus, the jump address is loaded into the microprogram address counter on the next clock cycle and an UNCONDITIONAL JUMP is executed. This load select control function definition is shown in Table 1.

**TABLE 1.
LOAD SELECT CONTROL FUNCTION.**

S_1 S_0	Function
0 0	Continue
0 1	Jump Condition 1 True
1 0	Jump Condition 2 True
1 1	Jump Unconditional

OVERLAPPING THE MICROPROGRAM INSTRUCTION FETCH

Now that a few basic microprogram address control instructions have been defined, let us examine the control instructions used in a microprogram control unit featuring the overlap fetching of the next microinstruction. This technique is also known as "pipelining". The block diagram for such a microprogram control unit is shown in Figure 2. The key difference when compared with previous microprogrammed architectures is the existence of the "pipeline register" at the output of the microprogram memory. By definition, the pipeline register (or microword register) contains the microinstruction currently being executed by the machine. Simultaneously, while this microinstruction is being executed, the address of the next microinstruction is applied to the microprogram memory and the contents of that memory word are being fetched and set-up at the inputs to the pipeline register. This technique of pipelining can be used to improve the performance of the microprogram control unit. This results because the contents of the microprogram memory word required for the next cycle are being fetched on an overlapping basis with the actual execution of the current microprogram word. It should be realized that when the pipeline approach is used, the design engineer must be aware of the fact that some registers contain the results of the previous microinstruction executed, some registers contain the current microinstruction being executed, and some registers contain data for the next microinstruction to be executed.

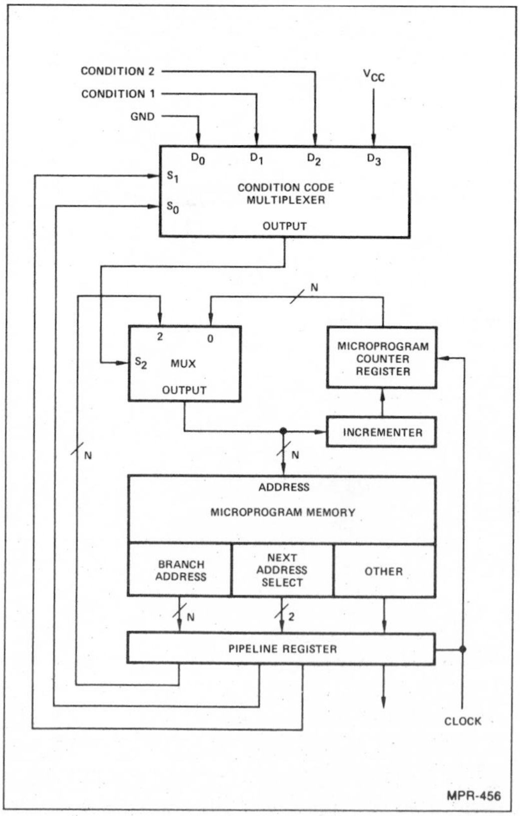

Figure 2. Overlapping (or Pipelining) the Fetch of the Next Microinstruction.

Let us now compare the block diagram of Figure 2 with that shown in Figure 1. The major difference, of course, is the addition of the pipeline register at the output of the microprogram control memory. Also, notice the addition of the address multiplexer at the source of the microprogram memory address. This address multiplexer is used to select the microprogram counter register or the pipeline register as the source of the next address for the microprogram memory. The condition code multiplexer is used to control the address multiplexer in this address selection. By placing an incrementer at the output of the address multiplexer, is is possible to always generate the current microprogram address "plus one" at the input of the microprogram counter register.

In Figure 1, the microprogram address counter was described as a counter and could be a device such as the Am25LS161 counter. In the implementation as shown in Figure 2, the Am25LS161 counter is not appropriate. Instead, an incrementer and register are used to give the equivalent effect of a counter.

The key difference between using a true binary counter and the incrementer register described here is as follows. When the jump address from the pipeline register is selected by the multiplexer, the incrementer will combinatorially prepare that address plus one for entry into the microprogram counter register. This entry will occur on the LOW-to-HIGH transition of the clock. Thus, the microprogram counter register can always be made to contain address plus one, independent of the selection of the next microinstruction address. When the address multiplexer is switched so that the microprogram counter register is selected as the source of the microprogram memory address, the incrementer will again set-up address plus one for entry into the microprogram counter register. Thus, when the address multiplexer selects the microprogram counter register, the address multiplexer, incrementer and microprogram counter register appear to operate as a normal binary counter.

The condition code multiplexer S_0S_1 operates in exactly the same fashion as described for the condition code multiplexer of Figure 1. That is, binary zero in the pipeline register (the current microinstruction being executed) forces an unconditional selection of the microprogram register via D_0. Binary one or binary two in the next address select control bits of the pipeline register cause a conditional selection at the address multiplexer via D_1 or D_2. Thus, a CONDITIONAL JUMP can be executed. Binary three in the next address select portion of the pipeline register causes an UNCONDITIONAL JUMP instruction to be executed via D_3.

When the overall machine timing is studied, it will be observed that the key difference between overlap fetching and non-overlap fetching involves the propagation delay of the microprogram memory. In the non-pipelined architecture, the microprogram memory propagation delay must be added to the propagation delay of all the other elements of the machine. In the overlap fetch architecture, the propagation delay associated with the next microprogram memory address fetch is a separate loop independent of the other portion of the machine.

SUBROUTINING IN MICROPROGRAMMING CONTROL

Thus far, we have examined the CONTINUE instruction as well as the CONDITIONAL and UNCONDITIONAL JUMP instructions for overlap fetch. Just as in the programming of minicomputers and microcomputers, the advantages of SUBROUTINING can be realized in microprogramming. The idea here, of course, is that the same block of microcode (or even a single microinstruction) can be shared by several microinstruction sequences. This results in an overall reduction in the total number of microprogram memory words required by the design. If we are to jump to a subroutine, what is required is the ability to store an address to which the subroutine should return when it has completed its execution. Examining the block diagram of Figure 3, we see the addition of a subroutine and loop (push/pop) stack (also called the file) and its associated stack pointer. The control signals required by the stack are an enable stack signal (FILE ENABLE = FE) which will be used to tell the file whenever we wish to perform a push or a pop, and a push/pop control (PUP) used to control the direction of the stack pointer (push or pop).

In this architecture, the stack pointer always points to the address of the last microinstruction written on the stack. This allows the "next address multiplexer" to read the stack at any time via port F. When this selection is performed, the last word written on the stack will be the word applied to the microprogram memory. The condition code multiplexer of the previous example has also been replaced by a next address control unit. This next address control unit (Am29811A) can execute 16 different next address control functions where most of these functions are conditional. Thus, the device has four instruction inputs as well as one condition code test input which is connected to the condition code multiplexer. Note also that the next address control field of the microprogram word has been expanded to a four-bit field. Outputs from the Am29811A next address control block are used to control the stack pointer and the next address multiplexer of the Am2911. In addition, the device has outputs to control the three-state enable of the pipeline register and the three-state enable of the starting address decode PROM. Also, the architecture has a counter that can be used as a loop-counter or event counter.

The 16 instructions associated with the Am29811A are listed in Table 2. As is easily seen by referring to Table 2, three of the instructions in this set are associated with subroutining in microprogram memory. The first instruction of this set, is a simple conditional JUMP-TO-SUBROUTINE where the source of the subroutine address is in the pipeline register. The RETURN-FROM-SUBROUTINE instruction is also conditional and is used to return to the next microinstruction following the JUMP-TO-SUBROUTINE instruction. There is also a conditional JUMP-TO-ONE-OF-TWO-SUBROUTINES, where the subroutine address is either in the PIPELINE register or in the internal REGISTER in the Am2911. This instruction will be explained in more detail later.

TYPICAL COMPUTER CONTROL UNIT ARCHITECTURE USING THE Am2911 AND Am29811A

The microprogram memory control unit block diagram of Figure 3 is easily implemented using the Am2911 and Am29811A. This architecture provides a structured state machine design capable of executing many highly sophisticated next address control instructions. The Am2911 contains a next address multiplexer that provides four different inputs from which the address of the next microinstruction can be selected. These are the direct input (D), the register input (R), the program counter (PC), and the file (F). The starting address decoder (mapping PROM) output and the pipeline register output are connected together at the D input to the Am2911 and are operated in the three-state mode.

The architecture of Figure 3 shows an instruction register capable of being loaded with a machine instruction word from the data bus. The op code portion of the instruction is decoded using a mapping PROM to arrive at a starting address for the

TABLE 2. FUNCTIONAL DESCRIPTION OF Am29811A INSTRUCTION SET.

MNEMONIC	INPUTS: INSTRUCTION I_3 I_2 I_1 I_0	FUNCTION	TEST INPUT	OUTPUTS: NEXT ADDR SOURCE	FILE	COUNTER	MAP-E	PL-E
JZ	L L L L	JUMP ZERO	X	D	HOLD	L L	H	L
CJS	L L L H	COND JSB PL	L	PC	HOLD	HOLD	H	L
			H	D	PUSH	HOLD	H	L
JMAP	L L H L	JUMP MAP	X	D	HOLD	HOLD	L	H
CJP	L L H H	COND JUMP PL	L	PC	HOLD	HOLD	H	L
			H	D	HOLD	HOLD	H	L
PUSH	L H L L	PUSH/COND LD CNTR	L	PC	PUSH	HOLD	H	L
			H	PC	PUSH	LOAD	H	L
JSRP	L H L H	COND JSB R/PL	L	R	PUSH	HOLD	H	L
			H	D	PUSH	HOLD	H	L
CJV	L H H L	COND JUMP VECTOR	L	PC	HOLD	HOLD	H	H
			H	D	HOLD	HOLD	H	H
JRP	L H H H	COND JUMP R/PL	L	R	HOLD	HOLD	H	L
			H	D	HOLD	HOLD	H	L
RFCT	H L L L	REPEAT LOOP, CNTR ≠ 0	L	F	HOLD	DEC	H	L
			H	PC	POP	HOLD	H	L
RPCT	H L L H	REPEAT PL, CNTR ≠ 0	L	D	HOLD	DEC	H	L
			H	PC	HOLD	HOLD	H	L
CRTN	H L H L	COND RTN	L	PC	HOLD	HOLD	H	L
			H	F	POP	HOLD	H	L
CJPP	H L H H	COND JUMP PL & POP	L	PC	HOLD	HOLD	H	L
			H	D	POP	HOLD	H	L
LDCT	H H L L	LOAD CNTR & CONTINUE	X	PC	HOLD	LOAD	H	L
LOOP	H H L H	TEST END LOOP	L	F	HOLD	HOLD	H	L
			H	PC	POP	HOLD	H	L
CONT	H H H L	CONTINUE	X	PC	HOLD	HOLD	H	L
JP	H H H H	JUMP PL	X	D	HOLD	HOLD	H	L

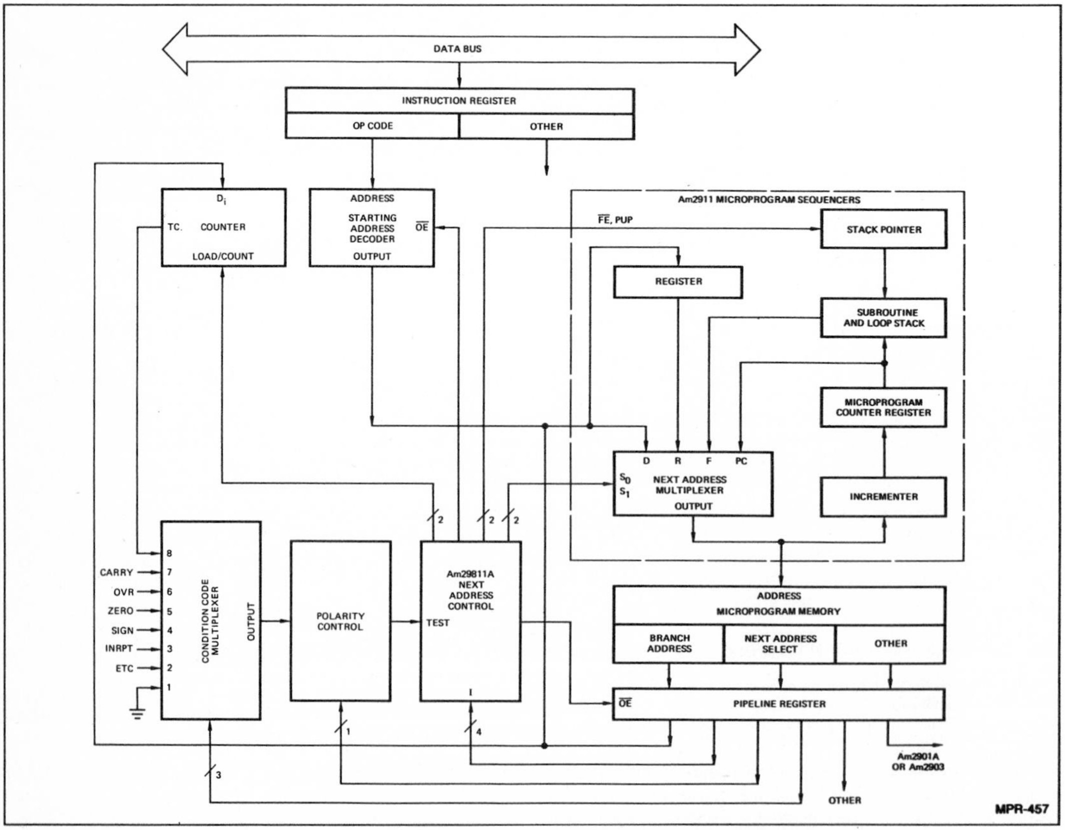

Figure 3. A Typical Computer Control Unit Using the Am2911 and Am29811A.

TABLE 3. PIN FUNCTIONS.

Abbreviation	Name	Function
D_i	Direct Input Bit i	Direct input to register/counter and multiplexer. D_0 is LSB
I_i	Instruction Bit i	Selects one-of-sixteen instructions for the Am2910
$\overline{CC}$	Condition Code	Used as test criterion. Pass test is a LOW on $\overline{CC}$.
$\overline{CCEN}$	Condition Code Enable	Whenever the signal is HIGH, $\overline{CC}$ is ignored and the part operates as though $\overline{CC}$ were true (LOW).
CI	Carry-In	Low order carry input to incrementer for microprogram counter
$\overline{RLD}$	Register Load	When LOW forces loading of register/counter regardless of instruction or condition
$\overline{OE}$	Output Enable	Three-state control of Y_i outputs
CP	Clock Pulse	Triggers all internal state changes at LOW-to-HIGH edge
V_{CC}	+5 Volts	
GND	Ground	
Y_i	Microprogram Address Bit i	Address to microprogram memory. Y_0 is LSB, Y_{11} is MSB
$\overline{FULL}$	Full	Indicates that five items are on the stack
$\overline{PL}$	Pipeline Address Enable	Can select #1 source (usually Pipeline Register) as direct input source
$\overline{MAP}$	Map Address Enable	Can select #2 source (usually Mapping PROM or PLA) as direct input source
$\overline{VECT}$	Vector Address Enable	Can select #3 source (for example, Interrupt Starting Address) as direct input source

microinstruction sequence required to execute the machine instruction. When the microprogram memory address is to be the first microinstruction of the machine instruction sequence, the Am29811A next address control unit selects the multiplexer D input and enables the three-state output from the mapping PROM. When the current microinstruction being executed is selecting the next microinstruction address as a JUMP function, the JUMP address will be available at the multiplexer D input. This is accomplished by having the Am29811A select the next address multiplexer D input and also enabling the three-state output of the pipeline register branch address field. The register enable input to the Am2911 is connected to ground so that this register will always load the value at the Am2911 D input. The value at D is clocked into the Am2911's register (R) at the end of the current microcycle, which makes the D value of *this* microcycle available as the R value of the *next* microcycle. Thus, by using the branch address field of two sequential microinstructions, a conditional JUMP-TO-ONE-OF-TWO-SUBROUTINES or a conditional JUMP-TO-ONE-OF-TWO-BRANCH-ADDRESSES can be executed by either selecting the D input or the R input of the next address multiplexer.

When sequencing through continuous microinstructions in microprogram memory, the program counter in the Am2911 is used. Here, the Am29811A simply selects the PC input of the next address multiplexer. In addition, most of these instructions enable the three-state outputs of the pipeline register associated with the branch address field, which allows the register within the Am2911 to be loaded.

The 4 x 4 stack in the Am2911 is used for looping and subroutining in microprogram operations. Up to four levels of subroutines or loops can be nested. Also, loops and subroutines can be intermixed as long as the four-word depth of the stack is not exceeded.

ARCHITECTURE OF THE Am2910

The Am2910 is a bipolar microprogram controller intended for use in high-speed microprocessor applications. It allows addressing of up to 4K words of microprogram. A block diagram is shown in Figure 4.

The controller contains a four-input multiplexer that is used to select either the register/counter, direct input, microprogram counter, or stack as the source of the next microinstruction address.

The register/counter consists of 12 D-type, edge-triggered flip-flops, with a common clock enable. When its load control, $\overline{RLD}$, is LOW, new data is loaded on a positive clock transition. A few instructions include load; in most systems, these instructions will be sufficient, simplifying the microcode. The output of the register/counter is available to the multiplexer as a source for the next microinstruction address. The direct input furnishes a source of data for loading the register/counter.

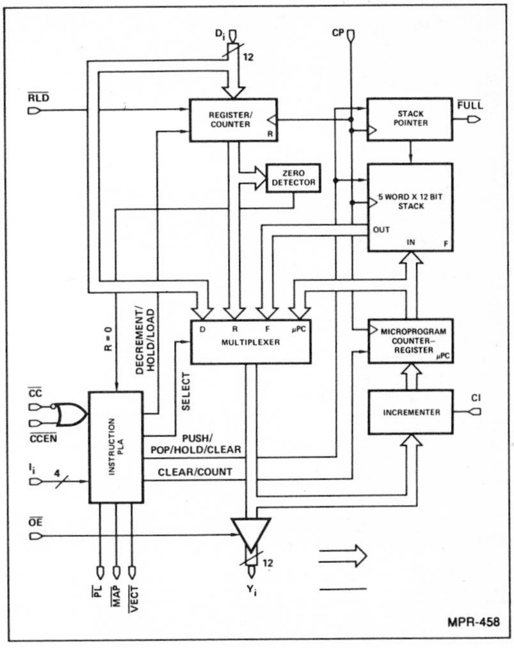

Figure 4. Am2910 Block Diagram.

The Am2910 contains a microprogram counter (μPC) that is composed of a 12-bit incrementer followed by a 12-bit register. The μPC can be used in either of two ways. When the carry-in to the incrementer is HIGH, the microprogram register is loaded on the next clock cycle with the current Y output word plus one (Y+1→μPC). Sequential microinstructions are thus executed. When the carry-in is LOW, the incrementer passes the Y output word unmodified so that μPC is reloaded with the same Y word on the next clock cycle (Y→μPC). The same microinstruction is thus executed any number of times.

The third source for the multiplexer is the direct (D) inputs. This source is used for branching.

The fourth source available at the multiplexer input is a 5-word by 12-bit stack (file). The stack is used to provide return address linkage when executing microsubroutines or loops. The stack contains a build-in stack pointer (SP) which always points to the last file word written. This allows stack reference operations (looping) to be performed without a pop. The stack pointer operates as an up/down counter. During microinstructions 2, 4 and 5, the PUSH operation is performed. This causes the stack pointer to increment and the file to be written with the required return linkage. On the cycle following the PUSH, the return data is at the new location pointed to by the stack pointer.

During six other microinstructions, a POP operation occurs. This places the information at the top of the stack onto the Y outputs. The stack pointer decrements at the next rising clock edge following a POP, effectively removing old information from the top of the stack.

The stack pointer linkage is such that any sequence of pushes, pops or stack references can be achieved. At RESET (Instruction 0), the depth of nesting becomes zero. For each PUSH, the nesting depth increases by one; for each POP, the depth decreases by one. The depth can grow to five. After a depth of five is reached, FULL goes LOW. Any further PUSHes onto a full stack overwrites information at the top of the stack, but leaves the stack pointer unchanged. This operation will usually destroy useful information and is normally avoided. A POP from an empty stack places non-meaningful data on the Y outputs, but is otherwise safe. The stack pointer remains at zero whenever a POP is attempted from a stack already empty.

The register/counter is operated during three microinstructions (8, 9, 15) as a 12-bit down counter, with result = zero available as a microinstruction branch test criterion. This provides efficient iteration of microinstructions. The register/counter is arranged such that if it is preloaded with a number N and then used as a loop termination counter, the sequence will be executed exactly N+1 times. During instruction 15, a three-way branch under combined control of the loop counter and the condition code is available.

The device provides three-state Y outputs. These can be particularly useful in designs requiring automatic checkout of the processor. The microprogram controller outputs can be forced into the high-impedance state, and pre-programmed sequences of microinstructions can be executed via external access to the address lines.

OPERATION

Table 4 shows the result of each instruction in controlling the multiplexer which determines the Y outputs, and in controlling the three enable signals $\overline{PL}$, $\overline{MAP}$ and $\overline{VECT}$. The effect on the μPC, the register/counter, and the stack after the next positive-going clock edge is also shown. The multiplexer determines which internal source drives the Y outputs. The value loaded into μPC is either identical to the Y output, or else one greater, as determined by CI. For each instruction, one and only one of the three outputs $\overline{PL}$, $\overline{MAP}$ and $\overline{VECT}$ is LOW. If these outputs control three-state enables for the primary source of microprogram jumps (usually part of a pipeline register), a PROM which maps the instruction to a microinstruction starting location, and an optional third source (often a vector from a DMA or interrupt source), respectively, the three-state sources can drive the D inputs without further logic.

Several inputs, as shown in Table 4 can modify instruction execution. The combination $\overline{CC}$ HIGH and $\overline{CCEN}$ LOW is used as a test in 10 of the 16 instructions. $\overline{RLD}$, when LOW, causes the D input to be loaded into the register/counter, overriding any HOLD or DEC operation specified in the instruction. $\overline{OE}$, normally LOW, may be forced HIGH to remove the Am2910 Y outputs from a three-state bus.

TABLE 4. Am2910 MICROINSTRUCTION SET.

HEX I_3-I_0	MNEMONIC	NAME	REG/CNTR CONTENTS	FAIL $\overline{CCEN}$ = LOW and $\overline{CC}$ = HIGH: Y	FAIL: STACK	PASS $\overline{CCEN}$ = HIGH or $\overline{CC}$ = LOW: Y	PASS: STACK	REG/CNTR	ENABLE
0	JZ	JUMP ZERO	X	0	CLEAR	0	CLEAR	HOLD	PL
1	CJS	COND JSB PL	X	PC	HOLD	D	PUSH	HOLD	PL
2	JMAP	JUMP MAP	X	D	HOLD	D	HOLD	HOLD	MAP
3	CJP	COND JUMP PL	X	PC	HOLD	D	HOLD	HOLD	PL
4	PUSH	PUSH/COND LD CNTR	X	PC	PUSH	PC	PUSH	Note 1	PL
5	JSRP	COND JSB R/PL	X	R	PUSH	D	PUSH	HOLD	PL
6	CJV	COND JUMP VECTOR	X	PC	HOLD	D	HOLD	HOLD	VECT
7	JRP	COND JUMP R/PL	X	R	HOLD	D	HOLD	HOLD	PL
8	RFCT	REPEAT LOOP, CNTR ≠ 0	≠0	F	HOLD	F	HOLD	DEC	PL
			=0	PC	POP	PC	POP	HOLD	PL
9	RPCT	REPEAT PL, CNTR ≠ 0	≠0	D	HOLD	D	HOLD	DEC	PL
			=0	PC	HOLD	PC	HOLD	HOLD	PL
A	CRTN	COND RTN	X	PC	HOLD	F	POP	HOLD	PL
B	CJPP	COND JUMP PL & POP	X	PC	HOLD	D	POP	HOLD	PL
C	LDCT	LD CNTR & CONTINUE	X	PC	HOLD	PC	HOLD	LOAD	PL
D	LOOP	TEST END LOOP	X	F	HOLD	PC	POP	HOLD	PL
E	CONT	CONTINUE	X	PC	HOLD	PC	HOLD	HOLD	PL
F	TWB	THREE-WAY BRANCH	≠0	F	HOLD	PC	POP	DEC	PL
			=0	D	POP	PC	POP	HOLD	PL

Note: If $\overline{CCEN}$ = LOW and $\overline{CC}$ = HIGH, hold; else load. X = Don't Care.

The stack, a five-word last-in, first-out 12-bit memory, has a pointer which addresses the value presently on the top of the stack. Explicit control of the stack pointer occurs during instruction 0 (RESET), which makes the stack empty by resetting the SP to zero. After a RESET, and whenever else the stack is empty, the content of the top of stack is undefined until a PUSH occurs. Any POPs performed while the stack is empty put undefined data on the F outputs and leave the stack pointer at zero. Any time the stack is full (five more PUSHes than POPs have occurred since the stack was last empty), the $\overline{FULL}$ warning output occurs. No additional PUSH should be attempted onto a full stack; if tried, information at the top of the stack will be overwritten and lost.

THE Am2910 INSTRUCTION SET

The Am2910 provides 16 instructions which select the address of the next microinstruction to be executed. Four of the instructions are unconditional – their effect depends only on the instruction. Ten of the instructions have an effect which is partially controlled by an external, data-dependent condition. Three of the instructions have an effect which is partially controlled by the contents of the internal register/counter. The instruction set is shown in Table 4. In this discussion it is assumed that CI is tied HIGH.

In the ten conditional instructions, the result of the data-dependent test is applied to $\overline{CC}$. If the $\overline{CC}$ input is LOW, the test is considered to have been passed, and the action specified in the name occurs; otherwise, the test has failed and an alternate (often simply the execution of the next sequential microinstruction) occurs. Testing of $\overline{CC}$ may be disabled for a specific microinstruction by setting $\overline{CCEN}$ HIGH, which unconditionally forces the action specified in the name; that is, it forces a pass. Other ways of using $\overline{CCEN}$ include (1) tying it HIGH, which is useful if no microinstruction is data-dependent; (2) tying it LOW if data-dependent instructions are never forced unconditionally; or (3) tying it to the source of Am2910 instruction bit I_0, which leaves instructions 4, 6 and 10 as data-dependent but makes others unconditional. All of these tricks save one bit of microcode width.

The effect of three instructions depends on the contents of the register/counter. Unless the counter holds a value of zero, it is decremented; if it does hold zero, it is held and a different microprogram next address is selected. These instructions are useful for executing a microinstruction loop a known number of times. Instruction 15 is affected both by the external condition code and the internal register/counter.

Perhaps the best technique for understanding the Am2910 is to simply take each instruction and review its operation. In order to provide some feel for the actual execution of these instructions, Figure 5 is included and depicts examples of all 16 instructions.

The examples given in Figure 5 should be interpreted in the following manner: The intent is to show microprogram flow as various microprogram memory words are executed. For example, the CONTINUE instruction, instruction number 14, as shown in Figure 5, simply means that the contents of microprogram memory word 50 is executed, then the contents of word 51 is executed. This is followed by the contents of microprogram memory word 52 and the contents of microprogram memory word 53. The microprogram addresses used in the examples were arbitrarily chosen and have no meaning other than to show instruction flow. The exception to this is the first example, JUMP ZERO, which forces the microprogram location counter to address ZERO. Each dot refers to the time that the contents of the microprogram memory word is in the pipeline register. While no special symbology is used for the conditional instructions, the text to follow will explain what the conditional choices are in each example.

It might be appropriate at this time to mention that AMD has a microprogram assembler called AMDASM, which has the capability of using the Am2910 instructions in symbolic representation. AMDASM's Am2910 instruction symbolics (or mnemonics) are given in Figure 5 for each instruction and are also shown in Table 4.

Instruction 0, JZ (JUMP and ZERO, or RESET) unconditionally specifies that the address of the next microinstruction is zero. Many designs use this feature for power-up sequences and provide the power-up firmware beginning at microprogram memory word location 0.

Instruction 1 is a CONDITIONAL JUMP-TO-SUBROUTINE via the address provided in the pipeline register. As shown in Figure 5, the machine might have executed words at address 50, 51 and 52. When the contents of address 52 is in the pipeline register, the next address control function is the CONDITIONAL JUMP-TO-SUBROUTINE. Here, if the test is passed, the next instruction executed will be the contents of microprogram memory location 90. If the test failed, the JUMP-TO-SUBROUTINE will not be executed; the contents of microprogram memory location 53 will be executed instead. Thus, the CONDITIONAL JUMP-TO-SUBROUTINE instruction at location 52 will cause the instruction either in location 90 or in location 53 to be executed next. If the TEST input is such that location 90 is selected, value 53 will be pushed onto the internal stack. This provides the return linkage for the machine when the subroutine beginning at location 90 is completed. In this example, the subroutine was completed at location 93 and a RETURN-FROM-SUBROUTINE would be found at location 93.

Instruction 2 is the JUMP MAP instruction. This is an unconditional instruction which causes the $\overline{MAP}$ output to be enabled so that the next microinstruction location is determined by the address supplied via the mapping PROMs. Normally the JUMP MAP instruction is used at the end of the instruction fetch sequence for the machine. In the example of Figure 5, microinstructions at locations 50, 51, 52 and 53 might have been the fetch sequence and at its completion at location 53, the jump map function would be contained in the pipeline register. This example shows the mapping PROM outputs to be 90; therefore, an unconditional jump to microprogram memory address 90 is performed.

Instruction 3, CONDITIONAL JUMP PIPELINE, derives its branch address from the pipeline register branch address value (BR_0-BR_{11} in Figure 6). This instruction provides a technique for branching to various microprogram sequences depending upon the test condition inputs. Quite often, state machines are designed which simply execute tests on various inputs waiting for the condition to come true. When the true condition is reached, the machine then branches and executes a set of microinstructions to perform some function. This usually has the effect of resetting the input being tested until some point in the future. Figure 5 shows the conditional jump via the pipeline register address at location 52. When the contents of microprogram memory word 52 are in the pipeline register, the next address will be either location 53 or location 30 in this example. If the test is passed, the value currently in the pipeline register (3) will be selected. If the test fails, the next address selected will be contained in the microprogram counter which, in this example, is 53.

Instruction 4 is the PUSH/CONDITIONAL LOAD COUNTER instruction and is used primarily for setting up loops in microprogram firmware. In Figure 5, when instruction 52 is in the pipeline register, a PUSH will be made onto the stack and the counter will be loaded based on the condition. When a PUSH occurs, the value pushed is always the next sequential instruction address. In this case, the address is 53. If the test fails, the counter is not

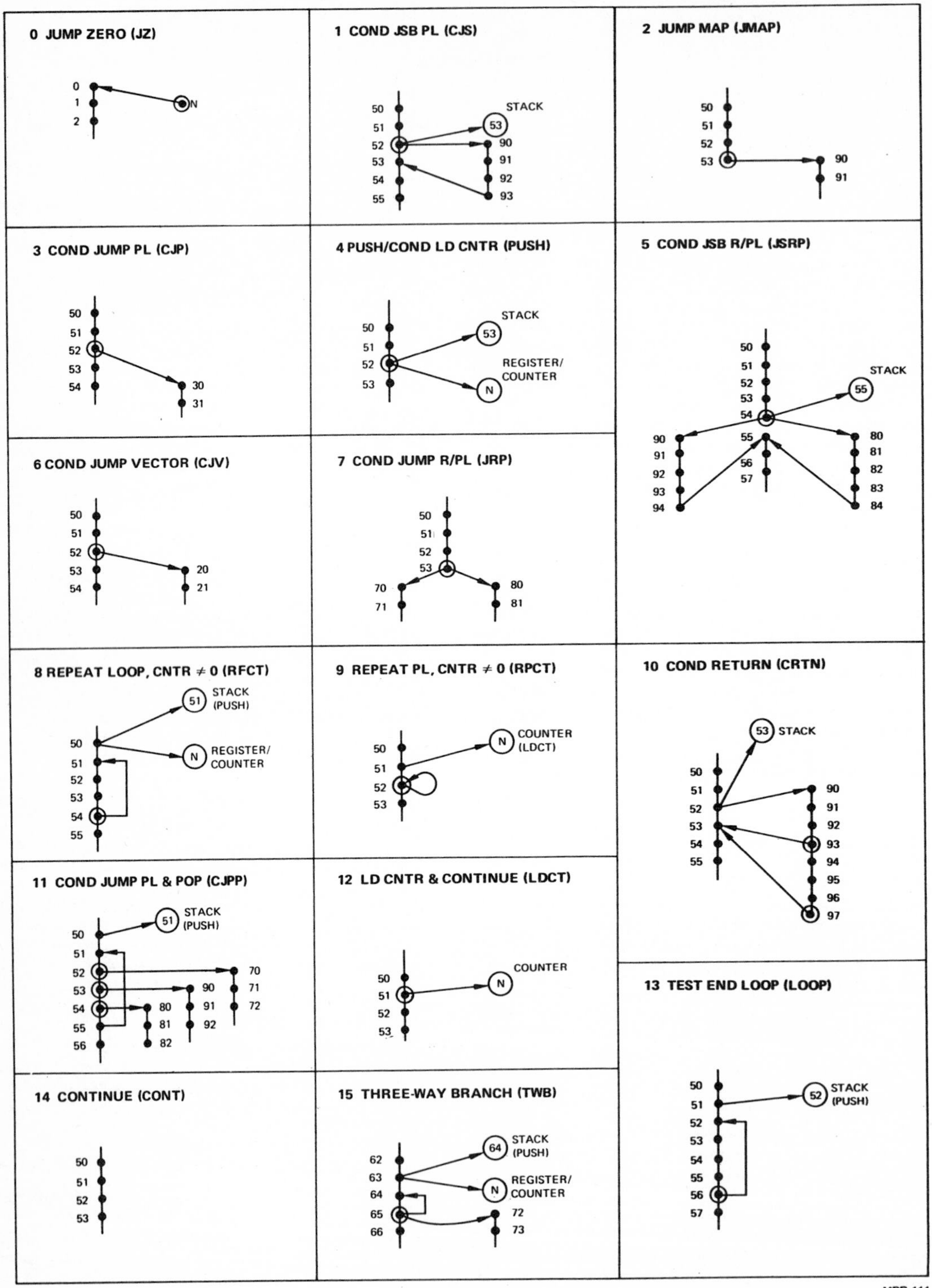

Figure 5. Am2910 Execution Examples.

loaded; if it is passed, the counter is loaded with the value contained in the pipeline register branch address field. Thus, a single microinstruction can be used to set up a loop to be executed a specific number of times. Instruction 8 will describe how to use the pushed value and the register/counter for looping.

Instruction 5 is a CONDITIONAL JUMP-TO-SUBROUTINE via the register/counter or the contents of the PIPELINE register. As shown in Figure 5, a PUSH is always performed and one of two subroutines executed. In this example, either the subroutine beginning at address 80 or the subroutine beginning at address 90 will be performed. A return-from-subroutine (instruction number 10) returns the microprogram flow to address 55. In order for this microinstruction control sequence to operate correctly, both the next address fields of instruction 53 and the next address fields of instruction 54 would have to contain the proper value. Let's assume that the branch address fields of instruction 53 contain the value 90 so that it will be in the Am2910 register/counter when the contents of address 54 are in the pipeline register. This requires that instruction at address 53 load the register/counter. Now, during the execution of instruction 5 (at address 54), if the test failed, the contents of the register (value = 90) will select the address of the next microinstruction. If the test input passes, the pipeline register contents (value = 80) will determine the address of the next microinstruction. Therefore, this instruction provides the ability to select one of two subroutines to be executed based on a test condition.

Instruction 6 is a CONDITIONAL JUMP VECTOR instruction which provides the capability to take the branch address from a third source heretofore not discussed. In order for this instruction to be useful, the Am2910 output, $\overline{\text{VECT}}$, is used to control a three-state control input of a register, buffer, or PROM containing the next microprogram address. This instruction provides one technique for performing interrupt type branching at the microprogram level. Since this instruction is conditional, a pass causes the next address to be taken from the vector source, while failure causes the next address to be taken from the microprogram counter. In the example of Figure 5, if the CONDITIONAL JUMP VECTOR instruction is contained at location 52, execution will continue at vector address 20 if the TEST input is HIGH and the microinstruction at address 53 will be executed if the TEST input is LOW.

Instruction 7 is a CONDITIONAL JUMP via the contents of the Am2910 REGISTER/COUNTER or the contents of the PIPELINE register. This instruction is very similar to instruction 5; the conditional jump-to-subroutine via R or PL. The major difference between instruction 5 and instruction 7 is that no push onto the stack is performed with 7. Figure 5 depicts this instruction as a branch to one of two locations depending on the test condition. The example assumes the pipeline register contains the value 70 when the contents of address 52 is being executed. As the contents of address 53 is clocked into the pipeline register, the value 70 is loaded into the register/counter in the Am2910. The value 80 is available when the contents of address 53 is in the pipeline register. Thus, control is transferred to either address 70 or address 80 depending on the test condition.

Instruction 8 is the REPEAT LOOP, COUNTER ≠ ZERO instruction. This microinstruction makes use of the decrementing capability of the register/counter. To be useful, some previous instruction, such as 4, must have loaded a count value into the register/counter. This instruction checks to see whether the register/counter contains a non-zero value. If so, the register/counter is decremented, and the address of the next microinstruction is taken from the top of the stack. If the register counter contains zero, the loop exit condition is occurring; control falls through to the next sequential microinstruction by selecting μPC; the stack is POP'd by decrementing the stack pointer, but the contents of the top of the stack are thrown away.

An example of the REPEAT LOOP, COUNTER ≠ ZERO instruction is shown in Figure 5. In this example, location 50 most likely would contain a PUSH/CONDITIONAL LOAD COUNTER instruction which would have caused address 51 to be PUSHed on the stack and the counter to be loaded with the proper value for looping the desired number of times.

In this example, since the loop test is made at the end of the instructions to be repeated (microaddress 54), the proper value to be loaded by the instruction at address 50 is one less than the desired number of passes through the loop. This method allows a loop to be executed from 0 to 4095 times.

Single-microinstruction loops provide a highly efficient capability for executing a specific microinstruction a fixed number of times. Examples include fixed rotates, byte swap, fixed point multiply, and fixed point divide.

Instruction 9 is the REPEAT PIPELINE REGISTER, COUNTER ≠ ZERO instruction. This instruction is similar to instruction 8 except that the branch address now comes from the pipeline register rather than the file. In some cases, this instruction may be thought of as a one-word file extension; that is, by using this instruction, a loop with the counter can still be performed when subroutines are nested five deep. This instruction's operation is very similar to that of instruction 8. The differences are that on this instruction, a failed test condition causes the source of the next microinstruction address to be the D inputs; and, when the test condition is passed, this instruction does not perform a POP because the stack is not being used.

In the example of Figure 5, the REPEAT PIPELINE, COUNTER ≠ ZERO instruction is instruction 52 and is shown as a single microinstruction loop. The address in the pipeline register would be 52. Instruction 51 in this example could be the LOAD COUNTER AND CONTINUE instruction (number 12). While the example shows a single microinstruction loop, by simply changing the address in a pipeline register, multi-instruction loops can be performed in this manner for a fixed number of times as determined by the counter.

Instruction 10 is the conditional RETURN-FROM-SUBROUTINE instruction. As the name implies, this instruction is used to branch from the subroutine back to the next microinstruction address following the subroutine call. Since this instruction is conditional, the return is performed only if the test is passed. If the test is failed, the next sequential microinstruction is performed. The example in Figure 5 depicts the use of the conditional RETURN-FROM-SUBROUTINE instruction in both the conditional and the unconditional modes. This example first shows a jump-to-subroutine at instruction location 52 where control is transferred to location 90. At location 93, a conditional RETURN-FROM-SUBROUTINE instruction is performed. If the test is passed, the stack is accessed and the program will transfer to the next instruction at address 53. If the test is failed, the next microinstruction at address 94 will be executed. The program will continue to address 97 where the subroutine is complete. To perform an unconditional RETURN-FROM-SUBROUTINE, the conditional RETURN-FROM-SUBROUTINE instruction is executed unconditionally; the microinstruction at address 97 is programmed to force $\overline{\text{CCEN}}$ HIGH, disabling the test and the forced PASS causes an unconditional return.

Instruction 11 is the CONDITIONAL JUMP PIPELINE register address and POP stack instruction. This instruction provides another technique for loop termination and stack maintenance.

The example in Figure 5 shows a loop being performed from address 55 back to address 51. The instructions at locations 52, 53 and 54 are all conditional JUMP and POP instructions. At address 52, if the TEST input is passed, a branch will be made to address 70 and the stack will be properly maintained via a POP. Should the test fail, the instruction at location 53 (the next sequential instruction) will be executed. Likewise, at address 53, either the instruction at 90 or 54 will be subsequently executed, respective to the test being passed or failed. The instruction at 54 follows the same rules, going to either 80 or 55. An instruction sequence as described here, using the CONDITIONAL JUMP PIPELINE and POP instruction, is very useful when several inputs are being tested and the microprogram is looping waiting for any of the inputs being tested to occur before proceeding to another sequence of instructions. This provides the powerful jump-table programming technique at the firmware level.

Instruction 12 is the LOAD COUNTER AND CONTINUE instruction, which simply enables the counter to be loaded with the value at its parallel inputs. These inputs are normally connected to the pipeline branch address field which (in the architecture being described here) serves to supply either a branch address or a counter value depending upon the microinstruction being executed. There are altogether three ways of loading the counter – the explicit load by this instruction 12; the conditional load included as part of instruction 4; and the use of the $\overline{\text{RLD}}$ input along with any instruction. The use of $\overline{\text{RLD}}$ with any instruction overrides any counting or decrementation specified in the instruction, calling for a load instead. Its use provides additional microinstruction power, at the expense of one bit of microinstruction width. This instruction 12 is exactly equivalent to the combination of instruction 14 and $\overline{\text{RLD}}$ LOW. Its purpose is to provide a simple capability to load the register/counter in those implementations which do not provide microprogrammed control for $\overline{\text{RLD}}$.

Instruction 13 is the TEST END-OF-LOOP instruction, which provides the capability of conditionally exiting a loop at the bottom; that is, this is a conditional instruction that will cause the microprogram to loop, via the file, if the test is failed else to continue to the next sequential instruction. The example in Figure 5 shows the TEST END-OF-LOOP microinstruction at address 56. If the test fails, the microprogram will branch to address 52. Address 52 is on the stack because a PUSH instruction had been executed at address 51. If the test is passed at instruction 56, the loop is terminated and the next sequential microinstruction at address 57 is being executed, which also causes the stack to be POPd; thus, accomplishing the required stack maintenance.

Instruction 14 is the CONTINUE instruction, which simply causes the microprogram counter to increment so that the next sequential microinstruction is executed. This is the simplest microinstruction of all and should be the default instruction which the firmware requests whenever there is nothing better to do.

Instruction 15, THREE-WAY BRANCH, is the most complex. It provides for testing of both a data-dependent condition and the counter during one microinstruction and provides for selecting among one of three microinstruction addresses as the next microinstruction to be performed. Like instruction 8, a previous instruction will have loaded a count into the register/counter while pushing a microbranch address onto the stack. Instruction 15 performs a decrement-and-branch-until-zero function similar to instruction 8. The next address is taken from the top of the stack until the count reaches zero; then the next address comes from the pipeline register. The above action continues as long as the test condition fails. If at any execution of instruction 15 the test condition is passed, no branch is taken; the microprogram counter register furnishes the next address. When the loop is ended, either by the count becoming zero, or by passing the conditional test, the stack is POP'd by decrementing the stack pointer, since interest in the value contained at the top of the stack is then complete.

The application of instruction 15 can enhance performance of a variety of machine-level instructions. For instance, (1) a memory search instruction to be terminated either by finding a desired memory content or by reaching the search limit; (2) variable-field-length arithmetic terminated early upon finding that the content of the portion of the field still unprocessed is all zeroes; (3) key search in a disc controller processing variable length records; (4) normalization of a floating point number.

As one example, consider the case of a memory search instruction. As shown in Figure 5, the instruction at microprogram address 63 can be Instruction 4 (PUSH), which will push the value 64 onto the microprogram stack and load the number N, which is one less than the number of memory locations to be searched before giving up. Location 64 contains a microinstruction which fetches the next operand from the memory area to be searched and compares it with the search key. Location 65 contains a microinstruction which tests the result of the comparison and also is a THREE-WAY BRANCH for microprogram control. If no match is found, the test fails and the microprogram goes back to location 64 for the next operand address. When the count becomes zero, the microprogram branches to location 72, which does whatever is necessary if no match is found. If a match occurs on any execution of the THREE-WAY BRANCH at location 65, control falls through to location 66 which handles this case. Whether the instruction ends by finding a match or not, the stack will have been POP'd once, removing the value 64 from the top of the stack.

Am29811A Instruction Set Difference

The Am29811A instruction set is identical to the Am2910 except for instruction number 15. In the Am29811A, instruction number 15 is an unconditional JUMP PIPELINE REGISTER instruction. This provides the ability to unconditionally branch to any address contained in the branch address field of the microprogram. Thus, an unconditional N-way branch can be performed. Use of this instruction as opposed to a forced conditional jump pipeline instruction simply allows the condition code multiplexer select field to be shared (formatted) with other functions.

TYPICAL COMPUTER CONTROL UNIT ARCHITECTURE USING THE Am2910

The microprogram memory control unit block diagram of Figure 6 is easily implemented using the Am2910. This architecture provides a structured state machine design capable of executing many highly sophisticated next address control instructions.

The architecture of Figure 6 shows an instruction register capable of being loaded with a machine instruction word from the data bus. The op code portion of the instruction is decoded using a mapping PROM to arrive at a starting address for the microinstruction sequence required to execute the machine instruction. When the microprogram memory address is to be the first microinstruction of the machine instruction sequence, the Am2910 next address control selects the multiplexer D input and enables the three-state output from the mapping PROM. When the current microinstruction being executed is selecting the next microinstruction address as a JUMP function, the JUMP address will be available at the multiplexer D input. This is accomplished by having the Am2910 select the next address multiplexer D input and also enabling the three-state output of the pipeline register branch address field. The register enable input to the Am2910 can be grounded so that this register will load the value at the

Am2910 D input. The value at D is clocked into the Am2910's register (R) at the end of the current microcycle, which makes the D value of this microcycle available as the R value of the next microcycle. Thus, by using the branch address field of two sequential microinstructions, a conditional JUMP-TO-ONE-OF-TWO-SUBROUTINES or a conditional JUMP-TO-ONE-OF-TWO-BRANCH-ADDRESSES can be executed by either selecting the D input or the R input of the next address multiplexer.

When sequencing through continuous microinstructions in microprogram memory, the program counter in the Am2910 is used. Here, the control logic simply selects the PC input of the next address multiplexer. In addition, most of these instructions enable the three-state outputs of the pipeline register associated with the branch address field, which allows the register within the Am2910 to be loaded. The 5 x 12 stack in the Am2910 is used for looping and subroutining in microprogram operations. Up to five levels of subroutines or loops can be nested. Also, loops and subroutines can be intermixed as long as the five word depth of the stack is not exceeded.

CCU TIMING

The minimum clock cycle that can be used in a CCU design is usually determined by the component delays along the longest "pipeline-register-clock to logic to pipeline-register-clock" path. At the beginning of any given clock cycle, data available at the output of the microprogram memory, counter status, and any other data and/or status fields, are latched into their associated pipeline registers. At this point, all delay paths begin. Visual inspection will not always point out the longest signal delay path.

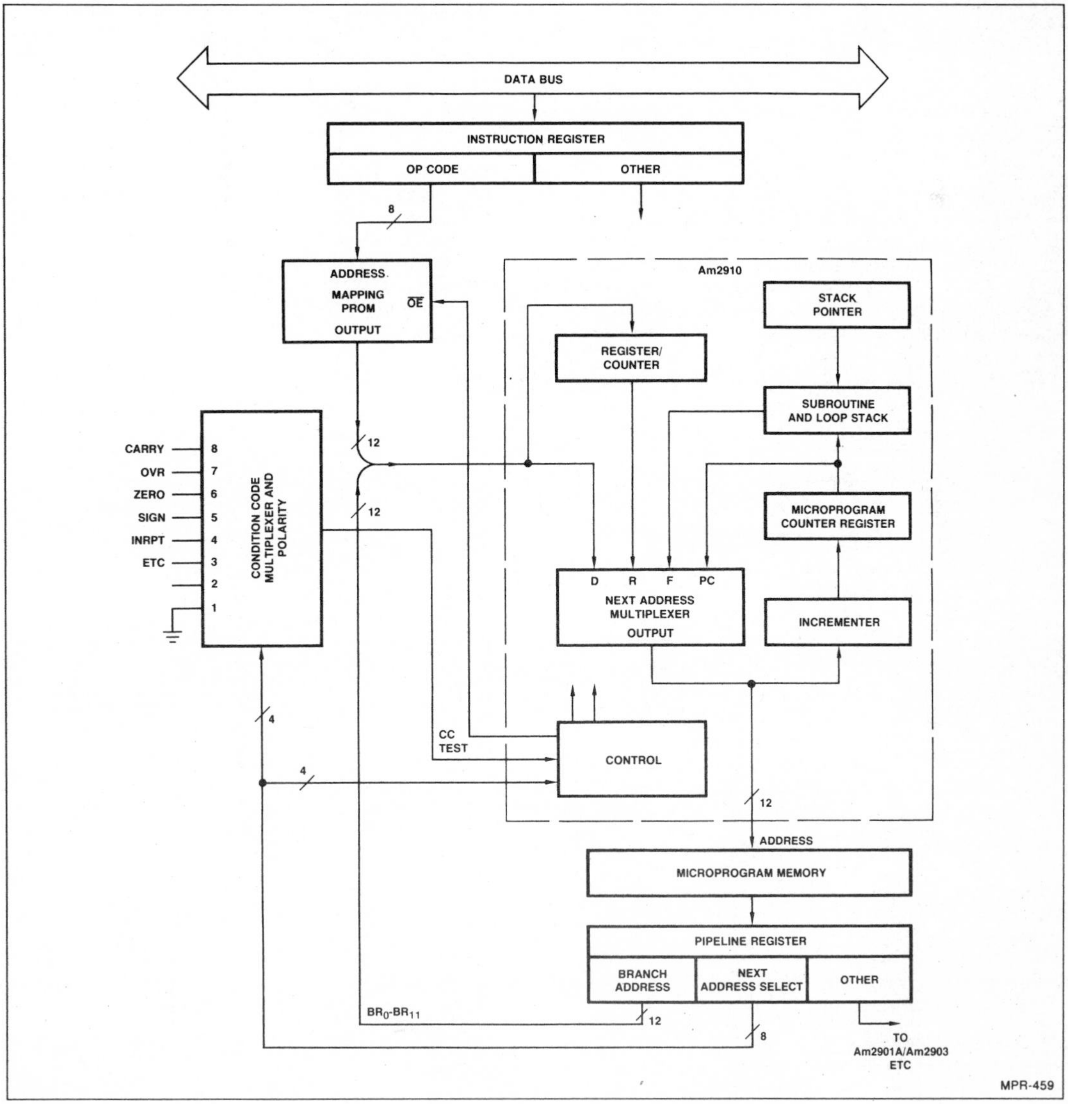

Figure 6. A Typical Computer Control Unit Using the Am2910.

The obviously long paths are a good place to start, but each definable path should be calculated on a component by component basis until the truly longest logic signal path is found.

Referring to Figure 6, a number of potentially long paths can be identified. These include the instruction register to pipeline register time, the pipeline register to pipeline register time via the condition code multiplexer and the status to pipeline register time. In order to demonstrate the technique for calculating the AC performance of the Am2910 state machine design, the timing diagrams of Figure 7 are presented. Here, a number of propagation delay paths are evaluated such that the reader can learn the technique for performing these computations.

All of the propagation delays have been calculated using typical propagation delays because at the time of this writing, the characterization of the Am2910 has not been completed. When the final data sheet is published, the user need only select the appropriate worst case specifications and he can compute the desired maximum propagation delays for his design. Also, by looking at the typical propagation delay numbers, the designer will be able to evaluate the design margin in the system after he has completed all of the worst case calculations. These typical propagation delays represent the expected values if a system were set up on the bench and actual measurements would be taken at 5V and 25°C operating temperature.

While Figure 6 and Figure 7 deal with the Am2910 microprogram sequencer, it is also instructive to evaluate the AC performance of a typical computer control unit using the Am2911 and Am29811A. Figure 3 shows such a connection and will be used as the basis for performing the propagation delay path calculations. The calculations for the various propagation delay paths are demonstrated in Figure 8 and are intended to show the technique for computing these delays. As before, the typical propagation delays have been used in the computation for comparison purposes. The user can derive the maximum numbers at 25°C and 5V, commercial temperature range and power supply variations or military temperature range and power supply variations as required for his design.

When Figure 7 and Figure 8 are reviewed in detail, the reader will recognize that the longest propagation delay paths in the case of the Am2910 as well as the Am2911 and Am29811A involve the three-state enables on the map PROM or the pipeline register for the branch address. If absolute maximum speed is desired, these paths can be eliminated by using one of several techniques. One technique is to simply allocate one or more bits in the pipeline register to control the three-state enables of the various devices connected to the D input of the Am2910. For the example of Figure 6, one bit would be sufficient and the pipeline register could be implemented using an Am74S175 register. This would allow the true and complement outputs to be used to drive the pipeline register branch address output enable and the mapping PROM output enable. Thus, these longest paths would be eliminated and an improvement of about 30ns would be achieved. A second technique for eliminating these propagation delay paths would be to use a four input NAND gate and a four input NOR gate to encode the equivalent function of the $\overline{\text{MAP}}$ enable and the $\overline{\text{PL}}$ enable. This technique is demonstrated in Figure 9. Again, an Am74S175 register would be used as the pipeline register to provide the instruction inputs to the Am2910 sequencer. This would allow instruction 2 to be decoded to provide the MAP enable signal and "NOT INSTRUCTION 2" to be decoded as the pipeline enable signal. This technique can be applied as well to the computer control unit of Figure 3 to accomplish the same longest path elimination.

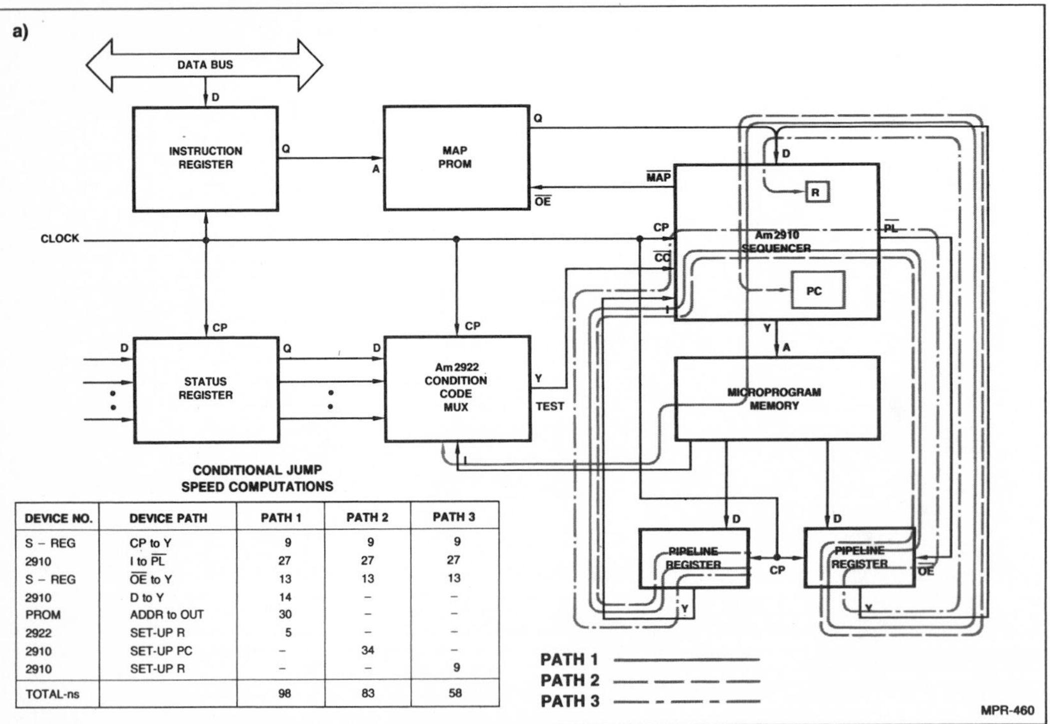

CONDITIONAL JUMP SPEED COMPUTATIONS

DEVICE NO.	DEVICE PATH	PATH 1	PATH 2	PATH 3
S – REG	CP to Y	9	9	9
2910	I to $\overline{\text{PL}}$	27	27	27
S – REG	$\overline{\text{OE}}$ to Y	13	13	13
2910	D to Y	14	–	–
PROM	ADDR to OUT	30	–	–
2922	SET-UP R	5	–	–
2910	SET-UP PC	–	34	–
2910	SET-UP R	–	–	9
TOTAL-ns		98	83	58

Figure 7. Propagation Delay Calculations on the Am2910 Microprogram Sequencer.

b)

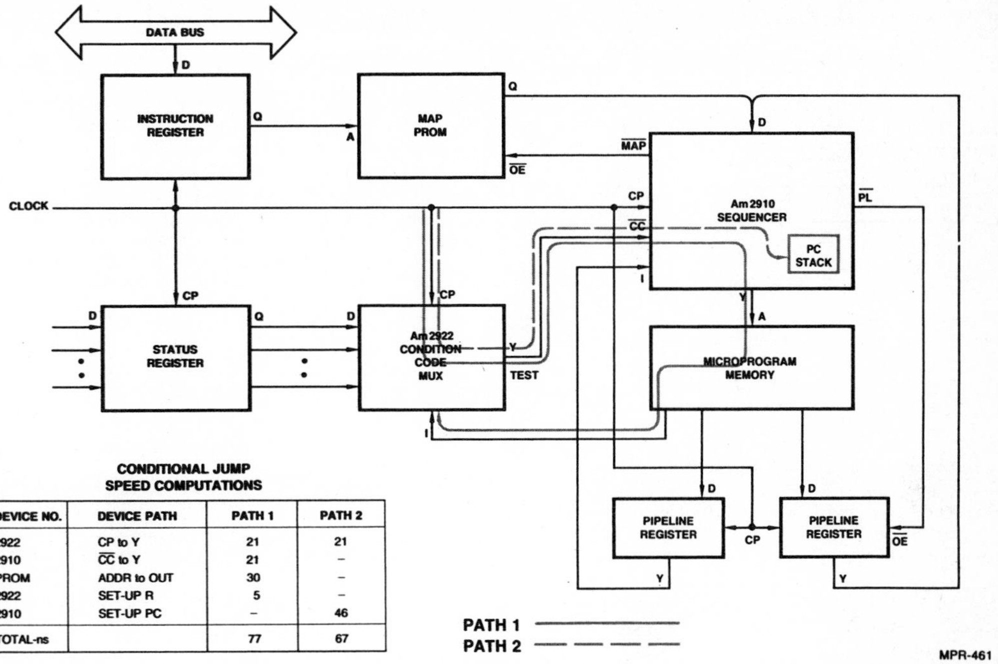

CONDITIONAL JUMP SPEED COMPUTATIONS

DEVICE NO.	DEVICE PATH	PATH 1	PATH 2
2922	CP to Y	21	21
2910	$\overline{CC}$ to Y	21	–
PROM	ADDR to OUT	30	–
2922	SET-UP R	5	–
2910	SET-UP PC	–	46
TOTAL-ns		77	67

c)

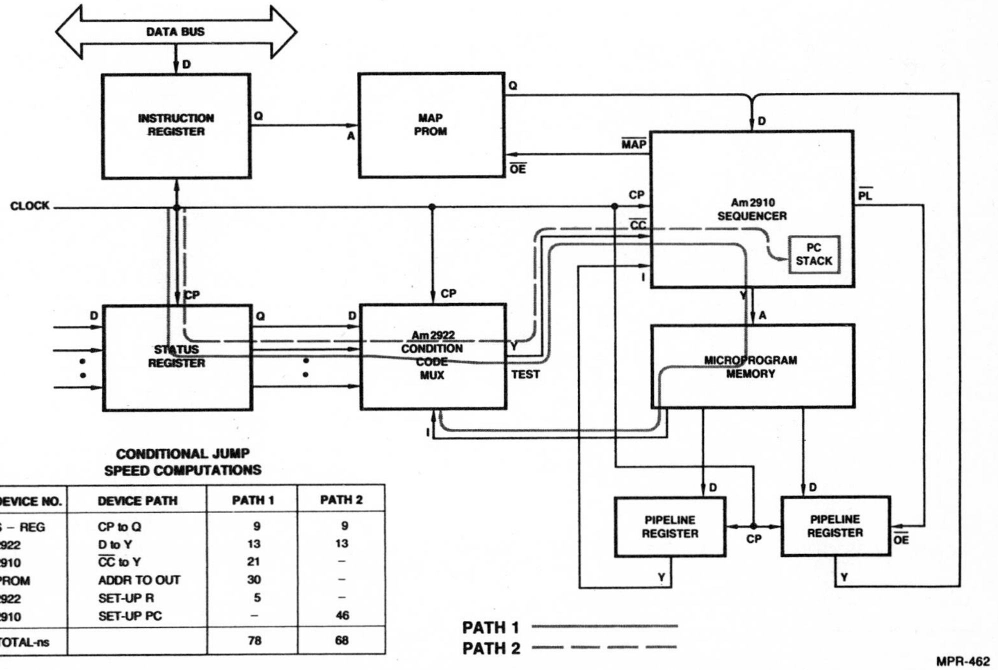

CONDITIONAL JUMP SPEED COMPUTATIONS

DEVICE NO.	DEVICE PATH	PATH 1	PATH 2
S – REG	CP to Q	9	9
2922	D to Y	13	13
2910	$\overline{CC}$ to Y	21	–
PROM	ADDR TO OUT	30	–
2922	SET-UP R	5	–
2910	SET-UP PC	–	46
TOTAL-ns		78	68

Figure 7. Propagation Delay Calculations on the Am2910 Microprogram Sequencer (Cont.).

d)

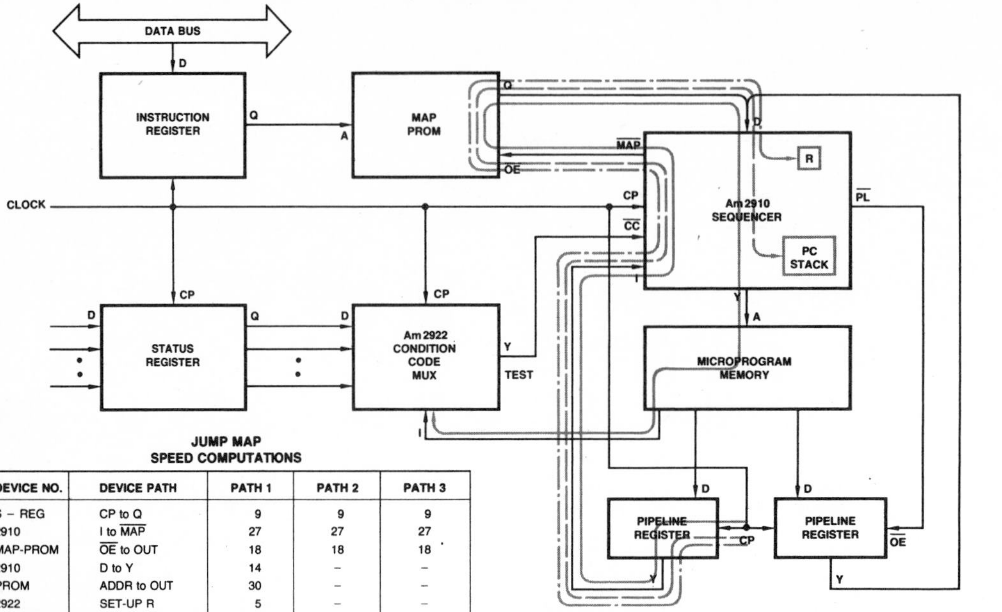

JUMP MAP
SPEED COMPUTATIONS

DEVICE NO.	DEVICE PATH	PATH 1	PATH 2	PATH 3
S – REG	CP to Q	9	9	9
2910	I to $\overline{MAP}$	27	27	27
MAP-PROM	$\overline{OE}$ to OUT	18	18	18
2910	D to Y	14	–	–
PROM	ADDR to OUT	30	–	–
2922	SET-UP R	5	–	–
2910	SET-UP PC	–	34	–
2910	SET-UP R	–	–	9
TOTAL-ns		103	88	63

PATH 1 ————————
PATH 2 — — — —
PATH 3 — - — - —

MPR-463

e)

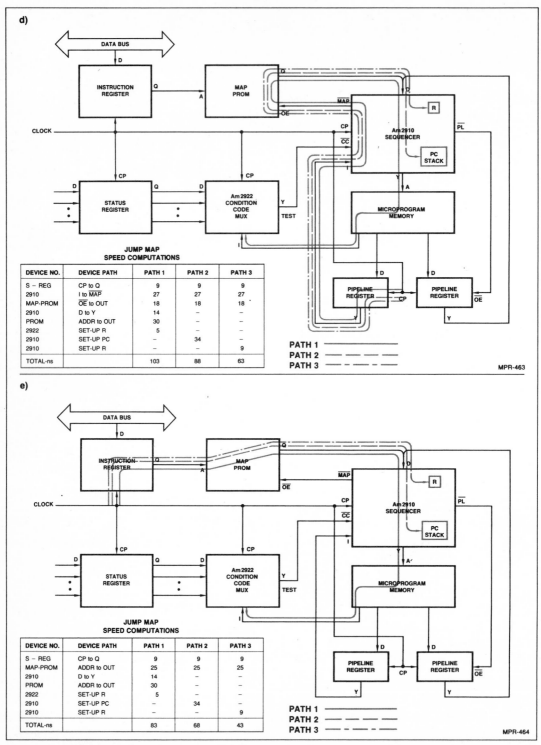

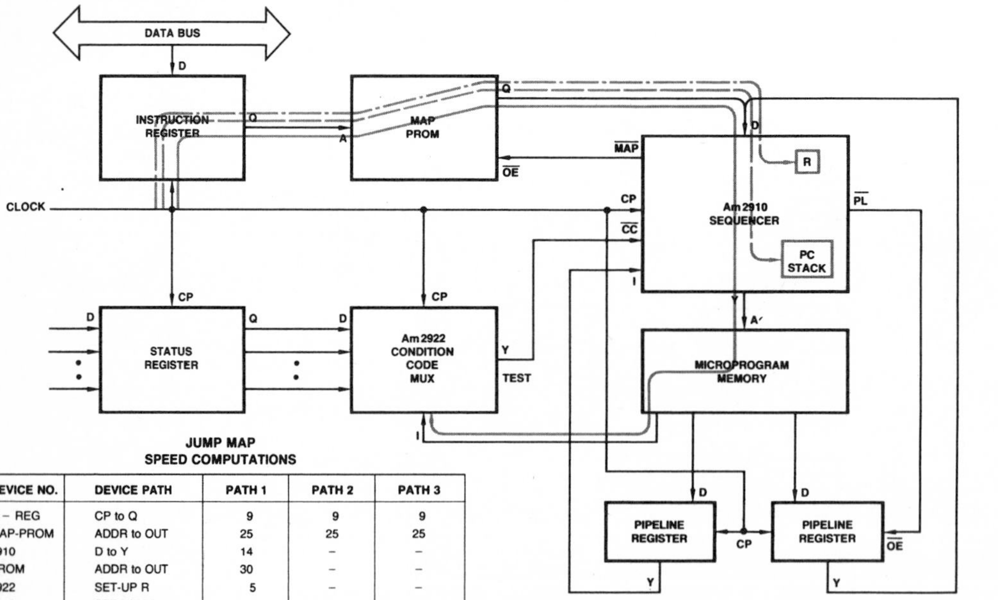

JUMP MAP
SPEED COMPUTATIONS

DEVICE NO.	DEVICE PATH	PATH 1	PATH 2	PATH 3
S – REG	CP to Q	9	9	9
MAP-PROM	ADDR to OUT	25	25	25
2910	D to Y	14	–	–
PROM	ADDR to OUT	30	–	–
2922	SET-UP R	5	–	–
2910	SET-UP PC	–	34	–
2910	SET-UP R	–	–	9
TOTAL-ns		83	68	43

PATH 1 ————————
PATH 2 — — — —
PATH 3 — - — - —

MPR-464

Figure 7. Propagation Delay Calculations on the Am2910 Microprogram Sequencer (Cont.).

f)

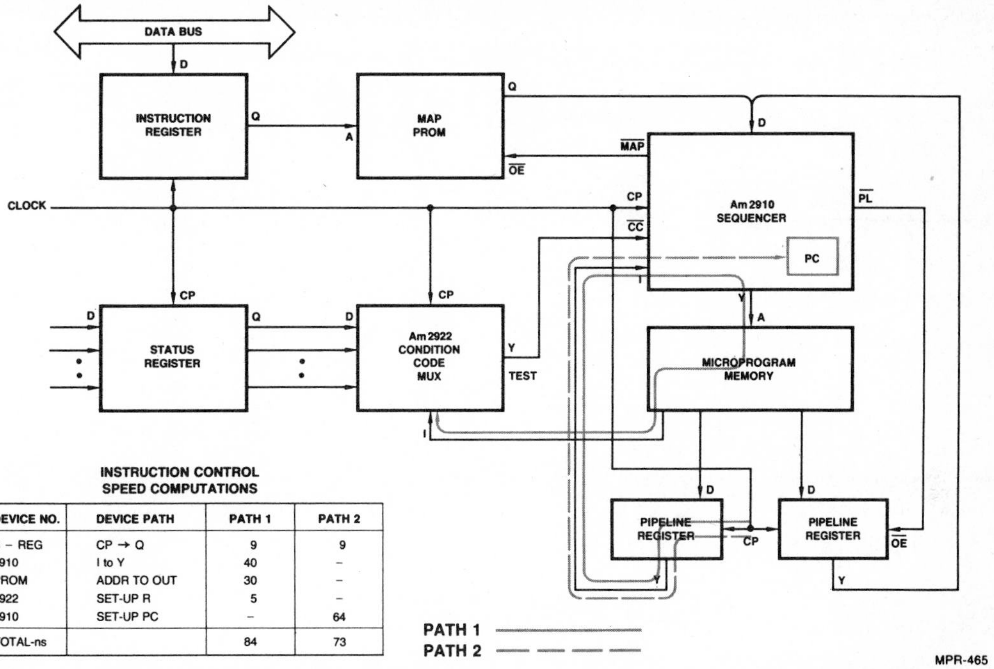

INSTRUCTION CONTROL SPEED COMPUTATIONS

DEVICE NO.	DEVICE PATH	PATH 1	PATH 2
S – REG	CP → Q	9	9
2910	I to Y	40	–
PROM	ADDR TO OUT	30	–
2922	SET-UP R	5	–
2910	SET-UP PC	–	64
TOTAL-ns		84	73

g)

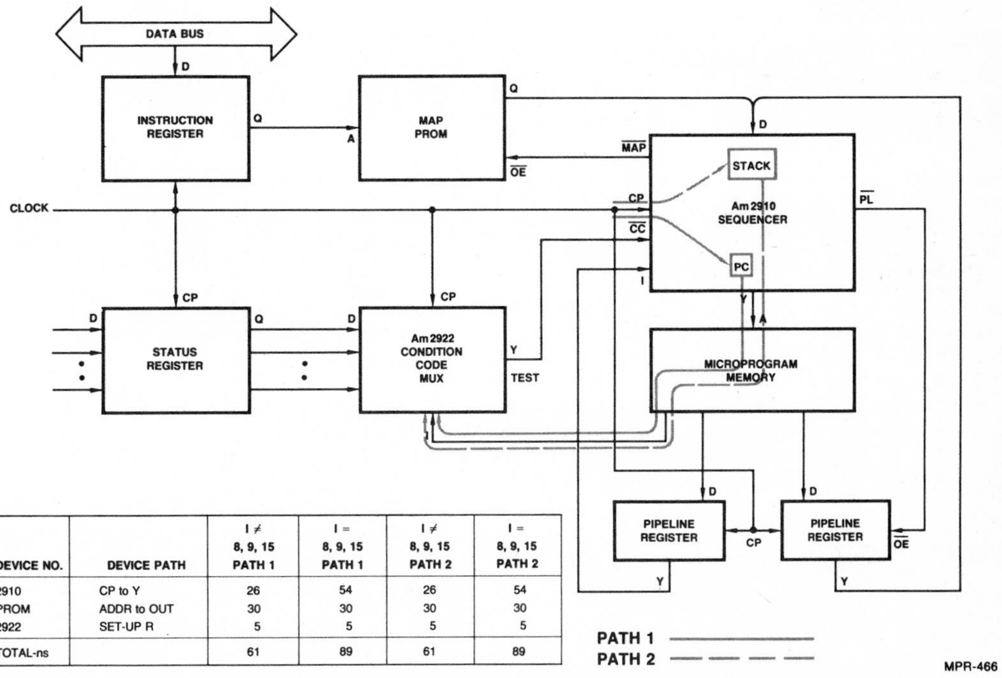

DEVICE NO.	DEVICE PATH	I ≠ 8, 9, 15 PATH 1	I = 8, 9, 15 PATH 1	I ≠ 8, 9, 15 PATH 2	I = 8, 9, 15 PATH 2
2910	CP to Y	26	54	26	54
PROM	ADDR to OUT	30	30	30	30
2922	SET-UP R	5	5	5	5
TOTAL-ns		61	89	61	89

Figure 7. Propagation Delay Calculations on the Am2910 Microprogram Sequencer (Cont.).

a)

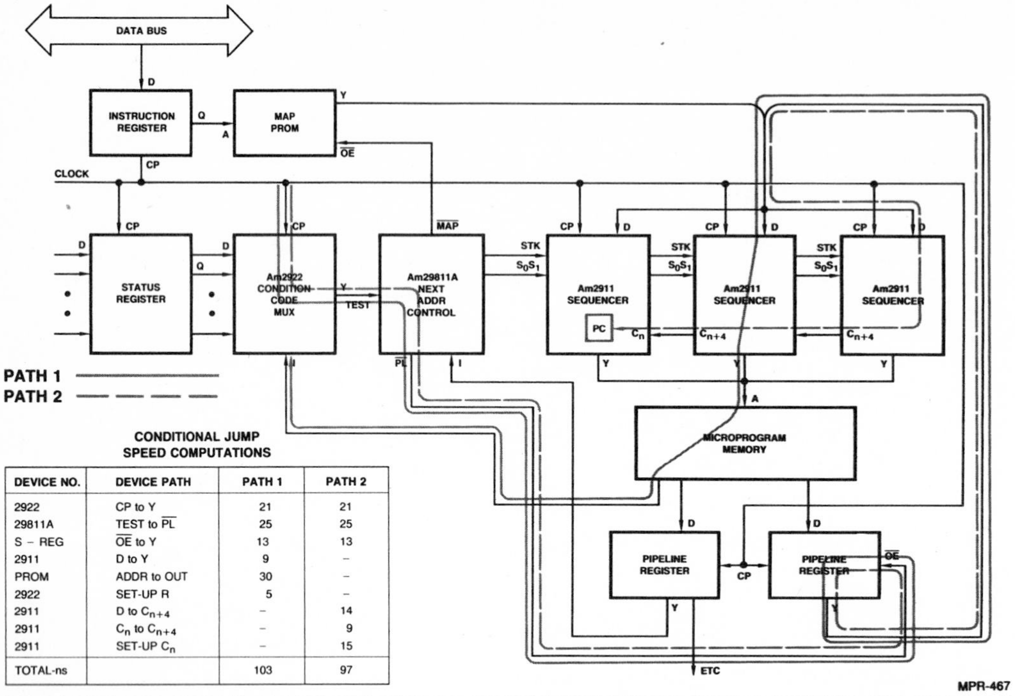

CONDITIONAL JUMP SPEED COMPUTATIONS

DEVICE NO.	DEVICE PATH	PATH 1	PATH 2
2922	CP to Y	21	21
29811A	TEST to $\overline{PL}$	25	25
S – REG	$\overline{OE}$ to Y	13	13
2911	D to Y	9	–
PROM	ADDR to OUT	30	–
2922	SET-UP R	5	–
2911	D to C_{n+4}	–	14
2911	C_n to C_{n+4}	–	9
2911	SET-UP C_n	–	15
TOTAL-ns		103	97

b)

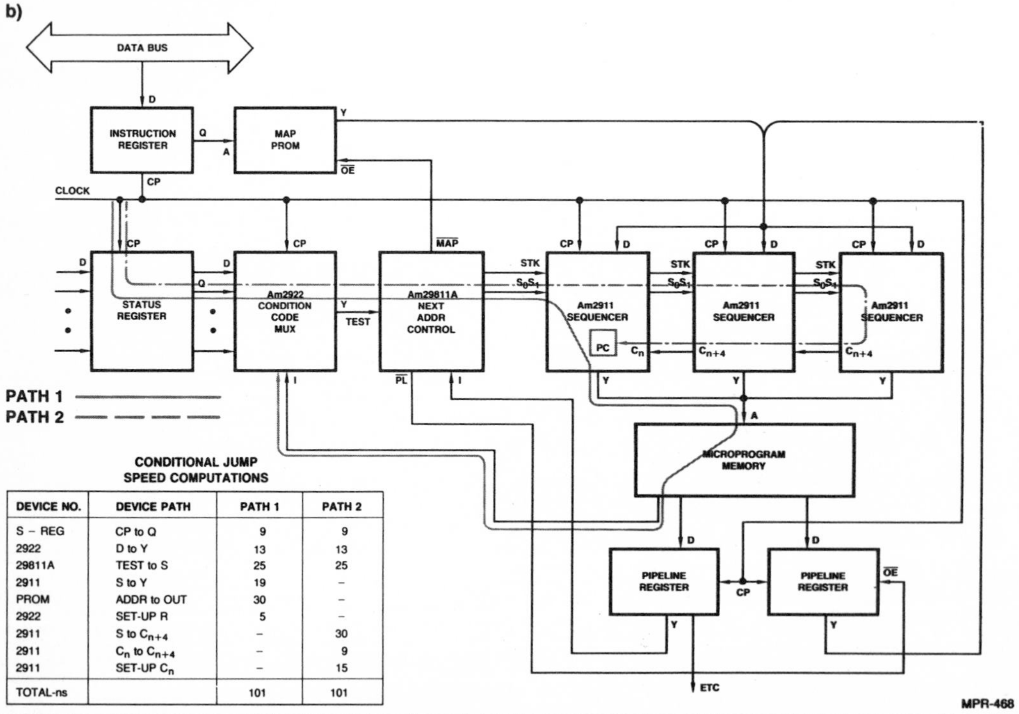

CONDITIONAL JUMP SPEED COMPUTATIONS

DEVICE NO.	DEVICE PATH	PATH 1	PATH 2
S – REG	CP to Q	9	9
2922	D to Y	13	13
29811A	TEST to S	25	25
2911	S to Y	19	–
PROM	ADDR to OUT	30	–
2922	SET-UP R	5	–
2911	S to C_{n+4}	–	30
2911	C_n to C_{n+4}	–	9
2911	SET-UP C_n	–	15
TOTAL-ns		101	101

Figure 8. Propagation Delay Calculations for the Am2911 and Am29811A Design.

c)

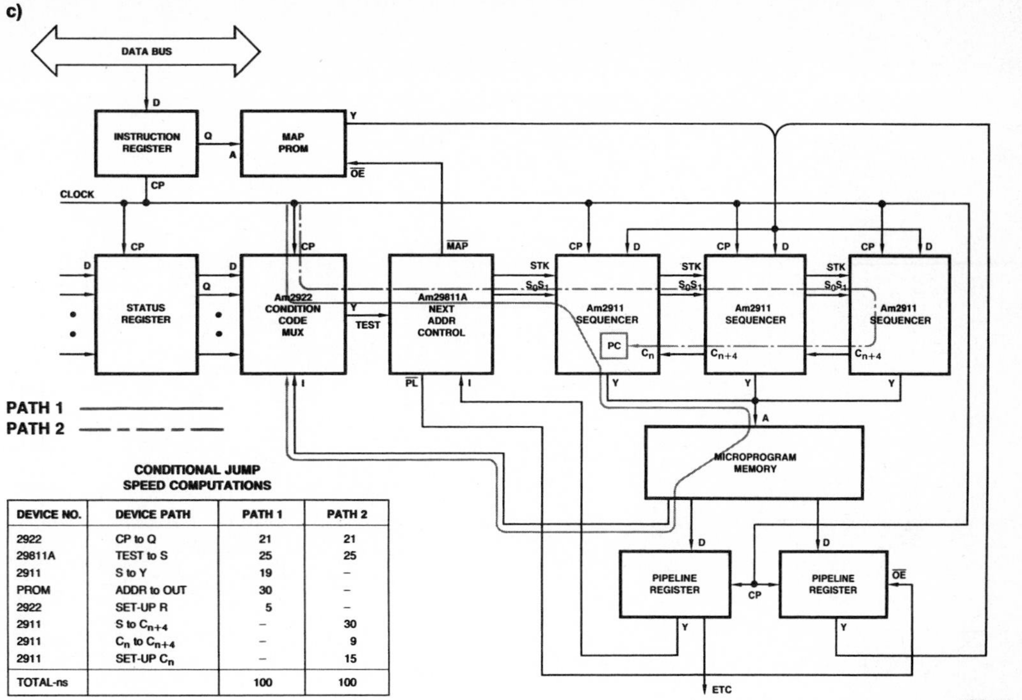

CONDITIONAL JUMP SPEED COMPUTATIONS

DEVICE NO.	DEVICE PATH	PATH 1	PATH 2
2922	CP to Q	21	21
29811A	TEST to S	25	25
2911	S to Y	19	–
PROM	ADDR to OUT	30	–
2922	SET-UP R	5	–
2911	S to C_{n+4}	–	30
2911	C_n to C_{n+4}	–	9
2911	SET-UP C_n	–	15
TOTAL-ns		100	100

MPR-469

d)

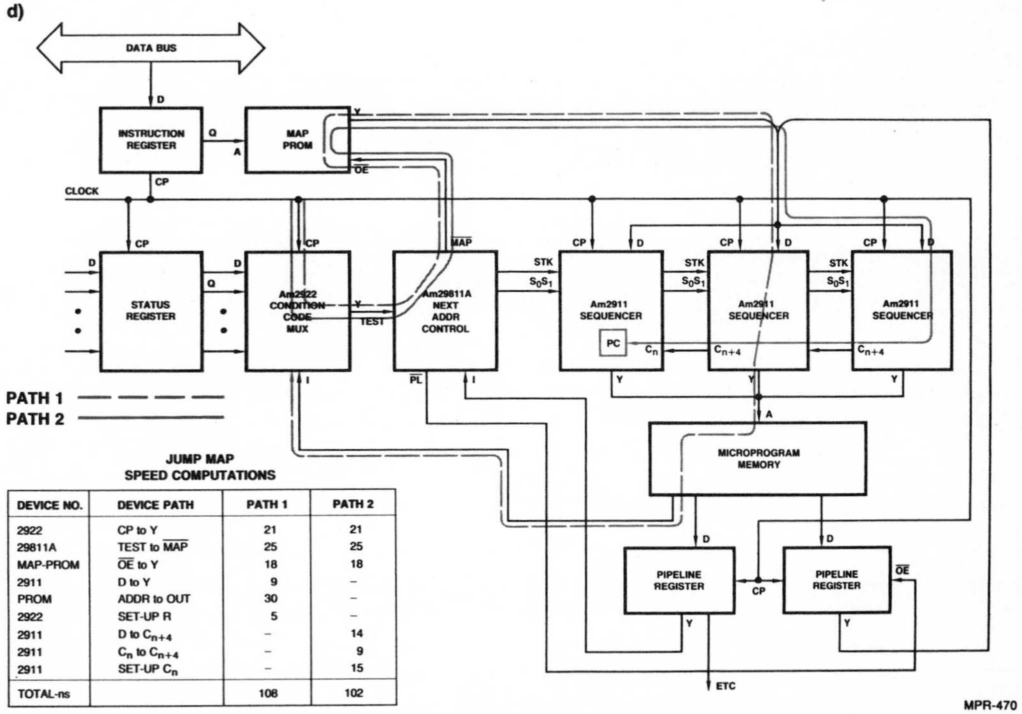

JUMP MAP SPEED COMPUTATIONS

DEVICE NO.	DEVICE PATH	PATH 1	PATH 2
2922	CP to Y	21	21
29811A	TEST to $\overline{MAP}$	25	25
MAP-PROM	$\overline{OE}$ to Y	18	18
2911	D to Y	9	–
PROM	ADDR to OUT	30	–
2922	SET-UP R	5	–
2911	D to C_{n+4}	–	14
2911	C_n to C_{n+4}	–	9
2911	SET-UP C_n	–	15
TOTAL-ns		108	102

MPR-470

Figure 8. Propagation Delay Calculations for the Am2911 and Am29811A Design (Cont.).

e)

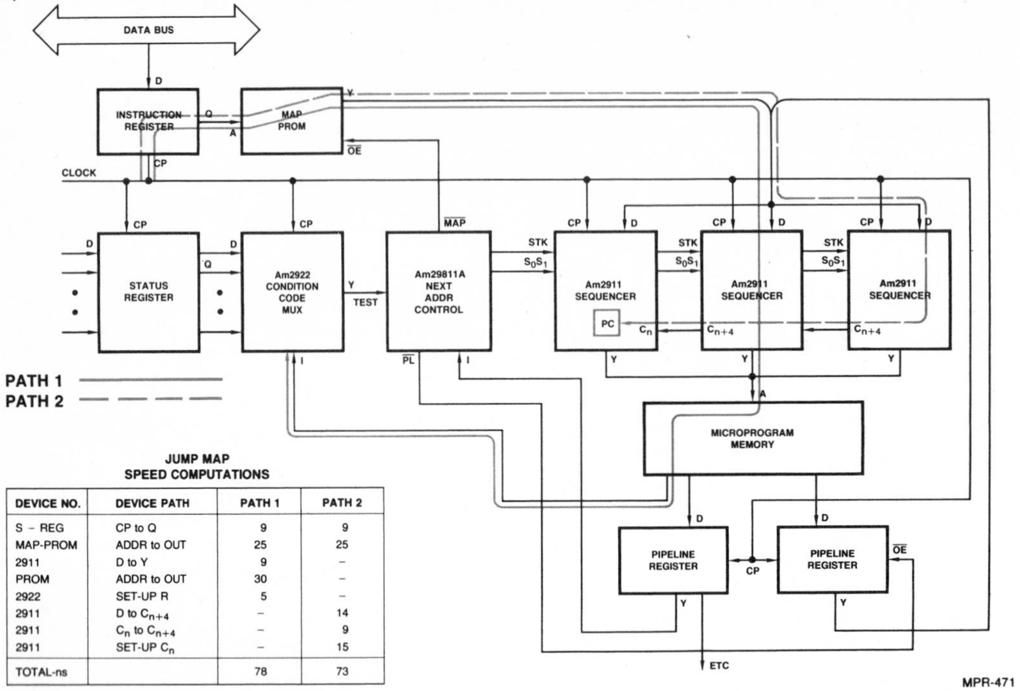

JUMP MAP
SPEED COMPUTATIONS

DEVICE NO.	DEVICE PATH	PATH 1	PATH 2
S – REG	CP to Q	9	9
MAP-PROM	ADDR to OUT	25	25
2911	D to Y	9	–
PROM	ADDR to OUT	30	–
2922	SET-UP R	5	–
2911	D to C_{n+4}	–	14
2911	C_n to C_{n+4}	–	9
2911	SET-UP C_n	–	15
TOTAL-ns		78	73

MPR-471

f)

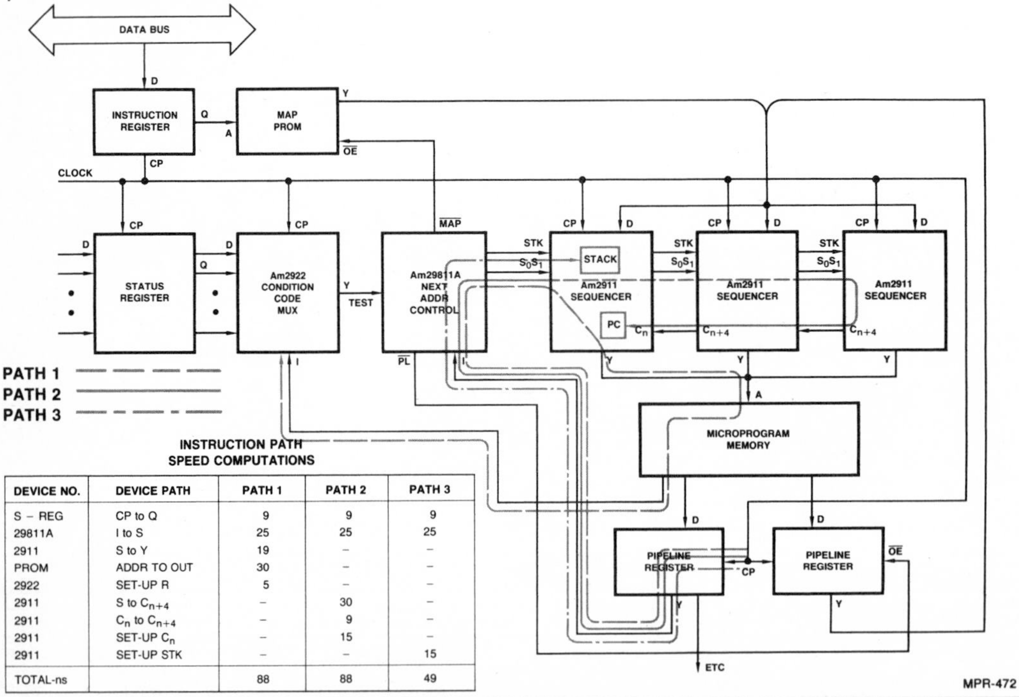

INSTRUCTION PATH
SPEED COMPUTATIONS

DEVICE NO.	DEVICE PATH	PATH 1	PATH 2	PATH 3
S – REG	CP to Q	9	9	9
29811A	I to S	25	25	25
2911	S to Y	19	–	–
PROM	ADDR TO OUT	30	–	–
2922	SET-UP R	5	–	–
2911	S to C_{n+4}	–	30	–
2911	C_n to C_{n+4}	–	9	–
2911	SET-UP C_n	–	15	–
2911	SET-UP STK	–	–	15
TOTAL-ns		88	88	49

MPR-472

Figure 8. Propagation Delay Calculations for the Am2911 and Am29811A Design (Cont.).

g)

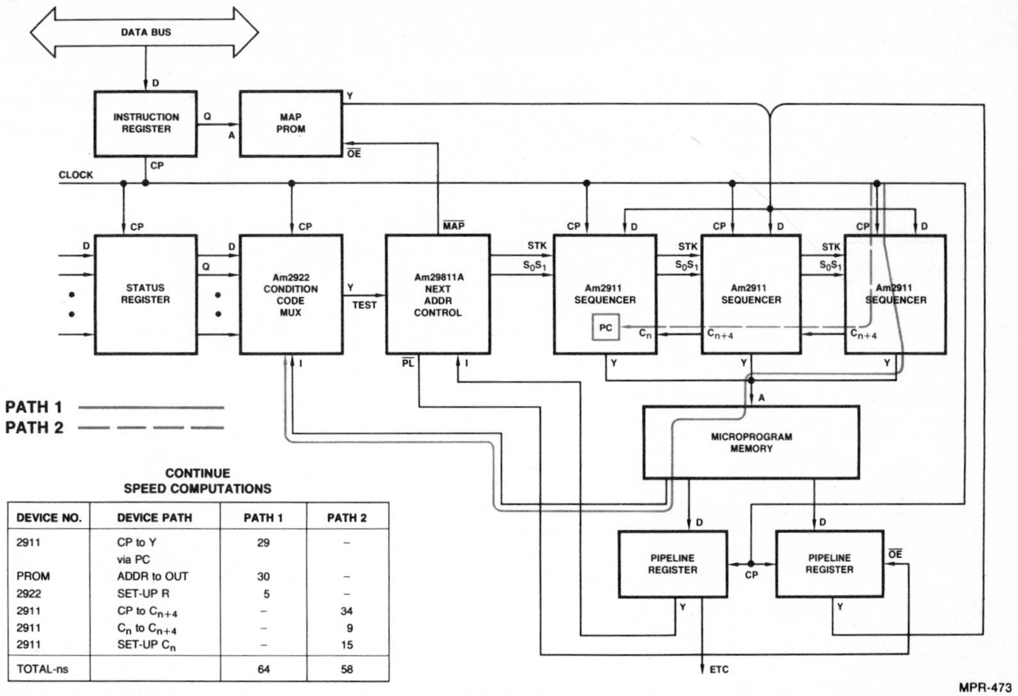

CONTINUE
SPEED COMPUTATIONS

DEVICE NO.	DEVICE PATH	PATH 1	PATH 2
2911	CP to Y via PC	29	–
PROM	ADDR to OUT	30	–
2922	SET-UP R	5	–
2911	CP to C_{n+4}	–	34
2911	C_n to C_{n+4}	–	9
2911	SET-UP C_n	–	15
TOTAL-ns		64	58

h)

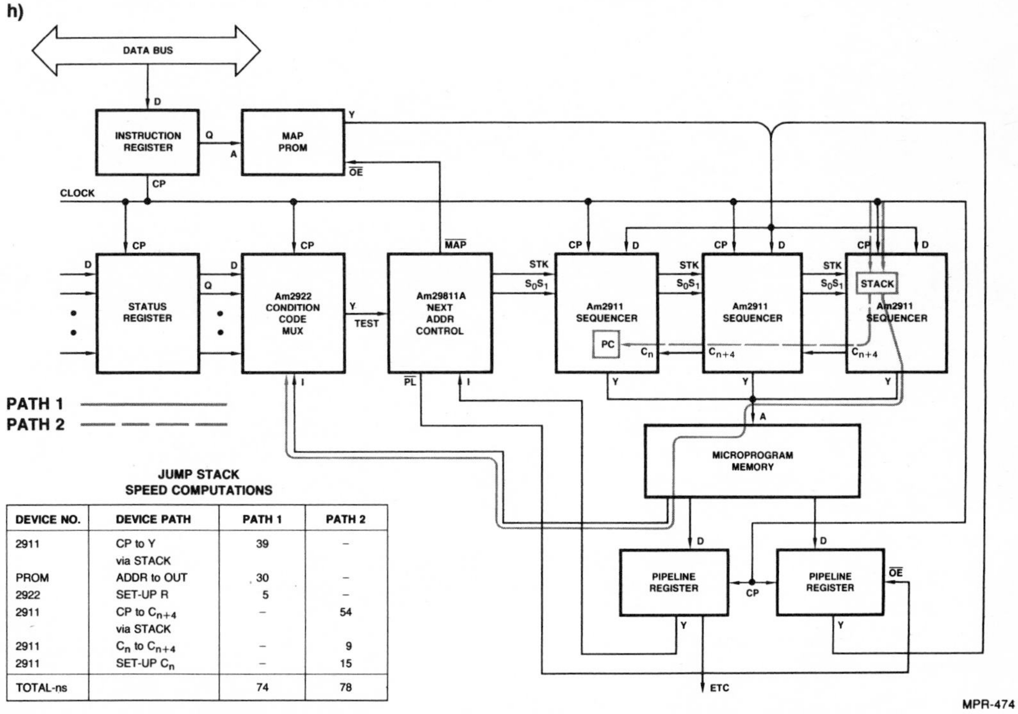

JUMP STACK
SPEED COMPUTATIONS

DEVICE NO.	DEVICE PATH	PATH 1	PATH 2
2911	CP to Y via STACK	39	–
PROM	ADDR to OUT	30	–
2922	SET-UP R	5	–
2911	CP to C_{n+4} via STACK	–	54
2911	C_n to C_{n+4}	–	9
2911	SET-UP C_n	–	15
TOTAL-ns		74	78

Figure 8. Propagation Delay Calculations for the Am2911 and Am29811A Design (Cont.).

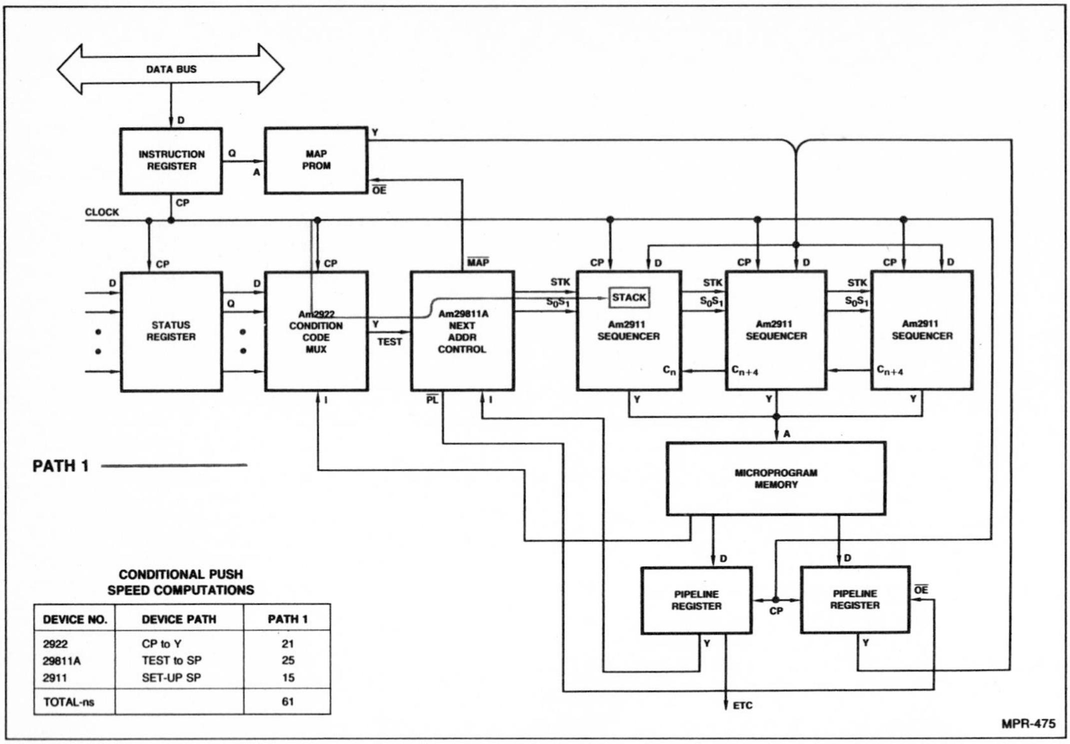

CONDITIONAL PUSH
SPEED COMPUTATIONS

DEVICE NO.	DEVICE PATH	PATH 1
2922	CP to Y	21
29811A	TEST to SP	25
2911	SET-UP SP	15
TOTAL-ns		61

Figure 8. Propagation Delay Calculations for the Am2911 and Am29811A Design (Cont.).

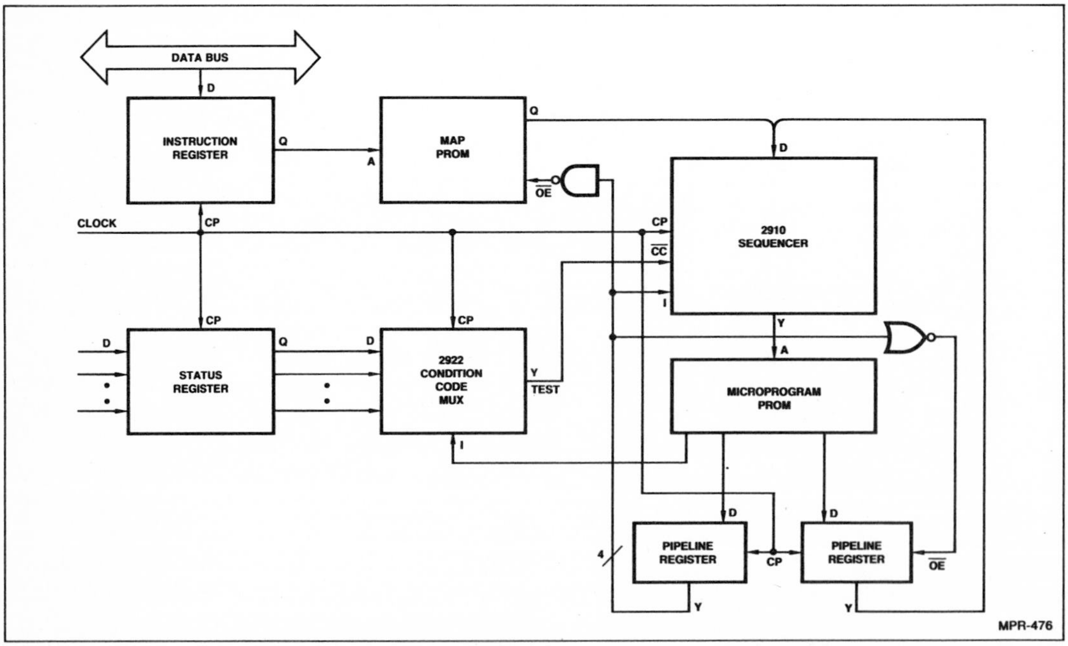

Figure 9. Using NAND and NOR Gates to Improve Am2910 Speed.

In order to compare the performance of the Am2910 with the Am2911 and Am29811A, Table 5 is presented. Here the propagation delays for the Am2911 and Am29811A are for a 12-bit wide microprogram sequencer configuration. If a wider configuration is used, only one additional carry input to carry output delay must be added to the appropriate paths of these calculations. A 12-bit wide Am2911/29811A configuration has been evaluated so that an "apples to apples" comparison can be made.

As is shown in Table 5, a number of combinations are possible for the longest AC propagation delay paths for these microprogram sequencers. First, the continue instruction can be executed the fastest of any of the microprogram instructions if the continues are sequential. That is, from the second continue on, the typical microcycle can be either 61 or 64ns respectively. To achieve this speed, it is required that various signals throughout the architecture be stable such that the only paths that enter into the propagation delay calculation are the clock-to-output of the microprogram counter, the microprogram memory and the pipeline register setup.

The second group of instructions shown in Table 5 show some examples of instruction execution and jumping. These examples assume that the $\overline{\text{MAP}}$ and $\overline{\text{OE}}$ outputs are not used as described earlier. These calculations apply to several of the instructions but not to all the instructions. For the Am2910 sequencer all of the propagation delays are around 80 to 85ns; while for the Am2911/Am29811A combination, the propagation delays range from about 80ns to 100ns, depending on the instruction. It should be noted that certain other instructions such as push and conditional load counter should be evaluated to determine the speed at which they can be executed.

The last two instructions shown in Table 5 are for jumps where the output enable of the field supplying the address to the D inputs of the microprogram sequencers are controlled by either the Am2910 or Am29811A. Notice that for Am2910 configuration, the jump map represents the longest propagation delay path and is 103ns typical. Also, for the Am2911/Am29811A combination, the jump map instruction also represents the longest propagation delay path and is 109ns typical.

It is not the purpose of this exercise to show every possible propagation delay path; but rather, to show the reader the technique for computing propagation delays such that any design can be evaluated and the worst case past derived. Even here, not all of the worst case numbers shown in Table 5 have been derived in Figures 7 and 8. This was done intentionally and is left as an exercise for the student.

If the Am2909 or Am2911 and the Am29811A are combined into microprogram sequencers of either 8 bits in width or 16 bits in width, the calculations need only be modified slightly to determine the microcycle times. Obviously, if two Am2911s are used, the worst case propagation delay paths do not change. However, if four Am2911s are used, the carry path will become the longer propagation delay path on several of the computations. This may be offset however since larger microprogram PROMs may be used if 64K of microcode is actually being addressed or high power buffers may be placed between the Am2911 outputs and the microprogram memory to provide sufficient drive for such a large microprogram store.

In addition, the Am2909 and Am2911 may be used without the Am29811A where the user wishes to generate a special purpose instruction set or very high speed control of the internal multiplexer and push pop stack. In some, designs as much as 25 to 30ns, typical, can be removed from the longest propagation delay paths of the design by using high speed Schottky SSI. While this has not been the typical case, some designers have used it to provide a performance improvement not achievable with a standard Schottky condition code multiplexer and the Am29811A next address control unit.

APPLICATIONS

It should be understood that the microprogram state machine built using either the Am2910 or the Am2911/29811A represents a general purpose state machine controller. Applications for this type of microprogrammed control include uses in minicomputers, communications, instrumentation, controllers and peripherals as well as special purpose processors. Typically, the microprogrammed approach provides a more structured organization to the design and allows the design engineer the greatest flexibility in implementation.

It is important to understand that microprogrammed machines need not be part of a typical minicomputer type structure. That is, a general purpose minicomputer usually has a machine instruction set that is totally different from its microprogram instruction control. As such, it is essential that the designer new to computer design and microprogram design understand the difference between a machine instruction and a microprogram instruction. This differentiation is shown in Figure 10 where a typical 16-bit machine level instruction is demonstrated as compared with a typical microprogram instruction. The machine level instruction usually consists of 16 bits and in this example, these bits are used to provide the op code, source register definition and destination register definition. The microprogram instruction on the other hand usually consists of anywhere from 32 to 128 bits in a typical minicomputer type design. Here, the bits are used to control the elemental functions of a machine such as the Am2910 instruction control and condition code multiplexer, the Am2903 source, ALU function and destination control and so forth. For purposes of this explanation, let us assume that the machine level instruction is available to the machine programmer while the microprogram

TABLE 5. SUMMARY OF LONGEST AC PATHS FOR MICROPROGRAM SEQUENCERS.

Instruction	Am2910	Am2911 Am29811A	Comments
Continue	61	64	The fastest instruction. Assumes sequential continues!
Instruction Execute	84	88	If the $\overline{\text{MAP}}$ and $\overline{\text{PL}}$ outputs are not used.
Jump Map (no $\overline{\text{OE}}$)	83	78	
Jump PL (No $\overline{\text{OE}}$)	78	101	
Jump Map (via $\overline{\text{OE}}$)	103	109	If the $\overline{\text{MAP}}$ and $\overline{\text{PL}}$ outputs are used.
Jump PL (via $\overline{\text{OE}}$)	98	104	

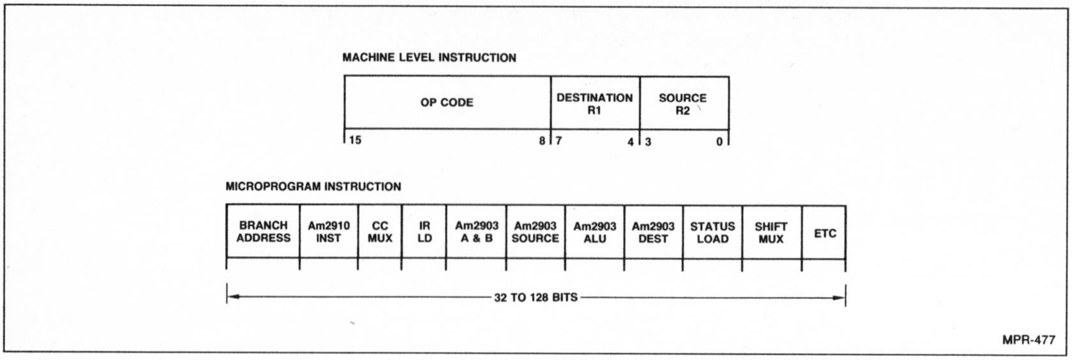

Figure 10. Understanding Machine and Microprogram Instructions.

instruction is not available to the machine programmer at the assembly language level. Let it suffice to say that this assumption is not necessarily valid in machines being designed today.

Perhaps one of the most typical applications of the microprogrammed computer control unit state machine design is as the controller for a minicomputer. Here, the function of the microprogrammed controller is to fetch and execute machine level instructions. The flow required to perform this function is depicted in Figure 11 which should be representative for all general purpose type machines. Figure 11 shows that after initialization, the computer control unit simply fetches machine instructions, decodes these instructions and then fetches the required operands such that the original instruction can be executed. This cycle of fetching and executing instructions is performed without end. Such things as hardware halts or resets are ignored and should be assumed to only cause re-initialization.

Once the flow of a typical computer control unit is understood, it is possible to evaluate a number of architectures using the Am2910 or Am2911/Am29811A such that the flow diagram of Figure 11 can be implemented.

STATE MACHINE ARCHITECTURES

After a machine instruction is fetched from memory, it is normally placed in the machine instruction register as described in Figure 6. Then the op code portion of the instruction is decoded so that a sequence of microinstructions in the microprogram memory can be selected for execution. Each microinstruction is fetched and its contents placed in the pipeline register as shown in Figure 6 for execution.

While the architecture of Figure 6 is recommended and has been used throughout the preceding portion of this chapter, it should be understood that a number of architectures are possible using these microprogram sequencers. The normal flow in fetching microinstructions is to determine the address of the next microinstruction, fetch the contents at that address and set up this data at the input of the pipeline register such that it can be clocked into the pipeline register for execution. If we assume that a clock is being used to clock the pipeline register, the Am2910, the machine instruction register and the Am2903 microprocessor bit slices, it is possible to define a number of computer control unit designs where the relationship between the clock edges is different.

There seem to be a minimum of seven different architectures that can be defined based on placing registers in the appropriate signal paths and storing data on the low-to-high transition of the

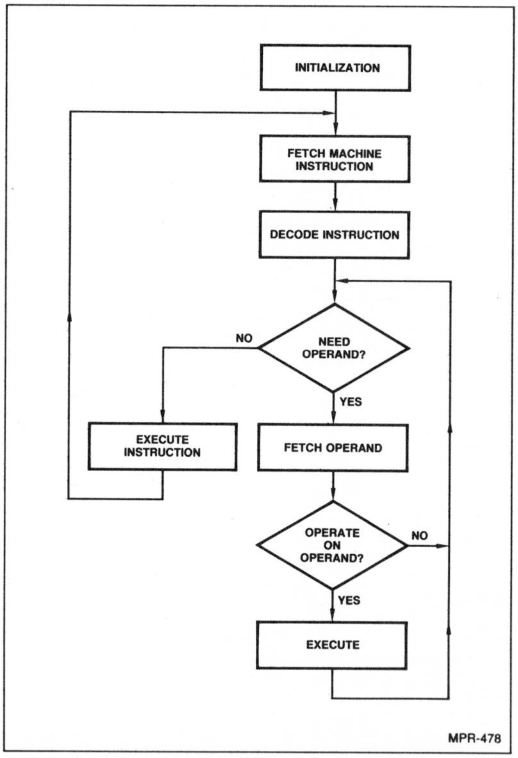

Figure 11. Computer Control Flow Diagram.

clock. For purposes of this discussion, we will assume that all clocked devices will operate using the same clock such that changes will occur on the LOW-to-HIGH transition of the clock. While it is possible to use multiphase clocks and tie different clock phases to different devices, that type of system operation will not be described here. In all cases, we will be talking about the flow of signals between LOW-to-HIGH transitions of the clock. Typically, a cycle is started by a clock edge at a device and the signals begin to flow from one device to the next until a set-up time to a clock edge results. Then, the next microinstruction is executed in exactly the same manner. There are three different identifiable types of microinstruction sequences where only one register is in the signal flow loop. The first of these we shall call an Address-Based microinstruction cycle. It usually starts with the address of a microprogram memory word being stored in a register by the clock. This address has been determined by the previous microinstruction. This address then accesses the microprogram memory to fetch its contents which are presented at its outputs to control the Arithmetic Logic Unit and the results of the Arithmetic Logic Unit function may be used to determine the next address selected that will be stored in this microprogram address register. This is shown as Figure 12a. The second type of microprogram architecture is called Instruction-Based. Here, the register is placed at the output of the microprogram memory as shown in Figure 12b. Again, the cycle consists of executing the microinstruction in the ALU; perhaps using the results of the operation to determine the address of the next microinstruction and then fetching the contents of that microinstruction and setting this new data up at the input to the register. The third basic architecture for microprogram control is called Data-Based. Here, a register is used to hold the status data from the ALU and this is the determining clock point for the cycle. Here, the status register initiates the selection of the next address from which the microprogrammed data is fetched and this microprogram instruction is used to execute a new function in the ALU thereby setting up the results for the status register. This scheme is shown in Figure 12c. Note that this scheme requires an additional register at the output of the microprogram memory to hold a portion of the microprogram instruction for controlling the condition code multiplexer and Am2910 instruction set. These primitive architectures for microprogrammed control demonstrate the three points at which a register can be placed to provide a start and an end for the microcycle. In a general sense, each of these three architectures is one level pipelined. This, however, is not the definition normally associated with pipelining of microprogram control.

If combinations of the above described architectures are implemented, an improvement in performance will be realized. In each of the three architectures thus described (address-based, instruction-based, and data-based), all of the signal paths are in series and must be transcended before a microcycle can be completed. They are quite easy to program, however, since all of the tasks are completed in the loop before proceeding to the next microinstruction. As stated earlier, these tend to be the slowest of the possible architectures for microprogram control. This disadvantage can be overcome by using a technique referred to as pipelining in microprogram control. In a pipeline architecture, we overlap the fetch of the next microinstruction while we are executing the current microinstruction. This is achieved by inserting additional registers in the overall path such that we can hold the signals step-by-step. There are three possible combinations of the above mentioned architectures that can be utilized in microprogram control. These are address-instruction-based, address-data-based, and instruction-data-based. While each of these represent two stages of pipelining, we normally refer to these as the pipelined architectures. These are shown in Figure 12d, 12e and 12f. It is the instruction-data based architecture that is recommended for the Am2910 and provides the overall best trade-off in cost versus performance.

The last possible architecture using registers in the signal path is a combination of all three architectures and is called address-instruction-data-based microprogram control and is shown in Figure 12g. Here, three stages of pipeline are involved and we normally refer to this as two-level pipelined archiecture. Needless to say, if no pipelining were involved at all, we would have a ring oscillator.

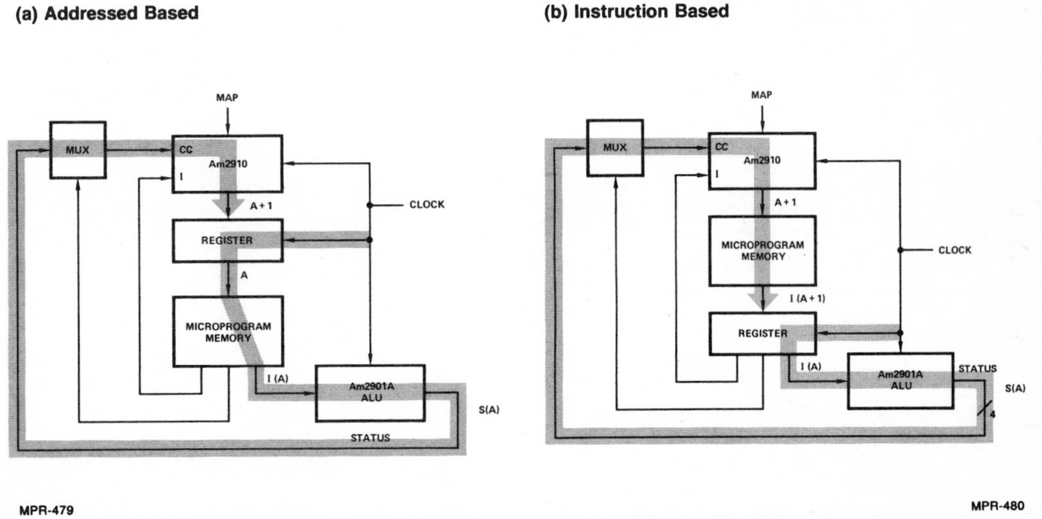

Shaded Lines Show Required Signal Flow to Complete a Microcycle: Determine Address, Fetch Instruction and Execute.

Figure 12. Standard Microprogram Control Architectures.

(c) Data Based

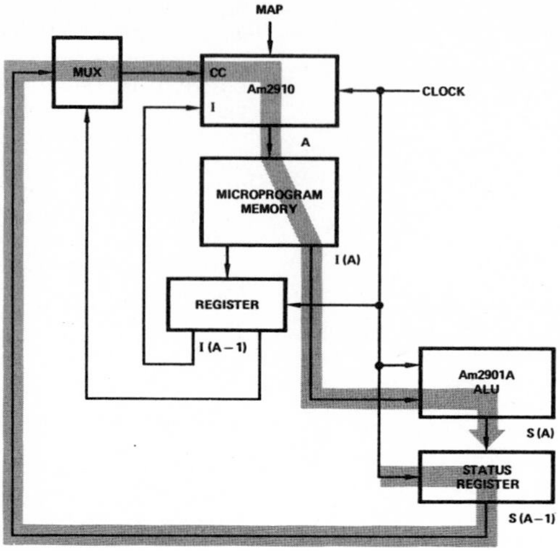

MPR-481

(d) Instruction-Data Based

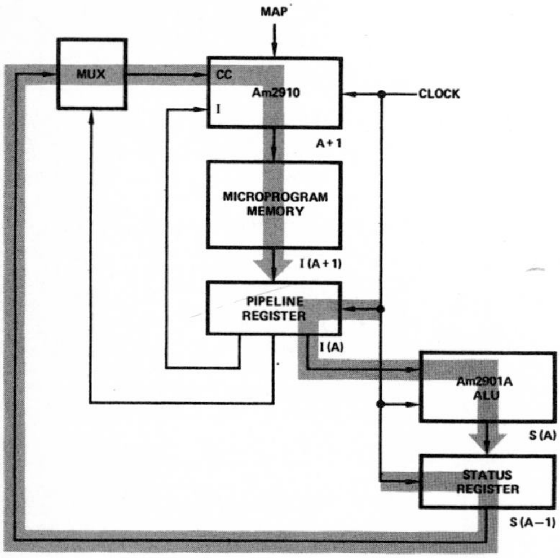

MPR-482

(e) Instruction-Address Based

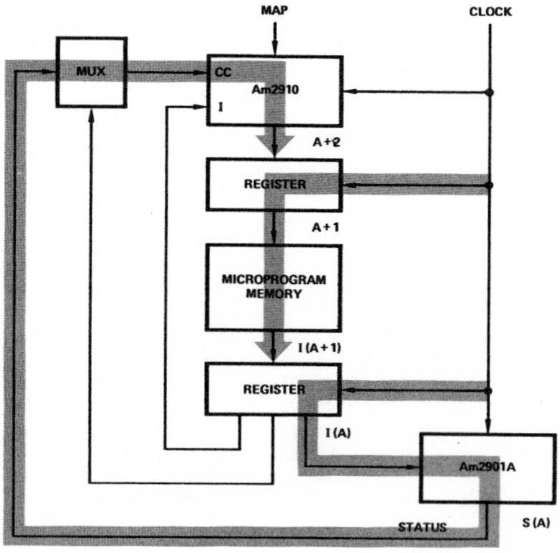

MPR-483

Shaded Lines Show Required Signal Flow to Complete a Microcycle: Determine Address, Fetch Instruction and Execute.

Figure 12. Standard Microprogram Control Architectures (Cont.).

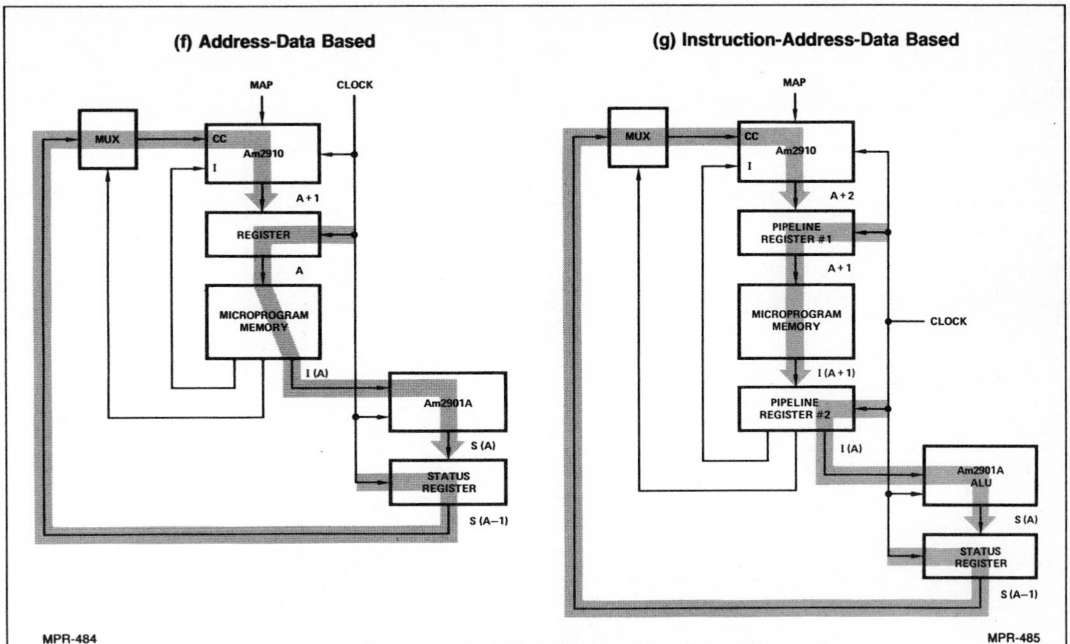

Shaded Lines Show Required Signal Flow to Complete a Microcycle: Determine Address, Fetch Instruction and Execute.

Figure 12. Standard Microprogram Control Architectures (Cont.).

The advantage of the instruction-data-based architecture is that the address and contents of the next microinstruction are being fetched while the current microinstruction in the pipeline register (Figure 6) is being executed. This allows a shorter microcycle since the microprogram memory fetch and ALU execution can be operated in parallel. The results of this type operation are demonstrated in Figure 13 where we see a typical timing diagram of the microprogram execution of the address-data-based instruction architecture. It should be noted that when the computational aspects of a microinstruction are not completed in the same microcycle, they obviously cannot be used to determine the address of another microcycle until the computation has been completed and stored in the status register. Thus, this pipelined architecture offers significant speed improvement except in the case of certain conditional jumps. In other words, the conditional jump may not use the status register information of the immediately preceding microinstruction because the computation is just being performed. For this architecture, the conditional jump fetch must be executed on the cycle after the status register contains the proper execution results. This can be seen by studying Figure 13. In most microprogram designs this is not a disadvantage because other housekeeping and ALU operations can be performed while the address of the next microinstruction is being determined using the current contents of the status register. While it is not directly pertinent to the discussion at this time, let us point out that the Am2904 has been designed such that the machine architect can utilize both instruction-data-based architecture as well as instruction-based architecture if no housekeeping is required. Thus, the Am2910 and Am2904 can be used in a variable architecture cycle to achieve maximum performance for the machine.

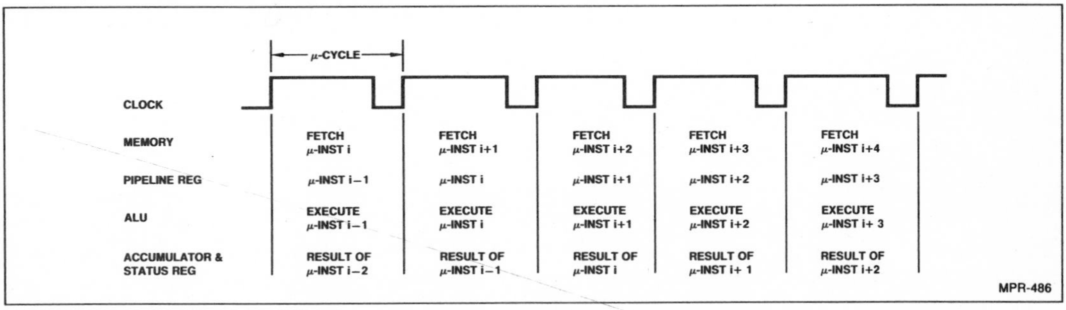

Figure 13. Timing Diagram of Microprogram Execution.

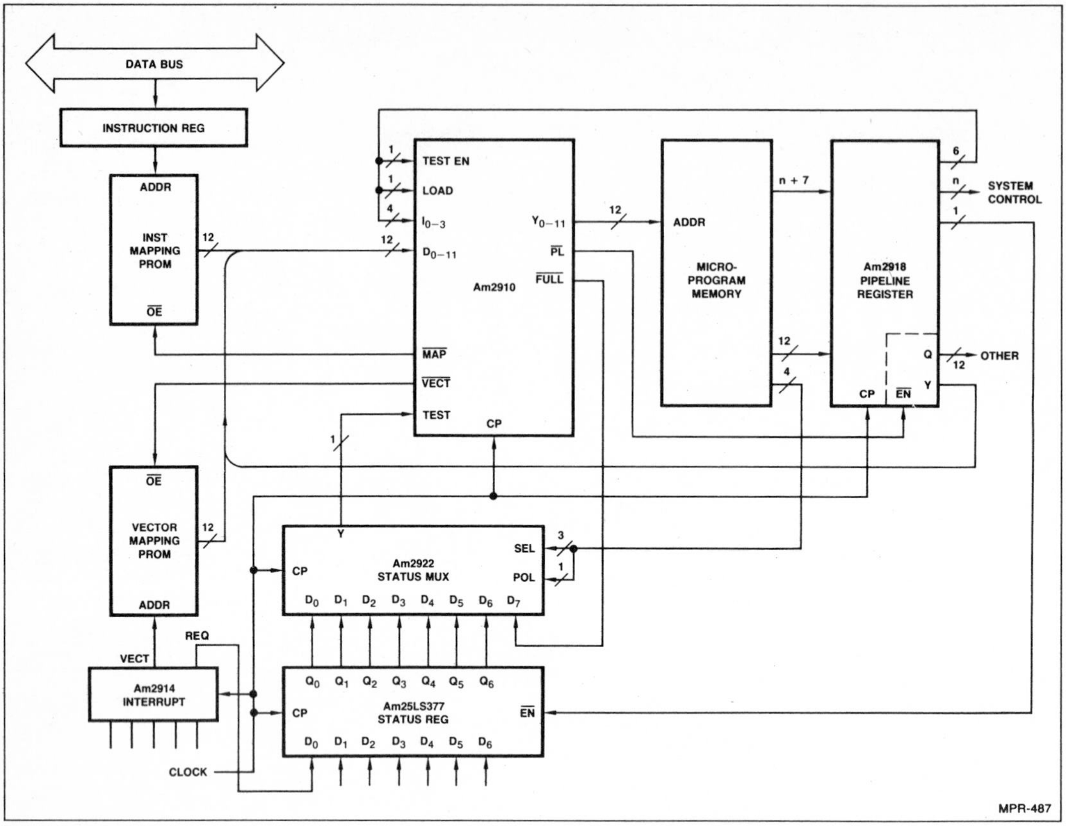

Figure 14. Typical Am2910 Microprogram Control Unit.

The Am2910 in Computer Control

A general state machine design using the Am2910 is shown in Figure 14. Here, all three output enables are used to advantage in order to control the mapping PROM, pipeline register and vector PROM in this design. This design is very straightforward and in fact is identical to that shown earlier.

One area that should not be overlooked is that of initializing the Am2910 at power up. One technique for accomplishing this is to use a pipeline register with a clear input to provide all LOWs to the instruction inputs of the Am2910. This will cause a reset of the stack in the Am2910 and force the outputs to the zero word and microcode which can be used for the initialization routine. Typically, power up will result in the firing of a timer which can be connected to the clear input of the register. Figure 15 shows the technique for initializing the Am2910 using this method.

One advantage of the Am2909 when compared to either the Am2910 or Am2911 is the OR inputs to the microprogram address field. These OR inputs allow two, four, eight or 16-way branching for each device if proper control is used. This control can be accomplished using the Am29803A, 16-way branch control unit. A typical computer control unit using the Am2909, Am2911, Am29803A and Am29811A is shown in Figure 16. In this example, the least significant microprogram control sequencer is an Am2909 and the two more significant sequencers are Am2911s.

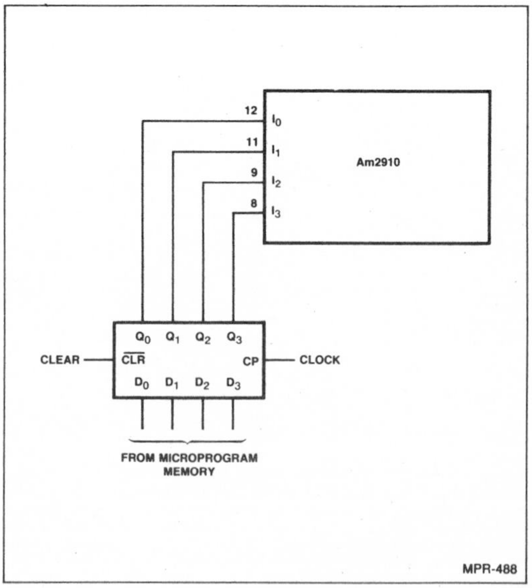

Figure 15. Initializing the Am2910.

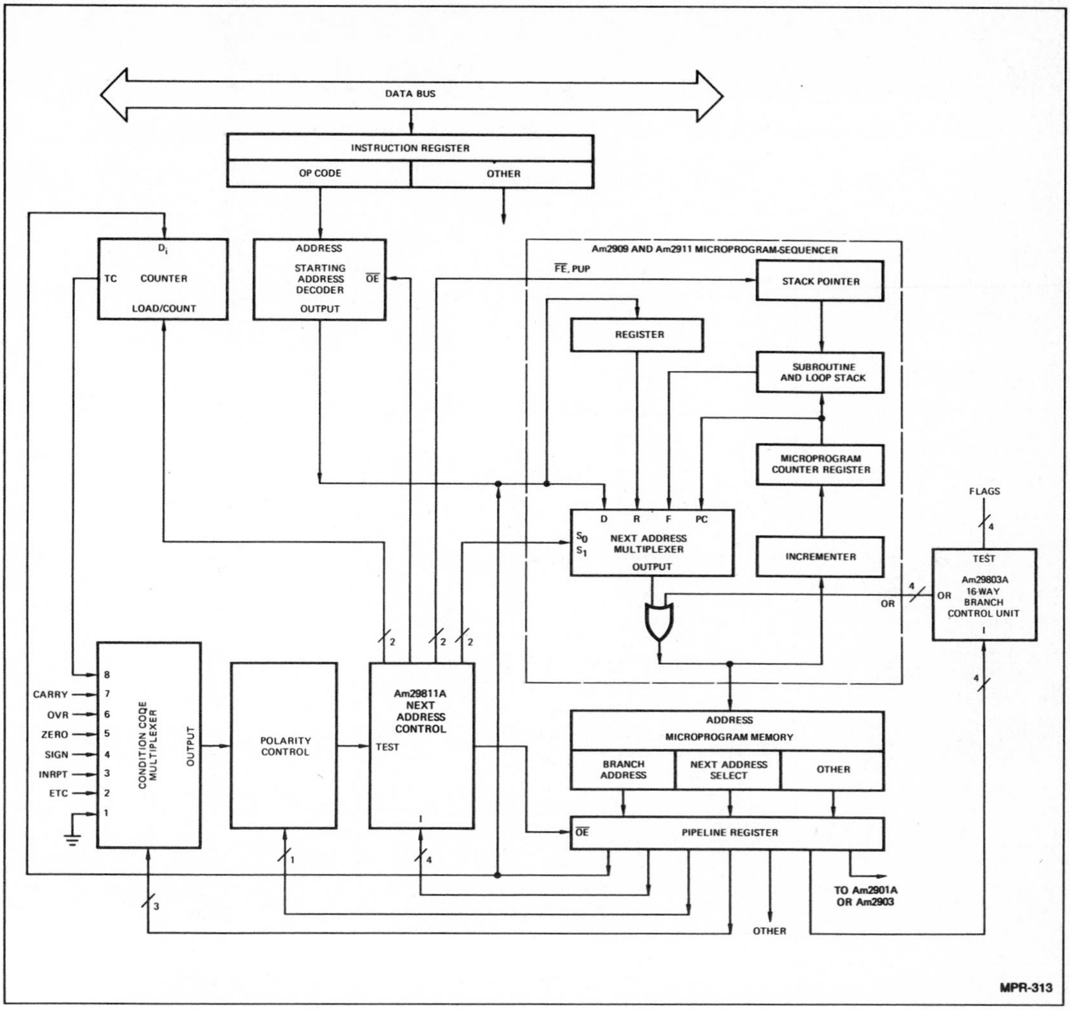

Figure 16. A High Performance Microprogram Controller Using the Am2909, Am29811A and Am29803A.

DETAILED DESCRIPTION OF THE Am2911 AND Am29811A IN A COMPUTER CONTROL UNIT

The detailed connection diagram of a straight-forward computer control unit is shown in Figure 17. This design features all of the next address control functions described previously and a few features have also been added.

Referring to Figure 17, the instruction register consists of two Am25LS377 Eight-Bit Registers with Clock Enable. These registers are designated as U1 and U2 and provide ability to selectively load a 16-bit instruction. This particular design assumes that the instruction word consists of an eight-bit op code as well as eight bits of other data. Therefore, the op code is decoded using three 256-word by 4-bit PROMs. The Am29761 has been selected for this function and is shown in Figure 17 as U3, U4 and U5.

The basic control function for the microprogram memory is provided by the Am2911s. In this design, three Am2911s (U6, U7, and U8) are used so that up to 4K words of microprogram memory can be addressed. The microprogram memory can consist of PROMs, ROMs, or RAMs, depending on the particular design and the point of its development. This particular design shows the capability of a 64-bit microword; however, the actual number of bits used will vary from design to design.

The pipeline register associated with the computer control unit consists of five integrated circuits designated U16, U17, U18, U19 and U20.

One of the features of the architecture depicted in Figure 17 is the event counter shown as U9, U10 and U11. This event counter consists of three Am25LS163s connected as a 12-bit counter. The counter can be parallel loaded with a 12-bit word from pipeline registers U18, U19 and U20. The multiplexer and D-type flip-flop (U21 and U22) at the counter overflow output (U9) is present to improve system cycle time and will be described in detail later.

Note: Figures 17, 18, 20, and 24 are at back of the book.

MULTIPLEXER SELECT

R_{20}	R_{19}	R_{18}	R_{17}	SELECT
0	0	0	0	TEST 0
0	0	0	1	TEST 1
0	0	1	0	TEST 2
•				•
•				•
•				•
1	1	1	1	TEST 15

POLARITY CONTROL

R_{16}	OUTPUT
0	COMPLEMENT OF TEST
1	TRUE TEST

NEXT ADDRESS CONTROL

R_{15}	R_{14}	R_{13}	R_{12}	FUNCTION
X	X	X	X	NEXT INSTRUCTION

MACHINE INSTRUCTION REGISTER

R_{21}	FUNCTION
0	LOAD
1	HOLD

CONTROL VALUE

R_{11}–R_0	FUNCTION
XXX---XXX	VALUE

JUMP ADDRESS

BR_{11}–BR_0	FUNCTION
XXX---XXX	JUMP ADDRESS

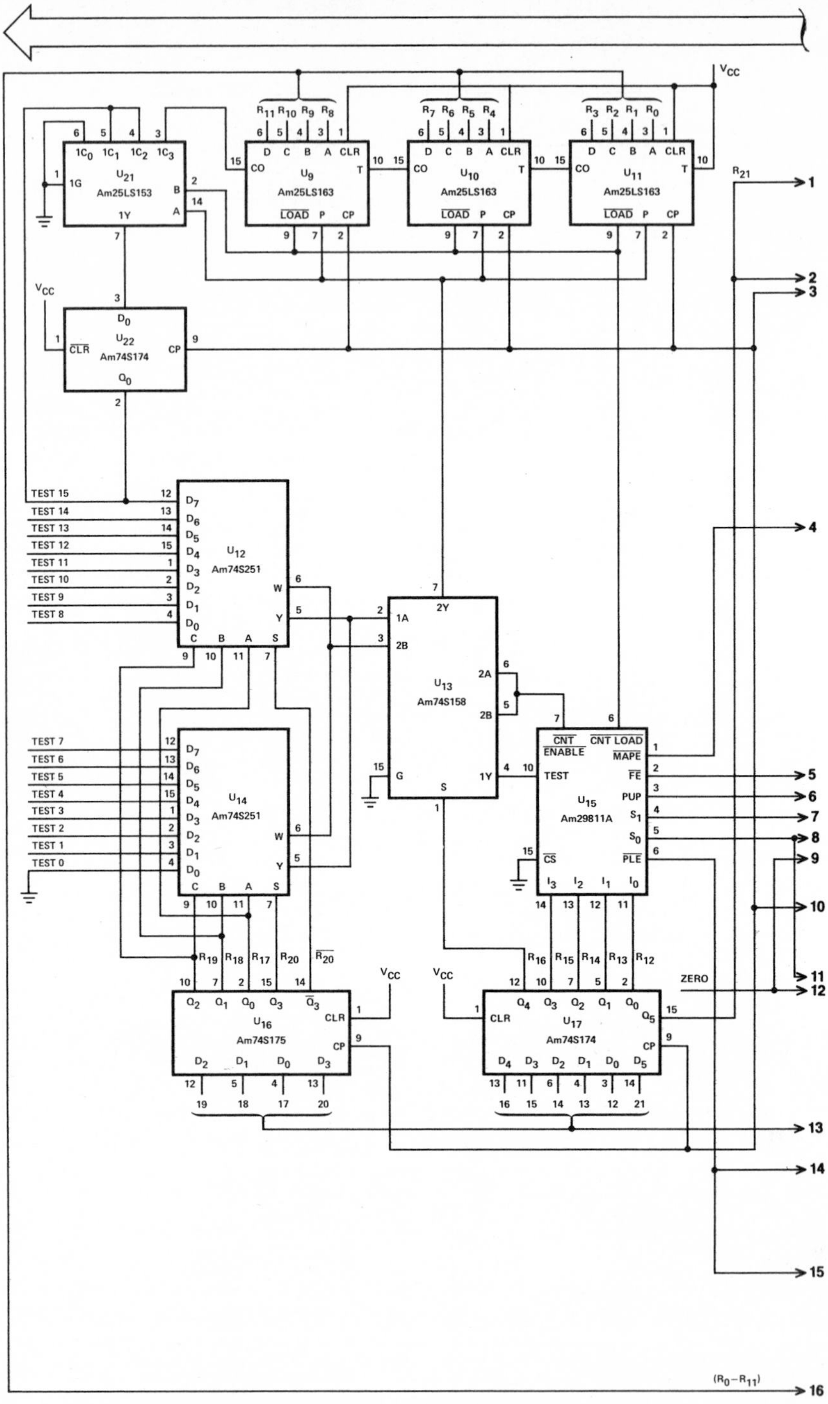

Figure 17. Computer Control Unit with Am2911.

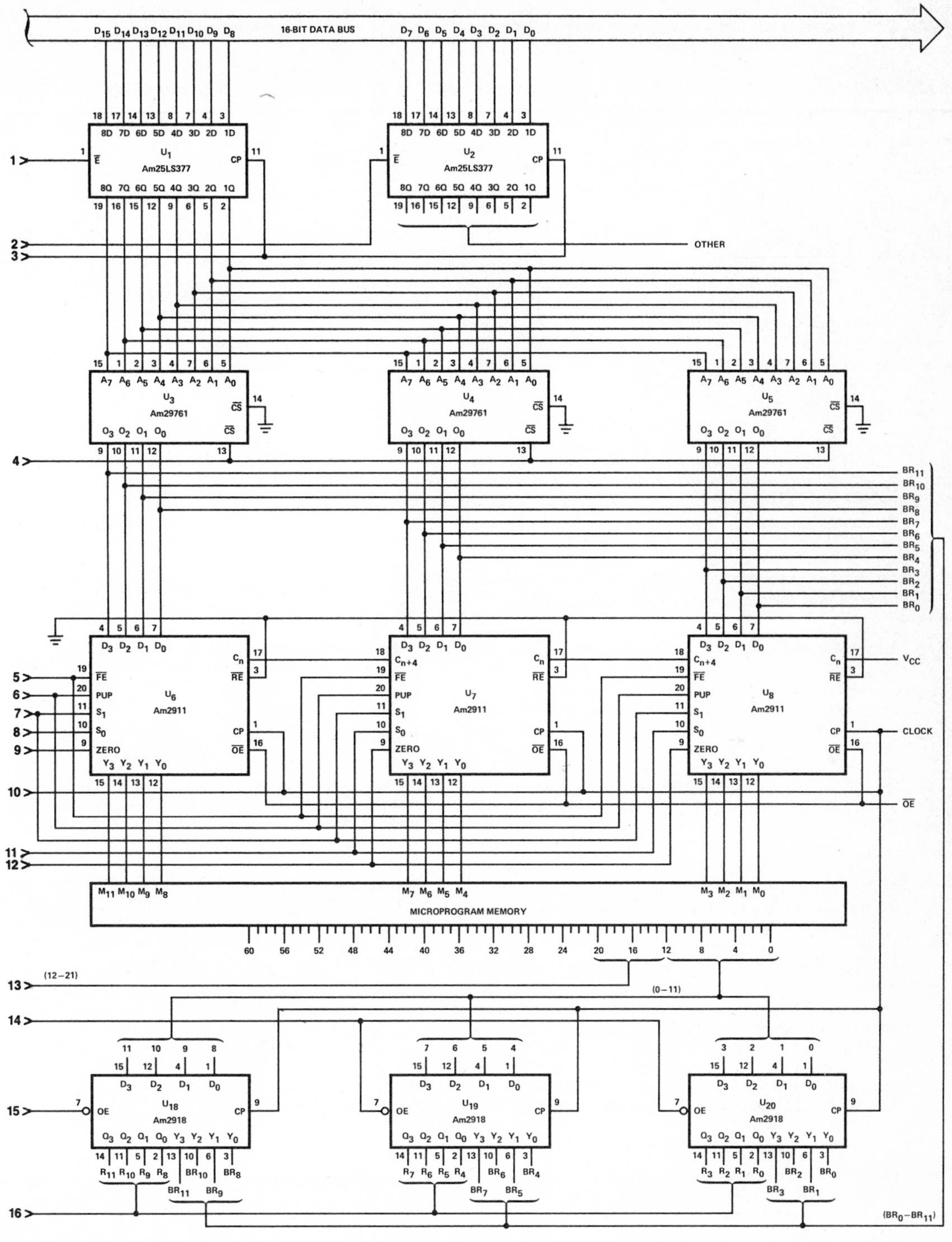
16-BIT DATA BUS
D_{15} D_{14} D_{13} D_{12} D_{11} D_{10} D_9 D_8
D_7 D_6 D_5 D_4 D_3 D_2 D_1 D_0
U_1
Am25LS377
U_2
Am25LS377
OTHER
U_3
Am29761
U_4
Am29761
U_5
Am29761
BR_{11} BR_{10} BR_9 BR_8 BR_7 BR_6 BR_5 BR_4 BR_3 BR_2 BR_1 BR_0
U_6
Am2911
U_7
Am2911
U_8
Am2911
V_{CC}
CLOCK
$\overline{OE}$
MICROPROGRAM MEMORY
M_{11} M_{10} M_9 M_8
M_7 M_6 M_5 M_4
M_3 M_2 M_1 M_0
60 56 52 48 44 40 36 32 28 24 20 16 12 8 4 0
(12–21)
(0–11)
U_{18}
Am2918
U_{19}
Am2918
U_{20}
Am2918
$(BR_0–BR_{11})$

This design also features a 16-input condition code multiplexer using two Am74S251s, which are designated U12 and U14. Condition code polarity control capability has been added to the design by using an Am74S158 Two-Input Multiplexer designated as U13. The W outputs and Y outputs from U12 and U14 have been connected together but only one set of outputs will be enabled at a time via the three-state control signal designated as R_{20} and $\overline{R_{20}}$. Since the Y output is inverting and the W output is non-inverting, the two-input multiplexer, U13, can be used to select the test condition as either inverting or non-inverting. This allows the test input on the Am29811A Next Address Control Unit, U15, to execute conditional instructions on either the inverted or non-inverted polarity of the test signal. For example, a CONDITIONAL BRANCH may be performed on either carry set or carry reset. Likewise, the same CONDITIONAL BRANCH might be performed on either the *sign* bit as a logic one or the *sign* bit as a logic zero. Note that the Am29811A Next Address Control Unit has eight outputs. Four outputs to control the Am2911's S_0, S_1, PUP and $\overline{FE}$ inputs. Two outputs to control the three-state enables of the devices connected to the D inputs, i.e., a map enable ($\overline{MAP\ E}$) to select the mapping PROMs and a pipeline enable ($\overline{PL\ E}$) to enable the three-state Am2918 outputs which make up a 12-bit wide branch address field. The remaining two Am29811A outputs are for loading and enabling the Am25LS163 counters. $\overline{\text{CNT ENABLE}}$ from the Am29811A is active-LOW while the Am25LS163 counter requires an active-HIGH enable, therefore $\overline{\text{CNT ENABLE}}$ from the Am29811A is passed through one section of the Two-Input Multiplexer (U13) for inversion. An alternative counter, the Am25LS169, has enable as active-LOW; therefore, this inversion through U13 is not required.

At this point, a discussion of the typical operation of this computer control unit is in order. First, bits 0-11 of the microprogram memory output word, are connected to the pipeline register designated U18, U19 and U20. The Am2918 has been selected for this portion of the pipeline register because of its continuous outputs and three-state outputs. The three-state outputs are connected to the D inputs of the Am2911 to provide a branch address whenever needed. These 12 bits are designated BR_0-BR_{11}. The Q outputs of these same Am2918s are designated R_0-R_{11} and are connected to the parallel load input of the Am25LS163 Counters. Thus, the counter can be loaded with any value between 0 and 4,095. Many designs will take advantage of R_0-R_{11} and use it as a general purpose field whenever the counter is not being loaded or a jump pipeline is not being performed. Using a microprogram memory field for more than one function (branch address and counter load value in this example) is called FORMATTING and will be covered in greater detail later. The other two devices in the pipeline register shown on the architecture of Figure 17 are U16 and U17. First, U17 receives four bits (12, 13, 14 and 15) from the microprogram memory to provide four-bit instruction field to the Am29811A. This four-bit field, designated R_{12}-R_{15}, provides the actual next address control instruction for the computer control unit. R_{16} is the polarity control bit for the test input and is connected to the select input of the Am74S158 Two-Input Multiplexer. When R_{16} is LOW, the signal at the Am29811A test input will be inverted, but when R_{16} is HIGH, the test input will be non-inverted.

The Am74S175 has been used as part of the pipeline register (U16) because it has both inverting and non-inverting outputs. Signals R_{17}, R_{18} and R_{19} are used to control the One-of-Eight Multiplexer (U12 and U14) A, B and C inputs. Pipeline register output R_{20} and $\overline{R_{20}}$ are used to enable either the U12 outputs or the U14 outputs such that a one-of-sixteen multiplexer function is implemented. In this design, the TEST 0 input of U14 is connected to ground. This provides a convenient path for converting any of the conditional instructions to non-conditional instructions. That is, any of the conditional instructions can be executed unconditionally by selecting the TEST 0 input which is connected to ground and forcing the polarity control to either the inverting or non-inverting condition. This allows the execution of unconditional JUMP, unconditional JUMP-TO-SUBROUTINE, and unconditional RETURN-FROM-SUBROUTINE instructions.

Bit 21 from the microprogram memory utilizes a flip-flop in U17 as part of the pipeline register. This output, R_{21}, is used as the enable input to the instruction register. Needless to say, other techniques for encoding this enable function in a formatted field could be provided.

A HIGH PERFORMANCE COMPUTER CONTROL UNIT USING THE Am2909 AND Am29803A

The high performance CCU (Figure 18) is of a similar basic design as the previously described CCU. The major differences are, referring to Figure 18, the addition of an extended enable control (U16), a vector input (U24 and U25), and an Am29803A 16-way Branch Control Unit (U23). These performance enhancements are more related to function than to actual circuit speed. The use of these enhancements by the microprogram provides greater flexibility in controlling a machine's environment, and can reduce the microinstruction count required to perform a particular task, which has the effect of increasing overall system throughput.

In describing this high performance CCU design, those sections which remain unchanged from the previous description (Figure 17), will not be covered again. This includes the mapping PROMs, sequencer, Am29811A, counter, condition test inputs and associated polarity control, and the pipeline register. The areas that will be covered are: extended enable control (U16), Vector inputs (U24 and U25), and the Am29803A 16-way Branch Control Unit (U23).

Extended Enable Control

Extended enable control is accomplished via an Am74S139 dual two-to-four line decoder in conjunction with the Am29811A next address control unit. In Figure 17, PL E and MAP E of the Am29811A were connected directly to the components that they are to control (pipeline registers and mapping PROMs, respectively). Likewise, $\overline{\text{CNT LOAD}}$ and $\overline{\text{CNT ENABLE}}$ are connected directly to the counters that they control (with the exception that $\overline{\text{CNT ENABLE}}$ requires inversion when using Am25LS163 counters). In Figure 18, $\overline{PL\ E}$, $\overline{MAP\ E}$, $\overline{\text{CNT LOAD}}$ and $\overline{\text{CNT ENABLE}}$ go to the inputs of the Am74S139 two-to-four line decoder (U16). When either $\overline{PL\ E}$ or $\overline{MAP\ E}$ is LOW, then either $2Y_1$ or $2Y_2$ of U16 is LOW and either the pipeline branch address registers or mapping PROMs are enabled. If both PL E and MAP E are HIGH, then output $2Y_3$ of U16 is LOW enabling the three-state outputs of U24 and U25 which are alternate microprogram starting address decoders (alternate mapping PROMs), and called VECTOR INPUT in this design. Likewise, $\overline{\text{CNT LOAD}}$ and $\overline{\text{CNT ENABLE}}$ follow the same rules, enabling the counter to load or count via $1Y_1$ and $1Y_2$ of U16.

Vector Input

The "Vector Input" provides the system designer with a powerful next starting address control. For example, one possible use might be as an interrupt vector. For instance, use the "Interrupt Request" output of an Am2914 Vectored Priority Interrupt Controller (or group of Am2914s) as an input to one of the conditional test inputs of multiplexers (U12 or U14). Then connect the Am2914 Vector Out lines to the vector mapping PROMs (Vector input U24 and U25). The microprogram then could, at the appro-

Note: Figures 17, 18, 20, and 24 are at back of the book.

priate time, test for a pending interrupt and if present, jump in microprogram memory directly to the routine which handles the specific interrupt as requested via the Am2914 Vector Output lines. This routine will take the proper steps to preserve the status of the interrupt system, and then will service the interrupt. This is one of many possible uses for the Vector Input. Other possible uses include both hardware and software "TRAP" routines and so forth. As can be seen, the design presented here uses the Vector Enable line (output $2Y_3$ or U16) to enable an alternate starting address input at the Am2911. This, however, does not preclude the use of other devices in place of mapping PROMs as the D-input vector source.

It should be understood that this does not accomplish a "micro-interrupt" function in that it is not a random possibility. Instead a microprogrammed test is made and an alternate microroutine is performed. A true "microprogram interrupt" is one that could occur at any microinstruction. The Am2910 does not handle this case internally.

Am29803A 16-Way Branch Control Unit

The Am29803A provides 16-way branch control when used in conjunction with the Am2909 bipolar microprocessor sequencer, and is shown as U23 in Figure 18 with its pipeline register U22. The Am29803A has four TEST-inputs, four INSTRUCTION-inputs, four OR-outputs, and an enable control. The four OR-outputs connect directly to the Am2909 OR-inputs (U8 in Figure 18). The four INSTRUCTION-inputs to the Am29803A provide control over the TEST-inputs and OR-outputs, and are provided by the microprogram via the pipeline register U22 (Figure 18).

Basically, the INSTRUCTION-inputs (I_0-I_3) provide sixteen instructions (0-F_{16}) which can select sixteen possible combinations of the TEST-inputs and provide a specific output on the OR-outputs depending upon the state of the inputs being tested. (The subscript 16 refers to basic 16.) All possible combinations of instruction-inputs, TEST-inputs and OR-outputs are shown in Figure 19.

Note that instruction zero does not test any inputs (a disable instruction). Instructions 1, 2, 4 and 8 test one input and can cause a branch to one of two words. Instructions 3, 5, 6, 9, 10 and 12 test two inputs and can jump to one of four words (a 4-word page). Instructions 7, 11, 13 and 14 test three inputs and can jump on an eight word page. Instruction number 15 tests all four inputs and the result can jump to any word on a sixteen word page.

USING THE Am29803A

In the architecture of Figure 18, the Am29803A allows 2-way, 4-way, 8-way or 16-way branching as determined by selectable combinations of the TEST-inputs. Referring to Figure 19, the ZERO instruction (all instruction bits LOW) inhibits the testing of any TEST-inputs, thus providing LOW OR-outputs. Any single TEST-input selected (T_0, T_1, T_2 or T_3) will result in OR_0 being HIGH or LOW in correspondence with the polarity of the selected TEST-input. Selecting any combination of two TEST inputs results in the outputs OR_0 and/or OR_1 being HIGH or LOW, following a mapped one-to-one relationship, i.e., OR_0 and OR_1 will follow the TEST-inputs, but no matter which pair of TEST-inputs are selected, their HIGH/LOW condition is mapped to the OR_0 and OR_1 outputs. Likewise, selecting any three TEST inputs, will map their HIGH/LOW condition to the OR_0, OR_1 and OR_2 outputs. Selecting all four TEST-inputs, of course, causes a one-to-one relationship to exist between the HIGH/LOW conditions of the TEST-inputs and the corresponding OR-outputs. Refer to Figure 19 to verify the relationships between INSTRUCTION-inputs, TEST-input, and OR-output. It is very important that the mapping relationship between these signals be completely understood. When using the Am29803A TEST-OR capability as shown in Figure 18, the microprogrammer must position the applicable microcode within microprogram memory so that the low-order address bits are available for ORing. Sequencer instructions using the Am2909/2911 D-inputs (JRP, JSRP, JP and CJS in particular) are ideally suited for the Am29803A TEST-OR capability. The jump-to-location, available via pipeline BR_0-BR_{11} or the Am2909/2911 register, can contain the address of a branch table. A branch table is merely a sequential series of unconditional jump instructions. The particular jump instruction executed is determined by the low-order address bits; that is, the first jump instruction in a branch table must start at a location in microprogram memory whose low-order address bit (or bits) is zero. If a single Am29803A TEST-input is selected (2-way branching) then only the least significant bit in the beginning branch table address needs to be zero. Two Am29803A TEST-inputs selected (4-way branching) requires that the branch table start on an address with the low-order two bits equal to zero; 8-way branching requires three low-order zero bits, and 16-way branching requires four low-order zero address bits. Understanding this branch control concept is really quite simple. The branch table is located in microprogram memory beginning at a location whose address has sufficient low-order zero bits to accommodate the number of selected Am29803A TEST-inputs. If, for instance, three TEST-inputs were selected, the first jump instruction in the branch table must be at an address whose low-order three bits are zero, such as address $0F8_{16}$. The second jump instruction in the branch table would begin in microprogram memory address $0F9_{16}$. The third jump at location $0FA_{16}$, the fourth at $0FB_{16}$, etc. Through all eight locations ($0F8_{16}$-$0FF_{16}$). Assume the following pipeline instruction (referring to Figure 18): (1) U22 selects three Am29803A TEST-inputs, (2) U18 instructs the Am29811A Next Address Controller to select the Am2909/2911 D-inputs, (3) U16 enables the pipeline branch address as the D source, and (4) U19, U20 and U21 supplies the address $0F8_{16}$ as the branch address. The Am29803A TEST-inputs will be ORed into the low-order three bit positions, thus providing a jump entry into the branch table *indexed* by the value of the OR bits. Each instruction in the branch table is usually a jump instruction, which allows the selection of a particular microcode routine determined by the value presented at the Am29803A TEST-inputs. These jump instructions are the first instruction of the particular sequence. There are, of course, many other ways to use the Am29803A 16-way Branch Control Unit.

The microprogram memory address supplied via an Am2909 sequencer can be modified by the Am29803A 16-way Branch Control Unit. Remember, however, that the microcode associated with this address modification relies on certain address bits being zero, therefore this microcode is not arbitrarily relocatable. The above discussion describes using the D-input and branching to provide low-order zeroes to use the OR inputs. Through proper design, the Register, PC Counter, or File can be used equally well.

THE COMPLETE COMPUTER CONTROL UNIT USING THE Am2910

A detailed connection diagram for a straightforward computer control unit using the Am2910 is shown in Figure 20. This design utilizes the Am25LS377 as U1 and U2 to implement a 16-bit instruction register. The op code outputs from the instruction register drive three Am29761 PROMs to perform the op code decoding function. These are shown in the diagram of Figure 20 as U3, U4 and U5. The Am2910 sequencer (U6) is used to perform the basic microprogram sequencing function.

Note: Figures 17, 18, 20, and 24 are at back of the book.

MULTIPLEXER SELECT

R_{20}	R_{19}	R_{18}	R_{17}	SELECT
0	0	0	0	TEST 0
0	0	0	1	TEST 1
0	0	1	0	TEST 2
•				•
•				•
•				•
1	1	1	1	TEST 15

POLARITY CONTROL

R_{16}	OUTPUT
0	COMPLEMENT OF TEST
1	TRUE TEST

NEXT ADDRESS CONTROL

R_{15}	R_{14}	R_{13}	R_{12}	FUNCTION
X	X	X	X	NEXT INSTRUCTION

MACHINE INSTRUCTION REGISTER

R_{21}	FUNCTION
0	LOAD
1	HOLD

COUNTER VALUE

R_{11}–R_0	FUNCTION
XXX---XXX	VALUE

JUMP ADDRESS

BR_{11}–BR_0	FUNCTION
XXX---XXX	JUMP ADDRESS

OR BRANCH CONTROL

R_{25}	R_{24}	R_{23}	R_{22}	FUNCTION
X	X	X	X	TEST INSTRUCTION

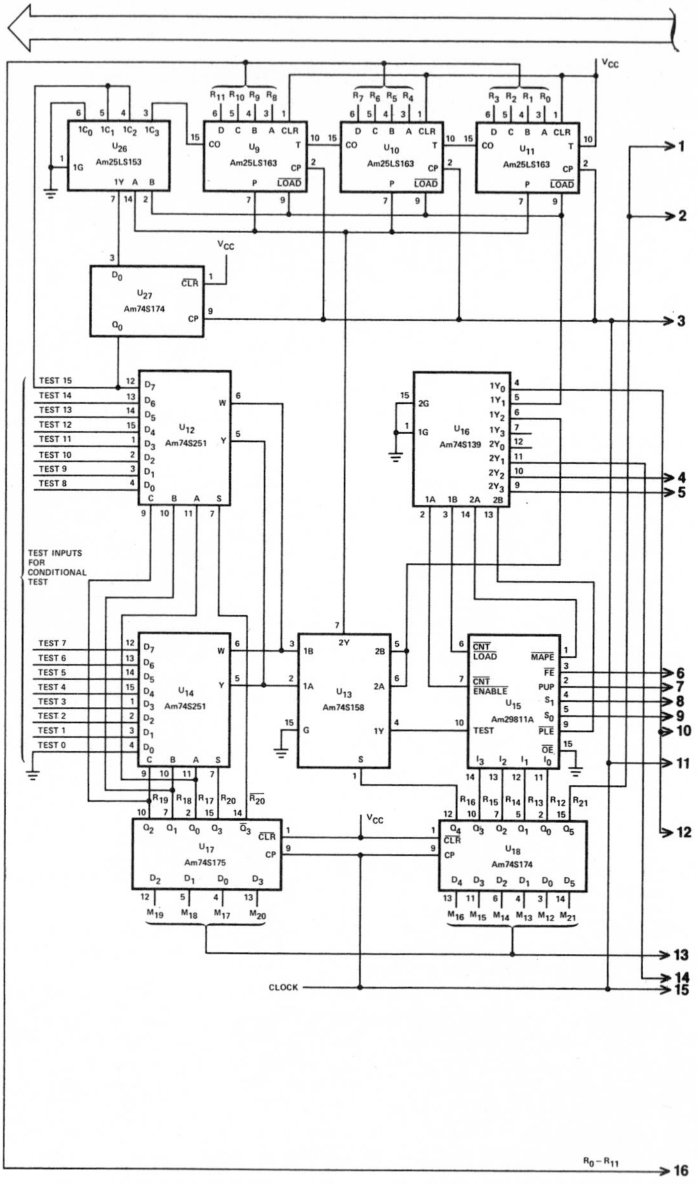

Figure 18. High Performance Computer Control Unit with Am2909/2911.

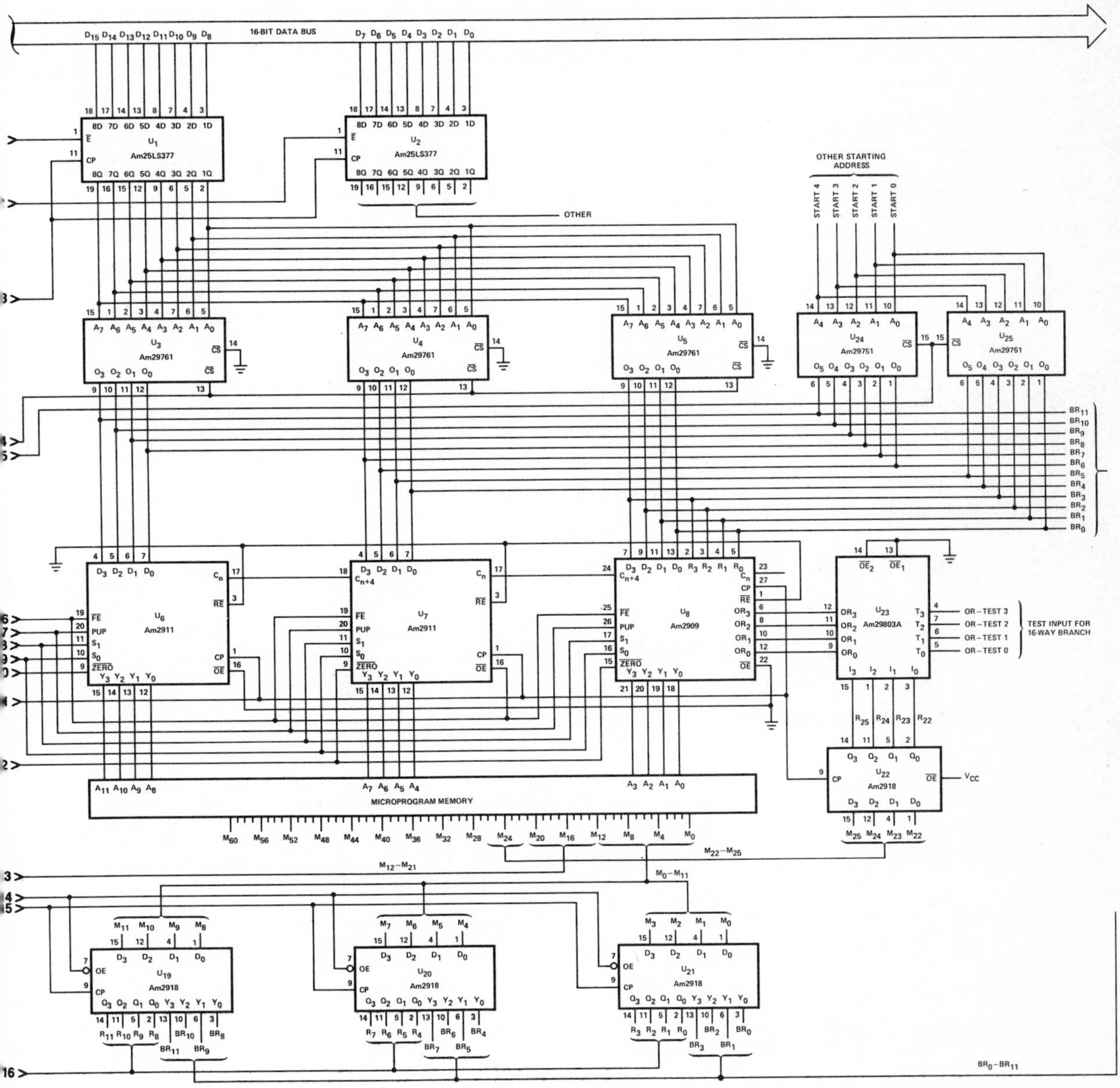
16-BIT DATA BUS
D_{15} D_{14} D_{13} D_{12} D_{11} D_{10} D_9 D_8
D_7 D_6 D_5 D_4 D_3 D_2 D_1 D_0
U_1
Am25LS377
U_2
Am25LS377
OTHER
OTHER STARTING ADDRESS
START 4
START 3
START 2
START 1
START 0
U_3
Am29761
U_4
Am29761
U_5
Am29761
U_{24}
Am29751
U_{25}
Am29751
BR_{11}
BR_{10}
BR_9
BR_8
BR_7
BR_6
BR_5
BR_4
BR_3
BR_2
BR_1
BR_0
U_6
Am2911
U_7
Am2911
U_8
Am2909
U_{23}
Am29803A
OR – TEST 3
OR – TEST 2
OR – TEST 1
OR – TEST 0
TEST INPUT FOR 16-WAY BRANCH
U_{22}
Am2918
V_{CC}
A_{11} A_{10} A_9 A_8
A_7 A_6 A_5 A_4
A_3 A_2 A_1 A_0
MICROPROGRAM MEMORY
M_{60} M_{56} M_{52} M_{48} M_{44} M_{40} M_{36} M_{32} M_{28} M_{24} M_{20} M_{16} M_{12} M_8 M_4 M_0
M_{22}–M_{25}
M_{12}–M_{21}
M_0–M_{11}
U_{19}
Am2918
U_{20}
Am2918
U_{21}
Am2918
BR_0–BR_{11}

Function	I_3	I_2	I_1	I_0	T_3	T_2	T_1	T_0	OR_3	OR_2	OR_1	OR_0
No Test	L	L	L	L	X	X	X	X	L	L	L	L
Test T_0	L	L	L	H	X	X	X	L	L	L	L	L
					X	X	X	H	L	L	L	H
Test T_1	L	L	H	L	X	X	L	X	L	L	L	L
					X	X	H	X	L	L	L	H
Test T_0 & T_1	L	L	H	H	X	X	L	L	L	L	L	L
					X	X	L	H	L	L	L	H
					X	X	H	L	L	L	H	L
					X	X	H	H	L	L	H	H
Test T_2	L	H	L	L	X	L	X	X	L	L	L	L
					X	H	X	X	L	L	L	H
Test T_0 & T_2	L	H	L	H	X	L	X	L	L	L	L	L
					X	L	X	H	L	L	L	H
					X	H	X	L	L	L	H	L
					X	H	X	H	L	L	H	H
Test T_1 & T_2	L	H	H	L	X	L	L	X	L	L	L	L
					X	L	H	X	L	L	L	H
					X	H	L	X	L	L	H	L
					X	H	H	X	L	L	H	H
Test T_0, T_1 & T_2	L	H	H	H	X	L	L	L	L	L	L	L
					X	L	L	H	L	L	L	H
					X	L	H	L	L	L	H	L
					X	L	H	H	L	L	H	H
					X	H	L	L	L	H	L	L
					X	H	L	H	L	H	L	H
					X	H	H	L	L	H	H	L
					X	H	H	H	L	H	H	H
Test T_3	H	L	L	L	L	X	X	X	L	L	L	L
					H	X	X	X	L	L	L	H
Test T_0 & T_3	H	L	L	H	L	X	X	L	L	L	L	L
					L	X	X	H	L	L	L	H
					H	X	X	L	L	L	H	L
					H	X	X	H	L	L	H	H
Test T_1 & T_3	H	L	H	L	L	X	L	X	L	L	L	L
					L	X	H	X	L	L	L	H
					H	X	L	X	L	L	H	L
					H	X	H	X	L	L	H	H
Test T_0, T_1 & T_3	H	L	H	H	L	X	L	L	L	L	L	L
					L	X	L	H	L	L	L	H
					L	X	H	L	L	L	H	L
					L	X	H	H	L	L	H	H
					H	X	L	L	L	H	L	L
					H	X	L	H	L	H	L	H
					H	X	H	L	L	H	H	L
					H	X	H	H	L	H	H	H
Test T_2 & T_3	H	H	L	L	L	L	X	X	L	L	L	L
					L	H	X	X	L	L	L	H
					H	L	X	X	L	L	H	L
					H	H	X	X	L	L	H	H
Test T_0, T_2 & T_3	H	H	L	H	L	L	X	L	L	L	L	L
					L	L	X	H	L	L	L	H
					L	H	X	L	L	L	H	L
					L	H	X	H	L	L	H	H
					H	L	X	L	L	H	L	L
					H	L	X	H	L	H	L	H
					H	H	X	L	L	H	H	L
					H	H	X	H	L	H	H	H
Test T_1, T_2 & T_3	H	H	H	L	L	L	L	X	L	L	L	L
					L	L	H	X	L	L	L	H
					L	H	L	X	L	L	H	L
					L	H	H	X	L	L	H	H
					H	L	L	X	L	H	L	L
					H	L	H	X	L	H	L	H
					H	H	L	X	L	H	H	L
					H	H	H	X	L	H	H	H
Test T_0, T_1, T_2 & T_3	H	H	H	H	L	L	L	L	L	L	L	L
					L	L	L	H	L	L	L	H
					L	L	H	L	L	L	H	L
					L	L	H	H	L	L	H	H
					L	H	L	L	L	H	L	L
					L	H	L	H	L	H	L	H
					L	H	H	L	L	H	H	L
					L	H	H	H	L	H	H	H
					H	L	L	L	H	L	L	L
					H	L	L	H	H	L	L	H
					H	L	H	L	H	L	H	L
					H	L	H	H	H	L	H	H
					H	H	L	L	H	H	L	L
					H	H	L	H	H	H	L	H
					H	H	H	L	H	H	H	L
					H	H	H	H	H	H	H	H

L = LOW, H = HIGH, X = Don't care

Figure 19. Function Table.

A 16 input condition code multiplexer function is provided by using two Am2922s as U7 and U8. These devices allow one of sixteen inputs to be tested and the polarity of the test can also be determined. The pipeline register consists of U9, U10, U11, U12 and U13. These devices are edge triggered D type registers and have been selected to provide unique functions as required depending on their bit positions in the pipeline register. An Am74S175 was selected for U9 because both a true and complement output were desired to provide control to the condition code multiplexer three state enables. An Am74S174 register was selected as U10 because it provides a clear input for initializing the Am2910 microprogram sequencer. Three Am2918s were selected for U11, U12 and U13 because they have a three state output that can be used to provide the branch address field to the D inputs of the Am2910 and they also have a set of outputs that can be used to provide other control signals via this field when it does not contain a branch address. No specific devices are shown for the microprogram memory as the user should select the desired width and depth depending on his design.

ANOTHER DESIGN EXAMPLE

The Am2909, Am2910, Am2911, Am29811A and Am29803A have been designed to operate in the microprogram sequencing section of any digital state machine. Typically, the examples shown are for performing the computer control unit function of a typical minicomputer class machine. The design engineer should not limit his thinking for the use of these devices simply to that of microprogram sequencing in a computer control unit. These devices can be successfully used in other areas of designing such as memory control, DMA control, interrupt control and special purpose microprogrammed machine architectures. In order to provide an example of a design using these devices in something other than a typical computer control unit, a microprogrammed CRT controller is described in the following.

In order to provide some basis for the design of a CRT controller, the requirements of this controller must be spelled out. These are given as follows:

A) Character size: 5 x 7 dot matrix. The character field will be 7 dots by 10 horizontal lines thereby providing ample space for the 5 x 7 character and the intervening space between characters and lines of characters.
B) 80 characters per line. A standard 80 character per line display will be utilized and there will be 18 character periods allowed for horizontal retrace time.
C) 24 lines of characters per frame. This provides a total of 240 visible lines per frame (24 lines of characters by 10 horizontal lines per character). There are a total of 24 lines provided for vertical retrace bringing the total number of lines per frame to 264.
D) Refresh rate: 60 frames per second. Therefore, the horizontal line rate will be 264 x 60 = 15,840Hz. As there are a total of 80 + 18 = 98 character periods in a line, the character rate will be 98 x 15.84 = 1,552.32KHz, and the dot rate will be 7 x 1.5288 = 10.86624MHz. (Note: No interlace is used.)
E) It is assumed that there is a 2K word deep x 8-bit wide character RAM available to the host computer in which it can write the ASCII equivalent of the characters to be displayed. If scrolling is to be used, the host computer must also write the first visible character's address divided by 16_{10} into the Am25LS374 "First Address Register".
F) This CRT controller must generate an 11-bit character address that is used by the 2K word deep character RAM. It must also generate the required video enable signals and the horizontal and vertical blanking signals.

Principle of Operation

A detailed block diagram of the CRT controller is shown in Figure 21. The block diagram shows an interface to an SBC-80/10 data bus, address bus and control bus. The outputs of the CRT controller are connected to a CRT monitor on the block diagram. Otherwise the block diagram shows a straightforward use of the Am2910 and three Am2911s to implement the CRT control function using microprogrammed techniques. The SBC-80/10 was selected for this example since it is well known.

A logic diagram of the CRT controller is shown in Figure 22. Three Am29775 512-word x 8-bit registered PROMs are used to contain the 23-bit wide microprogram. While only a minimum number of words are used in the design as shown, many additional words can be used to add various options (as described later). The address for these Am29775 registered PROMs is provided by an Am2910 microprogram sequencer. Three Am2911 sequencers are used to generate the character address for the character RAM. The least significant Am2911 sequencer is connected as a divide by 16 counter. This RAM address is compared with the desired last character address (80 x 24 = 1920) value using an Am25LS2521 8-bit equal to detector. When the last address is detected, it can be sensed at the condition code multiplexer (Am25LS153) that is used to select the condition code for the Am2910 sequencer.

The data derived from the 2K word character RAM is decoded by a character generator (6061) in this design and the character output is parallel loaded into an Am25LS23 shift register. This shift register is used to provide the video signal from its Q_0 output to eventually drive the display via an Am74S240 buffer. The diagram of Figure 22 depicts an oscillator input source to supply the dot frequency. In this design, a 10.86624MHz oscillator should be connected to this oscillator input point. This oscillator input signal is used to clock the shift register containing the individual dot bits (dot-on or dot-off) and also drives an Am25LS169 counter which divides this frequency by 7 to generate the character rate clock. This character rate clock is used throughout the controller to provide a timing signal for the state machine design.

An Am25LS168 decade counter is used to generate the line inputs for the character generator and to count 10 horizontal lines per character space. This counter is clocked by the horizontal blanking signal (HB) and its $\overline{\text{RCO}}$ output is used as one of the condition code multiplexer inputs. The $\overline{\text{RCO}}$ output can be tested to determine when 10 counts have been executed by the counter and it is also used to enable the last address comparator during the 10th horizontal line time.

When the host computer accesses the character RAM, the $\overline{\text{HOST-ACCESS}}$ line is pulled LOW. This removes the Am2911 outputs from the character RAM address bus. When this access occurs, improper data may be present at the shift register inputs. Thus, the character generator PROM output is disabled by the $\overline{\text{HOST-ACCESS}}$ signal during this time.

When power is applied to this CRT controller or whenever it is reset, the RESET line is driven LOW. This signal is inverted through an Am25LS240 and then disables a part of the pipeline register outputs as well as enabling one half of an Am25LS241. This Am25LS241 inserts LOWs onto the instruction (I) inputs of the Am2910 sequencer. Then, the next character rate clock will force the microprogram address outputs to zero and the microprogram for the CRT controller as shown in Figure 23 will be executed starting at address zero.

MULTIPLEXER SELECT

R_{20}	R_{19}	R_{18}	R_{17}	SELECT
0	0	0	0	TEST 0
0	0	0	1	TEST 1
0	0	1	0	TEST 2
	•			•
	•			•
	•			•
1	1	1	1	TEST 15

NEXT ADDRESS CONTROL

R_{15}	R_{14}	R_{13}	R_{12}	FUNCTION
X	X	X	X	NEXT INSTRUCTION

CONTROL VALUE

R_{11}-R_0	FUNCTION
XXX - - - XXX	VALUE

POLARITY CONTROL

R_{16}	OUTPUT
0	COMPLEMENT TEST
1	TRUE TEST

MACHINE INSTRUCTION REGISTER

R_{21}	FUNCTION
0	LOAD
1	HOLD

JUMP ADDRESS

BR_{11}-BR_0	FUNCTION
XXX - - - XXX	JUMP ADDRESS

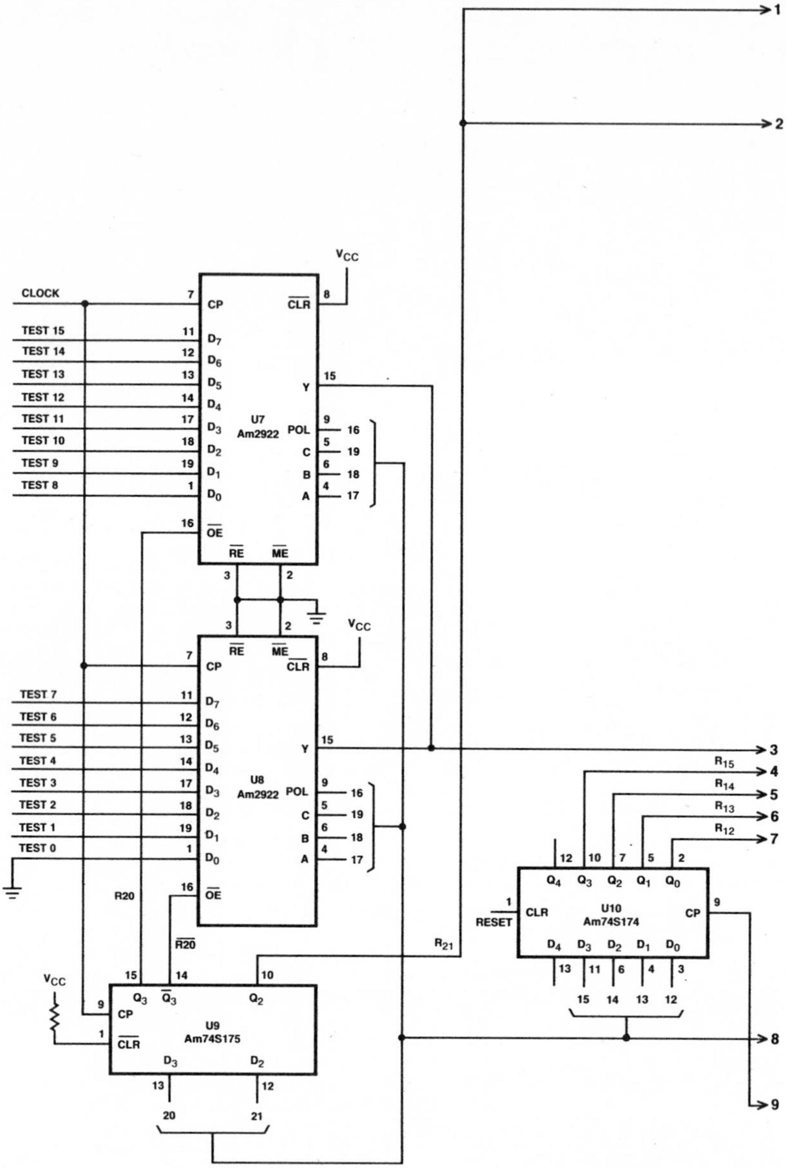

Figure 20. Computer Control Unit with Am2910.

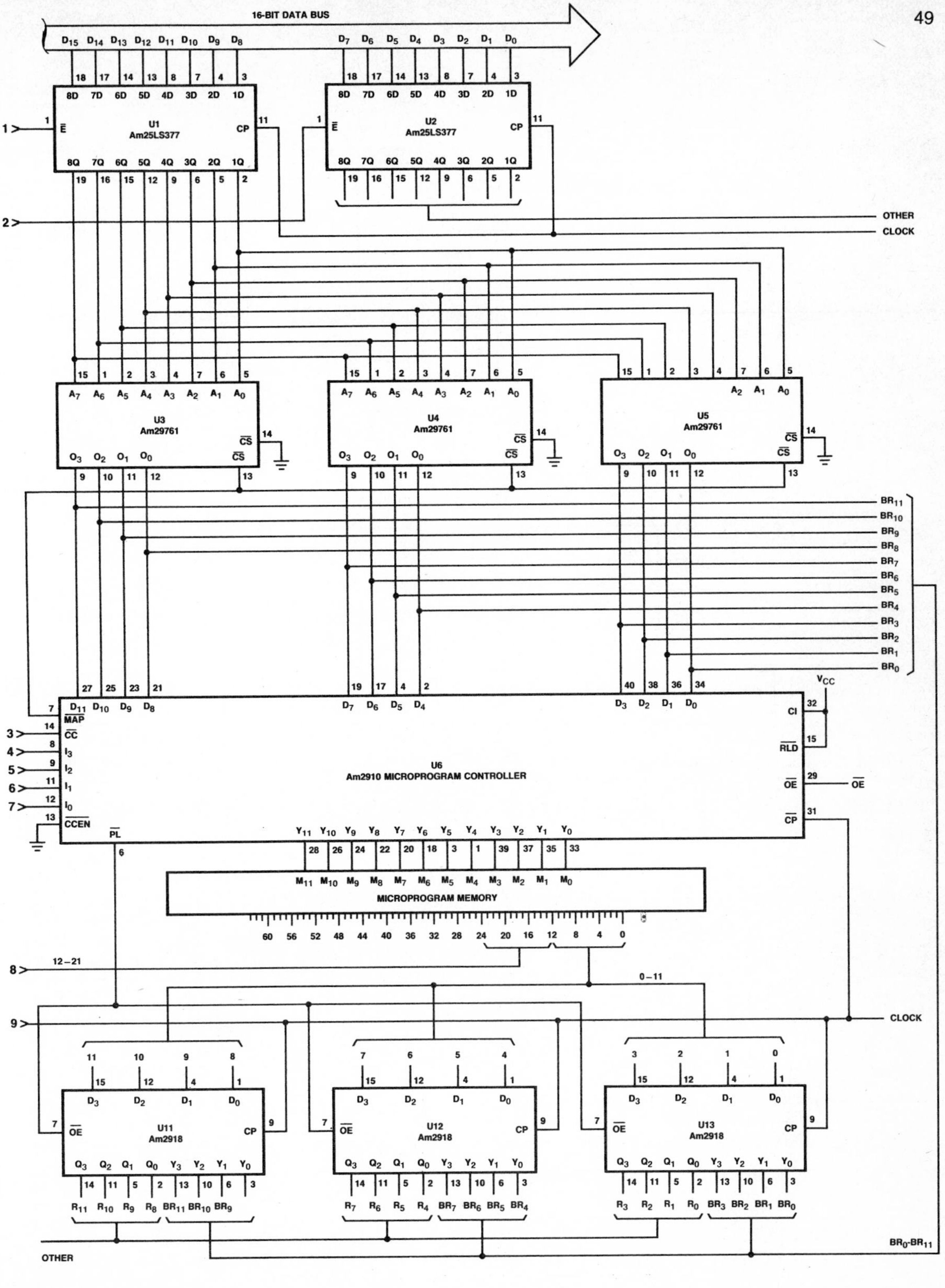
16-BIT DATA BUS
D_{15} D_{14} D_{13} D_{12} D_{11} D_{10} D_9 D_8
D_7 D_6 D_5 D_4 D_3 D_2 D_1 D_0
U1
Am25LS377
U2
Am25LS377
8D 7D 6D 5D 4D 3D 2D 1D
8Q 7Q 6Q 5Q 4Q 3Q 2Q 1Q
$\overline{E}$
CP
OTHER
CLOCK
U3
Am29761
U4
Am29761
U5
Am29761
A_7 A_6 A_5 A_4 A_3 A_2 A_1 A_0
O_3 O_2 O_1 O_0
$\overline{CS}$
BR_{11} BR_{10} BR_9 BR_8 BR_7 BR_6 BR_5 BR_4 BR_3 BR_2 BR_1 BR_0
V_{CC}
U6
Am2910 MICROPROGRAM CONTROLLER
D_{11} D_{10} D_9 D_8 D_7 D_6 D_5 D_4 D_3 D_2 D_1 D_0
$\overline{MAP}$
$\overline{CC}$
I_3 I_2 I_1 I_0
$\overline{CCEN}$
$\overline{PL}$
CI
$\overline{RLD}$
$\overline{OE}$
CP
Y_{11} Y_{10} Y_9 Y_8 Y_7 Y_6 Y_5 Y_4 Y_3 Y_2 Y_1 Y_0
M_{11} M_{10} M_9 M_8 M_7 M_6 M_5 M_4 M_3 M_2 M_1 M_0
MICROPROGRAM MEMORY
60 56 52 48 44 40 36 32 28 24 20 16 12 8 4 0
12–21
0–11
CLOCK
U11
Am2918
U12
Am2918
U13
Am2918
D_3 D_2 D_1 D_0
$\overline{OE}$
CP
Q_3 Q_2 Q_1 Q_0 Y_3 Y_2 Y_1 Y_0
R_{11} R_{10} R_9 R_8 BR_{11} BR_{10} BR_9
R_7 R_6 R_5 R_4 BR_7 BR_6 BR_5 BR_4
R_3 R_2 R_1 R_0 BR_3 BR_2 BR_1 BR_0
OTHER
BR_0-BR_{11}

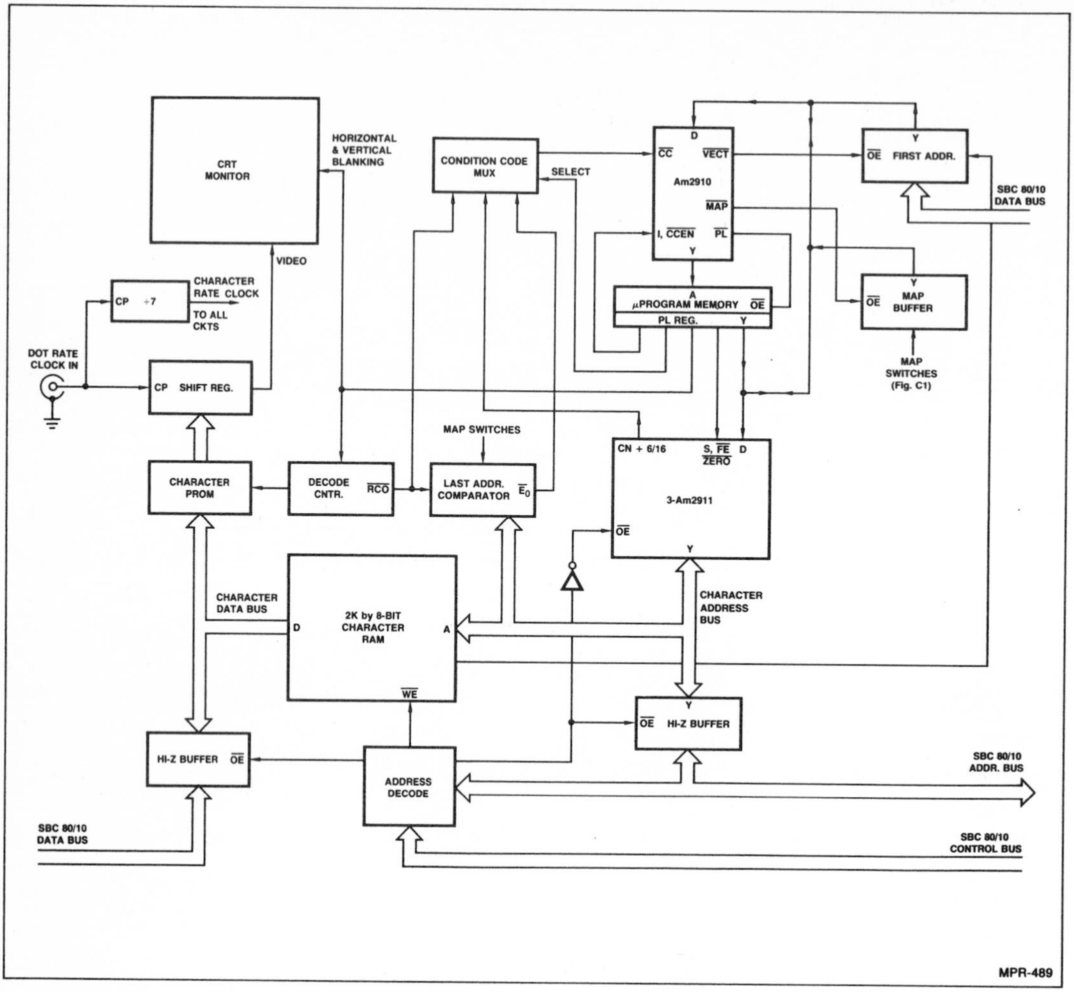

Figure 21. CRT Controller Block Diagram.

The Microprogram for the CRT Controller

Table 6 shows a complete description of the microprogrammed CRT controller microcode. Execution of these microinstructions is controlled by the Am2910 sequencer.

As can be seen in Table 6, several techniques were used in this short microprogram to provide the different counting requirements of this CRT controller. Although only one format (80 characters per line, 24 lines per frame) was shown here, the designer can easily configure his own format by simply changing some constants in the microprogram. As an exercise, the reader is encouraged to find a means to program the CRT controller for different formats. The host computer software could configure the controller format by using an additional register similar to the "First Address Register". This will be discussed in an appendix at the end of this chapter.

A complete wiring diagram for the microprogrammed CRT controller is shown in Figure 24. This can be used directly with the interface shown in Appendix A such that the CRT controller can be connected directly to an Am9080A based microprocessor system. Appendix A also depicts the use of a 2K word x 8 bit character RAM as described previously.

Note: Figure 24 is at back of the book.

CRT Controller Timing Considerations

As was discussed earlier, the character clock frequency for the CRT controller is 1,552.32KHz. Thus, it is desirable to calculate the longest path of the design to ensure that none exceed this clock period of 644.1ns. The timing diagrams of Figure 25 depict a number of different paths with the associated propagation delay calculations.

When all of the timing diagrams of Figure 25 are examined, it will be found that only three show propagation delay times of over 200ns typical. Of these, the worst case is 318ns as shown in Figure 25(i). Since the requirement of the design is to insure that none exceed 644.1ns, we have more than a 2 to 1 margin in the design based on the typicals. Thus, we can see that the design will operate properly even over the full military temperature range and power supply variations based on this analysis.

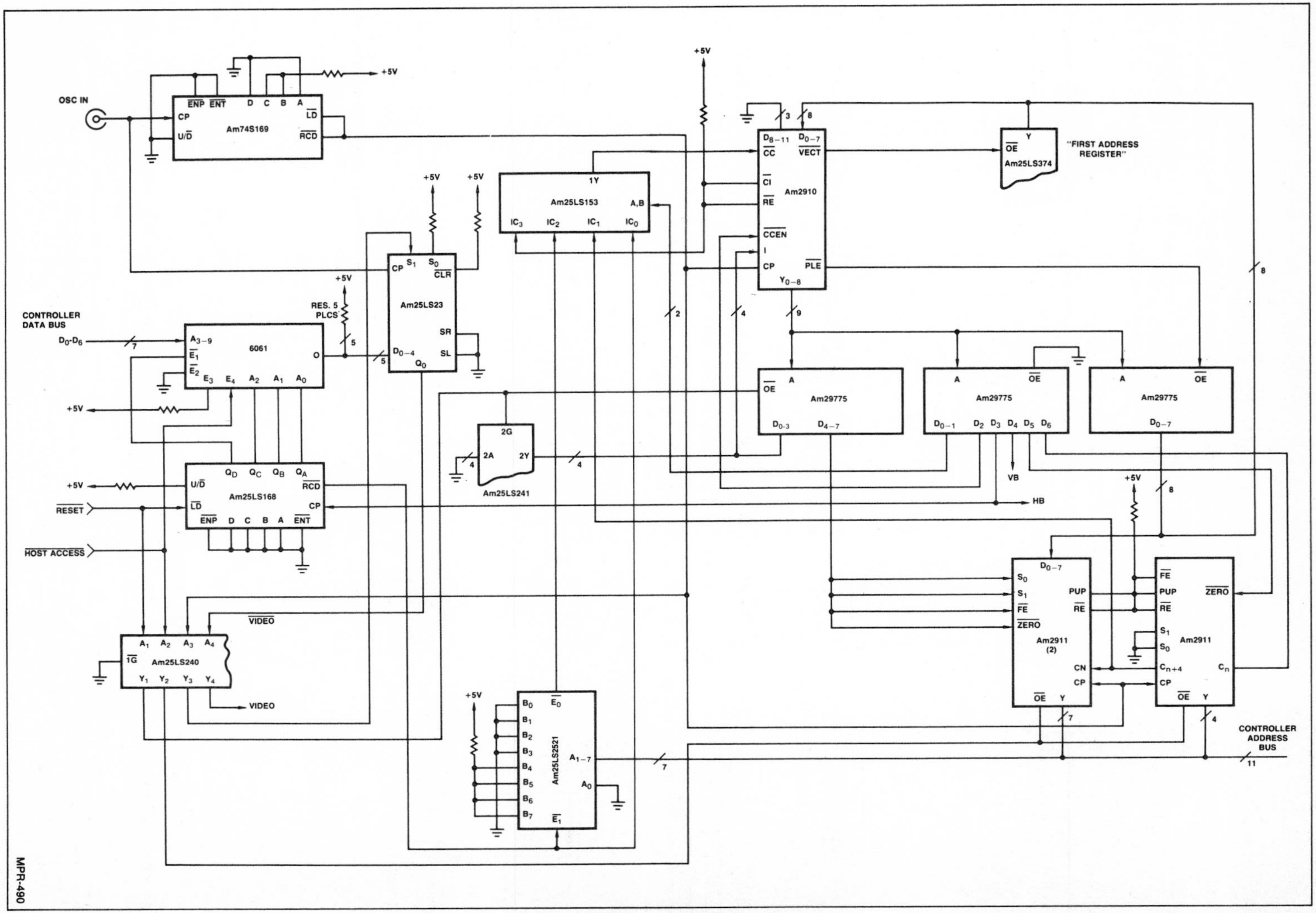

Figure 22. CRT Controller.

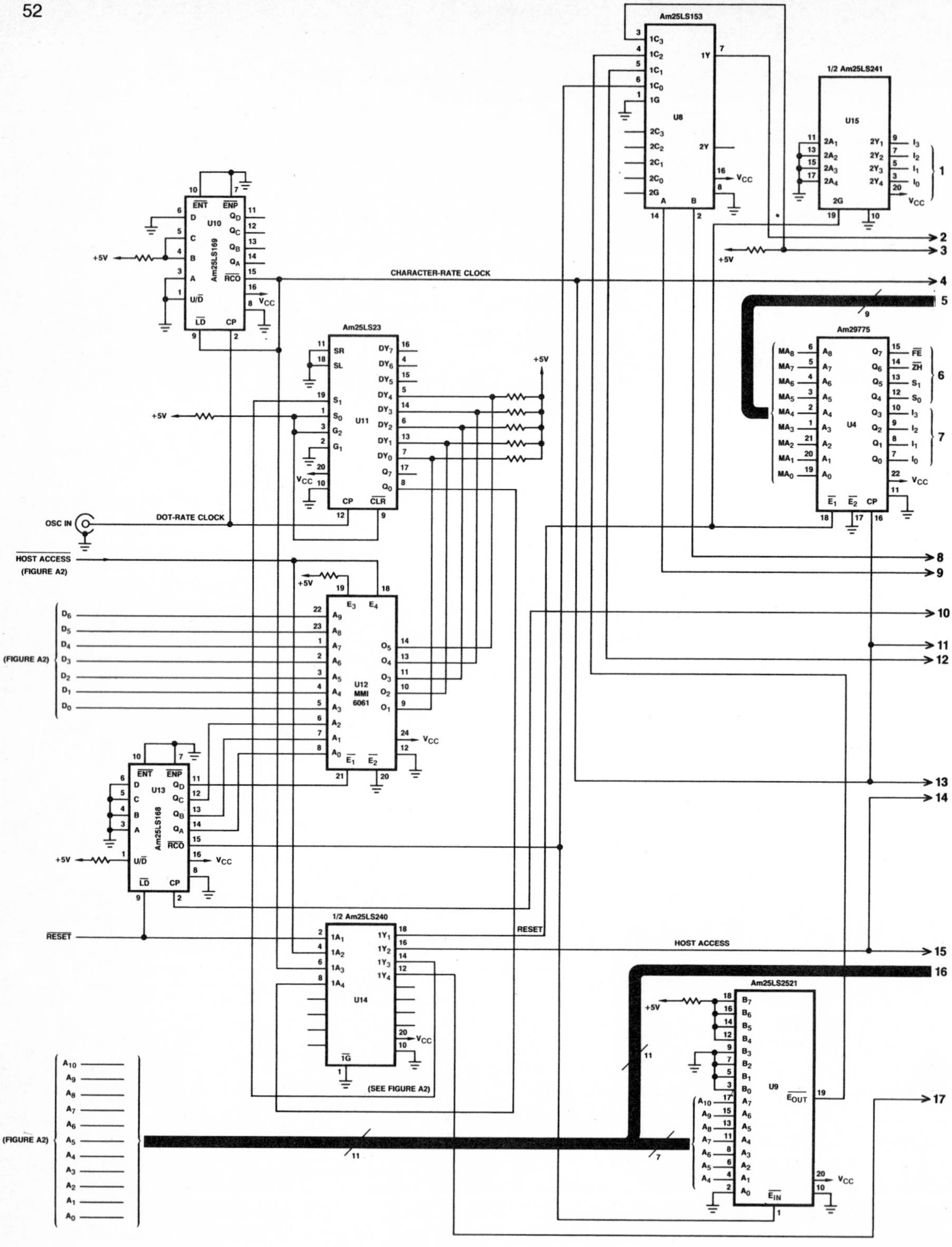

Figure 24. CRT Controller.

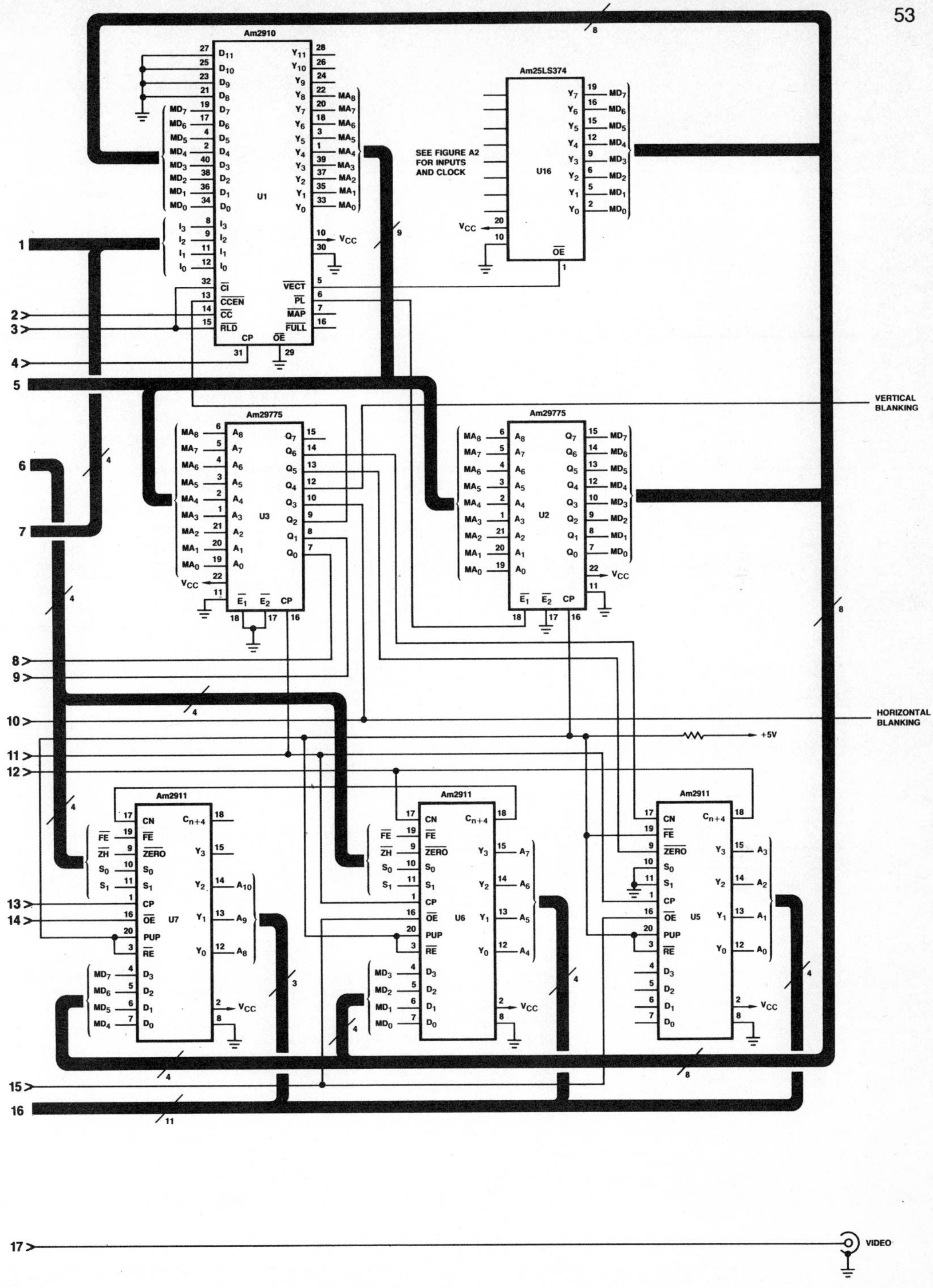
Am2910
U1
Am25LS374
U16
SEE FIGURE A2
FOR INPUTS
AND CLOCK
Am29775
U3
Am29775
U2
VERTICAL
BLANKING
HORIZONTAL
BLANKING
+5V
Am2911
U7
Am2911
U6
Am2911
U5
VIDEO

ADDR (Hex)	Label	Am2910 I	$\overline{CCEN}$	MUX	Am2911 S_1	S_0	$\overline{FE}$	$\overline{ZEROH}$	$\overline{ZEROL}$	C_n	HB	VB	NUM	Comments
0	INIT	CJV	L	3	H	H	L	H	L	L	H	L	X	;Load first address from Register to 2911's file
1		LDCT	X	X	L	L	H	H	L	L	H	L	23_{10}	;Load 2910's counter with member of rows/frame − 1
2	MAIN	CONT	X	X	H	L	H	H	L	H	H	L	X	;Address supplied by 2911's file
3		CJP	L	1	L	L	H	H	H	H	L	L	$	
4		CJP	L	1	L	L	H	H	H	H	L	L	$	
5		CJP	L	1	L	L	H	H	H	H	L	L	$	;One row: 5 x 16 = 80 characters
6		CJP	L	1	L	L	H	H	H	H	L	L	$	
7		CJP	L	1	L	L	H	H	H	H	L	L	$	
8		CJS	L	0	L	L	H	H	H	H	H	L	TENTH	;If tenth (last) line of a row: jump to "TENTH" subroutine
9		CJS	L	2	L	L	H	H	H	H	H	L	LASTA	;If last character: jump to "LASTA" subroutine
A		CJP	L	1	L	L	H	H	H	H	H	L	$	;Wait, until horizontal invisible counts done
B		CJP	H	X	L	L	H	H	X	X	H	L	MAIN	;Then do the Main routine again
C	TENTH	RPCT	X	X	L	L	L	H	H	H	H	L	GOBACK	;Push next addr on 2911's file: jump to "GOBACK" if not End of Frame
D		CJV	L	3	H	H	L	H	L	X	H	H	X	;Load 2911's file from First Address Register
E		LDCT	X	Y	L	L	H	H	X	X	H	H	146_{10}	;Load 2910's counter with number of invisible characters during Vert retrace divided by 16, minus 1
F		PUSH	L	3	L	L	H	H	H	H	H	H	X	;Push next PC to 2910's file for double
10		CJP	L	1	L	L	H	H	H	H	H	H	$	;Wait for LS2911 to count 16
11		RFCT	X	X	L	L	H	H	H	H	H	H	X	;Decrement 2910's counter and jump one line back if = 0
12		LDCT	X	X	L	L	H	H	H	H	H	H	23_{10}	;Load 2910's counter again with number of rows/frame − 1
13		CRTN	H	X	L	L	H	H	H	H	H	H	X	;Return from subroutine
14	GOBACK	CRTN	H	X	L	L	H	H	H	H	H	L	X	;Return
15	LASTA	CRTN	H	X	X	X	L	L	H	H	H	L	X	;Load zero to 2911's file and return.

Figure 23. Microprogram for the CRT Controller.

TABLE 6. DESCRIPTION OF THE MICROPROGRAM FOR THE CRT CONTROLLER.

Micro-program Address	Low Order Am2911	High Order Am2911s	Am2910	Comments
0	Since $\overline{ZERO}$ is low, its output will be LOW. The C_n input (from the Pipeline Register) is LOW so that the micro-program incrementer will not increment.	Both S_1 and S_0 are HIGH so that the D inputs will be routed to the Y outputs. These inputs will come from the First Address Register (the Am2910 $\overline{VECT}$ is LOW). C_n is LOW (see left column); therefore the micro-program counter will not incre-ment. $\overline{FE}$ is LOW (and PUP is always HIGH) causing the pre-sent output to be pushed on the stack. The character ad-dress is already the "First Character Address".	The CJV instruction is selected. Therefore, $\overline{VECT}$ output will be LOW, enabling the "First Ad-dress Register onto the internal 8-bit bus. $\overline{CCEN}$ is LOW; the MUX is selecting a constant HIGH, and the sequencer will address the next consecutive microprogram address (word 1).	This instruction pushes the "First Character Address" more signif-icant bits onto the Am2911's file, and continues to the next micro-instruction.
1	$\overline{ZERO}$ and C_n are still LOW, so no change in this device.	S_1 and S_2 are LOW; thus, the Y outputs will be the current PC, (the same as the Y out-puts were in the previous step). C_n is still LOW, therefore no change will occur in the PC.	LDCT is selected and the num-ber of character-rows per frame minus 1 (23_{10}) is loaded into the Am2910 register/counter. The sequencer addresses the next microinstruction.	
2 "MAIN"	Maintaining $\overline{ZERO}$ LOW assures the proper starting address. C_n is HIGH; there-fore, the internal PC will be incremented.	With S_1 = HIGH, S_0 = LOW and $\overline{FE}$ = HIGH, the Am2911 will refer to its internal file (the starting address of this particular character-row) without popping.	The Am2910 will generate the next microprogram address.	This is the starting location for the main loop.

Note: Figure 24 is at back of the book.

TABLE 6. DESCRIPTION OF THE MICROPROGRAM FOR THE CRT CONTROLLER (Cont.).

Micro-program Address	Low Order Am2911	High Order Am2911s	Am2910	Comments
3	This Am2911 now counts up using its PC incrementer. At the final count (moving from F_{16} to 0) its C_{n+4} output will be HIGH.	Initially these two Am2911s will not change their Y outputs since their C_n input is LOW. However, when the C_n input goes HIGH, the internal PC will increment	With the MUX selecting the C_{n+4} output from the least significant Am2911 slice, the CC input to the Am2910 sequencer will be LOW until the Am2911 counts 16. $\overline{CC}$ = LOW will cause the next microprogram address to be the pipeline register contents; this is also the current microprogram address (word 3). When C_{n+4} goes HIGH, $\overline{CC}$ will go HIGH and together with $\overline{CCEN}$ = LOW, will force the Am2910 to address the next consecutive microprogram address (4).	This microstep will be executed 16 times. (Note that 80 = 5 x 16.)
4 through 7	Same as 3.	Same as 3.	Same as 3, except that at each address, the current microprogram address is written.	The microprogram itself is used as a counter in this application since the count is only 5, the microprogram is relatively short versus the memory's depth and this is a convenient means to economize on chip count.
8	Continues to count (note that it enters this line with an output of zero).	Since C_n is LOW (see left column) no change occurs in these devices. Note that the Y outputs contain the more significant bits of the address of the first character of the *next* character row.	The MUX selects the Am25LS168 ten-line-counters $\overline{RCO}$ as the condition code input to the Am2910 (CC). If the line count is less than 10, $\overline{CC}$ will be HIGH and the next microinstruction will be addressed. If the tenth line of a character row is executed, $\overline{CC}$ will be LOW and a JUMP-TO-SUBROUTINE to an address, supplied by the pipeline register ("TENTH") will be executed.	We are now at the end of a TV line. Therefore, the Horizontal Blanking Signal (HB) is HIGH. The least significant Am2911 slice now counts the invisible characters during the horizontal retrace.
9	Continues to count through the internal PC incrementer.	No change.	The MUX now selects the Last Address Comparator output for $\overline{CC}$. If the current more significant bits of the character-address coincide with the last address + 1 ($1920_{10}/16$) a subroutine call will be performed to "LASTA". Otherwise, the microprogram will continue consecutively.	Note that 80 characters/row and 24 rows/frame requires a 1920_{10} word memory. When the last memory location (1920_{10}) is read out, the scan will begin at 0.
A	Continues to count. At count 15, C_{n+4} goes HIGH.	No change until C_n goes HIGH, then count.	Same as at address 3.	Waiting for the least significant Am2911 to count to 15. This microstep will be executed as many times as necessary to accomplish this.
B	It doesn't matter what this device does at this microstep because at the next microstep it will receive LOW on its $\overline{ZERO}$ input.	No change.	Unconditionally ($\overline{CCEN}$ = HIGH) steers the microprogram to the address supplied by the pipeline register ("MAIN" = 2).	Performing a JUMP to the beginning of the main-loop (address 2).
C "TENTH"	Continues to count.	No change.	If internal counter is equal to zero, it means that 24 character rows were already displayed and we are at the bottom of the CRT display. A vertical retrace period is needed and the microprogram will continue sequentially. If the counter is not yet zero, we do not need to execute the vertical retrace routine and the next address will be supplied by the pipe-register ("GOBACK" = 14_{16}) while the internal counter is decremented.	The decision whether the bottom of the CRT (End of Frame) is reached or not is made internally in the Am2910, using its counter.

TABLE 6. DESCRIPTION OF THE MICROPROGRAM FOR THE CRT CONTROLLER (Cont.).

Micro-program Address	Low Order Am2911	High Order Am2911s	Am2910	Comments
D	$\overline{ZERO}$ = LOW, therefore, output Y = 0. This is necessary to assure that C_{n+4} is LOW.	Same as at address 0.	Same as at address 0.	As we are at the End of Frame, the "First-Address-Register" contents (enabled by the Am2910's $\overline{VECT}$ output) is pushed onto the Am2911's file. Note that the Vertical Blanking Signal (VB) goes HIGH.
E	Same as at address B.	No change.	The internal counter is loaded with 146_{10}, supplied by the pipeline register. The next consecutive microstep is addressed.	$(146_{10} + 1) \times 16_{10} = 2352_{10}$ equals the number of character-periods during vertical retrace. Loading 2352_{10} directly into the Am2910's counter would require 7 bits. Usingthis scheme we reduce the microprogram width.
F	Counts.	No change.	With $\overline{CCEN}$ = LOW and $\overline{CC}$ = HIGH (supplied from a constant HIGH by the MUX), the next address (10_{16}) will be pushed onto the Am2910 file, the counter will not be affected and the next consecutive microstep will be addressed.	This is a preparatory step for the 2 step "Vertical Retrace" double-nested loop.
10_H	Counts. When final count is reached, C_{n+4} = HIGH.	No change with C_n = LOW; increments with C_n = HIGH. This has no practical affect as the HB signal is HIGH, and at the beginning of the next visible line, the correct address will be fetched from the file (address 2).	The MUX supplies the C_{n+4} output of the less significant Am2911 slice to the Am2910 $\overline{CC}$ input. While this signal is low, the Am2910 will select the pipeline register as the source of the next microinstruction address. The current address (10_H) being written there, this instruction will be executed until $\overline{CC}$ goes HIGH. Then the next consecutive instruction will be selected through the Am2910 internal PC.	Again, this is a possible way to dwell on a certain microstep waiting a condition to change its status (like address 3 through 7). This is the internal loop of a double-nested loop system.
11_H	Counts.	No change.	If the final count has been reached, the next microinstruction will be addressed and the internal stack will be popped (adjusted). Otherwise, the next microinstruction address will be the one residing on the top of the stack (which is 10_{16}).	This is the external loop of the double-nested loop system, which counts the vertical retrace interval. By adding a single microinstruction the chip count was reduced.
12_H	Counts.	No change.	Same as at address 1.	Reinitializes the Am2910 internal counter with the number of character rows per frame.
13_H	Counts.	No change.	Unconditional return from subroutine. ($\overline{CCEN}$ = HIGH).	End of "TENTH" subroutine at End of Frame (with vertical retrace).
14_H "GOBACK"	Counts.	No change.	Unconditional return from subroutine.	End of "TENTH" subroutine without vertical retrace.
15_H "LASTA"	Counts.	Pushes zero into file.	Unconditional return from subroutine.	A one-line subroutine to reinitialize character address to zero.

a)

DEVICE NO.	DEVICE PATH	PATH 1	PATH 2	PATH 3	PATH 4
29775	CP to D	15	15	15	15
2911 (A)	C_n to C_{n+4}	9	–	–	–
2911 (A)	ZERO to C_{n+4}	–	30	–	–
2911 (B)	C_n to C_{n+4}	9	9	–	–
2911 (C)	C_n (t_S)	15	15	–	–
2911 (B, C)	FE (t_S)	–	–	14	–
2911 (B)	S_0, S_1 to C_{n+4}	–	–	–	30
2911 (C)	C_n (t_S)	–	–	–	15
TOTAL-ns		48	69	29	60

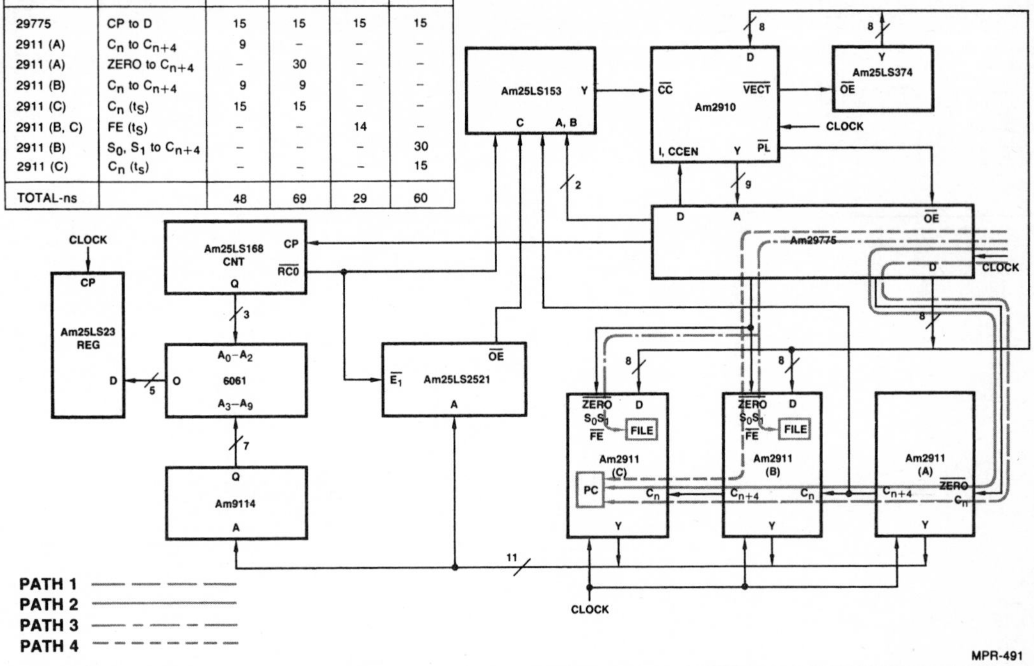

b)

DEVICE NO.	DEVICE PATH	PATH 1	PATH 2	PATH 3
29775	CP to D	15	15	15
2911 (A)	ZERO to Y	19	–	–
2911 (B, C)	ZERO to Y	–	19	–
2911 (B, C)	S_0, S_1 to Y	–	–	19
9114	A to D	150	150	150
6061	A to Out	70	70	70
25LS23	D to CP (t_S)	23	23	23
TOTAL-ns		277	277	277

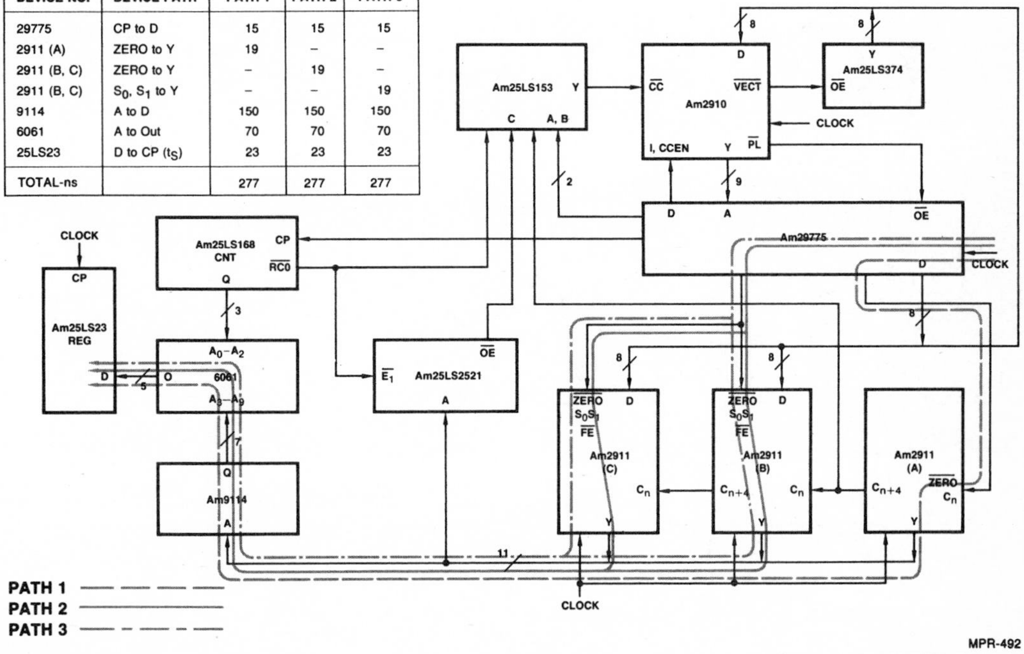

Figure 25.

c)

DEVICE NO.	DEVICE PATH	PATH 1	PATH 2	PATH 3
29775	CP to D	15	15	–
2910	I to Y	40	–	–
2910	CCEN to Y	–	23	–
2910	CP to Y	–	–	54
29775	A (t_S)	40	40	40
TOTAL-ns		95	78	94

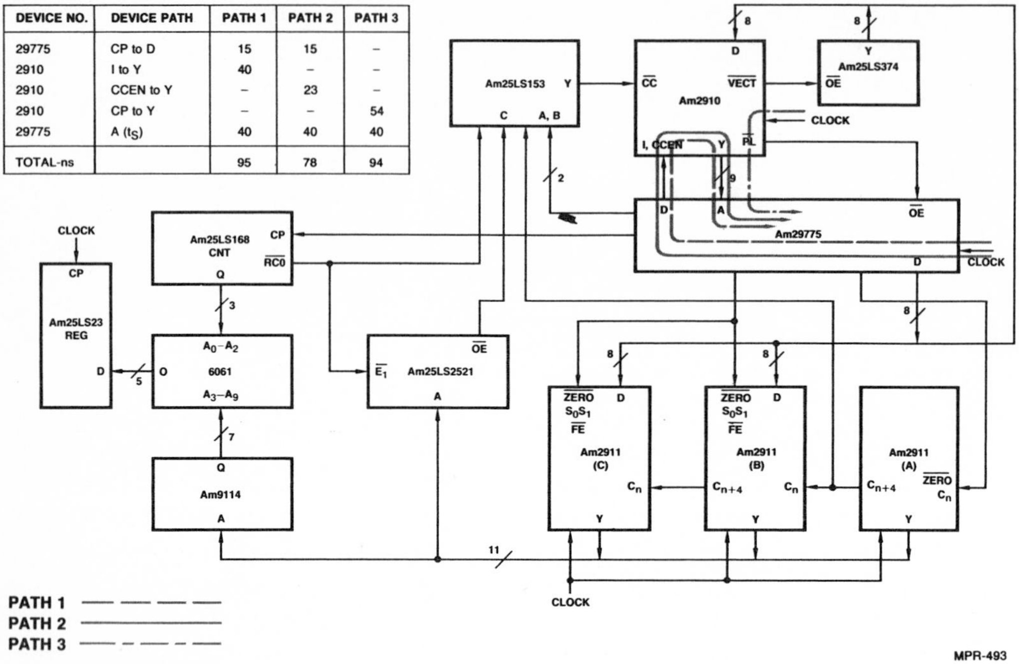

d)

DEVICE NO.	DEVICE PATH	PATH 1
29775	CP to D	15
25LS153	A, B to Y	19
2910	CC to Y	21
29775	A (t_S)	40
TOTAL-ns		95

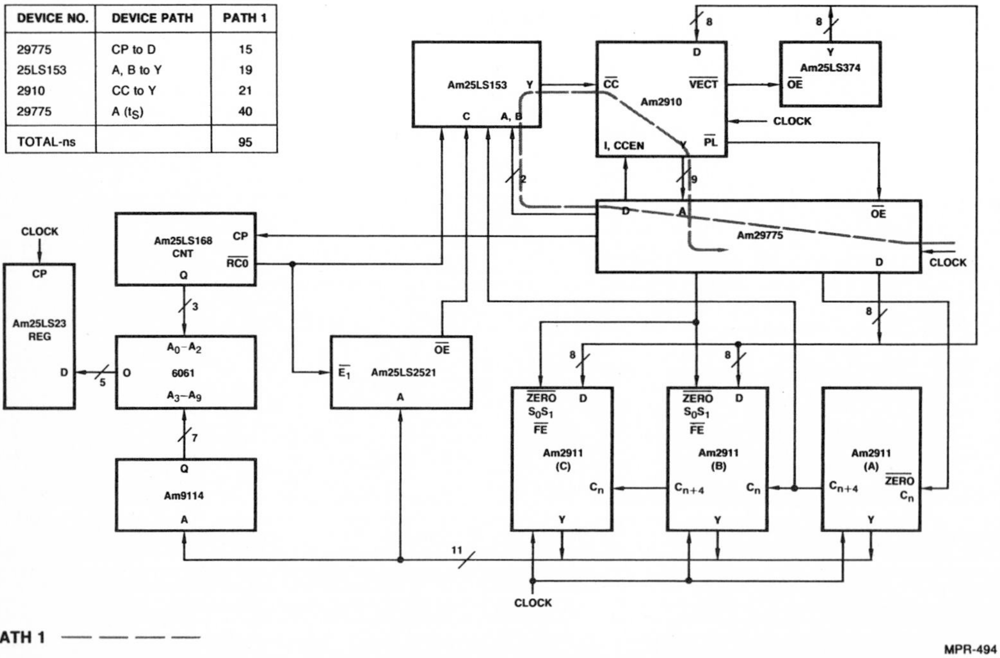

Figure 25. (Cont.)

e)

DEVICE NO.	DEVICE PATH	PATH 1	PATH 2
29775	CP to D	15	15
2910	I to PL, VECT	27	27
29775	E_1 to D	–	15
25LS374	OE to Y	14	–
2910	PC (t_S)	–	34
2911	D (t_S)	17	–
TOTAL-ns		73	91

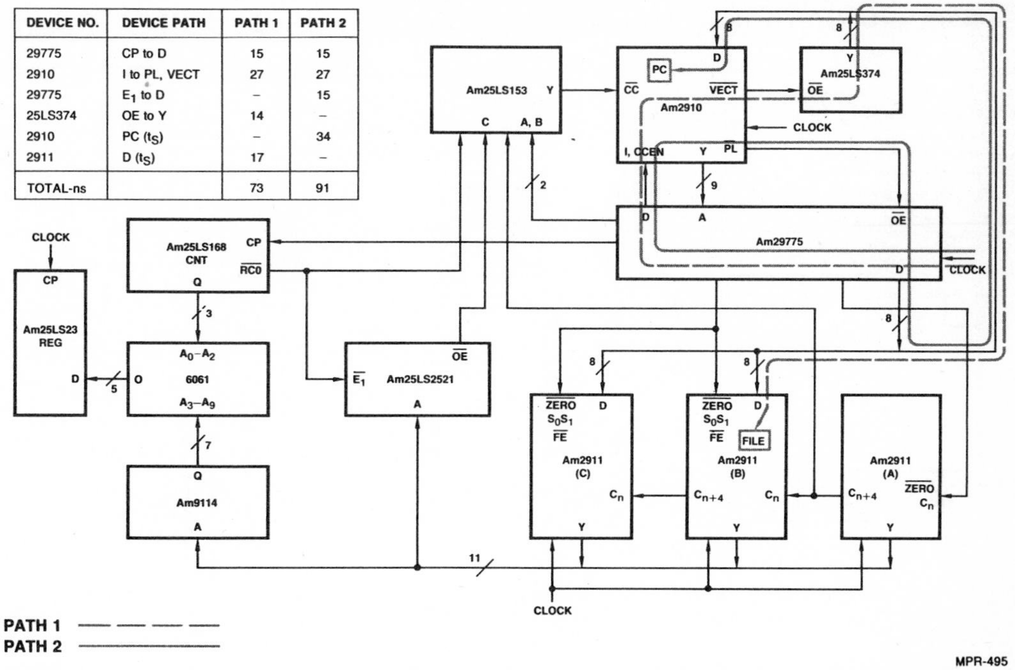

MPR-495

f)

DEVICE NO.	DEVICE PATH	PATH 1	PATH 2	PATH 3
29775	CP to D	15	15	15
2911	ZERO to C_{n+4}	–	–	30
2911	C_n to C_{n+4}	–	9	–
25LS168	CP to $\overline{RCO}$	19	–	–
25LS153	D to Y	20	20	20
2910	CC to Y	21	21	21
29775	A (t_S)	40	40	40
TOTAL-ns		115	105	126

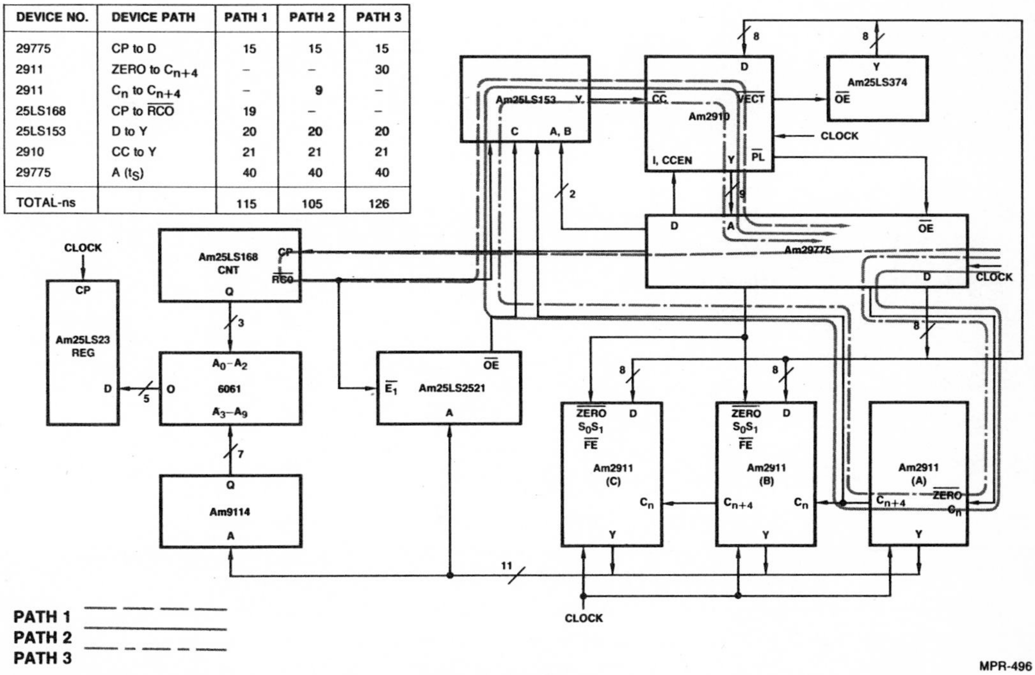

MPR-496

Figure 25. (Cont.)

g)

DEVICE NO.	DEVICE PATH	PATH 1	PATH 2	PATH 3
29775	CP to D	15	15	–
2911	S_0, S_1 to Y	–	19	–
2911	CP to Y (S_1S_0 = HL)	–	–	54
25LS168	CP to $\overline{RCO}$	19	–	–
25LS2521	A to E_0	–	9	9
25LS2521	E_1 to E_0	6	–	–
25LS153	D to Y	20	20	20
2910	CC to Y	21	21	21
29775	A (t_S)	40	40	40
TOTAL-ns		121	124	144

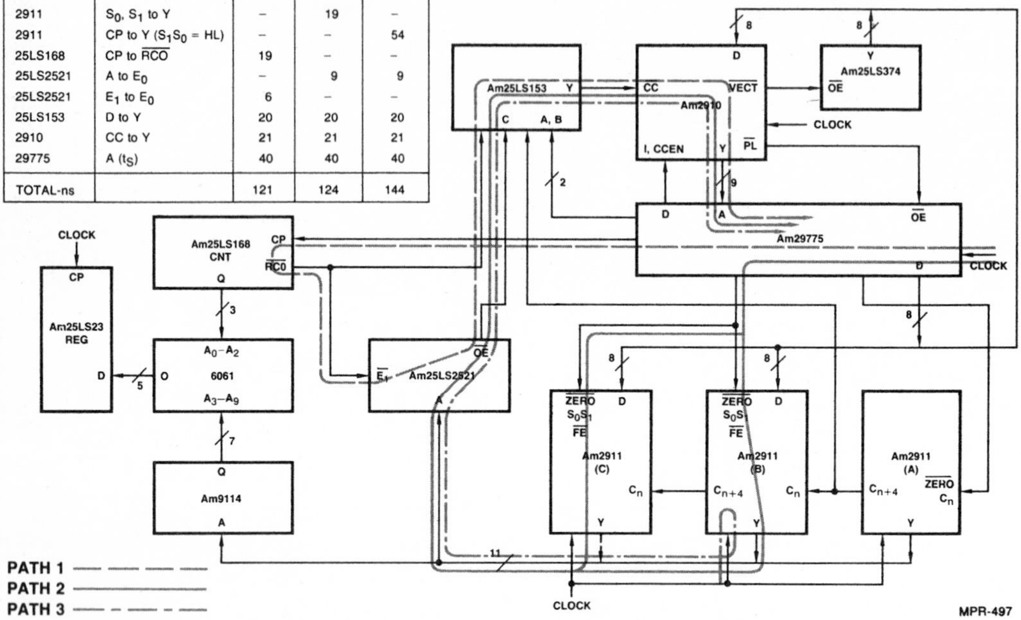

h)

DEVICE NO.	DEVICE PATH	PATH 1	PATH 2
2911	CP to Y (S_1S_0 = HL)	39	–
2911	CP to C_{n+4} (S_1S_0 = HL)	–	54
2911	C_n (t_S)	–	15
9114	A to D	150	–
6061	A to OUT	70	–
25LS23	D (t_S)	23	–
TOTAL-ns		282	69

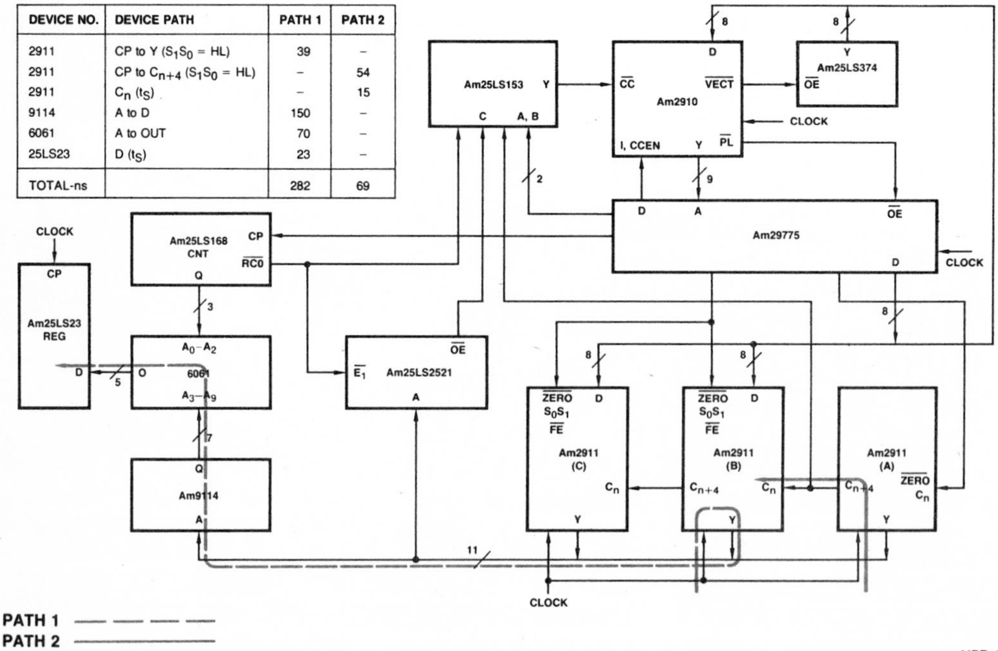

Figure 25. (Cont.)

i)

DEVICE NO.	DEVICE PATH	PATH 1	PATH 2	PATH 3
29775	CP to D	15	15	15
2910	I to PL	36	36	36
29775	E_1 to D	15	–	–
25LS374	OE to Y	–	14	14
2911	D to Y	9	9	–
9114	A to D	150	150	–
6061	A to D	70	70	–
25LS23	t_S (D)	23	23	–
2911	t_S (D)	–	–	17
TOTAL-ns		318	317	82

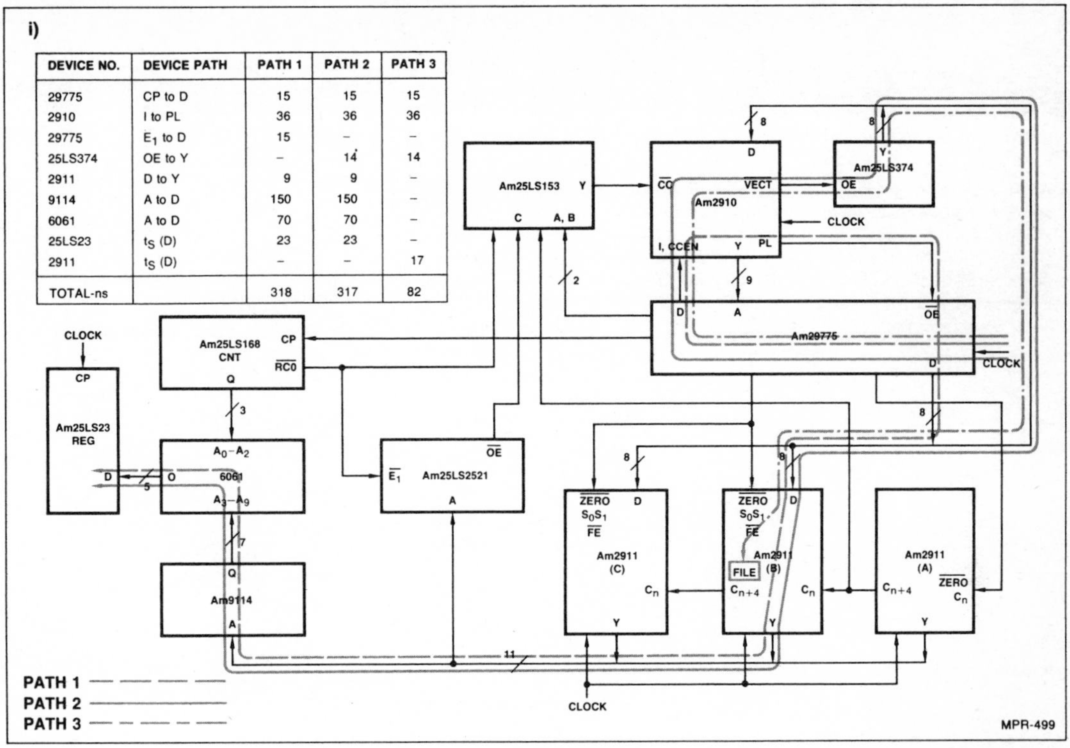

Figure 25. (Cont.)

SUMMARY

The Am2910 provides a powerful solution to the microprogram memory sequence control problem. The Am2910 is a fixed instruction set, 12-bit wide microprogram sequencer. In addition, the Am2909, Am2911, Am29811A and Am29803A provide another solution to the microprogram sequencing problem. These devices are bit slice oriented and provide more potential flexibility to the microprogram sequencing solution. All of these devices are particularly well suited for the high performance computer control unit and structured state machine designs using overlap fetch of the next microinstruction – also referred to as instruction-data-based microprogram architecture.

These Am2900 family microprogram control devices offer the highest performance LSI solution to the problem of microprogram control. They provide a number of conditional-branch source addresses as well as conditional jump-to-subroutine and conditional-return instructions. In addition, several techniques for timed and untimed looping are provided such that loops from one to several microinstructions can be executed. All of the devices described in this chapter are competitively priced and currently available. In addition, all of these devices are available with specifications guaranteed over the full commercial temperature range and power supply tolerance as well as the full military temperature range and power supply tolerance. All of these devices undergo 100% reliability assurance testing in compliance with MIL-STD-883.

APPENDIX A

Figure A1 shows the logic diagram of an interface circuit used to connect the microprogrammed CRT controller to any Am9080A type processor. Sixteen address-lines, eight data lines, a memory-read, a memory write and an I/O write signal are assumed to be used in an active LOW polarity.

An Am25LS2521 8-bit comparator is used to decode the addresses of the 2K by 8 character memory. This memory can be placed anywhere in the memory space in increments of 2K by using 5 DIP-switches. The comparator is enabled by the presence of either the $\overline{\text{MMR}}$ or the $\overline{\text{MMW}}$ signal. The output of this comparator is the $\overline{\text{HOST ACCESS}}$ signal.

The $\overline{\text{HOST ACCESS}}$ signal enables the two Am25LS240 buffers which connect the processor address bus to the character memory address bus. It also enables one half of an Am25LS241 buffer transferring the $\overline{\text{MMR}}$ or $\overline{\text{MMR}}$ active LOW signal to the proper data buffer enable (Am25LS240's) and to the $\overline{\text{WE}}$ pins of the four Am9114 memories in case of a memory write operation. The $\overline{\text{CS}}$ of two of these memories are driven by A_{10} while the $\overline{\text{CS}}$ of the other two memories are driven by A_{10}, thus forming a 2K by 8 memory space.

An Am25LS2521 8-bit comparator is enabled by the $\overline{\text{I/OW}}$ control line. If n matches the settings of the DIP switches at the B inputs of the comparator, an OUT n instruction will write the data into the Am25LS374 "First Address Register".

Figure A2 shows the complete wiring diagram of this interface circuit.

Note: Figure A2 is at back of the book.

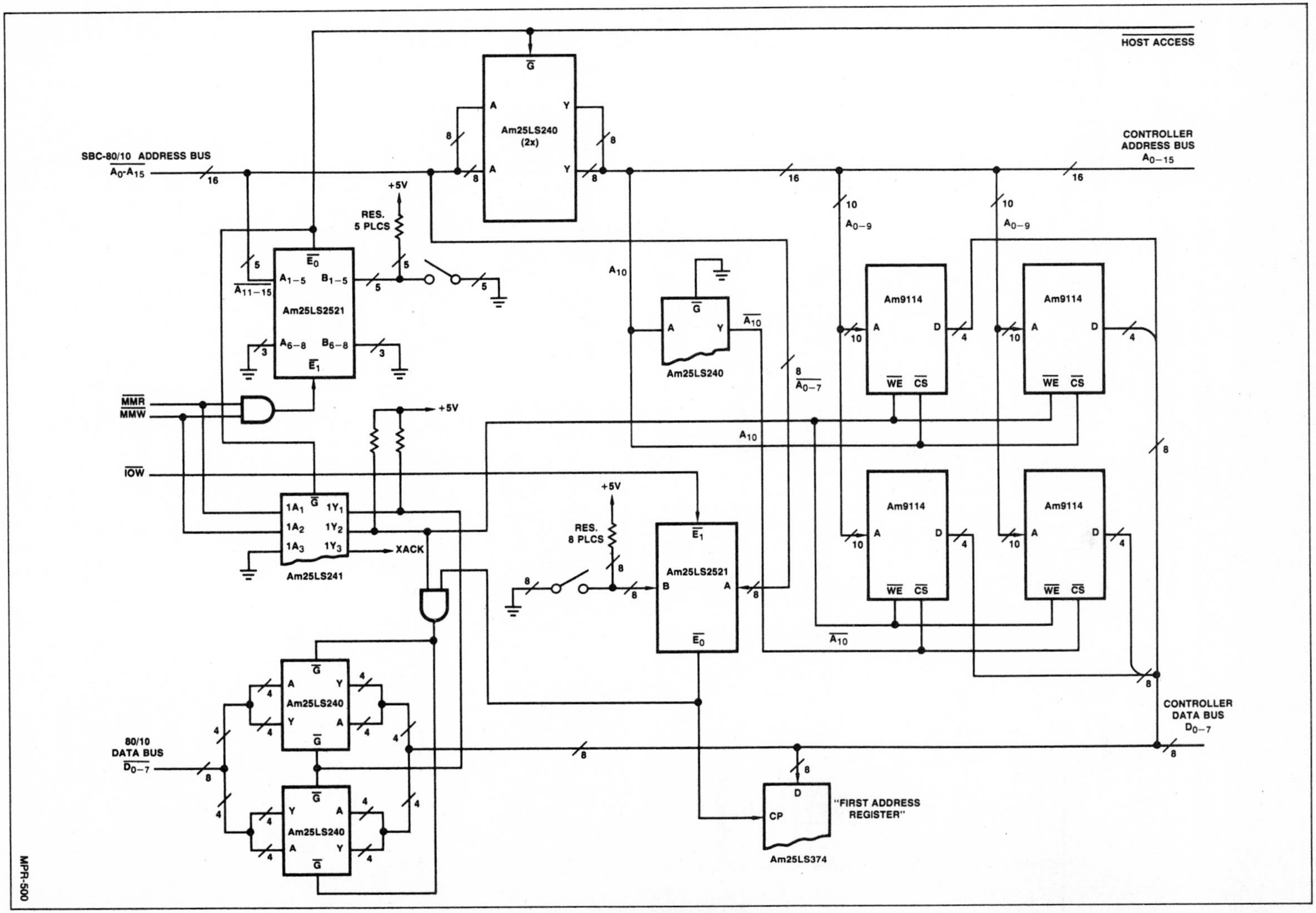

Figure A1. CRT Controller.

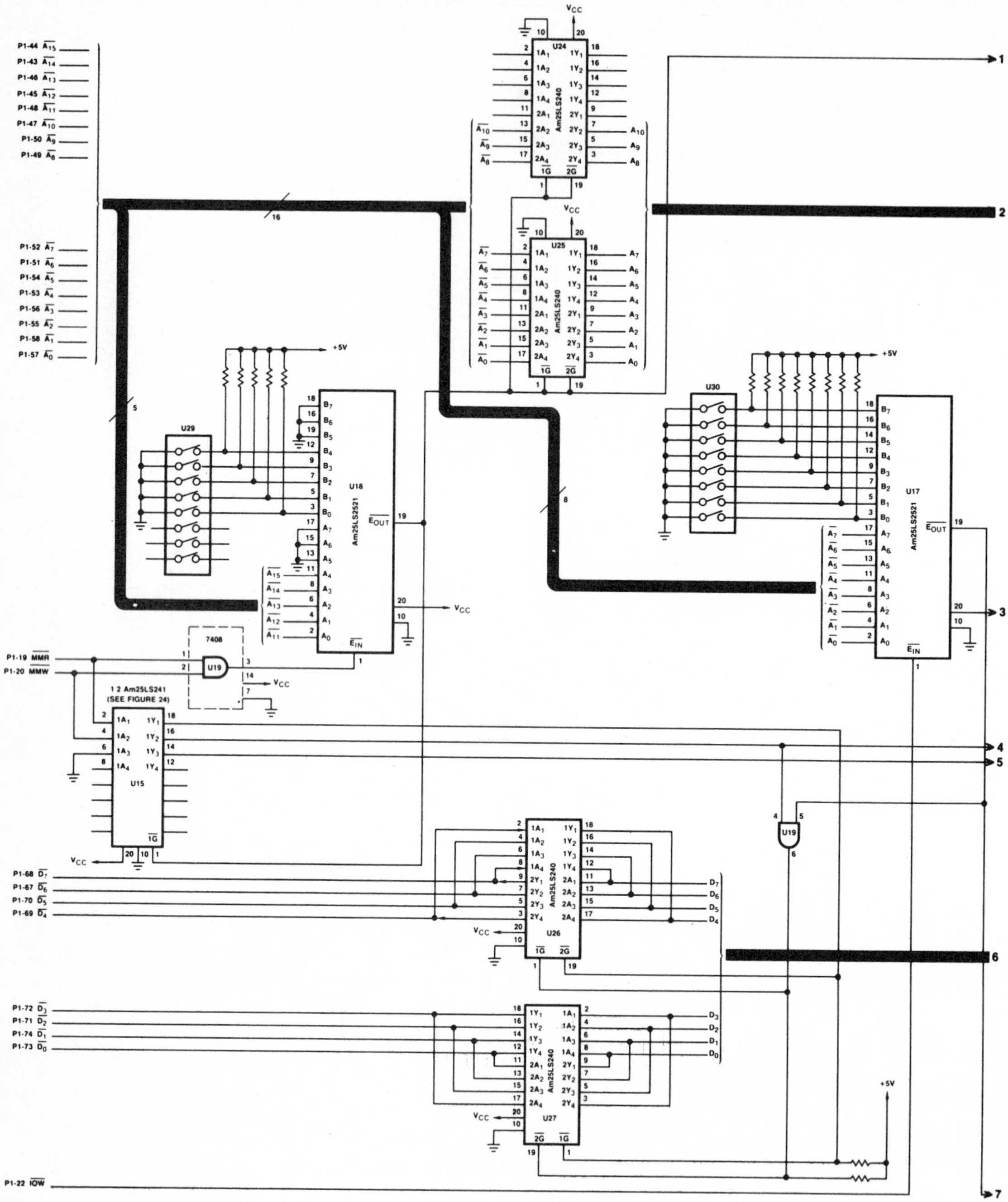

Figure A2. CRT Controller.

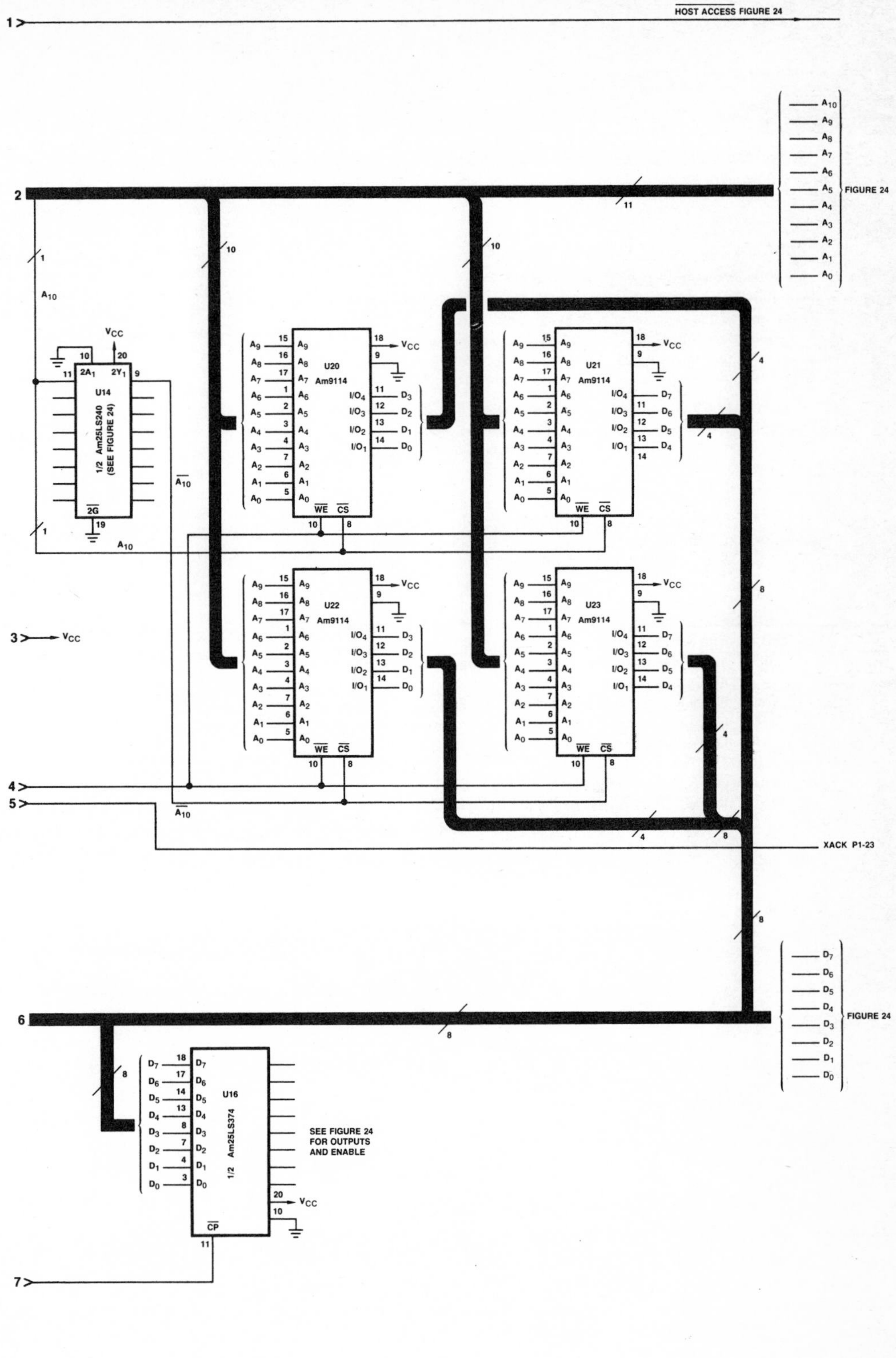
HOST ACCESS FIGURE 24
FIGURE 24
A10
U14
1/2 Am25LS240 (SEE FIGURE 24)
U20
Am9114
U21
Am9114
U22
Am9114
U23
Am9114
VCC
XACK P1-23
FIGURE 24
U16
1/2 Am25LS374
SEE FIGURE 24 FOR OUTPUTS AND ENABLE

APPENDIX B

General

A software emulation of the CRT controller was written in BASIC-E and run on the System 29 support processor. Figure B1 is a printout of this program.

Notations

For reference purposes, each clock pulse (CP) in the program is numbered. The clocks are character-rate clocks. A subscript "10" signifies that this variable belongs to the Am2910 (e.g. R10 = the contents of the Am2910 Register Counter) and similarly a subscript 11 signifies the Am2911 dependent variables (e.g. Y11 – the Y outputs of the two more significant Am2911s).

Usually the normal function names were used though for the active LOW functions the bar was deleted for simplicity. A 0 signifies always a LOW and 1 signifies HIGH. Other abbreviations used in the program:

MA =	Microprogram Address (Y output of the Am2910)
CA =	Character Address
PC =	Program Counter (internal)
R =	Register (internal)
F =	File (internal)
SP =	Stack Pointer (internal)
TENC =	The Am25LS168 decade counter
L4B =	The 4 least significant bits of CA (the Y outputs of the less significant Am2911
CN =	Carry-in into the less significant Am2911
CN4 =	Carry-out from the less significant Am2911
CN4 =	Carry-in to the next significant Am2911
I10 =	The Am2910 instruction
HB =	Horizontal Blanking signal (active HIGH)
VB =	Vertical Blanking signal (active HIGH)
CPM =	Maximum Clock Pulse (at which the program stops)

Description

The different groups and subroutines of the emulation program are as follows: (See Figure B1).

<1000 series:	The microcode. Subroutine 50 is the Am25LS168 decade counter clocking routine. TENTH is the RCO output of this device.
1000 series:	This is essentially the Am2910 emulation. Note the definition of the two functions FNFAIL and FNPASS at the beginning of the program, compare to the Am2910 instruction definitions in its data sheet.
2000 series:	The Am25LS153 multiplexer emulation.
2500 series:	The less significant Am2911 emulation. Note that the only input to this device is ZEROL. CN and the internal PC (called L4B) are controlled in the CLOCK Subroutine (4000 series).
3000 series:	The two more significant Am2911's emulation, S_0 and S_1 are treated as a single number (ranging from 0 through 3) and denoted by S11.
4000 series:	The Clocking routine.
5000 series:	The main emulation routine. It includes the Am25LS2521 comparator routine and checks the Clock Pulse against CPM to determine end of run.
5500 series:	Emulation parameter setup (initialization). The starting and ending CP numbers, MA, TENC, R10 and VECTOR (The "First Address Register") can be set.
6000 series:	Sets up the print-out parameters
7000 series:	Printout subroutine
9000 series:	Sets the program mode: RUN, PRINT or QUIT (return to CP/M)

The emulation was exercised to evaluate fifteen different performance aspects of the CRT Controller. The results indicated that in all cases, the design operated as desired.

```
REM
REV=12
PRINT REV
9000    REM     HEADER
        PRINT
        PRINT
        PRINT " ******************************************************"
        PRINT
        PRINT
        PRINT "    A MICROPROGRAMMED CRT CONTROLLER EMULATION"
        PRINT
        PRINT
        PRINT " ******************************************************"
        PRINT
        PRINT
        PRINT "                              BY MOSHE M. SHAVIT"
        PRINT "                            ADVANCED MICRO DEVICES"
        PRINT "                               FEBRUARY 27, 1978"
        PRINT
        PRINT
REM
        DIM F10(6)
        DEF     FNFAIL=CCEN=0 AND CC=1
        DEF     FNPASS=CCEN=1  OR CC=0
REM
REM
REM     GOTO 6000       REM     PROGRAM PARAMETERS (REMOVED REV 6)
REM
REM     <--REV 6
REM
9100    PRINT
        PRINT
        PRINT
        INPUT "R-UN, P-RINT OR Q-UIT ";MODE$
        IF LEN(MODE$)=0 THEN GOTO 9100
        MODE=ASC(MODE$)-79
        IF MODE<1 OR MODE > 3 \
                THEN    PRINT MODE$; " IS INVALID":\
                        GOTO 9100
        ON MODE GOTO 9110,9120,9130
REM
9120    RETURN
REM
9130    REM     RUN
        PRINT
        INPUT "PUT RESULTS ON FILE (0 IF DIRECT PRINTOUT)= ";WFILE$
        PRINT "CP= ";CP;"MA= ";MA;"VECTOR= ";VECTOR;\
                "CPM= ";CPM;"ROW= ";24-R10
        INPUT "INITIALIZE (Y OR N; CP,MA=0 IF N)";S$
        IF S$="Y" \
                THEN GOSUB 5500 \       REM     INIT.
                ELSE    CP=0 : MA=0
        IF WFILE$="0" \
                THEN    GOTO 6010 \     REM DIRECT PRINTOUT
                ELSE    FILE WFILE$ : GOTO 5000 REM MAIN
REM
9110    REM     PRINT
        PRINT
        INPUT "GET RESULTS FROM FILE=";RFILE$
        FILE RFILE$
REM
6000    REM PRINT PARAMETERS
        PRINT
6010    PRINT "OUTPUT FORMATS:"
```

Figure B1.

```
        PRINT '             A=CP AND CA ONLY'
        PRINT '             B=CP,CA,HB,VB,MA'
        PRINT '             C=CP,CA,MA,TENC,R10'
        PRINT '             D=ALL'
        PRINT
        INPUT 'FORMAT=';FORMAT$
        IF LEN(FORMAT$)=0 THEN GOTO 6010
        IF ASC(FORMAT$)<65 OR ASC(FORMAT$)>68 \
                THEN PRINT FORMAT$;' IS ILLEGAL' :\
                        GOTO 6010
        PRINT
REM
6020    REM
        IF WFILE$ NE '0' \
        THEN    CONTROL$='A' :\
                GOTO 6030
        PRINT 'CLOCK CONTROL'
        PRINT '             A=CONTINOUS'
        PRINT '             B=STEP'
        INPUT 'CONTROL=';CONTROL$
        IF LEN(CONTROL$)=0 THEN GOTO 6020
        IF ASC(CONTROL$)<65 OR ASC(CONTROL$)>66 \
                THEN    PRINT CONTROL$;' IS ILLEGAL' :\
                        GOTO 6020
        PRINT
REM
6030    PRINT 'OUTPUT CONTROL'
        PRINT '             A=AT EACH CP'
        PRINT '             B=AT EVERY N-TH CP'
        PRINT '             C=MANUAL CONTROL'
        PRINT '             D=STARTING AT CPS AT EVERY CP'
        PRINT '             E=STARTING AT CPS AT EVERY N-TH CP'
        INPUT 'OUTPUT=';OUTPUT$
        IF LEN(OUTPUT$)=0 THEN GOTO 6030
        IF ASC(OUTPUT$)<65 OR ASC(OUTPUT$)>69 \
                THEN    PRINT OUTPUT$;' IS ILLEGAL' :\
                        GOTO 6030
        O.CTL=ASC(OUTPUT$)-64
        ON O.CTL GOTO 6090,6032,6090,6034,6036
6032    INPUT 'N=';N
        M=0
        GOTO 6090
6034    INPUT 'CPS= ';CPS
        GOTO 6090
6036    INPUT 'CPS= ';CPS
        INPUT 'N= ';N
        M=0
        GOTO 6090
REM
6090    FORMAT = ASC(FORMAT$)-64
        ON FORMAT GOSUB 6190,6300,6200,6100
        IF WFILE$='0' THEN GOTO 5000    REM     MAIN
REM
6900    PRINT
        IF END #1 THEN 6910
        FOR I=1 TO 2 STEP 0     REM DO UNTIL END OF FILE
        READ #1; CP,R10,F1,SP10,PC10,CA,MUX,CC,CCEN,MA,TENC,\
                CN4,F11,HB,VB
        F10(SP10)=F1
        GOSUB 7000      REM PRINT
        GOSUB 5200      REM ESCAPE      (REV 7)
        IF S=155 THEN PRINT:PRINT 'ABORTED AT ';CP : GOTO 6910
        NEXT I
```

Figure B1 (Cont.)

```
REM
6910    CLOSE 1
        OUT 100,12       REM      PRINTER PAGE EJECT (REV 7)
        GOTO 9100
REM
6100    PRINT
        PRINT "CP","R10","F10","SP10","PC10"
        PRINT "CA","MUX","CC","CCEN","MA"
        PRINT "TENC","CN4","F11","HB","VB"
        PRINT
6190    RETURN
REM
6200    PRINT
        PRINT "CLOCK","CHAR.ADDR","2910 REG.","LINE CNTR.","NEXT MA"
        RETURN
REM
6300    PRINT
        PRINT "CLOCK","CHAR.ADDR","H.BLANKING","V.BLANKING","NEXT MA"
        RETURN
REM
REM
7000    REM      PRINT SUBROUTINE
        ON O.CTL GOTO 7010,7005,7002,7003,7004
REM
7002    INPUT "OUTPUT (Y OR N)";S$
        IF S$="Y" \
                THEN     GOTO 7010 \
                ELSE     RETURN
REM
7003    IF CP<CPS THEN RETURN ELSE GOTO 7010
REM
7004    IF CP<CPS THEN RETURN ELSE GOTO 7005
REM
7005    M=M+1
        IF M=N THEN M=0 : GOTO 7010 ELSE RETURN
REM
7010    ON FORMAT GOTO 7100,7200,7300,7400
REM
7100    PRINT "CP= ";CP,"CA= ";CA
        RETURN
REM
7200    IF HB=0 THEN HB$="L" ELSE HB$="         H"
        IF VB=0 THEN VB$="L" ELSE VB$="         H"
        PRINT CP,CA,HB$,VB$,MA
        RETURN
REM
7300    PRINT
        PRINT CP,CA,R10,TENC,MA
        RETURN
REM
7400    PRINT
        PRINT CP,R10,F10(SP10),SP10,PC10
        PRINT CA,MUX,CC,CCEN,MA
        PRINT TENC,CN4,F11,HB,VB
        RETURN
REM
REM
5000    REM      MAIN ROUTINE
        REM
        GOSUB 4000        REM      CLOCK
        REM      FETCH MICROCODE
        ON MA+1 GOSUB 30,2,3,4,5,6,7,8,9,10,11,12,13,14,15,16,17,18,19,20,21,22
        GOSUB 2500        REM      2911L
        GOSUB 3000        REM      2911H
```

Figure B1 (Cont.)

```
        CA=Y11*16+L4B     REM      CHARACTER ADDRESS
                          REM      COMPARATOR NEXT
        IF Y11=120 AND TENTH=0 \           REM REV 8
                THEN      COMP=0 \
                ELSE      COMP=1
        GOSUB 2000        REM      MUX
        GOSUB 1000        REM      2910
REM     REV 6
        IF WFILE$="0" THEN GOSUB 7000 \ REM DIRECT PRINTOUT
                ELSE PRINT #1;CP,R10,F10(SP10),SP10,PC10,CA,MUX,\
                          CC,CCEN,MA,TENC,CN4,F11,HB,VB
        IF CONTROL$="B" THEN INPUT S$    REM      SINGLE STEP
        REM     CHECK END OF RUN
        GOSUB 5200        REM      ESCAPE   (REV 7)
        IF S=155 THEN PRINT:PRINT "ABORTED AT ";CP : GOTO 5100
        IF CP<CPM THEN GOTO 5000          REM      REPEAT MAIN
REM
5100    IF WFILE$ NE "0" THEN CLOSE (1)
        OUT 100,12        REM PRINTER PAGE EJECT (REV 7)
        GOTO 9100
REM
REM     5200 SUB REV 7
5200    REM     ESCAPE SUBROUTINE
        S=INP(97)
        S=INT(S/2)
        S=S/2-INT(S/2)
        IF S NE 0 THEN S = INP(96)
        RETURN
REM
5500    REM     INITIALIZATION
        PRINT
        SP10=1
        PRINT "MA= ";MA
5505    INPUT "NEW MA (Y OR N)";S$
        IF S$="N" THEN GOTO 5510
        INPUT "MA=(0<=MA<22)";MA
        MA=INT(MA)
        IF MA<0 OR MA>21 \
                THEN     PRINT MA;" IS ILLEGAL" :\
                         GOTO 5505
        IF MA=0 THEN TENC=0 : HB=1 : TENTH=1
REM
5510    PRINT
        PRINT "VECTOR= ";VECTOR
5515    INPUT "NEW VECTOR (Y OR N)";S$
        IF S$="N" THEN GOTO 5520
        INPUT "VECTOR=(0<=VECTOR<120)";VECTOR
        VECTOR=INT(VECTOR)
        IF VECTOR<0 OR VECTOR>119 \
                THEN     PRINT VECTOR;" IS ILLEGAL" :\
                         GOTO 5515
REM
5520    PRINT
        PRINT "CP= ";CP
        INPUT "NEW CP (Y OR N) ";S$
        IF S$="N" THEN GOTO 5530
5525    INPUT "CP(>=0)= ";CP
        CP=INT(CP)
        IF CP<0 THEN PRINT CP;" IS ILLEGAL" : GOTO 5525
REM
5530    PRINT
        PRINT "CPM= ";CPM
5535    INPUT "NEW CPM (Y OR N)";S$
        IF S$="N" THEN GOTO 5540
```

Figure B1. (Cont.)

```
        INPUT "CPM=(CP+1<CPM)";CPM
        CPM=INT(CPM)
        IF CPM<CP+1 THEN PRINT CPM;" IS ILLEGAL";"CP= ";CP :GOTO 5535
REM
5540    PRINT
        PRINT "TENC= ";TENC
        IF MA=0 THEN GOTO 5550
5545    INPUT "NEW TENC (Y OR N)";S$
        IF S$="N" THEN GOTO 5550
        INPUT "TENC=(0<=TENC<10)";TENC
        TENC=INT(TENC)
        IF TENC<0 OR TENC>9 \
                THEN    PRINT TENC;" IS ILLEGAL" :\
                        GOTO 5545
        IF TENC=9 THEN TENTH=0 ELSE TENTH=1
REM
5550    PRINT
        PRINT "R10= ";R10
5555    INPUT "NEW R10 (Y OR N)";S$
        IF S$="N" THEN GOTO 5560
        INPUT "R10 (0<=R10<25)=";R10
        R10=INT(R10)
        IF R10<0 OR R10>24 THEN PRINT R10;" IS ILLEGAL" : GOTO 5555
REM
5560    REM
        RETURN
REM
REM
REM
30      I10=6
        CCEN=0
        MUX=3
        S11=3
        FE=0
        ZEROH=1
        ZEROL=0
        CN=0
        HB=1    REM     REV 2
        VB=0
        PL=0
        RETURN
REM
2       I10=12
        S11=0
        FE=1
        ZEROH=1
        ZEROL=0
        CN=0
        HB=1    REM     REV 2
        VB=0
        PL=23
        RETURN
REM
3       I10=14
        S11=2
        FE=1
        ZEROH=1
        ZEROL=0
        CN=1
        HB=1    REM     REV 2
        VB=0
        RETURN
REM
4       I10=3
```

Figure B1 (Cont.)

```
        CCEN=0
        MUX=1
        S11=0
        FE=1
        ZEROH=1
        ZEROL=1
        CN=1
        HB=0
        VB=0
        PL=3
        RETURN
REM
5       I10=3
        CCEN=0
        MUX=1
        S11=0
        FE=1
        ZEROH=1
        ZEROL=1
        CN=1
        HB=0
        VB=0
        PL=4
        RETURN
REM
6       I10=3
        CCEN=0
        MUX=1
        S11=0
        FE=1
        ZEROH=1
        ZEROL=1
        CN=1
        HB=0
        VB=0
        PL=5
        RETURN
REM
7       I10=3
        CCEN=0
        MUX=1
        S11=0
        FE=1
        ZEROH=1
        ZEROL=1
        CN=1
        HB=0
        VB=0
        PL=6
        RETURN
REM
8       I10=3
        CCEN=0
        MUX=1
        S11=0
        FE=1
        ZEROH=1
        ZEROL=1
        CN=1
        HB=0
        VB=0
        PL=7
        RETURN
REM
9       I10=1
        CCEN=0
        MUX=0
        S11=0
        FE=1
        ZEROH=1
        ZEROL=1
        CN=1
        GOSUB 50 REM TENC
        VB=0
        PL=12
        RETURN
REM
10      I10=1
        CCEN=0
        MUX=2
        S11=0
        FE=1
        ZEROH=1
        ZEROL=1
        CN=1
        GOSUB 50
        VB=0
        PL=21
        RETURN
REM
11      I10=3
        CCEN=0
        MUX=1
        S11=0
        FE=1
        ZEROH=1
        ZEROL=1
        CN=1
        GOSUB 50
        VB=0
        PL=10
        RETURN
REM
12      I10=3
        CCEN=1
        S11=0
        FE=1
        ZEROH=1
        GOSUB 50
        VB=0
        PL=2
        RETURN
REM
13      I10=9
        S11=0
        FE=0    REM     REV 5
        ZEROH=1
        ZEROL=1
        CN=1
        GOSUB 50
        VB=0
        PL=20
        RETURN
REM
14      I10=6
        CCEN=0
        MUX=3
        S11=3
```

Figure B1 (Cont.)

```
        FE=0    REM      REV 10
        ZEROH=1
        ZEROL=0
        GOSUB 50
        VB=1
        RETURN
REM
15      I10=12
        S11=0   REM      REV 10
        FE=1    REM      REV 10
        ZEROH=1
REM     ZEROH=1          REM      REMOVED REV 10
        GOSUB 50
        VB=1
        PL=119
        RETURN
REM
16      I10=4
        CCEN=0
        MUX=3
        S11=0
        FE=1
        ZEROH=1
        ZEROL=1
        CN=1
        GOSUB 50
        VB=1
        RETURN
REM
17      I10=3
        CCEN=0
        MUX=1
        S11=0
        FE=1
        ZEROH=1
        ZEROL=1
        CN=1
        GOSUB 50
        VB=1
        PL=16
        RETURN
REM
18      I10=8
        S11=0
        FE=1
        ZEROH=1
        ZEROL=1
        CN=1
        GOSUB 50
        VB=1
        RETURN
REM
19      I10=12
        S11=0
        FE=1
        ZEROH=1
        ZEROL=1
        CN=1
        GOSUB 50
        VB=1
        PL=23
        RETURN
REM
20      I10=10
```

Figure B1 (Cont.)

```
        CCEN=1
        S11=0
        FE=1
        ZEROH=1
        ZEROL=1
        CN=1
        GOSUB 50
        VB=1
        RETURN
REM
21      I10=10
        CCEN=1
        S11=0
        FE=1
        ZEROH=1
        ZEROL=1
        CN=1
        GOSUB 50
        VB=0
        RETURN
REM
22      I10=10
        CCEN=1
        FE=0            REM     REV 9
        ZEROH=0
        ZEROL=1         REM     REV 9
        CN=1
        GOSUB 50
        VB=0
        RETURN
REM
50      REM TEN-LINE-COUNTER CLOCKING SUBROUTINE
        IF HB=1 THEN RETURN
        HB=1
        TENC=TENC+1
        IF TENC=9 THEN TENTH=0 ELSE TENTH=1
        IF TENC=10 THEN TENC=0
        RETURN
REM     PUSH AND POP SUBROUTINES REMOVED REV 3
1000    REM     2910 INSTRUCTIONS SUBROUTINE
        ON I10+1 GOTO 1100,1110,1120,1130,1140,1150,1160,1170,1180, \
        1190,1200,1210,1220,1230,1240,1250
REM
1100    REM     JZ
        MA=0    REM     2910 Y
        SP10=0  REM     2910 STACK POINTER (=0 REV 3)
        RETURN
REM
1110    REM     CJS
        IF FNFAIL \
                THEN    MA=PC10 \
                ELSE    MA=PL :\
                        PUSH=1          REM     REV 3
        RETURN
REM
1120    REM     JMAP
        PRINT "JMAP NOT PROGRAMMED"
        RETURN
REM
1130    REM     CJP
        IF FNFAIL \
                THEN    MA=PC10 \
                ELSE    MA=PL
        RETURN
```

Figure B1 (Cont.)

```
REM
1140    REM     PUSH
        IF FNPASS THEN R10=PL   REM     LOAD COUNTER
        MA=PC10
        PUSH=1          REM     REV 3
        RETURN
REM
1150    REM     JSRP
        PRINT "JSRP NOT PROGRAMMED"
        RETURN
REM
1160    REM     CJV
        IF FNFAIL \
                THEN    MA=PC10 \
                ELSE    MA=VECTOR
        RETURN
REM
1170    REM     JRP
        IF FNFAIL \
                THEN MA=R10 \
                ELSE MA=PL
        RETURN
REM
1180    REM     RFCT
        IF R10=0 \
                THEN    MA=PC10 :\
                        POP=1 \
                ELSE    MA=F10(SP10) :\
                        R10=R10-1
        RETURN
REM
1190    REM     RPCT
        IF R10=0 \
                THEN    MA=PC10 \
                ELSE    MA=PL :\
                        R10=R10-1
        RETURN
REM
1200    REM     CRTN
        IF FNFAIL \
                THEN    MA=PC10 \
                ELSE    MA=F10(SP10) :\
                        POP=1           REM     REV 3
        RETURN
REM
1210    REM     CJPP

        PRINT "CJPP NOT PROGRAMMED"
        RETURN
REM
1220    REM     LDCT
        R10=PL
        MA=PC10
        RETURN
REM
1230    REM     LOOP
        IF FNFAIL \
                THEN    MA=F10(SP10) \
                ELSE    MA=PC10 :\
                        POP=1           REM REV 3
        RETURN
REM
1240    REM     CONT
        MA=PC10
        RETURN
```

Figure B1. (Cont.)

```
REM
1250    REM     TWB
        PRINT "TWB NOT PROGRAMMED"
        RETURN
REM
REM
2000    REM     MUX SUBROUTINE
        ON MUX+1 GOTO 2100,2200,2300,2400
REM
2100    IF TENTH=0 \
                THEN    CC=0 \
                ELSE    CC=1
        RETURN
REM
2200    IF CN4=0 \
                THEN    CC=0 \
                ELSE    CC=1
        RETURN
REM
2300    IF COMP=0 \
                THEN    CC=0 \
                ELSE    CC=1
        RETURN
REM
2400    CC=1
        RETURN
REM
REM
2500    REM     LEAST SIGNIFICANT 2911 (2911L) SUBROUTINE
        IF ZEROL=0 THEN L4B=0
        RETURN
REM
REM
REM
REM
3000    REM     MORE SIGNIFICANT 2911S (2911H) SUBROUTINE
        ON S11+1 GOSUB 3100,3200,3300,3400
        IF ZEROH=0 THEN Y11=0
        RETURN
REM
3100    Y11=PC11
        RETURN
REM
3200    Y11=R11
        RETURN
REM
3300    Y11=F11
        RETURN
REM
3400    IF I10=6 \
                THEN    Y11=VECTOR \
                ELSE    Y11=PL
        RETURN
REM
REM
4000    REM     CLOCK SUBROUTINE
REM     PC10=MA+1       REMOVED REV 4
        IF CN=1 THEN L4B=L4B+1
        IF L4B>15 THEN L4B=0 : CN4=1 ELSE CN4=0
        IF CN4=1 \
                THEN    PC11=Y11+1 \
                ELSE    PC11=Y11
        IF FE=0 THEN F11=PC11
REM     <--REV 3
```

Figure B1 (Cont.)

```
        IF PUSH=1 \
                THEN     SP10=SP10+1 :\
                         F10(SP10)=PC10 :\
                         PUSH=0
        IF SP10>4 \
                THEN     PRINT "2910 STACK FULL " :\
                         SP10=3
        IF POP=1 \
                THEN     SP10=SP10-1 :\
                         POP=0
        IF SP10<0 \
                THEN     PRINT "POP EMPTY FILE? ";CP :\
                         SP10=0
REM     REV 3 -->
        PC10=MA+1        REM     REV 4
        CP=CP+1
        RETURN
REM
REM
```

Figure B1 (Cont.)

APPENDIX C

A simple circuit was designed to accommodate five different display formats and also to comply with the European 50Hz TV standard. Figure C1 is the circuit diagram of this additional circuit.

The following parameters change when the format is changed:

1) The number of characters/line.
2) The number of lines/frame.
3) The number of characters to display (i.e., the address of the last character).
4) The line frequency and therefore the dot frequency.

The number of characters/line is counted by the least significant Am2911 sequencer via the microcode. Therefore, the microcode can be changed to change the number of characters/line. The number of lines/frame is counted by a constant, loaded into the Am2910 internal counter by the microcode. The microcode can be changed to vary the number of lines/frame.

The scan is reinitialized to zero when the last address +1 is attained. U_9 (Am25LS2521) detects this address by comparing bits A_4 through A_{10} of the character address bus to a constant supplied to its B inputs. A table listing these constants is shown in Figure C1. By setting the DIP switches according to that table, the character scan will reinitialize correctly. The same constant is routed through one half of an Am25LS240 (U24) to the internal data bus. At microprogram address zero, a JUMP MAP instruction enables these outputs thereby putting a starting address on the bus according to the table in Figure C1.

The microprogram is shown on Figure C2.

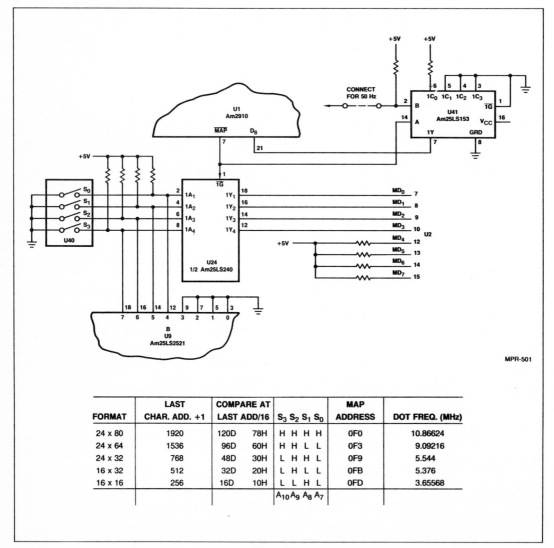

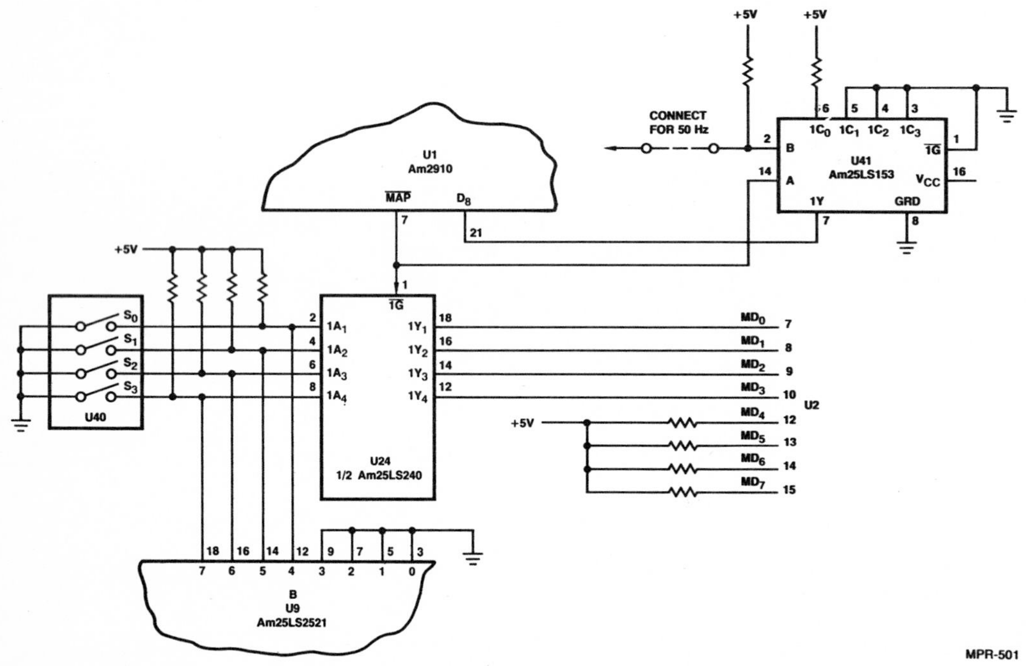

FORMAT	LAST CHAR. ADD. +1	COMPARE AT LAST ADD/16		S_3 S_2 S_1 S_0	MAP ADDRESS	DOT FREQ. (MHz)
24 x 80	1920	120D	78H	H H H H	0F0	10.86624
24 x 64	1536	96D	60H	H H L L	0F3	9.09216
24 x 32	768	48D	30H	L H H L	0F9	5.544
16 x 32	512	32D	20H	L H L L	0FB	5.376
16 x 16	256	16D	10H	L L H L	0FD	3.65568
				A_{10} A_9 A_8 A_7		

Figure C1.

```
A>TYPE CRT.DEF
;
;CRT DEFINITION FILE
;BY MOSHE M. SHAVIT
;REV Ø 3/8/78
;
TITLE    CRT CONTROLLER --DEFINITIONS
WORD     24
;
FE:      DEF      1VB#1,23X
ZEROH:   DEF      1X,1VB#1,22X
S11:     DEF      2X,2V%:Q#,2ØX
I1Ø:     DEF      4X,4VH#,16X
CN:      DEF      9X,1VB#1,14X
ZEROL:   DEF      1ØX,1VB#1,13X
VB:      DEF      11X,1VB#Ø,12X
HB:      DEF      12X,1VB#Ø,11X
CCEN:    DEF      13X,1VB#,1ØX
MUXØ:    DEF      14X,B#ØØ,8X
MUX1:    DEF      14X,B#1Ø,8X
MUX2:    DEF      14X,B#Ø1,8X
MUX3:    DEF      14X,B#11,8X
PL:      DEF      16X,8V%:
;
L:       EQU      B#Ø
H:       EQU      B#1
;
COUNT:   DEF      B#1,B#1,B#ØØ,5X,B#1,B#1,B#Ø,B#Ø,1X,2X,8X
COUNTH:  DEF      B#1,B#1,B#ØØ,5X,B#1,B#1,B#Ø,B#1,1X,2X,8X
COUNTV:  DEF      B#1,B#1,B#ØØ,5X,B#1,B#1,B#1,B#1,1X,2X,8X
;
END

A>
```

Figure C2. AMDASM Definition and Assembly Files for the CRT Controller.

```
AMDOS/29 AMDASM MICRO ASSEMBLER, V1.1
CRT CONTROLLER

       ;CRT CONTROLLER MICROPROGRAM
       ;
       ;BY MOSHE M. SHAVIT
       ;REV 2 5/3/78
       ;
       ;
 ØØØØ            I1Ø H#2 ;JUMP MAP
       ;
       ;         24 ROWS 8Ø CHARACTERS 6Ø F/S
       ;
       ;
 ØØØ1 S248Ø:  I1Ø H#6 & CCEN L & MUX3 & S11 3 & FE L & ZEROH & ZEROL L &
        / CN L & HB H & VB
 ØØØ2         I1Ø H#C & S11 Ø & FE & ZEROH & ZEROL L & CN L & HB H &
       /VB & PL D#23
 ØØØ3 M248Ø:  I1Ø H#E & S11 2 & FE & ZEROH & ZEROL L & CN & HB H & VB
 ØØØ4         I1Ø H#3 & CCEN L & MUX1 & COUNT & PL $
 ØØØ5         I1Ø H#3 & CCEN L & MUX1 & COUNT & PL $
 ØØØ6         I1Ø H#3 & CCEN L & MUX1 & COUNT & PL $
 ØØØ7         I1Ø H#3 & CCEN L & MUX1 & COUNT & PL $
 ØØØ8         I1Ø H#3 & CCEN L & MUX1 & COUNT & PL $
 ØØØ9         I1Ø H#1 & CCEN L & MUXØ & COUNTH & PL T248Ø
 ØØØA         I1Ø H#1 & CCEN L & MUX2 & COUNTH & PL LASTA
 ØØØB         I1Ø H#3 & CCEN L & MUX1 & COUNTH & PL $
 ØØØC         I1Ø H#3 & CCEN H & S11 Ø & FE & ZEROH & HB H & VB & PL M248Ø
 ØØØD T248Ø:  I1Ø H#9 & S11 Ø & FE L & ZEROH & ZEROL & CN H & HB H & VB & PL GOB
ACK
 ØØØE         I1Ø H#6 & CCEN L & MUX3 & S11 3 & FE L & ZEROH & ZEROL L &
        / HB H & VB H
 ØØØF         I1Ø H#C & S11 Ø & FE & ZEROH & HB H & VB H & PL D#146
 ØØ1Ø         I1Ø H#4 & CCEN L & MUX3 & COUNTV
 ØØ11         I1Ø H#3 & CCEN L & MUX1 & COUNTV & PL $
 ØØ12         I1Ø H#8 & COUNTV
 ØØ13         I1Ø H#C & COUNTV & PL D#23
 ØØ14         I1Ø H#A & CCEN H & COUNTV
       ;
 ØØ15 GOBACK: I1Ø H#A & CCEN H & COUNTH
 ØØ16 LASTA:  I1Ø H#A & CCEN H & FE L & ZEROH L & ZEROL & CN H & HB H & VB
       ;
       ;
       ;         24 ROWS 64 CHARACTERS 6Ø F/S
       ;
       ;
 ØØ17 S2464:  I1Ø H#6 & CCEN L & MUX3 & S11 3 & FE L & ZEROH & ZEROL L &
        / CN L & HB H & VB
 ØØ18         I1Ø H#C & S11 Ø & FE & ZEROH & ZEROL L & CN L & HB H &
       /VB & PL D#23
 ØØ19 M2464:  I1Ø H#E & S11 2 & FE & ZEROH & ZEROL L & CN & HB H & VB
 ØØ1A         I1Ø H#3 & CCEN L & MUX1 & COUNT & PL $
 ØØ1B         I1Ø H#3 & CCEN L & MUX1 & COUNT & PL $
 ØØ1C         I1Ø H#3 & CCEN L & MUX1 & COUNT & PL $
 ØØ1D         I1Ø H#3 & CCEN L & MUX1 & COUNT & PL $
 ØØ1E         I1Ø H#1 & CCEN L & MUXØ & COUNTH & PL T2464
 ØØ1F         I1Ø H#1 & CCEN L & MUX2 & COUNTH & PL LASTA
 ØØ2Ø         I1Ø H#3 & CCEN L & MUX1 & COUNTH & PL $
 ØØ21         I1Ø H#3 & CCEN H & S11 Ø & FE & ZEROH & HB H & VB & PL M2464
 ØØ22 T2464:  I1Ø H#9 & S11 Ø & FE L & ZEROH & ZEROL & CN H & HB H & VB & PL GOB
ACK
 ØØ23         I1Ø H#6 & CCEN L & MUX3 & S11 3 & FE L & ZEROH & ZEROL L &
        / HB H & VB H
 ØØ24         I1Ø H#C & S11 Ø & FE & ZEROH & HB H & VB H & PL D#122
 ØØ25         I1Ø H#4 & CCEN L & MUX3 & COUNTV
 ØØ26         I1Ø H#3 & CCEN L & MUX1 & COUNTV & PL $
 ØØ27         I1Ø H#8 & COUNTV
```

Figure C2 (Cont.)

```
AMDOS/29 AMDASM MICRO ASSEMBLER, V1.1
CRT CONTROLLER
 0028          I10 H#C & COUNTV & PL D#23
 0029          I10 H#A & CCEN H & COUNTV
       ;
       ;
       ;
       ;       24 ROWS 32 CHARACTERS 60 F/S
       ;
       ;
 002A S2432:   I10 H#6 & CCEN L & MUX3 & S11 3 & FE L & ZEROH & ZEROL L &
       / CN L & HB H & VB
 002B          I10 H#C & S11 0 & FE & ZEROH & ZEROL L & CN L & HB H &
       /VB & PL D#23
 002C M2432:   I10 H#E & S11 2 & FE & ZEROH & ZEROL L & CN & HB H & VB
 002D          I10 H#3 & CCEN L & MUX1 & COUNT & PL $
 002E          I10 H#3 & CCEN L & MUX1 & COUNT & PL $
 002F          I10 H#1 & CCEN L & MUX0 & COUNTH & PL T2432
 0030          I10 H#1 & CCEN L & MUX2 & COUNTH & PL LASTA
 0031          I10 H#3 & CCEN L & MUX1 & COUNTH & PL $
 0032          I10 H#3 & CCEN H & S11 0 & FE & ZEROH & HB H & VB & PL M2432
 0033 T2432:   I10 H#9 & S11 0 & FE L & ZEROH & ZEROL & CN H & HB H & VB & PL GOB
ACK
 0034          I10 H#6 & CCEN L & MUX3 & S11 3 & FE L & ZEROH & ZEROL L &
       / HB H & VB H
 0035          I10 H#C & S11 0 & FE & ZEROH & HB H & VB H & PL D#74
 0036          I10 H#4 & CCEN L & MUX3 & COUNTV
 0037          I10 H#3 & CCEN L & MUX1 & COUNTV & PL $
 0038          I10 H#8 & COUNTV
 0039          I10 H#C & COUNTV & PL D#23
 003A          I10 H#A & CCEN H & COUNTV
       ;
       ;
       ;       16 ROWS 32 CHARACTERS 60 F/S
       ;
       ;
 003B S1632:   I10 H#6 & CCEN L & MUX3 & S11 3 & FE L & ZEROH & ZEROL L &
       / CN L & HB H & VB
 003C          I10 H#C & S11 0 & FE & ZEROH & ZEROL L & CN L & HB H &
       /VB & PL D#15
 003D M1632:   I10 H#E & S11 2 & FE & ZEROH & ZEROL L & CN & HB H & VB
 003E          I10 H#3 & CCEN L & MUX1 & COUNT & PL $
 003F          I10 H#3 & CCEN L & MUX1 & COUNT & PL $
 0040          I10 H#1 & CCEN L & MUX0 & COUNTH & PL T1632
 0041          I10 H#1 & CCEN L & MUX2 & COUNTH & PL LASTA
 0042          I10 H#3 & CCEN L & MUX1 & COUNTH & PL $
 0043          I10 H#3 & CCEN H & S11 0 & FE & ZEROH & HB H & VB & PL M1632
 0044 T1632:   I10 H#9 & S11 0 & FE L & ZEROH & ZEROL & CN H & HB H & VB & PL GOB
ACK
 0045          I10 H#6 & CCEN L & MUX3 & S11 3 & FE L & ZEROH & ZEROL L &
       / HB H & VB H
 0046          I10 H#C & S11 0 & FE & ZEROH & HB H & VB H & PL D#250
 0047          I10 H#4 & CCEN L & MUX3 & COUNTV
 0048          I10 H#3 & CCEN L & MUX1 & COUNTV & PL $
 0049          I10 H#8 & COUNTV
 004A          I10 H#C & COUNTV & PL D#48
 004B          I10 H#4 & CCEN L & MUX3 & COUNTV
 004C          I10 H#3 & CCEN L & MUX1 & COUNTV & PL $
 004D          I10 H#8 & COUNTV
 004E          I10 H#C & COUNTV & PL D#15
 004F          I10 H#A & CCEN H & COUNTV
       ;
       ;
       ;       16 ROWS 16 CHARACTERS 60 F/S
       ;
       ;
```

Figure C2 (Cont.)

```
AMDOS/29 AMDASM MICRO ASSEMBLER, V1.1
CRT CONTROLLER

 ØØ5Ø S1616:  I1Ø H#6 & CCEN L & MUX3 & S11 3 & FE L & ZEROH & ZEROL L &
        / CN L & HB H & VB
 ØØ51         I1Ø H#C & S11 Ø & FE & ZEROH & ZEROL L & CN L & HB H &
       /VB & PL D#15
 ØØ52 M1616:  I1Ø H#E & S11 2 & FE & ZEROH & ZEROL L & CN & HB H & VB
 ØØ53         I1Ø H#3 & CCEN L & MUX1 & COUNT & PL $
 ØØ54         I1Ø H#1 & CCEN L & MUXØ & COUNTH & PL T1616
 ØØ55         I1Ø H#1 & CCEN L & MUX2 & COUNTH & PL LASTA
 ØØ56         I1Ø H#3 & CCEN L & MUX1 & COUNTH & PL $
 ØØ57         I1Ø H#3 & CCEN H & S11 Ø & FE & ZEROH & HB H & VB & PL M1616
 ØØ58 T1616:  I1Ø H#9 & S11 Ø & FE L & ZEROH & ZEROL & CN H & HB H & VB & PL GOB
ACK
 ØØ59         I1Ø H#6 & CCEN L & MUX3 & S11 3 & FE L & ZEROH & ZEROL L &
       / HB H & VB H
 ØØ5A         I1Ø H#C & S11 Ø & FE & ZEROH & HB H & VB H & PL D#2Ø3
 ØØ5B         I1Ø H#4 & CCEN L & MUX3 & COUNTV
 ØØ5C         I1Ø H#3 & CCEN L & MUX1 & COUNTV & PL $
 ØØ5D         I1Ø H#8 & COUNTV
 ØØ5E         I1Ø H#C & COUNTV & PL D#15
 ØØ5F         I1Ø H#A & CCEN H & COUNTV
      ;
 ØØFØ         ORG     H#ØFØ   ;24*8Ø
 ØØFØ         I1Ø H#3 & CCEN H & PL S248Ø
      ;
      ;
 ØØF3         ORG     H#ØF3   ;24*64
 ØØF3         I1Ø H#3 & CCEN H & PL S2464
      ;
      ;
 ØØF9         ORG     H#ØF9   ;24*32
 ØØF9         I1Ø H#3 & CCEN H & PL S2432
      ;
      ;
 ØØFB         ORG     H#ØFB   ;16*32
 ØØFB         I1Ø H#3 & CCEN H & PL S1632
      ;
      ;
 ØØFD         ORG     H#ØFD   ;16*16
 ØØFD         I1Ø H#3 & CCEN H & PL S1616
      ;
      ;
      ;
      ;5Ø F/S ROUTINES
      ;
 Ø1ØØ         ORG     H#1ØØ
      ;
      ;       24 ROWS 8Ø CHARACTERS 5Ø F/S
      ;
      ;
 Ø1ØØ S248ØE: I1Ø H#6 & CCEN L & MUX3 & S11 3 & FE L & ZEROH & ZEROL L &
       / CN L & HB H & VB
 Ø1Ø1         I1Ø H#C & S11 Ø & FE & ZEROH & ZEROL L & CN L & HB H &
       /VB & PL D#23
 Ø1Ø2 M248ØE: I1Ø H#E & S11 2 & FE & ZEROH & ZEROL L & CN & HB H & VB
 Ø1Ø3         I1Ø H#3 & CCEN L & MUX1 & COUNT & PL $
 Ø1Ø4         I1Ø H#3 & CCEN L & MUX1 & COUNT & PL $
 Ø1Ø5         I1Ø H#3 & CCEN L & MUX1 & COUNT & PL $
 Ø1Ø6         I1Ø H#3 & CCEN L & MUX1 & COUNT & PL $
 Ø1Ø7         I1Ø H#3 & CCEN L & MUX1 & COUNT & PL $
 Ø1Ø8         I1Ø H#1 & CCEN L & MUXØ & COUNTH & PL T248ØE
 Ø1Ø9         I1Ø H#1 & CCEN L & MUX2 & COUNTH & PL LASTA
 Ø1ØA         I1Ø H#3 & CCEN L & MUX1 & COUNTH & PL $
 Ø1ØB         I1Ø H#3 & CCEN H & S11 Ø & FE & ZEROH & HB H & VB & PL M248ØE
 Ø1ØC T248ØE: I1Ø H#9 & S11 Ø & FE L & ZEROH & ZEROL & CN H & HB H & VB & PL GOB
ACK
```

Figure C2 (Cont.)

```
AMDOS/29 AMDASM MICRO ASSEMBLER, V1.1
CRT CONTROLLER

 Ø10D          I1Ø H#6 & CCEN L & MUX3 & S11 3 & FE L & ZEROH & ZEROL L &
         / HB H & VB H
 Ø10E          I1Ø H#C & S11 Ø & FE & ZEROH & HB H & VB H & PL D#2ØØ   ;ITERATES
201 TIMES
 Ø10F          I1Ø H#4 & CCEN L & MUX3 & COUNTV
 Ø11Ø          I1Ø H#3 & CCEN L & MUX1 & COUNTV & PL $
 Ø111          I1Ø H#8 & COUNTV
      ;
 Ø112          I1Ø H#C & COUNTV & PL D#239
 Ø113          I1Ø H#4 & CCEN L & MUX3 & COUNTV
 Ø114          I1Ø H#3 & CCEN L & MUX1 & COUNTV & PL $
 Ø115          I1Ø H#8 & COUNTV
      ;
 Ø116          I1Ø H#C & COUNTV & PL D#23
 Ø117          I1Ø H#A & CCEN H & COUNTV
      ;
      ;
      ;        24 ROWS 64 CHARACTERS 5Ø F/S
      ;
      ;
 Ø118 S2464E: I1Ø H#6 & CCEN L & MUX3 & S11 3 & FE L & ZEROH & ZEROL L &
         / CN L & HB H & VB
 Ø119          I1Ø H#C & S11 Ø & FE & ZEROH & ZEROL L & CN L & HB H &
         /VB & PL D#23
 Ø11A M2464E: I1Ø H#E & S11 2 & FE & ZEROH & ZEROL L & CN & HB H & VB
 Ø11B          I1Ø H#3 & CCEN L & MUX1 & COUNT & PL $
 Ø11C          I1Ø H#3 & CCEN L & MUX1 & COUNT & PL $
 Ø11D          I1Ø H#3 & CCEN L & MUX1 & COUNT & PL $
 Ø11E          I1Ø H#3 & CCEN L & MUX1 & COUNT & PL $
 Ø11F          I1Ø H#1 & CCEN L & MUXØ & COUNTH & PL T2464E
 Ø12Ø          I1Ø H#1 & CCEN L & MUX2 & COUNTH & PL LASTA
 Ø121          I1Ø H#3 & CCEN L & MUX1 & COUNTH & PL $
 Ø122          I1Ø H#3 & CCEN H & S11 Ø & FE & ZEROH & HB H & VB & PL M2464E
 Ø123 T2464E: I1Ø H#9 & S11 Ø & FE L & ZEROH & ZEROL & CN H & HB H & VB & PL GOB
ACK
 Ø124          I1Ø H#6 & CCEN L & MUX3 & S11 3 & FE L & ZEROH & ZEROL L &
         / HB H & VB H
 Ø125          I1Ø H#C & S11 Ø & FE & ZEROH & HB H & VB H & PL D#2ØØ
 Ø126          I1Ø H#4 & CCEN L & MUX3 & COUNTV
 Ø127          I1Ø H#3 & CCEN L & MUX1 & COUNTV & PL $
 Ø128          I1Ø H#8 & COUNTV
      ;
 Ø129          I1Ø H#C & COUNTV & PL D#167      ;369
 Ø12A          I1Ø H#4 & CCEN L & MUX3 & COUNTV
 Ø12B          I1Ø H#3 & CCEN L & MUX1 & COUNTV & PL $
 Ø12C          I1Ø H#8 & COUNTV
      ;
 Ø12D          I1Ø H#C & COUNTV & PL D#23
 Ø12E          I1Ø H#A & CCEN H & COUNTV
      ;
      ;
      ;
      ;        24 ROWS 32 CHARACTERS 5Ø F/S
      ;
      ;
 Ø12F S2432E: I1Ø H#6 & CCEN L & MUX3 & S11 3 & FE L & ZEROH & ZEROL L &
         / CN L & HB H & VB
 Ø13Ø          I1Ø H#C & S11 Ø & FE & ZEROH & ZEROL L & CN L & HB H &
         /VB & PL D#23
 Ø131 M2432E: I1Ø H#E & S11 2 & FE & ZEROH & ZEROL L & CN & HB H & VB
 Ø132          I1Ø H#3 & CCEN L & MUX1 & COUNT & PL $
 Ø133          I1Ø H#3 & CCEN L & MUX1 & COUNT & PL $
 Ø134          I1Ø H#1 & CCEN L & MUXØ & COUNTH & PL T2432E
 Ø135          I1Ø H#1 & CCEN L & MUX2 & COUNTH & PL LASTA
 Ø136          I1Ø H#3 & CCEN L & MUX1 & COUNTH & PL $
```

Figure C2 (Cont.)

```
AMDOS/29 AMDASM MICRO ASSEMBLER, V1.1
CRT CONTROLLER

 0137          I10 H#3 & CCEN H & S11 0 & FE & ZEROH & HB H & VB & PL M2432E
 0138 T2432E: I10 H#9 & S11 0 & FE L & ZEROH & ZEROL & CN H & HB H & VB & PL GOB
ACK
 0139          I10 H#6 & CCEN L & MUX3 & S11 3 & FE L & ZEROH & ZEROL L &
      / HB H & VB H
 013A          I10 H#C & S11 0 & FE & ZEROH & HB H & VB H & PL D#224
 013B          I10 H#4 & CCEN L & MUX3 & COUNTV
 013C          I10 H#3 & CCEN L & MUX1 & COUNTV & PL $
 013D          I10 H#8 & COUNTV
 013E          I10 H#C & COUNTV & PL D#23
 013F          I10 H#A & CCEN H & COUNTV
      ;
      ;
      ;        16 ROWS 32 CHARACTERS 50 F/S
      ;
      ;
 0140 S1632E: I10 H#6 & CCEN L & MUX3 & S11 3 & FE L & ZEROH & ZEROL L &
      / CN L & HB H & VB
 0141          I10 H#C & S11 0 & FE & ZEROH & ZEROL L & CN L & HB H &
      /VB & PL D#15
 0142 M1632E: I10 H#E & S11 2 & FE & ZEROH & ZEROL L & CN & HB H & VB
 0143          I10 H#3 & CCEN L & MUX1 & COUNT & PL $
 0144          I10 H#3 & CCEN L & MUX1 & COUNT & PL $
 0145          I10 H#1 & CCEN L & MUX0 & COUNTH & PL T1632E
 0146          I10 H#1 & CCEN L & MUX2 & COUNTH & PL LASTA
 0147          I10 H#3 & CCEN L & MUX1 & COUNTH & PL $
 0148          I10 H#3 & CCEN H & S11 0 & FE & ZEROH & HB H & VB & PL M1632E
 0149 T1632E: I10 H#9 & S11 0 & FE L & ZEROH & ZEROL & CN H & HB H & VB & PL GOB
ACK
 014A          I10 H#6 & CCEN L & MUX3 & S11 3 & FE L & ZEROH & ZEROL L &
      / HB H & VB H
 014B          I10 H#C & S11 0 & FE & ZEROH & HB H & VB H & PL D#250
 014C          I10 H#4 & CCEN L & MUX3 & COUNTV
 014D          I10 H#3 & CCEN L & MUX1 & COUNTV & PL $
 014E          I10 H#8 & COUNTV
 014F          I10 H#C & COUNTV & PL D#223      ;475
 0150          I10 H#4 & CCEN L & MUX3 & COUNTV
 0151          I10 H#3 & CCEN L & MUX1 & COUNTV & PL $
 0152          I10 H#8 & COUNTV
 0153          I10 H#C & COUNTV & PL D#15
 0154          I10 H#A & CCEN H & COUNTV
      ;
      ;
      ;        16 ROWS 16 CHARACTERS 50 F/S
      ;
      ;
 0155 S1616E: I10 H#6 & CCEN L & MUX3 & S11 3 & FE L & ZEROH & ZEROL L &
      / CN L & HB H & VB
 0156          I10 H#C & S11 0 & FE & ZEROH & ZEROL L & CN L & HB H &
      /VB & PL D#15
 0157 M1616E: I10 H#E & S11 2 & FE & ZEROH & ZEROL L & CN & HB H & VB
 0158          I10 H#3 & CCEN L & MUX1 & COUNT & PL $
 0159          I10 H#1 & CCEN L & MUX0 & COUNTH & PL T1616E
 015A          I10 H#1 & CCEN L & MUX2 & COUNTH & PL LASTA
 015B          I10 H#3 & CCEN L & MUX1 & COUNTH & PL $
 015C          I10 H#3 & CCEN H & S11 0 & FE & ZEROH & HB H & VB & PL M1616E
 015D T1616E: I10 H#9 & S11 0 & FE L & ZEROH & ZEROL & CN H & HB H & VB & PL GOB
ACK
 015E          I10 H#6 & CCEN L & MUX3 & S11 3 & FE L & ZEROH & ZEROL L &
      / HB H & VB H
 015F          I10 H#C & S11 0 & FE & ZEROH & HB H & VB H & PL D#200
 0160          I10 H#4 & CCEN L & MUX3 & COUNTV
 0161          I10 H#3 & CCEN L & MUX1 & COUNTV & PL $
 0162          I10 H#8 & COUNTV
```

Figure C2 (Cont.)

```
AMDOS/29 AMDASM MICRO ASSEMBLER, V1.1
CRT CONTROLLER

        ;
 Ø163         I1Ø H#C & COUNTV & PL D#121      ;323
 Ø164         I1Ø H#4 & CCEN L & MUX3 & COUNTV
 Ø165         I1Ø H#3 & CCEN L & MUX1 & COUNTV & PL $
 Ø166         I1Ø H#8 & COUNTV
        ;
 Ø167         I1Ø H#C & COUNTV & PL D#15
 Ø168         I1Ø H#A & CCEN H & COUNTV
        ;
 Ø1FØ         ORG      H#1FØ   ;24*8Ø
 Ø1FØ         I1Ø H#3 & CCEN H & PL S248ØE
        ;
        ;
 Ø1F3         ORG      H#1F3   ;24*64
 Ø1F3         I1Ø H#3 & CCEN H & PL S2464E
        ;
        ;
 Ø1F9         ORG      H#1F9   ;24*32
 Ø1F9         I1Ø H#3 & CCEN H & PL S2432E
        ;
        ;
 Ø1FB         ORG      H#1FB   ;16*32
 Ø1FB         I1Ø H#3 & CCEN H & PL S1632E
        ;
        ;
 Ø1FD         ORG      H#1FD   ;16*16
 Ø1FD         I1Ø H#3 & CCEN H & PL S1616E
        ;
        ;
        END
   ØØØØ XXXXØØ1ØXXXXXXXX XXXXXXXX    ØØ22 Ø1ØØ1ØØ1X11Ø1XXX ØØØ1Ø1Ø1
   ØØØ1 Ø111Ø11ØXØØØ1Ø11 XXXXXXXX    ØØ23 Ø111Ø11ØXXØ11Ø11 XXXXXXXX
   ØØØ2 11ØØ11ØØXØØØ1XXX ØØØ1Ø111    ØØ24 11ØØ11ØØXXX11XXX Ø1111Ø1Ø
   ØØØ3 111Ø111ØX1ØØ1XXX XXXXXXXX    ØØ25 11ØØØ1ØØX1111Ø11 XXXXXXXX
   ØØØ4 11ØØØØ11X11ØØØ1Ø ØØØØØ1ØØ    ØØ26 11ØØØØ11X1111Ø1Ø ØØ1ØØ11Ø
   ØØØ5 11ØØØØ11X11ØØØ1Ø ØØØØØ1Ø1    ØØ27 11ØØ1ØØØX1111XXX XXXXXXXX
   ØØØ6 11ØØØØ11X11ØØØ1Ø ØØØØØ11Ø    ØØ28 11ØØ11ØØX1111XXX ØØØ1Ø111
   ØØØ7 11ØØØØ11X11ØØØ1Ø ØØØØØ111    ØØ29 11ØØ1Ø1ØX11111XX XXXXXXXX
   ØØØ8 11ØØØØ11X11ØØØ1Ø ØØØØ1ØØØ    ØØ2A Ø111Ø11ØXØØØ1Ø11 XXXXXXXX
   ØØØ9 11ØØØØØ1X11Ø1ØØØ ØØØØ11Ø1    ØØ2B 11ØØ11ØØXØØØ1XXX ØØØ1Ø111
   ØØØA 11ØØØØØ1X11Ø1ØØ1 ØØØ1Ø11Ø    ØØ2C 111Ø111ØX1ØØ1XXX XXXXXXXX
   ØØØB 11ØØØØ11X11Ø1Ø1Ø ØØØØ1Ø11    ØØ2D 11ØØØØ11X11ØØØ1Ø ØØ1Ø11Ø1
   ØØØC 11ØØØØ11XXXØ11XX ØØØØØØ11    ØØ2E 11ØØØØ11X11ØØØ1Ø ØØ1Ø111Ø
   ØØØD Ø1ØØ1ØØ1X11Ø1XXX ØØØ1Ø1Ø1    ØØ2F 11ØØØØØ1X11Ø1ØØØ ØØ11ØØ11
   ØØØE Ø111Ø11ØXXØ11Ø11 XXXXXXXX    ØØ3Ø 11ØØØØØ1X11Ø1ØØ1 ØØØ1Ø11Ø
   ØØØF 11ØØ11ØØXXX11XXX 1ØØ1ØØ1Ø    ØØ31 11ØØØØ11X11Ø1Ø1Ø ØØ11ØØØ1
   ØØ1Ø 11ØØØ1ØØX1111Ø11 XXXXXXXX    ØØ32 11ØØØØ11XXXØ11XX ØØ1Ø11ØØ
   ØØ11 11ØØØØ11X1111Ø1Ø ØØØ1ØØØ1    ØØ33 Ø1ØØ1ØØ1X11Ø1XXX ØØØ1Ø1Ø1
   ØØ12 11ØØ1ØØØX1111XXX XXXXXXXX    ØØ34 Ø111Ø11ØXXØ11Ø11 XXXXXXXX
   ØØ13 11ØØ11ØØX1111XXX ØØØ1Ø111    ØØ35 11ØØ11ØØXXX11XXX Ø1ØØ1Ø1Ø
   ØØ14 11ØØ1Ø1ØX11111XX XXXXXXXX    ØØ36 11ØØØ1ØØX1111Ø11 XXXXXXXX
   ØØ15 11ØØ1Ø1ØX11Ø11XX XXXXXXXX    ØØ37 11ØØØØ11X1111Ø1Ø ØØ11Ø111
   ØØ16 ØØXX1Ø1ØX11Ø11XX XXXXXXXX    ØØ38 11ØØ1ØØØX1111XXX XXXXXXXX
   ØØ17 Ø111Ø11ØXØØØ1Ø11 XXXXXXXX    ØØ39 11ØØ11ØØX1111XXX ØØØ1Ø111
   ØØ18 11ØØ11ØØXØØØ1XXX ØØØ1Ø111    ØØ3A 11ØØ1Ø1ØX11111XX XXXXXXXX
   ØØ19 111Ø111ØX1ØØ1XXX XXXXXXXX    ØØ3B Ø111Ø11ØXØØØ1Ø11 XXXXXXXX
   ØØ1A 11ØØØØ11X11ØØØ1Ø ØØØ11Ø1Ø    ØØ3C 11ØØ11ØØXØØØ1XXX ØØØØ1111
   ØØ1B 11ØØØØ11X11ØØØ1Ø ØØØ11Ø11    ØØ3D 111Ø111ØX1ØØ1XXX XXXXXXXX
   ØØ1C 11ØØØØ11X11ØØØ1Ø ØØØ111ØØ    ØØ3E 11ØØØØ11X11ØØØ1Ø ØØ11111Ø
   ØØ1D 11ØØØØ11X11ØØØ1Ø ØØØ111Ø1    ØØ3F 11ØØØØ11X11ØØØ1Ø ØØ111111
   ØØ1E 11ØØØØØ1X11Ø1ØØØ ØØ1ØØØ1Ø    ØØ4Ø 11ØØØØØ1X11Ø1ØØØ Ø1ØØØ1ØØ
   ØØ1F 11ØØØØØ1X11Ø1ØØ1 ØØØ1Ø11Ø    ØØ41 11ØØØØØ1X11Ø1ØØ1 ØØØ1Ø11Ø
   ØØ2Ø 11ØØØØ11X11Ø1Ø1Ø ØØ1ØØØØØ    ØØ42 11ØØØØ11X11Ø1Ø1Ø Ø1ØØØØ1Ø
   ØØ21 11ØØØØ11XXXØ11XX ØØØ11ØØ1    ØØ43 11ØØØØ11XXXØ11XX ØØ1111Ø1
```

Figure C2 (Cont.)

```
AMDOS/29 AMDASM MICRO ASSEMBLER, V1.1
CRT CONTROLLER

0044 01001001X1101XXX 00010101
0045 01110110XX011011 XXXXXXXX
0046 11001100XXX11XXX 11111010
0047 11000100X1111011 XXXXXXXX
0048 11000011X1111010 01001000
0049 11001000X1111XXX XXXXXXXX
004A 11001100X1111XXX 00110000
004B 11000100X1111011 XXXXXXXX
004C 11000011X1111010 01001100
004D 11001000X1111XXX XXXXXXXX
004E 11001100X1111XXX 00001111
004F 11001010X11111XX XXXXXXXX
0050 01110110X0001011 XXXXXXXX
0051 11001100X0001XXX 00001111
0052 11101110X1001XXX XXXXXXXX
0053 11000011X1100010 01010011
0054 11000001X1101000 01011000
0055 11000001X1101001 00010110
0056 11000011X1101010 01010110
0057 11000011XXX011XX 01010010
0058 01001001X1101XXX 00010101
0059 01110110XX011011 XXXXXXXX
005A 11001100XXX11XXX 11001011
005B 11000100X1111011 XXXXXXXX
005C 11000011X1111010 01011100
005D 11001000X1111XXX XXXXXXXX
005E 11001100X1111XXX 00001111
005F 11001010X11111XX XXXXXXXX
00F0 XXXX0011XXXXX1XX 00000001
00F3 XXXX0011XXXXX1XX 00010111
00F9 XXXX0011XXXXX1XX 00101010
00FB XXXX0011XXXXX1XX 00111011
00FD XXXX0011XXXXX1XX 01010000
0100 01110110X0001011 XXXXXXXX
0101 11001100X0001XXX 00010111
0102 11101110X1001XXX XXXXXXXX
0103 11000011X1100010 00000011
0104 11000011X1100010 00000100
0105 11000011X1100010 00000101
0106 11000011X1100010 00000110
0107 11000011X1100010 00000111
0108 11000001X1101000 00001100
0109 11000001X1101001 00010110
010A 11000011X1101010 00001010
010B 11000011XXX011XX 00000010
010C 01001001X1101XXX 00010101
010D 01110110XX011011 XXXXXXXX
010E 11001100XXX11XXX 11001000
010F 11000100X1111011 XXXXXXXX
0110 11000011X1111010 00010000
0111 11001000X1111XXX XXXXXXXX
0112 11001100X1111XXX 11101111
0113 11000100X1111011 XXXXXXXX
0114 11000011X1111010 00010100
0115 11001000X1111XXX XXXXXXXX
0116 11001100X1111XXX 00010111
0117 11001010X11111XX XXXXXXXX
0118 01110110X0001011 XXXXXXXX
0119 11001100X0001XXX 00010111
011A 11101110X1001XXX XXXXXXXX
011B 11000011X1100010 00011011
011C 11000011X1100010 00011100
011D 11000011X1100010 00011101
011E 11000011X1100010 00011110
011F 11000001X1101000 00100011
0120 11000001X1101001 00010110
0121 11000011X1101010 00100001
0122 11000011XXX011XX 00011010
0123 01001001X1101XXX 00010101
0124 01110110XX011011 XXXXXXXX
0125 11001100XXX11XXX 11001000
0126 11000100X1111011 XXXXXXXX
0127 11000011X1111010 00100111
0128 11001000X1111XXX XXXXXXXX
0129 11001100X1111XXX 10100111
012A 11000100X1111011 XXXXXXXX
012B 11000011X1111010 00101011
012C 11001000X1111XXX XXXXXXXX
012D 11001100X1111XXX 00010111
012E 11001010X11111XX XXXXXXXX
012F 01110110X0001011 XXXXXXXX
0130 11001100X0001XXX 00010111
0131 11101110X1001XXX XXXXXXXX
0132 11000011X1100010 00110010
0133 11000011X1100010 00110011
0134 11000001X1101000 00111000
0135 11000001X1101001 00010110
0136 11000011X1101010 00110110
0137 11000011XXX011XX 00110001
0138 01001001X1101XXX 00010101
0139 01110110XX011011 XXXXXXXX
013A 11001100XXX11XXX 11100000
013B 11000100X1111011 XXXXXXXX
013C 11000011X1111010 00111100
013D 11001000X1111XXX XXXXXXXX
013E 11001100X1111XXX 00010111
013F 11001010X11111XX XXXXXXXX
0140 01110110X0001011 XXXXXXXX
0141 11001100X0001XXX 00001111
0142 11101110X1001XXX XXXXXXXX
0143 11000011X1100010 01000011
0144 11000011X1100010 01000100
0145 11000001X1101000 01001001
0146 11000001X1101001 00010110
0147 11000011X1101010 01000111
0148 11000011XXX011XX 01000010
0149 01001001X1101XXX 00010101
014A 01110110XX011011 XXXXXXXX
014B 11001100XXX11XXX 11111010
014C 11000100X1111011 XXXXXXXX
014D 11000011X1111010 01001101
014E 11001000X1111XXX XXXXXXXX
014F 11001100X1111XXX 11011111
0150 11000100X1111011 XXXXXXXX
0151 11000011X1111010 01010001
0152 11001000X1111XXX XXXXXXXX
0153 11001100X1111XXX 00001111
0154 11001010X11111XX XXXXXXXX
0155 01110110X0001011 XXXXXXXX
0156 11001100X0001XXX 00001111
0157 11101110X1001XXX XXXXXXXX
0158 11000011X1100010 01011000
0159 11000001X1101000 01011101
015A 11000001X1101001 00010110
015B 11000011X1101010 01011011
015C 11000011XXX011XX 01010111
```

Figure C2 (Cont.)

```
AMDOS/29 AMDASM MICRO ASSEMBLER, V1.1
CRT CONTROLLER

  015D 01001001X1101XXX 00010101
  015E 01110110XX011011 XXXXXXXX
  015F 11001100XXX11XXX 11001000
  0160 11000100X1111011 XXXXXXXX
  0161 11000011X1111010 01100001
  0162 11001000X1111XXX XXXXXXXX
  0163 11001100X1111XXX 01111001
  0164 11000100X1111011 XXXXXXXX
  0165 11000011X1111010 01100101
  0166 11001000X1111XXX XXXXXXXX
  0167 11001100X1111XXX 00001111
  0168 11001010X11111XX XXXXXXXX
  01F0 XXXX0011XXXXX1XX 00000000
  01F3 XXXX0011XXXXX1XX 00011000
  01F9 XXXX0011XXXXX1XX 00101111
  01FB XXXX0011XXXXX1XX 01000000
  01FD XXXX0011XXXXX1XX 01010101

 ENTRY POINTS

 SYMBOLS

  GOBACK   0015
  H        0001
  L        0000
  LASTA    0016
  M1616    0052
  M1616E   0157
  M1632    003D
  M1632E   0142
  M2432    002C
  M2432E   0131
  M2464    0019
  M2464E   011A
  M2480    0003
  M2480E   0102
  S1616    0050
  S1616E   0155
  S1632    003B
  S1632E   0140
  S2432    002A
  S2432E   012F
  S2464    0017
  S2464E   0118
  S2480    0001
  S2480E   0100
  T1616    0058
  T1616E   015D
  T1632    0044
  T1632E   0149
  T2432    0033
  T2432E   0138
  T2464    0022
  T2464E   0123
  T2480    000D
  T2480E   010C

 TOTAL PHASE 2 ERRORS =   0
```

Figure C2 (Cont.)

APPENDIX D

The Microprogrammed CRT Controller was built on a System 29 universal card and exercised by the System 29 support processor. An Am9080A program was written to fill the character memory. Figure D1 is the listing of this program. In order to observe the correct output of the controller, an oscilloscope or CRT monitor can be connected through an adaptation circuit shown in Figure D2.

```
                   ;
                   ;PROGRAMM TO WRITE INTO CHARACTER MEMORY
                   ;BY MOSHE M. SHAVIT
                   ;REV 0 3/6/78
                   ;
01FF =             STACK   EQU     1FFH      ;STACK POINTER
00FF =             FAR     EQU     0FFH      ;FIRST ADDRESS REGISTER O/P PORT
8000 =             CHARAD  EQU     8000H     ;CHARACTER MEMORY STARTS HERE

                   ;
0200                       ORG     STACK+1   ;WORKING SPACE ABOVE STACK
0200               FA      DS      1         ;FIRST ADDRESS
0201               CURAD   DS      2         ;CURRENT ADDRRESS
0203               FIL     DS      2         ;A(FIRST CHARACTER IN LINE)
                   ;
0100                       ORG     100H      ;PROGRAM STARTS HERE
0100 31FF01                LXI     SP,STACK
0103 213087                LXI     H,730H+CHARAD    ;LAST LINE, FIRST CHARACTER
0106 220302                SHLD    FIL       ;IN "FIRST CHARACTER IN LINE" BUFFER
0109 220102                SHLD    CURAD     ;AND IN CURRENT ADDRESS BUFFER
010C AF                    XRA     A         ;CLEAR A
010D D3FF                  OUT     FAR       ;START ADDRESS=0
010F 320002                STA     FA        ;SAVE IN BUFFER
0112 CD1B01                CALL    CLEAR     ;CLEAR ALL CHAR. MEMORY
0115 CD2C01        MAIN    CALL    CHARIN    ;READ CHARACTER AND PUT IN CHAR. MEMORY
0118 C31501                JMP     MAIN      ;DO IT AGAIN
                   ;
                   ;
011B 0600          CLEAR   MVI     B,0       ;DATA=0
011D 210080                LXI     H,CHARAD          ;FIRST CHARACTER ADDRESS
0120 110008                LXI     D,2048D   ;COUNTER
0123 70            CLEAR1  MOV     M,B       ;CLEAR THAT ADDRESS
0124 1B                    DCX     D         ;COUNT
0125 23                    INX     H         ;NEXT ADDRESS
0126 7A                    MOV     A,D       ;CHECK
0127 B3                    ORA     E         ;         IF DONE
0128 C22301                JNZ     CLEAR1    ;NO. CONTINUE
012B C9                    RET               ;YES. BACK TO CALLER
                   ;
                   ;
012C 0E01          CHARIN  MVI     C,1       ;CP/M READ CODE
012E CD0500                CALL    5         ;CP/M READ ROUTINE
0131 FE1A                  CPI     1AH       ;CTL-Z?
0133 CA0000                JZ      0         ;RETURN TO CPM IF YES
0136 2A0102                LHLD    CURAD     ;FETCH CURRENT ADDRESS
0139 FE0D                  CPI     0DH       ;CR?
013B CA4401                JZ      CRLF      ;YES.
013E 77                    MOV     M,A       ;WRITE  CHARACTER
013F 23                    INX     H         ;INCREMENT
0140 220102                SHLD    CURAD     ;STORE IN BUFFER
0143 C9                    RET               ;BACK TO CALLER
                   ;
                   ;
0144 E5            CRLF    PUSH    H
0145 D5                    PUSH    D
0146 C5                    PUSH    B
0147 F5                    PUSH    PSW
0148 1E0A                  MVI     E,0AH
014A 0E02                  MVI     C,2
014C CD0500                CALL    5
014F F1                    POP     PSW
0150 C1                    POP     B
0151 D1                    POP     D
0152 E1                    POP     H         ;ROUTINE TO ECHO LF
0153 EB                    XCHG              ;SAVE  CURRENT ADDRESS IN DE
```

Figure D1

```
0154 015000              LXI    B,80D     ;80 CHARACTERS/LINE
0157 2A0302              LHLD   FIL       ;FETCH FIRST CH. IN LINE ADDRESS
015A 09                  DAD    B         ;HL= A(NEXT LINE'S FIRST CH. ADD.)
015B EB                  XCHG             ;HL=CURRENT ADDR.,DE=A(NEXT LINE FIRST CH. ADDR)
015C 0600                MVI    B,0       ;DATA=0
015E 7C         CRLF2    MOV    A,H       ;MORE SIGNIFICANT CURRENT ADDRESS
015F BA                  CMP    D         ;=NEXT LINE FIRST ADDRESS?
0160 C26801              JNZ    CRLF3     ;NO
0163 7D                  MOV    A,L       ;LESS SIGNIFICANT CURRENT ADDRESS
0164 BB                  CMP    E         ;IS CURRENT LINE FULL?
0165 CA6D01              JZ     CRLF4     ;YES
0168 70         CRLF3    MOV    M,B       ;STORE 0 AT THAT ADDRESS
0169 23                  INX    H         ;INCREMENT ADDRESS
016A C35E01              JMP    CRLF2     ;GO CHECK AGAIN
016D 7C         CRLF4    MOV    A,H       ;MORE SIGNIFICANT PART OF ADDRESS
016E E607                ANI    7         ;ONLY 3 LESS SIGNIFICANT BITS
0170 FE07                CPI    7         ;LAST LINE PASSED?
0172 C27E01              JNZ    CRLF5     ;NOT YET
0175 7D                  MOV    A,L       ;LESS SIGNIFICANT BYTE OF ADDRESS
0176 FE80                CPI    80H       ;ARE WE AT 780H=1920D?
0178 C27E01              JNZ    CRLF5     ;NOT YET, SKIP
017B 210080              LXI    H,CHARAD            ;YES, START WRITING AT BEGINNING OF CH. MEM.
017E 220302     CRLF5    SHLD   FIL       ;STORE IN FIRST CH. IN LINE BUFFER
0181 220102              SHLD   CURAD     ;AND IN CURRENT ADDRESS BUFFER
0184 3A0002              LDA    FA        ;FETCH FIRST VISIIBLE CHARACTER ADDRESS
0187 C605                ADI    5         ;SCROLL
0189 FE78                CPI    120D      ;TOO MUCH?
018B CC9401              CZ     CRLF0     ;YES
018E 320002              STA    FA        ;STORE IN FIRST ADDRESS BUFFER
0191 D3FF                OUT    FAR       ;LOAD REGISTER
0193 C9                  RET              ;RETURN TO CALLER
                ;
                ;
0194 AF         CRLF0    XRA    A         ;FIRST ADDRESS=0
0195 C9                  RET
                ;
                ;
```

Figure D1 (Cont.)

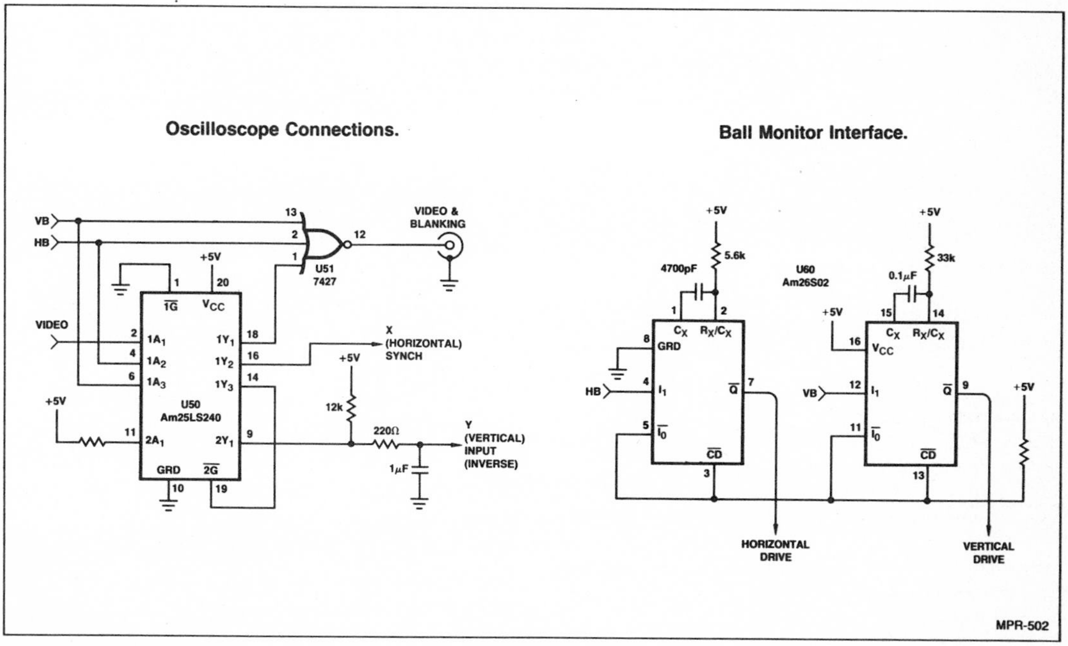

Figure D2.

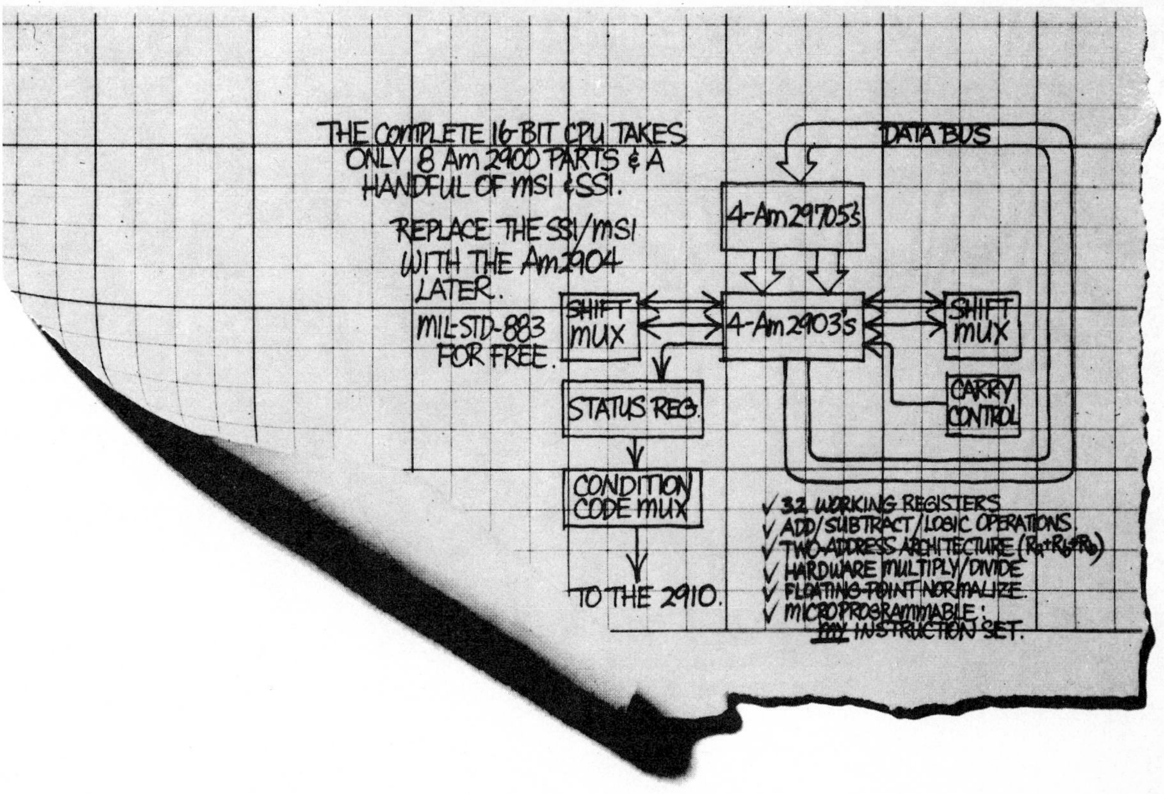

Chapter III
The Data Path

INTRODUCTION

The heart of most digital arithmetic processors is the arithmetic logic unit (ALU). The ALU can be thought of as a digital subsystem that performs various arithmetic and logic operations on two digital input variables. The Am2901A and Am2903 are Low Power Schottky TTL arithmetic logic unit/function generators that perform arithmetic/logic operations on two four-bit input variables. In most ALUs, speed is generally a key ingredient. Therefore, as much parallelism in the operation of the arithmetic logic unit as possible is desired.

The Am2901A and Am2903 ALUs are designed to operate with an Am2902A carry lookahead generator to perform multi-level full carry lookahead over any number of bits. Therefore, the devices have both the carry generate and carry propagate outputs required by the Am2902A carry lookahead generator. The devices also have the carry output (C_{n+4}) and a two's complement overflow detection signal (OVR) available at the output. The net result is that a very high-speed 16-bit arithmetic logic unit/function generator can be designed and assembled using four of these bit slice devices and one Am2902A (the Am2902A is a high-speed version of the '182 carry lookahead generator). In addition, the Am2901A and Am2903 provide a minimum of 16 working registers for providing source operands to the ALU.

UNDERSTANDING THE BASIC FULL ADDER

The results of an arithmetic operation in any position in a word depends not only on the two-input operand bits at that position, but also on all the lesser significant operand bits of the two input variables. The final result for any bit, therefore, is not available until the carries of all the previous bits have rippled through the logic array starting from the least significant bit and propagating through to the most significant bit. A full adder is a device that accepts two individual operand bits at the same binary weight, and also accepts a carry input bit from the next lesser significant weight full adder. The full adder then produces the sum bit for this bit position and also produces a carry bit to be used in the next more significant weight full adder carry input. The truth table for a full adder is shown in Figure 1. From this truth table, the equations for the full adder:

$$S = A \oplus B \oplus C$$
$$C_O = AB + BC + AC,$$

where A and B are the input operands to the full adder and C is the carry input into the adder.

Inputs			Outputs	
A	B	C	S	C_O
0	0	0	0	0
0	0	1	1	0
0	1	0	1	0
0	1	1	0	1
1	0	0	1	0
1	0	1	0	1
1	1	0	0	1
1	1	1	1	1

Figure 1. Full Adder Truth Table.

The sum output, S, represents the sum of the A and B operand inputs and the carry input. The carry output, C_O, represents the carry out of this cell and can be used in the next more significant cell of the adder. Full adder cells can be cascaded as depicted in Figure 2 to form a four-bit ripple carry parallel adder.

Note that once we have cascaded devices as shown in Figure 2, we may wish to discuss the equations for the i-th bit of the adder. In so doing, we might describe the equations of the full adder as follows:

$$S_i = A_i \oplus B_i \oplus C_i$$
$$C_{i+1} = A_iB_i + B_iC_i + A_iC_i$$

where the A_i and B_i are the input operands at the i-th bit, and the C_i is the carry input to the i-th bit. (Note that the equations for this adder are iterative in nature and each depends on the result of the previous lesser significant bits of the adder array.)

The connection scheme shown in Figure 2 requires a ripple propagation time through each full adder cell. If a 16-bit adder is to be assembled, the carry will have to propagate through all 16 full adder cells. What is desired is some technique for anticipating the carry such that we will not have to wait for a ripple carry to propagate through the entire network. By using some additional logic, such an adder array can be constructed. This type of adder is usually called a carry lookahead adder.

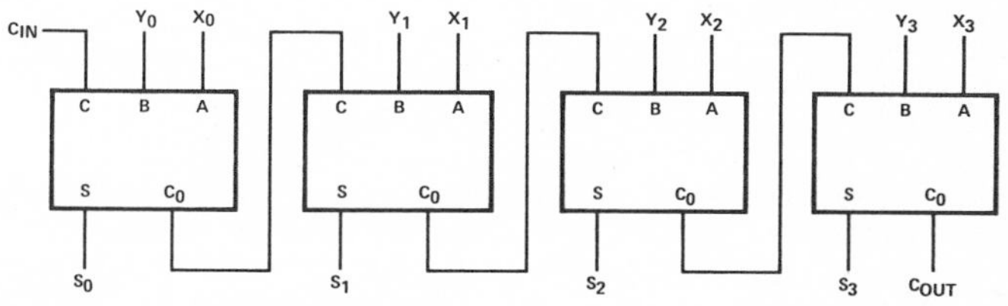

Figure 2. Cascaded Full Adder Cells Connected as a Four-Bit Ripple-Carry Full Adder.

A FOUR-BIT CARRY LOOKAHEAD ADDER

Looking back to the equations developed for i-th bit of an adder, let us now rewrite the carry equation in a slightly different form. When we factor the C_i in this equation, the new equation becomes:

$$C_{i+1} = A_iB_i + C_i(A_i + B_i)$$

From the above equation, let us now define two additional equations. These are:

$$G_i = A_iB_i$$
$$P_i = A_i + B_i$$

With these two new auxiliary equations, we can now rewrite the carry equation for the i-th bit as follows:

$$C_{i+1} = G_i + P_iC_i$$

Note that we have now developed two terms: the P_i term is known as carry propagate and the G_i term is known as carry generate. An anticipated carry can be generated at any stage of the adder by implementing the above equations and using the auxiliary functions P_i and G_i as required.

It is interesting to note that the sum equation can also be written in terms of these two auxiliary equations, P_i and G_i. For this case, the equation is:

$$S_i = (A_i + B_i)(\overline{A_iB_i}) \oplus C_i$$

The auxiliary function G_i is called carry generate, because if it is true, then a carry is immediately produced for the next adder stage. The function P_i is called carry propagate because it implies there will be a carry into the next stage of the adder if there is a carry into this stage of the adder. That is, G_i, causes a carry signal at the i-th stage of the adder to be generated and presented to the next stage of the adder while P_i causes an existing carry at the input to the i-th stage of the adder to propagate to the next stage of the adder.

Let us now write all of the sum and carry equations required for a full four-bit lookahead carry adder.

$$S_0 = A_0 \oplus B_0 \oplus C_0$$
$$S_1 = A_1 \oplus B_1 \oplus (G_0 + P_0C_0)$$
$$S_2 = A_2 \oplus B_2 \oplus (G_1 + P_1G_0 + P_1P_0C_0)$$
$$S_3 = A_3 \oplus B_3 \oplus (G_2 + P_2G_1 + P_2P_1G_0 + P_2P_1P_0C_0)$$
$$C_{i+4} = G_3 + P_3G_2 + P_3P_2G_1 + P_3P_2P_1G_0 + P_3P_2P_1P_0C_0$$

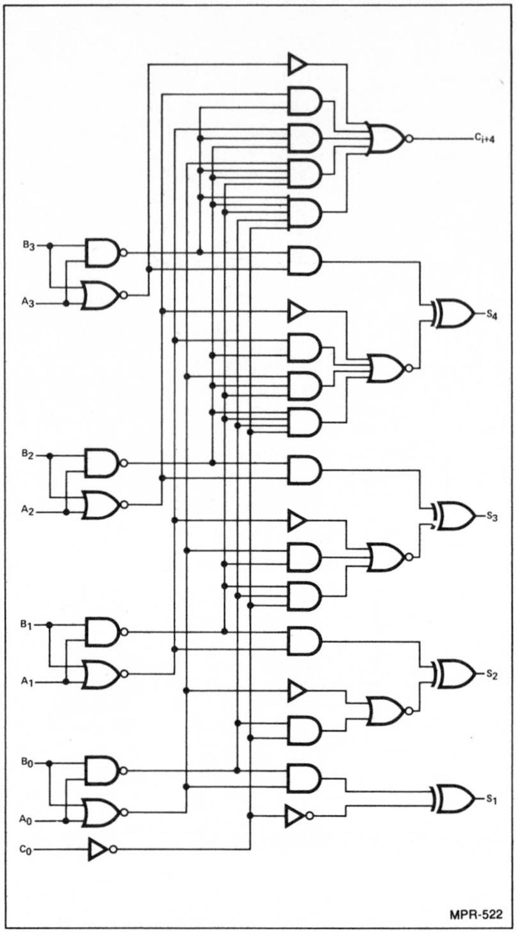

Figure 3. Full Four-Bit Carry-Lookahead Adder.

An important point to note is that ALL of the sum equations and the final carry output equation, C_{i+4}, can be written in terms of the A_i, B_i, and C_0 inputs to the four-bit adder. The configuration as described above is shown in Figure 3. This figure is divided into two parts – the upper blocks show the auxiliary function generator circuitry required to implement the P_i and G_i equations while the lower block implements the logic required to generate the sum output at each bit position.

A serious drawback to the lookahead carry adder is that as the word length is increased, the carry functions become more and more complex, eventually becoming impractical due to the large number of interconnections and heavy loading of the G_i and P_i functions. The auxiliary function concept can be extended, however, by dividing the word length into fairly small increments and defining blocks of auxiliary functions G and P.

It is possible for a given block to define a function G as the carry out generated with the block; and P can be defined as the carry propagate over the block. If the block size is set at four bits, then the functions for G and P for this block can be defined as follows:

$$G = G_3 + P_3G_2 + P_3P_2G_1 + P_3P_2P_1G_0$$
$$P = P_3P_2P_1P_0$$

It is important to note that neither of these terms involves a carry-in (C_0) to the block, so no matter how many blocks are tied in an adder, all the blocks have stable G and P functions available in a minimum number of gate delays.

The G and P functions can be gated to produce a carry-in to each four-bit block, as a function of the lesser significant blocks. The carry-in to a block is therefore:

$$C_n = G_{n-1} + P_{n-1}G_{n-2} + P_{n-1}P_{n-2}G_{n-3} + \ldots$$
$$+ P_{n-1}P_{n-2}P_{n-3} \ldots P_2P_1P_0C_0$$

Finally, the carry-in to each of the bits in a four-bit block must include a term for the actual least significant carry-in; note, therefore, that the equations for the four-bit full adder presented above include a term for carry-in at each bit position.

Figure 4 shows the technique for cascading typical bit slice ALUs such as the Am2901A or Am2903 and one Am2902A in a full 16-bit high-speed carry lookahead connection. Figure 5 shows a connection scheme using only four bit slices in a 16-bit arithmetic logic unit connection where the carries are rippled between the devices. Each bit slice does use internal carry lookahead over the four-bit block.

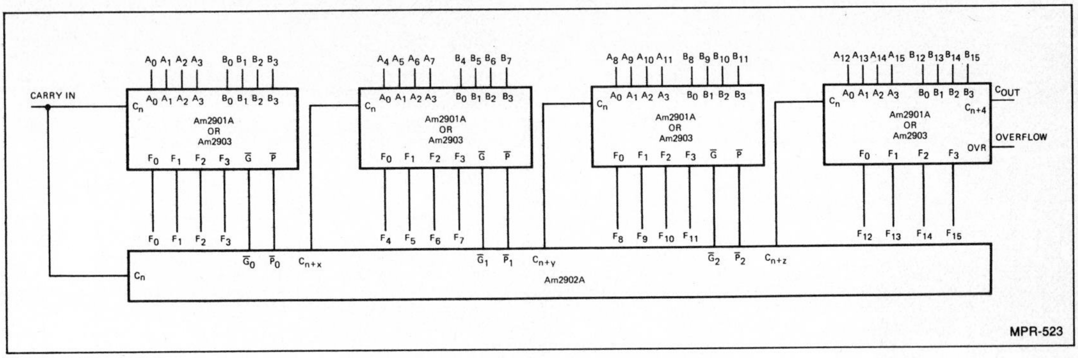

Figure 4. Full Lookahead Carry 16-Bit Adder.

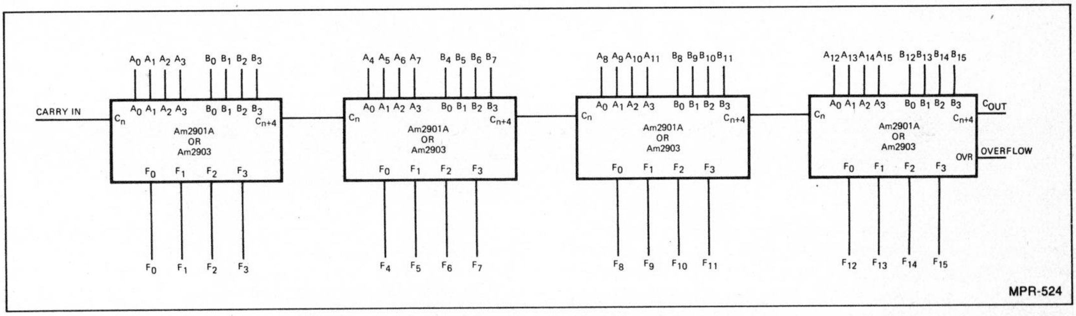

Figure 5. Connection of 16-Bit ALU Using Ripple Carry.

In summary, the ripple carry method can be used in conjunction with the lookahead technique in several ways.

1. Lookahead carry over sections of the adder and ripple carry between these sections of the adder can be used. This method is often the most efficient in terms of hardware for a given speed requirement. It does not require the use of a lookahead carry generator such as the Am2902A.
2. Lookahead carry across 16-bit blocks with a ripple carry between 16-bit blocks can be used. This technique is usually called two-level carry lookahead addition. This technique results in very high-speed arithmetic function generation and makes a reasonable tradeoff between the speed and hardware for word lengths greater than 16 bits.
3. Full lookahead carry across all levels and all block sizes can be used. This is the highest speed arithmetic logic unit connection scheme. For word sizes up to 64 bits, it is referred to as three-level lookahead carry addition. Such a 64-bit ALU requires the use of five Am2902A carry lookahead generator units in addition to the 16 bit slice ALU devices as shown in Figure 6.

OVERFLOW

When two's complement numbers are added or subtracted, the result must lie within the range of the numbers that can be handled by the operand word length. Numbers are normally represented either as fractions with a binary point between the sign bit and the rest of the word, or as integers where the binary point is after the least significant bit. The actual choice for the location of the binary point is really up to the design engineer, as the hardware configuration required for either technique is identical. It is also possible to use number notations that include both integer and fractional representations in the same numbering scheme. Overflow is defined as the situation in which the result of an arithmetic operation lies outside of the number range that can be represented by the number of bits in the word. For example, if two eight-bit numbers are added and the result does not lie within the number range that can be represented by an eight-bit word, we say that an overflow has occurred. This can happen at either the positive end of the number range or at the negative end of the number range. The logic function that indicates that the result of an operation is outside of the representable number range is:

$$OVR = C_s \oplus C_{s+1}$$

where C_s is the carry-in to the sign bit and C_{s+1} is the carry-out of the sign bit.

Thus, for a four-bit ALU with the sign bit in the most significant bit position, the two's complement overflow can be defined as the C_{n+4} term exclusive OR'ed with the C_{n+3} term.

Putting the ALU in the Data Path of a Simple Computer

Once the Design Engineer understands the basic configuration and operation of a simple high speed carry lookahead adder, he can begin to understand the configuration required to implement the data handling section of a typical computing machine. The simplest architecture for the data handling path of a minicomputer is shown in Figure 7. Here, an accumulator is used in conjunction with an ALU to perform a basic arithmetic/storage capability for data handling. The computer control unit of Figure 7 can be a simple or sophisticated state machine as described in Chapter 2.

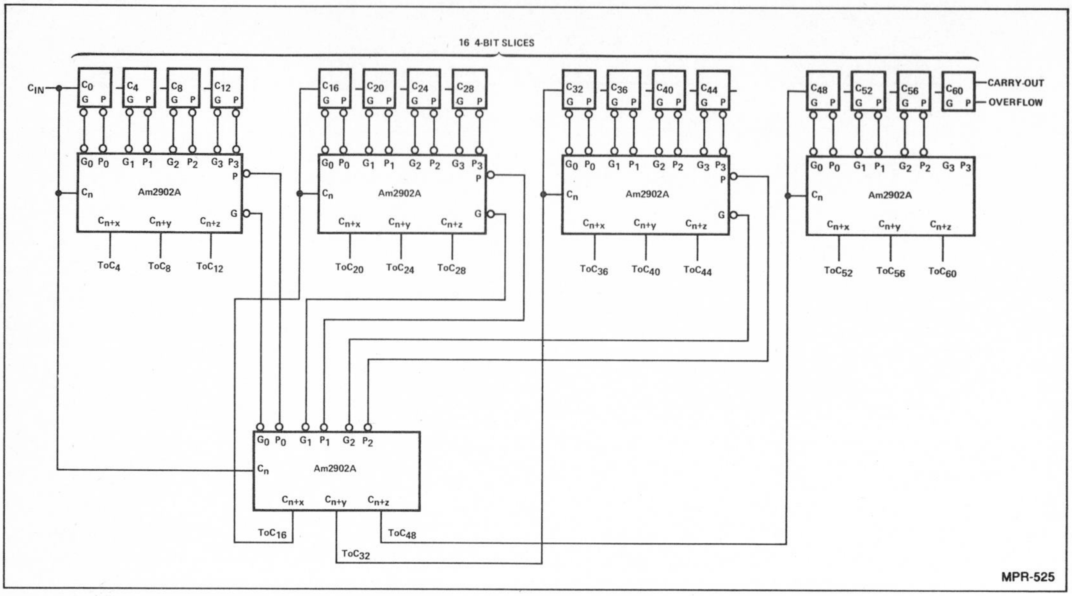

Figure 6. 64-Bit ALU with Full Carry Lookahead Using 5 Am2902s and 16 4-Bit Slices.

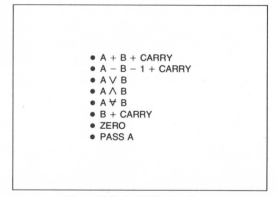

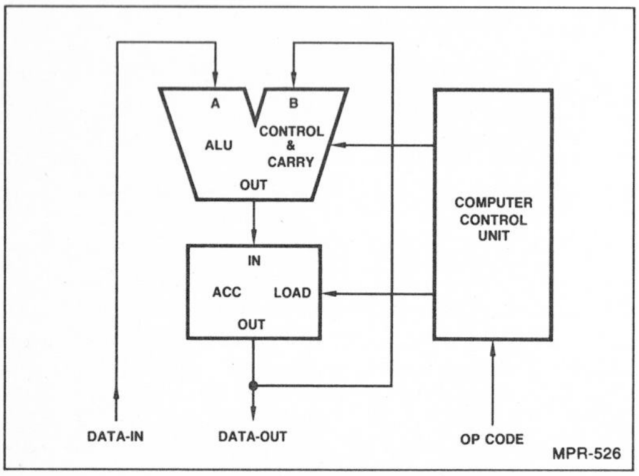

Figure 7. Basic Computer Data Path.

- A + B + CARRY
- A − B − 1 + CARRY
- A ∨ B
- A ∧ B
- A ∀ B
- B + CARRY
- ZERO
- PASS A

Figure 8. Basic ALU Instructions.

While the introductory material of this chapter concentrated on full adders, it should be understood that more ALU functions than addition are required if we are in to implement the data path of a typical minicomputer. Typically, some or all of the functions shown in Figure 8 are needed if we are to implement a powerful data handling capability.

The operation of the ALU/accumulator configuration shown in Figure 7 can be described as follows. The accumulator can be loaded by bringing data in from the data-in port through the A input of the ALU, passed through the ALU and loaded into the accumulator. A second word of data can be presented at the data-in port to the A input of the ALU and the ALU can be used to perform an operation such as A + B, A OR B, A AND B, A − B and so forth. The results of this ALU operation can then be placed into the accumulator. The accumulator output is available at the data-out port for use elsewhere. Additional ALU functions such as those shown in Figure 8 are easily implemented by adding some additional circuitry to the four-bit carry look ahead adder shown in Figure 3. If this circuitry is added, we will arrive at a logic diagram as shown in Figure 9. This diagram certainly is familiar to most CPU designers and is the well known Am74S181 four-bit arithmetic logic unit/function generator.

Once the operation of the simple computer data path as shown in Figure 7 is understood, the Design Engineer will soon recognize the need for additional registers if our machine is to be general purpose and execute instructions. Very rapidly the need arises for a register to hold a program counter (PC) and a memory address register (MAR). The purpose of the program counter is to point to the address of the next instruction in main memory. Typically it is loaded into the memory address register which actually provides the address on to the address bus of the machine. Then, the program counter is incremented through the ALU and stored until

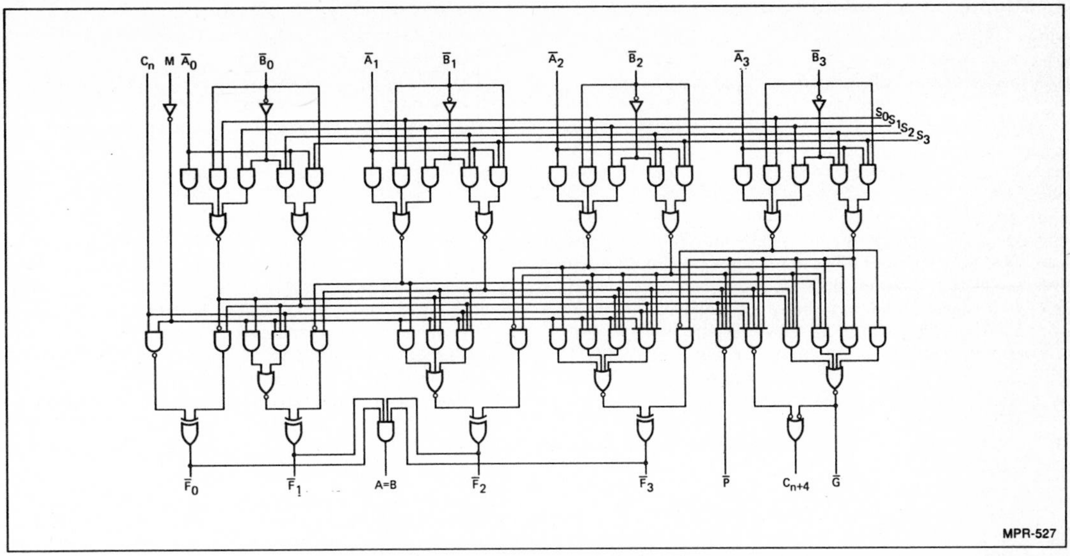

Figure 9. Logic Diagram for Am25LS181.

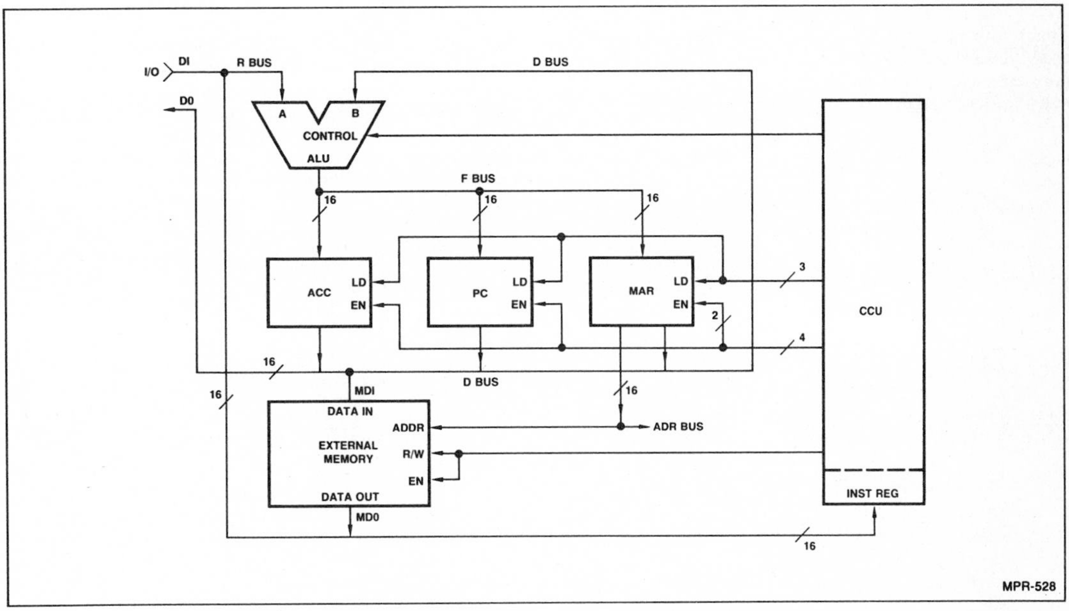

Figure 10.Three Register Computer Data Path.

it is needed again. The block diagram of Figure 10 shows these additional registers connected in parallel at the output of the ALU. This ALU output is called the F bus. Each of these registers (the accumulator, the PC, and the MAR) has an enable input from the CCU so that they can selectively be loaded with data from the ALU. In addition, each of these registers has an output enable such that they can be selectively enabled onto the D bus. The D bus represents the data output path from the basic computer data path and also is used as one of the inputs to the actual ALU/function generator. The other input in this example is called the R bus and comes directly from the main memory data output as well as from the I/O data input. As shown in Figure 10, the memory address register (MAR) has a second output that is used to drive the address bus. In this example, this register always contains the address to be applied to the external memory whether it be the address of data or the address of an instruction.

The best way to understand the operation of this single ALU/three register machine is to take an example. Let us assume we have just completed the execution of one machine instruction and are ready to fetch the next instruction. The first operation would be to transfer the current value of the program counter onto the D bus through the ALU onto the F bus and into the memory address register. This might be accomplished during one microcycle. The second operation might be to again put the PC on the D bus, pass it through the ALU B port and increment the value at the B port and reload it into the PC register. Thus, the PC has again been updated to point to the address of the next intruction. During this time, the address from the MAR is on the address bus and we are fetching data from the external memory and placing it on the R bus. The third microcycle would be to bring the data out of the external memory and pass it to the instruction register in the CCU. The next microcycle might be to decode this instruction and determine that the next word after the current instruction in memory (an immediate operation) is to be added to the value currently in the accumulator. Thus, we would again need to place the PC into the MAR on one cycle and then increment the PC on the next cycle. Following this, the data from the external memory could be brought to the R bus through the A port of the ALU and added to the accumulator value which is placed on the D bus and brought through the B port of the ALU. The result would be placed in the accumulator. This operation would complete the example and we would be ready to fetch the next instruction. As can be seen, a number of microcycles are required to fetch the instruction, decode it, fetch the data and execute the instruction. One of the best ways to understand the flow needed to implement a typical instruction set is shown in Figure 11. Here, we see the basic instruction fetch and decode operation followed by the path used to execute each of the various instructions. Then, we see a return to the fetch operation to fetch the next instruction.

Certainly from this discussion we can see how three registers have enhanced the performance of the simple ALU/accumulator data path shown in Figure 7. Typically, even more registers than shown in Figure 10 are needed if we are to increase the power of our machine. If we examine the block diagram of Figure 12, we see a similar architecture to that as shown in Figure 10. Here, the number of working registers has been expanded to sixteen at the output of the ALU. These can be used to provide a program counter function and a number of accumulator functions simultaneously. In addition, note that the registers have two output ports such that the simultaneous selection of any two of the sixteen registers is possible. Both of these registers can be presented to the ALU so that operations on two registers simultaneously can be executed. In addition, a data input multiplexer is available at the A port of the ALU such that external data can be brought in to the configuration. Likewise, there is an output multiplexer such that either the A output of the registers or the ALU output can be selected. This output multiplexer is used to provide a data out port and the output can also be loaded into memory address register to provide an address as required. Thus, the architecture of Figure 12 is quite similar to that of Figure 10 except that the number of registers has been increased to provide additional flexibility.

If we assume that one of the sixteen registers inside of this register file is to be used as the program counter, we see that the program counter can be brought out of the A output port and loaded into the memory address register and at the same time it can also be brought out the B output port and incremented in ALU and reloaded into the register file. In this architecture it appears the A output of the register stack can also be brought to the input multiplexer and the A port of the ALU and incremented via that path and reloaded into the registers. While this is possible in the architecture of Figure 12, we are leading up to the implementation of an Am2901A and this path is not needed in the Am2901A. Thus, we can implement functions and operations in the diagram of Figure 12 just as we could in the diagram of Figure 10. However, what was previously performed in two microcycles can now be performed in one microcycle. That is, the MAR can be loaded with the current value of the PC and at the same time the PC can be incremented and the new value restored in the PC register.

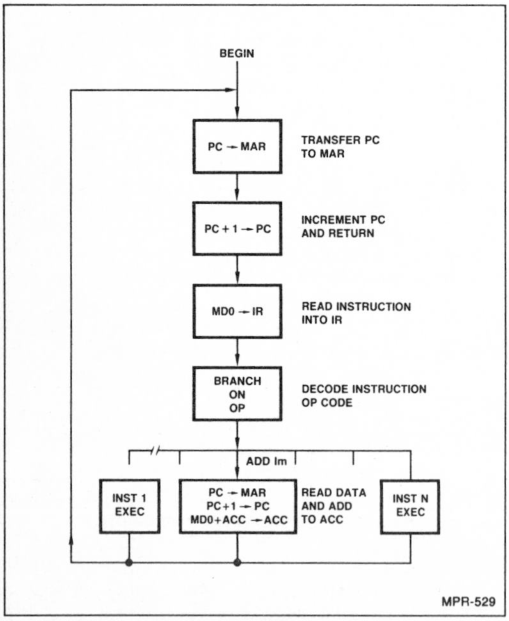

Figure 11. Steps for ADD Instruction.

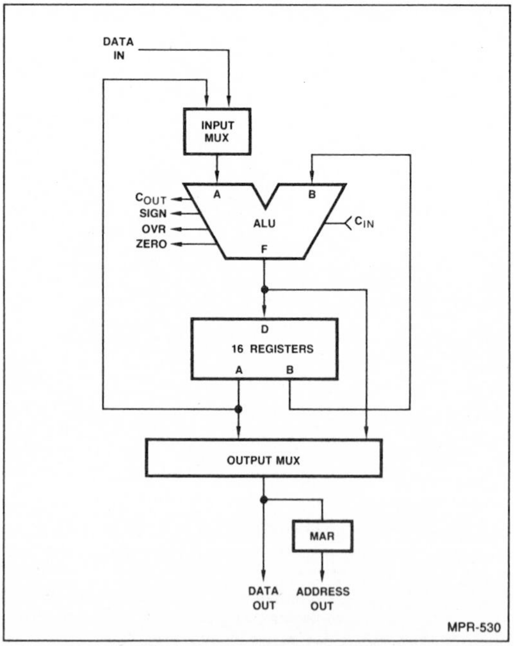

Figure 12. Multi-Register ALU.

Another feature of the block diagram of Figure 12 is the depiction of the carry in bit to the ALU and the four output flags associated with the ALU. Here, carry in is the normal carry in as needed in any adder such that the device is cascadable. In addition, certain kinds of arithmetic functions such two's complement arithmetic also need the ability to provide a carry in for certain operations. The most common is two's complement subtract which is usually performed by complementing the operand to be subtracted, adding and adding one at the carry in. Also, the ALU shows the four output flags usually associated with a typical minicomputer. These are the carry output, the sign bit, the overflow detect, and the zero detect. These four status flags are used to determine various things about the operation being performed. The carry out flag and overflow flag are as described in the previous sections of this chapter. They provide the carry and overflow information about the addition.

The sign bit is simply the most significant bit of the ALU and represents the sign of a two's complement number. That is, when the sign bit is LOW, we assume the two's complement number is positive and when the sign bit is HIGH, we assume the two's complement number is negative. Thus, the sign bit is active HIGH and carries negative weight as we assume in any standard two's complement number representation. If the reader is unfamiliar with two's complement number notations, a discussion of this topic can be found in an application note entitled "The Am25S05, Am2505 and Am25L05 Schottky, Standard and Low Power TTL Two's Complement Digital Multipliers" as found in Advanced Micro Devices' Schottky and Low Power Schottky Data Book dated 10/77. This application note begins on page 5-49 and fully details two's complement number notation and gives examples.

The fourth status flag is called the zero flag and again is just what the name implies. This flag represents the fact that all of the ALU outputs are at logic zero. In this design, a logic zero means that all of the ALU output bits are LOW.

If the architecture of Figure 12 is extended a little more, we will arrive at the Am2901A as depicted in Figure 13. Here, we have redrawn the structure so that the registers are placed above the ALU; however, the function is identical. Two new functions have been added to this block diagram that have not previously been discussed. These are the RAM shift matrix located directly above the sixteen registers now described as a 16 x 4 dual port RAM. The purpose of the RAM shift network is to allow the ability of shifting the data word to be written into the register either up one bit position or down one bit position. The second function added to the block diagram is that of the Q register and shift network. Here, the Q register is used as an auxiliary register such that double length operations can be performed and it is also used in the multiply and divide algorithms. In addition, the shift network allows the Q register contents to be shifted up one bit position or shifted down one bit position. In addition, it should be pointed out that the memory address register is not part of the Am2901A. This is because there were not enough pins on the package to implement the function and the additional power required by the output buffers would have reduced the performance of the ALU and register stack. Instead, this function is being designed into other 2900 family products.

Am2901A ARCHITECTURE

A detailed block diagram of the Am2901A bipolar microprogrammable microprocessor structure is shown in Figure 14. The circuit is a four-bit slice cascadable to any number of bits. Therefore, all data paths within the circuit are four bits wide. The two key elements in the Figure 14 block diagram are the 16-word by 4-bit 2-port RAM and the high-speed ALU.

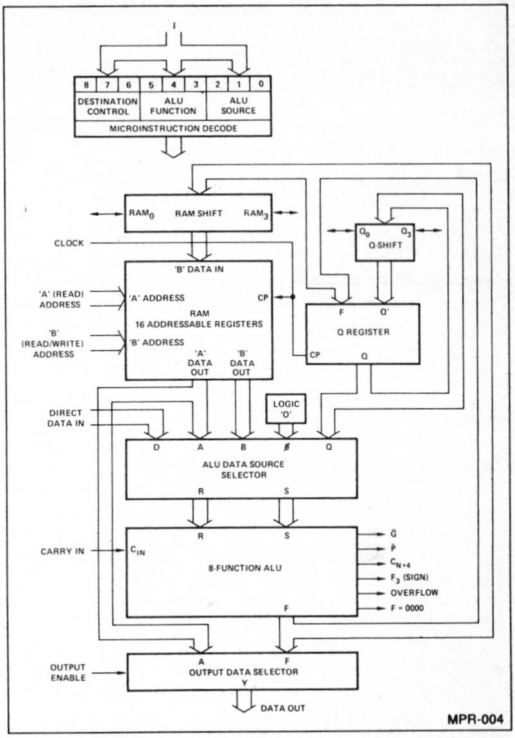

Figure 13. Am2901A Block Diagram.

Data in any of the 16 words of the Random Access Memory (RAM) can be read from the A-port of the RAM as controlled by the 4-bit A address field input. Likewise, data in any of the 16 words of the RAM as defined by the B address field input can be simultaneously read from the B-port of the RAM. The same code can be applied to the A select field and B select field in which case the identical file data will appear at both the RAM A-port and B-port outputs simultaneously.

When enabled by the RAM write enable (RAM EN), new data is always written into the file (word) defined by the B address field of the RAM. The RAM data input field is driven by a 3-input multiplexer. This configuration is used to shift the ALU output data (F) if desired. This three-input multiplexer scheme allows the data to be shifted up one bit position, shifted down one bit position, or not shifted in either direction.

The RAM A-port data outputs and RAM B-port data outputs drive separate 4-bit latches. These latches hold the RAM data while the clock input is LOW. This eliminates any possible race conditions that could occur while new data is being written into the RAM.

The high-speed Arithmetic Logic Unit (ALU) can perform three binary arithmetic and five logic operations on the two 4-bit input words R and S. The R input field is driven from a 2-input multiplexer, while the S input field is driven from a 3-input multiplexer. Both multiplexers also have an inhibit capability; that is, no data is passed. This is equivalent to a "zero" source operand.

Referring to Figure 14, the ALU R-input multiplexer has the RAM A-port and the direct data inputs (D) connected as inputs. Likewise, the ALU S-input multiplexer has the RAM A-port, the RAM B-port and the Q register connected as inputs.

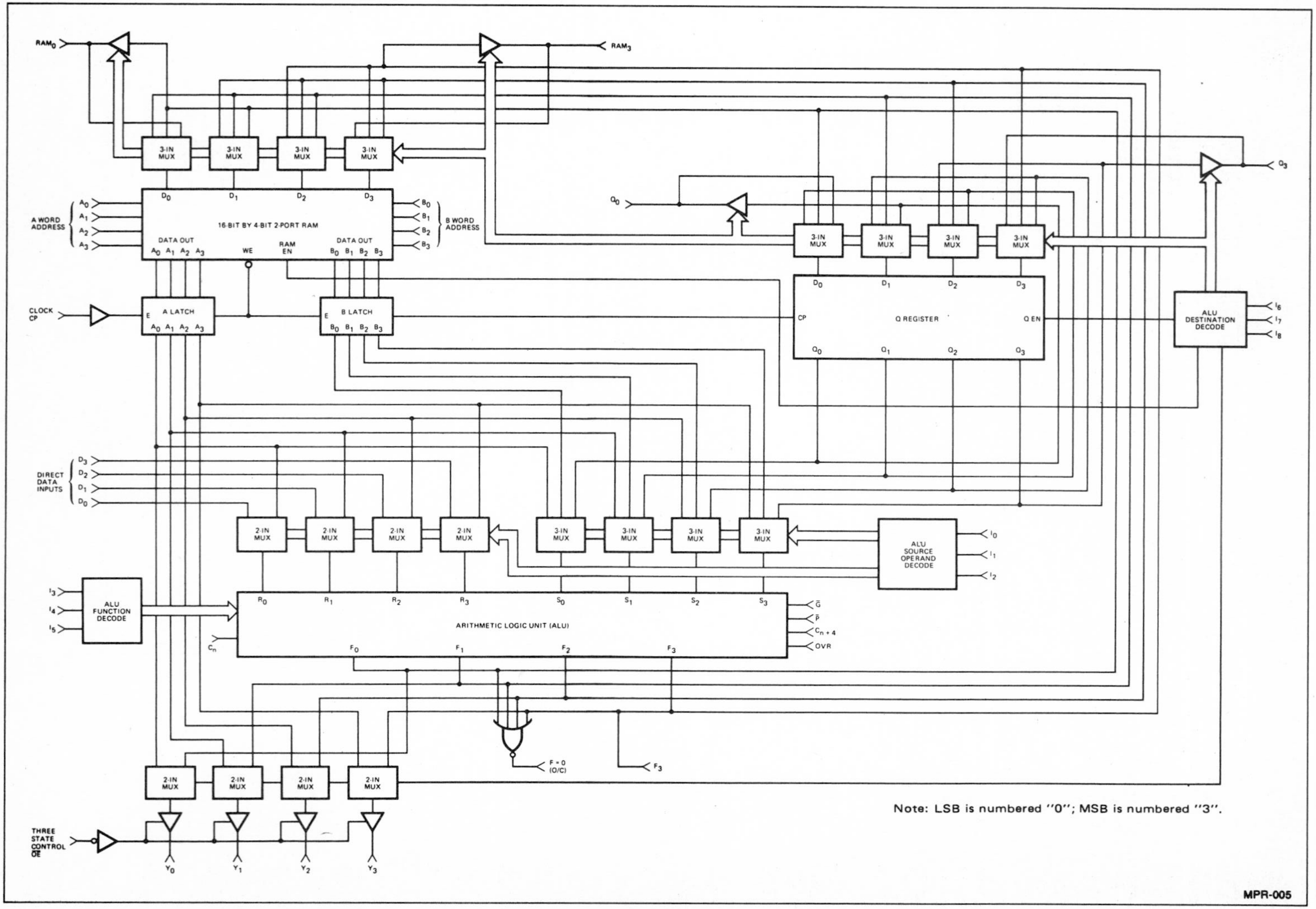
RAM0
RAM3
3-IN MUX
16-BIT BY 4-BIT 2-PORT RAM
DATA OUT
A WORD ADDRESS
B WORD ADDRESS
WE
RAM EN
CLOCK CP
A LATCH
B LATCH
Q REGISTER
Q EN
ALU DESTINATION DECODE
DIRECT DATA INPUTS
2-IN MUX
ALU SOURCE OPERAND DECODE
ALU FUNCTION DECODE
ARITHMETIC LOGIC UNIT (ALU)
OVR
F = 0 (O/C)
THREE STATE CONTROL OE
Note: LSB is numbered "0"; MSB is numbered "3".
MPR-005

Figure 14.

This multiplexer scheme gives the capability of selecting various pairs of the A, B, D, Q and "0" inputs as source operands to the ALU. These five inputs, when taken two at a time, result in ten possible combinations of source operand pairs. These combinations include AB, AD, AQ, A0, BD, BQ, B0, DQ, D0 and Q0. It is apparent that AD, AQ and A0 are somewhat redundant with BD, BQ and B0 in that if the A address and B address are the same, the identical function results. Thus, there are only seven completely non-redundant source operand pairs for the ALU. The Am2901A microprocessor implements eight of these pairs. The microinstruction inputs used to select the ALU source operands are the I_0, I_1 and I_2 inputs.

The two source operands not fully described as yet are the D input and Q input. The D input is the four-bit wide direct data field input. This port is used to insert all data into the working registers inside the device. Likewise, this input can be used in the ALU to modify any of the internal data files. The Q register is a separate 4-bit file intended primarily for multiplication and division routines but it can also be used as an accumulator or holding register for some applications.

The ALU itself is a high-speed arithmetic/logic operator capable of performing three binary arithmetic and five logic functions. The I_3, I_4 and I_5 microinstruction inputs are used to select the ALU function. The definition of these functions is shown in Figure 15. The normal technique for cascading the ALU of several devices is in a look-ahead carry mode. Carry generate, $\overline{G}$, and carry propagate, $\overline{P}$, are outputs of the device for use with a carry-look-ahead-generator such as the Am2902A ('182). A carry-out, C_{n+4}, is also generated and is available as an output for use as the carry flag in a status register. Both carry-in (C_n) and carry-out (C_{n+4}) are active HIGH.

SOURCE OPERANDS

A, B	B, 0
A, D	D, 0
A, Q	Q, 0
A, 0	D, Q

ALU FUNCTIONS

R+S	R OR S
R–S	R AND S
S–R	R EXOR S
	R EXNOR S
	R AND S

DESTINATION

SHIFT	LOAD	Y-OUT
UP	RAM	F
UP	RAM & Q	F
DOWN	RAM	F
DOWN	RAM & Q	F
NONE	NONE	F
NONE	Q	F
NONE	RAM	F
NONE	RAM	A

Figure 15. Am2901A Microinstruction Control.

The ALU has three other status-oriented outputs. These are F_3, F = 0, and overflow (OVR). The F_3 output is the most significant (sign) bit of the ALU and can be used to determine positive or negative results without enabling the three-state data outputs. F_3 is non-inverted with respect to the sign bit output Y_3. The F = 0 output is used for zero detect. It is an open-collector output and can be wire OR'ed between microprocessor slices. F = 0 is HIGH when all F outputs are LOW. The overflow output (OVR) is used to flag arithmetic operations that exceed the available two's complement number range. The overflow output (OVR) is HIGH when overflow exists; that is, when C_{n+3} and C_{n+4} are not the same polarity.

The ALU data output is routed to several destinations. It can be a data output of the device and it can also be stored in the RAM or the Q register. Eight possible combinations of ALU destination functions are available as defined by the I_6, I_7 and I_8 microinstruction inputs. These combinations are shown in Figure 15.

The four-bit data output field (Y) features three-state outputs and can be directly bus organized. An output control ($\overline{OE}$) is used to enable the three-state outputs. When $\overline{OE}$ is HIGH, the Y outputs are in the high-impedance state.

A two-input multiplexer is also used at the data output such that either the A-port of the RAM or the ALU outputs (F) are selected at the device Y outputs. This selection is controlled by the I_6, I_7 and I_8 microinstruction inputs.

As was discussed previously, the RAM inputs are driven from a three-input multiplexer. This allows the ALU outputs to be entered non-shifted, shifted up one position (X2) or shifted down one position (÷2). The shifter has two ports; one is labeled RAM_0 and the other is labeled RAM_3. Both of these ports consist of a buffer-driver with a three-state output and an input to the multiplexer. Thus, in the shift up mode, the RAM_3 buffer is enabled and the RAM_0 multiplexer input is enabled. Likewise, in the shift down mode, the RAM_0 buffer and RAM_3 input are enabled. In the no-shift mode, both buffers are in the high-impedance state and the multiplexer inputs are not selected. This shifter is controlled from the I_6, I_7 and I_8 microinstruction inputs.

Similarly, the Q register is driven from a 3-input multiplexer. In the no-shift mode, the multiplexer enters the ALU data into the Q register. In either the shift-up or shift-down mode, the multiplexer selects the Q register data appropriately shifted up or down. The Q shifter also has two ports; one is labeled Q_0 and the other is Q_3. The operation of these two ports is similar to the RAM shifter and is also controlled from I_6, I_7 and I_8.

The clock input to the Am2901A controls the RAM, the Q register, and the A and B data latches. When enabled, data is clocked into the Q register on the LOW-to-HIGH transition of the clock. When the clock input is HIGH, the A and B latches are open and will pass whatever data is present at the RAM outputs. When the clock input is LOW, the latches are closed and will retain the last data entered. If the RAM-EN is enabled, new data will be written into the RAM file (word) defined by the B address field when the clock input is LOW.

Am2903 GENERAL DESCRIPTION

The Am2903 is a four-bit expandable bipolar microprocessor slice that performs all functions performed by the industry standard Am2901A. In addition, it provides a number of significant enhancements that are especially useful in arithmetic oriented processors. The Am2903 contains sixteen internal working registers arranged in a two address architecture and it also provides all of the necessary signals to expand the register file externally using the Am29705 register stack. Any number of registers can be cascaded to the Am2903 using this technique. In addition to its complete arithmetic and logic instruction set, the Am2903 provides a special set of instructions which facilitate the implementation of multiplication, division, normalization and other previously time consuming operations such as parity generation and sign extension. A block diagram of the Am2903 is shown in Figure 16.

ARCHITECTURE OF THE Am2903

The Am2903 is a high-performance, cascadable, four-bit bipolar microprocessor slice designed for use in CPU's, peripheral controllers, microprogrammable machines, and numerous other applications. The microinstruction flexibility of the Am2903 allows the efficient emulation of almost any digital computing machine.

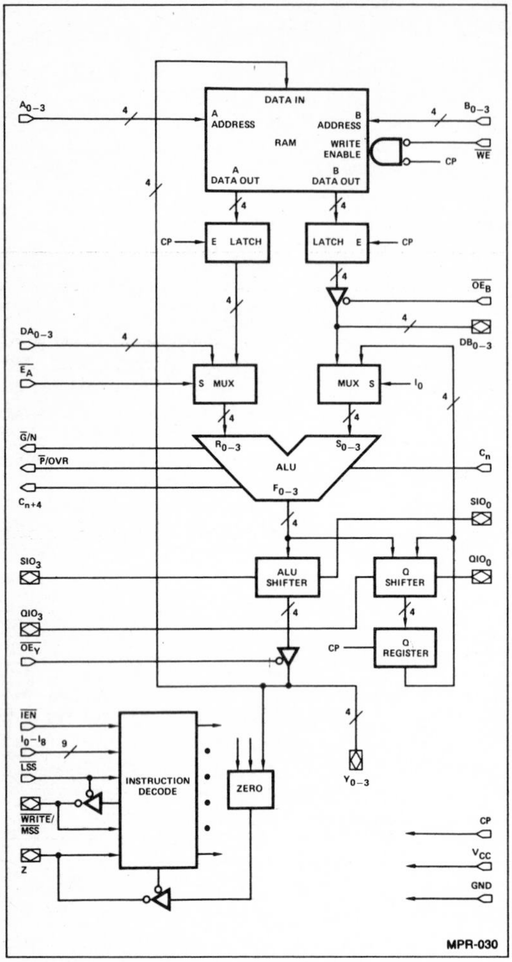

Figure 16. Basic Am2903 Block Diagram.

The nine-bit microinstruction selects the ALU sources, function, and destination. The Am2903 is cascadable with full lookahead or ripple carry, has three-state outputs, and provides various ALU status flag outputs. Advanced Low-Power Schottky processing is used to fabricate this 48-pin LSI circuit.

All data paths within the device are four bits wide. As shown in the block diagram of Figure 16, the device consists of a 16-word by 4-bit, two-port RAM with latches on both output ports, a high-performance ALU and shifter, a multi-purpose Q Register with shifter input, and a nine-bit instruction decoder.

Two-Port RAM

Any two RAM words addressed at the A and B address ports can be read simultaneously at the respective RAM A and B output ports. Identical data appear at the two output ports when the same address is applied to both address ports. The latches at the RAM output ports are transparent when the clock input, CP, is HIGH and they hold the RAM output data when CP is LOW. Under control of the $\overline{OE}_B$ three-state output enable, RAM data can be read directly at the Am2903 DB I/O port.

External data at the Am2903 Y I/O port can be written directly into the RAM, or ALU shifter output data can be enabled onto the Y I/O port and entered into the RAM. Data is written into the RAM at the B address when the write enable input, $\overline{WE}$, is LOW and the clock input, CP, is LOW.

Arithmetic Logic Unit

The Am2903 high-performance ALU can perform seven arithmetic and nine logic operations on two 4-bit operands. Multiplexers at the ALU inputs provide the capability to select various pairs of ALU source operands. The $\overline{E}_A$ input selects either the DA external data input or RAM output port A for use as one ALU operand and the $\overline{OE}_B$ and I_0 inputs select RAM output port B, DB external data input, or the Q Register content for use as the second ALU operand. Also, during some ALU operations, zeros are forced at the ALU operand inputs. Thus, the Am2903 ALU can operate on data from two external sources, from an internal and external source, or from two internal sources.

When instruction bits I_4, I_3, I_2, I_1 and I_0 are LOW, the Am2903 executes special functions. Figure 17 defines these special functions and the operation which the ALU performs for each. When the Am2903 executes instructions other than the nine special functions, the ALU operation is determined by instruction bits I_4, I_3, I_2 and I_1. Figure 18 defines the ALU operation as a function of these four instruction bits.

Am2903s may be cascaded in either a ripple carry or lookahead carry fashion. When a number of Am2903s are cascaded, each slice must be programmed to be a most significant slice (MSS), intermediate slice (IS), or least significant slice (LSS) of the array. The carry generate, $\overline{G}$, and carry propagate, $\overline{P}$, signals required for a lookahead carry scheme are generated by the Am2903 and are available as ontputs of the least significant and intermediate slices.

The Am2903 also generates a carry-out signal, C_{n+4}, which is generally available as an output of each slice. Both the carry-in, C_n, and carry-out, C_{n+4}, signals are active HIGH. The ALU generates two other status outputs. These are negative, N, and overflow, OVR. The N output is generally the most significant (sign) bit of the ALU output and can be used to determine positive or negative results. The OVR output indicates that the arithmetic operation being performed exceeds the available two's complement number range. The N and OVR signals are available as outputs of the most significant slice. Thus, the multi-purpose $\overline{G}$/N and $\overline{P}$/OVR outputs indicate $\overline{G}$ and $\overline{P}$ at the least significant and intermediate slices, and sign and overflow at the most significant slice. To some extent, the meaning of the C_{n+4}, $\overline{P}$/OVR, and $\overline{G}$/N signals vary with the ALU function being performed.

ALU Shifter

Under instruction control, the ALU shifter passes the ALU output (F) non-shifted, shifts it up one bit position (2F), or shifts it down one bit position (F/2). Both arithmetic and logical shift operations are possible. An arithmetic shift operation shifts data around the most significant (sign) bit position of the most significant slice, and a logical shift operation shifts data through this bit position (see Figure 19). SIO_0 and SIO_3 are bidirectional serial shift inputs/outputs. During a shift-up operation, SIO_0 is generally a serial shift input and SIO_3 a serial shift output. During a shift-down operation, SIO_3 is generally a serial shift input and SIO_0 a serial shift output.

The ALU shifter also provides the capability to sign extend at slice boundaries. Under instruction control, the SIO_0 (sign) input can be extended through Y_0, Y_1, Y_2, Y_3 and propagated to the SIO_3 output.

I_8	I_7	I_6	I_5	Hex Code	Special Function	ALU Function	ALU Shifter Function	SIO_3 Most Sig. Slice	SIO_3 Other Slices	SIO_0	Q Reg & Shifter Function	QIO_3	QIO_0	$\overline{WRITE}$
L	L	L	L	0	Unsigned Multiply	$F = S + C_n$ if $Z = L$ $F = R + S + C_n$ if $Z = H$	Log. $F/2 \rightarrow Y$ (Note 1)	Hi-Z	Input	F_0	Log. $Q/2 \rightarrow Q$	Input	Q_0	L
L	L	H	L	2	Two's Complement Multiply	$F = S + C_n$ if $Z = L$ $F = R + S + C_n$ if $Z = H$	Log. $F/2 \rightarrow Y$ (Note 2)	Hi-Z	Input	F_0	Log. $Q/2 \rightarrow Q$	Input	Q_0	L
L	H	L	L	4	Increment by One or Two	$F = S + 1 + C_n$	$F \rightarrow Y$	Input	Input	Parity	Hold	Hi-Z	Hi-Z	L
L	H	L	H	5	Sign/Magnitude-Two's Complement	$F = S + C_n$ if $Z = L$ $F = \overline{S} + C_n$ if $Z = H$	$F \rightarrow Y$ (Note 3)	Input	Input	Parity	Hold	Hi-Z	Hi-Z	L
L	H	H	L	6	Two's Complement Multiply, Last Cycle	$F = S + C_n$ if $Z = L$ $F = S - R - 1 + C_n$ if $Z = H$	Log. $F/2 \rightarrow Y$ (Note 2)	Hi-Z	Input	F_0	Log. $Q/2 \rightarrow Q$	Input	Q_0	L
H	L	L	L	8	Single Length Normalize	$F = S + C_n$	$F \rightarrow Y$	F_3	F_3	Hi-Z	Log. $2Q \rightarrow Q$	Q_3	Input	L
H	L	H	L	A	Double Length Normalize and First Divide Op.	$F = S + C_n$	Log $2F \rightarrow Y$	$R_3 \veebar F_3$	F_3	Input	Log. $2Q \rightarrow Q$	Q_3	Input	L
H	H	L	L	C	Two's Complement Divide	$F = S + R + C_n$ if $Z = L$ $F = S - R - 1 + C_n$ if $Z = H$	Log. $2F \rightarrow Y$	$\overline{R_3 \veebar F_3}$	F_3	Input	Log. $2Q \rightarrow Q$	Q_3	Input	L
H	H	H	L	E	Two's Complement Divide, Correction and Remainder	$F = S + R + C_n$ if $Z = L$ $F = S - R - 1 + C_n$ if $Z = H$	$F \rightarrow Y$	F_3	F_3	Hi-Z	Log. $2Q \rightarrow Q$	Q_3	Input	L

NOTES: 1. At the most significant slice only, the C_{n+4} signal is internally gated to the Y_3 output.
2. At the most significant slice only, $F_3 \veebar OVR$ is internally gated to the Y_3 output.
3. At the most significant slice only, $S_3 \veebar F_3$ is generated at the Y_3 output.
4. Op codes 1, 3, 7, 9, B, D, and F are reserved for future use.

L = LOW
H = HIGH
X = Don't Care

Hi-Z = High Impedance
$\veebar$ = Exclusive OR
Parity = $SIO_3 \veebar F_3 \veebar F_2 \veebar F_1 \veebar F_0$

Figure 17. Special Functions: $I_0 = I_1 = I_2 = I_3 = I_4$ = LOW, $\overline{IEN}$ = LOW.

I_4	I_3	I_2	I_1	Hex Code	ALU Functions	
L	L	L	L	0	$I_0 = L$	Special Functions
					$I_0 = H$	F_i = HIGH
L	L	L	H	1	F = S Minus R Minus 1 Plus C_n	
L	L	H	L	2	F = R Minus S Minus 1 Plus C_n	
L	L	H	H	3	F = R Plus S Plus C_n	
L	H	L	L	4	F = S Plus C_n	
L	H	L	H	5	F = $\overline{S}$ Plus C_n	
L	H	H	L	6	F = R Plus C_n	
L	H	H	H	7	F = $\overline{R}$ Plus C_n	
H	L	L	L	8	F_i = LOW	
H	L	L	H	9	$F_i = \overline{R_i}$ AND S_i	
H	L	H	L	A	$F_i = R_i$ EXCLUSIVE NOR S_i	
H	L	H	H	B	$F_i = R_i$ EXCLUSIVE OR S_i	
H	H	L	L	C	$F_i = R_i$ AND S_i	
H	H	L	H	D	$F_i = R_i$ NOR S_i	
H	H	H	L	E	$F_i = R_i$ NAND S_i	
H	H	H	H	F	$F_i = R_i$ OR S_i	

L = LOW H = HIGH i = 0 to 3

Figure 18. ALU Functions.

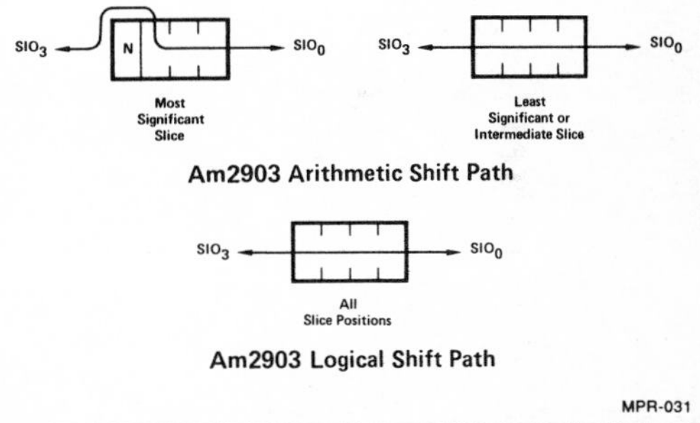

Figure 19.

A cascadable, five-bit parity generator/checker is designed into the Am2903 ALU shifter and provides ALU error detection capability. Parity for the F_0, F_1, F_2, F_3 ALU outputs and SIO_3 input is generated and, under instruction control, is made available at the SIO_0 output.

The instruction inputs determine the ALU shifter operation. Figure 17 defines the special functions and the operation the ALU shifter performs for each. When the Am2903 executes instructions other than the nine special functions, the ALU shifter operation is determined by instruction bits $I_8I_7I_6I_5$. Figure 20 defines the ALU shifter operation as a function of these four bits.

Q Register

The Q Register is an auxiliary four-bit register which is clocked on the LOW-to-HIGH transition of the CP input. It is intended primarily for use in multiplication and division operations; however, it can also be used as an accumulator or holding register for some applications. The ALU output, F, can be loaded into the Q Register, and/or the Q Register can be selected as the source for the ALU S operand. The shifter at the input to the Q Register provides

I_8	I_7	I_6	I_5	Hex Code	ALU Shifter Function	SIO_3 Most Sig. Slice	SIO_3 Other Slices	Y_3 Most Sig. Slice	Y_3 Other Slices	Y_2 Most Sig. Slice	Y_2 Other Slices	Y_1	Y_0	SIO_0	$\overline{Write}$	Q Reg & Shifter Function	QIO_3	QIO_0
L	L	L	L	0	Arith. F/2→Y	Input	Input	F_3	SIO_3	SIO_3	F_3	F_2	F_1	F_0	L	Hold	Hi-Z	Hi-Z
L	L	L	H	1	Log. F/2→Y	Input	Input	SIO_3	SIO_3	F_3	F_3	F_2	F_1	F_0	L	Hold	Hi-Z	Hi-Z
L	L	H	L	2	Arith. F/2→Y	Input	Input	F_3	SIO_3	SIO_3	F_3	F_2	F_1	F_0	L	Log. Q/2→Q	Input	Q_0
L	L	H	H	3	Log. F/2→Y	Input	Input	SIO_3	SIO_3	F_3	F_3	F_2	F_1	F_0	L	Log. Q/2→Q	Input	Q_0
L	H	L	L	4	F→Y	Input	Input	F_3	F_3	F_2	F_2	F_1	F_0	Parity	L	Hold	Hi-Z	Hi-Z
L	H	L	H	5	F→Y	Input	Input	F_3	F_3	F_2	F_2	F_1	F_0	Parity	H	Log. Q/2→Q	Input	Q_0
L	H	H	L	6	F→Y	Input	Input	F_3	F_3	F_2	F_2	F_1	F_0	Parity	H	F→Q	Hi-Z	Hi-Z
L	H	H	H	7	F→Y	Input	Input	F_3	F_3	F_2	F_2	F_1	F_0	Parity	L	F→Q	Hi-Z	Hi-Z
H	L	L	L	8	Arith. 2F→Y	F_2	F_3	F_3	F_2	F_1	F_1	F_0	SIO_0	Input	L	Hold	Hi-Z	Hi-Z
H	L	L	H	9	Log. 2F→Y	F_3	F_3	F_2	F_2	F_1	F_1	F_0	SIO_0	Input	L	Hold	Hi-Z	Hi-Z
H	L	H	L	A	Arith. 2F→Y	F_2	F_3	F_3	F_2	F_1	F_1	F_0	SIO_0	Input	L	Log. 2Q→Q	Q_3	Input
H	L	H	H	B	Log. 2F→Y	F_3	F_3	F_2	F_2	F_1	F_1	F_0	SIO_0	Input	L	Log. 2Q→Q	Q_3	Input
H	H	L	L	C	F→Y	F_3	F_3	F_3	F_3	F_2	F_2	F_1	F_0	Hi-Z	H	Hold	Hi-Z	Hi-Z
H	H	L	H	D	F→Y	F_3	F_3	F_3	F_3	F_2	F_2	F_1	F_0	Hi-Z	H	Log. 2Q→Q	Q_3	Input
H	H	H	L	E	SIO_0→Y_0, Y_1, Y_2, Y_3	SIO_0	SIO_0	SIO_0	SIO_0	SIO_0	SIO_0	SIO_0	SIO_0	Input	L	Hold	Hi-Z	Hi-Z
H	H	H	H	F	F→Y	F_3	F_3	F_3	F_3	F_2	F_2	F_1	F_0	Hi-Z	L	Hold	Hi-Z	Hi-Z

Parity = $F_3 \forall F_2 \forall F_1 \forall F_0 \forall SIO_3$
∀ = Exclusive OR

L = LOW
H = HIGH

Hi-Z = High Impedance

Figure 20a. ALU Destination Control for I_0 or I_1 or I_2 or I_3 or I_4 = HIGH, $\overline{IEN}$ = LOW.

OPERATION		ALU SHIFTER	RAM WRITE	Q
SINGLE LENGTH SHIFT		UP DOWN ARITH UP ARITH DOWN	YES	NC
DOUBLE LENGTH SHIFT		UP DOWN ARITH UP ARITH DOWN	YES	UP DOWN UP DOWN
Q-SHIFT		PASS	NO	UP DOWN
LOAD	RAM	PASS	YES	NC
	RAM & Q		YES	LOAD
	Q		NO	LOAD
	NONE		NO	NC
SIGN EXTEND		SIO_0	YES	NC

NC = No Change

Figure 20b. Am2903 ALU Destination Control Summary.

the capability to shift the Q Register contents up one bit position (2Q) or down one bit position (Q/2). Only logical shifts are performed. QIO_0 and QIO_3 are bidirectional shift serial inputs/outputs. During a Q Register shift-up operation, QIO_0 is a serial shift input and QIO_3 is a serial shift output. During a shift-down operation, QIO_3 is a serial shift input and QIO_0 is a serial shift output.

Double-length arithmetic and logical shifting capability is provided by the Am2903. The double-length shift is performed by connecting QIO_3 of the most significant slice to SIO_0 of the least significant slice, and executing an instruction which shifts both the ALU output and the Q Register.

The Q Register and shifter operation is controlled by instruction bits $I_8I_7I_6I_5$. Figures 17 and 20 define the Q Register and shifter operation as a function of these four bits.

Output Buffers

The DB and Y ports are bidirectional I/O ports driven by three-state output buffers with external output enable controls. The Y output buffers are enabled when the $\overline{OE_Y}$ input is LOW and are in the high-impedance state when $\overline{OE_Y}$ is HIGH. Likewise, the DB output buffers are enabled when the $\overline{OE_B}$ input is LOW and in the high-impedance state when $\overline{OE_B}$ is HIGH.

The zero, Z, pin is an open collector input/output that can be wire-OR'ed between slices. As an output it can be used as a zero detect status flag and generally indicates that the $Y_{0\text{-}3}$ pins are all LOW, whether they are driven from the Y output buffers or from an external source connected to the $Y_{0\text{-}3}$ pins. To some extent the meaning of this signal varies with the instruction being performed.

Instruction Decoder

The Instruction Decoder generates required internal control signals as a function of the nine Instruction inputs, $I_{0\text{-}8}$; the Instruction Enable input, $\overline{IEN}$; the $\overline{LSS}$ input; and the $\overline{WRITE}/\overline{MSS}$ input/output. The $\overline{WRITE}$ output is LOW when an instruction which writes data into the RAM is being executed.

When $\overline{IEN}$ is LOW, the $\overline{WRITE}$ output is enabled and the Q Register and Sign Compare Flip-Flop can be written according to the Am2903 instruction. The Sign Compare Flip-Flop is an on-chip flip-flop which is used during an Am2903 divide operation.

Programming the Am2903 Slice Position

Tying the $\overline{LSS}$ input LOW programs the slice to operate as a least significant slice (LSS) and enables the $\overline{WRITE}$ output signal onto the $\overline{WRITE}/\overline{MSS}$ bidirectional I/O pin. When $\overline{LSS}$ is tied HIGH, the $\overline{WRITE}/\overline{MSS}$ pin becomes an input pin; tying the $\overline{WRITE}/\overline{MSS}$ pin HIGH programs the slice to operate as an intermediate slice (IS) and tying it LOW programs the slice to operate as a most significant slice (MSS). This is shown in Figure 21.

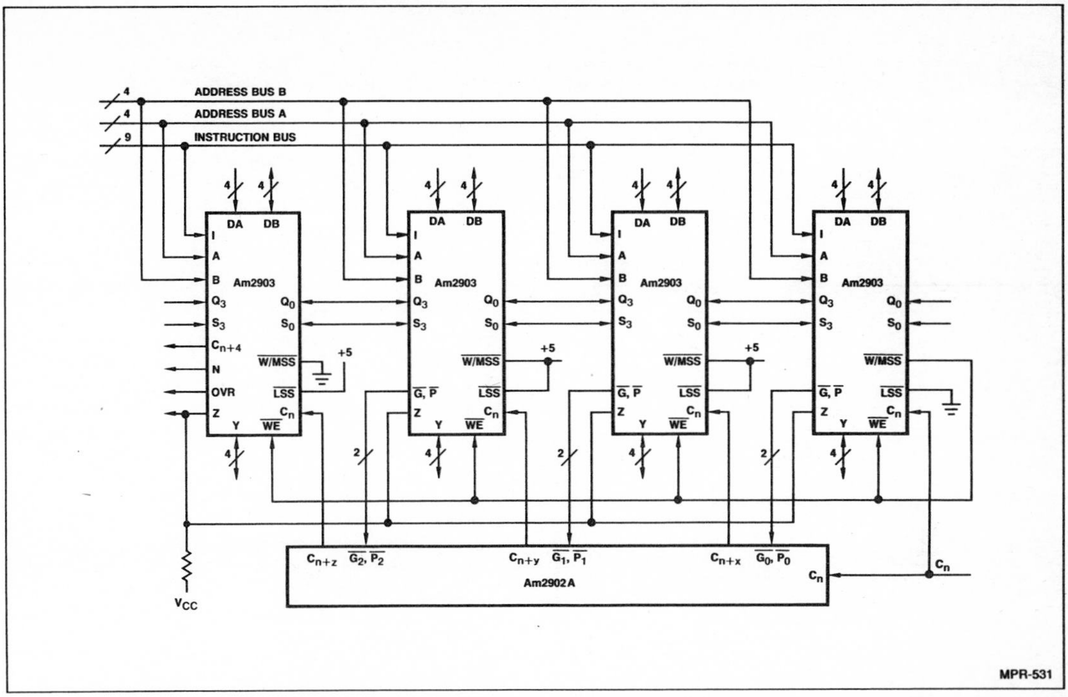

Figure 21. Am2903 – 16-Bit CPU with Carry Look Ahead.

EXPANDING THE NUMBER OF Am2903 REGISTERS

The Am2903 contains 16 internal working registers configured in a standard two port architecture. The number of working registers in the ALU configuration can be increased by utilizing the Am29705 16-word by 4-bit two-port RAM. Any number of Am29705's can be connected to the Am2903 to increase the number of working registers. Figure 22 shows a block diagram of the basic Am29705. As is seen, the device consists of a 16 word by 4 bit two port RAM with latches at the A and B outputs similar to the RAM contained within the Am2903. Each of the latch outputs has three state drivers capable of driving the DA and DB inputs of the Am2903. The Am29705 is a non-inverting device. That is, data presented at the inputs is stored in the RAM and when brought to the RAM outputs, it is non-inverted from when it was orginally brought into the device.

The technique for using the Am29705 to expand the number of registers in the Am2903 can best be visualized by referring to Figures 23 and 24 simultaneously. In Figure 23, the data bus connections are shown such that the Am2903 Y output is used to drive the Am29705 inputs. Here, we also assume this bus may be tied to a data bus through a bi-directional buffer. In Figure 23, the A outputs of the Am29705 are connected together and also connected to the DA input of the Am2903. Likewise, the B outputs from the Am29705 are also shown connected to the DB inputs of the Am2903. In all cases, we are assuming 16-bit data busses. Thus, four Am2903's are assumed and eight Am29705's are assumed. As shown in Figure 23, one of the write enable inputs to the Am29705 is tied to the latch enable input of the Am29705 and these pins are also tied to the clock input of the Am2903. This allows the latches in the Am29705 to perform identically to those in the Am2903.

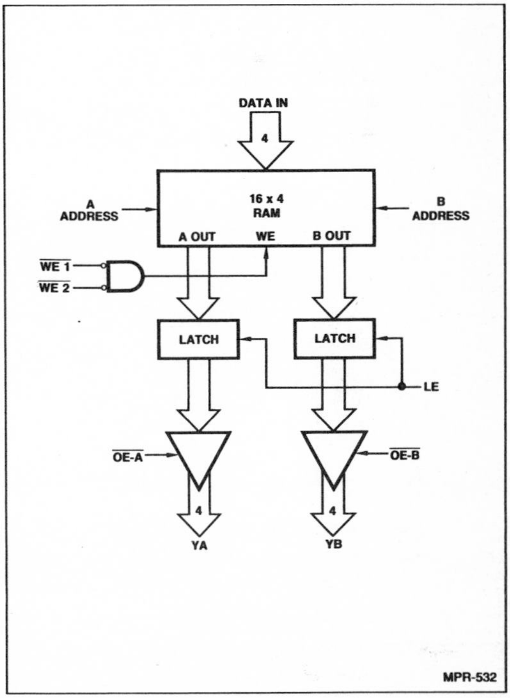

Figure 22. Am29705 Block Diagram.

If we refer to Figure 24, we see the connections required to set up the addressing for additional registers associated with the Am2903. Here, three two-line to four-line decoders are used to properly control the A address, B address and write enable signals to the devices. As shown in Figure 24, the four A address lines are all tied in parallel between the Am2903 and the Am29705's. The two-line to four-line decoder is used to enable the appropriate output enable from the Am29705's or switch the EA MUX inside the Am2903 such that the proper register is selected. The B address operates in a similar fashion in that the four B address lines are also all tied together. Likewise, a two-line to four-line decoder is used to properly select the output enable of either the Am29705's or the Am2903 such that the correct source

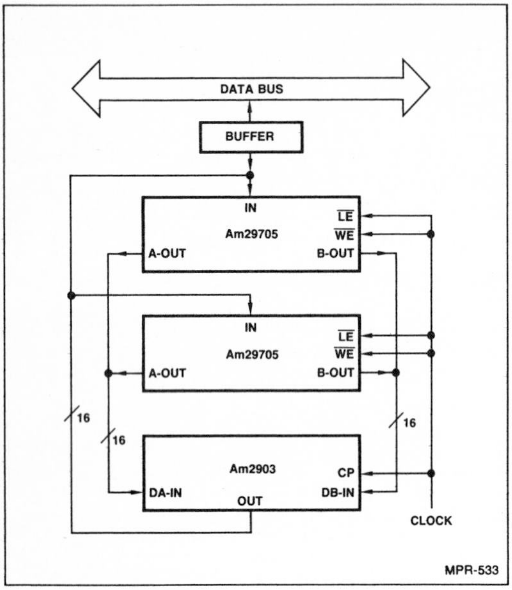

Figure 23. Am2903 – Data Bus Cascading.

operand register is selected. In addition, a two-line to four-line decoder is used to control the write enable signal such that only one register is written into as a destination. This is controlled by properly selecting the write enable of either the Am2903 or the Am29705 as determined by the two most significant bits of the B address.

If this technique is used properly, any number of Am29705's can be used in conjunction with the Am2903. It may be necessary to use either a three-line to eight-line decoder or perhaps even a larger circuit to decode the more significant bits of the A and B addresses. Likewise, the write enable signal must be controlled so that the correct destination register will be written.

UNDERSTANDING BIT SLICE TIMING

Perhaps one of the most important aspects of designing with either the Am2901A or the Am2903 is understanding the calculations required to compute the worst case AC performance. In order to perform these calculations, we have selected a number of standard Schottky devices and assigned minimum, typical and maximum speeds at 25°C and 5V for use in these calculations as shown in Figure 25. Certainly the design engineer should use the exact specifications of the devices he has selected for his design in order to perform the worst case calculations. What is intended here is an understanding of the technique to perform these calculations and some method to allow a comparison of the Am2901A and Am2903 in terms of their AC performance. Since at the time of this writing the Am2903 is still being characterized, only the typical AC data is currently available. Thus, all calculations will be made using the typical AC times such that we can compare the Am2901A with the Am2903. When final characterization data on the Am2903 is available, the designer can then compute his performance by selecting the appropriate temperature range and power supply variations as required by his design.

Figure 26 shows the typical AC calculations for the functions usually considered in an Am2901A design. These functions are usually the speed for a logic operation, arithmetic operation, logic operation with shift and arithmetic operation with shift. In each case, we are computing speeds from the LOW-to-HIGH transition of a clock through an entire microcycle to the next LOW-to-HIGH transition of a clock.

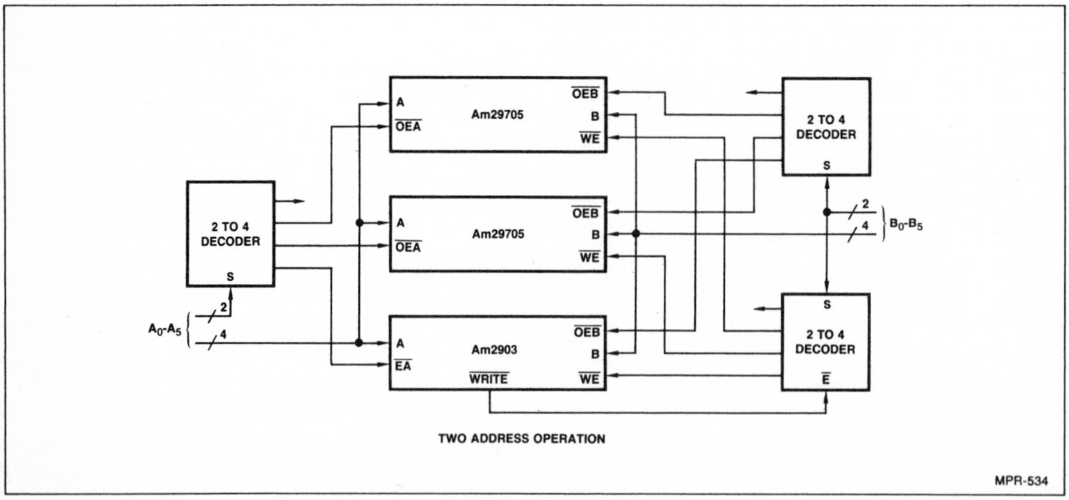

Figure 24. Am2903 – RAM Address Cascading.

DEVICE & PATH	MIN.	TYP.	MAX.
S Register			
Clock to Output		9	15
$\overline{OE}$ to Output		13	20
Set-Up	5	2	
S MUX			
Data to Output		5	8
Select to Output		12	18
$\overline{OE}$ to Output		13	20
Microprogram PROM			
Address to Output		30	50
$\overline{OE}$ to Output		18	25
Mapping PROM			
Address to Output		25	45
$\overline{OE}$ to Output		18	25
Decoder			
Select to Output		8	12
Counter			
Clock to Q		9	13
Clock to TC		12	18
CET to TC		8	12
Data Set-Up	8	4	
Load Set-Up	16	10	
CEP or CET Set-Up	12	7	
S-EXOR			
IN to OUT		7	11
Am2922			
Clock to Output		21	32
Data to Output		13	19
$\overline{OE}$ to Output		10	17
Data Set-Up	10	5	
Am29811A			
Input to Output		25	35
Am29803A			
Input to Output		25	35
Am2902A			
C_n to $C_{n+x,y,z}$		7	11
G, P to G, P		7	10
G, P to $C_{n+x,y,z}$		5	7

Figure 25. Standard Device Schottky Speeds.

Similarly, Figure 27 shows the same type of computations for an Am2903 system. There is one very important distinction that should be made in computing the timing of an Am2903 16-bit ALU when compared with an Am2901A ALU in that in the Am2903, the shifter is at the output of the ALU and is followed by the zero detector. Thus, in an Am2903 design, the flags are no longer independent of the shift operation. This is easily seen in Figure 27.

By way of comparison, Figure 28 shows speeds for the four types of operations for the Am2901A 16-bit system as compared with the Am2903 16-bit system.

a)

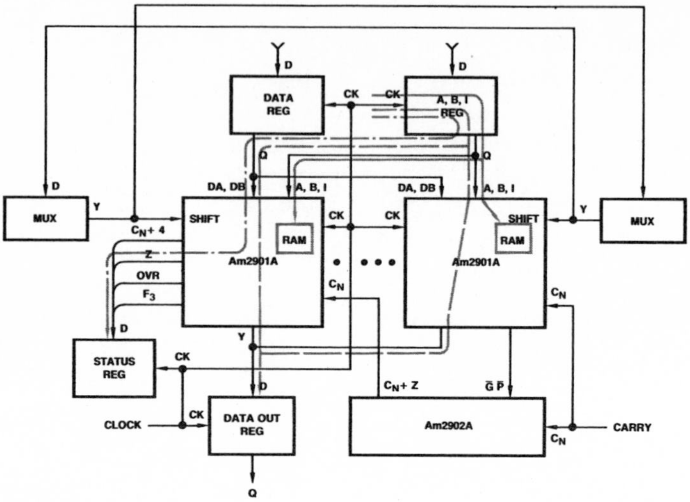

LOGIC OPERATION SPEED COMPUTATIONS

DEVICE NO.	DEVICE PATH	PATH 1	PATH 2	PATH 3
S – REG	CP to Q	9	9	9
2901A	READ-MODIFY-WRITE	55	–	–
2901A	AB – Y	–	45	–
2901A	AB – Zero	–	–	65
S-REG	SET-UP D	–	2	2
TOTAL-ns		64	56	76

PATH 1 ————————

PATH 2 — — — —

PATH 3 — - — - —

MPR-535

b)

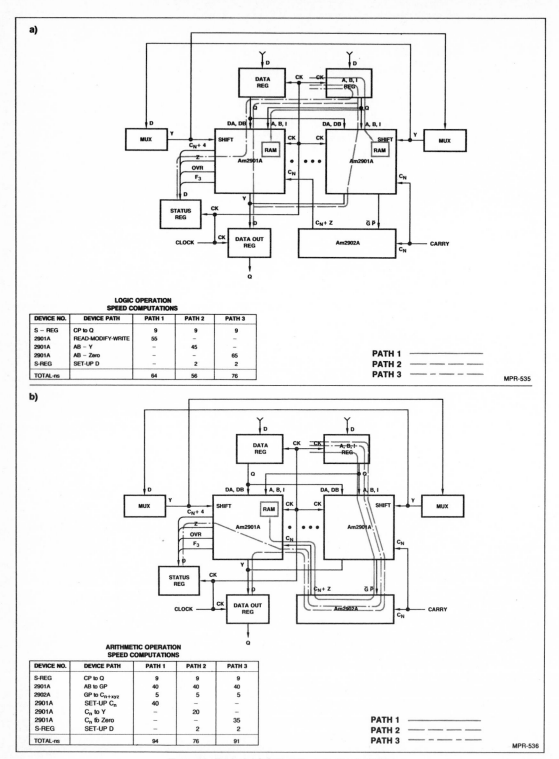

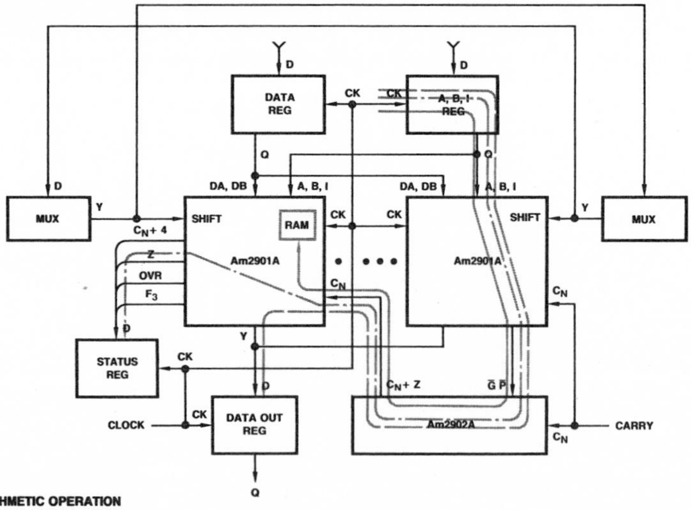

ARITHMETIC OPERATION SPEED COMPUTATIONS

DEVICE NO.	DEVICE PATH	PATH 1	PATH 2	PATH 3
S-REG	CP to Q	9	9	9
2901A	AB to GP	40	40	40
2902A	GP to C_{n+xyz}	5	5	5
2901A	SET-UP C_n	40	–	–
2901A	C_n to Y	–	20	–
2901A	C_n to Zero	–	–	35
S-REG	SET-UP D	–	2	2
TOTAL-ns		94	76	91

PATH 1 ————————

PATH 2 — — — —

PATH 3 — - — - —

MPR-536

Figure 26. Typical AC Calculations for the Am2901A.

c)

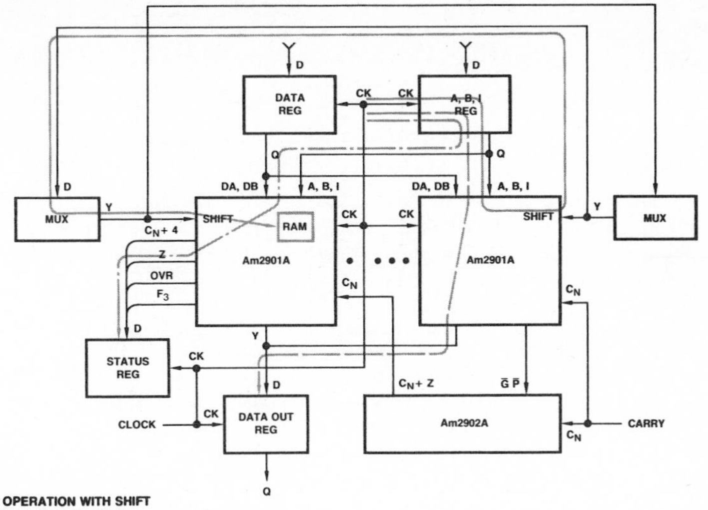

LOGIC OPERATION WITH SHIFT SPEED COMPUTATIONS

DEVICE NO.	DEVICE PATH	PATH 1	PATH 2	PATH 3
S – REG	CP to Q	9	9	9
2901A	AB to RAM_{03}	60	–	–
S-MUX	D to Y	5	–	–
2901A	SET-UP RAM_{03}	15	–	–
2901A	AB to Y	–	45	–
2901A	AB to Z	–	–	65
S-REG	SET-UP D	–	2	2
TOTAL-ns		89	56	76

PATH 1 ————
PATH 2 — — — —
PATH 3 — - — - —

MPR-537

d)

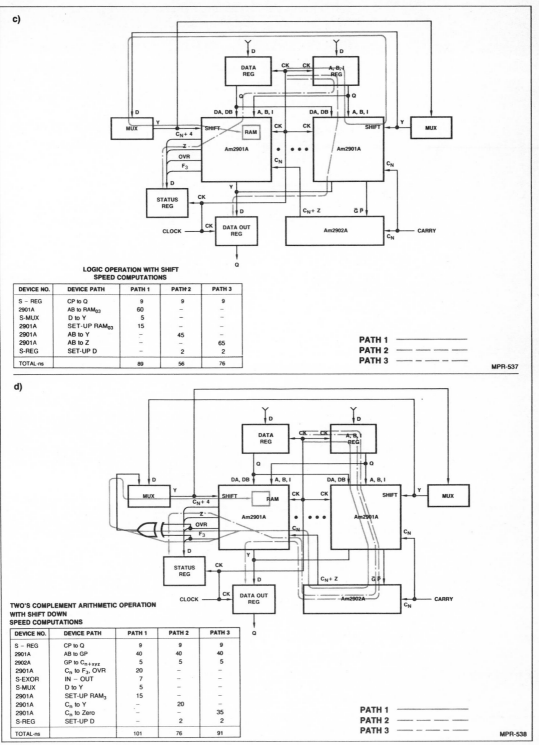

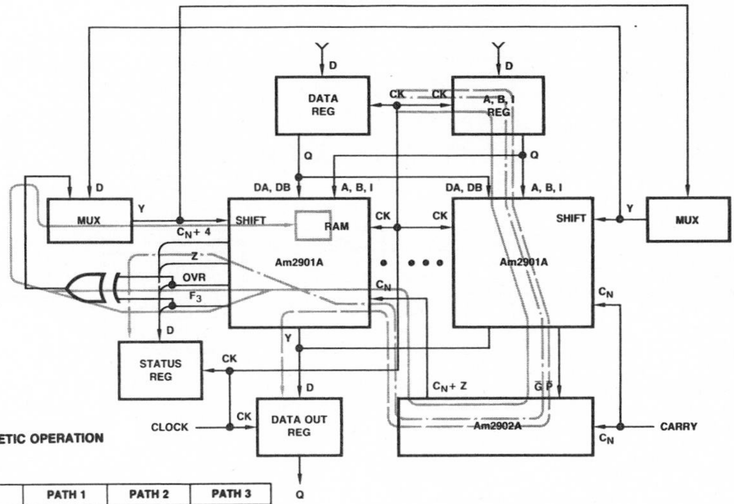

TWO'S COMPLEMENT ARITHMETIC OPERATION WITH SHIFT DOWN SPEED COMPUTATIONS

DEVICE NO.	DEVICE PATH	PATH 1	PATH 2	PATH 3
S – REG	CP to Q	9	9	9
2901A	AB to GP	40	40	40
2902A	GP to C_{n+xyz}	5	5	5
2901A	C_n to F_3, OVR	20	–	–
S-EXOR	IN – OUT	7	–	–
S-MUX	D to Y	5	–	–
2901A	SET-UP RAM_3	15	–	–
2901A	C_n to Y	–	20	–
2901A	C_n to Zero	–	–	35
S-REG	SET-UP D	–	2	2
TOTAL-ns		101	76	91

PATH 1 ————
PATH 2 — — — —
PATH 3 — - — - —

MPR-538

Figure 26. (Cont.)

e)

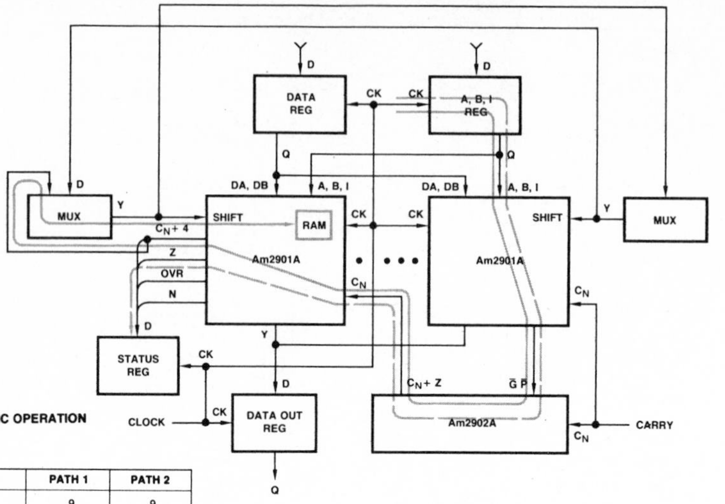

MAGNITUDE ONLY ARITHMETIC OPERATION WITH SHIFT DOWN SPEED COMPUTATIONS

DEVICE NO.	DEVICE PATH	PATH 1	PATH 2
S – REG	CP to Q	9	9
2901A	AB to GP	40	40
2902A	GP to C_{n+xyz}	5	5
2901A	C_n to C_{n+4}	10	–
S-MUX	D to Y	5	–
2901A	SET-UP RAM_3	15	–
2901A	C_n to Zero	–	35
S-REG	SET-UP D	–	2
TOTAL-ns		84	91

PATH 1 ————————
PATH 2 — — — —

MPR-539

Figure 26. (Cont.)

a)

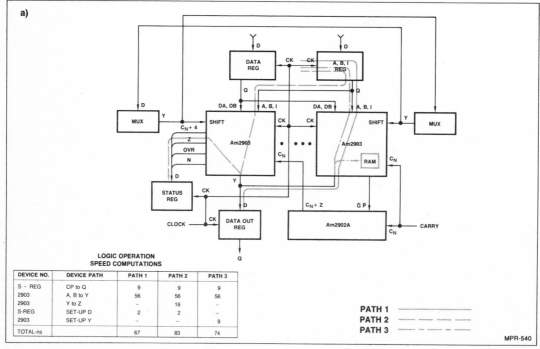

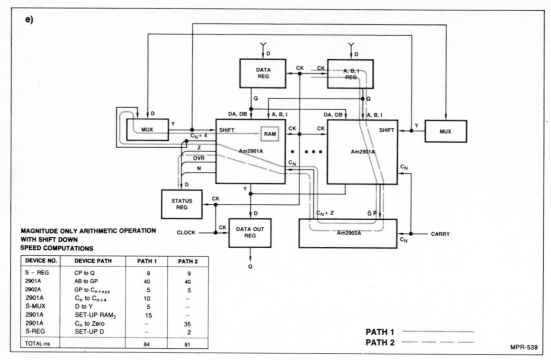

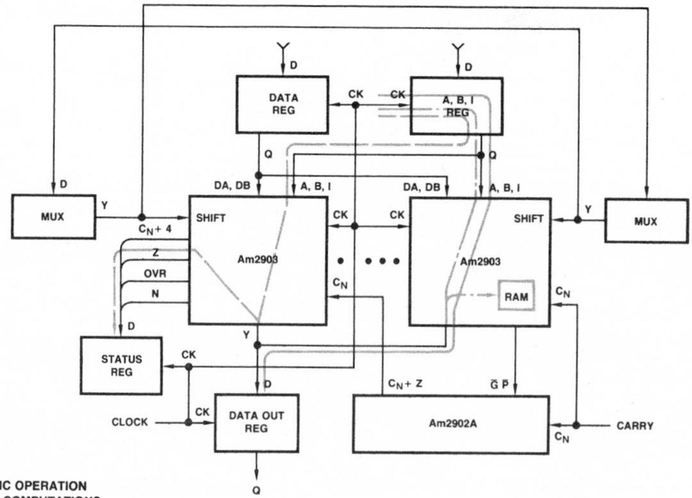

LOGIC OPERATION SPEED COMPUTATIONS

DEVICE NO.	DEVICE PATH	PATH 1	PATH 2	PATH 3
S – REG	CP to Q	9	9	9
2903	A, B to Y	56	56	56
2903	Y to Z	–	16	–
S-REG	SET-UP D	2	2	–
2903	SET-UP Y	–	–	9
TOTAL-ns		67	83	74

PATH 1 ————————
PATH 2 — — — —
PATH 3 — - — - —

MPR-540

Figure 27. Typical AC Calculations for the Am2903.

b)

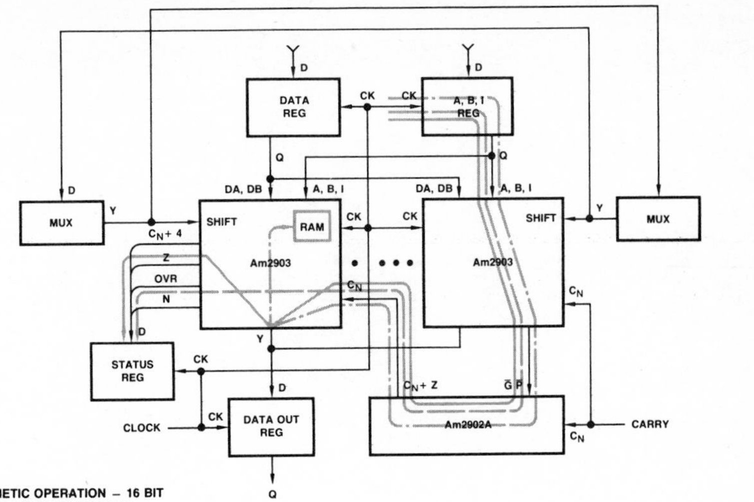

ARITHMETIC OPERATION – 16 BIT
SPEED COMPUTATIONS

DEVICE NO.	DEVICE PATH	PATH 1	PATH 2	PATH 3
S-REG	CP to Q	9	9	9
2903	A, B to G, P	56	56	56
2902A	G, P to C_{n+xyz}	5	5	5
2903	C_n to Y	25	–	25
2903	C_n to FLAG	–	38	–
2903	Y to Z	16	–	–
S-REG	SET-UP D	2	2	–
2903	SET-UP Y	–	–	9
TOTAL-ns		113	110	104

PATH 1 ————
PATH 2 — — — —
PATH 3 — - — - —

MPR-541

c)

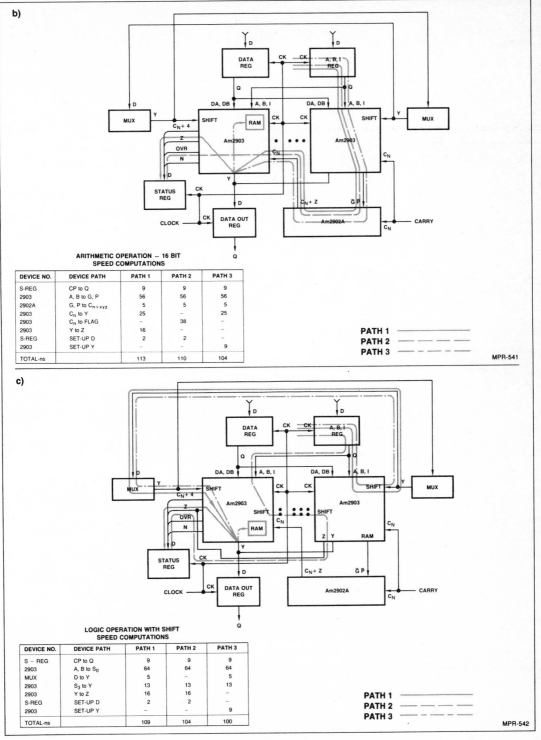

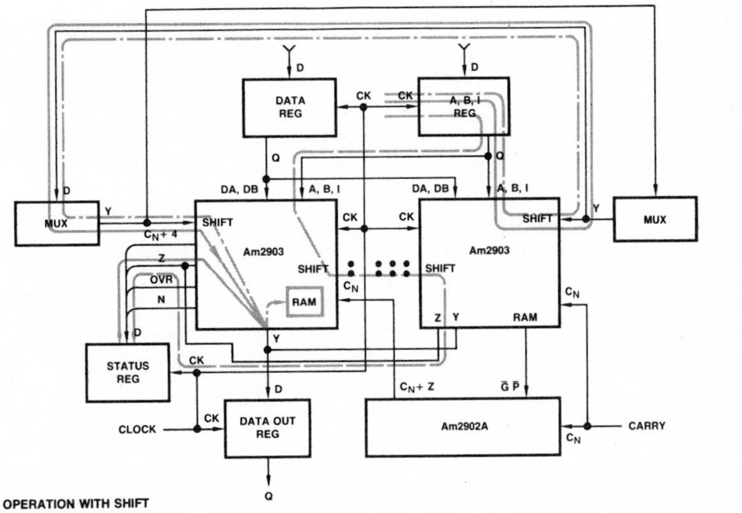

LOGIC OPERATION WITH SHIFT
SPEED COMPUTATIONS

DEVICE NO.	DEVICE PATH	PATH 1	PATH 2	PATH 3
S – REG	CP to Q	9	9	9
2903	A, B to S_0	64	64	64
MUX	D to Y	5	–	5
2903	S_3 to Y	13	13	13
2903	Y to Z	16	16	–
S-REG	SET-UP D	2	2	–
2903	SET-UP Y	–	–	9
TOTAL-ns		109	104	100

PATH 1 ————
PATH 2 — — — —
PATH 3 — - — - —

MPR-542

Figure 27. (Cont.)

d)

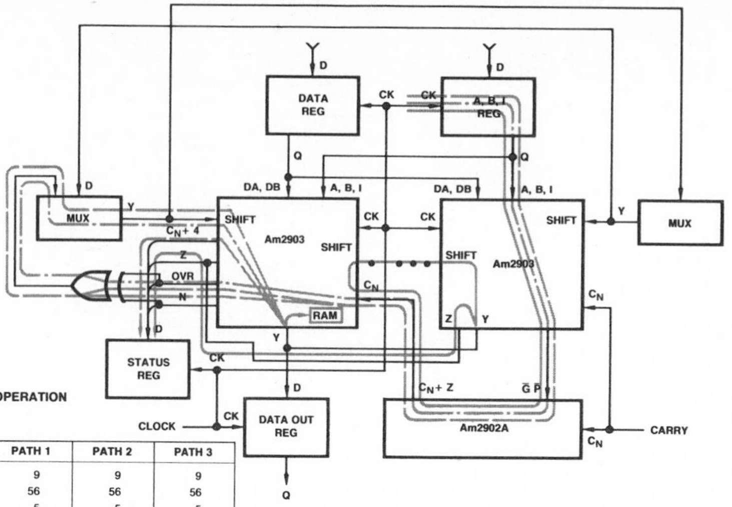

TWO'S COMPLEMENT ARITHMETIC OPERATION
WITH SHIFT DOWN – 16 BIT
SPEED COMPUTATIONS

DEVICE NO.	DEVICE PATH	PATH 1	PATH 2	PATH 3
S – REG	CP to Q	9	9	9
2903	A, B to G, P	56	56	56
2902A	GP to C_{n+xyz}	5	5	5
2903	C_n to SIO_0	21	–	–
2903	SIO_3 to Y	13	–	–
2903	C_n to N, OVR	–	38	38
S-EXOR	IN to OUT	–	7	7
S-MUX	D to Y	–	5	5
2903	SIO_3 to Y	–	13	13
2903	Y to Z	16	16	–
2903	SET-UP Y	–	–	9
S-REG	SET-UP D	2	2	–
TOTAL-ns		122	151	142

PATH 1 ————
PATH 2 — — — —
PATH 3 — - — - —

MPR-543

e)

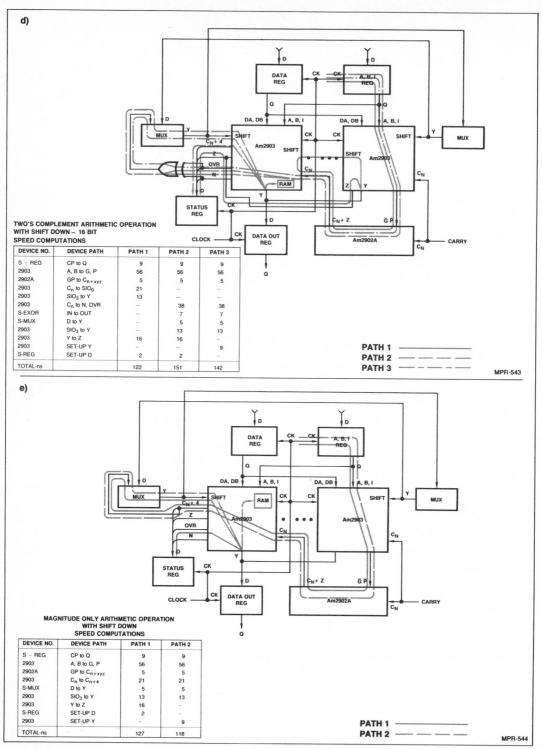

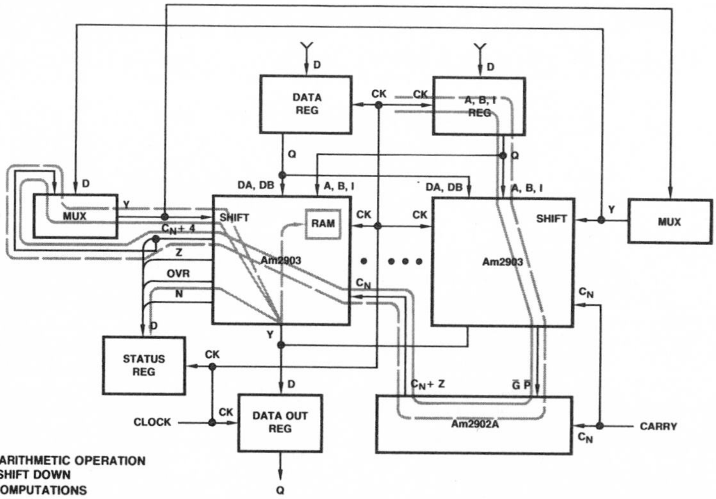

MAGNITUDE ONLY ARITHMETIC OPERATION
WITH SHIFT DOWN
SPEED COMPUTATIONS

DEVICE NO.	DEVICE PATH	PATH 1	PATH 2
S – REG	CP to Q	9	9
2903	A, B to G, P	56	56
2902A	GP to C_{n+xyz}	5	5
2903	C_n to C_{n+4}	21	21
S-MUX	D to Y	5	5
2903	SIO_3 to Y	13	13
2903	Y to Z	16	–
S-REG	SET-UP D	2	–
2903	SET-UP Y	–	9
TOTAL-ns		127	118

PATH 1 ————
PATH 2 — — — —

MPR-544

Figure 27. (Cont.)

Functional Operation	Am2901A	Am2903
Logic	76	83
Arithmetic	94	113
Logic with Shift	89	109
Two's Complement Arithmetic with Shift Down	101	151
Magnitude Only Arithmetic with Shift Down	91	127

Figure 28. Summary of Am2901A and Am2903 AC Performance in a 16-Bit Configuration.

USING THE Am2903 IN A 16-BIT DESIGN

Perhaps the best technique for understanding the design of the 16-bit ALU is to simply take an example. Figure 29 shows a block diagram overview of four Am2903's with the appropriate shift matrix control, status register, MAR and the usual interface to a CCU and main memory. This block diagram represents the normal data handling path associated with a simple 16-bit minicomputer. If we expand this block diagram to show what would normally be considered to be the complete 16-bit central processing unit, the block diagram of Figure 30 results. Here, we see the Am2903's surrounded by a typical set of MSI support chips. In addition, the block diagram shows a typical computer control unit as described in Chapter 2 of this series. Thus, all of the blocks are now in place to show a simple 16-bit microcomputer built using the Am2900 family devices. The full design for such a machine is shown in Figure 31.

Figures 31A, Figure 31B and Figure 31C detail the connection of each IC used in this design. Quite simply, the design can be described as follows. Figure 31A represents the microprogram sequencer portion of the design. U1, U2 and U3 are the instruction register that receive a 16-bit instruction from main memory. U4, U5 and U6 are the mapping PROMs used to decode the OP code portion of the instruction to arrive at a starting address for the microprogram sequencer. The microprogram sequencer is the Am2910 and is shown as U7. The branch address pipeline register is U8, U9 and U10 and can be enabled to the D inputs of the Am2910 sequencer to provide the jump address from microcode. The pipeline register for the instruction inputs to the Am2910 is U14. This machine also has the ability to select the A and B addresses for the Am2903 devices from the microprogram as well as the instruction register and U11 and U12 provide this capability as a part of the pipeline register. U13 is a two line to four line decoder used as part of the control for the A and B address select for the Am2903's. U15 is part of the pipeline register and provides both true and complement outputs for bit 11. U16 and U17 represent a one of sixteen decoder whose output can be applied to the DA bus to allow the implementation of all the bit operations. These include bit set, bit clear, bit toggle and bit test. U18 and U19 are PROM's that provide the ability to enter one of thirty-two preprogrammed constants onto the DA bus.

Figure 31B is predominately the data handling portion of the design. Here, U20 and U21 represent a data register that receives data from the data bus. U26, U27, U28 and U29 are the four Am2903's that form a 16-bit register/ALU combination. U30 is the carry look ahead generator for the ALU section. U22, U23

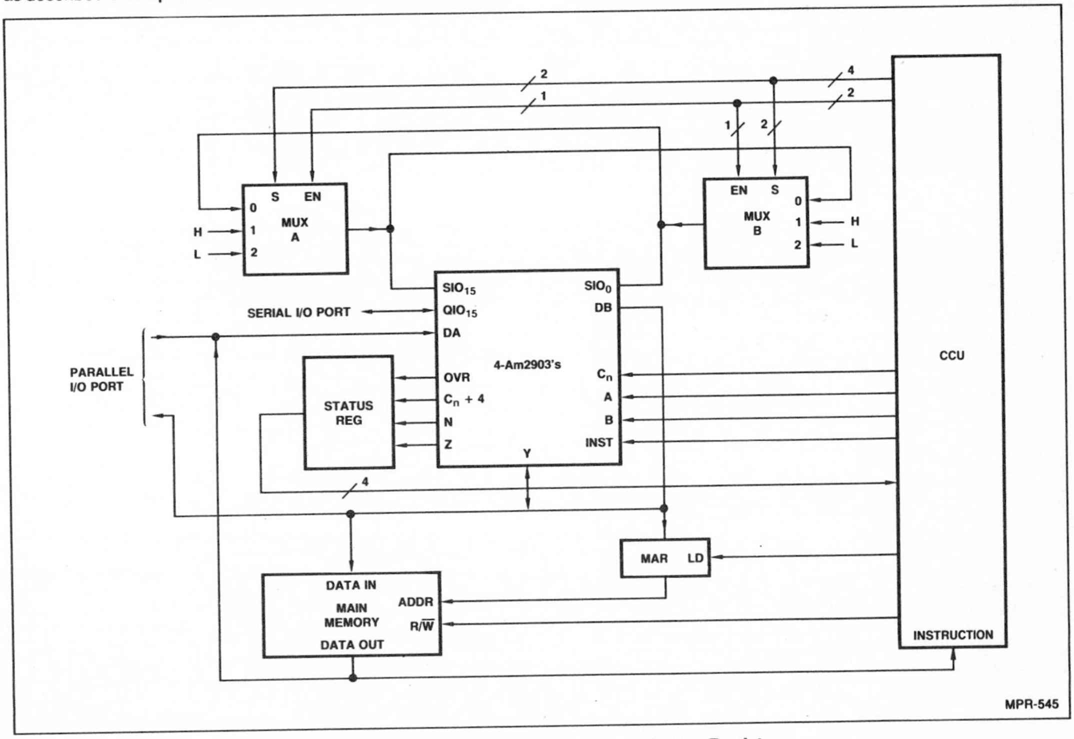

Figure 29. Am2903 with Shift Mux and Status Register.

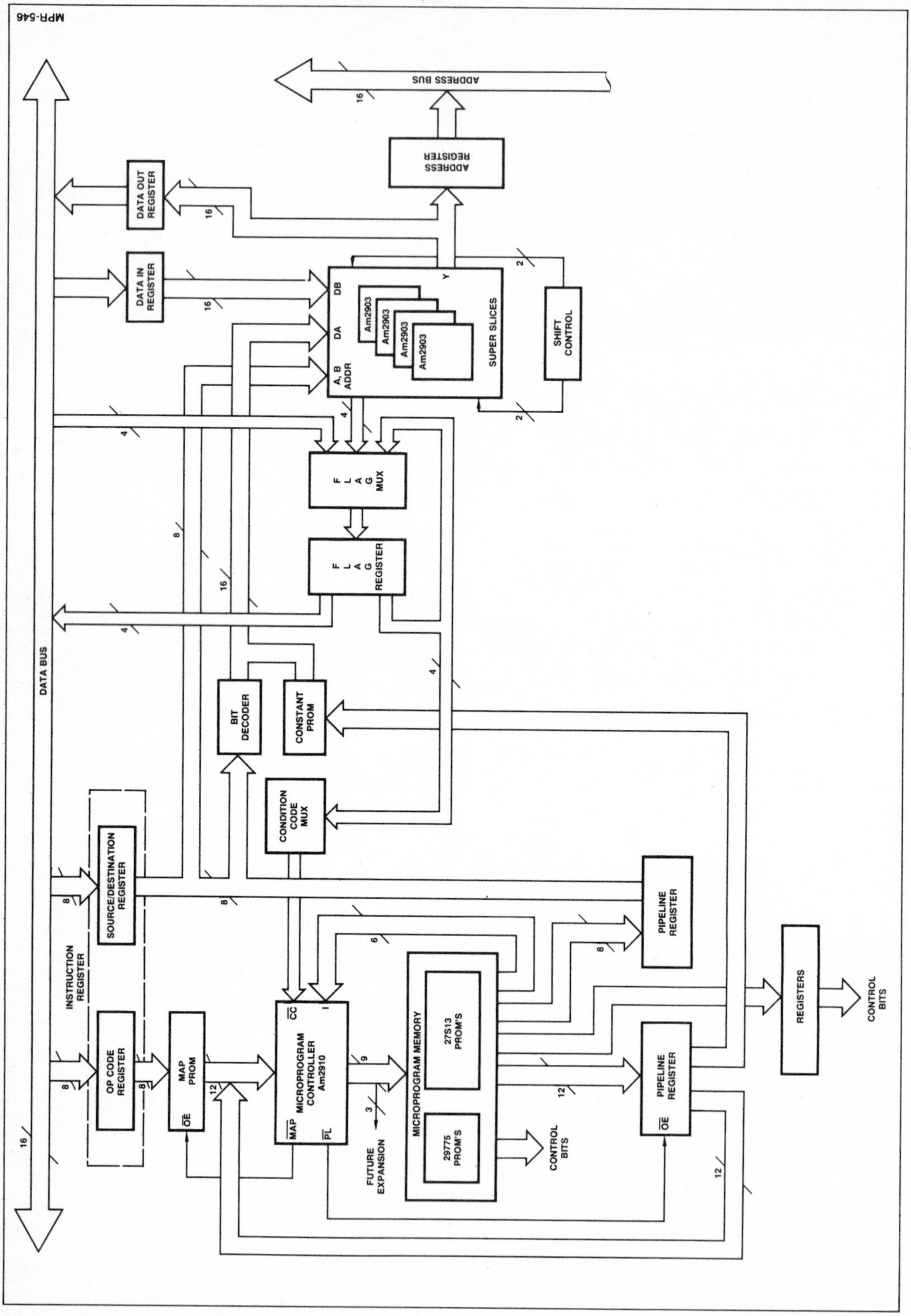
MPR-546
DATA BUS
ADDRESS BUS
ADDRESS REGISTER
DATA OUT REGISTER
DATA IN REGISTER
DB
DA
A, B ADDR
Y
Am2903
Am2903
Am2903
Am2903
SUPER SLICES
SHIFT CONTROL
FLAG MUX
FLAG REGISTER
BIT DECODER
CONSTANT PROM
CONDITION CODE MUX
INSTRUCTION REGISTER
SOURCE/DESTINATION REGISTER
OP CODE REGISTER
MAP PROM
OE
MICROPROGRAM CONTROLLER Am2910
MAP
CC
I
PL
FUTURE EXPANSION
MICROPROGRAM MEMORY
27S13 PROM'S
29775 PROM'S
CONTROL BITS
PIPELINE REGISTER
PIPELINE REGISTER
OE
REGISTERS
CONTROL BITS
16
16
16
16
16
4
4
4
4
8
8
8
8
8
6
9
3
12
12
12
2
2

Figure 30.

and U24 represent the status register with the ability to save and restore the flags in main memory. U25 is the condition code multiplexer for the microprogram sequencer. U33, U34, U35 and U36 represent the shift linkage multiplexers that tie together the internal shifters within the Am2903's. U37 is part of the pipeline register and provides both true and complement outputs of a number of the microprogram bits. U38 is part of the carry in logic control such that double length arithmetic operations can be performed. U31 and U32 are the data out register that can be used to accept data from the Am2903s and enable this data onto the data bus. U39 and U40 represent the memory address register and are used to hold the address provided from the CPU to main memory.

The microprogram store is shown in Figure 31C. Here, we have used both the 512 x 8 registered PROM's and 512 x 4 non-registered PROM's in this design. A total of 68 microprogram bits have been depicted in this design. These are shown so that maximum flexibility is achieved. In most typical designs some 10 to 20 of these bits would not be used. Figure 31C shows four 512-word by 8-bit registered PROM's (U41, U42, U43 and U44). It also shows nine 512-word by 4-bit PROM's represented as U45 through U53.

Perhaps the best way to review the design is to simply understand the function of each of the microprogram control bits. If the purpose of each of these bits is well understood, the design engineer will be well along in understanding the design of the simple minicomputer CPU presented here.

The Microprogram Structure

The microprogram for the design shown in Figure 31 is 68 bits wide. The functions of the microprogram control bits are as follows:

Bits PL0 through PL8 — The 9 instruction bits of the Am2903 superslices.

Bits PL9, PL10, PL11 — The $\overline{IEN}$, $\overline{EA}$, $\overline{OEB}$ control inputs of the Am2903 superslices, respectively. PL11 is also connected to the data-in registers (U20 and U21) output-enable. This connection assures that there will be no conflict on the DB pins.

Bits PL12 through PL14 (μ12 through μ14) — Select the source for SIO of the Am2903, both for shift-up and for shift-down operations. The following table summarizes the functions of these bits.

Microprogram Bits 14	13	12	SIO_n (Shift-down)	SIO_0 (Shift-up)
L	L	L	0	0
L	L	H	SIO_0	SIO_n
L	H	L	QIO_0	QIO_n
L	H	H	Carry	Carry
H	L	L	Zero	Zero
H	L	H	Sign	Sign
H	H	L	Not allocated	Not allocated
H	H	H	1	1

Bits PL15 through PL17 (μ15 through μ17) — Select the source for QIO of the Am2903, both for shift-up and shift-down operations. The following table summarizes the functions of these bits.

Microprogram Bits 17	16	15	QIO_n (Shift-down)	QIO_0 (Shift-up)
L	L	L	0	0
L	L	H	SIO_0	SIO_n
L	H	L	QIO_0	QIO_n
L	H	H	Carry	Carry
H	L	L	Zero	Zero
H	L	H	Sign	Sign
H	H	L	Not allocated	Not allocated
H	H	H	1	1

Bit PL18 — When LOW, enables the MAR clock input, i.e. the data appearing on the Y output pins of the Am2903 Superslices™ will be clocked into the MAR at the LOW-to-HIGH transition of the clock pulse.

Bit PL19 — When LOW, enables the MAR output onto the Memory Address Bus.

Bit PL20 — When LOW, enables the data output register clock, i.e. the data appearing in the Y output pins of the Am2903 Superslices™ will be clocked into the data output registers (U31 and U32) at the LOW-to-HIGH transition of the clock pulse.

Bit PL21 — When LOW, enables the data output registers onto the Data Bus.

Bit PL22 — When LOW, enables the data-in register clock, i.e. the data appearing in the Data-Bus will be clocked into the data-in registers at the LOW-to-HIGH transition of the clock pulse.

Bit PL23 — This is the CI input of the Am2910 microprogram sequencer.

Bits PL24 through PL27 — This is a 4-bit wide field which can be used either for the A-address, for the B-address or for both A and B addresses of the Am2903 superslices.

Bits PL28 through PL31 — This is a 4-bit wide field, which can be used for either the A-address of the Am2903 superslice or to designate one of sixteen bits to the DA inputs of the Am2903 superslice via the Am2921's (μ16 and μ17).

Bits PL32 and PL33 — Select the source for the Am2903 A-address, according to the table below:

Bits 33	32	A-Address Source
L	L	Data Bus bits 0 through 3
L	H	Microprogram bits 28 through 31
H	L	Data Bus bits 4 through 7
H	H	Microprogram bits 24 through 27

Bit PL34 — Selects the source of the Am2903 B-address, according to the table below:

Bit 34	B-Address Source
L	Data Bus bits 4 through 7
H	Microprogram bits 24 through 27

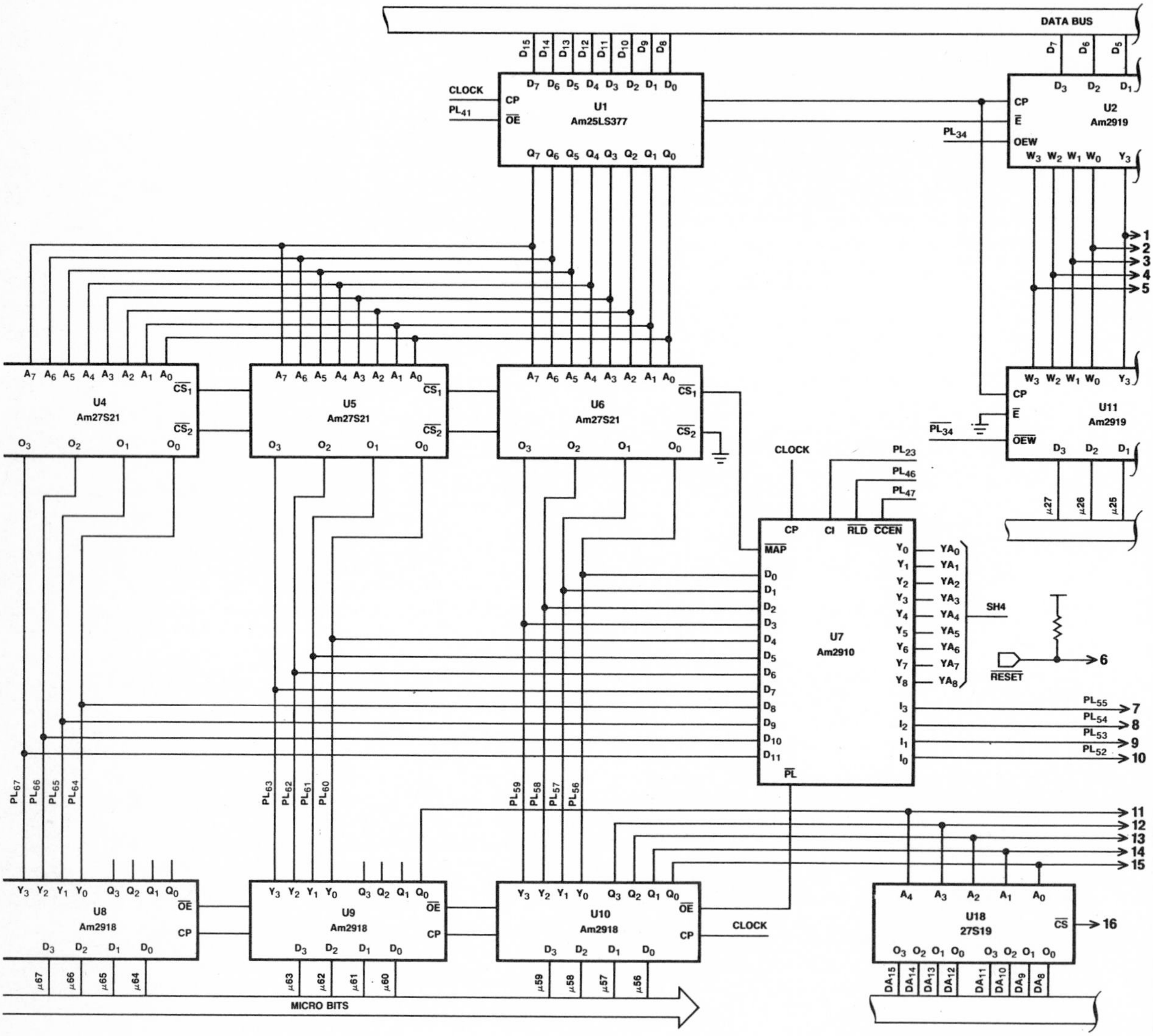
DATA BUS
CLOCK
PL41
CP
OE
U1
Am25LS377
U2
Am2919
PL34
OEW
U4
Am27S21
U5
Am27S21
U6
Am27S21
U11
Am2919
CLOCK
PL23
PL46
PL47
CP
CI
RLD
CCEN
MAP
U7
Am2910
SH4
RESET
PL55
PL54
PL53
PL52
PL
U8
Am2918
U9
Am2918
U10
Am2918
CLOCK
U18
27S19
CS
MICRO BITS

Figure 31a.

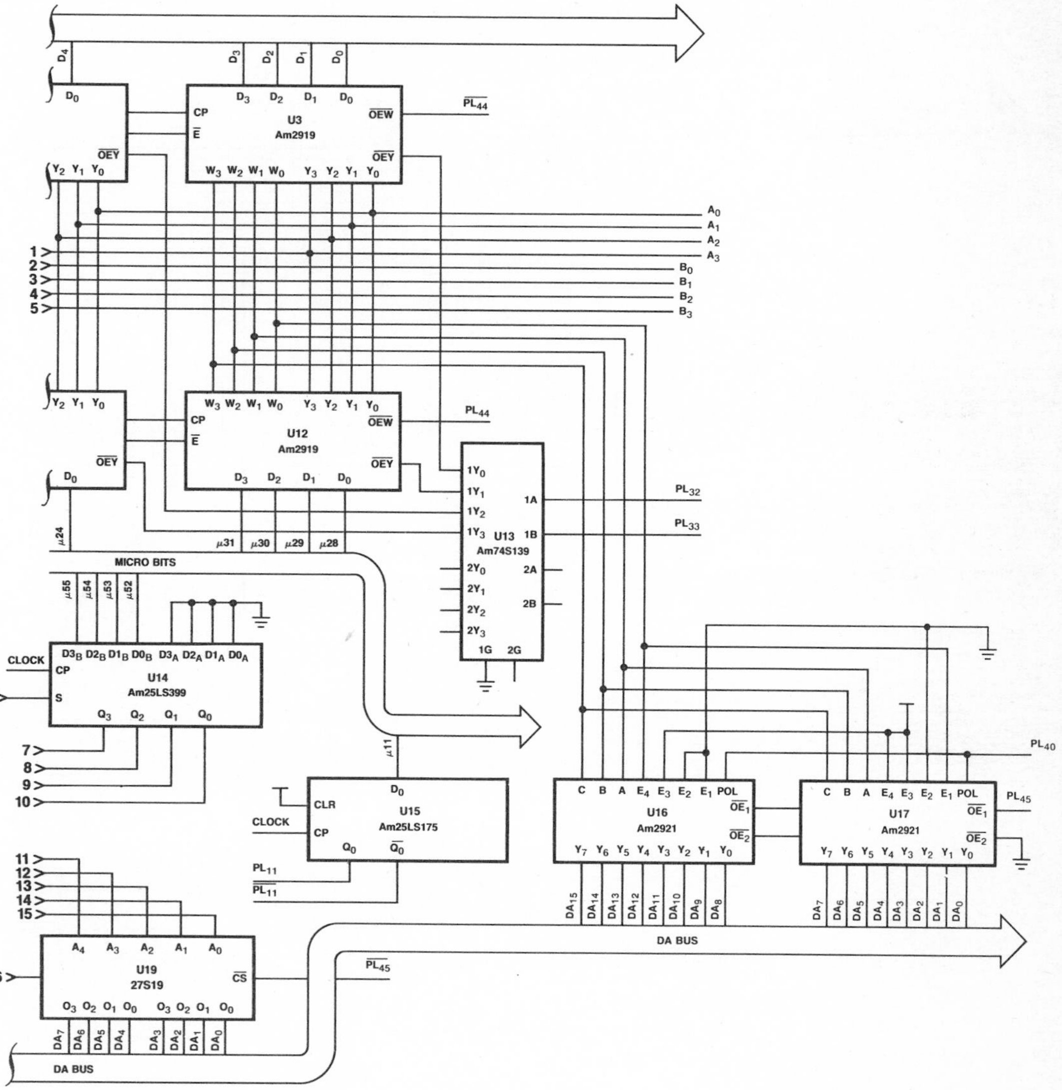
U3
Am2919
CP
OEW
OEY
PL44
U12
Am2919
U13
Am74S139
PL32
PL33
MICRO BITS
U14
Am25LS399
CLOCK
U15
Am25LS175
CLR
CP
PL11
U16
Am2921
U17
Am2921
POL
PL40
PL45
DA BUS
U19
27S19
CS
A0
A1
A2
A3
B0
B1
B2
B3

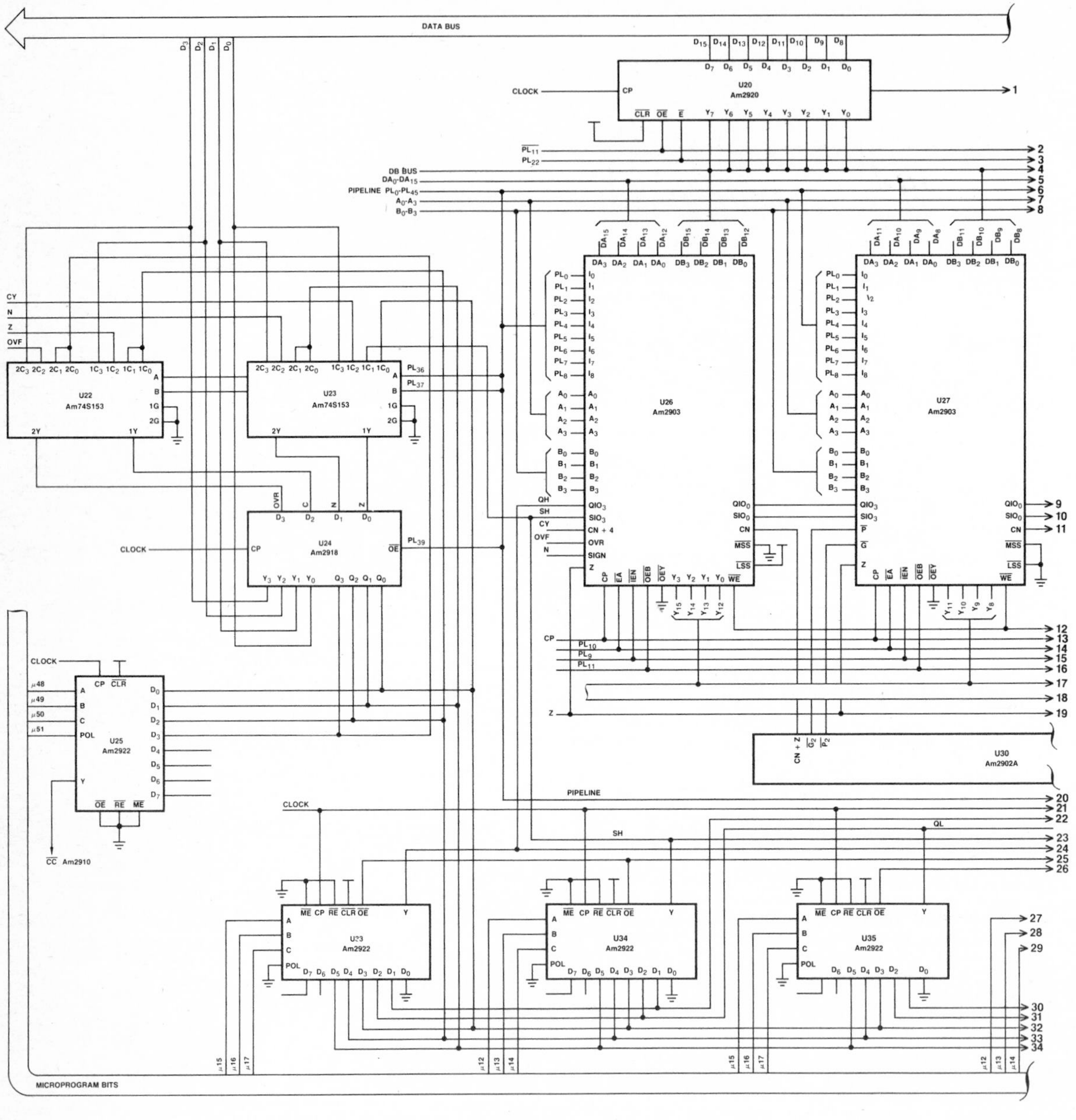
DATA BUS
U20
Am2920
CLOCK
DB BUS
PIPELINE
U22
Am74S153
U23
Am74S153
U24
Am2918
U25
Am2922
U26
Am2903
U27
Am2903
U30
Am2902A
U33
Am2922
U34
Am2922
U35
Am2922
PIPELINE
SH
QL
CC Am2910
MICROPROGRAM BITS

Figure 31b.

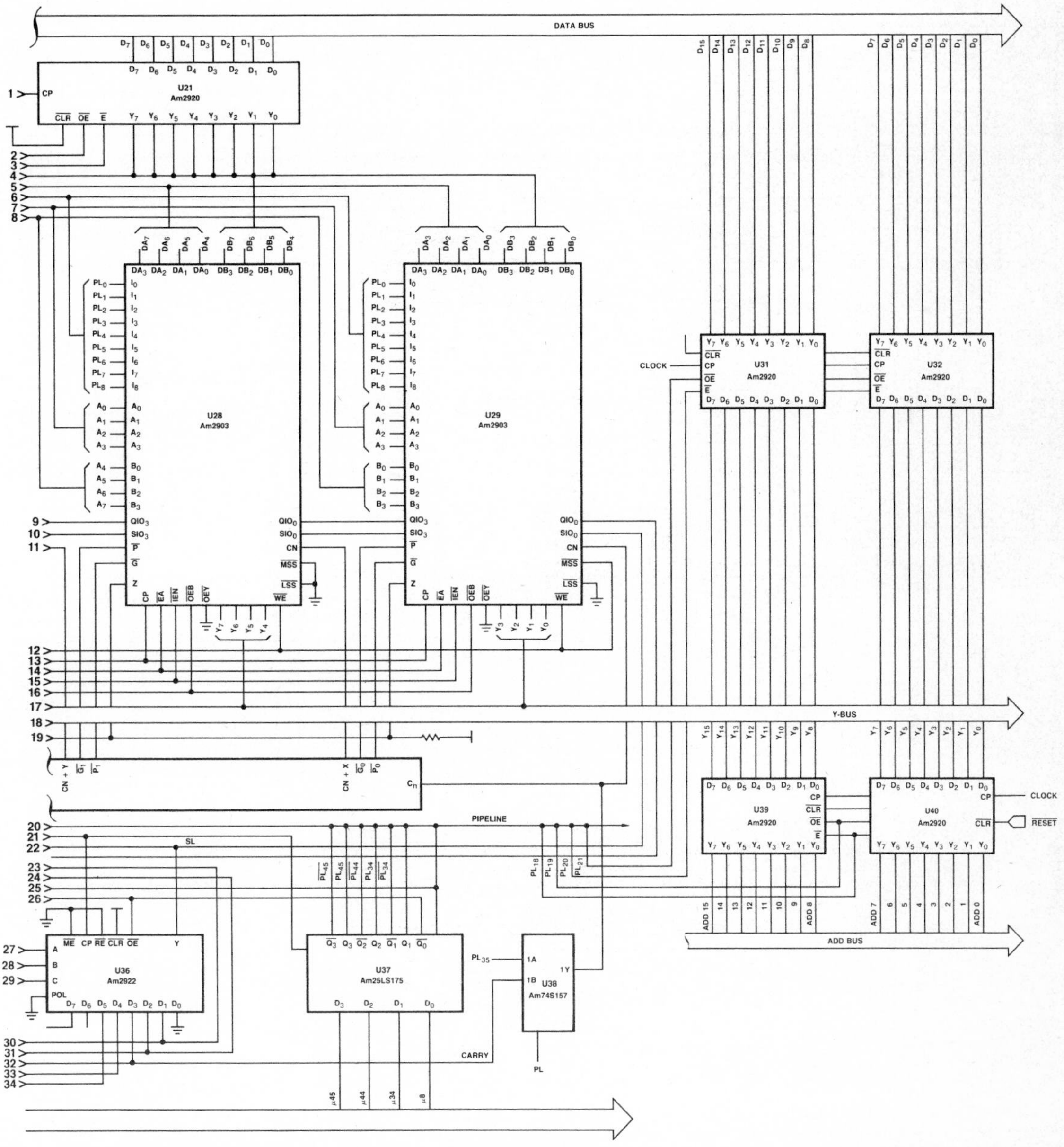
DATA BUS
U21
Am2920
U28
Am2903
U29
Am2903
U31
Am2920
U32
Am2920
CLOCK
Y-BUS
PIPELINE
SL
U39
Am2920
U40
Am2920
RESET
ADD BUS
U36
Am2922
U37
Am25LS175
U38
Am74S157
CARRY
PL

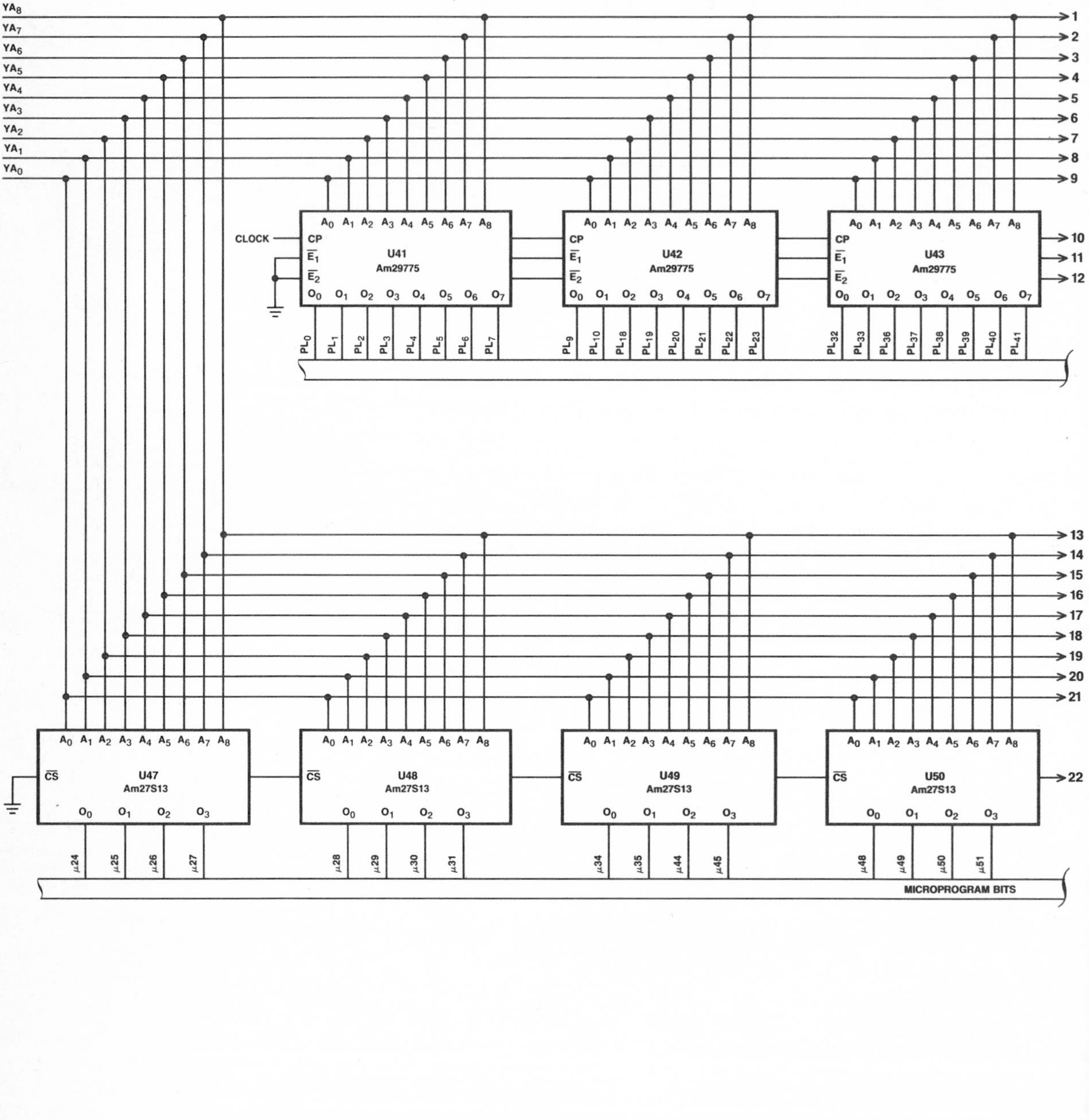
YA8
YA7
YA6
YA5
YA4
YA3
YA2
YA1
YA0
CLOCK
CP
U41
Am29775
U42
Am29775
U43
Am29775
PL0 PL1 PL2 PL3 PL4 PL5 PL6 PL7
PL9 PL10 PL18 PL19 PL20 PL21 PL22 PL23
PL32 PL33 PL36 PL37 PL38 PL39 PL40 PL41
U47
Am27S13
U48
Am27S13
U49
Am27S13
U50
Am27S13
μ24 μ25 μ26 μ27
μ28 μ29 μ30 μ31
μ34 μ35 μ44 μ45
μ48 μ49 μ50 μ51
MICROPROGRAM BITS

Figure 31c.

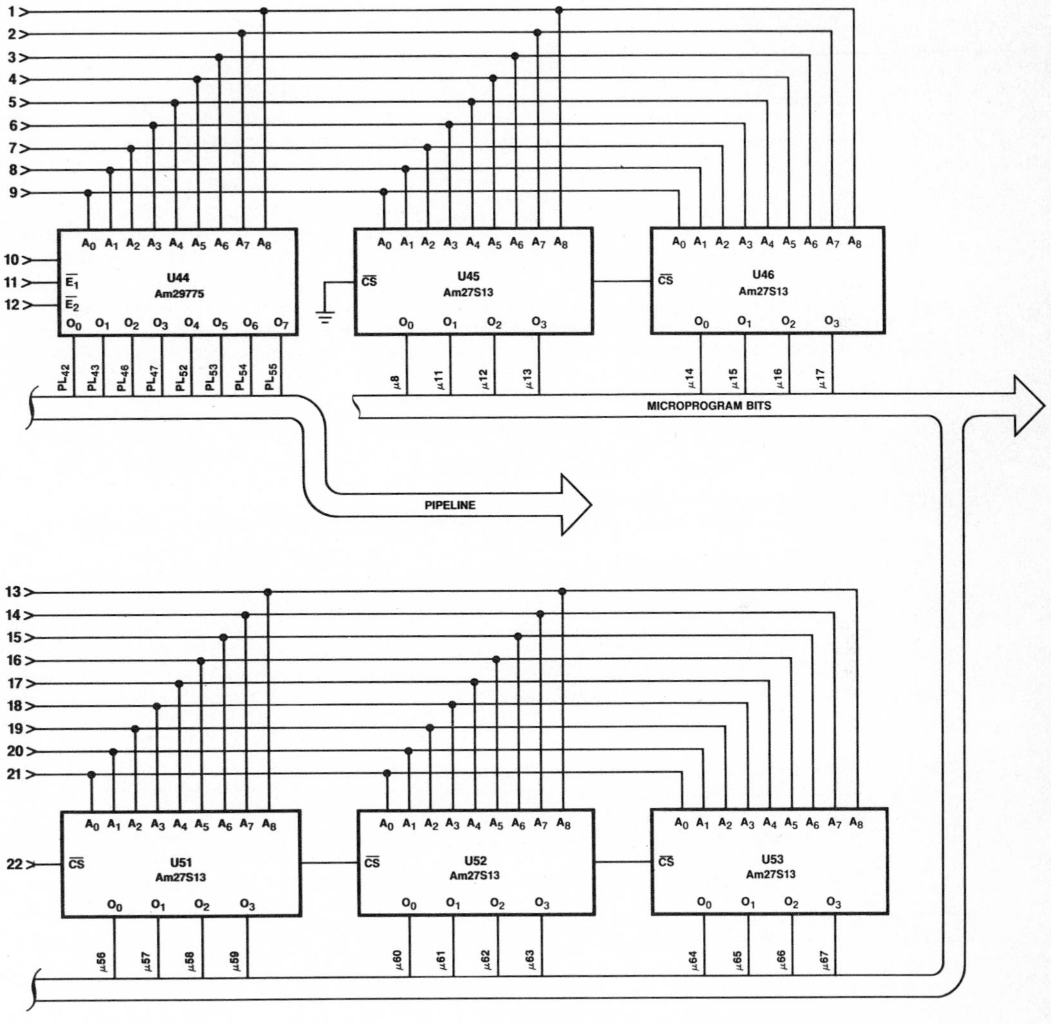

U44
Am29775
U45
Am27S13
U46
Am27S13
U51
Am27S13
U52
Am27S13
U53
Am27S13
PIPELINE
MICROPROGRAM BITS
PL42 PL43 PL46 PL47 PL52 PL53 PL54 PL55
μ8 μ11 μ12 μ13 μ14 μ15 μ16 μ17
μ56 μ57 μ58 μ59 μ60 μ61 μ62 μ63 μ64 μ65 μ66 μ67

Bit PL35 — Is the C_n input of the least significant Am2903 via an Am74S157 mux (μ38).

Bits PL36 and PL37 — Affect the status register input signals, according to the table below:

Bits 37	Bits 36	Next Carry	Next Zero, Sign, Overflow
L	L	Previous Carry	Previous Zero, Sign, Overflow
L	H	Previous SIO_{15}	Previous Zero, Sign, Overflow
H	L	Am2903 superslices' Output	
H	H	Data Bus bits 0 through 3	

Bit PL38 — Selects either the carry flip-flop or the PL35 bit for carry in.

Bit PL39 — When LOW, enables the status register output to the data bus bits 0 through 3.

Bit PL40 — Controls the output polarity of the one-of-sixteen bit select logic.

Bit PL41 — When LOW, enables the Instruction register (U1, U2, U3) clock. The data present at bits 0 through 15 of the Data-Bus will be latched into the Instruction register at the next LOW-to-HIGH transition of the clock pulse.

Bit PL42 — This is an output signal. When HIGH, it signals the main memory that a memory read is requested.

Bit PL43 — This is an output signal. When HIGH, it signals to the main memory that a memory write is requested.

Bit PL44 — Selects the source of the one of sixteen bit decoders (U16 and U17). When LOW, the output of the Am2919 register (U12) containing the previously latched microprogram bits 28 through 31 will be applied to the decoders. When HIGH, the output of the Am2919 register (U3) containing the previously latched Data-Bus bits 0 through 3 will be applied to the decoders.

Bit PL45 — Selects the Am2903 Superslices™' DA port source. When LOW, the output of the one of sixteen bit decoder (U16 and U17) will be applied to that port. When HIGH, the output of the Am29771 PROM's (U18 and U19) will be applied to the Am2903 DA ports.

Bit PL46 and PL47 — These are the $\overline{RLD}$ and $\overline{CCEN}$ control inputs of the Am2910 sequencer, respectively.

Bits PL48 through PL50 — These select the condition code according to the following table:

Bits 50	Bits 49	Bits 48	Condition Code Selected
L	L	L	Carry
L	L	H	Sign
L	H	L	Zero
L	H	H	Overflow
H	L	L	Not Allocated
H	L	H	Not Allocated
H	H	L	Not Allocated
H	H	H	Not Allocated

Bit PL51 — Is the condition code polarity control. When HIGH, the condition code selected will pass non-inverted. When LOW, the selected condition code will be complemented.

Bits PL52 through PL55 — Are the I inputs of the Am2910 sequencer.

Bits PL56 through PL67 — This is a 12-bit wide field and it serves, usually as the next microprogram address. However, the 5 least significant bits of this field (bits 56-60) serve also as an address field of the Am29771 "constant" PROM's (U18 and U19).

Some Sample Microroutines

Figure 32 shows the microprogram code for a few sample microroutines. Different addressing schemes are demonstrated with the "ADD" operation. All the other arithmetic or logic operations can be easily programmed by substituting the I_1-I_4 field of the Am2903 with the appropriate function. Since the main memory address is generated by the Am2903 superslices, the internal register No. 15 serves as the program counter.

The following is a description of some sample microroutines. The reader should refer to the description of the microprogram bits given earlier in this chapter and to the data sheets of the Am2910 sequencer and of the Am2903 superslice.

Microword INIT.

This microword should be at address 0 and when the machine is reset, the Am2910 will start executing from here. The purpose of this location is to reset the machine program counter (Register 15) to zero. Ultimately more microinstructions can be added, should the necessity of other reset functions arise.

Bits 1-4 (Am2903 I_1-I_4) being 8_H will cause the superslices to generate all zeroes at the F-points (internal). Bits 5-8 (Am2903 I_5-I_8) being F_H will cause this data (all zeroes) to appear on the Y outputs. Bit 9 ($\overline{IEN}$) is LOW and therefore, $\overline{WRITE}$ will be LOW and this data will be written into the internal register selected by the B-address inputs. Bit 34 is HIGH; therefore, microprogram bits 24-27 will be selected as B address source. Since F_H is in these bits, all zeroes will be written into the program counter (Register 15). Bit 18 is LOW; therefore, the data at the Y outputs (all zeroes) wil be latched into the MAR at the next clock pulse. Bits 36 and 37 are set such that the flags will be updated, namely CY=N=OVF=0, Z=1.

Bits 42, 43 are both LOW so no memory reference signal is sent to the main memory (the MAR is still in an undetermined state). Bits 52-55 (Am2910 I) are set to E_H which will force the sequencer to continue to the next sequential address (1) as the CI (bit 23) is HIGH.

Bits 21 and 39 are both HIGH to ensure that there is no conflict on the data bus though in this case one of them could be a DON'T-CARE. Bit 38 could also be a DON'T-CARE as the carry is zeroed by the ALU. Making a HIGH in bit 46 enables executing this microstep without disturbing the Am2910 sequencer's internal register which at power-up has no significance but may be important, should a software restart be issued.

All the other bits are DON'T-CAREs.

Microword FETCH

This is the first step in the machine instruction fetch routine. In this step, the main memory is addressed by the MAR, a read signal is issued (bit 42 = HIGH), and the machine instruction (macroinstruction) is placed on the data bus by the memory. It is

		2910					DA								
	PL	I	CCP	$\overline{CC}$	$\overline{CLEN}$	$\overline{RLD}$	CONS	BIT	MMW	MMR	$\overline{IRE}$	POL	FDOE	CY=0	Flags
Number of Bits	12	4	1	3	1	1	1	1	1	1	1	1	1	1	2
Bit No.	56-67	52-55	51	48-50	47	46	45	44	43	42	41	40	39	38	36-37
INIT	X	E	X	X	X	1	X	X	0	0	X	X	1	0	2
FETCH	X	E	X	X	X	1	X	X	0	1	0	X	1	0	0
FETCH + 1	X	2	X	X	X	1	X	X	0	0	1	X	1	0	0
ADD	FETCH + 1	7	X	X	1	1	X	X	0	1	0	X	1	0	2
ADDIMM	X	E	X	X	X	1	X	X	0	1	1	X	1	0	0
ADDIMM + 1	FETCH + 1	7	X	X	1	1	X	X	0	1	0	X	1	0	2
ADD DIR	X	E	X	X	X	1	X	X	0	1	1	X	1	0	0
ADD DIR + 1	X	E	X	X	X	1	X	X	0	0	1	X	1	0	0
ADD DIR + 2	ADDIMM + 1	7	X	X	1	1	X	X	0	1	1	X	1	0	0
ADD RR1	X	E	X	X	X	1	X	X	0	0	1	X	1	0	0
ADD RR1 + 1	X	E	X	X	X	1	X	X	0	1	1	X	1	0	0
ADD RR1 + 2	FETCH + 1	7	X	X	1	1	X	X	0	1	0	X	1	0	2

	2903					2910	Y-D			MAR		2903							
	C_n	B	A	R_2	R_1	CI	$\overline{DDBE}$	$\overline{OE}$	$\overline{E}$	$\overline{OE}$	$\overline{E}$	Q	S	$\overline{OEB}$	$\overline{EA}$	$\overline{IEN}$	I_{5-8}	I_{1-4}	I_0
Number of Bits	1	1	2	4	4	1	1	1	1	1	1	3	3	1	1	1	4	4	1
Bit No.	35	34	32-33	28-31	24-27	23	22	21	20	19	18	15-17	12-14	11	10	9	5-8	1-4	0
INIT	X	1	X	X	F	1	X	1	X	X	0	X	X	X	X	0	F	8	X
FETCH	X	X	X	X	X	1	1	1	1	0	1	X	X	0	X	1	X	X	X
FETCH + 1	1	1	X	X	F	1	1	1	1	0	0	X	X	0	X	0	F	4	0
ADD	0	0	0	X	X	1	1	1	1	0	1	X	X	0	0	0	F	3	0
ADDIMM	1	1	X	X	F	1	0	1	1	0	0	X	X	0	X	0	F	4	0
ADDIMM + 1	0	0	0	X	X	1	1	1	1	0	1	X	X	1	0	0	F	3	0
ADD DIR	1	1	X	X	F	1	0	1	1	0	X	X	X	0	X	0	F	4	0
ADD DIR + 1	0	X	X	X	X	1	1	1	1	X	0	X	X	1	X	1	X	4	0
ADD DIR + 2	0	X	3	X	F	1	0	1	1	0	0	X	X	X	0	1	F	6	X
ADD RR1	0	X	0	X	X	1	X	1	1	X	0	X	X	X	0	1	F	6	X
ADD RR1 + 1	0	X	3	X	F	1	0	1	1	0	0	X	X	X	0	1	F	6	X
ADD RR1 + 2	0	0	2	X	X	1	1	1	1	0	1	X	X	1	0	0	F	3	0

1. 4-bit fields in hex, others in octal.
2. X = Don't Care.

Figure 32. Example Microcode for Figure 31 Design.

latched into the instruction register (U1, U2, and U3) at the next clock LOW-to-HIGH transition (bit 41 = LOW). It is assumed that if a relatively slow main memory is used, the clock is halted until the data is stable on the data bus and the register set up times are met. We will see in a later chapter how easy it is to implement this requirement using the Am2925 clock generator. The same assumption will also be made in a memory write cycle.

Bit 9 (Am2903 $\overline{IEN}$) is HIGH; thus, we don't care what the ALU does during this microstep. We prevent the flags from changing by setting bits 36-38 LOW. Also, the registers at the Y output have the $\overline{E}$ input HIGH (bits 18, 20). Bits 21 and 39 are both HIGH; thus, the data bus is free to accept data from the main memory (bit 42 is HIGH, signaling memory read request). The MAR is enabled to the address bus (bit 19 = LOW) and at the next clock, the macroinstruction will be latched into the instruction registers (bit 41 = LOW). The Am2910 sequencer will continue to the next instruction (bits 52-55 = E_H).

Microword FETCH + 1

This is the second step in the macroinstruction fetch routine. The instruction already resides in the instruction registers U1, U2 and U3).

The Am2910 sequencer receives a JUMP MAP instruction (bits 52 though 55 = 2). The next microinstruction will begin to execute the present macroinstruction – according to the mapping PROM.

We use this microstep to update (increment) the program counter (Register 15). Bit 34 being HIGH, microprogram bits 24-27 (=F_H) will be the B address. The Am2903 $\overline{OEB}$ and I_0 are LOW, therefore, the contents of Register 15 will serve as the S operand for the ALU. C_n being HIGH, a 4 in the I_1-I_4 field will increment this value. $\overline{IEN}$ = LOW with I_5-I_8 = F will write this (incremented) value into the same register (R15). At the same time, the MAR is also updated (bit 18 = LOW).

We could update the program counter and the MAR in the previous microstep (location FETCH), but then we had to leave the ALU idle during this microcycle. By adopting the present scheme, we can overlap the first step of the macroinstruction fetch routine (the memory-read cycle) with the execution of the last step of the previous macroinstruction – provided the memory and the data bus are free to perform it. The JUMP MAP cycle is always necessary – and that is why we prefer to update the PC at this step.

Microword ADD

This is a sample register-to-register operation. The two operands reside in the internal registers pointed to by the two 4-bit fields of the macroinstruction:

15 … 8	7 … 4	3 … 0
OPCODE	1st Operand and Destination Register Number	2nd Operand Register Number

Bits 32-33 are set LOW, instruction register bits 0-3 are selected as A address. Bit 34 = LOW selects instruction register bits 4-7 as B address (see Fig. above). Bit 1 (I_0), bit 10 ($\overline{EA}$) and bit 11 ($\overline{OEB}$) are also LOW; therefore, the contents of the selected registers will be presented to the ALU's R and S inputs. Bits 1-4 (I_1-I_4) = 3, the ALU will perform:

$F = R \text{ plus } S \text{ plus } C_n.$

Note that bit 35 and 38 are LOW. With I_5-I_8 (bits 5-8) = F_H and $\overline{IEN}$ (bit 0) = LOW, the result will be written into the internal register pointed at by the B address lines.

Bits 18 and 20 are HIGH and inhibit the MAR and the data out registers from being affected, while bits 36, 37 (=2) allow the flags to assume values according to the result of the operation.

During the execution of the function required (ADD in this example) we fetch the next OP CODE from the main memory. The MAR is enabled to the address bus (bit 19 = LOW) and a memory read is requested (bit 42 = HIGH). At the end of this microstep the next macroinstruction will be latched into the instruction registers (bit 41 = LOW).

The Am2910 sequencer is instructed to select the pipeline register bits 56-67 as the next microprogram address (bits 52-57 = 7, bit 47 = HIGH) where the location of FETCH + 1 (2 in this example) is written. The next step will be JUMP MAP and update PC.

Microword ADD IMMEDIATE

This 2 step microroutine adds the contents of an internal register, pointed at by bits 0-3 of the macroinstruction with its second word, placing the result into the internal register pointed at by bits 4-7 of the OPCODE.

15 … 8	7 … 4	3 … 0
OPCODE	Result Register Number	2nd Operand Register Number

First word of the macroinstruction

15 … 0
DATA (1st Operand)

Second (next consecutive) word of the macroinstruction

The first step is to read the first operand from the memory (bit 19 = LOW, bit 42 = HIGH) and to latch it into the data-in register (U20 and U21) (bit 22 = LOW). At the same time the ALU updates (increments) the program counter (register 15) and the MAR (bit 18 = LOW). (Compare the location FETCH + 1). The Am2910 sequencer will continue to the next microprogram address (compare to location FETCH).

Location ADDIMM + 1 is the second step of this macroinstruction. It is very similar to location ADD, the only difference is that bit 11 ($\overline{OEB}$) is HIGH, selecting the Data-in register as source for the ALU's S operand. The same macroinstruction fetch overlap technique is used again.

Microword ADD DIRect

This is the starting location to execute a macroinstruction where the second word is the address of the operand:

15 … 8	7 … 4	3 … 0
OPCODE	Result Register Number	2nd Operand Register Number

First word of the macroinstruotion

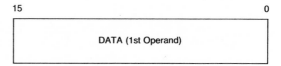

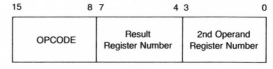

15	0
Address of the 1st operand	

Second (next consecutive) word of the macroinstruction

The first step is to read the second word of the macroinstruction into the Data-in register. This microword is identical to the one written at location ADDIMM.

Microword ADD DIR + 1

The Data-in register now contains the address of the operand. We have to transfer it into the MAR.

With I_0 (bit 0) LOW and $\overline{OEB}$ (bit 11) HIGH, the ALU's operand will be the DB bus, i.e., the Data-in register. I_1-I_4 (bits 1-4) = 4 will pass this input to its output, as C_n (bit 3) is LOW. With $\overline{IEN}$ (bit 9) = HIGH, the $\overline{WRITE}$ line will be HIGH too, assuring that the internal registers maintain their contents. Since I_5-I_8 (bits 5-8) = F_H, the ALU output will appear on the Am2903 Y pins. This data which is actually the operand address and will be transferred into the MAR at the next clock cycle. The Am2910 sequencer continues to the next consecutive microstep.

Microword ADD DIR + 2

Now we read in the operand from the main memory. The MAR is enabled to address bus (bit 19 = LOW), a memory read signal is issued (bit 42 = HIGH) and the data-in register's clock is enabled (bit 22 = LOW). At the next LOW-to-HIGH transition of the clock, the operand will be placed in the data-in register.

Meanwhile, we need to restore the address of the next macroinstruction in the MAR. Bits 32-33 = 3 select microprogram bits 24-27 as the A address (an F_H is written there); therefore, the internal program counter will be addressed, as $\overline{EA}$ (bit 10) = LOW. The ALU performs an F = R + C_n with C_n (bit 35) LOW, thus passing the program counter contents to the output. $\overline{IEN}$ (bit 9) = HIGH prevents disturbance of internal Am2903 registers and bit 18 will enable the MAR to receive the next macroinstruction address.

Note that the situation now is exactly the same as after the first step of ADD IMMediate. The operand is in the data register and the MAR points to the next macroinstruction. Therefore, the Am2910 sequencer will address, as the next microstep, location ADDIMM + 1. The step after this will, of course, be FETCH + 1. A total of 5 microsteps were needed to execute this macroinstruction but it occupies only 3 microprogram locations.

It is worthwhile to note here that by adding two more Am2920 registers between the Data-bus and the Address-bus and a couple of control-bits in the microprogram, we could shorten the microprogram by one step. In this design we chose not to do so in order to demonstrate the Data-bus to Address-bus path through the ALU.

Microword ADD RR1

The macroinstruction to be excuted here points to the register in which the first operand is written, and also into which the result should be written. The second 4-bit field of the OP-CODE (bits 0-3) points to the register in which the address of the second operand is stored.

15 8	7 4	3 0
OPCODE	1st Operand and Result Register Number	2nd Operand's Address Register Number

Bits 32 and 33 are LOW. Therefore, instruction register bits 0-3 will form the A-address. Now we take the contents of this register and place it in the MAR exactly the same way as we did in location ADD DIR + 2 with the program counter. The Am2910 continues.

Microword ADD RR1 + 1

Here we fetch the operand and place it in the Data-in register. At the same time, we restore the program counter into the MAR.

Microword ADD RR1 + 2

Bits 32, 33 = 2 and instruction register bits 4-7 serve as the A-address. Bit 34 = LOW; the same instruction register bits serve as B-address, too. Note, that $\overline{OEB}$ (bit 11) is HIGH; therefore, the ALU R-source will be the Data-in register and the S-source will be the register addressed by A-address. The result (sum), however, will be written to the correct register, as $\overline{IEN}$ (bit 9) is LOW.

At the same time, the next macroinstruction is fetched in the usuall oooverlapping way and the next microinstruction to be excuted will be at location FETCH + 1.

Summary

In this design shown in Figure 31, we have demonstrated some of the addressing schemes mentioned in Chapter 1. We used the ADD instruction throughout these examples, but any other arithmetic or logic instruction can be executed, in *exactly* the same manner by changing the microcode bits 1-4 to the appropriate ALU code.

The reader is encouraged to write several microcode-lines to execute the other addressing modes mentioned in Chapter 1. He will discover that when the result of the macroinstruction is to be written into main memory, the overlapping instruction-fetch is not feasible. In some cases, when the MAR no longer contains the Program Counter value, an additional microstep is needed in order to restore the Program Counter into the MAR. The reader is again encouraged to modify location FETCH in order to save this additional microstep.

Appendix

Throughout Chapter 3, a number of AC calculations have been made to show typical speeds for an Am2901A and Am2903 16-bit ALU configuration. This Appendix shows the latest SWITCHING CHARACTERISTICS for the Am2901A and Am2903.

The typical data on the Am2901A shown in this Appendix supersedes that shown on page 2-12 of the Am2900 Family Data Book dated 4-78 (AM-PUB003). The only difference between the data shown in the typical column of the switching characteristic and this Appendix appears in Table 3. The typical carry in set-up time should be 40ns.

The typical switching characteristic data for the Am2903 as shown in this Appendix supersedes the data presented in the Am2903 Bipolar Microprocessor Slice/Am2910 Microprogram Controller Data Booklet dated 3-78. Here, a number changes have been made to the table for both the combinatorial propagation delays and the set-up and hold times.

Should any questions arise concerning the switching characteristics for either the Am2901A or Am2903, please do not hesitate to contact the AMD factory and ask for Bipolar Microprocessor Marketing or Bipolar Microprocessor Applications.

Am2901A – (MAY 18, 1978)

ROOM TEMPERATURE SWITCHING CHARACTERISTICS

(See next page for AC Characteristics over operating range.)

Tables I, II, and III below define the timing characteristics of the Am2901A at 25°C. The tables are divided into three types of parameters; clock characteristics, combinational delays from inputs to outputs, and set-up and hold time requirements. The latter table defines the time prior to the end of the cycle (i.e., clock LOW-to-HIGH transition) that each input must be stable to guarantee that the correct data is written into one of the internal registers.

All values are at 25°C and 5.0V. Measurements are made at 1.5V with V_{IL} = 0V and V_{IH} = 3.0V. For three-state disable tests, C_L = 5.0pF and measurement is to 0.5V change on output voltage level. All outputs fully loaded.

TABLE I

CYCLE TIME AND CLOCK CHARACTERISTICS

TIME	TYPICAL	GUARANTEED
Read-Modify-Write Cycle (time from selection of A, B registers to end of cycle)	55ns	93ns
Maximum Clock Frequency to Shift Q Register (50% duty cycle)	40MHz	20MHz
Minimum Clock LOW Time	30ns	30ns
Minimum Clock HIGH Time	30ns	30ns
Minimum Clock Period	75ns	93ns

TABLE II

COMBINATIONAL PROPAGATION DELAYS (all in ns, C_L = **50pF** (except output disable tests))

	TYPICAL 25°C, 5.0V								GUARANTEED 25°C, 5.0V							
From Input \ To Output	Y	F_3	C_{n+4}	$\overline{G}, \overline{P}$	F=0 R_L= 270	OVR	Shift Outputs RAM_0 RAM_3	Shift Outputs Q_0 Q_3	Y	F_3	C_{n+4}	$\overline{G}, \overline{P}$	F=0 R_L= 270	OVR	Shift Outputs RAM_0 RAM_3	Shift Outputs Q_0 Q_3
A, B	45	45	45	40	65	50	60	–	75	75	70	59	85	76	90	–
D (arithmetic mode)	30	30	30	25	45	30	40	–	39	37	41	31	55	45	59	–
D (I = X37) (Note 5)	30	30	–	–	45	–	40	–	36	34	–	–	51	–	53	–
C_n	20	20	10	–	35	20	30	–	27	24	20	–	46	26	45	–
I_{012}	35	35	35	25	50	40	45	–	50	50	46	41	65	57	70	–
I_{345}	35	35	35	25	45	35	45	–	50	50	50	42	65	59	70	–
I_{678}	15	–	–	–	–	–	20	20	26	–	–	–	–	–	26	26
$\overline{OE}$ Enable/Disable	20/20	–	–	–	–	–	–	–	30/33	–	–	–	–	–	–	–
A bypassing ALU (I = 2xx)	30	–	–	–	–	–	–	–	35	–	–	–	–	–	–	–
Clock $\uparrow$ (Note 6)	40	40	40	30	55	40	55	20	52	52	52	41	70	57	71	30

TABLE III

SET-UP AND HOLD TIMES (all in ns) (Note 1)

From Input	Notes	TYPICAL 25°C, 5.0V Set-Up Time	TYPICAL 25°C, 5.0V Hold Time	GUARANTEED 25°C, 5.0V Set-Up Time	GUARANTEED 25°C, 5.0V Hold Time
A, B Source	2, 4 3, 5	40 $t_{pw}L$ + 15	0	93 $t_{pw}L$ + 25	0
B Dest.	2, 4	$t_{pw}L$ + 15	0	$t_{pw}L$ + 15	0
D (arithmetic mode)		25	0	70	0
D (I = X37) (Note 5)		25	0	60	0
C_n		40	0	55	0
I_{012}		30	0	64	0
I_{345}		30	0	70	0
I_{678}	4	$t_{pw}L$ + 15	0	$t_{pw}L$ + 25	0
$RAM_{0,3}$, $Q_{0,3}$		15	0	20	0

Notes: 1. See next page.
2. If the B address is used as a source operand, allow for the "A, B source" set-up time; if it is used only for the destination address, use the "B dest." set-up time.
3. Where two numbers are shown, both must be met.
4. "$t_{pw}L$" is the clock LOW time.
5. DV0 is the fastest way to load the RAM from the D inputs. This function is obtained with I = 337.
6. Using Q register as source operand in arithmetic mode. Clock is not normally in critical speed path when Q is not a source.

A. Am2903 SWITCHING CHARACTERISTICS (TYPICAL ROOM TEMPERATURE PERFORMANCE) – (MAY 18, 1978)

Tables IA, IIA, and IIIA define the nominal timing characteristics of the Am2903 at 25°C and 5.0V. The Tables divide the parameters into three types: pulse characteristics for the clock and write enable, combinational delays from input to output, and set-up and hold times relative to the clock and write pulse.

Measurements are made at 1.5V with V_{IL} = 0V and V_{IH} = 3.0V. For three-state disable tests, C_L = 5.0pF and measurement is to 0.5V change on output voltage level.

TABLE IA – Write Pulse and Clock Characteristics

Time	
Minimum Time CP and $\overline{WE}$ both LOW to write	15ns
Minimum Clock LOW Time	15ns
Minimum Clock HIGH Time	35ns

TABLE IIA – Combinational Propagation Delays (All in ns)
Outputs Fully Loaded. CL = 50pF (except output disable tests)

From Input \ To Output	Y	C_{n+4}	$\overline{G}, \overline{P}$	(S) Z	N	OVR	DB	$\overline{WRITE}$	QIO_0, QIO_3	SIO_0	SIO_3	SIO_0 (Parity)
A, B Addresses (Arith. Mode)	65	60	56	–	64	70	33	–	–	65	69	87
A, B Addresses (Logic Mode)	56	–	46	–	56	–	33	–	–	55	64	81
DA, DB Inputs	39	38	30	–	40	56	–	–	–	39	47	60
$\overline{EA}$	38	33	26	–	36	41	–	–	–	36	41	58
C_n	25	21	–	–	20	38	–	–	–	21	25	48
I_0	40	31	24	–	37	42	–	15(1)	–	41	39	63
I_{4321}	45	45	32	–	44	52	–	17(1)	–	45	51	68
I_{8765}	25	–	–	–	–	–	–	21	22/29(2)	24/17(2)	27/17(2)	24/17(2)
$\overline{IEN}$	–	–	–	–	–	–	–	10	–	–	–	–
$\overline{OEB}$ Enable/Disable	–	–	–	–	–	–	12/15(2)	–	–	–	–	–
$\overline{OEY}$ Enable/Disable	14/14(2)	–	–	–	–	–	–	–	–	–	–	–
SIO_0, SIO_3	13	–	–	–	–	–	–	–	–	–	19	20
Clock	58	57	40	–	56	72	24	–	28	56	63	76
Y	–	–	–	16	–	–	–	–	–	–	–	–
$\overline{MSS}$	25	–	25	–	25	25	–	–	–	24	27	24

Notes: 1. Applies only when leaving special functions.
2. Enable/Disable. Enable is defined as output active and correct. Disable is a three-state output turning off.
3. For delay from any input to Z, use input to Y plus Y to Z.

TABLE IIIA – Set-Up and Hold Times (All in ns)
CAUTION: READ NOTES TO TABLE III. NA = Not Applicable; no timing constraint.

Input	With Respect to to this Signal	HIGH-to-LOW		LOW-to-HIGH		Comment
		Set-up	Hold	Set-up	Hold	
Y	Clock	NA	NA	9	−3	To store Y in RAM or Q
$\overline{WE}$ HIGH	Clock	5	Note 2	Note 2	0	To Prevent Writing
$\overline{WE}$ LOW	Clock	NA	NA	15	0	To Write into RAM
A,B as Sources	Clock	19	−3	NA	NA	See Note 3
B as a Destination	Clock and $\overline{WE}$ both LOW	−4	Note 4	Note 4	−3	To Write Data only into the Correct B Address
QIO_0, QIO_3	Clock	NA	NA	10	−4	To Shift Q
I_{8765}	Clock	2	Note 5	Note 5	−18	
$\overline{IEN}$ HIGH	Clock	10	Note 2	Note 2	0	To Prevent Writing into Q
$\overline{IEN}$ LOW	Clock	NA	NA	10	−5	To Write into Q

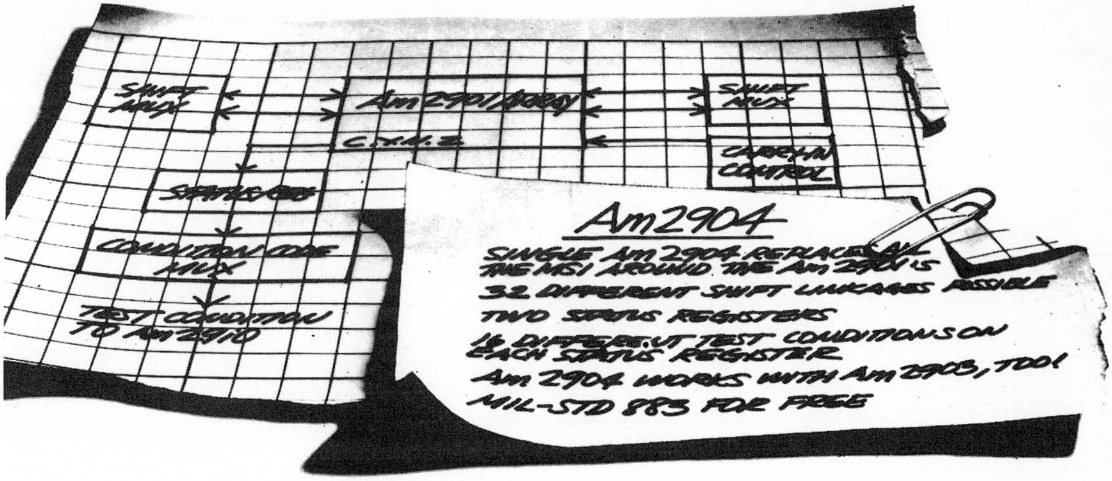

Chapter IV
The Data Path — Part II

CHAPTER IV
THE DATA PATH

The previous CPU example (See Chapter III) utilized SSI and MSI components to accomplish the shift-linkage, carry control, and status register functions associated with the ALU. These functions can all be implemented with the Am2904 status and shift control unit.

The Am2904 is an LSI device that contains all the logic necessary to perform the shift and status control operations associated with the ALU portion of a microcomputer. These operations include storage for ALU status flags; carry-in generation and selection; data-path, carry bit linkage for shift/rotate instructions; and status condition code generation and selection. The ALU status flags: carry, zero, negative, and overflow; may be stored in either of two registers, a machine status register or a micro status register. The carry-in multiplexer can select the true or complement of the microstatus carry flag or machine status carry flag, as well as an external carry, a logical one, or a logical zero. The shift linkage multiplexers provide paths to rotate/shift single and double length words up, down, around the carry flag, and through the carry flag. The status condition code multiplexer provides tests on the true or complement of any status flag, as well as more complicated logical combinations of these flags to facilitate magnitude comparisons on unsigned and two's complement numbers, and normalization operations.

STATUS REGISTERS

The status registers contained in the Am2904 are shown in the upper portion of Figure 1. Each register is independently controlled by a combination of instruction signals and enable signals.

MICRO STATUS REGISTER (μSR)

The μSR is enabled when the $\overline{CE}\mu$ signal is low. When $\overline{CE}\mu$ is low the instruction present on I_5 through I_0 will be executed on the LOW to HIGH transition of the Clock input. These instructions fall into three main categories: Bit Operations, Register Operations and Load Operations.

The bit operations allow individual bits of the μSR to be set or reset. (See Table 1.1).

The register operations allow the μSR to be loaded from the machine status register, to be set to all one's, reset to all zero's, or swapped with the machine status register. (See Table 1.2).

The load operations allow the μSR to be loaded from the I inputs directly, from the I inputs with I_C complemented, or from the I inputs with overflow retained, $I_{OVR} + \mu_{OVR} \rightarrow \mu_{OVR}$ (See Table 1.3). The load operation with I_C complemented can be used to emulate machines which use direct subtraction and thus need to complement the carry to obtain a borrow. The load with overflow retained allows a series of arithmetic instructions to be executed without the need for a check for overflow after each instruction. If an overflow occurred at any time during the series it will be "trapped." Thus a single test for overflow, at the end of the series, is all that is required.

MACHINE STATUS REGISTER (MSR)

The MSR is enabled when $\overline{CE}_M$ is low. If $\overline{CE}_M$ is low the instruction present on I_5 through I_0 will be executed on the LOW to HIGH transition of the Clock input. Additionally the individual bits of the MSR may be selectively enabled through the use of the Enable inputs $\overline{E}_Z$, $\overline{E}_C$, $\overline{E}_N$ and $\overline{E}_{OVR}$ (See Figure 1). This allows all possible combinations of the four status flags to be selectively operated on for maximum flexibility. Thus the instruction specified by I_5-I_0 only effect the enabled status flags.

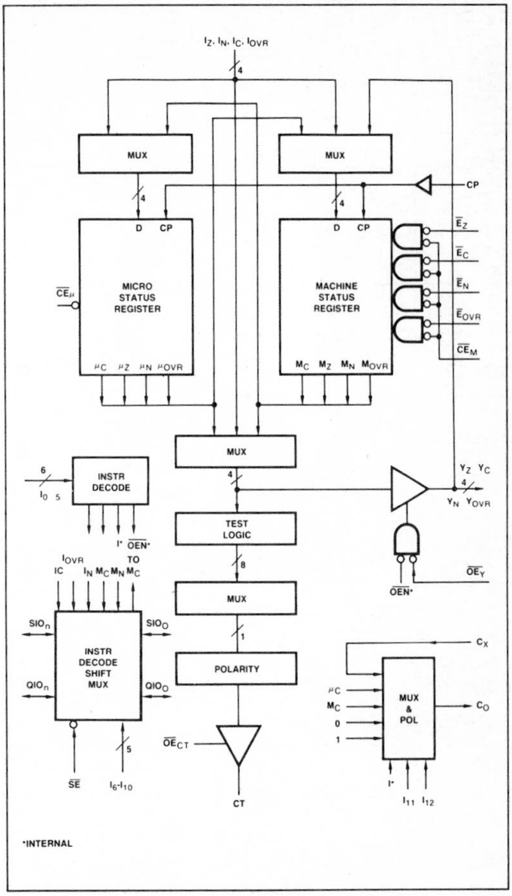

Figure 1. Am2904 Block Diagram.

The MSR instructions fall into two main categories: register operations and load operations (bit operations can be implemented through the use of the selective enable control lines).

The register operations allow the MSR to be loaded from the bi-directional Y port, or the μSR. Additionally the MSR may be set, reset, or complemented (See Table 2.1). These three instructions, combined with the selective enables, allow any combination of MSR bits to be set, reset, or complemented.

The load operations allow the MSR to be loaded directly from the I inputs, from the I inputs with I_C complemented, or from the I inputs for shift through overflow (See Table 2.2). The load with I_C complemented can be used to produce a borrow. The load for shift through overflow loads the zero flag and the negative flag from the I inputs while swapping the overflow and carry flags. This allows the shift through overflow operation to be easily implemented.

SHIFT LINKAGE MULTIPLEXERS

The shift linkage multiplexers control bi-directional shift lines SIOn, SIO_0 (RAM shifter on the Am2903) and QIOn, QIO_0 (Q register shifter on the Am2903). To enable the shift linkage multiplexers the shift enable line $\overline{SE}$ must be low. When $\overline{SE}$ is low the

TABLE 1. MICRO STATUS REGISTER INSTRUCTION CODES.

Table 1-1. Bit Operations.

I_{543210} Octal	μSR Operation	Comments
10	$0 \rightarrow \mu_Z$	RESET ZERO BIT
11	$1 \rightarrow \mu_Z$	SET ZERO BIT
12	$0 \rightarrow \mu_C$	RESET CARRY BIT
13	$1 \rightarrow \mu_C$	SET CARRY BIT
14	$0 \rightarrow \mu_N$	RESET SIGN BIT
15	$1 \rightarrow \mu_N$	SET SIGN BIT
16	$0 \rightarrow \mu_{OVR}$	RESET OVERFLOW BIT
17	$1 \rightarrow \mu_{OVR}$	SET OVERFLOW BIT

Table 1-2. Register Operations.

I_{543210} Octal	μSR Operation	Comments
00	$M_X \rightarrow \mu_X$	LOAD MSR TO μSR
01	$1 \rightarrow \mu_X$	SET μSR
02	$M_X \rightarrow \mu_X$	REGISTER SWAP
03	$0 \rightarrow \mu_X$	RESET μSR

Table 1-3. Load Operations.

I_{543210} Octal	μSR Operation	Comments
06, 07	$I_Z \rightarrow \mu_Z$ $I_C \rightarrow \mu_C$ $I_N \rightarrow \mu_N$ $I_{OVR} + \mu_{OVR} \rightarrow \mu_{OVR}$	LOAD WITH OVERFLOW RETAIN
30, 31 50, 51 70, 71	$I_Z \rightarrow \mu_Z$ $I_C \rightarrow \mu_C$ $I_N \rightarrow \mu_N$ $I_{OVR} \rightarrow \mu_{OVR}$	LOAD WITH CARRY INVERT
04, 05 20-27 32-47 52-67 72-77	$I_Z \rightarrow \mu_Z$ $I_C \rightarrow \mu_C$ $I_N \rightarrow \mu_N$ $I_{OVR} \rightarrow \mu_{OVR}$	LOAD DIRECTLY FROM I_Z, I_C, I_N, I_{OVR}

Note: The above tables assume $\overline{CE}$ is LOW.

shift linkage data path will be set-up depending on the state of instruction lines I_{10} through I_6 (See Table 3). These instructions allow single length or double length shifts/rotates either up, or down. Additionally shifts/rotates may be done through or around the MSR carry and negative flag. Special operations exist to provide support for add and shift (multiply) instructions. These instructions select the present carry I_C (for unsigned multiply), or the Exclusive-OR of the sign flag I_n with the overflow flag I_{OVR} (for two's complement multiplication).

CONDITION CODE MULTIPLEXER

The condition code multiplier selects one of sixteen possible logical combinations of the μSR, MSR or I inputs, depending on the state of the I_5-I_0 input lines. These combinations include the true or complement form of any individual bit in the μSR, MSR or I inputs. Additionally several more complicated logical operations may be performed to provide magnitude tests on both two's complement numbers and unsigned numbers. Table 5 lists the conditional test outputs (CT) corresponding to the state of the I_5-I_0 instruction lines. Table 6 lists the possible relations between two unsigned or two's complement numbers and the corresponding status and instruction codes. The three-state conditional test output CT is active only if $\overline{OE}_{CT}$ is low.

CARRY IN MULTIPLEXER

The Carry output can be selected from one of seven different sources depending on the state of instruction input lines. The seven possible sources are: logical zero, logical one, the μSR carry flag, the complement of the μSR carry flag, the MSR carry flag, the complement of the MSR carry flag, or the external carry input C_X (See Table 4).

TABLE 2. MACHINE STATUS REGISTER INSTRUCTION CODES.

Table 2-1. Register Operations.

I_{543210} Octal	MSR Operation	Comments
00	$Y_X \rightarrow M_X$	LOAD Y_Z, Y_C, Y_N, Y_{OVR} TO MSR
01	$1 \rightarrow M_X$	SET MSR
02	$\mu_X \rightarrow M_X$	REGISTER SWAP
03	$0 \rightarrow M_X$	RESET MSR
05	$\overline{M}_X \rightarrow M_X$	INVERT MSR

Table 2-2. Load Operations.

I_{543210} Octal	MSR Operation	Comments
04	$I_Z \rightarrow M_Z$ $M_{OVR} \rightarrow M_C$ $I_N \rightarrow M_N$ $M_C \rightarrow M_{OVR}$	LOAD FOR SHIFT THROUGH OVERFLOW OPERATION
10, 11 30, 31 50, 51 70, 71	$I_Z \rightarrow M_Z$ $I_C \rightarrow M_C$ $I_N \rightarrow M_N$ $I_{OVR} \rightarrow M_{OVR}$	LOAD WITH CARRY INVERT
06, 07 12-17 20-27 32-37 40-47 52-67 72-77	$I_Z \rightarrow M_Z$ $I_C \rightarrow M_C$ $I_N \rightarrow M_N$ $I_{OVR} \rightarrow M_{OVR}$	LOAD DIRECTLY FROM I_Z, I_C I_N, I_{OVR}

Note: 1. The above tables assume $\overline{CE}_M$, $\overline{E}_Z$, $\overline{E}_C$, $\overline{E}_N$, $\overline{E}_{OVR}$ are LOW.

Y INPUT/OUTPUT LINES

The bi-directional Y data lines may be used for extra data input lines when the Y output buffer is disabled ($\overline{OE}_Y$ high). Additionally, when I_5-I_0 are low, the Y buffer is disabled, irrespective of the $\overline{OE}_Y$ signal. When the Y buffer is enabled ($\overline{OE}_Y$ is low) the Y data lines are selected from the MSR, μSR, or I input lines depending on the state of instruction lines I_5 and I_4 (See Table 7).

TABLE 3. SHIFT LINKAGE MULTIPLEXER INSTRUCTION CODES.

I_{10}	I_9	I_8	I_7	I_6	M_C RAM Q	SIO_0	SIO_n	QIO_0	QIO_n	Loaded into M_C
0	0	0	0	0	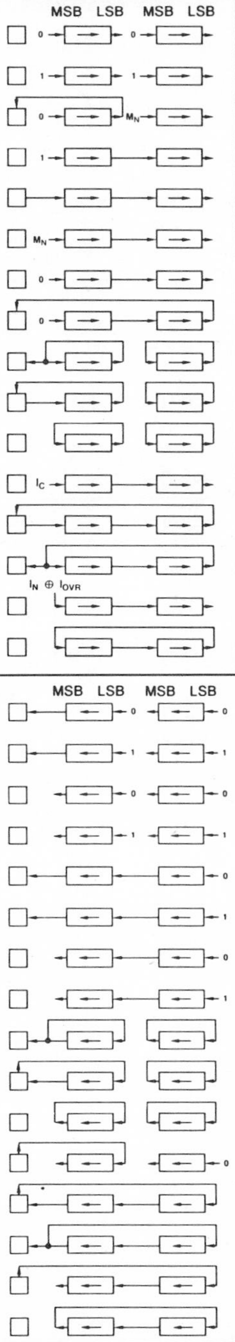	Z	0	Z	0	
0	0	0	0	1		Z	1	Z	1	
0	0	0	1	0		Z	0	Z	M_N	SIO_0
0	0	0	1	1		Z	1	Z	SIO_0	
0	0	1	0	0		Z	M_C	Z	SIO_0	
0	0	1	0	1		Z	M_N	Z	SIO_0	
0	0	1	1	0		Z	0	Z	SIO_0	
0	0	1	1	1		Z	0	Z	SIO_0	QIO_0
0	1	0	0	0		Z	SIO_0	Z	QIO_0	SIO_0
0	1	0	0	1		Z	M_C	Z	QIO_0	SIO_0
0	1	0	1	0		Z	SIO_0	Z	QIO_0	
0	1	0	1	1		Z	I_C	Z	SIO_0	
0	1	1	0	0		Z	M_C	Z	SIO_0	QIO_0
0	1	1	0	1		Z	QIO_0	Z	SIO_0	QIO_0
0	1	1	1	0		Z	$I_N \oplus I_{OVR}$	Z	SIO_0	
0	1	1	1	1		Z	QIO_0	Z	SIO_0	
1	0	0	0	0		0	Z	0	Z	SIO_n
1	0	0	0	1		1	Z	1	Z	SIO_n
1	0	0	1	0		0	Z	0	Z	
1	0	0	1	1		1	Z	1	Z	
1	0	1	0	0		QIO_n	Z	0	Z	SIO_n
1	0	1	0	1		QIO_n	Z	1	Z	SIO_n
1	0	1	1	0		QIO_n	Z	0	Z	
1	0	1	1	1		QIO_n	Z	1	Z	
1	1	0	0	0		SIO_n	Z	QIO_n	Z	SIO_n
1	1	0	0	1		M_C	Z	QIO_n	Z	SIO_n
1	1	0	1	0		SIO_n	Z	QIO_n	Z	
1	1	0	1	1		M_C	Z	0	Z	
1	1	1	0	0		QIO_n	Z	M_C	Z	SIO_n
1	1	1	0	1		QIO_n	Z	SIO_n	Z	SIO_n
1	1	1	1	0		QIO_n	Z	M_C	Z	
1	1	1	1	1		QIO_n	Z	SIO_n	Z	

Notes: 1. Z = High impedance (outputs off) state.
2. Outputs enabled and M_C loaded only if $\overline{SE}$ is LOW.
3. Loading of M_C from I_{10-6} overrides control from I_{5-0}, $\overline{CE}_M$, $\overline{E}_C$.

TABLE 4. CARRY-IN CONTROL MULTIPLEXER INSTRUCTION CODES.

I_{12}	I_{11}	I_5	I_3	I_2	I_1	C_0
0	0	X	X	X	X	0
0	1	X	X	X	X	1
1	0	X	X	X	X	C_X
1	1	0	0	X	X	μ_C
1	1	0	X	1	X	μ_C
1	1	0	X	X	1	μ_C
1	1	0	1	0	0	$\bar{\mu}_C$
1	1	1	0	X	X	M_C
1	1	1	X	1	X	M_C
1	1	1	X	X	1	M_C
1	1	1	1	0	0	$\bar{M}_C$

TABLE 5. CONDITION CODE OUTPUT (CT) INSTRUCTION CODES.

I_{3-0} HEX	I_3	I_2	I_1	I_0	$I_5 = I_4 = 0$	$I_5 = 0, I_4 = 1$	$I_5 = 1, I_4 = 0$	$I_5 = I_4 = 1$
0	0	0	0	0	$(\mu_N \oplus \mu_{OVR}) + \mu_Z$	$(\mu_N \oplus \mu_{OVR}) + \mu_Z$	$(M_N \oplus M_{OVR}) + M_Z$	$(I_N \oplus I_{OVR}) + I_Z$
1	0	0	0	1	$(\mu_N \odot \mu_{OVR}) \cdot \bar{\mu}_Z$	$(\mu_N \odot \mu_{OVR}) \cdot \bar{\mu}_Z$	$(M_N \odot M_{OVR}) \cdot \bar{M}_Z$	$(I_N \odot I_{OVR}) \cdot \bar{I}_Z$
2	0	0	1	0	$\mu_N \oplus \mu_{OVR}$	$\mu_N \oplus \mu_{OVR}$	$M_N \oplus M_{OVR}$	$I_N \oplus I_{OVR}$
3	0	0	1	1	$\mu_N \odot \mu_{OVR}$	$\mu_N \odot \mu_{OVR}$	$M_N \odot M_{OVR}$	$I_N \odot I_{OVR}$
4	0	1	0	0	μ_Z	μ_Z	M_Z	I_Z
5	0	1	0	1	$\bar{\mu}_Z$	$\bar{\mu}_Z$	$\bar{M}_Z$	$\bar{I}_Z$
6	0	1	1	0	μ_{OVR}	μ_{OVR}	M_{OVR}	I_{OVR}
7	0	1	1	1	$\bar{\mu}_{OVR}$	$\bar{\mu}_{OVR}$	$\bar{M}_{OVR}$	$\bar{I}_{OVR}$
8	1	0	0	0	$\mu_C + \mu_Z$	$\mu_C + \mu_Z$	$M_C + M_Z$	$\bar{I}_C + I_Z$
9	1	0	0	1	$\bar{\mu}_C \cdot \bar{\mu}_Z$	$\bar{\mu}_C \cdot \bar{\mu}_Z$	$\bar{M}_C \cdot \bar{M}_Z$	$I_C \cdot \bar{I}_Z$
A	1	0	1	0	μ_C	μ_C	M_C	I_C
B	1	0	1	1	$\bar{\mu}_C$	$\bar{\mu}_C$	$\bar{M}_C$	$\bar{I}_C$
C	1	1	0	0	$\bar{\mu}_C + \mu_Z$	$\bar{\mu}_C + \mu_Z$	$\bar{M}_C + M_Z$	$\bar{I}_C + I_Z$
D	1	1	0	1	$\mu_C \cdot \bar{\mu}_Z$	$\mu_C \cdot \bar{\mu}_Z$	$M_C \cdot \bar{M}_Z$	$I_C \cdot \bar{I}_Z$
E	1	1	1	0	$I_N \oplus M_N$	μ_N	M_N	I_N
F	1	1	1	1	$I_N \odot M_N$	$\bar{\mu}_N$	$\bar{M}_N$	$\bar{I}_N$

Notes: 1. $\oplus$ Represents EXCLUSIVE-OR $\odot$ Represents EXCLUSIVE-NOR or coincidence.

TABLE 6. CRITERIA FOR COMPARING TWO NUMBERS FOLLOWING "A MINUS B" OPERATIONS.

	For Unsigned Numbers			For 2's Complement Numbers		
		I_{3-0}			I_{3-0}	
Relation	**Status**	**CT = H**	**CT = L**	**Status**	**CT = H**	**CT = L**
A = B	Z = 1	4	5	Z = 1	4	5
A = B	Z = 0	5	4	Z = 0	5	4
A ≥ B	C = 1	A	B	$N \odot OVR = 1$	3	2
A < B	C = 0	B	A	$N \oplus OVR = 1$	2	3
A > B	$C \cdot \bar{Z} = 1$	D	C	$(N \odot OVR) \cdot \bar{Z} = 1$	1	0
A ≤ B	$\bar{C} + Z = 1$	C	D	$(N \oplus OVR) + Z = 1$	0	1

$\oplus$ = Exclusive OR H = HIGH Note: For Am2910, the CC input is active LOW, so use I_{3-0} code to produce
$\odot$ = Exclusive NOR L = LOW CT = L for the desired test.

TABLE 7. Y OUTPUT INSTRUCTION CODES.

$\overline{OE}_Y$	I_5	I_4	Y Output	Comment
1	X	X	Z	Output Off High Impedance
O	O	X	$\mu_i \rightarrow Y_i$	See Note 1
O	1	O	$M_i \rightarrow Y_i$	
O	1	1	$I_i \rightarrow Y_i$	

Notes: 1. For the conditions:
$I_5, I_4, I_3, I_2, I_1, I_0$ are LOW, Y is an input.
$\overline{OE}_Y$ is "Don't Care" for this condition.
2. X is "Don't Care" condition.

TIMING ANALYSIS

In the previous chapter a timing analysis was presented with the shift-linkage, carry-control, and status registers implemented in SSI and MSI. This timing analysis will be repeated with the SSI and MSI logic replaced with the Am2904. Tables 8.1, 8.2, 8.4 and 8.5 list the typical AC characteristics of the registers, Am2902A, Am2901A, Am2903, and Am2904 used in these calculations. Table 8.3 lists the assumed AC characteristics for the set-up time of the Am2904.

Figure 2 illustrates the timing analysis for an Am2901A based design. The analysis begins with the LOW to HIGH transition of the system clock. All signals must be valid for the next LOW to HIGH transition of the system clock, i.e. one-microcycle later.

Figure 3 illustrates a similar timing analysis for the Am2903. The results of both analysis are listed in Table 9.

USING THE Am2904 IN A 16-BIT DESIGN

Perhaps the best technique for understanding the Am2904 is to simply compare 16-bit ALU designs with and without the Am2904. The first design, Figure 4a, is an example of a 16-bit CPU design using SSI/MSI parts instead of the Am2904. In Figure 4b, the second 16-bit CPU design, the Am2904 is shown replacing the SSI/MSI. The Am2904 substitutes for the appropriate shift matrix control and status registers. A more detailed comparison may be obtained by referring to the 16-bit ALU designs in Chapter III and the one in Appendix C of this chapter. To understand the Am2904 further, the usage of the Am2904 is described through the microprogram bits in the microprogram structure and shown later in the actual microprograms.

TABLE 8-1. STANDARD DEVICE SCHOTTKY SPEEDS.

Device and Path	Min.	Typ.	Max.
S-REGISTER			
Clock to Output		9	15
$\overline{OE}$ to Output		13	20
Set-up	5	2	
Am2902A			
Cn to Cn+x, Y, Z		7	11
G, P to G, P		7	10
G, P to Cn+x, Y, Z		5	7

TABLE 8-2.
PRELIMINARY SWITCHING CHARACTERISTICS.
Combinational Delays (ns)

From (Input)	To (Output)	t_{pd}
I_Z I_C I_N I_{OVR}	Y_Z Y_C Y_N Y_{OVR}	20
CP	Y_Z, Y_C, Y_N, Y_{OVR}	30
I_4, I_5	Y_Z, Y_C, Y_N, Y_{OVR}	23
I_Z, I_C, I_N, I_{OVR}	CT	30
CP	CT	30
I_0-I_5	CT	30
C_X	C_O	12
CP	C_O	20
$I_{1,2,3,5,11,12}$	C_O	24
SIO_n, QIO_n	SIO_o	16
SIO_o, QIO_o	SIO_n	16
I_C, I_N, I_{OVR}	SIO_n	20
SIO_n, QIO_n	QIO_o	16
SIO_o, QIO_o	QIO_n	16
CP	SIO_o, SIO_n QIO_o, QIO_n	21
I_6-I_{10}	SIO_o, SIO_n QIO_o, QIO_n	19

TABLE 8-3. ASSUMED SET-UP TIME.*

Input	TS
IOVR, IZ, IN, IC	20ns

*The actual set-up times where not available at the time this was written. See current data sheets for correct timing on these signals.

TABLE 8-4.

Am2901A – (MAY 18, 1978)

ROOM TEMPERATURE SWITCHING CHARACTERISTICS

Tables I, II, and III below define the timing characteristics of the Am2901A at 25°C. The tables are divided into three types of parameters; clock characteristics, combinational delays from inputs to outputs, and set-up and hold time requirements. The latter table defines the time prior to the end of the cycle (i.e., clock LOW-to-HIGH transition) that each input must be stable to guarantee that the correct data is written into one of the internal registers.

All values are at 25°C and 5.0V. Measurements are made at 1.5V with V_{IL} = 0V and V_{IH} = 3.0V. For three-state disable tests, C_L = 5.0pF and measurement is to 0.5V change on output voltage level. All outputs fully loaded.

TABLE I

CYCLE TIME AND CLOCK CHARACTERISTICS

TIME	TYPICAL	GUARANTEED
Read-Modify-Write Cycle (time from selection of A, B registers to end of cycle)	55ns	93ns
Maximum Clock Frequency to Shift Q Register (50% duty cycle)	40MHz	20MHz
Minimum Clock LOW Time	30ns	30ns
Minimum Clock HIGH Time	30ns	30ns
Minimum Clock Period	75ns	93ns

TABLE II

COMBINATIONAL PROPAGATION DELAYS (all in ns, C_L = **50pF** (except output disable tests))

	TYPICAL 25°C, 5.0V								GUARANTEED 25°C, 5.0V							
From Input / To Output	Y	F_3	C_{n+4}	$\overline{G}, \overline{P}$	F=0 R_L= 270	OVR	Shift Outputs		Y	F_3	C_{n+4}	$\overline{G}, \overline{P}$	F=0 R_L= 270	OVR	Shift Outputs	
							RAM_0 RAM_3	Q_0 Q_3							RAM_0 RAM_3	Q_0 Q_3
A, B	45	45	45	40	65	50	60	–	75	75	70	59	85	76	90	–
D (arithmetic mode)	30	30	30	25	45	30	40	–	39	37	41	31	55	45	59	–
D (I = X37) (Note 5)	30	30	–	–	45	–	40	–	36	34	–	–	51	–	53	–
C_n	20	20	10	–	35	20	30	–	27	24	20	–	46	26	45	–
I_{012}	35	35	35	25	50	40	45	–	50	50	46	41	65	57	70	–
I_{345}	35	35	35	25	45	35	45	–	50	50	50	42	65	59	70	–
I_{678}	15	–	–	–	–	–	20	20	26	–	–	–	–	–	26	26
$\overline{OE}$ Enable/Disable	20/20	–	–	–	–	–	–	–	30/33	–	–	–	–	–	–	–
A bypassing ALU (I = 2xx)	30	–	–	–	–	–	–	–	35	–	–	–	–	–	–	–
Clock ↑ (Note 6)	40	40	40	30	55	40	55	20	52	52	52	41	70	57	71	30

TABLE III

SET-UP AND HOLD TIMES (all in ns) (Note 1)

From Input	Notes	TYPICAL 25°C, 5.0V		GUARANTEED 25°C, 5.0V	
		Set-Up Time	Hold Time	Set-Up Time	Hold Time
A, B Source	2, 4 3, 5	40 $t_{pw}L$ + 15	0	93 $t_{pw}L$ + 25	0
B Dest.	2, 4	$t_{pw}L$ + 15	0	$t_{pw}L$ + 15	0
D (arithmetic mode)		25	0	70	0
D (I = X37) (Note 5)		25	0	60	0
C_n		40	0	55	0
I_{012}		30	0	64	0
I_{345}		30	0	70	0
I_{678}	4	$t_{pw}L$ + 15	0	$t_{pw}L$ + 25	0
$RAM_{0,3}$, $Q_{0,3}$		15	0	20	0

Notes: 1. See next page.
2. If the B address is used as a source operand, allow for the "A, B source" set-up time; if it is used only for the destination address, use the "B dest." set-up time.
3. Where two numbers are shown, both must be met.
4. "$t_{pw}L$" is the clock LOW time.
5. DV0 is the fastest way to load the RAM from the D inputs. This function is obtained with I = 337.
6. Using Q register as source operand in arithmetic mode. Clock is not normally in critical speed path when Q is not a source.

TABLE 8-5.

A. Am2903 SWITCHING CHARACTERISTICS (TYPICAL ROOM TEMPERATURE PERFORMANCE) – (MAY 18, 1978)

Tables IA, IIA, and IIIA define the nominal timing characteristics of the Am2903 at 25°C and 5.0V. The Tables divide the parameters into three types: pulse characteristics for the clock and write enable, combinational delays from input to output, and set-up and hold times relative to the clock and write pulse.

Measurements are made at 1.5V with V_{IL} = 0V and V_{IH} = 3.0V. For three-state disable tests, C_L = 5.0pF and measurement is to 0.5V change on output voltage level.

TABLE IA – Write Pulse and Clock Characteristics

Time	
Minimum Time CP and $\overline{WE}$ both LOW to write	15ns
Minimum Clock LOW Time	15ns
Minimum Clock HIGH Time	35ns

TABLE IIA – Combinational Propagation Delays (All in ns)
Outputs Fully Loaded. CL = 50pF (except output disable tests)

From Input \ To Output	Y	C_{n+4}	$\overline{G}, \overline{P}$	(S) Z	N	OVR	DB	$\overline{WRITE}$	QIO_0, QIO_3	SIO_0	SIO_3	SIO_0 (Parity)
A, B Addresses (Arith. Mode)	65	60	56	–	64	70	33	–	–	65	69	87
A, B Addresses (Logic Mode)	56	–	46	–	56	–	33	–	–	55	64	81
DA, DB Inputs	39	38	30	–	40	56	–	–	–	39	47	60
$\overline{EA}$	38	33	26	–	36	41	–	–	–	36	41	58
C_n	25	21	–	–	20	38	–	–	–	21	25	48
I_0	40	31	24	–	37	42	–	15(1)	–	41	39	63
I_{4321}	45	45	32	–	44	52	–	17(1)	–	45	51	68
I_{8765}	25	–	–	–	–	–	–	21	22/29(2)	24/17(2)	27/17(2)	24/17(2)
$\overline{IEN}$	–	–	–	–	–	–	–	10	–	–	–	–
$\overline{OEB}$ Enable/Disable	–	–	–	–	–	–	12/15(2)	–	–	–	–	–
$\overline{OEY}$ Enable/Disable	14/14(2)	–	–	–	–	–	–	–	–	–	–	–
SIO_0, SIO_3	13	–	–	–	–	–	–	–	–	–	19	20
Clock	58	57	40	–	56	72	24	–	28	56	63	76
Y	–	–	–	16	–	–	–	–	–	–	–	–
$\overline{MSS}$	25	–	25	–	25	25	–	–	–	24	27	24

Notes: 1. Applies only when leaving special functions.
2. Enable/Disable. Enable is defined as output active and correct. Disable is a three-state output turning off.
3. For delay from any input to Z, use input to Y plus Y to Z.

TABLE IIIA – Set-Up and Hold Times (All in ns)
CAUTION: READ NOTES TO TABLE III. NA = Note Applicable; no timing constraint.

Input	With Respect to to this Signal	HIGH-to-LOW Set-up	HIGH-to-LOW Hold	LOW-to-HIGH Set-up	LOW-to-HIGH Hold	Comment
Y	Clock	NA	NA	9	−3	To store Y in RAM or Q
$\overline{WE}$ HIGH	Clock	5	Note 2	Note 2	0	To Prevent Writing
$\overline{WE}$ LOW	Clock	NA	NA	15	0	To Write into RAM
A,B as Sources	Clock	19	−3	NA	NA	See Note 3
B as a Destination	Clock and $\overline{WE}$ both LOW	−4	Note 4	Note 4	−3	To Write Data only into the Correct B Address
QIO_0, QIO_3	Clock	NA	NA	10	−4	To Shift Q
I_{8765}	Clock	2	Note 5	Note 5	−18	
$\overline{IEN}$ HIGH	Clock	10	Note 2	Note 2	0	To Prevent Writing into Q
$\overline{IEN}$ LOW	Clock	NA	NA	10	−5	To Write into Q

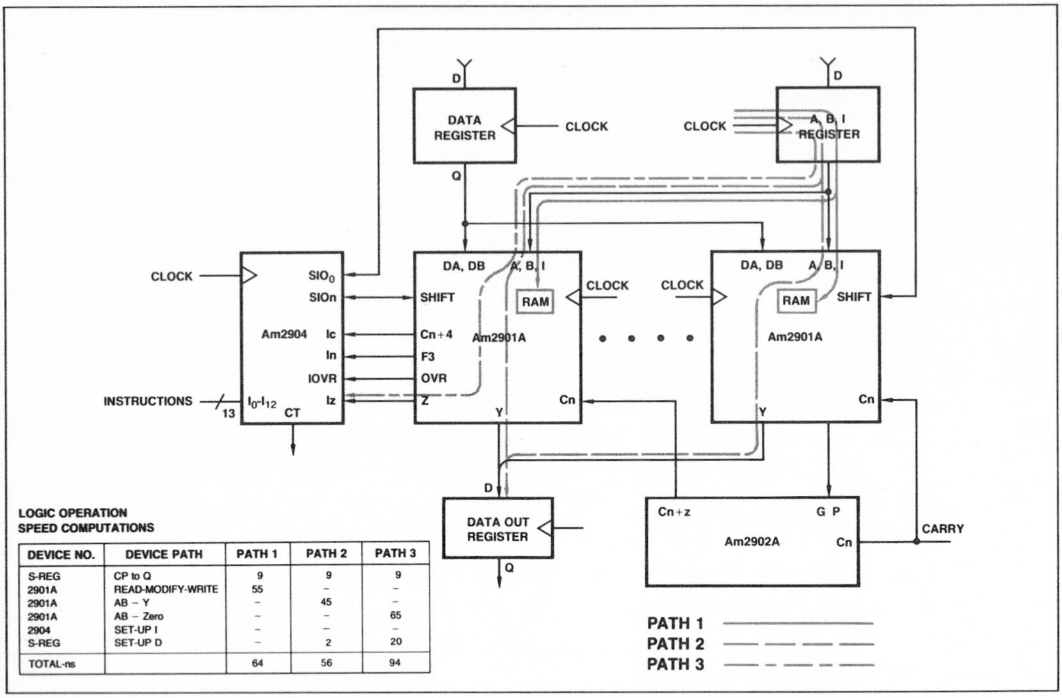

LOGIC OPERATION SPEED COMPUTATIONS

DEVICE NO.	DEVICE PATH	PATH 1	PATH 2	PATH 3
S-REG	CP to Q	9	9	9
2901A	READ-MODIFY-WRITE	55	–	–
2901A	AB – Y	–	45	–
2901A	AB – Zero	–	–	65
2904	SET-UP I	–	–	–
S-REG	SET-UP D	–	2	20
TOTAL-ns		64	56	94

Figure 2-1.

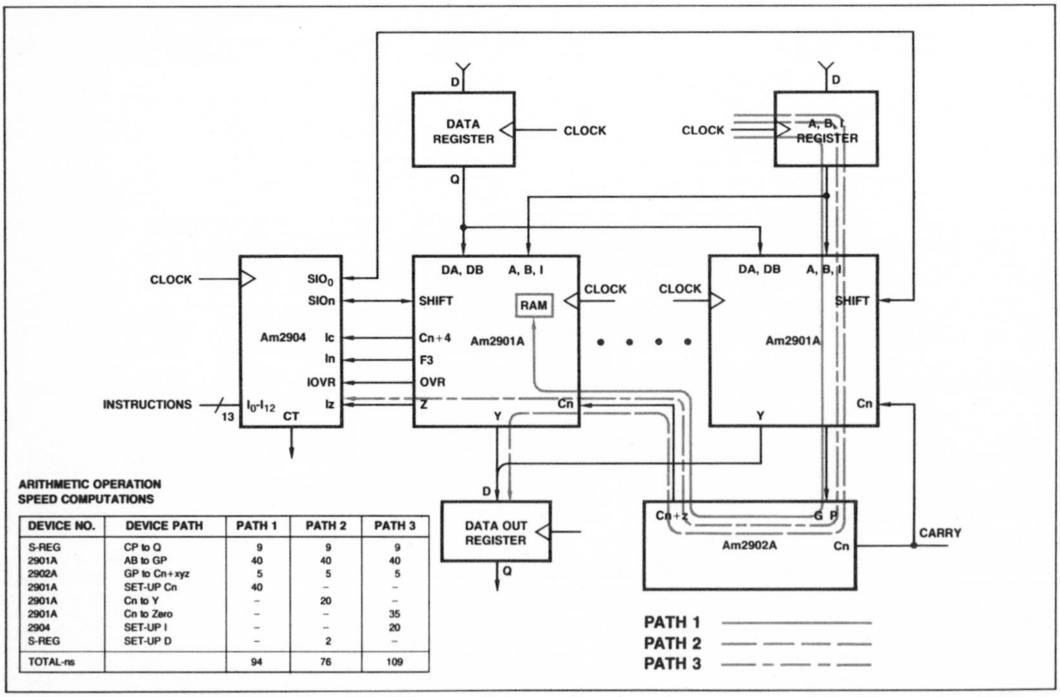

ARITHMETIC OPERATION SPEED COMPUTATIONS

DEVICE NO.	DEVICE PATH	PATH 1	PATH 2	PATH 3
S-REG	CP to Q	9	9	9
2901A	AB to GP	40	40	40
2902A	GP to Cn+xyz	5	5	5
2901A	SET-UP Cn	40	–	–
2901A	Cn to Y	–	20	–
2901A	Cn to Zero	–	–	35
2904	SET-UP I	–	–	20
S-REG	SET-UP D	–	2	–
TOTAL-ns		94	76	109

Figure 2-2.

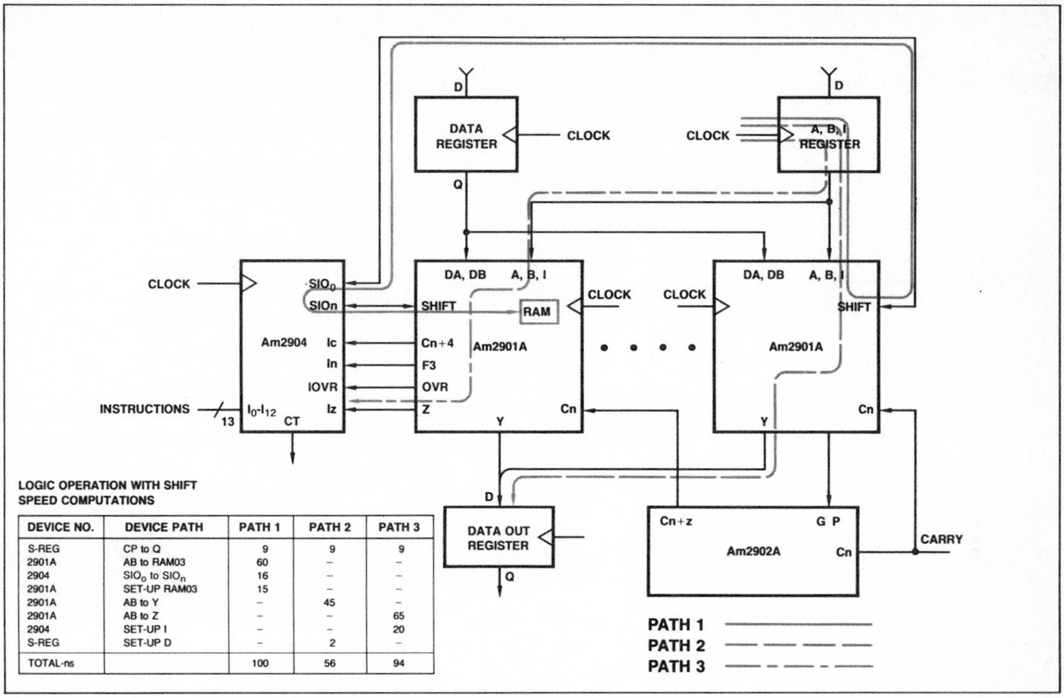

LOGIC OPERATION WITH SHIFT
SPEED COMPUTATIONS

DEVICE NO.	DEVICE PATH	PATH 1	PATH 2	PATH 3
S-REG	CP to Q	9	9	9
2901A	AB to RAM03	60	–	–
2904	SIO_0 to SIO_n	16	–	–
2901A	SET-UP RAM03	15	–	–
2901A	AB to Y	–	45	–
2901A	AB to Z	–	–	65
2904	SET-UP I	–	–	20
S-REG	SET-UP D	–	2	–
TOTAL-ns		100	56	94

Figure 2-3.

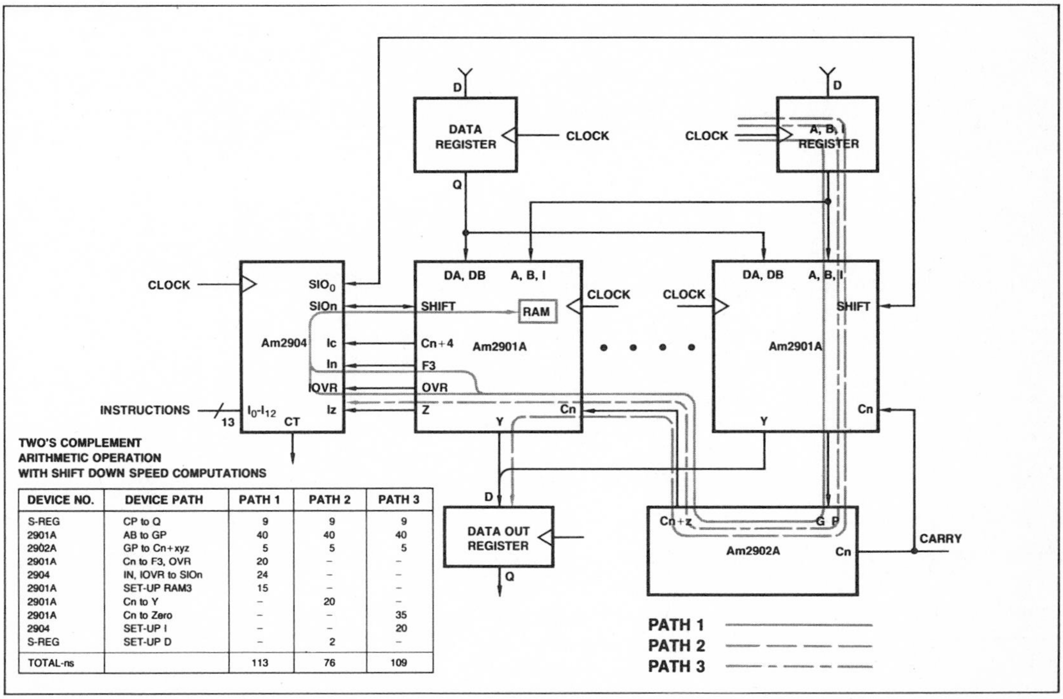

TWO'S COMPLEMENT
ARITHMETIC OPERATION
WITH SHIFT DOWN SPEED COMPUTATIONS

DEVICE NO.	DEVICE PATH	PATH 1	PATH 2	PATH 3
S-REG	CP to Q	9	9	9
2901A	AB to GP	40	40	40
2902A	GP to Cn+xyz	5	5	5
2901A	Cn to F3, OVR	20	–	–
2904	IN, IOVR to SIOn	24	–	–
2901A	SET-UP RAM3	15	–	–
2901A	Cn to Y	–	20	–
2901A	Cn to Zero	–	–	35
2904	SET-UP I	–	–	20
S-REG	SET-UP D	–	2	–
TOTAL-ns		113	76	109

Figure 2-4.

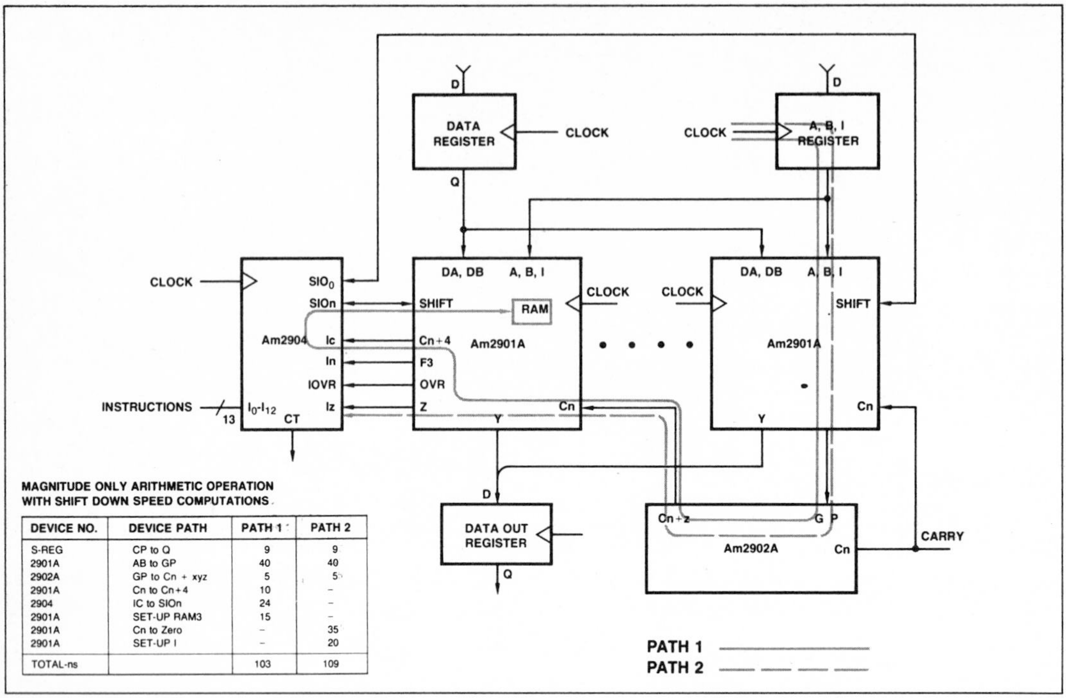

MAGNITUDE ONLY ARITHMETIC OPERATION WITH SHIFT DOWN SPEED COMPUTATIONS

DEVICE NO.	DEVICE PATH	PATH 1	PATH 2
S-REG	CP to Q	9	9
2901A	AB to GP	40	40
2902A	GP to Cn + xyz	5	5
2901A	Cn to Cn+4	10	–
2904	IC to SIOn	24	–
2901A	SET-UP RAM3	15	–
2901A	Cn to Zero	–	35
2901A	SET-UP I	–	20
TOTAL-ns		103	109

Figure 2-5.

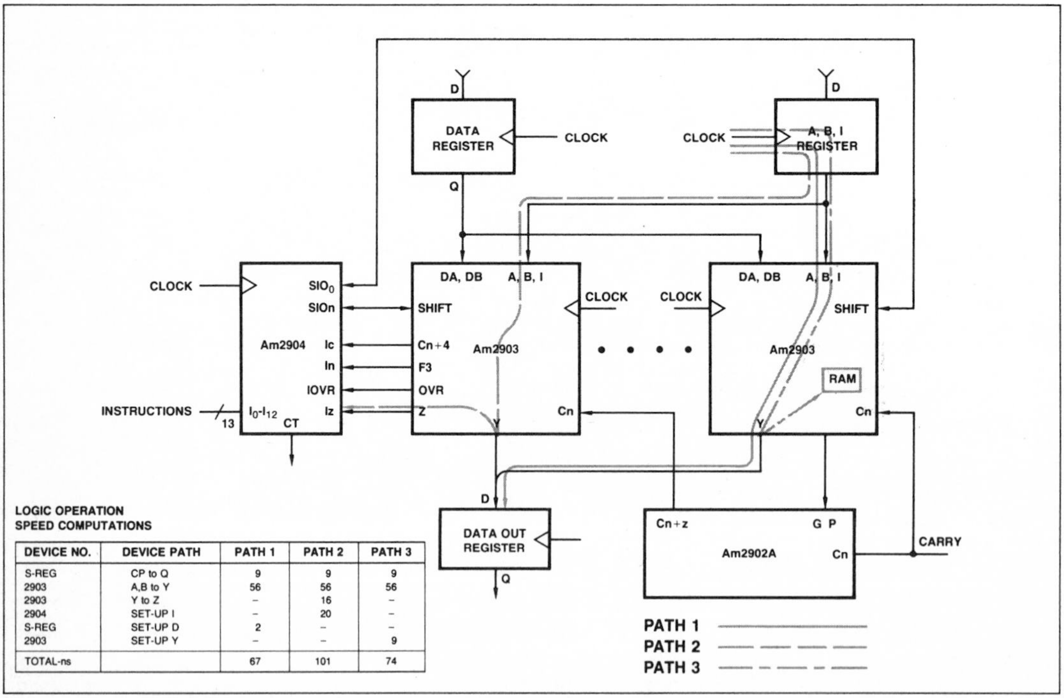

LOGIC OPERATION SPEED COMPUTATIONS

DEVICE NO.	DEVICE PATH	PATH 1	PATH 2	PATH 3
S-REG	CP to Q	9	9	9
2903	A,B to Y	56	56	56
2903	Y to Z	–	16	–
2904	SET-UP I	–	20	–
S-REG	SET-UP D	2	–	–
2903	SET-UP Y	–	–	9
TOTAL-ns		67	101	74

Figure 3-1.

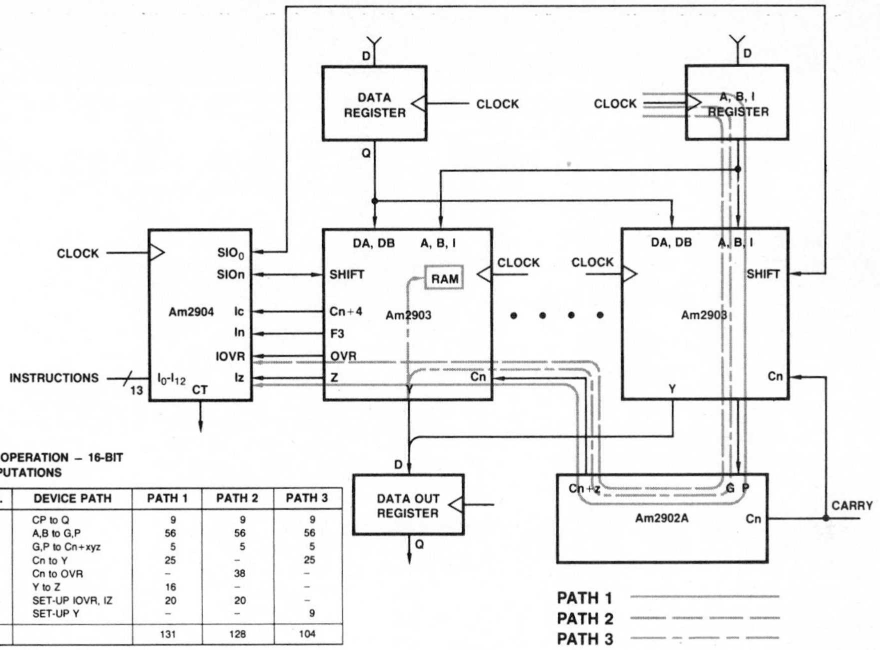

ARITHMETIC OPERATION – 16-BIT SPEED COMPUTATIONS

DEVICE NO.	DEVICE PATH	PATH 1	PATH 2	PATH 3
S-REG	CP to Q	9	9	9
2903	A,B to G,P	56	56	56
2902A	G,P to Cn+xyz	5	5	5
2903	Cn to Y	25	–	25
2903	Cn to OVR	–	38	–
2903	Y to Z	16	–	–
2904	SET-UP IOVR, IZ	20	20	–
2903	SET-UP Y	–	–	9
TOTAL-ns		131	128	104

Figure 3-2.

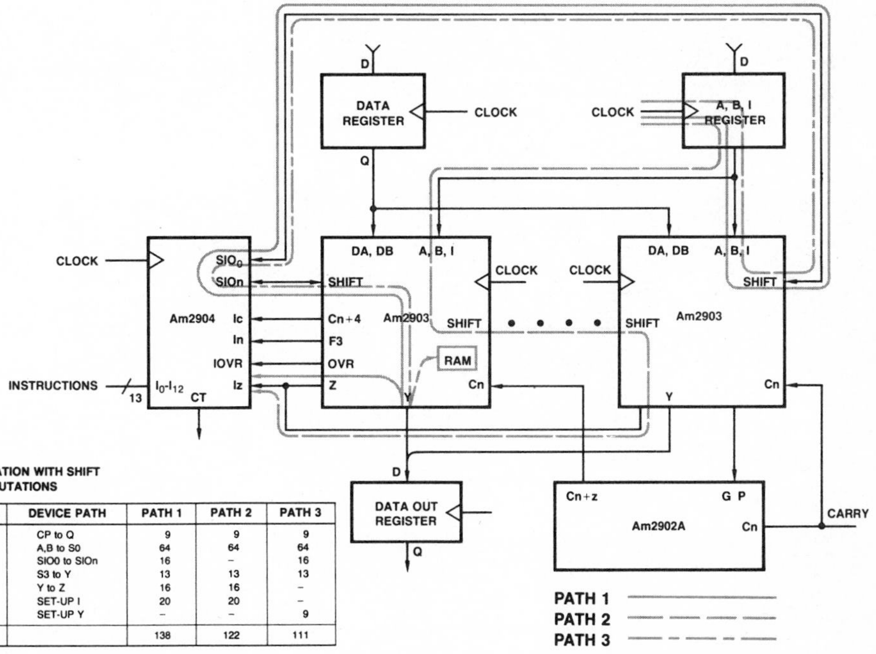

LOGIC OPERATION WITH SHIFT SPEED COMPUTATIONS

DEVICE NO.	DEVICE PATH	PATH 1	PATH 2	PATH 3
S-REG	CP to Q	9	9	9
2903	A,B to S0	64	64	64
2909	SIO0 to SIOn	16	–	16
2903	S3 to Y	13	13	13
2903	Y to Z	16	16	–
2904	SET-UP I	20	20	–
2903	SET-UP Y	–	–	9
TOTAL-ns		138	122	111

Figure 3-3.

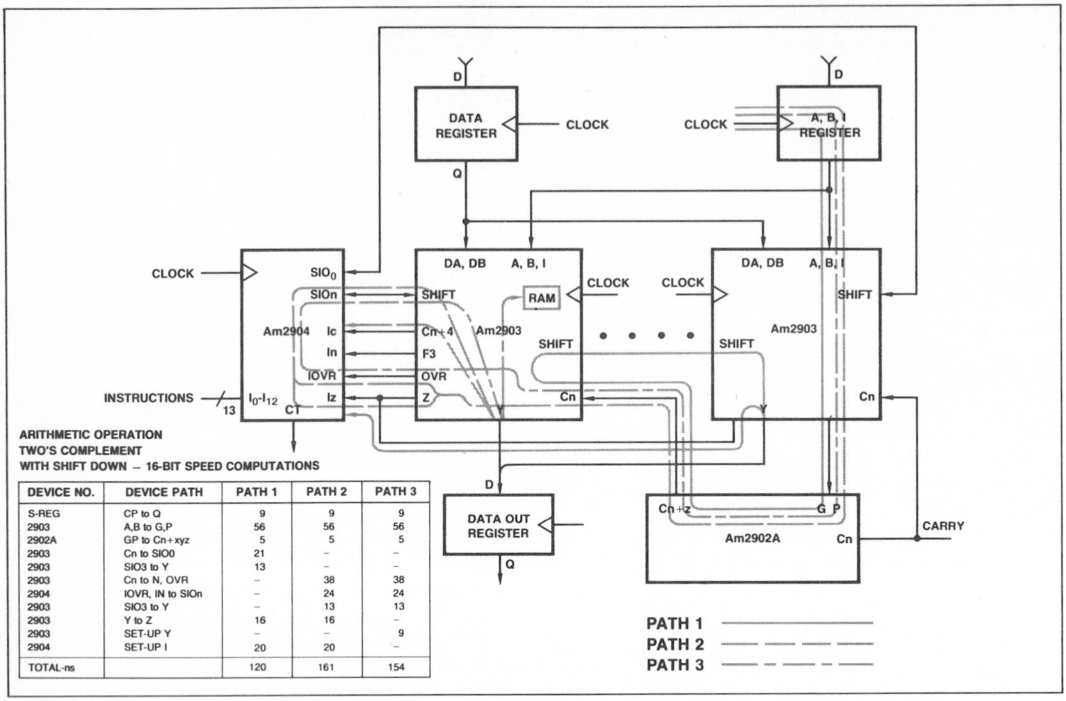

ARITHMETIC OPERATION
TWO'S COMPLEMENT
WITH SHIFT DOWN – 16-BIT SPEED COMPUTATIONS

DEVICE NO.	DEVICE PATH	PATH 1	PATH 2	PATH 3
S-REG	CP to Q	9	9	9
2903	A,B to G,P	56	56	56
2902A	GP to Cn+xyz	5	5	5
2903	Cn to SIO0	21	–	–
2903	SIO3 to Y	13	–	–
2903	Cn to N, OVR	–	38	38
2904	IOVR, IN to SIOn	–	24	24
2903	SIO3 to Y	–	13	13
2903	Y to Z	16	16	–
2903	SET-UP Y	–	–	9
2904	SET-UP I	20	20	–
TOTAL-ns		120	161	154

Figure 3-4.

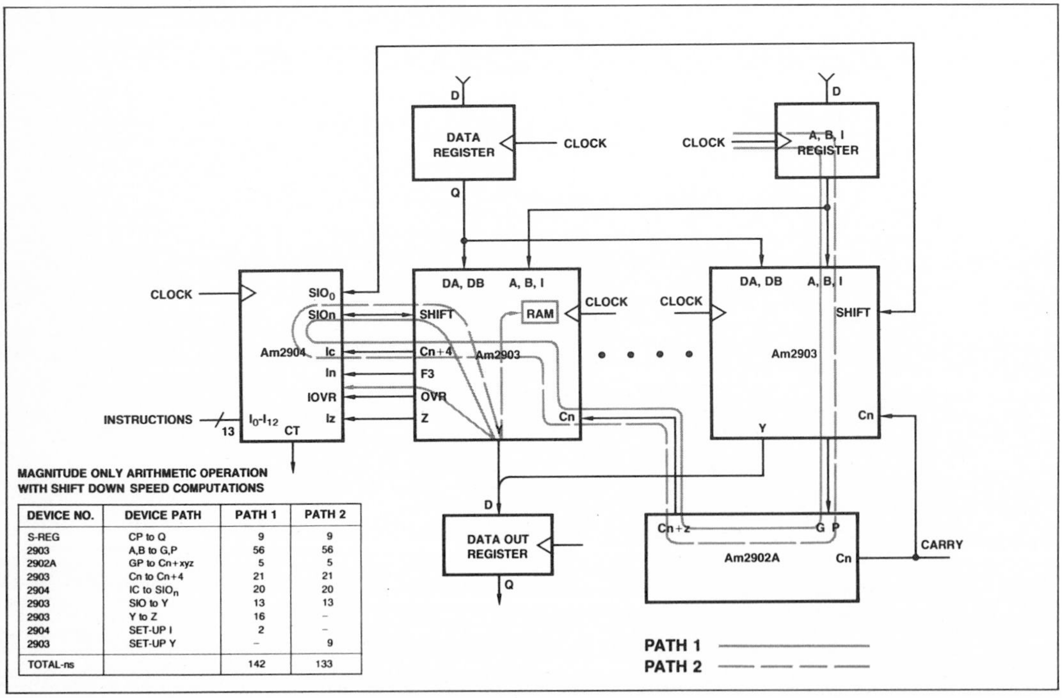

MAGNITUDE ONLY ARITHMETIC OPERATION
WITH SHIFT DOWN SPEED COMPUTATIONS

DEVICE NO.	DEVICE PATH	PATH 1	PATH 2
S-REG	CP to Q	9	9
2903	A,B to G,P	56	56
2902A	GP to Cn+xyz	5	5
2903	Cn to Cn+4	21	21
2904	IC to SIO_n	20	20
2903	SIO to Y	13	13
2903	Y to Z	16	–
2904	SET-UP I	2	–
2903	SET-UP Y	–	9
TOTAL-ns		142	133

Figure 3-5.

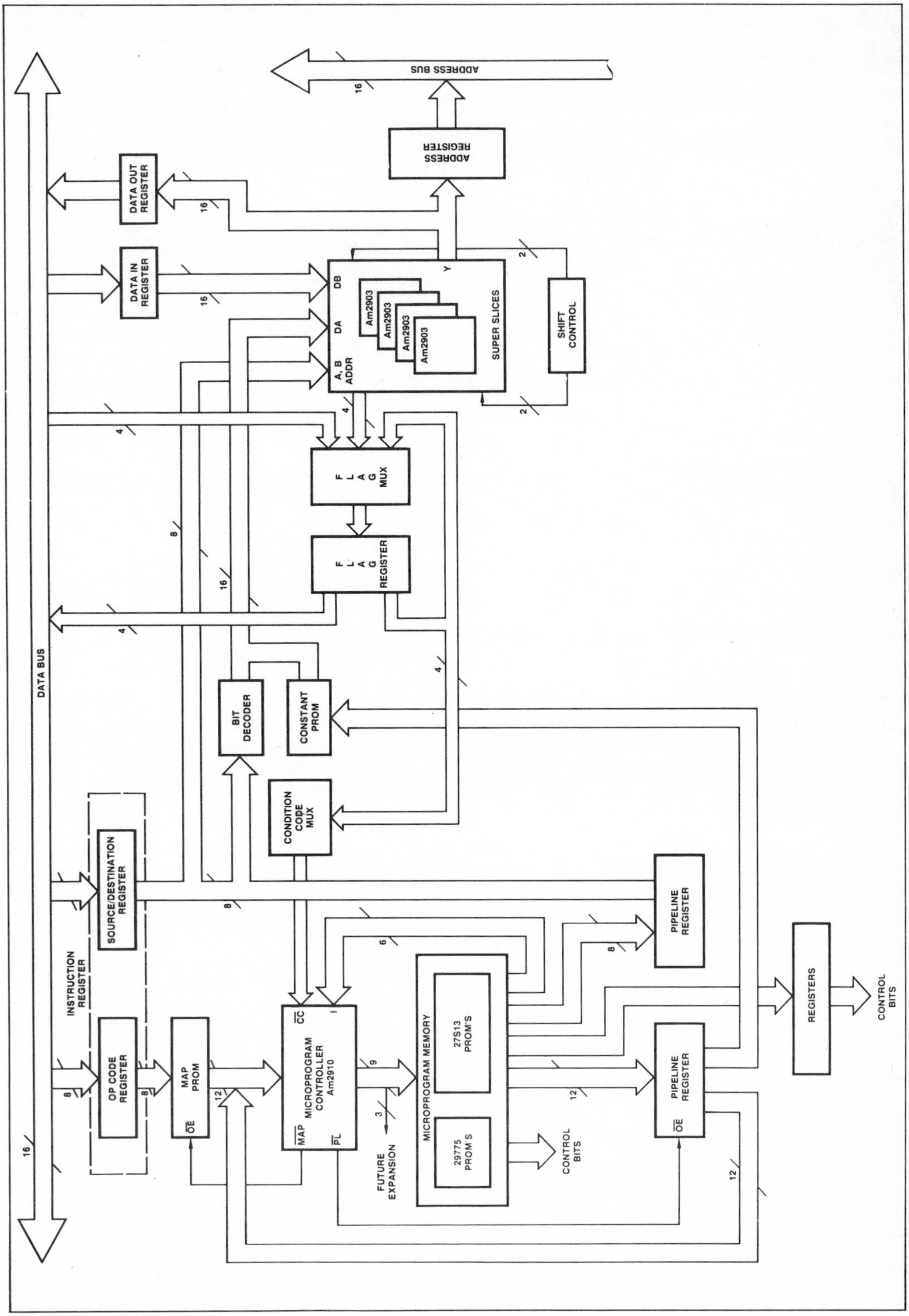
DATA BUS
ADDRESS BUS
16
DATA OUT REGISTER
DATA IN REGISTER
ADDRESS REGISTER
DB
DA
A, B ADDR
Y
Am2903
SUPER SLICES
SHIFT CONTROL
2
4
FLAG MUX
FLAG REGISTER
8
BIT DECODER
CONSTANT PROM
CONDITION CODE MUX
INSTRUCTION REGISTER
SOURCE/DESTINATION REGISTER
OP CODE REGISTER
MAP PROM
OE
MICROPROGRAM CONTROLLER Am2910
CC
I
MAP
PL
9
3
FUTURE EXPANSION
MICROPROGRAM MEMORY
27S13 PROM'S
29775 PROM'S
CONTROL BITS
6
12
PIPELINE REGISTER
REGISTERS

Figure 4a.

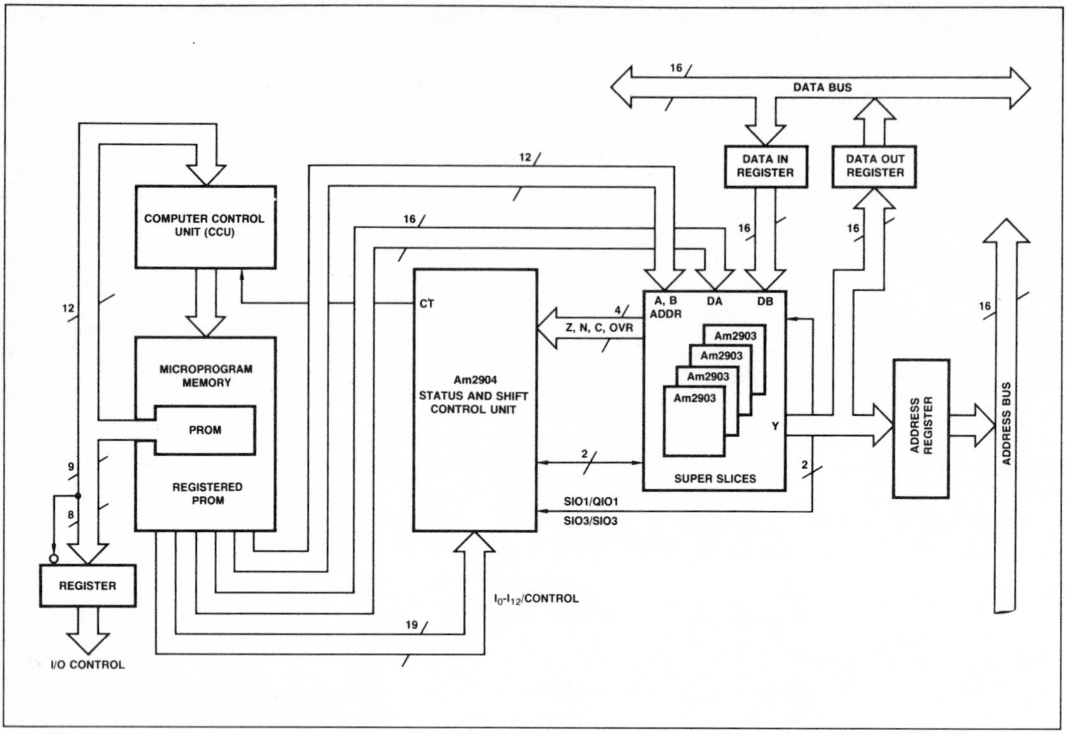

Figure 4b.

TABLE 9. TIMING ANALYSIS SUMMARY (ns).

Operation	Am2901A	Am2903
Logic	94	101
Arithmetic	109	131
Logic w/Shift	100	138
Two's Complement Arithmetic with Shift Down	113	161
Magnitude only Arithmetic with Shift Down	109	142

THE MICROPROGRAM STRUCTURE

The functions of the pipelined (PL) microprogram bits are illustrated in Figure 5 and as follows:

Bits PL0 through PL11 This is a shared control field. The field is used for branching to a microprogram address or to load the CCU counter or control bits for I/O.

Bit PL12 The shared control field is determined by PL12, LOW for branching and counting or HIGH for I/O control.

Bit PL13 When LOW, enables the $\overline{WRITE}$ output and allows the Q Register and Sign Compare flip-flop to be written into.

Bits PL14 and PL15 The $\overline{CE\mu}$ and $\overline{SE}$ control inputs of the Am2904, respectively. $\overline{CE\mu}$ enables the Micro Status Register. $\overline{SE}$ enables the Am2904 shift operations.

Bits PL16 through PL19 CCU Next Address.

Bits PL20 through PL23 CCU Multiplex test select.

Bit PL24 This bit determines the polarity of the incoming test signal to the CCU.

Bit PL25 Active LOW Instruction Register enable.

Bits PL26 through PL29 CCU multi-way branching select.

Bits PL30 through PL32 Selects the ALU operand sources.

PL30	PL31	PL32	ALU Operand R	ALU Operand S
L	L	L	RAM Output A	RAM Output B
L	L	H	RAM Output A	DB_{0-3}
L	H	X	RAM Output A	Q Register
H	L	L	DA_{0-3}	RAM Output B
H	L	H	DA_{0-3}	DB_{0-3}
H	H	X	DA_{0-3}	Q Register

L = LOW H = HIGH X = Don't Care

Bits PL33 through PL36 — Selects the ALU functions.

I_4	I_3	I_2	I_1	Hex Code	ALU Functions	
L	L	L	L	0	I_0 = L	Special Functions
					I_0 = H	F_i = HIGH
L	L	L	H	1	F = S Minus R Minus 1 Plus C_n	
L	L	H	L	2	F = R Minus S Minus 1 Plus C_n	
L	L	H	H	3	F = R Plus S Plus C_n	
L	H	L	L	4	F = S Plus C_n	
L	H	L	H	5	F = $\overline{S}$ Plus C_n	
L	H	H	L	6	F = R Plus C_n	
L	H	H	H	7	F = $\overline{R}$ Plus C_n	
H	L	L	L	8	F_i = LOW	
H	L	L	H	9	F_i = $\overline{R}_i$ AND S_i	
H	L	H	L	A	F_i = R_i EXCLUSIVE NOR S_i	
H	L	H	H	B	F_i = R_i EXCLUSIVE OR S_i	
H	H	L	L	C	F_i = R_i AND S_i	
H	H	L	H	D	F_i = R_i NOR S_i	
H	H	H	L	E	F_i = R_i NAND S_i	
H	H	H	H	F	F_i = R_i OR S_i	

L = LOW H = HIGH i = 0 to 3

Bits PL37 through 40 — Selects the ALU destination controls.

I_8	I_7	I_6	I_5	Hex Code	Special Function
L	L	L	L	0	Unsigned Multiply
L	L	H	L	2	Two's Complement Multiply
L	H	L	L	4	Increment by One or Two
L	H	L	H	5	Sign/Magnitude-Two's Complement
L	H	H	L	6	Two's Complement Multiply, Last Cycle
H	L	L	L	8	Single Length Normalize
H	L	H	L	A	Double Length Normalize and First Divide Op.
H	H	L	L	C	Two's Complement Divide
H	H	H	L	E	Two's Complement Divide, Correction and Remainder

Bits PL41 through PL44 — This 4-bit wide field is used for the A-address source.

Bits PL45 through PL48 — This 4-bit wide field is used for the B-address source.

Bits PL49 through PL52 — This 4-bit wide field is the B destination address into which new data is written.

Bit PL53 — Am2903 control input $\overline{OE}_Y$. When LOW enables the ALU shifter output data onto the Y bus.

Bits PL54 through PL59 — Am2904 instruction code field.

Bits PL60 through PL63 — Am2904 shift linkage multiplexer instruction code field.

Bits PL64 and PL65 — Am2904 "carry-in" control multiplexer field.

Bits PL66 through PL68 — The $\overline{CE}_M$, $\overline{OE}_{CT}$, $\overline{OE}_Y$ control inputs of the Am2904, respectively.

Bit PL69 — This bit when LOW, enables bits PL74 through PL89 onto the Am2903 DA Bus.

Bit PL70 — When LOW, zeros the carry in's to the Am2903 slices.

Bit PL71 — When HIGH, enables a status register used in BCD calculations.

Bit PL72 — When LOW, clears the status register.

Bit PL73 — When LOW, enables Am2909/11 registers.

Bits PL74 through PL89 — This field contains a 16-bit constant from microcode that is passed to the Am2903's via the DA bus. Constant is enabled by PL69.

I_0 OR I_1 OR I_2 OR I_4 = HIGH, $\overline{I_{EN}}$ = LOW

I_8	I_7	I_6	I_5	Hex Code	ALU Shifter Function	SIO_3 Most Sig. Slice	SIO_3 Other Slices	Y_3 Most Sig. Slice	Y_3 Other Slices	Y_2 Most Sig. Slice	Y_2 Other Slices	Y_1	Y_0	SIO_0	$\overline{Write}$	Q Reg & Shifter Function	QIO_3	QIO_0
L	L	L	L	0	Arith. F/2→Y	Input	Input	F_3	SIO_3	SIO_3	F_3	F_2	F_1	F_0	L	Hold	Hi-Z	Hi-Z
L	L	L	H	1	Log. F/2→Y	Input	Input	SIO_3	SIO_3	F_3	F_3	F_2	F_1	F_0	L	Hold	Hi-Z	Hi-Z
L	L	H	L	2	Arith. F/2→Y	Input	Input	F_3	SIO_3	SIO_3	F_3	F_2	F_1	F_0	L	Log. Q/2→Q	Input	Q_0
L	L	H	H	3	Log. F/2→Y	Input	Input	SIO_3	SIO_3	F_3	F_3	F_2	F_1	F_0	L	Log. Q/2→Q	Input	Q_0
L	H	L	L	4	F→Y	Input	Input	F_3	F_3	F_2	F_2	F_1	F_0	Parity	L	Hold	Hi-Z	Hi-Z
L	H	L	H	5	F→Y	Input	Input	F_3	F_3	F_2	F_2	F_1	F_0	Parity	H	Log. Q/2→Q	Input	Q_0
L	H	H	L	6	F→Y	Input	Input	F_3	F_3	F_2	F_2	F_1	F_0	Parity	H	F→Q	Hi-Z	Hi-Z
L	H	H	H	7	F→Y	Input	Input	F_3	F_3	F_2	F_2	F_1	F_0	Parity	L	F→Q	Hi-Z	Hi-Z
H	L	L	L	8	Arith. 2F→Y	F_2	F_3	F_3	F_2	F_1	F_1	F_0	SIO_0	Input	L	Hold	Hi-Z	Hi-Z
H	L	L	H	9	Log. 2F→Y	F_3	F_3	F_2	F_2	F_1	F_1	F_0	SIO_0	Input	L	Hold	Hi-Z	Hi-Z
H	L	H	L	A	Arith. 2F→Y	F_2	F_3	F_3	F_2	F_1	F_1	F_0	SIO_0	Input	L	Log. 2Q→Q	Q_3	Input
H	L	H	H	B	Log. 2F→Y	F_3	F_3	F_2	F_2	F_1	F_1	F_0	SIO_0	Input	L	Log. 2Q→Q	Q_3	Input
H	H	L	L	C	F→Y	F_3	F_3	F_3	F_3	F_2	F_2	F_1	F_0	Hi-Z	H	Hold	Hi-Z	Hi-Z
H	H	L	H	D	F→Y	F_3	F_3	F_3	F_3	F_2	F_2	F_1	F_0	Hi-Z	H	Log. 2Q→Q	Q_3	Input
H	H	H	L	E	SIO_0→Y_0, Y_1, Y_2, Y_3	SIO_0	SIO_0	SIO_0	SIO_0	SIO_0	SIO_0	SIO_0	SIO_0	Input	L	Hold	Hi-Z	Hi-Z
H	H	H	H	F	F→Y	F_3	F_3	F_3	F_3	F_2	F_2	F_1	F_0	Hi-Z	L	Hold	Hi-Z	Hi-Z

The Am2903 special functions can be selected by the following conditions: $I_0 = I_1 = I_2 = I_3 = I_4$ = LOW, $\overline{I_{EN}}$ = LOW

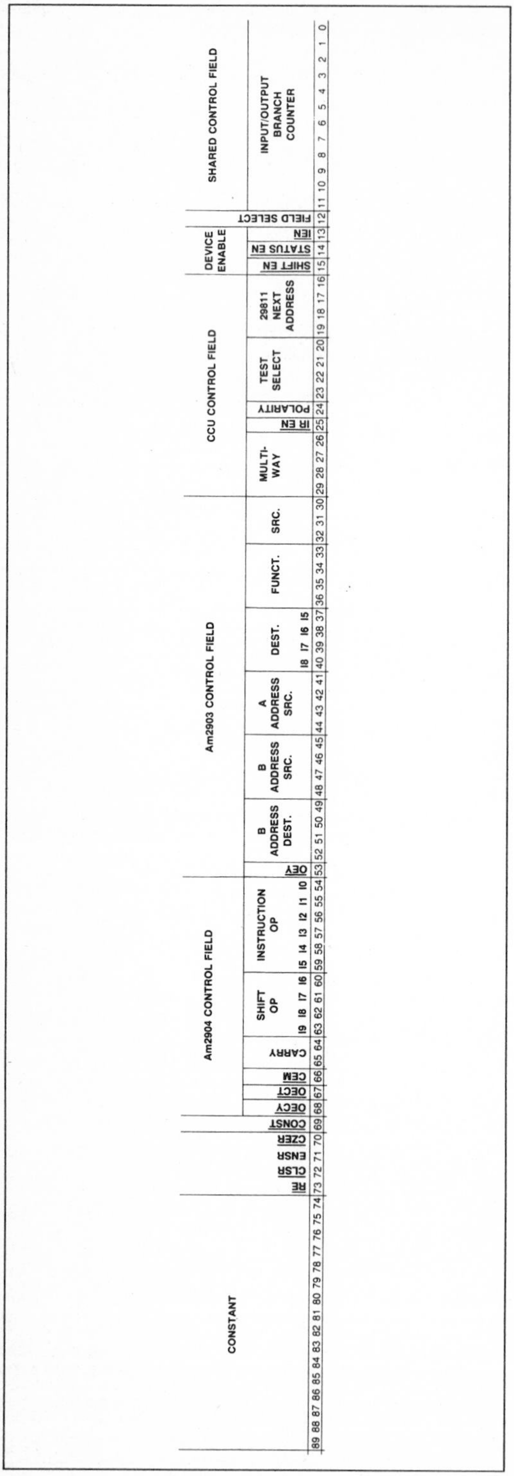

Figure 5.

SOME SAMPLE MICROROUTINES

The following algorithms are implemented using the Am2903 Superslices™ and Am2904 status and shift control unit. The algorithms were developed with the aid of AMDASM on System 29. All algorithms assume values and constants to be initialized prior to the entrance of the algorithms. Appendix A relates the actual microcode to the microword fields. Appendix B is the AMDASM Phase 1 and Phase 2 listings of the microprograms and the definitions of mnemonics. Figure 4b is a block diagram of the CPU hardware including the Am2904 Status and Shift Control Unit from which the microroutines were developed. A detailed diagram of the CPU hardware is in Appendix C.

Normalization, Single- and Double-Length

Normalization is used as a means of referencing a number to a fixed radix point. Normalization strips out all leading sign bits such that the two bits immediately adjacent to the radix point are of opposite polarity.

Normalization is commonly used in such operations as fixed-to-floating point conversion and division. The Am2903 provides for normalization by using the Single-Length and Double-Length Normalize commands. Figure 6a represents the Q Register of a 16-bit processor which contains a positive number. When the Single-Length Normalize command is applied, each positive edge of the clock will cause the bits to shift toward the most significant bit (bit 15) of the Q Register. Zeros are shifted in via the QIO0 port. When the bits on either side of the radix point (bits 14 and 15) are of opposite value, the number is considered to be normalized as shown in Figure 6b. The event of normalization is externally indicated by a HIGH level on the Cn+4 pin of the most significant slice (Cn+4 MSS = Q3 MSS ⊻ Q2 MSS).

There are also provisions made for a normalization indication via the OVR pin one microcycle before the same indication is available on the Cn+4 pin (OVR = Q2 MSS ⊻ Q1 MSS). This is for use in applications that require a stage of register buffering of the normalization indication.

Since a number comprised of all zeros is not considered for normalization, the Am2903 indicates when wuch a condition arises. If the Q Register is zero and the Single-Length Normalization command is given, a HIGH level will be present on the Z line.

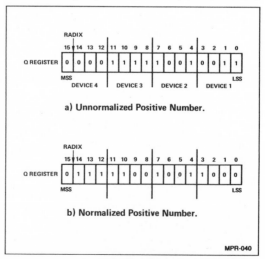

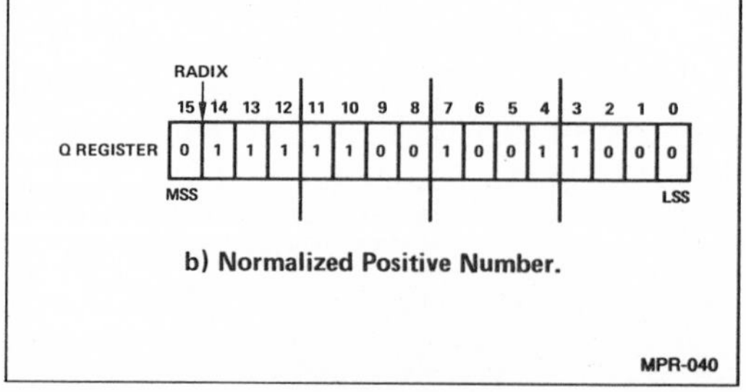

Figure 6.

The sign output, N, indicates the sign of the number stored in the Q register, Q3 MSS. An unnormalized negative number (Figure 7a) is normalized in the same manner as a positive number. The results of single-length normalization are shown in Figure 7b. The device interconnection for single-length normalization is outlined in Figure 8. During single-length normalization, the number of shifts performed to achieve normalization can be counted and stored in one of the working registers. This can be achieved by forcing a HIGH at the Cn input of the least significant slice, since during this special function the ALU performs the function [B] + Cn and the result is stored in B. Figure 9 illustrates the single-length normalize. However, the microcode is shown in Figure 10. Microcode for both single and double normalization can be reduced by one step by testing for zero during passing of number into Q.

Normalizing a double-length word can be done with the Double-Length Normalize command which assumes that a user-selected RAM Register contains the most significant portion of the word to be normalized while the Q Register holds the least significant half (Figure 11.) The device interconnection for double-length normalization is shown in Figure 12. The Cn+4, OVR, N, and Z outputs of the most significant slice perform the same functions in double-length normalization as they did in single-length normalization except that Cn+4, OVR, and N are derived from the output of the ALU of the most significant slice in the case of double-length normalization, instead of the Q Register of the most significant slice as in single-length normalization. A high-level Z line in double-length normalization reveals that the outputs of the ALU and Q Register are both zero, hence indicating that the double-length word is zero.

When double-length normalization is being performed, shift counting is done either with an extra microcycle or with an external counter. Figure 13 illustrates the double-length normalize flowchart and Figure 14 shows the microcode.

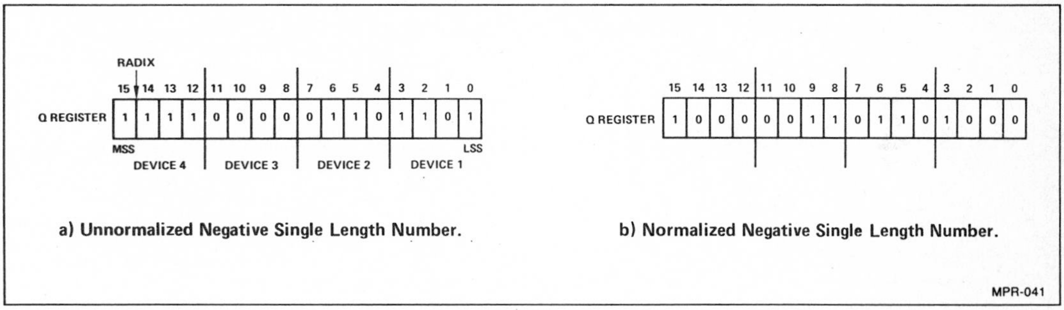

Figure 7.

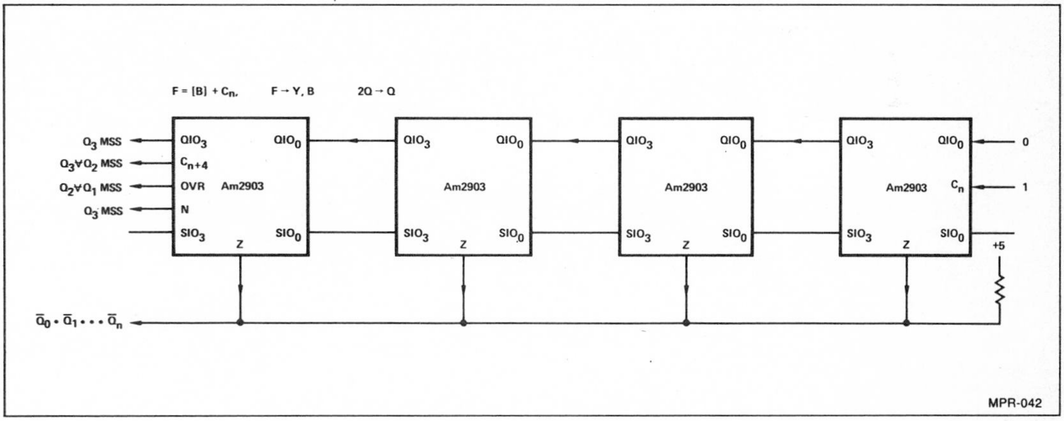

Figure 8. Single Length Normalize.

Unsigned Multiply

This Special Function allows for easy implementation of unsigned multiplication. Figure 15 is the unsigned multiply flow chart. The algorithm requires that initially the RAM word addressed by Address port B be zero, that the multiplier be in the Q Register, and that the multiplicand be in the register addressed by Address port A. The initial conditions for the execution of the algorithm are that: 1) register R_1 be reset to zero; 2) the multiplicand be in R_0 and 3) the multiplier be in R_{15}. The first operation transfers the multiplier, R_{15}, to the Q Register. The Unsigned Multiply instruction is then executed 16 times. During the Unsigned Multiply instruction, R1 is addressed by RAM address port B and the multiplicand is addressed by RAM address port A.

When the unsigned Multiply command is given, the Z pin of device 1 becomes an output while the Z pins of the remaining devices are specified as inputs as shown in Figure 18. The Z output of device 1 is the same state as the least significant bit of the multiplier in the Q Register. The Z output of device 1 informs

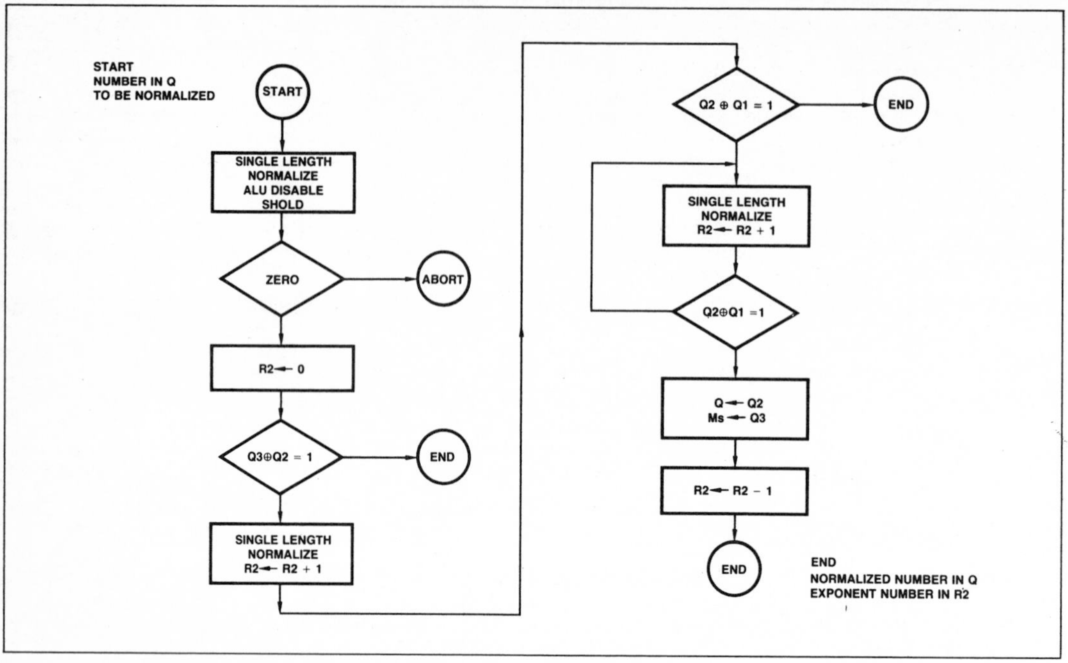

Figure 9. Single Length Normalize.

```
013C          SLN R2,R2,OFF & CONT & SHOLD
013D          MAZ & T & CJP & GOTO ABORT
013E          MAC & T & LOW R0 & CJP & GOTO END
013F          SLN R2,R2 & MAO & T & CJP ONE & GOTO END & SUL
0140  AGAIN:  SLN R2,R2 & MIO & T & CJP ONE & GOTO AGAIN & SUL
0141          SDQP & SMS & CONT
0142          SRS R2,R2,R0 & CONT
```

Figure 10.

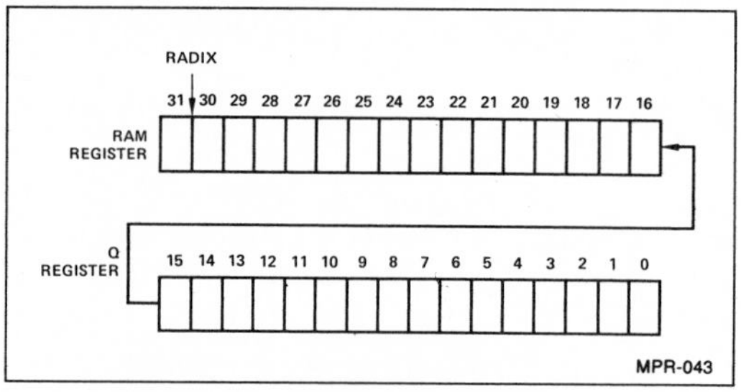

Figure 11. Double Length Word.

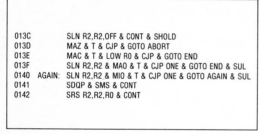

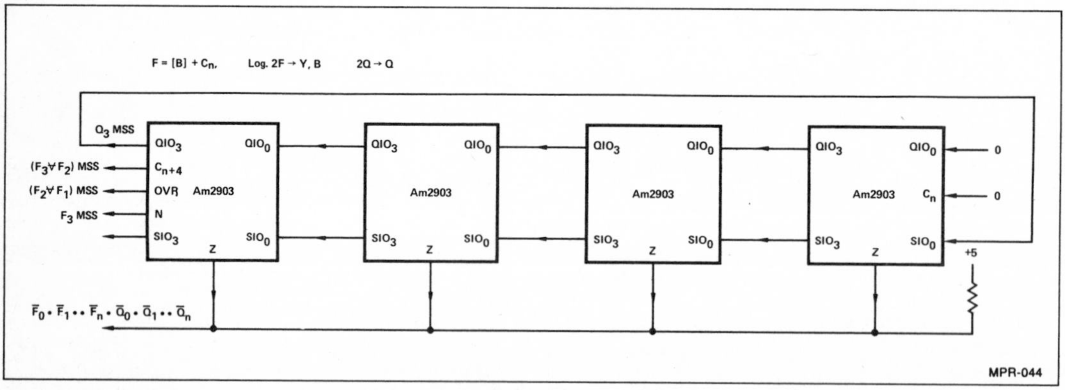

Figure 12. Double Length Normalize.

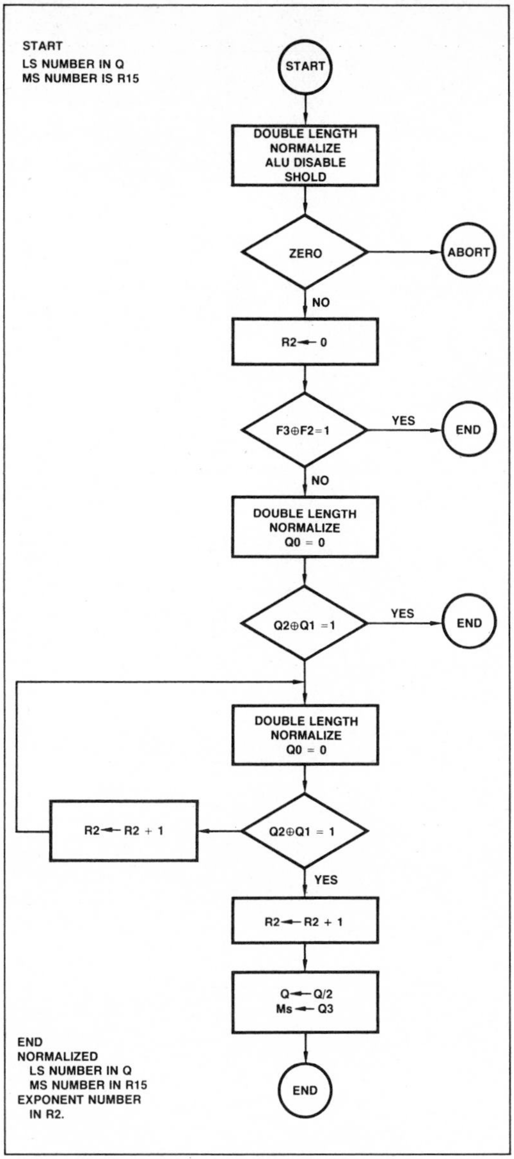

Figure 13. Double Length Normalize.

```
0148           DLN R15,R15,OFF & CONT & SHOLD
0149           MAZ & T & CJP & GOTO ABORT
014A           LOW R2 & MAC & T & CJP & GOTO END2
014B           DLN R15,R15 & SDUL & MAO & T & CJP & GOTO JUMP1
014C  LOOP4:   DLN R15,R15 & SDUL & MIO & T & CJP & GOTO JUMP1
014D           PAR R2,R2 & JP ONE & GOTO LOOP4
014E  JUMP1:   PAR R2,R2 & CONT ONE
014F           SDRQ R15, R15 & SDMS & END
```

Figure 14.

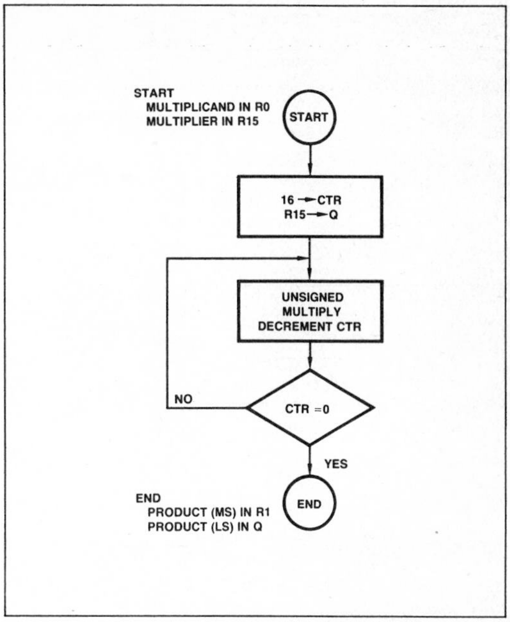

Figure 15. Unsigned 16 X 16 Multiply.

the ALUs of all the slices, via their Z pins, to add the partial product (referenced by the B address port) to the multiplicand (referenced by the A address port) if Z = 1. If Z = 0, the output of the ALU is simply the partial product (referenced by the B address port). Since Cn is held LOW, it is not a factor in the computation. Each positive-going edge of the clock will internally shift the ALU outputs toward the least significant bit and simultaneously store the shifted results in the register selected by the B address port, thus becoming the new partial sum. During the down shifting process, the Cn+4 generated in device 4 is internally shifted into the Y_3 position of device 4. At this time, one bit of the multiplier will down shift out of the QIO_0 ports of each device into the QIO_3 port of the next less significant slice. The partial product is shifted down between chips in a like manner, between the SIO_0 and SIO_3 ports, with SIO_0 of device 1 being connected to QIO_3 of device 4 for purposes of constructing a 32-bit long register to hold the 32-bit product. Shifting of the partial product between the B address and Q registers are accomplished via the Am2904. At the finish of the 16 x 16 multiply, the most significant 16 bits of the product will be found in the register referenced by the B address lines while the least significant 16 bits are stored in the Q Register. Using a typical Computer Control Unit (CCU), as shown in Appendix C, the unsigned multiply operation requires only two lines of microcode, as shown in Figure 16, and is executed in 17 microcycles.

```
010C        LQPT R15 & F & GRD & PUSH & COUNT 00E
010D        UMUL R1,R1,R0 & F & CNT & SDDL & RFCT
```

Figure 16.

Two's Complement Multiplication

The algorithm for two's complement multiplication is illustrated by Figure 17. The initial conditions for two's complement multiplication are the same as for the unsigned multiply operation. The Two's Complement Multiply Command is applied for 15 clock cycles in the case of a 16 x 16 multiply. During the down shifting process the term N ∀ OVR generated in device 4 is internally shifted into the Y_3 position of device 4. The data flow shown in Figure 18a is still valid. After 15 cycles, the sign bit of the multiplier is present at the Z output of device 1. At this time, the user must place the Two's Complement Multiply Last cycle command on the instruction lines. The interconnection for this instruction is shown in Figure 18b. On the next positive edge of the clock, the Am2903 will adjust the partial product, if the sign of the multiplier is negative, by subtracting out the two's complement representation of the multiplicand. If the sign bit is positive, the partial product is not adjusted. At this point, two's complement multiplication is completed. Using a typical CCU, as shown in Appendix C, the two's complement multiply operation requires only three lines of microcode, as shown in Figure 19, and is executed in 17 microcycles.

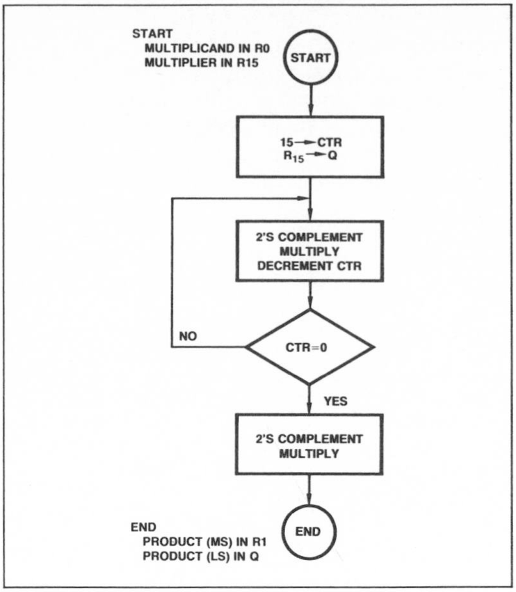

Figure 17. 2's Complement 16 X 16 Multiply.

TWO'S COMPLEMENT DIVISION

The division process is accomplished using a four quadrant non-restoring algorithm which yields an algebraically correct answer such that the divisor times the quotient plus the remainder equals the dividend. The algorithm works for both single precision and

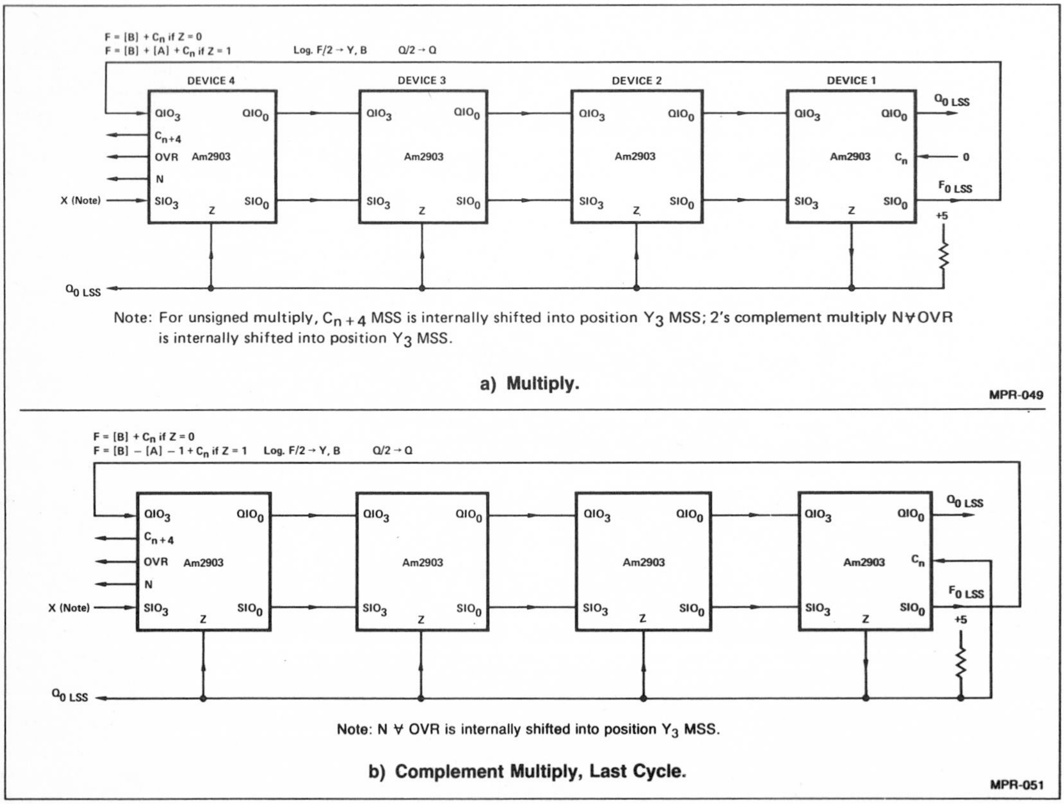

Figure 18.

```
0113    LQPT R15 & F & GRD & PUSH & COUNT 00D
0114    TCM R1,R1,R0 & F & CNT & SDDL & RFCT
0115    TCMC R1,R1,R0 & SDDL & CONT CZ
```

Figure 19.

multi-precision divide operations. The only condition that needs to be met is that the absolute magnitude of the divisor be greater than the absolute magnitude of the dividend. For multi-precision divide operations the least significant bit of the dividend is truncated. This is necessary if the answer is to be algebraically correct. Bias correction is automatically provided by forcing the least significant bit of the quotient to a one, yet an algebraically correct answer is still maintained. Once the algorithm is completed, the answer may be modified to meet the user's format requirements, such as rounding off or converting the remainder so that its sign is the same as the dividend. These format modifications are accomplished using the standard Am2903 instructions.

The true value of the remainder is equal to the value stored in the working register times 2^{n-1} when n is the number of quotient digits.

The following paragraphs describe a double precision divide operator.

Referring to the flow chart outlined in Figure 20, we begin the algorithm with the assumption that the divisor is contained in R_0, while the most significant and least significant halves of the dividend reside in R_1 and R_4 respectively. The first step is to duplicate the divisor by copying the contents of R_0 into R_3. Next the most significant half of the dividend is copied by transferring the contents of R_1 into R_2 while simultaneously checking to ascertain if the divisor (R_0) is zero. If the divisor is zero then division is aborted. If the divisor is not zero, the copy of the most significant half of the dividend in R_2 is converted from its two's complement to its sign magnitude representation. The divisor in R_3 is converted in like manner in

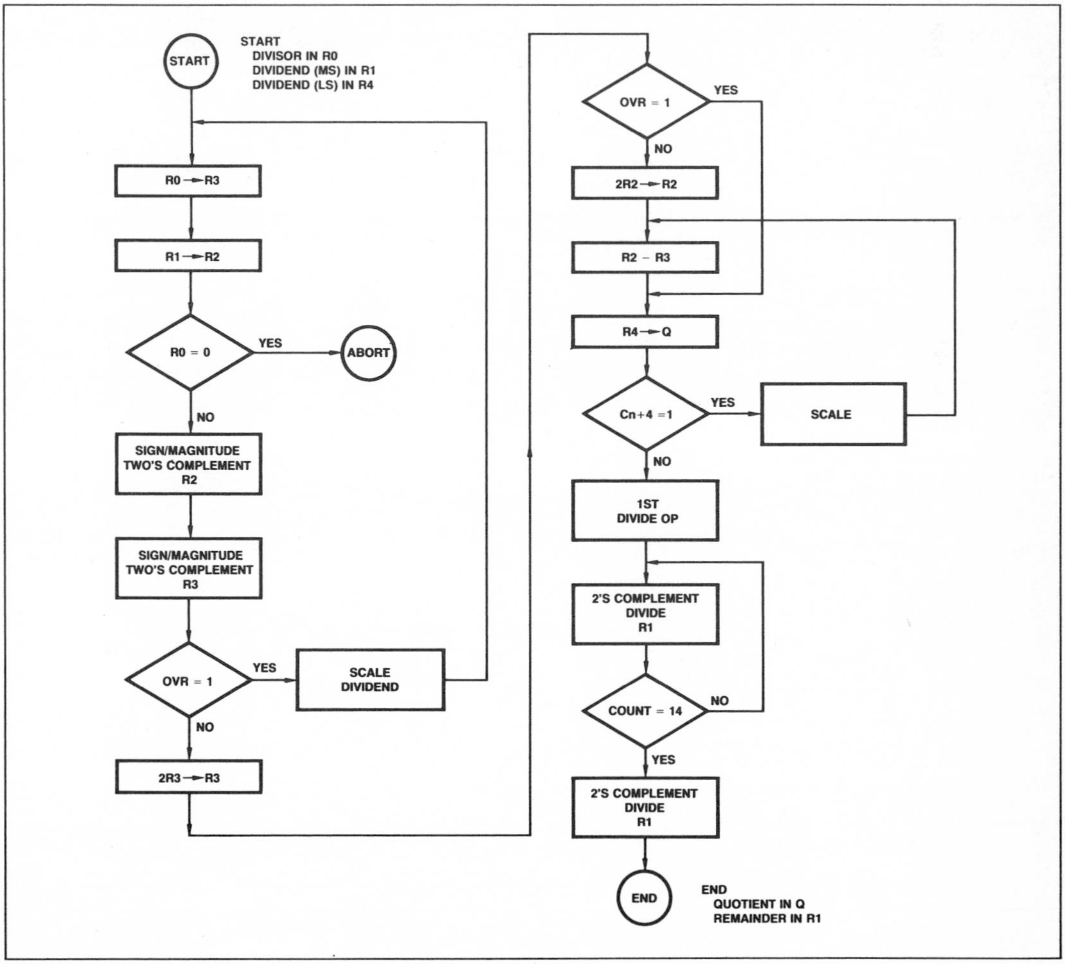

Figure 20. Two's Complement Division.

the next step, while testing to see if the results of the dividend conversion yielded an indication on the overflow pin of the Am2903. If the output of the overflow pin is 'one' then the dividend is -2^n and hence is the largest possible number, meaning that it cannot be less than the divisor. What must be done in this case is to scale the dividend by down shifting the upper and lower halves stored in R_1 and R_4 respectively. After scaling, the routine requires that the algorithm be reinitiated at the beginning.

Conversely, if the output of the overflow pin is not a one, the sign magnitude representation of the divisor (R_3) is shifted up in the Am2903, removing the sign while at the same time testing the results of two's complement to sign magnitude conversion of the divisor in the Am2910. If the results of the test indicate that the divisor is -2^n i.e., overflow equals one, then the lower half of the dividend is placed in the Q register and division may proceed. This is possible because the divisor is now guaranteed to be greater than the dividend. If overflow is not a one then we must proceed by shifting out the sign of the sign magnitude representation of the dividend stored in R_2. At this point we are able to check if the divisor is greater than the dividend by subtracting the absolute value of the divisor (R_3) from the absolute value of the upper half of the dividend (R_2) and storing the results in R_3. Next, the least significant half of the dividend is transferred from R_4 to the Q register while simultaneously testing the carry from the result of the divisor/dividend subtraction. If the carry (Cn+4) is one, indicating the divisor is not greater than the dividend then a scaling operation must occur. This involves either shifting up the divisor or shifting down the dividend. If the carry is not one then the divisor is greater than the dividend and division may now begin.

The first divide operation is used to ascertain the sign bit of the quotient. The two's complement divide instruction is then executed repetitively, fourteen times in the case of a sixteen bit divisor and a thirty-two bit dividend. The final step is the two's complement correction command which adjusts the quotient by allowing the least significant bit of the quotient to be set to one. At the end of the division algorithm the sixteen bit quotient is found in the Q register while the remainder now replaces the most significant half of the dividend in R_1. It should be noted that the remainder must be shifted down fifteen places to represent its true value. The interconnections for these instructions are shown in Figures 21, 22, 23. Using a typical CCU as shown in Appendix C, the double precision divide operation microcode, is shown in Figure 24.

For those applications that require truncation instead of bias correction, the same algorithm as above should be implemented except one additional Two's Complement Divide instruction should be used in lieu of the Two's Complement Divide Correction and Remainder instruction. However, this technique results in an invalid remainder.

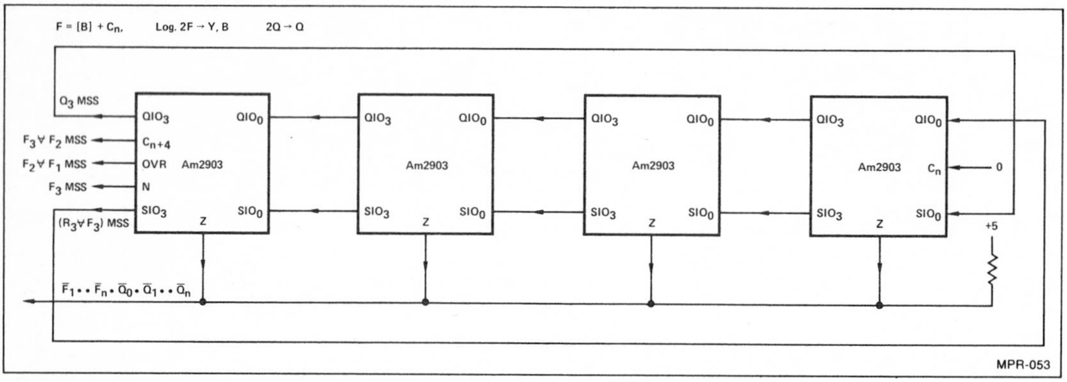

Figure 21. Double Length Normalize/First Divide Operation.

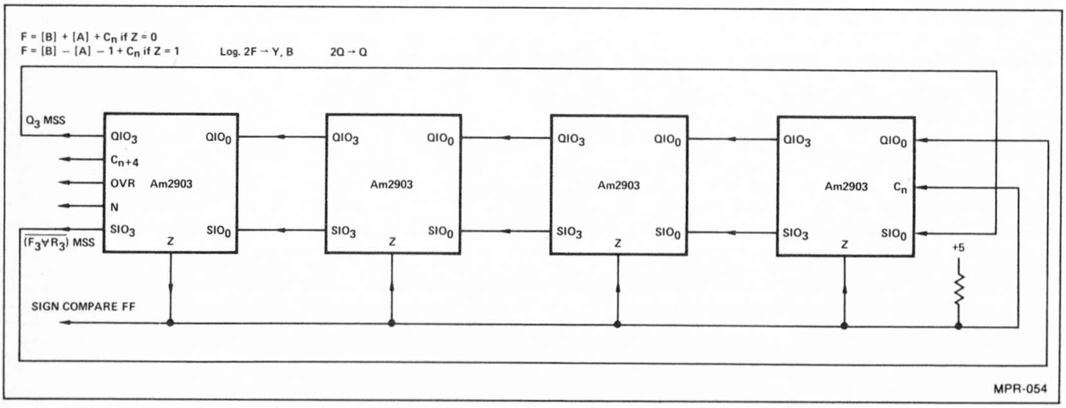

Figure 22. 2's Complement Divide.

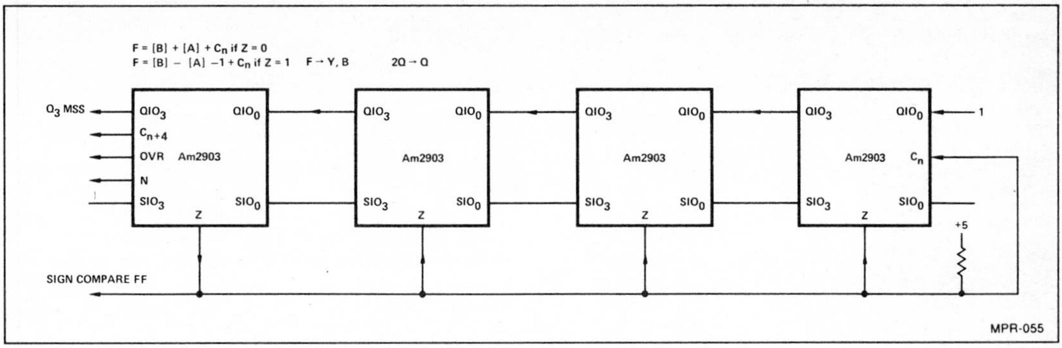

Figure 23. 2's Complement Divide Correction.

```
0119  DIV:     LOW R10 & JSR & GOTO INP
011A           PAR R7,R15 & JSR & GOTO INP
011B           PAR R1,R15, & JSR & GOTO INP
011C           PAR R4,R15 & CONT
011D  LOOP1:   PAR R3,R7 & CONT
011E           PAR R2,R1 & T & MIZ & CJP & GOTO ABORT
011F           SMTC R2,R2 & CONT Z
0120           SMTC R3,R3 & T & MIO & CJP CZ & GOTO SCALE1
0121           ALUOFF & T & MIO & CJP & GOTO SKIP6
0122           SURL R3,R3 & SUL & CONT
0123           SURL R2,R2 & SUL & CONT
0124           ALUOFF & JP & GOTO LOOP2
0125  SCALE1:  LQPT R4 & JSR & GOTO SDIVD
0126           ALUOFF & JP LOOP1
0127  LOOP2:   SSR R3,R2,YBUS & CONT ONE
0128  SKIP6:   LQPT R4 & F & MIC & CJP & GOTO SKIP3
0129           ALUOFF & JSR & GOTO SDIVD
012A           SURL R2,R2 & SDL & CONT
012B           ALUOFF & JP & GOTO LOOP2
012C  SKIP3:   ALUOFF & F & GRD & LDCT & COUNT 00C
012D           DLN R1,R1,R7 & T & GRD & SDUL & PUSH
012E           TDIV R1,R1,R7 & F & CNT & SDUL & RFCT CZ
012F           TDC R1,R1,R7 & SUH & CONT CZ
0130           QMOV R15 & JSR & GOTO OUTP
0131           PAR R15,R1 & JSR & GOTO OUTP
0132           ALUOFF & JP & GOTO DIV
0133  SDIVD:   PAR R1,R1 & CONT
0134           ALUOFF & T & MIS & CJP & GOTO NEG
0135           PAR R1,R1,ADRQ & SDDL & CONT
0136           ALUOFF & JP & GOTO RET
0137  NEG:     PAR R1,R1,ADRQ & SDDL & CONT
0138  RET:     QMOV R4 & CONT
0139           PAR R10,R10 & RTN ONE
```

Figure 24.

NON-RESTORING BINARY ROOTS

The algorithm for Non-Restoring Binary Roots is illustrated in Figure 25. The initial conditions required are: 1) the non-negative number to be rooted in the radicand register, R_1; 2) R_2 has the positive append bits 101_B; 3) R_3 has the negative append bits 011_B; 4) R_4 is the mask register with $BFFF_H$; 5) R_5 is the partial register with 4000_H; and 6) the counter register, R_6, with the value 08_H.

An example of the Non-Restoring Binary Root algorithm is shown in Figure 26. Starting at the binary point, the number to be rooted is partitioned into pairs. The partial value is subtracted from the first pair. An intermediate remainder and sign are then produced.

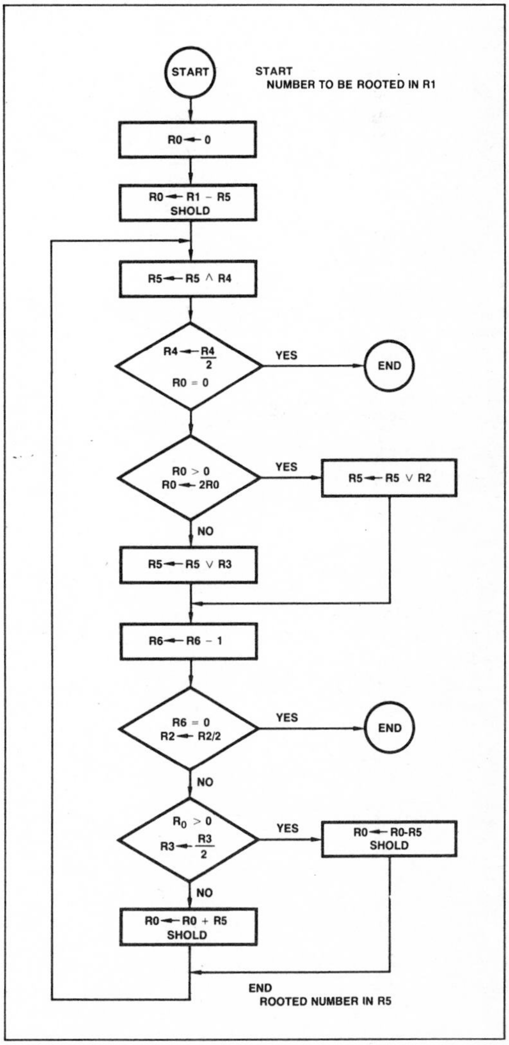

Figure 25. Non-Restoring Binary Root.

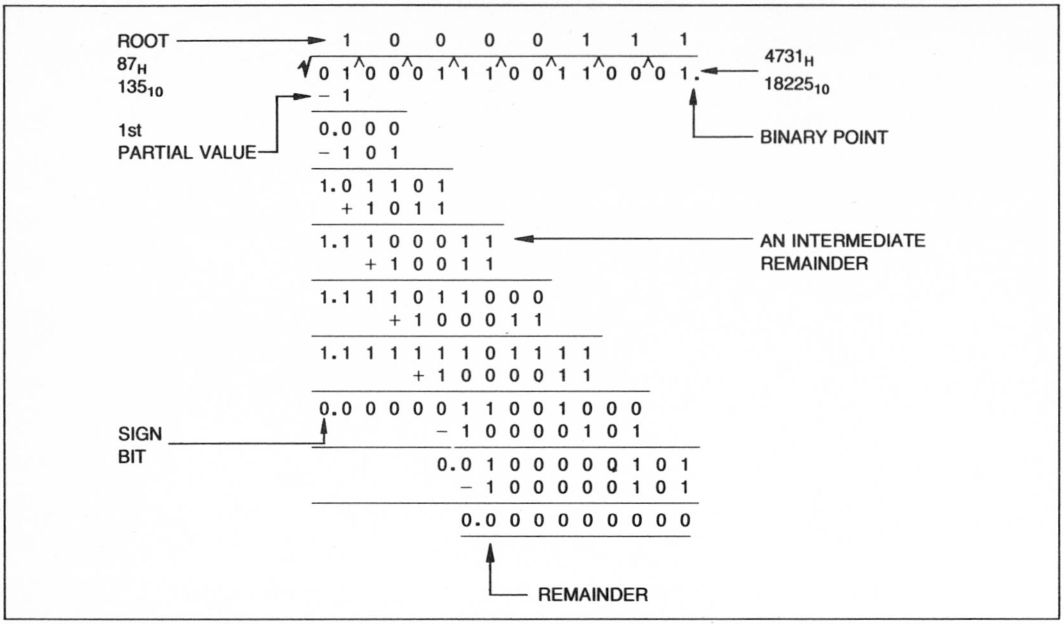

Figure 26. Non-Restoring Binary Root Example.

If the remainder is positive, a 1 is entered in the corresponding root bit. Then a 01 is appended to the partial, shifted and subtracted from the present remainder to produce the next remainder. When the remainder becomes negative, the present remainder is not restored. A 0 is entered in the next corresponding root bit. Then an 11 is appended to the partial, shifted and added to the present remainder. The entire process is repeated until the partial root has developed into 8 bits or the remainder is zero.

Referring to Figure 26, the same method of finding the root applies. A starting partial value, R_5, is subtracted from the radicand, R_1, which produces the intermediate remainder R_0. During this time, the sign of the remainder is stored within the Am2904. Then R_5 is masked by R_4 to obtain the next partial value and R_4 is shifted to obtain a new mask for the next cycle. Status is obtained from the Am2904 and tested. If the remainder is positive, a root bit of 1 is developed and bits 01 appended by R_2. When negative, a root bit of 0 is developed and bits 11 appended by R_3. At this point R_6 is decremented and tested for zero. If $R_6 \neq 0$, then addition or subtraction is performed on the remainder depending on the sign bit stored in the Am2904. A new remainder is produced and cycled through the procedure again. Figure 27 illustrates the microcode.

```
0152  SQRT:   LOW R10 & CONT
0153          LOW R0 & CONT
0154          PAR R1,R15 & CONT
0155          PAR R2,R0,,DARB & CONST 0005 & CONT
0156          PAR R3,R0,,DARB & CONST 0003 & CONT
0157          PAR R4,R0,,DARB & CONST H#BFFF & CONT
0158          PAR R4,R0,,DARB & CONST 4000 & CONT
0159          PAR R6,R0,,DARB & CONST 0008 & CONT
015A          SRS R0,R1,R5 & CONT & SHOLD
015B  CYCLE:  AND R5,R5,R4 & CONT
015C          SDRL R4,R4 & MAS & CJP & GOTO END3
015D          SDRL R0,R0, & T & MAS & CJP & GOTO POS
015E          OR R5,R3 & JP & GOTO CNT
015F  POS:    OR R5,R2 & CONT
0160  CNT:    SRS R6,R6,RIO & CONT
0161          SDRL R2,R2, & T & MIZ & CJP & GOTO END3
0162          SDRL R3,R3 & T & MAS & CJP & GOTO SUB
0163          ADD R0,R0,R5 & JP & GOTO CYCLE & SHOLD
0164  SUB:    SRS R0,R0,R5 & JP & GOTO CYCLE & SHOLD
0165  END3:   JP & GOTO SQRT
```

Figure 27.

BCD HARDWARE ADDITIONS

In applications where fast BCD operations are needed the designer has the option of using a slight amount of additional hardware to dramatically increase the performance of these operations. These firmware/hardware trade-off's are very application sensitive. The hardware-firmware examples given below are specifically for an intensive BCD system with a large fraction of conventional logic-arithmetic operations. The designer is willing to reduce cycle time slightly to increase BCD thru-put. Small hardware additions are acceptable as long as flexibility is retained.

The hardware additions finally decided on were chosen to increase the performance of BCD to binary conversion, binary to BCD conversion and BCD addition. The performance increases were approximately an order of magnitude in the first two cases, and a factor of 4 or 5 in the last case. A diagram of the additions (3¼ ICs) is given in Figure 28.

The 74S08 AND gates normally pass the carry from the Am2902A to the Am2903s. When microbit $\overline{CZER}$ is low the Carries-in are forced to zero. This is used to "disconnect" the carry so that a test may be done on each slice simultaneously. For example if a test for 5 or greater is desired a HEX B is added and

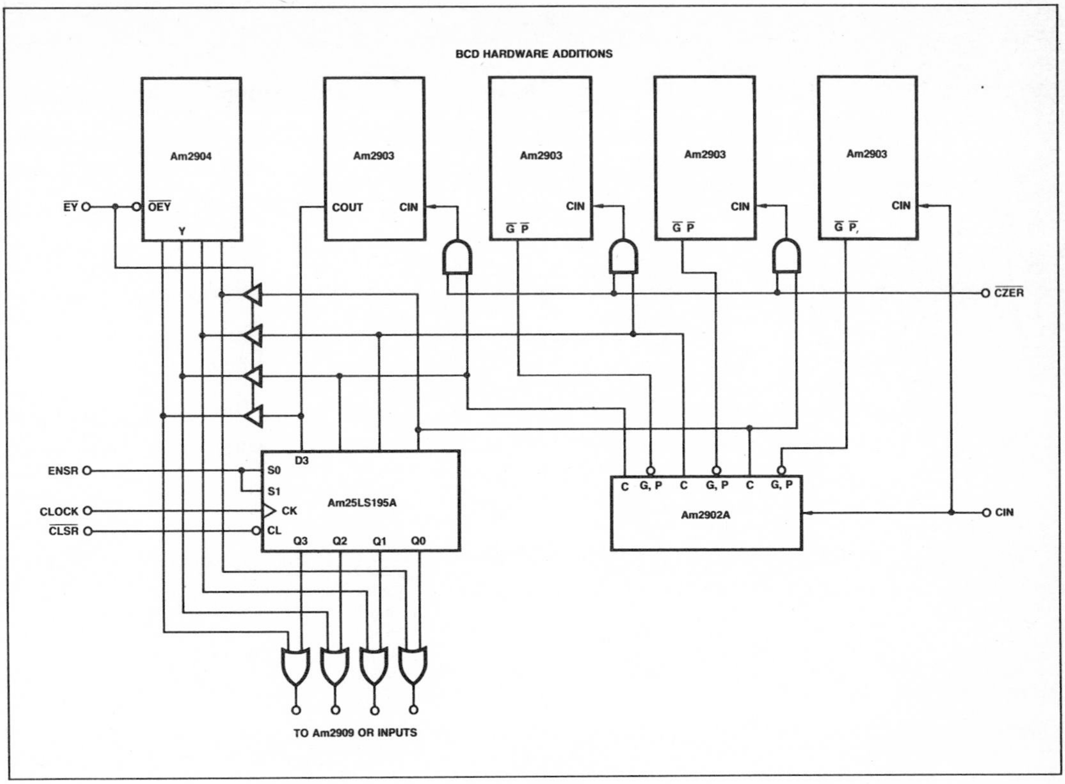

Figure 28.

the carry out of each slice will indicate the result of the test. This allows simultaneous tests on each individual slice and greatly increases thru-put. This addition increases the performance of BCD to binary conversion and binary to BCD conversion by at least an order of magnitude. The drawback to this addition is that the AND-gates introduce an extra gate delay in a critical path. The machine cycle time may be increased by about 8ns. The increase in BCD performance will more than offset this delay for BCD intensive systems.

Another hardware addition is the Am25LS241 three-state buffer. This buffer allows the Am2904 to be used to store the carry-out status bits via the bi-directional Y bus.

The 25LS195A is wired as a 4-bit register with clear and enable. This register is used to store the carry-out bits from a test cycle. The outputs of the 25LS195A are ORed with the output of the Am2904 Y-bus and connected to the Am2909 OR inputs in the CCU. This allows a multi-way branch on the OR of two test cycles, greatly increasing the performance of BCD addition.

BCD TO BINARY CONVERSION

The usual method of BCD to binary conversion is to divide the BCD number by 2. The 1-bit remainder will indicate if a 1 existed in the BCD number. The previous division result is divided by 2 again and the remainder will indicate if a 2 existed in the BCD number. In general the remainder from a division by 2^n will indicate if a 2^{n-1} existed in the BCD number. These remainders can be used to construct the binary representation, $b_n 2^n + b_{n-1} 2^{n-1} + b_{n-2} 2^{n-2} + \ldots + b_1 2^1 + b_0 2^0$. The b_n bit is thus the remainder from division step n + 1. The binary representation may thus be created by shifting the remainders down until the m-bit BCD number has been divided by 2 m times.

To divide a BCD number by 2 a down shift is executed. The 4, 2 and 1-bit positions will contain the correct result, but the 8-bit position is incorrect. Its value has changed from 10 to 8 instead of from 10 to 5. This means the resulting BCD number will have a value 3 greater than it should for the division by 2 to be correct. A 3 must be subtracted from any digit in which a 1 entered its 8-bit.

A sample conversion is given in Table 10. The BCD number is gradually shifted down and corrected when necessary. The binary number is finally correct after 16 cycles.

A flow diagram for the algorithm is given in Figure 29. The BCD input, A, is shifted down into the binary output B, to start the loop. The constant 0888 is added to A with the carries-in forced to zero. The resulting carries-out will indicate if A contained a 1 in any of the 8-bit positions. These carries are saved in status register SR1. A multi-way branch is then executed to enter the adjust table. The digits are adjusted depending on the previous test. At the same time a shift can be executed to prepare for the next test instruction. A test for end of loop is also done in this cycle to provide an exit if 16 iterations of the loop are complete. Finally a shift up of B is needed to cancel the extra right shift when the loop is exited. The microcode for this algorithm is given in Figure 30.

TABLE 10.

Digit 3	Digit 2	Digit 1	Digit 0	BCD → Binary Result	Operation	
0010	1001	0000	0100			
0001	0100	1000	0010	0	SHIFT	
0001	0100	0101	0010		ADJUST	DIGIT 1
0000	1010	0010	1001	00	SHIFT	
0000	0111	0010	0110		ADJUST	DIGITS 2, 0
0000	0011	1001	0011	000	SHIFT	
0000	0011	0110	0011		ADJUST	DIGIT 1
0000	0001	1011	0001	1000	SHIFT	
0000	0001	1000	0001		ADJUST	DIGIT 1
0000	0000	1100	0000	11000	SHIFT	
0000	0000	1001	0000		ADJUST	DIGIT 1
0000	0000	0100	1000	011000	SHIFT	
0000	0000	0100	0101		ADJUST	DIGIT 0
0000	0000	0010	0010	1011000	SHIFT	
0000	0000	0010	0010		ADJUST	NONE
0000	0000	0001	0001	01011000	SHIFT	
0000	0000	0001	0001		ADJUST	NONE
0000	0000	0000	1000	101011000	SHIFT	
0000	0000	0000	0101		ADJUST	DIGIT 0
0000	0000	0000	0010	1101011000	SHIFT	
0000	0000	0000	0010		ADJUST	NONE
0000	0000	0000	0001	01101011000	SHIFT	
			0001		ADJUST	NONE
			0000	101101011000	SHIFT	
			0000		ADJUST	NONE
			000	0101101011000	SHIFT	
			000		ADJUST	NONE
			00	00101101011000	SHIFT	
			00		ADJUST	NONE
			0	000101101011000	SHIFT	
			0		ADJUST	NONE
				0000101101011000	SHIFT	
					ADJUST	NONE

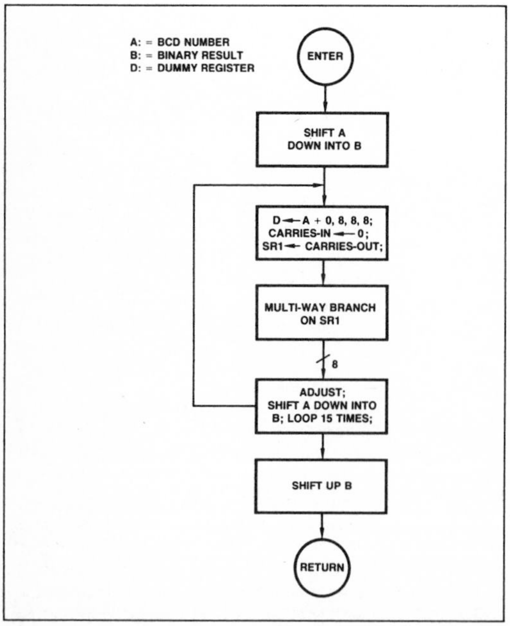

Figure 29. BCD to Binary Conversion (16 Bits to 14 Bits).

BINARY TO BCD CONVERSION

A method very similar to the one used for BCD to binary conversion may be used for binary to BCD conversion. The BCD number is created by shifting the binary number up, into a partial BCD result. The BCD number is adjusted to provide a multiplication by 2. The shift adjust process continues until the least significant binary bit is shifted into the BCD result.

The adjustment is needed when a 1 is shifted from the 8-bit position to the 1-bit position of the next digit. the value has increased from 8 to 10, instead of from 8 to 16. To correct this a 6 must be added to any digit that has a 1 shifted out of its 8-bit position. Alternately a 3 could be added before the shift to any digit that has a 1 in its 8-bit position.

Another correction is needed whenever an invalid BCD digit is encountered. If a number greater than 9 is detected in any digit a 10 must be subtracted from that digit and a 1 added to the next highest digit. The same correction can be accomplished if a 6 is added to the invalid digit after the shift. To correct before the shift a 3 is added to any digit which contains a 5, 6 or 7. These adjustments are summarized in Table 11. Both adjustments may be accomplished by adding a 3 to any digit which is greater than 4.

Table 12 shows an example conversion. The binary number is gradually shifted up and the BCD partial result adjusted. After 14 iterations the conversion is complete. A flow diagram for the algorithm is given in Figure 31.

```
A:  = R0
B:  = Q

                 1   ENR & COUNT LOOP & CONT
                 2   PAS R0, R0 LDRQ & SDDL & LDCT & CONST 15
LOOP:            3   ADD R1, R0, R0, DARB & ALUOFF & CONST 0888 & CZERO & ENSUR1 & CLSR2 & RPCT
                 4   ALUOFF & MULTI 8WAY
                     ALIGN 8
                 5   ALUOFF & CJRP & CNTR & GOTO EXIT
                 6   SUB R0, R0, R0, LDRQ,DARB & CONST 0003 & CJRP & CNTR & GOTO EXIT
                 7   SUB R0, R0, R0, LDRQ,DARB & CONST 0003 & CJRP & CNTR & GOTO EXIT
                 8   SUB R0, R0, R0, LDRQ,DARB & CONST 0003 & CJRP & CNTR & GOTO EXIT
                 9   SUB R0, R0, R0, LDRQ,DARB & CONST 0003 & CJRP & CNTR & GOTO EXIT
                10   SUB R0, R0, R0, LDRQ,DARB & CONST 0003 & CJRP & CNTR & GOTO EXIT
                11   SUB R0, R0, R0, LDRQ,DARB & CONST 0003 & CJRP & CNTR & GOTO EXIT
                12   SUB R0, R0, R0, LDRQ,DARB & CONST 0003 & CJRP & CNTR & GOTO EXIT
EXIT:           13   PAS R0, R0, R0, LURQ & SDUL & RTN
```

Figure 30.

TABLE 11.

Present #	Adjustment Before Shift	Reason
0000	NONE	–
0001	NONE	–
0010	NONE	–
0011	NONE	–
0100	NONE	–
0101	+3	
0110	+3	Illegal BCD
0111	+3	
1000	+3	
1001	+3	
1010	+3	
1011	+3	Shift Thru
1100	+3	Correction
1101	+3	
1110	+3	
1111	+3	

Initially the 14-bit binary number is left justified by two shift up operations. To start the loop the binary input, B, is shifted up, into the partial BCD result, A. The constant BBBB is added to A, with the carries-in forced to zero. The resulting carries-out are stored in status register SR1. A multi-way branch is used to enter the adjust table. The digits are adjusted depending on the result of the previous test. In the same instruction a shift is executed to prepare for the next test cycle. Additionally an end of loop test is used to provide an exit if 16 iterations of the loop are complete. Before the exit a fix-up cycle is used to cancel the extra shift executed in the loop. The microcode for this algorithm is given in Figure 32.

BCD ADD

One method of performing a 4-digit BCD add is to do a 16-bit binary add, with the carries-in forced to zero, and adjust the resulting sum. The adjustments are necessary to change invalid BCD digits to valid BCD digits. When an invalid digit is modified a carry to the next highest digit is generated. This could cause a

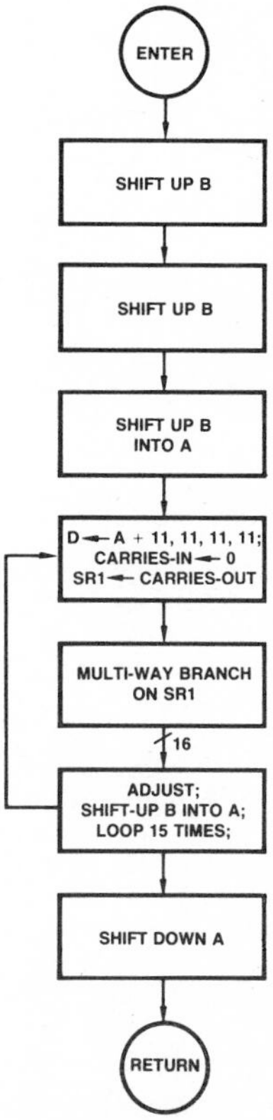

Figure 31. Binary to BCD Conversion (14 Bits to 16 Bits).

```
Q: =Binary Input
R0: = BCD Result
         SURL R0, R0 & SUL & CONT
         SURL R0, R0, & SUL & ENR & COUNT LOOP & CONT
         PAS R0, R0, ,LURQ & SDUL & LDCT & COUNT 15
LOOP:    ADD R1,R0, R0, DARB & ALUOFF & CONST BBBB & CZERO & ENSR1 & CLSR2 & RPCT
         ALUOFF & MULTI 16WAY
         ALIGN 16
         ALUOFF & CJRP & GOTO EXIT
         ADD R1, R0, R0, LURQ,DARB & CONST 0003 & CJRP & CNTR & GOTO EXIT
         ADD R1, R0, R0, LURQ,DARB & CONST 0003 & CJRP & CNTR & GOTO EXIT
         ADD R1, R0, R0, LURQ,DARB & CONST 0003 & CJRP & CNTR & GOTO EXIT
         ADD R1, R0, R0, LURQ,DARB & CONST 0003 & CJRP & CNTR & GOTO EXIT
         ADD R1, R0, R0, LURQ,DARB & CONST 0003 & CJRP & CNTR & GOTO EXIT
         ADD R1, R0, R0, LURQ,DARB & CONST 0003 & CJRP & CNTR & GOTO EXIT
         ADD R1, R0, R0, LURQ,DARB & CONST 0003 & CJRP & CNTR & GOTO EXIT
         ADD R1, R0, R0, LURQ,DARB & CONST 0003 & CJRP & CNTR & GOTO EXIT
         ADD R1, R0, R0, LURQ,DARB & CONST 0003 & CJRP & CNTR & GOTO EXIT
         ADD R1, R0, R0, LURQ,DARB & CONST 0003 & CJRP & CNTR & GOTO EXIT
         ADD R1, R0, R0, LURQ,DARB & CONST 0003 & CJRP & CNTR & GOTO EXIT
         ADD R1, R0, R0, LURQ,DARB & CONST 0003 & CJRP & CNTR & GOTO EXIT
         ADD R1, R0, R0, LURQ,DARB & CONST 0003 & CJRP & CNTR & GOTO EXIT
         ADD R1, R0, R0, LURQ,DARB & CONST 0003 & CJRP & CNTR & GOTO EXIT
         ADD R1, R0, R0, LURQ,DARB & CONST 0003 & CJRP & CNTR & GOTO EXIT
EXIT:    SDRL R0, R0, & SDL & RTN
```

Figure 32. Binary to BCD Conversion Microcode (14 Bits to 16 Bits).

TABLE 12.

Result Digit 3	Digit 2	Digit 1	Digit 0	Binary → BCD Conversion	Operation	
				00101101011000		
			0	0101101011000	SHIFT	
			0		ADJUST	NONE
			00	101101011000	SHIFT	
			00		ADJUST	NONE
			001	01101011000	SHIFT	
			001		ADJUST	NONE
			0010	1101011000	SHIFT	
			0010		ADJUST	NONE
		0	0101	101011000	SHIFT	
		0	1000		ADJUST	DIGIT 0
		01	0001	01011000	SHIFT	
		01	0001		ADJUST	NONE
		010	0010	1011000	SHIFT	
		010	0010		ADJUST	NONE
		0100	0101	011000	SHIFT	
		0100	1000		ADJUST	DIGIT 0
	0	1001	0000	11000	SHIFT	
	0	1100	0000		ADJUST	DIGIT 1
	01	1000	0001	1000	SHIFT	
	01	1011	0001		ADJUST	DIGIT 1
	011	0110	0011	000	SHIFT	
	011	1001	0011		ADJUST	DIGIT 1
	0111	0010	0110	00	SHIFT	
	1010	0010	1001		ADJUST	DIGIT 2
1	0100	0101	0010	0	SHIFT	
1	0100	1000	0010		ADJUST	DIGIT 1
10	1001	0000	0100		SHIFT	
10	1001	0000	0100		ADJUST	NONE
2	9	0	4			

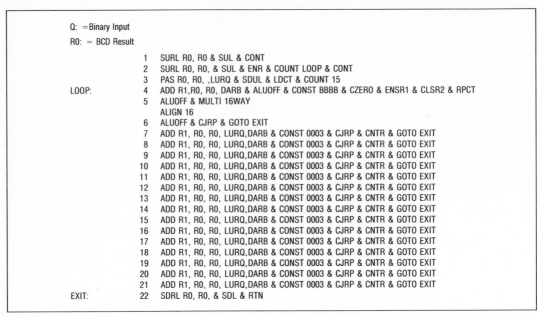

previously valid digit to become invalid. The word must be checked and modified until all digits are valid (up to four modification cycles could be necessary).

Initially the two BCD numbers are added with the carries-in to each digit forced to zero. The carries out are saved. Next the hex number 6666 is added to the sum, with the carries-in forced to zero, and the resulting carries out are saved. This tests each digit for validity, a carry-out indicating an invalid BCD digit (greater than 9). If a carry was generated in either cycle a 6 is added to the invalid digit, with carries-in forced to zero, to create the valid BCD digit. Additionally a 1 must be added to the next highest digit to provide the BCD carry-out. Each time a digit is adjusted the carry-out may invalidate the next highest digit. Thus adjustment cycles must be followed by validity tests until all digits are valid. A flow diagram for this algorithm is given in Figure 33. The microcode for this algorithm is given in Figure 34.

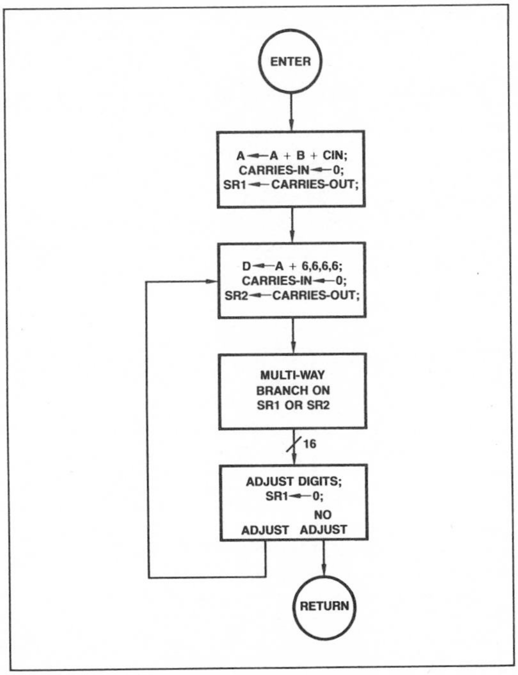

Figure 33. BCD Add.

```
A: = R1
B: = R0

 1 ADD R1,R1,R0 & CZERO & ENSR1 & CONT Z
 2 ADD R1,R1,R0,,DARB & ALUOFF & CZERO & ENSR2 & CONST 6666
 3 ALUOFF & MULTI 16WAY & RMAC
   ALIGN 16
 4 ALUOFF & JMP & GOTO EXIT & ENSR1
 5 ADD R1,R1,R0,,DARB & CONST 0016 & GOTO LOOP & CLRSR1
 6 ADD R1,R1,R0,,DARB & CONST 0160 & GOTO LOOP & CLRSR1
 7 ADD R1,R1,R0,,DARB & CONST 0176 & GOTO LOOP & CLRSR1
 8 ADD R1,R1,R0,,DARB & CONST 1600 & GOTO LOOP & CLRSR1
 9 ADD R1,R1,R0,,DARB & CONST 1616 & GOTO LOOP & CLRSR1
10 ADD R1,R1,R0,,DARB & CONST 1760 & GOTO LOOP & CLRSR1
11 ADD R1,R1,R0,,DARB & CONST 1776 & GOTO LOOP & CLRSR1
12 ALUOFF & JMP & GOTO LOOP & SMAC & CLRSR1
13 ADD R1,R1,R0,,DARB & CONST 0016 & GOTO LOOP & SMAC & CLRSR1
14 ADD R1,R1,R0,,DARB & CONST 0160 & GOTO LOOP & SMAC & CLRSR1
15 ADD R1,R1,R0,,DARB & CONST 0176 & GOTO LOOP & SMAC & CLRSR1
16 ADD R1,R1,R0,,DARB & CONST 1600 & GOTO LOOP & SMAC & CLRSR1
17 ADD R1,R1,R0,,DARB & CONST 1616 & GOTO LOOP & SMAC & CLRSR1
18 ADD R1,R1,R0,,DARB & CONST 1760 & GOTO LOOP & SMAC & CLRSR1
19 ADD R1,R1,R0,,DARB & CONST 1776 & GOTO LOOP & SMAC & CLRSR1

EXIT:
```

Figure 34. BCD Add Microcode.

SUMMARY

In this chapter, a detailed description of the Am2904 was presented, along with an example timing analysis. Several microcode algorithms were discussed to show how the Am2904 operates in a 2903 based CPU. As can be seen, the Am2904 provides a powerful, single-chip LSI solution to the shift multiplexer, status register, and carry multiplexer design portion of a CPU using either the Am2901B or the Am2903.

The Appendix includes a full microcode listing. The interested reader is encouraged to study these listings to gain a better understanding of the hardware organization (Appendix C). An additional microcode listing (Appendix B) gives the AMDASM™ definition file and source file for the microcode. The reader should study these listings while referring to the AMDASM Manual. (The Am2900 Family Data Book contains an AMDASM Reference Manual, document AM-PUB003, 4-78 FRODO.)

COMMENTS	ADDRESS	LABEL	CONSTANT																$\overline{\text{RE}}$	$\overline{\text{CLSR}}$	$\overline{\text{ENSR}}$	$\overline{\text{CZER}}$	$\overline{\text{CONST}}$	$\overline{\text{OECY}}$	$\overline{\text{OECT}}$	$\overline{\text{CEM}}$	CARRY		SHIFT OP I_9	I_8	I_7	I_6	INSTRUCTION OP I_5	I_4	I_3	I_2	I_1	I_0	$\overline{\text{OEY}}$
			89	88	87	86	85	84	83	82	81	80	79	78	77	76	75	74	73	72	71	70	69	68	67	66	65	64	63	62	61	60	59	58	57	56	55	54	53
UNSIGN MULTIPLY	0 1 0 C		X	X	X	X	X	X	X	X	X	X	X	X	X	X	X	X	X	X	X	X	X	X	X	X	0	0	X	X	X	X	X	X	X	X	X	X	0
	0 1 0 D		X	X	X	X	X	X	X	X	X	X	X	X	X	X	X	X	X	X	X	X	X	X	X	X	0	0	0	1	1	0	X	X	X	X	X	X	0
TWO'S COMPLEMENT MULTIPLY	0 1 1 3		X	X	X	X	X	X	X	X	X	X	X	X	X	X	X	X	X	X	X	X	X	X	X	X	0	0	X	X	X	X	X	X	X	X	X	X	0
	0 1 1 4		X	X	X	X	X	X	X	X	X	X	X	X	X	X	X	X	X	X	X	X	X	X	X	X	0	0	0	1	1	0	X	X	X	X	X	X	0
	0 1 1 5		X	X	X	X	X	X	X	X	X	X	X	X	X	X	X	X	X	X	X	X	X	X	X	X	1	1	0	1	1	0	X	X	X	X	X	X	0
TWO'S COMPLEMENT DIVIDE	0 1 1 9		X	X	X	X	X	X	X	X	X	X	X	X	X	X	X	X	X	X	X	X	X	X	X	X	0	0	X	X	X	X	X	X	X	X	X	X	0
	0 1 1 A		X	X	X	X	X	X	X	X	X	X	X	X	X	X	X	X	X	X	X	X	X	X	X	X	0	0	X	X	X	X	X	X	X	X	X	X	0
	0 1 1 B		X	X	X	X	X	X	X	X	X	X	X	X	X	X	X	X	X	X	X	X	X	X	X	X	0	0	X	X	X	X	X	X	X	X	X	X	0
	0 1 1 C		X	X	X	X	X	X	X	X	X	X	X	X	X	X	X	X	X	X	X	X	X	X	X	X	0	0	X	X	X	X	X	X	X	X	X	X	0
	0 1 1 D	LOOP 1:	X	X	X	X	X	X	X	X	X	X	X	X	X	X	X	X	X	X	X	X	X	X	X	X	0	0	X	X	X	X	X	X	X	X	X	X	0
	0 1 1 E		X	X	X	X	X	X	X	X	X	X	X	X	X	X	X	X	X	X	X	X	X	X	0	X	0	0	X	X	X	X	0	1	0	1	0	0	0
	0 1 1 F		X	X	X	X	X	X	X	X	X	X	X	X	X	X	X	X	X	X	X	X	X	X	X	X	1	0	X	X	X	X	X	X	X	X	X	X	0
	0 1 2 0		X	X	X	X	X	X	X	X	X	X	X	X	X	X	X	X	X	X	X	X	X	X	0	X	1	0	X	X	X	X	0	1	0	1	1	0	0
	0 1 2 1		X	X	X	X	X	X	X	X	X	X	X	X	X	X	X	X	X	X	X	X	X	X	0	X	0	0	X	X	X	X	0	1	0	1	1	0	X
	0 1 2 2		X	X	X	X	X	X	X	X	X	X	X	X	X	X	X	X	X	X	X	X	X	X	X	X	0	0	0	0	1	0	X	X	X	X	X	X	0
	0 1 2 3		X	X	X	X	X	X	X	X	X	X	X	X	X	X	X	X	X	X	X	X	X	X	X	X	0	0	0	0	1	0	X	X	X	X	X	X	0
	0 1 2 4		X	X	X	X	X	X	X	X	X	X	X	X	X	X	X	X	X	X	X	X	X	X	X	X	0	0	X	X	X	X	X	X	X	X	X	X	X
	0 1 2 5	SCALE 1:	X	X	X	X	X	X	X	X	X	X	X	X	X	X	X	X	X	X	X	X	X	X	X	X	0	0	X	X	X	X	X	X	X	X	X	X	0
	0 1 2 6		X	X	X	X	X	X	X	X	X	X	X	X	X	X	X	X	X	X	X	X	X	X	X	X	0	1	X	X	X	X	X	X	X	X	X	X	X
	0 1 2 7	LOOP 2:	X	X	X	X	X	X	X	X	X	X	X	X	X	X	X	X	X	X	X	X	X	X	X	X	0	1	X	X	X	X	X	X	X	X	X	X	0
	0 1 2 8	SKIP 6:	X	X	X	X	X	X	X	X	X	X	X	X	X	X	X	X	X	X	X	X	X	X	0	X	0	0	X	X	X	X	0	1	1	0	1	0	0
	0 1 2 9		X	X	X	X	X	X	X	X	X	X	X	X	X	X	X	X	X	X	X	X	X	X	X	X	0	0	X	X	X	X	X	X	X	X	X	X	X
	0 1 2 A		X	X	X	X	X	X	X	X	X	X	X	X	X	X	X	X	X	X	X	X	X	X	X	X	0	0	0	0	0	0	X	X	X	X	X	X	0
	0 1 2 B		X	X	X	X	X	X	X	X	X	X	X	X	X	X	X	X	X	X	X	X	X	X	X	X	0	0	X	X	X	X	X	X	X	X	X	X	X
	0 1 2 C	SKIP 3:	X	X	X	X	X	X	X	X	X	X	X	X	X	X	X	X	X	X	X	X	X	X	X	X	0	0	X	X	X	X	X	X	X	X	X	X	X
	0 1 2 D		X	X	X	X	X	X	X	X	X	X	X	X	X	X	X	X	X	X	X	X	X	X	X	X	0	0	1	1	1	1	X	X	X	X	X	X	0
	0 1 2 E		X	X	X	X	X	X	X	X	X	X	X	X	X	X	X	X	X	X	X	X	X	X	X	X	1	0	1	1	1	1	X	X	X	X	X	X	0
	0 1 2 F		X	X	X	X	X	X	X	X	X	X	X	X	X	X	X	X	X	X	X	X	X	X	X	X	1	0	0	0	1	1	X	X	X	X	X	X	0
	0 1 3 0		X	X	X	X	X	X	X	X	X	X	X	X	X	X	X	X	X	X	X	X	X	X	X	X	0	0	X	X	X	X	X	X	X	X	X	X	0
	0 1 3 1		X	X	X	X	X	X	X	X	X	X	X	X	X	X	X	X	X	X	X	X	X	X	X	X	0	0	X	X	X	X	X	X	X	X	X	X	0
	0 1 3 2		X	X	X	X	X	X	X	X	X	X	X	X	X	X	X	X	X	X	X	X	X	X	X	X	0	0	X	X	X	X	X	X	X	X	X	X	X
	0 1 3 3		X	X	X	X	X	X	X	X	X	X	X	X	X	X	X	X	X	X	X	X	X	X	X	X	0	0	X	X	X	X	X	X	X	X	X	X	0
	0 1 3 4		X	X	X	X	X	X	X	X	X	X	X	X	X	X	X	X	X	X	X	X	X	X	0	X	0	0	X	X	X	X	0	1	1	1	1	0	X
	0 1 3 5		X	X	X	X	X	X	X	X	X	X	X	X	X	X	X	X	X	X	X	X	X	X	X	X	0	0	0	1	1	0	X	X	X	X	X	X	0
	0 1 3 6		X	X	X	X	X	X	X	X	X	X	X	X	X	X	X	X	X	X	X	X	X	X	X	X	0	0	X	X	X	X	X	X	X	X	X	X	X
	0 1 3 7		X	X	X	X	X	X	X	X	X	X	X	X	X	X	X	X	X	X	X	X	X	X	X	X	0	0	0	1	1	0	X	X	X	X	X	X	0
	0 1 3 8		X	X	X	X	X	X	X	X	X	X	X	X	X	X	X	X	X	X	X	X	X	X	X	X	0	0	X	X	X	X	X	X	X	X	X	X	0
	0 1 3 9		X	X	X	X	X	X	X	X	X	X	X	X	X	X	X	X	X	X	X	X	X	X	X	X	0	1	X	X	X	X	X	X	X	X	X	X	0

Am2903 CONTROL FIELD																							CCU CONTROL FIELD														DEVICE ENABLE				SHARED CONTROL FIELD											
B ADDRESS DEST.				B ADDRESS SRC.				A ADDRESS SRC.				DEST.				FUNCT.				SRC.			MULTI-WAY				IR EN	POLARITY	TEST SELECT				29811 NEXT ADDRESS				SHIFT EN	STATUS EN	IEN	FIELD SELECT	INPUT/OUTPUT BRANCH COUNTER											
												I_8	I_7	I_6	I_5																																					
52	51	50	49	48	47	46	45	44	43	42	41	40	39	38	37	36	35	34	33	32	31	30	29	28	27	26	25	24	23	22	21	20	19	18	17	16	15	14	13	12	11	10	9	8	7	6	5	4	3	2	1	0
X	X	X	X	X	X	X	X	1	1	1	1	0	1	1	0	0	1	1	0	0	0	0	0	0	0	0	1	0	0	0	0	0	0	1	0	0	X	0	0	1	0	0	0	0	0	0	0	0	1	1	1	0
0	0	0	1	0	0	0	1	0	0	0	0	0	0	0	0	0	0	0	0	0	0	0	0	0	0	0	1	0	1	1	1	1	1	0	0	0	0	0	0	X	X	X	X	X	X	X	X	X	X	X	X	X
X	X	X	X	X	X	X	X	1	1	1	1	0	1	1	0	0	1	1	0	0	0	0	0	0	0	0	1	0	0	0	0	0	0	1	0	0	X	0	0	1	0	0	0	0	0	0	0	0	1	1	0	1
0	0	0	1	0	0	0	1	0	0	0	0	0	0	1	0	0	0	0	0	0	0	0	0	0	0	0	1	0	1	1	1	1	1	0	0	0	0	0	0	X	X	X	X	X	X	X	X	X	X	X	X	X
0	0	0	1	0	0	0	1	0	0	0	0	0	1	1	0	0	0	0	0	0	0	0	0	0	0	0	1	X	1	1	1	1	1	0	0	0	0	0	0	X	X	X	X	X	X	X	X	X	X	X	X	X
1	0	1	0	X	X	X	X	X	X	X	X	1	1	1	1	1	0	0	0	X	X	X	0	0	0	0	1	0	0	0	0	0	0	0	0	1	X	0	0	1	0	0	0	1	0	0	0	0	0	0	0	0
0	1	1	1	X	X	X	X	1	1	1	1	1	1	1	1	0	1	1	0	0	0	0	0	0	0	0	1	0	0	0	0	0	0	0	0	1	X	0	0	1	0	0	0	1	0	0	0	0	0	0	0	0
0	0	0	1	X	X	X	X	1	1	1	1	1	1	1	1	0	1	1	0	0	0	0	0	0	0	0	1	0	0	0	0	0	0	0	0	1	X	0	0	1	0	0	0	1	0	0	0	0	0	0	0	0
0	1	0	0	X	X	X	X	1	1	1	1	1	1	1	1	0	1	1	0	0	0	0	0	0	0	0	1	X	X	X	X	X	1	1	1	0	X	0	0	X	X	X	X	X	X	X	X	X	X	X	X	X
0	0	1	1	X	X	X	X	0	1	1	1	1	1	1	1	0	1	1	0	0	0	0	0	0	0	0	1	X	X	X	X	X	1	1	1	0	X	0	0	X	X	X	X	X	X	X	X	X	X	X	X	X
0	0	1	0	X	X	X	X	0	0	0	1	1	1	1	1	0	1	1	0	0	0	0	0	0	0	0	1	1	1	0	1	1	0	0	1	1	X	0	0	1	0	0	0	1	0	1	1	0	0	1	1	0
0	0	1	0	0	0	1	0	X	X	X	X	0	1	0	1	0	0	0	0	0	0	0	0	0	0	0	1	X	X	X	X	X	1	1	1	0	X	0	0	X	X	X	X	X	X	X	X	X	X	X	X	X
0	0	1	1	0	0	1	1	X	X	X	X	0	1	0	1	0	0	0	0	0	0	0	0	0	0	0	1	1	1	0	1	1	0	0	1	1	X	0	0	1	0	0	0	1	0	0	1	0	0	1	0	1
X	X	X	X	X	X	X	X	X	X	X	X	X	X	X	X	X	X	X	X	X	X	X	0	0	0	0	1	1	1	0	1	1	0	0	1	1	X	0	1	1	0	0	0	1	0	0	1	0	1	0	0	0
0	0	1	1	0	0	1	1	X	X	X	X	1	0	0	1	0	1	0	1	0	0	0	0	0	0	0	1	X	X	X	X	X	1	1	1	0	0	0	0	X	X	X	X	X	X	X	X	X	X	X	X	X
0	0	1	0	0	0	1	0	X	X	X	X	1	0	0	1	0	1	0	1	0	0	0	0	0	0	0	1	X	X	X	X	X	1	1	1	0	0	0	0	X	X	X	X	X	X	X	X	X	X	X	X	X
X	X	X	X	X	X	X	X	X	X	X	X	X	X	X	X	X	X	X	X	X	X	X	0	0	0	0	1	X	X	X	X	X	1	1	1	1	X	0	1	1	0	0	0	1	0	0	1	0	0	1	1	1
X	X	X	X	X	X	X	X	0	1	0	0	0	1	1	0	0	1	1	0	0	0	0	0	0	0	0	1	0	0	0	0	0	0	0	0	1	X	0	0	1	0	0	0	1	0	0	1	1	0	0	1	1
X	X	X	X	X	X	X	X	X	X	X	X	X	X	X	X	X	X	X	X	X	X	X	0	0	0	0	1	X	X	X	X	X	1	1	1	1	X	0	1	X	X	X	X	X	X	X	X	X	X	X	X	X
1	1	1	1	0	0	1	1	0	0	1	0	1	1	0	0	0	0	1	0	0	0	0	0	0	0	0	1	X	X	X	X	X	1	1	1	0	X	0	0	X	X	X	X	X	X	X	X	X	X	X	X	X
X	X	X	X	X	X	X	X	0	1	0	0	0	1	1	0	0	1	1	0	0	0	0	0	0	0	0	1	0	1	0	1	1	0	0	1	1	X	0	0	1	0	0	0	1	0	0	1	0	1	1	0	0
X	X	X	X	X	X	X	X	X	X	X	X	X	X	X	X	X	X	X	X	X	X	X	0	0	0	0	1	0	0	0	0	0	0	0	0	1	X	0	1	1	0	0	0	1	0	0	1	1	0	0	1	1
0	0	1	0	0	0	1	0	X	X	X	X	0	0	0	1	0	1	0	1	0	0	0	0	0	0	0	1	X	X	X	X	X	1	1	1	0	0	0	0	X	X	X	X	X	X	X	X	X	X	X	X	X
X	X	X	X	X	X	X	X	X	X	X	X	X	X	X	X	X	X	X	X	X	X	X	0	0	0	0	1	X	X	X	X	X	1	1	1	1	X	0	1	1	0	0	0	1	0	0	1	0	0	1	1	1
X	X	X	X	X	X	X	X	X	X	X	X	X	X	X	X	X	X	X	X	X	X	X	0	0	0	0	1	0	0	0	0	0	1	1	0	0	X	0	1	1	0	0	0	0	0	0	0	0	1	1	0	0
0	0	0	1	0	0	0	1	0	1	1	1	1	0	1	0	0	0	0	0	0	0	0	0	0	0	0	X	X	X	X	X	X	X	X	X	X	X	X	X	X	X	X	X	X	X	X	X	X	X	X	X	X
0	0	0	1	0	0	0	1	0	1	1	1	1	1	0	0	0	0	0	0	0	0	0	0	0	0	0	1	0	1	1	1	1	1	0	0	0	0	0	0	X	X	X	X	X	X	X	X	X	X	X	X	X
0	0	0	1	0	0	0	1	0	1	1	1	1	1	1	0	0	0	0	0	0	0	0	0	0	0	0	1	X	X	X	X	X	1	1	1	0	0	0	0	X	X	X	X	X	X	X	X	X	X	X	X	X
1	1	1	1	X	X	X	X	X	X	X	X	1	1	1	1	0	1	0	0	0	1	0	0	0	0	0	1	0	0	0	0	0	0	0	0	1	X	0	0	1	0	0	0	1	0	0	0	0	0	1	0	0
1	1	1	1	X	X	X	X	0	0	0	1	1	1	1	1	0	1	1	0	0	0	0	0	0	0	0	1	0	0	0	0	0	0	0	0	1	X	0	0	1	0	0	0	1	0	0	0	0	0	1	0	0
X	X	X	X	X	X	X	X	X	X	X	X	X	X	X	X	X	X	X	X	X	X	X	0	0	0	0	1	X	X	X	X	X	1	1	1	1	X	0	1	1	0	0	0	1	0	0	0	1	1	0	0	1
0	0	0	1	X	X	X	X	0	0	0	1	1	1	1	1	0	1	1	0	0	0	0	0	0	0	0	1	X	X	X	X	X	1	1	1	0	X	0	0	X	X	X	X	X	X	X	X	X	X	X	X	X
X	X	X	X	X	X	X	X	X	X	X	X	X	X	X	X	X	X	X	X	X	X	X	0	0	0	0	1	1	1	0	1	1	0	0	1	1	X	0	1	1	0	0	0	1	0	0	1	1	0	1	1	1
0	0	0	1	X	X	X	X	0	0	0	1	0	0	1	1	0	0	0	0	0	0	0	0	0	0	0	1	X	X	X	X	X	1	1	1	0	0	0	0	X	X	X	X	X	X	X	X	X	X	X	X	X
X	X	X	X	X	X	X	X	X	X	X	X	X	X	X	X	X	X	X	X	X	X	X	0	0	0	0	1	X	X	X	X	X	1	1	1	1	X	0	1	1	0	0	0	1	0	0	1	1	1	0	0	0
0	0	0	1	X	X	X	X	0	0	0	1	0	0	1	0	0	1	1	0	0	0	0	0	0	0	0	1	X	X	X	X	X	1	1	1	0	0	0	0	X	X	X	X	X	X	X	X	X	X	X	X	X
0	1	0	0	X	X	X	X	X	X	X	X	1	1	1	1	0	1	0	0	0	1	0	0	0	0	0	1	X	X	X	X	X	1	1	1	0	X	0	0	X	X	X	X	X	X	X	X	X	X	X	X	X
1	0	1	0	X	X	X	X	1	0	1	0	1	1	1	1	0	1	1	0	0	0	0	0	0	0	0	1	0	0	0	0	0	1	0	1	0	X	0	0	X	X	X	X	X	X	X	X	X	X	X	X	X

COMMENTS	ADDRESS	LABEL	CONSTANT 89 88 87 86 85 84 83 82 81 80 79 78 77 76 75 74	73 72 71 70	$\overline{CONST}$ 69	$\overline{OECY}$ 68 (Am2904 CONTROL FIELD)	$\overline{OECT}$ 67	$\overline{CEM}$ 66	CARRY 65 64	SHIFT OP I_9 I_8 I_7 I_6 (63 62 61 60)	INSTRUCTION OP I_5 I_4 I_3 I_2 I_1 I_0 (59 58 57 56 55 54)	$\overline{OEY}$ 53
SINGLE LENGTH NORMALIZE	0 1 3 C		X X X X X X X X X X X X X X X X	X X X X	X	X	X	X	0 0	X X X X	X X X X X X	0
	0 1 3 D		X X X X X X X X X X X X X X X X	X X X X	X	X	0	X	0 0	X X X X	0 1 0 1 0 0	X
	0 1 3 E		X X X X X X X X X X X X X X X X	X X X X	X	X	0	X	0 0	X X X X	0 1 0 1 1 0	0
	0 1 3 F		X X X X X X X X X X X X X X X X	X X X X	X	X	0	X	0 1	X X X X	0 1 0 1 1 0	0
	0 1 4 0	AGAIN:	X X X X X X X X X X X X X X X X	X X X X	X	X	0	X	0 1	X X X X	0 1 0 1 1 0	0
	0 1 4 1		X X X X X X X X X X X X X X X X	X X X X	X	X	X	X	0 0	0 0 1 0	X X X X X X	0
	0 1 4 2		X X X X X X X X X X X X X X X X	X X X X	X	X	X	X	0 0	X X X X	X X X X X X	0
DOUBLE LENGTH NORMALIZE	0 1 4 8		X X X X X X X X X X X X X X X X	X X X X	X	X	X	X	0 0	X X X X	X X X X X X	0
	0 1 4 9		X X X X X X X X X X X X X X X X	X X X X	X	X	0	X	0 0	X X X X	0 1 0 1 0 0	X
	0 1 4 A		X X X X X X X X X X X X X X X X	X X X X	X	X	0	X	0 0	X X X X	0 1 0 1 1 0	0
	0 1 4 B		X X X X X X X X X X X X X X X X	X X X X	X	X	0	X	0 0	0 1 1 0	0 1 0 1 1 0	0
	0 1 4 C	LOOP4:	X X X X X X X X X X X X X X X X	X X X X	X	X	0	X	0 0	0 1 1 0	0 1 0 1 1 0	0
	0 1 4 D		X X X X X X X X X X X X X X X X	X X X X	X	X	X	X	0 1	X X X X	X X X X X X	0
	0 1 4 E	JUMP1:	X X X X X X X X X X X X X X X X	X X X X	X	X	X	X	0 1	X X X X	X X X X X X	0
	0 1 4 F		X X X X X X X X X X X X X X X X	X X X X	X	X	X	X	0 0	0 1 0 1	X X X X X X	0
BINARY ROOTS	0 1 5 2		X X X X X X X X X X X X X X X X	X X X X	X	X	X	X	0 0	X X X X	X X X X X X	0
	0 1 5 3		X X X X X X X X X X X X X X X X	X X X X	X	X	X	X	0 0	X X X X	X X X X X X	0
	0 1 5 4		X X X X X X X X X X X X X X X X	X X X X	X	X	X	X	0 0	X X X X	X X X X X X	0
	0 1 5 5		0 0 0 0 0 0 0 0 0 0 0 0 0 1 0 1	X X X X	0	X	X	X	0 0	X X X X	X X X X X X	0
	0 1 5 6		0 0 0 0 0 0 0 0 0 0 0 0 0 0 1 1	X X X X	0	X	X	X	0 0	X X X X	X X X X X X	0
	0 1 5 7		1 0 1 1 1 1 1 1 1 1 1 1 1 1 1 1	X X X X	0	X	X	X	0 0	X X X X	X X X X X X	0
	0 1 5 8		0 1 0 0 0 0 0 0 0 0 0 0 0 0 0 0	X X X X	0	X	X	X	0 0	X X X X	X X X X X X	0
	0 1 5 9		0 0 0 0 0 0 0 0 0 0 0 0 1 0 0 0	X X X X	0	X	X	X	0 0	X X X X	X X X X X X	0
	0 1 5 A		X X X X X X X X X X X X X X X X	X X X X	X	X	X	X	0 0	X X X X	X X X X X X	0
	0 1 5 B	CYCLE:	X X X X X X X X X X X X X X X X	X X X X	X	X	X	X	0 0	X X X X	X X X X X X	0
	0 1 5 C		X X X X X X X X X X X X X X X X	X X X X	X	X	0	X	0 0	X X X X	1 0 1 1 1 0	0
	0 1 5 D		X X X X X X X X X X X X X X X X	X X X X	X	X	0	X	0 0	X X X X	1 0 1 1 1 0	0
	0 1 5 E		X X X X X X X X X X X X X X X X	X X X X	X	X	X	X	0 0	X X X X	X X X X X X	0
	0 1 5 F	POS:	X X X X X X X X X X X X X X X X	X X X X	X	X	X	X	0 0	X X X X	X X X X X X	0
	0 1 6 0	CNT:	X X X X X X X X X X X X X X X X	X X X X	X	X	X	X	0 0	X X X X	X X X X X X	0
	0 1 6 1		X X X X X X X X X X X X X X X X	X X X X	X	X	0	X	0 0	X X X X	0 1 0 1 0 0	0
	0 1 6 2		X X X X X X X X X X X X X X X X	X X X X	X	X	0	X	0 0	X X X X	0 1 1 1 1 0	0
	0 1 6 3		X X X X X X X X X X X X X X X X	X X X X	X	X	X	X	0 0	X X X X	X X X X X X	0
	0 1 6 4	SUB:	X X X X X X X X X X X X X X X X	X X X X	X	X	X	X	0 0	X X X X	X X X X X X	0

Am2903 CONTROL FIELD																							CCU CONTROL FIELD														DEVICE ENABLE				SHARED CONTROL FIELD											
B ADDRESS DEST.				B ADDRESS SRC.				A ADDRESS SRC.				DEST.				FUNCT.				SRC.			MULTI-WAY				IR EN	POLARITY	TEST SELECT				29811 NEXT ADDRESS				$\overline{\text{SHIFT EN}}$	$\overline{\text{STATUS EN}}$	$\overline{\text{IEN}}$	FIELD SELECT	INPUT/OUTPUT BRANCH COUNTER											
												I_8	I_7	I_6	I_5																																				
52	51	50	49	48	47	46	45	44	43	42	41	40	39	38	37	36	35	34	33	32	31	30	29	28	27	26	25	24	23	22	21	20	19	18	17	16	15	14	13	12	11	10	9	8	7	6	5	4	3	2	1	0
0	0	1	0	0	0	1	0	X	X	X	X	1	0	0	0	0	0	0	0	0	0	0	0	0	0	0	1	X	X	X	X	X	1	1	1	0	X	0	1	X	X	X	X	X	X	X	X	X	X	X	X	X
X	X	X	X	X	X	X	X	X	X	X	X	X	X	X	X	X	X	X	X	X	X	X	0	0	0	0	1	1	1	0	1	1	0	0	1	1	X	0	X	1	0	0	0	1	0	1	1	0	0	1	1	0
0	0	0	0	X	X	X	X	X	X	X	X	1	1	1	1	1	0	0	0	X	X	X	0	0	0	0	1	1	1	0	1	1	0	0	1	1	X	0	0	1	0	0	0	1	0	1	0	0	0	1	0	1
0	0	1	0	0	0	1	0	X	X	X	X	1	0	0	0	0	0	0	0	0	0	0	0	0	0	0	1	1	1	0	1	1	0	0	1	1	X	0	0	1	0	0	0	1	0	1	0	0	0	1	0	1
0	0	1	0	0	0	1	0	X	X	X	X	1	0	0	0	0	0	0	0	0	0	0	0	0	0	0	1	0	1	0	1	1	0	0	1	1	X	0	0	1	0	0	0	1	0	1	0	0	0	0	0	0
X	X	X	X	X	X	X	X	X	X	X	X	0	1	0	1	X	X	X	X	0	0	0	0	0	0	0	1	X	X	X	X	X	1	1	1	0	0	0	0	X	X	X	X	X	X	X	X	X	X	X	X	X
0	0	1	0	0	0	1	0	0	0	0	0	1	1	1	1	0	0	0	1	0	0	0	0	0	0	0	1	X	X	X	X	X	1	1	1	0	X	0	0	X	X	X	X	X	X	X	X	X	X	X	X	X
1	1	1	1	1	1	1	1	X	X	X	X	1	0	1	0	0	0	0	0	0	0	0	0	0	0	0	1	X	X	X	X	X	1	1	1	0	X	0	1	X	X	X	X	X	X	X	X	X	X	X	X	X
X	X	X	X	X	X	X	X	X	X	X	X	X	X	X	X	X	X	X	X	X	X	X	0	0	0	0	1	1	1	0	1	1	0	0	1	1	X	0	X	1	0	0	0	1	0	1	1	0	0	1	1	0
0	0	1	0	X	X	X	X	X	X	X	X	1	1	1	1	1	0	0	0	X	X	X	0	0	0	0	1	1	1	0	1	1	0	0	1	1	X	0	0	1	0	0	0	1	0	1	0	1	0	0	0	1
1	1	1	1	1	1	1	1	X	X	X	X	1	0	1	0	0	0	0	0	0	0	0	0	0	0	0	1	1	1	0	1	1	0	0	1	1	0	0	0	1	0	0	0	1	0	1	0	0	1	1	1	0
1	1	1	1	1	1	1	1	X	X	X	X	1	0	1	0	0	0	0	0	0	0	0	0	0	0	0	1	1	1	0	1	1	0	0	1	1	0	0	0	1	0	0	0	1	0	1	0	0	1	1	1	0
0	0	1	0	X	X	X	X	0	0	1	0	1	1	1	1	0	1	1	0	0	0	0	0	0	0	0	1	X	X	X	X	X	1	1	1	1	X	0	0	1	0	0	0	1	0	1	0	0	1	1	0	0
0	0	1	0	X	X	X	X	0	0	1	0	1	1	1	1	0	1	1	0	0	0	0	0	0	0	0	1	X	X	X	X	X	1	1	1	0	X	0	0	X	X	X	X	X	X	X	X	X	X	X	X	X
X	X	X	X	X	X	X	X	X	X	X	X	0	1	0	1	X	X	X	X	0	0	0	0	0	0	0	1	0	0	0	0	0	0	0	0	1	0	0	0	1	0	0	0	1	0	0	0	0	0	1	0	0
1	0	1	0	X	X	X	X	X	X	X	X	1	1	1	1	1	0	0	0	X	X	X	0	0	0	0	1	X	X	X	X	X	1	1	1	0	X	0	0	X	X	X	X	X	X	X	X	X	X	X	X	X
0	0	0	0	X	X	X	X	X	X	X	X	1	1	1	1	1	0	0	0	X	X	X	0	0	0	0	1	X	X	X	X	X	1	1	1	0	X	0	0	X	X	X	X	X	X	X	X	X	X	X	X	X
0	0	0	1	X	X	X	X	1	1	1	1	1	1	1	1	0	1	1	0	0	0	0	0	0	0	0	1	X	X	X	X	X	1	1	1	0	X	0	0	X	X	X	X	X	X	X	X	X	X	X	X	X
0	0	1	0	X	X	X	X	0	0	0	0	1	1	1	1	0	1	1	0	1	0	0	0	0	0	0	1	X	X	X	X	X	1	1	1	0	X	0	0	X	X	X	X	X	X	X	X	X	X	X	X	X
0	0	1	1	X	X	X	X	0	0	0	0	1	1	1	1	0	1	1	0	1	0	0	0	0	0	0	1	X	X	X	X	X	1	1	1	0	X	0	0	X	X	X	X	X	X	X	X	X	X	X	X	X
0	1	0	0	X	X	X	X	0	0	0	0	1	1	1	1	0	1	1	0	1	0	0	0	0	0	0	1	X	X	X	X	X	1	1	1	0	X	0	0	X	X	X	X	X	X	X	X	X	X	X	X	X
0	1	0	1	X	X	X	X	0	0	0	0	1	1	1	1	0	1	1	0	1	0	0	0	0	0	0	1	X	X	X	X	X	1	1	1	0	X	0	0	X	X	X	X	X	X	X	X	X	X	X	X	X
0	1	1	0	X	X	X	X	0	0	0	1	1	1	1	1	0	1	1	0	1	0	0	0	0	0	0	1	X	X	X	X	X	1	1	1	0	X	0	0	X	X	X	X	X	X	X	X	X	X	X	X	X
0	0	0	1	0	0	0	1	0	1	0	1	1	1	1	1	0	0	0	1	0	0	0	0	0	0	0	1	X	X	X	X	X	1	1	1	0	X	0	0	X	X	X	X	X	X	X	X	X	X	X	X	X
0	1	0	1	0	1	0	1	0	1	0	0	1	1	1	1	1	1	0	0	0	0	0	0	0	0	0	1	X	X	X	X	X	1	1	1	0	X	0	0	X	X	X	X	X	X	X	X	X	X	X	X	X
0	1	0	0	0	1	0	0	X	X	X	X	0	0	0	1	0	0	0	1	0	0	0	0	0	0	0	1	X	1	0	1	1	0	0	1	1	X	0	0	1	0	0	0	1	0	1	1	0	0	1	0	1
0	0	0	0	0	0	0	0	X	X	X	X	1	0	0	1	1	0	0	1	0	0	0	0	0	0	0	1	1	1	0	1	1	0	0	1	1	X	0	0	1	0	0	0	1	0	1	0	1	1	1	1	1
0	1	0	1	0	0	1	1	X	X	X	X	1	1	1	1	1	1	1	1	0	0	0	0	0	0	0	1	X	X	X	X	X	1	1	1	1	X	0	0	1	0	0	0	1	0	1	1	0	0	0	0	0
0	1	0	1	0	0	1	0	X	X	X	X	1	1	1	1	1	1	1	1	0	0	0	0	0	0	0	1	X	X	X	X	X	1	1	1	0	X	0	0	X	X	X	X	X	X	X	X	X	X	X	X	X
0	1	1	0	0	1	1	0	1	0	1	0	1	1	1	1	0	0	0	1	0	0	0	0	0	0	0	1	X	X	X	X	X	1	1	1	0	X	0	0	X	X	X	X	X	X	X	X	X	X	X	X	X
0	0	1	0	0	0	1	0	X	X	X	X	0	0	0	1	0	1	0	0	0	0	0	0	0	0	0	1	1	1	0	1	1	0	0	1	1	X	0	0	1	0	0	0	1	0	1	1	0	0	1	0	1
0	0	1	1	0	0	1	1	X	X	X	X	0	0	0	1	0	1	0	0	0	0	0	0	0	0	0	1	1	1	0	1	1	0	0	1	1	X	0	0	1	0	0	0	1	0	1	1	0	0	1	0	0
0	0	0	0	0	0	0	0	0	1	0	1	1	1	1	1	0	0	1	1	0	0	0	0	0	0	0	1	X	X	X	X	X	1	1	1	1	X	0	0	1	0	0	0	1	0	1	0	1	1	0	1	1
0	0	0	0	0	0	0	0	0	1	0	1	1	1	1	1	0	0	0	1	0	0	0	0	0	0	0	1	X	X	X	X	X	1	1	1	1	X	0	0	1	0	0	0	1	0	1	0	1	1	0	1	1

COMMENTS			CONSTANT																					Am2904 CONTROL FIELD														
	ADDRESS	LABEL																	$\overline{ENR}$	$\overline{CZERO}$	ENSR	$\overline{CLRSR}$	$\overline{CONST}$	$\overline{OECY}$	$\overline{OECT}$	$\overline{CEM}$	CARRY		SHIFT OP I_9	I_8	I_7	I_6	INSTRUCTION OP I_5	I_4	I_3	I_2	I_1	I_0
			89	88	87	86	85	84	83	82	81	80	79	78	77	76	75	74	73	72	71	70	69	68	67	66	65	64	63	62	61	60	59	58	57	56	55	54
	0	ENTER	X	X	X	X	X	X	X	X	X	X	X	X	X	X	X	X	0	1	0	1	1	0	1	1	X	X	X	X	X	X	X	X	X	X	X	X
BCD TO BINARY	1		X	X	X	X	X	X	X	X	X	X	X	X	X	X	X	X	1	1	0	1	1	0	1	1	X	X	0	1	1	0	X	X	X	X	X	X
CONVERSION	2		0	0	0	0	1	0	0	0	1	0	0	0	1	0	0	0	1	0	0	0	0	1	1	0	0	0	X	X	X	X	0	0	0	0	0	0
ROUTINE	3	LOOP	X	X	X	X	X	X	X	X	X	X	X	X	X	X	X	X	1	1	0	1	1	0	1	1	X	X	X	X	X	X	X	X	X	X	X	X
BRANCH	8		0	0	0	0	0	0	0	0	0	0	0	0	0	0	0	0	1	1	0	1	0	0	1	1	0	1	0	1	1	1	X	X	X	X	X	X
TABLE	9		0	0	0	0	0	0	0	0	0	0	0	0	0	0	1	1	1	1	0	1	0	0	1	1	0	1	0	1	1	1	X	X	X	X	X	X
	10		0	0	0	0	0	0	0	0	0	0	1	1	0	0	0	0	1	1	0	1	0	0	1	1	0	1	0	1	1	1	X	X	X	X	X	X
	11		0	0	0	0	0	0	0	0	0	0	1	1	0	0	1	1	1	1	0	1	0	0	1	1	0	1	0	1	1	1	X	X	X	X	X	X
	12		0	0	0	0	0	0	1	1	0	0	0	0	0	0	0	0	1	1	0	1	0	0	1	1	0	1	0	1	1	1	X	X	X	X	X	X
	13		0	0	0	0	0	0	1	1	0	0	0	0	0	0	1	1	1	1	0	1	0	0	1	1	0	1	0	1	1	1	X	X	X	X	X	X
	14		0	0	0	0	0	0	1	1	0	0	1	1	0	0	0	0	1	1	0	1	0	0	1	1	0	1	0	1	1	1	X	X	X	X	X	X
	15		0	0	0	0	0	0	1	1	0	0	1	1	0	0	1	1	1	1	0	1	0	0	1	1	0	1	0	1	1	1	X	X	X	X	X	X
	16	EXIT	X	X	X	X	X	X	X	X	X	X	X	X	X	X	X	X	1	1	0	1	1	0	1	1	X	X	1	1	1	0	X	X	X	X	X	X
BINARY TO BCD	0	ENTER	X	X	X	X	X	X	X	X	X	X	X	X	X	X	X	X	1	1	0	1	1	0	1	1	0	0	0	0	0	0	X	X	X	X	X	X
CONVERSION	1		X	X	X	X	X	X	X	X	X	X	X	X	X	X	X	X	0	1	0	1	1	0	1	1	0	0	0	0	0	0	X	X	X	X	X	X
ROUTINE	2		X	X	X	X	X	X	X	X	X	X	X	X	X	X	X	X	1	1	0	1	1	0	1	1	0	0	0	1	0	0	X	X	X	X	X	X
	3	LOOP	1	0	1	1	1	0	1	1	1	0	1	1	1	0	1	1	1	0	0	0	0	1	1	0	0	0	X	X	X	X	0	0	0	0	0	0
	4		X	X	X	X	X	X	X	X	X	X	X	X	X	X	X	X	1	1	0	1	1	0	1	1	X	X	X	X	X	X	X	X	X	X	X	X
BRANCH	16		0	0	0	0	0	0	0	0	0	0	0	0	0	0	0	0	1	1	0	1	0	0	1	1	0	0	0	1	0	0	X	X	X	X	X	X
TABLE	17		0	0	0	0	0	0	0	0	0	0	0	0	0	0	1	1	1	1	0	1	0	0	1	1	0	0	0	1	0	0	X	X	X	X	X	X
	18		0	0	0	0	0	0	0	0	0	0	1	1	0	0	0	0	1	1	0	1	0	0	1	1	0	0	0	1	0	0	X	X	X	X	X	X
	19		0	0	0	0	0	0	0	0	0	0	1	1	0	0	1	1	1	1	0	1	0	0	1	1	0	0	0	1	0	0	X	X	X	X	X	X
	20		0	0	0	0	0	0	1	1	0	0	0	0	0	0	0	0	1	1	0	1	0	0	1	1	0	0	0	1	0	0	X	X	X	X	X	X
	21		0	0	0	0	0	0	1	1	0	0	0	0	0	0	1	1	1	1	0	1	0	0	1	1	0	0	0	1	0	0	X	X	X	X	X	X
	22		0	0	0	0	0	0	1	1	0	0	1	1	0	0	0	0	1	1	0	1	0	0	1	1	0	0	0	1	0	0	X	X	X	X	X	X
	23		0	0	0	0	0	0	1	1	0	0	1	1	0	0	1	1	1	1	0	1	0	0	1	1	0	0	0	1	0	0	X	X	X	X	X	X
	24		0	0	1	1	0	0	0	0	0	0	0	0	0	0	0	0	1	1	0	1	0	0	1	1	0	0	0	1	0	0	X	X	X	X	X	X
	25		0	0	1	1	0	0	0	0	0	0	0	0	0	0	1	1	1	1	0	1	0	0	1	1	0	0	0	1	0	0	X	X	X	X	X	X
	26		0	0	1	1	0	0	0	0	0	0	1	1	0	0	0	0	1	1	0	1	0	0	1	1	0	0	0	1	0	0	X	X	X	X	X	X
	27		0	0	1	1	0	0	0	0	0	0	1	1	0	0	1	1	1	1	0	1	0	0	1	1	0	0	0	1	0	0	X	X	X	X	X	X
	28		0	0	1	1	0	0	1	1	0	0	0	0	0	0	0	0	1	1	0	1	0	0	1	1	0	0	0	1	0	0	X	X	X	X	X	X
	29		0	0	1	1	0	0	1	1	0	0	0	0	0	0	1	1	1	1	0	1	0	0	1	1	0	0	0	1	0	0	X	X	X	X	X	X
	30		0	0	1	1	0	0	1	1	0	0	1	1	0	0	0	0	1	1	0	1	0	0	1	1	0	0	0	1	0	0	X	X	X	X	X	X
	31		0	0	1	1	0	0	1	1	0	0	1	1	0	0	1	1	1	1	0	1	0	0	1	1	0	0	0	1	0	0	X	X	X	X	X	X
	32	EXIT	X	X	X	X	X	X	X	X	X	X	X	X	X	X	X	X	1	1	0	1	1	0	1	1	X	X	0	1	0	0	X	X	X	X	X	X

Am2903 CONTROL FIELD																								CCU CONTROL FIELD														DEVICE ENABLE				SHARED CONTROL FIELD											
$\overline{OEY}$	B ADDRESS DEST.				B ADDRESS SRC.				A ADDRESS SRC.				DEST. I_8	I_7	I_6	I_5	FUNCT.				SRC.			MULTI-WAY				$\overline{IR\ EN}$	POLARITY	TEST SELECT				29811 NEXT ADDRESS				$\overline{SHIFT\ EN}$	$\overline{STATUS\ EN}$	$\overline{IEN}$	FIELD SELECT	INPUT/OUTPUT BRANCH COUNTER											
53	52	51	50	49	48	47	46	45	44	43	42	41	40	39	38	37	36	35	34	33	32	31	30	29	28	27	26	25	24	23	22	21	20	19	18	17	16	15	14	13	12	11	10	9	8	7	6	5	4	3	2	1	0
1	X	X	X	X	X	X	X	X	X	X	X	X	X	X	X	X	X	X	X	X	X	X	X	0	0	0	0	1	X	X	X	X	X	1	1	1	0	1	1	1	1	0	0	0	0	0	0	0	0	0	0	1	1
0	0	0	0	0	0	0	0	0	0	0	0	0	0	0	1	1	0	1	1	0	0	0	0	0	0	0	0	1	X	X	X	X	X	1	1	0	0	0	1	0	1	0	0	0	0	0	0	0	0	1	1	1	1
1	0	0	0	0	0	0	0	0	0	0	0	0	0	1	0	0	0	0	1	1	1	0	0	0	0	0	0	1	X	X	X	X	X	1	0	0	1	1	1	0	1	X	X	X	X	X	X	X	X	X	X	X	X
1	X	X	X	X	X	X	X	X	X	X	X	X	X	X	X	X	X	X	X	X	X	X	X	0	1	1	1	1	X	X	X	X	X	1	1	1	1	1	1	1	1	0	0	0	0	0	0	0	0	1	0	0	0
0	0	0	0	0	0	0	0	0	0	0	0	0	0	0	1	1	0	0	0	1	1	0	0	0	0	0	0	1	1	1	1	1	1	0	1	1	1	0	1	0	1	0	0	0	0	0	0	0	1	0	0	0	0
0	0	0	0	0	0	0	0	0	0	0	0	0	0	0	1	1	0	0	0	1	1	0	0	0	0	0	0	1	1	1	1	1	1	0	1	1	1	0	1	0	1	0	0	0	0	0	0	0	1	0	0	0	0
0	0	0	0	0	0	0	0	0	0	0	0	0	0	0	1	1	0	0	0	1	1	0	0	0	0	0	0	1	1	1	1	1	1	0	1	1	1	0	1	0	1	0	0	0	0	0	0	0	1	0	0	0	0
0	0	0	0	0	0	0	0	0	0	0	0	0	0	0	1	1	0	0	0	1	1	0	0	0	0	0	0	1	1	1	1	1	1	0	1	1	1	0	1	0	1	0	0	0	0	0	0	0	1	0	0	0	0
0	0	0	0	0	0	0	0	0	0	0	0	0	0	0	1	1	0	0	0	1	1	0	0	0	0	0	0	1	1	1	1	1	1	0	1	1	1	0	1	0	1	0	0	0	0	0	0	0	1	0	0	0	0
0	0	0	0	0	0	0	0	0	0	0	0	0	0	0	1	1	0	0	0	1	1	0	0	0	0	0	0	1	1	1	1	1	1	0	1	1	1	0	1	0	1	0	0	0	0	0	0	0	1	0	0	0	0
0	0	0	0	0	0	0	0	0	0	0	0	0	0	0	1	1	0	0	0	1	1	0	0	0	0	0	0	1	1	1	1	1	1	0	1	1	1	0	1	0	1	0	0	0	0	0	0	0	1	0	0	0	0
0	0	0	0	0	0	0	0	0	0	0	0	0	0	0	1	1	0	0	0	1	1	0	0	0	0	0	0	1	1	1	1	1	1	0	1	1	1	0	1	0	1	0	0	0	0	0	0	0	1	0	0	0	0
0	0	0	0	0	0	0	0	0	0	0	0	0	1	0	1	1	0	1	1	0	0	0	0	0	0	0	0	1	0	0	0	0	0	1	0	1	0	0	1	0	1	X	X	X	X	X	X	X	X	X	X	X	X
0	0	0	0	0	0	0	0	0	0	0	0	0	1	0	0	1	0	1	1	0	0	0	0	0	0	0	0	1	X	X	X	X	X	1	1	1	0	0	1	1	1	X	X	X	X	X	X	X	X	X	X	X	X
0	0	0	0	0	0	0	0	0	0	0	0	0	1	0	0	1	0	1	1	0	0	0	0	0	0	0	0	1	X	X	X	X	X	1	1	1	0	0	1	1	1	0	0	0	0	0	0	0	0	0	0	1	1
0	0	0	0	0	0	0	0	0	0	0	0	0	1	0	1	1	0	1	1	0	0	0	0	0	0	0	0	1	X	X	X	X	X	1	1	0	0	0	1	0	1	0	0	0	0	0	0	0	0	1	1	1	1
1	0	0	0	0	0	0	0	0	0	0	0	0	0	1	0	0	0	0	1	1	1	0	0	0	0	0	0	1	X	X	X	X	X	1	0	0	1	1	1	1	1	X	X	X	X	X	X	X	X	X	X	X	X
0	X	X	X	X	X	X	X	X	X	X	X	X	X	X	X	X	X	X	X	X	X	X	X	1	1	1	1	1	X	X	X	X	X	1	1	1	1	1	1	1	1	0	0	0	0	0	0	0	1	0	0	0	0
0	0	0	0	0	0	0	0	0	0	0	0	0	1	0	1	1	0	0	1	1	1	0	0	0	0	0	0	1	1	1	1	1	1	0	1	1	1	0	1	0	1	0	0	0	0	0	0	1	0	0	0	0	0
0	0	0	0	0	0	0	0	0	0	0	0	0	1	0	1	1	0	0	1	1	1	0	0	0	0	0	0	1	1	1	1	1	1	0	1	1	1	0	1	0	1	0	0	0	0	0	0	1	0	0	0	0	0
0	0	0	0	0	0	0	0	0	0	0	0	0	1	0	1	1	0	0	1	1	1	0	0	0	0	0	0	1	1	1	1	1	1	0	1	1	1	0	1	0	1	0	0	0	0	0	0	1	0	0	0	0	0
0	0	0	0	0	0	0	0	0	0	0	0	0	1	0	1	1	0	0	1	1	1	0	0	0	0	0	0	1	1	1	1	1	1	0	1	1	1	0	1	0	1	0	0	0	0	0	0	1	0	0	0	0	0
0	0	0	0	0	0	0	0	0	0	0	0	0	1	0	1	1	0	0	1	1	1	0	0	0	0	0	0	1	1	1	1	1	1	0	1	1	1	0	1	0	1	0	0	0	0	0	0	1	0	0	0	0	0
0	0	0	0	0	0	0	0	0	0	0	0	0	1	0	1	1	0	0	1	1	1	0	0	0	0	0	0	1	1	1	1	1	1	0	1	1	1	0	1	0	1	0	0	0	0	0	0	1	0	0	0	0	0
0	0	0	0	0	0	0	0	0	0	0	0	0	1	0	1	1	0	0	1	1	1	0	0	0	0	0	0	1	1	1	1	1	1	0	1	1	1	0	1	0	1	0	0	0	0	0	0	1	0	0	0	0	0
0	0	0	0	0	0	0	0	0	0	0	0	0	1	0	1	1	0	0	1	1	1	0	0	0	0	0	0	1	1	1	1	1	1	0	1	1	1	0	1	0	1	0	0	0	0	0	0	1	0	0	0	0	0
0	0	0	0	0	0	0	0	0	0	0	0	0	1	0	1	1	0	0	1	1	1	0	0	0	0	0	0	1	1	1	1	1	1	0	1	1	1	0	1	0	1	0	0	0	0	0	0	1	0	0	0	0	0
0	0	0	0	0	0	0	0	0	0	0	0	0	1	0	1	1	0	0	1	1	1	0	0	0	0	0	0	1	1	1	1	1	1	0	1	1	1	0	1	0	1	0	0	0	0	0	0	1	0	0	0	0	0
0	0	0	0	0	0	0	0	0	0	0	0	0	1	0	1	1	0	0	1	1	1	0	0	0	0	0	0	1	1	1	1	1	1	0	1	1	1	0	1	0	1	0	0	0	0	0	0	1	0	0	0	0	0
0	0	0	0	0	0	0	0	0	0	0	0	0	1	0	1	1	0	0	1	1	1	0	0	0	0	0	0	1	1	1	1	1	1	0	1	1	1	0	1	0	1	0	0	0	0	0	0	1	0	0	0	0	0
0	0	0	0	0	0	0	0	0	0	0	0	0	1	0	1	1	0	0	1	1	1	0	0	0	0	0	0	1	1	1	1	1	1	0	1	1	1	0	1	0	1	0	0	0	0	0	0	1	0	0	0	0	0
0	0	0	0	0	0	0	0	0	0	0	0	0	1	0	1	1	0	0	1	1	1	0	0	0	0	0	0	1	1	1	1	1	1	0	1	1	1	0	1	0	1	0	0	0	0	0	0	1	0	0	0	0	0
0	0	0	0	0	0	0	0	0	0	0	0	0	1	0	1	1	0	0	1	1	1	0	0	0	0	0	0	1	1	1	1	1	1	0	1	1	1	0	1	0	1	0	0	0	0	0	0	1	0	0	0	0	0
0	0	0	0	0	0	0	0	0	0	0	0	0	1	0	1	1	0	0	1	1	1	0	0	0	0	0	0	1	1	1	1	1	1	0	1	1	1	0	1	0	1	0	0	0	0	0	0	1	0	0	0	0	0
0	0	0	0	0	0	0	0	0	0	0	0	0	0	0	1	1	0	1	1	0	0	0	0	0	0	0	0	1	0	0	0	0	0	1	0	1	0	0	1	0	1	X	X	X	X	X	X	X	X	X	X	X	X

APPENDIX A

COMMENTS	ADDRESS	LABEL	CONSTANT																$\overline{ENR}$	$\overline{CZERO}$	ENSR	$\overline{CLRSR}$	$\overline{CONST}$	Am2904 CONTROL FIELD: $\overline{OECY}$	$\overline{OECT}$	$\overline{CEM}$	CARRY		SHIFT OP: I_9	I_8	I_7	I_6	INSTRUCTION OP: I_5	I_4	I_3	I_2	I_1	I_0
			89	88	87	86	85	84	83	82	81	80	79	78	77	76	75	74	73	72	71	70	69	68	67	66	65	64	63	62	61	60	59	58	57	56	55	54
	0	ENTER	X	X	X	X	X	X	X	X	X	X	X	X	X	X	X	X	1	0	0	1	1	1	1	0	1	1	X	X	X	X	0	0	0	0	0	0
BCD ADD	1		0	1	1	0	0	1	1	0	0	1	1	0	0	1	1	0	1	0	1	1	0	1	1	1	0	0	X	X	X	X	X	X	X	X	X	X
ROUTINE	2		X	X	X	X	X	X	X	X	X	X	X	X	X	X	X	X	1	1	0	1	1	0	1	0	X	X	X	X	X	X	0	0	0	0	1	1
ADJUST	16	TAB	0	0	0	0	0	0	0	0	0	0	0	0	0	0	0	0	1	1	0	0	0	1	1	1	0	0	X	X	X	X	X	X	X	X	X	X
TABLE	17		0	0	0	0	0	0	0	0	0	0	0	1	0	1	1	0	1	1	0	0	0	1	1	1	0	0	X	X	X	X	X	X	X	X	X	X
	18		0	0	0	0	0	0	0	1	0	1	1	0	0	0	0	0	1	1	0	0	0	1	1	1	0	0	X	X	X	X	X	X	X	X	X	X
	19		0	0	0	0	0	0	0	1	0	1	1	1	0	1	1	0	1	1	0	0	0	1	1	1	0	0	X	X	X	X	X	X	X	X	X	X
	20		0	0	0	1	0	1	1	0	0	0	0	0	0	0	0	0	1	1	0	0	0	1	1	1	0	0	X	X	X	X	X	X	X	X	X	X
	21		0	0	0	1	0	1	1	0	0	0	0	1	0	1	1	0	1	1	0	0	0	1	1	1	0	0	X	X	X	X	X	X	X	X	X	X
	22		0	0	0	1	0	1	1	1	0	1	1	0	0	0	0	0	1	1	0	0	0	1	1	1	0	0	X	X	X	X	X	X	X	X	X	X
	23		0	0	0	1	0	1	1	1	0	1	1	1	0	1	1	0	1	1	0	0	0	1	1	1	0	0	X	X	X	X	X	X	X	X	X	X
	24		0	0	0	0	0	0	0	0	0	0	0	0	0	0	0	0	1	1	0	0	0	1	1	0	0	0	X	X	X	X	0	0	0	0	0	1
	25		0	0	0	0	0	0	0	0	0	0	0	1	0	1	1	0	1	1	0	0	0	1	1	0	0	0	X	X	X	X	0	0	0	0	0	1
	26		0	0	0	0	0	0	0	1	0	1	1	0	0	0	0	0	1	1	0	0	0	1	1	0	0	0	X	X	X	X	0	0	0	0	0	1
	27		0	0	0	0	0	0	0	1	0	1	1	1	0	1	1	0	1	1	0	0	0	1	1	0	0	0	X	X	X	X	0	0	0	0	0	1
	28		0	0	0	1	0	1	1	0	0	0	0	0	0	0	0	0	1	1	0	0	0	1	1	0	0	0	X	X	X	X	0	0	0	0	0	1
	29		0	0	0	1	0	1	1	0	0	0	0	1	0	1	1	0	1	1	0	0	0	1	1	0	0	0	X	X	X	X	0	0	0	0	0	1
	30		0	0	0	1	0	1	1	1	0	1	1	0	0	0	0	0	1	1	0	0	0	1	1	0	0	0	X	X	X	X	0	0	0	0	0	1
	31		0	0	0	1	0	1	1	1	0	1	1	1	0	1	1	0	1	1	0	0	0	1	1	0	0	0	X	X	X	X	0	0	0	0	0	1
		EXIT																																				

	Am2903 CONTROL FIELD																								CCU CONTROL FIELD															DEVICE ENABLE				SHARED CONTROL FIELD											
$\overline{OEY}$	B ADDRESS DEST.				B ADDRESS SRC.				A ADDRESS SRC.				DEST.				FUNCT.				SRC.			MULTI-WAY				$\overline{IR\ EN}$	POLARITY	TEST SELECT				29811 NEXT ADDRESS				$\overline{SHIFT\ EN}$	$\overline{STATUS\ EN}$	$\overline{IEN}$	FIELD SELECT	INPUT/OUTPUT BRANCH COUNTER											
													I_8	I_7	I_6	I_5																																					
53	52	51	50	49	48	47	46	45	44	43	42	41	40	39	38	37	36	35	34	33	32	31	30	29	28	27	26	25	24	23	22	21	20	19	18	17	16	15	14	13	12	11	10	9	8	7	6	5	4	3	2	1	0
0	0	0	0	1	0	0	0	1	0	0	0	0	1	1	1	1	0	0	1	1	0	0	0	0	0	0	0	1	X	X	X	X	X	1	1	1	0	1	1	0	1	X	X	X	X	X	X	X	X	X	X	X	X
1	0	0	0	1	0	0	0	1	0	0	0	0	1	1	1	1	0	0	1	1	1	0	0	0	0	0	0	1	X	X	X	X	X	1	1	1	0	1	1	1	1	X	X	X	X	X	X	X	X	X	X	X	X
1	X	X	X	X	X	X	X	X	X	X	X	X	X	X	X	X	X	X	X	X	X	X	X	1	1	1	1	1	X	X	X	X	X	1	1	1	1	1	1	1	1	0	0	0	0	0	0	0	1	0	0	0	0
0	0	0	0	1	0	0	0	1	0	0	0	0	1	1	1	1	0	0	1	1	1	0	0	0	0	0	0	1	X	X	X	X	X	1	1	1	1	1	0	0	1	0	0	0	0	0	1	0	0	0	0	0	0
0	0	0	0	1	0	0	0	1	0	0	0	0	1	1	1	1	0	0	1	1	1	0	0	0	0	0	0	1	X	X	X	X	X	1	1	1	1	1	0	0	1	0	0	0	0	0	0	0	0	0	0	0	1
0	0	0	0	1	0	0	0	1	0	0	0	0	1	1	1	1	0	0	1	1	1	0	0	0	0	0	0	1	X	X	X	X	X	1	1	1	1	1	0	0	1	0	0	0	0	0	0	0	0	0	0	0	1
0	0	0	0	1	0	0	0	1	0	0	0	0	1	1	1	1	0	0	1	1	1	0	0	0	0	0	0	1	X	X	X	X	X	1	1	1	1	1	0	0	1	0	0	0	0	0	0	0	0	0	0	0	1
0	0	0	0	1	0	0	0	1	0	0	0	0	1	1	1	1	0	0	1	1	1	0	0	0	0	0	0	1	X	X	X	X	X	1	1	1	1	1	0	0	1	0	0	0	0	0	0	0	0	0	0	0	1
0	0	0	0	1	0	0	0	1	0	0	0	0	1	1	1	1	0	0	1	1	1	0	0	0	0	0	0	1	X	X	X	X	X	1	1	1	1	1	0	0	1	0	0	0	0	0	0	0	0	0	0	0	1
0	0	0	0	1	0	0	0	1	0	0	0	0	1	1	1	1	0	0	1	1	1	0	0	0	0	0	0	1	X	X	X	X	X	1	1	1	1	1	0	0	1	0	0	0	0	0	0	0	0	0	0	0	1
0	0	0	0	1	0	0	0	1	0	0	0	0	1	1	1	1	0	0	1	1	1	0	0	0	0	0	0	1	X	X	X	X	X	1	1	1	1	1	0	0	1	0	0	0	0	0	0	0	0	0	0	0	1
0	0	0	0	1	0	0	0	1	0	0	0	0	1	1	1	1	0	0	1	1	1	0	0	0	0	0	0	1	X	X	X	X	X	1	1	1	1	1	0	0	1	0	0	0	0	0	0	0	0	0	0	0	1
0	0	0	0	1	0	0	0	1	0	0	0	0	1	1	1	1	0	0	1	1	1	0	0	0	0	0	0	1	X	X	X	X	X	1	1	1	1	1	0	0	1	0	0	0	0	0	0	0	0	0	0	0	1
0	0	0	0	1	0	0	0	1	0	0	0	0	1	1	1	1	0	0	1	1	1	0	0	0	0	0	0	1	X	X	X	X	X	1	1	1	1	1	0	0	1	0	0	0	0	0	0	0	0	0	0	0	1
0	0	0	0	1	0	0	0	1	0	0	0	0	1	1	1	1	0	0	1	1	1	0	0	0	0	0	0	1	X	X	X	X	X	1	1	1	1	1	0	0	1	0	0	0	0	0	0	0	0	0	0	0	1
0	0	0	0	1	0	0	0	1	0	0	0	0	1	1	1	1	0	0	1	1	1	0	0	0	0	0	0	1	X	X	X	X	X	1	1	1	1	1	0	0	1	0	0	0	0	0	0	0	0	0	0	0	1
0	0	0	0	1	0	0	0	1	0	0	0	0	1	1	1	1	0	0	1	1	1	0	0	0	0	0	0	1	X	X	X	X	X	1	1	1	1	1	0	0	1	0	0	0	0	0	0	0	0	0	0	0	1
0	0	0	0	1	0	0	0	1	0	0	0	0	1	1	1	1	0	0	1	1	1	0	0	0	0	0	0	1	X	X	X	X	X	1	1	1	1	1	0	0	1	0	0	0	0	0	0	0	0	0	0	0	1
0	0	0	0	1	0	0	0	1	0	0	0	0	1	1	1	1	0	0	1	1	1	0	0	0	0	0	0	1	X	X	X	X	X	1	1	1	1	1	0	0	1	0	0	0	0	0	0	0	0	0	0	0	1
0	0	0	0	1	0	0	0	1	0	0	0	0	1	1	1	1	0	0	1	1	1	0	0	0	0	0	0	1	X	X	X	X	X	1	1	1	1	1	0	0	1	0	0	0	0	0	0	0	0	0	0	0	1

APPENDIX B

```
AMDOS/29 AMDASM MICRO ASSEMBLER, V1.1
CPUII DEFINITIONS

 ;ADVANCE MICRO DEVICES
 ; AM29Ø3 AND AM29Ø4 DEFINITION FILE FOR CPUII
 ;
 ;REV. OCTOBER 17, 1978


 WORD 9Ø

 ;EQUATES

 MEM:     EQU H#F
 SPF:     EQU H#Ø
 OFF:     EQU B#1


 ;29Ø3 DESTINATION MODIFIERS

 ADR:     EQU H#Ø
 LDR:     EQU H#1
 ADRQ:    EQU H#2
 LDRQ:    EQU H#3
 RPT:     EQU H#4
 LDQP:    EQU H#5
 QPT:     EQU H#6
 RQPT:    EQU H#7
 AUR:     EQU H#8
 LUR:     EQU H#9
 AURQ:    EQU H#A
 LURQ:    EQU H#B
 YBUS:    EQU H#C
 LUQ:     EQU H#D
 SINX:    EQU H#E


 ;CONSTANTS

 RØ:      EQU H#Ø
 R1:      EQU H#1
 R2:      EQU H#2
 R3:      EQU H#3
 R4:      EQU H#4
 R5:      EQU H#5
 R6:      EQU H#6
 R7:      EQU H#7
 R8:      EQU H#8
 R9:      EQU H#9
 R1Ø:     EQU H#A
 R11:     EQU H#B
 R12:     EQU H#C
 R13:     EQU H#D
 R14:     EQU H#E
 R15:     EQU H#F
```

```
AMDOS/29 AMDASM MICRO ASSEMBLER, V1.1
CPUII DEFINITIONS


 ;2903 SOURCE MODIFIERS

 RADB:    EQU 3B#001
 RAQ:     EQU 3B#010
 DARB:    EQU 3B#100
 DADB:    EQU 3B#101
 DAQ:     EQU 3B#110

 ;I/O

 IOIN:    EQU 12H#01
 BIN:     EQU 12H#10
 BOUT:    EQU 12H#08
 LMAR:    EQU 12H#10
 YREG:    EQU 12H#02
 AOUT:    EQU 12H#40
 IOUT:    EQU 12H#04


 ;CARRY SELECT

 ONE:     EQU 2B#01
 CZ:      EQU 2B#10

 ;SUB DEFINITIONS



 SUB0:    SUB 36X,1B#0,4VX,4VX,4VX
 SUB1:    SUB 36X,1B#0,4VX,4VX,4VX,4VH#F
 SUB2:    SUB 36X,1B#0,4VX,4VX,4X,4VH#F
 SUB3:    SUB 3VB#000,16X,1B#0,13X
 SUB4:    SUB 36X,1B#0,12X
 SUB5:    SUB 44X,1B#0,15X
 SUB6:    SUB 44X,1B#0,15X
 SUB7:    SUB 26X
 SUB8:    SUB 36X,1B#0,4VX,8X,4VH#F
 SUB9:    SUB 36X,1B#0,4VX,4X,4VX,4VH#F
 SUB10:   SUB 36X,1B#0,4VX,4VX,4X
 SUB11:   SUB 24X,2VB#00,34X,4B#0000,1B#1,5X
 SUB12:   SUB 77X,1B#1,12VXH#0%
 SUB13:   SUB SPF,3VB#000,16X,1B#0,13X
 SUB14:   SUB 24X,2VB#00,34X,4B#0000,2B#10
 SUB15:   SUB 23X,1B#0,6X
 SUB16:   SUB SPF,3B#000,16X,1VB#0,13X
 SUB17:   SUB 54X
 SUB18:   SUB 22X,1B#0,7X
 SUB19:   SUB 16X,1B#0,13X
 SUB20:   SUB 1X,1VB#0,14X
 SUB21:   SUB 30X,H#B,20X



 ;CCU CONTROL
```

```
AMDOS/29 AMDASM MICRO ASSEMBLER, V1.1
CPUII DEFINITIONS

 ACK:     DEF 66X,H#9,20X
 OBF:     DEF 66X,H#A,20X
 CNT:     DEF 66X,H#F,20X
 GRD:     DEF 66X,H#0,20X
 JZ:      DEF SUB11,H#0,SUB20
 CJS:     DEF SUB11,H#1,SUB20
 JMAP:    DEF SUB11,H#2,SUB20
 CJP:     DEF SUB11,H#3,SUB20
 PUSH:    DEF SUB11,H#4,SUB20
 JSRP:    DEF SUB11,H#5,SUB20
 CJV:     DEF SUB11,H#6,SUB20
 JRP:     DEF SUB11,H#7,SUB20
 RFCT:    DEF SUB11,H#8,SUB20
 RPCT:    DEF SUB11,H#9,SUB20
 CRTN:    DEF SUB11,H#A,SUB20
 CJPP:    DEF SUB11,H#B,SUB20
 LDCT:    DEF SUB11,H#C,SUB20
 LOOP:    DEF SUB11,H#D,SUB20
 CONT:    DEF SUB11,H#E,SUB20
 JP:      DEF SUB11,H#F,SUB20
 JSR:     DEF SUB14,H#01,SUB20
 RTN:     DEF SUB14,H#0A,SUB20

 ;SHARED CONTROL FIELD

 GOTO:    DEF SUB12
 COUNT:   DEF SUB12
 PUT:     DEF 77X,1B#0,12VXH#0%

 ;POLARITY CONTROL

 T:       DEF 65X,1B#1,24X
 F:       DEF 65X,1B#0,24X

 ;2903 CONTROL/FUNCTIONS

 IN:      DEF 36X,1B#1,H#F,8X,H#F,H#0,19X,1B#0,13X
 OUT:     DEF 36X,1B#0,8X,H#F,H#C,H#6,SUB3
 YOFF:    DEF 36X,1B#1,53X
 HIGH:    DEF SUB8,H#0,3B#010,SUB19
 SRS:     DEF SUB1,H#1,SUB3
 SSR:     DEF SUB1,H#2,SUB3
 ADD:     DEF SUB1,H#3,SUB3
 PAS:     DEF SUB2,H#4,SUB3
 COMS:    DEF SUB2,H#5,SUB3
 PAR:     DEF SUB9,H#6,SUB3
 COMR:    DEF SUB9,H#7,SUB3
 LOW:     DEF SUB8,H#8,3X,SUB19
 CRAS:    DEF SUB1,H#9,SUB3
 XNRS:    DEF SUB1,H#A,SUB3
 XOR:     DEF SUB1,H#B,SUB3
 AND:     DEF SUB1,H#C,SUB3
 NOR:     DEF SUB1,H#D,SUB3
 NAND:    DEF SUB1,H#E,SUB3
 OR:      DEF SUB1,H#F,SUB3

 ;2903 SPECIAL FUNCTIONS
```

AMDOS/29 AMDASM MICRO ASSEMBLER, V1.1
CPUII DEFINITIONS

```
UMUL:    DEF SUBØ,H#Ø,SUB16
TCM:     DEF SUBØ,H#2,SUB16
SMTC:    DEF SUB1Ø,H#5,SUB16
TCMC:    DEF SUBØ,H#6,SUB16
SLN:     DEF SUB1Ø,H#8,SUB16
DLN:     DEF SUBØ,H#A,SUB16
TDIV:    DEF SUBØ,H#C,SUB16
TDC:     DEF SUBØ,H#E,SUB16
INC:     DEF SUB1Ø,H#4,SUB16
SDQP:    DEF SUB4,H#5,4X,SUB3
SUQP:    DEF SUB4,H#D,4X,SUB3
LQPT:    DEF 36X,1B#Ø,8X,4VX,H#6,H#6,SUB3
RMOV:    DEF SUB2,H#4,SUB3
QMOV:    DEF 36X,1B#Ø,4VX,8X,MEM,H#4,3B#Ø1Ø,SUB19
SDRL:    DEF SUB1Ø,H#1,H#4,SUB3
SURL:    DEF SUB1Ø,H#9,H#4,SUB3

    .

;29Ø4 SHIFT CONTROL

SDDH:    DEF SUB7,H#3,SUB6
SDUH:    DEF SUB7,H#7,SUB5
SDDL:    DEF SUB7,H#6,SUB6
SDUL:    DEF SUB7,H#6,SUB5
RDD:     DEF SUB7,H#F,SUB6
RDU:     DEF SUB7,H#F,SUB5
SSXO:    DEF SUB7,H#E,SUB6
RSD:     DEF SUB7,H#A,SUB6
RSU:     DEF SUB7,H#A,SUB5
SUL:     DEF SUB7,H#2,SUB5
SUH:     DEF SUB7,H#3,SUB5
SDL:     DEF SUB7,H#Ø,SUB6
SDH:     DEF SUB7,H#1,SUB6
SDMS:    DEF SUB7,H#5,SUB6
SMS:     DEF SUB7,H#2,SUB6
SDDC:    DEF SUB7,H#7,SUB6
SDUC:    DEF SUB7,H#4,SUB5

;29Ø4 MICRO INSTRUCTION CODES

RSTI:    DEF 3ØX,6B#ØØØØ11,SUB17
SWAP:    DEF 3 X,6B#ØØØØ1Ø,SUB17
SHLD:    EQU 1B#1


;29Ø4 MACHINE INSTRUCTION CODES

LMA:     DEF SUB15,6B#ØØØØØØ,SUB17
RSTA:    DEF SUB15,6B#ØØØØ11,SUB17
SHOLD:   DEF 23X,1B#Ø,66X


;29Ø4 MICRO STATUS SELECT
```

```
AMDOS/29 AMDASM MICRO ASSEMBLER, V1.1
CPUII DEFINITICNS

 MIZ:     DEF SUB18,6B#010100,SUB21
 MIO:     DEF SUB18,6B#010110,SUB21
 MIC:     DEF SUB18,6B#011010,SUB21
 MIS:     DEF SUB18,6B#011110,SUB21

 ;2904 MACHINE STATUS SELECT

 MAZ:     DEF SUB18,6B#100100,SUB21
 MAO:     DEF SUB18,6B#100110,SUB21
 MAC:     DEF SUB18,6B#101010,SUB21
 MAS:     DEF SUB18,6B#101110,SUB21

 ;DEVICE DISABLE


 ALUCFF: DEF 7 X,1B#1,13X
 ALLOFF: DEF 7 X,3B#111,13X


 ;LOAD CONSTANT

 CONST:   DEF 16 VXH#0%,4X,1B#0,69X

 ;BCD STATUS REGISTER CONTROL

 ENR:     DEF 16X,1B#0,73X
 CLSR2:   DEF 17X,1B#0,72X
 ENSR1:   DEF 18X,1B#1,71X
 CZERO:   DEF 19X,1B#0,70X




 END

 TOTAL PHASE 1 ERRORS =   0
```

AMDOS/29 AMDASM MICRO ASSEMBLER, V1.1

```
       ;ADVANCE MICRO DEVICES
       ;  AM2903 AND AM2904 CPUII SOURCE FILE

 Ø1ØØ            ORG H#1ØØ
 Ø1ØØ INP:       ALUOFF & T & OBF & CJP & GOTO INP
 Ø1Ø1            ALUOFF & PUSH
 Ø1Ø2            IN & T & OBF & LOOP & PUT IOIN
 Ø1Ø3            ALUOFF & RTN

 Ø1Ø4 OUTP:      OUT & CONT & PUT YREG
 Ø1Ø5            ALUOFF & PUSH
 Ø1Ø6            ALUOFF & F & ACK & LOOP & PUT IOUT
 Ø1Ø7            ALUOFF & PUSH
 Ø1Ø8            ALUOFF & T & ACK & LOOP
 Ø1Ø9            ALUOFF & RTN

 Ø1ØA USM:       LOW R1 & JSR & GOTO INP
 Ø1ØB            PAR RØ,R15 & JSR & GOTO INP
 Ø1ØC            LQPT R15 & F & GRD & PUSH & COUNT ØØE
 Ø1ØD            UMUL R1,R1,RØ & F & CNT & SDDL & RFCT
 Ø1ØE            PAR R15,R1 & JSR & GOTO OUTP
 Ø1ØF            QMOV R15 & JSR & GOTO OUTP
 Ø11Ø            JP & GOTO USM

 Ø111 SM:        LOW R1 & JSR & GOTO INP
 Ø112            PAR RØ,R15 & JSR & GOTO INP
 Ø113            LQPT R15 & F & GRD & PUSH & COUNT ØØD
 Ø114            TCM R1,R1,RØ & F & CNT & SDDL & RFCT
 Ø115            TCMC R1,R1,RØ & SDDL & CONT CZ
 Ø116            PAR R15,R1 & JSR & GOTO OUTP
 Ø117            QMOV R15 & JSR & GOTO OUTP
 Ø118            ALUOFF & JP & GOTO SM

 Ø119 DIV:       LOW R1Ø & JSR & GOTO INP
 Ø11A            PAR R7,R15 & JSR & GOTO INP
 Ø11B            PAR R1,R15 & JSR & GOTO INP
 Ø11C            PAR R4,R15 & CONT
 Ø11D LOOP1:     PAR R3,R7 & CONT
 Ø11E            PAR R2,R1 & T & MIZ & CJP & GOTO ABORT
 Ø11F            SMTC R2,R2 & CONT CZ
 Ø12Ø            SMTC R3,R3 & T & MIO & CJP CZ & GOTO SCALE1
 Ø121            ALUOFF & T & MIO & CJP & GOTO SKIP6
 Ø122            SURL R3,R3 & SUL & CONT
 Ø123            SURL R2,R2 & SUL & CONT
 Ø124            ALUOFF & JP & GOTO LOOP2
 Ø125 SCALE1:    LQPT R4 & JSR & GOTO SDIVD
 Ø126            ALUOFF & JP LOOP1
 Ø127 LOOP2:     SSR R15,R3,R2,YBUS & CONT ONE
 Ø128 SKIP6:     LQPT R4 & F & MIC & CJP & GOTO SKIP3
 Ø129            ALUOFF & JSR & GOTO SDIVD
 Ø12A            SDRL R2,R2 & SDL & CONT
 Ø12B            ALUOFF & JP & GOTO LOOP2
 Ø12C SKIP3:     ALUOFF & F & GRD & LDCT & COUNT ØØC
 Ø12D            DLN R1,R1,R7 & T & GRD & RDU & PUSH
 Ø12E            TDIV R1,R1,R7 & F & CNT & RDU & RFCT CZ
 Ø12F            TDC R1,R1,R7 & SUH & CONT CZ
 Ø13Ø            QMOV R15 & JSR & GOTO OUTP
```

AMDOS/29 AMDASM MICRO ASSEMBLER, V1.1

```
Ø131          PAR R15,R1 & JSR & GOTO OUTP
Ø132          ALUOFF & JP & GOTO DIV
Ø133 SDIVD:   PAR R1,R1 & CONT
Ø134          ALUOFF & T & MIS & CJP & GOTO NEG
Ø135          PAR R1,R1,ADRQ & SDDL & CONT
Ø136          ALUOFF & JP & GOTO RET
Ø137 NEG:     PAR R1,R1,ADRQ & SDDL & CONT
Ø138 RET:     QMOV R4 & CONT
Ø139          PAR R1Ø,R1Ø & RTN ONE

Ø13A SLNORM:  JSR & GOTO INP
Ø13B          LQPT R15 & CONT
Ø13C          SLN R2,R2,OFF & CONT & SHOLD
Ø13D          MAZ & T & CJP & GOTO ABORT
Ø13E          MAC & T & LOW RØ & CJP & GOTO END
Ø13F          SLN R2,R2 & MAC & T & CJP ONE & GOTO END & SUL
Ø14Ø AGAIN:   SLN R2,R2 & MIO & F & CJP ONE & GOTO AGAIN & SUL
Ø141          SDQP & SMS & CONT
Ø142          SRS R2,R2,RØ & CONT
Ø143          QMOV R15 & JSR & GOTO OUTP
Ø144          PAR R15,R2 & JSR & GOTO OUTP
Ø145 END:     JP & GOTO SLNORM

Ø146 DLNORM:  JSR & GOTO INP
Ø147          LQPT R15 & JSR & GOTO INP
Ø148          DLN R15,R15,R15,OFF & CONT & SHOLD
Ø149          MAZ & T & CJP & GOTO ABORT
Ø14A          LOW R2 & MAC & T & CJP & GOTO END2
Ø14B          DLN R15,R15,R15 & SDUL & MAO & T & CJP & GOTO JUMP1
Ø14C LOOP4:   DLN R15,R15,R15 & SDUL & MIO & T & CJP & GOTO JUMP1
Ø14D          PAR R2,R2 & JP ONE & GOTO LOOP4
Ø14E JUMP1:   PAR R2,R2 & CONT ONE
Ø14F          SDRQ R15,R15 & SDMS & JSR & GOTO OUTP
Ø15Ø          QMOV R15 & JSR & GOTO OUTP
Ø151 END2:    JP & GOTO DLNORM

Ø152 SQRT:    LOW R1Ø & CONT
Ø153          LOW RØ & JSR & GOTO INP
Ø154          PAR R1,R15 & CONT
Ø155          PAR R2,RØ,,DARB & CONST ØØØ5 & CONT
Ø156          PAR R3,RØ,,DARB & CONST ØØØ3 & CONT
Ø157          PAR R4,RØ,,DARB & CONST H#BFFF & CONT
Ø158          PAR R5,RØ,,DARB & CONST 4ØØØ & CONT
Ø159          PAR R6,RØ,,DARB & CONST ØØØ8 & CONT
Ø15A          SRS RØ,R1,R5 & CONT & SHOLD
Ø15B CYCLE:   AND R5,R5,R4 & CONT
Ø15C          SDRL R4,R4 & MAS & CJP & GOTO END3
Ø15D          SURL RØ,RØ & T & MAS & CJP & GOTO POS
Ø15E          OR R5,R3 & JP & GOTO CNT
Ø15F POS:     OR R5,R2 & CONT
Ø16Ø CNT:     SRS R6,R6,R1Ø & CONT
Ø161          SDRL R2,R2 & T & MIZ & CJP ,SHLD & GOTO END3
Ø162          SDRL R3,R3 & T & MAS & CJP & GOTO SUB
Ø163          ADD R2,RØ,R5 & JP & GOTO CYCLE & SHOLD
Ø164 SUB:     SRS RØ,RØ,R5 & JP & GOTO CYCLE & SHOLD
Ø165 END3:    JP & GOTO SQRT
```

AMDOS/29 AMDASM MICRO ASSEMBLER, V1.1

```
 0166 ABORT:  ALUOFF & JP & GOTO ABORT
 0167         JP & GOTO DIV


      END
```

AMDOS/29 AMDASM MICRO ASSEMBLER, V1.1

```
0100 XXXXXXXXXXXXXXXX XXXXXXXX00XXXXXX XXXXXXXXXXXXXXXX XXXXXXXXXXXX0000
     1110100011X01100 0100000000
0101 XXXXXXXXXXXXXXXX XXXXXXXX00XXXXXX XXXXXXXXXXXXXXXX XXXXXXXXXXXX0000
     1XXXXX0100X01XXX XXXXXXXXXX
0102 XXXXXXXXXXXXXXXX XXXXXXXX00XXXXXX XXXX11111XXXXXXX X11110000XXX0000
     1110101101X00000 0000000001
0103 XXXXXXXXXXXXXXXX XXXXXXXX00XXXXXX XXXXXXXXXXXXXXXX XXXXXXXXXXXX0000
     1000001010X01XXX XXXXXXXXXX
0104 XXXXXXXXXXXXXXXX XXXXXXXX00XXXXXX XXXX0XXXXXXXX111 1110011000000000
     1XXXXX1110X00000 0000000010
0105 XXXXXXXXXXXXXXXX XXXXXXXX00XXXXXX XXXXXXXXXXXXXXXX XXXXXXXXXXXX0000
     1XXXXX0100X01XXX XXXXXXXXXX
0106 XXXXXXXXXXXXXXXX XXXXXXXX00XXXXXX XXXXXXXXXXXXXXXX XXXXXXXXXXXX0000
     1010011101X01000 0000000100
0107 XXXXXXXXXXXXXXXX XXXXXXXX00XXXXXX XXXXXXXXXXXXXXXX XXXXXXXXXXXX0000
     1XXXXX0100X01XXX XXXXXXXXXX
0108 XXXXXXXXXXXXXXXX XXXXXXXX00XXXXXX XXXXXXXXXXXXXXXX XXXXXXXXXXXX0000
     1110011101X01XXX XXXXXXXXXX
0109 XXXXXXXXXXXXXXXX XXXXXXXX00XXXXXX XXXXXXXXXXXXXXXX XXXXXXXXXXXX0000
     1000001010X01XXX XXXXXXXXXX
010A XXXXXXXXXXXXXXXX XXXXXXXX00XXXXXX XXXX00001XXXXXXX X11111000XXX0000
     1000000001X00100 0100000000
010B XXXXXXXXXXXXXXXX XXXXXXXX00XXXXXX XXXX00000XXXX111 1111101100000000
     1000000001X00100 0100000000
010C XXXXXXXXXXXXXXXX XXXXXXXX00XXXXXX XXXX0XXXXXXXX111 1011001100000000
     1000000100X00100 0000001110
010D XXXXXXXXXXXXXXXX XXXXXXXX000110XX XXXX000010001000 0000000000000000
     1011111000000XXX XXXXXXXXXX
010E XXXXXXXXXXXXXXXX XXXXXXXX00XXXXXX XXXX01111XXXX000 1111101100000000
     1000000001X00100 0100000100
010F XXXXXXXXXXXXXXXX XXXXXXXX00XXXXXX XXXX01111XXXXXXX X111101000100000
     1000000001X00100 0100000100
0110 XXXXXXXXXXXXXXXX XXXXXXXX00XXXXXX XXXXXXXXXXXXXXXX XXXXXXXXXXXX0000
     1XXXXX1111X0X100 0100001010
0111 XXXXXXXXXXXXXXXX XXXXXXXX00XXXXXX XXXX00001XXXXXXX X11111000XXX0000
     1000000001X00100 0100000000
0112 XXXXXXXXXXXXXXXX XXXXXXXX00XXXXXX XXXX00000XXXX111 1111101100000000
     1000000001X00100 0100000000
0113 XXXXXXXXXXXXXXXX XXXXXXXX00XXXXXX XXXX0XXXXXXXX111 1011001100000000
     1000000100X00100 0000001101
0114 XXXXXXXXXXXXXXXX XXXXXXXX000110XX XXXX000010001000 0001000000000000
     1011111000000XXX XXXXXXXXXX
0115 XXXXXXXXXXXXXXXX XXXXXXXX100110XX XXXX000010001000 0011000000000000
     1XXXXX1110000XXX XXXXXXXXXX
0116 XXXXXXXXXXXXXXXX XXXXXXXX00XXXXXX XXXX01111XXXX000 1111101100000000
     1000000001X00100 0100000100
0117 XXXXXXXXXXXXXXXX XXXXXXXX00XXXXXX XXXX01111XXXXXXX X111101000100000
     1000000001X00100 0100000100
0118 XXXXXXXXXXXXXXXX XXXXXXXX00XXXXXX XXXXXXXXXXXXXXXX XXXXXXXXXXXX0000
     1XXXXX1111X01100 0100010001
0119 XXXXXXXXXXXXXXXX XXXXXXXX00XXXXXX XXXX01010XXXXXXX X11111000XXX0000
     1000000001X00100 0100000000
011A XXXXXXXXXXXXXXXX XXXXXXXX00XXXXXX XXXX00111XXXX111 1111101100000000
     1000000001X00100 0100000000
011B XXXXXXXXXXXXXXXX XXXXXXXX00XXXXXX XXXX00001XXXX111 1111101100000000
     1000000001X00100 0100000000
011C XXXXXXXXXXXXXXXX XXXXXXXX00XXXXXX XXXX00100XXXX111 1111101100000000
     1XXXXX1110X00XXX XXXXXXXXXX
```

AMDCS/29 AMDASM MICRO ASSEMBLER, V1.1

```
0110 XXXXXXXXXXXXXXXX XXXXXXXX00XXXXXX XXXX00011XXXX011 1111101100000000
     1XXXXX1110X00XXX XXXXXXXXXX
011E XXXXXXXXXXXXXXXX XXXXXX0X00XXXX01 010000010XXXX000 1111101100000000
     1110110011X00100 0101100110
011F XXXXXXXXXXXXXXXX XXXXXXXX10XXXXXX XXXX000100010XXX X010100000000000
     1XXXXX1110X00XXX XXXXXXXXXX
0120 XXXXXXXXXXXXXXXX XXXXXX0X10XXXX01 0110001100011XXX X010100000000000
     1110110011X00100 0100100101
0121 XXXXXXXXXXXXXXXX XXXXXX0X00XXXX01 0110XXXXXXXXXXXX XXXXXXXXXXXX0000
     1110110011X01100 0100101000
0122 XXXXXXXXXXXXXXXX XXXXXXXX000010XX XXXX000110011XXX X100101000000000
     1XXXXX1110000XXX XXXXXXXXXX
0123 XXXXXXXXXXXXXXXX XXXXXXXX000010XX XXXX000100010XXX X100101000000000
     1XXXXX1110000XXX XXXXXXXXXX
0124 XXXXXXXXXXXXXXXX XXXXXXXX00XXXXXX XXXXXXXXXXXXXXXX XXXXXXXXXXXX0000
     1XXXXX1111X01100 0100100111
0125 XXXXXXXXXXXXXXXX XXXXXXXX00XXXXXX XXXX0XXXXXXXX010 0011001100000000
     1000000001X00100 0100110011
0126 XXXXXXXXXXXXXXXX XXXXXXXX01XXXXXX XXXXXXXXXXXXXXXX XXXXXXXXXXXX0000
     1XXXXX1111X01XXX XXXXXXXXXX
0127 XXXXXXXXXXXXXXXX XXXXXXXX01XXXXXX XXXX011110011001 0110000100000000
     1XXXXX1110X00XXX XXXXXXXXXX
0128 XXXXXXXXXXXXXXXX XXXXXX0X00XXXX01 10100XXXXXXXX010 0011001100000000
     1010110011X00100 0100101100
0129 XXXXXXXXXXXXXXXX XXXXXXXX00XXXXXX XXXXXXXXXXXXXXXX XXXXXXXXXXXX0000
     1000000001X01100 0100110011
012A XXXXXXXXXXXXXXXX XXXXXXXX000000XX XXXX000100010XXX X000101000000000
     1XXXXX1110000XXX XXXXXXXXXX
012B XXXXXXXXXXXXXXXX XXXXXXXX00XXXXXX XXXXXXXXXXXXXXXX XXXXXXXXXXXX0000
     1XXXXX1111X01100 0100100111
012C XXXXXXXXXXXXXXXX XXXXXXXX00XXXXXX XXXXXXXXXXXXXXXX XXXXXXXXXXXX0000
     1000001100X01100 0000001100
012D XXXXXXXXXXXXXXXX XXXXXXXX001111XX XXXX000010001011 1101000000000000
     1100000100000XXX XXXXXXXXXX
012E XXXXXXXXXXXXXXXX XXXXXXXX101111XX XXXX000010001011 1110000000000000
     1011111000000XXX XXXXXXXXXX
012F XXXXXXXXXXXXXXXX XXXXXXXX100011XX XXXX000010001011 1111000000000000
     1XXXXX1110000XXX XXXXXXXXXX
0130 XXXXXXXXXXXXXXXX XXXXXXXX00XXXXXX XXXX01111XXXXXXX X111101000100000
     1000000001X00100 0100000100
0131 XXXXXXXXXXXXXXXX XXXXXXXX00XXXXXX XXXX01111XXXX000 1111101100000000
     1000000001X00100 0100000100
0132 XXXXXXXXXXXXXXXX XXXXXXXX00XXXXXX XXXXXXXXXXXXXXXX XXXXXXXXXXXX0000
     1XXXXX1111X01100 0100011001
0133 XXXXXXXXXXXXXXXX XXXXXXXX00XXXXXX XXXX00001XXXX000 1111101100000000
     1XXXXX1110X00XXX XXXXXXXXXX
0134 XXXXXXXXXXXXXXXX XXXXXX0X00XXXX01 1110XXXXXXXXXXXX XXXXXXXXXXXX0000
     1110110011X01100 0100110111
0135 XXXXXXXXXXXXXXXX XXXXXXXX000110XX XXXX00001XXXX000 1001001100000000
     1XXXXX1110000XXX XXXXXXXXXX
0136 XXXXXXXXXXXXXXXX XXXXXXXX00XXXXXX XXXXXXXXXXXXXXXX XXXXXXXXXXXX0000
     1XXXXX1111X01100 0100111000
0137 XXXXXXXXXXXXXXXX XXXXXXXX000110XX XXXX00001XXXX000 1001001100000000
     1XXXXX1110000XXX XXXXXXXXXX
0138 XXXXXXXXXXXXXXXX XXXXXXXX00XXXXXX XXXX00100XXXXXXX X111101000100000
     1XXXXX1110X00XXX XXXXXXXXXX
0139 XXXXXXXXXXXXXXXX XXXXXXXX01XXXXXX XXXX01010XXXX101 0111101100000000
     1000001010X00XXX XXXXXXXXXX
```

```
AMDOS/29 AMDASM MICRO ASSEMBLER, V1.1

 Ø13A XXXXXXXXXXXXXXXX XXXXXXXXØØXXXXXX XXXXXXXXXXXXXXXX XXXXXXXXXXXXØØØØ
      1ØØØØØØØØ1XØX1ØØ Ø1ØØØØØØØØ
 Ø13B XXXXXXXXXXXXXXXX XXXXXXXXØØXXXXXX XXXXØXXXXXXXX111 1Ø11ØØ11ØØØØØØØØ
      1XXXXX111ØXØØXXX XXXXXXXXXX
 Ø13C XXXXXXXXXXXXXXXX XXXXXXXØØØXXXXXX XXXXØØØ1ØØØ1ØXXX X1ØØØØØØØØØØØØØØ
      1XXXXX111ØXØ1XXX XXXXXXXXXX
 Ø13D XXXXXXXXXXXXXXXX XXXXXXØXØØXXXX1Ø Ø1ØØXXXXXXXXXXXX XXXXXXXXXXXXØØØØ
      111Ø11ØØ11XØX1ØØ Ø1Ø11ØØ11Ø
 Ø13E XXXXXXXXXXXXXXXX XXXXXXØXØØXXXX1Ø 1Ø1ØØØØØØXXXXXXX X11111ØØØXXXØØØØ
      111Ø11ØØ11XØØ1ØØ Ø1Ø1ØØØ1Ø1
 Ø13F XXXXXXXXXXXXXXXX XXXXXXØXØ1ØØ1Ø1Ø Ø11ØØØØ1ØØØ1ØXXX X1ØØØØØØØØØØØØØØ
      111Ø11ØØ11ØØØ1ØØ Ø1Ø1ØØØ1Ø1
 Ø14Ø XXXXXXXXXXXXXXXX XXXXXXØXØ1ØØ1ØØ1 Ø11ØØØØ1ØØØ1ØXXX X1ØØØØØØØØØØØØØØ
      1Ø1Ø11ØØ11ØØØ1ØØ Ø1Ø1ØØØØØØ
 Ø141 XXXXXXXXXXXXXXXX XXXXXXXXØØØØ1ØXX XXXXØXXXXXXXXXXX XØ1Ø1XXXXØØØØØØØ
      1XXXXX111ØØØØXXX XXXXXXXXXX
 Ø142 XXXXXXXXXXXXXXXX XXXXXXXXØØXXXXXX XXXXØØØ1ØØØ1ØØØØ Ø1111ØØØ1ØØØØØØØ
      1XXXXX111ØXØØXXX XXXXXXXXXX
 Ø143 XXXXXXXXXXXXXXXX XXXXXXXXØØXXXXXX XXXXØ1111XXXXXXX X1111Ø1ØØØ1ØØØØØ
      1ØØØØØØØØ1XØØ1ØØ Ø1ØØØØØ1ØØ
 Ø144 XXXXXXXXXXXXXXXX XXXXXXXXØØXXXXXX XXXXØ1111XXXXØØ1 Ø1111Ø11ØØØØØØØØ
      1ØØØØØØØØ1XØØ1ØØ Ø1ØØØØØ1ØØ
 Ø145 XXXXXXXXXXXXXXXX XXXXXXXXØØXXXXXX XXXXXXXXXXXXXXXX XXXXXXXXXXXXØØØØ
      1XXXXX1111XØX1ØØ Ø1ØØ111Ø1Ø
 Ø146 XXXXXXXXXXXXXXXX XXXXXXXXØØXXXXXX XXXXXXXXXXXXXXXX XXXXXXXXXXXXØØØØ
      1ØØØØØØØØ1XØX1ØØ Ø1ØØØØØØØØ
 Ø147 XXXXXXXXXXXXXXXX XXXXXXXXØØXXXXXX XXXXØXXXXXXXX111 1Ø11ØØ11ØØØØØØØØ
      1ØØØØØØØØ1XØØ1ØØ Ø1ØØØØØØØØ
 Ø148 XXXXXXXXXXXXXXXX XXXXXXXØØØXXXXXX XXXXØ11111111111 11Ø1ØØØØØØØØØØØØ
      1XXXXX111ØXØ1XXX XXXXXXXXXX
 Ø149 XXXXXXXXXXXXXXXX XXXXXXØXØØXXXX1Ø Ø1ØØXXXXXXXXXXXX XXXXXXXXXXXXØØØØ
      111Ø11ØØ11XØX1ØØ Ø1Ø11ØØ11Ø
 Ø14A XXXXXXXXXXXXXXXX XXXXXXØXØØXXXX1Ø 1Ø1ØØØØ1ØXXXXXXX X11111ØØØXXXØØØØ
      111Ø11ØØ11XØØ1ØØ Ø1Ø1Ø1ØØØ1
 Ø14B XXXXXXXXXXXXXXXX XXXXXXØXØØØ11Ø1Ø Ø11ØØ11111111111 11Ø1ØØØØØØØØØØØØ
      111Ø11ØØ11ØØØ1ØØ Ø1Ø1ØØ111Ø
 Ø14C XXXXXXXXXXXXXXXX XXXXXXØXØØØ11ØØ1 Ø11ØØ11111111111 11Ø1ØØØØØØØØØØØØ
      111Ø11ØØ11ØØØ1ØØ Ø1Ø1ØØ111Ø
 Ø14D XXXXXXXXXXXXXXXX XXXXXXXXØ1XXXXXX XXXXØØØ1ØXXXXØØ1 Ø1111Ø11ØØØØØØØØ
      1XXXXX1111XØØ1ØØ Ø1Ø1ØØ11ØØ
 Ø14E XXXXXXXXXXXXXXXX XXXXXXXXØ1XXXXXX XXXXØØØ1ØXXXXØØ1 Ø1111Ø11ØØØØØØØØ
      1XXXXX111ØXØØXXX XXXXXXXXXX
 Ø14F XXXXXXXXXXXXXXXX XXXXXXXXØØØ1Ø1XX XXXXØ11111111XXX XØØ11Ø1ØØØØØØØØØ
      1ØØØØØØØØ1ØØØ1ØØ Ø1ØØØØØ1ØØ
 Ø15Ø XXXXXXXXXXXXXXXX XXXXXXXXØØXXXXXX XXXXØ1111XXXXXXX X1111Ø1ØØØ1ØØØØØ
      1ØØØØØØØØ1XØØ1ØØ Ø1ØØØØØ1ØØ
 Ø151 XXXXXXXXXXXXXXXX XXXXXXXXØØXXXXXX XXXXXXXXXXXXXXXX XXXXXXXXXXXXØØØØ
      1XXXXX1111XØX1ØØ Ø1Ø1ØØØ11Ø
 Ø152 XXXXXXXXXXXXXXXX XXXXXXXXØØXXXXXX XXXXØ1Ø1ØXXXXXXX X11111ØØØXXXØØØØ
      1XXXXX111ØXØØXXX XXXXXXXXXX
 Ø153 XXXXXXXXXXXXXXXX XXXXXXXXØØXXXXXX XXXXØØØØØXXXXXXX X11111ØØØXXXØØØØ
      1ØØØØØØØØ1XØØ1ØØ Ø1ØØØØØØØØ
 Ø154 XXXXXXXXXXXXXXXX XXXXXXXXØØXXXXXX XXXXØØØØ1XXXX111 11111Ø11ØØØØØØØØ
      1XXXXX111ØXØØXXX XXXXXXXXXX
 Ø155 ØØØØØØØØØØØØØ1Ø1 XXXXØXXXØØXXXXXX XXXXØØØ1ØXXXXØØØ Ø1111Ø11Ø1ØØØØØØ
      1XXXXX111ØXØØXXX XXXXXXXXXX
 Ø156 ØØØØØØØØØØØØØØ11 XXXXØXXXØØXXXXXX XXXXØØØ11XXXXØØØ Ø1111Ø11Ø1ØØØØØØ
      1XXXXX111ØXØØXXX XXXXXXXXXX
```

AMDCS/29 AMDASM MICRO ASSEMBLER, V1.1

```
0157 1011111111111111 XXXX0XXX00XXXXXX XXXX00100XXXX000 0111101101000000
     1XXXXX1110X00XXX XXXXXXXXXX
0158 0100000000000000 XXXX0XXX00XXXXXX XXXX00101XXXX000 0111101101000000
     1XXXXX1110X00XXX XXXXXXXXXX
0159 0000000000001000 XXXX0XXX00XXXXXX XXXX00110XXXX000 0111101101000000
     1XXXXX1110X00XXX XXXXXXXXXX
015A XXXXXXXXXXXXXXXX XXXXXXX000XXXXXX XXXX000000001010 1111100010000000
     1XXXXX1110X00XXX XXXXXXXXXX
015B XXXXXXXXXXXXXXXX XXXXXXXX00XXXXXX XXXX001010101010 0111111000000000
     1XXXXX1110X00XXX XXXXXXXXXX
015C XXXXXXXXXXXXXXXX XXXXXX0X00XXXX10 1110001000100XXX X000101000000000
     1X10110011X00100 0101100101
015D XXXXXXXXXXXXXXXX XXXXXX0X00XXXX10 1110000000000XXX X100101000000000
     1110110011X00100 0101011111
015E XXXXXXXXXXXXXXXX XXXXXXXX00XXXXXX XXXX001010011XXX X111111110000000
     1XXXXX1111X00100 0101100000
015F XXXXXXXXXXXXXXXX XXXXXXXX00XXXXXX XXXX001010010XXX X111111110000000
     1XXXXX1110X00XXX XXXXXXXXXX
0160 XXXXXXXXXXXXXXXX XXXXXXXX00XXXXXX XXXX001100110101 0111100010000000
     1XXXXX1110X00XXX XXXXXXXXXX
0161 XXXXXXXXXXXXXXXX XXXXXX0X00XXXX01 0100001000010XXX X000101000000000
     1110110011X10100 0101100101
0162 XXXXXXXXXXXXXXXX XXXXXX0X00XXXX10 1110000110011XXX X000101000000000
     1110110011X00100 0101100100
0163 XXXXXXXXXXXXXXXX XXXXXXX000XXXXXX XXXX000000000010 1111100110000000
     1XXXXX1111X00100 0101011011
0164 XXXXXXXXXXXXXXXX XXXXXXX000XXXXXX XXXX000000000010 1111100010000000
     1XXXXX1111X00100 0101011011
0165 XXXXXXXXXXXXXXXX XXXXXXXX00XXXXXX XXXXXXXXXXXXXXXX XXXXXXXXXXXX0000
     1XXXXX1111X0X100 0101010010
0166 XXXXXXXXXXXXXXXX XXXXXXXX00XXXXXX XXXXXXXXXXXXXXXX XXXXXXXXXXXX0000
     1XXXXX1111X01100 0101100110
0167 XXXXXXXXXXXXXXXX XXXXXXXX00XXXXXX XXXXXXXXXXXXXXXX XXXXXXXXXXXX0000
     1XXXXX1111X0X100 0100011001
```

Am2903 MNEMONICS

I_0 FUNCTION

RAMB	RAM B – OUTPUT
Q	Q REGISTER
SPF	SPECIAL FUNCTIONS

ALU Functions

SPF	Special Functions	
HIGH	Fi = HIGH	HIGHS
SRS	Subtract R from S	$S - R - 1 + C_n$
SSR	Subtract S from R	$R - S - 1 + C_n$
ADD	Add R and S	$R + S + C_n$
PAS	Pass S	$S + C_n$
COMS	2's Complement S	$\overline{S} + C_n$
PAR	Pass R	$R + C_n$
COMR	2's Complement R	$\overline{R} + C_n$
LOW	Fi = LOW	LOW'S
CRAS	Complement R AND with S	$\overline{R}AS$
XNRS	Exclusive NOR R with S	$\overline{RVS}$
XOR	Exclusive OR R with S	RVS
AND	AND R with S	RAS
NOR	NOR R with S	$\overline{RVS}$
NAND	NAND R with S	$\overline{RAS}$
OR	OR R with S	RVS

ALU Destination Control

ADR	Arithmetic Shift Down, Results Into RAM
LDR	Logical Shift Down, Results Into RAM
ADRQ	Arithmetic Shift Down, Results Into RAM and Q Register
LDRQ	Logical Shift Down, Results Into RAM and Q Register
RPT	Results Into RAM, Generate Parity
* LDQP	Logical Shift Down Contents of Q Register, Generate Parity
* QPT	Results Into Q Register, Generate Parity
RQPT	Results Into RAM and Q Register, Generate Parity
AUR	Arithmetic Shift Up, Results Into RAM
LUR	Logical Shift Up, Results Into RAM
AURQ	Arithmetic Shift Up, Results Into RAM and Q Register
LURQ	Arithmetic Shift Up, Results Into RAM and Q Register
* YBUS	Results to Y BUS Only
* LUQ	Logical Shift Up the Contents of the Q Register
SINX	Sign Extend
REG	Results to RAM, Sign Extend

* = $\overline{\text{WRITE}}$ = H

Special Functions

UMUL	Unsigned Multiply
TCM	Two's Complement Multiply
INC	Increment by One or Two
SMTC	Sign Magnitude ⟷ Two's Complement
TCMC	Two's Complement Multiply Last Step
SLN	Single Length Normalize
DLN	Double Length Normalize
TDN	Two's Complement Multiply Division
TDC	Two Complement Division Correction

Am2904 Mnemonics

SHIFT INSTRUCTIONS

	I_{10}	I_9	I_8	I_7	I_6	M_C RAM Q	SIO_0	SIO_n	QIO_0	QIO_n	Loaded into M_C
SDL	0	0	0	0	0	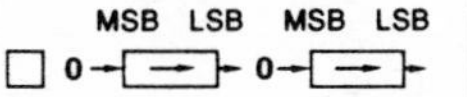	Z	0	Z	0	
SUH	0	0	0	0	1	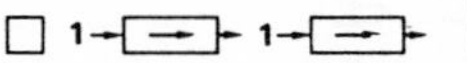	Z	1	Z	1	
SUL	1	0	0	1	0	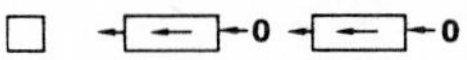	0	Z	0	Z	
SUH	1	0	0	1	1	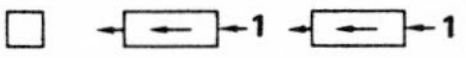	1	Z	1	Z	
SDDH	0	0	0	1	1	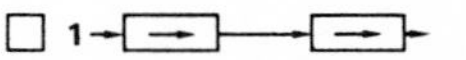	Z	1	Z	SIO_0	
SDDL	0	0	1	1	0	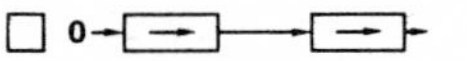	Z	0	Z	SIO_0	
SDUL	1	0	1	1	0	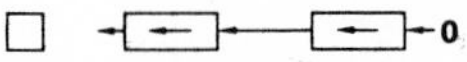	QIO_n	Z	0	Z	
SDUH	1	0	1	1	1	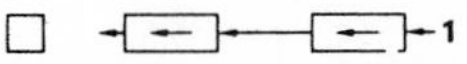	QIO_n	Z	1	Z	
RSD	0	1	0	1	0		Z	SIO_0	Z	QIO_0	
RSU	1	1	0	1	0		SIO_n	Z	QIO_n	Z	
SSXO	0	1	1	1	0	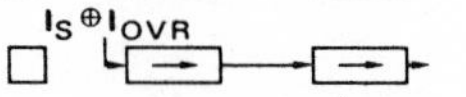	Z	$I_N \oplus I_{OVR}$	Z	SIO_0	
RDD	0	1	1	1	1	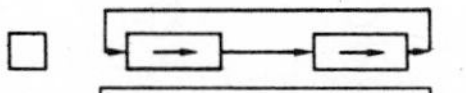	Z	QIO_0	Z	SIO_0	
RDU	1	1	1	1	1	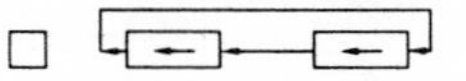	QIO_n	Z	SIO_n	Z	
SDMS	0	0	1	0	1	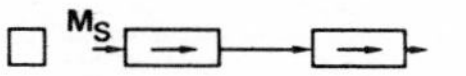	Z	M_N	Z	SIO_0	
SMS	0	0	0	1	0		Z	0	Z	M_N	SIO_0
SDDC	0	0	1	1	1	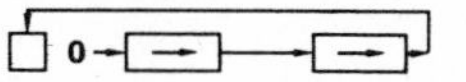	Z	0	Z	SIO_0	QIO_0
SDUC	1	0	1	0	0	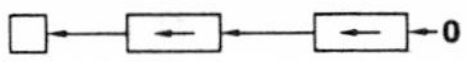	QIO_n	Z	0	Z	SIO_n

Microstatus Register Instruction Codes

RSTI	Reset μSR	$0 \rightarrow \mu_X$
SWAP	Register Swap	$M_X \rightarrow \mu_X$
SHLD	Hold Status	

Microregister Condition Code Output (CT)

MIZ	Zero	$\mu_Z \rightarrow C_T$
MIO	Overflow	$\mu_{OVR} \rightarrow C_T$
MIC	Carry	$\mu_C \rightarrow C_T$
MIS	Sign	$\mu_N \rightarrow C_T$

Machine Status Register Instruction Codes

LMA	Load Y_Z, Y_C, Y_N, Y_{OVR} To MSR	$Y_X \rightarrow M_X$
RSTA	Reset MSR	$0 \rightarrow M_X$
SHOLD	Hold Status	

Machine Register Condition Code Output (CT)

MAZ	Zero	$M_Z \rightarrow C_T$
MAO	Overflow	$M_{OVR} \rightarrow C_T$
MAC	Carry	$M_C \rightarrow C_T$
MAS	Sign	$M_N \rightarrow C_T$

APPENDIX C

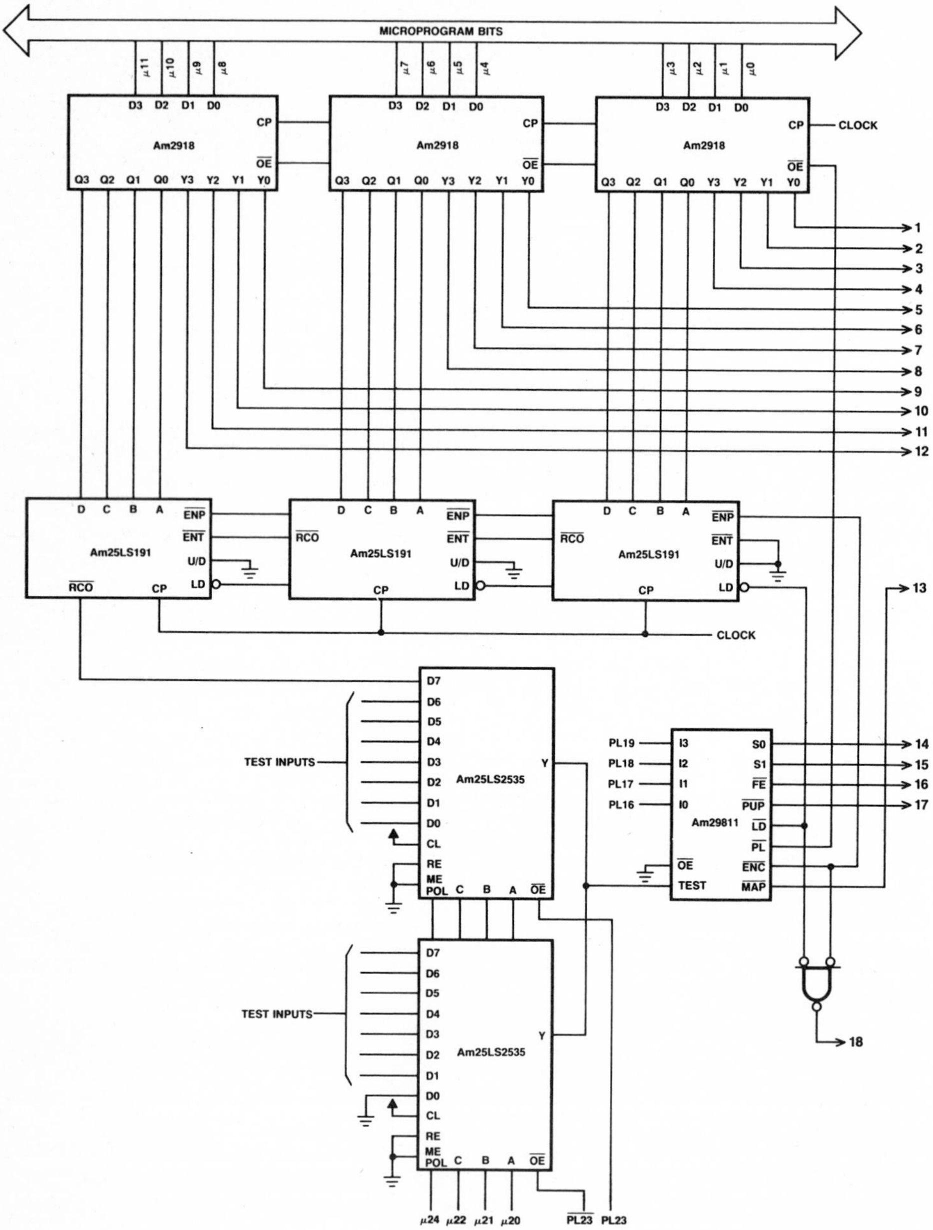
MICROPROGRAM BITS
μ11 μ10 μ9 μ8
μ7 μ6 μ5 μ4
μ3 μ2 μ1 μ0
D3 D2 D1 D0
CP
Am2918
OE
Q3 Q2 Q1 Q0 Y3 Y2 Y1 Y0
CLOCK
1
2
3
4
5
6
7
8
9
10
11
12
D C B A
ENP
ENT
U/D
LD
RCO
CP
Am25LS191
13
CLOCK
D7
D6
D5
D4
D3
D2
D1
D0
CL
RE
ME
POL
C B A
OE
Y
Am25LS2535
TEST INPUTS
PL19
PL18
PL17
PL16
I3
I2
I1
I0
Am29811
S0
S1
FE
PUP
LD
PL
ENC
MAP
TEST
14
15
16
17
18
μ24 μ22 μ21 μ20
PL23 PL23

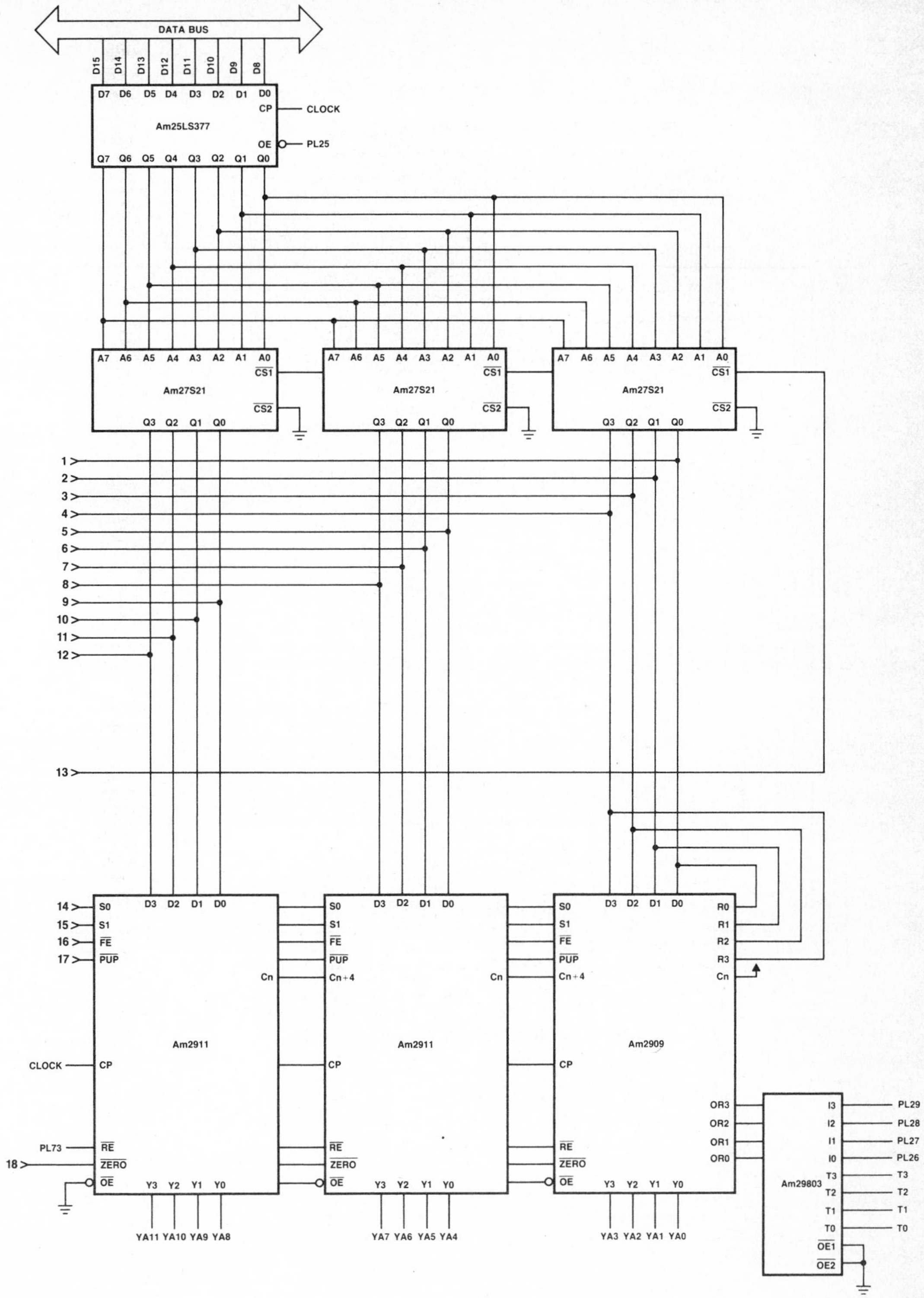
DATA BUS
D15 D14 D13 D12 D11 D10 D9 D8
Am25LS377
CLOCK
PL25
Am27S21
Am27S21
Am27S21
1 2 3 4 5 6 7 8 9 10 11 12
13
14 15 16 17
18
Am2911
Am2911
Am2909
CLOCK
PL73
Am29803
PL29 PL28 PL27 PL26
T3 T2 T1 T0
YA11 YA10 YA9 YA8
YA7 YA6 YA5 YA4
YA3 YA2 YA1 YA0

APPENDIX C

MICROPROGRAM MEMORY

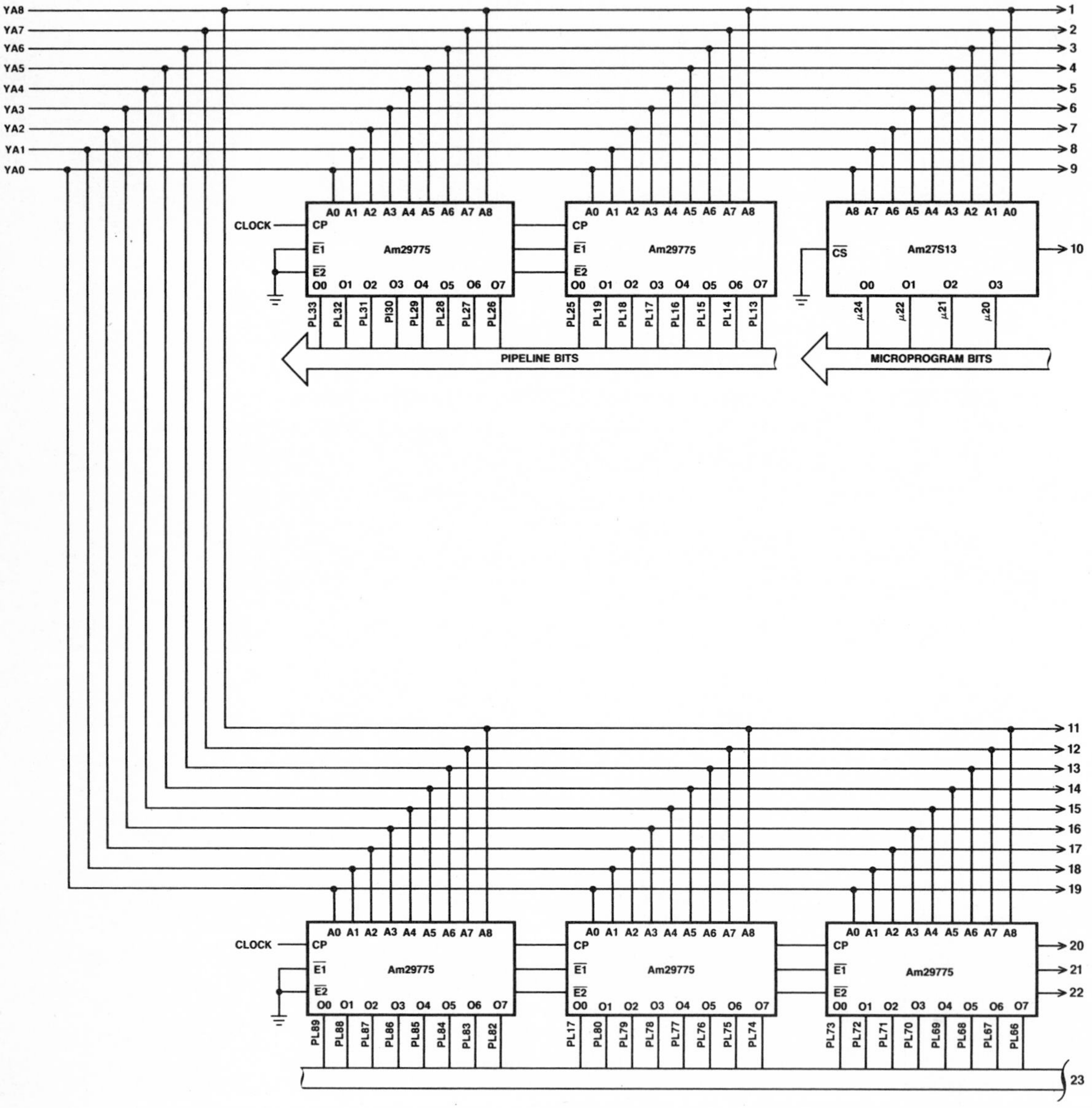

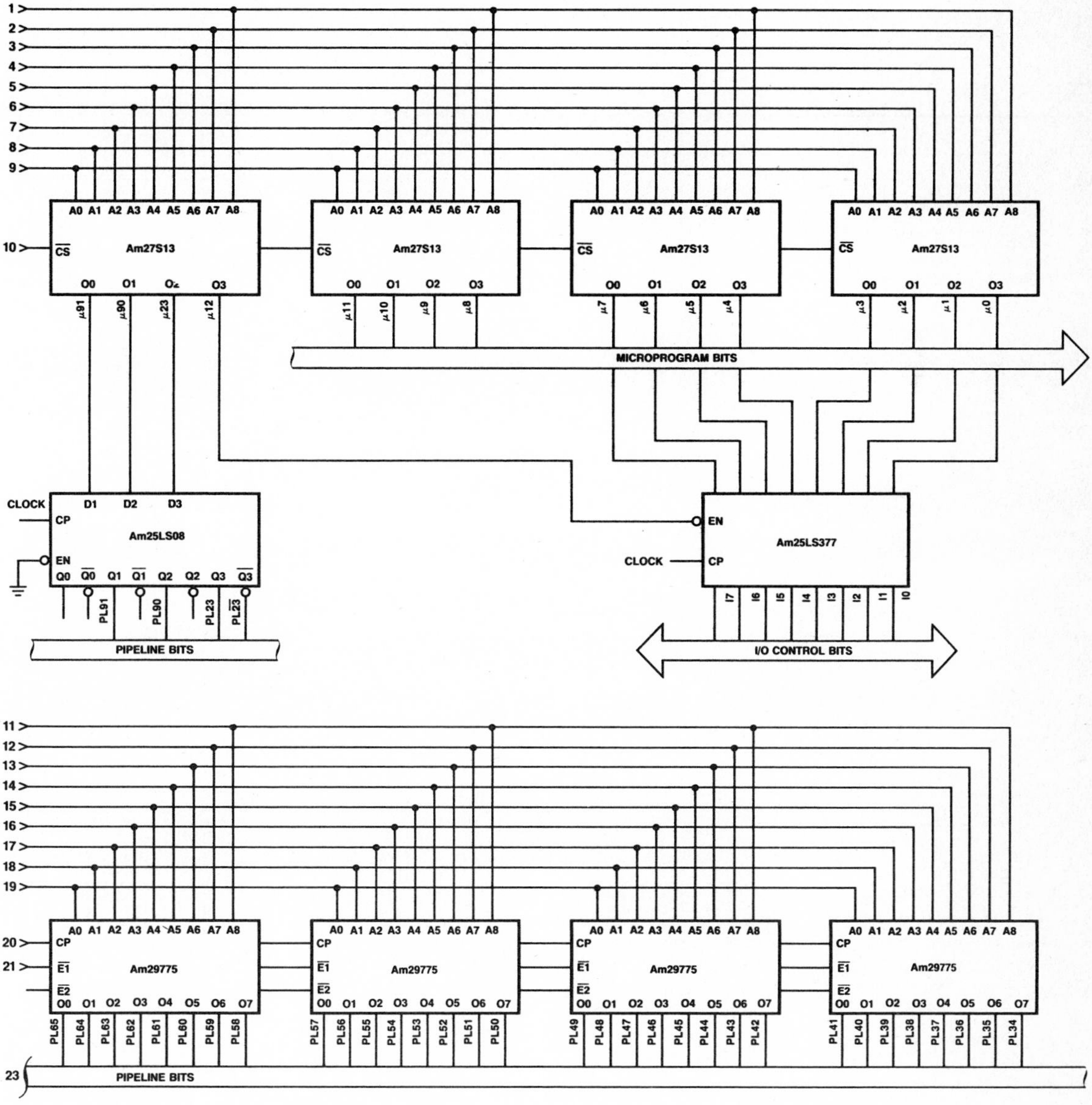

Am27S13
A0 A1 A2 A3 A4 A5 A6 A7 A8
CS
O0 O1 O2 O3
μ91 μ90 μ23 μ12
μ11 μ10 μ9 μ8
μ7 μ6 μ5 μ4
μ3 μ2 μ1 μ0
MICROPROGRAM BITS
CLOCK
Am25LS08
CP
EN
D1 D2 D3
Q0 Q0 Q1 Q1 Q2 Q2 Q3 Q3
PL91 PL90 PL23 PL23
PIPELINE BITS
Am25LS377
EN
CP
I7 I6 I5 I4 I3 I2 I1 I0
I/O CONTROL BITS
Am29775
CP
E1
E2
O0 O1 O2 O3 O4 O5 O6 O7
PL65 PL64 PL63 PL62 PL61 PL60 PL59 PL58
PL57 PL56 PL55 PL54 PL53 PL52 PL51 PL50
PL49 PL48 PL47 PL46 PL45 PL44 PL43 PL42
PL41 PL40 PL39 PL38 PL37 PL36 PL35 PL34
PIPELINE BITS

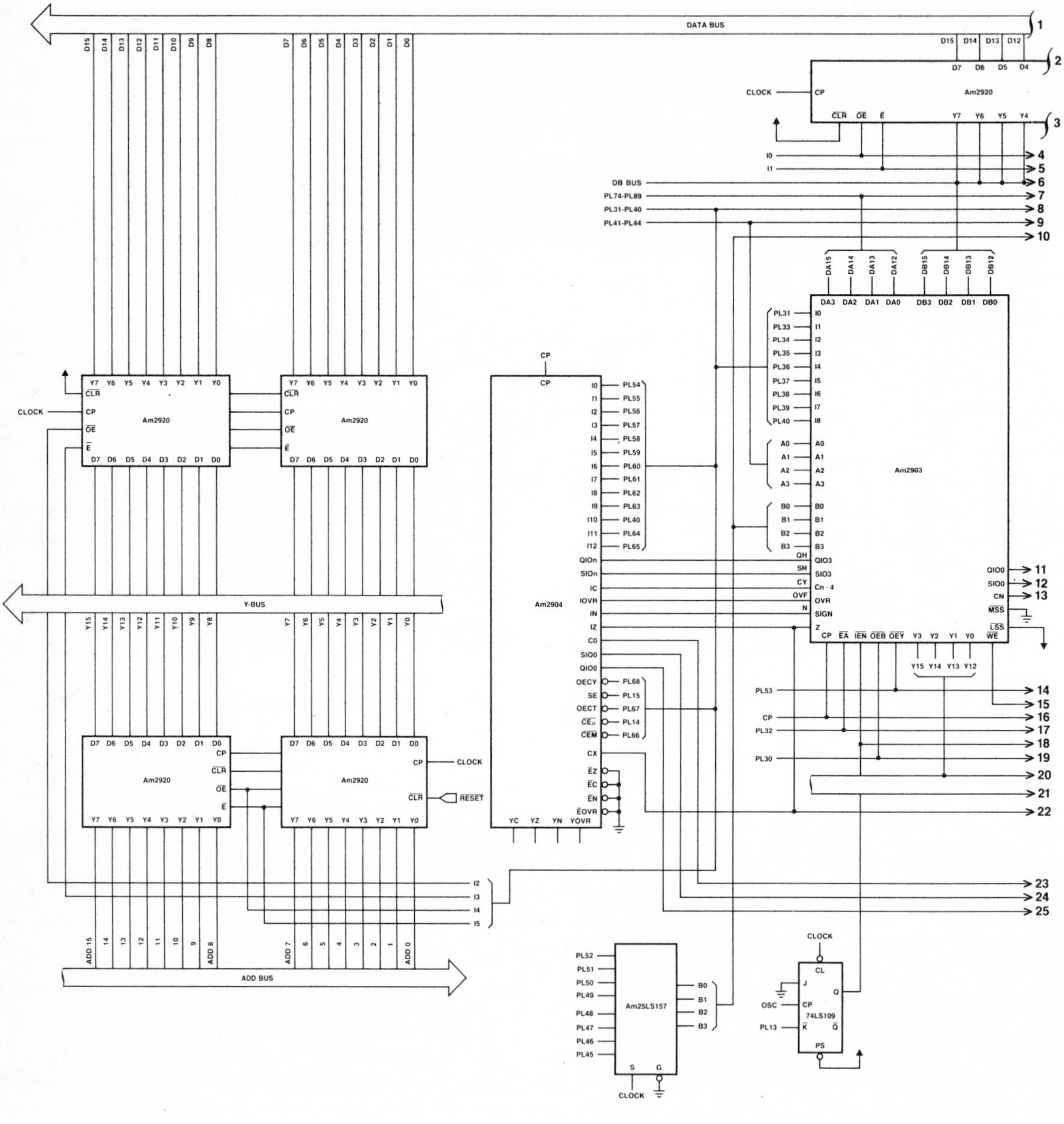
DATA BUS
Am2920
CLOCK
DB BUS
PL74-PL89
PL31-PL40
PL41-PL44
Am2903
Am2904
Y-BUS
ADD BUS
RESET
Am25LS157
74LS109
OSC
PL13

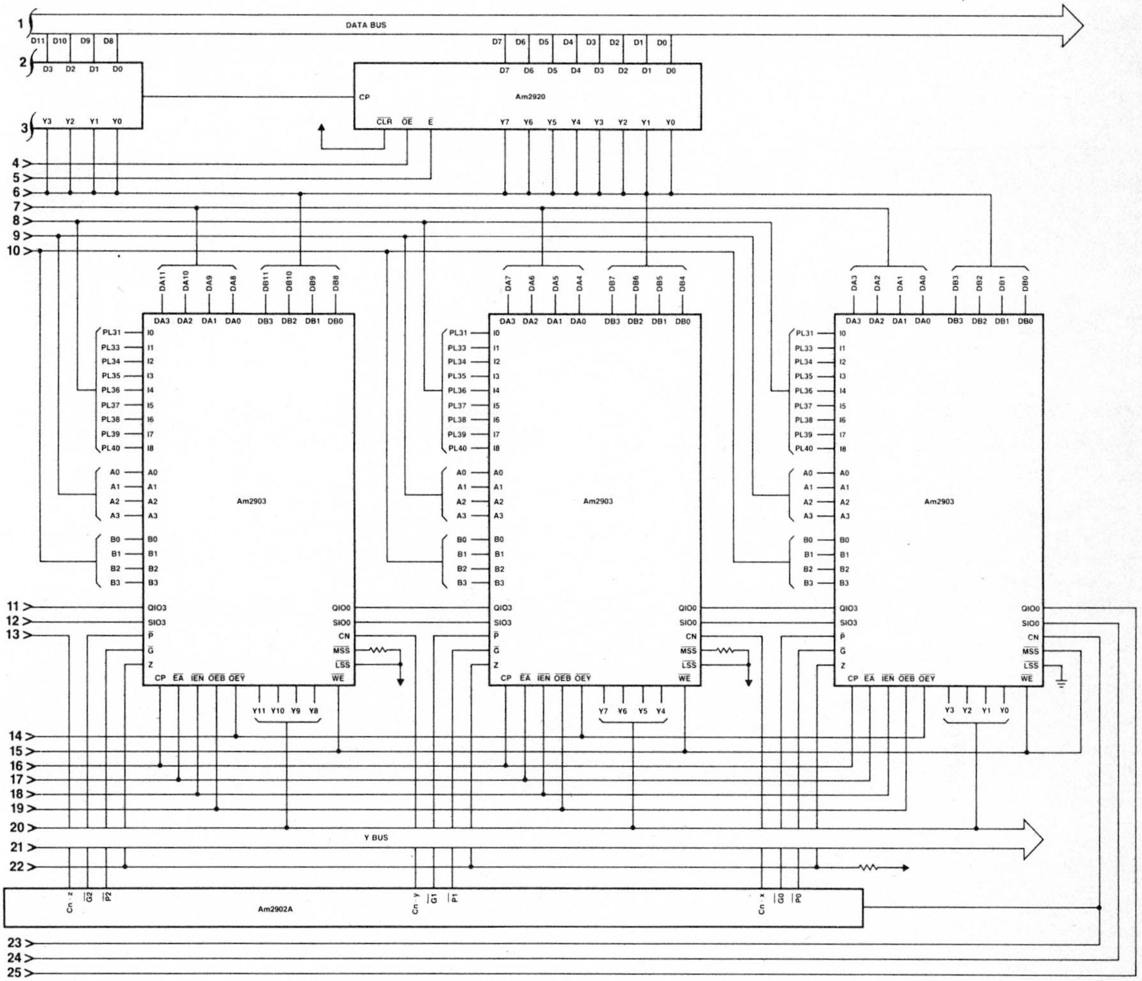

Central Processing Unit

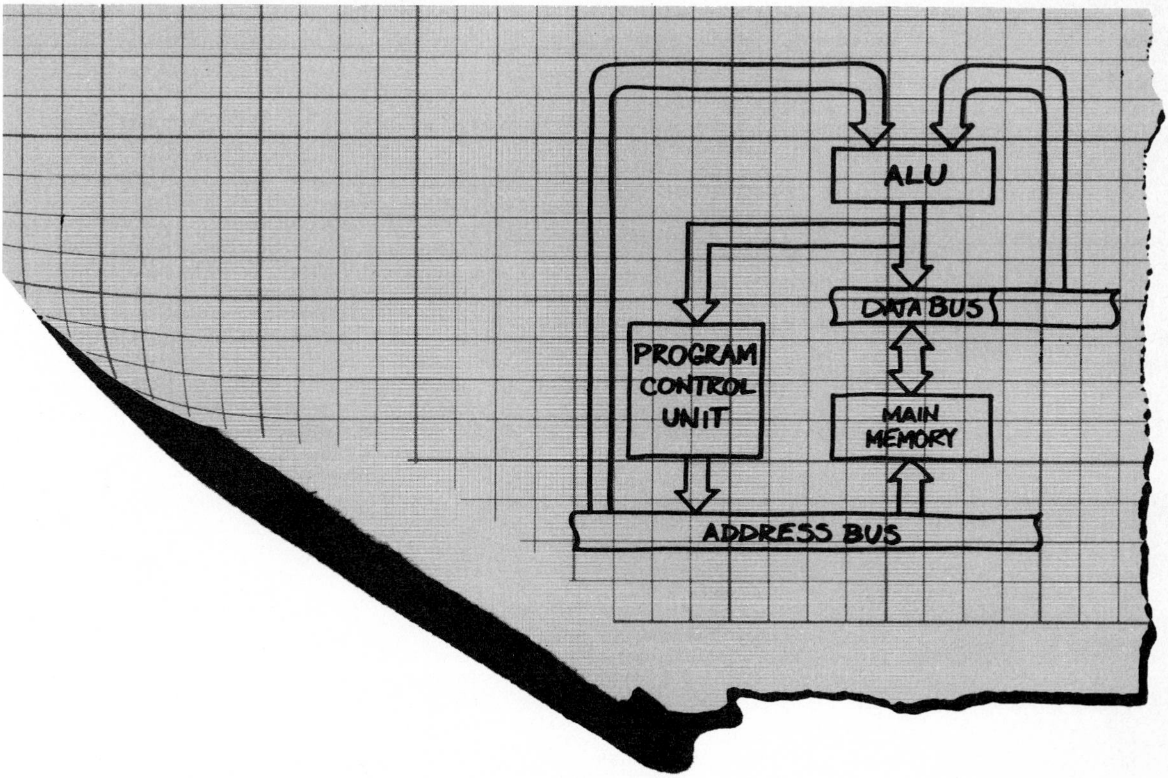

Chapter V
Program Control Unit

Introduction

In order to access instructions and data in an orderly manner within a computer, a Program Control Unit is usually used to provide the most efficient mechanism for program control. A program is a set of instructions which direct the processor to perform a specific task. Ordinarily, program instructions are stored in sequential memory locations. During the normal processing of a program, an instruction is fetched from the location specified by the program counter, the instruction is executed, the program counter is incremented, and another fetch and execute cycle begins. The addressing mechanisms that such control unit might employ are various. Indeed there are some machines that literally use dozens of addressing modes to fetch instructions and data. In this discussion of program control units, several of the addressing modes and their common implementation techniques will be discussed. The addressing modes used commonly in today's machines include register, immediate, direct, indirect, index, and relative and various combinations thereof.

Data Formats

Technically, an instruction set manipulates data of various length words. Generally speaking, most 16 bit minicomputers can manipulate data of three different word lengths: 8-bit bytes, 16-bit words and 32-bit double words. This data may represent fixed point numbers, floating point numbers, or logical data. The data is used as operands for the instructions, and is manipulated as indicated by the particular instruction being executed.

Typically, fixed point data is treated as signed 15-bit integers in the 16-bit representation or as signed 31-bit integers in the 32-bit double length notation. Positive and negative numbers are represented in the ordinary 2's complement notation with the sign bit carrying negative weight. Positive numbers have a sign bit of zero and negative numbers have a sign of one. The numerical value of zero is always represented with all bits LOW.

Floating point numbers consist of a signed exponent and a signed fraction. Many different formats are used by manufacturers in expressing floating point data and these variations will not be described here. Let it simply suffice to say that the floating point number represents a quantity expressed as the product of a fraction times the number 2 raised to the power of the exponent. In some cases, the number 16 is raised to the power of the exponent. Typically, all floating point numbers are assumed to be normalized prior to their use as operands. No pre-normalization is performed and all results are post-normalized. Usually, the floating point instruction set will normalize un-normalized floating point numbers.

Logical operations are used to manipulate 8-bit bytes, 16-bit words or 32-bit double words. All bits participate in the logical operations.

Instruction Formats

Various minicomputers use different types of instruction formats ranging from the very simple straight forward formats to the more complicated difficult to decode formats. For example, a register to register format can consist of a simple 8-bit opcode and two 4-bit source operand specifiers. On the other hand, it may consist of a byte or word specifier, an opcode specifier, source and destination register specifiers, and mode specifiers for each of the source and destination register selections. Again, it is not the purpose of this application note to describe all of the trade-offs in selecting instruction formats but rather to select a simple format such that the student of bipolar microprogrammed microprocessors can understand the techniques used by instructions for operating the machine.

Thus, we will use a few 16-bit and 32-bit formats in this application note to demonstrate the function of the program control unit in various types of instruction execution.

Instruction Types

For purposes of this application note, we will define nine different instruction types using various addressing modes. As we define these instruction types, we will use the basic ADD instruction as the example in all cases. It should be recognized that the operations of the instructions are similar for all the arithmetic as well as logical type operations. However, by using the ADD instruction it will be easier to describe the operation of each of these instructions rather than to try to be very general in their description. Figure 1 shows all nine instruction types with their appropriate names. As is seen, four of the instruction types are single 16-bit word instructions while five of the instruction types are double word or 32-bit, instructions. The advantage of the double word instructions is that a second word can be used as an address whereby it provides an index value or a second word can be used for data which is used as an immediate value.

Register-to-Register Instructions

When the register-to-register (RR) instruction is executed, it is simply a technique for selecting two of the machine's internal working registers in order to execute the desired operation. The instruction is fetched from memory and placed in the instruction register and the source register R2 and second source register R1 are selected as the two source operands for the ALU. Register R1 is the destination register in addition to being a source register and the results of the ALU operation will be placed in the register specified by the R1 field. In the instruction format shown in Figure 1 for the register-to-register instruction, the 8-bit opcode field specifies the machine operation to be performed. The next 4-bit field, R1, in the instruction format specifies the address of the first operand. In most machines, the R1 field is normally the address of a general register. The 4-bit R2 field in the register-to-register instruction format specifies the address of the second operand; this also is normally the address of a general register. in most machines, the R1 field also in addition to being a source operand is the destination general register select. Thus, the results of the operation are stored in the register selected by the R1 field.

The RR instructions are used for operations between registers. We are assuming in this discussion that the machine contains 16 general registers which function as accumulators or index registers in all arithmetic and logical operations. Each general register contains a 16-bit word consisting of two 8-bit bytes. For arithmetic operations, the most significant bit is considered the sign bit using 2's complement representation. The general registers of the machine are usually numbered from 0 to 15 (decimal) and written in hexadecimal notation as 0 through F. In this example, the general registers have not been given specific functional assignments. However, in some machines certain registers are assumed to perform specific functions. These can include specific stack pointer registers and program counter registers. Figure 2 depicts the typical signal path for executing the RR instruction in a bit-slice system.

The actual operation of the Register-to-Register Instruction is as follows. First, the instruction is fetched and placed in the instruction register as shown in Figure 2. This is part of the fetch routine. Next, the instruction is decoded via the mapping PROM and the appropriate microinstruction in the microprogram memory selected and placed in the pipeline register. Then, the instruction is executed where the two registers in the general purpose registers of the Am2903 are selected by the contents of the R1 and R2 fields of the instruction register. The actual microcode required to

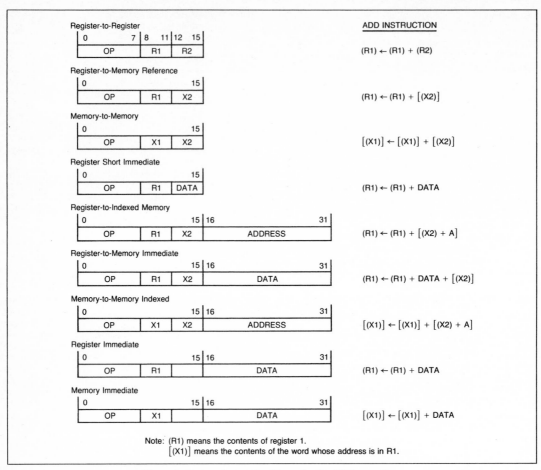

Figure 1. Various Instruction Types for the ADD operation.

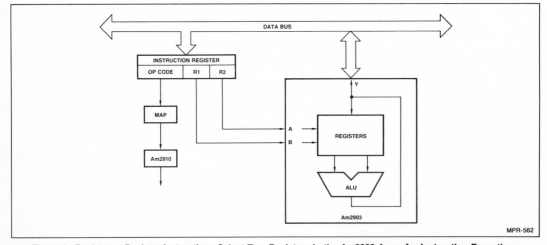

Figure 2. Register-to-Register Instructions Select Two Registers in the Am2903 Array for Instruction Execution.

execute this instruction is shown in Figure 3. Here, we assume the Program Counter (PC) value is contained in one of the general registers and can be selected by microcode as well as the R1 and R2 fields. This was shown in Chapter 3.

Register-to-Memory-Reference

The register-to-memory-reference instruction is one whereby the contents of the memory location pointed to by the register identified with the X2 value is fetched from memory and then added to the register value specified in the R1 field. The result of this operation is placed in the register specified by the R1 field.

Figure 4 shows a general block diagram of the hardware used to implement the instruction types described in the first part of this application note. As shown, the memory address register can be driven by either the Y outputs or the DB outputs of the Am2903s.

In addition, the Y outputs of the Am2903s can be placed onto the memory data bus by means of a three-state buffer. The computer control unit is intended to be representative of that described in Chapter 2 of this application note series. For purposes of this discussion, we assume the program counter (PC) is one of the general purpose registers within the Am2903 register stack. Later, we will change this concept and use the PC external to Am2903.

The operation of the register-to-memory-reference instruction as depicted in Figure 1 can best be described by referring to Figure 5. Here, we see the first three microinstructions that represent the fetch routine for the currently described machine. First, the program counter is placed in the memory address register and the program counter is incremented and returned to the PC register.

Microinstruction Operation	Microcycle Time												
	T0	T1	T2	T3	T4	T5	T6	T7	T8	T9	T10	T11	T12
PC → MAR; PC + 1 → PC	X												
Fetch Inst to IR		X											
Decode			X										
R1+R2 → R1				X									

Figure 3. Register-to-Register Instruction Microcode.

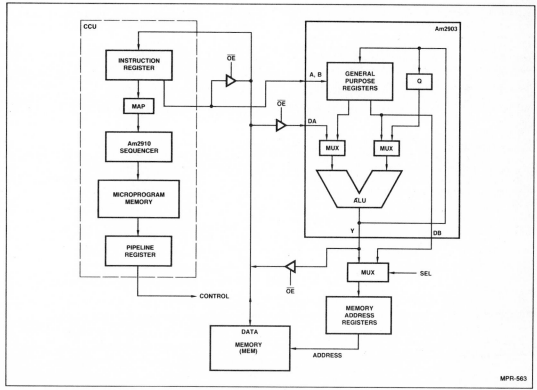

Figure 4. Simple Memory Addressing Scheme with PC in the ALU.

Microinstruction Operation	Microcycle Time												
	T0	T1	T2	T3	T4	T5	T6	T7	T8	T9	T10	T11	T12
PC → MAR; PC + 1 → PC	X												
Fetch Inst to IR		X											
Decode			X										
(X2) → MAR				X									
MEM + R1 → R2					X								

Figure 5. Register to Memory Reference Instruction Microcode.

Next, the instruction is fetched from memory and placed in the instruction register within the CCU. Thirdly, the instruction is decoded via the mapping PROM and the appropriate micro-instruction selected and placed in the pipeline register. To execute this particular register-to-memory-reference instruction, it is necessary to place the contents of the register specified by the X2 field into the memory address register. Then the contents of memory can be fetched and the operand added to the value currently contained in the register specified by the R1 field. The result of this operation is placed in the register specified by the R1 field. All totaled, the execution of this register to memory reference instruction requires five microcycles as depicted in this example.

Memory to Memory

This instruction is one whereby the memory location pointed to by the contents of the register specified in the X2 field is fetched and the memory location pointed to by the contents of the register locations specified in the X1 is fetched and these two operands are added together. At the completion of the instruction, the resultant is placed in the memory location as defined by the contents of the register specified in the X1 field.

The Memory to Memory Instruction operation is also depicted by the block diagram shown in Figure 4. In fact, all of the next six instructions to be defined utilize the block diagram of Figure 4 to represent the hardware required for implementing these instructions.

The microcode required for the memory to memory instruction is detailed in Figure 6. The first three microinstructions represent the fetch routine. In the fourth microinstruction, the contents of the register specified by the X2 field are placed in the memory address register. Then, in the fifth microinstruction the contents of

this memory location is loaded into the Q register within the Am2903. This value is temporarily held for use later. In the sixth microinstruction, the contents of the register specified by the X1 field in the instruction is placed in the memory address register. On the seventh microinstruction, this operand is fetched from memory and added to the contents of the Q register with the result being placed in the Q register. In the eighth microinstruction, the current contents of the Q register is returned to the memory location. This memory location is specified by the contents of the register specified by the X1 field and is still in the memory address register. Thus, we have used the Q register as a temporary holding register for the data used in this instruction.

Register with Short-Immediate

This instruction is a technique whereby a 4-bit field is added to the contents of the register specified by the R1 field. Thus, short jumps or branches can be executed within a range of zero to fifteen memory locations. The more significant 12-bits of the word are zero filled.

The register with short immediate instruction operates very similar to the register-to-register instruction. The microcode for this instruction is shown in Figure 7. The only difference between the register-to-register instruction and the register short-immediate instruction is that instead of adding operands specified by the R1 and R2 fields, we take a data value contained in a four-bit field in the instruction as depicted in Figure 1 and add it to the contents of the register specified in the R1 field. The results of the operation are returned to the register specified by the R1 field. This addition is performed by taking the 4-bit data value shown in Figure 1 as the DATA and zero filling the twelve most significant bits. This gives us a 16-bit word ranging in value between zero and fifteen. Thus, short jumps can be implemented using this technique.

Microinstruction Operation	Microcycle Time												
	T0	T1	T2	T3	T4	T5	T6	T7	T8	T9	T10	T11	T12
PC → MAR; PC + 1 → PC	X												
Fetch Inst to IR		X											
Decode			X										
(X2) → MAR				X									
MEM → Q					X								
(X1) → MAR						X							
MEM + Q → Q							X						
Q → MEM								X					

Figure 6. Memory to Memory Instruction Microcode.

Microinstruction Operation	T0	T1	T2	T3	T4	T5	T6	T7	T8	T9	T10	T11	T12
PC → MAR; PC + 1 → PC	X												
Fetch Inst to IR		X											
Decode			X										
R1 + Data → R1				X									

Figure 7. Register Short Immediate Instruction Microcode.

Register to Indexed Memory

The 16-bit word in the register defined by X2 in the instruction is added to the address that is the second word of memory. Then, this address is used to fetch an operand from memory which is added to the contents of the register pointed to by R1. The results of this operation are then placed in R1. The instruction format for this instruction was shown in Figure 1.

The Register to Indexed Memory Instruction is shown is Figure 8 and executed in the following manner. First, the current PC value is placed in the MAR and PC + 1 is returned to the PC register. Next, the instruction at this memory location is fetched and placed in the instruction register. On the third cycle this instruction is decoded and the contents of the microprogram memory placed in the pipeline register. On the fourth microinstruction, the PC value is again placed in the MAR and PC + 1 is returned to the PC register. On the fifth microinstruction, the value at this location in memory is fetched and added to the contents of the X2 register with the result being placed in the MAR. And on the sixth microinstruction, the operand pointed to by this address is fetched and added to the contents of R1 with the result being placed in the register pointed to by the R1 field of the instruction.

Register to Memory Immediate

In the register to memory immediate instruction, the contents of the memory location pointed to by the register specified in the X2 field is fetched from the memory and the data value which is in the second word of the instruction is also fetched from memory and added to it. This result is then added to the contents of the R1 register and the final result replaces the value currently in R1.

The register to memory immediate instruction as shown in Figure 1 is implemented using the microcode shown in Figure 9. Again, the first three microinstructions are the fetch routine. The fourth microinstruction is used to take the contents of the register specified by the X2 field and place it in the memory address

Microinstruction Operation	T0	T1	T2	T3	T4	T5	T6	T7	T8	T9	T10	T11	T12
PC → MAR; PC + 1 → PC	X												
Fetch Inst to IR		X											
Decode			X										
PC → MAR; PC + 1 → PC				X									
MEM + X2 → MAR					X								
MEM + R1 → R1						X							

Figure 8. Register to Indexed Memory Instruction Microcode.

Microinstruction Operation	T0	T1	T2	T3	T4	T5	T6	T7	T8	T9	T10	T11	T12
PC → MAR; PC + 1 → PC	X												
Fetch Inst to IR		X											
Decode			X										
(X2) → MAR				X									
MEM + R1 → R1					X								
PC → MAR; PC + 1 → PC						X							
MEM + R1 → R1							X						

Figure 9. Register to Memory Immediate Instruction Microcode.

register. Next, the operand at this memory location is brought into the Am2903's and added to the contents of the register specified by the R1 field with the results returned to that register. The sixth microinstruction is used to set up the memory address register to fetch the second word of the instruction. The seventh microinstruction brings this data value into the Am2903 ALU via the data bus and adds this value to the contents of the register specified by the R1 field. The result of the operation is placed into the register specified by the R1 field.

Memory to Memory Indexed

The memory to memory indexed instruction is one whereby the contents of the register specified in the X2 field are added to the second word of the instruction to form a new address. This address is then used to fetch an operand which is added to the operand selected by taking the contents of the register specified in the R1 field and using that as a memory address to fetch an operand. The result of this addition is then replaced in the memory location pointed to by the contents of the register specified in the X1 field.

The memory to memory indexed instruction is probably the most complicated of the instruction formats described in the application note. In all, nine microinstructions are required for its implementation. Basically, the first three microinstructions are used to fetch the instruction from memory, place it in the instruction register, and decode the instruction for initial operation. Again, the basic fetch routine. Microinstruction number 4 sets up the memory address register to fetch the second word of the instruction and microinstruction number 5 is used to bring this value from memory into the Am2903 ALU where it is added to the X2 register. The results of the addition are placed into the memory address register during this microinstruction. This value is used to fetch a value from memory which is placed in the Q register using microinstruction number 6. In the seventh microinstruction, the contents of the register pointed to by the X1 field are placed in the memory address register so that microinstruction eight can be utilized to bring this memory value into the Am2903s where it is added to the contents of the Q register with the result being placed into the Q register. Microinstruction number 9 is used to place this value back into the memory location as specified by the contents of the register pointed to by the X1 field. This memory address is still contained in the memory address register so that no updating is required. The total microcode required to implement this instruction routine is shown in Figure 10.

Register Immediate

The register immediate instruction is a very useful instruction which allows data to be added to the contents of the register. In this example, the second word of the instruction is fetched and added to the contents of the register specified in the R1 field.

Figure 11 depicts the microcode used to implement the register immediate instruction. Here, the first three microinstructions are the fetch routine for the instruction. The fourth microinstruction of this routine sets up the MAR to fetch the second word of the two word instruction. The contents of this memory location is brought into the Am2903 ALU and added to the contents of the register specified by the R1 field. The result of this operation is placed in the register specified by the R1 field.

Microinstruction Operation	Microcycle Time												
	T0	T1	T2	T3	T4	T5	T6	T7	T8	T9	T10	T11	T12
PC → MAR; PC + 1 → PC	X												
Fetch Inst to IR		X											
Decode			X										
PC → MAR; PC + 1 → PC				X									
MEM + X2 → MAR					X								
MEM → Q						X							
(X1) → MAR							X						
MEM + Q → Q								X					
Q → MEM									X				

Figure 10. Memory to Memory Indexed Instruction Microcode.

Microinstruction Operation	Microcycle Time												
	T0	T1	T2	T3	T4	T5	T6	T7	T8	T9	T10	T11	T12
PC → MAR; PC + 1 → PC	X												
Fetch Inst to IR		X											
Decode			X										
PC → MAR; PC + 1 → PC				X									
MEM + R1 → R1					X								

Figure 11. Register Immediate Instruction Microcode.

Memory Immediate

The memory immediate instruction is used to add immediate data contained in the second word of the instruction to a location in memory. The memory location is contained in the register specified in the X1 field of the instruction.

The memory immediate instruction is similar to the register immediate instruction except that an indirect addressing scheme is used. Again, the first three microinstructions fetch and decode the memory immediate instruction. The fourth and fifth microinstructions are used to fetch the data value which is the second word of this memory immediate instruction. Microinstruction number 4 sets up the memory address register and microinstruction number 5 brings the data into the Am2903 Q register. Microinstruction number 6 places the contents of the register specified by the X1 field into the memory address register so that the contents of this memory location can be brought into the Am2903 during microinstruction number 7. Here, during microinstruction 7 the contents of the Q register are added to this value and returned to the Q register. At microinstruction 8, the Q register is written back to the memory location as specified by the contents of the register pointed to by the X1 field. This value was already in the memory address register because it was used to fetch the operand originally at this location. The microcode for this instruction is detailed in Figure 12.

Improving Program Control Unit Performance

If we examine the microcode as shown for the various instruction types depicted in Figure 1, we find that all of these microroutines have several things in common. First, the very first microinstruction simply sets up the memory address register with the current value of the program counter. In addition, this microinstruction increments the current program counter value. The second microinstruction simply fetches the contents of memory and places it in the instruction register. The third microinstruction is used to decode the microinstruction, select the appropriate micromemory word and set it into the pipeline register. Finally, the fourth microinstruction begins actual execution of the desired instruction. In all of these examples and using the block diagram of Figure 4, we find that a bottle neck occurs in the ALU because of our need to be operating on program counter data and operand data intermixed. We can improve the performance of the program control unit by making the program counter an external register and using a multiplexer to select either the program counter or the Am2903 output to load the memory address register. This is depicted in block diagram form in Figure 13.

The first effect of implementing a program control unit with this architecture is that one of the instruction types is shortened by one microcycle. This is the register-to-memory-immediate instruction. The new microcode flowcharts for this instruction is

Microinstruction Operation	Microcycle Time T0	T1	T2	T3	T4	T5	T6	T7	T8	T9	T10	T11	T12
PC → MAR; PC + 1 → PC	X												
Fetch Inst to IR		X											
Decode			X										
PC → MAR; PC + 1 → PC				X									
MEM → Q					X								
(X1) → MAR						X							
MEM + Q → Q							X						
Q → MEM								X					

Figure 12. Memory Immediate Instruction Microcode.

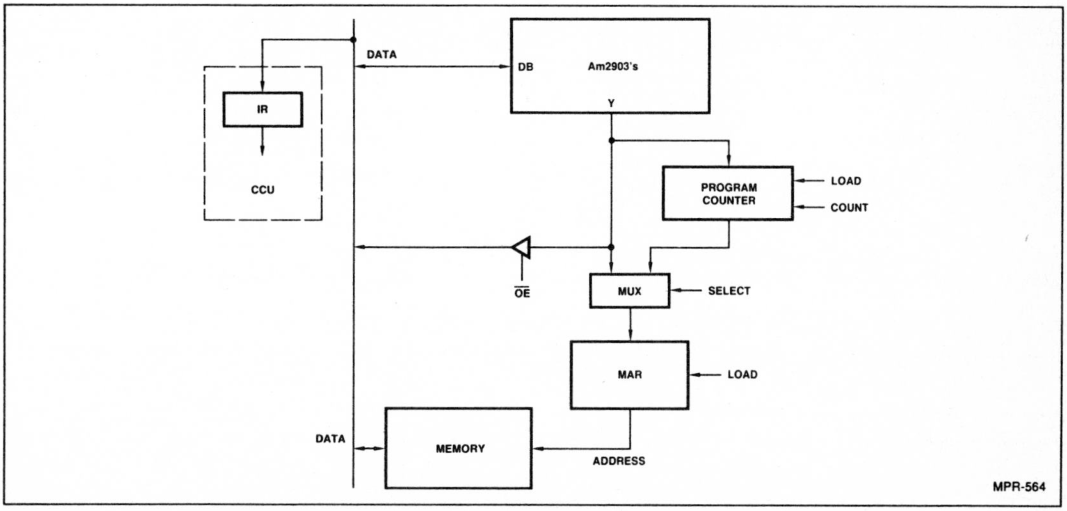

Figure 13. Memory Addressing Scheme with PC Outside of the ALU.

shown in Figure 14. In this case, we see that a PC value can be placed into the memory address register and the PC incremented while the ALU within the Am2903 is being used to perform either a pass or an addition. Thus, this architectural change has made some improvement in the thru-put of our machine.

The most important improvement in thru-put realized by the architecture shown in Figure 13 can be seen by evaluating the timing for sequential instructions. That is, what happens when several instructions are executed sequentially?

To keep the examples simple, let's visualize the microcycle timing chart for three register-to-register instructions executed sequentially. The most obvious timing chart would simply be to take the register-to-register microinstruction flows as shown in Figure 3 and concatenate three examples of this timing chart. If we do this, we will see that the final execution of the values of R1 + R2 return to R1 utilize the ALU, but the program counter is not in operation. However, the next microcycle requires placing the program counter into the memory address register. Thus, the architecture of Figure 13 allows us to do these two micro-operations during the same microinstruction. If we assume three register-to-register instructions in sequence in memory; let's call them instruction A, B and C; the timing chart of Figure 15 results. What we see in this diagram is that the execution of instruction A can be overlapped with the set up the program counter in memory address register for fetching instruction B. Thus, instead of instruction B starting at time T4, it may be started at time T3. This can be accomplished by simply having the execution microinstruction also load the MAR with the current PC value and increment the PC. From this discussion, we can see that instead of twelve microcycle times being required to execute three register-to-register instructions, only nine microcycle times will be required. We should caution that if the reader counts the microcycles in Figure 15, he will arrive at 10 microcycle times being required. This leads us to our next point.

If we examine all of the instructions described earlier in this application note, we will find that in all cases, the execution of the instruction (the last microcycle) can be overlapped with the first microinstruction of the fetch routine. Thus, the architectural change shown in Figure 13 not only allows three of the instructions to execute faster during their total microcode, but in fact all microinstructions can be executed at least one microcycle faster because of the ability to overlap the first microcycle of the fetch routine with the execution of the instruction. This architectural change therefore saves one or two microcycles depending on the instruction.

In Chapter 9 we will show how further overlapping at the machine instruction level can allow us to execute a register-to-register instruction during every microcycle, effectively; rather than every three microcycles as shown in Figure 15. At the present time, let us simply leave the discussion at this point.

Subroutining

An implementation technique that is common to the different addressing modes is the subroutine (also called stack and link). The subroutine allows sections of main program to access a common subsection of the program. The general effect is to allow less lines of machine code to be written for any given program that employs subroutines.

Figure 16 shows an example of a subroutine within the program. The main program executes instructions until it gets to instruction 52 which is a call to subroutine. This instruction puts address 80 in the program counter while saving address 53 in a separate register called Return Register. The program continues on from address 80 to address 85 where it encounters the return from subroutine command. The return-from-subroutine command takes a value out of the return register and puts that into the program counter. At that point the program counter continues down in the main body of the program until it reaches address 57. At this time, another call to subroutine may occur forcing the program counter back to the value of 80 while putting the value 58 into the return address. The subroutine is executed and at address 85 the return command is again encountered. At this point,

Microinstruction Operation	Microcycle Time T0	T1	T2	T3	T4	T5	T6	T7	T8	T9	T10	T11	T12
PC → MAR; PC + 1 → PC	X												
Fetch Inst to IR		X											
Decode			X										
(X2) → MAR				X									
MEM + R1 → R1					X								
PC → MAR; PC + 1 → PC					X								
MEM + R1 → R1						X							

Figure 14. Register to Memory Immediate Instruction Improved Microcode.

Microinstruction Operation	Microcycle Time T0	T1	T2	T3	T4	T5	T6	T7	T8	T9	T10	T11	T12
PC → MAR; PC + 1 → PC	A			B			C						
Fetch Inst to IR		A			B			C					
Decode			A			B			C				
R1 + R2 → R1				A			B			C			

Figure 15. Register to Register Instruction with Overlap of Execute and PC Control.

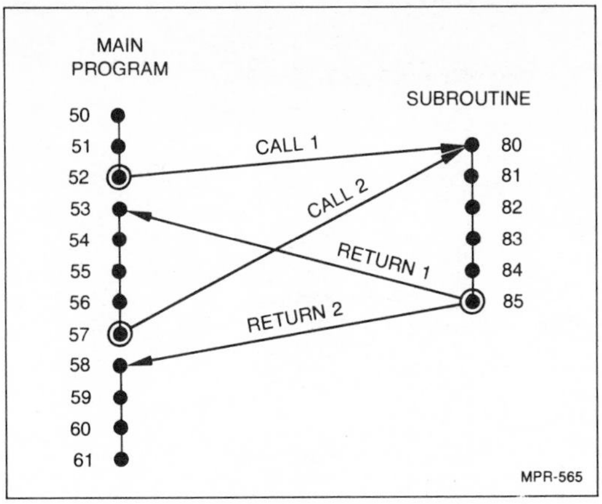

Figure 16. Subroutine Execution.

the subroutine will return control of the program to address 58 of the instruction stream and the main program continues to sequence through its instructions.

In many systems, one subroutine may very well call another subroutine which may in turn call yet another subroutine and so on. To accomplish this the return address linkage must now be "nested" using a last-in first-out (LIFO) stacking arrangement. Figure 17 illustrates subroutine nesting. In this example, the main program contains a subroutine call or jump-to-subroutine command (JSB) at address 53. Program control is passed to the first subroutine at address 88, while the return address 54 is placed in the stack. At address 89 the of the subroutine 1 another JSB command is encountered passing the program control to Subroutine 2 at address 502. The return address value 90 is pushed onto the top of the stack. This continues in like fashion for calls to Subroutine 3 and 4 with return address 506 and 723 being placed on the stack. At address 785 of Subroutine 4, a Return from Subroutine (RTS) command is decoded causing the return address 723 on the top of the stack to be placed in the program counter and the contents of the stack are "poped" up one place. At address 725 another RTS command is found, causing the top of the stack, address 506, to be placed in the program counter and the stack is poped. The identical action occurs for the RTS commands at address 507 and 92 such that control is eventually returned to the main program and the stack is empty.

The LIFO or subroutine stack in the program control hardware is shown in Figure 18. When the call from subroutine command is decoded by the computer control unit, the pipeline register outputs cause the stack control to accept the output of the program counter register and place it at the top of the stack. Next the subroutine address is brought in from the memory passed through the multiplexer and placed in the MAR. The subroutine address is also brought through the multiplexer incrementer, through the incrementer and placed in the program counter register to be used as a possible next source of address. The subroutine return address is recovered from the stack when the pipeline register instructs the stack control logic to place the return address at the multiplexer. The return address is passed through the multiplexer and clocked into the MAR. The return address is also clocked into the PC register via the incrementer multiplexer and the incrementer, for use as the next sequential address. Figure 19 shows the jump to subroutine instruction and Figure 20 shows the microcycles that are used in a typical call to subroutine command using the program control hardware shown in Figure 18. At T0 the program counter is placed into the MAR and updated. Time T1 finds the MAR accessing the subroutine call instruction, with the instruction being placed into the instruction register. At T2 the opcode is decoded by the CCU, and the first instruction microcode bits are clocked into the pipeline register. At time T3, the PC is placed in the MAR. At T4 the starting address of the subroutine is being fetched and placed into the MAR; the stack pointer is incremented; the current program counter is placed on the LIFO stack; and the starting address of the Subroutine plus one is placed into the program counter.

Figure 21 details the microcycle timing for a return-from-subroutine execution. At time zero the current program counter is placed into the MAR, then incremented by one. During time one the contents of the MAR fetches the return from subroutine command, which is then clocked into the instruction register at the end of the microcycle. At time 2 the contents of the instruction register is decoded in the CCU with the control bits being clocked into the pipeline register. During time 3 the return address on the top of

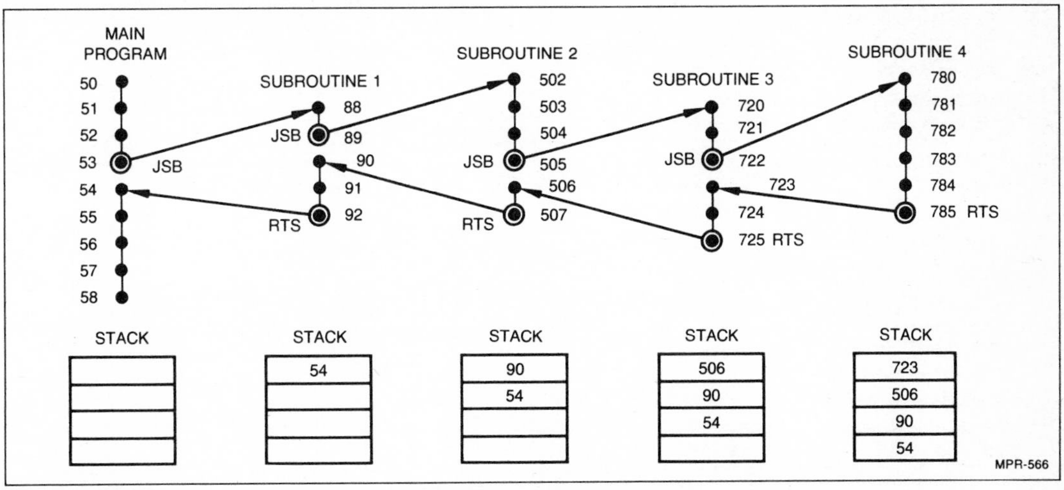

Figure 17. Nested Subroutine Example.

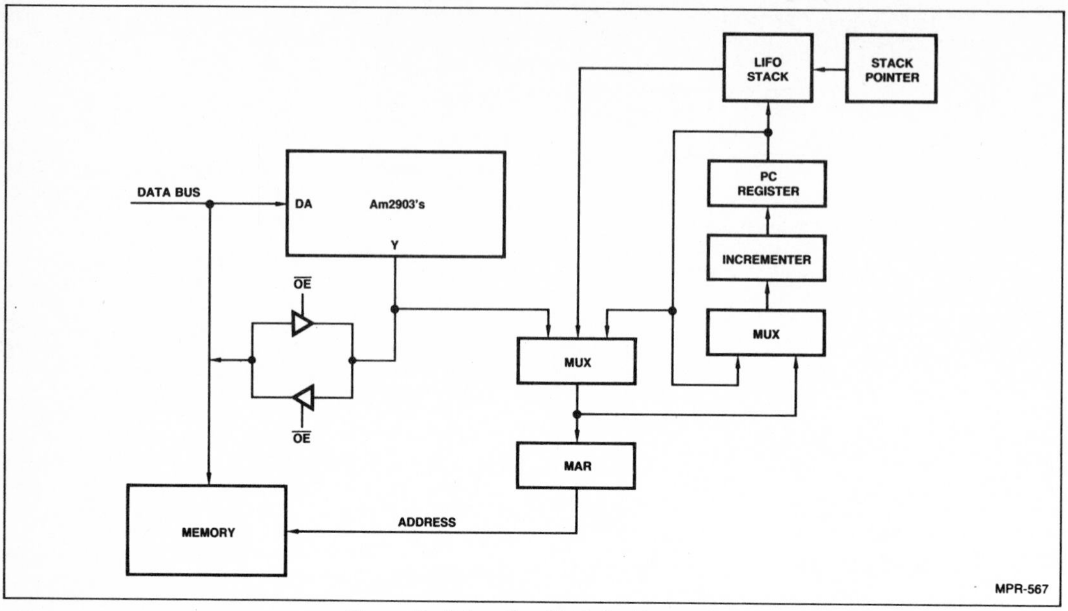

Figure 18. Subroutine Stack Architecture.

| OP | | | BRANCH ADDRESS |

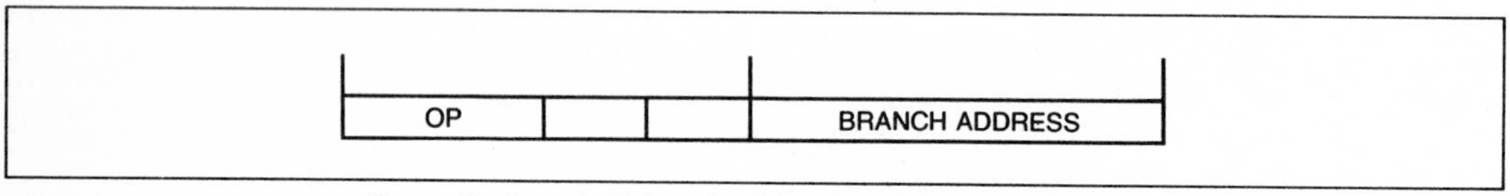

Figure 19. Jump to Subroutine (Branch and Stack) Instruction.

Microinstruction Operation	Microcycle Time												
	T0	T1	T2	T3	T4	T5	T6	T7	T8	T9	T10	T11	T12
PC → MAR; PC + 1 → PC	X												
Fetch Inst to IR		X											
Decode			X										
PC → MAR; PC + 1 → PC				X									
MEM → MAR; PC → STACK / MEM + 1 → PC; SP + 1 → SP					X								

Figure 20. Branch and Stack Instruction Microcode.

Microinstruction Operation	Microcycle Time												
	T0	T1	T2	T3	T4	T5	T6	T7	T8	T9	T10	T11	T12
PC → MAR; PC + 1 → PC	X												
Fetch Inst to IR		X											
Decode			X										
Stack → MAR; Stack + 1 → SP / SP − 1 → SP				X									

Figure 21. Return from Subroutine Instruction Microcode.

the LIFO stack is placed into the MAR, while that value plus one is stored into program counter. The stack pointer is then decremented.

The basic program control hardware thus developed with some embellishments added are contained within the Am2930 program control unit as shown in Figure 22. The Am2930 is a 4-bit slice of the program control unit. It therefore easily allows the address bus to be virtually independent of the data bus in terms of width. The Am2930 has a general purpose auxiliary register which has two sources and two destinations. One source being the D inputs which flow through the R multiplexer and hence into the auxiliary register and the other source being the output of the full adder which is the second input to the R multiplexer. The two outputs of the auxiliary register go to the A and B multiplexers which in turn source the A and B inputs to the full adder. The register enable pin ($\overline{RE}$) allows the auxiliary register to be unconditionally loaded from the D Inputs of the Am2930. The A multiplexer selects as its sources a logical zero, the output of the auxiliary register, or the D inputs. The B multiplexer accepts the outputs of the auxiliary register, a logical zero, the output of the subroutine stack file, or the output of the program counter register as its sources.

In the Am2930 design the LIFO stack is 17 words deep, allowing up to seventeen levels of subroutine. The LIFO stack is controlled by the stack pointer logic which gives a FULL indication when the stack is full and an EMPTY indication when the stack has emptied. The input to the LIFO stack is fed through a stack multiplexer whose inputs may be D inputs or the output of the program counter. Thus, depending upon the application, the stack may be used as either a subroutine stack or a general purpose LIFO stack which resides on the D bus. The incrementer and the full adder are controlled by the Ci and Cn carry-in bits respectively. Figure 23 details the ripple carry connections between Am2930s in a 16-bit array. The Ci input of the least significant slice (LSS) is controlled from the pipeline register.

The Ci signal is internally propagated through the incrementer of each device using carry look ahead logic. The microprogram memory, using the Ci input may now cause the Am2930s to repeatedly access the same main memory instruction if so desired. The full adder has its Cn input tied to ground for the LSS device of the Am2930 array. The Cn signal is progagated in parallel through the Am2930s.

For a faster propagation of the Cn signal the interconnection shown in Figure 24 should be employed. The generate and propagate pins ($\overline{G}$, $\overline{P}$) of the Am2902A carry look ahead generator. The look ahead carries (Cn + x, y, z) are connected to the Cn inputs of their respective devices. The output of the Am2930 is three-state and is controlled by the output enable pin

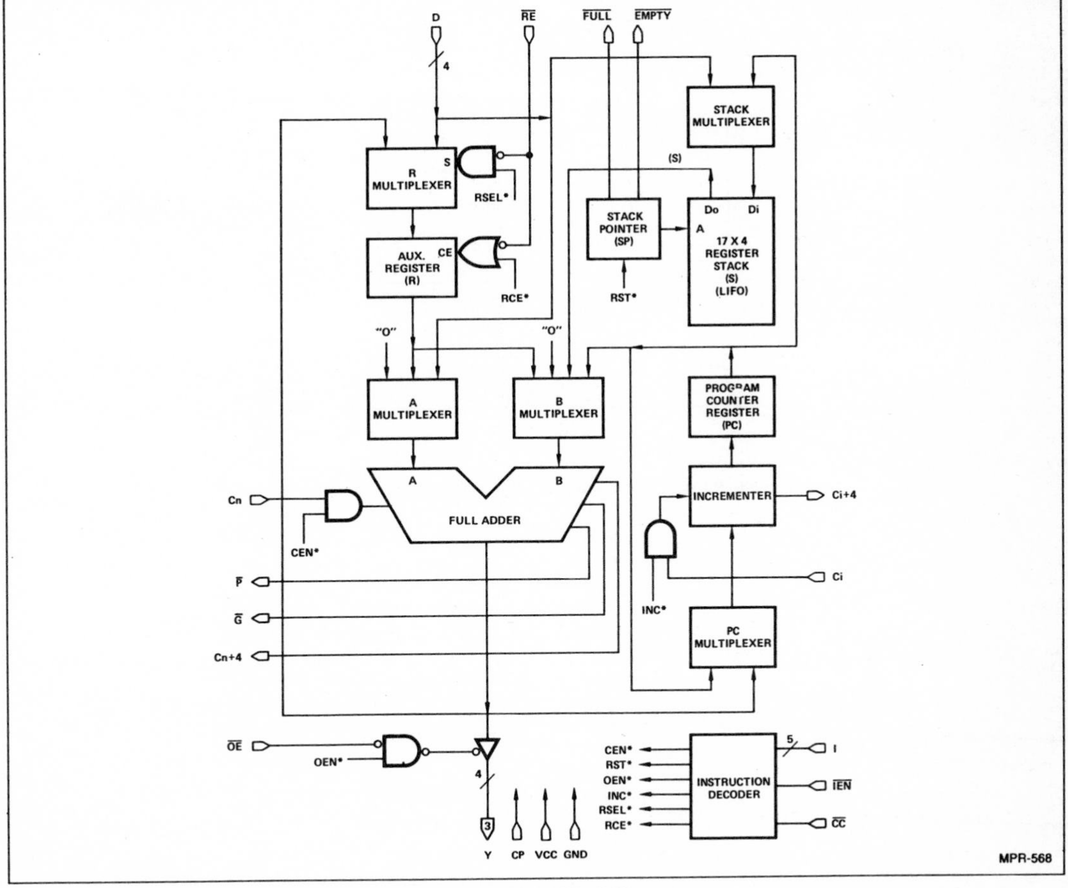

Figure 22. Am2930 Block Diagram.

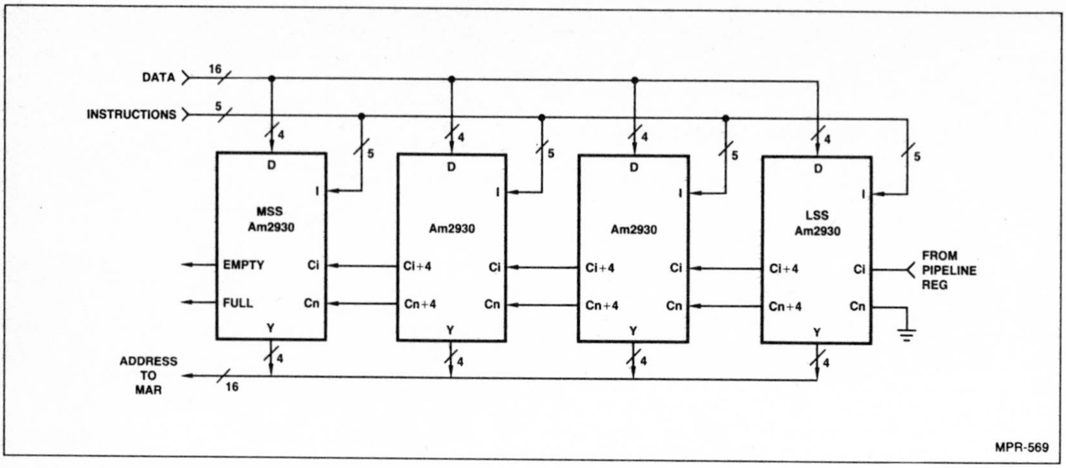

Figure 23. Ripple Expansion Scheme for Am2930's.

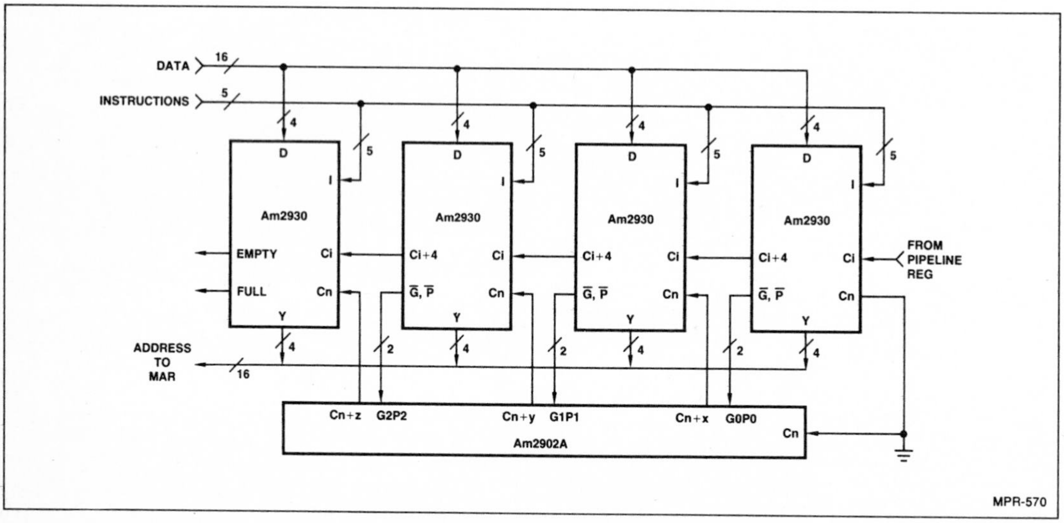

Figure 24. Parallel Look-Ahead Expansion Scheme for Am2930's.

($\overline{OE}$). Other features of the Am2930 include an Instruction Enable pin ($\overline{IEN}$). This pin allows the Am2930 array to be taken off of the microprogram data bus thus allowing the bits that were formerly committed to the Am2930 to be used in conjunction with other devices. The Am2930 also includes a condition code input ($\overline{CC}$). The Condition Code input permits the conditional testing of a single bit. This allows the feasibility of such techniques as conditional branching at the macroprogram level. For more detailed explanation of the Am2930, its instructions and its applications, see the Am2930 Data Sheet. Figure 25 shows a typical system interconnection using the Am2930. The instruction lines, Ci, $\overline{RE}$ and the $\overline{OE}$ control pins are connected directly to the outputs of the combination microprogram memory and pipeline registers contained in the Am24775 devices. The condition code inputs are obtained from the Am2904 status and control device, thus allowing conditional jumps on status. Status from the Am2904 is also fed into the test mux for use by the Am2910 for its conditional code input. Likewise the full and empty indications from the Am2930 are fed into the test MUX for use by the Am2910 to ascertain the current status of the stack. If the stack is full and the user wishes to push the data onto the stack then the current data must be emptied from the stack under microprogram control, using additional hardware.

Another feature of the Am2930 Program Control Unit as shown in Figure 22 is the full adder between the program counter and Y outputs. This allows for the execution of PC relative addressing types of instructions. While this can be an effective addressing scheme, it will not be covered in detail in this application note.

While the Am2930 offers advantages in small high performance systems requiring a small LIFO stack, it is not intended to be the solution for all program counter requirements.

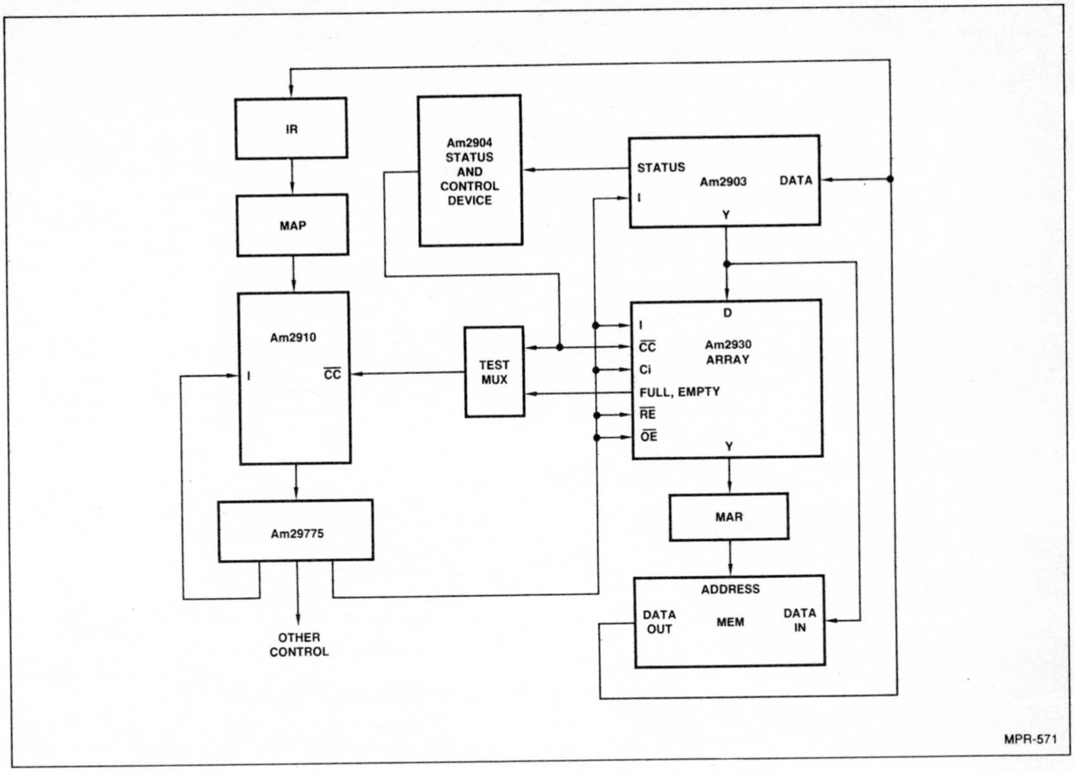

Figure 25. System Interconnection Using the Am2930.

Using the Am2901A as a Program Control Unit

Up to this point, the discussion has concerned a general architecture which includes 16 general registers in the ALU section and the LIFO stack is a program control section as shown in Figure 18. An alternative architecture and that used by most general purpose machines, is to place the LIFO stack in main memory. The stack pointer for the main memory LIFO stack can be contained in the program control unit to be described in this section. If the program control unit is built using Am2901A's it now has the capability of using its internal registers as the program counter, stack pointer, upper stack bound pointer, lower stack bound pointer, and internal temporary registers. This of course provides considerable flexibility in the architecture and also allows for a much greater repertoire of instructions to be executed. Particularly, several stack instructions can be included in the instruction set, most of which will use the form of the register-to-indexed-memory instruction format as shown in Figure 1.

Another advantage of the architecture shown in Figure 25 is speed. The Am2901A's slightly surpass the Am2903 in speed. Thus, a 16-bit Am2901A program control unit architecture can be implemented and it will perform well within the microcycle times budgeted for the system.

Looking at Figure 26 which shows the Am2901A used as a program control unit and the Am2903 used for the general register stacks/ALU section, we see a three-state buffer on the Y outputs of the Am2903 connected to the data bus as well as a three-state buffer at the input of the Am2903's from the data bus. This provides isolation and buffering for the bus as well as allowing appropriate disconnects so that certain microcycles can be combined to improve the overall performance of the machine. In addition a transfer register is used between the Am2903's and Am2901s to allow a microcycle to be terminated if an ALU operation is taking place within the Am2903's. This provides higher performance operation for the machine. In addition, a bi-directional buffer (such as the Am8304B) is used between the Am2901A Y-outputs and the Am2903 Y-outputs. This gives the ability to push the program counter contained in the Am2901A on the stack for interrupt handling. In addition, values coming from the Am2903 can be placed in the memory address register.

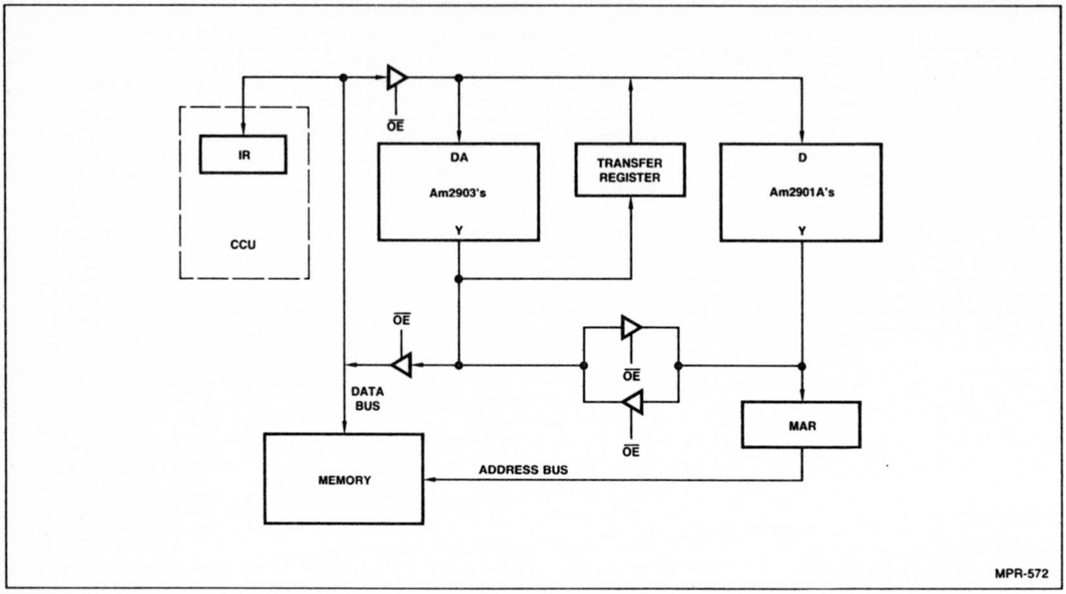

Figure 26. PCU Architecture Using the Am2901A.

Summary

The thrust of this discussion has been aimed at defining and implementing hardware to accomplish addressing of main memory. We have shown that a speed advantage is realized if the program counter is kept separate from the main general purpose register stack/ALU hardware. The most general purpose program control unit is the Am2901A. It offers several advantages in terms of program control, stack pointer control, and stack pointer boundary conditions. The Am2930 can be used in program control units occupying less space and including a built-in stack, but has some speed and performance limitations. Both devices can be used to implement the basic addressing modes associated with the instructions described in this application note.

Another purpose of this application note is to set the stage for Chapter 9 where we will overlap machine instructions such that register to register instructions can be executed in a single 200ns microcycle and the memory reference instructions can be executed in 600ns (3 microcycles) as the effective execution time. Also, we will expand on the use of the Am2901A as a Program Control Unit.

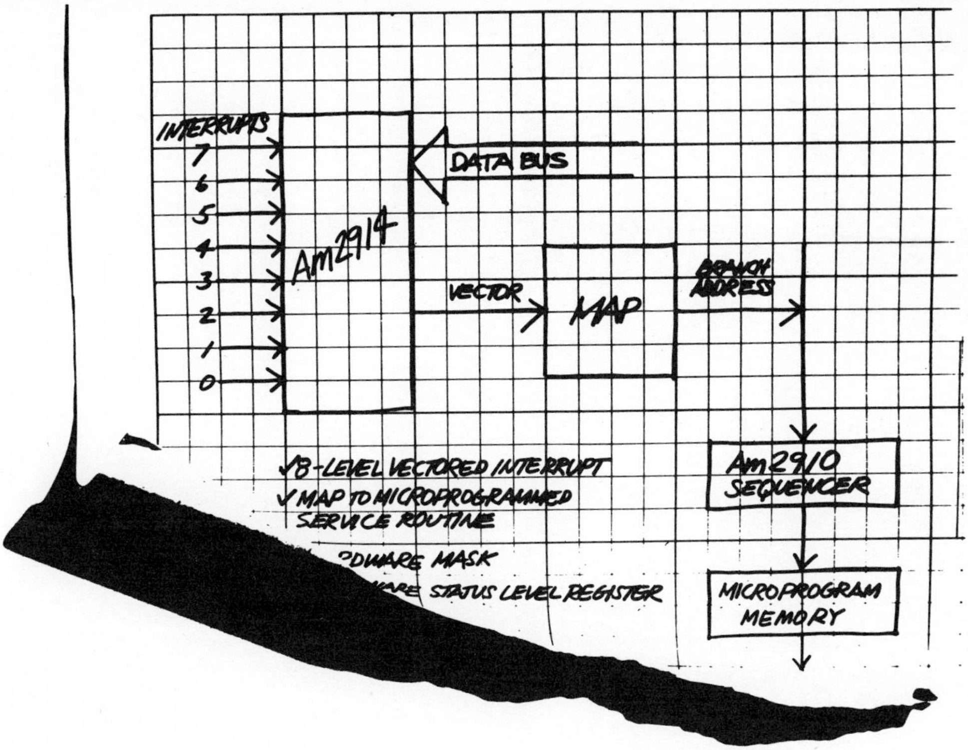
INTERRUPTS
7
6
5
4
3
2
1
0
Am2914
DATA BUS
VECTOR
MAP
BRANCH ADDRESS
Am2910 SEQUENCER
MICROPROGRAM MEMORY
✓8-LEVEL VECTORED INTERRUPT
✓MAP TO MICROPROGRAMMED SERVICE ROUTINE
MASK
STATUS LEVEL REGISTER

Chapter VI
Interrupt

INTRODUCTION

A digital computer can be viewed as a finite state machine that moves from state to state via the execution of a program. Interrupt mechanisms provide a well-defined way of altering the flow of states in response to outside asynchronous events (interrupts). There is a wide variety of ways of handling interrupts depending upon the system requirements. The choice of a particular interrupt mechanism can have a large impact on the through-put and flexibility of a system. Therefore, time should be spent carefully defining the interrupt mechanism of a new computer design.

POLLING VS. NON-POLLING

One of the simplest ways to handle asynchronous events is the polling method. With each possible event there is an associated flag that can be accessed by the program. The processor then interrogates each flag in order to determine if service is required. This method trades simple hardware for software. This not only uses memory space but also uses time for polling the flags when no service is required. The polling method has low system through-put, high real time overhead and slow response time.

In non-polling systems, the asynchronous event generates an interrupt request signal which is passed to the processor. The processor in turn suspends the execution of the current process and starts execution of an interrupt service routine. When the interrupt routine is completed, the processor resumes execution of the suspended process. This system is called an interrupt driven system because it executes interrupt service routines that are initiated by interrupt requests.

Although the non-polling method requires more hardware, it has many advantages. Because the execution of interrupt service routines is transparent to the current process, less thought and time is required of the programmer of the current process. The response time is faster because no time is spent interrogating the other non-active interrupts, which in turn increases the system throughput. There is less real time overhead and less memory space required because only the service routine exists in memory and no polling routine is required.

MACHINE VS. MICROPROGRAM LEVEL INTERRUPTS

There are two levels on which interrupts may be handled. The first and most common is the machine level interrupt. In this method possible interrupt requests are checked for during the machine instruction fetch cycle. This guarantees that an interrupt can only happen when a machine instruction is complete and before a new instruction starts.

The second level of handling interrupts is on the microprogram level. In the machine level interrupt system, the microprogram has complete control of when to recognize an interrupt but in the microprogram level system the microprogram can be interrupted at any time. This method has a smaller response time for servicing interrupt requests but requires that restrictions may be placed on the microprogram and the interrupt mechanism. These restrictions come from setting aside space on the finite microprogram stack in the sequencer for possible interrupt requests. Special consideration may also have to be given to loop counters.

TYPES OF INTERRUPTS

There are basically four types of interrupts based on the relationship of the source of the interrupt to the processor: within the processor, within the system, between software, and between processors. A multiprocessor has to be able to handle all four levels of interrupts. Therefore, the interrupt structure that is picked will have these design tradeoffs to consider.

A. *Intraprocessor* interrupts are those asynchronous events that happen within the processor during the execution of a machine instruction. This group includes such things as zero divide, overflow, accessing restricted memory, execution of a privileged instruction, machine failure, etc.

B. *Intrasystem* interrupts are interrupts created by system peripherals such as disks, CRT's and printers that require service.

C. *Executive* interrupts are those interrupts caused by the current program that is executing. This provides a way for the current program to make a request of the executive (operating system) program. These requests might include such things as starting new tasks, allocating hardware resources (disks, line printers), communication with other tasks, etc. A good example would be the supervisor call (SVC) in the IBM 360/370 computers.

D. *Interprocessor* interrupts include those interrupts between two intelligent processors. For example, this class of interrupts would be used to initiate data and status transfer between a local processor and a processor at a remote site.

SEQUENCE OF EVENTS FOR INTERRUPT HANDLING

When an interrupt occurs there is a sequence of six events that happen. These events, which can be implemented in microcode or machine code, integrated together with the hardware comprise the interrupt mechanism. The sequence of events describes the steps that occur to provide for a smooth transfer from the current process environment to an interrupt servicing environment and back again. The sequence ensures that the processor status will be the same immediately after an interrupt is serviced as immediately before the interrupt occurred. The events listed in the next few paragraphs may differ in order or overlap depending upon the machine design and application.

Interrupt Recognition

This step consists of the recognition of an interrupt request by the processor via an interrupt request line. In this step the processor can determine which device made the request. The method that is used to determine which device to service is directly related to the interrupt structure of the machine. The different types of interrupt structures will be discussed in more detail below.

Save Status

The goal of this step is to make the interrupt sequence transparent to the interrupted process. Therefore, the processor saves a minimum set of flags and registers that may be changed by the interrupt service routine, so that after the service routine is finished they may be restored.

The minimum set of flags and registers would be those which will be destroyed in the transfer of control from the current process to the interrupt service routine. It is then the responsibility of the service routine to save any other registers which it might change. The minimum set of flags and registers might include the Program Counter, Overflow Flag, Sign Flag, Interrupt Mask, etc. The minimum set also includes any register or flag that needs to be saved that the interrupt service routine cannot access.

Interrupt Masking

This step can overlap some of the other steps. For the first few steps of the sequence all interrupts are masked out so that no interrupt may occur before the processor status is saved. The mask is then usually set to accept interrupts of higher priority.

Some machines allow the service routine to selectively enable or disable interrupts also. There may be different variations to this step depending upon the application.

Interrupt Acknowledge

At some point the processor must acknowledge the interrupt being serviced so that the interrupting device knows that it is free to continue its task. The processor can acknowledge several different ways. One of the ways is to have a line devoted to interrupt acknowledge. Another method relies upon the interrupting device recognizing an acknowledge when the cause of the interrupt is serviced.

Some processor designs also use this signal as a request for the interrupting device to send an I.D. down the data bus. This aspect will be discussed in more detail below.

Interrupt Service Routine

At this point the processor can call the interrupt service routine. The address of the routine can be obtained several ways depending upon the system architecture. The most trivial is when there is only one routine which polls each device to find out which one interrupted. Some designs require that the interrupting device put an address on the data bus so that the processor can store it in its program counter and branch to it. Other designs use an I.D. number derived from the priority of the interrupt and put it through a mapping PROM or look-up table in memory in order to obtain the address of the service routine.

Restore and Return

After the interrupt service routine has returned via some variation of an Interrupt Return instruction, the processor should restore all the registers and flags that were saved previous to the interrupt routine. If this is done correctly, the processor should have the same status as before the interrupt was recognized.

INTERRUPT STRUCTURES

There are several interrupt structures that can be implemented. As usual there is a trade-off between hardware and software (or firmware). Listed below are some of the more common structures used. The particular structures vary in the way that the processor determines which device made the interrupt request.

Single Request, Multiple Poll

In this structure there is one request line which is shared among all interrupting devices. When the processor recognizes an interrupt request it polls all the devices to find the interrupting device (see Figure 1). Priority is introduced via the order in which the devices are polled. This scheme also allows dynamic reallocation of priority.

Single Request, Daisy Chain Acknowledge

In this structure there is one request line which is shared. When the processor receives an interrupt it sends out a signal acknowledging the interrupt. The acknowledge signal is passed from I/O device to I/O device until the interrupting device receives the signal. At this point the interrupting device identifies itself by putting an I.D. number on the data bus (see Figure 2). This structure requires less software, but has a static priority associated with each interrupting device. There is also a time delay associated with daisy chain acknowledge structure because in each device INTA signal has to pass through several gate delays.

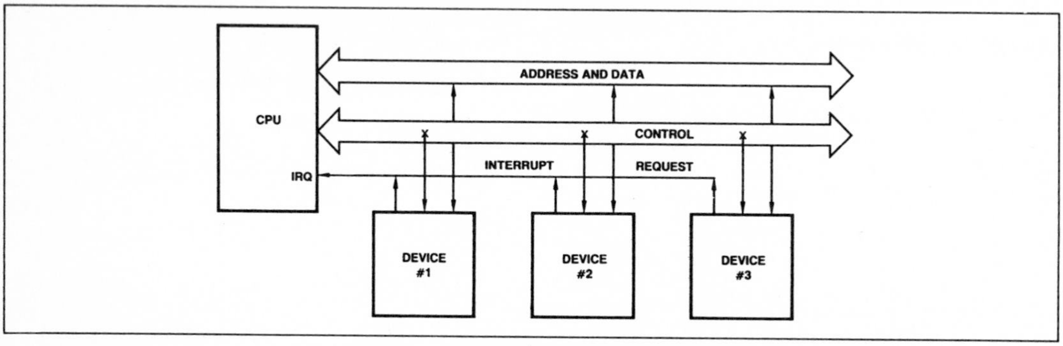

Figure 1. Single Request, Multiple Poll.

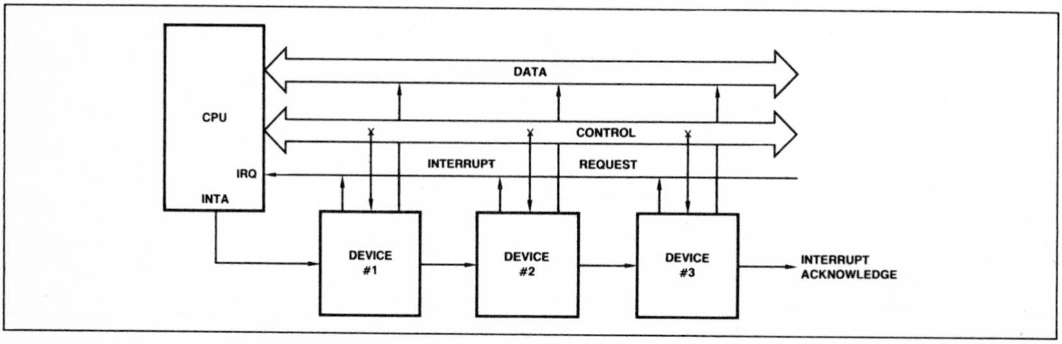

Figure 2. Single Request, Daisy Chain Acknowledge.

Multiple Request

This structure features one line per priority level (see Figure 3). The multiple line structure gives the fastest response time since the interrupting device can be identified immediately. It also results in simpler interfaces in the peripheral units, in general, a single interrupt request flip-flop. This structure allows for the possibility of having a mask bit associated with each priority level (device). The trade-off of this circuit is a wider bus and a limit of one peripheral per priority level.

Multiple Request, Daisy Chain Acknowledge

This structure combines the Single Request/Daisy Chain Acknowledge with the Multiple Request structure (see Figure 4). For each interrupt request line there is an interrupt acknowledge line which is connected to a string of devices in a daisy chain fashion. When the appropriate device receives the interrupt acknowledge, it puts an I.D. number on the data bus.

The advantage of this structure is that a lot (more than available interrupt levels) of devices may be handled by breaking them up into short daisy chains. This gives a shorter access time than a pure daisy chain with less hardware than an interrupt request line per device. This advantage is that each device must be intelligent to pass on the acknowledge signal which requires more hardware in each device.

PRIORITY SCHEMES

When handling asynchronous requests one must assume that sometimes two or more requests can happen simultaneously. In order to handle this situation, there must be some sort of priority scheme implemented to pick which request is serviced first.

The two most common priority schemes are the static and the rotating structures. In the static structure, all the interrupt levels are ordered from the lowest priority to the highest priority. This can be fixed in software or hardware and is usually permanent.

In the rotating structure the possible interrupt requests are arranged in a circle. There is a pointer which points to the lowest priority interrupt. The priority of each interrupt increases as one travels around the circle, with the highest priority interrupt being

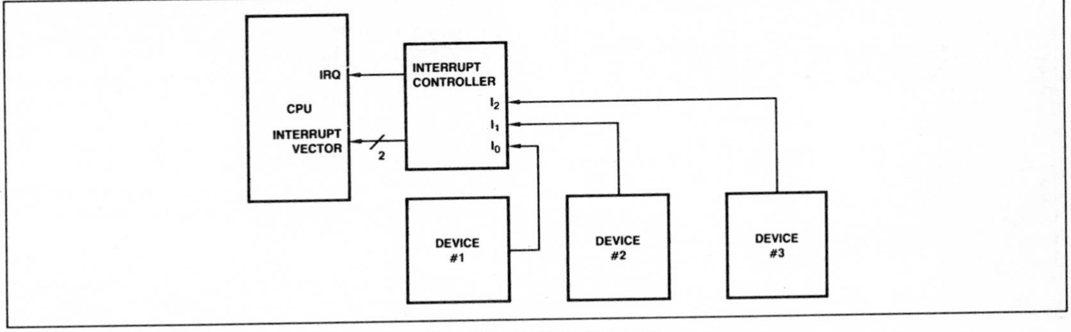

Figure 3. Multiple Request.

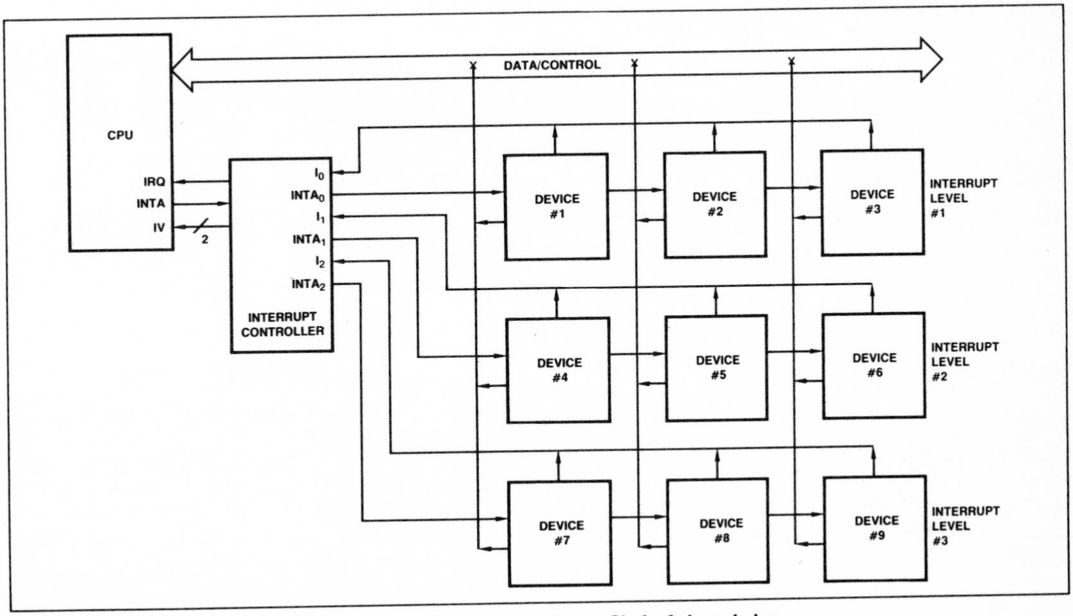

Figure 4. Multiple Requests, Daisy Chain Acknowledge.

adjacent to the lowest priority interrupt. The lowest priority interrupt pointer is changed to point at the interrupt that was just serviced. This structure is advantageous when all interrupts have similar priority and service bandwidth requirements.

NESTING

Nesting allows only higher priority interrupts to interrupt a processing interrupt service routine. Nesting requires fencing off equal and lower level interrupts. Fencing requires that the interrupt structure hold the value of the highest priority interrupt being serviced. This can be implemented with a Status Register that holds the value as a binary encoded number or in other systems as an In-Service Register with a different bit associated with each interrupt.

Whether nesting is performed in microcode or not, all computers must have machine instructions to enable and disable interrupts and set and clear mask bits. With these instructions, interrupt handlers can be written to accomplish nesting of interrupts although less efficiently than when done with microcode and hardware. In low-end computers, the interrupt structure only prioritizes interrupts leaving nesting to the software interrupt handlers.

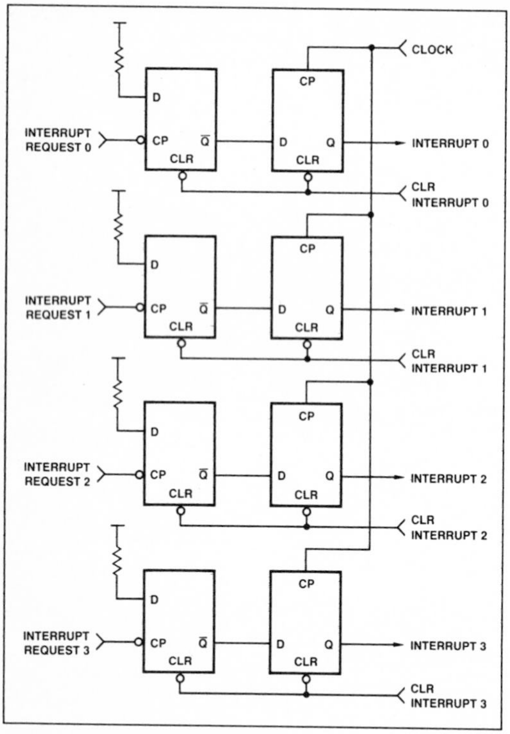

Figure 5.

A UNIVERSAL HARDWARE INTERRUPT STRUCTURE

While designing a hardware interrupt structure, the designer should consider the specific functions that are to be achieved. This provides for system optimization in not only hardware but also software. In the following paragraphs is a step by step development of a general purpose interrupt structure as related to the design concepts involved.

Multiple Interrupt Request Handling

Since interrupt requests are generated from a number of sources, the interrupt structures ability to handle interrupt requests from several sources is important.

As implemented in Figure 5, the register configuration allows the hardware to handle interrupt requests from several sources. The first column of registers catches the asynchronous interrupt request. The second column of registers synchronizes the requests with respect to the system. After the interrupt is serviced, one of the CLR lines can be used to selectively clear the interrupt request.

Interrupt Request Prioritization

Since the processor can service only one interrupt request at a time, the interrupt structure should have the ability to prioritize the requests and determine which has the highest priority. As shown in Figure 6, a priority encoder can be put on the output of the interrupt storage registers. The priority encoder will identify the highest interrupt request as a binary encoded number.

Dynamic Interrupt Request Masking

The ability to selectively inhibit or "mask" individual interrupt requests under program control is desirable. For example at times it may be important to inhibit all interrupts except Power Failure. As shown in Figure 7 this is realized by ANDing the output of a mask register with the output of the interrupt storage registers. Therefore, the mask register can be used to select which interrupt requests will pass through to the rest of the hardware.

Interrupt Request Clearing

Flexibility in the method of clearing the interrupt allows different modes of interrupt system operation. Of particular value are the abilities to clear the interrupt currently being serviced or clear all interrupts.

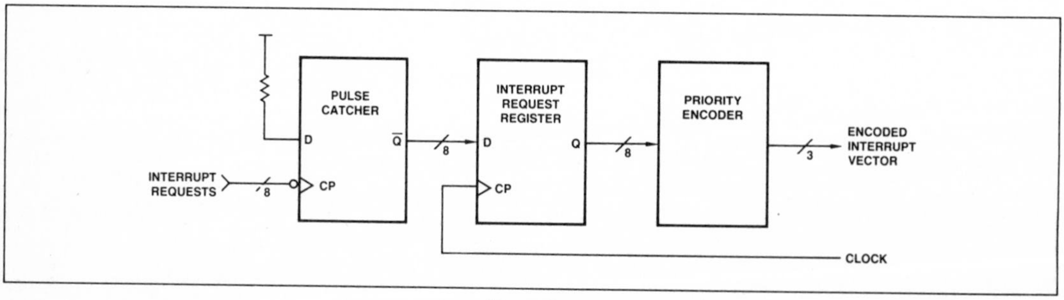

Figure 6.

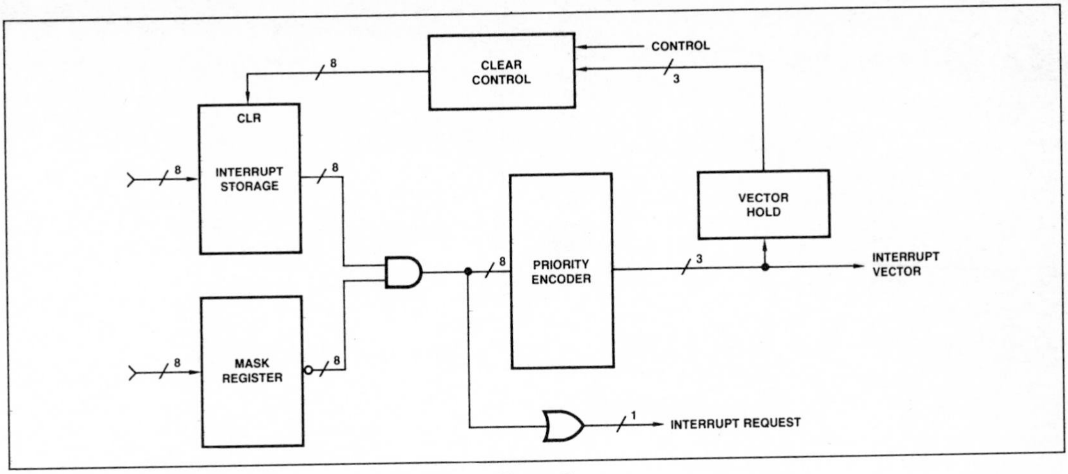

Figure 7.

This is implemented in Figure 8 by use of the Vector Hold register on the output of the Priority Encoder. This register holds the latest interrupt request that was recognized. Before another interrupt request is recognized, the output of the Vector Hold register can be fed through some clear control logic to selectively clear the old interrupt.

Interrupt Request Priority Threshold

The ability to establish a priority threshold is valuable. In this type of operation, only those interrupt requests which have higher priority than a specified threshold priority are accepted. The threshold priority can be defined by microprogram or can be automatically established by hardware at the interrupt currently being serviced plus one. This automatic threshold prevents multiple interrupts from the same source.

This feature is implemented in Figure 8 using an incrementer and status register which is compared with the current request. Each time an interrupt is recognized, the status register is updated with one plus the current level.

Interrupt Service Routine "Nesting"

This feature allows an interrupt service routine for a given priority request to be interrupted in turn by a higher priority interrupt request. This can be achieved by saving the status register before each interrupt is serviced and restoring it afterwards.

Microprogrammability and Hardware Modularity

These last two design concepts bring us to the Vectored Priority Interrupt controller, the Am2914. The Am2914 is a modular interrupt system block which is beneficial in two ways. First,

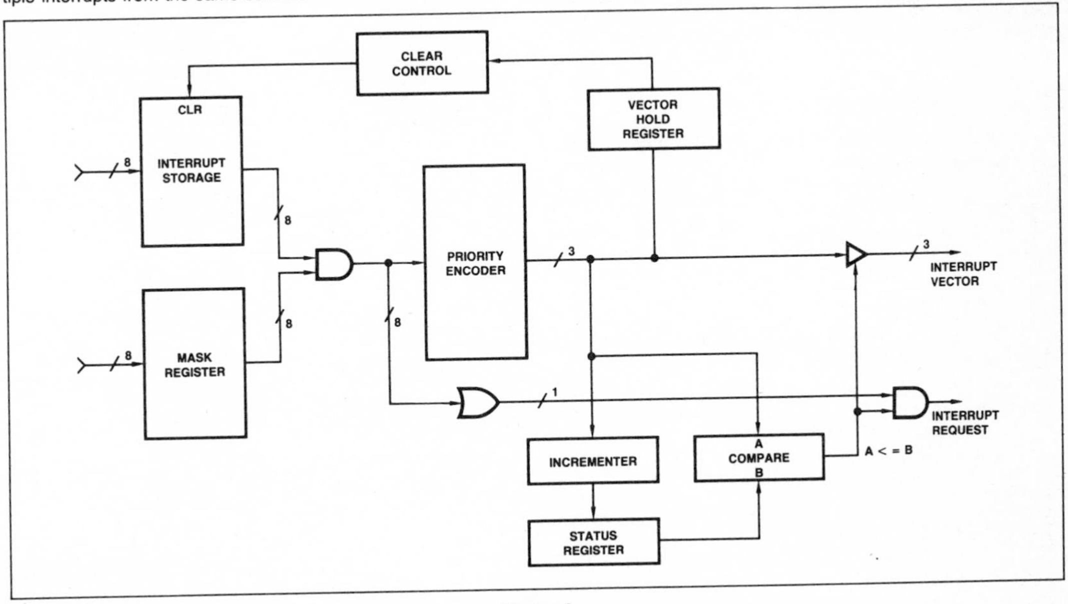

Figure 8.

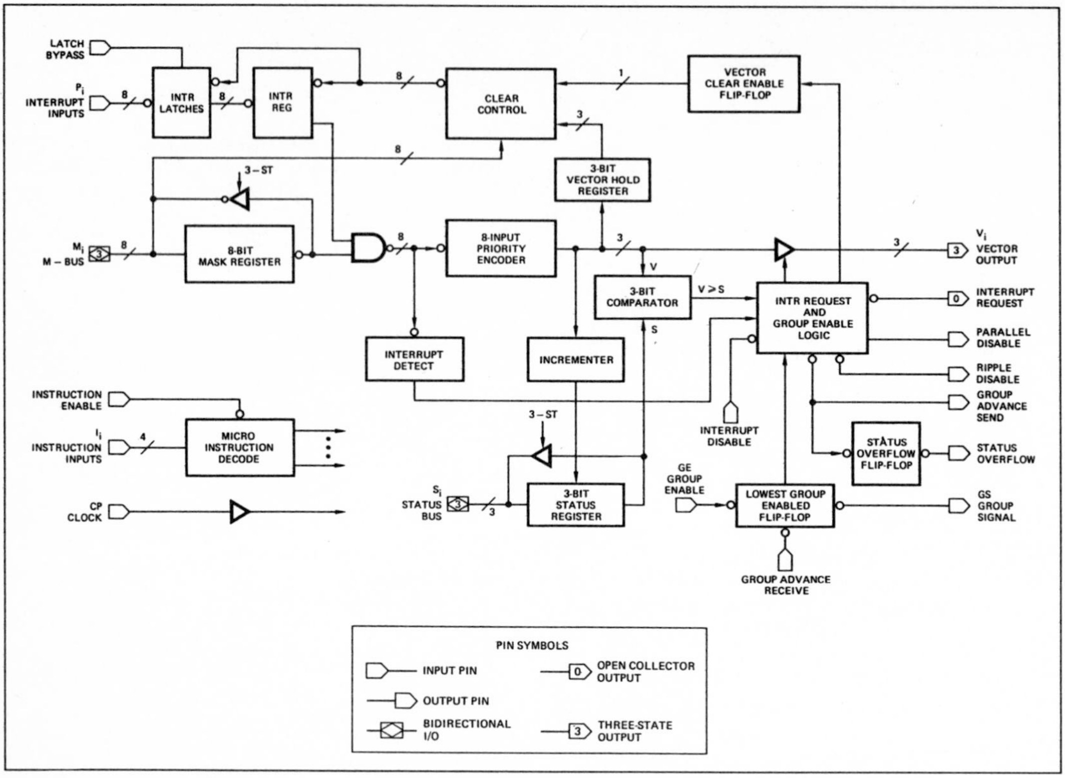

Figure 9. Am2914 Block Diagram.

hardware modularity provides expansion capability. Additional modules may be added as the need to service additional requests arises. Secondly, hardware modularity provides a structural regularity which simplifies the system structure and also reduces the number of hardware part numbers.

The Am2914 is microprogrammable, which permits the construction of a general purpose or "universal" interrupt structure which can be microprogrammed to meet a specific application's requirement. The universality of the structure allows standardization of the hardware and amortization of the hardware development costs across a much broader user base. The end result is a flexible, low cost interrupt structure as shown in Figure 9.

PROGRAMMING THE Am2914

The Am2914 is controlled by a four-bit microinstruction field I_0-I_3. The microinstruction is executed if $\overline{IE}$ (Instruction Enable) is LOW and is ignored if $\overline{IE}$ is HIGH, allowing the four I bits to be shared with other functions. Sixteen different microinstructions are executed. Figure 11 shows the microinstructions and the microinstruction codes.

In this microinstruction set, the *Master Clear* microinstruction is selected as binary zero so that during a power-up sequence, the microinstruction register in the microprogram control unit of the central processor can be cleared to all zeros. Thus, on the next clock cycle, the Am2914 will execute the *Master Clear* function.

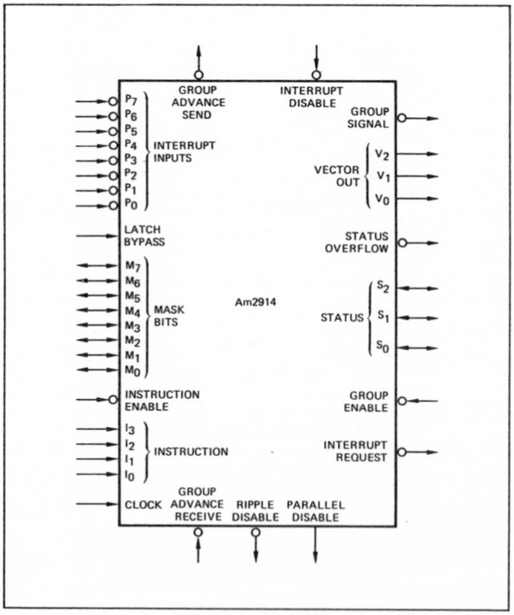

Figure 10. Am2914 Logic Symbol.

MICROINSTRUCTION DESCRIPTION	MICROINSTRUCTION CODE $I_3I_2I_1I_0$
MASTER CLEAR	0000
CLEAR ALL INTERRUPTS	0001
CLEAR INTERRUPTS FROM M-BUS	0010
CLEAR INTERRUPTS FROM MASK REGISTER	0011
CLEAR INTERRUPT, LAST VECTOR READ	0100
READ VECTOR	0101
READ STATUS REGISTER	0110
READ MASK REGISTER	0111
SET MASK REGISTER	1000
LOAD STATUS REGISTER	1001
BIT CLEAR MASK REGISTER	1010
BIT SET MASK REGISTER	1011
CLEAR MASK REGISTER	1100
DISABLE INTERRUPT REQUEST	1101
LOAD MASK REGISTER	1110
ENABLE INTERRUPT REQUEST	1111

Figure 11. Am2914 Microinstruction Set.

This includes clearing the Interrupt Latches and Register as well as the Mask Register and Status Register. The LGE flip-flop of the least significant group is set LOW because the Group Advance Receive input is tied LOW. All other Group Advance Receive inputs are tied to Group Advance Send outputs and these are forced HIGH during this instruction. This clear instruction also sets the Interrupt Request Enable flip-flop so that a fully interrupt driven system can be easily initiated from any interrupt.

The *Clear All Interrupts* microinstruction clears the Interrupt Latches and Register.

The *Clear Interrupts from M-Bus* microinstruction clears those Interrupt Latches and Register bits which have corresponding M-Bus bits set equal to one.

The *Clear Interrupts from Mask Register* microinstruction clears those Interrupt Latches and Register bits which have corresponding Mask Register bits set equal to one. The M-Bus is used by the Am2914 during the execution of this microinstruction and must be floating.

The *Clear Interrupt, Last Vector Read* microinstruction clears the Interrupt Latch and Register bit associated with the last vector read.

The *Read Vector* microinstruction is used to read the vector value of the highest priority request causing the interrupt. The vector outputs are three-state drivers that are enabled onto the is instruction. This microinstruction also automatically loads the value "vector plus one" into the Status Register. In addition, this instruction sets the Vector Clear Enable flip-flop and loads the current vector value into the Vector Hold Register so that this value can be used by the *Clear Interrupt, Last Vector Read* microinstruction. This allows the user to read the vector associated with the interrupt, and at some later time clear the Interrupt Latch and Register bit associated with the vector read.

During the *Read Status Register* microinstruction, the Status Register outputs are enabled onto the Status Bus (S_0-S_2). The Status Bus is a three-bit, bi-directional, three-state bus.

The *Read Mask Register* microinstruction enables the Mask Register outputs onto the bi-directional, three-state M-Bus.

The *Set Mask Register* microinstruction sets all the bits in the Mask Register to one. This results in all interrupts being inhibited.

The *Load Status Register* microinstruction loads S-Bus data into the Status Register and also loads the LGE flip-flop from the Group Enable input.

The *Bit Clear Mask Register* microinstruction may be used to selectively clear individual Mask Register bits. This microinstruction clears those Mask Register bits which have corresponding M-Bus bits equal to one. Mask Register bits with corresponding M-Bus bits equal to zero are not affected.

The *Bit Set Mask Register* microinstruction sets those Mask Register bits which have corresponding M-Bus bits equal to one. Other Mask Register bits are not affected.

The entire Mask Register is cleared by the *Clear Mask Register* microinstruction. This enables all interrupts subject to the Interrupt Enable flip-flop and the Status Register.

All Interrupt Requests may be disabled by execution of the *Disable Interrupt Request* microinstruction. This microinstruction resets an Interrupt Request Enable flip-flop on the chip.

The *Load Mask Register* microinstruction loads data from the three-state, bi-directional M-Bus into the Mask Register.

The *Enable Interrupt Request* microinstruction sets the Interrupt Enable flip-flop. Thus, Interrupt Requests are enabled subject to the contents of the Mask and Status Registers.

Am2914 BLOCK DIAGRAM DESCRIPTION

The Am2914 block diagram is shown in Figure 9. The Microinstruction Decode circuitry decodes the Interrupt Microinstructions and generates required control signals for the chip.

The Interrupt Register holds the Interrupt Inputs and is an eight-bit, edge-triggered register which is set on the rising edge of the CP Clock signal if the Interrupt Input is LOW.

The Interrupt latches are set/reset latches. When the Latch Bypass signal is LOW, the latches are enabled and act as negative pulse catchers on the inputs to the Interrupt Register. When the Latch Bypass signal is HIGH, the Interrupt latches are transparent.

The Mask Register holds the eight mask bits associated with the eight interrupt levels. The register may be loaded from or read to the M-Bus. Also, the entire register or individual mask bits may be set or cleared.

The Interrupt Detect circuitry detects the presence of any unmasked Interrupt Input. The eight-input Priority Encoder determines the highest priority, non-masked Interrupt Input and forms a binary coded interrupt vector. Following a Vector Read, the three-bit Vector Hold Register holds the binary coded interrupt vector. This stored vector can be used later for clearing interrupts.

The three-bit Status Register holds the status bits and may be loaded from or read to the S-Bus. During a Vector Read, the Incrementer increments the interrupt vector by one, and the result is clocked into the Status Register. Thus, the Status Register points to a level one greater than the vector just read.

The three-bit Comparator compares the Interrupt Vector with the contents of the Status Register and indicates if the Interrupt Vector is greater than or equal to the contents of the Status Register.

The Lowest Group Enabled Flip-Flop is used when a number of Am2914's are cascaded. In a cascaded system, only one Lowest Group Enabled Flip-Flop is LOW at a time. It indicates the eight interrupt group, which contains the lowest priority interrupt level which will be accepted and is used to form the higher order status bits.

The Interrupt Request and Group Enable logic contain various gating to generate the Interrupt Request, Parallel Disable, Ripple Disable, and Group Advance Send signals.

The Status Overflow signal is used to disable all interrupts. It indicates the highest priority interrupt vector has been read and the Status Register has overflowed.

The Clear Control logic generates the eight individual clear signals for the bits in the Interrupt Latches and Register. The Vector Clear Enable Flip-Flop indicates if the last vector read was from this chip. When it is set it enables the Clear Control Logic.

The CP clock signal is used to clock the Interrupt Register, Mask Register, Status Register, Vector Hold Register, and the Lowest Group Enabled, Vector Clear Enable and Status Overflow Flip-Flops, all on the clock LOW-to-HIGH transition.

CASCADING THE Am2914

A number of input/output signals are provided for cascading the Am2914 Vectored Priority Interrupt Encoder. A definition of these I/O signals and their required connections follows:

Group Signal ($\overline{GS}$) – This signal is the output of the Lowest Group Enabled flip-flop and during a Read Status microinstruction is used to generate the high order bits of the Status word.

Group Enable ($\overline{GE}$) – This signal is one of the inputs to the Lowest Group Enable flip-flop and is used to load the flip-flop during the Load Status microinstruction.

Group Advance Send ($\overline{GAS}$) – During a Read Vector microinstruction, this output signal is LOW when the highest priority vector (vector seven) of the group is being read. In a cascaded system Group Advance Send must be tied to the Group Advance Receive input of the next higher group in order to transfer status information.

Group Advance Receive ($\overline{GAR}$) – During a Master Clear or Read Vector microinstruction, this input signal is used with other internal signals to load the Lowest Group Enabled flip-flop. The Group Advance Receive input of the lowest priority group must be tied to ground.

Status Overflow ($\overline{SV}$) – This output signal becomes LOW after the highest priority vector (vector seven) of the group has been read and indicates the Status Register has overflowed. It stays LOW until a Master Clear or Load Status microinstruction is executed. The Status Overflow output of the highest priority group should be connected to the Interrupt Disable input of the same group and serves to disable all interrupts until new status is loaded or the system is master cleared. The Status Overflow outputs of lower priority groups should be left open (see Figure 14).

Interrupt Disable ($\overline{ID}$) – When LOW, this input signal inhibits the Interrupt Request output from the chip and also generates a Ripple Disable output.

Ripple Disable ($\overline{RD}$) – This output signal is used only in the Ripple Cascade Mode (see below). The Ripple Disable output is LOW when the Interrupt Disable input is LOW, the Lowest Group Enabled flip-flop is LOW, or an Interrupt Request is generated in the group. In the ripple cascade mode, the Ripple Disable output is tied to the Interrupt Disable input of the next lower priority group (see Figure 13).

Parallel Disable (PD) – This output is used only in the parallel cascade mode (see below). It is LOW when the Lowest Group Enabled flip-flop is LOW or an Interrupt Request is generated in the group. It is not affected by the Interrupt Disable input.

CASCADING CONFIGURATIONS

A single Am2914 chip may be used to prioritize and encode up to eight interrupt inputs. Figure 12 shows how the above cascade lines should be connected in such a single chip system.

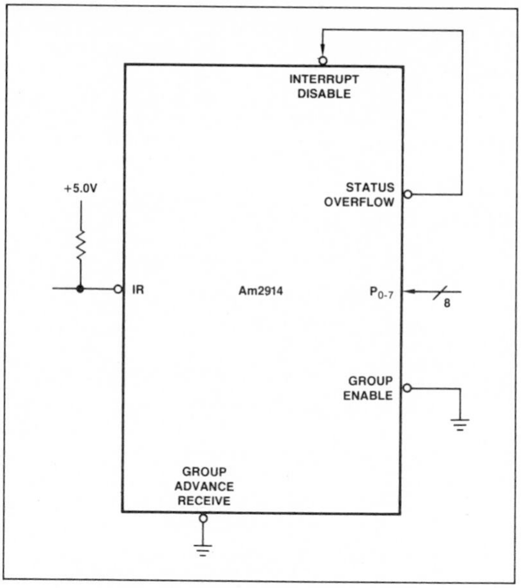

Figure 12. Cascade Lines Connection for Single Chip System.

The Group Advance Receive and Group Enable inputs should be connected to ground so that the Lowest Group Enabled flip-flop is forced LOW during a *Master Clear* or *Load Status* microinstruction. Status Overflow should be connected to Interrupt Disable in order to disable interrupts when vector seven is read. The Group Advance Send, Ripple Disable, Group Signal and Parallel Disable pins should be left open.

The Am2914 may be cascaded in either a Ripple Cascade Mode or a Parallel Cascade Mode. In the Ripple Cascade Mode, the Interrupt Disable signal, which disables lower priority interrupts, is allowed to ripple through lower priority groups. Figures 13, 16, and 17 show the cascade connections required for a ripple cascade 32 input interrupt system.

In the parallel cascade mode, a parallel lookahead scheme is employed using the high-speed Am2902 Lookahead Carry Generator. Figures 14, 15, and 17 show the cascade connections required for a parallel cascade 32-input interrupt system. For this application, the Am2902 is used as a lookahead interrupt disable

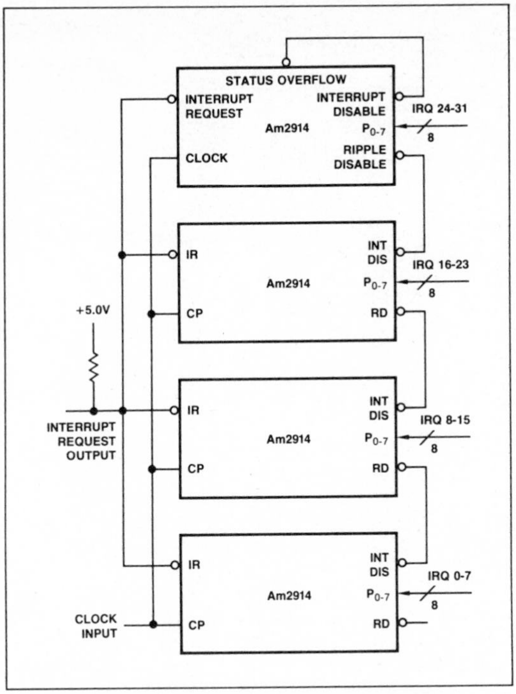

Figure 13. Interrupt Disable Connections for Ripple Cascade Mode.

generator. A Parallel Disable output from any group results in the disabling of all lower priority groups in parallel. Figure 15 shows the Am2902 logic diagram and equations.

In Figures 16 and 17 the Am2913 Priority Interrupt Expander is shown forming the high order bits of the vector and status, respectively. The Am2913 is an eight-line to three-line priority encoder with three-state outputs which are enabled by the five output control signals G1, G2, $\overline{G3}$, $\overline{G4}$, and $\overline{G5}$. In Figure 16, the Am2913 is connected so that its outputs are enabled during a Read Vector instruction, and in Figure 17 the Am2913 is connected to microinstruction bits so that its outputs are enabled during a Read Status Instruction. The Am2913 logic diagram and truth table are shown in Figure 18.

The Am25LS138 three-line to eight-line Decoder also is shown in Figure 17. It is used to decode the three high order status bits during a Load Status instruction. The Am25LS138 logic diagram and truth table are shown in Figure 19.

Am2914 IN THE Am2900 SYSTEM

The block diagram of Figure 20 shows a typical 16-bit minicomputer architecture. The Am2914 is the heart of the Interrupt Control Unit as shown at the bottom of the block diagram. It receives its microinstructions from the Computer Control Unit. The mask, Status and Interrupt vector information are passed on the data bus. The interrupt request line from the Am2914 input into the next microprogram Address Control unit where it can be tested to determine if an interrupt request has been made.

Figures 21 and 22 show the detailed hardware design of two example interrupt control units (ICU's) for an Am2900 Computer

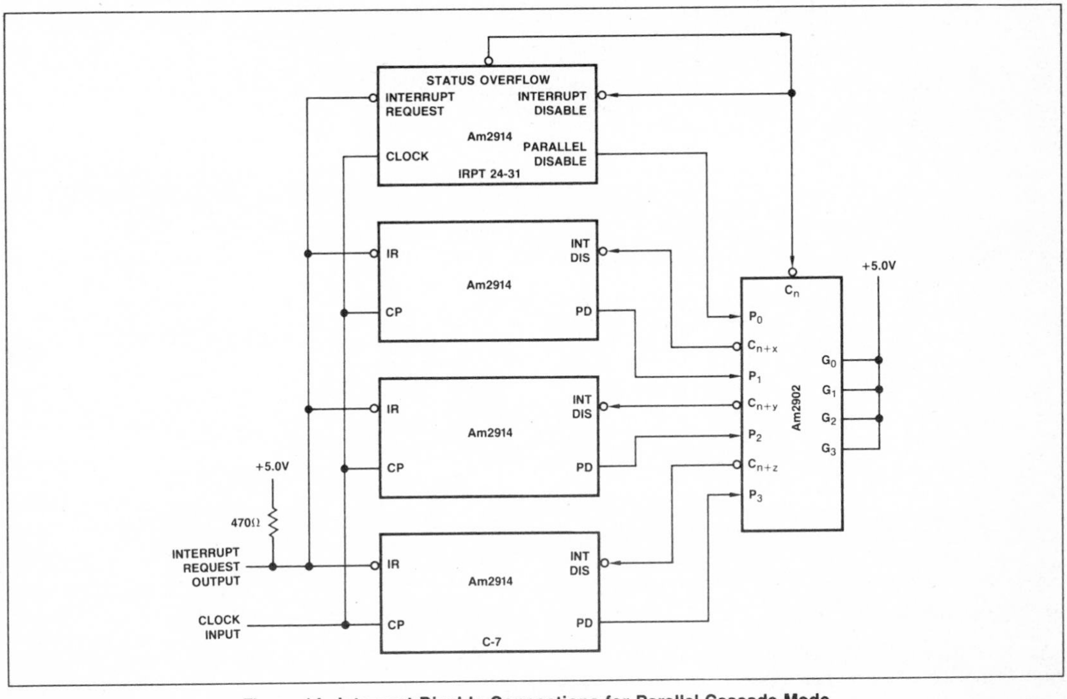

Figure 14. Interrupt Disable Connections for Parallel Cascade Mode.

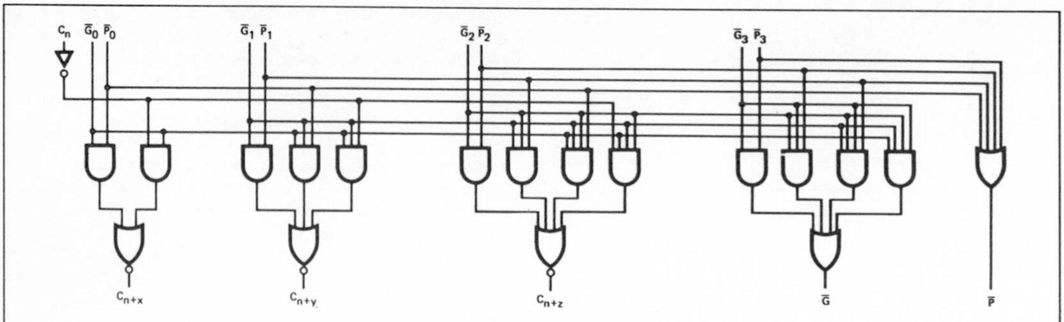

$$C_{n+x} = G_0 + P_0C_n$$
$$C_{n+y} = G_1 + P_1G_0 + P_1P_0C_n$$
$$C_{n+z} = G_2 + P_2G_1 + P_2P_1G_0 + P_2P_1P_0C_n$$
$$G = G_3 + P_3G_2 + P_3P_2G_1 + P_3P_2P_1G_0$$
$$P = P_3P_2P_1P_0$$

Figure 15. Am2902 Carry Look-Ahead Generator Logic Diagram and Equations.

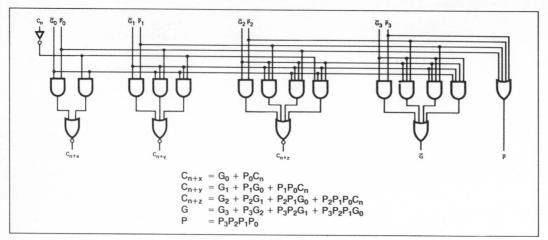

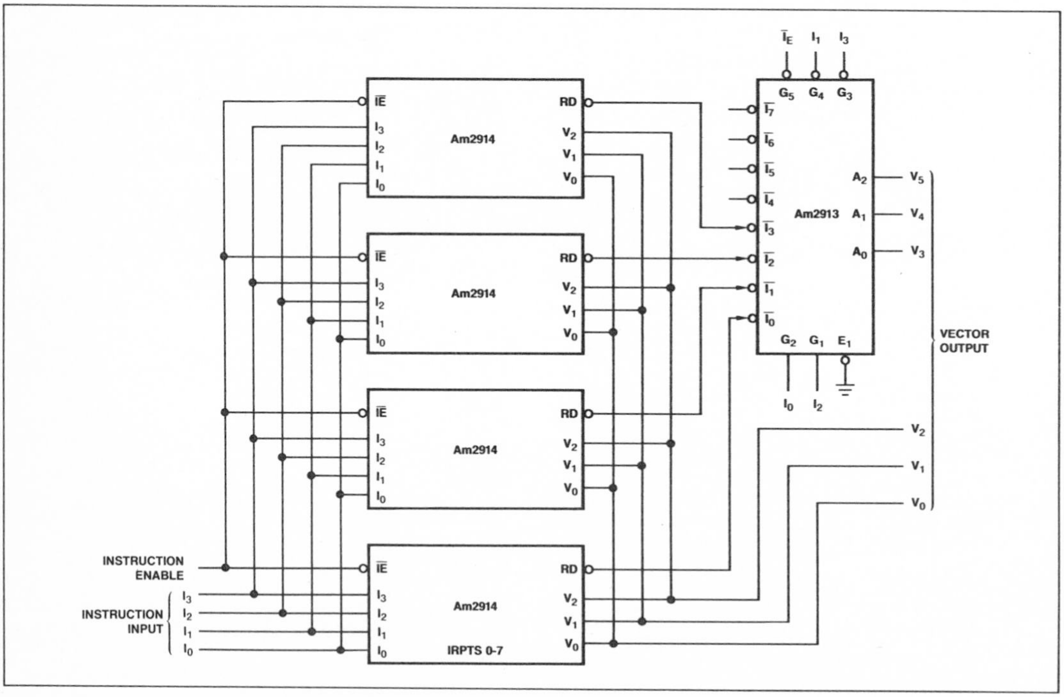

Figure 16. Vector Connections for both the Parallel and Ripple Cascade Modes.

System. Figure 21 shows an eight interrupt level ICU, and Figure 22 shows an ICU which has sixteen levels. In both designs, the Am2914 Instruction inputs and Instruction Enable input are driven by the $I_{0\text{-}3}$ field and $\overline{\text{IE}}$ bit, respectively, of the Microinstruction Register. Note that Am2914 Instruction inputs are enabled only when the $\overline{\text{IE}}$ bit is LOW. Therefore, the $I_{0\text{-}3}$ field of the Microinstruction Register may be shared with another functional unit of the computer such as the ALU.

The Latch Bypass input is shown connected to ground so that a Low-going pulse will be detected at any of the Interrupt Inputs. The designer has the option of connecting the Latch Bypass input to a pull up resistor connected to +5 volts. This makes the inputs low level sensitive. They are clocked in by each system clock. It is therefore implied that the processor will have to acknowledge the interrupt so that the interrupting device will know when to release the interrupt request line.

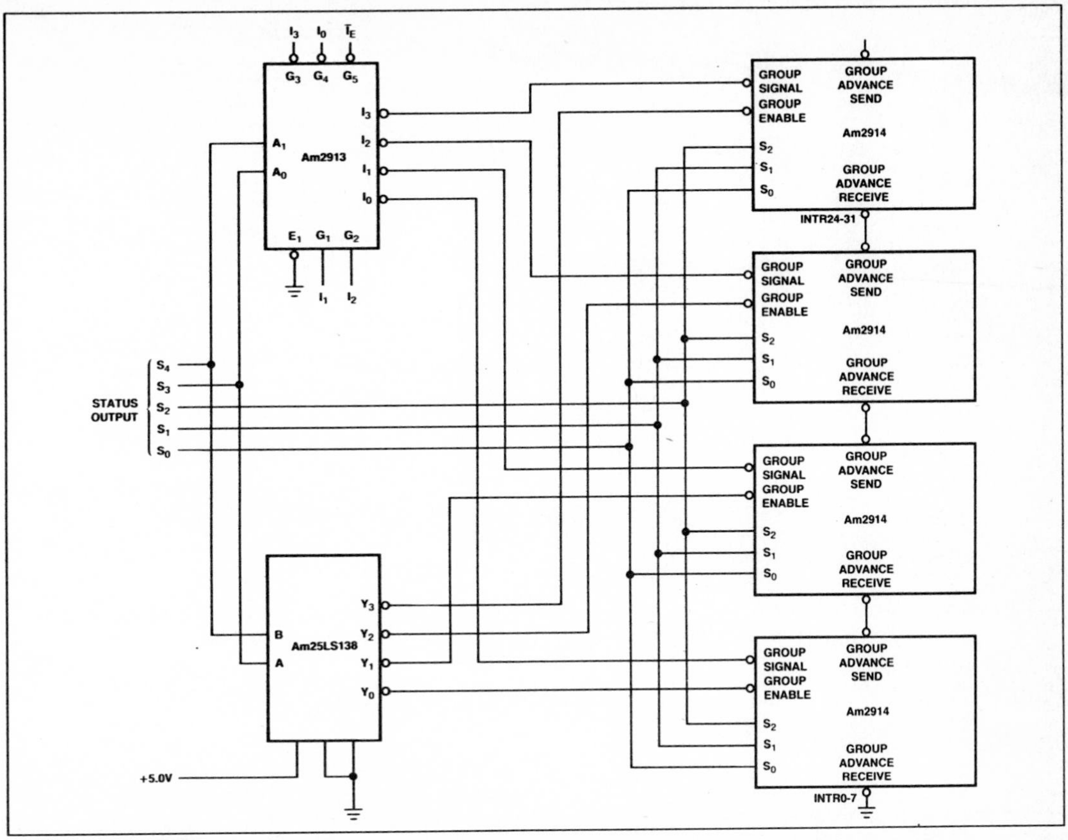

Figure 17. Group Signal, Group Enable, Group Advance Send, Group Advance Receive and Status Connections for Both the Parallel and Ripple Cascade Modes.

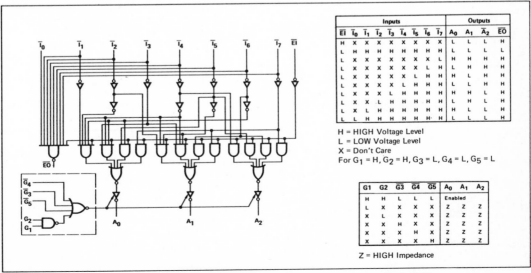

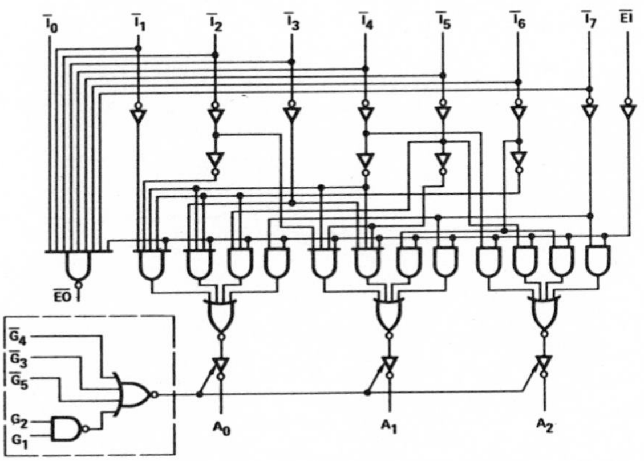

Inputs									Outputs			
$\overline{EI}$	$\overline{I}_0$	$\overline{I}_1$	$\overline{I}_2$	$\overline{I}_3$	$\overline{I}_4$	$\overline{I}_5$	$\overline{I}_6$	$\overline{I}_7$	A_0	A_1	$\overline{A}_2$	$\overline{EO}$
H	X	X	X	X	X	X	X	X	L	L	L	H
L	H	H	H	H	H	H	H	H	L	L	L	L
L	X	X	X	X	X	X	X	L	H	H	H	H
L	X	X	X	X	X	X	L	H	L	H	H	H
L	X	X	X	X	X	L	H	H	H	L	H	H
L	X	X	X	X	L	H	H	H	L	L	H	H
L	X	X	X	L	H	H	H	H	H	H	L	H
L	X	X	L	H	H	H	H	H	L	H	L	H
L	X	L	H	H	H	H	H	H	H	L	L	H
L	L	H	H	H	H	H	H	H	L	L	L	H

H = HIGH Voltage Level
L = LOW Voltage Level
X = Don't Care
For G_1 = H, G_2 = H, G_3 = L, G_4 = L, G_5 = L

G1	G2	$\overline{G3}$	$\overline{G4}$	$\overline{G5}$	A_0	A_1	A_2
H	H	L	L	L	Enabled		
L	X	X	X	X	Z	Z	Z
X	L	X	X	X	Z	Z	Z
X	X	H	X	X	Z	Z	Z
X	X	X	H	X	Z	Z	Z
X	X	X	X	H	Z	Z	Z

Z = HIGH Impedance

Figure 18. Am2913 Priority Interrupt Expander Logic Diagram and Truth Table.

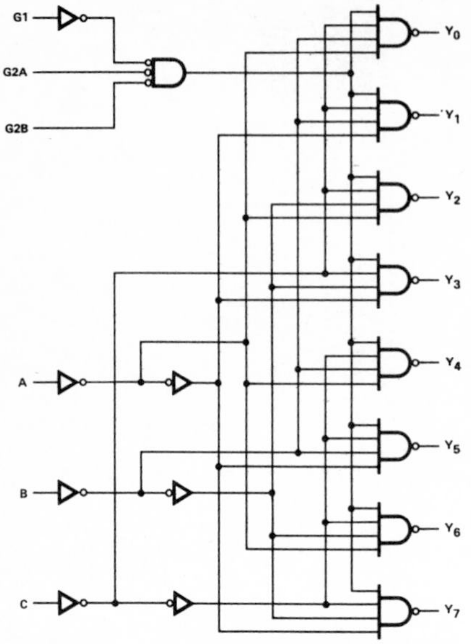

Inputs				Outputs							
Enable			Select								
G1	G2A	G2B	C B A	Y_0	Y_1	Y_2	Y_3	Y_4	Y_5	Y_6	Y_7
L	X	X	X X X	H	H	H	H	H	H	H	H
X	H	X	X X X	H	H	H	H	H	H	H	H
X	X	H	X X X	H	H	H	H	H	H	H	H
H	L	L	L L L	L	H	H	H	H	H	H	H
H	L	L	L L H	H	L	H	H	H	H	H	H
H	L	L	L H L	H	H	L	H	H	H	H	H
H	L	L	L H H	H	H	H	L	H	H	H	H
H	L	L	H L L	H	H	H	H	L	H	H	H
H	L	L	H L H	H	H	H	H	H	L	H	H
H	L	L	H H L	H	H	H	H	H	H	L	H
H	L	L	H H H	H	H	H	H	H	H	H	L

H = HIGH
L = LOW
X = Don't Care

Figure 19. Am25LS138 3 to 8 Line Decoder Logic Diagram and Truth Table.

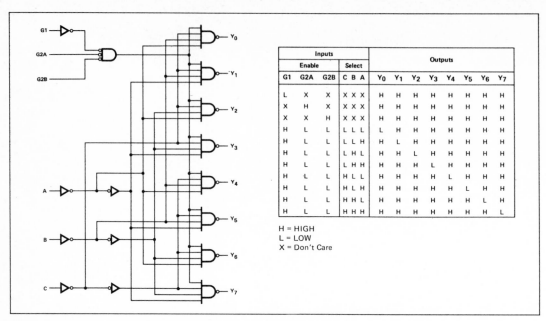

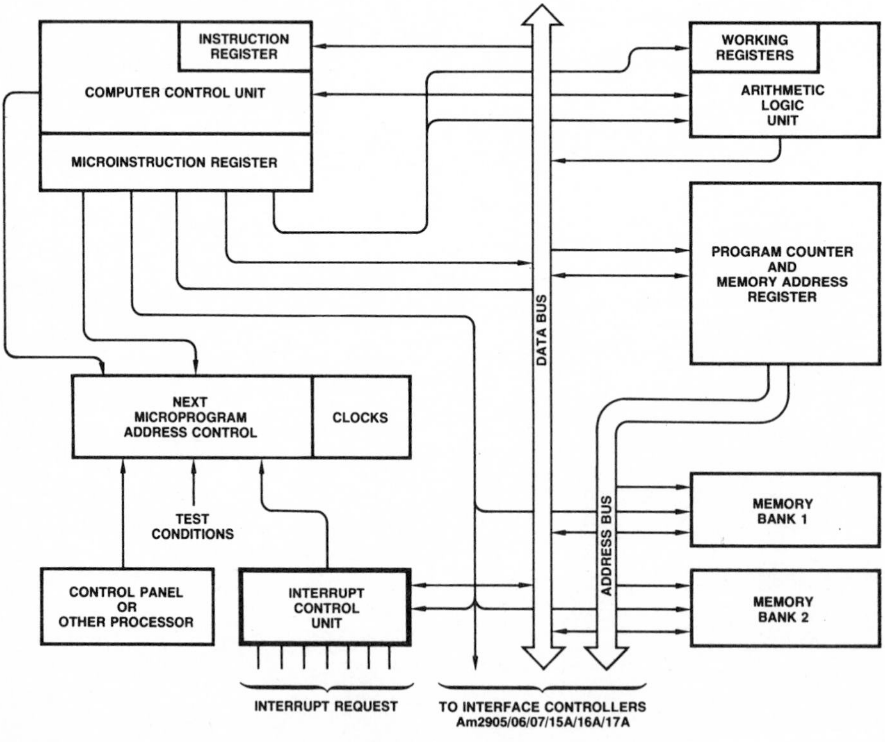

Figure 20. A Generalized Computer Architecture.

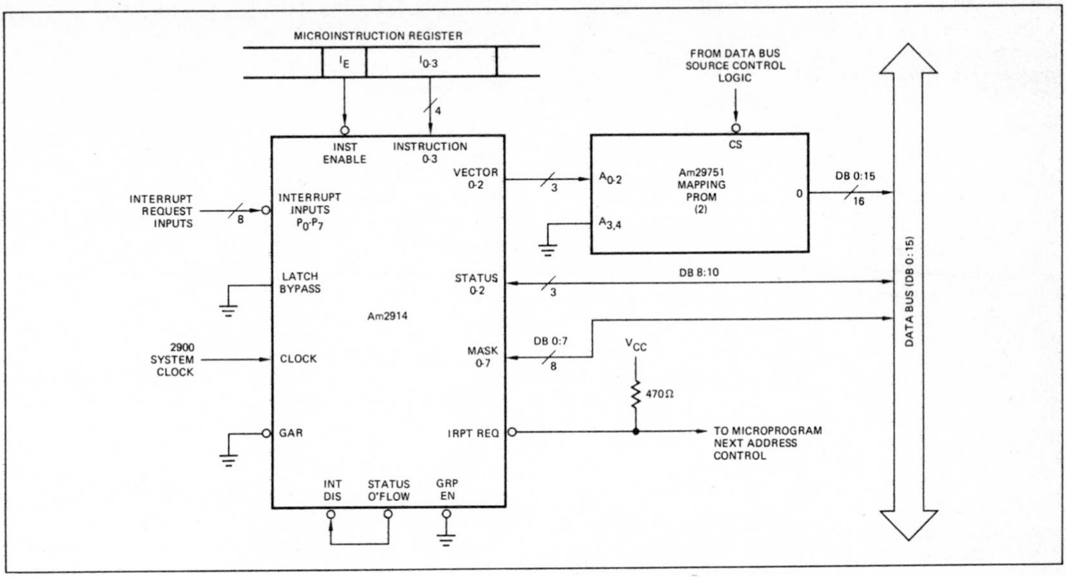

Figure 21. 8 Level Interrupt Control Unit for Am2900 System.

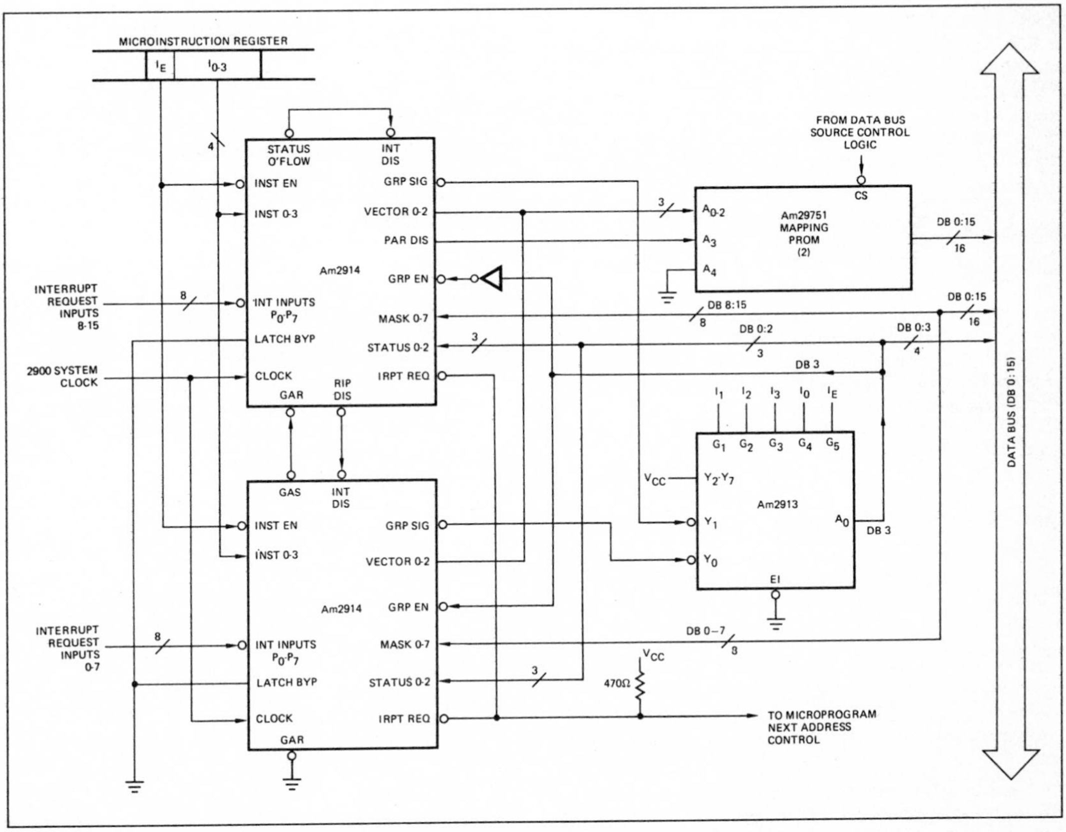

Figure 22. 16 Level Interrupt Control Unit for Am2900 System.

In Figures 21 and 22, the Status and Mask inputs/outputs are connected to the data bus in a bi-directional configuration so that Status and Mask Registers may be loaded from or read to the data bus with appropriate Am2914 instructions. This gives the designer two possibilities which could be very advantageous.

Number one is the ability to store the Status and Mask information on a stack in memory. This is very advantageous when doing nested interrupts. Secondly, it allows the designer to construct machine instruction that can modify these two registers. This is very important to the system programmer who is involved in writing software to manage the interrupts.

For the eight level ICU of Figure 21, the Status Overflow output is connected to the Interrupt Disable input, and the Group Advance Receive and Group Enable inputs are connected to ground, as previously described.

For the 16 interrupt level ICU of Figure 22, the Parallel Disable output of the higher priority group serves as the high order vector bit. An Am2913 Priority Interrupt Expander is gated by the Am2914 instruction lines so that its output is enabled only during a Read Status instruction, and is used to encode the high order bit of the status. An inverter suffices to decode the high order bit of the status bit during a Load Status instruction. As described previously for a ripple cascade system, the Group Advance Receive input of the next higher priority group; the Ripple Disable output is connected to the Interrupt Disable input of the next lower priority group; the Status Overflow output of the highest priority group is connected to the Interrupt Disable input of the same group, and the Group Advance Receive input of the lowest priority group is connected to ground.

In both designs, two Am29751 32-word by 8-bit PROM's with three-state outputs are used to map the Am2914 Vector outputs into a 16-bit address vector. The PROM outputs are connected to the data bus. When a Read Vector Instruction (Am2914) is executed, the address vector is available to be used either as the address of the next instruction or a location to find the address of the next instruction to execute.

Figure 23 shows a design where the address vector from the mapping PROM can be clocked into a register in the Am2903's. The registers in the Am2903's would be split between general purpose, scratch, stack pointers and Program Counter registers.

The address vector also may be gated directly to the "D" inputs of the Am2911 Microprogram Sequencer as shown in Figure 24, and used as the start PROM address of a microinstruction interrupt service routine. This method would be most useful in a controller application. This method would trade faster service for a bigger microprogram that accommodates all the code to service each individual interrupt.

FIRMWARE EXAMPLE FOR Am2914 INTERRUPT SYSTEM

The software for handling interrupt requests is on two levels. The first level to come into play is the microprogram level. This is the level at which the request is recognized and the program counter is manipulated to start execution of a machine level interrupt service routine which is the second level. When the machine level interrupt service routine is finished, some form of a Return Interrupt instruction is executed. The microcode for the return instruction manipulates the program counter so that execution of the current machine program previous to the request is restored as shown in Figure 25.

This example is concerned with the microprogram level. This microcode goes along with the hardware shown in Figure 23. In this example the code is shown in the form of Flow Charts because the actual microprogram format will vary from machine to machine.

The important features to notice that have a direct relevance to the firmware are the Latch Bypass and where the Mask, Status and Vector busses go. For this example, the Latch Bypass is LOW making the Interrupt Latches latch up on a negative going pulse. The Mask and Status busses go to the data bus allowing the Status and Mask data to be transferred to and from memory. The Vector bus passes through a mapping PROM to the data bus where it can be read into the Program Counter contained in the Am2903's. The PROM contains addresses of service routines which correspond to the different interrupt levels.

Another relevant fact, important to understanding the firmware is that the interrupt mechanism is limited to handle interrupts on the machine level.

As shown in Figure 26a, the first thing that happens in the fetch routine (written in microcode) is a conditional subroutine call that will be taken if an interrupt request is present. This happens before the current machine instruction is fetched and the program counter is incremented.

In the Interrupt routine (shown in Figure 26b) a microprogram subroutine is first called to push the program counter onto the system stack. This is done so that the program counter can be restored in order to resume execution of the machine program after the interrupt service routine is done. The next thing that is saved on the system stack is the contents of the Am2914 Status Register. This is done because the status register which contains the priority level that would be serviced prior to the interrupt, will be restored after the interrupt is serviced. This maintains a nested interrupt structure (fence).

After saving the program counter and status register, the vector is read out of the Am2914 through the mapping PROM to obtain the address of the machine interrupt service routine. The address is then read into the program counter which resides in the Am2903's. When the Vector is read, the interrupt request priority plus one is automatically put into the status register by the Am2914 so that all interrupt requests of lower priority than the one being serviced are ignored. This is often referred to as moving the fence up. Since the vector has been read and the new address is in the program counter, the interrupt request can be cleared from the interrupt register via the Clear Interrupt/Last Vector Read instruction. At this point a jump is made to the Fetch routine which will now fetch the first instruction of the machine Interrupt Service routine.

The last instruction that the machine level interrupt service executes is an Interrupt Return. This will in turn call Return Interrupt microprogram. The status is first popped off the system stack and loaded back into the status register. This restores the Interrupt Fence. The program counter is then popped off the system stack and loaded into the program counter register. This restores the program counter to point to the instruction that was going to be executed when the interrupt request occurred.

TIME DELAY WHEN USING THE Am2914

An aspect that should be covered when using any part is how it will fit into the system timing; because the cycle time of the system will be as long as the longest delay path in the machine. Shown in Figure 27 is the longest delay path through the Am2914 for the previous 16-bit computer example. The calculations were using both typical and worst case values at 25°C and 5.0V.

The longest delay path for the system where the vector from the mapping PROM feeds into the "D" inputs of the Am2910 is

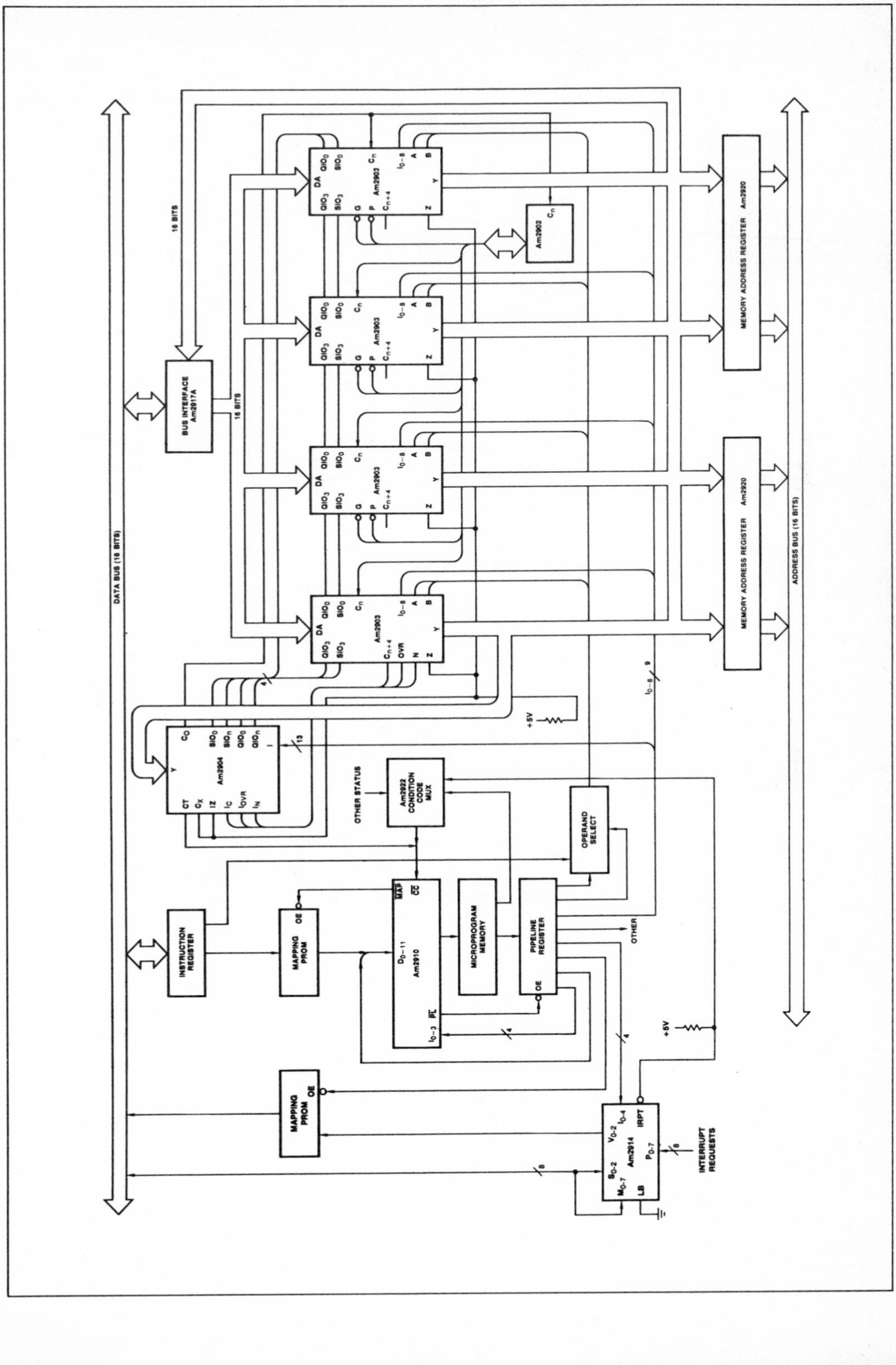

Figure 23. Example of a 16-Bit Computer #1.

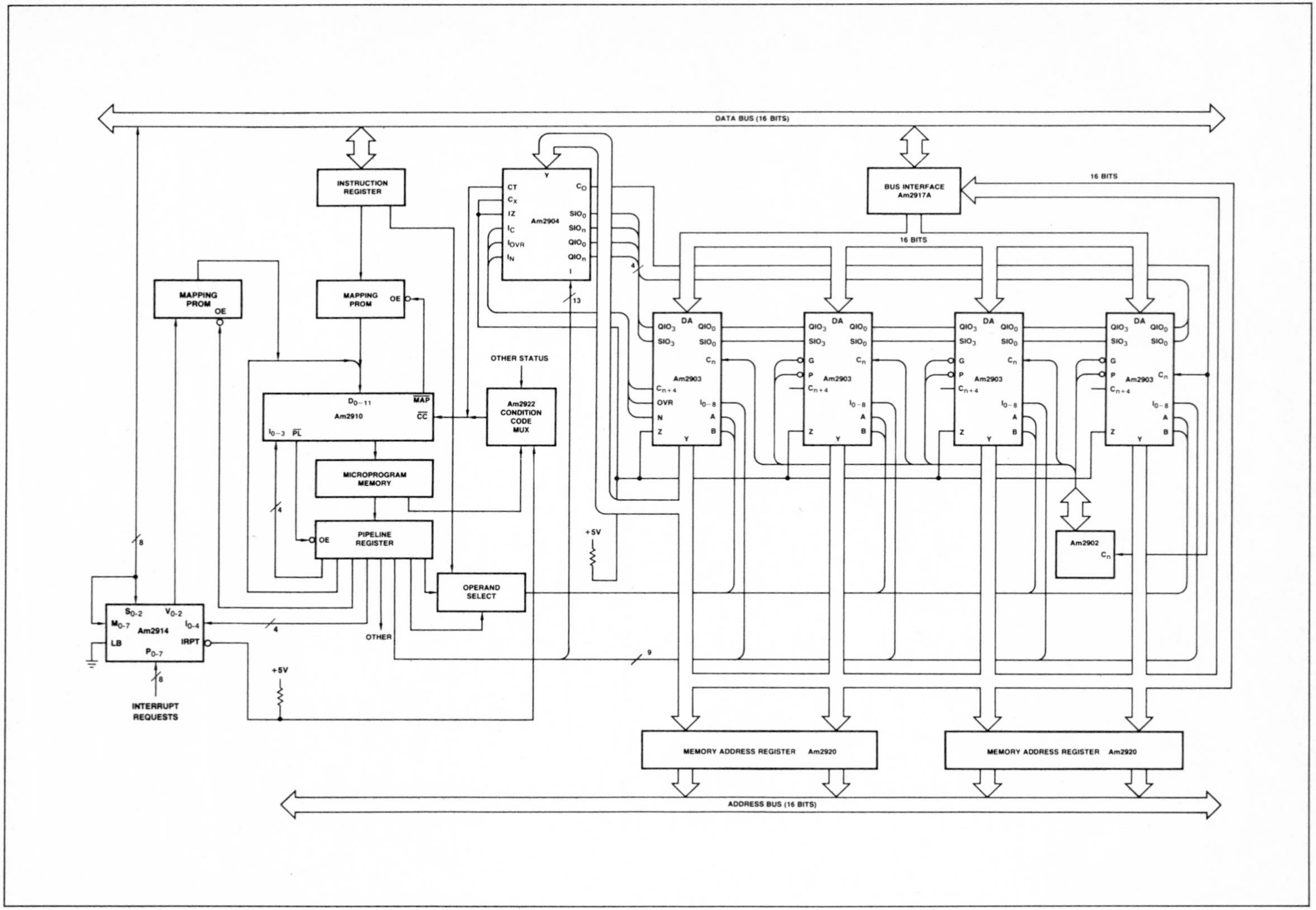
DATA BUS (16 BITS)
INSTRUCTION REGISTER
Am2904
BUS INTERFACE Am2917A
16 BITS
16 BITS
MAPPING PROM
MAPPING PROM
OTHER STATUS
Am2910
Am2922 CONDITION CODE MUX
Am2903
Am2903
Am2903
Am2903
MICROPROGRAM MEMORY
PIPELINE REGISTER
Am2902
+5V
OPERAND SELECT
Am2914
OTHER
+5V
INTERRUPT REQUESTS
MEMORY ADDRESS REGISTER Am2920
MEMORY ADDRESS REGISTER Am2920
ADDRESS BUS (16 BITS)

Figure 24.

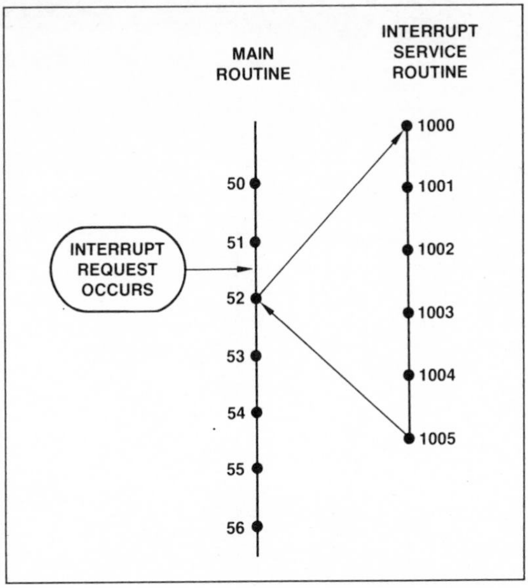

Figure 25. Machine Level Instruction Flow During Interrupt Request.

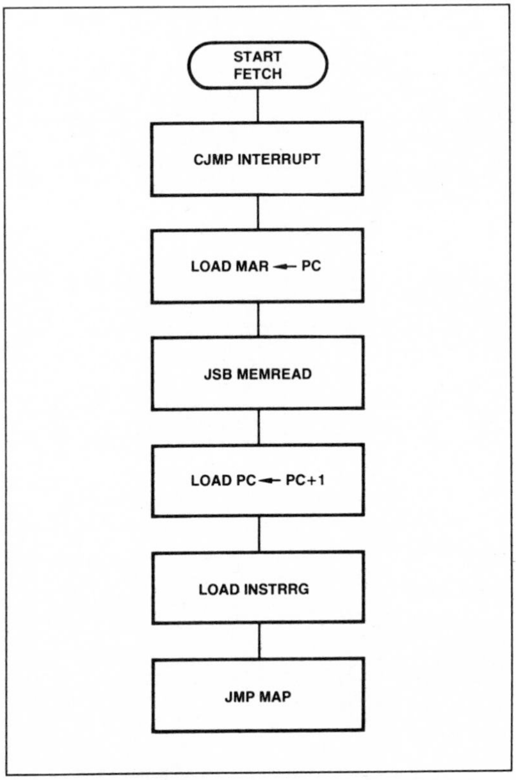

Figure 26a. Flow Chart for a Simplified Microprogram Fetch Routine.

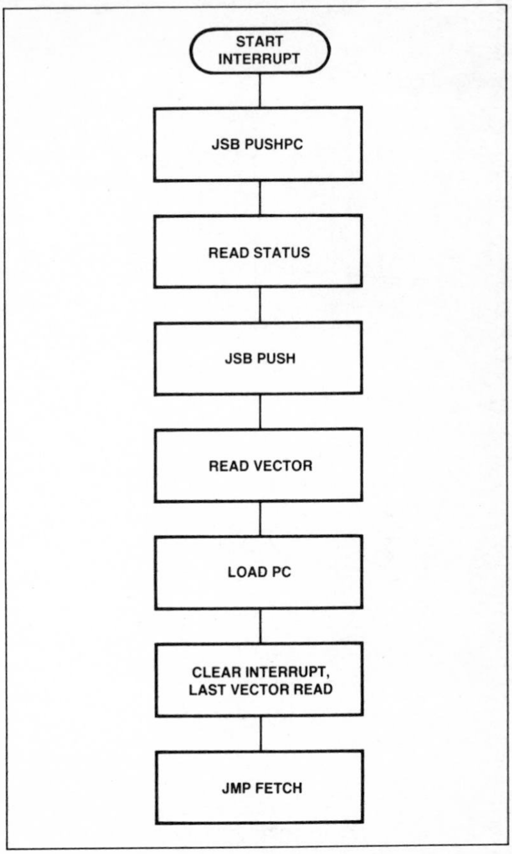

Figure 26b. Call Interrupt Service Routine Microprogram Flow Chart.

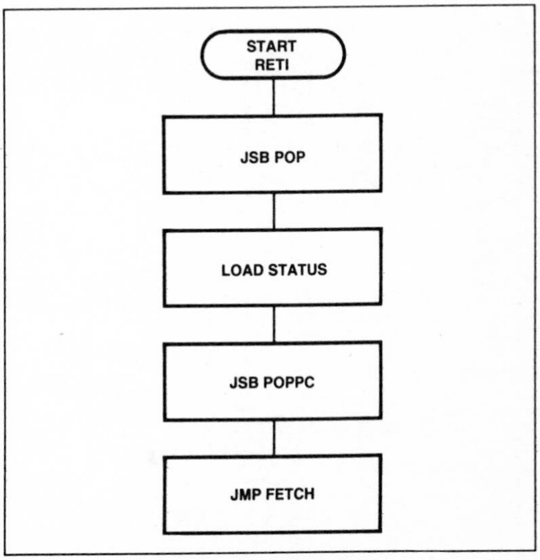

Figure 26c. Return Interrupt Microprogram Flow Chart.

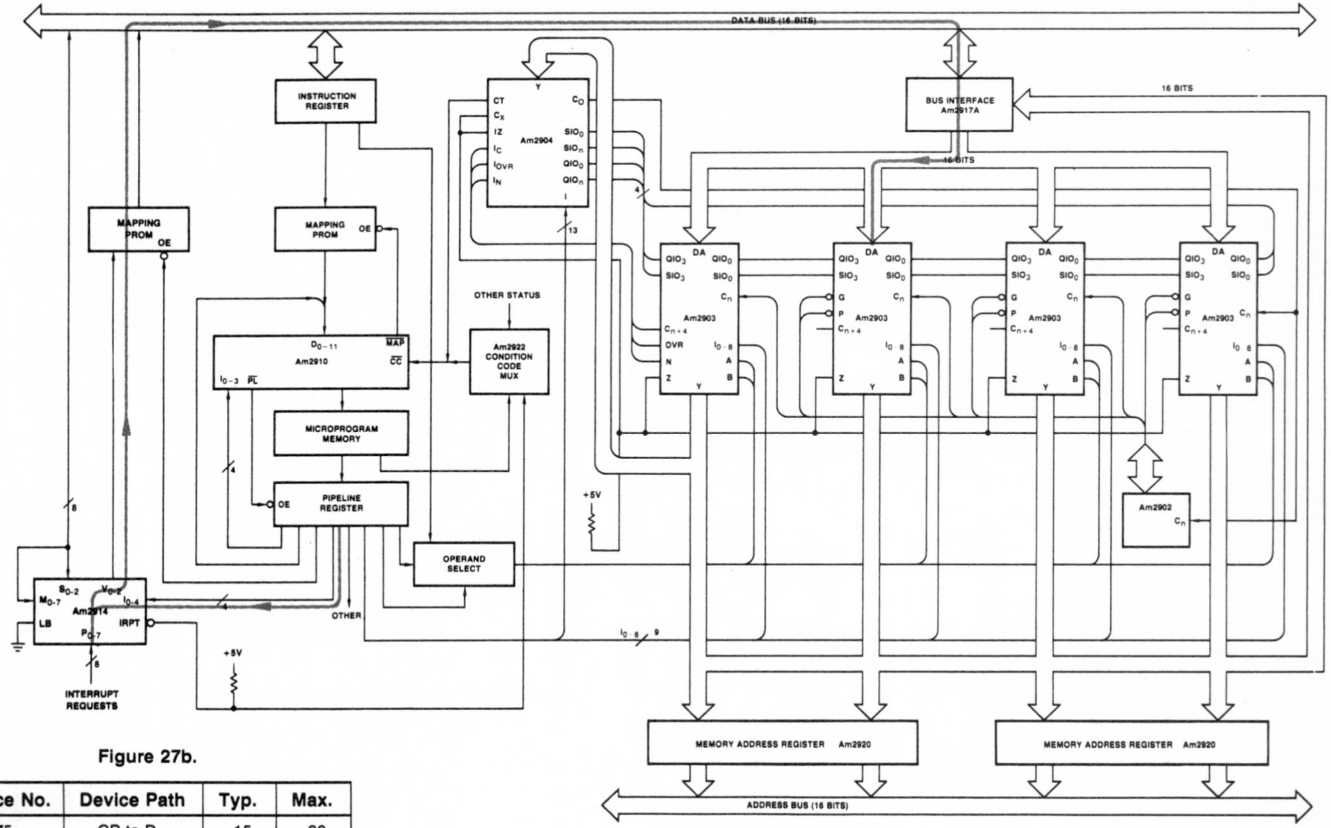

Figure 27b.

Device No.	Device Path	Typ.	Max.
29775	CP to D	15	20
2914	I to V_{012}	40	55
27S19	A to O	25	40
2917A	Bus to R	18	30
2903	t_s to (Y)	10	16
Total-ns		108	161

DELAY PATH ———

Figure 27a. AC Calculations.

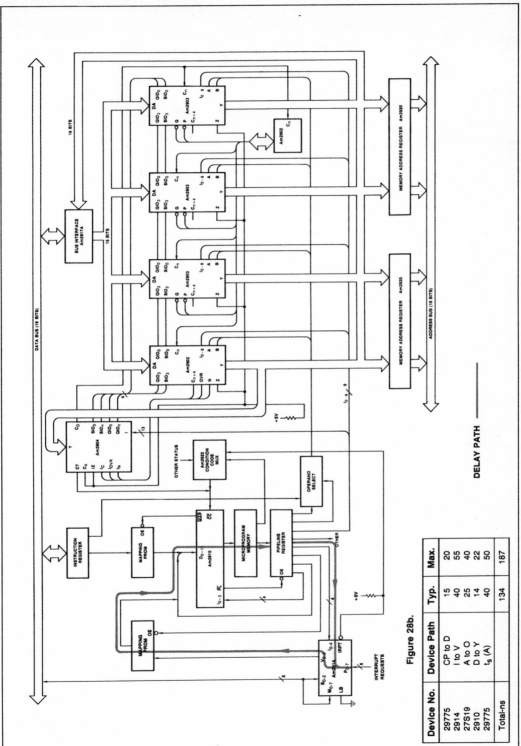

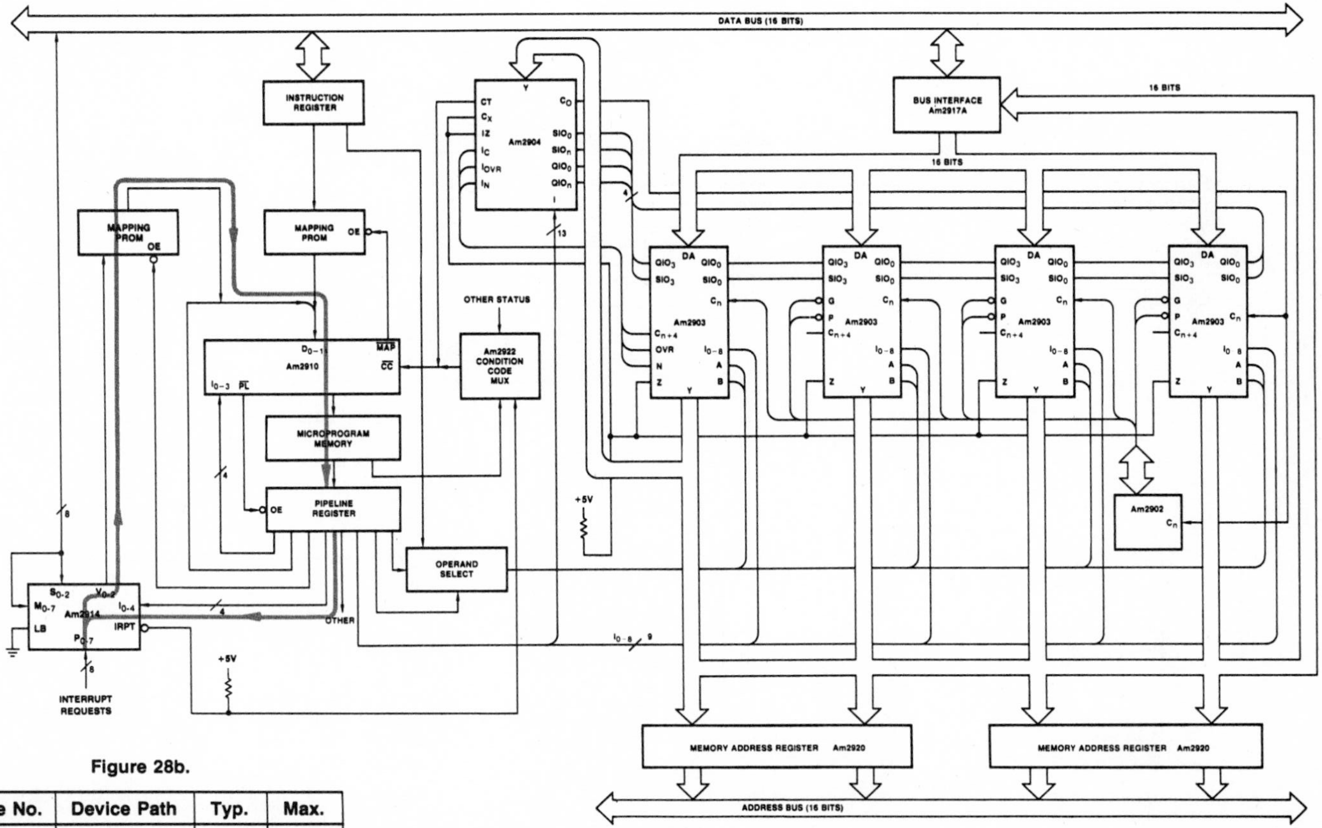

Figure 28b.

Device No.	Device Path	Typ.	Max.
29775	CP to D	15	20
2914	I to V	40	55
27S19	A to O	25	40
2910	D to Y	14	22
29775	t_s (A)	40	50
Total-ns		134	187

DELAY PATH ———

Figure 28a.

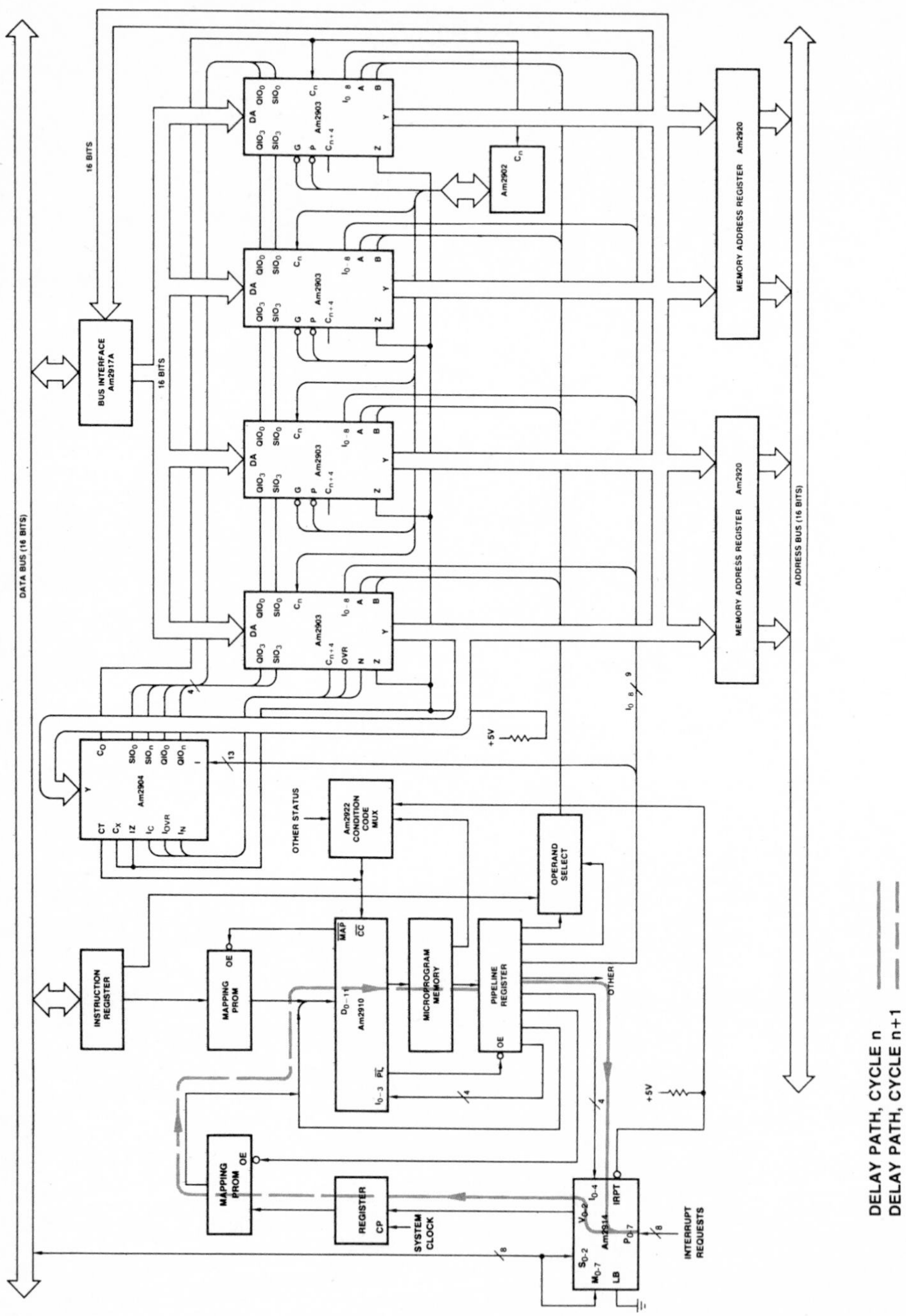
DATA BUS (16 BITS)
ADDRESS BUS (16 BITS)
16 BITS
BUS INTERFACE Am2917A
Am2903
Am2902
MEMORY ADDRESS REGISTER Am2920
Am2904
Am2922 CONDITION CODE MUX
OTHER STATUS
OPERAND SELECT
INSTRUCTION REGISTER
MAPPING PROM
Am2910
MICROPROGRAM MEMORY
PIPELINE REGISTER
REGISTER
SYSTEM CLOCK
Am2914
INTERRUPT REQUESTS
+5V
DELAY PATH, CYCLE n
DELAY PATH, CYCLE n+1

Figure 28c.

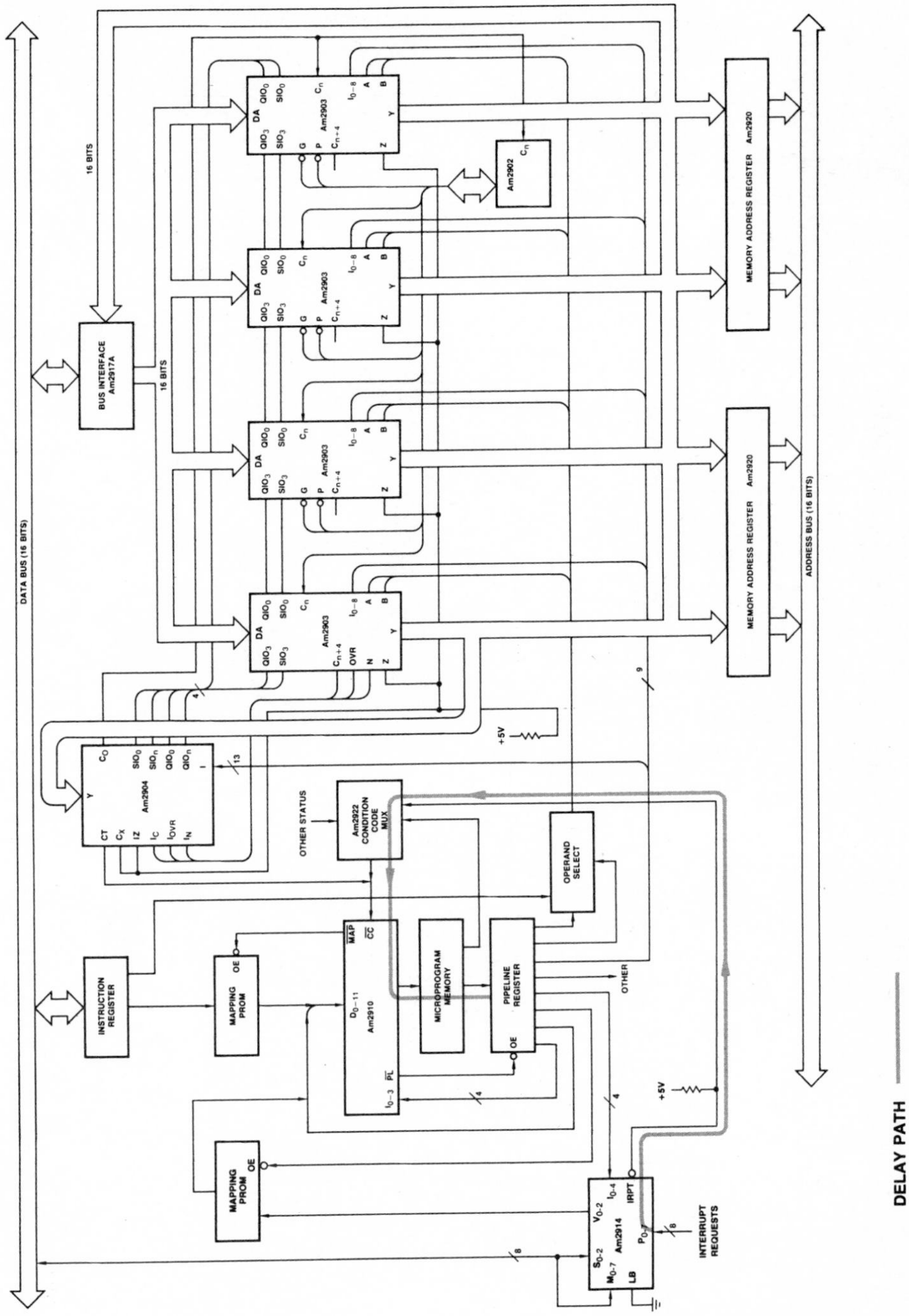
DATA BUS (16 BITS)
ADDRESS BUS (16 BITS)
16 BITS
16 BITS
BUS INTERFACE Am2917A
Am2903
Am2903
Am2903
Am2903
Am2902
MEMORY ADDRESS REGISTER Am2920
MEMORY ADDRESS REGISTER Am2920
Am2904
Am2922 CONDITION CODE MUX
OTHER STATUS
OPERAND SELECT
INSTRUCTION REGISTER
MAPPING PROM
MAPPING PROM
Am2910
MICROPROGRAM MEMORY
PIPELINE REGISTER
OTHER
Am2914
INTERRUPT REQUESTS
+5V
DELAY PATH

Figure 28d.

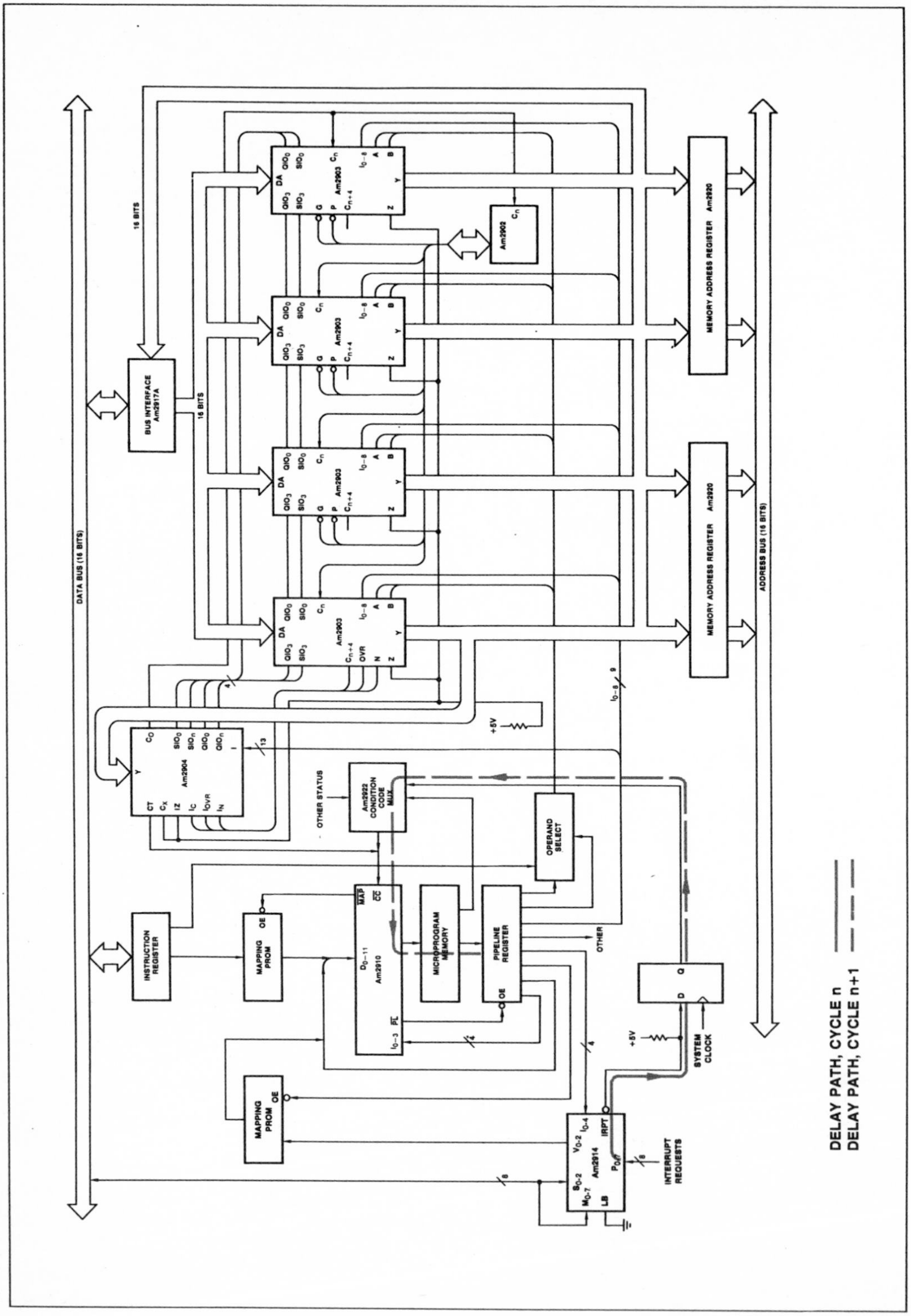
DATA BUS (16 BITS)
ADDRESS BUS (16 BITS)
16 BITS
BUS INTERFACE Am2917A
Am2903
Am2902
MEMORY ADDRESS REGISTER Am2920
Am2904
Am2922 CONDITION CODE MUX
OTHER STATUS
OPERAND SELECT
INSTRUCTION REGISTER
MAPPING PROM
Am2910
MICROPROGRAM MEMORY
PIPELINE REGISTER
OTHER
SYSTEM CLOCK
Am2914
INTERRUPT REQUESTS
+5V
DELAY PATH, CYCLE n
DELAY PATH, CYCLE n+1

Figure 28e.

Device No.	Device Path	Typ.	Max.
29775	CP to D	15	20
2914	I to V	40	55
2918	t_S (Data)	5	5
Cycle n Total-ns		60	80
2918	CP to Q	8.5	13
27S19	A to O	25	40
2910	D to Y	14	22
29775	t_S (A)	40	50
Cycle n+1 Total-ns		97.5	125

Figure 28f.

Device No.	Device Path	Typ.	Max.
2914	CP to IRQ	65	82
2922	D_n to Y	13	19
2910	$\overline{CC}$ to Y	27	44
29775	t_S (A)	40	50
Total-ns		145	195

Figure 28g.

Device No.	Device Path	Typ.	Max.
2914	CP to IRQ	65	82
74S74	t_S (Data)	3	3
Cycle n Total-ns		68	85
74S74	CP to Q	6	9
2922	D_n to Y	13	19
2910	$\overline{CC}$ to Y	27	44
29775	t_S (A)	40	50
Cycle n+1 Total-ns		86	122

Figure 28h.

shown in Figure 28. This path is much longer because of the two PROM's that have to be accessed. Therefore, there may be a trade-off of slightly longer system cycle time for faster service of interrupts via service routines in microcode.

For some systems the delay time shown in Figure 28b may be too long. Therefore, the designer can split the delay time into parts by putting a register between the Am2914 and the mapping PROM as shown in Figure 28c. When done in two system clock cycles, the delay time will be as shown in Figure 28f.

Figure 28d shows the delay path from the Interrupt Request Register through the Condition Code MUX to the Am2910. The time calculations are shown in Figure 28g. Again, for some systems, this path may be too long. Therefore, as shown above, this path may be broken in two, which is shown in Figure 28e. This will result in two system clock cycles. The delay involved in each cycle is shown in Figure 28h.

ANOTHER EXAMPLE OF Am2900 SYSTEM USING THE Am2914

As shown in Figure 29, this example varies in the way that the interrupt request is recognized by the microprogrammed machine. In this example the interrupt request line for the Am2914 enables or disables the $\overline{MAP}$ signal going to the mapping PROM. When an interrupt request is present and a Jump Map instruction is executed, the output of the mapping PROM remains tri-stated; and the bus connected to the "D" inputs of the Am2910 is HIGH because of the pull-up resistors. Therefore, the microprogram will start executing at the highest location in microprogram memory when an interrupt request is present. At this location a Jump Instruction to the microprogram interrupt service routine could be placed. The microcode is written so that the only time a Jump Map instruction is executed is at the end of the Fetch microprogram routine as shown in Figure 30a.

In the previous example the interrupt request was recognized before the program counter is incremented after which the Jump Map instruction is executed. When the Jump Map is executed, either the instruction is executed or an interrupt request is serviced. Therefore, when the Return Interrupt machine instruction is executed, the program counter needs to be backed up via microcode, as shown in Figure 30b, in order to refetch the machine instruction which was lost. This also dictates that the program counter have a path to an incrementer/decrementer or ALU, which in this example is handled by putting the program counter in the Am2903's.

MICROPROGRAM LEVEL INTERRUPT EXAMPLE

Some high-speed control applications require extremely fast interrupt response. While it may ordinarily be desirable to complete an entire processing sequence (such as executing a microprogram for a macroinstruction) prior to testing for the interrupt and allowing it to occur, it is not always possible to achieve the required interrupt response time desired. If this is the case, microinstruction level interrupt handling must be employed. The technique described below has a maximum latency of three microcycles which can be 450-600ns total. Implementation is straightforward using the Am2910 Microsequencer, a 40-pin LSI device that can control 4096 words of microprogram at a 150ns cycle time, and a few extra MSI and SSI packages. In this application, the Am2910 is configured in its standard architecture. The additional logic does not influence the normal system cycle time.

If microlevel interrupt handling is to be employed, logic must be provided to generate a substitute microprogram address corresponding to the location of the interrupt service routine. In the event of a microlevel interrupt, the sequencer address outputs are tri-stated and the substitute address is placed on the microprogram address bus, causing the next microinstruction fetch to be determined by the interrupt control vector generator. While this is happening, steps must be taken with the Am2910 to insure that the interrupted routine can be properly restored. To understand this procedure, it will be necessary to examine the Am2910 in more detail.

Referring to Figure 31, the microprogram address bus is driven by the Y outputs of the Am2910 through a tri-state buffer than can be disabled by means of the $\overline{OE}$ input. The address is selected in a multiplexer from a direct input, from a register/counter, from a push/pop stack, or from a microprogram counter register. The microprogram counter register is commonly used as the address source when executing the next microinstruction in sequence. Whenever an address appears at the multiplexer outputs, it is incremented and presented to the microprogram counters inputs. At the rising edge of the clock, this new address that is current address-plus-1 is loaded into the microprogram counter and a microprogram access begins at this address.

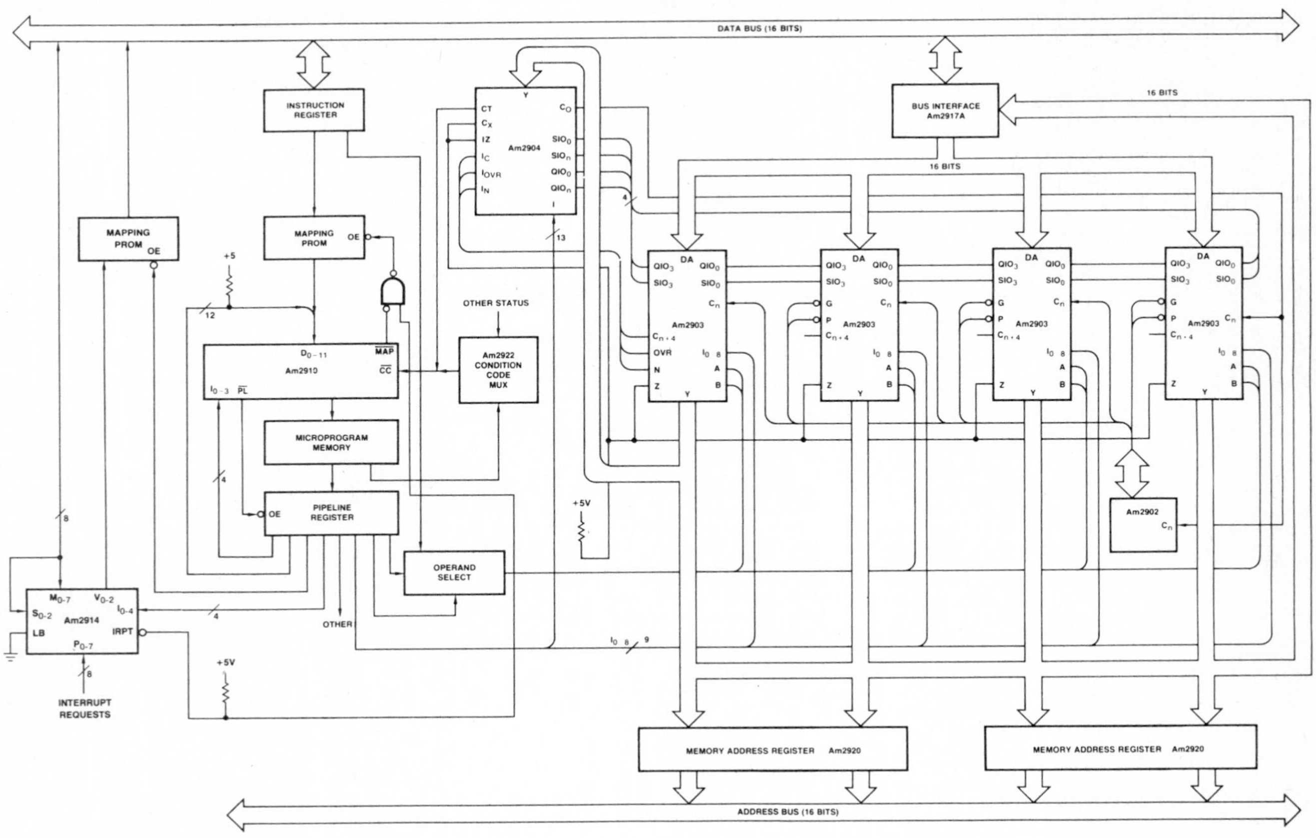

Figure 29. Example of a 16-Bit Computer #2.

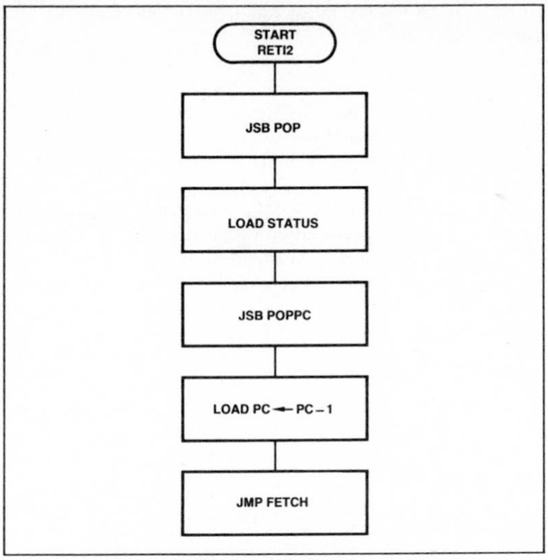

Figure 30a. Return Interrupt Microprogram for Second Example.

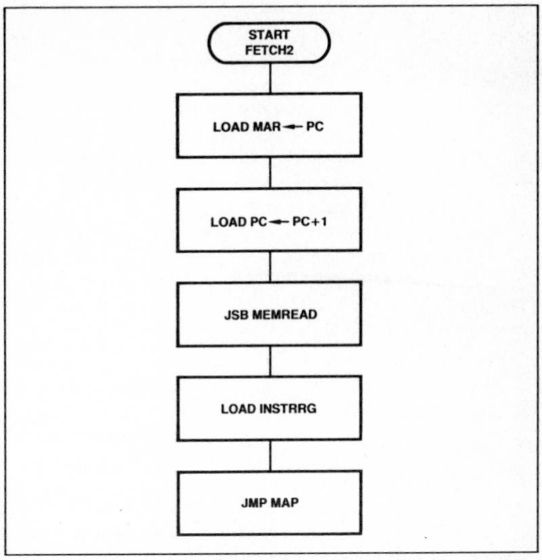

Figure 30b. Fetch Microprogram for the Second Example.

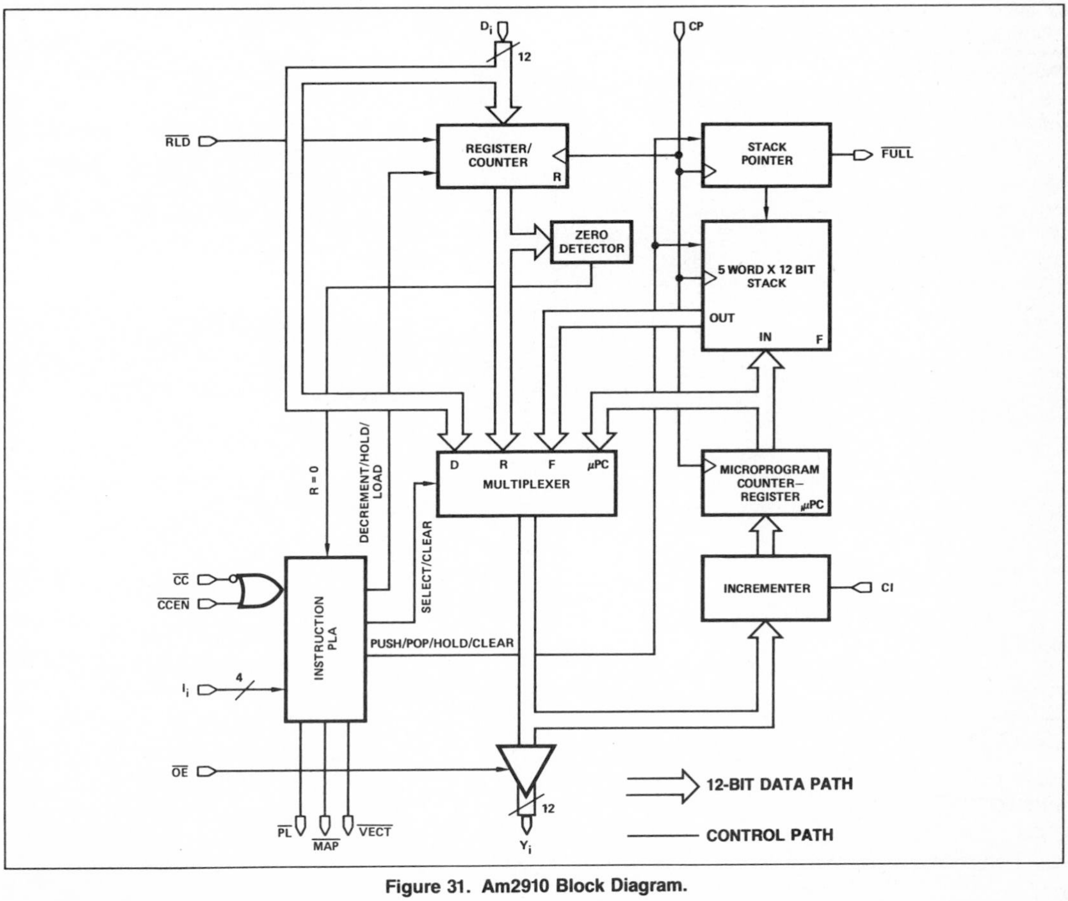

Figure 31. Am2910 Block Diagram.

Note that at this time, whatever was fetched at the previous address was loaded into the microword register for execution. Thus, the microprogram sequencer is always looking for the address of the next microinstruction to be executed (while a previously fetched microinstruction is residing in the microword register). Subroutine and microprogram loops may be accomplished by using the stack and the register counter. *Regardless of what is selected as source of next address, the selected address will be incremented and presented to the microprogram counter.* So to accomplish a microprogram branch, one would simply select the D inputs for a branch address for one cycle, then the next address source could be switched back to the program counter on the next cycle which would then contain the branch address plus 1.

This is a carry input to the incrementer which is normally tied HIGH. In the case of a microlevel interrupt, the microprogram sequencer will not determine the address of the next microinstruction to be executed. Instead the sequencer output will be tri-stated and a substitute address will be placed on the bus. The sequencer continues to operate in a normal fashion with its multiplexer output being incremented and presented to the microprogram counter register. It must now be noted that the instruction located at the address then coming out of the multiplexer outputs *will not be executed* but rather the next microinstruction to be executed will be determined by the interrupt vector generator. It would therefore, be wrong to increment this microprogram address but rather it must be saved intact in order to push it onto the stack for access during interrupt return. This is easily accomplished in the Am2910 by grounding the carry input to the incrementer simultaneously with three-stating the sequencer output. Then the multiplexer output will be stored in the microprogram counter register and on the next microcycle the Am2910 must be told to push in order to preserve this address on the stack.

This carry-in input is all important and exists on all Advanced Micro Devices' microprogram sequencers. Unless the carry-in is grounded, whatever address was in the multiplexer output when the sequencer output was tri-stated is incremented and an instruction is missed in the interrupted routine. This, of course, would likely be disastrous. The key to this microinterrupt technique is that the address of the unexecuted instruction (when the Am2910 was tri-stated and a substitute address supplied) is preserved by inhibiting the increment via the carry input, so the address is passed on intact to the microprogram counter. If the microinterrupt is to be more than one cycle long, the microprogram counter must be pushed so as to save the return address. Otherwise, a "continue" may be used to return from the interrupt on the very next cycle. In this event the microinterrupt effectively inserts one instruction in the stream.

Figure 32 is the block diagram of a hardware design that implements the above concept. The SYNC/CONTROL and INTERRUPT CONTROL/VECTOR GENERATOR logic are shown in detail in Figure 33. Part of the Am2918 and both 'LS74 Flip-Flops are used to synchronize the recognition of the asynchronous interrupt request as shown in Figure 34. The interrupt request arrives at the interrupt input. On the next clock cycle it is clocked into the Am2918. In the following clock cycle a pulse that is one system clock cycle long is put out by the flip-flop pair FF1 and FF2. The pulse is used to disable the carry input of the Am2910, tri-state the output of the Am2910, and enable the jump vector onto the input of the PROM. The vector indexes into a table in microprogram memory that contains "JUMP SUBROUTINE" instructions to different interrupt service routines.

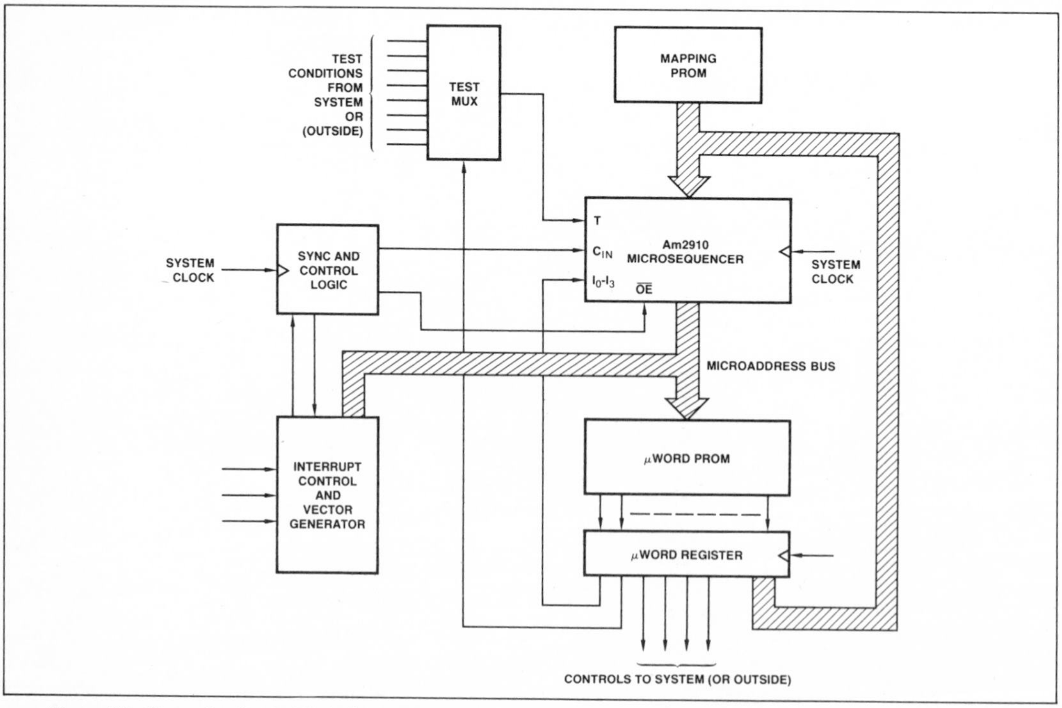

Figure 32. Computer Control Unit Set-up for High-Speed Micro-Level Interrupt Handling. Latency is a Maximum of Two Microcycles (i.e., about 300 to 500ns).

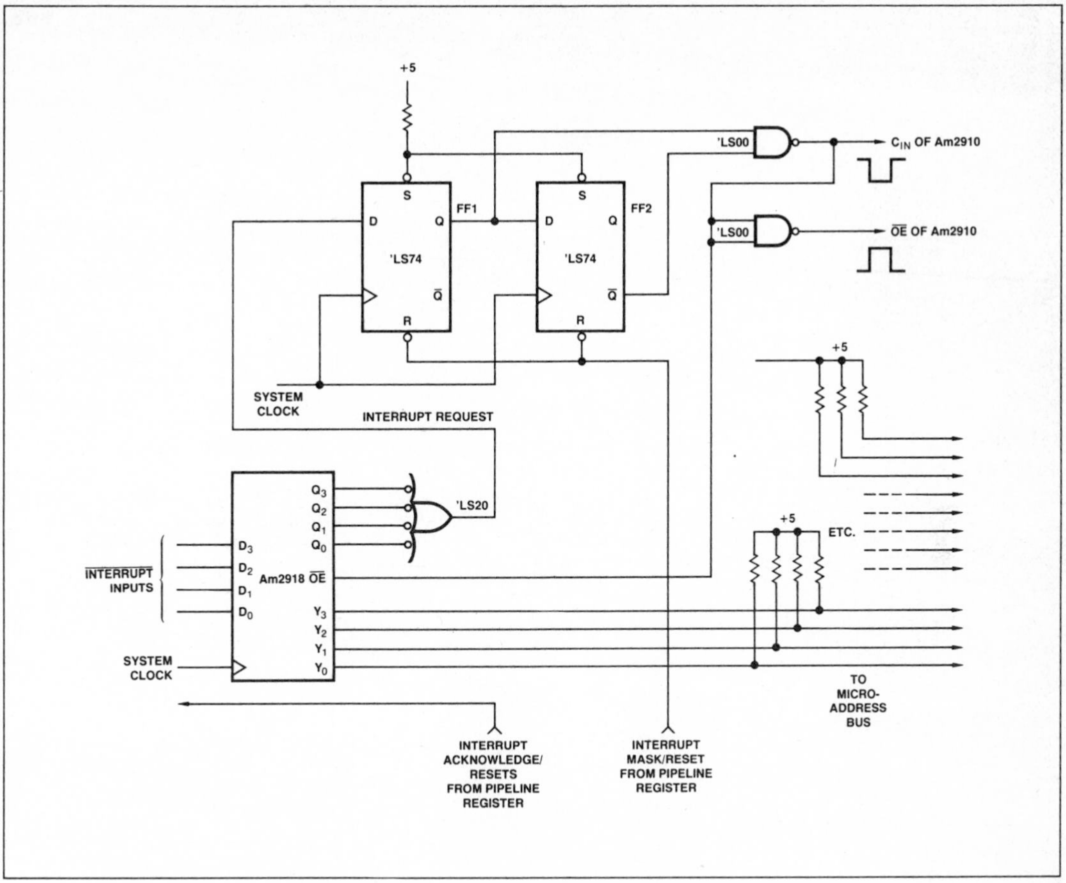

Figure 33. Example of Sync Control Logic and Vector Generator.

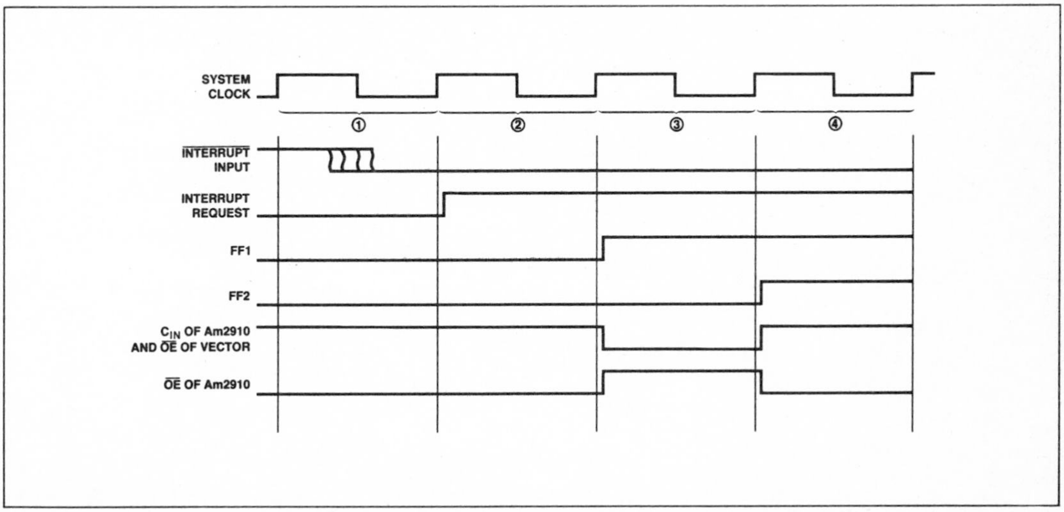

Figure 34. Timing of Vector Generator and Sync Control Logic.

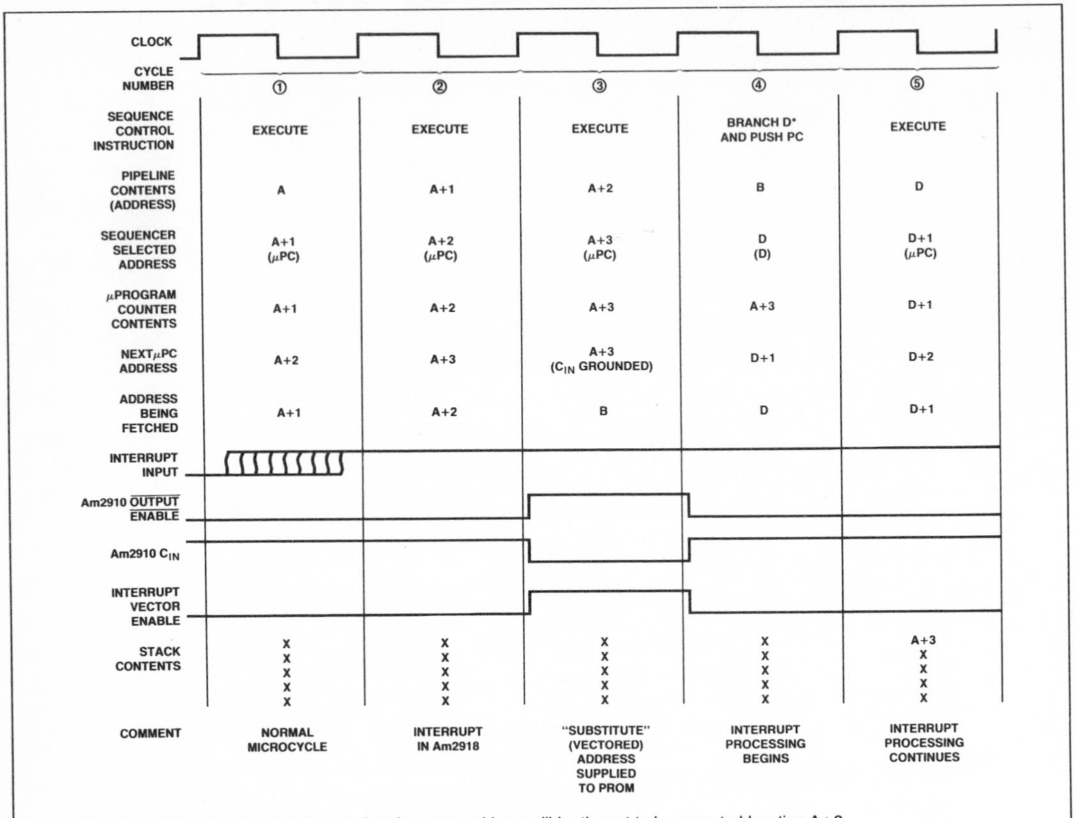

*This is a JSB instruction, but observe that the return address will be the yet-to-be executed location A+3.

Figure 35. Interrupt Sequence Timing.

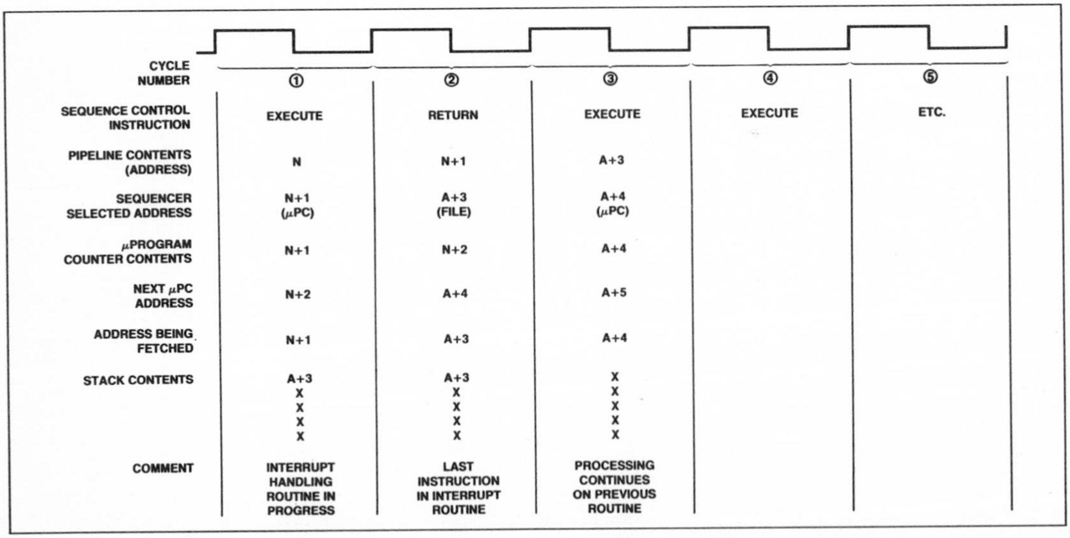

Figure 36. Return-From-Interrupt Sequence Timing.

Figure 35 shows how the interrupt sequence timing fits into the normal flow of microprogram address in the Am2910. Note how the stack is used. This demonstrates the need for always reserving room on the stack to allow for interrupts. This applies to any room that the interrupt service routine may require as well as the return address. This limitation may require that only one interrupt request be serviced at a time.

Figure 36 shows how the return from the interrupt service routine fits into the microprogram flow. Notice that a Return instruction is used to accomplish this.

SUMMARY

In this chapter, Interrupts were discussed beginning with a definition of the Interrupt Mechanism and proceeding to a classification of different interrupts and how they are handled. A discussion of the concepts that go into designing the "Universal Interrupt" hardware was given which culminated with the Am2914. The chapter ends with several Interrupt Mechanism applications using the Am2914 and Am2910.

In this chapter it was shown how interrupts can be handled using parts from the Am2900 family. Because of their hardware modularity and universal architecture, they may be used in a variety of applications. Since the Am2900 Family parts are microprogrammable, they allow the user's system to grow with time as system requirements change. Together these attributes make the Am2900 Family the flexible cost effective family that it is.

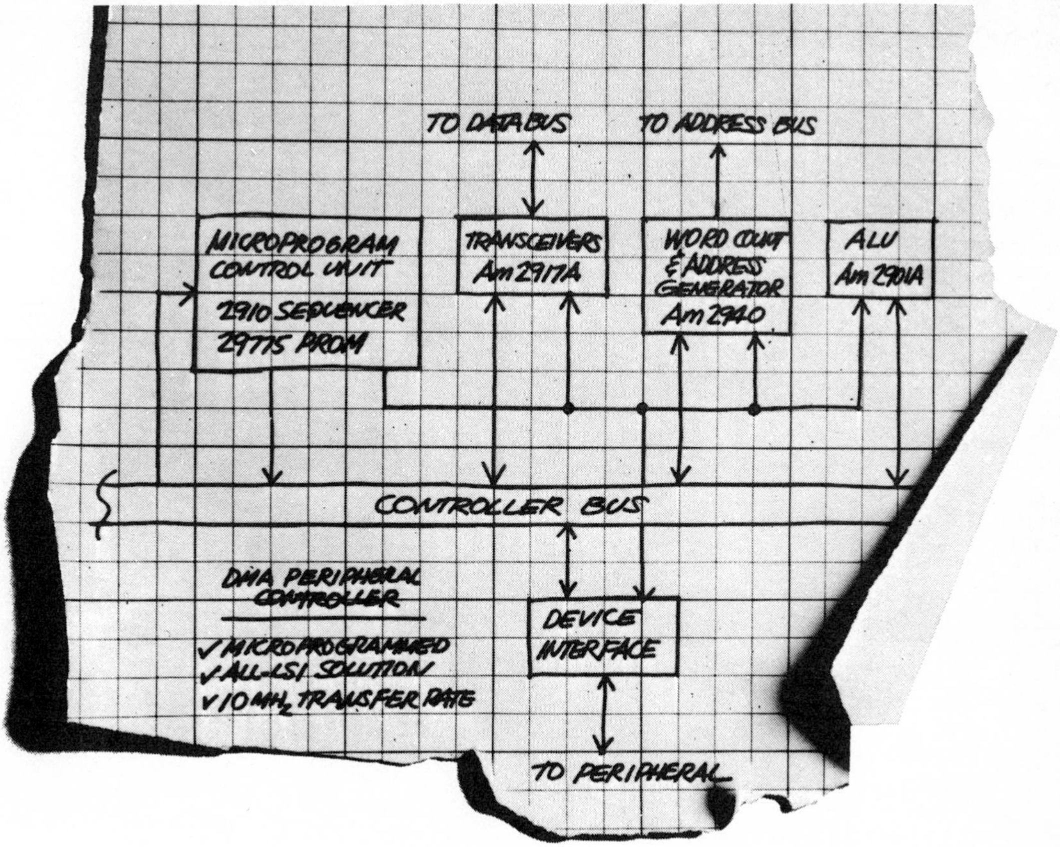

Chapter VII
Direct Memory Access

Introduction

The transfer of data between the microcomputer and the peripheral devices is generally referred to as Input/Output (I/O). What is desired is a high speed technique of transferring data between the peripherals and the memory. Generally speaking, there is a minimum of three types of I/O. These are, Programmed I/O, Memory Mapped I/O and Direct Memory Access I/O. All of these schemes are common in today's currently available minicomputers. A basic understanding of these I/O techniques is helpful in fully comprehending DMA. The first two of these types of I/O can be interrupt driven. That is, programmed I/O or memory mapped I/O can be initiated by an interrupt from the peripheral device.

Programmed I/O

In this type of I/O, all operations are controlled by the CPU program. In other words, the peripheral device performs the functions of inputting or outputting data as it is controlled by the CPU. Normally, the machine will include a set of I/O instructions which are used to transfer data to or from the peripheral devices via an Input/Output port. All data for the peripheral devices passes through these I/O ports to the CPU and the resources of the CPU must be utilized in order to effect an I/O transfer. Figure 1 shows the Block Diagram of a programmed I/O system used in a typical microcomputer. Figure 2 shows an example of that portion of the program used to output data to the peripheral device.

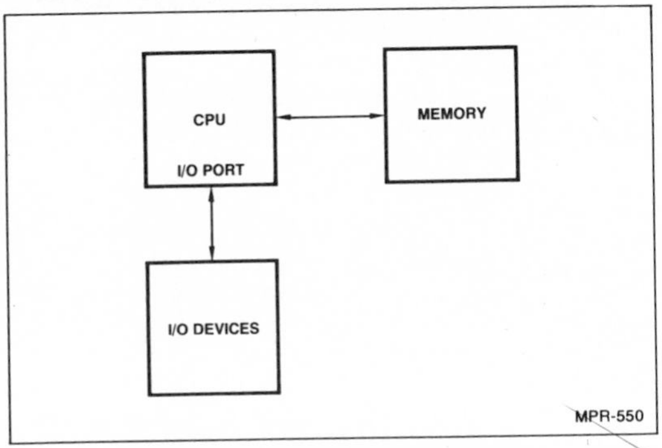

Figure 1. Programmed I/O System.

CPU Program	Comments
–	–
–	–
Load R, M	Load CPU Register R with the Contents of Memory Address M
Out D, R	Transfer the Contents of CPU Register R to I/O Device D via the I/O port.
–	–

Figure 2. Example Output Program – Programmed I/O.

Programmed I/O is simple to implement and does not require the utilization of any memory addresses for its realization. In addition, special instructions are available to the programmer to execute the peripheral data transfers. Programmed I/O is also low cost relative to other types of I/O; however, it has the following disadvantages. Since I/O device operation is asynchronous with respect to CPU operation, the CPU has no way of knowing when a peripheral device is ready to transfer data and must periodically poll the device to determine its readiness. This results in an inefficient I/O transfer. Also, since the CPU must be used to effect the I/O transfer, the CPU resources are tied up during the time of transfer and the time of polling and cannot be used for other tasks. For these reasons, Programmed I/O is generally limited to use with low speed devices.

Perhaps, one of the best known programmed I/O microcomputers in the industry today is the Am9080A. This device features two instructions for either inputting data or outputting data to any one of 256 Input/Output ports.

Memory Mapped I/O

Memory Mapped I/O is a technique whereby the transfer of data to and from peripheral devices is accomplished by using some of the normally available memory space. In this technique, memory addresses are decoded within the peripheral devices and are thus used to determine when a specific device is being addressed. Usually, each type of function within the peripheral device is assigned a memory address and can then be accessed by the CPU. For example, the peripheral device may contain a command register, a status register, a data in register and a data out register. Thus, four memory addresses might be utilized in performing I/O to this peripheral. Figure 1 is also the block diagram for a Memory Mapped I/O scheme.

The chief advantage of Memory Mapped I/O is that all of the memory reference instructions are usually available to perform the I/O function. Consequently, no special I/O instructions are required in the machine. The key disadvantage of this technique is that a block of the memory addressing range must be set aside for assignment to the peripheral devices. Thus, the overall memory addressing range of the machine is reduced by the size of this block. Again, the resources of the CPU are tied up while the I/O is being performed. A well known machine using only Memory Mapped I/O is the PDP 11. In it the upper 4k of memory space is usually used for the I/O devices.

Interrupt Driven I/O

Interrupts are means by which a peripheral device can stop the normal flow of the CPU instruction execution and force the CPU to temporarily suspend its current program. Then, the program "jumps" to a different program which executes an I/O transfer. Typically, this eliminates the need for polling the peripheral devices to determine if an I/O transfer is ready. Thus, the interrupt driven scheme provides a more efficient I/O transfer technique. However, there is an overhead burden associated with interrupts in that the CPU must store away and later restore all of the parameters required to resume the interrupted program. This overhead degrades the CPU performance. Depending on the overall interrupt structure, the CPU still may have to do some polling of devices which may be tied to the same interrupt level.

It should be pointed out that both Programmed I/O and Memory Mapped can take advantage of the interrupt technique. That is, an interrupt can be used to initiate the peripheral data transfer in either type of system. The CPU still must control the transfer of the data between the memory and the peripheral device and the CPU resources are unavailable for executing other instructions during this time.

What is DMA?

DMA is a technique for data transfer which provides a direct path between the I/O device and the memory without CPU intervention. With this path, a peripheral device has "Direct Memory Access" and can transfer data directly to or from the memory. The

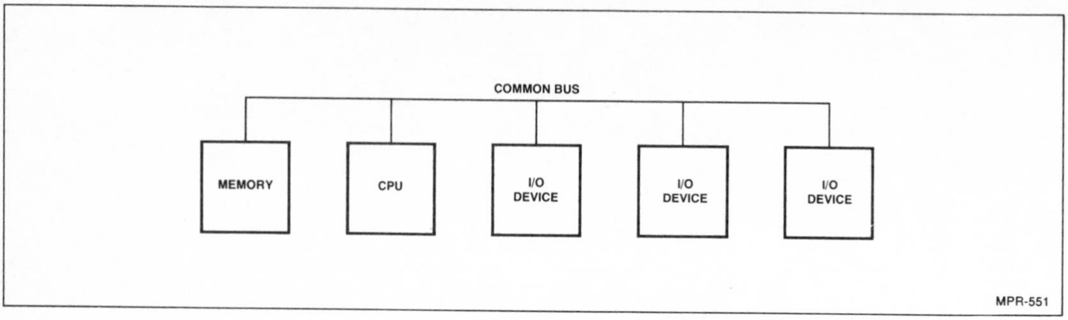

Figure 3. DMA I/O System.

purpose of the DMA is to relieve the CPU of the task of controlling the I/O transfer, thereby freeing it to perform other tasks during this time, and to provide a means by which data can be transferred between an I/O device and memory at very high speed. Figure 3 shows the Block Diagram of a system where several I/O devices can perform DMA transfers into memory. Note that the CPU and peripheral devices share a common bus to the memory and that the CPU and peripheral devices cannot access memory during the same cycle. DMA can also be designed to perform memory-to-memory transfers or I/O-to-I/O transfers.

Several DMA transfer methods exist, such as the CPU halt method, the memory timeslice method, and the "cycle steal" method. In the CPU halt method, the CPU is halted and switched off the bus while a DMA transfer occurs. This is the most straightforward method. However, it takes a relatively long time to switch the CPU on and off the bus, and the CPU cannot do anything during the transfer.

The memory timeslice method works by splitting each memory cycle into two timeslots; one is reserved for the CPU and the other for DMA. This method provides the highest CPU execution rate as well as the highest DMA transfer rate because both the CPU and DMA are guaranteed access to memory during every memory cycle. The disadvantage of this method is that high speed, costly memories must be used.

The "cycle steal" method is a cost/performance compromise between the low cost of the CPU halt method and the high performance of the memory timeslice method. Cycle stealing refers to a DMA device "stealing" a CPU memory cycle in order to execute a DMA transfer. CPU program execution continues during the DMA transfer (the CPU is not halted), resulting in an overlap of CPU program execution with DMA transfer. If the CPU and a DMA device require a memory cycle at the same time, priority is granted to the DMA device and the CPU waits until the DMA cycle is completed. DMA causes CPU performance degradation only in those applications where the CPU uses the entire memory bandwidth. In many applications the CPU is slow relative to memory cycle time and "cycle stealing" provides satisfactory performance at relatively low cost.

How is DMA Implemented?

In order to relieve the CPU of the I/O transfer control task, circuitry external to the CPU must be added. This circuitry is called the DMA Controller and performs the following functions.

Address Line Control – In a DMA system, the memory address lines are driven by either the CPU or a DMA device, depending on which is using the memory during a given cycle. The DMA controller must switch the appropriate address onto the memory address lines.

Data Transfer Control – The DMA Controller must provide the control signals required to transfer data directly between memory and an I/O device. As with the address lines, these control signals must be switched onto and off of the memory control lines appropriately.

Address Maintenance – Just as the CPU has the program counter and one or more other registers for memory address pointers, the DMA controller must also maintain an address pointer that indicates where the next word of data will be read or written in memory. This pointer must be incremented or decremented after each word transfer.

Word Count Maintenance – At the initialization of a DMA transfer, the CPU specifies to the DMA Controller the total number of words to be transferred. During the transfer, the DMA controller must maintain a count of the number of words that have been transferred and terminate the transfer when the specified number of words has been reached.

Mode Control – Certain aspects of a DMA transfer, such as direction of data flow, method of termination, etc., may vary from one DMA transfer to the next. For this reason, a number of DMA modes may be required. Mode control logic contained in the DMA controller, is set by the CPU at the initialization of a DMA transfer.

A DMA Controller can be placed in each I/O device (Distributed DMA) or DMA control circuitry for a number of I/O devices can be placed in a separate unit (Centralized DMA). The former provides the advantage of incremental cost; DMA control circuitry is added only as I/O devices are added. The latter provides the advantages of consolidation.

At DMA initialization, the CPU normally specifies the mode, the starting memory address and the number of words to be transferred (word count) to the DMA controller. In some applications, it is desirable to repeat a DMA transfer over and over again without disturbing the CPU. This capability is called Repetitive DMA, and can be implemented by adding two registers to the DMA controller. One register saves the starting address and the other the starting word count. This allows the DMA Controller to automatically reinitialize itself after the transfer of the data has been completed, thereby eliminating the need for CPU intervention.

The Am2940 DMA ADDRESS GENERATOR

The design of the Address Line Control, Data Transfer Control and Mode Control circuitry of a DMA Controller is dependent upon system architecture and timing; therefore, it varies considerably from system to system. However, the address maintenance and word count maintenance circuitry is independent of these variables, and is common to almost all DMA Controllers. The Am2940 DMA Address Generator is designed for use in DMA Controllers and provides the Address and Word Count maintenance circuitry that is common to most. It combines the advantages of high speed bipolar LSI with the flexibility and general purpose usefulness of microprogrammed control.

Am2940 GENERAL DESCRIPTION

The Am2940, a 28-pin member of Advanced Micro Devices Am2900 family of Low-Power Schottky bipolar LSI chips, is a high-speed, cascadable, eight-bit wide Direct Memory Access Address Generator slice. Any number of Am2940s can be cascaded to form larger addresses.

The primary function of the device is to generate sequential memory addresses for use in the sequential transfer of data to or from a memory. It also maintains a data word count and generates a DONE signal when a programmable terminal count has been reached. The device is designed for use in peripheral controllers with DMA capability or in any other system which transfers data to or from sequential locations of a memory.

The Am2940 can be programmed to increment or decrement the memory address in any of four control modes, and executes eight different instructions. The initial address and word count are saved internally by the Am2940 so that they can be restored later in order to repeat the data transfer operation.

Am2940 ARCHITECTURE

As shown in the Block Diagram of Figure 4, the Am2940 consists of the following:

- A three-bit Control Register.
- An eight-bit Address Counter with input multiplexer.
- An eight-bit Address Register.
- An eight-bit Word Counter with input multiplexer.
- An eight-bit Word Count Register.
- Transfer complete circuitry.
- An eight-bit wide data multiplexer with three-state output buffers.
- Three-state address output buffers with external output enable control.
- An instruction decoder.

Control Register

Under instruction control, the Control Register can be loaded or read from the bidirectional DATA lines D_0-D_7. Control Register bits 0 and 1 determine the Am2940 Control Mode, and bit 2 determines whether the Address Counter increments or decrements. Figure 5 defines the Control Register format.

Address Counter

The Address Counter, which provides the current memory address, is an eight-bit, binary, up/down counter with full look-ahead carry generation. The Address Carry Input ($\overline{ACI}$) and Address Carry Output ($\overline{ACO}$) allow cascading to accommodate larger addresses. Under instruction control, the Address Counter can be enabled, disabled, and loaded from the DATA inputs, D_0-D_7, or the Address Register. When enabled and the $\overline{ACI}$ input is LOW, the Address Counter increments/decrements on the LOW to HIGH transition of the CLOCK input, CP. The Address Counter output can be enabled onto the three-state ADDRESS outputs A_0-A_7 under control of the Output Enable input, $\overline{OE}_A$.

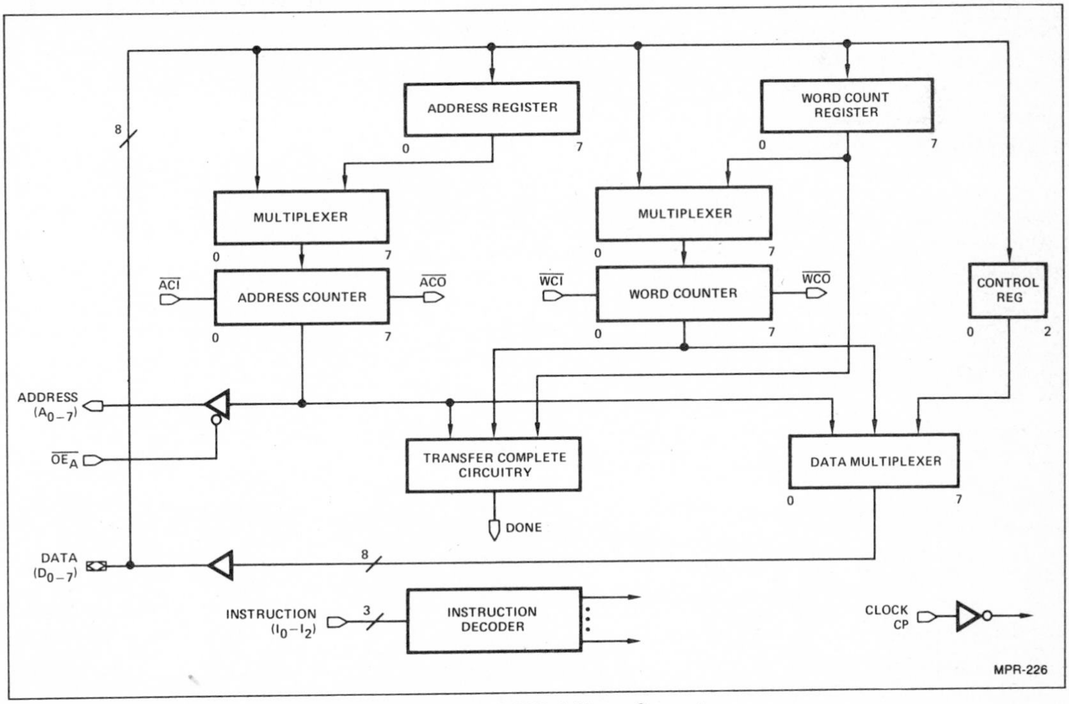

Figure 4. Am2940 DMA Address Generator.

Control Register

CR_2	CR_1	CR_0

CR_1	CR_0	Control Mode Number	Control Mode Type	Word Counter	Done Output Signal	
					$\overline{WCI}$ = LOW	$\overline{WCI}$ = HIGH
L	L	0	Word Count Equals Zero	Decrement	HIGH when Word Counter = 1	HIGH when Word Counter = 0
L	H	1	Word Count Compare	Increment	HIGH when Word Counter + 1 = Word Count Register	HIGH when Word Counter = Word Count Register
H	L	2	Address Compare	Hold	HIGH when Word Counter = Address Counter	
H	H	3	Word Counter Carry Out	Increment	Always LOW	

CR_2	Address Counter
L	Increment
H	Decrement

H = HIGH
L = LOW

Figure 5. Control Register Format Definition.

Address Register

The eight-bit Address Register saves the initial address so that it can be restored later in order to repeat a transfer operation. When the LOAD ADDRESS instruction is executed, the Address Register and Address Counter are simultaneously loaded from the DATA inputs, D_0-D_7.

Word Counter and Word Count Register

The Word Counter and Word Count Register, which maintain and save a word count, are similar in structure and operation to the Address Counter and Address Register, with the exception that the Word Counter increments in Control Modes 1 and 3, decrements in Control Mode 0, and is disabled in Control Mode 2. The LOAD WORD COUNT instruction simultaneously loads the Word Counter and Word Count Register.

Transfer Complete Circuitry

The Transfer Complete Circuitry is a combinational logic network which detects the completion of the data transfer operation in three Control Modes and generates the DONE output signal. The DONE signal is an open-collector output, which can be dot-anded between chips.

Data Multiplexer

The Data Multiplexer is an eight-bit wide, 3-input multiplexer which allows the Address Counter, Word Counter, and Control Register to be read at the DATA lines, D_0-D_7. The Data Multiplexer and three-state Data output buffers are instruction controlled.

Address Output Buffers

The three-state Address Output Buffers allow the Address Counter output to be enabled onto the ADDRESS lines, A_0-A_7, under external control. When the Output Enable input, $\overline{OE}_A$, is LOW, the Address output buffers are enabled; when $\overline{OE}_A$ is HIGH, the ADDRESS lines are in the high-impedance state. The address and Data Output Buffers can sink 24mA output current over the commercial operating range.

Instruction Decoder

The Instruction Decoder generates required internal control signals as a function of the INSTRUCTION inputs, I_0-I_2 and Control Register bits 0 and 1.

Clock

The CLOCK input, CP, is used to clock the Address Register, Address Counter, Word Count Register, Word Counter, and Control Register, all on the LOW to HIGH transition of the CP signal.

Am2940 CONTROL MODES

Control Mode 0 – Word Count Equals Zero Mode

In this mode, the LOAD WORD COUNT instruction loads the word count into the Word Count Register and Word Counter. When the Word Counter is enabled and the Word Counter Carry-in, $\overline{WCI}$, is LOW, the Word Counter decrements on the LOW to HIGH transition of the CLOCK input, CP. Figure 5 specifies when the DONE signal is generated in this mode.

Control Mode 1 – Word Count Compare Mode.

In this mode the LOAD WORD COUNT instruction loads the word count into the Word Count Register and clears the Word Counter. When the Word Counter is enabled and the Word Counter Carry-in, $\overline{WCI}$, is LOW, the Word Counter increments on the LOW to HIGH transition of the clock input, CP. Figure 5 specifies when the DONE signal is generated.

Control Mode 2 – Address Compare Mode

In this mode, only an initial and final memory address need be specified. The initial Memory Address is loaded into the Address Register and Address Counter and the final memory address is loaded into the Word Count Register and Word Counter. The Word Counter is always disabled in this mode and serves as a holding register for the final memory address. When the Address Counter is enabled and the $\overline{ACI}$ input is LOW, the Address Counter increments or decrements (depending on Control Register bit 2) on the LOW to HIGH transition of the CLOCK input, CP. The Transfer Complete Circuitry compares the Address Counter with the Word Counter and generates the DONE signal during the last word transfer, i.e., when the Address Counter equals the Word Counter.

Control Mode 3 – Word Counter Carry Out Mode

For this mode of operation, the user can load the Word Count Register and Word Counter with the two's complement of the number of data words to be transferred. When the Word Counter is enabled and the $\overline{WCI}$ input is LOW, the Word Counter increments on the LOW to HIGH transition of the CLOCK input, CP. A Word Counter Carry Out signal, $\overline{WCO}$, indicates the last data word is being transferred. The DONE signal is not required in this mode and, therefore, is always LOW.

Am2940 INSTRUCTIONS

The Am2940 instruction set consists of eight instructions. Six instructions load and read the Address Counter, Word Counter and Control Register, one instruction enables the Address and Word Counters, and one instruction reinitializes the Address and Word Counters. The function of the REINITIALIZE COUNTERS, LOAD WORD COUNT, and ENABLE COUNTERS instructions vary with the Control Mode being utilized. Table 1 defines the Am2940 Instructions as a function of Instruction inputs I_0-I_2 and the four Am2940 Control Modes.

The WRITE CONTROL REGISTER instruction writes DATA input D_0-D_2 into the Control Register; DATA inputs D_3-D_7 are "don't care" inputs for this instruction. The READ CONTROL REGISTER instruction gates the Control Register outputs to DATA lines, D_0-D_2. DATA lines D_3-D_7 are in the HIGH state during this instruction.

The Word Counter can be read using the READ WORD COUNTER instruction, which gates the Word Counter ouputs to DATA lines D_0-D_7. The LOAD WORD COUNT instruction is Control Mode dependent. In Control Modes 0, 2, and 3, DATA inputs D_0-D_7 are written into both the Word Count Register and Word Counter. In Control Mode 1, DATA inputs D_0-D_7 are written into the Word Count Register and the Word Counter is cleared.

The READ ADDRESS COUNTER instruction gates the Address Counter outputs to DATA lines D_0-D_7, and the LOAD ADDRESS instruction writes DATA inputs D_0-D_7 into both the Address Register and Address Counter.

In Control Modes 0, 1, and 3, the ENABLE COUNTERS instruction enables both the Address and Word Counters; in Control Mode 2, the Address Counter is enabled and the Word Counter holds its contents. When enabled and the carry input is active, the counters increment on the LOW to HIGH transition of the CLOCK input, CP. Thus, with this instruction applied, counting can be controlled by the carry inputs.

The REINITIALIZE COUNTERS instruction also is Control Mode dependent. In Control Modes 0, 2, and 3, the contents of the Address Register and Word Count Register are transferred to the respective Address Counter and Word Counter; in Control Mode 1, the content of the Address Register is transferred to the Address Counter and the Word Counter is cleared. The REINITIALIZE COUNTERS instruction allows a data transfer operation to be repeated without reloading the address and word count from the DATA lines.

Am2940 Timing

Various computations must be performed by the designer to determine how fast the Am2940 can be operated reliably in a given design. The exercises of this section demonstrate how these computations are performed.

Worst case A.C. characteristics, over the full temperature and voltage operating range should be used in these computations. Since, at the time of this writing, the Am2940 is still being characterized, only typical A.C. characteristics are available. These typicals are used here merely to demonstrate how the computations are performed; the designer must use worst-case characteristics. Figure 6 shows the characteristics of a Schottky register and a memory which are assumed for this exercise.

Figures 7A, B, and C show the typical cycle time calculations for the 16-bit Am2940 configuration. The typical delay along the longest path for any of the eight Am2940 instructions determines the typical cycle time. In each case, delays are computed from the LOW to HIGH transition of a clock through an entire microcycle to the next LOW to HIGH transition of a clock. The typical cycle time for a 16-bit Am2940 configuration is 64ns.

TABLE I. Am2940 INSTRUCTIONS

I_2 I_1 I_0	Octal Code	Function	Mnemonic	Control Mode	Word Reg.	Word Counter	Address Reg.	Address Counter	Control Register	Data D_0-D_7
L L L	0	WRITE CONTROL REGISTER	WRCR	0, 1, 2, 3	HOLD	HOLD	HOLD	HOLD	D_0-D_2→CR	INPUT
L L H	1	READ CONTROL REGISTER	RDCR	0, 1, 2, 3	HOLD	HOLD	HOLD	HOLD	HOLD	CR→D_0-D_2 (Note 1)
L H L	2	READ WORD COUNTER	RDWC	0, 1, 2, 3	HOLD	HOLD	HOLD	HOLD	HOLD	WC→D
L H H	3	READ ADDRESS COUNTER	RDAC	0, 1, 2, 3	HOLD	HOLD	HOLD	HOLD	HOLD	AC→D
H L L	4	REINITIALIZE COUNTERS	REIN	0, 2, 3	HOLD	WCR→WC	HOLD	AR→AC	HOLD	Z
				1	HOLD	ZERO→WC	HOLD	AR→AC	HOLD	Z
H L H	5	LOAD ADDRESS	LDAD	0, 1, 2, 3	HOLD	HOLD	D→AR	D→AC	HOLD	INPUT
H H L	6	LOAD WORD COUNT	LDWC	0, 2, 3	D→WR	D→WC	HOLD	HOLD	HOLD	INPUT
				1	D→WR	ZERO→WC	HOLD	HOLD	HOLD	INPUT
H H H	7	ENABLE COUNTERS	ENCT	0, 1, 3	HOLD	ENABLE COUNT	HOLD	ENABLE COUNT	HOLD	Z
				2	HOLD	HOLD	HOLD	ENABLE COUNT	HOLD	Z

CR = Control Reg.
AR = Address Reg.
AC = Address Counter

WCR = Word Count Reg.
WC = Word Counter
D = Data

L = LOW
H = HIGH
Z = High Impedance

Note 1:
Data Bits D_3-D_7 are high during this instruction.

	Min.	Typ.	Max.
Schottky Register			
Clock to Output Delay		9	15
Input Set-Up Time	5	2	
Memory			
Address Set-Up Time	20	10	

Figure 6. Assumed AC Characteristics.

Figure 8 shows the address output enable time computations. Since the Am2940 has an asynchronous address output enable control, the address output enable time may not be related to the Am2940 cycle time.

Figure 9 shows the typical cycle time calculation for an 8-bit Am2940 configuration. The path shown is the longest path and determines an 8-bit typical cycle time of 52ns.

The typical cycle time calculation for a 24-bit Am2940 configuration is shown in Figure 10. The path shown is the longest path and determines a 24-bit typical cycle time of 76ns.

Figure 11 is a summary of typical Am2940 cycle times for the 8, 16 and 24-bit configurations.

a)

**CALCULATIONS FOR
READ CONTROL REG,
READ ADDRESS COUNTER,
READ WORD COUNTER
INSTRUCTIONS**

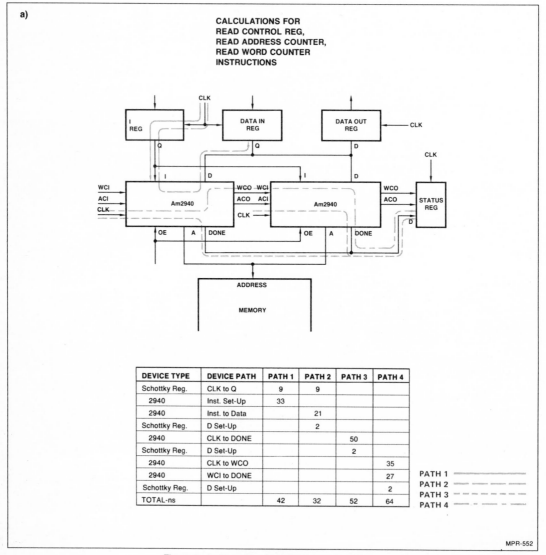

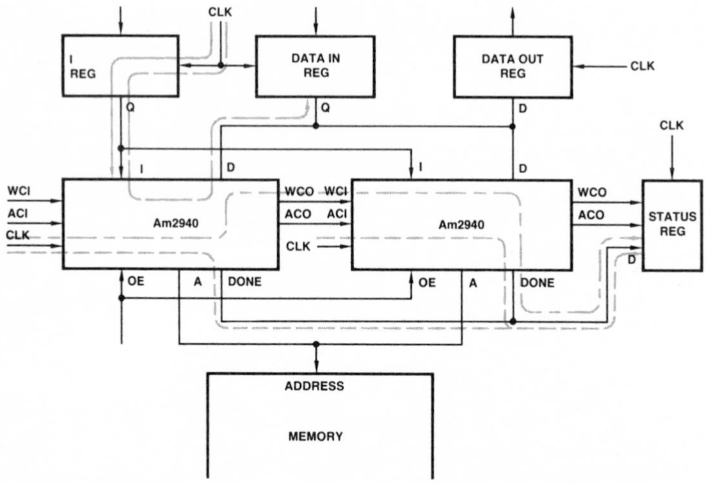

DEVICE TYPE	DEVICE PATH	PATH 1	PATH 2	PATH 3	PATH 4
Schottky Reg.	CLK to Q	9	9		
2940	Inst. Set-Up	33			
2940	Inst. to Data		21		
Schottky Reg.	D Set-Up		2		
2940	CLK to DONE			50	
Schottky Reg.	D Set-Up			2	
2940	CLK to WCO				35
2940	WCI to DONE				27
Schottky Reg.	D Set-Up				2
TOTAL-ns		42	32	52	64

PATH 1
PATH 2
PATH 3
PATH 4

MPR-552

Figure 7. 16-Bit Typical Cycle Time Computations.

b)

CALCULATIONS FOR WRITE CONTROL REG, LOAD WORD COUNT, LOAD ADDRESS INSTRUCTIONS

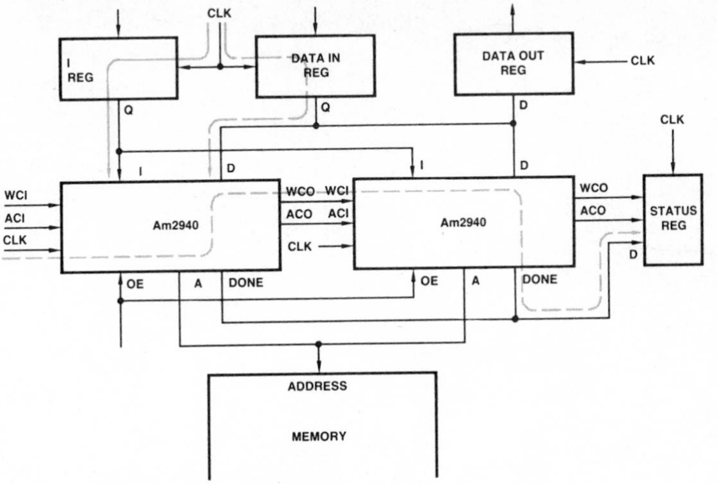

MPR-553

DEVICE TYPE	DEVICE PATH	PATH 1	PATH 2	PATH 3
Schottky Reg.	CLK to Q	9	9	
2940	Inst. Set-Up	33		
2940	Data Set-Up		13	
2940	CLK to WCO			35
2940	WCI to DONE			27
Schottky Reg.	D Set-Up			2
TOTAL-ns		42	22	64

PATH 1 ———
PATH 2 — — —
PATH 3 - - - - -

c)

CALCULATIONS FOR REINITIALIZE COUNTERS, ENABLE COUNTERS INSTRUCTIONS

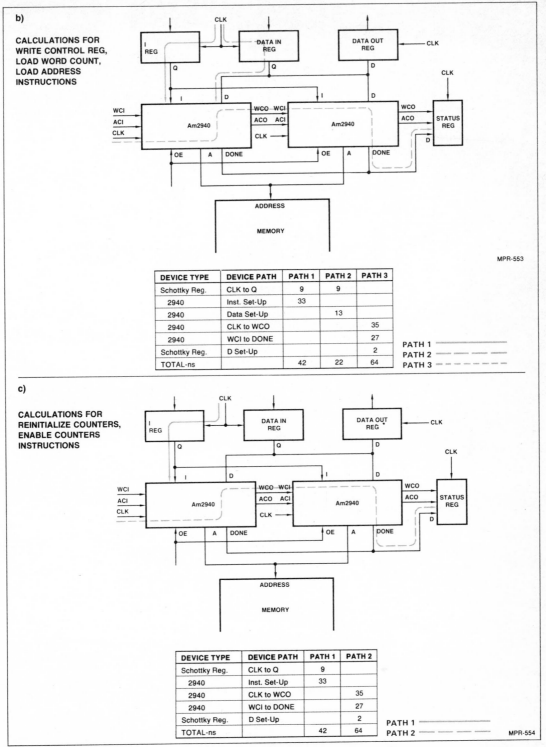

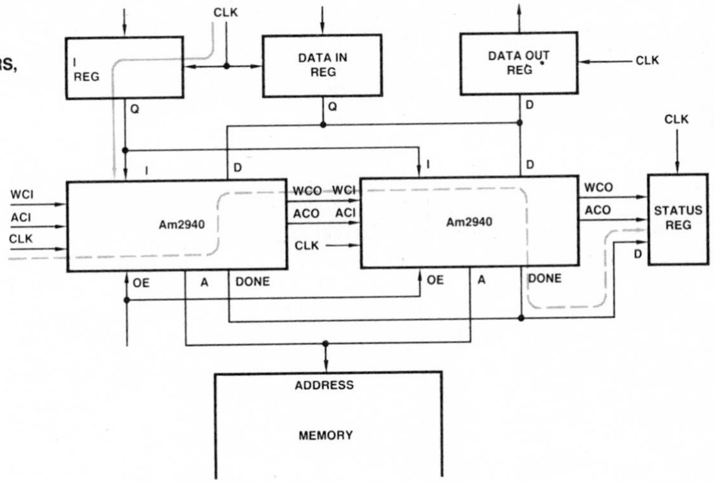

DEVICE TYPE	DEVICE PATH	PATH 1	PATH 2
Schottky Reg.	CLK to Q	9	
2940	Inst. Set-Up	33	
2940	CLK to WCO		35
2940	WCI to DONE		27
Schottky Reg.	D Set-Up		2
TOTAL-ns		42	64

PATH 1 ———
PATH 2 — — —

MPR-554

Figure 7. 16-Bit Typical Cycle Time Computations. (Cont.)

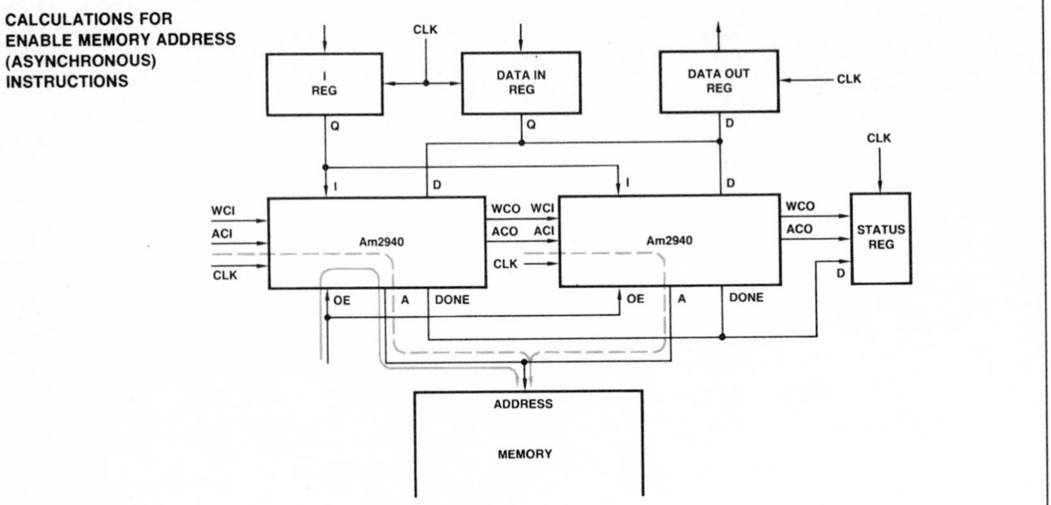

DEVICE TYPE	DEVICE PATH	PATH 1	PATH 2
2940	OE to A	19	
2940	CLK to A		35
Memory	ADR Set-Up	10	10
TOTAL-ns		29	45

PATH 1
PATH 2

MPR-555

Figure 8. Speed Computations.

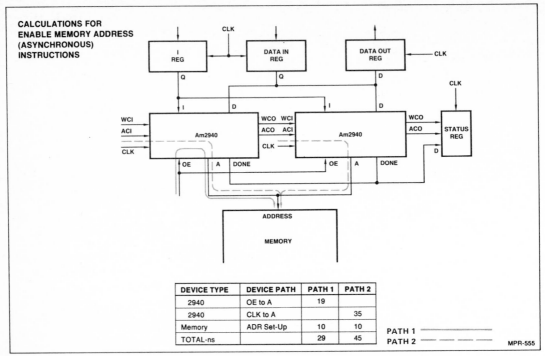

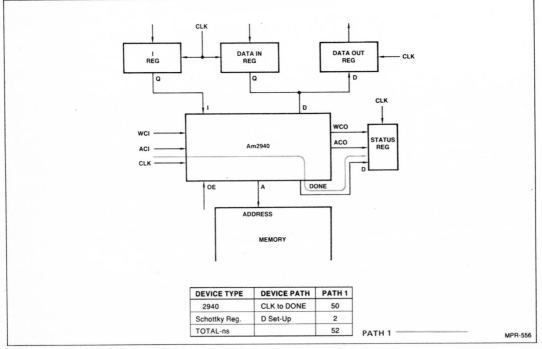

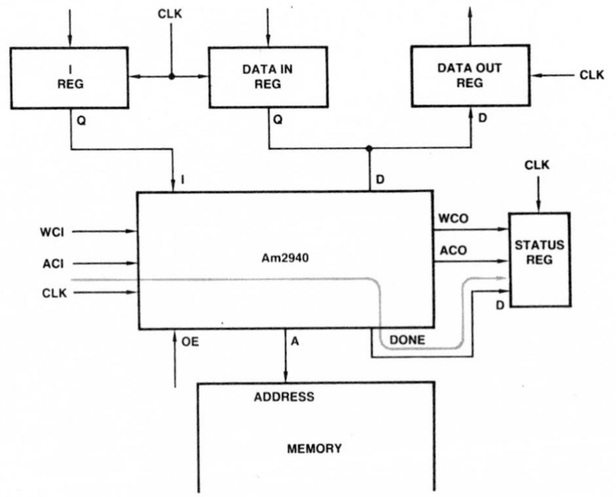

DEVICE TYPE	DEVICE PATH	PATH 1
2940	CLK to DONE	50
Schottky Reg.	D Set-Up	2
TOTAL-ns		52

PATH 1

MPR-556

Figure 9. 8-Bit Typical Cycle Time Computation.

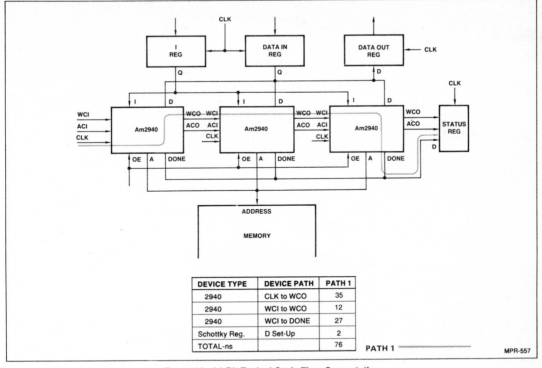

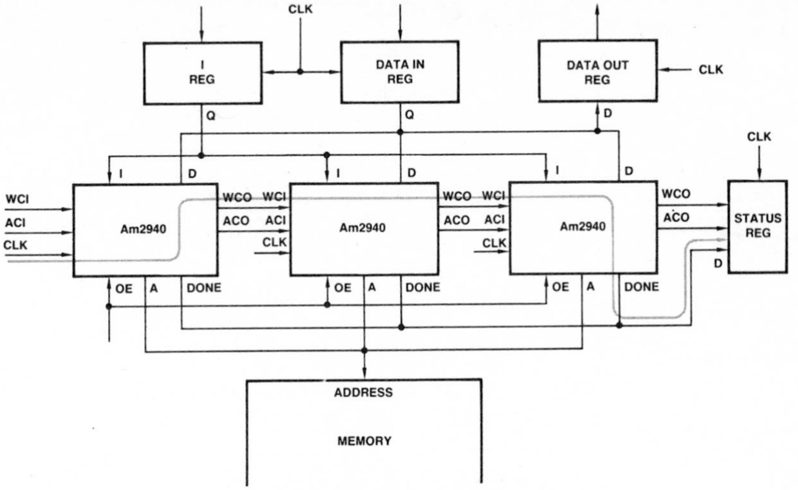

DEVICE TYPE	DEVICE PATH	PATH 1
2940	CLK to WCO	35
2940	WCI to WCO	12
2940	WCI to DONE	27
Schottky Reg.	D Set-Up	2
TOTAL-ns		76

Figure 10. 24-Bit Typical Cycle Time Computation.

	Typical Cycle Time
8-Bit Configuration	52ns
16-Bit Configuration	64ns
24-Bit Configuration	76ns

Figure 11. Summary of Am2940 Cycle Times.

AN EXAMPLE DESIGN

The Am2940 is designed for use in high speed peripheral Controllers using DMA and provides the address and word count maintenance circuitry that is common to most. As indicated previously, DMA Control can be placed in each I/O Controller (Distributed DMA) or DMA Control for a number of I/O devices can be centralized in a separate unit.

Figure 12 shows a block diagram of a microprogrammed I/O Controller which is designed for use in a Distributed DMA system. The Am2910 Microprogram Sequencer, Microprogram Memory and the Microinstruction Register form the microprogram control portion of this I/O Controller. The Am2940 maintains the memory address and word count required for DMA operation. An internal three-state bus provides the communication path between the Microinstruction Register, the Am2917 Data Transceivers, the Am2940, the Am2901A Microprocessor, and the Device Interface Circuitry. The Address Line Control, Data Transfer Control and Mode Control functions of this DMA Controller are incorporated into the I/O Controller Microprogram and the Asynchronous Interface Control Circuitry. The I/O Controller Microprogram also controls the Am2940.

The Am2940 interconnections are shown in detail in Figure 13. Two Am2940s are cascaded to generate a sixteen-bit address. The Am2940 ADDRESS and DATA output current sink capability is 24mA over the commercial operating range. This allows the Am2940s to drive the System Address Bus and Internal Three-State Bus directly, thereby eliminating the need for separate bus drivers. Three bits in the Microinstruction Register provide the Am2940 Instruction Inputs, I_0-I_2. The microprogram clock is used to clock the Am2940s and, when the ENABLE COUNTERS instruction is applied, address and word counting is controlled by the CNT bit of the Microinstruction Register.

Asynchronous interface control circuitry generates System Bus control signals and enables the Am2940 Address onto the System Address Bus at the appropriate time. The open-collector DONE outputs are dot-anded and used as a test input to the Am2910 Microprogram Sequencer.

The I/O controller read operation is flowcharted in Figure 14. The CPU initializes the I/O controller by sending a read command, the starting memory address, the word count and any other parameters required to perform the operation. The I/O Controller then obtains a word of data from the I/O device and requests use of the system bus for a DMA transfer. When the bus is granted, the I/O Controller requests a memory data transfer. Upon receipt of the memory acknowledge signal, which indicates the memory trans-

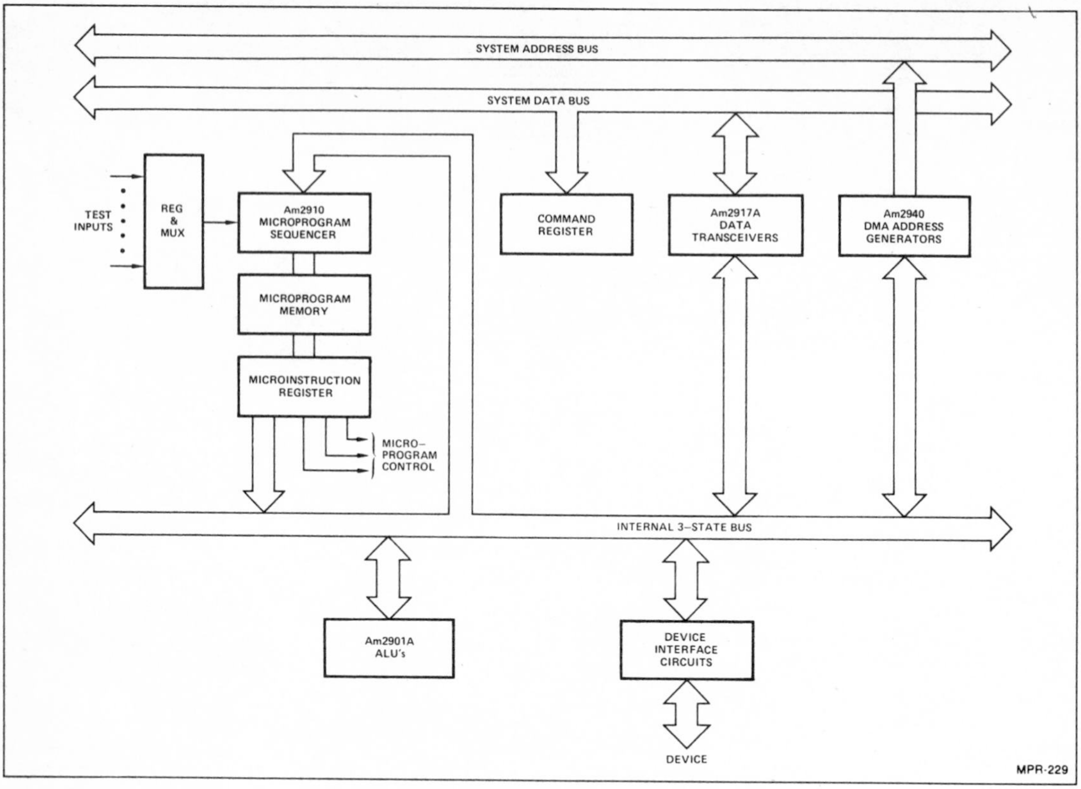

Figure 12. DMA Peripheral Controller Block Diagram.

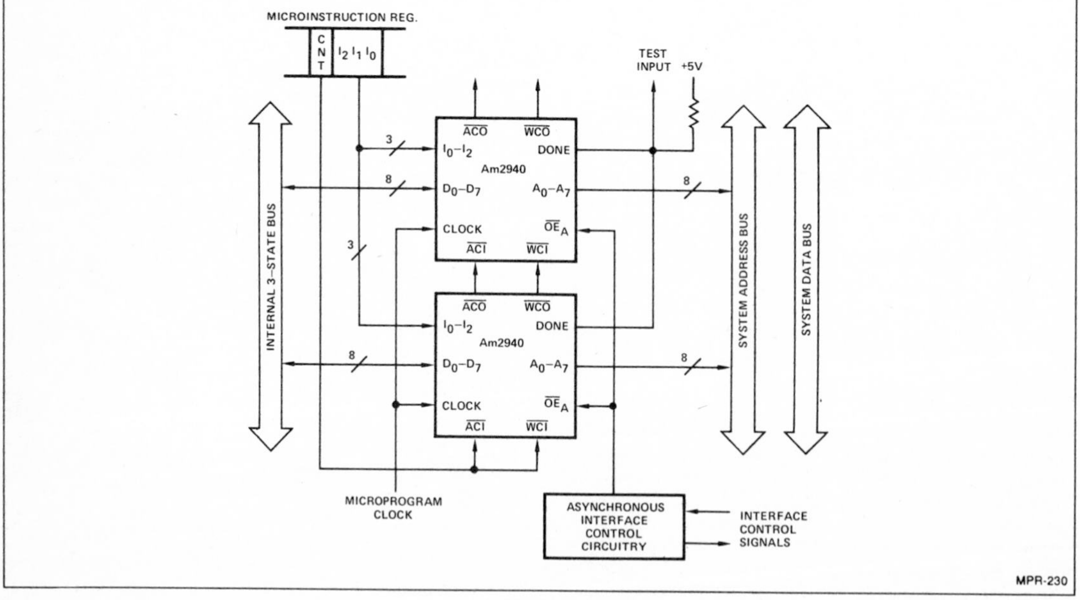

Figure 13. Am2940 Interconnections.

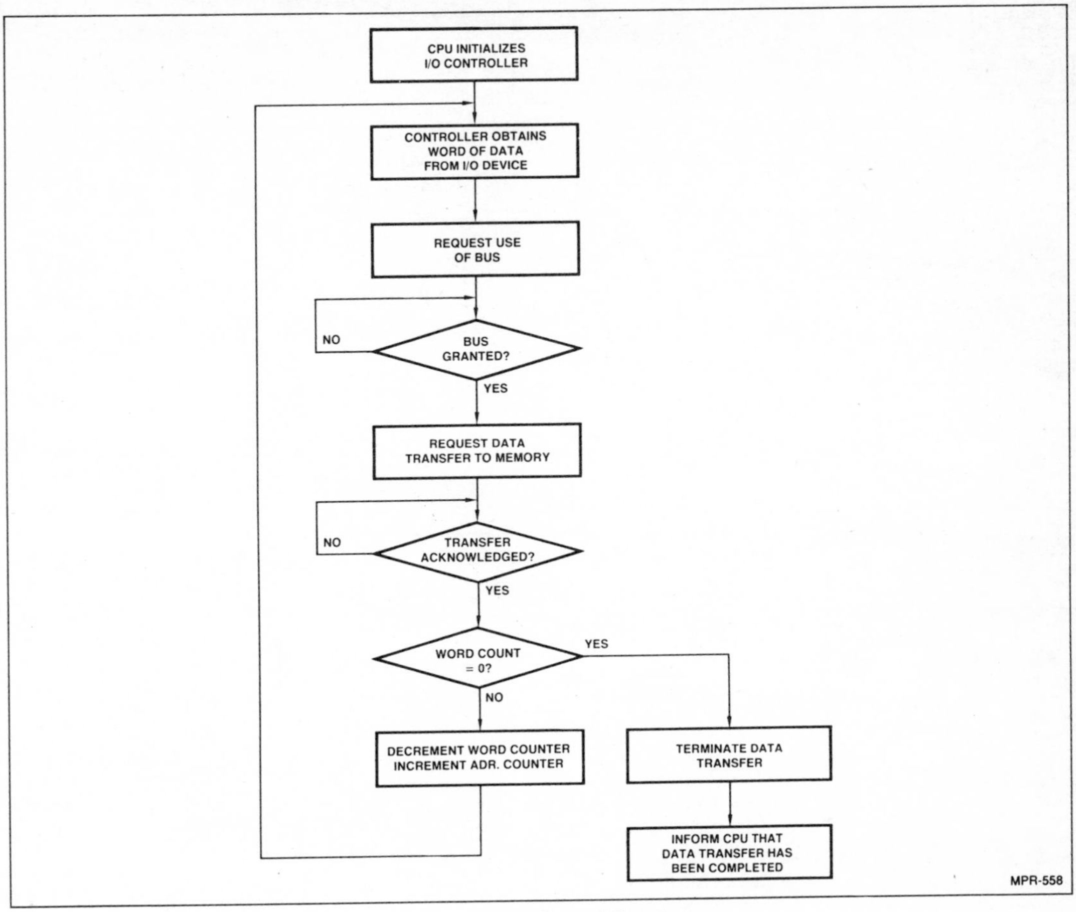

Figure 14. Read Control Flowchart.

fer is complete, the I/O Controller tests the word count. If the word count is not equal to zero, the word counter is decremented, the address counter is incremented and another data word is transferred. When the word count reaches zero, the I/O Controller terminates the data transfer and informs the CPU that the transfer has been completed.

THE Am2942 PROGRAMMABLE TIMER/COUNTER, DMA ADDRESS GENERATOR.

GENERAL DESCRIPTION

The Am2942, a 22-pin version of the Am2940, can be used as a high-speed DMA address Generator or Programmable Timer/Counter. It provides multiplexed Address and Data lines, for use with a common bus, and additional Instruction Input and Instruction Enable pins. The Am2942 executes 16 instructions; eight are the same as the Am2940 instructions, and eight instructions facilitate the use of the Am2942 as a Programmable Timer/Counter. The Instruction Enable input allows the sharing of the Am2942 instruction field with other devices.

When used as a Timer/Counter, the Am2942 provides two independent, programmable, eight-bit, up-down counters in a 22-pin package. The two on-chip counters can be cascaded to form a single chip, 16-bit counter. Also, any number of chips can be cascaded – for example three cascaded Am2942s form a 48-bit timer/counter.

Reinitialization instructions provide the capability to reinitialize the counters from on-chip registers. Am2942 Programmable Control Modes, identical to those of the Am2940, offer four different types of programmable control.

Am2942 ARCHITECTURE

As shown in the Block Diagram, the Am2942 consists of the following:

- A three-bit Control Register.
- An eight-bit Address Counter with input multiplexer.
- An eight-bit Address Register.
- An eight-bit Word Counter with input multiplexer.
- An eight-bit Word Count Register.
- Transfer complete circuitry.
- An eight-bit wide data multiplexer with three-state output buffers.
- An instruction decoder.

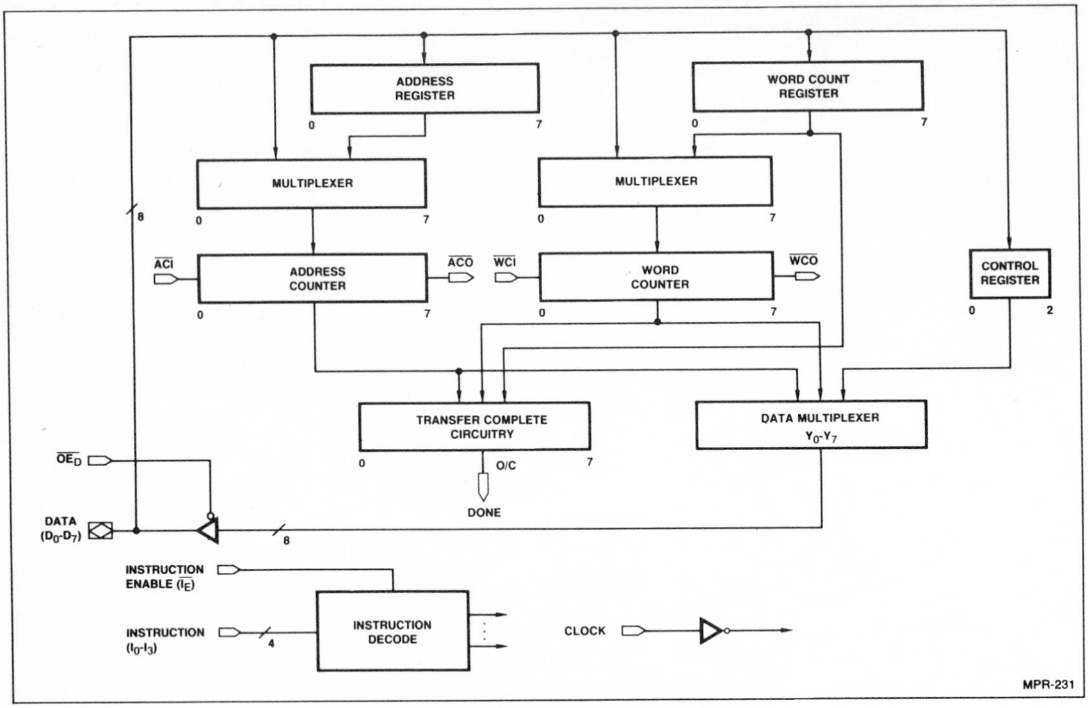

Figure 15. Am2942 Block Diagram.

Control Register

Under instruction control, the Control Register can be loaded or read from the bidirectional DATA lines, D_0-D_7. Control Register bits 0 and 1 determine the Am2942 Control Mode, and bit 2 determines whether the Address Counter increments or decrements. Figure 16 defines the Control Register format.

Address Counter

The Address Counter, which provides the current memory address, is an eight-bit, binary, up/down counter with full look-ahead carry generation. The Address Carry input ($\overline{ACI}$) and Address Carry Output ($\overline{ACO}$) allow cascading to accommodate larger addresses. Under instruction control, the Address Counter can be enabled, disabled, and loaded from the DATA inputs, D_0-D_7, or the Address Register. When enabled and the ACI input is LOW, the Address Counter increments/decrements on the LOW to HIGH transition of the CLOCK input, CP.

Address Register

The eight-bit Address Register saves the initial address so that it can be restored later in order to repeat a transfer operation. When the LOAD ADDRESS instruction is executed, the Address Register and Address Counter are simultaneously loaded from the DATA inputs, D_0-D_7.

Control Register

CR_2	CR_1	CR_0

CR_1	CR_0	Control Mode Number	Control Mode Type	Word Counter	Done Output Signal: $\overline{WCI}$ = LOW	Done Output Signal: $\overline{WCI}$ = HIGH
L	L	0	Word Count Equals Zero	Decrement	HIGH when Word Counter = 1	HIGH when Word Counter = 0
L	H	1	Word Count Compare	Increment	HIGH when Word Counter + 1 = Word Count Register	HIGH when Word Counter = Word Count Register
H	L	2	Address Compare	Decrement	HIGH when Word Counter = Address Counter	
H	H	3	Word Counter Carry Out	Increment	Always LOW	

CR_2	Address Counter
L	Increment
H	Decrement

H = HIGH
L = LOW

Figure 16. Control Register Format Definition.

Word Counter And Word Count Register

The Word Counter and Word Count Register, which maintain and save a word count, are similar in structure and operation to the Address Counter and Address Register, with the exception that the Word Counter increments in Control Modes 1 and 3 and decrements in Control Modes 0 and 2. The LOAD WORD COUNT instruction simultaneously loads the Word Counter and Word Count Register.

Transfer Complete Circuitry

The Transfer Complete Circuitry is a combinational logic network which detects the completion of the data transfer operation in three Control Modes and generates the DONE output signal. The DONE signal is an open-collector output, which can be dot-anded between chips.

Data Multiplexer

The Data Multiplexer is an eight-bit wide, three-input multiplexer which allows the Address Counter, Word Counter and Control Register to be read at DATA lines D_0-D_7. The Data Multiplexer output, Y_0-Y_7, is enabled onto DATA lines D_0-D_7 if, and only if, the Output Enable input, OE_D, is LOW. (Refer to Figure 17.)

$\overline{OE}_D$	D_0-D_7
L	DATA MULTIPLEXER OUTPUT, Y_0-Y_7
H	HIGH Z

Figure 17. Data Bus Output Enable Function.

Instruction Decoder

The Instruction Decoder generates required internal control signals as a function of the INSTRUCTION inputs, I_0-I_3 Control Register bits 0 and 1, and the INSTRUCTION ENABLE input, I_E.

Clock

The clock input, CP, is used to clock the Address Register, Address Counter, Word Count Register, Word Counter, and Control Register, all on the LOW to HIGH transition of the CP signal.

Am2942 CONTROL MODES

Control Mode 0 – Word Count Equals Zero Mode

In this mode, the LOAD WORD COUNT instruction loads the word count into the Word Count Register and Word Counter. When the Word Counter is enabled and the Word Counter Carry-in, $\overline{WCI}$, is LOW, the Word Counter decrements on the LOW to HIGH transition of the CLOCK input, CP. Figure 16 specifies when the DONE signal is generated in this mode.

Control Mode 1 – Word Count Compare Mode

In this mode the LOAD WORD COUNT instruction loads the word count into the Word Count Register and clears the Word Counter. When the Word Counter is enabled and the Word Counter Carry-in, $\overline{WCI}$, is LOW, the Word Counter increments on the LOW to HIGH transition of the clock input, CP. Figure 16 specifies when the DONE signal is generated.

Control Mode 2 – Address Compare Mode

In this mode, only an initial and final memory address need to be specified. The initial Memory Address is loaded into the Address Register and Address Counter and the final memory address is loaded into the Word Count Register and Word Counter. The Word Counter serves as a holding register for the final memory address. When the Address Counter is enabled and the $\overline{ACI}$ input is LOW, the Address Counter increments or decrements (depending on Control Register bit 2) on the LOW to HIGH transition of the CLOCK input, CP. The Transfer Complete Circuitry compares the Address Counter with the Word Counter and generates the DONE signal during the last word transfer, i.e., when the Address Counter equals the Word Counter.

Control Mode 3 – Word Counter Carry Out Mode

For this mode of operation, the user can load the Word Count Register and Word Counter with the two's complement of the number of data words to be transferred. When the Word Counter is enabled and the $\overline{WCI}$ input is LOW, the Word Counter increments on the LOW to HIGH transition of the CLOCK input, CP. A Word Counter Carry Out signal, $\overline{WCO}$, indicates the last data word is being transferred. The DONE signal is not required in this mode and, therefore, is always LOW.

Am2942 INSTRUCTIONS

The Am2942 instruction set consists of sixteen instructions. Eight are DMA instructions and are the same as the Am2940 instructions. The remaining eight instructions are designed to facilitate the use of the Am2942 as a Programmable Timer/Counter. Figures 18 and 19 define the Am2942 Instructions.

Instructions 0-7 are DMA instructions. The WRITE CONTROL REGISTER instruction writes DATA input D_0-D_2 into the Control Register; DATA inputs D_3-D_7 are "don't care" inputs for this instruction. The READ CONTROL REGISTER instruction gates the Control Register to Data Multiplexer outputs Y_0-Y_2. Outputs Y_3-Y_7 are HIGH during this instruction.

The Word Counter can be read using the READ WORD COUNTER instruction, which gates the Word Counter to Data Multiplexer outputs, Y_0-Y_7. The LOAD WORD COUNT instruction is Control Mode dependent. In Control Modes 0, 2 and 3, DATA inputs D_0-D_7 are written into both the Word Count Register and Word Counter. In Control Mode 1, DATA inputs D_0-D_7 are written into the Word Count Register and the Word Counter is cleared.

The READ ADDRESS COUNTER instruction gates the Address Counter to Data Multiplexer outputs, Y_0-Y_7, and the LOAD ADDRESS instruction writes DATA inputs D_0-D_7 into both the Address Register and Address Counter.

In Control Modes 0, 1, and 3, the ENABLE COUNTERS instruction enables both the Address and Word Counters; in Control Mode 2, the Address Counter is enabled and the Word Counter holds its contents. When enabled and the carry input is active, the counters increment on the LOW to HIGH transition of the CLOCK input, CP. Thus, with this instruction applied, counting can be controlled by the carry inputs.

The REINITIALIZE COUNTERS instruction also is Control Mode dependent. In Control Modes 0, 2, and 3, the contents of the Address Register and Word Count Register are transferred to the respective Address Counter and Word Counter; in Control Mode 1, the content of the Address Register is transferred to the Address Counter and the Word Counter is cleared. The REINITIALIZE COUNTERS instruction allows a data transfer operation to be repeated without reloading the address and word count from the DATA lines.

$\overline{I_E}$	I_3	I_2	I_1	I_0	HEX CODE		
0	0	0	0	0	0	WRITE CONTROL REGISTER	DMA INSTRUCTIONS
0	0	0	0	1	1	READ CONTROL REGISTER	
0	0	0	1	0	2	READ WORD COUNTER	
0	0	0	1	1	3	READ ADDRESS COUNTER	
0	0	1	0	0	4	REINITIALIZE COUNTERS	
0	0	1	0	1	5	LOAD ADDRESS	
0	0	1	1	0	6	LOAD WORD COUNT	
0	0	1	1	1	7	ENABLE COUNTERS	
1	0	X	X	X	0-7	INSTRUCTION DISABLE	
0	1	0	0	0	8	WRITE CONTROL REGISTER, T/C	TIMER/COUNTER INSTRUCTIONS
0	1	0	0	1	9	REINITIALIZE ADDRESS COUNTER	
0	1	0	1	0	A	READ WORD COUNTER, T/C	
0	1	0	1	1	B	READ ADDRESS COUNTER, T/C	
0	1	1	0	0	C	REINITIALIZE ADDRESS & WORD COUNTERS	
0	1	1	0	1	D	LOAD ADDRESS, T/C	
0	1	1	1	0	E	LOAD WORD COUNT, T/C	
0	1	1	1	1	F	REINITIALIZE WORD COUNTER	
1	1	X	X	X	8-F	INSTRUCTION DISABLE, T/C	

0 = LOW 1 = HIGH X = DON'T CARE

Notes: 1. When I_3 is tied LOW, the Am2942 acts as a DMA circuit: When I_3 is tied HIGH, the Am2942 acts as a Timer/Counter circuit.
2. Am2942 instructions 0 through 7 are the same as Am2940 instructions.

Figure 18. Am2942 Instructions

When $\overline{I_E}$ is HIGH, Instruction inputs, I_0-I_2, are disabled. If I_3 is LOW, the function performed is identical to that of the ENABLE COUNTERS instruction. Thus, counting can be controlled by the carry inputs with the ENABLE COUNTERS instruction applied or with Instruction Inputs I_0-I_2 disabled.

Instructions 8-F facilitate the use of the Am2942 as a Programmable Timer/Counter. They differ from instructions 0-7 in that they provide independent control of the Address Counter, Word Counter and Control Register.

The WRITE CONTROL REGISTER, T/C instruction writes DATA input D_0-D_2 into the Control Register. DATA inputs D_3-D_7 are "don't care" inputs for this instruction. The Address and Word Counters are enabled, and the Control Register contents appear at the Data Multiplexer output.

The REINITIALIZE ADDRESS COUNTER instruction allows the independent reinitialization of the Address Counter. The Word Counter is enabled and the contents of the Address Counter appear at the Data Multiplexer output.

The Word Counter can be read, using the READ WORD COUNTER, T/C instruction. Both counters are enabled when this instruction is executed.

When the READ ADDRESS COUNTER, T/C instruction is executed, both counters are enabled and the address counter contents appear at the Data Multiplexer output.

The REINITIALIZE ADDRESS and WORD COUNTERS instruction provides the capability to reinitialize both counters at the same time. The Address Counter contents appear at the Data Multiplexer output.

DATA inputs D_0-D_7 are loaded into both the Address Register and Counter when the LOAD ADDRESS, T/C instruction is executed. The Word Counter is enabled and its contents appear at the Data Multiplexer output.

The LOAD WORD COUNT, T/C instruction is identical to the LOAD WORD COUNT instruction with the exception that Address Counter is enabled.

The Word Counter can be independently reinitialized using the REINITIALIZE WORD COUNTER instruction. The Address Counter is enabled and the Word Counter contents appear at the Data Multiplexer output.

When the $\overline{I_E}$ input is HIGH, Instruction inputs, I_0-I_2, are disabled. The function performed when I_3 is HIGH is identical to that performed when I_3 is LOW, with the exception that the Word Counter contents appear at the Data Multiplexer output.

EXAMPLE DESIGNS

Figure 20 shows an Am2942 used as two independent, programmable eight-bit timer/counters. In this example, an Am2910 Microprogram Sequencer provides an address to Am29775 512 x 8 Registered PROMs. The on-chip PROM output register is used as the Microinstruction Register.

The Am2942 Instruction input, I_3 is tied HIGH to select the eight Timer/Counter instructions. The $\overline{I_E}$, I_0-I_2, and $\overline{OE_D}$ inputs are provided by the microinstruction, and the D_0-D_7 data lines are connected to a common Data Bus. GATE WC and GATE AC are separate enable controls for the respective Word Counter and Address Counter. The DONE, $\overline{ACO}$ and $\overline{WCO}$ output signals indicate that a pre-programmed time or count has been reached.

$\overline{I_E}$	$I_3I_2I_1I_0$ (Hex)	Function	Mnemonic	Control Mode	Word Reg.	Word Counter	Adr. Reg.	Adr. Counter	Control Reg.	Data Multiplexer Output
L	0	WRITE CONTROL REGISTER	WRCR	0, 1, 2, 3	HOLD	HOLD	HOLD	HOLD	$D_{0\text{-}2} \rightarrow$ CR	FORCED HIGH
L	1	READ CONTROL REGISTER	RDCR	0, 1, 2, 3	HOLD	HOLD	HOLD	HOLD	HOLD	CONTROL REG.
L	2	READ WORD COUNTER	RDWC	0, 1, 2, 3	HOLD	HOLD	HOLD	HOLD	HOLD	WORD COUNTER
L	3	READ ADDRESS COUNTER	RDAC	0, 1, 2, 3	HOLD	HOLD	HOLD	HOLD	HOLD	ADR. COUNTER
L	4	REINITIALIZE COUNTERS	REIN	0, 2, 3	HOLD	WR → WC	HOLD	AR → AC	HOLD	ADR. CNTR.
				1	HOLD	ZERO → WC	HOLD	AR → AC	HOLD	ADR. CNTR.
L	5	LOAD ADDRESS	LDAD	0, 1, 2, 3	HOLD	HOLD	D → AR	D → AC	HOLD	WORD COUNTER
L	6	LOAD WORD COUNT	LDWC	0, 2, 3	D → WR	D → WC	HOLD	HOLD	HOLD	FORCED HIGH
				1	D → WR	ZERO → WC	HOLD	HOLD	HOLD	FORCED HIGH
L	7	ENABLE COUNTERS	ENCT	0, 1, 3	HOLD	ENABLE	HOLD	ENABLE	HOLD	ADR. CNTR.
				2	HOLD	HOLD	HOLD	ENABLE	HOLD	ADR. CNTR.
H	0-7	INSTRUCTION DISABLE	–	0, 1, 3	HOLD	ENABLE	HOLD	ENABLE	HOLD	ADR. CNTR.
				2	HOLD	HOLD	HOLD	ENABLE	HOLD	ADR. CNTR.
L	8	WRITE CONTROL REGISTER, T/C	WCRT	0, 1, 2, 3	HOLD	ENABLE	HOLD	ENABLE	$D_{0\text{-}2} \rightarrow$ CR	CONTROL REG.
L	9	REINITIALIZE ADR. COUNTER	REAC	0, 1, 2, 3	HOLD	ENABLE	HOLD	AR → AC	HOLD	ADR. COUNTER
L	A	READ WORD COUNTER, TC	RWCT	0, 1, 2, 3	HOLD	ENABLE	HOLD	ENABLE	HOLD	WORD COUNTER
L	B	READ ADDRESS COUNTER, T/C	RACT	0, 1, 2, 3	HOLD	ENABLE	HOLD	ENABLE	HOLD	ADR. COUNTER
L	C	REINITIALIZE ADDRESS AND WORD COUNTERS	RAWC	0, 2, 3	HOLD	WR → WC	HOLD	AR → AC	HOLD	ADR. CNTR.
				1	HOLD	ZERO → WC	HOLD	AR → AC	HOLD	ADR. CNTR.
L	D	LOAD ADDRESS, T/C	LDAT	0, 1, 2, 3	HOLD	ENABLE	D → AR	D → AC	HOLD	WORD COUNTER
L	E	LOAD WORD COUNT, T/C	LWCT	0, 2, 3	D → WR	D → WC	HOLD	ENABLE	HOLD	FORCED HIGH
				1	D → WR	ZERO → WC	HOLD	ENABLE	HOLD	FORCED HIGH
L	F	REINITIALIZE WORD COUNTER	REWC	0, 2, 3	HOLD	WR → WC	HOLD	ENABLE	HOLD	WD. CNTR.
				1	HOLD	ZERO → WC	HOLD	ENABLE	HOLD	WD. CNTR.
H	8-F	INSTRUCTION DISABLE, T/C	–	0, 1, 3	HOLD	ENABLE	HOLD	ENABLE	HOLD	WD. CNTR.
				2	HOLD	HOLD	HOLD	ENABLE	HOLD	WD. CNTR.

WR = WORD REGISTER AC = ADDRESS COUNTER
WC = WORD COUNTER CR = CONTROL REGISTER
AR = ADDRESS REGISTER D = DATA

Figure 19. Am2942 Function Table.

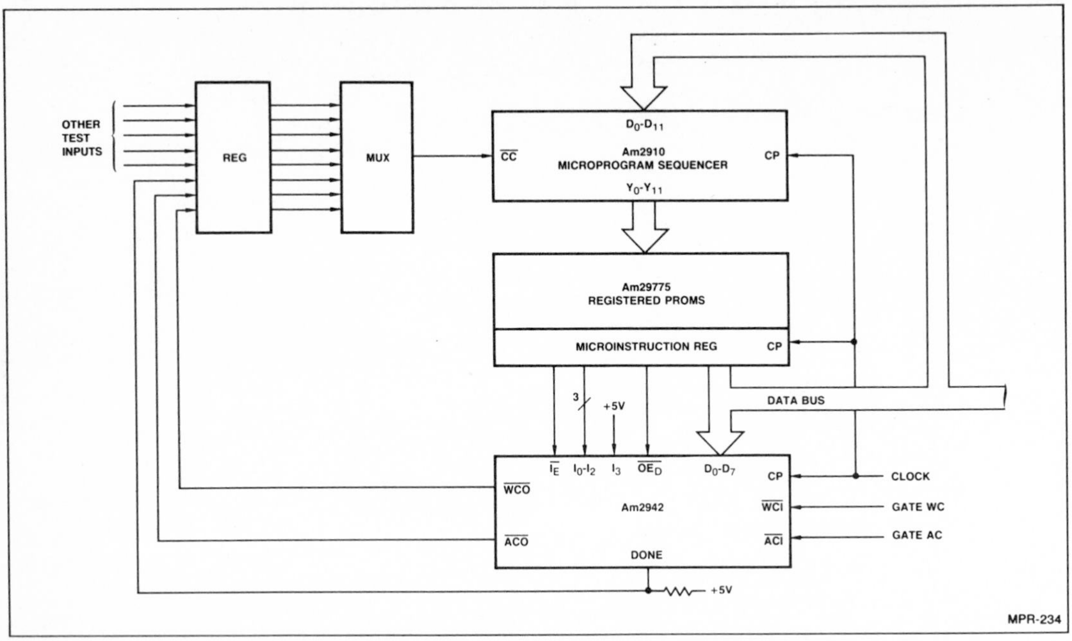

Figure 20. Two 8-Bit Programmable Counters/Timers in a 22-Pin Package.

Figure 21 shows an Am2942 used as a single 16-bit, programmable timer/counter. In this example, the Word Counter carry-out, $\overline{WCO}$, is connected to the Address Counter carry-in, $\overline{ACI}$, to form a single 16-bit counter which is enabled by the GATE signal.

Figure 22 shows two Am2942s cascaded to form a 32-bit programmable timer/counter. The two Word Counters form the low order 16 bits, and the two Address Counters form the high order bits. This allows the timer/counter to be loaded and read 16 bits at a time.

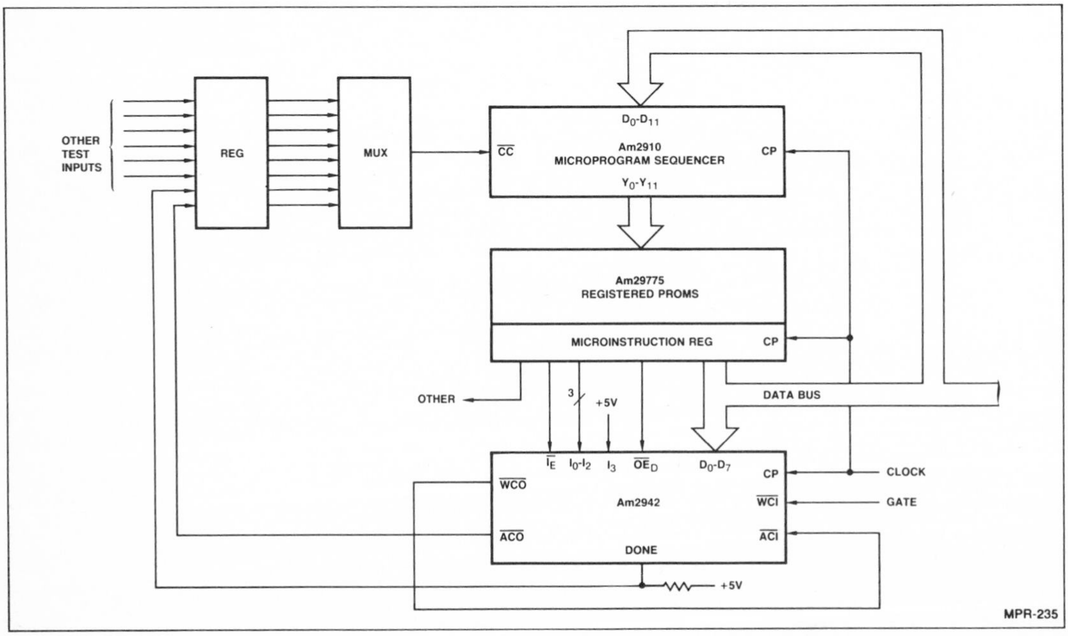

Figure 21. 16-Bit Programmable Counter/Timer Using a Single Am2942.

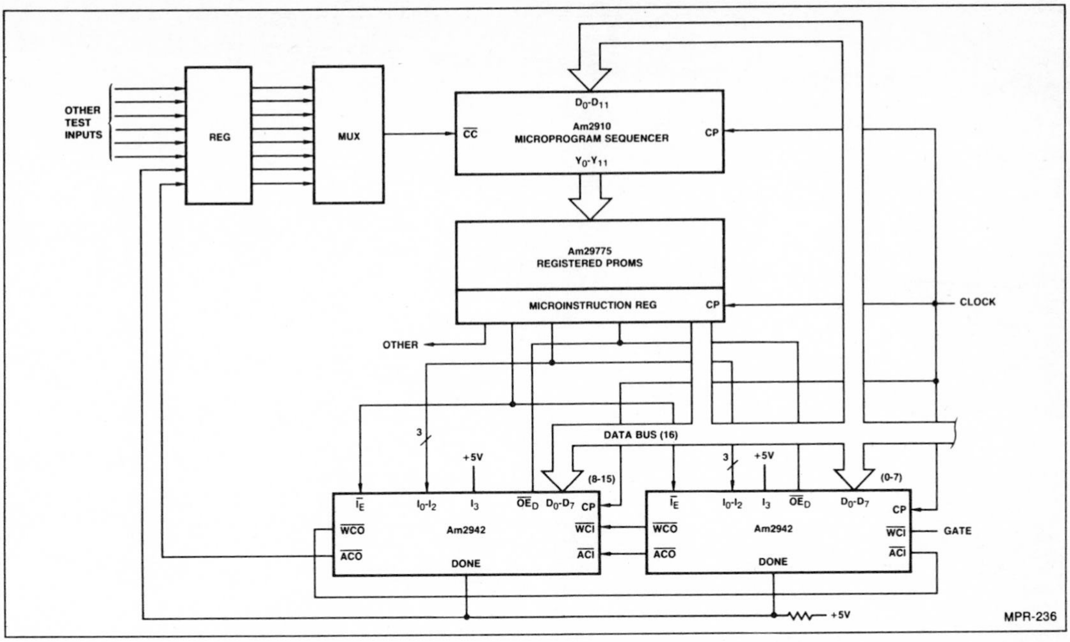

Figure 22. 32-Bit Programmable Counter/Timer Using Two Am2942s.

In Figure 23, two Am2942s are shown cascaded to form dual 16-bit counters/timers. GATE WC and GATE AC are separate enable controls for the respective Word Counter and Address Counter. Using the 16-bit Data Bus, each 16-bit counter can be loaded or read in parallel.

Figure 24 shows two Am2942s used as DMA address Generators on a common DATA/ADDRESS bus. The common bus allows the use of the Am2942 multiplexed data and address pins, D_0-D_7. The Am2942 is in a 22 pin package whereas the Am2940, which has separate address and data pins, requires a 28 pin package.

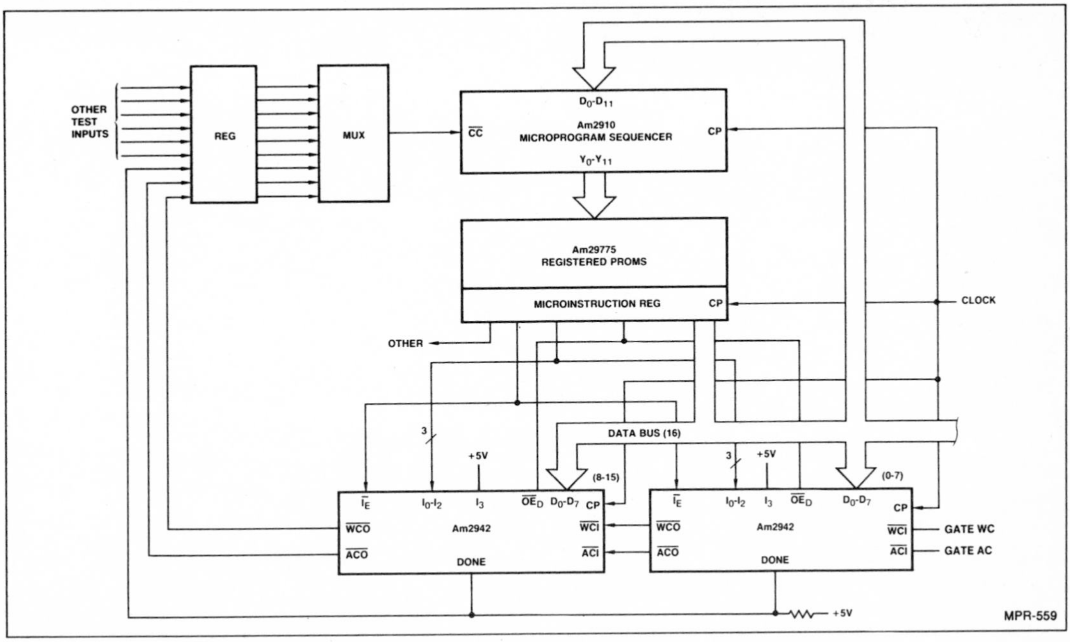

Figure 23. Dual 16-Bit Programmable Counters/Timers.

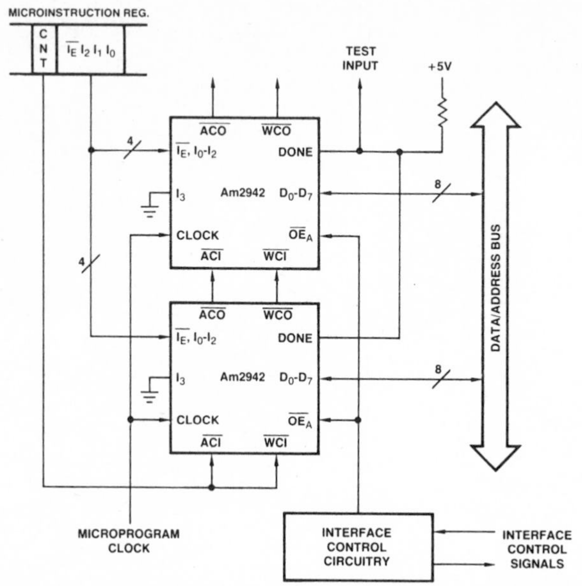

Figure 24. Am2942s Used as DMA Address Generator on Common Bus.

In this example the Am2942 Address Counter, Word Counter and Control Register are loaded and read directly from the CPU via the DATA/ADDRESS bus. Since the bus carries addresses as well as data, the D_0-D_7 pins can be used also to enable the address onto the bus.

Four bits in the Microinstruction Register provide the Am2942 Instruction Inputs, I_0-I_2 and the Instruction Enable input $\overline{I_E}$. The I_4 input is tied LOW, selecting the eight DMA instructions. The microprogram clock is used to clock the Am2942s, and when the ENABLE COUNTERS instruction is applied or the instruction is disabled ($\overline{I_E}$ = HIGH), address and word counting is controlled by the CNT bit of the Microinstruction Register.

Interface control circuitry generates bus control signals and enables the Am2942 address onto the bus at the appropriate. The open-collector DONE outputs are dot-anded and used as a test input to the microprogram sequencer.

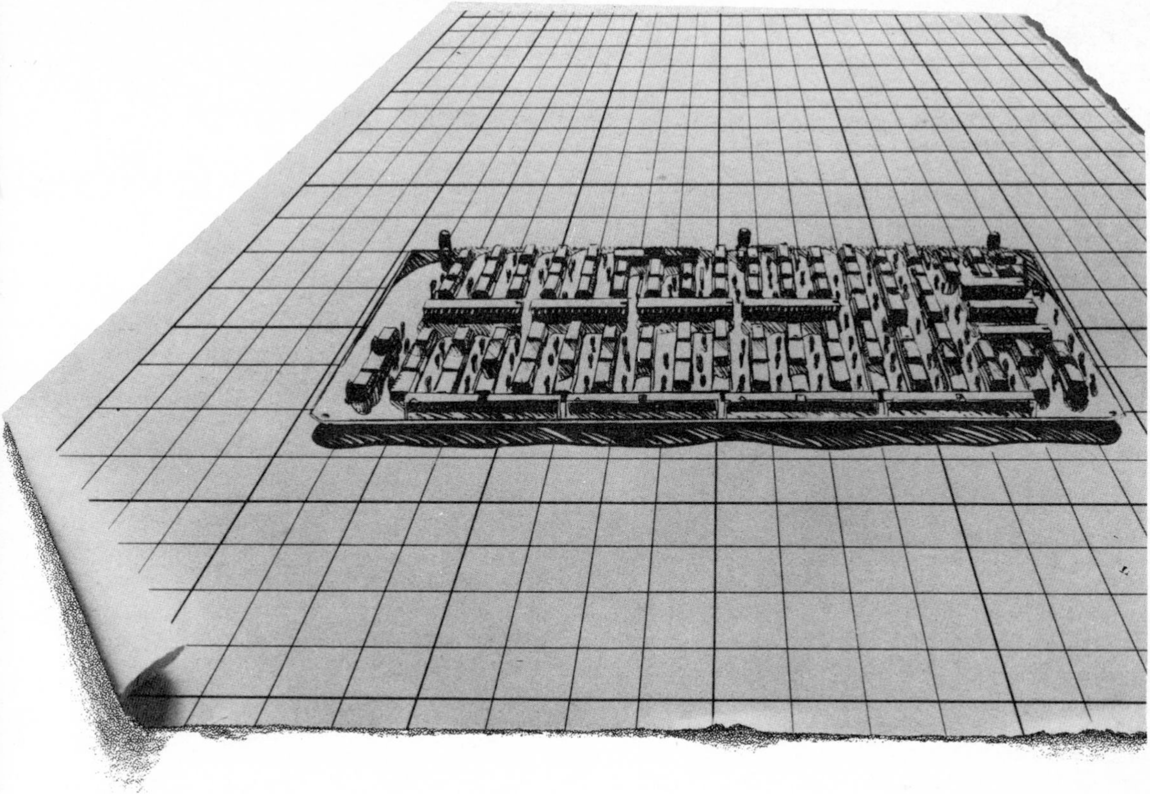

Chapter VIII
HEX-29

INTRODUCTION

Modern digital systems are becoming faster and increasingly complex. As a result, more is being demanded of digital design engineers. Fortunately, there is a design technique that can greatly simplify the design process. It can also lead to cleaner, more efficient, more reliable finished devices. This technique is called MICROPROGRAMMING. Do not be confused by this word; it has nothing whatever to do with machine level language or programming a microprocessor. Microprogramming is inherently more powerful than programming in a processor's instruction set for many reasons, not the least of which is the access to the entire functional resources of the hardware on a machine cycle by machine cycle basis. An excellent treatment of microprogramming and microprogrammed machines is available from AMD in previous application notes. Perhaps the easiest to comprehend introduction to this subject is in AMD's *Microprogramming Handbook.* This is highly recommended reading for any newcomer to this area of digital design.

Though microprogramming has always been an inherently more powerful design technique since its invention in 1955, it has been little used until recently (1976), and with some justification. The reason is quite simple. The very large majority of IC's available until the 1976-1978 time frame were specifically designed to be used with 'random logic' design techniques. Since these random logic IC's were poorly suited to the highly structured nature of well designed microprogrammed systems, the potential advantages of microprogrammed systems could not be realized easily.

Fortunately for all of us, in the mid 1970's AMD made a significant decision to develop a very extensive family of Schottky technology IC's specifically optimized for use in microprogrammed systems. These circuits belong to the Am2900 family as well as the Am25S, Am26S, Am27S, and Am25LS families. The acceptance has been so great that many of the other large IC manufacturers are now second sourcing many of these parts and introducing others. So, in just three to four years, microprogrammed machine design has come of age. Now, for most any job of medium to very high complexity, a microprogrammed system is the only way to go if a microprocessor isn't fast or versatile enough.

The purpose of this application note is to illustrate the use of microprogramming and 'bit-slice' technology in a high performance 16-bit time-sharing CPU.This application note is unique in that the CPU being described is the heart of a new commercially available minicomputer system. Thus, it is possible to examine the nature of the CPU as it relates to a complete basic minicomputer system. For this reason, a very short section follows that describes the basic system elements and the system goals toward which the CPU was designed.

The product described herein is called the "HEX-29" CPU. Information on the AMD devices embodied in this application note should be directed to AMD via your local AMD representatives. Inquiries about the HEX-29 CPU and minicomputer system for OEM and/or end user applications should be directed to:

HEX-29
Digital Microsystems, Inc.
4448 Piedmont
Oakland, CA 94661
(415) 658-8532

SYSTEM DESIGN GOALS

In any significant project it is mandatory that reasonable, coherent system design goals be spelled out before serious work is begun. This can be a surprisingly short list of general specifications, but a well thought out system philosophy can make all the difference. Most important, everyone involved should have a copy so everyone will be pulling in the same direction.

The following list represents the system design goals for the HEX-29 CPU and system.

1. Compact, reliable, easy to use.
2. Multi-user, multi-task, timesharing.
3. Fast, code-efficient high level language processing.
4. Low cost for complete system.
5. Intelligent microprogrammed channel controllers for high speed I/O.

Indeed, this seems like a short list, but it is the list from which the more detailed specifications were developed. For example, in order to be compact, switching power supply technology is employed. Reliability evolves from many factors including burn in and testing cycles. Probably the single largest cause of 'flakiness' in digital systems is insufficient cooling. An oversize fan moves about five times the volume of air past the IC's as is normally recommended. This large, slower speed fan has the additional advantage that the lower frequency 'white noise' it generates is far less annoying than the 'whine' from smaller high speed fans.

So, it is easy to see that many of the more specific details of system design will fall readily out of these overall design goals. The features of the final HEX-29 system are shown below. It should be instructive to trace each of these features to one (or more) of the design goals listed above. Reviewing this list will also prepare the context for the more detailed sections to follow in later sections.

HEX-29 FEATURES

VERY FAST
- 160ns basic machine cycle
- Only two machine cycles for many instructions
- Microprogrammed clock for increased through-put

COMPLETE SET OF DATA TYPES
- Bit operations
- Nibble operations
- Byte operations
- Word operations
- Double word operations
- Quad word operations
- Variable field operations

EXTENSIVE REGISTER SET
- 16 general purpose/defined purpose registers
- 16 memory management registers
- Extended function condition code register
- 4 interrupt control/status registers

MICROPROGRAMMED
- Expandable instruction set (on board)
- Writable/fixed control store capability
- Integral fixed/floating point processor
- Highly structured, comprehendible, modular design

SOPHISTICATED MEMORY MANAGEMENT
- Multi-user and multi-task timesharing structure
- Complete intertask protection and security
- Megabyte addressing space (expandable)
- Software protectable pages for shared re-entrant coding
- Dual mode operating capability

MULTIPLE STACK PROCESSOR
- Sophisticated program linkage through defined control stack pointer
- Multiple, general register, data stack processing

SOPHISTICATED INTERRUPT STRUCTURE
- 8 level maskable vectored prioritized hardware interrupts
- Second level prioritized expansion on each hardware level
- 256 levels of program controlled software interrupts
- Invalid memory access trap is a vectored interrupt
- Non-existent instruction trap is a vector interrupt
- Breakpoint instruction is a special vectored interrupt
- Automatic mode switching on all interrupts

HIGH THRU-PUT DMA/REFRESH CONTROL
- 8 level prioritized DMA requests and acknowledges
- Up to four Mega-byte/second DMA transfer rate without slowing program execution
- Up to 12 Mega-byte/second DMA transfer rate
- Integral transparent dynamic memory refresh control

EXTENSIVE HIGH LEVEL INSTRUCTION SET
- Multitude of data types handled
- Enormous variety of addressing modes
- General register and defined register classes of instructions
- Many very fast numeric and string macroinstructions
- Integral 16 and 32-bit integer and 64-bit floating point ADD, SUB, MUL, DIV, CMP, NEG, etc.
- Advanced character, byte and word string processing
- Microcoded high level language primitives

VERY HIGH QUALITY PHYSICAL DESIGN
- Four layer P.C. cards throughout system (internal GND and V_{CC})
- All bus signals interleaved with direct return ground path
- All bus signals active low; three-state to inactive level

INTELLIGENT CHANNEL CONTROLLERS
- Microprogrammed floppy disk and hard disk controllers
- Services multiple users I/O simultaneously and transparent to CPU program execution
- Reduces executive program complexity and speeds execution

SOFTWARE SUPPORT
- Multi-user/multi-task time sharing operating system includes sophisticated file management features
- Sophisticated resident macro-assembler
- Customized micro-assembler
- Superfast, super extended BASIC interpreter
- True PASCAL compiler (not interpreter)
- Advanced editor and word processor package
- More software coming

It should be clear from this list that the HEX-29 minicomputer is a powerful/sophisticated design. This is DIRECTLY attributable to the availability of the excellent Schottky technology I.C.'s available from AMD for use in microprogrammed digital systems.

In a well designed microprogrammed system there should be VERY few random logic gate packages required. In the HEX-29 CPU, there are only a few gates used as such. If anywhere near 20% of a microprogrammed system is composed of gate packages, it is probable that the design can be further simplified to replace the random logic with microcode and/or structured logic techniques. It is important to note that the more functions that are implemented with structured logic and controlled by microcode bits, the more versatile and general is the whole design.

MICROPROGRAMMED MACHINES

It is highly recommended that AMD's MICROPROGRAMMING HANDBOOK be studied before this application note if a detailed understanding of the HEX-29 CPU is desired. The idea is, of course, that the basic principles of microprogrammed machines be familiar before this specific example is examined. The Am2900 Learning and Evaluation Kit is also recommended as a practical introduction tool. For those only interested in the capabilities of a well designed microprogrammed CPU, that reading is not entirely necessary, and Section V of this Application note will be superfluous. Section IV is a more general discussion for these readers, but is also necessary for those going on to Section V.

A short discussion of microprogrammed systems appears here only as a short refresher for those who have studied the MICROPROGRAMMING HANDBOOK by John Mick and Jim Brick of AMD.

Any microprogrammed machine can be divided into the following two discrete parts:

1. Control store and microprogram control
2. Data routing and function logic

These two sections of a microprogrammed machine are really quite nearly independent. In effect, the control store and microprogram control section is the 'boss and brains' of the operation. It issues all of the orders and makes all the decisions. The data routing and function logic devices are merely puppets that carry out the commands selected by the microprogram control logic from the control store. Note that 'microword memory' and 'microcode' are used interchangeably with 'control store' and are synonomous.

Control Store and Microprogram Control

The control store is simply a number of PROM's. The number of locations in this memory is chosen to be large enough to hold the desired number of microprogram routines. The width of the word is chosen to have sufficient bits to control all of the possible functions in the data routing and function logic. Admittedly, RAM or EPROM could be used as the memory devices, but it is best to think of it as an array of read only memory devices. So, schematically an example of a control store array looks like Figure 1.

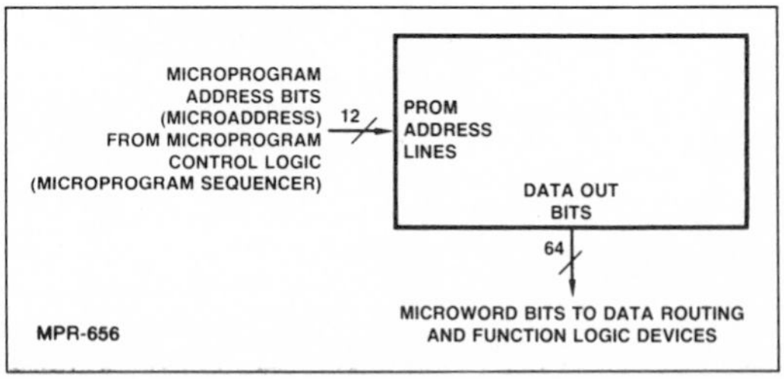

Figure 1.

In practice, there is a register between the microword data bits and the actual data routing and function control devices. This register assures that all bits change simultaneously at the beginning of each new microinstruction cycle and allows the execution of one microinstruction with the fetching of the next. The addition of this 'pipeline register' is shown in the Figure 2 expansion of our block schematic.

The remaining part of this section is the microprogram control unit, more commonly called the microprogram sequencer. The microprogram sequencer is nothing more than a presettable binary counter with a few extra functions. Figure 3 shows this device in place.

We show the sequencer as a 12-bit binary counter with a few other inputs. The outputs (Y) drive the address lines of the control store PROMs. So, each time the system clock rises, the counters increment and sequential addresses are accessed from the PROM. Note that the current output of the control store is captured in the pipeline register on this same LOW-to-HIGH transition. Thus, the sequencer is always fetching the NEXT control store word which will control the fetching of the next, and so on and so on.

Note that there are several bits from the pipeline register that are routed back to the sequencer. In our example, 12 bits are used as a microword branch address and another bit is used as a preset enable (load) line. Normally, each cycle of the system clock increments the sequencer outputs and the next microword is fetched from the control store. However, somewhere down the line we are going to want to branch to a microcode sequence that is not 'in line' with the code that is currently executing. It is very easy to see how this is done.

The microaddress of the routine to which we want to branch is imbedded in the current microword, 12 bits in our example. The microword bit that is connected to the load input of the sequencer is coded to be low on this cycle. So, the sequencer, which is really just a 12-bit counter with a unique load control in our example, will cause the branch address we selected to pass through to the output of the counters and fetch the microword from the microaddress to which we branched. The routine will now continue to execute sequentially addressed microwords until we execute another branch code.

The only other really necessary function we need from our sequencer is the ability to do conditional branches. In other words, we want to be able to branch to some microcode routine, but only if a certain condition exists. As usual, this capability is easily added; only one multiplexer is needed. Figure 4 shows the new configuration.

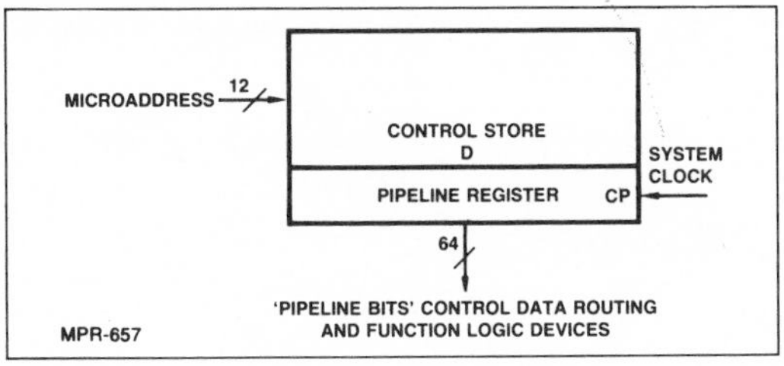

Figure 2.

Now two additional microword bits control the conditions under which a microbranch will take place. If input 0 is selected, a branch will always take place since the logic LOW level on input 0 will appear at the load input of the sequencer. Conversely, if input 3 is selected, a HIGH logic level is always routed through the multiplexer to the load input and a load is not performed. Thus the next sequential microinstruction is fetched. So far we can do branch and continue functions with the multiplexer.

If we select inputs 1 or 2 on the condition select multiplexer, we may get one of two conditions. If the selected input is HIGH, it will be routed to the load input of the sequencer and no load will take place. But if the selected condition is at a LOW logic level, the load input of the sequencer is pulled LOW, a load is performed, and a branch has been accomplished. Since a branch only occurs when the condition bit is LOW, this function is called a 'branch on condition = 0'. Clearly a 'branch on condition = 1' can be implemented simply by inverting the condition bit before it enters the multiplexer.

So as far as controlling the flow of microprograms goes, it is clear that we can make it look very much like assembly language programming of a microcomputer. We can execute sequential microinstructions (in line code), branch conditionally, or branch unconditionally. If we use real live sequencers like the Am2909, Am2910 or Am2911 instead of binary counters we get several other very important functions including micro-subroutining and looping.

When we substitute Am2909's, Am2910's or Am2911's as our sequencers, the final element of our complete microprogram memory and control section is in place. Figure 5 shows this configuration.

The next address PROM of Figure 5 converts the microcode branch function bits into one of two sets of bits that control the function performed by the Am2911's. Which of the two is chosen depends upon the logic level of the particular condition bit that is selected.

This is the basic structure of any microprogram control unit regardless of what the rest of the system looks like. The width of the microword data word, the microaddress field, the condition select field, etc., will change as needed, but the structure remains the same. Note that some of the microword data bits are used to control the microprogram sequencing logic. The bits left over are used to control the data routing and function logic in the device; i.e., everything else!

Data Routing and Function Logic

The data routing and function logic section of a microprogrammed machine closely reflects the job the device is to perform. In this respect there is some similarity with random logic

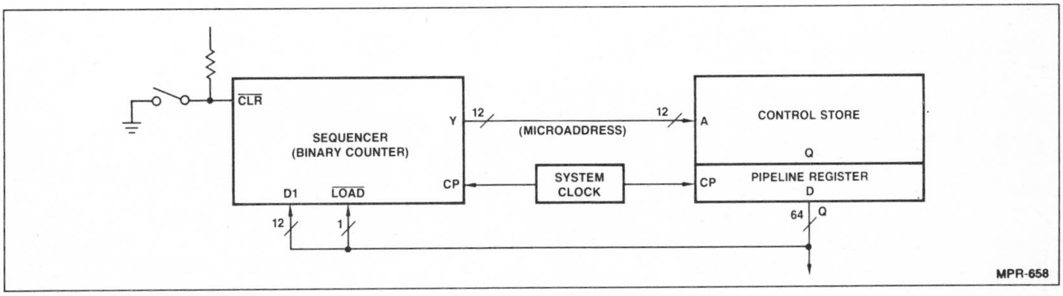

Figure 3.

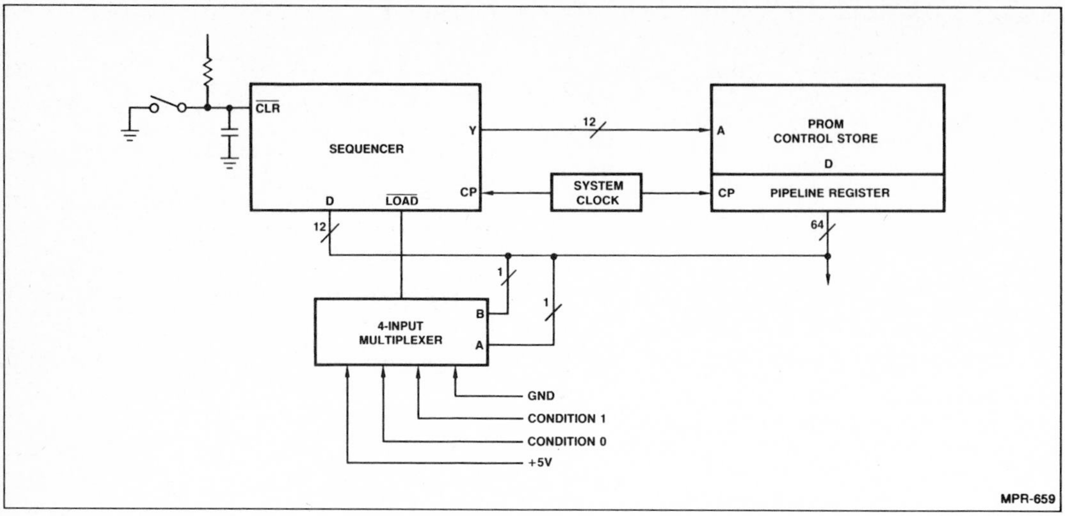

Figure 4.

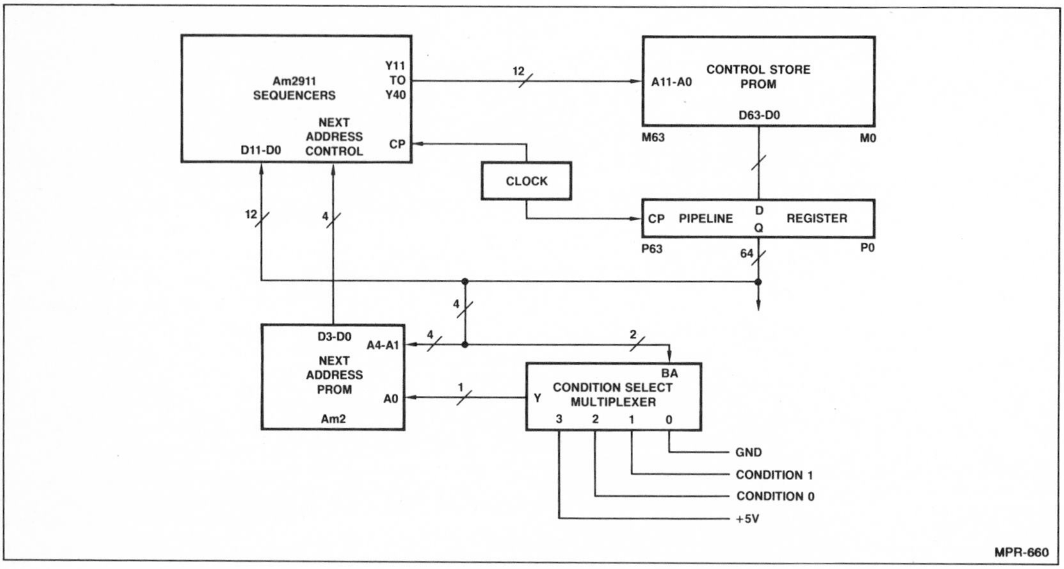

Figure 5.

designs. The key difference is the glue that binds all of the small functional units that make a device work. In a random logic design it is a more or less random array of gates and flip-flops that interconnect and control these functional units.

The chief advantage of a microprogrammed machine is that this random logic is largely replaced by the coherent sequences of control bits that is the microprogram. Problems such as race conditions, undesirable interactions between functional elements and marginal timing nearly disappear in a microprogrammed design. Often there are one or two internal data buses on which all transfers of internal data between functional units take place.

Think of several possible sources of information that may be needed in a particular design. If they are all three-statable devices, microword bits could be tied to the output enable of each and the desired device enabled onto the internal bus on a microcycle by microcycle basis. Likewise one or more devices may capture this data. Microword bits attached to the clock pulse (CP) inputs of registers and the like can achieve this function.

Further, microword bits select other functions to be performed, for example an ALU or shift function. Much of Section V of this application note will demonstrate the use of these data routing and function logic control bits.

GENERAL SPECIFICATIONS

The following section of this application note explores the design of the HEX-29 CPU on an intermediate level. It will be similar in detail to the detailed hardware and software specifications given for most microprocessors by the manufacturers. In other words, all the information needed to use the HEX-29 CPU, including bus timing and instruction set, are examined. This will serve to demonstrate what can be achieved in a medium level microprogrammed machine. It will also serve as a necessary transition for those planning to study the more detailed internal structure of the CPU in the next section of this application note.

It is very important, when designing a microprogrammed machine, that the target device be specified in detail approaching that given in this section. Only then can an intelligent attempt at hardware design begin. It is especially important to define a clean, simple, reliable interface between the microprogrammed device and other system elements. Considerable attention should also be paid to defining data types, instruction formats, interrupt requirements, etc.

Internal CPU Registers

The HEX-29 CPU has 36 internal registers. Of these, 16 are memory management (map) registers, 16 are general purpose registers, three are associated with the interrupt structure, and one is the condition code register.

Table 1 shows the functions associated with the 16 general purpose registers of the HEX-29. It is most significant that all 16 general purpose registers have alternate functions. This should not imply that they are not true general purpose registers however. Any register can be used as an accumulator, stack pointer, index register, memory pointer, data counter, etc., in most instructions. To increase coding efficiency and execution speed, however, some instructions use the defined register assignments in Table 1.

TABLE 1.

Name	Alternate Name	Alternate Function			
RF	PC	Program Counter			
RE	SP	Stack Pointer			
RD	RD	Data Passing			
RC	Y	Y Index Register			
RB	X	X Index Register			
RA	A	Accumulator			
R9	CT	Counter			
R8	SC	Scratchpad			
R7	R7	FP1	(LSW)		
R6	R6	FP1			
R5	R5	FP1	(MSW)		
R4	R4	FP1	(EXP)		
R3	R3	FP0	(LSW)	DW1	(LSW)
R2	R2	FP0		DW1	(MSW)
R1	R1	FP0	(MSW)	DW0	(LSW)
R0	R0	FP0	(EXP)	DW0	(MSW)

Notes: FP1 = Floating Point Register 1.
FP0 = Floating Point Register 0.
DW1 = Double Word Register 1.
DW0 = Double Word Register 0.

For example, the instruction set of the HEX-29 CPU can load immediate, push, pop, and move indexed and direct any of the multiple register combinations (FP1, FP0, DW1, DW0) in one instruction. One mode of indexed addressing and many byte processing instructions benefit greatly from the alternate use of some registers.

Condition Code Register

The condition code register contains all zeros in its upper byte. The bit assignments in the low byte are shown in Table 2.

TABLE 2. CONDITION CODE REGISTER BITS.

Position	Name	Function
Bit 7	U2	User Flag #2
Bit 6	U1	User Flag #1
Bit 5	U0	User Flag #0
Bit 4	H	Half Sign Flag (Bit 7; MSb of low byte)
Bit 3	Z	Zero Flag
Bit 2	N	Negative Flag (MSb of result)
Bit 1	V	2's Complement overflow flag
Bit 0	C	Carry Flag (arithmetic and shift carry)

The user flags (U2, U1, U0) are an extra feature of the HEX-29 CPU. They are not altered by any but five special flag modification instructions (SETF, CLRF, COMF, POPF, LDF). These op codes set, clear, complement, pop, or load the flags respectively. Since the user flags are immune to change except by these special purpose flag altering instuctions, they are excellent for passing status information between routines.

The half sign flag (H) is set if the result of an operation contains a 1 in the most significant bit of the low byte; otherwise it is cleared. This flag is useful in many byte processing and loop counting routines.

If the result of an operation is zero, the zero flag (Z) is set, or else it is cleared. This is the most useful of all the flags and is used on comparisons, arithmetic and logical operations, loop counting, etc. . . .

When the most significant bit of the result of an operation is a logic 1, the negative flag (N) is set. Otherwise it is cleared. Note that in two's complement notation, the most significant bit of a number determines the sign of the number. If it is a logic 1, the number is negative; if it is a logic 0, the number is positive.

If the two's complement result of an arithmetic operation results in a two's complement overflow, the V flag is set. This flag is also used as a general error flag by the HEX-29 CPU. For example, the V flag is set if a divide by zero instruction is attempted. In floating point notation, if the exponent becomes too large or small, (arithmetic overflow/underflow), the V flag is set to so indicate.

The carry flag (C) is used for two purposes. It is a source and/or destination bit in shift and rotate instructions, and as a carry-out bit when an arithmetic function result is too large to fit in the appropriate destination register. The convention with regard to the carry flag on addition and subtraction follows:

C flag = 1 if
1. Binary add results in a carry out.
2. Binary subtract results in no borrow.

C flag = 0 if
1. Binary add results in no carry out.
2. Binary subtract results in a borrow.

All of the condition code flags, except the user flags, have some special meanings in some of the complex 'macro' instructions. These are described in the detailed section on the HEX-29 instruction set.

Interrupt Registers

There are three special purpose interrupt registers in the HEX-29 CPU. They are:

1. Mask Register
2. Status Register
3. Vector Register

These registers are command driven, that is, the register selected is a function of the interrupt command being executed. More detailed information on the nature of these registers appears later in this application note.

Memory Management Registers

A sophisticated memory management structure is embodied in the HEX-29 CPU. Integral to this structure is the set of 16 memory map registers. These 8-bit registers contain transformation values that allow multiple users and tasks to share the processing time of the CPU without interacting with each other. Each task logged onto the HEX-29 is unique from all others through its memory map image. When it is chosen to run on the CPU, its memory map image becomes synonomous with the CPU memory map registers. More detailed information on this aspect of the HEX-29 CPU appears later in this application note.

Instruction Formats

The instruction formats of the HEX-29 CPU are simple and few in number. For this reason, the HEX-29 instruction set is not difficult to learn and use, even though it is very extensive and quite sophisticated.

Emphasis on the use of 4-bit (hexadecimal), and 8-bit (byte) fields in the instruction formats simplify the organization of the instruction set. All of the instruction formats used in the HEX-29 are shown in Figure 6.

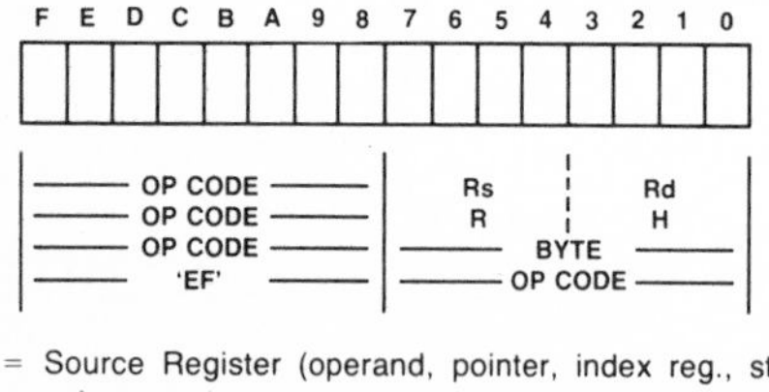

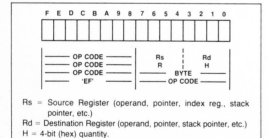

Rs = Source Register (operand, pointer, index reg., stack pointer, etc.)
Rd = Destination Register (operand, pointer, stack pointer, etc.)
H = 4-bit (hex) quantity.
Byte = 8-bit byte (data, index, offset, address, etc.)

MPR-661

Figure 6. Instruction Formats.

Most instructions involve operations on 16-bit words. However, the HEX-29 instruction set also includes op-codes that operate on the following data types:

1. 1 Bit (Bit)
2. 4 Bits (Hex or Nibble)
3. 8 Bits (Byte)
4. 16 Bits (Word)
5. 32 Bits (Double Word)
6. 64 Bits (Quad Word: Floating Point)
7. N Bits (Variable Format)

In addition to working on the fixed length data types, there are many 'macro' instructions that operate on variable length character, byte, and word strings in memory. These strings can be either contiguous in memory or in the form of linked lists. Several of these 'macro' instructions are highly optimized microcoding of the most critical routines used in high level language processing.

The multiplicity of data types processed efficiently by the HEX-29 increases its ability to meet the diverse demands of modern computing.

Addressing Modes and Assembly Language

Much of the power and simplicity of the HEX-29 instruction set is derived from the large number of useful addressing modes available for the most used basic functions such as MOV, ADD, SUB, INC, DEC, CMP, etc. Addressing modes specify where operands of an instruction are to be found and where the result is to be stored.

The 16 general purpose 16-bit registers are designated R0, R1, R2 . . . RC, RD, RE, RF. These are the primary names of the 16 registers and refer directly to the corresponding registers. In other words, when 'RD' is written in a HEX-29 Assembly Language (HAL) program, the contents of this register are used as an operand or destination in the instruction.

The use of a register as a pointer to memory is called memory pointer addressing. The names M0, M1, M2, . . . MC, MD, ME, MF apply to the 16 general purpose registers when they are used as memory pointers.

When a register points to a memory location which contains the address of the memory location holding the value of interest, the register is said to be an "indirect pointer". The names I0, I1, I2, . . . IC, ID, IE, IF are used to specify the 16 general purpose registers when they are being used with this type of addressing.

Indexed addressing is possible using the names Z0, Z1, Z2, . . . , ZC, ZD, ZE. The use of one of these names means that the data is at the address formed by adding the contents of the register referenced to the contents of word following the instruction in main memory.

Most often, when a register is used as a memory pointer (MD for example), or as an indirect pointer (I9 for example), it is extremely desirable that the register auto-increment or perhaps auto-decrement since programs, lists, and stacks are ordered in a positive direction through memory.

In HEX-29 Assembly Language (HAL) it is quite simple to specify that a memory, indirect pointer register, etc. is auto-incremented or auto-decremented by appending a '+' or '−' character to the respective register specification.

For example:

MOV M7+, R6 — The contents of memory pointed to by R7 is moved into R6. R7 is then incremented.

MOV RA, ME− — Decrement RE. Then move the contents of RA into the memory location pointed to by RE.

It is significant that auto-incrementing takes place after the operation while auto-decrementing takes place before the operation; (auto-post-increment and auto-pre-decrement.)

Several very fundamental addressing modes arise from auto-incrementing memory and indirect pointers. Consider the following examples:

A. Program Counter (RF) as an auto-incrementing pointer yields 'immediate addressing'.
   MOV MF+, RA = Move immediate into RA.
   ADD MF+, R6 = Add immediate to R6.
   MOV MF+, RF = Jump to address in immediate word.

B. Stack Pointer (RE) as an auto-incrementing pointer yields 'stack addressing'.
   MOV ME+, R2 = Pop top of stack into R2.
   XOR ME+, R1 = Pop top of stack and XOR into R1.
   MOV ME+, RF = Return from subroutine!

C. General registers used as data stack pointers.
   ADD MD+, MD = Add top two members of data stack + leave result on top of the stack.
   CMP MD+, M8+ = Compare top members of two stacks + remove these values from the stacks.
   AND MF+, M6 = AND immediate word with the top member of stack pointed to by R6.

D. Program Counter (RF) as an auto-incrementing indirect pointer yields 'direct addressing'.
   MOV IF+, R7 = Move direct into R7.
   ADD IF+, RC = Add direct into RC.
   MOV IF+, IF+ = Move direct to direct.

It should be clear that these examples represent only a few of the most useful of many possible uses of auto-incrementing and auto-decrementing with memory and indirect pointers. Careful study of the HEX-29 instruction set will reveal many more uses not examined in these examples.

Classes of Instructions

The instruction set of the HEX-29 includes many different functions and a multitude of addressing modes. Nonetheless, all instructions fall into one of two classes of instructions. The general register class of instructions are extremely flexible because of the enormous number of variations inherent in each op-code. The defined register class of instructions permits extremely fast and memory efficient code for often used functions and register sets. The power of the HEX-29 instruction set is derived from an extensive combination of the most powerful and efficient instructions from each class.

General Register Instructions

In a general register instruction, the function and addressing mode are specified in the op-code field (upper byte). The lower byte then holds two 4-bit (hex) values that specify the registers used in the instruction. It should be clear, therefore, that for every general register instruction there are 256 possible specific actions that can be performed.

The full power of these instructions may not be evident without an example. A discussion of just 5 of the 256 possible variations on the MOV M+, R instruction will demonstrate the extreme flexibility of each and every general register instruction. Execution of the MOV M+, R instruction proceeds as follows:

1. Contents of Rs are moved to the address bus.
2. Rs is auto-incremented by one.
3. The data addressed by Rs is loaded into Rd.

In this instruction, Rs is used as an auto-incrementing memory pointer, hence the M+ notation. Rs and Rd are the source on destination registers. Below is the set of 5 examples of how the one op-code can be used to implement a number of important functions.

1. MOV MF+, R3 (W) = Load immediate word (W) into R3.
2. MOV MF+, RF (W) = Jump direct to address (W).
3. MOV ME+, R6 = Pop top of control stack into R6.
4. MOV MD+, R4 = Load next member of list into R4.
5. MOV ME+, RF = Return from subroutine.

Taking a few minutes to review this section and understand how all of these functions are achieved with the single MOV M+, R op-code should reveal the nature of the power and flexibility of the general register class of instructions.

Defined Register Instructions

A defined register instruction is an instruction whose function, addressing mode, and register assignments are all defined in the op-code field (upper byte). The low byte is then available for use as an offset for short relative branching instructions, an immediate byte or character, an 8-bit index value, an 8-bit logical mask, etc. With this class of instructions, often only one word is required for the entire instruction. This speeds execution and improves coding efficiency markedly in most applications. It is for this class of instruction that the alternate register function assignments appear in the model of the HEX-29 register set. An example of a one word defined register instruction with the two word instruction it can replace follows:

ADC X, A	26	Defined Register Instruction
ADC ZB, RA	0026	General Register Instruction

Both of the instructions accomplish the same thing. In both cases RB (X index register) is used as an index register and RA (Accumulator) is the destination operand. The value in memory at the address pointed to by the sum of the X index register (RB) plus the hex constant 26 is added to the contents of the Accumulator (RA) and the sum left in Accumulator (RA).

The significant difference between the two instructions is that the defined register instruction takes only half as much code (one word vs. two), and executes faster since there are fewer memory accesses and fewer machine cycles. Very often the defined register instruction will be adequate for the job. But when the choices of registers RB and RA are not acceptable or if an 8-bit index offset is not large enough, the general register instruction would be the proper choice. It allows any register pair to be specified as the index register and destination/accumulator and has a 16-bit index offset in the word following the instruction.

As mentioned earlier, it is largely the ability of mixing defined and general purpose instructions freely that makes programs written in HEX-29 Assembly Language very code efficient and fast.

HEX-29 Instruction Set

The HEX-29 instruction set is quite extensive. It not only offers all of the basic functions in a wide variety of addressing modes, it also includes a multitude of special purpose instructions. These special purpose instructions cover many important aspects of programming including program control, numeric processing, string manipulation and searching, list processing, etc.

Fortunately, all of these types of instructions fall into one of only four different instruction formats. These were shown in Figure 6. Table 3 shows all of the instructions for the HEX-29 machine.

TABLE 3. SUMMARY OF MNEMONICS ARITHMETIC OPERATIONS.

ADC	Add words plus carry
ADD	Add words w/o carry
ADDB	Add byte to word
ADDH	Add hex value (nibble) to word
DADD	Add double word values (32 bits + 32 bits → 32 bits)
FADD	Add floating point values (64-bit FP + 64-bit FP → 64-bit FP)
SBB	Subtract with borrow
SUB	Subtract w/o borrow
SUBB	Subtract byte from word
SUBH	Subtract hex value from word
RSUB	Subtract words in reverse order
DSUB	Subtract double word values (32 bits − 32 bits → 32 bits)
FSUB	Subtract floating point values (64-bit FP − 64-bit FP → 64-bit FP)
UMUL	Unsigned word multiply (16 bits * 16 bits → 32 bits)
SMUL	Signed word multiply (16 bits * 16 bits → 32 bits)
DMUL	Double word signed multiply (32 bits * 32 bits → 64 bits)
FMUL	Floating point multiply (64-bit FP * 64-bit FP → 64-bit FP)
UDIV	Unsigned word divide (16 bits ÷ 16 bits → 16 bits + 16-bit remainder)
SDIV	Signed word divide (16 bits ÷ 16 bits → 16 bits + 16-bit remainder)
DDIV	Double word signed divide (32 bits ÷ 32 bits → 32-bit + 32-bit remainder)
FDIV	Floating point divide (64-bit FP ÷ 64-bit FP → 64-bit FP)
CMP	Compare words
CMPB	Compare byte with word
CMPBA	Compare byte with byte
CMPH	Compare positive hex value (nibble) with a word
CMPHN	Compare negative hex value (nibble) with a word
CMPHA	Compare hex value (nibble) with another nibble
DCMP	Compare signed double word values
FCMP	Compare floating point values
NEG	Negate word (2's complement)
DNEG	Negate signed double word value
FNRM	Normalize floating point number
DTST	Test signed double word value for zero + sign
FTST	Test floating point value for zero + sign
INC	Increment word by one
DEC	Decrement word by one

Shifts & Rotates

ASR	Arithmetic shift right
ASL	Arithmetic shift left
CSL	Count and shift left (until MSb=1)
DSL	Double word shift left
DSR	Double word shift right
LSR	Logical shift right
RCL	Rotate closed left
ROL	Rotate left (through carry flag)
ROR	Rotate right (through carry flag)
VSL	Variable shift left (0 to 15 places)
VSR	Variable shift right (0 to 15 places)

TABLE 3. SUMMARY OF MNEMONICS ARITHMETIC OPERATIONS. (Cont.)

Logical Operations

AND	Boolean AND words
ANDB	Boolean AND byte with word
IOR	Boolean inclusive OR words
IORB	Boolean inclusive OR byte with word
XOR	Boolean exclusive OR words
XORB	Boolean exclusive OR byte with word
COM	Complement word
CLR2	Clear the specified 2 registers
BTS	Bit set
BTC	Bit clear
BTI	Bit invert
BTT	Bit test
CLRF	Clear specified flags
SETF	Set specified flags
COMF	Complement specified flags

Data Movement

MVN	Move, no flags altered
MOV	Move, update flags
MVM	Move multiple words
MVB	Move a byte
LDB	Load a byte
STB	Store a byte
MVH	Move a positive nibble
MVHN	Move a negative nibble
LDI2	Load immediate 2 registers
XCH	Exchange contents of two registers
DXCH	Exchange contents of DW1 and DW0
FXCH	Exchange contents of FP1 and FP0
XCHM	Exchange top two members of any stack
DUP	Duplicate top member of any stack
SWT	'Switch'. Store register indexed and reload indexed
JAM	Move any bit field from one word to another
SWP	Swap high and low bytes in a word
PSH2	Push any two registers onto control stack
POP2	Pop top two words on control stack into two registers
PSHF	Push flags (condition code register) onto control stack
POPF	Pop top of control stack into condition code register
PSH8	Push 8 registers onto control stack
POP8	Pop 8 registers from control stack
PSHD	Push R8, R9, RA, RB, RC, RD onto control stack
POPD	Pop R8, R9, RA, RBRC, RD from control stack
LDINT	Load interrupt register
RDINT	Read interrupt register
RMM	Read a memory map location
LMM	Load a memory map location
FMM	Fill memory map
BMBF	Block move bytes forward in memory
BMBR	Block move bytes reverse in memory
BMWF	Block move words forward in memory
BMWR	Block move words reverse in memory

PROGRAM CONTROL

EXR	Execute contents of register as an instruction
RTI	Return from interrupt
BPT	Breakpoint trap
JFS	Jump if specified flags are set
JFC	Jump if specified flags are clear
CFS	Call subroutine if specified flags are set
CFC	Call subroutine if specified flags are clear
JIFS	Jump indirect if specified flags are set
JIFC	Jump indirect if specified flags are clear
CIFS	Call subroutine if specified flags are set
CIFC	Call subroutine if specified flags are clear
RTFS	Return from subroutine if specified flags are set
RTFC	Return from subtoutine if specified flags are clear
JMP	Jump to the address specified
CALL	Call subroutine
CEX	Call executive (software interrupt)
BGT	Branch if greater than
BGE	Branch if greater than or equal
BLT	Branch if less than
BLE	Branch if less than or equal
*TTWB	Transition table word branch
*TTBB	Transition table byte branch
DBNZ	Decrement and Branch Non-Zero
BZD	Branch on zero or decrement
*CBB	Compare and branch if in bounds
BR	Branch
BSR	Branch to subroutine
BC	Branch if carry flag set
BNC	Branch if carry flag not set
BV	Branch if overflow flag set
BNV	Branch if overflow flag not set
BN	Branch if negative flag set
BNN	Branch if negative flag not set
BZ	Branch if zero flag set
BNZ	Branch if zero flag not set
BH	Branch if half sign flag set
BNH	Branch if half sign flag not set

Miscellaneous Instructions

NOP	No operation for 2 to 256 cycles
*SCNB	Scan for match with specified byte
*SCNW	Scan for match with specified word
*SEAF	Basic fixed entry length list search
*SEAL	Basic variable entry length linked list search

*These 'macro' instructions are examined in more detail on the following pages.

SUMMARY OF SELECTED 'MACRO' INSTRUCTIONS

UMUL	Unsigned 16-bit multiply 16 bits 16 bits → 32-bit answer R3 R2 → R3 (MSW of answer) → R2 (LSW of answer) → R1 (LSW of answer) → R0 (MSW of answer) If V=1 then R0 is not zero (Answer is longer than 16 bits) If N=1 then MSb of R0 = 1. (No particular significance) If Z=1 then answer is zero (R1 and R0 are cleared)
SMUL	Signed 16-bit multiply (Two's complement notation) 16 bits 16 bits → 32-bit answer R3 R2 → R3 (MSW of answer) → R2 (LSW of answer) → R1 (LSW of answer) → R0 (MSW of answer) If V=1 then answer is longer than 16 bits (overflowed LSW) If N=1 then answer is negative If Z=1 then answer is zero (R1 and R0 are cleared)
UDIV	Unsigned 16-bit divide 16 bits / 16 bits → 16-bit answer and 16-bit remainder R3 / R2 → R2 R3 holds remainder If V=1 then an attempt to divide by zero was refused If N=1 then MSB of answer = 1 If Z=1 then answer is zero (R2 = 0 R3 need not be zero)
SDIV	Signed 16-bit divide (Two's complement notation) 16 bits / 16 bits → 16-bit answer and 16-bit remainder R3 / R2 → R2 R3 holds remainder If V=1 then an attempt to divide by zero was refused, or overflow If N=1 then the answer is negative If Z=1 then the answer is zero (R2 = 0 R3 need not be zero R3 has sign of numerator
DADD	Double word signed add 32 bits + 32 bits → 32 bits DW1 + DW0 → DW0 ie. R3,R2 + R1,R0 → R1,R0 The C flag is treated the same as in Rngle word addition If V=1 then a two's complement overflow occurred If N=1 then the answer is negative If Z=1 then the answer is zero
DSUB	Double word signed subtract (Two's complement notation) 32 bits − 32 bits → 32 bits DW1 − DW0 → DW0 ie. R3,R2 − R1,R0 → R1,R0 The C flag is treated the same as in single word subtract IF V=1 then a two's complement overflow occurred If N=1 then the answer is negative If Z=1 then the answer is zero If one divides "8000" by "FFFF" (−32768 ÷ −1) the answer is "8000" (+32768). However, 8000 is a negative number in two's complement, so an overflow has occurred
DMUL	Double word signed multiply 32 bits = 32 bits → 64 bits DW1 DW0 → DW0,DW1 ie. R3,R2 R1,R0 → R1,R0,R3,R NOTE: The order of the answer words is as follows: MSW → R2 MSW − 1 → R3 MSW − 2 → R0 MSW − 3 → R1 (LSW)

SUMMARY OF SELECTED 'MACRO' INSTRUCTIONS (Cont.)

The reason for this seemingly unnecessary odd order concerns the results that are desired in DW0 (R0,R1) at the end of the operation. The desired result of 32-bit math operations are nearly always 32-bit answers. However, a 32-bit * 32-bit multiply can generate up to 64 bits. Therefore, the least significant 32 bits of the answer are stored in DW0 where the answer is expected on all double word (DW) instructions. The most significant 32 bits must be stored in DW1, therefore the seemingly reversed order of storage. If the V flag = 0 at the completion of an operation, then only the 32 bits in DW0 are significant and the user program can store this 32-bit double word without fear of losing significant bits. So, in the normal situation where only the least significant 32 bits of the answer is desired and the more significant 32 bits of the answer does not contain significant bits, the answer is where the normal convention specifies; in DW0. If the V flag is found set and it is desirable to save the 64-bit result rather than go to an error routine, a simple DXCH will exchange the contents of DW1 and DW0 and leave the 64-bit answer in a logical order with the MSW in R0 and the LSW in R3. It can then be buffered with any of the floating point register 0 buffer instructions. If V=1 then the answer has greater than 32 bits of significance.
If N=1 then the answer is negative
If Z=1 then the answer is zero

DDIV	Double word signed divide (Two's complement notation) 32 bits / 32 bits → 32-bit answer and 32-bit remainder DW1 / DW0 → DW0 Remainder → DW1 If V=1 then attempted divide by zero was refused, or overflow If N=1 then answer is negative If Z=1 then answer is zero (DW0 = 0. DW1 not tested)
DCMP	Double word compare (Two's complement notation) 32 bits − 32 bits → Nowhere (Update V,N,Z flags) DW1 − DW0 → Nowhere The C flag is treated the same as in a single word compare If V=1 then a two's complement overflow occurred If N=1 then the difference is a negative value If Z=1 then the difference is zero
DXCH	Double word exchange Operates on any contents of DW1 and DW0 DW1 → TEMP DW0 → DW1 TEMP → DW0 DW1 = R3 and R2 DW0 = R1 and R0 No flags are altered
DNEG	Double word negate (Two's complement notation) 0000 0000 − 32 bits → 32 bits 0000 0000 − DW0 → DW0 If V=1 then a two's complement overflow occurred DW0 = 8 0000 0000 If N=1 then the final value in DW0 is negative If Z=1 then the final value in DW0 is zero
TST DW0	Double word test value (Two's complement notation) Set flags based upon the contents of DW0 0000 0000 + DW0 → Nowhere (Update V,N,Z) If V=1 then a valid 2's complement value overflows the LSW If N=1 then the value in DW0 is negative If Z=1 then the value in DW0 is zero
FPADD	Floating point add Double Precision (64 bits) Standard HEX-29 floating point format FP1 + FP0 → FP0 If V=1 then an overflow in the 2's complement exponent occurred If N=1 then the answer is negative If Z=1 then the answer is zero
FPSUB	Floating point subtract Double Precision (64 bits) Standard HEX-29 floating point format FP1 − FP0 → FP0 If V=1 then an overflow in the 2's complement exponent occurred If N=1 then the answer is negative If Z=1 then the answer is zero

SUMMARY OF SELECTED 'MACRO' INSTRUCTIONS (Cont.)

FPMUL Floating point multiply Double Precision (64 bits)
Standard HEX-29 floating point format
FP1 FP0 → FP0
If V=1 then an overflow in the 2's complement exponent occurred
If N=1 then the answer is negative
If Z=1 then the answer is zero

FPDIV Floating point divide Double Precision (64 bits)
Standard HEX-29 floating point format
FP1 / FP0 → FP0
If V=1 then an overflow in the 2's complement exponent occurred or negative zero refused.
If N=1 then the answer is negative
If Z=1 then the answer is zero

FPCMP Floating point compare Double Precision (64 bits)
Standard HEX-29 floating point format
Compare the magnitudes of FP1 and FP0
If N XOR V = 1, then FP1 < FP0
If Z=1 then FP1 = FP0

NOTE: WE HAVE TO FURTHER DEFINE THE WAY THIS WORKS, BUT THIS INSTRUCTION WILL SET THE FLAGS SUCH THAT THE 2's COMPLEMENT BRANCH ON THE EF PAGE WILL WORK!!!

FPNRM Floating point normalize Double Precision (64 bits)
Standard HEX-29 floating point format
The sign of the mantissa must be in the MSb of the exponent word before this instruction is executed
Shift mantissa left and increment exponent until MSb of the MSW of the mantissa is one. (Operates on FP0 only)
If V=1 there was a 2's complement overflow of the exponent
The C flag is trashed
N=1 result is negative
Z=1 result is zero

FPXCH Floating point exchange Double Precision (64 bits)
Operates on any contents of FP1 & FP0 (R7 thru R0)
FP1 → TEMP FP0 → FP1 TEMP → FP0
FP1 = R7, R6, R5, R4
FP0 = R3, R2, R1, R0
No flags are altered

TST FP0 Floating point test Double Precision (64 bit)
Standard HEX-29 floating point format
Set the flags based upon the contents of FP0
If N=1 then the value in FP0 is negative
If Z=1 then the value in FP0 is zero

SEAL BASIC string variable / numeric or string matrix element search
The SEAL instruction provides a very flexible way to rapidly and efficiently search linked lists for a particular entry. In each entry in the list, the first two 16-bit words are ordered as follows: The first word of each entry is the link offset to the next entry in the linked list. The second word is the entry name word. Any 16-bit value can be used in this field.

The name of the entry to be searched for must be put in the accumulator (RA) before this instruction is executed. The format of the instruction is as follows:

SEAL F,Md where F is the literal binary value 1111.

The destination field of the instruction (Md) specifies the register that must point to the beginning of the linked list. Starting at this point, this instruction will link its way thru the list looking for a match between the word after the link offset word (the entry name) and the contents of the accumulator (RA).

At the completion of the instruction, the Z flag indicates the results of the instruction in the following manner:

Z=1 No match was found in list (End of list reached)
Z=0 A match was found and Md is pointing to the word after the entry name that matched the accumulator

SUMMARY OF SELECTED 'MACRO' INSTRUCTIONS (Cont.)

Since the link offset word is a two's complement value, it can link to any other location in memory. The link offset is equal to the difference between the address of the next link offset word and the address of the current link offset word, minus one.

Note that this instruction can be used to search linked lists with entry names that are much longer than 16 bits with ease. For example, if the entry names to be matched are 2 words long, all that need be done is to compare the word at which the pointer is aimed with the second word of the desired variable name. If it matches, then the pointer now points to the first element in the list after the double word entry name. If it does not match, the search can be continued by backing up the pointer to the link offset of the current entry and re-executing the SEAL instruction.

At the completion of the instruction, the contents of the register specified by the Md field in the instruction will contain the address of the word AFTER the variable name in the list entry that matched the one in the accumulator (RA). At the completion of the instruction the Z flag will indicate the results of the instruction execution. If the Z flag is at a zero level, the search was successful and the pointer to the table (Md) contains the appropriate value. On the other hand, if the Z flag is set to a one level, no match to the variable name in the accumulator was found anywhere in the linked list.

LO VN da da ... da da LO VN da ... da da LO VN ...

LO = Link Offset word
VN = Variable Name word
da = data entries irrelevant to instruction

SEAF — Basic fixed link offset variable search

The SEAF instruction provides a very flexible way to rapidly and efficiently search lists for a particular entry. It is slightly different from the SEAF instruction in that the link offset word is not imbedded in the list entries. Instead, this instruction assumes that all list entries are of the same length (even though the internal formats may vary). The value of the link offset is the immediate word following the BASF op code word.

Perhaps the most obvious use of this instruction is for searching a numeric variable list for a specific variable name followed by the value. The lists entries can be any length, so single and double word integers and floating point lists can all be handled with equal ease, but not all with the same instruction since the list entries will not be the same length for all of these.

The link offset word following the instruction is a two's complement number. Therefore, any fixed length can be searched forwards or backwards in memory. The link offset constant equals the number of words in each list entry, or its 2's complement for a backwards search.

Again the variable name word to be searched for must be put into the accumulator (RA) before the BASF instruction is executed. And the contents of the destination field register (specified by Md) points to the first element of the list. The form of this instruction is shown below:

SEAF 0,Md where 0 = binary 0000

SCNW — Scan for word

The SCNW instruction is of the following form:

SCNW Ms,Md

This instruction scans a table of words (pointed to by Rs) for a match with the contents of the accumulator. Each time a word is fetched from the table, Rd is incremented. If Rd contains zero at the beginning of the instruction, then it will contain the number of the words searched in the source table before a match with the accumulator occurred.

Alternatively Rd may contain a pointer to another table. When a match between the accumulator and the source table occurs, Rd will point to a corresponding entry in the 'destination' table.

If the source list pointer and the destination list pointer are the same, then the two tables are interleaved; ie. the combined list would start:

Source list word #1
Destination list word #1
Source list word #2
Destination list word #2
Source list word #3
etc.
etc.

SUMMARY OF SELECTED 'MACRO' INSTRUCTIONS (Cont.)

This instruction can be very useful in command processing routines and for searching lists that are not linked within the list itself (see BASS and BASF).

The last entry in the source list must be a zero. If no matches were found previous to this zero word, then the Z flag is set. If the Z flag was not set, then a match was found and the pointers are valid. This instruction is interruptable on a word by word basis.

SCNB Scan for byte

The scan for byte instruction (SCNB) works identically to the scan for word instruction except that the source list contains bytes packed into words. Thus the source list is only half as long as the destination list (if there is one).

Note that both lists must start on word boundaries. Only the low byte of the accumulator is used in the compare with the source bytes. The contents of the accumulator are not affected by the instruction. This instruction is interruptable on every other byte that is compared. The Z flag has the same meaning as for the SCNW instruction.

Instruction Matrix

A convenient way to present all of the basic op-codes of the HEX-29 CPU is by way of an 'instruction matrix'. The eight-bit op-code in the upper byte is broken into two nibbles. The most significant nibble of the op-code appears on the left side of the matrix shown in Figure 7. The lower nibble appears along the top row. The second matrix shown in Figure 8, is called the 'extended function' matrix. In the HEX-29 CPU, the low byte of the instruction word is interpreted as an 'extended function' op-code if the upper byte is an 'EF' hex.

Memory Management

The HEX-29 incorporates a sophisticated memory management structure. Though very clean and elegant in implementation, the capabilities of the processor are greatly extended by this circuitry. Transparent to the user not requiring its many features, this structure is vital to many very important applications; most significantly the support of multi-user, multi-task, time-sharing operations.

To all programs executing on the HEX-29, all memory addresses are 16 bits long. But before these 16 lines reach the system bus, they pass through the memory management section of the HEX-29 CPU. In this circuitry, the most significant four bits (A15-A12) are 'mapped' into eight bits on the bus (a 'write-protect' bit (WP) and seven address lines (A18-A12)). The net increase of three address bits expands the total addressable memory space to 512k words or 1 Megabyte. The WP bit is used to write protect the memory in blocks as desired by the executive program.

Since each of the 16 locations in the memory map represents a 4k word block (or page), up to 64k words can be addressed by a program at any time. Any location in the memory may contain any 8-bit value, so memory that is contiguous to a program need not be contiguous in physical memory. For clarity, Figure 9 shows schematically how this 'memory mapping' works.

The low 4k words of physical address space is reserved for the nucleus of an operating system; also called an executive or supervisor program. This is called physical page zero. The contents of the memory map can only be altered if the low location of the memory map contains all zeros. Since this is synonymous with the physical page zero address block, only the executive program is able to change the contents of the memory map. And since all I/O devices and channel control blocks are located in physical page zero, all I/O must also be done through the executive program. Likewise, all hardware and software interrupts invoke the supervisor automatically.

Because of this simple but fool-proof security scheme, complete protection of all users memory space and I/O devices can easily be maintained by the executive program.

Also note that the supervisor program can safely make programs that are re-entrant available to several users simultaneously as long as it write protects the code. Since user programs are often no larger than the host program under which it is running, this technique can result in a savings of 30% to 50% in system memory usage.

Occasionally, for special purposes, a single user may wish sole access to the entire resources of the system. Examples would include programs too large to run in a single user's 128k bytes of memory. Or perhaps a new I/O access method. In any case, it is possible for a single user on the system to gain complete control

	0	1	2	3	4	5	6	7	8	9	A	B	C	D	E	F
0	MVN R, R	MOV R, R	ADD R, R	ADC R, R	SUB R, R	SBC R, R	AND R, R	IOR R, R	XOR R, R	CMP R, R	RSUB R, R	INC R, R	DEC R, R	COM R, R	NEG R, R	SWP R, R
1	MVN M+R	MOV M+R	ADD M+R	ADC M+R	SUB M+R	SBC M+R	AND M+R	IOR M+R	XOR M+R	CMP M+R	RSUB M+R	INC M, R	DEC M, R	COM M, R	NEG M, R	SWP M, R
2	MVN I+R	MOV I+R	ADD I+R	ADC I+R	SUB I+R	SBC I+R	AND I+R	IOR I+R	XOR I+R	CMP I+R	RSUB I+R	INC I+R	DEC I+R	COM I+R	NEG I+R	SWP I+R
3	MVN Z, R	MOV Z, R	ADD Z, R	ADC Z, R	SUB Z, R	SBC Z, R	AND Z, R	IOR Z, R	XOR Z, R	CMP Z, R	RSUB Z, R	INC Z, R	DEC Z, R	COM Z, R	NEG Z, R	SWP Z, R
4	MVN X, A	MOV X, A	ADD X, A	ADC X, A	SUB X, A	SBC X, A	AND X, A	IOR X, A	XOR X, A	CMP X, A	RSUB X, A	INC X, SC	DEC X, SC	COM X, SC	NEG X, SC	SWP X, SC
5	MVN M+M	MOV M+M	ADD M+M	ADC M+M	SUB M+M	SBC M+M	AND M+M	IOR M+M	XOR M+M	CMP M+M+	RSUB M+M					
6	LDI2 R, R	CLR2 R, R	PSH2 R, R	POP2 R, R	XCH R, R	ASR R, R	ASL R, R	ROR R, R	ROL R, R	LSR R, R	RCL R, R	CSL R, R	VSR R, R	VSL R, R	DSR R, R	DSL R, R
7	BTS R, H	BTC R, H	BTI R, H	BTT R, H	MVH R, H	MVHN R, H	ADDH R, H	SUBH R, H	CMPHA R, H	CMPH R, H	CMPHN R, H	FMM R, H	VSR R, H	VSL R, H	EXR R	JAM R, R, W
8	BTS Z, H	BTC Z, H	BTI Z, H	BTT Z, H	ANDB B, A	IORB B, A	XORB B, A	SWT R, Z	MOV A, Y	MOV Y, A	LDBI R, R	STBI R, R	XCH M DUP M	COMF B	MVN CC, R	MOV R, CC
9	MVB B, A	MVB Z, Z	MVB Z, R	MVB R, Z	LDB M, M	STB M, M	ADDB B, A	SUBB B, A	CMPBA B, A	CMPB B, A	CMPB Z, Z	CMPB R, Z	CMPB R, R	CMPB M, M	SETF B	CLRF B
A	MOV M, R	MOV I, R	MOV M+M+	MOV M+I+	MOV M+Z	MOV M+M−	MOV A, X	MOV Z, I+	MOV Z, Z	MOV Z, M−	MOV RD, Y	MOV RB, Y	MOV R9, Y	MVM RR, Y	LDINT M+H	LDINT R, H
B	MOV R, M	MOV R, I	MOV R, M+	MOV R, I+	MOV R, Z	MVN R, M−	MOV R, M−	MOV I+I+	MOV I+, Z	MOV I+M−	MOV Y, RD	MOV Y, RB	MOV Y, R9	MVM Y, R, R	RMM R, R	RDINT R, H
C	MVM FP0 M+, DW0	MVM FP1 M+DW1	MVM FP0 DW0, M−	MVM FP1 DW1, M−	MVM FP0 Z, DW0	MVM FP1 Z, DW1	MVM FP0 DW0, Z	MVM FP1 DW1, Z	MVM X, FP0	MVM X, FP1	MVM FP0, X	MVM FP1, X	MVM X, DW0	MVM X, DW1	MVM DW0, X	MVM DW1, X
D	JFS B	JFC B	CFS B	CFC B	JIFS B	JIFC B	CIFS B	CIFC B	RTFS B	RTFC B	JMP R	CALL R	CALL X	CALL Y	CALL Z	CEX B
E	BR +L	B−R +L	BC ±B	BNC ±B	BV ±B	BNV ±B	BN ±B	BNN ±B	BZ ±B	BNZ ±B	BH ±B	BNH ±B	DBNZ ±B	BZD ±B	CBB ±B	EF
F	BR −L	BSR −L	CALLO B	JMPO B					BMWF M, M	BMWR M, M	SEAL M SEAF M	SCNW M, M	SCNB M, M	TTWB M, M	TTBB M, M	NOP B

Figure 7. HEX-29 Instructions.

	0	1	2	3	4	5	6	7	8	9	A	B	C	D	E	F
0	FADD	FSUB	FMUL	FDIV	FCMP	FXCH	FNRM FP0	FTST FP0								
1	DADD	DSUB	DMUL	DDIV	DCMP	DXCH	DNEG DW0	DTST DW0								
2	SMUL	SDIV	UMUL	UDIV												
3	PSHF	PSH8	PSHD	LMM A	RTI											
4	POPF	POP8	POPD		BPT											
B	MVM FP0, FP1	MVM FP1, FP0	MVM ABS, FP0	MVM ABS, FP1	MVM FP0, ABS	MVM FP1, ABS										
C	MVM DW0, DW1	MVM DW1, DW0	MVM ABS, DW0	MVM ABS, DW1	MVM DW0, ABS	MVM DW1, ABS										
D	CALL REL	CALL ABS														
E	BGT	BGE	BLT	BLE												
F	BMBF	BMBR	SRCH													

Figure 8. HEX-29 EF Instructions.

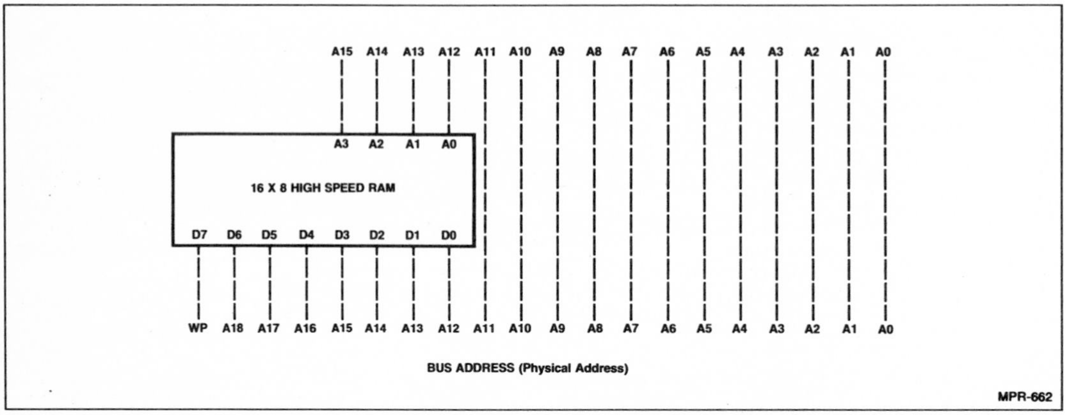

Figure 9. Memory Mapping Program Address (Logical Address).

and access to the system by assigning himself as the executive program. This can only be accomplished after a system reset. Hence only those with physical access to the computer (and who have a reset key) can accomplish this operation. This user is then empowered with all of the features and capabilities of the machine with no limitations. Direct access to all of the system I/O devices, the entire interrupt structure, the memory map, etc., is then at the command of the single user in the executive or supervisor mode.

Most often, each user needs only one or two 4k pages of memory in addition to the host program which is probably shared. Thus it would be very wasteful if each user were to have access to a full 65k words of physical memory space. For this reason, a page of physical memory has a special designation in the system.

The highest possible physical address block when write protected is called the 'invalid access' block. Whenever a user accesses memory that the supervisor has mapped into the invalid access block, the processor 'traps' to a special location in the supervisor program called the 'invalid access trap'. This occurs before the current machine cycle is completed. This is treated identically to an interrupt by the processor except that the current instruction is not completed.

Any number of actions can be taken by the supervisor at this time. This will usually depend upon the resources of the machine and the circumstances under which the problem arose. For example, the executive program could inform the program that its memory space had been exceeded, or perhaps just allocate another block of memory to that user's memory map and continue the execution of the offending program. A more detailed discussion of the sequence of events that takes place upon an invalid access appears in the section on the interrupt structure of the HEX-29 CPU.

The highest physical address page, when not write protected, is called the 'dead page'. No action of any kind takes place in this block and there is no memory there for the program to reference. Any number of pages from any number of users may be assigned to this physical page without fear of interaction. This is the block that will normally be assigned by the executive program to all user areas that are not needed or are not to be used.

Interrupt Structure

The HEX-29 CPU contains a powerful interrupt structure. As with memory management, this aspect of the CPU operation is largely transparent to users of the system. In most applications the HEX OPERATING SYSTEM FOR TIMESHARING (HOST) program services all interrupts. Nonetheless, it is useful to know the basic structure of the interrupt system. The three types of interrupts serviced by the HEX-29 CPU are examined in the following paragraphs.

The hardware interrupts are caused by signals from physical devices outside of the processor. These signals, generated by peripherals, their controllers, or the real time clock, serve to notify the CPU of some condition or requirement of the interrupting device.

The HEX-29 CPU has eight hardware interrupts. They are individually maskable and are prioritized into eight levels. Each priority level has its own vector associated with it. In other words, each interrupt level has a corresponding memory location through which program control is passed upon that level interrupt. These memory locations are within the defined executive page (physical page 0) and thus all interrupts cause the HEX-29 to switch into executive mode automatically. The eight hardware interrupt levels and the associated memory locations are shown below.

Hardware Interrupt Level	Memory Location of Vector
Highest Priority 7	0407_H
6	0406_H
5	0405_H
4	0404_H
3	0403_H
2	0402_H
1	0401_H
Lowest Priority 0	0400_H

So, for example, when an interrupt occurs on level 3, the HEX-29 CPU will enter supervisor mode, save the users PC and SP, and call the appropriate service routine at the address stored in memory location 0403_H.

Normally, each hardware interrupt level is reserved for a class of devices such as hard disc controllers, floppy disc controllers, serial channels, etc. If, for example, there are eight serial devices that are interrupting on level 0, the service routine is required to locate the one (or more) devices that are requesting service on that interrupt level and processes them accordingly. This could be done by polling all the serial devices whenever the interrupt was received. A more efficient technique, used in the HEX-29 system, is to further prioritize the like devices on a given interrupt level. Then when an interrupt occurs, a vector is read by the executive program that instantly informs it of the highest priority device requesting service on that level. When that device is serviced, the vector is read again to locate any other devices in need of service (if any), and finally resumes normal program execution when all devices are serviced.

A software interrupt is an instruction that, when executed, causes an interrupt to occur. The mnemonic used for this op-code in the HEX-29 CPU is 'CEX', which stands for 'call executive'. This instruction passes an 8-bit vector to the 'HOST' operating system which is used to determine the action requested by the program executing the CEX. Except that this interrupt is caused by a program rather than a physical device, the CEX operates in the same manner as a hardware interrupt. It vectors through memory location 040C. A pseudo software interrupt is the breakpoint 'BPT' instruction which vectors through memory location 040B. The BPT instruction does not pass an 8-bit vector to the executive and is thus useful in program debugging.

The third type of interrupt is called a 'trap'. A trap takes place when certain conditions occur that require the processor's immediate attention. For example, if the program currently running on the CPU tries to execute an op-code for which there is no defined instruction, an 'invalid instruction trap' occurs. This is essentially a service to notify a user that his program was defective and that an attempt was made to execute an op-code which has no meaning. These locations are left blank in the instruction matrix since they can subsequently be defined as new instructions. This 'trap' vectors through memory address 040D and acts identically to all other interrupts. The only other trap in the HEX-29 CPU is the 'invalid memory access' condition. This is discussed in more detail in the previous section on memory management. The 'invalid memory access' trap vectors through memory address 0408.

Table 4 shows the memory locations that are defined in the HEX-29 for interrupt handling.

TABLE 4. INTERRUPT MEMORY LOCATIONS.

Memory Location	System Defined Uses
040F	Reserved
040E	Reserved
040D	Vector for invalid instruction trap
040C	Vector for call executive (CEX) instruction
040B	Vector for breakpoint (BPT) instruction
040A	Temperature storage for user stack pointer
0409	Temperature storage for executive stack pointer
0408	Vector for invalid memory access trap
0407	Vector for hardware interrupt level 7
0406	Vector for hardware interrupt level 6
0405	Vector for hardware interrupt level 5
0404	Vector for hardware interrupt level 4
0403	Vector for hardware interrput level 3
0402	Vector for hardware interrupt level 2
0401	Vector for hardware interrupt level 1
0400	Vector for hardware interrupt level 0

Again, note that all interrupts are processed identically so that the one return from interrupt (RTI) instruction properly terminates all interrupt service routines.

DMA/REFRESH CONTROL

In order that an efficient multi-user or multi-task system be implemented, it is necessary that the processor not be burdened with the relatively slow transfer of programs and data between system memory and mass storage devices such as floppy and hard disks. For this reason, the controllers for these devices are designed with a high degree of intelligence and self-reliance. These controllers take virtually all of the burden of mass storage transfers upon themselves. This frees the HEX-29 CPU to execute programs for all users not waiting for these mass storage transfers to take place. Because these controllers are essentially separate special purpose microprogrammed CPUs, they are often called 'peripheral processors', 'channel processors', or just 'channels'.

For this scheme to be effective, both the CPU and the channel processors must be accessing system memory concurrently. Fortunately, the inherent structure and operation of the HEX-29 CPU is eminently suited to this requirement.

In every instruction there is at least one machine cycle during which the HEX-29 CPU is decoding or internally executing an instruction. During these machine cycles the CPU does not use the system bus; the system bus and memory are available for access by devices other than the HEX-29 CPU. This is called a 'Free DMA cycle' or 'bus available' cycle. During these machine cycles a channel processor may read or write memory without interfering with, or assistance from the HEX-29 CPU. The act of accessing system memory by any device other than the CPU is called 'direct memory access' or DMA since the channel processor is directly accessing system memory without CPU assistance or intervention.

Resident in the HEX-29 CPU is a very clean, very powerful multi-level prioritized DMA structure. Within this structure up to ten groups of devices can share the system bus on a priority basis. Normally the priority levels are assigned on the basis of transfer speeds . . . the faster the device is able to support memory transfers, the higher the priority it is assigned. In this manner several channel processors can access system memory concurrently at the intervals they require. The DMA structure of the HEX-29 CPU can support very high combined transfer rates with multiple DMA devices using this technique. With high speed memory, the HEX-29 CPU need not even slow down its program execution to support a concurrent combined DMA transfer rate of 4 Megabytes per second. With slower memory, this figure drops to about 2 to 3 Megabytes per second. Even this slower rate corresponds to concurrent DMA by one high speed hard disk plus several floppy disks plus room to spare. Still, the CPU can be halted, if necessary, to achieve combined DMA rates of up to 12 Megabytes per second maximum.

The support of dynamic memory in the HEX-29 system is simplified by signals associated with this DMA structure. Whenever there are no devices requesting the bus for DMA, a signal on the bus indicates this condition. Dynamic memory refresh controllers can take advantage of these unused free DMA cycles to refresh internal dynamic RAM chips if desired. Even when very heavy use of the bus by DMA devices occurs, it is unlikely that too few of these unused free DMA cycles will be available for the dynamic memory refresh controllers. In this event, however, another signal can be used to disable all other DMA priorities and allow the refresh controllers as much time as is required.

SYSTEM BUS AND TIMING

When specifying the bus signals and their timing relationships during the early design stage of the HEX-29 CPU, utmost attention was paid to simplicity and reliability. The result is that there are very few signals required to interface to the bus properly, and the timing requirements are quite straight forward and easy to meet.

The following section is a description of the mnemonic names and functions of the HEX-29 system bus signals:

System Bus

A18-A0 (Address Bus) Three-state outputs. A18-A0 are the 19 physical address lines of the HEX-29 system address bus. A18 is the most significant bit, A0 is the least significant bit. These outputs are three-stated whenever the bus is available ($\overline{\text{BA}}$ is low).

D15-D0 (Data Bus) Three-state and bi-directional input/outputs. D15-D0 are the 16 lines that make up the HEX-29 system data bus. D15 is the most significant bit, D0 is the least significant bit.

WP (also $\overline{\text{WE}}$) (Write Protect) Three-state output. WP is used to protect areas of memory from being written. Practically speaking this signal is active-LOW and would have been called $\overline{\text{WE}}$ (Write Enable) if not for possible confusion with the read/$\overline{\text{write}}$ signal which also must be LOW to write memory.

R/$\overline{\text{W}}$ (Read/$\overline{\text{Write}}$) Three-state output. The R/$\overline{\text{W}}$ signal determines whether a read or write operation is performed. A LOW level of the R/$\overline{\text{W}}$ line indicates a write memory is to be performed if VMA (valid memory access) is also LOW when the system clock (CLK) goes LOW.

$\overline{\text{VMA}}$ (Valid Memory Access) Three-state output. $\overline{\text{VMA}}$ is LOW during all cycles that a memory access (read or write) will be performed by the processor.

CLK Output, not three-state. CLK is the system clock. All timing in the HEX-29 system is defined relative to this signal. For convenience, the period of each machine cycle that the clock is high is called ϕ_1 (phase 1) and the period that it is low is called ϕ_2 (phase 2). All system 'chip selects' are derived from this signal.

$\overline{\text{SDMA}}$ Output, not three-state. $\overline{\text{SDMA}}$ is mnemonic for 'synchronize direct memory access'. This bus signal is LOW the cycle before DMA is permissible. The sole purpose of this signal is to notify DMA devices early of an upcoming 'free DMA' cycle. This will make it easier to 'grab the bus' very early in a 'free DMA' cycle to improve the address generation timing.

$\overline{\text{BA}}$ (Bus Available) Output, not three-state. $\overline{\text{BA}}$ is LOW on all cycles during which DMA is permitted by the CPU. When $\overline{\text{BA}}$ is LOW, all three-stateable outputs from the HEX-29 CPU card are turned off and control is relinquished to DMA devices for the current cycle. $\overline{\text{BA}}$ is mnemonic for 'bus available'.

$\overline{\text{STR}}$ (Stretch Clock) Input to HEX-29 CPU. When an addressed device is not fast enough to be reliably accessed (read or written) within the minimum access time of the HEX-29 CPU, it should pull the $\overline{\text{STR}}$ signal LOW. For each 40ns that $\overline{\text{STR}}$ is held LOW, the system clock is lengthened by 40ns and thus the access time required of the addressed device. This signal can be held LOW for as many as 40ns increments as required to meet the access time of the addressed memory or I/O device.

$\overline{\text{CLR}}$ (Clear) Output, not three-state. $\overline{\text{CLR}}$ is a LOW level pulse which is just a 'cleaned up' $\overline{\text{RESET}}$ signal. Any device that requires an initialization pulse should use this line.

$\overline{\text{I7}}$-$\overline{\text{I0}}$ (Interrupts) Inputs to HEX-29 CPU. $\overline{\text{I7}}$-$\overline{\text{I0}}$ are the eight hardware interrupt inputs. $\overline{\text{I7}}$ is the highest priority and $\overline{\text{I0}}$ is the lowest. These inputs are negative edge catching; that is, an interrupt signal is recognized by the interrupt circuitry in the HEX-29 CPU when the line goes LOW. These lines should be driven by open collector outputs so that multiple devices can interrupt on the same priority level.

$\overline{R7}$-$\overline{R0}$ (DMA Requests) — Inputs to HEX-29 CPU. $\overline{R7}$-$\overline{R0}$ are the eight DMA request inputs. $\overline{R7}$ is the highest priority, $\overline{R0}$ is the lowest. These lines are active-LOW; i.e., a LOW level requests DMA time.

$\overline{Q7}$-$\overline{Q0}$ (DMA Acknowledge) — Outputs, not three-state. $\overline{Q7}$-$\overline{Q0}$ are the eight DMA acknowledge lines that reply to the corresponding DMA request lines ($\overline{R7}$-$\overline{R0}$). A reply to the highest requesting priority is acknowledged by a LOW level on the corresponding acknowledge line. Only one of these lines will be LOW at any given time; i.e., the highest priority request gets the acknowledge.

$\overline{NRQ}$ (No DMA Request) — Output, not three-state. $\overline{NRQ}$ is LOW when no DMA requests ($\overline{R7}$-$\overline{R0}$) are being received. This is used primarily as a signal to dynamic memory refresh controllers that a refresh may be performed on any 'free DMA' cycle.

$\overline{DDMA}$ (Disable DMA) — Input to HEX-29 CPU. When $\overline{DDMA}$ is pulled LOW, no DMA requests are acknowledged. Essentially this line is just the highest priority DMA request line – except there is no corresponding acknowledge signal. This signal is normally reserved for dynamic memory refresh controllers. If the refresh interval is about to expire and some locations have not yet been refreshed, this line can be pulled LOW to disable all other DMA devices and assure adequate time to refresh the remaining locations. Note that $\overline{NRQ}$ is not LOW when $\overline{DDMA}$ is active (LOW). The $\overline{DDMA}$ line should be driven by open collector outputs.

$\overline{HALT}$ — Input to HEX-29 CPU. When pulled LOW, the $\overline{HALT}$ input will cause the processor to terminate program execution at the conclusion of the current instruction. At this time the bus will become continuously available for DMA as all three-state outputs of the HEX-29 CPU will turn off and $\overline{BA}$ will go active (LOW). This line can be held LOW indefinitely. When released, the processor will continue program execution. This line should be driven by open collector outputs.

$\overline{FETCH}$ (Fetch Instruction) — Output, not three-state. This signal is LOW only on memory read cycles when an instruction is being fetched from system memory. Otherwise this signal is normally not used except during system development and debugging for single instruction execution.

$\overline{RESET}$ — Input to HEX-29 CPU. This is the signal from which system reset ($\overline{CLR}$) is derived. Normally this input is simply grounded with a pushbutton or keyswitch to reset the HEX-29 system.

OSC (Oscillator) — Output, not three-state. This is the crystal controlled master oscillator from which the system clock is derived. The period of this oscillator is normally 40ns. (25MHz).

System Timing

In any microprogrammed system which must interface to a number of external devices (as a CPU must), it is critical that considerable forethought be given to the methods of inter-device communication. It is quite common to design and build devices that operate with very high degrees of reliability – only to find that overall system reliability is inadequate when the various devices are interfaced.

One of the utmost goals in designing the HEX-29 CPU was to develop an extremely reliable, easy to use, system bus definition. Simplicity and reliability go hand in hand and this is reflected in the HEX-29 system bus. Perhaps the single most important decision in this regard was to define that all memory and I/O device accesses by the processor or DMA devices would share one set of timing rules. In other words, one set of timing specifications applies to any kind of access of any device by any other device. Some systems have different timing requirements for all sorts of reasons; a few examples are listed here.

1. Memory read timing is more critical (shorter) if the memory being fetched is an instruction.
2. Variations exist in the set-up and hold times required on read memory vs. write memory cycles.
3. Memory devices and I/O devices use some different signals and timing specifications.
4. DMA devices are required to meet a different set of timing requirements than the processor.
5. Interrupt processing routines violate the normal memory access techniques.

Special cases carry special problems and should be avoided like the plague. It is always best and easiest to have all devices and situations share one set of control signals and one set of timing relationships. Another good practice put into effect on the HEX-29 CPU is the exclusive use of active-LOW bus signals. This is important in many respects. First, bipolar logic IC's can sink (pull LOW) far more current than they can source. Thus any noise spikes need to carry far more energy to force the signal into an invalid level. Secondly, all signals that three-state (turn-off) will be pulled-up (float) to the inactive level. Furthermore, this scheme tends to reduce the power required by bus signal drivers and therefore reduce heat dissipation.

Physical design is also important to system reliability. It is wise to use four layer PC cards with GND and V_{CC} planes as the internal layers, as do all of the HEX-29 system cards. An additional feature of the HEX-29 system bus is that all signals are interlaced with GND traces that return directly to the internal GND plane next to each bus signal. System termination should also be provided whenever signals must travel more than 18". Bypass capacitors should abound on all system cards, one per three IC's as a minimum. The HEX-29 averages one per IC.

The timing of each machine cycle in a HEX-29 system is a combination of synchronous and asynchronous characteristics. Actually, all signals are synchronous with – or are synchronized by – the master oscillator from which the system clock is derived. Thus, despite the fact that some signals seem to be asynchronous, they are actually synchronized automatically with the system clock. The simplicity of this approach will become clear once the relationship of all signals to the system clock is explained.

The conventions regarding the HEX-29 system clock are very simple. All machine cycles begin when the system clock goes HIGH and end simultaneously with the begining of the next machine cycle. The period of time that the system clock (CLK) is HIGH is called ϕ_1 (phase 1) and the period of time that it is LOW is called ϕ_2 (phase 2). See Figure 10 for clarification.

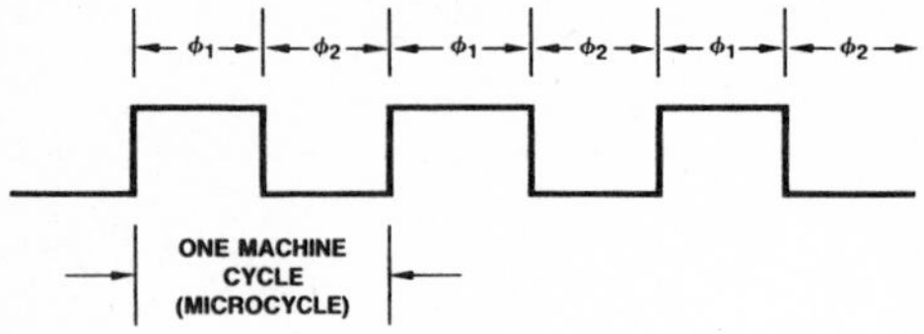

Figure 10.

During all memory and I/O accesses, the processor (or DMA controller) must guarantee that all address lines and control signals are valid for at least 20ns before the end of ϕ_1 (falling edge of clock). Depending upon the addressing mode, the processor will require a variable period of time to generate a valid address. Thus it is the responsibity of the processor to control the period of ϕ_1 to meet its requirements. If no external accesses are made by the CPU, ϕ_1 and ϕ_2 will last only 80ns each unless a DMA device takes control of the bus on that cycle and requires longer times.

Similarly, ϕ_2 is controlled by the memory and I/O devices on the bus. If none are being accessed on a particular machine cycle, no control need be exercised on the system clock and ϕ_2 will last for 80ns. However, when accessed, many memory and I/O devices more than 80ns to perform a successful read or write operation. They must be able to lengthen ϕ_2 of the system clock to increase the access time appropriately. This is accomplished with the $\overline{STR}$ bus signal. When a device is accessed that requires that ϕ_2 be longer than 80ns, it must bring $\overline{STR}$ LOW within 50ns of the falling edge of system clock (i.e., 50ns into ϕ_2). For every 40ns that $\overline{STR}$ is held LOW, the system clock is held in its present state for an additional 40ns. ϕ_2 can thus be extended indefinitely as required by the access time of the addressed device. ϕ_1 can also be extended in 40ns increments with the STR signal if so required by DMA devices with slow address generation times, or the like.

A DMA device must gain access to the bus before it can access the memory location that it desires. This is very simple. It simply pulls its DMA request line LOW and waits for the corresponding DMA acknowledge signal to go LOW in reply. Then, at the beginning of the first machine cycle which finds these signals plus SDMA LOW, the DMA device has been granted access to the bus and may immediately generate the appropriate signals on the address, data, and control buses to accomplish the transfer. The memory device being accessed does not care whether it is the processor or a DMA device on the bus since the bus signals and timing used by the memory card is identical for both. Thus it controls ϕ_2 with the $\overline{STR}$ signal as necessary and the access is completed in exactly the same manner as if it had been the processor controlling the bus. The Boolean equation for a DMA device gaining access to the bus follows – and Figure 11 is a schematic showing how easy the implementation can be.

$\overline{Q_X} \cdot \overline{R_X} \cdot \overline{SDMA} \cdot CLK$ = DMA device has access for the current cycle

X = any DMA priority level

The timing relationships for the HEX-29 bus are shown in Figure 12.

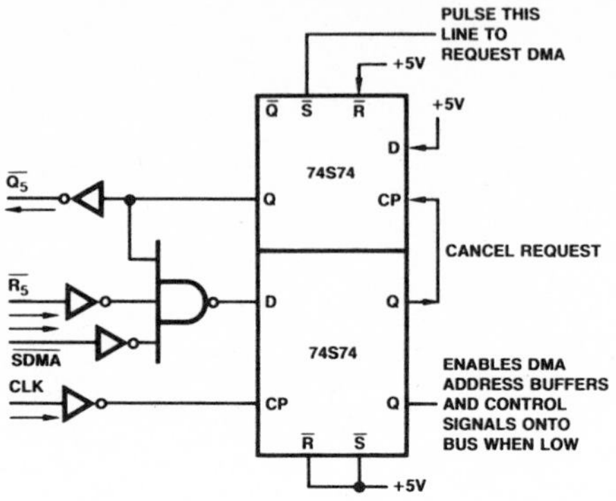

Figure 11. DMA Bus Signals.

INTERNAL OPERATION

Block Diagram

The block diagram of the HEX-29 CPU (Figure 13) shows the following functional modules:

1. System Clock
2. Microprogram Control
3. μWord Memory (Control Store)
4. Am2901A Bit Slice ALU/Register Sets
5. ALU Arithmetic Carry In Control
6. Shift and Rotate Linkages
7. Condition Code Control
8. Am2901A Output Bus
   a. Data Output Latches
   b. Address Latches
   c. Memory Management RAM
   d. Condition Code Register
9. Am2901A Input Bus
   a. Data Bus Input Registers
   b. Byte Swap Input Registers
   c. Microword Data Registers
   d. Clear Byte/Bit Set Logic
   e. Instruction Decode PROMs
   f. Condition Code Register
10. Interrupt Control
11. DMA/Refresh Control

Sections 8 and 9 are more difficult to isolate on the block diagram since they are the buses that connect many function modules together. A full detailed schematic of the HEX-29 is shown in Figure 14; a fold out drawing at the back of the chapter. A discussion of the function of each of the above modules follows.

System Clock (Figure 15)

All timing in the HEX-29 CPU is controlled by the system clock. The positive going edge of the system clock (LOW-to-HIGH transition) marks the end of one machine cycle and the beginning of the next. All input signals to the HEX-29 CPU from the system bus are captured on this edge. The next microinstruction is clocked into the pipeline register on this edge.

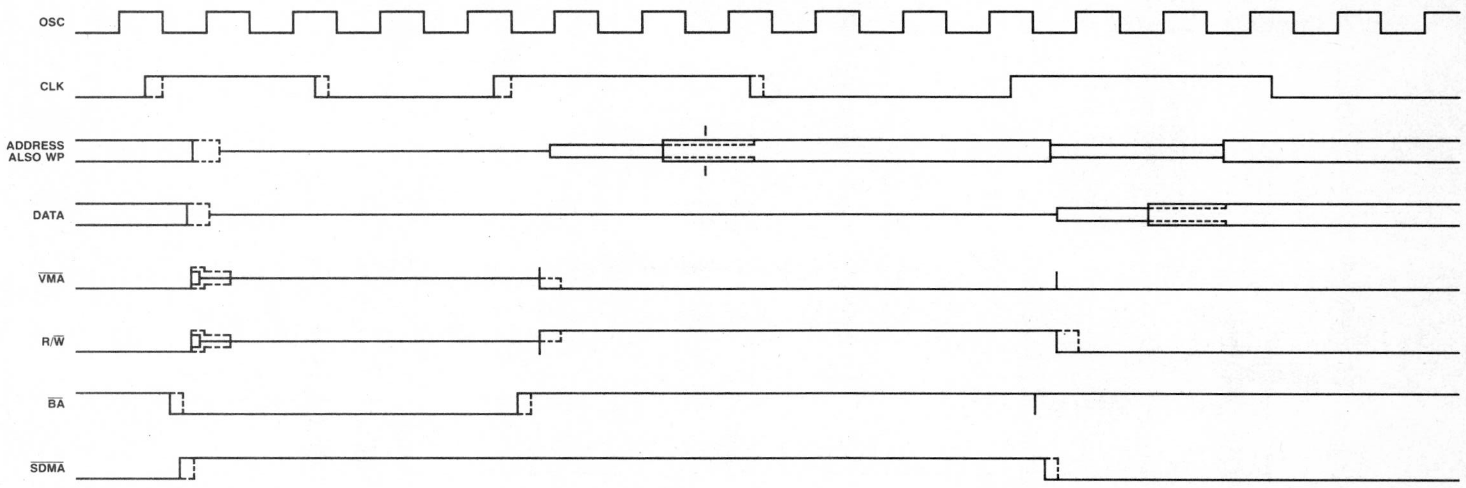
OSC
CLK
ADDRESS
ALSO WP
DATA
$\overline{VMA}$
R/$\overline{W}$
$\overline{BA}$
$\overline{SDMA}$

Figure 12.

Figure 13. System Block Diagram.

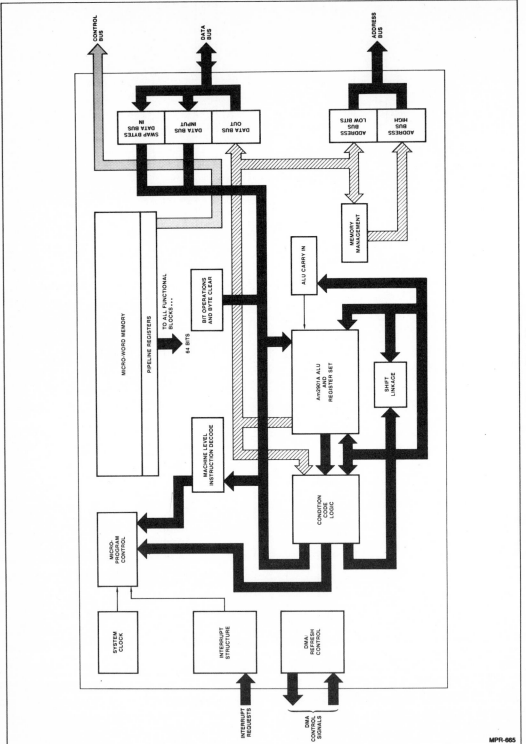

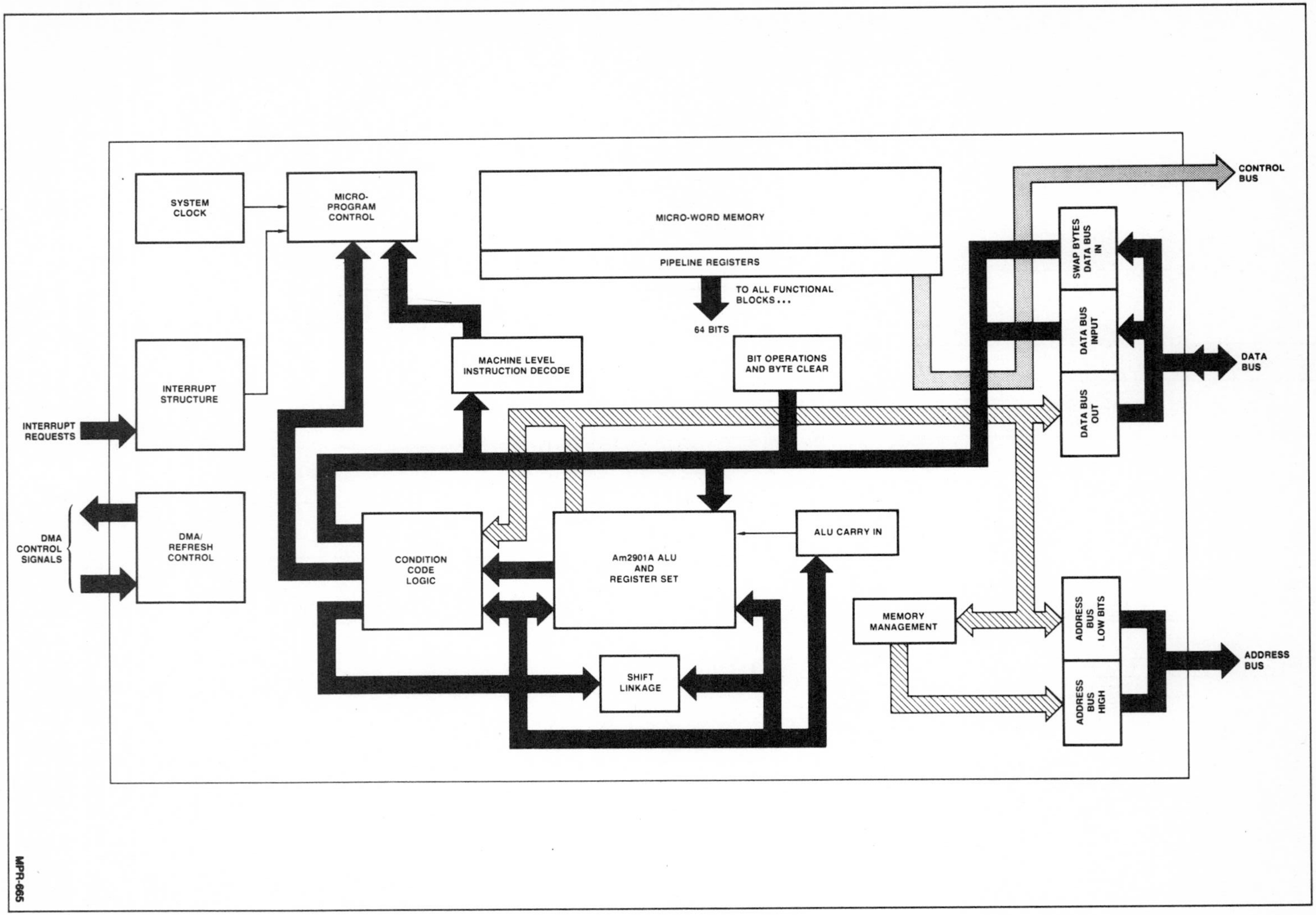

Normally a system clock is a simple square wave or more complex waveform with a fixed period and duty cycle. But the system clock of the HEX-29 CPU is microprogrammed. In other words, the period and duty cycle are selected by microword bits in each microcycle. The advantage of this approach is one of through-put (speed).

In any CPU, some internal operations require longer to execute reliably than others. And one or more of these operations requires the maximum length of time to complete reliably. This is called the worst case delay path or "critical path". Normally the period of time required to perform this "critical path" operation is chosen as the clock period for all instructions.

Since the "critical path" operation may take a factor of 30% to 100% longer to execute than typical operations, it is clear that much processor time is being wasted in any typical program. Two microword bits are used to control the HEX-29 microprogrammed system clock so that each microcycle lasts only as long as necessary for the operation being performed. An overall speed gain of about 30% to 40% is realized with this technique. This was discussed in detail in Chapter II and Chapter III.

The master oscillator from which the system clock is derived is a 25MHz crystal controlled oscillator. Phase 1 (ϕ_1) of the system clock cycle (Figures 10 and 12) is programmed to be 2, 3, 4 or 5 times the 40ns fundamental period of the oscillator. The duration of ϕ_2 of the system clock is 80ns. Since main memory will rarely be as fast as 80ns access time, a method to allow system memory cards to lengthen ϕ_2 is also provided with the $\overline{STR}$ bus signal. When the $\overline{STR}$ signal is low, the Am74S161 is disabled from counting and the state of the clock will not change until it is released and it counts out normally.

The conventions regarding the system clock are very simple and were chosen as the easiest to interface with a variety of memory and I/O devices.

All machine cycles begin when the system clock goes HIGH. The period of time that the clock remains at a HIGH logic level is called ϕ_1. ϕ_2 is the period that it is LOW. During all memory access (and I/O since I/O is memory mapped), the processor guarantees that all address lines and control bus signals (R/$\overline{W}$, $\overline{VMA}$,WP, etc.) are valid and stable at least 20ns before the end of ϕ_1. In other words, the CPU must make all bus signals valid at least 20ns before ϕ_2 begins.

Depending upon the addressing mode being used, the processor will require more or less time to make all necessary signals to the system bus and memory cards valid.

For example, indexed addressing requires an arithmetic operation from the Am2901B's rather than logical operations or a direct pass, therefore indexed addressing is bound to take slightly longer than immediate, direct, or pointer addressing.

It is for these indexed operations and some others that ϕ_1 can be lengthened in 40ns increments by microword bits ST_1 and ST_0. So the processor controls the system clock during ϕ_1 to meet its requirements. When there is no memory access, the minimum 80ns for ϕ_1 is generally more than adequate. Simple addressing modes require 80ns-120ns. The most complex addressing modes can take 160ns to 190ns using the worst case specs for all IC's in the address generation path.

At the end of ϕ_1 (the beginning of ϕ_2), the processor relinquishes control of the system clock to the memory or I/O device that is being accessed. Since I/O is mapped into normal memory space, there is only one set of timing rules for both memory and I/O accesses. If no more than 80ns is required to properly complete the read or write operation, then ϕ_2 will last only 80ns. But the access time of most main memory cards will be greater than 80ns so a way of increasing the duration of ϕ_2 is provided with $\overline{STR}$ bus signals.

If this signal ($\overline{STR}$) is pulled LOW within the first 50ns of ϕ_2, ϕ_2 will be lengthened by 40ns for every 40ns that $\overline{STR}$ is held LOW. Thus ϕ_2 can be extended indefinitely to match the access time of the device being addressed. Naturally this input should be driven by open collector outputs so that all cards can share the one $\overline{STR}$ line.

Though the $\overline{STR}$ signal is intended to be used during ϕ_2 on memory reference cycles, it works in an identical fashion during ϕ_1. This can be used to advantage by DMA controllers that require more than 60ns to generate valid address, data, or control signals on transparent DMA cycles.

A jumper option on the microprogrammable system clock allows the default period of ϕ_2 to be increased from 80ns to 120ns on memory reference cycles only. This is useful in systems where no memory or I/O devices have access times of 80ns or less, and/or when more than 50ns is required to pull $\overline{STR}$ LOW to lengthen ϕ_2. Figure 16 is a table of the ϕ_1 and default ϕ_2 periods available with the microprogrammed clock on the HEX-29 CPU.

ST1	ST0	$\overline{VMA}$	ϕ_1 Period	Default ϕ_2 Period	Default ϕ_2 Period with VMA Option Jumpered
1	1	1	80ns	80ns	80ns
1	1	0	80ns	80ns	120ns
1	0	1	120ns	80ns	80ns
1	0	0	120ns	80ns	120ns
0	1	1	160ns	80ns	80ns
0	1	0	160ns	80ns	120ns
0	0	1	200ns	80ns	80ns
0	0	0	200ns	80ns	120ns

Figure 16. Microprogrammed System Clock Timing.

Microprogram Control

The microprogram control section (Figure 17) of the HEX-29 CPU performs several functions; they are:

1. System reset and initialization
2. Interrupt and halt control
3. Machine level instruction to microinstruction mapping
4. Microinstruction sequencing and microsubroutining
5. Invalid Access Memory Management Trap

When the system reset button or keyswitch is closed, the input to a one-shot is pulled LOW. When it is released, the rising edge triggers a 500 μs pulse. This is synchronized with the system by gating it through a flip-flop driver by system clock. The resulting signal is used to zero the outputs of the Am2909 microprocessor sequencer. Thus, when the one-shot times out, the microprogram will begin execution at microaddress 000. The microcode needed to initialize the system is stored at this and the following several microaddresses and assures the proper system start-up.

Each time a machine level instruction is fetched, the microprogram control logic checks for a hardware interrupt or halt signal from the system bus. If either signal is active, the microprogram branches to the appropriate microinstruction address to execute the appropriate microcode to service the request. The interrupt routine will buffer user registers, switch to supervisor mode, and call a machine level routine through a vector table element as defined by the priority level of the interrupt. If the halt

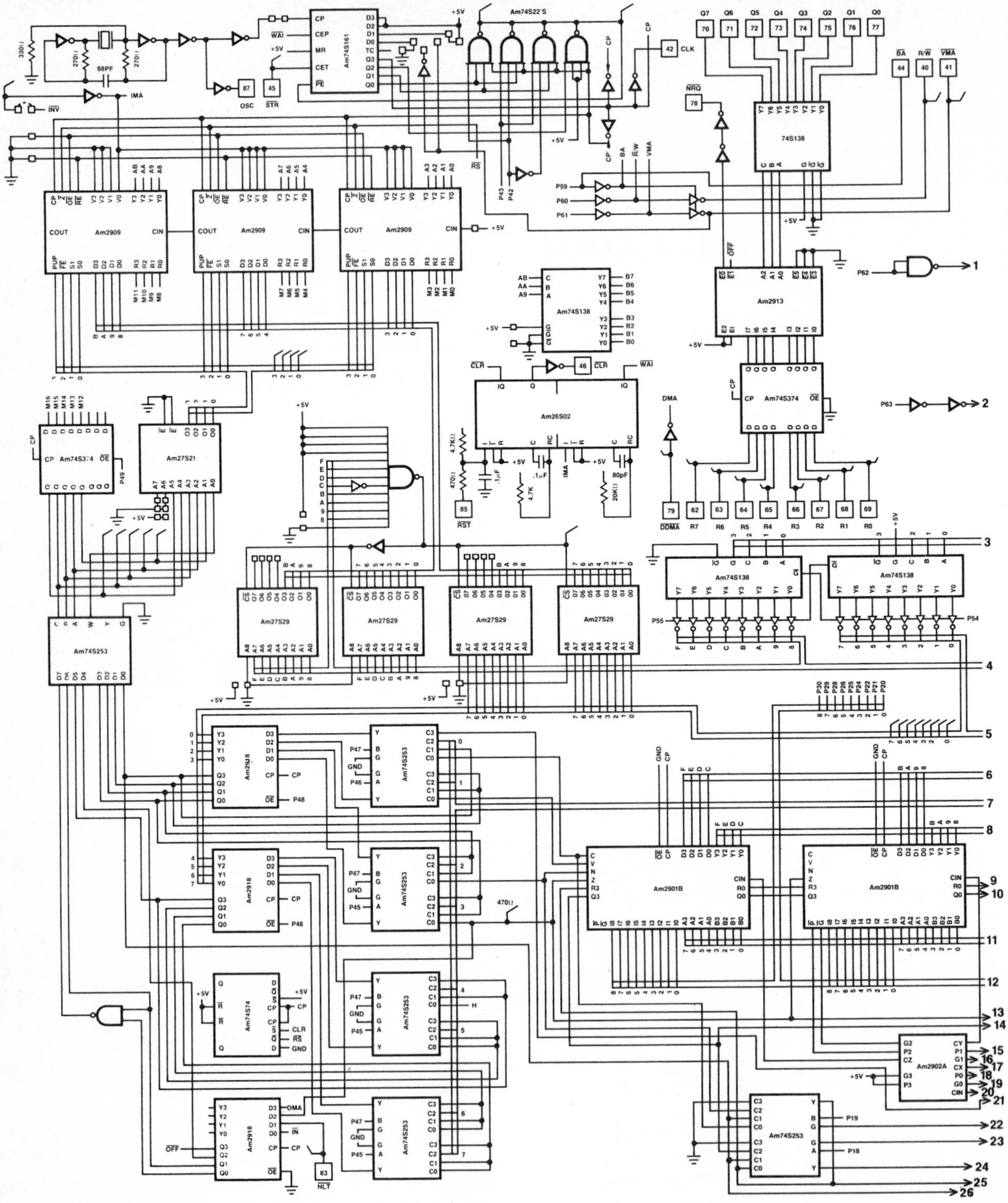
Am74S22'S
Am74S161
74S138
Am2909
Am2909
Am2909
Am74S138
Am2913
Am26S02
Am74S374
Am27S21
Am74S374
Am74S253
Am27S29
Am27S29
Am27S29
Am27S29
Am74S138
Am74S138
Am2918
Am74S253
Am2918
Am74S253
Am74S74
Am74S253
Am2918
Am74S253
Am2901B
Am2901B
Am2902A
Am74S253
OSC
STR
CLK
IMA
INV
RST
HLT
DDMA
DMA
BA
R/W
VMA
NRQ
CLR
WAI
OFF
+5V
68PF
330Ω
270Ω
470Ω
4.7KΩ
.1μF
80pF
20KΩ
4.7K

Figure 14a.

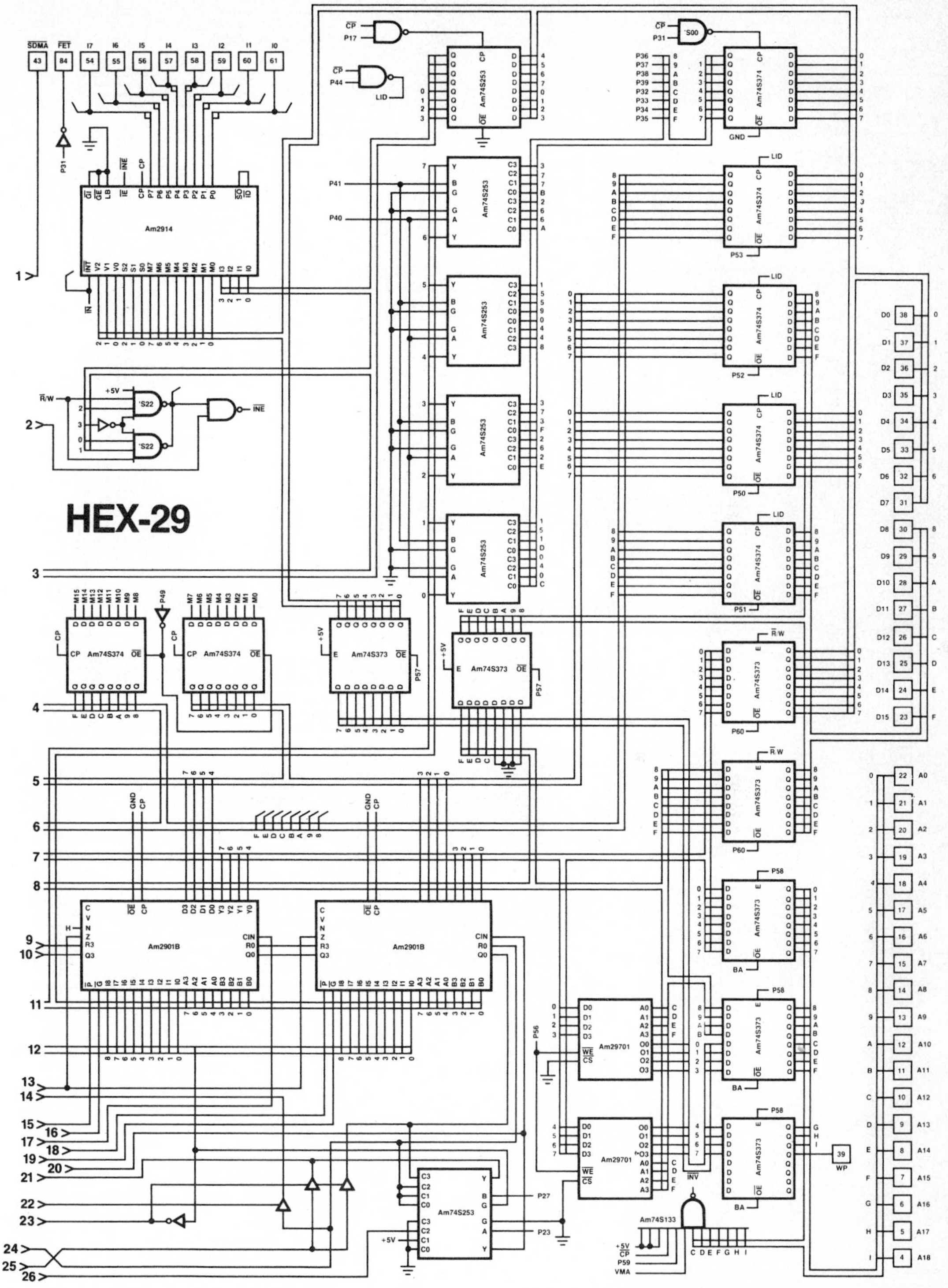
HEX-29
Am2914
Am74S253
Am74S374
Am74S373
Am2901B
Am29701
Am74S133
'S22
'S00
SDMA
FET
R/W
INE
LID
WP
VMA
INV

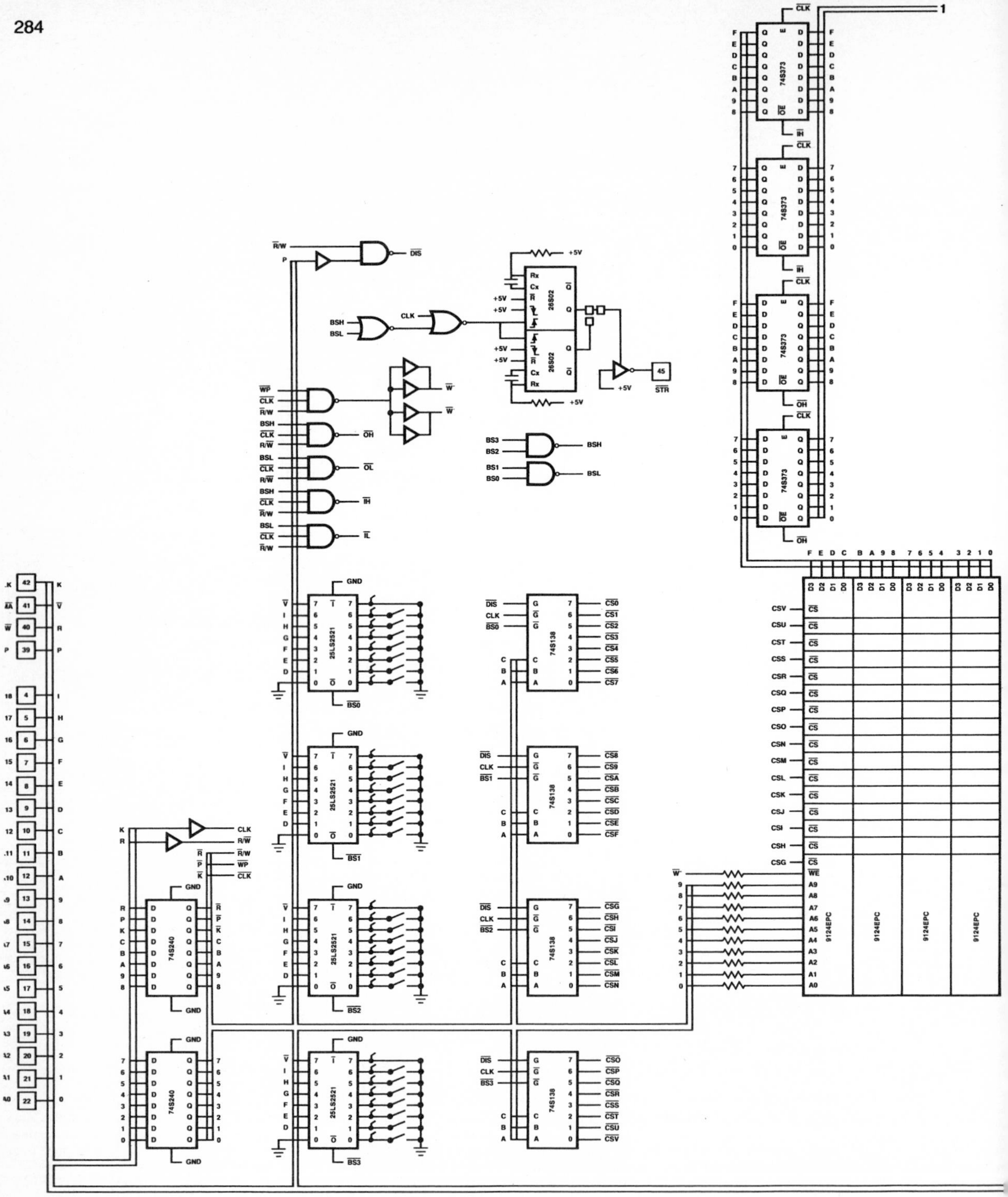

Figure 14b.

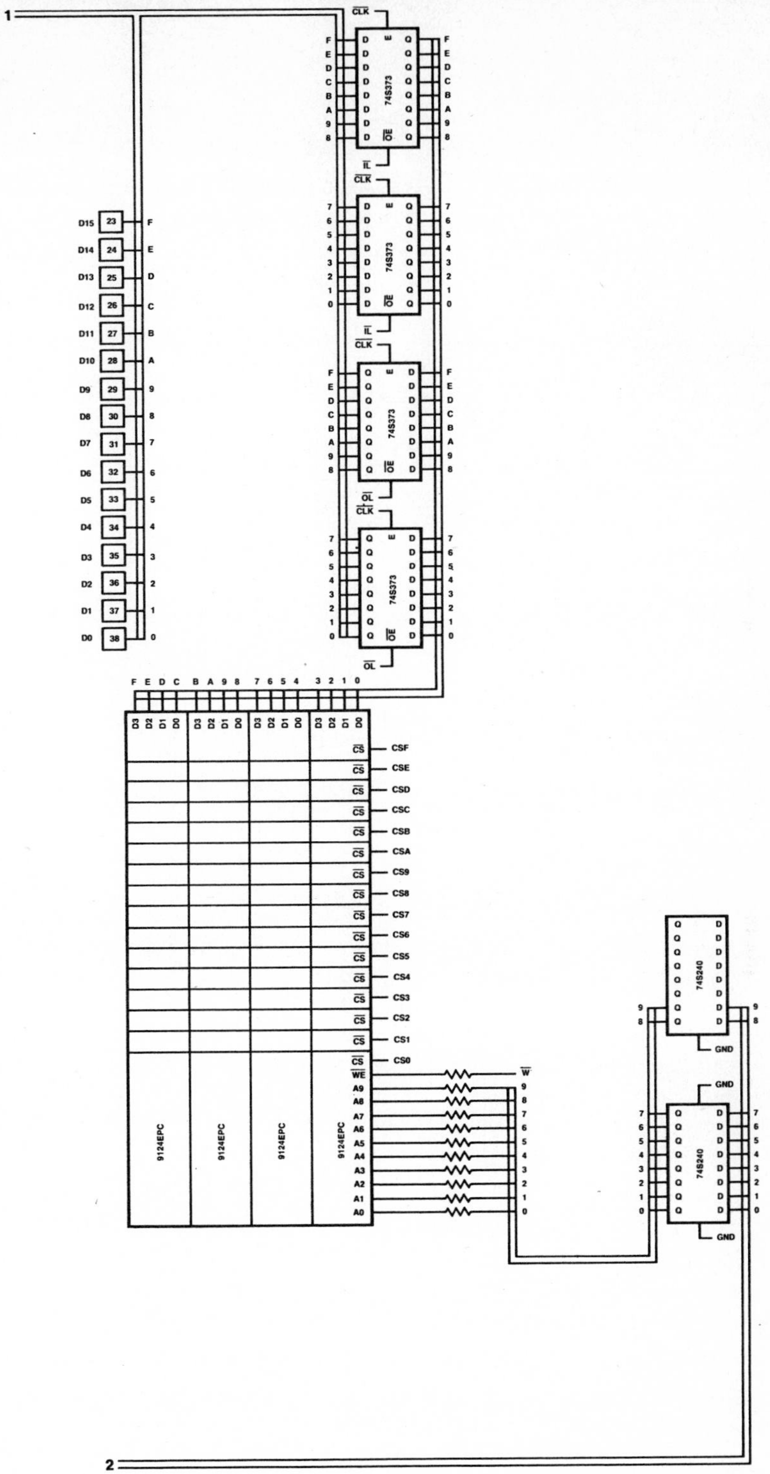
1
CLK
74S373
D
Q
OE
E
IL
OL
D15
D14
D13
D12
D11
D10
D9
D8
D7
D6
D5
D4
D3
D2
D1
D0
23
24
25
26
27
28
29
30
31
32
33
34
35
36
37
38
F E D C B A 9 8 7 6 5 4 3 2 1 0
D3 D2 D1 D0
CS
CSF
CSE
CSD
CSC
CSB
CSA
CS9
CS8
CS7
CS6
CS5
CS4
CS3
CS2
CS1
CS0
WE
W
A9
A8
A7
A6
A5
A4
A3
A2
A1
A0
9124EPC
74S240
GND
2

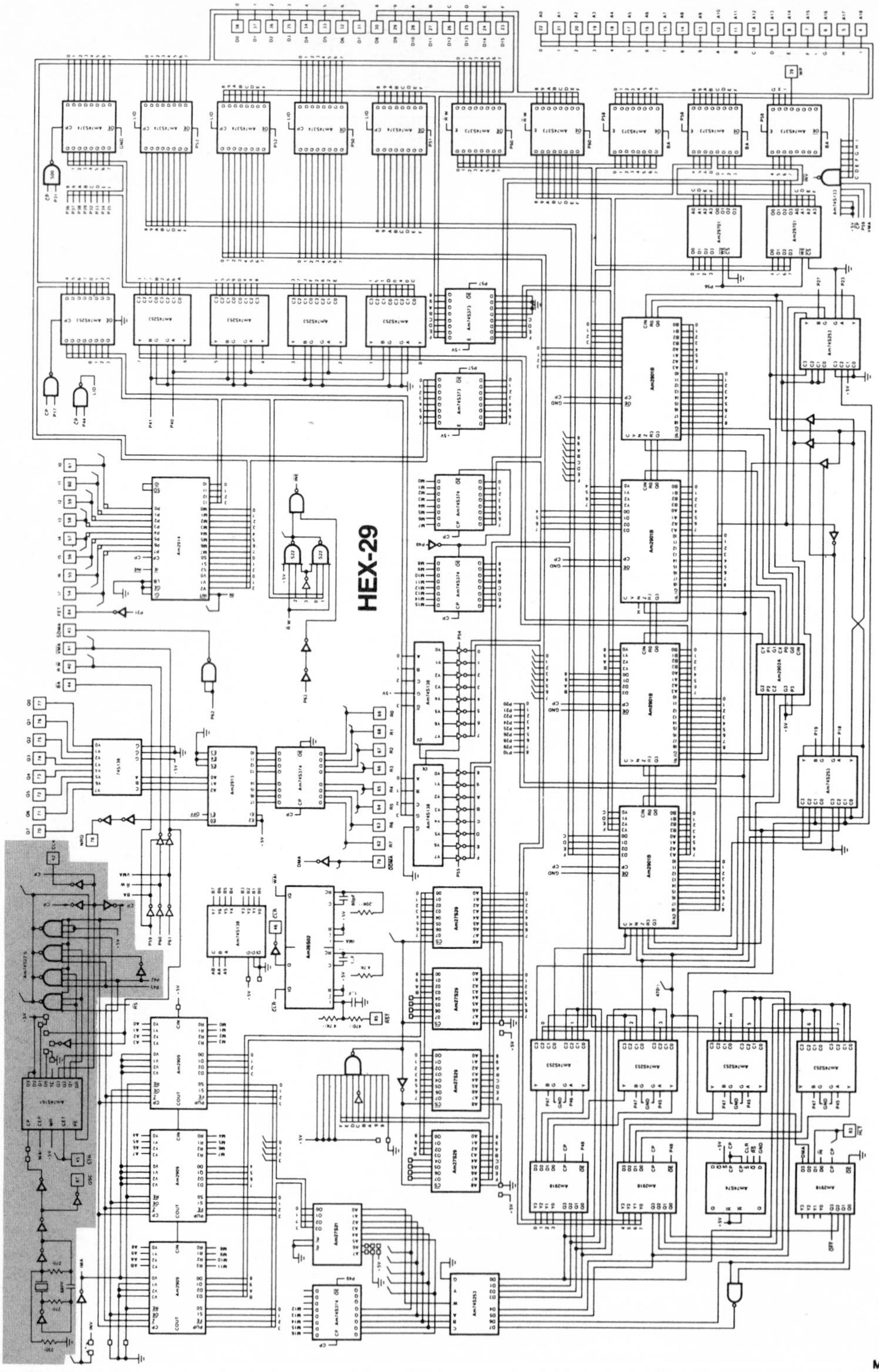

Figure 15.

MPR-666

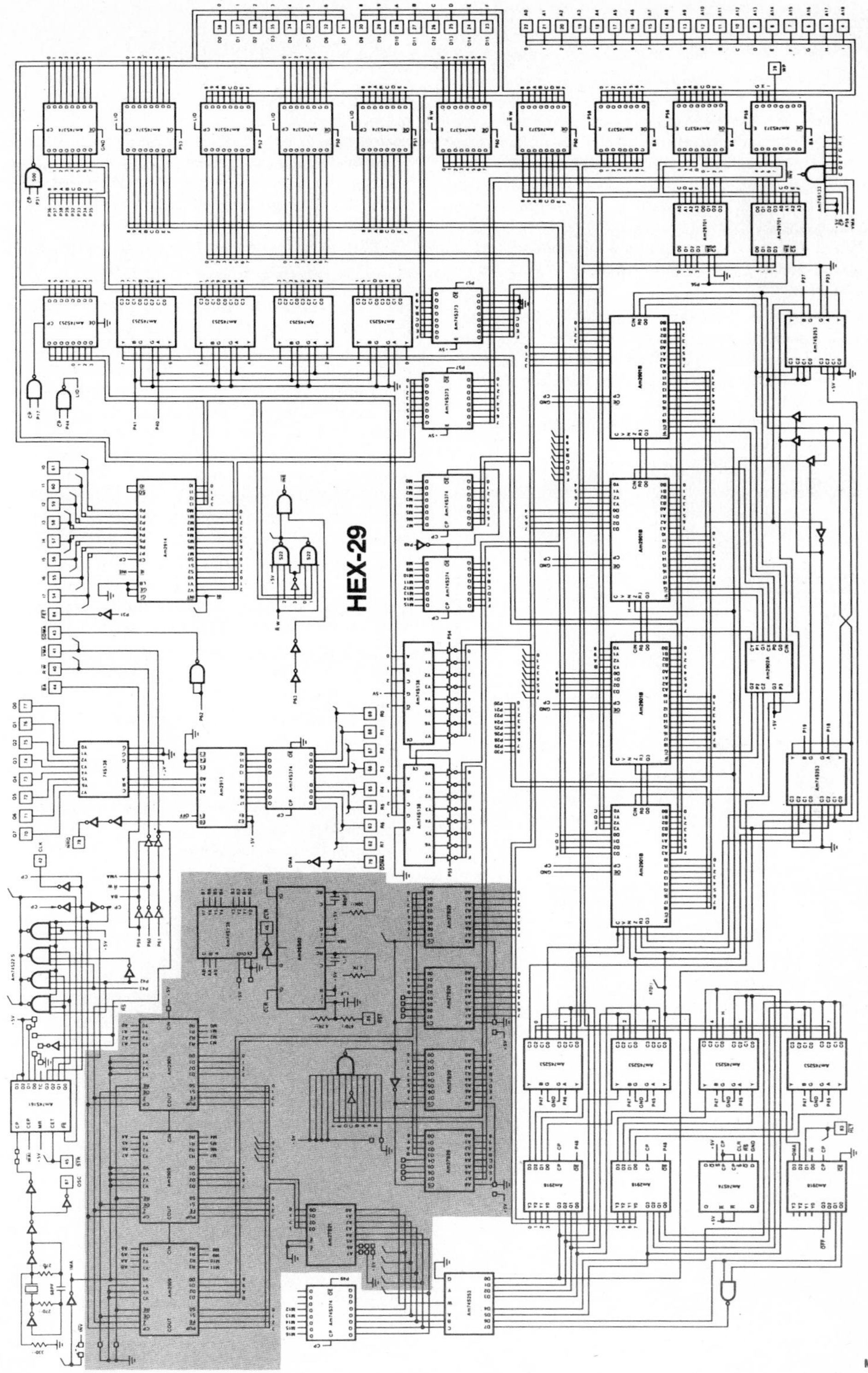

Figure 17.

MPR-667

signal is pulled LOW, the external system bus is released to DMA devices or refresh controllers until the halt bus line is released and the program continues execution.

When an instruction has been fetched and there are no interrupts or halt signals pending, the microprogram must begin executing microinstructions at a new microaddress. This microaddress is a function of the machine instruction to be executed. The "mapping" of the machine level instruction into a microaddress is done courtesy of the Am27S29 instruction decode PROM's. The op-code is placed on the PROM address lines and the microaddress appears at the outputs which are connected to the direct inputs to the Am2909's. The Am2909's simply pass this microaddress to the microword memory by executing a Branch to Address on direct inputs function.

This, and all other microprogram sequencer operations are selected by the outputs of the microprogram branch PROM which is driven by microword bits. This PROM, an AM27S21 contains the output combinations required to execute a variety of microprogram control functions including microbranching, microsubroutining, and two-way microbranching either unconditionally or upon condition code bits selected by microword bits. The function code for this PROM is shown in Figure 18.

As part of the multi-user, multi-task time sharing capabilities, the HEX-29 CPU provides an invalid memory access trap. In this structure, the executive program can assign any unused page of user memory space as either non-existent (transparent) or as an invalid access area. If any user instruction attempts to access memory in a page that has been assigned as an invalid access page, the microprogram control logic takes action.

Address	Function
0	BR C = 0 or continue
1	BR C = 1 or continue
2	BR V = 0 or continue
3	BR V = 1 or continue
4	BR N = 0 or continue
5	BR N = 1 or continue
6	BR Z = 0 or continue
7	BR Z = 1 or continue
8	BR H = 0 or continue
9	BR H = 1 or continue
A	BR LZ = 0 or continue
B	BR LZ = 1 or continue
C	BR HLT = 0 or continue
D	BR HLT = 1 or continue
E	BR IH = 0 or continue
F	BR IH = 1 or continue
10	BR
11	Not used
12	CALL
13	Not used
14	CALL N = 0
15	Not used
16	RTS Z = 1
17	Not used
18	RTS
19	Not used
1A	Not used
1B	Not used
1C	Not used
1D	Not used
1E	BRMAP IH = 0 or BR
1F	CONTINUE

Figure 18. Microprogram Sequencer Branch Code.

Before the current machine cycle completes, the next instruction address is forced to the highest value in the current 512-word microword block using the Am2909 OR inputs. At this point a microbranch to the invalid access trap microroutine is performed. The invalid access is processed just like another (highest) level of hardware vectored interrupt except that the current machine level instruction does not complete before the microprogram recognizes and acts upon the condition.

MICROWORD MEMORY

Any number of memory device types could have been chosen for the microword memory in the HEX-29 CPU. RAM has the advantage that it is dynamically alterable, but if this feature is utilized much more hardware support would have been necessary and the overall cost increased significantly. Besides, the effect of writable control store can be simulated with fixed memory devices by microcode bank switching at much lower cost and complexity if the feature is desirable. For development of new microcode routines, RAM writable control store in the address space of another computer system offers many advantages. This is particularly true if the other computer happens to support a micro-assembler and file management system as does the System 29.*

Though EROM's and EAROM's are also viable microword memory devices for microcode development, they are much too slow to make efficient use of the rest of the high speed microprogrammed processor in the production device.

Fuse-link bipolar PROM's are the only viable microword memory devices for production systems for a variety of reasons. They are very fast, (45ns maximum access on the HEX-29 CPU), small (512 x 8 in 20 pins), less expensive than fast RAM, and more flexible than a mask ROM would be. It is a simple matter to alter or extend the microprogram of commercial systems with fuse-link PROM microword memory.

As mentioned, the microword memory of the HEX-29 is composed of AM27S29 512 x 8 fuse-link PROM's and is shown in Figure 19. These space efficient 20 pin parts have worst case access times of 45ns over the commercial temperature and voltage range. Up to 4k of microword memory can be addressed by the set of three Am2909 microprogram sequencers on the CPU card. Space for up to 2k of microword memory PROM's is available on the HEX-29 CPU card. Though a perfectly adequate instruction set can be coded in less than 512-words of microword memory, the HEX-29 has a very extensive high level instruction set including 16 and 32-bit integer and 64-bit floating point ADD, SUB, MUL, DIV, CMP, and extensive buffering instructions. In addition to the extremely complete numeric processing package, numerous nibble, character, byte, and word macroinstructions are implemented with scans, linked and unlinked searches, block moves, and etc. A stack processor is a subset of this more than complete instruction set. For all of the capabilities of the HEX-29 CPU, less than 1.5k of microword memory was required. Thus, more than 0.5k of space remains for future expansion by the user before a larger PC card is needed (extremely unlikely).

Connections for the microword data, address and select lines are available at connectors at the top of the HEX-29 CPU card. Thus, it is quite straightforward to support off-board microword memory.

* System 29 is a development system for microprogrammed systems available from Advanced Micro Computers.

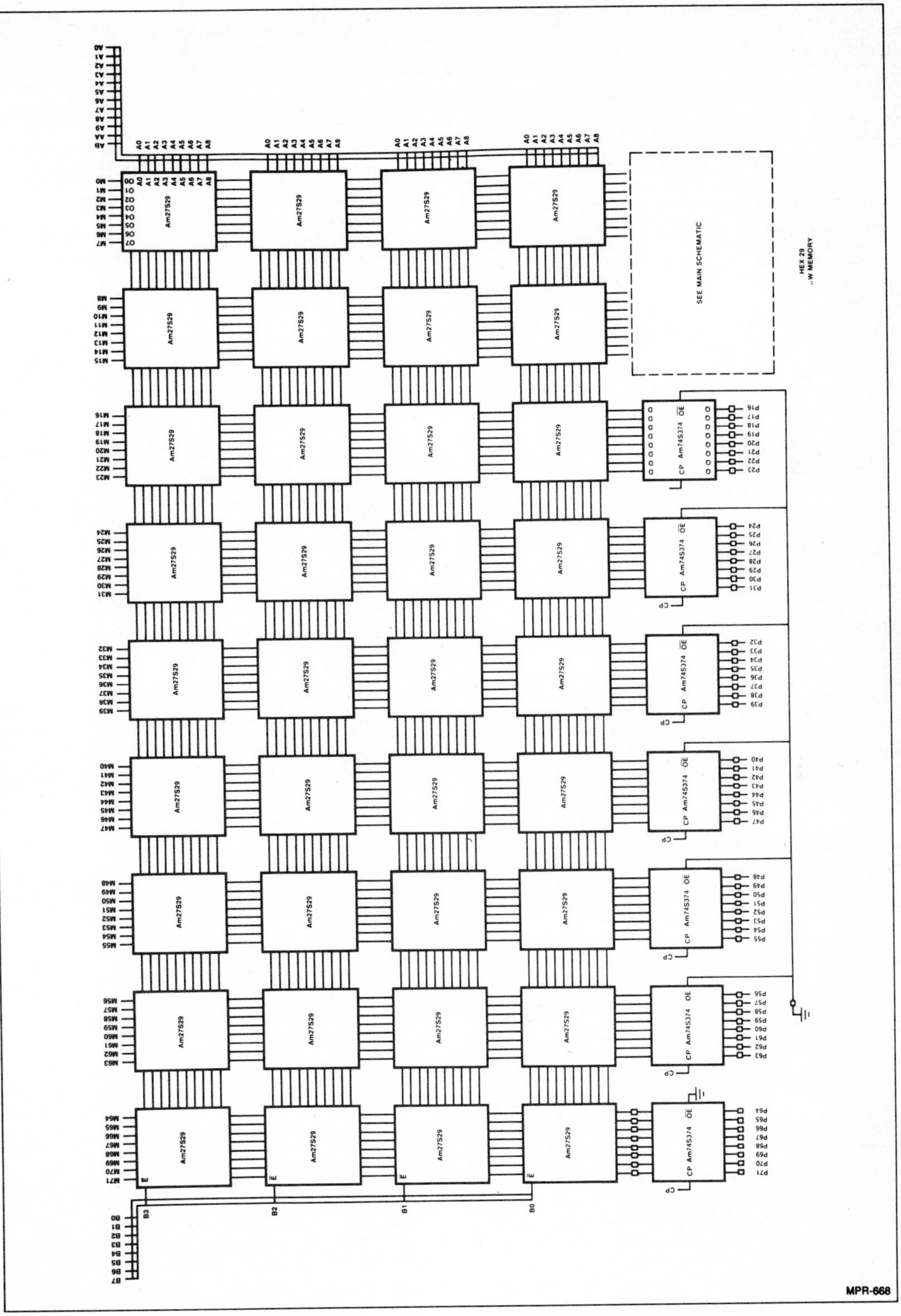

Figure 19.

It is even perfectly reasonable to use an off-board writable control store with up to 2k of microword RAM concurrently with up to 2k of PROM resident on the PC card.

If the on board PROM contains an instruction set, it is then a simple matter to use the off board writable control store to develop new microcode for the machine interactively on the one HEX-29 system!

The outputs of the microword memory devices are attached to the inputs of Am74S374 registers. These registers are called the pipeline registers since they allow the fetching of the next micro-instruction concurrently with execution of the current one. Clocking of the pipeline registers occurs on the LOW-to-HIGH transition of the system clock. The outputs of the pipeline registers are the 64 microword (or pipeline) bits that control every aspect of the processor.

These 64 bits can be logically grouped into several functional fields a follows:

1. Microword Data/Microbranch Address and Control
2. ALU Source Select
3. ALU Destination Select
4. ALU Function Select
5. ALU Carry In Select
6. Shift Linkage Select
7. ALU A and B Specifications
8. A and B Fields Select
9. Enable onto ALU inputs Select
10. Latch External Data Inputs
11. Latch CPU Outputs
12. Control Bus Signals
13. Microprogrammed Clock
14. Condition Code Controls
15. Enable Interrupt Circuitry
16. Memory Map Control

Notice that with the exception of the microword data and microbranch address and control fields, no other fields are overlapped. This is a 'horizontally' structured design. Overlapping several fields leads to 'vertically' structured systems. This latter class of machines can save some microword memory, but only at the expense of through-put and increased hardware complexity. Now that the cost of the PROM's has come down significantly, the savings accrued from using a vertically structured design approach is generally insignificant when compared with the overall system cost.

A summary of the functions of the microword bits is shown in Figure 20.

Am2901B ALU/REGISTER SETS

The heart of the HEX-29 CPU is the set of four Am2901B bit slice ALU/Register Sets depicted in Figure 21. All arithmetic and logical operations are performed in these bipolar LSI IC's, including address generation. The user accessible set of 16 registers and routing functions are also internal to these remarkable and extremely versatile chips.

The operation of these units, though very elegant and comprehendible, is too lengthy to include here and the user is referred to the *Am2900 Family Data Book* by AMD.

Carry lookahead is accomplished by the Am2901B's and an external IC, the Am2902A. Shift control is partially within the Am2901B's and is supported by other external circuitry to be discussed later.

A summary sheet of the Am2901B ALU functions appears on page 29 but should be supplemented by studying the AMD literature already mentioned. A good supplement is the AMD *Schottky and Low Power Schottky Handbook.*

The A and B input fields to the Am2901B's are multiplexed by 4 Am74S253's in the following four ways.

Am2901B B Inputs	Am2901B A Inputs
μword Memory	μword Memory
Upper Nibble ABL	Upper Nibble ABL
Lower Nibble ABL	Lower Nibble ABL
Upper Nibble ABL	Lower Nibble ABL

ABL = A,B Latch (On data bus bits 27-20.)

CARRY IN CONTROL

The arithmetic carry-in (C_N) signal (Figure 22) to the Am2901B bit slices can be selected from four sources as follows:

1. Logic 0 (No carry-in add instruction, borrow in subtract instruction.)
2. Logic 1 (Carry-in in add instruction, no borrow in subtract.)
3. Carry Flag (C bit in condition code register.)
4. Q Shift Bit (Double length shifts.)

Note that the natural state of the Carry Flag output from the Am2901B is 1 for carry on add, 0 for no carry on add, 1 for no borrow on subtract, and 0 for borrow on subtract. This convention has been maintained in the condition code and carry in logic. Some other machines operate differently with respect to this convention, but others do not and the HEX-29 maintains the faster convention for lack of a good reason to alter it. Some programmers will be required to remember this convention while others will be used to it.

SHIFT AND ROTATE LINKAGE

The shift and rotate linkage (Figure 23a) of the HEX-29 is composed of an Am74S253 and an Am74LS125 plus the internal shift control structure of the Am2901B's. The functions that can be performed by this circuitry are shown in Figure 23b.

The solid lines in Figure 23b delineate the basic shift linkages. The dotted lines are optional linkages which can also be enabled. With these linkages, all of the normal shifts and rotates can be performed plus a number of double word shifts including special shifts for high speed multiplies and divides.

CONDITION CODE CONTROL

The condition code register shown in Figure 24 of the HEX-29 has eight flags. The definitions and placement of these flags are defined in Figure 25.

In addition to the very useful and fairly common C, V, N, Z flags, a half sign is provided for easier byte processing. The three user flags are not changed by any of the normal arithmetic or logical operations. However, they can be read by the processor and written by the processor with special instructions such as load flags, read flags, set bits in flags, clear bits in flags, invert bits in flags. The fact that none of the user flags is changed by any but this type of special routine is very significant. It means that various routines and program segments can pass flags back and forth freely without fear of modification or restriction on the instructions that can be executed. Reading the condition code flags into the processor, or branching or subroutining upon combinations of bits set or clear does not alter the flags.

Name		Function		
0. μD0	BRA0			
1. μD1	BRA1			
2. μD2	BRA2			
3. μD3	BRA3			
4. μD4	BRA4	Microprogram		
5. μD5	BRA5	Branch		
6. μD6	BRA6	Address		
7. μD7	BRA7		Microword data to Internal	
8. μD8	BRA8		data bus to Am2901B's	
9. μD9	BRA9			
10. μDA	BRAA			
11. μDB	BRAB			
12. μDC	BRC0			
13. μDD	BRC1	Microprogram		
14. μDE	BRC2	Branch		
15. μDF	BRC3	Control		
16.	BRC4			
17. LIN		Latch in low nibble of data bus		
18. ROT0		Control Bits		A
19. ROT1		Shift and Rotate MUX		B
20. SRC0				
21. SRC1		Am2901 Source Select Code		
22. SRC2				
23. CIA		Carry-In MUX Select Bit A		
24. ALU0				
25. ALU1		Am2901 ALU Function Code		
26. ALU2				
27. CIB		Carry-In MUX Select Bit B		
28. DST0				
29. DST1		Am2901 Destination Code		
30. DST2				
31. FET		Fetch Instruction this cycle		
32. B0				
33. B1		Am2901 'B' field register specification		
34. B2				
35. B3				
36. A0				
37. A1		Am2901 'A' field register specification		
38. A2				
39. A3				
40. ABM0		A, B fields MUX Select Bit 0 (A, B fields on Am2901)		
41. ABM1		A, B fields MUX Select Bit 1 (A, B fields on Am2901)		
42. ST0		Microprogrammed system clock stretch bit 0		
43. ST1		Microprogrammed system clock stretch bit 1		
44. LDI		Latch Data In – Both Swapped and Unswapped		
45. LNZ		Latch N, Z, H flags – MUX Select		
46. LCV		Latch C, V flags – MUX Select		
47. LCC		Latch Condition Codes – U2, U1, U0, H, Z, N, V, C MUX Select		
48. $\overline{RCC}$		Read Condition Codes onto internal bus, low byte		
49. SDA		Select Microword bits 15-0 to internal bus, else branch code		
50. $\overline{DIL}$		Data In Low Byte Enable onto internal bus		
51. $\overline{DIH}$		Data In High Byte Enable onto internal bus		
52. $\overline{SWPL}$		Swapped Data In Low Byte Enabled onto internal bus		
53. $\overline{SWPH}$		Swapped Data In High Byte Enabled onto internal bus		
54. $\overline{CLL}$		Clear Low Byte on internal bus – Bit Set Enable HIGH		
55. $\overline{CLH}$		Clear High Byte on internal bus – Bit Set Enable LOW		
56. $\overline{LMM}$		Load Memory Map – Write into Memory Map RAM		
57. $\overline{RMM}$		Read Memory Map – Enable Memory Map to data bus		
58. $\overline{LAD}$		Latch Address – Enable Transparent Address Latch		
59. $\overline{BA}$		Bus Available – Busses available for DMA this cycle		
60. R/$\overline{W}$		REad/Write Memory (Write if low)		
61. $\overline{VMA}$		Valid Memory Address (Read or Write) this cycle		
62. SDMA		Sync. DMA – Active cycle before bus is available		
63. INE		Interrupt Logic Enable		

Figure 20A. Microword Bits.

0	BR C = 0		10	BR
1	BR C = 1		11	
2	BR V = 0		12	BSR
3	BR V = 1		13	
4	BR N = 0		14	BSR N = 0
5	BR N = 1		15	
6	BR Z = 0		16	RTS Z = 1
7	BR Z = 1		17	
8	BR HS = 0		18	RTS
9	BR HS = 1		19	
A	BR LZ = 0		1A	
B	BR LZ = 1		1B	
C	BR HLT = 0		1C	
D	BR HLT = 1		1D	
E	BR IH = 0		1E	BR IH = 1 or MAP
F	BR IH = 1		1F	CONTINUE

Figure 20B. Am2909 Microprogram Branch Control, Bits 12-16.

	LCC	LCU	LNZ	
LCN	0	0	0	New CVNZH
LC	0	0	1	New CV Old NZH
LN	0	1	0	Old CV New NZH
(Nom.)	0	1	1	Old CVNZH
BCC	1	0	0	Bus → CVNZHV
	1	0	1	Bus → CV Old NZH
	1	1	0	Shift Old V Bus → NZHU
LSC	1	1	1	Shift C Old V Old NZH

Figure 20C. Condition Code Manipulation, Bits 45-47.

ALU	CIB	CIA	0	1	2	3	4	5	6	7
0	0	0	A + Q	A + B	Q	B	A	D + A	D + Q	D
	0	1	A + Q + 1	A + B + 1	Q + 1	B + 1	A + 1	D + A + 1	D + Q + 1	D + 1
	1	0	A + Q + C	A + B + C	Q + C	B + C	A + C	D + A + C	D + Q + C	D + C
1	0	0	Q − A − 1	B − A − 1	Q − 1	B − 1	A − 1	A − D − 1	Q − D − 1	− D − 1
	0	1	Q − A	B − A	Q	B	A	A − D	Q − D	− D
	1	0	Q − A − C	B − A − C	Q − C	B − C	A − C	A − D − C	Q − D − C	− D − C
2	0	0	A − Q − 1	A − B − 1	− Q − 1	− B − 1	− A − 1	D − A − 1	D − Q − 1	D − 1
	0	1	A − Q	A − B	− Q	− B	− A	D − A	D − Q	D
	1	0	A − Q − C	A − B − C	− Q − C	− B − C	− A − C	D − A − C	D − Q − C	D − C
3	–	–	A∨Q	A∨B	Q	B	A	D∨A	D∨Q	D
4	–	–	A∧Q	A∧B	0	0	0	D∧A	D∧Q	0
5	–	–	A∧Q	A∧B	Q	B	A	D∧A	D∧Q	0
6	–	–	A∀Q	A∀B	Q	B	A	D∀A	D∀Q	D
7	–	–	A∀Q	A∀B	Q	B	A	D∀A	D∀Q	D

Figure 20D. Am2901 Source, Carry-in & Function Select, Bits 20-27.

DST	Rotates
0	F → Q
1	NONE
2	F → B A → Y
3	F → B
4	RIGHT F/2 → B Q/2 → Q
5	RIGHT F/2 → B
6	LEFT 2F → B 2Q → Q
7	LEFT 2F → B

Figure 20E. Am2901 Destination Codes, Bits 28-30.

ABMUX	A reg	B reg
0	μW_A	μW_B
1	R_S	R_D
2	R_S	R_S
3	R_D	R_D

Figure 20F. Am2901 A, B Field Selects, Bits 40-41.

	Right	Left
0	MUL	RCL
1	ROR	ROL
2	ASR	DRL
3	LSR	LSL

Figure 20G. Shift & Rotate Control, Bits 18-19.

STR	CLOCK
0	280ns
1	240ns
2	200ns
3	160ns

Figure 20H. Microprogrammed System Clock Stretch, Bits 42-43.

Figure 20 (Cont.).

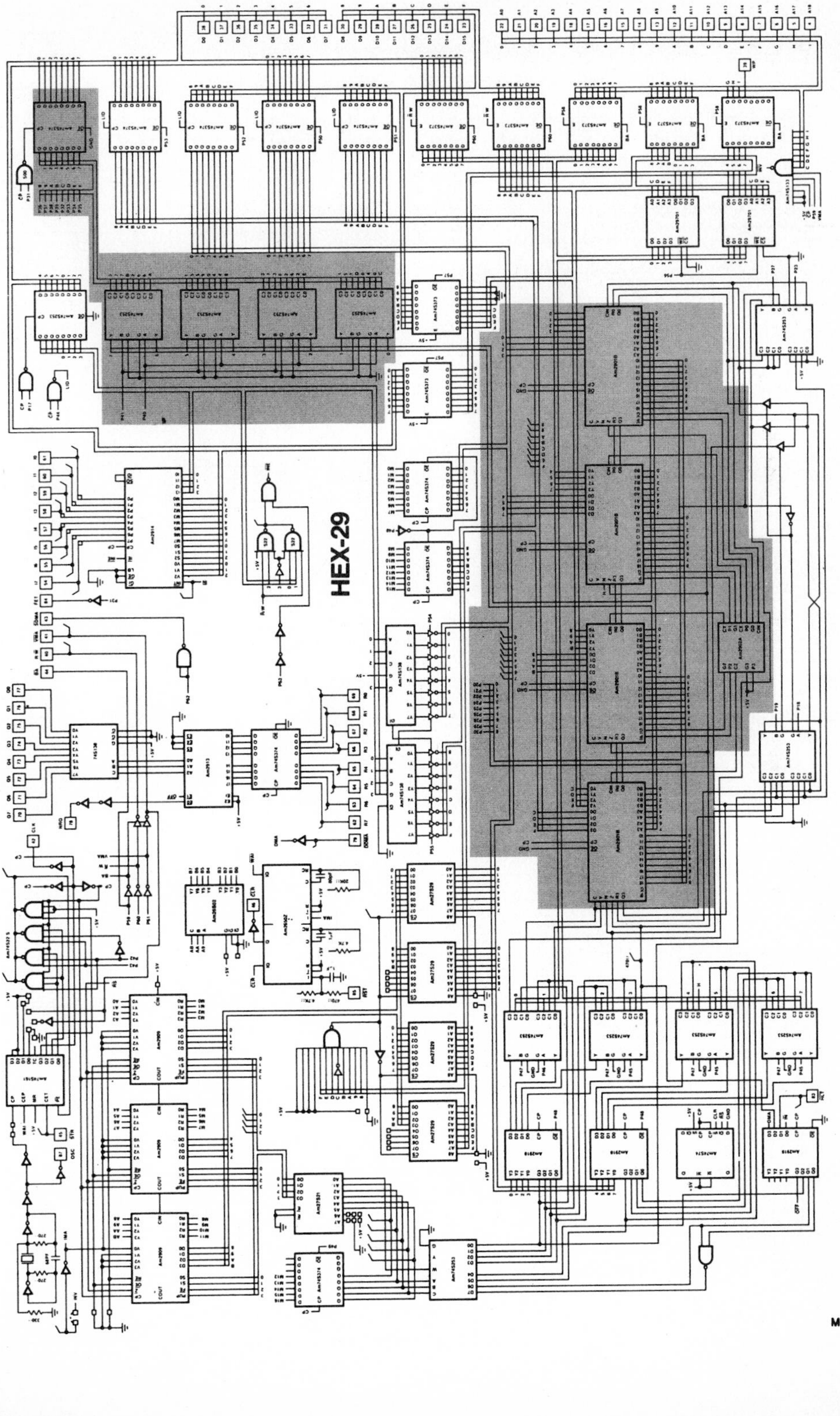

Figure 21.

MPR-669

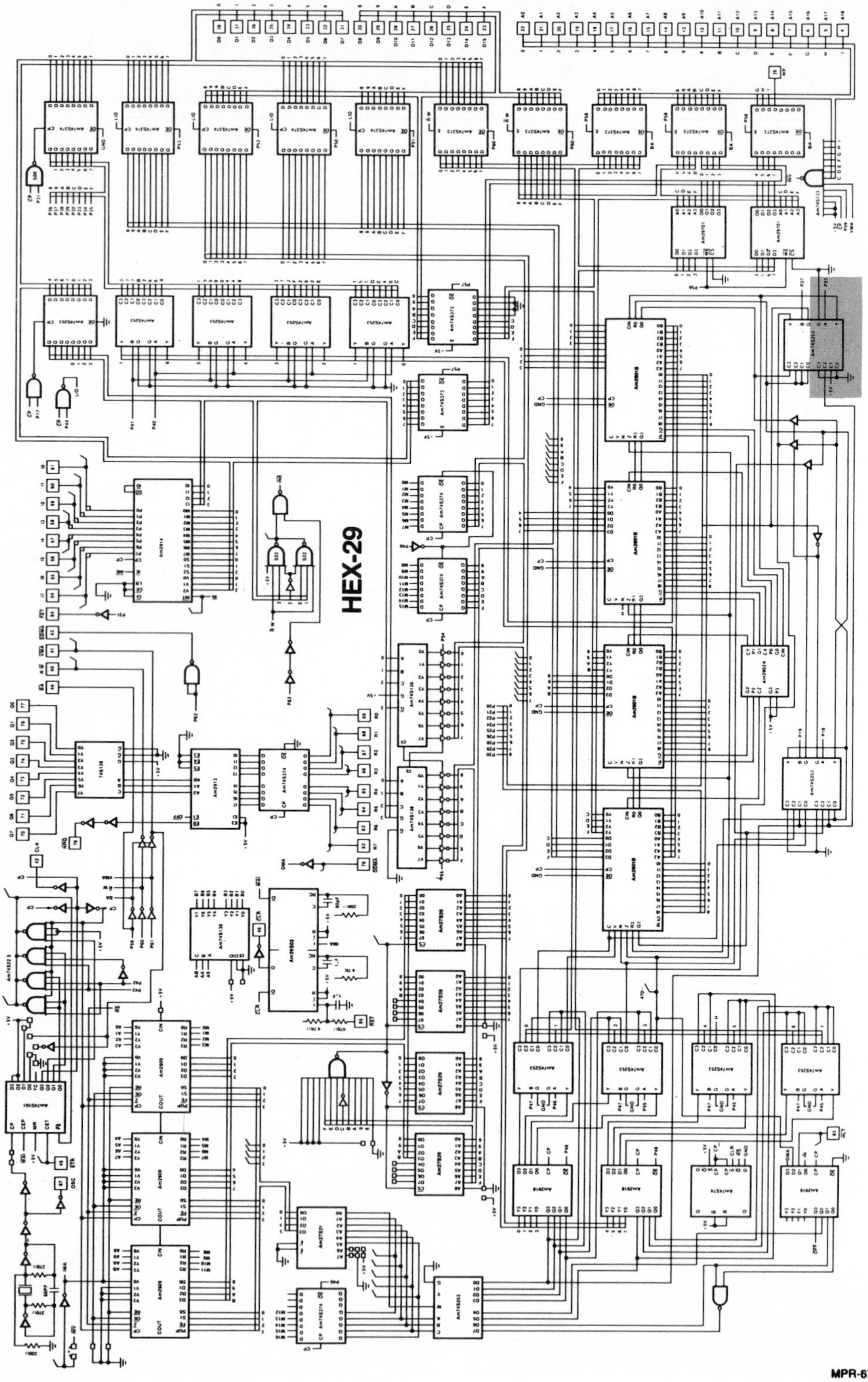

Figure 22.

MPR-670

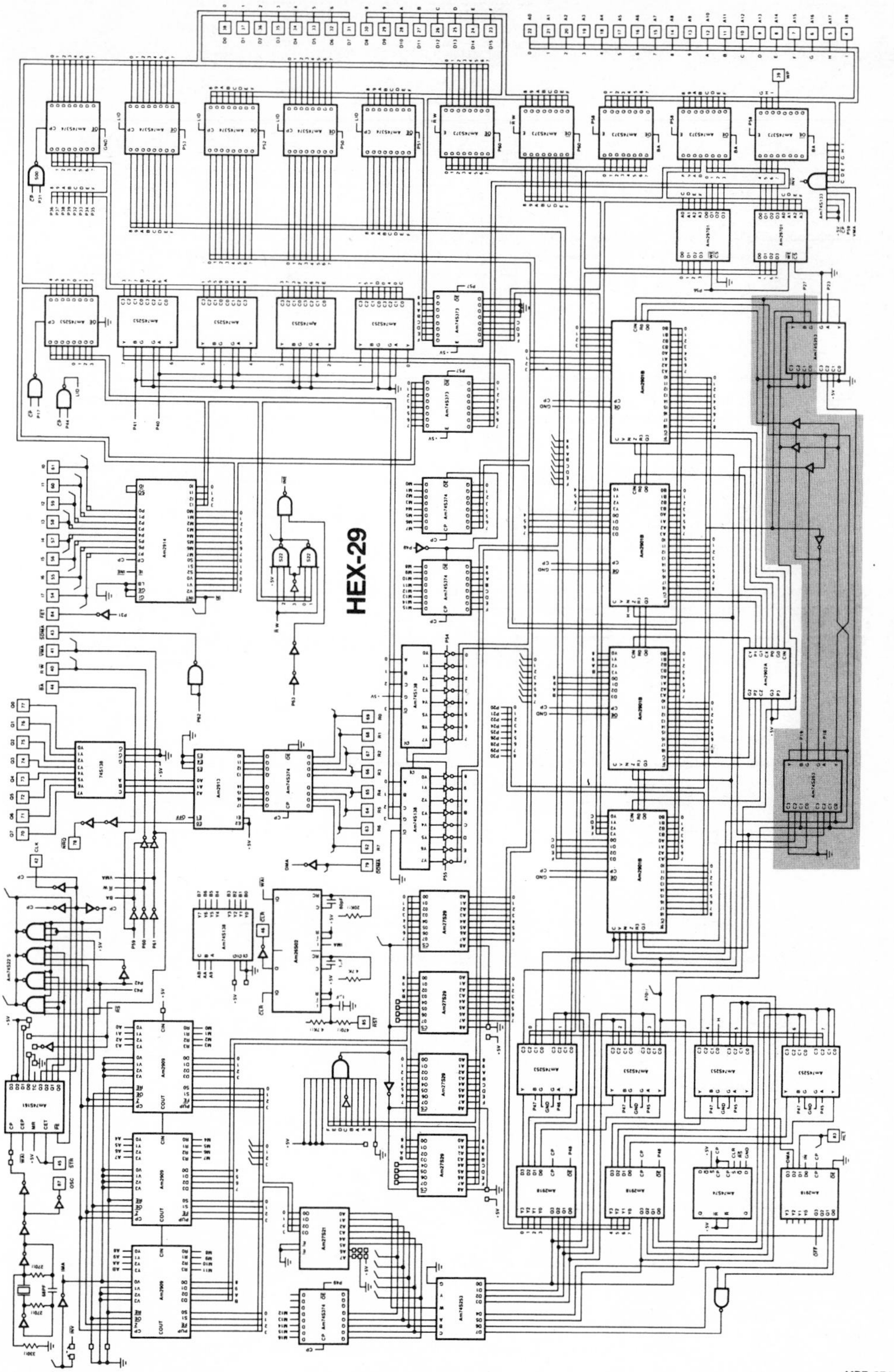

Figure 23A.

MPR-671

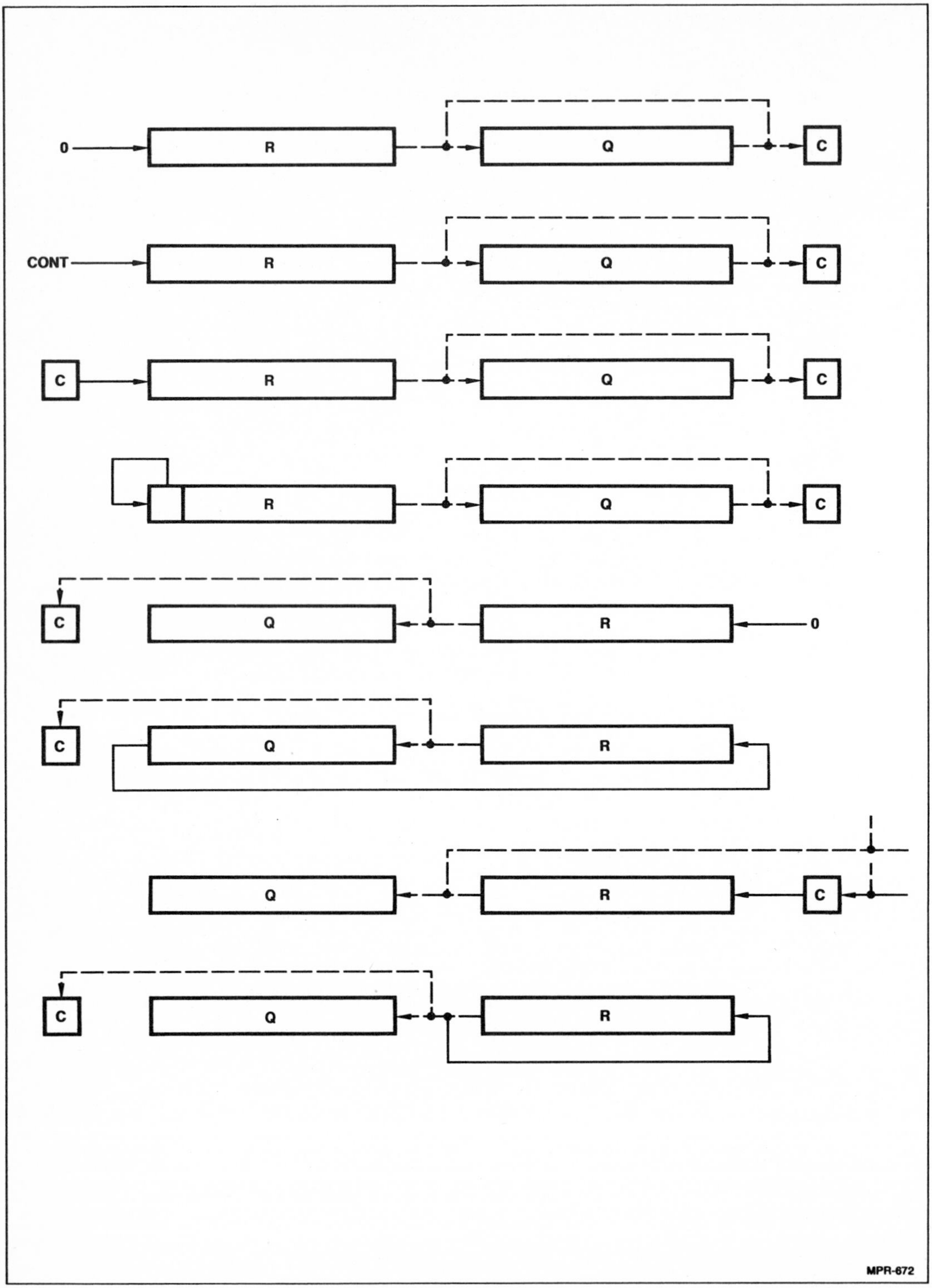

Figure 23B.

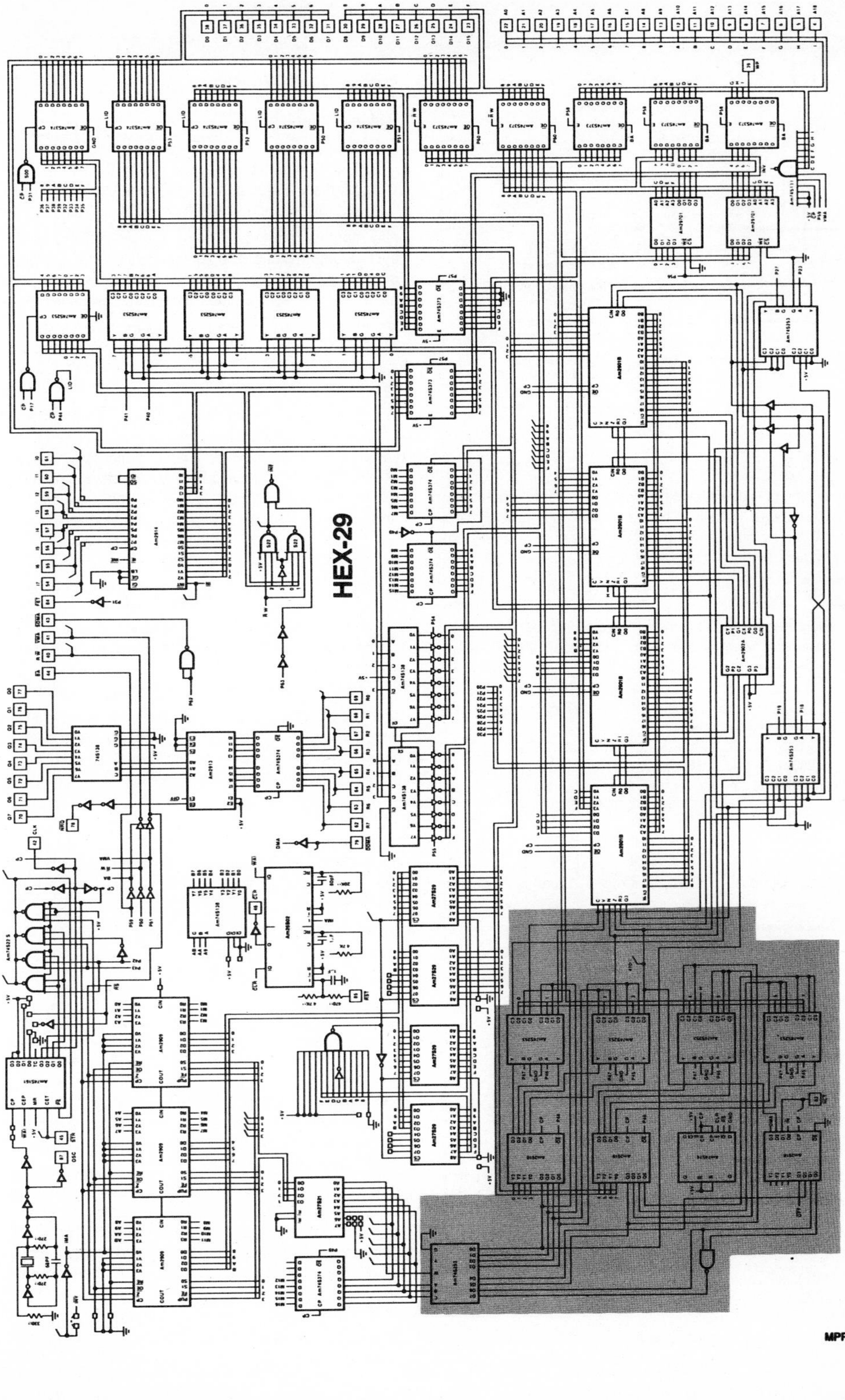

Figure 24.

MPR-673

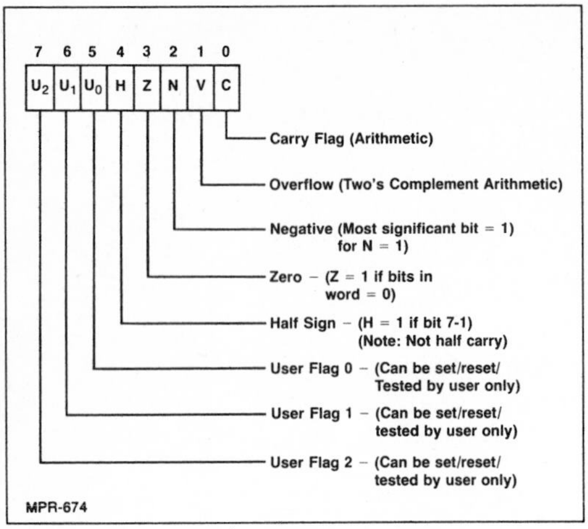

Figure 25.

Eight condition code operations provide all the useful operations needed for complete flexibility. They are shown in Figure 26a and 26b in two different formats. Note that the codes are grouped into three categories; arithmetic (C and V), logical/arithmetic (N, Z, H) and user (U_2, U_1, U_0).

These eight conditions include all the necessary and desirable features such as updating only the shift carry bit and the ability to do operations that read, operate on, and reload the condition code register all in one machine cycle (160ns). Also, a feature of immense importance where microcoded floating point or fixed point math is concerned is the ability to update flags on a cycle by cycle basis! An unusual feature.

	Carry/ Overflow C, V	Negative/Zero/ Half N, Z, H	User Flags U2, U1, U0
7	Shift Bit C,V V	No Change	No Change
*6	Shift Bit C,V V	Load From Bus	Load From Bus
*5	Load From Bus	No Change	No Change
4	Load From Bus	Load From Bus	Load From Bus
3	No Change	No Change	No Change
2	No Change	Update	No Change
1	Update	No Change	No Change
0	Update	Update	No Change

*Less useful than other codes but perfectly legal.

Figure 26A.

Name	U2	U1	U0	H	Z	N	V	C
Shift MSb or LSb into C	NC	NC	NC	NC	NC	NC	NC	S
*Shift into C –								
Bus Load Rest	B	B	B	B	B	B	NC	S
*Bus Load C & V Flags	NC	NC	NC	NC	NC	NC	B	B
Bus Load All Flags	B	B	B	B	B	B	B	B
No Changes	NC	NC	NC	NC	NC	NC	NC	NC
Update N, Z, H Flags	NC	NC	NC	μ	μ	μ	NC	NC
Update C and V Flags	NC	NC	NC	NC	NC	NC	μ	μ
Update C, V, N, Z, H	NC	NC	NC	μ	μ	μ	μ	μ

μ = updated, NC = unchanged, B = loaded from internal bus,
S = Shift Bit

Figure 26B.

Am2901B OUTPUT BUS

Being a highly structured, modular device, the HEX-29 CPU is very bus oriented. The output bus of the Am2901B's generate the addresses and data to the rest of the system devices as well as some internal function. The four logical units on this bus (shown in Figure 27) are:

1. Address Out Latches – (System Address bus)
2. Data Out Latches–(System data bus)
3. Memory Map/Latches–(Memory Management Features)
4. Condition Code MUX–(For updating flags from processor)

Any memory reference requires that an address be valid on the system address bus. The source of this address is generally one of the Am2901B internal registers or modifications thereof from previous fetch cycles (such as indexed addressing).

On a write cycle, data must be placed on the system data bus. This is accomplished in the same manner as address generation except that a different microword bit is used to activate the data latches.

In a multi-user/multi-task/timesharing environment, it is desirable to have a powerful memory management scheme. The HEX-29 CPU implements this via a flexible memory mapping system where the upper four bits of the 16-bit address generated by the Am2901B's are 'mapped' into seven address bits and a write protect bit. Invalid access traps and one Megabyte address space are integral features of this system. The loading of this MAP RAM (2 Am29701's) is also accomplished via the Am2901B output bus.

Another important characteristic of the HEX-29 CPU is its ability to read, write, test and operate upon the eight condition code flags in the byte form. All eight flags can be written to by the Am2901B's at one time, in one microcycle. This is very useful for many flag operations and is absolutely necessary for efficient updating of the user flags for interroutine parameter and condition passing.

The logic of these bussed systems is quite simple. A separate microword bit or bit field is used to cause each of these logical units on the bus to accept the data bus. Therefore, simple microprogramming techniques are applicable to this busing approach.

Am2901B INPUT BUS

Much of the power and modularity of the HEX-29 design is due to the highly structured bus approach on the Am2901B Data Inputs. The logical units that can drive this bus (Figure 28) are listed below:

1. Data Input Registers
2. Swap Input Registers
3. Microword Data Registers
4. Clear Upper Byte/Clear Lower Byte/Bit Op Logic
5. Condition Code Register

Data input from the system bus is captured in the data input registers and the swap input registers. The data input registers bring the upper and lower bytes of the data bus to the corresponding bytes in the Am2901B cascade while the swap input registers switch the upper byte of the data bus to the lower byte on the Am2901B cascade and the lower byte of the data bus to the upper byte of the Am2901B cascade.

Additionally, logic to set all bits in the upper or lower byte to zeros, (clear upper byte and clear lower byte), allow selecting arithmetic or logical zeros in either byte field. If the bit set option is enabled, all bits are pulled low except the one selected by the hexadecimal value in the low nibble of the nibble latch from an instruction or other data source.

All eight condition code bits can be enabled onto the low byte if desired. All flags can thus be sampled by the Am2901B's at once.

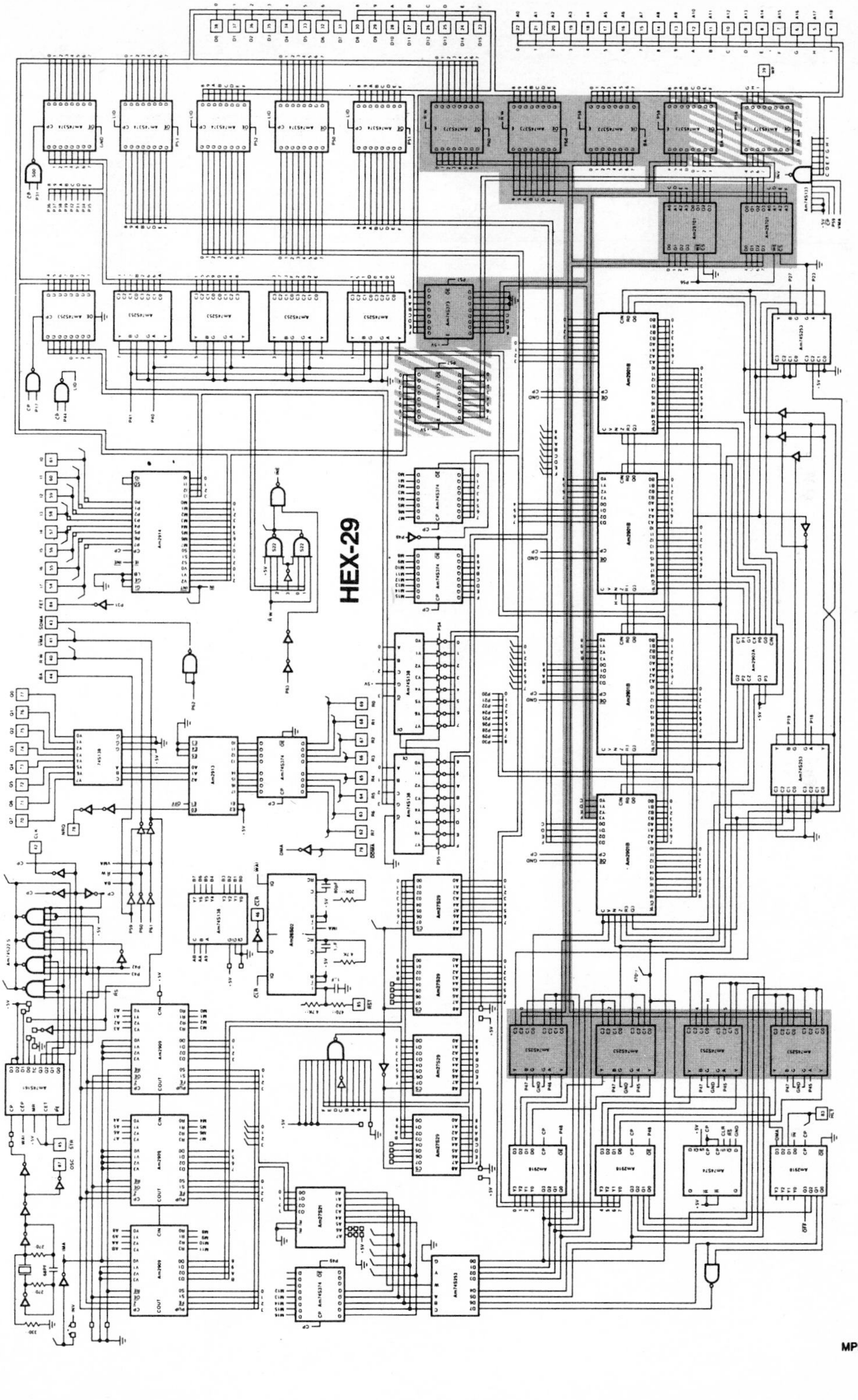

Figure 27.

MPR-675

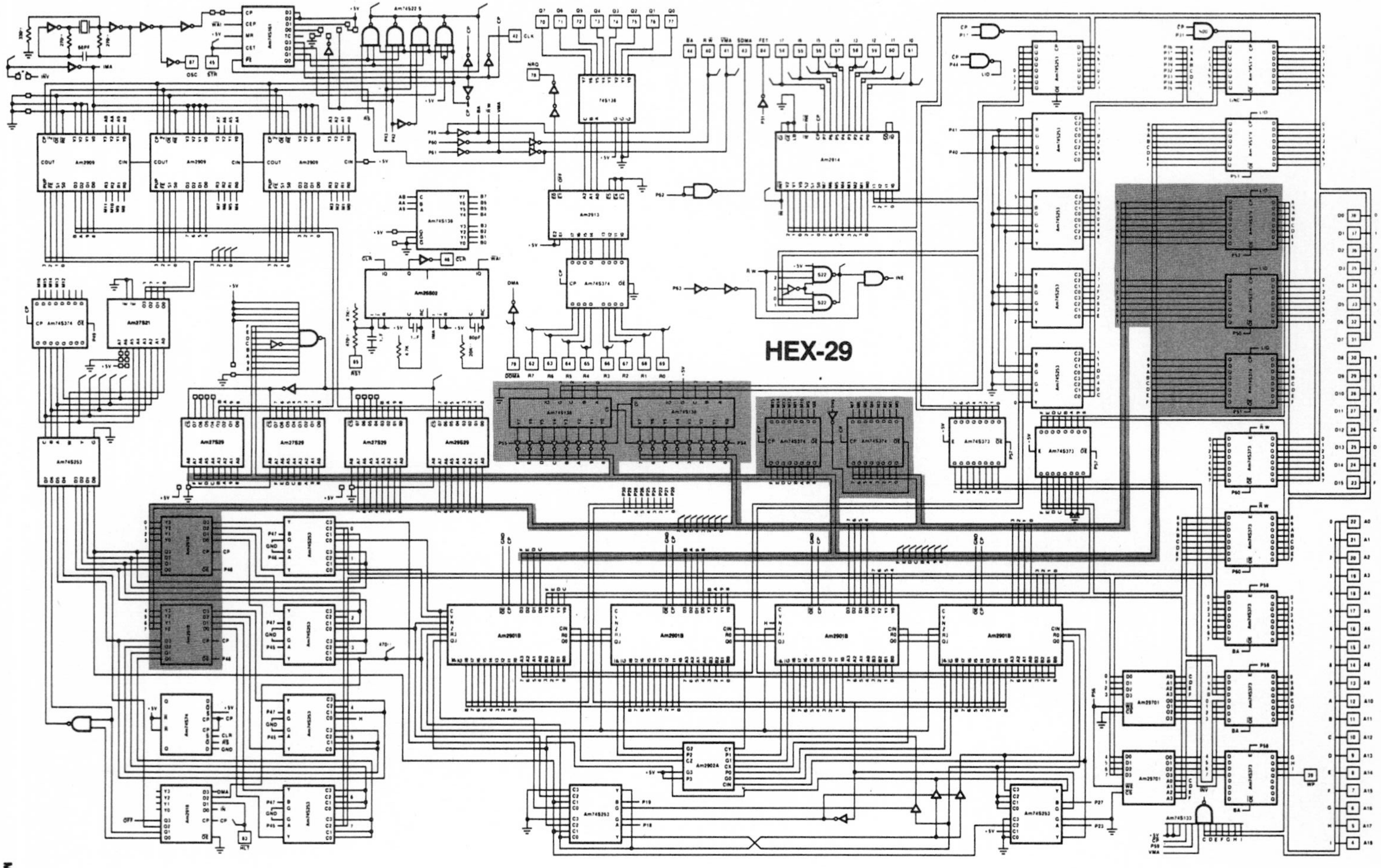

Figure 28.

MPR-676

Data from microword memory from three-state registers in parallel with the pipeline register can be enabled onto the upper and lower bytes for direct loading of the Am2901B's from microprograms.

In the absence of any device being enabled onto a particular byte on this bus, it will be pulled up into a logic 1 state. This can be useful for masking in logical operations and filling or biasing in arithmetic operations.

An important factor in the flexibility of this approach on the HEX-29 is that the upper and lower bytes of the data in registers, swap in registers, and the clear upper/lower byte logic are separately enabled. Also, the condition code register only drives the lower byte and the pull-up feature will operate on either byte individually. Thus the upper and lower bytes can be individually driven on a 'mix and match' basis from several sources.

The versatility so generated allows numerous fast processing modes. See Table 5 for a list of all of the possible combinations of high and low byte inputs to the 2901B's.

TABLE 5.

Into Upper Byte of Am2901's	Into Lower Byte of Am2901's
0. Microword memory bits P15-P8	Microword memory bits P7-P0
1. Bit set value (upper byte)	Bit set value (lower byte)
2. Upper byte – data bus	Lower byte – data bus
3. Upper byte – data bus	Upper byte – data bus
4. Upper byte – data bus	Clear lower byte
5. Upper byte – data bus	All high generator
6. Upper byte – data bus	Condition code register
7. Lower byte – data bus	Lower byte – data bus
8. Lower byte – data bus	Upper byte – data bus
9. Lower byte – data bus	Clear lower byte
10. Lower byte – data bus	All high generator
11. Lower byte – data bus	Condition code register
12. All high generator	Lower byte – data bus
13. All high generator	Upper byte – data bus
14. All high generator	Clear lower byte
15. All high generator	All high generator
16. All high generator	Condition code register
17. Clear upper byte	Lower byte – data bus
18. Clear upper byte	Upper byte – data bus
19. Clear upper byte	All high generator
20. Clear upper byte	Condition code register
*21. Clear upper byte	Clear lower byte

*Note: Interestingly enough this is the only case in the entire table that the hardware CANNOT generate on the bus, but IS the ONLY one of these codes that CAN be generated by the AMD 2901B slices! (How convenient!)

Examples of uses for some of these modes include:

1. Clearing upper byte for 8-bit index offset
2. Fast bit set/clear/test/invert operations
3. Set upper byte high to AND lower byte with upper byte change
4. Clear upper byte to AND off upper byte and operate lower
5. Upper byte of data bus to lower byte for all byte ops on upper byte
6. Load defined values from microcode for tamper-proof constants, vectors, etc.
7. Normal data input or address input without swap or modification.
8. Clear upper byte and data in low-bite immediate ops, etc.

INTERRUPT CONTROL

The powerful maskable priority vectored interrupt system (Figure 29) of the HEX-29 is a direct derivative of the incredible Am2914 bipolar LSI interrupt control IC. This circuit is so well integrated that it uses only one microword bit and requires very little support circuitry. The general set of operations that can be executed by the Am2914 is shown below. For more detailed information on this chip see the *Am2900 Family Data Book*.

F. Enable Request
E. Load Mask Register
D. Disable Request
C. Clear Mask Register
B. Bit Set Mask Register
A. Bit Clear Mask Register
9. Load Status Register
8. Set Mask Register
7. REad Mask Register
6. Read Status Register
5. Read Vector
4. Clear Interrupts Last Vector Read.
3. Clear Interrupts via M Register
2. Clear Interrupts via M Bus
1. Clear all Interrupts
0. Master Clear

Flow charts of the actions taken in microcode by the HEX-29 CPU are shown in Figure 30 and Figure 31.

DMA CONTROL

The DMA structure is quite straightforward. There are eight active-LOW DMA request lines and eight corresponding DMA acknowledge lines. The highest priority requesting a DMA cycle at the beginning of the microcycle before DMA will be allowed gets an acknowledge signal that lasts up until the DMA cycle – at least.

If no devices are requesting DMA, the $\overline{NRQ}$ (no request) bus signal goes LOW. This is an excellent opportunity for dynamic RAM circuitry to refresh sequential rows on each DMA cycle that $\overline{NRQ}$ is LOW.

Another input signal $\overline{DDMA}$, will override all priorities and not acknowledge any level of DMA request. This could be used by dynamic RAM refresh circuitry when it must be permitted to refresh itself soon or chance losing data.

Many schemes of DMA handling can be accomplished with this simple and uncomplicated priority controlled system. An Am74S374 captures the DMA requests (Figure 32) on a cycle by cycle basis. An Am2913 prioritizes these requests and acknowledges the highest level request with a three-bit binary code. An Am74S138 expands this to the eight bits of DMA acknowledge that correspond to the eight input bits. The Am2913 supplies the $\overline{NRQ}$ bus signal and provides for the $\overline{DDMA}$ bus signal.

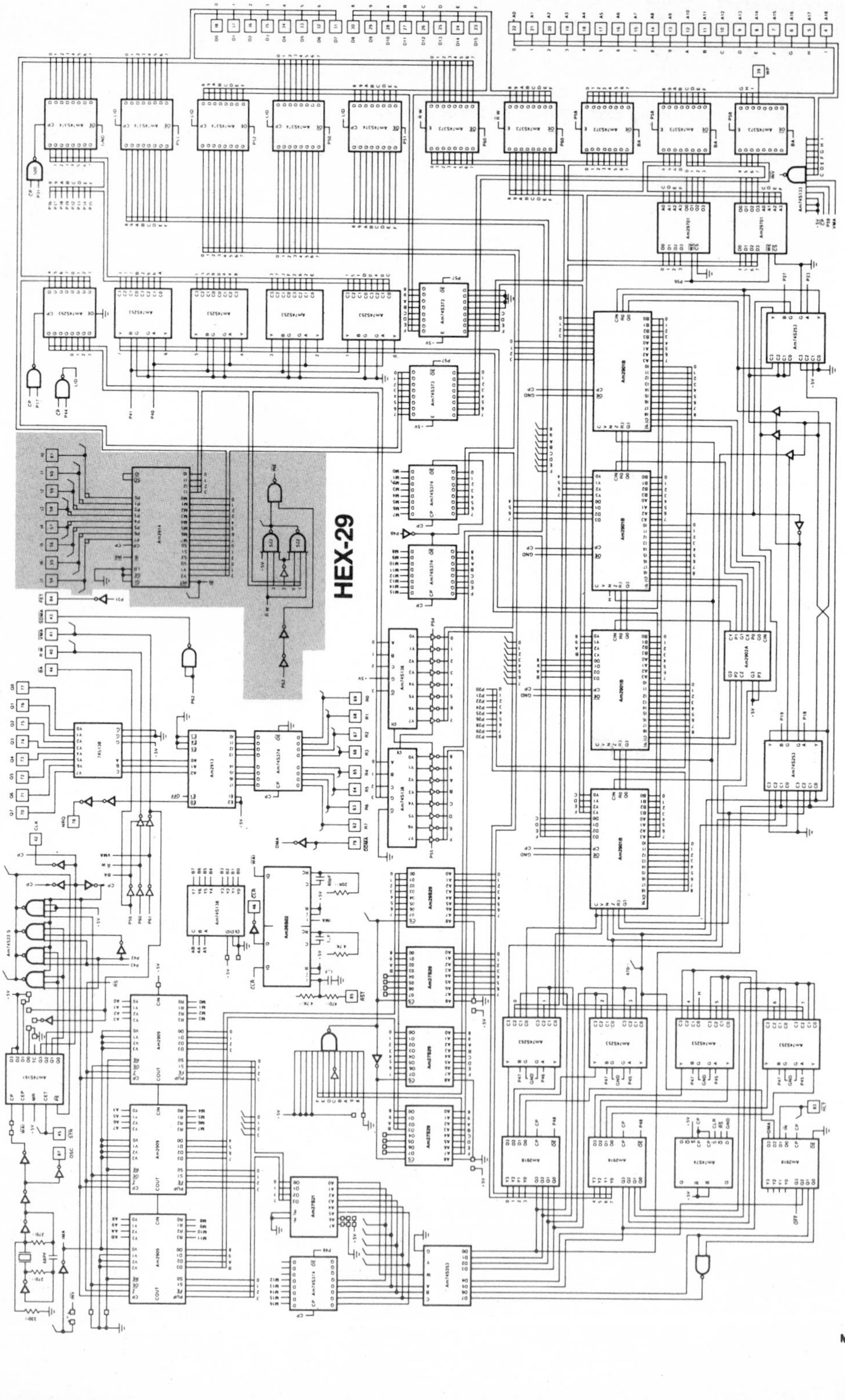

Figure 29.

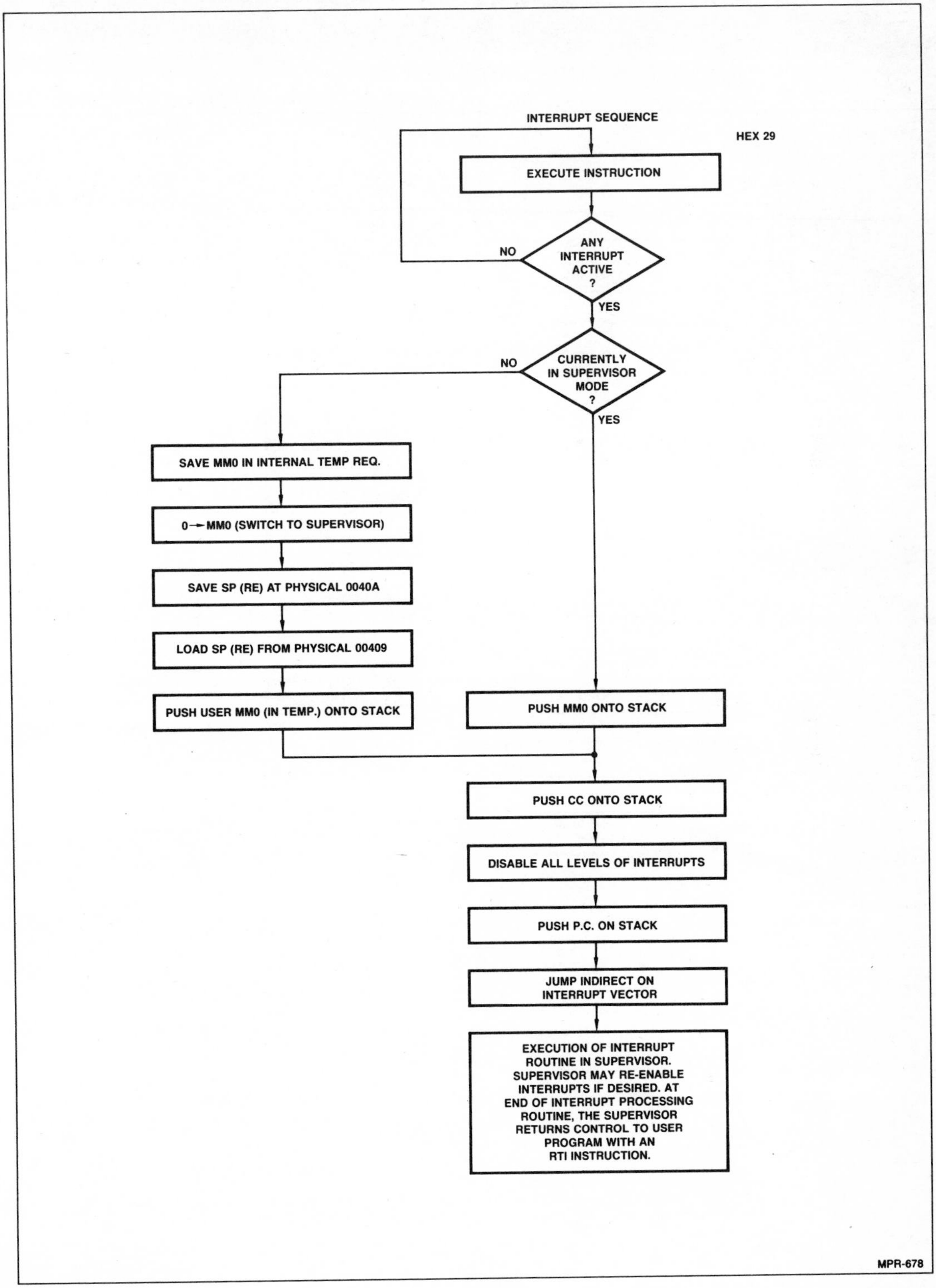
INTERRUPT SEQUENCE
HEX 29
EXECUTE INSTRUCTION
ANY INTERRUPT ACTIVE ?
NO
YES
CURRENTLY IN SUPERVISOR MODE ?
NO
YES
SAVE MM0 IN INTERNAL TEMP REQ.
0→MM0 (SWITCH TO SUPERVISOR)
SAVE SP (RE) AT PHYSICAL 0040A
LOAD SP (RE) FROM PHYSICAL 00409
PUSH USER MM0 (IN TEMP.) ONTO STACK
PUSH MM0 ONTO STACK
PUSH CC ONTO STACK
DISABLE ALL LEVELS OF INTERRUPTS
PUSH P.C. ON STACK
JUMP INDIRECT ON INTERRUPT VECTOR
EXECUTION OF INTERRUPT ROUTINE IN SUPERVISOR. SUPERVISOR MAY RE-ENABLE INTERRUPTS IF DESIRED. AT END OF INTERRUPT PROCESSING ROUTINE, THE SUPERVISOR RETURNS CONTROL TO USER PROGRAM WITH AN RTI INSTRUCTION.
MPR-678

Figure 30.

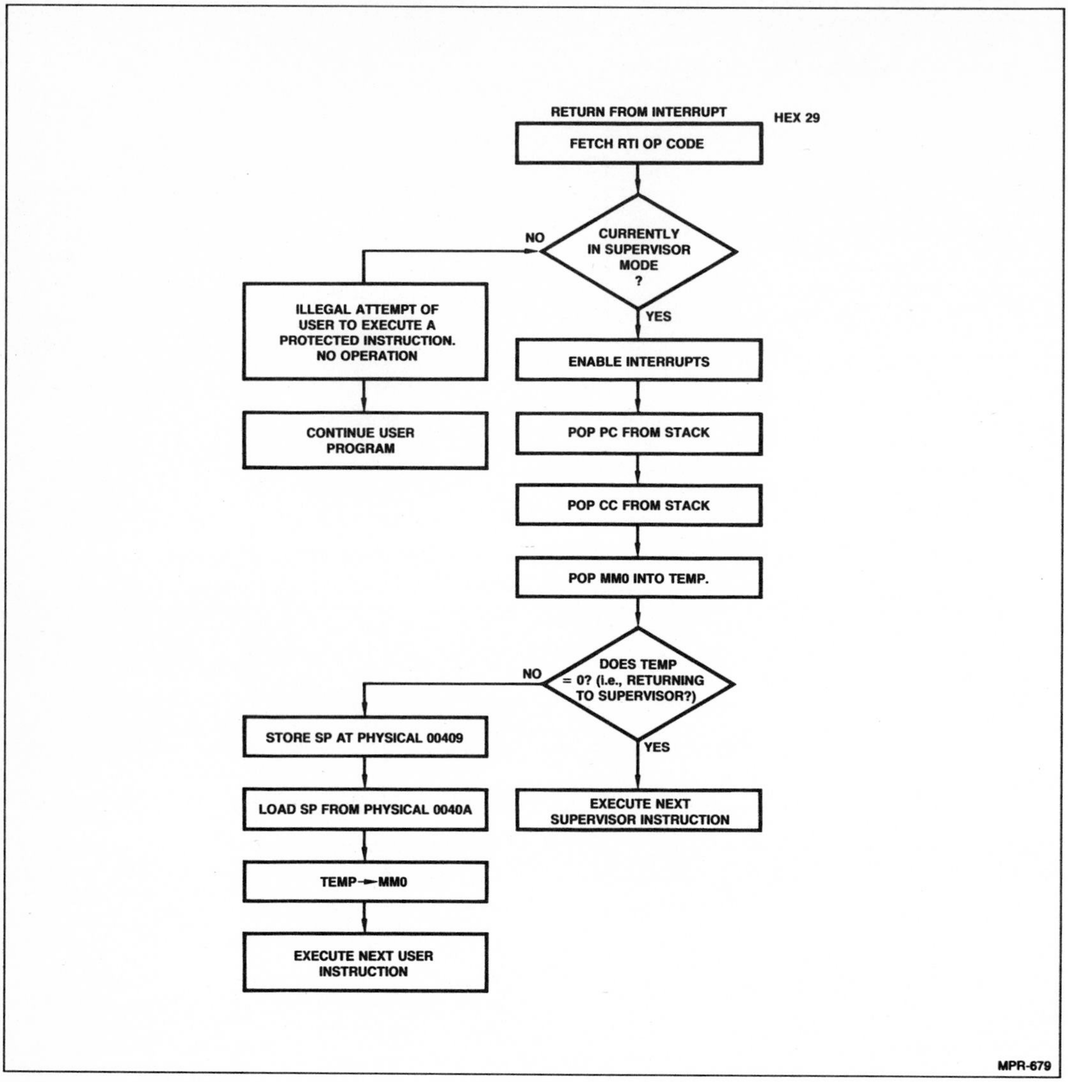
RETURN FROM INTERRUPT
HEX 29
FETCH RTI OP CODE
CURRENTLY IN SUPERVISOR MODE ?
NO
YES
ILLEGAL ATTEMPT OF USER TO EXECUTE A PROTECTED INSTRUCTION. NO OPERATION
CONTINUE USER PROGRAM
ENABLE INTERRUPTS
POP PC FROM STACK
POP CC FROM STACK
POP MM0 INTO TEMP.
DOES TEMP = 0? (i.e., RETURNING TO SUPERVISOR?)
NO
YES
STORE SP AT PHYSICAL 00409
LOAD SP FROM PHYSICAL 0040A
TEMP→MM0
EXECUTE NEXT USER INSTRUCTION
EXECUTE NEXT SUPERVISOR INSTRUCTION
MPR-679

Figure 31.

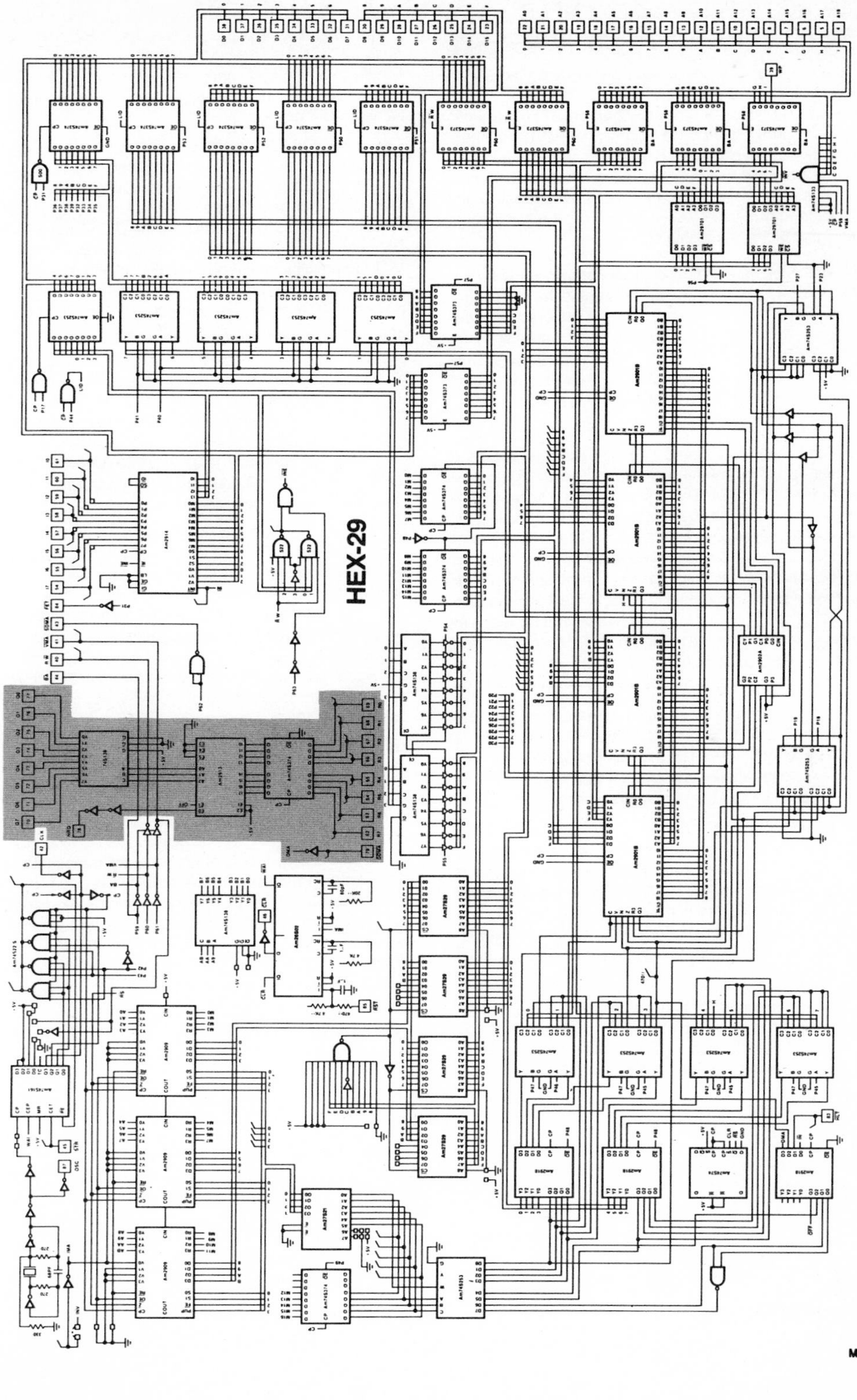

Figure 32.

SYSTEM BUS INTERFACE EXAMPLE HEX-64KBS STATIC MEMORY CARD

It was possible to design the system bus to be very simple to work with because the HEX-29 is a microprogrammed device. The following section discusses an implementation of a 64k byte static memory card for the HEX-29 system bus using Am9124 memory ICs. The purpose is to show that designing cards that interface with the HEX-29 system bus is relatively easy. Note that a design for I/O devices would be similar to this implementation since I/O devices are memory mapped and share exactly the same set of bus signals and timing requirements.

Starting from the left hand of the schematic shown in Figure 33, we find that the low 13 bits of the address bus and the four control bus signals (CLK, $\overline{\text{VMA}}$, R/$\overline{\text{W}}$, and WP) are buffered from the system bus by two Am74S240 ICs and three sections of an Am74S244. These are inverting and non-inverting buffers respectively, and offer extremely high current drive (64mA sink current) and very high speed (~4 to 6ns) with only very light bus loading (400μA low level).

Ten of the address lines buffered by these ICs then drive the address lines of half of the memory array through series type termination resistors. These resistors (~33 ohms) serve to prevent undershooting zero volts by more than the permissible 0.5V on negative edge transitions of the address lines. This type of termination has the advantage that it does not draw current from the driver ICs; it is highly recommended over split termination for memory arrays where current loading is negligible, but capacitive loading is significant. Note that to further reduce these capacitive loading effects, the address lines of only half of the memory array are driven by one set of buffers. (Find the second set of Am74S240 address buffers at the far right of the schematic.)

The remaining 3 address lines that were buffered by the Am74S240s drive the A, B, and C inputs of (4) Am74S138 one-of-eight decoders. These ICs develop the 32 1k word chip selects that enable the appropriate Am9124 memory ICs for read and write operations when they are addressed.

Of course only one of the Am74S138 ICs should be enabled when the board is addressed. This is a function of the higher address lines, A18-A13. Since each Am74S138 is able to select 1k word blocks of memory, each Am74S138 should be addressable on 8k word boundaries. Decoding the upper address lines (A18-A13) to match selectable 8k boundary addresses is accomplished with four Am25LS2521 8-bit equal to comparators, one for each Am74S138.

The DIP switches on the right hand side of each Am25LS2521 define the conditions under which the corresponding Am74S138 will be selected. When the eight inputs on the left hand side of these chips correspond to the values set on the DIP switch on the right, the Am74S138 is enabled. Note that the $\overline{\text{VMA}}$ bus signal (Valid Memory Access) must be LOW to enable the Am25LS2521. Also note that each 8k word bank can be unconditionally removed from the system memory space by leaving the lowest DIP switch open. Thus the board may be filled in 8k word increments if desired.

The Am74S138 ICs are also enabled by the system clock via the CLK signal. Therefore, memory chip selects can only occur during the time that the system clock is LOW (called ϕ_2). The importance of this will be discussed shortly. Another signal that must be valid for these ICs to be enabled is the DIS Signal. Whenever the R/W signal is LOW (indicating a write) and WP (write protect) is HIGH (protect the memory), then the DIS signal is brought LOW. This disables the Am74S138's and blocks the selecting of any memory ICs, thereby write protecting all on-board memory.

Above the memory array on the schematic are the data bus buffers, one set for each half. Again, this is done to reduce capacitive loading, this time on the data lines. Am74S373 octal tri-state latches are used for all eight of these data buffers. The enable inputs are driven by the inversion of the system clock bus signal so that they are transparent during all of ϕ_2, which is when the data is transferred. The appropriate Am74S373 latches are turned on ($\overline{\text{OE}}$ LOW) during read and write signals so that the data is buffered in the proper direction.

The Am26S02 one-shot is used to stretch ϕ_2 of the system clock to meet the access time of the memory. Without this signal, ϕ_2 would last only 80ns and the access time specifications of the Am9124 memory ICs would not be met. The Am26S02 is activated whenever memory ICs on the board are addressed when the system clock enters ϕ_2 (negative edge). Once fired, the duration of ϕ_2 is stretched by 40ns for every 40ns that the STR bus signal is held LOW. Since the Am9124 EPC memory devices have an access time of 200ns worst case, ϕ_2 must be stretched by 120ns.

Summary

As can be seen, the HEX-29 16-bit design represents a simple, straightforward design approach to building a high-performance 16-bit processor. This design takes advantage of many of the features of the Am2901 and Am2909. The instruction set shown in this application note is intended to be representative of the more common types of instructions to be executed on a machine of this class. In addition, microcode could be developed to execute a great many additional instructions as well as other classes of instruction such as entire floating point package. This design utilizes microprogram control throughout, and is a good demonstration of parallel microprogramming in a most straightforward application.

AMD wishes to thank Mr. Mike Simmons and Mr. Lee McDonald of HEX for their work on this invited paper as a part of this application note series.

APPENDIX

HEX-29 Microcode

This appendix contains 256 words of HEX-29 microcode. The first part is a definition file which defines the HEX-29 hardware structure for the AMDASM™ assembler. The various inputs to the Am2901 are defined via equates while all other microword fields are literally defined. The second part is the assembly file which symbolically, via terms defined in the definition phase, constructs each microword. Each microword begins with an optional label (such as RESET:). Next is the Am2909 branch control field, followed by all of the remaining control fields. This structure gives the appearance of a conventional assembler, i.e., LABEL, OPERATION, OPERANDS. A microinstruction which has no Am2909 branch control specified, such as microwords 3 and 4, uses microword bits 0-15 (which includes the branch control field) to place immediate data directly on the internal Am2901 bus. The Am2909 is then forced to "CONTINUE" by the "LIN" field. LIN, besides Latching IN the data on the Am2901 bus, disables the microprogram branch control register output, causing the "CONTINUE" function to be selected in the branch control PROM (see Figure 20B).

These 256 microwords represent a reasonable subset of the HEX-29 standard instructions, i.e., branch, conditional branch, data moves (MDV), and, or, add, sub, etc.

```
;
; HEX-29 DEFINITION PHASE (PHASE 1)
;
WORD 64
;
;AM2901 REGISTER EQUATES
;
R0:     EQU     H#0
R1:     EQU     H#1
R2:     EQU     H#2
R3:     EQU     H#3
R4:     EQU     H#4
R5:     EQU     H#5
R6:     EQU     H#6
R7:     EQU     H#7
R8:     EQU     H#8
R9:     EQU     H#9
R10:    EQU     H#A
R11:    EQU     H#B
R12:    EQU     H#C
R13:    EQU     H#D
R14:    EQU     H#E
R15:    EQU     H#F
;
;AM2901 SOURCE (R S) OPERAND EQUATES
;
AQ:     EQU     Q#0
AB:     EQU     Q#1
ZQ:     EQU     Q#2
ZB:     EQU     Q#3
ZA:     EQU     Q#4
DA:     EQU     Q#5
DQ:     EQU     Q#6
DZ:     EQU     Q#7
;
;AM2901 ALU FUNCTION (R FUNCTION S) EQUATES
;
ADD:    EQU     Q#0         ;R+S
SUBR:   EQU     Q#1         ;S-R
SUBS:   EQU     Q#2         ;R-S
OR:     EQU     Q#3         ;R S
AND:    EQU     Q#4         ;R S
NOT:    EQU     Q#5         ;R S
EXOR:   EQU     Q#6         ;R S
EXNOR:  EQU     Q#7         ;R S
;
;AM2901 DESTINATION CONTROL EQUATES
;
QREG:   EQU     Q#0         ;F Q , Y=F
NOOP:   EQU     Q#1         ;NOTHING , Y=F
RAMA:   EQU     Q#2         ;F B , Y=A
RAMF:   EQU     Q#3         ;F B , Y=F
RAMQD:  EQU     Q#4         ;F/2 B , Q/2 Q , Y=F
RAMD:   EQU     Q#5         ;F/2 B , Y=F
RAMQU:  EQU     Q#6         ;2F B , 2Q Q , Y=F
RAMU:   EQU     Q#7         ;2F B , Y=F
;
;
AM2901: DEF      24X,4VX,4VX,1X,3VX,1X,3VX,1X,3VX,20X
;
NOINE:  DEF      B#0,63X          ;INE = INTERRUPT LOGIC ENABLE
INE:    DEF      B#1,63X
;
NOSDMA: DEF      1X,B#0,62X       ;SDMA = SYNC DMA
SDMA:   DEF      1X,B#1,62X
;
VMA:    DEF      2X,B#0,61X       ;VALID MEMORY ACCESS THIS CYCLE
NOVMA:  DEF      2X,B#1,61X
;
WRITE:  DEF      3X,B#0,60X       ;READ/NOT-WRITE MEMORY
READ:   DEF      3X,B#1,60X
;
BA:     DEF      4X,B#0,59X       ;BUS AVAILABLE THIS CYCLE
NOBA:   DEF      4X,B#1,59X
;
NOLAD:  DEF      5X,B#0,58X       ;LAD = ENAB TRANSPARENT ADDR LATCH
LAD:    DEF      5X,B#1,58X
;
RMM:    DEF      6X,B#0,57X       ;READ MEMORY MAP
NORMM:  DEF      6X,B#1,57X
;
LMM:    DEF      7X,B#0,56X       ;LOAD MEMORY MAP
NOLMM:  DEF      7X,B#1,56X
;
CLRHL:  DEF      8X,B#00,54X      ;CLEAR HI/LO BYTE INTERNAL BUS
CLRLO:  DEF      8X,B#01,54X
CLRHI:  DEF      8X,B#10,54X
NOCLB:  DEF      8X,B#11,54X
;
SWPHL:  DEF      10X,B#00,52X     ;SWAP DATA HI/LO INTERNAL BUS
SWPLO:  DEF      10X,B#01,52X
SWPHI:  DEF      10X,B#10,52X
NOSWP:  DEF      10X,B#11,52X
;
DINHL:  DEF      12X,B#00,50X     ;DATA IN HI/LO INTERNAL BUS
DINLO:  DEF      12X,B#01,50X
DINHI:  DEF      12X,B#10,50X
NODIN:  DEF      12X,B#11,50X
;
NOSDA:  DEF      14X,B#0,49X      ;SDA = SELECT MICROWORD BITS 15-0
SDA:    DEF      14X,B#1,49X      ;      TO INTERNAL BUS
;
RCC:    DEF      15X,B#0,48X      ;READ CC TO INTERNAL BUS
NORCC:  DEF      15X,B#1,48X
;
NOLCC:  DEF      16X,Q#0,45X      ;CC MUX SELECT
LCC:    DEF      16X,Q#1,45X
LCV:    DEF      16X,Q#2,45X
LCCLCV: DEF      16X,Q#3,45X
LNZ:    DEF      16X,Q#4,45X
LNZCC:  DEF      16X,Q#5,45X
LNZCV:  DEF      16X,Q#6,45X
LNZCCV: DEF      16X,Q#7,45X
;
NOLDI:  DEF      19X,B#0,44X      ;LDI = LATCH DATA IN, SWAPPED & UNSWAPPED
LDI:    DEF      19X,B#1,44X
;
NOSTR:  DEF      20X,B#00,42X     ;STR = CLOCK STRETCH CONTROL
STR1:   DEF      20X,B#01,42X
STR2:   DEF      20X,B#10,42X
STR3:   DEF      20X,B#11,42X
;
MWAMWB: DEF      22X,B#00,40X     ;2901 A,B MUX SELECT
RSRD:   DEF      22X,B#01,40X
RSRS:   DEF      22X,B#10,40X
RDRD:   DEF      22X,B#11,40X
;
NOFTCH: DEF      32X,B#0,31X      ;FETCH = FETCH INSTRUCTION THIS CYCLE
FETCH:  DEF      32X,B#1,31X
;
NOCIB:  DEF      36X,B#0,27X      ;CIB = CARRY-IN MUX SELECT BIT B
CIB:    DEF      36X,B#1,27X
;
NOCIA:  DEF      40X,B#0,23X      ;CIA = CARRY-IN MUX SELECT BIT A
CIA:    DEF      40X,B#0,23X
;
RCLMUL: DEF      44X,B#00,18X     ;SHIFT & ROTATE MUX CTL BITS
ROLROR: DEF      44X,B#01,18X
DRLASR: DEF      44X,B#10,18X
LSLLSR: DEF      44X,B#11,18X
;
NOLIN:  DEF      46X,B#0,17X      ;LATCH-IN LOW NIBBLE OF DATA BUS
LIN:    DEF      46X,B#1,17X
;
BRC0:   DEF      47X,B#00000,12X ;2909 NEXT INSTRUCTION CONTROL
BRC1:   DEF      47X,B#00001,12X
BRV0:   DEF      47X,B#00010,12X
BRV1:   DEF      47X,B#00011,12X
BRN0:   DEF      47X,B#00100,12X
BRN1:   DEF      47X,B#00101,12X
BRZ0:   DEF      47X,B#00110,12X
BRZ1:   DEF      47X,B#00111,12X
BRHS0:  DEF      47X,B#01000,12X
BRHS1:  DEF      47X,B#01001,12X
BRLZ0:  DEF      47X,B#01010,12X
BRLZ1:  DEF      47X,B#01011,12X
BRHLT0: DEF      47X,B#01100,12X
BRHLT1: DEF      47X,B#01101,12X
BRIH0:  DEF      47X,B#01110,12X
BRIH1:  DEF      47X,B#01111,12X
BRANCH: DEF      47X,B#10000,12X
CALL:   DEF      47X,B#10010,12X
CN0:    DEF      47X,B#10100,12X
RTSZ1:  DEF      47X,B#10110,12X
RET:    DEF      47X,B#11000,12X
BRIHMAP: DEF     47X,B#11110,12X
CONTNUE: DEF     47X,B#11111,12X
;
DATA:   DEF      48X,16VH#0000    ;MICROWORD DATA
;
;
END
;
; HEX-29 MICROPROGRAM ASSEMBLY PHASE
;
;  (FIRST 256 MICROPROGRAM WORDS)
;
;
;
RESET:   CONTNUE        & AM2901  R0    , R0    , QREG  , ADD   , AQ
/                       & NOINE  & SDMA   & NOVMA  & READ
/                       & BA     & NOLAD  & NORMM  & LMM    & NOCLB
/                       & NOSWP  & NODIN  & NOSDA  & NORCC  & LCCLCV
/                       & NOLDI  & NOSTR  & MWAMWB & NOFTCH & NOCIB
/                       & NOCIA  & RCLMUL & NOLIN

         CONTNUE        & AM2901  R0    , R0    , QREG  , ADD   , AQ
/                       & NOINE  & NOSDMA & NOVMA  & READ
/                       & BA     & NOLAD  & NORMM  & LMM    & NOCIB
/                       & NOSWP  & NODIN  & NOSDA  & NORCC  & LCCLCV
/                       & NOLDI  & NOSTR  & MWAMWB & NOFTCH & NOCIB
/                       & NOCIA  & RCLMUL & NOLIN

         CONTNUE        & AM2901  R0    , R0    , NOOP  , AND   , DZ
/                       & NOINE  & NOSDMA & NOVMA  & WRITE
/                       & NOBA   & NOLAD  & NORMM  & NOLMM  & NOCLB
/                       & NOSWP  & NODIN  & NOSDA  & NORCC  & LCCLCV
/                       & NOLDI  & NOSTR  & MWAMWB & NOFTCH & NOCIB
/                       & NOCIA  & RCLMUL & NOLIN

                        & AM2901  R0    , R0    , NOOP  , OR    , DZ
/                       & INE    & SDMA   & NOVMA  & WRITE
/                       & NOBA   & NOLAD  & NORMM  & LMM    & NOCLB
/                       & NOSWP  & NODIN  & SDA    & NORCC  & LCCLCV
/                       & NOLDI  & NOSTR  & MWAMWB & NOFTCH & NOCIB
/                       & NOCIA  & RCLMUL & LIN    & DATA   H#000D

                        & AM2901  R15   , R15   , RAMF  , OR    , DZ
/                       & INE    & SDMA   & NOVMA  & READ
/                       & BA     & NOLAD  & NORMM  & LMM    & NOCLB
/                       & NOSWP  & NODIN  & SDA    & NORCC  & LCCLCV
/                       & NOLDI  & NOSTR  & MWAMWB & NOFTCH & NOCIB
/                       & NOCIA  & RCLMUL & LIN    & DATA   H#0200

         BRANCH IFETCH  & AM2901  R0    , R0    , QREG  , ADD   , AQ
/                       & NOINE  & NOSDMA & NOVMA  & READ
/                       & BA     & NOLAD  & NORMM  & LMM    & NOCLB
/                       & NOSWP  & NODIN  & NOSDA  & NORCC  & LCCLCV
/                       & NOLDI  & NOSTR  & MWAMWB & NOFTCH & NOCIB
/                       & NOCIA  & RCLMUL & NOLIN


          ORG    H#0008

IFETCH:                 & AM2901  R15   , R15   , RAMA  , ADD   , ZA
/                       & NOINE  & SDMA   &  VMA   & READ
/                       & NOBA   & LAD    & NORMM  & LMM    & NOCLB
/                       & NOSWP  & NODIN  & NOSDA  & NORCC  & LCCLCV
/                       & LDI    & NOSTR  & MWAMWB & FETCH  & NOCIB
/                       & NOCIA  & RCLMUL & LIN    & DATA   H#F000
INSTR:   BRIHMAP IHR    & AM2901  R15   , R15   , RAMF  , ADD   , ZB
/                       & NOINE  & NOSDMA & NOVMA  & READ
/                       & BA     & LAD    & NORMM  & LMM    & NOCLB
/                       & NOSWP  & DINHL  & NOSDA  & NORCC  & LCCLCV
/                       & NOLDI  & NOSTR  & MWAMWB & NOFTCH & NOCIB
/                       & CIA    & RCLMUL & NOLIN


          ORG    H#000C

BRA+:    BRANCH INSTR   & AM2901  R15   , R15   , RAMF  , ADD   , DA
/                       & NOINE  & SDMA   &  VMA   & READ
/                       & NOBA   & LAD    & NORMM  & LMM    & CLRLO
/                       & NOSWP  & DINHI  & NOSDA  & NORCC  & LCCLCV
/                       & LDI    & NOSTR  & MWAMWB & FETCH  & NOCIB
/                       & NOCIA  & RCLMUL & NOLIN

BRA-:    BRANCH INSTR   & AM2901  R15   , R15   , RAMF  , ADD   , DA
/                       & NOINE  & SDMA   &  VMA   & READ
/                       & NOBA   & LAD    & NORMM  & LMM    & NOCLB
```

```
/                       & NOSWP & DINHI & NOSDA & NORCC & LCCLCV
/                       & LDI   & NOSTR & MWAMWB & FETCH & NOCIB
/                       & NOCIA & RCLMUL & NOLIN

BSR+:  CONTNUE          & AM29Ø1 R14 , R14 , RAMF , SUBR , ZA
/                       & NOINE & NOSDMA & NOVMA & READ
/                       & BA    & LAD   & NORMM & LMM  & NOCLB
/                       & NOSWP & NODIN & NOSDA & NORCC & LCCLCV
/                       & NOLDI & NOSTR & MWAMWB & NOFTCH & NOCIB
/                       & NOCIA & RCLMUL & NOLIN

       BRANCH IFETCH    & AM29Ø1 R15 , R15 , RAMA , ADD , DA
/                       & NOINE & NOSDMA & VMA & WRITE
/                       & NOBA  & NOLAD & NORMM & LMM  & CLRLO
/                       & NOSWP & DINHI & NOSDA & NORCC & LCCLCV
/                       & NOLDI & NOSTR & MWAMWB & NOFTCH & NOCIB
/                       & NOCIA & RCLMUL & NOLIN

BSR-:  CONTNUE          & AM29Ø1 R14 , R14 , RAMF , SUBR , ZA
/                       & NOINE & NOSDMA & NOVMA & READ
/                       & BA    & LAD   & NORMM & LMM  & NOCLB
/                       & NOSWP & NODIN & NOSDA & NORCC & LCCLCV
/                       & NOLDI & NOSTR & MWAMWB & NOFTCH & NOCIB
/                       & NOCIA & RCLMUL & NOLIN

       BRANCH IFETCH    & AM29Ø1 R15 , R15 , RAMA , ADD , DA
/                       & NOINE & NOSDMA & VMA & WRITE
/                       & NOBA  & NOLAD & NORMM & LMM  & NOCLB
/                       & NOSWP & DINHI & NOSDA & NORCC & LCCLCV
/                       & NOLDI & NOSTR & MWAMWB & NOFTCH & NOCIB
/                       & NOCIA & RCLMUL & NOLIN

BC+:   BRCØ   IFETCH    & AM29Ø1 R15 , R15 , QREG , ADD , DA
/                       & NOINE & NOSDMA & NOVMA & READ
/                       & BA    & NOLAD & NORMM & LMM  & CLRLO
/                       & NOSWP & DINHI & NOSDA & NORCC & LCCLCV
/                       & NOLDI & NOSTR & MWAMWB & NOFTCH & NOCIB
/                       & NOCIA & RCLMUL & NOLIN
       BRANCH INSTR     & AM29Ø1 R15 , R15 , RAMF , ADD , ZQ
/                       & NOINE & SDMA  & VMA  & READ
/                       & NOBA  & LAD   & NORMM & LMM  & NOCLB
/                       & NOSWP & NODIN & NOSDA & NORCC & LCCLCV
/                       & LDI   & NOSTR & MWAMWB & FETCH & NOCIB
/                       & NOCIA & RCLMUL & NOLIN

BC-:   BRCØ   IFETCH    & AM29Ø1 R15 , R15 , QREG , ADD , DA
/                       & NOINE & NOSDMA & NOVMA & READ
/                       & BA    & NOLAD & NORMM & LMM  & NOCLB
/                       & NOSWP & DINHI & NOSDA & NORCC & LCCLCV
/                       & NOLDI & NOSTR & MWAMWB & NOFTCH & NOCIB
/                       & NOCIA & RCLMUL & NOLIN

       BRANCH INSTR     & AM29Ø1 R15 , R15 , RAMF , ADD , ZQ
/                       & NOINE & SDMA  & VMA  & READ
/                       & NOBA  & LAD   & NORMM & LMM  & NOCLB
/                       & NOSWP & NODIN & NOSDA & NORCC & LCCLCV
/                       & LDI   & NOSTR & MWAMWB & FETCH & NOCIB
/                       & NOCIA & RCLMUL & NOLIN

BNC+:  BRC1   IFETCH    & AM29Ø1 R15 , R15 , QREG , ADD , DA
/                       & NOINE & NOSDMA & NOVMA & READ
/                       & BA    & NOLAD & NORMM & LMM  & CLRLO
/                       & NOSWP & DINHI & NOSDA & NORCC & LCCLCV
/                       & NOLDI & NOSTR & MWAMWB & NOFTCH & NOCIB
/                       & NOCIA & RCLMUL & NOLIN

       BRANCH INSTR     & AM29Ø1 R15 , R15 , RAMF , ADD , ZQ
/                       & NOINE & SDMA  & VMA  & READ
/                       & NOBA  & LAD   & NORMM & LMM  & NOCLB
/                       & NOSWP & NODIN & NOSDA & NORCC & LCCLCV
/                       & LDI   & NOSTR & MWAMWB & FETCH & NOCIB
/                       & NOCIA & RCLMUL & NOLIN

BNC-:  BRC1   IFETCH    & AM29Ø1 R15 , R15 , QREG , ADD , DA
/                       & NOINE & NOSDMA & NOVMA & READ
/                       & BA    & NOLAD & NORMM & LMM  & NOCLB
/                       & NOSWP & DINHI & NOSDA & NORCC & LCCLCV
/                       & NOLDI & NOSTR & MWAMWB & NOFTCH & NOCIB
/                       & NOCIA & RCLMUL & NOLIN

       BRANCH INSTR     & AM29Ø1 R15 , R15 , RAMF , ADD , ZQ
/                       & NOINE & SDMA  & VMA  & READ
/                       & NOBA  & LAD   & NORMM & LMM  & NOCLB
/                       & NOSWP & NODIN & NOSDA & NORCC & LCCLCV
/                       & LDI   & NOSTR & MWAMWB & FETCH & NOCIB
/                       & NOCIA & RCLMUL & NOLIN

BV+:   BRVØ   IFETCH    & AM29Ø1 R15 , R15 , QREG , ADD , DA
/                       & NOINE & NOSDMA & NOVMA & READ
/                       & BA    & NOLAD & NORMM & LMM  & CLRLO
/                       & NOSWP & DINHI & NOSDA & NORCC & LCCLCV
/                       & NOLDI & NOSTR & MWAMWB & NOFTCH & NOCIB
/                       & NOCIA & RCLMUL & NOLIN

       BRANCH INSTR     & AM29Ø1 R15 , R15 , RAMF , ADD , ZQ
/                       & NOINE & SDMA  & VMA  & READ
/                       & NOBA  & LAD   & NORMM & LMM  & NOCLB
/                       & NOSWP & NODIN & NOSDA & NORCC & LCCLCV
/                       & LDI   & NOSTR & MWAMWB & FETCH & NOCIB
/                       & NOCIA & RCLMUL & NOLIN

BV-:   BRVØ   IFETCH    & AM29Ø1 R15 , R15 , QREG , ADD , DA
/                       & NOINE & NOSDMA & NOVMA & READ
/                       & BA    & NOLAD & NORMM & LMM  & NOCLB
/                       & NOSWP & DINHI & NOSDA & NORCC & LCCLCV
/                       & NOLDI & NOSTR & MWAMWB & NOFTCH & NOCIB
/                       & NOCIA & RCLMUL & NOLIN

       BRANCH INSTR     & AM29Ø1 R15 , R15 , RAMF , ADD , ZQ
/                       & NOINE & SDMA  & VMA  & READ
/                       & NOBA  & LAD   & NORMM & LMM  & NOCLB
/                       & NOSWP & NODIN & NOSDA & NORCC & LCCLCV
/                       & LDI   & NOSTR & MWAMWB & FETCH & NOCIB
/                       & NOCIA & RCLMUL & NOLIN

BNV+:  BRV1   IFETCH    & AM29Ø1 R15 , R15 , QREG , ADD , DA
/                       & NOINE & NOSDMA & NOVMA & READ
/                       & BA    & NOLAD & NORMM & LMM  & CLRLO
/                       & NOSWP & DINHI & NOSDA & NORCC & LCCLCV
/                       & NOLDI & NOSTR & MWAMWB & NOFTCH & NOCIB
/                       & NOCIA & RCLMUL & NOLIN

       BRANCH INSTR     & AM29Ø1 R15 , R15 , RAMF , ADD , ZQ
/                       & NOINE & SDMA  & VMA  & READ
/                       & NOBA  & LAD   & NORMM & LMM  & NOCLB
/                       & NOSWP & NODIN & NOSDA & NORCC & LCCLCV
/                       & LDI   & NOSTR & MWAMWB & FETCH & NOCIB
/                       & NOCIA & RCLMUL & NOLIN

BNV-:  BRV1   IFETCH    & AM29Ø1 R15 , R15 , QREG , ADD , DA
/                       & NOINE & NOSDMA & NOVMA & READ
/                       & BA    & NOLAD & NORMM & LMM  & NOCLB
/                       & NOSWP & DINHI & NOSDA & NORCC & LCCLCV
/                       & NOLDI & NOSTR & MWAMWB & NOFTCH & NOCIB
/                       & NOCIA & RCLMUL & NOLIN

       BRANCH INSTR     & AM29Ø1 R15 , R15 , RAMF , ADD , ZQ
/                       & NOINE & SDMA  & VMA  & READ
/                       & NOBA  & LAD   & NORMM & LMM  & NOCLB
/                       & NOSWP & NODIN & NOSDA & NORCC & LCCLCV
/                       & LDI   & NOSTR & MWAMWB & FETCH & NOCIB
/                       & NOCIA & RCLMUL & NOLIN

BN+:   BRNØ   IFETCH    & AM29Ø1 R15 , R15 , QREG , ADD , DA
/                       & NOINE & NOSDMA & NOVMA & READ
/                       & BA    & NOLAD & NORMM & LMM  & CLRLO
/                       & NOSWP & DINHI & NOSDA & NORCC & LCCLCV
/                       & NOLDI & NOSTR & MWAMWB & NOFTCH & NOCIB
/                       & NOCIA & RCLMUL & NOLIN

       BRANCH INSTR     & AM29Ø1 R15 , R15 , RAMF , ADD , ZQ
/                       & NOINE & SDMA  & VMA  & READ
/                       & NOBA  & LAD   & NORMM & LMM  & NOCLB
/                       & NOSWP & NODIN & NOSDA & NORCC & LCCLCV
/                       & LDI   & NOSTR & MWAMWB & FETCH & NOCIB
/                       & NOCIA & RCLMUL & NOLIN

BN-:   BRNØ   IFETCH    & AM29Ø1 R15 , R15 , QREG , ADD , DA
/                       & NOINE & NOSDMA & NOVMA & READ
/                       & BA    & NOLAD & NORMM & LMM  & NOCLB
/                       & NOSWP & DINHI & NOSDA & NORCC & LCCLCV
/                       & NOLDI & NOSTR & MWAMWB & NOFTCH & NOCIB
/                       & NOCIA & RCLMUL & NOLIN

       BRANCH INSTR     & AM29Ø1 R15 , R15 , RAMF , ADD , ZQ
/                       & NOINE & SDMA  & VMA  & READ
/                       & NOBA  & LAD   & NORMM & LMM  & NOCLB
/                       & NOSWP & NODIN & NOSDA & NORCC & LCCLCV
/                       & LDI   & NOSTR & MWAMWB & FETCH & NOCIB
/                       & NOCIA & RCLMUL & NOLIN

BNN+:  BRN1   IFETCH    & AM29Ø1 R15 , R15 , QREG , ADD , DA
/                       & NOINE & NOSDMA & NOVMA & READ
/                       & BA    & NOLAD & NORMM & LMM  & CLRLO
/                       & NOSWP & DINHI & NOSDA & NORCC & LCCLCV
/                       & NOLDI & NOSTR & MWAMWB & NOFTCH & NOCIB
/                       & NOCIA & RCLMUL & NOLIN

       BRANCH INSTR     & AM29Ø1 R15 , R15 , RAMF , ADD , ZQ
/                       & NOINE & SDMA  & VMA  & READ
/                       & NOBA  & LAD   & NORMM & LMM  & NOCLB
/                       & NOSWP & NODIN & NOSDA & NORCC & LCCLCV
/                       & LDI   & NOSTR & MWAMWB & FETCH & NOCIB
/                       & NOCIA & RCLMUL & NOLIN

BNN-:  BRN1   IFETCH    & AM29Ø1 R15 , R15 , QREG , ADD , DA
/                       & NOINE & NOSDMA & NOVMA & READ
/                       & BA    & NOLAD & NORMM & LMM  & NOCLB
/                       & NOSWP & DINHI & NOSDA & NORCC & LCCLCV
/                       & NOLDI & NOSTR & MWAMWB & NOFTCH & NOCIB
/                       & NOCIA & RCLMUL & NOLIN

       BRANCH INSTR     & AM29Ø1 R15 , R15 , RAMF , ADD , ZQ
/                       & NOINE & SDMA  & VMA  & READ
/                       & NOBA  & LAD   & NORMM & LMM  & NOCLB
/                       & NOSWP & NODIN & NOSDA & NORCC & LCCLCV
/                       & LDI   & NOSTR & MWAMWB & FETCH & NOCIB
/                       & NOCIA & RCLMUL & NOLIN

BZ+:   BRZØ   IFETCH    & AM29Ø1 R15 , R15 , QREG , ADD , DA
/                       & NOINE & NOSDMA & NOVMA & READ
/                       & BA    & NOLAD & NORMM & LMM  & CLRLO
/                       & NOSWP & DINHI & NOSDA & NORCC & LCCLCV
/                       & NOLDI & NOSTR & MWAMWB & NOFTCH & NOCIB
/                       & NOCIA & RCLMUL & NOLIN

       BRANCH INSTR     & AM29Ø1 R15 , R15 , RAMF , ADD , ZQ
/                       & NOINE & SDMA  & VMA  & READ
/                       & NOBA  & LAD   & NORMM & LMM  & NOCLB
/                       & NOSWP & NODIN & NOSDA & NORCC & LCCLCV
/                       & LDI   & NOSTR & MWAMWB & FETCH & NOCIB
/                       & NOCIA & RCLMUL & NOLIN

BZ-:   BRZØ   ØØØ8      & AM29Ø1 R15 , R15 , QREG , ADD , DA
/                       & NOINE & NOSDMA & NOVMA & READ
/                       & BA    & NOLAD & NORMM & LMM  & NOCLB
/                       & NOSWP & DINHI & NOSDA & NORCC & LCCLCV
/                       & NOLDI & NOSTR & MWAMWB & NOFTCH & NOCIB
/                       & NOCIA & RCLMUL & NOLIN

       BRANCH INSTR     & AM29Ø1 R15 , R15 , RAMF , ADD , ZQ
/                       & NOINE & SDMA  & VMA  & READ
/                       & NOBA  & LAD   & NORMM & LMM  & NOCLB
/                       & NOSWP & NODIN & NOSDA & NORCC & LCCLCV
/                       & LDI   & NOSTR & MWAMWB & FETCH & NOCIB
/                       & NOCIA & RCLMUL & NOLIN

BNZ+:  BRZ1   ØØØ8      & AM29Ø1 R15 , R15 , QREG , ADD , DA
/                       & NOINE & NOSDMA & NOVMA & READ
/                       & BA    & NOLAD & NORMM & LMM  & CLRLO
/                       & NOSWP & DINHI & NOSDA & NORCC & LCCLCV
/                       & NOLDI & NOSTR & MWAMWB & NOFTCH & NOCIB
/                       & NOCIA & RCLMUL & NOLIN

       BRANCH INSTR     & AM29Ø1 R15 , R15 , RAMF , ADD , ZQ
/                       & NOINE & SDMA  & VMA  & READ
/                       & NOBA  & LAD   & NORMM & LMM  & NOCLB
/                       & NOSWP & NODIN & NOSDA & NORCC & LCCLCV
/                       & LDI   & NOSTR & MWAMWB & FETCH & NOCIB
/                       & NOCIA & RCLMUL & NOLIN

BNZ-:  BRZ1   ØØØ8      & AM29Ø1 R15 , R15 , QREG , ADD , DA
/                       & NOINE & NOSDMA & NOVMA & READ
/                       & BA    & NOLAD & NORMM & LMM  & NOCLB
/                       & NOSWP & DINHI & NOSDA & NORCC & LCCLCV
/                       & NOLDI & NOSTR & MWAMWB & NOFTCH & NOCIB
/                       & NOCIA & RCLMUL & NOLIN

       BRANCH INSTR     & AM29Ø1 R15 , R15 , RAMF , ADD , ZQ
/                       & NOINE & SDMA  & VMA  & READ
/                       & NOBA  & LAD   & NORMM & LMM  & NOCLB
/                       & NOSWP & NODIN & NOSDA & NORCC & LCCLCV
```

```
/                      & LDI    & NOSTR  & MWAMWB & FETCH  & NOCIB
/                      & NOCIA  & RCLMUL & NOLIN

BH+:    BRHSØ  IFETCH  & AM2901  R15   , R15   , QREG  , ADD   , DA
/                      & NOINE  & NOSDMA & NOVMA  & READ
/                      & BA     & NOLAD  & NORMM  & LMM    & CLRLO
/                      & NOSWP  & DINHI  & NOSDA  & NORCC  & LCCLCV
/                      & NOLDI  & NOSTR  & MWAMWB & NOFTCH & NOCIB
/                      & NOCIA  & RCLMUL & NOLIN

        BRANCH INSTR   & AM2901  R15   , R15   , RAMF  , ADD   , ZQ
/                      & NOINE  & SDMA   &  VMA   & READ
/                      & NOBA   & LAD    & NORMM  & LMM    & NOCLB
/                      & NOSWP  & NODIN  & NOSDA  & NORCC  & LCCLCV
/                      & LDI    & NOSTR  & MWAMWB & FETCH  & NOCIB
/                      & NOCIA  & RCLMUL & NOLIN

BH-:    BRHSØ  IFETCH  & AM2901  R15   , R15   , QREG  , ADD   , DA
/                      & NOINE  & NOSDMA & NOVMA  & READ
/                      & BA     & NOLAD  & NORMM  & LMM    & NOCLB
/                      & NOSWP  & DINHI  & NOSDA  & NORCC  & LCCLCV
/                      & NOLDI  & NOSTR  & MWAMWB & NOFTCH & NOCIB
/                      & NOCIA  & RCLMUL & NOLIN

        BRANCH INSTR   & AM2901  R15   , R15   , RAMF  , ADD   , ZQ
/                      & NOINE  & SDMA   &  VMA   & READ
/                      & NOBA   & LAD    & NORMM  & LMM    & NOCLB
/                      & NOSWP  & NODIN  & NOSDA  & NORCC  & LCCLCV
/                      & LDI    & NOSTR  & MWAMWB & FETCH  & NOCIB
/                      & NOCIA  & RCLMUL & NOLIN

BNH+:   BRHS1  IFETCH  & AM2901  R15   , R15   , QREG  , ADD   , DA
/                      & NOINE  & NOSDMA & NOVMA  & READ
/                      & BA     & NOLAD  & NORMM  & LMM    & CLRLO
/                      & NOSWP  & DINHI  & NOSDA  & NORCC  & LCCLCV
/                      & NOLDI  & NOSTR  & MWAMWB & NOFTCH & NOCIB
/                      & NOCIA  & RCLMUL & NOLIN

        BRANCH INSTR   & AM2901  R15   , R15   , RAMF  , ADD   , ZQ
/                      & NOINE  & SDMA   &  VMA   & READ
/                      & NOBA   & LAD    & NORMM  & LMM    & NOCLB
/                      & NOSWP  & NODIN  & NOSDA  & NORCC  & LCCLCV
/                      & LDI    & NOSTR  & MWAMWB & FETCH  & NOCIB
/                      & NOCIA  & RCLMUL & NOLIN

BNH-:   BRHS1  IFETCH  & AM2901  R15   , R15   , QREG  , ADD   , DA
/                      & NOINE  & NOSDMA & NOVMA  & READ
/                      & BA     & NOLAD  & NORMM  & LMM    & NOCLB
/                      & NOSWP  & DINHI  & NOSDA  & NORCC  & LCCLCV
/                      & NOLDI  & NOSTR  & MWAMWB & NOFTCH & NOCIB
/                      & NOCIA  & RCLMUL & NOLIN

        BRANCH INSTR   & AM2901  R15   , R15   , RAMF  , ADD   , ZQ
/                      & NOINE  & SDMA   &  VMA   & READ
/                      & NOBA   & LAD    & NORMM  & LMM    & NOCLB
/                      & NOSWP  & NODIN  & NOSDA  & NORCC  & LCCLCV
/                      & LDI    & NOSTR  & MWAMWB & FETCH  & NOCIB
/                      & NOCIA  & RCLMUL & NOLIN

DBNZ+:  CONTNUE        & AM2901  R9    , R9    , RAMF  , SUBR  , ZA
/                      & NOINE  & SDMA   & NOVMA  & READ
/                      & BA     & NOLAD  & NORMM  & LMM    & NOCLB
/                      & NOSWP  & NODIN  & NOSDA  & NORCC  & LCCLCV
/                      & NOLDI  & NOSTR  & MWAMWB & NOFTCH & NOCIB
/                      & NOCIA  & RCLMUL & NOLIN

        BRLZ1  IFETCH  & AM2901  R15   , R15   , QREG  , ADD   , DA
/                      & NOINE  & NOSDMA & NOVMA  & READ
/                      & BA     & NOLAD  & NORMM  & LMM    & CLRLO
/                      & NOSWP  & DINHI  & NOSDA  & NORCC  & LCCLCV
/                      & NOLDI  & NOSTR  & MWAMWB & NOFTCH & NOCIB
/                      & NOCIA  & RCLMUL & NOLIN

        BRANCH INSTR   & AM2901  R15   , R15   , RAMF  , OR    , ZQ
/                      & NOINE  & SDMA   &  VMA   & READ
/                      & NOBA   & LAD    & NORMM  & LMM    & NOCLB
/                      & NOSWP  & NODIN  & NOSDA  & NORCC  & LCCLCV
/                      & LDI    & NOSTR  & MWAMWB & FETCH  & NOCIB
/                      & NOCIA  & RCLMUL & NOLIN

DBNZ-:  CONTNUE        & AM2901  R9    , R9    , RAMF  , SUBR  , ZA
/                      & NOINE  & SDMA   & NOVMA  & READ
/                      & BA     & NOLAD  & NORMM  & LMM    & NOCLB
/                      & NOSWP  & NODIN  & NOSDA  & NORCC  & LCCLCV
/                      & NOLDI  & NOSTR  & MWAMWB & NOFTCH & NOCIB
/                      & NOCIA  & RCLMUL & NOLIN
        BRLZ1  IFETCH  & AM2901  R15   , R15   , QREG  , ADD   , DA
/                      & NOINE  & NOSDMA & NOVMA  & READ
/                      & BA     & NOLAD  & NORMM  & LMM    & NOCLB
/                      & NOSWP  & DINHI  & NOSDA  & NORCC  & LCCLCV
/                      & NOLDI  & NOSTR  & MWAMWB & NOFTCH & NOCIB
/                      & NOCIA  & RCLMUL & NOLIN

        BRANCH INSTR   & AM2901  R15   , R15   , RAMF  , OR    , ZQ
/                      & NOINE  & SDMA   &  VMA   & READ
/                      & NOBA   & LAD    & NORMM  & LMM    & NOCLB
/                      & NOSWP  & NODIN  & NOSDA  & NORCC  & LCCLCV
/                      & LDI    & NOSTR  & MWAMWB & FETCH  & NOCIB
/                      & NOCIA  & RCLMUL & NOLIN

SQUEEZ: CONTNUE        & AM2901  RØ    , RØ    , QREG  , AND   , AQ
/                      & NOINE  & NOSDMA & NOVMA  & READ
/                      & BA     & NOLAD  & NORMM  & LMM    & NOCLB
/                      & NOSWP  & NODIN  & NOSDA  & NORCC  & LCCLCV
/                      & NOLDI  & NOSTR  & RSRS   & NOFTCH & NOCIB
/                      & NOCIA  & RCLMUL & NOLIN

        BRANCH INSTR   & AM2901  RØ    , RØ    , NOOP  , SUBR  , DQ
/                      & NOINE  & SDMA   &  VMA   & READ
/                      & NOBA   & NOLAD  & NORMM  & LMM    & CLRLO
/                      & NOSWP  & DINHI  & NOSDA  & NORCC  & NOLCC
/                      & LDI    & NOSTR  & MWAMWB & FETCH  & NOCIB
/                      & CIA    & RCLMUL & NOLIN

CBB+:   BRANCH  BIC    & AM2901  R15   , R15   , QREG  , ADD   , DA
/                      & NOINE  & SDMA   & NOVMA  & READ
/                      & BA     & NOLAD  & NORMM  & LMM    & CLRLO
/                      & NOSWP  & DINHI  & NOSDA  & NORCC  & LCCLCV
/                      & NOLDI  & NOSTR  & MWAMWB & NOFTCH & NOCIB
/                      & NOCIA  & RCLMUL & NOLIN

CBB-:   CONTNUE        & AM2901  R15   , R15   , QREG  , ADD   , DA
/                      & NOINE  & SDMA   & NOVMA  & READ
/                      & BA     & NOLAD  & NORMM  & LMM    & NOCLB
/                      & NOSWP  & DINHI  & NOSDA  & NORCC  & LCCLCV
/                      & NOLDI  & NOSTR  & MWAMWB & NOFTCH & NOCIB
/                      & NOCIA  & RCLMUL & NOLIN

BIC:                   & AM2901  R1Ø   , R8    , RAMF  , AND   , DA
/                      & NOINE  & NOSDMA & NOVMA  & READ
/                      & BA     & NOLAD  & NORMM  & LMM    & NOCLB
/                      & NOSWP  & NODIN  & SDA    & NORCC  & LCCLCV
/                      & NOLDI  & NOSTR  & MWAMWB & NOFTCH & NOCIB
/                      & NOCIA  & RCLMUL & LIN    & DATA   H#ØØFF

        CONTNUE        & AM2901  R15   , R15   , RAMA  , ADD   , ZA
/                      & NOINE  & SDMA   &  VMA   & READ
/                      & NOBA   & LAD    & NORMM  & LMM    & NOCLB
/                      & NOSWP  & NODIN  & NOSDA  & NORCC  & LCCLCV
/                      & LDI    & NOSTR  & MWAMWB & NOFTCH & NOCIB
/                      & CIA    & RCLMUL & NOLIN

        CONTNUE        & AM2901  R8    , R8    , NOOP  , SUBS  , DA
/                      & NOINE  & SDMA   & NOVMA  & READ
/                      & BA     & NOLAD  & NORMM  & LMM    & CLRLO
/                      & SWPHI  & NODIN  & NOSDA  & NORCC  & LCC
/                      & NOLDI  & NOSTR  & MWAMWB & NOFTCH & NOCIB
/                      & CIA    & RCLMUL & NOLIN

        BRCØ   IFETCH  & AM2901  R8    , R8    , NOOP  , SUBR  , DA
/                      & NOINE  & NOSDMA & NOVMA  & READ
/                      & BA     & NOLAD  & NORMM  & LMM    & CLRLO
/                      & NOSWP  & DINHI  & NOSDA  & NORCC  & LCC
/                      & NOLDI  & NOSTR  & MWAMWB & NOFTCH & NOCIB
/                      & CIA    & RCLMUL & NOLIN

        BRCØ   IFETCH  & AM2901  RØ    , RØ    , NOOP  , ADD   , AQ
/                      & NOINE  & NOSDMA & NOVMA  & READ
/                      & BA     & NOLAD  & NORMM  & LMM    & NOCLB
/                      & NOSWP  & NODIN  & NOSDA  & NORCC  & LCCLCV
/                      & NOLDI  & NOSTR  & MWAMWB & NOFTCH & NOCIB
/                      & NOCIA  & RCLMUL & NOLIN

        BRANCH INSTR   & AM2901  R15   , R15   , RAMF  , ADD   , ZQ
/                      & NOINE  & SDMA   &  VMA   & READ
/                      & NOBA   & LAD    & NORMM  & LMM    & NOCLB
/                      & NOSWP  & NODIN  & NOSDA  & NORCC  & LCCLCV
/                      & LDI    & NOSTR  & MWAMWB & FETCH  & NOCIB
/                      & NOCIA  & RCLMUL & NOLIN

ALSRR:  CONTNUE        & AM2901  RØ    , RØ    , RAMU  , ADD   , ZA
/                      & NOINE  & NOSDMA & NOVMA  & READ
/                      & BA     & NOLAD  & NORMM  & LMM    & NOCLB
/                      & NOSWP  & NODIN  & NOSDA  & NORCC  & LNZCCV
/                      & NOLDI  & NOSTR  & RSRD   & NOFTCH & NOCIB
/                      & NOCIA  & LSLLSR & NOLIN

RFLAG:  BRANCH INSTR   & AM2901  RØ    , RØ    , NOOP  , ADD   , ZB
/                      & NOINE  & SDMA   &  VMA   & READ
/                      & NOBA   & NOLAD  & NORMM  & LMM    & NOCLB
/                      & NOSWP  & NODIN  & NOSDA  & NORCC  & LCV
/                      & LDI    & NOSTR  & RSRD   & FETCH  & NOCIB
/                      & NOCIA  & RCLMUL & NOLIN

ASRRR:  BRANCH RFLAG   & AM2901  RØ    , RØ    , RAMD  , ADD   , ZA
/                      & NOINE  & NOSDMA & NOVMA  & READ
/                      & BA     & NOLAD  & NORMM  & LMM    & NOCLB
/                      & NOSWP  & NODIN  & NOSDA  & NORCC  & LNZCCV
/                      & NOLDI  & NOSTR  & RSRD   & NOFTCH & NOCIB
/                      & NOCIA  & DRLASR & NOLIN

ROLRR:  BRANCH RFLAG   & AM2901  RØ    , RØ    , RAMU  , ADD   , ZA
/                      & NOINE  & NOSDMA & NOVMA  & READ
/                      & BA     & NOLAD  & NORMM  & LMM    & NOCLB
/                      & NOSWP  & NODIN  & NOSDA  & NORCC  & LNZCCV
/                      & NOLDI  & NOSTR  & RSRD   & NOFTCH & NOCIB
/                      & NOCIA  & ROLROR & NOLIN

RORRR:  BRANCH RFLAG   & AM2901  RØ    , RØ    , RAMD  , ADD   , ZA
/                      & NOINE  & NOSDMA & NOVMA  & READ
/                      & BA     & NOLAD  & NORMM  & LMM    & NOCLB
/                      & NOSWP  & NODIN  & NOSDA  & NORCC  & LNZCCV
/                      & NOLDI  & NOSTR  & RSRD   & NOFTCH & NOCIB
/                      & NOCIA  & ROLROR & NOLIN

RLCRR:  BRANCH RFLAG   & AM2901  RØ    , RØ    , RAMU  , ADD   , ZA
/                      & NOINE  & NOSDMA & NOVMA  & READ
/                      & BA     & NOLAD  & NORMM  & LMM    & NOCLB
/                      & NOSWP  & NODIN  & NOSDA  & NORCC  & LNZCCV
/                      & NOLDI  & NOSTR  & RSRD   & NOFTCH & NOCIB
/                      & NOCIA  & RCLMUL & NOLIN

MVNCCR: BRANCH INSTR   & AM2901  RØ    , RØ    , RAMF  , OR    , DZ
/                      & NOINE  & SDMA   &  VMA   & READ
/                      & NOBA   & NOLAD  & NORMM  & LMM    & CLRLO
/                      & NOSWP  & NODIN  & NOSDA  & RCC    & LCCLCV
/                      & LDI    & NOSTR  & RDRD   & FETCH  & NOCIB
/                      & NOCIA  & RCLMUL & NOLIN

LSRRR:  BRANCH RFLAG   & AM2901  RØ    , RØ    , RAMD  , ADD   , ZA
/                      & NOINE  & NOSDMA & NOVMA  & READ
/                      & BA     & NOLAD  & NORMM  & LMM    & NOCLB
/                      & NOSWP  & NODIN  & NOSDA  & NORCC  & LNZCCV
/                      & NOLDI  & NOSTR  & RSRD   & NOFTCH & NOCIB
/                      & NOCIA  & LSLLSR & NOLIN

VLSRR:                 & AM2901  RØ    , RØ    , QREG  , AND   , DA
/                      & NOINE  & SDMA   & NOVMA  & READ
/                      & BA     & NOLAD  & NORMM  & LMM    & NOCLB
/                      & NOSWP  & NODIN  & SDA    & NORCC  & LCCLCV
/                      & NOLDI  & NOSTR  & RDRD   & NOFTCH & NOCIB
/                      & NOCIA  & RCLMUL & LIN    & DATA   H#ØØØF

VLSOOP: BRLZ1  IFETCH  & AM2901  RØ    , RØ    , NOOP  , ADD   , ZB
/                      & NOINE  & NOSDMA & NOVMA  & READ
/                      & BA     & NOLAD  & NORMM  & LMM    & NOCLB
/                      & NOSWP  & NODIN  & NOSDA  & NORCC  & LCV
/                      & NOLDI  & NOSTR  & RSRS   & NOFTCH & NOCIB
/                      & NOCIA  & RCLMUL & NOLIN

        CONTNUE        & AM2901  RØ    , RØ    , RAMU  , ADD   , ZA
/                      & NOINE  & SDMA   & NOVMA  & READ
/                      & BA     & NOLAD  & NORMM  & LMM    & NOCLB
/                      & NOSWP  & NODIN  & NOSDA  & NORCC  & LNZCCV
/                      & NOLDI  & NOSTR  & RSRS   & NOFTCH & NOCIB
/                      & NOCIA  & LSLLSR & NOLIN

        BRANCH VSLOOP  & AM2901  RØ    , RØ    , QREG  , SUBR  , ZQ
/                      & NOINE  & SDMA   & NOVMA  & READ
/                      & BA     & NOLAD  & NORMM  & LMM    & NOCLB
/                      & NOSWP  & NODIN  & NOSDA  & NORCC  & LCCLCV
/                      & NOLDI  & NOSTR  & MWAMWB & NOFTCH & NOCIB
```

```
/                         & NOCIA  & RCLMUL & NOLIN

VSLRH:                    & AM2901  R0     , R0     , QREG  , OR     , DZ
/                         & NOINE  & SDMA   & NOVMA  & READ
/                         & BA     & NOLAD  & NORMM  & LMM    & NOCLB
/                         & NOSWP  & NODIN  & SDA    & NORCC  & LCCLCV
/                         & NOLDI  & NOSTR  & MWAMWB & NOFTCH & NOCIB
/                         & NOCIA  & RCLMUL & LIN    & DATA   H#000F

          BRANCH VSLOOP   & AM2901  R0     , R0     , QREG  , AND    , DQ
/                         & NOINE  & SDMA   & NOVMA  & READ
/                         & BA     & NOLAD  & NORMM  & LMM    & CLRLO
/                         & NOSWP  & DINHI  & NOSDA  & NORCC  & LCCLCV
/                         & NOLDI  & NOSTR  & MWAMWB & NOFTCH & NOCIB
/                         & NOCIA  & RCLMUL & NOLIN

CSLRR:    CONTNUE         & AM2901  R8     , R8     , RAMF  , AND    , DZ
/                         & NOINE  & SDMA   & NOVMA  & READ
/                         & BA     & NOLAD  & NORMM  & LMM    & NOCLB
/                         & NOSWP  & NODIN  & NOSDA  & NORCC  & LCCLCV
/                         & NOLDI  & NOSTR  & MWAMWB & NOFTCH & NOCIB
/                         & NOCIA  & RCLMUL & NOLIN

                          & AM2901  R9     , R9     , QREG  , AND    , DA
/                         & NOINE  & SDMA   & NOVMA  & READ
/                         & BA     & NOLAD  & NORMM  & LMM    & NOCLB
/                         & NOSWP  & NODIN  & SDA    & NORCC  & LCCLCV
/                         & NOLDI  & NOSTR  & MWAMWB & NOFTCH & NOCIB
/                         & NOCIA  & RCLMUL & LIN    & DATA   H#001F

CSLOOP:   BRLZ1  IFETCH   & AM2901  R0     , R0     , NOOP  , ADD    , ZA
/                         & NOINE  & NOSDMA & NOVMA  & READ
/                         & BA     & NOLAD  & NORMM  & LMM    & NOCLB
/                         & NOSWP  & NODIN  & NOSDA  & NORCC  & LCV
/                         & NOLDI  & NOSTR  & RDRD   & NOFTCH & NOCIB
/                         & NOCIA  & RCLMUL & NOLIN

          BRN1   IFETCH   & AM2901  R0     , R0     , NOOP  , ADD    , AQ
/                         & NOINE  & NOSDMA & NOVMA  & READ
/                         & BA     & NOLAD  & NORMM  & LMM    & NOCLB
/                         & NOSWP  & NODIN  & NOSDA  & NORCC  & LCCLCV
/                         & NOLDI  & NOSTR  & MWAMWB & NOFTCH & NOCIB
/                         & NOCIA  & RCLMUL & NOLIN

          CONTNUE         & AM2901  R0     , R0     , RAMU  , ADD    , ZA
/                         & NOINE  & SDMA   & NOVMA  & READ
/                         & BA     & NOLAD  & NORMM  & LMM    & NOCLB
/                         & NOSWP  & NODIN  & NOSDA  & NORCC  & LNZCCV
/                         & NOLDI  & NOSTR  & RSRS   & NOFTCH & NOCIB
/                         & NOCIA  & LSLLSR & NOLIN

          CONTNUE         & AM2901  R0     , R0     , RAMU  , ADD    , ZA
/                         & NOINE  & SDMA   & NOVMA  & READ
/                         & BA     & NOLAD  & NORMM  & LMM    & NOCLB
/                         & NOSWP  & NODIN  & NOSDA  & NORCC  & LNZCCV
/                         & NOLDI  & NOSTR  & RDRD   & NOFTCH & NOCIB
/                         & NOCIA  & ROLROR & NOLIN

          CONTNUE         & AM2901  R8     , R8     , RAMF  , ADD    , ZB
/                         & NOINE  & SDMA   & NOVMA  & READ
/                         & BA     & NOLAD  & NORMM  & LMM    & NOCLB
/                         & NOSWP  & NODIN  & NOSDA  & NORCC  & LCCLCV
/                         & NOLDI  & NOSTR  & MWAMWB & NOFTCH & NOCIB
/                         & CIA    & RCLMUL & NOLIN

          BRANCH CSLOOP   & AM2901  R0     , R0     , QREG  , SUBR   , ZQ
/                         & NOINE  & SDMA   & NOVMA  & READ
/                         & BA     & NOLAD  & NORMM  & LMM    & NOCLB
/                         & NOSWP  & NODIN  & NOSDA  & NORCC  & LCCLCV
/                         & NOLDI  & NOSTR  & MWAMWB & NOFTCH & NOCIB
/                         & NOCIA  & RCLMUL & NOLIN

DSLRR:                    & AM2901  R9     , R9     , QREG  , AND    , DA
/                         & NOINE  & SDMA   & NOVMA  & READ
/                         & BA     & NOLAD  & NORMM  & LMM    & NOCLB
/                         & NOSWP  & NODIN  & SDA    & NORCC  & LCCLCV
/                         & NOLDI  & NOSTR  & MWAMWB & NOFTCH & NOCIB
/                         & NOCIA  & RCLMUL & NOLIN  & DATA   H#001F

DSLOOP:   BRLZ1  IFETCH   & AM2901  R0     , R0     , NOOP  , ADD    , ZA
/                         & NOINE  & NOSDMA & NOVMA  & READ
/                         & BA     & NOLAD  & NORMM  & LMM    & NOCLB
/                         & NOSWP  & NODIN  & NOSDA  & NORCC  & LCV
/                         & NOLDI  & NOSTR  & RDRD   & NOFTCH & NOCIB
/                         & NOCIA  & RCLMUL & NOLIN

          CONTNUE         & AM2901  R0     , R0     , RAMU  , ADD    , ZA
/                         & NOINE  & SDMA   & NOVMA  & READ
/                         & BA     & NOLAD  & NORMM  & LMM    & NOCLB
/                         & NOSWP  & NODIN  & NOSDA  & NORCC  & LNZCCV
/                         & NOLDI  & NOSTR  & RSRS   & NOFTCH & NOCIB
/                         & NOCIA  & LSLLSR & NOLIN

          CONTNUE         & AM2901  R0     , R0     , RAMU  , ADD    , ZA
/                         & NOINE  & SDMA   & NOVMA  & READ
/                         & BA     & NOLAD  & NORMM  & LMM    & NOCLB
/                         & NOSWP  & NODIN  & NOSDA  & NORCC  & LNZCCV
/                         & NOLDI  & NOSTR  & RDRD   & NOFTCH & NOCIB
/                         & NOCIA  & ROLROR & NOLIN

          BRANCH DSLOOP   & AM2901  R0     , R0     , QREG  , SUBR   , ZQ
/                         & NOINE  & SDMA   & NOVMA  & READ
/                         & BA     & NOLAD  & NORMM  & LMM    & NOCLB
/                         & NOSWP  & NODIN  & NOSDA  & NORCC  & LCCLCV
/                         & NOLDI  & NOSTR  & MWAMWB & NOFTCH & NOCIB
/                         & NOCIA  & RCLMUL & NOLIN

MOVRCC:   BRANCH INSTR    & AM2901  R0     , R0     , NOOP  , ADD    , ZB
/                         & NOINE  & SDMA   &  VMA   & READ
/                         & NOBA   & NOLAD  & NORMM  & LMM    & NOCLB
/                         & NOSWP  & NODIN  & NOSDA  & NORCC  & LNZ
/                         & LDI    & NOSTR  & RDRD   & FETCH  & NOCIB
/                         & NOCIA  & RCLMUL & NOLIN

XCHRR:    CONTNUE         & AM2901  R0     , R0     , QREG  , ADD    , ZA
/                         & NOINE  & SDMA   & NOVMA  & READ
/                         & BA     & NOLAD  & NORMM  & LMM    & NOCLB
/                         & NOSWP  & NODIN  & NOSDA  & NORCC  & LCCLCV
/                         & NOLDI  & NOSTR  & RDRD   & NOFTCH & NOCIB
/                         & NOCIA  & RCLMUL & NOLIN

          CONTNUE         & AM2901  R0     , R0     , RAMF  , ADD    , ZA
/                         & NOINE  & NOSDMA & NOVMA  & READ
/                         & BA     & NOLAD  & NORMM  & LMM    & NOCLB
/                         & NOSWP  & NODIN  & NOSDA  & NORCC  & LCCLCV
/                         & NOLDI  & NOSTR  & RSRD   & NOFTCH & NOCIB
```

```
/                         & NOCIA  & RCLMUL & NOLIN

          BRANCH INSTR    & AM2901  R0     , R0     , RAMF  , ADD    , ZQ
/                         & NOINE  & SDMA   &  VMA   & READ
/                         & NOBA   & NOLAD  & NORMM  & LMM    & NOCLB
/                         & NOSWP  & NODIN  & NOSDA  & NORCC  & LCCLCV
/                         & LDI    & NOSTR  & RSRS   & FETCH  & NOCIB
/                         & NOCIA  & RCLMUL & NOLIN
MVNRR:    BRANCH INSTR    & AM2901  R0     , R0     , RAMF  , ADD    , ZA
/                         & NOINE  & SDMA   &  VMA   & READ
/                         & NOBA   & NOLAD  & NORMM  & LMM    & NOCLB
/                         & NOSWP  & NODIN  & NOSDA  & NORCC  & LCCLCV
/                         & LDI    & NOSTR  & RSRD   & FETCH  & NOCIB
/                         & NOCIA  & RCLMUL & NOLIN

MOVRR:    BRANCH INSTR    & AM2901  R0     , R0     , RAMF  , ADD    , ZA
/                         & NOINE  & SDMA   &  VMA   & READ
/                         & NOBA   & NOLAD  & NORMM  & LMM    & NOCLB
/                         & NOSWP  & NODIN  & NOSDA  & NORCC  & LCV
/                         & LDI    & NOSTR  & RSRD   & FETCH  & NOCIB
/                         & NOCIA  & RCLMUL & NOLIN

ADDRR:    BRANCH INSTR    & AM2901  R0     , R0     , RAMF  , ADD    , AB
/                         & NOINE  & SDMA   &  VMA   & READ
/                         & NOBA   & NOLAD  & NORMM  & LMM    & NOCLB
/                         & NOSWP  & NODIN  & NOSDA  & NORCC  & NOLCC
/                         & LDI    & NOSTR  & RSRD   & FETCH  & NOCIB
/                         & NOCIA  & RCLMUL & NOLIN

ADCRR:    BRANCH INSTR    & AM2901  R0     , R0     , RAMF  , ADD    , AB
/                         & NOINE  & SDMA   &  VMA   & READ
/                         & NOBA   & NOLAD  & NORMM  & LMM    & NOCLB
/                         & NOSWP  & NODIN  & NOSDA  & NORCC  & NOLCC
/                         & LDI    & NOSTR  & RSRD   & FETCH  & CIB
/                         & NOCIA  & RCLMUL & NOLIN

SUBRR:    BRANCH INSTR    & AM2901  R0     , R0     , RAMF  , SUBR   , AB
/                         & NOINE  & SDMA   &  VMA   & READ
/                         & NOBA   & NOLAD  & NORMM  & LMM    & NOCLB
/                         & NOSWP  & NODIN  & NOSDA  & NORCC  & NOLCC
/                         & LDI    & NOSTR  & RSRD   & FETCH  & NOCIB
/                         & CIA    & RCLMUL & NOLIN

SBCRR:    BRANCH INSTR    & AM2901  R0     , R0     , RAMF  , SUBR   , AB
/                         & NOINE  & SDMA   &  VMA   & READ
/                         & NOBA   & NOLAD  & NORMM  & LMM    & NOCLB
/                         & NOSWP  & NODIN  & NOSDA  & NORCC  & NOLCC
/                         & LDI    & NOSTR  & RSRD   & FETCH  & CIB
/                         & NOCIA  & RCLMUL & NOLIN

ANDRR:    BRANCH INSTR    & AM2901  R0     , R0     , RAMF  , AND    , AB
/                         & NOINE  & SDMA   &  VMA   & READ
/                         & NOBA   & NOLAD  & NORMM  & LMM    & NOCLB
/                         & NOSWP  & NODIN  & NOSDA  & NORCC  & LCV
/                         & LDI    & NOSTR  & RSRD   & FETCH  & NOCIB
/                         & NOCIA  & RCLMUL & NOLIN

IORRR:    BRANCH INSTR    & AM2901  R0     , R0     , RAMF  , OR     , AB
/                         & NOINE  & SDMA   &  VMA   & READ
/                         & NOBA   & NOLAD  & NORMM  & LMM    & NOCLB
/                         & NOSWP  & NODIN  & NOSDA  & NORCC  & LCV
/                         & LDI    & NOSTR  & RSRD   & FETCH  & NOCIB
/                         & NOCIA  & RCLMUL & NOLIN

XORRR:    BRANCH INSTR    & AM2901  R0     , R0     , RAMF  , EXOR   , AB
/                         & NOINE  & SDMA   &  VMA   & READ
/                         & NOBA   & NOLAD  & NORMM  & LMM    & NOCLB
/                         & NOSWP  & NODIN  & NOSDA  & NORCC  & LCV
/                         & LDI    & NOSTR  & RSRD   & FETCH  & NOCIB
/                         & NOCIA  & RCLMUL & NOLIN

CMPRR:    BRANCH INSTR    & AM2901  R0     , R0     , NOOP  , SUBR   , AB
/                         & NOINE  & SDMA   &  VMA   & READ
/                         & NOBA   & NOLAD  & NORMM  & LMM    & NOCLB
/                         & NOSWP  & NODIN  & NOSDA  & NORCC  & NOLCC
/                         & LDI    & NOSTR  & RSRD   & FETCH  & NOCIB
/                         & CIA    & RCLMUL & NOLIN

INCRR:    BRANCH INSTR    & AM2901  R0     , R0     , RAMF  , ADD    , ZA
/                         & NOINE  & SDMA   &  VMA   & READ
/                         & NOBA   & NOLAD  & NORMM  & LMM    & NOCLB
/                         & NOSWP  & NODIN  & NOSDA  & NORCC  & LCV
/                         & LDI    & NOSTR  & RSRD   & FETCH  & NOCIB
/                         & CIA    & RCLMUL & NOLIN

DECRR:    BRANCH INSTR    & AM2901  R0     , R0     , RAMF  , SUBR   , ZA
/                         & NOINE  & SDMA   &  VMA   & READ
/                         & NOBA   & NOLAD  & NORMM  & LMM    & NOCLB
/                         & NOSWP  & NODIN  & NOSDA  & NORCC  & LCV
/                         & LDI    & NOSTR  & RSRD   & FETCH  & NOCIB
/                         & NOCIA  & RCLMUL & NOLIN

COMRR:    BRANCH INSTR    & AM2901  R0     , R0     , RAMF  , EXNOR  , ZA
/                         & NOINE  & SDMA   &  VMA   & READ
/                         & NOBA   & NOLAD  & NORMM  & LMM    & NOCLB
/                         & NOSWP  & NODIN  & NOSDA  & NORCC  & LCV
/                         & LDI    & NOSTR  & RSRD   & FETCH  & NOCIB
/                         & NOCIA  & RCLMUL & NOLIN

NEGRR:    BRANCH INSTR    & AM2901  R0     , R0     , RAMF  , SUBS   , ZA
/                         & NOINE  & SDMA   &  VMA   & READ
/                         & NOBA   & NOLAD  & NORMM  & LMM    & NOCLB
/                         & NOSWP  & NODIN  & NOSDA  & NORCC  & NOLCC
/                         & LDI    & NOSTR  & RSRD   & FETCH  & NOCIB
/                         & CIA    & RCLMUL & NOLIN

SWPRR:    CONTNUE         & AM2901  R0     , R0     , NOOP  , ADD    , ZA
/                         & NOINE  & NOSDMA & NOVMA  & WRITE
/                         & NOBA   & NOLAD  & NORMM  & LMM    & NOCLB
/                         & NOSWP  & NODIN  & NOSDA  & NORCC  & LCCLCV
/                         & LDI    & NOSTR  & RSRD   & NOFTCH & NOCIB
/                         & NOCIA  & RCLMUL & NOLIN

          BRANCH INSTR    & AM2901  R0     , R0     , RAMF  , OR     , DZ
/                         & NOINE  & SDMA   &  VMA   & READ
/                         & NOBA   & NOLAD  & NORMM  & LMM    & NOCLB
/                         & SWPHL  & NODIN  & NOSDA  & NORCC  & LCV
/                         & LDI    & NOSTR  & RSRD   & FETCH  & NOCIB
/                         & NOCIA  & RCLMUL & NOLIN

RSUBRR:   BRANCH INSTR    & AM2901  R0     , R0     , RAMF  , SUBS   , AB
/                         & NOINE  & SDMA   &  VMA   & READ
/                         & NOBA   & NOLAD  & NORMM  & LMM    & NOCLB
/                         & NOSWP  & NODIN  & NOSDA  & NORCC  & NOLCC
/                         & LDI    & NOSTR  & RSRD   & FETCH  & NOCIB
/                         & CIA    & RCLMUL & NOLIN
```

```
MOVAX:   CONTNUE        & AM2901  R11   , R11   , NOOP  , ADD   , DA
/                       & NOINE  & NOSDMA & NOVMA  & READ
/                       & BA     & LAD    & NORMM  & LMM    & CLRLO
/                       & NOSWP  & DINHI  & NOSDA  & NORCC  & LCCLCV
/                       & NOLDI  & NOSTR  & MWAMWB & NOFTCH & NOCIB
/                       & NOCIA  & RCLMUL & NOLIN

         BRANCH IFETCH  & AM2901  R10   , R10   , RAMA  , OR    , ZA
/                       & NOINE  & NOSDMA &  VMA   & WRITE
/                       & NOBA   & NOLAD  & NORMM  & LMM    & NOCLB
/                       & NOSWP  & NODIN  & NOSDA  & NORCC  & LCV
/                       & NOLDI  & NOSTR  & MWAMWB & NOFTCH & NOCIB
/                       & NOCIA  & RCLMUL & NOLIN

MVNXA:   CONTNUE        & AM2901  R11   , R11   , NOOP  , ADD   , DA
/                       & NOINE  & NOSDMA &  VMA   & READ
/                       & NOBA   & LAD    & NORMM  & LMM    & CLRLO
/                       & NOSWP  & DINHI  & NOSDA  & NORCC  & LCCLCV
/                       & LDI    & NOSTR  & MWAMWB & NOFTCH & NOCIB
/                       & NOCIA  & RCLMUL & NOLIN

         BRANCH INSTR   & AM2901  R15   , R10   , RAMA  , OR    , DZ
/                       & NOINE  & SDMA   &  VMA   & READ
/                       & NOBA   & LAD    & NORMM  & LMM    & NOCLB
/                       & NOSWP  & DINHL  & NOSDA  & NORCC  & LCCLCV
/                       & LDI    & NOSTR  & MWAMWB & FETCH  & NOCIB
/                       & NOCIA  & RCLMUL & NOLIN

MOVXA:   CONTNUE        & AM2901  R11   , R11   , NOOP  , ADD   , DA
/                       & NOINE  & NOSDMA &  VMA   & READ
/                       & NOBA   & LAD    & NORMM  & LMM    & CLRLO
/                       & NOSWP  & DINHI  & NOSDA  & NORCC  & LCCLCV
/                       & LDI    & NOSTR  & MWAMWB & NOFTCH & NOCIB
/                       & NOCIA  & RCLMUL & NOLIN

AIN:     BRANCH INSTR   & AM2901  R15   , R10   , RAMA  , OR    , DZ
/                       & NOINE  & SDMA   &  VMA   & READ
/                       & NOBA   & LAD    & NORMM  & LMM    & NOCLB
/                       & NOSWP  & DINHL  & NOSDA  & NORCC  & LCV
/                       & LDI    & NOSTR  & MWAMWB & FETCH  & NOCIB
/                       & NOCIA  & RCLMUL & NOLIN

ADDXA:   CONTNUE        & AM2901  R11   , R11   , NOOP  , ADD   , DA
/                       & NOINE  & SDMA   &  VMA   & READ
/                       & NOBA   & LAD    & NORMM  & LMM    & CLRLO
/                       & NOSWP  & DINHI  & NOSDA  & NORCC  & LCCLCV
/                       & LDI    & NOSTR  & MWAMWB & NOFTCH & NOCIB
/                       & NOCIA  & RCLMUL & NOLIN

         BRANCH IFETCH  & AM2901  R10   , R10   , RAMF  , ADD   , DA
/                       & NOINE  & NOSDMA & NOVMA  & READ
/                       & BA     & NOLAD  & NORMM  & LMM    & NOCLB
/                       & NOSWP  & DINHL  & NOSDA  & NORCC  & NOLCC
/                       & NOLDI  & NOSTR  & MWAMWB & NOFTCH & NOCIB
/                       & NOCIA  & RCLMUL & NOLIN

ADCXA:   CONTNUE        & AM2901  R11   , R11   , NOOP  , ADD   , DA
/                       & NOINE  & SDMA   &  VMA   & READ
/                       & NOBA   & LAD    & NORMM  & LMM    & CLRLO
/                       & NOSWP  & DINHI  & NOSDA  & NORCC  & LCCLCV
/                       & LDI    & NOSTR  & MWAMWB & NOFTCH & NOCIB
/                       & NOCIA  & RCLMUL & NOLIN

         BRANCH IFETCH  & AM2901  R10   , R10   , RAMF  , ADD   , DA
/                       & NOINE  & NOSDMA & NOVMA  & READ
/                       & BA     & NOLAD  & NORMM  & LMM    & NOCLB
/                       & NOSWP  & DINHL  & NOSDA  & NORCC  & NOLCC
/                       & NOLDI  & NOSTR  & MWAMWB & NOFTCH & CIB
/                       & NOCIA  & RCLMUL & NOLIN

SUBXA:   CONTNUE        & AM2901  R11   , R11   , NOOP  , ADD   , DA
/                       & NOINE  & SDMA   &  VMA   & READ
/                       & NOBA   & LAD    & NORMM  & LMM    & CLRLO
/                       & NOSWP  & DINHI  & NOSDA  & NORCC  & LCCLCV
/                       & LDI    & NOSTR  & MWAMWB & NOFTCH & NOCIB
/                       & NOCIA  & RCLMUL & NOLIN

         BRANCH IFETCH  & AM2901  R10   , R10   , RAMF  , SUBR  , DA
/                       & NOINE  & NOSDMA & NOVMA  & READ
/                       & BA     & NOLAD  & NORMM  & LMM    & NOCLB
/                       & NOSWP  & DINHL  & NOSDA  & NORCC  & NOLCC
/                       & NOLDI  & NOSTR  & MWAMWB & NOFTCH & NOCIB
/                       & CIA    & RCLMUL & NOLIN

SBCXA:   CONTNUE        & AM2901  R11   , R11   , NOOP  , ADD   , DA
/                       & NOINE  & SDMA   &  VMA   & READ
/                       & NOBA   & LAD    & NORMM  & LMM    & CLRLO
/                       & NOSWP  & DINHI  & NOSDA  & NORCC  & LCCLCV
/                       & LDI    & NOSTR  & MWAMWB & NOFTCH & NOCIB
/                       & NOCIA  & RCLMUL & NOLIN

         BRANCH IFETCH  & AM2901  R10   , R10   , RAMF  , SUBR  , DA
/                       & NOINE  & NOSDMA & NOVMA  & READ
/                       & BA     & NOLAD  & NORMM  & LMM    & NOCLB
/                       & NOSWP  & DINHL  & NOSDA  & NORCC  & NOLCC
/                       & NOLDI  & NOSTR  & MWAMWB & NOFTCH & CIB
/                       & NOCIA  & RCLMUL & NOLIN

ANDXA:   CONTNUE        & AM2901  R11   , R11   , NOOP  , ADD   , DA
/                       & NOINE  & SDMA   &  VMA   & READ
/                       & NOBA   & LAD    & NORMM  & LMM    & CLRLO
/                       & NOSWP  & DINHI  & NOSDA  & NORCC  & LCCLCV
/                       & LDI    & NOSTR  & MWAMWB & NOFTCH & NOCIB
/                       & NOCIA  & RCLMUL & NOLIN

         BRANCH IFETCH  & AM2901  R10   , R10   , RAMF  , AND   , DA
/                       & NOINE  & NOSDMA & NOVMA  & READ
/                       & BA     & NOLAD  & NORMM  & LMM    & NOCLB
/                       & NOSWP  & DINHL  & NOSDA  & NORCC  & LCV
/                       & NOLDI  & NOSTR  & MWAMWB & NOFTCH & NOCIB
/                       & NOCIA  & RCLMUL & NOLIN

ICRXA:   CONTNUE        & AM2901  R11   , R11   , NOOP  , ADD   , DA
/                       & NOINE  & SDMA   &  VMA   & READ
/                       & NOBA   & LAD    & NORMM  & LMM    & CLRLO
/                       & NOSWP  & DINHI  & NOSDA  & NORCC  & LCCLCV
/                       & LDI    & NOSTR  & MWAMWB & NOFTCH & NOCIB
/                       & NOCIA  & RCLMUL & NOLIN

         BRANCH IFETCH  & AM2901  R10   , R10   , RAMF  , OR    , DA
/                       & NOINE  & NOSDMA & NOVMA  & READ
/                       & BA     & NOLAD  & NORMM  & LMM    & NOCIB
/                       & NOSWP  & DINHL  & NOSDA  & NORCC  & LCV
/                       & NOLDI  & NOSTR  & MWAMWB & NOFTCH & NOCIB
/                       & NOCIA  & RCLMUL & NOLIN

XORXA:   CONTNUE        & AM2901  R11   , R11   , NOOP  , ADD   , DA
/                       & NOINE  & SDMA   &  VMA   & READ
/                       & NOBA   & LAD    & NORMM  & LMM    & CLRLO
/                       & NOSWP  & DINHI  & NOSDA  & NORCC  & LCCLCV
/                       & LDI    & NOSTR  & MWAMWB & NOFTCH & NOCIB
/                       & NOCIA  & RCLMUL & NOLIN

         BRANCH IFETCH  & AM2901  R10   , R10   , RAMF  , EXOR  , DA
/                       & NOINE  & NOSDMA & NOVMA  & READ
/                       & BA     & NOLAD  & NORMM  & LMM    & NOCLB
/                       & NOSWP  & DINHL  & NOSDA  & NORCC  & LCV
/                       & NOLDI  & NOSTR  & MWAMWB & NOFTCH & NOCIB
/                       & NOCIA  & RCLMUL & NOLIN

CMPXA:   CONTNUE        & AM2901  R11   , R11   , NOOP  , ADD   , DA
/                       & NOINE  & SDMA   &  VMA   & READ
/                       & NOBA   & LAD    & NORMM  & LMM    & CLRLO
/                       & NOSWP  & DINHI  & NOSDA  & NORCC  & LCCLCV
/                       & LDI    & NOSTR  & MWAMWB & NOFTCH & NOCIB
/                       & NOCIA  & RCLMUL & NOLIN

         BRANCH IFETCH  & AM2901  R10   , R10   , NOOP  , SUBR  , DA
/                       & NOINE  & NOSDMA & NOVMA  & READ
/                       & BA     & NOLAD  & NORMM  & LMM    & NOCLB
/                       & NOSWP  & DINHL  & NOSDA  & NORCC  & NOLCC
/                       & NOLDI  & NOSTR  & MWAMWB & NOFTCH & NOCIB
/                       & CIA    & RCLMUL & NOLIN

INCX:    CONTNUE        & AM2901  R11   , R11   , NOOP  , ADD   , DA
/                       & NOINE  & NOSDMA &  VMA   & READ
/                       & NOBA   & LAD    & NORMM  & LMM    & CLRLO
/                       & NOSWP  & DINHI  & NOSDA  & NORCC  & LCCLCV
/                       & LDI    & NOSTR  & MWAMWB & NOFTCH & NOCIB
/                       & NOCIA  & RCLMUL & NOLIN

         BRANCH IFETCH  & AM2901  R8    , R8    , RAMF  , ADD   , DZ
/                       & NOINE  & NOSDMA &  VMA   & WRITE
/                       & NOBA   & NOLAD  & NORMM  & LMM    & NOCLB
/                       & NOSWP  & DINHL  & NOSDA  & NORCC  & LCV
/                       & NOLDI  & NOSTR  & MWAMWB & NOFTCH & NOCIB
/                       & CIA    & RCLMUL & NOLIN

DECX:    CONTNUE        & AM2901  R11   , R11   , NOOP  , ADD   , DA
/                       & NOINE  & NOSDMA &  VMA   & READ
/                       & NOBA   & LAD    & NORMM  & LMM    & CLRLO
/                       & NOSWP  & DINHI  & NOSDA  & NORCC  & LCCLCV
/                       & LDI    & NOSTR  & MWAMWB & NOFTCH & NOCIB
/                       & NOCIA  & RCLMUL & NOLIN

         BRANCH IFETCH  & AM2901  R8    , R8    , RAMF  , SUBS  , DZ
/                       & NOINE  & NOSDMA &  VMA   & WRITE
/                       & NOBA   & NOLAD  & NORMM  & LMM    & NOCLB
/                       & NOSWP  & DINHL  & NOSDA  & NORCC  & LCV
/                       & NOLDI  & NOSTR  & MWAMWB & NOFTCH & NOCIB
/                       & NOCIA  & RCLMUL & NOLIN
COMX:    CONTNUE        & AM2901  R11   , R11   , NOOP  , ADD   , DA
/                       & NOINE  & NOSDMA &  VMA   & READ
/                       & NOBA   & LAD    & NORMM  & LMM    & CLRLO
/                       & NOSWP  & DINHI  & NOSDA  & NORCC  & LCCLCV
/                       & LDI    & NOSTR  & MWAMWB & NOFTCH & NOCIB
/                       & NOCIA  & RCLMUL & NOLIN

         BRANCH IFETCH  & AM2901  R8    , R8    , RAMF  , EXNOR , DZ
/                       & NOINE  & NOSDMA &  VMA   & WRITE
/                       & NOBA   & NOLAD  & NORMM  & LMM    & NOCIB
/                       & NOSWP  & DINHL  & NOSDA  & NORCC  & LCV
/                       & NOLDI  & NOSTR  & MWAMWB & NOFTCH & NOCIB
/                       & NOCIA  & RCLMUL & NOLIN

NEGX:    CONTNUE        & AM2901  R11   , R11   , NOOP  , ADD   , DA
/                       & NOINE  & NOSDMA &  VMA   & READ
/                       & NOBA   & LAD    & NORMM  & LMM    & CLRLO
/                       & NOSWP  & DINHI  & NOSDA  & NORCC  & LCCLCV
/                       & LDI    & NOSTR  & MWAMWB & NOFTCH & NOCIB
/                       & NOCIA  & RCLMUL & NOLIN

         BRANCH IFETCH  & AM2901  R8    , R8    , RAMF  , SUBR  , DZ
/                       & NOINE  & NOSDMA &  VMA   & WRITE
/                       & NOBA   & NOLAD  & NORMM  & LMM    & NOCLB
/                       & NOSWP  & DINHL  & NOSDA  & NORCC  & NOLCC
/                       & NOLDI  & NOSTR  & MWAMWB & NOFTCH & NOCIB
/                       & CIA    & RCLMUL & NOLIN

SWPX:    CONTNUE        & AM2901  R11   , R11   , NOOP  , ADD   , DA
/                       & NOINE  & NOSDMA &  VMA   & READ
/                       & NOBA   & LAD    & NORMM  & LMM    & CLRLO
/                       & NOSWP  & DINHI  & NOSDA  & NORCC  & LCCLCV
/                       & LDI    & NOSTR  & MWAMWB & NOFTCH & NOCIB
/                       & NOCIA  & RCLMUL & NOLIN

         BRANCH IFETCH  & AM2901  R8    , R8    , RAMF  , OR    , DZ
/                       & NOINE  & NOSDMA &  VMA   & WRITE
/                       & NOBA   & NOLAD  & NORMM  & LMM    & NOCLB
/                       & SWPHL  & NODIN  & NOSDA  & NORCC  & LCV
/                       & NOLDI  & NOSTR  & MWAMWB & NOFTCH & NOCIB
/                       & NOCIA  & RCLMUL & NOLIN

RSUBXA:  CONTNUE        & AM2901  R11   , R11   , NOOP  , ADD   , DA
/                       & NOINE  & SDMA   &  VMA   & READ
/                       & NOBA   & LAD    & NORMM  & LMM    & CLRLO
/                       & NOSWP  & DINHI  & NOSDA  & NORCC  & LCCLCV
/                       & LDI    & NOSTR  & MWAMWB & NOFTCH & NOCIB
/                       & NOCIA  & RCLMUL & NOLIN

         BRANCH IFETCH  & AM2901  R10   , R10   , RAMF  , SUBS  , DA
/                       & NOINE  & NOSDMA & NOVMA  & READ
/                       & BA     & NOLAD  & NORMM  & LMM    & NOCLB
/                       & NOSWP  & DINHL  & NOSDA  & NORCC  & NOLCC
/                       & NOLDI  & NOSTR  & MWAMWB & NOFTCH & NOCIB
/                       & CIA    & RCLMUL & NOLIN

MVNRM-:  CONTNUE        & AM2901  R0    , R0    , RAMF  , SUBR  , ZB
/                       & NOINE  & NOSDMA & NOVMA  & READ
/                       & BA     & LAD    & NORMM  & LMM    & NOCLB
/                       & NOSWP  & NODIN  & NOSDA  & NORCC  & LCCLCV
/                       & NOLDI  & NOSTR  & RDRD   & NOFTCH & NOCIB
/                       & NOCIA  & RCLMUL & NOLIN

MOUT:    BRANCH IFETCH  & AM2901  R0    , R0    , RAMA  , ADD   , ZB
/                       & NOINE  & NOSDMA &  VMA   & WRITE
/                       & NOBA   & NOLAD  & NORMM  & LMM    & NOCLB
/                       & NOSWP  & NODIN  & NOSDA  & NORCC  & LCCLCV
/                       & NOLDI  & NOSTR  & RSRS   & NOFTCH & NOCIB
/                       & NOCIA  & RCLMUL & NOLIN

MVNM+R:  CONTNUE        & AM2901  R0    , R0    , RAMA  , ADD   , ZA
```

```
/                      & NOINE  & SDMA   &  VMA   & READ
/                      & NOBA   & LAD    & NORMM  & LMM    & NOCLB
/                      & NOSWP  & NODIN  & NOSDA  & NORCC  & LCCLCV
/                      & LDI    & NOSTR  & RSRS   & NOFTCH & NOCIB
/                      & CIA    & RCLMUL & NOLIN

MVNIN:   BRANCH IFETCH & AM2901  RØ     , RØ     , RAMF  , OR    , DZ
/                      & NOINE  & NOSDMA & NOVMA  & READ
/                      & BA     & NOLAD  & NORMM  & LMM    & NOCLB
/                      & NOSWP  & DINHL  & NOSDA  & NORCC  & LCCLCV
/                      & NOLDI  & NOSTR  & RSRD   & NOFTCH & NOCIB
/                      & NOCIA  & RCLMUL & NOLIN

MVNI+R:  CONTNUE       & AM2901  RØ     , RØ     , RAMA  , ADD   , ZA
/                      & NOINE  & NOSDMA &  VMA   & READ
/                      & NOBA   & LAD    & NORMM  & LMM    & NOCLB
/                      & NOSWP  & NODIN  & NOSDA  & NORCC  & LCCLCV
/                      & LDI    & NOSTR  & RSRS   & NOFTCH & NOCIB
/                      & CIA    & RCLMUL & NOLIN

         BRANCH MVNIN  & AM2901  RØ     , RØ     , NOOP  , OR    , DZ
/                      & NOINE  & SDMA   &  VMA   & READ
/                      & NOBA   & LAD    & NORMM  & LMM    & NOCLB
/                      & NOSWP  & DINHL  & NOSDA  & NORCC  & LCCLCV
/                      & LDI    & NOSTR  & MWAMWB & NOFTCH & NOCIB
/                      & NOCIA  & RCLMUL & NOLIN

MVNZR:   CONTNUE       & AM2901  R15    , R15    , RAMA  , ADD   , ZA
/                      & NOINE  & NOSDMA &  VMA   & READ
/                      & NOBA   & LAD    & NORMM  & LMM    & NOCLB
/                      & NOSWP  & NODIN  & NOSDA  & NORCC  & LCCLCV
/                      & LDI    & NOSTR  & MWAMWB & NOFTCH & NOCIB
/                      & CIA    & RCLMUL & NOLIN

         BRANCH MVNIN  & AM2901  RØ     , RØ     , NOOP  , ADD   , DA
/                      & NOINE  & SDMA   &  VMA   & READ
/                      & NOBA   & LAD    & NORMM  & LMM    & NOCLB
/                      & NOSWP  & DINHL  & NOSDA  & NORCC  & LCCLCV
/                      & LDI    & NOSTR  & RSRD   & NOFTCH & NOCIB
/                      & NOCIA  & RCLMUL & NOLIN

MOVM+R:  CONTNUE       & AM2901  RØ     , RØ     , RAMA  , ADD   , ZA
/                      & NOINE  & SDMA   &  VMA   & READ
/                      & NOBA   & LAD    & NORMM  & LMM    & NOCLB
/                      & NOSWP  & NODIN  & NOSDA  & NORCC  & LCCLCV
/                      & LDI    & NOSTR  & RSRS   & NOFTCH & NOCIB
/                      & CIA    & RCLMUL & NOLIN

MOVIN:   BRANCH IFETCH & AM2901  RØ     , RØ     , RAMF  , OR    , DZ
/                      & NOINE  & NOSDMA & NOVMA  & READ
/                      & BA     & NOLAD  & NORMM  & LMM    & NOCLB
/                      & NOSWP  & DINHL  & NOSDA  & NORCC  & LCV
/                      & NOLDI  & NOSTR  & RSRD   & NOFTCH & NOCIB
/                      & NOCIA  & RCLMUL & NOLIN

MOVI+R:  CONTNUE       & AM2901  RØ     , RØ     , RAMA  , ADD   , ZA
/                      & NOINE  & NOSDMA &  VMA   & READ
/                      & NOBA   & LAD    & NORMM  & LMM    & NOCLB
/                      & NOSWP  & NODIN  & NOSDA  & NORCC  & LCCLCV
/                      & LDI    & NOSTR  & RSRS   & NOFTCH & NOCIB
/                      & CIA    & RCLMUL & NOLIN

IIN:     BRANCH MOVIN  & AM2901  RØ     , RØ     , NOOP  , OR    , DZ
/                      & NOINE  & SDMA   &  VMA   & READ
/                      & NOBA   & LAD    & NORMM  & LMM    & NOCLB
/                      & NOSWP  & DINHL  & NOSDA  & NORCC  & LCCLCV
/                      & LDI    & NOSTR  & MWAMWB & NOFTCH & NOCIB
/                      & NOCIA  & RCLMUL & NOLIN

MOVZR:   CONTNUE       & AM2901  R15    , R15    , RAMA  , ADD   , ZA
/                      & NOINE  & NOSDMA &  VMA   & READ
/                      & NOBA   & LAD    & NORMM  & LMM    & NOCLB
/                      & NOSWP  & NODIN  & NOSDA  & NORCC  & LCCLCV
/                      & LDI    & NOSTR  & MWAMWB & NOFTCH & NOCIB
/                      & CIA    & RCLMUL & NOLIN

         BRANCH MOVIN  & AM2901  RØ     , RØ     , NOOP  , ADD   , DA
/                      & NOINE  & SDMA   &  VMA   & READ
/                      & NOBA   & LAD    & NORMM  & LMM    & NOCLB
/                      & NOSWP  & DINHL  & NOSDA  & NORCC  & LCCLCV
/                      & LDI    & NOSTR  & RSRD   & NOFTCH & NOCIB
/                      & NOCIA  & RCLMUL & NOLIN

ADDM+R:  CONTNUE       & AM2901  RØ     , RØ     , RAMA  , ADD   , ZA
/                      & NOINE  & SDMA   &  VMA   & READ
/                      & NOBA   & LAD    & NORMM  & LMM    & NOCLB
/                      & NOSWP  & NODIN  & NOSDA  & NORCC  & LCCLCV
/                      & LDI    & NOSTR  & RSRS   & NOFTCH & NOCIB
/                      & CIA    & RCLMUL & NOLIN

ADDIN:   BRANCH IFETCH & AM2901  RØ     , RØ     , RAMF  , ADD   , DA
/                      & NOINE  & NOSDMA & NOVMA  & READ
/                      & BA     & NOLAD  & NORMM  & LMM    & NOCLB
/                      & NOSWP  & DINHL  & NOSDA  & NORCC  & NOLCC
/                      & NOLDI  & NOSTR  & RDRD   & NOFTCH & NOCIB
/                      & NOCIA  & RCLMUL & NOLIN

ADDI+R:  CONTNUE       & AM2901  RØ     , RØ     , RAMA  , ADD   , ZA
/                      & NOINE  & NOSDMA &  VMA   & READ
/                      & NOBA   & LAD    & NORMM  & LMM    & NOCLB
/                      & NOSWP  & NODIN  & NOSDA  & NORCC  & LCCLCV
/                      & LDI    & NOSTR  & RSRS   & NOFTCH & NOCIB
/                      & CIA    & RCLMUL & NOLIN

         BRANCH ADDIN  & AM2901  RØ     , RØ     , NOOP  , OR    , DZ
/                      & NOINE  & SDMA   &  VMA   & READ
/                      & NOBA   & LAD    & NORMM  & LMM    & NOCLB
/                      & NOSWP  & DINHL  & NOSDA  & NORCC  & LCCLCV
/                      & LDI    & NOSTR  & MWAMWB & NOFTCH & NOCIB
/                      & NOCIA  & RCLMUL & NOLIN

ADDZR:   CONTNUE       & AM2901  R15    , R15    , RAMA  , ADD   , ZA
/                      & NOINE  & NOSDMA &  VMA   & READ
/                      & NOBA   & LAD    & NORMM  & LMM    & NOCLB
/                      & NOSWP  & NODIN  & NOSDA  & NORCC  & LCCLCV
/                      & LDI    & NOSTR  & MWAMWB & NOFTCH & NOCIB
/                      & CIA    & RCLMUL & NOLIN

         BRANCH ADDIN  & AM2901  RØ     , RØ     , NOOP  , ADD   , DA
/                      & NOINE  & SDMA   &  VMA   & READ
/                      & NOBA   & LAD    & NORMM  & LMM    & NOCLB
/                      & NOSWP  & DINHL  & NOSDA  & NORCC  & LCCLCV
/                      & LDI    & NOSTR  & RSRS   & NOFTCH & NOCIB
/                      & NOCIA  & RCLMUL & NOLIN

ADCM+R:  CONTNUE       & AM2901  RØ     , RØ     , RAMA  , ADD   , ZA
/                      & NOINE  & SDMA   &  VMA   & READ
/                      & NOBA   & LAD    & NORMM  & LMM    & NOCLB
/                      & NOSWP  & NODIN  & NOSDA  & NORCC  & LCCLCV
/                      & LDI    & NOSTR  & RSRS   & NOFTCH & NOCIB
/                      & CIA    & RCLMUL & NOLIN

ADCIN:   BRANCH IFETCH & AM2901  RØ     , RØ     , RAMF  , ADD   , DA
/                      & NOINE  & NOSDMA & NOVMA  & READ
/                      & BA     & NOLAD  & NORMM  & LMM    & NOCLB
/                      & NOSWP  & DINHL  & NOSDA  & NORCC  & NOLCC
/                      & NOLDI  & NOSTR  & RDRD   & NOFTCH & CIB
/                      & NOCIA  & RCLMUL & NOLIN

ADCI+R:  CONTNUE       & AM2901  RØ     , RØ     , RAMA  , ADD   , ZA
/                      & NOINE  & NOSDMA &  VMA   & READ
/                      & NOBA   & LAD    & NORMM  & LMM    & NOCLB
/                      & NOSWP  & NODIN  & NOSDA  & NORCC  & LCCLCV
/                      & LDI    & NOSTR  & RSRS   & NOFTCH & NOCIB
/                      & CIA    & RCLMUL & NOLIN

         BRANCH ADCIN  & AM2901  RØ     , RØ     , NOOP  , OR    , DZ
/                      & NOINE  & SDMA   &  VMA   & READ
/                      & NOBA   & LAD    & NORMM  & LMM    & NOCLB
/                      & NOSWP  & DINHL  & NOSDA  & NORCC  & LCCLCV
/                      & LDI    & NOSTR  & MWAMWB & NOFTCH & NOCIB
/                      & NOCIA  & RCLMUL & NOLIN

ADCZR:   CONTNUE       & AM2901  R15    , R15    , RAMA  , ADD   , ZA
/                      & NOINE  & NOSDMA &  VMA   & READ
/                      & NOBA   & LAD    & NORMM  & LMM    & NOCLB
/                      & NOSWP  & NODIN  & NOSDA  & NORCC  & LCCLCV
/                      & LDI    & NOSTR  & MWAMWB & NOFTCH & NOCIB
/                      & CIA    & RCLMUL & NOLIN

         BRANCH ADCIN  & AM2901  RØ     , RØ     , NOOP  , ADD   , DA
/                      & NOINE  & SDMA   &  VMA   & READ
/                      & NOBA   & LAD    & NORMM  & LMM    & NOCLB
/                      & NOSWP  & DINHL  & NOSDA  & NORCC  & LCCLCV
/                      & LDI    & NOSTR  & RSRS   & NOFTCH & NOCIB
/                      & NOCIA  & RCLMUL & NOLIN

SUBM+R:  CONTNUE       & AM2901  RØ     , RØ     , RAMA  , ADD   , ZA
/                      & NOINE  & SDMA   &  VMA   & READ
/                      & NOBA   & LAD    & NORMM  & LMM    & NOCLB
/                      & NOSWP  & NODIN  & NOSDA  & NORCC  & LCCLCV
/                      & LDI    & NOSTR  & RSRS   & NOFTCH & NOCIB
/                      & CIA    & RCLMUL & NOLIN

SUBIN:   BRANCH IFETCH & AM2901  RØ     , RØ     , RAMF  , SUBR  , DA
/                      & NOINE  & NOSDMA & NOVMA  & READ
/                      & BA     & NOLAD  & NORMM  & LMM    & NOCLB
/                      & NOSWP  & DINHL  & NOSDA  & NORCC  & NOLCC
/                      & NOLDI  & NOSTR  & RDRD   & NOFTCH & NOCIB
/                      & CIA    & RCLMUL & NOLIN

SUBI+R:  CONTNUE       & AM2901  RØ     , RØ     , RAMA  , ADD   , ZA
/                      & NOINE  & NOSDMA &  VMA   & READ
/                      & NOBA   & LAD    & NORMM  & LMM    & NOCLB
/                      & NOSWP  & NODIN  & NOSDA  & NORCC  & LCCLCV
/                      & LDI    & NOSTR  & RSRS   & NOFTCH & NOCIB
/                      & CIA    & RCLMUL & NOLIN

         BRANCH SUBIN  & AM2901  RØ     , RØ     , NOOP  , OR    , DZ
/                      & NOINE  & SDMA   &  VMA   & READ
/                      & NOBA   & LAD    & NORMM  & LMM    & NOCLB
/                      & NOSWP  & DINHL  & NOSDA  & NORCC  & LCCLCV
/                      & LDI    & NOSTR  & MWAMWB & NOFTCH & NOCIB
/                      & NOCIA  & RCLMUL & NOLIN

SUBZR:   CONTNUE       & AM2901  R15    , R15    , RAMA  , ADD   , ZA
/                      & NOINE  & NOSDMA &  VMA   & READ
/                      & NOBA   & LAD    & NORMM  & LMM    & NOCLB
/                      & NOSWP  & NODIN  & NOSDA  & NORCC  & LCCLCV
/                      & LDI    & NOSTR  & MWAMWB & NOFTCH & NOCIB
/                      & CIA    & RCLMUL & NOLIN

         BRANCH SUBIN  & AM2901  RØ     , RØ     , NOOP  , ADD   , DA
/                      & NOINE  & SDMA   &  VMA   & READ
/                      & NOBA   & LAD    & NORMM  & LMM    & NOCLB
/                      & NOSWP  & DINHL  & NOSDA  & NORCC  & LCCLCV
/                      & LDI    & NOSTR  & RSRS   & NOFTCH & NOCIB
/                      & NOCIA  & RCLMUL & NOLIN

SUBCM+R: CONTNUE       & AM2901  RØ     , RØ     , RAMA  , ADD   , ZA
/                      & NOINE  & SDMA   &  VMA   & READ
/                      & NOBA   & LAD    & NORMM  & LMM    & NOCLB
/                      & NOSWP  & NODIN  & NOSDA  & NORCC  & LCCLCV
/                      & LDI    & NOSTR  & RSRS   & NOFTCH & NOCIB
/                      & CIA    & RCLMUL & NOLIN

SUBCIN:  BRANCH IFETCH & AM2901  RØ     , RØ     , RAMF  , SUBR  , DA
/                      & NOINE  & NOSDMA & NOVMA  & READ
/                      & BA     & NOLAD  & NORMM  & LMM    & NOCLB
/                      & NOSWP  & DINHL  & NOSDA  & NORCC  & NOLCC
/                      & NOLDI  & NOSTR  & RDRD   & NOFTCH & CIB
/                      & NOCIA  & RCLMUL & NOLIN

SUBCI+R: CONTNUE       & AM2901  RØ     , RØ     , RAMA  , ADD   , ZA
/                      & NOINE  & NOSDMA &  VMA   & READ
/                      & NOBA   & LAD    & NORMM  & LMM    & NOCLB
/                      & NOSWP  & NODIN  & NOSDA  & NORCC  & LCCLCV
/                      & LDI    & NOSTR  & RSRS   & NOFTCH & NOCIB
/                      & CIA    & RCLMUL & NOLIN
         BRANCH SUBCIN & AM2901  RØ     , RØ     , NOOP  , OR    , DZ
/                      & NOINE  & SDMA   &  VMA   & READ
/                      & NOBA   & LAD    & NORMM  & LMM    & NOCLB
/                      & NOSWP  & DINHL  & NOSDA  & NORCC  & LCCLCV
/                      & LDI    & NOSTR  & MWAMWB & NOFTCH & NOCIB
/                      & NOCIA  & RCLMUL & NOLIN

SUBCZR:  CONTNUE       & AM2901  R15    , R15    , RAMA  , ADD   , ZA
/                      & NOINE  & NOSDMA &  VMA   & READ
/                      & NOBA   & LAD    & NORMM  & LMM    & NOCLB
/                      & NOSWP  & NODIN  & NOSDA  & NORCC  & LCCLCV
/                      & LDI    & NOSTR  & MWAMWB & NOFTCH & NOCIB
/                      & CIA    & RCLMUL & NOLIN

         BRANCH SUBCIN & AM2901  RØ     , RØ     , NOOP  , ADD   , DA
/                      & NOINE  & SDMA   &  VMA   & READ
/                      & NOBA   & LAD    & NORMM  & LMM    & NOCLB
/                      & NOSWP  & DINHL  & NOSDA  & NORCC  & LCCLCV
/                      & LDI    & NOSTR  & RSRS   & NOFTCH & NOCIB
/                      & NOCIA  & RCLMUL & NOLIN

ANDM+R:  CONTNUE       & AM2901  RØ     , RØ     , RAMA  , ADD   , ZA
/                      & NOINE  & SDMA   &  VMA   & READ
```

```
/                          & NOBA   & LAD    & NORMM  & LMM    & NOCLB
/                          & NOSWP  & NODIN  & NOSDA  & NORCC  & LCCLCV
/                          & LDI    & NOSTR  & RSRS   & NOFTCH & NOCIB
/                          & CIA    & RCLMUL & NOLIN

ANDIN:    BRANCH IFETCH & AM2901  RØ    , RØ    , RAMF  , AND   , DA
/                          & NOINE  & NOSDMA & NOVMA  & READ
/                          & BA     & NOLAD  & NORMM  & LMM    & NOCLB
/                          & NOSWP  & DINHL  & NOSDA  & NORCC  & LCV
/                          & NOLDI  & NOSTR  & RDRD   & NOFTCH & NOCIB
/                          & NOCIA  & RCLMUL & NOLIN

ANDI+R:   CONTNUE       & AM2901  RØ    , RØ    , RAMA  , ADD   , ZA
/                          & NOINE  & NOSDMA &  VMA   & READ
/                          & NOBA   & LAD    & NORMM  & LMM    & NOCLB
/                          & NOSWP  & NODIN  & NOSDA  & NORCC  & LCCLCV
/                          & LDI    & NOSTR  & RSRS   & NOFTCH & NOCIB
/                          & CIA    & RCLMUL & NOLIN

          BRANCH ANDIN  & AM2901  RØ    , RØ    , NOOP  , OR    , DZ
/                          & NOINE  & SDMA   &  VMA   & READ
/                          & NOBA   & LAD    & NORMM  & LMM    & NOCLB
/                          & NOSWP  & DINHL  & NOSDA  & NORCC  & LCCLCV
/                          & LDI    & NOSTR  & MWAMWB & NOFTCH & NOCIB
/                          & NOCIA  & RCLMUL & NOLIN

ANDZR:    CONTNUE       & AM2901  R15   , R15   , RAMA  , ADD   , ZA
/                          & NOINE  & NOSDMA &  VMA   & READ
/                          & NOBA   & LAD    & NORMM  & LMM    & NOCLB
/                          & NOSWP  & NODIN  & NOSDA  & NORCC  & LCCLCV
/                          & LDI    & NOSTR  & MWAMWB & NOFTCH & NOCIB
/                          & CIA    & RCLMUL & NOLIN

          BRANCH ANDIN  & AM2901  RØ    , RØ    , NOOP  , ADD   , DA
/                          & NOINE  & SDMA   &  VMA   & READ
/                          & NOBA   & LAD    & NORMM  & LMM    & NOCLB
/                          & NOSWP  & DINHL  & NOSDA  & NORCC  & LCCLCV
/                          & LDI    & NOSTR  & RSRS   & NOFTCH & NOCIB
/                          & NOCIA  & RCLMUL & NOLIN

IORM+R:   CONTNUE       & AM2901  RØ    , RØ    , RAMA  , ADD   , ZA
/                          & NOINE  & SDMA   &  VMA   & READ
/                          & NOBA   & LAD    & NORMM  & LMM    & NOCLB
/                          & NOSWP  & NODIN  & NOSDA  & NORCC  & LCCLCV
/                          & LDI    & NOSTR  & RSRS   & NOFTCH & NOCIB
/                          & CIA    & RCLMUL & NOLIN

IORIN:    BRANCH IFETCH & AM2901  RØ    , RØ    , RAMF  , OR    , DA
/                          & NOINE  & NOSDMA & NOVMA  & READ
/                          & BA     & NOLAD  & NORMM  & LMM    & NOCLB
/                          & NOSWP  & DINHL  & NOSDA  & NORCC  & LCV
/                          & NOLDI  & NOSTR  & RDRD   & NOFTCH & NOCIB
/                          & NOCIA  & RCLMUL & NOLIN

IORI+R:   CONTNUE       & AM2901  RØ    , RØ    , RAMA  , ADD   , ZA
/                          & NOINE  & NOSDMA &  VMA   & READ
/                          & NOBA   & LAD    & NORMM  & LMM    & NOCLB
/                          & NOSWP  & NODIN  & NOSDA  & NORCC  & LCCLCV
/                          & LDI    & NOSTR  & RSRS   & NOFTCH & NOCIB
/                          & CIA    & RCLMUL & NOLIN

          BRANCH IORIN  & AM2901  RØ    , RØ    , NOOP  , OR    , DZ
/                          & NOINE  & SDMA   &  VMA   & READ
/                          & NOBA   & LAD    & NORMM  & LMM    & NOCLB
/                          & NOSWP  & DINHL  & NOSDA  & NORCC  & LCCLCV
/                          & LDI    & NOSTR  & MWAMWB & NOFTCH & NOCIB
/                          & NOCIA  & RCLMUL & NOLIN

IORZR:    CONTNUE       & AM2901  R15   , R15   , RAMA  , ADD   , ZA
/                          & NOINE  & NOSDMA &  VMA   & READ
/                          & NOBA   & LAD    & NORMM  & LMM    & NOCLB
/                          & NOSWP  & NODIN  & NOSDA  & NORCC  & LCCLCV
/                          & LDI    & NOSTR  & MWAMWB & NOFTCH & NOCIB
/                          & CIA    & RCLMUL & NOLIN

          BRANCH IORIN  & AM2901  RØ    , RØ    , NOOP  , ADD   , DA
/                          & NOINE  & SDMA   &  VMA   & READ
/                          & NOBA   & LAD    & NORMM  & LMM    & NOCLB
/                          & NOSWP  & DINHL  & NOSDA  & NORCC  & LCCLCV
/                          & LDI    & NOSTR  & RSRS   & NOFTCH & NOCIB
/                          & NOCIA  & RCLMUL & NOLIN

XORM+R:   CONTNUE       & AM2901  RØ    , RØ    , RAMA  , ADD   , ZA
/                          & NOINE  & SDMA   &  VMA   & READ
/                          & NOBA   & LAD    & NORMM  & LMM    & NOCLB
/                          & NOSWP  & NODIN  & NOSDA  & NORCC  & LCCLCV
/                          & LDI    & NOSTR  & RSRS   & NOFTCH & NOCIB
/                          & CIA    & RCLMUL & NOLIN

XORIN:    BRANCH IFETCH & AM2901  RØ    , RØ    , RAMF  , EXOR  , DA
/                          & NOINE  & NOSDMA & NOVMA  & READ
/                          & BA     & NOLAD  & NORMM  & LMM    & NOCLB
/                          & NOSWP  & DINHL  & NOSDA  & NORCC  & LCV
/                          & NOLDI  & NOSTR  & RDRD   & NOFTCH & NOCIB
/                          & NOCIA  & RCLMUL & NOLIN

XORI+R:   CONTNUE       & AM2901  RØ    , RØ    , RAMA  , ADD   , ZA
/                          & NOINE  & NOSDMA &  VMA   & READ
/                          & NOBA   & LAD    & NORMM  & LMM    & NOCLB
/                          & NOSWP  & NODIN  & NOSDA  & NORCC  & LCCLCV
/                          & LDI    & NOSTR  & RSRS   & NOFTCH & NOCIB
/                          & CIA    & RCLMUL & NOLIN

          BRANCH XORIN  & AM2901  RØ    , RØ    , NOOP  , OR    , DZ
/                          & NOINE  & SDMA   &  VMA   & READ
/                          & NOBA   & LAD    & NORMM  & LMM    & NOCLB
/                          & NOSWP  & DINHL  & NOSDA  & NORCC  & LCCLCV
/                          & LDI    & NOSTR  & MWAMWB & NOFTCH & NOCIB
/                          & NOCIA  & RCLMUL & NOLIN

XORZR:    CONTNUE       & AM2901  R15   , R15   , RAMA  , ADD   , ZA
/                          & NOINE  & NOSDMA &  VMA   & READ
/                          & NOBA   & LAD    & NORMM  & LMM    & NOCLB
/                          & NOSWP  & NODIN  & NOSDA  & NORCC  & LCCLCV
/                          & LDI    & NOSTR  & MWAMWB & NOFTCH & NOCIB
/                          & CIA    & RCLMUL & NOLIN

          BRANCH XORIN  & AM2901  RØ    , RØ    , NOOP  , ADD   , DA
/                          & NOINE  & SDMA   &  VMA   & READ
/                          & NOBA   & LAD    & NORMM  & LMM    & NOCLB
/                          & NOSWP  & DINHL  & NOSDA  & NORCC  & LCCLCV
/                          & LDI    & NOSTR  & RSRS   & NOFTCH & NOCIB
/                          & NOCIA  & RCLMUL & NOLIN

CMPM+R:   CONTNUE       & AM2901  RØ    , RØ    , RAMA  , ADD   , ZA
/                          & NOINE  & SDMA   &  VMA   & READ

/                          & NOBA   & LAD    & NORMM  & LMM    & NOCLB
/                          & NOSWP  & NODIN  & NOSDA  & NORCC  & LCCLCV
/                          & LDI    & NOSTR  & RSRS   & NOFTCH & NOCIB
/                          & CIA    & RCLMUL & NOLIN

CMPIN:    BRANCH IFETCH & AM2901  RØ    , RØ    , NOOP  , SUBR  , DA
/                          & NOINE  & NOSDMA & NOVMA  & READ
/                          & BA     & NOLAD  & NORMM  & LMM    & NOCLB
/                          & NOSWP  & DINHL  & NOSDA  & NORCC  & NOLCC
/                          & NOLDI  & NOSTR  & RDRD   & NOFTCH & NOCIB
/                          & CIA    & RCLMUL & NOLIN

CMPI+R:   CONTNUE       & AM2901  RØ    , RØ    , RAMA  , ADD   , ZA
/                          & NOINE  & NOSDMA &  VMA   & READ
/                          & NOBA   & LAD    & NORMM  & LMM    & NOCLB
/                          & NOSWP  & NODIN  & NOSDA  & NORCC  & LCCLCV
/                          & LDI    & NOSTR  & RSRS   & NOFTCH & NOCIB
/                          & CIA    & RCLMUL & NOLIN

          BRANCH CMPIN  & AM2901  RØ    , RØ    , NOOP  , OR    , DZ
/                          & NOINE  & SDMA   &  VMA   & READ
/                          & NOBA   & LAD    & NORMM  & LMM    & NOCLB
/                          & NOSWP  & DINHL  & NOSDA  & NORCC  & LCCLCV
/                          & LDI    & NOSTR  & MWAMWB & NOFTCH & NOCIB
/                          & NOCIA  & RCLMUL & NOLIN

CMPZR:    CONTNUE       & AM2901  R15   , R15   , RAMA  , ADD   , ZA
/                          & NOINE  & NOSDMA &  VMA   & READ
/                          & NOBA   & LAD    & NORMM  & LMM    & NOCLB
/                          & NOSWP  & NODIN  & NOSDA  & NORCC  & LCCLCV
/                          & LDI    & NOSTR  & MWAMWB & NOFTCH & NOCIB
/                          & CIA    & RCLMUL & NOLIN

          BRANCH CMPIN  & AM2901  RØ    , RØ    , NOOP  , ADD   , DA
/                          & NOINE  & SDMA   &  VMA   & READ
/                          & NOBA   & LAD    & NORMM  & LMM    & NOCLB
/                          & NOSWP  & DINHL  & NOSDA  & NORCC  & LCCLCV
/                          & LDI    & NOSTR  & RSRS   & NOFTCH & NOCIB
/                          & NOCIA  & RCLMUL & NOLIN

RSBM+R:   CONTNUE       & AM2901  RØ    , RØ    , RAMA  , ADD   , ZA
/                          & NOINE  & SDMA   &  VMA   & READ
/                          & NOBA   & LAD    & NORMM  & LMM    & NOCLB
/                          & NOSWP  & NODIN  & NOSDA  & NORCC  & LCCLCV
/                          & LDI    & NOSTR  & RSRS   & NOFTCH & NOCIB
/                          & CIA    & RCLMUL & NOLIN

RSUBIN:   BRANCH IFETCH & AM2901  RØ    , RØ    , RAMF  , SUBS  , DA
/                          & NOINE  & NOSDMA & NOVMA  & READ
/                          & BA     & NOLAD  & NORMM  & LMM    & NOCLB
/                          & NOSWP  & DINHL  & NOSDA  & NORCC  & NOLCC
/                          & NOLDI  & NOSTR  & RDRD   & NOFTCH & NOCIB
/                          & CIA    & RCLMUL & NOLIN

RSBI+R:   CONTNUE       & AM2901  RØ    , RØ    , RAMA  , ADD   , ZA
/                          & NOINE  & NOSDMA &  VMA   & READ
/                          & NOBA   & LAD    & NORMM  & LMM    & NOCLB
/                          & NOSWP  & NODIN  & NOSDA  & NORCC  & LCCLCV
/                          & LDI    & NOSTR  & RSRS   & NOFTCH & NOCIB
/                          & CIA    & RCLMUL & NOLIN

          BRANCH RSUBIN & AM2901  RØ    , RØ    , NOOP  , OR    , DZ
/                          & NOINE  & SDMA   &  VMA   & READ
/                          & NOBA   & LAD    & NORMM  & LMM    & NOCLB
/                          & NOSWP  & DINHL  & NOSDA  & NORCC  & LCCLCV
/                          & LDI    & NOSTR  & MWAMWB & NOFTCH & NOCIB
/                          & NOCIA  & RCLMUL & NOLIN

RSUBZR:   CONTNUE       & AM2901  R15   , R15   , RAMA  , ADD   , ZA
/                          & NOINE  & NOSDMA &  VMA   & READ
/                          & NOBA   & LAD    & NORMM  & LMM    & NOCLB
/                          & NOSWP  & NODIN  & NOSDA  & NORCC  & LCCLCV
/                          & LDI    & NOSTR  & MWAMWB & NOFTCH & NOCIB
/                          & CIA    & RCLMUL & NOLIN

          BRANCH RSUBIN & AM2901  RØ    , RØ    , NOOP  , ADD   , DA
/                          & NOINE  & SDMA   &  VMA   & READ
/                          & NOBA   & LAD    & NORMM  & LMM    & NOCLB
/                          & NOSWP  & DINHL  & NOSDA  & NORCC  & LCCLCV
/                          & LDI    & NOSTR  & RSRS   & NOFTCH & NOCIB
/                          & NOCIA  & RCLMUL & NOLIN

INCMR:    CONTNUE       & AM2901  RØ    , RØ    , RAMA  , ADD   , ZA
/                          & NOINE  & NOSDMA &  VMA   & READ
/                          & NOBA   & LAD    & NORMM  & LMM    & NOCLB
/                          & NOSWP  & NODIN  & NOSDA  & NORCC  & LCCLCV
/                          & LDI    & NOSTR  & RSRS   & NOFTCH & NOCIB
/                          & NOCIA  & RCLMUL & NOLIN

INCOUT:   BRANCH IFETCH & AM2901  RØ    , RØ    , RAMF  , ADD   , DZ
/                          & NOINE  & NOSDMA &  VMA   & WRITE
/                          & NOBA   & NOLAD  & NORMM  & LMM    & NOCLB
/                          & NOSWP  & DINHL  & NOSDA  & NORCC  & LCV
/                          & NOLDI  & NOSTR  & RDRD   & NOFTCH & NOCIB
/                          & CIA    & RCLMUL & NOLIN

INCI+R:   CONTNUE       & AM2901  RØ    , RØ    , RAMA  , ADD   , ZA
/                          & NOINE  & NOSDMA &  VMA   & READ
/                          & NOBA   & LAD    & NORMM  & LMM    & NOCLB
/                          & NOSWP  & NODIN  & NOSDA  & NORCC  & LCCLCV
/                          & LDI    & NOSTR  & RSRS   & NOFTCH & NOCIB
/                          & CIA    & RCLMUL & NOLIN

          BRANCH INCOUT & AM2901  RØ    , RØ    , NOOP  , OR    , DZ
/                          & NOINE  & NOSDMA &  VMA   & READ
/                          & NOBA   & LAD    & NORMM  & LMM    & NOCLB
/                          & NOSWP  & DINHL  & NOSDA  & NORCC  & LCCLCV
/                          & LDI    & NOSTR  & MWAMWB & NOFTCH & NOCIB
/                          & NOCIA  & RCLMUL & NOLIN

INCZR:    CONTNUE       & AM2901  R15   , R15   , RAMA  , ADD   , ZA
/                          & NOINE  & NOSDMA &  VMA   & READ
/                          & NOBA   & LAD    & NORMM  & LMM    & NOCLB
/                          & NOSWP  & NODIN  & NOSDA  & NORCC  & LCCLCV
/                          & LDI    & NOSTR  & MWAMWB & NOFTCH & NOCIB
/                          & CIA    & RCLMUL & NOLIN

          BRANCH INCOUT & AM2901  RØ    , RØ    , NOOP  , ADD   , DA
/                          & NOINE  & NOSDMA &  VMA   & READ
/                          & NOBA   & LAD    & NORMM  & LMM    & NOCLB
/                          & NOSWP  & DINHL  & NOSDA  & NORCC  & LCCLCV
/                          & LDI    & NOSTR  & RSRS   & NOFTCH & NOCIB
/                          & NOCIA  & RCLMUL & NOLIN

DECMR:    CONTNUE       & AM2901  RØ    , RØ    , RAMA  , ADD   , ZA
/                          & NOINE  & NOSDMA &  VMA   & READ
```

```
/                         & NOBA   & LAD    & NORMM  & LMM    & NOCLB
/                         & NOSWP  & NODIN  & NOSDA  & NORCC  & LCCLCV
/                         & LDI    & NOSTR  & RSRS   & NOFTCH & NOCIB
/                         & NOCIA  & RCLMUL & NOLIN

DECOUT:  BRANCH IFETCH & AM2901  R0    , R0    , RAMF  , SUBS  , DZ
/                         & NOINE  & NOSDMA &  VMA   & WRITE
/                         & NOBA   & NOLAD  & NORMM  & LMM    & NOCLB
/                         & NOSWP  & DINHL  & NOSDA  & NORCC  & LCV
/                         & NOLDI  & NOSTR  & RDRD   & NOFTCH & NOCIB
/                         & NOCIA  & RCLMUL & NOLIN

DECI+R:  CONTNUE       & AM2901  R0    , R0    , RAMA  , ADD   , ZA
/                         & NOINE  & NOSDMA &  VMA   & READ
/                         & NOBA   & LAD    & NORMM  & LMM    & NOCLB
/                         & NOSWP  & NODIN  & NOSDA  & NORCC  & LCCLCV
/                         & LDI    & NOSTR  & RSRS   & NOFTCH & NOCIB
/                         & CIA    & RCLMUL & NOLIN

         BRANCH DECOUT & AM2901  R0    , R0    , NOOP  , OR    , DZ
/                         & NOINE  & NOSDMA &  VMA   & READ
/                         & NOBA   & LAD    & NORMM  & LMM    & NOCLB
/                         & NOSWP  & DINHL  & NOSDA  & NORCC  & LCCLCV
/                         & LDI    & NOSTR  & MWAMWB & NOFTCH & NOCIB
/                         & NOCIA  & RCLMUL & NOLIN
DECZR:   CONTNUE       & AM2901  R15   , R15   , RAMA  , ADD   , ZA
/                         & NOINE  & NOSDMA &  VMA   & READ
/                         & NOBA   & LAD    & NORMM  & LMM    & NOCLB
/                         & NOSWP  & NODIN  & NOSDA  & NORCC  & LCCLCV
/                         & LDI    & NOSTR  & MWAMWB & NOFTCH & NOCIB
/                         & CIA    & RCLMUL & NOLIN

         BRANCH DECOUT & AM2901  R0    , R0    , NOOP  , ADD   , DA
/                         & NOINE  & NOSDMA &  VMA   & READ
/                         & NOBA   & LAD    & NORMM  & LMM    & NOCLB
/                         & NOSWP  & DINHL  & NOSDA  & NORCC  & LCCLCV
/                         & LDI    & NOSTR  & RSRS   & NOFTCH & NOCIB
/                         & NOCIA  & RCLMUL & NOLIN

COMMR:   CONTNUE       & AM2901  R0    , R0    , RAMA  , ADD   , ZA
/                         & NOINE  & NOSDMA &  VMA   & READ
/                         & NOBA   & LAD    & NORMM  & LMM    & NOCLB
/                         & NOSWP  & NODIN  & NOSDA  & NORCC  & LCCLCV
/                         & LDI    & NOSTR  & RSRS   & NOFTCH & NOCIB
/                         & NOCIA  & RCLMUL & NOLIN

COMOUT:  BRANCH IFETCH & AM2901  R0    , R0    , RAMF  , EXNOR , DZ
/                         & NOINE  & NOSDMA &  VMA   & WRITE
/                         & NOBA   & NOLAD  & NORMM  & LMM    & NOCLB
/                         & NOSWP  & DINHL  & NOSDA  & NORCC  & LCV
/                         & NOLDI  & NOSTR  & RDRD   & NOFTCH & NOCIB
/                         & NOCIA  & RCLMUL & NOLIN

COMI+R:  CONTNUE       & AM2901  R0    , R0    , RAMA  , ADD   , ZA
/                         & NOINE  & NOSDMA &  VMA   & READ
/                         & NOBA   & LAD    & NORMM  & LMM    & NOCLB
/                         & NOSWP  & NODIN  & NOSDA  & NORCC  & LCCLCV
/                         & LDI    & NOSTR  & RSRS   & NOFTCH & NOCIB
/                         & CIA    & RCLMUL & NOLIN

         BRANCH COMOUT & AM2901  R0    , R0    , NOOP  , OR    , DZ
/                         & NOINE  & NOSDMA &  VMA   & READ
/                         & NOBA   & LAD    & NORMM  & LMM    & NOCLB
/                         & NOSWP  & DINHL  & NOSDA  & NORCC  & LCCLCV
/                         & LDI    & NOSTR  & MWAMWB & NOFTCH & NOCIB
/                         & NOCIA  & RCLMUL & NOLIN

COMZR:   CONTNUE       & AM2901  R15   , R15   , RAMA  , ADD   , ZA
/                         & NOINE  & NOSDMA &  VMA   & READ
/                         & NOBA   & LAD    & NORMM  & LMM    & NOCLB
/                         & NOSWP  & NODIN  & NOSDA  & NORCC  & LCCLCV
/                         & LDI    & NOSTR  & MWAMWB & NOFTCH & NOCIB
/                         & CIA    & RCLMUL & NOLIN

         BRANCH COMOUT & AM2901  R0    , R0    , NOOP  , ADD   , DA
/                         & NOINE  & NOSDMA &  VMA   & READ
/                         & NOBA   & LAD    & NORMM  & LMM    & NOCLB
/                         & NOSWP  & DINHL  & NOSDA  & NORCC  & LCCLCV
/                         & LDI    & NOSTR  & RSRS   & NOFTCH & NOCIB
/                         & NOCIA  & RCLMUL & NOLIN

NEGMR:   CONTNUE       & AM2901  R0    , R0    , RAMA  , ADD   , ZA
/                         & NOINE  & NOSDMA &  VMA   & READ
/                         & NOBA   & LAD    & NORMM  & LMM    & NOCLB
/                         & NOSWP  & NODIN  & NOSDA  & NORCC  & LCCLCV
/                         & LDI    & NOSTR  & RSRS   & NOFTCH & NOCIB
/                         & NOCIA  & RCLMUL & NOLIN

NEGOUT:  BRANCH IFETCH & AM2901  R0    , R0    , RAMF  , SUBR  , DZ
/                         & NOINE  & NOSDMA &  VMA   & WRITE
/                         & NOBA   & NOLAD  & NORMM  & LMM    & NOCLB
/                         & NOSWP  & DINHL  & NOSDA  & NORCC  & NCLCC
/                         & NOLDI  & NOSTR  & RDRD   & NOFTCH & NOCIB
/                         & CIA    & RCLMUL & NOLIN

NEGI+R:  CONTNUE       & AM2901  R0    , R0    , RAMA  , ADD   , ZA
/                         & NOINE  & NOSDMA &  VMA   & READ
/                         & NOBA   & LAD    & NORMM  & LMM    & NOCLB
/                         & NOSWP  & NODIN  & NOSDA  & NORCC  & LCCLCV
/                         & LDI    & NOSTR  & RSRS   & NOFTCH & NOCIB
/                         & CIA    & RCLMUL & NOLIN

         BRANCH NEGOUT & AM2901  R0    , R0    , NOOP  , OR    , DZ
/                         & NOINE  & NOSDMA &  VMA   & READ
/                         & NOBA   & LAD    & NORMM  & LMM    & NOCLB
/                         & NOSWP  & DINHL  & NOSDA  & NORCC  & LCCLCV
/                         & LDI    & NOSTR  & MWAMWB & NOFTCH & NOCIB
/                         & NOCIA  & RCLMUL & NOLIN

NEGZR:   CONTNUE       & AM2901  R15   , R15   , RAMA  , ADD   , ZA
/                         & NOINE  & NOSDMA &  VMA   & READ
/                         & NOBA   & LAD    & NORMM  & LMM    & NOCLB
/                         & NOSWP  & NODIN  & NOSDA  & NORCC  & LCCLCV
/                         & LDI    & NOSTR  & MWAMWB & NOFTCH & NOCIB
/                         & CIA    & RCLMUL & NOLIN

         BRANCH NEGOUT & AM2901  R0    , R0    , NOOP  , ADD   , DA
/                         & NOINE  & NOSDMA &  VMA   & READ
/                         & NOBA   & LAD    & NORMM  & LMM    & NOCLB
/                         & NOSWP  & DINHL  & NOSDA  & NORCC  & LCCLCV
/                         & LDI    & NOSTR  & RSRS   & NOFTCH & NOCIB
/                         & NOCIA  & RCLMUL & NOLIN

SWPMR:   CONTNUE       & AM2901  R0    , R0    , RAMA  , ADD   , ZA
/                         & NOINE  & NOSDMA &  VMA   & READ
/                         & NOBA   & LAD    & NORMM  & LMM    & NOCLB
/                         & NOSWP  & NODIN  & NOSDA  & NORCC  & LCCLCV
/                         & LDI    & NOSTR  & RSRS   & NOFTCH & NOCIB
/                         & NOCIA  & RCLMUL & NOLIN

SWPOUT:  BRANCH IFETCH & AM2901  R0    , R0    , RAMF  , OR    , DZ
/                         & NOINE  & NOSDMA &  VMA   & WRITE
/                         & NOBA   & NOLAD  & NORMM  & LMM    & NOCLB
/                         & SWPHL  & NODIN  & NOSDA  & NORCC  & LCV
/                         & NOLDI  & NOSTR  & RDRD   & NOFTCH & NOCIB
/                         & NOCIA  & RCLMUL & NOLIN

SWPI+R:  CONTNUE       & AM2901  R0    , R0    , RAMA  , ADD   , ZA
/                         & NOINE  & NOSDMA &  VMA   & READ
/                         & NOBA   & LAD    & NORMM  & LMM    & NOCLB
/                         & NOSWP  & NODIN  & NOSDA  & NORCC  & LCCLCV
/                         & LDI    & NOSTR  & RSRS   & NOFTCH & NOCIB
/                         & CIA    & RCLMUL & NOLIN

         BRANCH SWPOUT & AM2901  R0    , R0    , NOOP  , OR    , DZ
/                         & NOINE  & NOSDMA &  VMA   & READ
/                         & NOBA   & LAD    & NORMM  & LMM    & NOCLB
/                         & NOSWP  & DINHL  & NOSDA  & NORCC  & LCCLCV
/                         & LDI    & NOSTR  & MWAMWB & NOFTCH & NOCIB
/                         & NOCIA  & RCLMUL & NOLIN

SWPZR:   CONTNUE       & AM2901  R15   , R15   , RAMA  , ADD   , ZA
/                         & NOINE  & NOSDMA &  VMA   & READ
/                         & NOBA   & LAD    & NORMM  & LMM    & NOCLB
/                         & NOSWP  & NODIN  & NOSDA  & NORCC  & LCCLCV
/                         & LDI    & NOSTR  & MWAMWB & NOFTCH & NOCIB
/                         & CIA    & RCLMUL & NOLIN

         BRANCH SWPOUT & AM2901  R0    , R0    , NOOP  , ADD   , DA
/                         & NOINE  & NOSDMA &  VMA   & READ
/                         & NOBA   & LAD    & NORMM  & LMM    & NOCLB
/                         & NOSWP  & DINHL  & NOSDA  & NORCC  & LCCLCV
/                         & LDI    & NOSTR  & RSRS   & NOFTCH & NOCIB
/                         & NOCIA  & RCLMUL & NOLIN

END
```

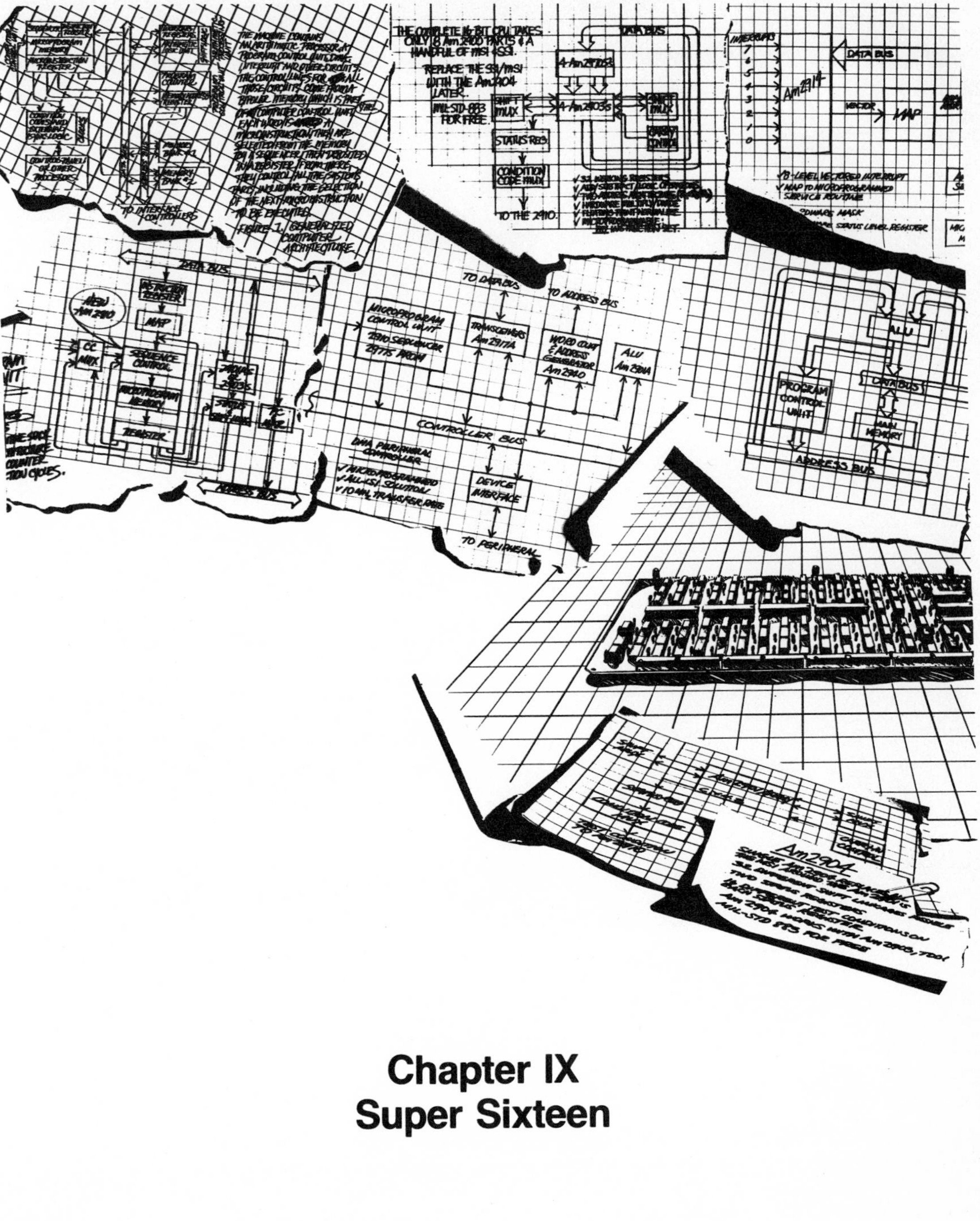

Chapter IX
Super Sixteen

INTRODUCTION

The AMD 16-Bit Computer design is an example of a high-speed microprocessor system which takes full advantage of AMD's Am2900 Family of Bipolar microprocessor circuits to provide an economical, high performance, self contained 16-bit computer. It was designed to demonstrate the principles of a microprogrammed system.

This design is intended to show some of the techniques used to achieve high performance. This includes pipelining at the microprogram level as well as pipelining at the macro or machine instruction program level. A powerful instruction set is demonstrated which allows the user to write efficient programs in a minimum amount of time.

One of the unique features of the design is that in addition to using the high performance Am2900 Bipolar microprocessor family, it takes advantage of the MOS peripherals normally associated with MOS microprocessors. These are used to perform the slower functions, particularly in the I/O interface area.

SYSTEM ORGANIZATION

The 16-Bit Computer is designed to perform in a system environment as shown in Figure 1. The system consists of a central processing unit (the 16-Bit Computer), memory units, I/O units (peripheral controllers), and a bus controller. These units communicate over the system bus consisting of a 16-bit wide address bus, 16-bit wide bi-directional data bus, and a control bus. The control bus is a collection of signals that include the memory and I/O interface controls and the interrupt request lines.

This organization allows systems to be configured with more than one CPU and multiple memory and I/O units. The bus controller arbitrates requests for bus use from the CPU's or I/O units that require DMA transfers.

This application note concentrates on the design of the CPU portion of the system.

INSTRUCTIONS

An instruction is either one or two 16-bit words in length and must be located in main memory on an integral word boundary. The left most eight bits of the instruction is always the operation code, followed by two, 4-bit register designation fields (Figure 2). The 16-bit (one word) instruction is always this format. The 32-bit (two words) instruction has the first (left most) word exactly like the 16-bit instruction. The second word of the 32-bit instruction is always full 16-bit value (d) which acts as a memory reference address or an immediate value (Figure 3). This architecturally simple instruction format becomes very powerful when implemented on a microprogrammed machine.

The 8-bit opcode provides for 256 primary instructions, which is usually more than enough for most general purpose computers. The 4-bit register fields (R_1 and R_2) each designate one of the sixteen, 16-bit registers (R_0-R_{15}). Depending upon the operation, each register can act as either an accumulator for arithmetic and logic operations, or an index register in modulo address arithmetic. On operations where the result is placed in a register, the R_1 field depicts the destination register and R_2 (or R_2+d) is, or points to the source field in main memory. On operations where the

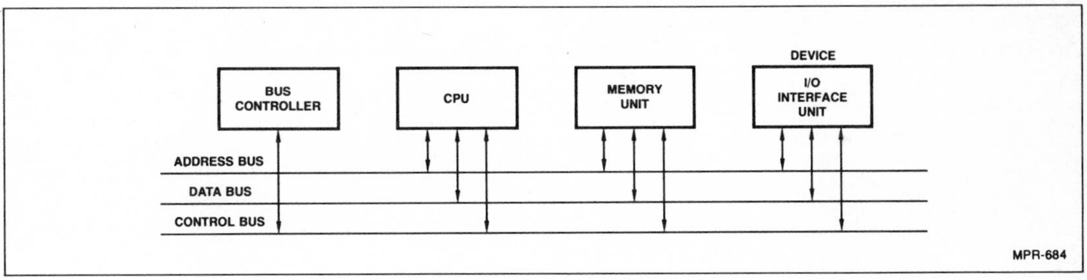

Figure 1. System Organization.

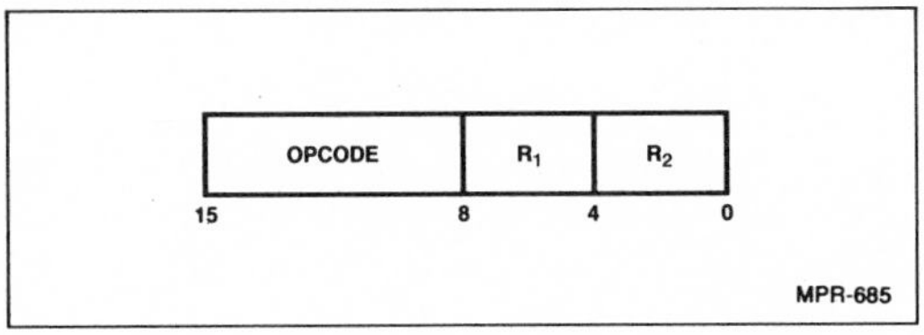

Figure 2. 16-Bit Instruction (RR, RS, SS).

result is transferred from a register to memory, the R_1 field depicts the source register and R_2 (or R_2+d) points to the destination memory location. Memory to memory transfers will have R_2 as the source pointer and R_1 as the destination pointer. Even though the R_1 and R_2 fields are architecturally wired to the Am2903 register address inputs, variations of the source/destination assignment may be implemented via microcode.

The complete defined standard instruction set is given in Table 1. This is a typical "machine level" instruction set. It allows manipu-

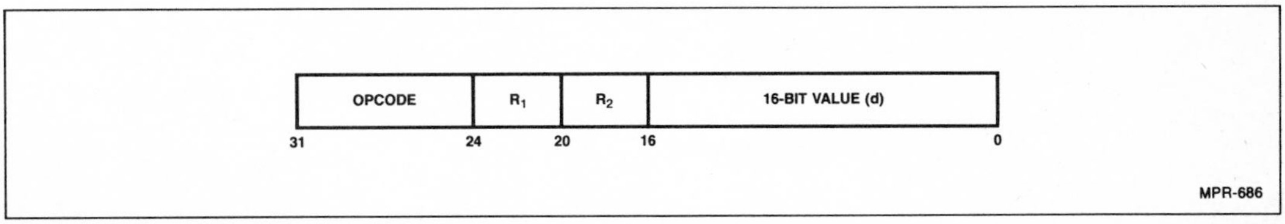

Figure 3. 32-Bit Instruction (RX, RSI).

Table 1. 16-Bit Computer Instruction Summary Mnemonic Instruction Format.

FIXED-POINT LOAD/STORE INSTRUCTIONS		
LD	LOAD	RR, RS, SS, RX, RSI
ST	STORE	RS, RX
FIXED-POINT ARITHMETIC INSTRUCTIONS		
ADD	ADD	RR, RS, SS, RX, RSI
ADC	ADD WITH CARRY	RR, RX
SUB	SUBTRACT	RR, RS, SS, RX, RSI
SBC	SUBTRACT WITH CARRY	RR, RX
AND	AND	RR, RS, SS, RX, RSI
OR	OR	RR, RS, SS, RX, RSI
XOR	XOR	RR, RS, SS, RX, RSI
TSTI	TEST IMMEDIATE	RSI
CMP	COMPARE	RR, RS, SS, RX, RSI
CMPL	COMPARE LOGICAL	RR, RS, SS, RX, RSI
MUL	MULTIPLY	RR, RX
MULU	MULTIPLY UNSIGNED	RR, RX
DIV	DIVIDE	RR, RX
COMP	ONES COMPLEMENT	RR, RS, SS, RX, RSI
BYTE INSTRUCTIONS		
LDB	LOAD BYTE	RR, RX, RSI
IC	INSERT CHARACTER	RR, RX, RSI
STC	STORE BYTE	RR, RX, RSI
XCHB	EXCHANGE	RR, RX, RSI
BS	BYTE SWAP	RR, RX
CLB	COMPARE LOGICAL BYTE	RR, RS, RX, RSI
ANDB	AND BYTE	RR, RS, RX, RSI
ORB	OR BYTE	RR, RS, RX, RSI
XORB	XOR BYTE	RR, RS, RX, RSI
SYSTEM INSTRUCTIONS		
LPSW	LOAD PROGRAM STATUS WORD	RX
SPSW	STORE PROGRAM STATUS WORD	RX
EPSW	EXCHANGE PROGRAM STATUS WORD	RR
SVC	SUPERVISOR CALL	RX
SETP	SET BIT PSW	RI
RSTP	RESET BIT PSW	RI
TSTP	TEST BIT PSW	RI
CMPP	COMPLEMENT BIT PSW	RI
STACK INSTRUCTIONS		
CALL	BRANCH AND STACK	RR, RX
RTN	RETURN	RR
PUSH	PUSH	RR
POP	POP	RR
PPUSH	PARTIAL PUSH	RR
PPOP	PARTIAL POP	RR
LDSP	LOAD STACK POINTER	RX
LDSLL	LOAD STACK LOWER LIMIT	RX
LDSUL	LOAD STACK UPPER LIMIT	RX
STSP	STORE STACK POINTER	RX
STSLL	STORE STACK LOWER LIMIT	RX
STSUL	STORE STACK UPPER LIMIT	RX
EXTENDED INSTRUCTIONS		
TR	TRANSLATE	RR
TRT	TRANSLATE AND TEST	RR
MVCL	MOVE LONG	RR
CLCL	COMPARE LONG	RR
EXEC	EXECUTE	RX
DA	DECIMAL ADD	RR, RX
DS	DECIMAL SUBTRACT	RR, RX
DI	DECREMENT INDEXES	RR
SHIFT/ROTATE		
SRL	SHIFT RIGHT LOGICAL	RX, RSI
SRA	SHIFT RIGHT ARITHMETIC	RX, RSI
RR	ROTATE RIGHT	RX, RSI
SLL	SHIFT LEFT LOGICAL	RX, RSI
RL	ROTATE LEFT	RX, RSI
SRDL	SHIFT RIGHT DOUBLE LOGICAL	RX, RSI
SRDA	SHIFT RIGHT DOUBLE ARITHMETIC	RX, RSI
SLDL	SHIFT LEFT DOUBLE LOGICAL	RX, RSI
SLDA	SHIFT LEFT DOUBLE ARITHMETIC	RX, RSI
RRD	ROTATE RIGHT DOUBLE	RX, RSI
RLD	ROTATE LEFT DOUBLE	RX, RSI
I/O INSTRUCTIONS		
IN	INPUT WORD	RR, RX
INB	INPUT BYTE	RR, RX
OUT	OUTPUT WORD	RR, RX
OUTB	OUTPUT BYTE	RR, RX
BRANCHES		
B	UNCONDITIONAL BRANCH	RX
BR	UNCONDITIONAL BRANCH REGISTER	RR
BC	BRANCH ON CONDITION TRUE	RX
BAL	BRANCH AND LINK	RX
BALR	BRANCH AND LINK REGISTER	RR
BXH	BRANCH ON INDEX HIGH	RX
BXLE	BRANCH ON INDEX LOW OR EQUAL	RX

lation of bit, byte, word and multibyte data; PUSH/POP single or multiple registers to/from stacks; maintain multiple stacks; decimal, binary and integer arithmetic; byte and word I/O; and maintain supervisory control over hardware and software generated interrupts.

Instruction Format

Many of the instructions have multiple formats. These formats depict addressing modes and determine where the source and destination fields are located. The defined instruction formats are shown in Figure 4.

The Program Control Unit

The Program Control Unit (PCU) under control of the microprogram is used to update the Program Counter and load this value into the Memory Address Register (MAR) for reading instructions/data from main memory. The PCU is also used to update the stack pointer and compare this value to the stack limits during stack operations. As can be seen in Figure 5, the Computer Block Diagram, data can be sent to the PCU from the ALU via the Transfer Register. The PCU can also output data onto the PCU bus to the Y-bus of the ALU via the bi-directional PCU transfer drivers.

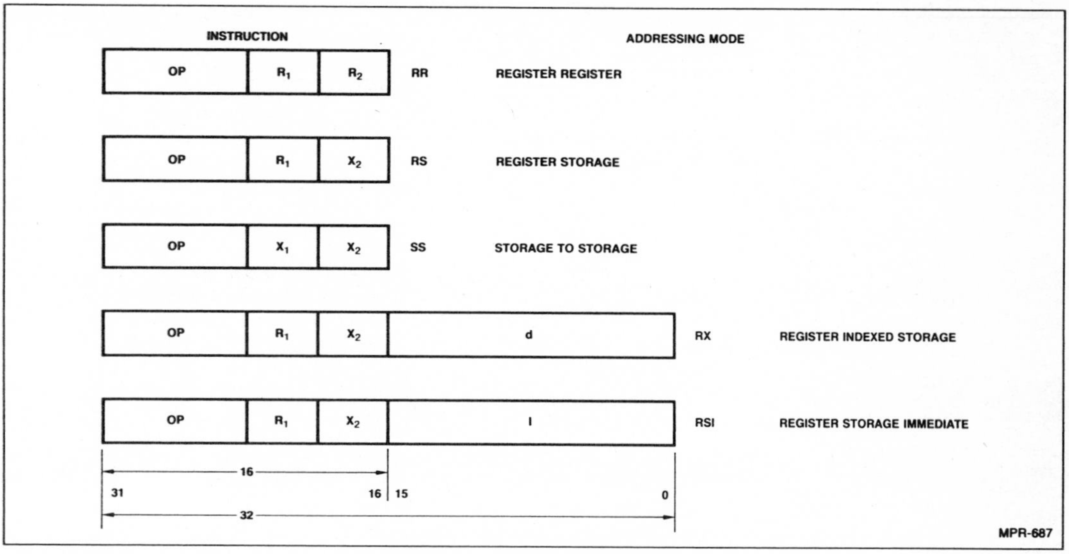

Figure 4. Instruction Formats.

The instructions set consists of nine instruction groups:

- Fixed-point load/store
- Fixed-point arithmetic
- Byte
- Shift/rotate
- Branch control
- I/O
- Stack
- Extended
- System

A complete description of each instruction is given in Appendix A.

CENTRAL PROCESSING UNIT ARCHITECTURE

Processor Organization

The organization of the computer is shown in Figure 5 (Computer Block Diagram). The computer is organized into several distinct sections, the Program Control Unit (PCU), the Arithmetic and Logic Unit (ALU), and the Computer Control Unit (CCU), the Data Path, the Memory Control and Clock Control, and Input/Output Interface and Interrupt Section. The logic diagrams for the CPU are located in Appendix F. Earlier chapters in the Build a Microcomputer series have described the principle sections of a computer and the Am2900 components used in these sections. This chapter describes how these components are used to implement a very high-speed low cost computer.

Note: Figure 5 is sheet 1 of the logic diagrams.

The PCU is organized around four Am2901's. The use of Am2901's allow the PCU to generate addresses with the flexibility of an ALU chip, to increment the Program Counter by two in one microcycle, and to provide the stack pointer registers for in main memory stack operations. The registers of these Am2901's are defined as shown in Figure 6. Register 0 holds the program counter and Registers 4 and 5 hold constants for incrementing. Byte addressing requires the address to be incremented by two every time 16 bits of instruction data are fetched.

The Arithmetic and Logic Unit (ALU)

The ALU shown in Figure 7 is organized around four Am2903's. The Am2903 performs all of the functions performed by the Am2901A but also provides the computer with separate DA bus and DB bus input ports as well as additional instructions to implement multiplication and division. Three major buses connect to the ALU: DA, DB and Y buses. The memory data from the Z_0 Register and microcode immediates are brought into the Am2903 through the DA port while Program Status Bits 16-23 enter via the DB port. The Am2903's output or receive data on the Y bus for loading into the RAM registers. The Am2903's zero decode logic detects zero on the Y port whether or not the Y port is receiving or sending data.

To implement the defined instruction set, the RAM register selection controls are sent from the Instruction (I) Register to the Am2903's. $I_{0\text{-}3}$ (used with instructions with the R_2 or X_2 field) are

Register Number	Register Assignment
0	Program Counter
1	Stack Pointer
2	Stack Lower Limit
3	Stack Upper Limit
4	+ 2
5	+ 4
6	Not used − available
7	Not used − available
8-15	Not used (wired disable)

Figure 6. PCU Register Assignments.

connected to the A address inputs on the Am2903 while I_{4-7} are connected to the B address inputs. The ALU operations performed are controlled by microcode bits M_{78-86} which are connected to the Am2903 I_{0-8} inputs.

The Am2904 provides the microcode and machine status registers holding the carry, negative, zero and overflow status. The machine status bits C, N, Z and OVR are defined as PSW bits 16-23. Logic in the Am2904 includes a condition code multiplexer to select the true or complement of any of the four status bits and combinations of status bits from either the machine or micro-status registers or directly from the ALU. This condition code multiplexer is controlled by Instruction Register bits I_{4-7} which are gated to the Am2904 I_{0-3} inputs during the execution of a conditional branch. The output of the multiplexer, labeled TEST is routed to the test tree for input into the Am2910. The Am2904 also provides the shift linkages and shift linkage control and selection of the type of carry signal to the ALU and lookahead carry unit.

The ALU is designed to work with byte operations as well as 16-bit operations. Byte operations operate only on the lower 8 bits of register data without affecting the upper 8 bits of data. During byte operations the WORD signal (M_{90}) goes inactive disabling the Write Enable and Output Y Enable for ALU bit slices 3 and 4. The word/byte multiplexer circuit will select C, N and OVR status bits from ALU bit slice 2 and at the same time ALU bit slice 2 has its MSS input pulled LOW to indicate most significant slice. The zero status bit being OR tied to all of the ALU bit slices cannot be multiplexed. Instead the Y bus signals 8-15 are forced to zero by gating zeroes from the PCU resulting in the Z signal line state being a function of ALU bit slices 1 and 2 only.

The Computer Control Unit

The Computer Control Unit controls the sequence of execution of the microinstructions. The Am2910 Microprogram Controller provides the sequencer for the microprogram (see logic diagrams Sheet 5). Branch addresses and counter values loaded into the Am2910 D_{0-11} inputs, originate from the Pipeline Register (M_{0-11}), the interrupt vector decoder, and the machine instruction decoder. The instruction decoder, also called Mapping ROM, (a 512 x 8 PROM) uses the Instruction Register I_{8-15} as address bits with the PROM outputs being the starting address of the micro-code sequence that executes each machine instruction. In this design the Am29775 Registered PROM's are used to provide both the microprogram memory (512 x 96 bits wide) and the Pipeline Register. The microcode bits M_{16-20} are output from Am29774 because these signals require open collector outputs rather than the standard tri-state outputs to allow the Am2910 inputs I_{0-3} to be pulled to zero.

The starting address generation for the interrupt service routine and initialization routine is accomplished with a minimum of extra logic. During the last microcode cycle of the previous machine instruction, the MAPEN signal is activated to enable the output of the Mapping ROM. However, if an interrupt request is pending, the Mapping ROM is disabled and the pull-up resistors force the eight least significant microprogram branch address lines to all ones, vectoring the microprogram to the interrupt service routine. After a reset, the microprogram should be vectored to address zero, the starting address of the initialization routine. This is accomplished by having the reset signal force zeroes into the Am2910 I_{0-3} inputs which causes the Am2910 to output address zero.

Clock and Memory Control

The architecture of this computer achieves its high throughput by being able to execute machine instructions in as little as one microcycle. This is accomplished by overlapping (also called pipelining) the fetch and decode with the execute microcycles. An essential part of this design is the memory control section. The clock and memory control circuits shown in Sheet 6 of the logic diagrams work together to provide a very efficient mechanism for integrating memory operations with the computer. The memory interface timing is a clocked handshaked protocol shown in Figure 8. Each memory transfer consists of a Bus Request, Bus Acknowledge response, Memory Request, Address Accept response, Data Request and a Data Sync response. At the maximum rate a memory interface response can occur 50ns after the computer activates a control line. This makes it possible to read from main memory once every microcycle (4 x 50ns = 200ns); however should a particular memory board require a longer cycle, it can delay sending Data Sync to the computer to extend the cycle.

The read and write timing are shown in more detail in Figures 9 and 10. Note that if a memory read is taking place during microcycle N, the Bus Request, Bus Acknowledge and the start of memory address are output from the computer in the previous N−1 cycle, and the data is sent to the computer during the first half of the following N+1 cycle. Now consider the case of back-to-back main memory read cycles. In this case, in the microcycle that the computer sends the address to the memory board, the memory board is sending data to the computer; but this is not the data associated with the address being received but the data associated with the address received during the previous microcycle.

A free running or uncontrolled 20MHz clock on the backplane is connected to all of the devices which effect memory transfers (CPU, bus controller, and memory modules). All of the signal handshaking that is required by the memory interface protocol is clocked with the same 20MHz clock to ensure no metastable conditions occur during memory transfer. Careful examination of this memory interface operation will reveal that not only does it solve the very serious metastable problem, but also that the clock synchronization and bus propagation delay occur during the memory read access time (or write time) and do not slow down the memory transfer rate.

The CPU clock generation is intimately related to the Memory Control Logic. The CPU clock signals Phase 1 (ϕ_1) and Phase 2 (ϕ_2) are shown along with the memory interface signals in Figure 8. Phase 1 is a square wave set high at the beginning of the microcycle and has a period of 200ns. Almost all operations of the computer are clocked with the leading edge of ϕ_1. The clock control logic will enable the next cycle only if a Bus Request has received a Bus Acknowledge and only if a Memory Request has

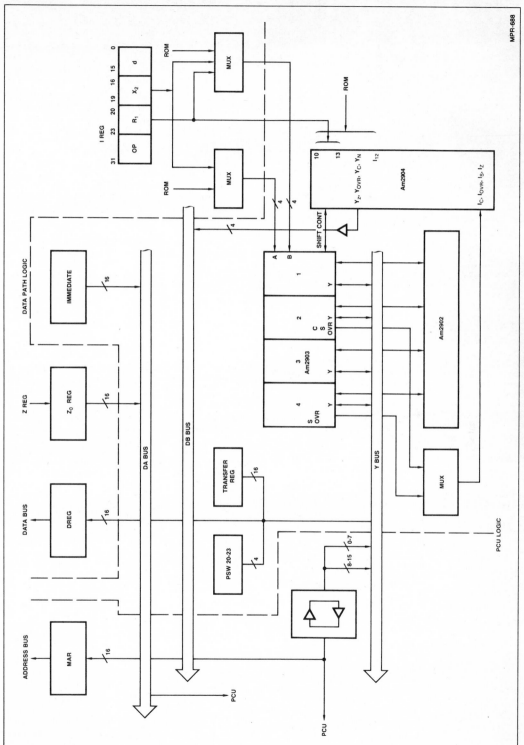

Figure 7. ALU Block Diagram.

MPR-688

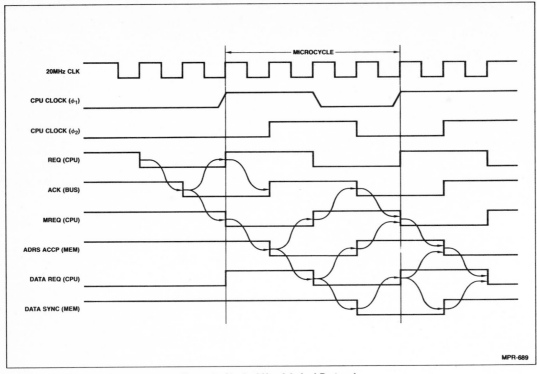

Figure 8. Clocked Handshaked Protocol.

received a Data Sync response. If the bus or memory resources of the system are temporarily being used by other processors, the computer will stop the clock and wait.

Data Path

The Data Path logic incorporates 8-bit wide devices wherever possible. The D Register drives directly onto the external data bus. Both main memory and I/O data are received through the Z Registers. Registers Z, Z_0 and Z_1 are actually latches implemented with Am74S373's. The Z Register enable latch signal, LDZ is derived from the memory control logic and main memory board logic both of which are clocked with the uncontrolled 20MHz clock (20MHzUNC). Using the uncontrolled clock allows the memory operation to go to completion at memory speed even when single stepping the microcode. This allows the system to use dynamic RAM's in the main memory since stopping the handshaking circuits during single step would prevent refresh operations from taking place.

Data from the main memory passes through the Z Register to the Z_0 and Z_1 Registers. The Z_0 and Z_1 Registers are enabled transparent at the beginning of the microcycle following the read main memory microcycle. This allows memory data to flow through the Z and Z_0 Registers (actually latches) to the ALU or flow through the Z and Z_1 Registers to the Instruction Decoder (Mapping ROM). The Z_1 and Z_0 Registers are locked down halfway through the microcycle guaranteeing the computer solid data and making it possible to send data from the D-Register out to the external Data Bus during the second half of the same microcycle. This is another example of how this design tightly dovetails data transfers in order to gain very high execution rates.

Interrupt and Input/Output

The interrupt and I/O section is shown in Sheet 7 of the logic diagrams.

The basic interrupt handling is controlled by the Am2914. In this design the Am2914 is used to prioritize and enable interrupts, provide the mask register, generate an Interrupt Request and Interrupt Vector. Interrupt nesting is done in the machine software interrupt handler. The external interrupt request signals (INT_0-INT_7) are input into the Am2914 from the external Control Bus (C Bus). When a peripheral controller requests computer servicing, it activates its assigned interrupt line. If this interrupt level is unmasked and interrupts are enabled, the Am2914 activates the INTERRUPT REQ signal that goes to the Computer Control Unit which causes the microprogram to vector to the microcode interrupt service routine. This microcode routine pushes the PSW onto the main memory stack, then reads the interrupt vector from the Am2914 and uses this value to vector the computer to the machine software routine that services the interrupt.

The Am9519 MOS Universal Interrupt Controller is incorporated into the design and its Group Interrupt signal is connected to the least significant INT_0 input of the Am2914. The Am9519 handles an additional eight interrupt levels for low speed requesting devices. This MOS LSI component offers the computer comprehensive interrupt handling capabilities at low cost. One feature the Am9519 offers is the capability of software generated interrupts. The console function, single instruction stepping, is implemented using a microcode routine that uses the software generated interrupt capability.

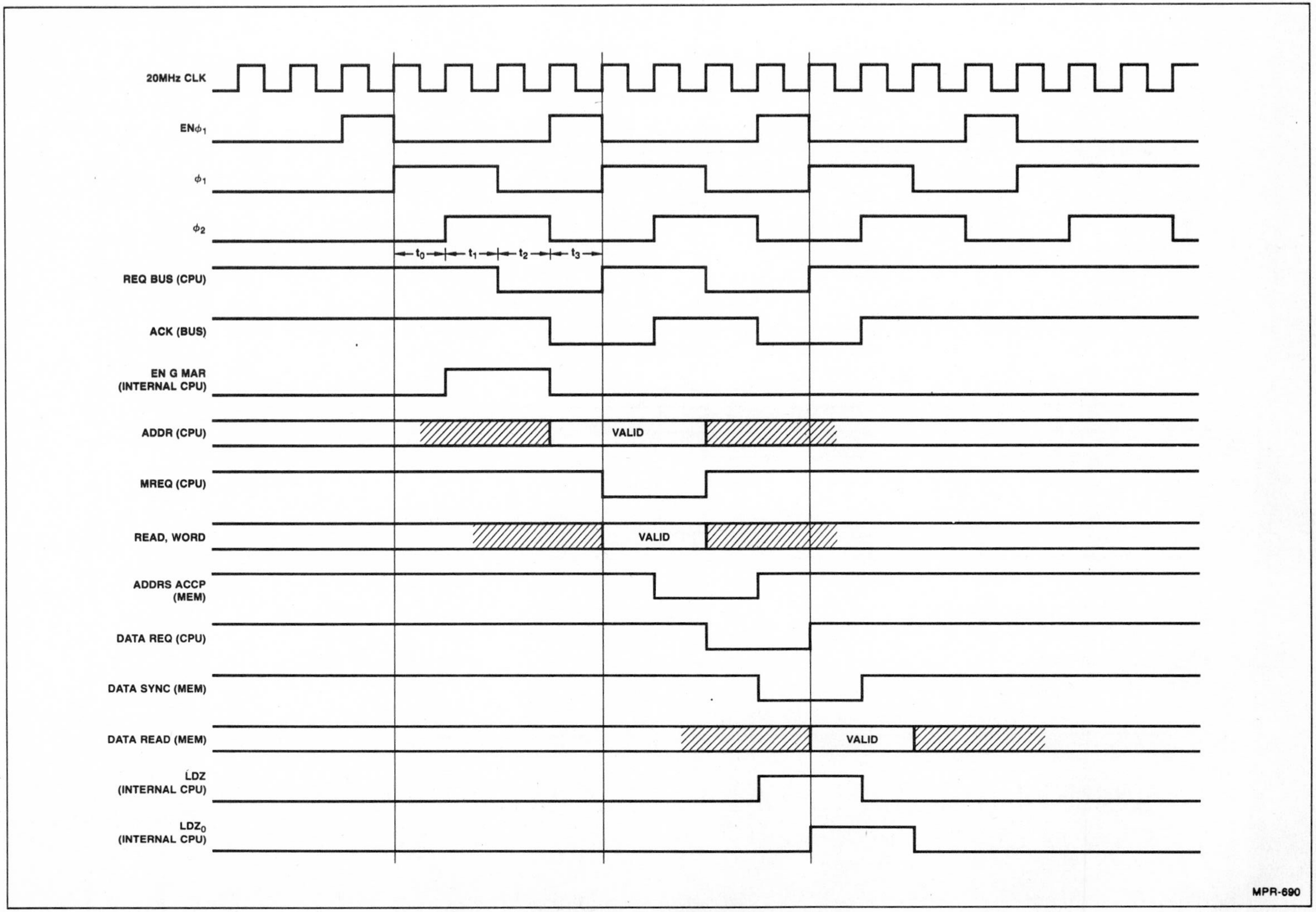

Figure 9. CPU Read Timing.

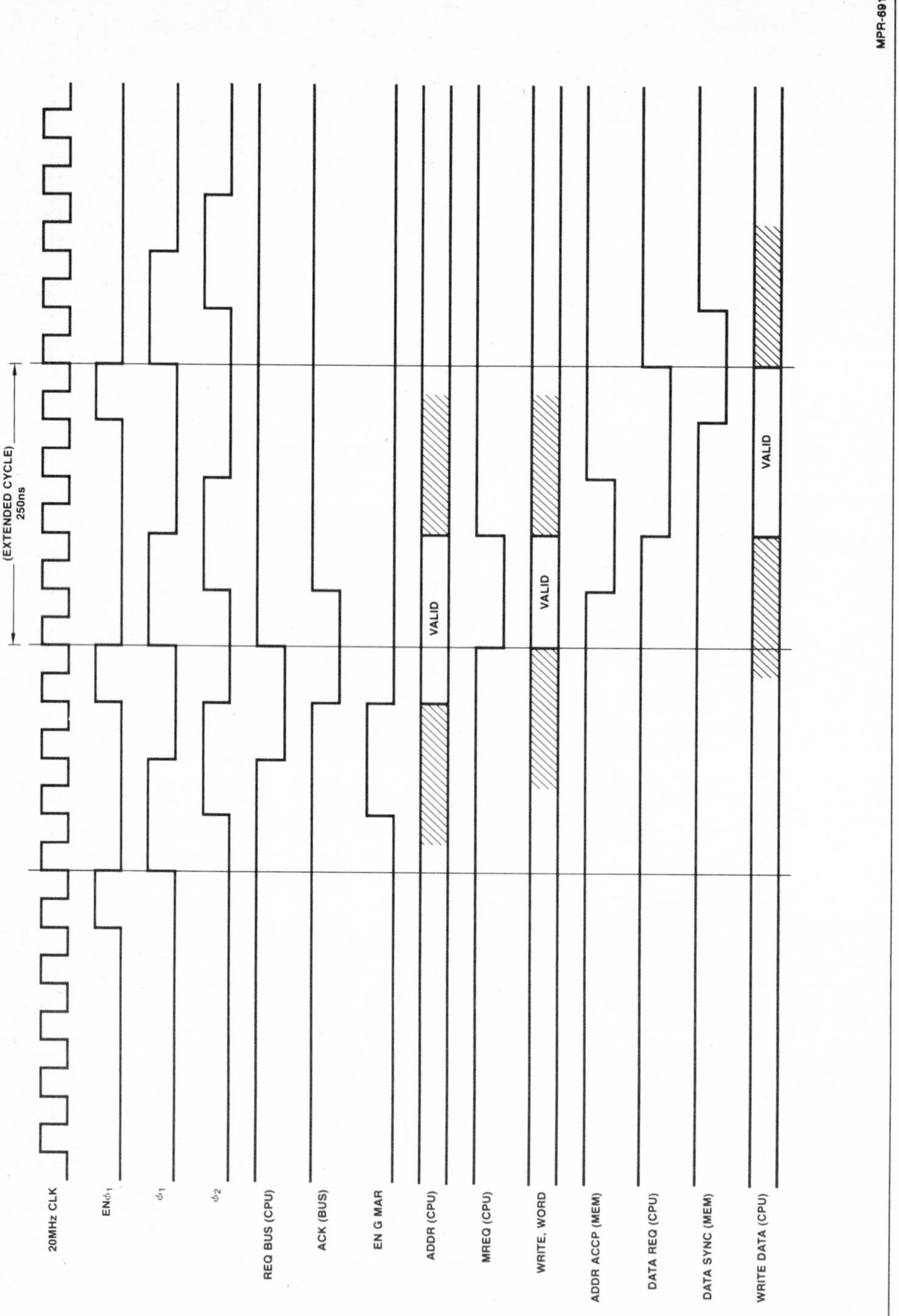

Figure 10. CPU Write Timing.

The I/O protocol for the AMD 16-Bit Computer is similar to that required to control Am8080/9080 peripheral circuits. As shown in Figures 11 and 12, the computer outputs the address over the system address bus, activates a control line (e.g., IORD) and holds these outputs until receiving a response, IOACK, from the peripheral controller. Execution of the I/O operation is done almost entirely in microcode with the I/O Control Register, a single Am2920, being the only additional hardware required. This is an example of a design precept followed in this computer which is to implement all features in microcode wherever possible. This results in a low cost computer, although sometimes slower, and a design that is flexible and easily modifiable to meet new requirements.

The I/O section has two Am8251/9551 Programmable Communication Interface components giving the computer two serial I/O Ports, one of which is reserved for the console. The console can be any standard RS-232 interface terminal.

Instruction Execution

To execute instructions, the main steps performed by the computer are: (1) form memory address, (2) instruction fetch, (3) decode, (4) displacement fetch, (5) form operand address, (6) operand fetch, and (7) execute. Every instruction type is made up of microinstructions that execute these basic steps, but most instructions require three steps or less. Instruction sequences for Register to Register (RR) and Register to Indexed Storage (RX) instructions are shown in Figures 13 and 14 to illustrate how the computer operates. These figures show the RR instruction requiring four microcycles and the typical RX instruction requiring seven microcycles. However, as will be explained later, in actual operation the effective time for an RR instruction is one microcycle and three for the RX.

Form Instruction Address

During this microcycle the instruction address is formed by having the Program Control Unit (PCU) under control of the microprogram increment the Program Counter by two. This address is then loaded into the MAR and back into the PC.

At the beginning of the cycle, Bus Request is activated causing the Bus Controller to respond with Bus Acknowledge. The address is then output from the MAR out on the Address Bus 50ns prior to the beginning of the next cycle.

Instruction Fetch

During this cycle, the main memory is fetching the contents of the address previously generated. The computer is designed to work with high-speed main memory capable of reading a memory location in one microcycle so that the instruction will be sent back to the computer at the beginning of the next cycle.

Decode Cycle

The instruction fetched from main memory during the previous cycle is sent to the computer at the beginning of the cycle. The instruction falls through the Z and Z_1 Registers (actually transparent latches) and is routed to the Instruction Decoder (Mapping PROM). The Instruction Decoder translates the 8-bit operation code of the instruction into an 8-bit address used as the starting address for the microprogram that will execute this instruction.

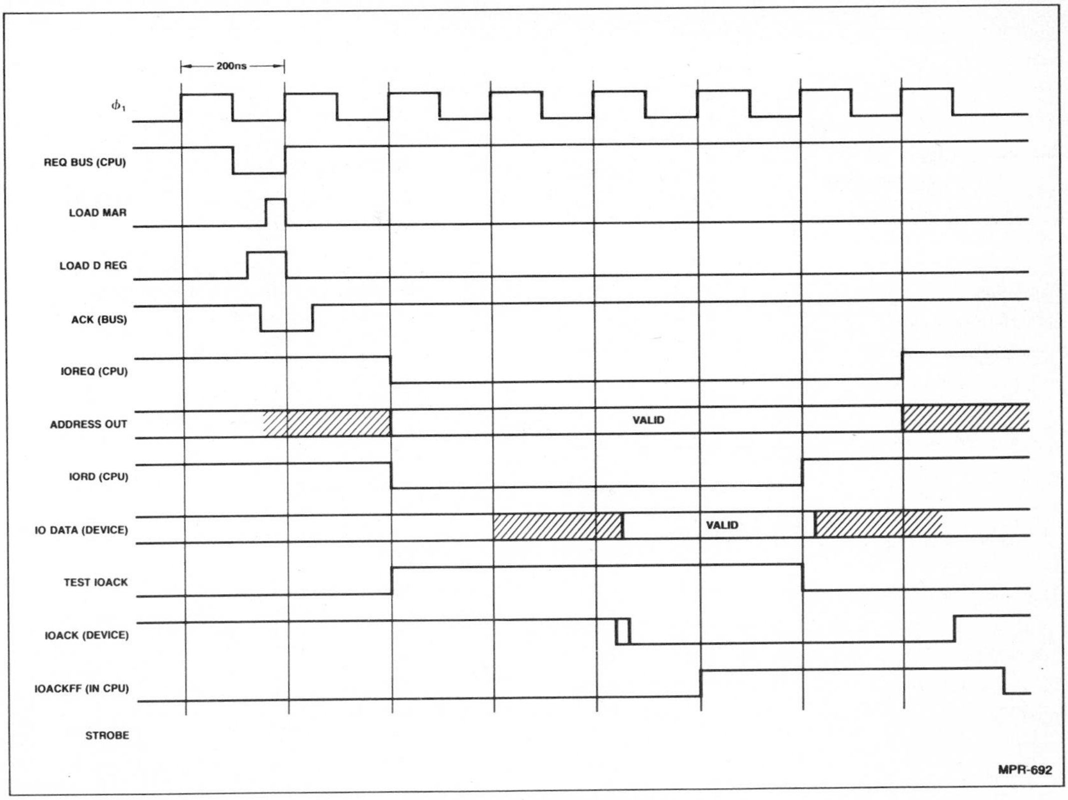

Figure 11. I/O Read Timing.

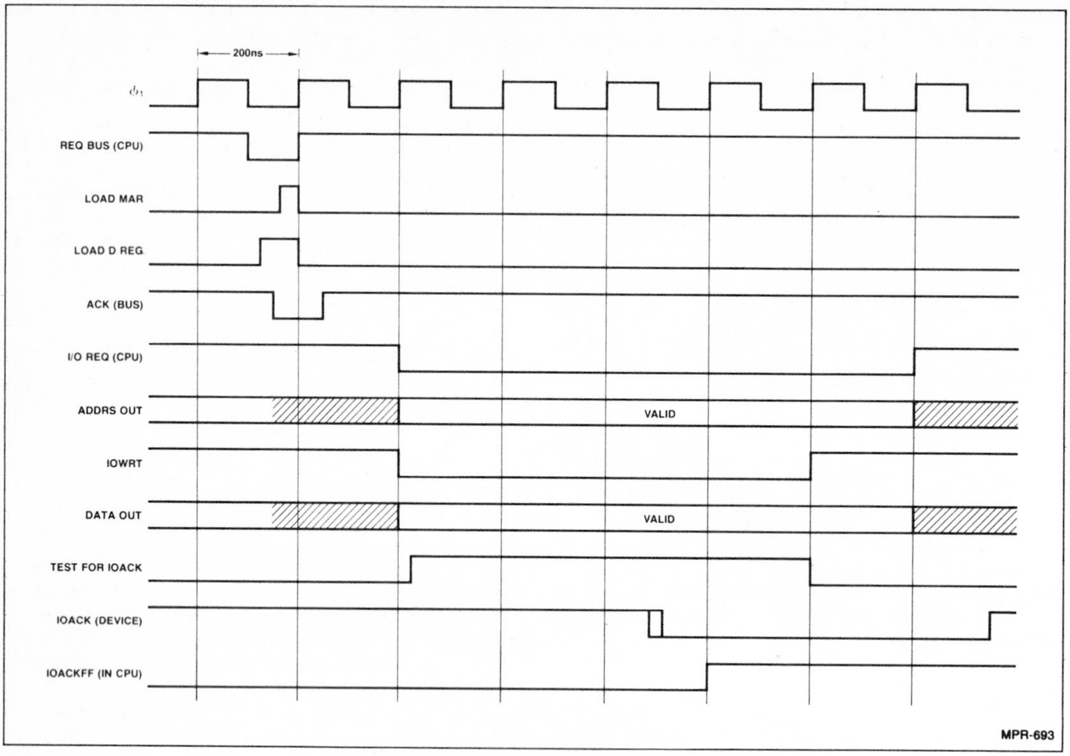

Figure 12. I/O Write Timing.

Microinstruction Operation	Microcycle Time			
	T_0	T_1	T_2	T_3
Form Instruction Address	A			
Instruction Fetch		A		
Decode			A	
Displacement Fetch				
Form Operand Address				
Operand Fetch				
Execute				A

Figure 13. RR Instruction Sequence.

Microinstruction Operation	Microcycle Time						
	T_0	T_1	T_2	T_3	T_4	T_5	T_6
Form Instruction Address	B						
Instruction Fetch		B					
Decode			B				
Displacement Fetch				B			
Form Operand Address					B		
Operand Fetch						B	
Execute							B

Figure 14. RX Instruction Sequence.

Displacement Fetch Cycle

After every instruction fetch another read cycle takes place. The second memory read will be another instruction fetch or an operand displacement fetch. The computer does not know what kind of a read out it is until the instruction decode is finished. For an RX instruction, after the memory read is completed, the computer identifies it as a displacement.

Form Operand Address Cycle

The memory word is sent from the main memory at the beginning of this cycle and then passes through the Z and Z_0 Register and goes to the ALU (Am2903's). The ALU adds the displacement and the contents of the register specified by X_2 field in the opcode and forms an operand address which is then loaded into the MAR. This has to be completed 50ns before the end of the cycle.

Operand Fetch Cycle

The memory read cycle is performed and the operand is sent to the computer at the beginning of the next cycle.

Execute Cycles

As the name implies, these are the microcycles that perform the task of the instruction but with the Am2903's normally only one execute cycle is required; however, some instructions (e.g., I/O instructions) take as many as seven execute cycles.

Simultaneously with the last execute cycle the Instruction Decoder is enabled.

Pipelined Operations

If the architecture of the computer executed each of the instructions and each microstep sequentially, this computer would be just another computer relying on a high-speed clock to gain high throughput. However, the 16-Bit Computer becomes an exceptional machine by using pipelining techniques. In this approach, the instruction steps for the following instructions are done during the decode and execute steps of the current instruction. The pipelining operation for a Register to Register class of instructions is shown in Figure 15. With the pipeline full, note that when instruction A is being executed, instruction B is being decoded, instruction C is being fetched from Main Memory and the MAR is being loaded with the address for instruction D. In the following cycle, RR instruction B is executed and RR instructions C, D and E proceed through the pipeline. The pipelining technique results in an RR instruction effectively being executed in one microcycle. As illustrated in Figure 16, a new RX instruction can be executed every three microcycles.

Pipelining is great for throughput, but it is a bear to microcode especially the first time through since during any one cycle up to four instruction sequences have to be considered. It is not as bad as it first appears. Note that an instruction decode cannot take place until the last execute cycle of the current instruction. The major pipelining takes place during the first three steps: form memory address, instruction fetch, and decode. Execute and operand fetch steps allow full overlapped operation only during the last execute cycle. Instructions that require many execute microcycles (e.g., I/O instructions) cause the computer performance to drop down to nearly that of a non-pipelined machine.

Pipeline Operation with Regard to Branching and Interrupts

Pipeline operations greatly reduce instruction execution time if machine instructions are executed in sequential order; however, if a branch is taken this advantage is lost because the steps set up in preparation for a decode cycle become useless. The pipeline is said to be "flushed out" when a branch is taken. The RX Branch on Condition instruction has the form:

WORD 1	OP	M	X_2
WORD 2	DISPLACEMENT		

Where: M is a 4-bit field specifying the conditions for the jump.
(X_2) + displacement is the branch address

Figure 17 shows the sequence chart for a RX Branch on Condition instruction. During the microcycle A_1 the target address K for the branch is formed and loaded into the MAR and also the instruction B is fetched for the no branch case. By microcycle A_2, it has been determined to take or not take the branch. If the branch is not taken, the MAR is loaded with address B+2, while if the branch is taken, an instruction fetch is performed for K and the MAR is loaded with K+2. Finally in A_3 the next instruction is decoded. By proper microcoding, the conditional branch is executed in only three microsteps even though the pipeline was "flushed out".

A, B, C, D are RR instructions

Action													
Form Instruction Address	A	B	C	D									
Fetch Instruction		A	B	C	D								
Decode			A	B	C	D							
Fetch Displacement													
Form Operand Address													
Fetch Operand													
Execute				A	B	C	D						

Figure 15. Register-to-Register Pipeline Operation.

A, B, C, D are RX instructions

Action													
Form Instruction Address	A		B			C							
Fetch Instruction		A		B			C						
Decode			A			B			C				
Fetch Displacement			A			B			C				
Form Operand Address				A			B			C			
Fetch Operand					A			B			C		
Execute						A			B			C	

Figure 16. Register-to-Indexed Storage Pipeline Operation.

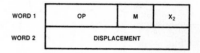

A = RX Branch Instruction
B = Next RX Instruction if branch is not taken
K = next RX Instruction if branch is taken

Action													
Form Instruction Address	A		B	K	B+2 K+2								
Fetch Instruction		A		B	K	B+2 K+2							
Decode			A			B K	etc.						
Fetch Displacement			A				B K						
Form Operand Address								B K					
Fetch Operand									B K				
Execute				A_1	A_2	A_3				B K			

Figure 17. Branch on Condition RX Pipeline Operation.

As with branching, an interrupt response alters the sequence of execution and "flushes" the pipeline. As was discussed previously in the Interrupt and Input/Output section, an interrupt request blocks the decoding of the next machine instruction and causes the Computer Control Unit to vector to the interrupt service routine. This microcode service routine pushes the PSW consisting of flags and Program Counter (PC) value onto the stack. The PC value is the current PC value minus 4. It is necessary to back the PC up to two instruction words (4 bytes), because the fetch instruction and form instruction address steps in the pipeline at the time of the jump to the interrupt microcode sequence have to be repeated when returning to the main machine program.

MICROINSTRUCTION FORMAT

All operations of the AMD 16-Bit Computer are under control of the microinstruction. Each microinstruction is 96 bits in length. The microinstruction format is summarized in Figure 18. The microinstruction definition is summarized in Figures 19a and 19b and is detailed in Table 2.

Figure 20 illustrates the AMDASM® Definition file for the 16-Bit Computer. AMDASM® is a meta-assembler developed by AMD for writing microprogams. The definition file defines microword length (WORD statement), formats (DEF statements) and constants (EQU statements) for the use of the actual microprogram (Figure 31).

The definition file is divided into 8 parts:

1. Am2910 sequencer opcode definitions
2. Am2903 ALU opcode definitions
3. Am2901A PCU opcode definitions
4. Am2904 shift mux and status control definitions
5. Datapath control bits definitions
6. Memory control bits definitions
7. Control strobe and control bits definitions
8. Immediate operand field definition

Am2910 Sequencer

Bit 91 of the microword is the input of CCEN of the Am2910. When bit 91 is a logical 1, the conditional operations are forced to unconditional operations. Bits 19-16 are the input to the instruction inputs to the Am2910. Bits 11-0 are the jump address field for instructions that need an address operand.

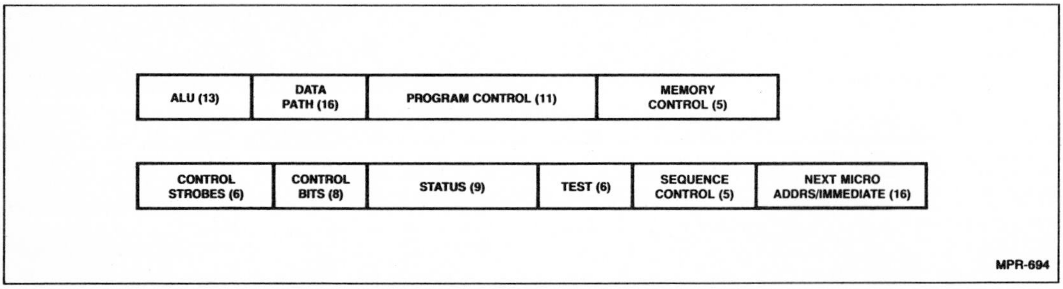

Figure 18. Summary of Microinstruction Word Fields.

16-BIT COMPUTER: MICRO CONTROL WORD BIT DEFINITIONS	Bits	Signal	Description
MISC	95	$\overline{RTB}$	ROUTE TO B
	92 91	(BP) Z → ZI	TRANSFER Z TO ZI
		$\overline{CCEN}$	Am2910
ALU (13)	90 89 88 87 86 85 84 83 82 81 80 79 78	$\overline{WORD}$	Am2903 IEU WORD/BYTE
		$\overline{EA}$	Am2903
		$\overline{OEY}$	Am2903
		$\overline{OEB}$	Am2903
		I_8	Am2903
		I_7	Am2903
		I_6	Am2903
		I_5	Am2903
		I_4	Am2903
		I_3	Am2903
		I_2	Am2903
		I_1	Am2903
		I_0	Am2903
Data Path (13)	77 76 75 74 73 72 71 70 69 68 67 66 65	$\overline{ENTREG}$	ENABLE TRANSFER REG.
		$\overline{LDTREG}$	LOAD TRANSFER REG.
		$\overline{ENCTR}$	I-REG EN CTR
		INC	I-REG INC/$\overline{DEC}$
		PCUCD	PCU TRANS CHIP DISABLE
		PCU → Y	PCU TRANSFER REG.
		LDMAR	LOAD MEMORY ADDR. REG.
		LDD	LOAD D-REG.
		$\overline{ZI \rightarrow I}$	LOAD ZI INTO I REG.
		$\overline{ENZ0}$	ENABLE Z0 → DA
		$\overline{PSW}$	ENABLE PSW
		$\overline{SHTCNTEN}$	SHIFT CNT Am2910 ADDR.
		$\overline{BRIEN}$	BRANCH INSTR. EN
Program Control (11)	64 63 62 61 59 58 57 56 55 54	$PCUI_7$	Am2901 F → B/$\overline{Q}$
		$PCUI_3$	Am2901
		$PCUI_2$	Am2901
		$PCUI_1$	Am2901
		$PCUI_0$	Am2901
		$PCUA_2$	Am2901
		$PCUA_1$	Am2901
		$PCUA_0$	Am2901
		$PCUB_2$	Am2901
		$PCUB_1$	Am2901
		$PCUB_0$	Am2901
Memory Control (5)	53 52 51 50 49	REQB	BUS REQUEST
		$\overline{MREQ}$	MEMORY REQUEST
		$\overline{HREQ}$	HOLD REQUEST
		WRITE	MEMORY WRITE/$\overline{READ}$
		MWORD	MEMORY WORD/$\overline{BYTE}$

Figure 19a. Micro Control Word Bit Definitions.

16-BIT COMPUTER

MICRO CONTROL WORD BIT DEFINITIONS

Field	Bits	Mnemonic	Definition
Control Strobes (6)	X X 48 47 46 45 44 43		
		$\overline{IMMD}$	EN IMMEDIATE → DA BUS
		$\overline{ROM/I}$	ROM/IREGEN
		$\overline{IOEN}$	I/O CONTROL REG. EN
		$\overline{INTDIS}$	Am2914 INTERRUPTS DISABLE
		$\overline{INTRIEN}$	Am2914 ENI_0-ENI_3
		$\overline{SHFTEN}$	Am2904 SHIFT EN
Control Bits (8)	42 41 40 39 38 37 36 35	$CNTLB_7$, $CNTLB_6$, $CNTLB_5$, $CNTLB_4$, $CNTLB_3$, $CNTLB_2$, $CNTLB_1$, $CNTLB_0$	GENERAL USE CONTROL BITS
Status (9)	X X 34 33 32 31 30 29 28 27 26		
		$\overline{OECT}$	Am2904 OUT EN CONDITIONAL TEST
		$\overline{EZ}$	Am2904 EN ZERO
		$\overline{EC}$	Am2904 EN CARRY
		$\overline{ES}$	Am2904 EN SIGN
		$\overline{EOVR}$	Am2904 EN OVERFLOW
		$\overline{CEM}$	Am2904 EN MACHINE STATUS
		$\overline{CE\mu}$	Am2904 EN MICRO STATUS
		I_{12}	Am2904 I_{12} CARRY OUT CNTL
		I_{11}	Am2904 I_{11} CARRY OUT CNTL
Test (6)	25 24 23 22 21 20		
		$TEST_5$	Am2904
		$TEST_4$	Am2904
		$TEST_3$	Am2904
		$TEST_2$	Am2904 & Am25LS251
		$TEST_1$	Am2904 & Am25LS251
		$TEST_0$	Am2904 & Am25LS251
Sequences CNTL (4)	19 18 17 16		
		NAC_3	Am2910 I_3
		NAC_2	Am2910 I_2
		NAC_1	Am2910 I_1
		NAC_0	Am2910 I_0
Next Micro Addr & Immed (16)	15 14 13 12 11 10 9 8 7 6 5 4 3 2 1 0	M_{15}, M_{14}, M_{13}, M_{12}, M_{11}, M_{10}, M_9, M_8, M_7, M_6, M_5, M_4, M_3, M_2, M_1, M_0	

Figure 19a. Micro Control Word Bit Definitions (Cont.)

Control Strobes / Control Bits (35-42)	ROM/IREGEN Bit 47	I/O Control Register Bit 46	Am2914 I_0-I_3 Bit 44	Am2904 Shift Enable Bit 43
$CNTLB_7$	B_3	I/O7		
$CNTLB_6$	B_2	I/O6		
$CNTLB_5$	B_1	I/O5		
$CNTLB_4$	B_0	I/O4		I_{10}
$CNTLB_3$	A_3	I/O3	I_3	I_9
$CNTLB_2$	A_2	I/O2	I_2	I_8
$CNTLB_1$	A_1	I/O1	I_1	I_7
$CNTLB_0$	A_0	I/O0	I_0	I_6

Figure 19b. Detailed Description of Bits 34 through 47.

Table 2. Microinstruction Definition.

		Definition
95	$\overline{RTB}$	Routes second register field to B-RAM of Am2903.
92	$Z \rightarrow Z_1$	Loads the value in the Z register into the Z_1 Register at the beginning of the microcycle.
91	$\overline{CCEN}$	Enables the CC input of the Am2910.
ALU		
90	$\overline{WORD}$	These bits control the four Am2903's. The function of EA, OEY, OEB, and I_{8-0} is listed in Figure 20. WORD when enabled (LOW) causes the Am2903's to operate on words (16-bits). When disabled (HIGH) the ALU operates on bytes (the least significant byte). This bit disabled blocks WE to the upper two Am2903's and turns off their Y outputs. Zeroes should be forced to the upper 8 bits of the Y bus via the PCU to allow the zero status to operate correctly when the WORD bit is disabled. Also, when disabled the status (C, OVR, S) sent to the Am2904 is taken from the second Am2903 (numbering 0-3 least significant to most significant slice) instead of the most significant Am2903.
89	$\overline{EA}$	
88	$\overline{OEY}$	
87	$\overline{OEB}$	
86	I_8	
85	I_7	
84	I_6	
84	I_6	
83	I_5	
82	I_4	
81	I_3	
80	I_2	
79	I_1	
78	I_0	
77	$\overline{ENTREG}$	Enable Transfer Register – enables the Transfer Register onto the DA input bus of the Am2901A's and Am2903's.
76	LDTREG	Load Transfer Register – loads the Transfer Register from the Y bus.
75	$\overline{ENCTR}$	Enable I Register Counter – enables the I Register Counter (I_{7-14}) to count. This value is used to address the general registers during stack instructions and by incrementing or decrementing this value the microprogram can read or write successive registers.
74	INC	I Register INC/DEC – the value in I_{7-14} can be either incremented (if this bit is HIGH) or decremented.
73	PCUCD	PCU Transceiver Disable – when HIGH this bit disables the PCU Transceivers from receiving or transmitting data.
72	PCU → Y	PCU Transceiver Control – when HIGH this bit allows the PCU Transceivers to pass data from PCU to the Y bus. [WORD high (microbit 90) disables the least significant 8 bits of these transceivers.] When LOW data passes from the Y bus to the MAR.
71	LDMAR	Load Memory Address Register (MAR) – this bit loads the Memory Address Register.
70	LDD	Load D Register – this bit loads the D Register with data from the Y bus.
69	$Z_1 \rightarrow I$	Load Z_1 into I Register – this bit loads data from Z_1 into the I Register. The I Register holds only the upper 16 bits of the instruction.
68	$\overline{ENZ_0}$	Enable $Z_0 \rightarrow$ DA – this bit LOW enables the Z_0 Register onto the ALU DA.

Table 2. Microinstruction Definition. (Cont.)

		Definition
67	$\overline{\text{PSW}}$	Enable PSW – this bit LOW enables the PSW onto the ALU DA.
66	$\overline{\text{SHTCNTEN}}$	Shift Count to Am2910 – this bit LOW enables the least significant four bits of the instruction ($I_{0\text{-}3}$) onto the D input to the Am2910 sequencer. This allows the value to be entered into the Am2910 internal counter to be used during shift instructions.
65	$\overline{\text{BRIEN}}$	Branch Instruction Enable – this bit LOW enables $I_{4\text{-}7}$ of the Instruction Register onto the Am2904 $I_{0\text{-}3}$ input. The $I_{0\text{-}3}$ inputs control the tests of the status register.
PCU		
64 63 62 61 60 59 58 57 56 55 54	$PCUI_7$ $PCUI_3$ $PCUI_2$ $PCUI_1$ $PCUI_0$ $PCUA_2$ $PCUA_1$ $PCUA_0$ $PCUB_2$ $PCUB_1$ $PCUB_0$	These bits control the PCU which is designed around four Am2901's. The $PCUI_7$, $PCUI_3$, $PCUI_2$, $PCUI_1$ and $PCUI_0$ bits connect directly to the Am2901 I_7, I_3, I_2, I_1 and I_0 respectively. The $PCUA_2$-$PCUA_0$ and $PCUB_2$-$PCUB_0$ connect to the A and B Address inputs of the Am2901. I_4, I_5, I_8, A_3 and B_3 are tied to ground. I_6 is tied to I_7.
53	REQB	Request Bus – this bit requests use of the system bus. This request is made the microcycle preceding a Memory Request or use of the bus for an I/O transfer. If the request is not honored, the processing of the next microinstruction is halted until the acknowledge is issued.
52	MREQ	Memory Request – this bit requests the memory to do a read or write operation.
51	$\overline{\text{HREQ}}$	Hold Request – this bit LOW blocks the bus controller from releasing the system bus to another device. Normally a Bus Request is cleared as soon as the Bus Acknowledge is issued. HREQ holds Bus Request and prevents any other device from using the bus.
50	WRITE	Memory Write/READ – this bit indicates to the memory the MREQ is for a write operation (if HIGH) and a read operation (if LOW).
49	MWORD	Memory Word/BYTE – the Memory Word/BYTE microbit specifies whether the memory operation will be a word operation or a byte operation. If the operation specified is a byte operation the least significant address bit determines which byte of the two byte pair in memory is affected. If the LSBit is a zero, the most significant byte is read or written, and the LSBit is a one, the least significant byte is read or written.
48	$\overline{\text{IMMD}}$	EN Immediate DA Bus – this bit LOW enables the 16-bit immediate value (least significant 16 bits of the microinstruction) to the ALU DA bus.
47	ROM/I	ROM/I REG Enable – this bit enables either the ROM bits 42-35 or the I register bits $I_{0\text{-}7}$ onto the A/B address inputs of the ALU according to the following: 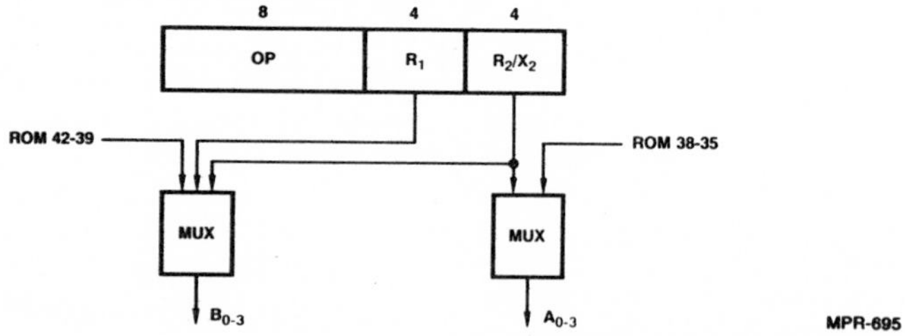
46	$\overline{\text{IOEN}}$	I/O Control Register Enable – this bit loads the I/O Control Register with microbits 42-35.
45	INTDIS	Am2914 Interrupt Disable – this bit disables the Am2914 Interrupt Controller from recognizing interrupt requests.
44	$\overline{\text{INTRIEN}}$	Am2914 ENI_0-ENI_3 – this bit is the instruction enable for the Am2914. The instruction inputs $I_{0\text{-}3}$ are connected to microbits 35-38 respectively.
43	$\overline{\text{SHFTEN}}$	Am2904 Shift Enable – this bit is connected to the shift enable of the Am2904. The shift controls $I_{6\text{-}10}$ are connected to microbits 35-39 respectively.

Table 2. Microinstruction Definition. (Cont.)

		Definition	
42	$CNTLB_7$	This control field is used to provide several different functions as defined by the previously described control strobes (microbits 47-43).	
41	$CNTLB_6$		
40	$CNTLB_5$		
39	$CNTLB_4$		
38	$CNTLB_3$		
37	$CNTLB_2$		
36	$CNTLB_1$		
35	$CNTLB_0$		
34	$\overline{OECT}$	OUT EN CONDITIONAL TEST	These bits are used to control the Am2904. Their functions are defined in Figure 21. OECT is used to enable the test output of the Am2904 to the CC input of the Am2910.
33	$\overline{EZ}$	EN ZERO	
32	$\overline{EC}$	EN CARRY	
31	$\overline{ES}$	EN SIGN	
30	$\overline{EOVR}$	EN OVERFLOW	
29	$\overline{CEM}$	EN MACRO STATUS	
28	$\overline{CE}$	EN MICRO STATUS	
27	I_{12}	CARRY OUT CONTROL	
26	I_{11}	CARRY OUT CONTROL	
25	$TEST_5$	These bits determine which test is to be performed for the conditional branch and stack functions. The various tests are listed in Figure 25. The testing is done both in the Am2904 and an 8 to 1 multiplexer.	
24	$TEST_4$		
23	$TEST_3$		
22	$TEST_2$		
21	$TEST_1$		
20	$TEST_0$		
19	NAC_3	291013	These bits are connected to the I_{3-0} inputs of the Am2910 to control the sequencing of the microprogram. Their definitions are listed in Figure 26.
18	NAC_2	291012	
17	NAC_1	291011	
16	NAC_0	291010	
15	M_{15}	These bits provide the branch address for the Am2910 and the 16-bit immediate field.	
14	M_{14}		
13	M_{13}		
12	M_{12}		
11	M_{11}		
10	M_{10}		
9	M_9		
8	M_8		
7	M_7		
6	M_6		
5	M_5		
4	M_4		
3	M_3		
2	M_2		
1	M_1		
0	M_0		

Am2903 ALU

The first 16 equates assign mnemonics for the I8-I5 of the Am2903 which controls the destination of the ALU result. The next 16 equates assign mnemonics for I4-I1 of the Am2903 which control the operations of the ALU. The ALU definition indicates the default is the Y bus forced to zero with no operation on destination. The next group of definition selects the source operand, followed by the special function definitions of the Am2903.

Am2901A PCU

The PCU definitions include a group of often used PC instructions such as PCU. NEXT, PCU. JUMP etc. The PCU definition itself allows a not predefined instruction be accessible to the microprogrammer.

AM2904 Shift Linkage Multiplexer and Status Register

The group of equates control the updating of the status register and the TEST definition controls the shift linkage multiplexer. The carry control controls the carry into the least significant Am2903 slice.

Datapath Control

The data control equates assign mnemonics to different datapath control bits.

```
AMDOS/29 AMDASM MICRO ASSEMBLER, V1.1
DEFINITION FILE FOR 16 BIT COMPUTER

 ;
 ;       AMDASM DEFINTION FILE FOR 16-BIT COMPUTER
 ;       USING AM2901A, AM2903, AM29Ø4 & AM291Ø
 ;       FILE CREATED BY STEVE CHENG 8/25/78
 ;
 ;       REVISION 2.Ø    12/6/78
 ;
         WORD 96
 ;
 ;       DEFINITIONS FOR AM291Ø SEQUENCER
 ;
JZ:      DEF 4X,B#Ø,71X,H#Ø,16X               ;JUMP ZERO
CJS:     DEF 4X,B#Ø,71X,H#1,4X,12V%           ;COND JSB PL
JSB:     DEF 4X,B#1,71X,H#1,4X,12V%           ;UNCONDITIONAL JSB PL
JMAP:    DEF 4X,B#Ø,71X,H#2,15X               ;JUMP MAP
CJP:     DEF 4X,B#Ø,71X,H#3,4X,12V%           ;COND JUMP PL
JMP:     DEF 4X,B#1,71X,H#3,4X,12V%           ;UNCONDITONAL JUMP PL
PUSH:    DEF 4X,B#Ø,71X,H#4,4X,12V%           ;PUSH/COND LD CNTR
PHLC:    DEF 4X,B#1,71X,H#4,4X,12V%           ;PUSH AND LD CNTR
JSRP:    DEF 4X,B#Ø,71X,H#5,4X,12V%           ;COND JSB R/PL
CJV:     DEF 4X,B#Ø,71X,H#6,16X               ;COND JUMP VECTOR
JMPV:    DEF 4X,B#1,71X,H#6,16X               ;UNCONDTIONAL JUMP VECTOR
JRP:     DEF 4X,B#Ø,71X,H#7,4X,12V%           ;COND JUMP R/PL
RFCT:    DEF 4X,B#Ø,71X,H#8,4X,12V%           ;REPEAT LOOP, CNTR <> Ø
RPCT:    DEF 4X,B#Ø,71X,H#9,4X,12V%           ;REPEAT PL, CNTR <> Ø
CRTN:    DEF 4X,B#Ø,71X,H#A,16X               ;COND RTN
RTN:     DEF 4X,B#1,71X,H#A,16X               ;UNCONDTIONAL RETURN
CJPP:    DEF 4X,B#Ø,71X,H#B,4X,12V%           ;COND JUMP PL & POP
LDCT:    DEF 4X,B#Ø,71X,H#C,4X,12V%H#FFF ;LD CNTR & CONT
LOOP:    DEF 4X,B#Ø,71X,H#D,16X               ;TEST END LOOP
CONT:    DEF 4X,B#Ø,71X,H#E,16X               ;CONTINUE
TWB:     DEF 4X,B#Ø,71X,H#F,4X,12V%           ;THREE-WAY BRANCH
 ;
 ;       DEFINITIONS FOR AM29Ø3 ALU
 ;
 ;       THE ALU DEFINTION IS OF THE FOLLOWING FORMAT
 ;       ALU DESTINATION CONTROL, FUNCTION
 ;
 ;       EQUATES FOR ALU DESTINATION CONTROL
 ;
ADR:     EQU H#Ø          ;ARITHMETIC SHIFT DOWN, RESULTS INTO RAM
LDR:     EQU H#1          ;LOGICAL SHIFT DOWN, RESULTS INTO RAM
ADRQ:    EQU H#2          ;ARITH. SHIFT DOWN, RESULTS INTO RAM AND Q
LDRQ:    EQU H#3          ;LOGICAL SHIFT DOWN, RESULTS INTO RAM AND Q
RPT:     EQU H#4          ;RESULTS INTO RAM, GENERATE PARITY
LDQP:    EQU H#5          ;LOGICAL SHIFT DOWN Q, GENERATE PARITY
QPT:     EQU H#6          ;RESULTS INTO Q, ;GENERATE PARITY
RQPT:    EQU H#7          ;RESULTS INTO RAM AND Q, GENERATE PARITY
AUR:     EQU H#8          ;ARITH. SHIFT UP, RESULTS INTO RAM
LUR:     EQU H#9          ;LOGICAL SHIFT UP, RESULTS INTO RAM
AURQ:    EQU H#A          ;ARITH. SHIFT UP, RESULTS INTO RAM AND Q
LURQ:    EQU H#B          ;LOGICAL SHIFT UP, RESULTS INTO RAM AND Q
YBUS:    EQU H#C          ;RESULTS TO Y BUS ONLY
LUQ:     EQU H#D          ;LOGICAL SHIFT UP Q
SINEX:   EQU H#E          ;SIGN EXTEND
REG:     EQU H#F          ;RESULTS TO RAM, SIGN EXTEND
 ;
 ;       EQUATES FOR ALU FUCNTIONS
 ;
HIGH:    EQU H#Ø          ;FI = 1
SUBR:    EQU H#1          ;SUBTRACT R FROM S
SUBS:    EQU H#2          ;SUBTRACT S FROM R
ADD:     EQU H#3          ;ADD R AND S
PASS:    EQU H#4          ;PASS S
COMPLS:  EQU H#5          ;2'S COMPLEMENT OF S
PASSR:   EQU H#6          ;PASS R
COMPLR:  EQU H#7          ;2'S COMPLEMENT OF R
LOW:     EQU H#8          ;FI = Ø
NOTRS:   EQU H#9          ;COMPLEMENT R AND WITH S
EXNOR:   EQU H#A          ;EXCLUSIVE NOR R WITH S
EXOR:    EQU H#B          ;EXCLUSIVE OR R WITH S
AND:     EQU H#C          ;AND R WITH S
NOR:     EQU H#D          ;NOR R WITH S
NAND:    EQU H#E          ;NAND R WITH S
OR:      EQU H#F          ;OR R WITH S
 ;
 ;       ALU DEFINTION
 ;
ALU:     DEF 9X,4VH#C,4VH#8,79X
 ;
 ;       ALU OPERAND SOURCES
 ;
AB:      DEF 6X,B#Ø,1X,B#Ø,8X,B#Ø,78X      ;R = RAM A, S = RAM B
ADB:     DEF 6X,B#Ø,1X,B#1,8X,B#Ø,78X      ;R = RAM A, S = DB
AQ:      DEF 6X,B#Ø,10X,B#1,78X            ;R = RAM A, S = Q
DAB:     DEF 6X,B#1,1X,B#Ø,8X,B#Ø,78X      ;R = DA, S = RAM B
DADB:    DEF 6X,B#1,1X,B#1,8X,B#Ø,78X      ;R = DA, S = DB
DAQ:     DEF 6X,B#1,1ØX,B#1,78X            ;R = DA, S = Q
 ;
 ;       WORD/BYTE CONTROL
 ;
WORD:    DEF 5X,B#Ø,9ØX
 ;
 ;       OUTPUT Y ENABLE
 ;
OEY:     DEF 7X,B#Ø,88X
 ;
 ;       SPECIAL FUNCTIONS FOR AM29Ø3
 ;
 ;       TO USE THE SPECIAL FUNCTIONS, THE DESTINATION
 ;       CONTROL MUST NOT BE AQ OR DAQ
 ;
 ;       SPECIAL FUNCTION EQUATES
 ;
USMUL:   EQU H#ØØ         ;UNSIGNED MULTIPLY
TCMUL:   EQU H#2Ø         ;TWO'S COMPLEMENT MULTIPLY
INCTWO:  EQU H#4Ø         ;INCREMENT BY ONE OR TWO
SMTC:    EQU H#5Ø         ;SIGN-MAGNITUDE/TWO'S COMPLEMENT
TCMLS:   EQU H#6Ø         ;TWO'S COMPLEMENT MULT. LAST STEP
SLN:     EQU H#8Ø         ;SINGLE LENGTH NORMALIZE
DLN:     EQU H#AØ         ;DOUBLE LENGTH NORMALIZE AND 1ST DIVIDE OP.
TCDIV:   EQU H#CØ         ;TWO'S COMPLEMENT DIVIDE
TCDC:    EQU H#EØ         ;TWO'S COMPLEMENT DIVISION CORRECTION
 ;
 ;       SPECIAL FUNCTION DEFINITION
 ;
SPF14:   DEF 9X,8VH#,79X
 ;
 ;       DEFINITION FOR AM29Ø1 PROGRAM CONTROL UNIT (PCU)
 ;
 ;       PCU REGISTER DEFINITIONS:
 ;       RØ = PC           PROGRAM COUNTER
 ;       R1 = SP           STACK POINTER
 ;       R2 = SPLL         STACK POINTER LOWER LIMIT
 ;       R3 = SPUL         STACK POINTER UPPER LIMIT
 ;       R4 = 2            CONSTANT Ø
 ;       R5 = 4            CONSTANT 2
 ;
 ;       EQUATES FOR PCU DEFINITIONS
 ;
QEU:     EQU B#Ø          ;Q REG = ZERO, B-RAM = ONE DEFAULT
 ;
 ;       EQUATE FOR PCU FUNCTIONS
 ;
SUB:     EQU B#1          ;SUB = ONE, ADD = ZERO DEFAULT
 ;
 ;       EQUATES FOR SOURCE CONTROL
 ;
PCUAQ:   EQU Q#Ø
PCUAB:   EQU Q#1
PCUZQ:   EQU Q#2
PCUZB:   EQU Q#3
PCUZA:   EQU Q#4
PCUDA:   EQU Q#5
PCUDQ:   EQU Q#6
PCUDZ:   EQU Q#7
 ;
 ;       EQUATES FOR PCU A-RAM
 ;
AØ:      EQU Q#Ø
A1:      EQU Q#1
A2:      EQU Q#2
A3:      EQU Q#3
A4:      EQU Q#4
A5:      EQU Q#5
A6:      EQU Q#6
A7:      EQU Q#7
 ;
 ;       EQUATES FOR PCU B-RAM
 ;
BØ:      EQU Q#Ø
B1:      EQU Q#1
B2:      EQU Q#2
B3:      EQU Q#3
B4:      EQU Q#4
B5:      EQU Q#5
B6:      EQU Q#6
B7:      EQU Q#7
 ;
 ;       PCU DEFINITION
 ;
PCU:     DEF 31X,1VB#1,1VB#Ø,3VQ#1,3VQ#,3VQ#,54X
 ;
PCU.NEXT:        DEF 31X,B#1ØØØ11ØØØØØ,54X       ;PC = PC + 2
PCU.PUSH:        DEF 31X,B#11ØØ11ØØØØ1,54X       ;SP = SP - 2
PCU.POP:         DEF 31X,B#1ØØØ11ØØØØ1,54X       ;SP = SP + 2
PCU.JUMP:        DEF 31X,B#1Ø111ØØØØØØ,54X       ;PC = D
PCU.TR2:         DEF 31X,B#1Ø1Ø11ØØØØØ,54X       ;PC = TREG + 2
PCU.NOP:         DEF 31X,B#1ØØ11ØØØØØØ,54X       ;PC TO OUTPUT
PCU.SP:          DEF 31X,B#1ØØ11ØØ1ØØ1,54X       ;SP TO OUTPUT
PCU.DEC4:        DEF 31X,B#11ØØ11Ø1ØØØ,54X       ;PC = PC - 4
 ;
 ;       DEFINTIONS FOR AM29Ø4 RELATED CONTROL BITS
 ;
 ;       AM29Ø4 BIT DEFINITIONS ARE AS FOLLOWS:
 ;       BITS 95-44 = DON'T CARES
 ;       BIT 43 = SHIFT ENABLE
 ;       BITS 42-35 = GENERAL PURPOSE CONTROL BITS
 ;       BIT 34 = OUT EN CONDITIONAL TEST
 ;       BIT 33 = ENABLE ZERO
 ;       BIT 32 = ENABLE CARRY
 ;       BIT 31 = ENABLE SIGN
 ;       BIT 3Ø = ENABLE OVERFLOW
 ;       BIT 29 = ENABLE MACHINE STATUS
 ;       BIT 28 = ENABLE MICRO STATUS
 ;       BITS 27-26 = CARRY OUT CONROL
 ;       BITS 25-2Ø= CONDTIONAL BRANCH TEST
 ;
SHIFTEN:         EQU B#Ø          ;SHIFT ENABLE
OECT:            EQU B#Ø          ;OUT EN CONDITIONAL TEST
EZ:              EQU B#Ø          ;ENABLE ZERO
EC:              EQU B#Ø          ;ENABLE CARRY
ES:              EQU B#Ø          ;ENABLE SIGN
EOVR:            EQU B#Ø          ;ENABLE OVERFLOW
CEM:             EQU B#Ø          ;ENABLE MACHINE STATUS
CEU:             EQU B#Ø          ;ENABLE MICRO STATUS
 ;
AM29Ø4:  DEF 52X,1VB#1,8X,1VB#1,1VB#1,1VB#1,1VB#1,1VB#1,1VB#1,1VB#1,28X
 ;
 ;       TEST BITS DEFINTION
 ;
TEST:    DEF 7ØX,6VQ#,2ØX
 ;
 ;       EQUATES FOR AM29Ø4 CARRY-OUT CONTROL
 ;
COEQØ:   EQU B#ØØ         ;CARRY-OUT = Ø
COEQ1:   EQU B#Ø1         ;CARRY-OUT = 1
COEQCI:  EQU B#1Ø         ;CARRY-OUT = CARRY-IN
COEQST:  EQU B#11         ;CARRY-OUT = CARRY OF STATUS REGISTER
 ;
 ;       CARRY-OUT CONTROL DEFINITION
 ;
CARRYCTL:        DEF 68X,2VB#ØØ,26X
 ;
 ;       REGISTER MUX SELECT
 ;
```

Figure 20. Definition File for 16-Bit Computer.

```
AMDOS/29 AMDASM MICRO ASSEMBLER, V1.1
DEFINITION FILE FOR 16 BIT COMPUTER

 RTB:     DEF B#0,95X       ;ROUTE R1 TO RAM B
 ;
 ;        EQUATES FOR DATAPATH DEFINITION
 ;
 ZZI:     EQU B#1           ;Z REG TO ZI REG
 ENTREG:  EQU B#0           ;ENABLE TRANSFER REGISTER
 LDTREG:  EQU B#1           ;LOAD TRANSFER REGISTER
 ENCTR:   EQU B#0           ;I-REG EN CTR
 INC:     EQU B#1           ;I-REG INC/DEC*
 PCUY:    EQU B#01          ;PCU TRANSCEIVER TO Y-BUS
 YMAR:    EQU B#00          ;PCU TRANSCEIVER TO MAR BUS
 PCUMAR:  EQU B#11          ;PCU TRANSCEIVER CEIP DISABLE
 LDMAR:   EQU B#1           ;LOAD MAR
 LDD:     EQU B#1           ;LOAD D REG
 ZII:     EQU B#1           ;LOAD ZI INTO I-REG
 ENZ0:    EQU B#0           ;ENABLE Z0 TO DA
 PSW:     EQU B#0           ;ENABLE PSW
 SHTCNTEN:EQU B#0           ;SHIFT CNT 2910 ADDR
 BRIEN:   EQU B#0           ;BRANCH INSTRUCTION ENABLE
 ;
 ;              DATAPATH DEFINITION
 ;
 DATAPATH:      DEF 3X,1VB#0,14X,1VB#1,1VB#0,1VB#1,1VB#0,2VB#11,1VB#0,
 /                  1VB#0,1VB#0,1VB#1,1VB#1,1VB#1,1VB#1,65X
 ;
 ;        EQUATES FOR MEMORY CONTROL
 ;
 REQB:    EQU B#1           ;BUS REQUEST
MREQ:    EQU B#1           ;MEMORY REQUEST
HREQ:    EQU B#0           ;HOLD REQUEST
WRITE:   EQU B#1           ;MEMORY WRITE
MWORD:   EQU B#1           ;MEMORY WORD/BYTE*
;
;        DEFINTION FOR MEMORY CONTROL
;
MEM.CONT:DEF 42X,1VB#0,1VB#0,1VB#1,1VB#0,1VB#0,49X
;
;        EQUATES FOR CONTROL STROBES
;
ROM:     EQU B#1           ;ROM/IREGEN*
IOEN:    EQU B#0           ;I/O CONTROL REG. ENABLE
INTDIS:  EQU B#0           ;INTERRUPT DISABLE
INTRIEN:EQU B#0            ;ENABLE I0-I3 ON AM2914
;
;        CONTROL STROBE DEFINTION
;
CONTROL:        DEF 48X,1VB#0,1VB#1,1VB#1,1VB#1,44X
;
;        CONROL BITS DEFINITION
;
CNTLB:   DEF 53X,8VH#,35X
;
;        IMMEDIATE ROM DEFINITION
;
IMMD:    DEF 47X,B#0,32X,16VH#    ;ENABLE IMMEDIATE OPERAND
;
         END

TOTAL PHASE 1 ERRORS =    0
```

Figure 20. Definition File for 16-Bit Computer (Cont.).

Memory Control

The memory control equates assign mnemonics to different memory control bits.

Control Strobe and Control Bits

The control strobe equates assign mnemonics to the control bit strobe signals. The control bit definition defines a hexadecimal bit pattern for the 8 control bits.

Immediate Operand

When the Am2910 sequencer is executing an instruction which does not require an address operand, bits 15-0 in the microword can be used as a 16-bit constant to load ALU, PCU etc. This is accomplished by putting the constant in bits 15-0 and force bit 48 to logic 0.

MICROCODE

Flowcharts

The flowcharts of the major instruction types are shown in the following figures.

Figure 21 illustrates the basic microprogram flowchart and demonstrates how the pipelining is done in microcode. This figure illustrates the sequencing of the computer starting with no instructions in the pipeline. By the fourth microinstruction, the pipeline is full and the CPU can execute for example a macroinstruction every microcycle.

Figure 22 illustrates the execution of an RR instruction. During an RR instruction, PC+6 is loaded into the MAR and a bus request is issured for the content of PC+6. The contents of PC+4 are read into the Z register. The Z_1 and I Registers are loaded with the contents of PC+2. The instruction at PC is executed. The input to the mapping PROM is loaded with the contents of PC+2. Thus in a stream of RR instructions, four instructions are in progress concurrently.

Figure 23 illustrates the execution of an RX instruction. In this figure the decode operation takes the microprogram to the microstep where the form address operation is done. Since the decode of the instruction has been completed in the previous step, the form address microinstructions are unique to each RX instruction in spite of the fact the operation performed is identical.

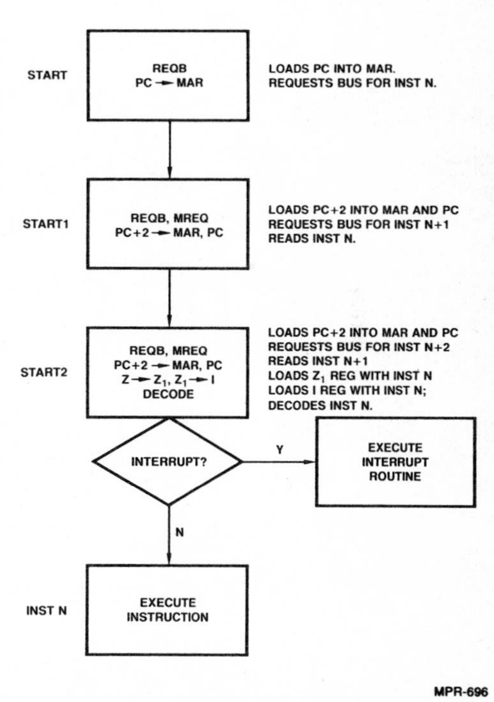

Figure 21. Microprogram Start Up Flow Chart.

From the form address step, the microprogram jumps to FETCHOP where the operand is fetched. This step returns to where the instruction is actually executed.

Figure 24 illustrates the execution of an RSI instruction. At the first microstep, the immediate operand is already in the Z_0 register. So the instruction is executed in the first step. The microprogram is then jumped to START2 to refill the pipeline.

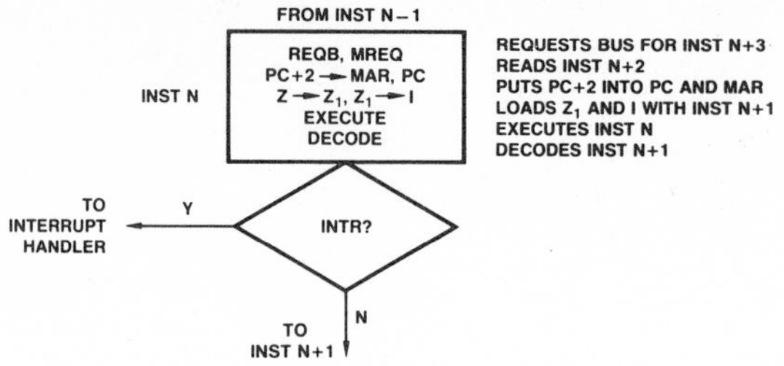

RR INSTRUCTIONS IMPLEMENTED

OPCODE	R1, R2	
LR	Load Register	R1 = (R2)
AR	Add Register	R1 = (R1) + (R2), Set CC
SR	Subtract Register	R1 = (R1) − (R2), Set CC
NR	AND Register	R1 = (R1) AND (R2), Set CC
ORR	OR Register	R1 = (R1) OR (R2), Set CC
CLR	Compare Logical Register	Set CC with (R1) − (R2)
XORR	Exclusive OR Register	R1 = (R1) XOR (R2), Set CC

MPR-697

Figure 22. RR Instruction Flow Chart.

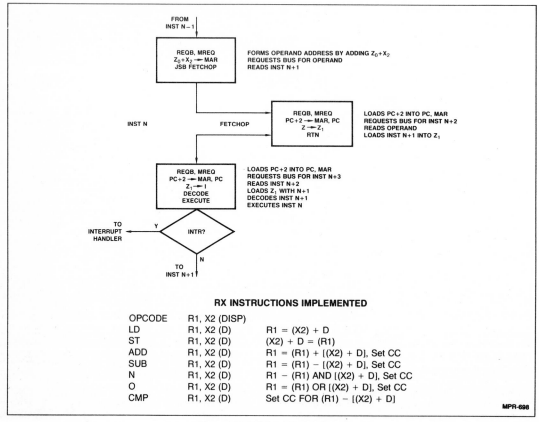

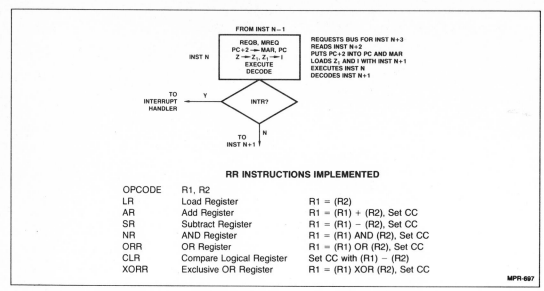

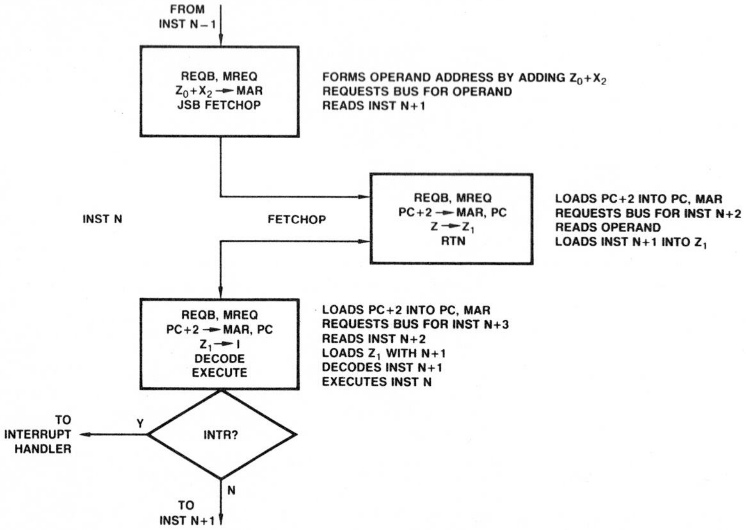

RX INSTRUCTIONS IMPLEMENTED

OPCODE	R1, X2 (DISP)	
LD	R1, X2 (D)	R1 = (X2) + D
ST	R1, X2 (D)	(X2) + D = (R1)
ADD	R1, X2 (D)	R1 = (R1) + [(X2) + D], Set CC
SUB	R1, X2 (D)	R1 = (R1) − [(X2) + D], Set CC
N	R1, X2 (D)	R1 − (R1) AND [(X2) + D], Set CC
O	R1, X2 (D)	R1 = (R1) OR [(X2) + D], Set CC
CMP	R1, X2 (D)	Set CC FOR (R1) − [(X2) + D]

MPR-698

Figure 23. RX Type Instruction.

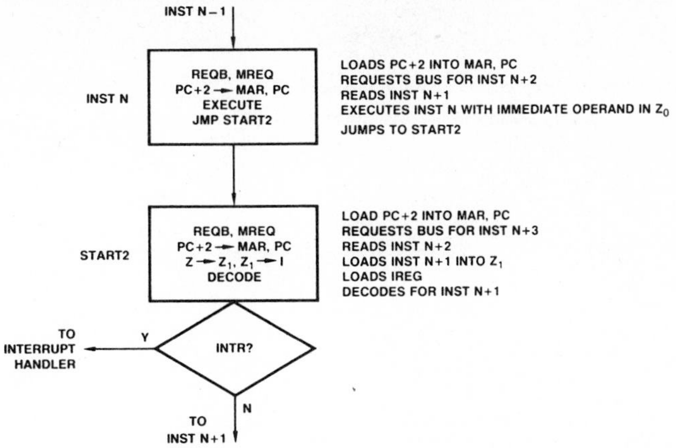

IMMEDIATE INSTRUCTIONS IMPLEMENTED

OP CODE	R1, DATA	
LI	Load Immediate	R1 = DATA
NI	AND Immediate	R1 = (R1) AND DATA, Set CC
OI	OR Immediate	R1 = (R1) OR DATA, Set CC
XI	Exclusive or Immediate	R1 = (R1) XOR DATA, Set CC
AI	Add Immediate	R1 = (R1) + DATA, Set CC
SI	Subtract Immediate	R1 = (R1) − DATA, Set CC
CI	Compare Immediate	Set CC with (R1) − DATA

MPR-699

Figure 24. Immediate Instructions.

Figure 25 illustrates the execution of an unconditional branch instruction. At the first microstep the displacement is already in the Z_0 register. The branch address is formed by adding the contents of the Z_0 register to the contents of the index register X_1. The MAR is loaded with the branch address and a bus request is issued for the contents of the branch address. The branch address is also loaded into the transfer register for subsequent loading of PC. In the next step, the contents of the transfer register+2 is loaded into the PC and MAR. A bus request is issued to BA+2. The content of BA is read. The microprogram is then transferred to START2 to fill up the pipeline.

Figure 26 illustrates the Conditional Branch instruction. In step 1, unlike the Unconditional Branch instruction, the contents of the memory (instruction N+1) is read, in case the test condition fails and the macro program falls through. The condition test is enabled in this step. If the test passes, the microprogram transfers to Unconditional Branch routine. If the test fails, the microprogram proceeds to fill the pipeline and continue.

Figure 27 illustrates the branch and link instruction. The flowchart is similar to Unconditional Branch except an extra step (STEP 2) is inserted. This step saves PC in R_1.

Figure 28 illustrates a shift or rotate instruction. In STEP 1 the opcode of the next instruction is loaded into Z_1 registers and the shift count of the shift instruction is loaded into the loop counter of Am2910. STEP 2 executes the shift instruction N+1 times, where N is the shift count in the instruction. It should be noted that since Am2910 detects −1 as the stop condition, the shift count loaded should be one less than the desired count. Step 3 is the same as the RNI (request next instruction). It is duplicated because the fail condition of RPCT in Am2910 can only fall through.

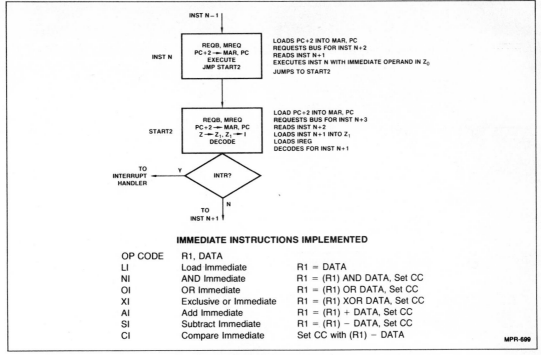

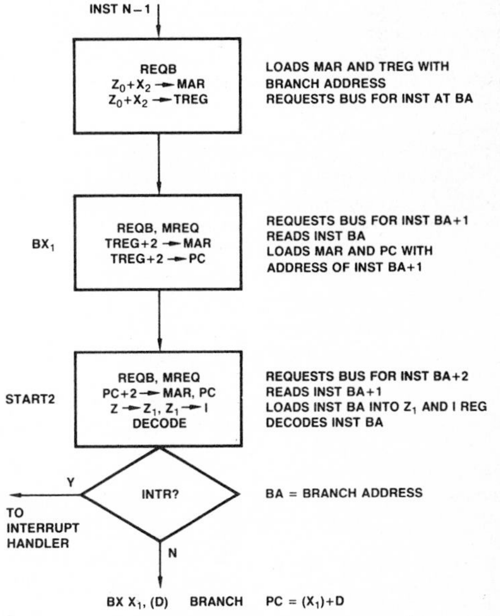

Figure 25. Unconditional Branch.

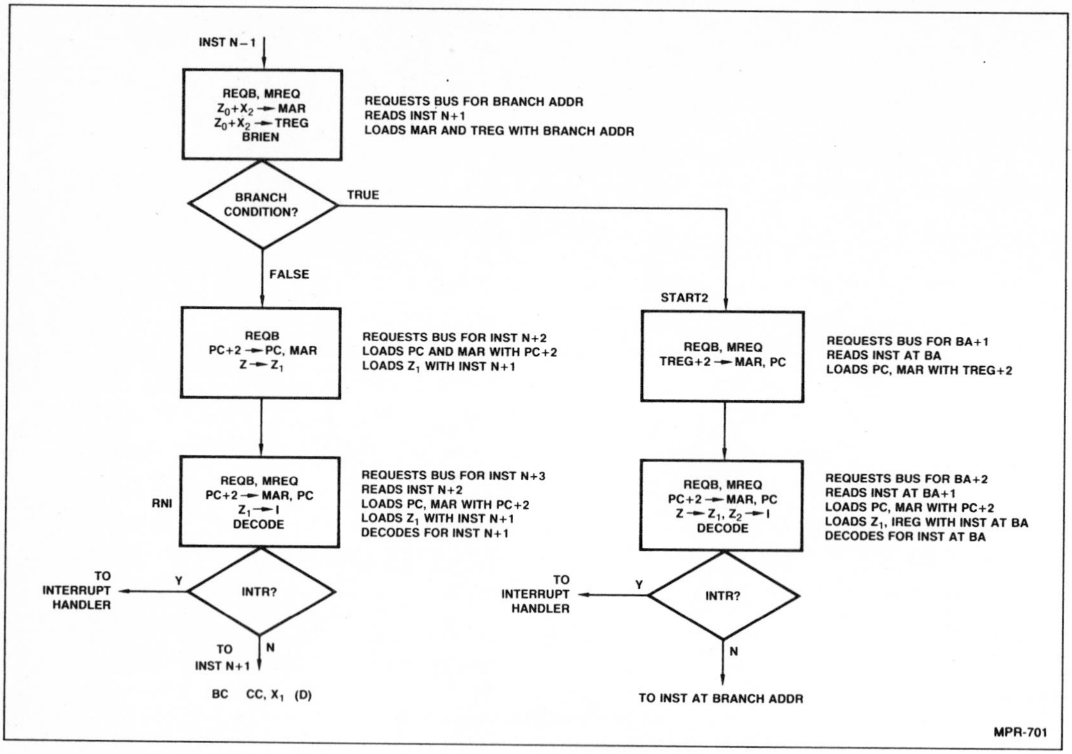

Figure 26. Conditional Branch.

Figure 29 illustrates the input instruction. In STEP 1, the I/O Port Address is formed by adding Z_0 and X_2. Bus request is issued for the I/O Port. The desired width of the I/O read pulse is loaded into the Am2910 Loop Counter. The width of the I/O read pulse is (N+2) X cycle time where N is the number loaded. The I/O read signal is turned on. In STEP 2, the bus is held for the I/O address and the loop counter is decremented until it becomes −1. In STEP 3, I/O read pulse is turned off but I/O address is held for possible address hold time requirement of the I/O device. On the trailing edge of the I/O read pulse, the content of the I/O Port is strobed into the Z_0 register. In STEP 4, the content of Z_0 register is loaded into R_1, thus completing the I/O read. Bus request is issued for the next instruction and microprogram jumps to START1 to refill the pipeline.

Figure 30 illustrates the output instruction. In STEP 1, bus request is ussued for the I/O Port Address. In STEP 1, the content of R_1 is transferred to the D register for outputting to the data bus. The I/O write pulse is set and the width of the write pulse is loaded into the Am2910 Loop Counter as in the input instruction. In STEP 3, the I/O address is held until loop counter becomes −1. In STEP 4, the content of the D register is strobed into the I/O Port by turning off the I/O Write Pulse. The microprogram jumps to START to refill the pipeline.

The Figures 21-30 illustrate the major instruction types implemented. These are by no means the only possible instructions for the 16-bit computer described. Some other instructions such as stack instructions are shown in the microcode but not in the figures and should be easily understood with the above examples as a guide.

Figure 31 illustrates the implementation of some typical instructions. Instruction 0 is the restart instruction. It jumps to INIT which is located in location H#180 because the mapping PROM maps only into the first 256 locations. So it is desirable to preserve these locations for Macro instructions. The initialization routine does the following:

1. Turn on I/O reset signal and jump (Inst H#0)
2. Set R_0 in ALU to 0 (Inst H#180)
3. Set R_0 in PCU (PC) to 0 (Inst H#181)
4. Set R_1 in PCU (SP) to H#4000 (Inst H#182)
5. Set R_4 in PCU to 2 (Inst H#183)
6. Set R_5 in PCU to 4 (Inst H#184)
7. Turn off I/O reset signal (Inst H#185)
8. Initialize console USART (Inst H#186-H#190)

The microinstruction that executes macroinstructions are grouped as follows:

Type	Figure	Microinst # (Hex)
RR Instructions	22	005-00B
RX Instructions	23	00C-01B
RSI Instructions	24	01C-022
Branch Instructions	25-27	023-02A
Shift Instructions	28	02B-042
Input Instruction	29	043-046
Output Instruction	30	047-04A
Stack Instructions	–	04B-059
Interrupt Instructions	–	05A-061

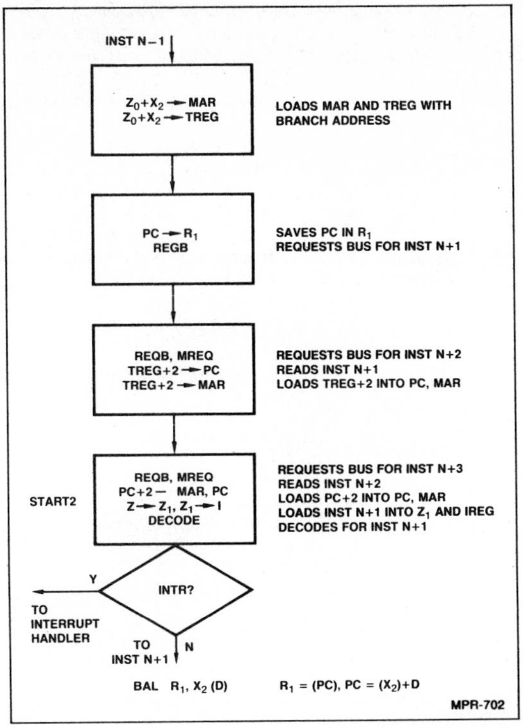

Figure 27. Branch and Link.

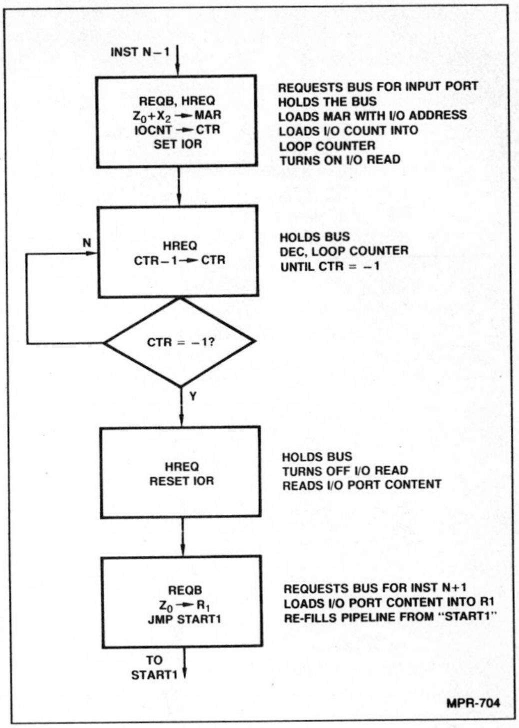

Figure 29. Input Instruction.

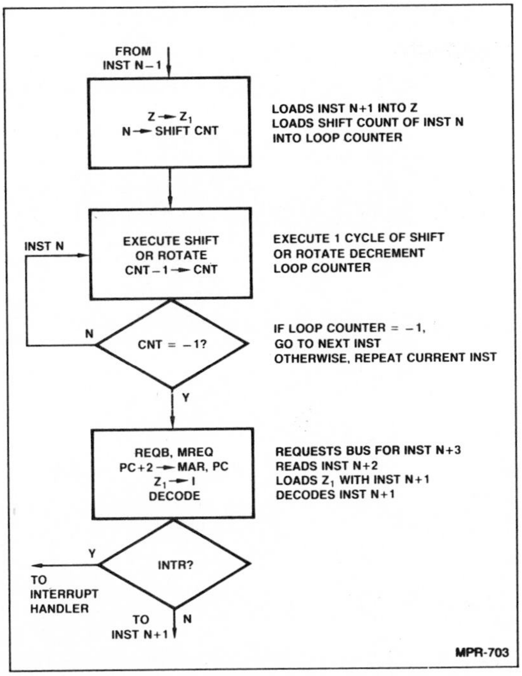

Figure 28. Shift and Rotate Instructions.

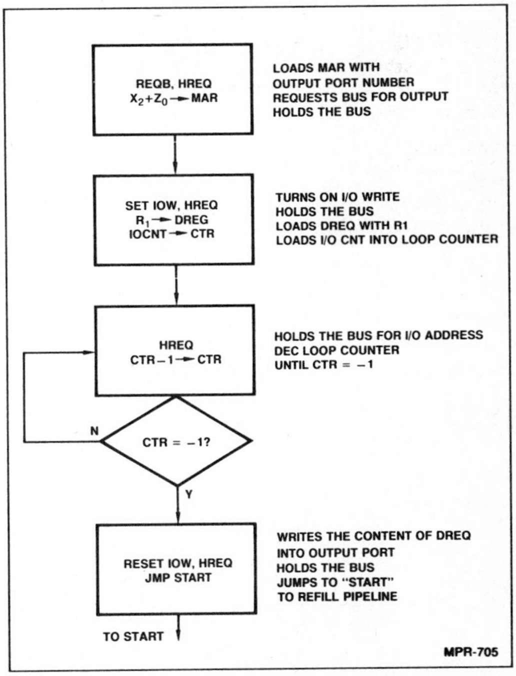

Figure 30. Output Instruction.

Upon an interrupt, the 16-Bit Computer finishes its current instruction and jumps to microinstruction H#1FF. The interrupt handler works as follows:

1. Current PSW is stored in DREG and SP = SP−2 (Inst H#1FF).
2. The content of PSW is written onto the stack in memory. PC = PC−4 to flush out the pipeline (Inst H#1F0).
3. SP = SP−2 (Inst H#1F1).
4. The content of the adjusted PC is written to the DREG (Inst H#1F2).
5. The content of the PC is written onto the stack in memory and the vector in the Am2914 is output to the interrupt vector PROM. A vector jump is made following this instruction depending on the interrupt number (Inst H#1F3).
6. The vector jump directs to 1 of 8 locations labelled INT_0-INT_7. For INT_1-INT_7, the first instruction disables interrupt in the Am2914 and forces new PC value into PC. INT_0 requires an extra instruction to clear the Am9519. The interrupt vector in the Am9519 is to be determined by the macro interrupt handler.
7. This next instruction is the same as the START instruction. The previous instruction cannot jump to START directly because the immediate operand uses the jump address field. The macroprogram resumes at the new PC value.

The instructions implemented cover only a small portion of all possible instructions. Only 137 or 512 microinstructions are used. The rest of the instruction space could be used to vastly enhance the instruction set such as byte operations, storage to storage instructions, etc.

```
AMDOS/29 AMDASM MICRO ASSEMBLER, V1.1
MICROPROGRAM FOR 16 BIT COMPUTER

          ;          *************************************
          ;
          ;          MICROPROGRAM FOR AMD 16-BIT COMPUTER
          ;            WRITTEN BY STEVE CHENG  9/78
          ;              REVISION 1.1  12/15/78
          ;
          ;          *************************************
          ;
          ;
          ;          RESET SEQUENCE STARTS HERE
          ;
 0000 RESET:  ALU & WORD & CONTROL ,IOEN,INTDIS, & CNTLB H#7F & DATAPATH &
      /       MEM.CONT REQB,,HREQ,,MWORD & AM2904 & PCU.NOP & JMP INIT
      ;
      ;       REQUEST BUS FOR INSTRUCTION N
      ;
 0001 START:  ALU YBUS,PASS & AB & WORD & OEY & CARRYCTL & CONTROL &
      /       DATAPATH ,,,,,,LDMAR,,,,,, & MEM.CONT REQB,,,,MWORD &
      /       AM2904 & PCU.NOP & CONT
      ;
      ;       REQUEST BUS FOR INSTRUCTION N+1. READ INSTRUCTION N
      ;
 0002 START1: ALU YBUS,PASS & AB & WORD & OEY & CARRYCTL & CONTROL &
      /       DATAPATH ,,,,,,LDMAR,,,,,, & MEM.CONT REQB,MREQ,,,MWORD &
      /       AM2904 & PCU.NEXT & CONT
      ;
      ;       REQUEST BUS FOR INSTRUCTION N+2. READ INTRUCTION N+1.
      ;       LOAD Z1 REGISTER WITH INSTRUCTION N.
      ;       DECODE FOR INSTRUCTION N
      ;
 0003 START2: ALU YBUS,PASS & DAB & CARRYCTL & OEY & WORD & CONTROL &
      /       DATAPATH ZZI,,,,,,LDMAR,,ZII,,,, & MEM.CONT REQB,MREQ,,,MWORD &
      /       AM2904 & PCU.NEXT & JMAP
      ;
      ;       REQUEST NEXT INSTRUCTION
      ;
 0004 RNI:    ALU YBUS,PASS & DAB & CARRYCTL & OEY & WORD & CONTROL &
      /       .DATAPATH ,,,,,,LDMAR,,ZII,,,, & MEM.CONT REQB,MREQ,,,MWORD &
      /       AM2904 & PCU.NEXT & JMAP
      ;       ======================================
      ;
      ;               RR TYPE INSTRUCTIONS
      ;
      ;       ======================================
      ;
      ;       LOAD REGISTER                   18      RR      CC: NONE
      ;       LR R1,R2          R1 = (R2)
      ;
 0005 LR:     ALU REG,PASSR & AB & CARRYCTL & OEY & WORD &
      /       DATAPATH ZZI,,,,,,LDMAR,,ZII,,,, & MEM.CONT REQB,MREQ,,,MWORD &
      /       AM2904 & CONTROL & PCU.NEXT & JMAP
      ;
      ;       ADD REGISTERS                   1A      RR      CC: CSVZ
      ;       AR R1,R2          R1 = (R1) + (R2)
      ;
 0006 AR:     ALU REG,ADD & AB & CARRYCTL & OEY & WORD &
      /       DATAPATH ZZI,,,,,,LDMAR,,ZII,,,, & MEM.CONT REQB,MREQ,,,MWORD &
      /       AM2904 ,,EZ,EC,ES,EOVR,CEM, & CONTROL & PCU.NEXT & JMAP
      ;
      ;       SUBTRACT REGISTERS              1B      RR      CC: CSVZ
      ;       SR R1,R2          R1 = (R1) - (R2)
      ;
 0007 SR:     ALU REG,SUBR & AB & CARRYCTL COEQ1 & OEY & WORD &
      /       DATAPATH ZZI,,,,,,LDMAR,,ZII,,,, & MEM.CONT REQB,MREQ,,,MWORD &
      /       AM2904 ,,EZ,EC,ES,EOVR,CEM, & CONTROL & PCU.NEXT & JMAP
      ;
      ;       AND REGISTERS                   14      RR      CC: CSVZ
      ;       NR R1,R2          R1 = (R1) AND (R2)
      ;
 0008 NR:     ALU REG,AND & AB & CARRYCTL & OEY & WORD &
      /       DATAPATH ZZI,,,,,,LDMAR,,ZII,,,, & MEM.CONT REQB,MREQ,,,MWORD &
      /       AM2904 ,,EZ,EC,ES,EOVR,CEM, & CONTROL & PCU.NEXT & JMAP
      ;
      ;       OR REGISTERS                    16      RR      CC: CSVZ
      ;       OR R1,R2          R1 = (R1) OR (R2)
      ;
 0009 ORR:    ALU REG,OR & AB & CARRYCTL & OEY & WORD &
      /       DATAPATH ZZI,,,,,,LDMAR,,ZII,,,, & MEM.CONT REQB,MREQ,,,MWORD &
      /       AM2904 ,,EZ,EC,ES,EOVR,CEM, & CONTROL & PCU.NEXT & JMAP
      ;
      ;       COMPARE LOGICAL REGISTERS       15      RR      CC: CSVZ
      ;       CLR R1,R2         CC = RESULT OF (R1) - (R2)
      ;                         CONTENTS OF R1 AND R2 ARE NOT AFFECTED
      ;
 000A CLR:    ALU YBUS,SUBR & AB & CARRYCTL COEQ1 & OEY & WORD &
      /       DATAPATH ZZI,,,,,,LDMAR,,ZII,,,, & MEM.CONT REQB,MREQ,,,MWORD &
      /       AM2904 ,,EZ,EC,ES,EOVR,CEM, & CONTROL & PCU.NEXT & JMAP
      ;
      ;       EXCLUSIVE OR REGISTERS          17      RR      CC: CSVZ
      ;       XOR R1,R2         R1 = (R1) XOR (R2)
      ;
 000B XORR:   ALU REG,EXOR & AB & CARRYCTL & OEY & WORD &
      /       DATAPATH ZZI,,,,,,LDMAR,,ZII,,,, & MEM.CONT REQB,MREQ,,,MWORD &
      /       AM2904 ,,EZ,EC,ES,EOVR,CEM, & CONTROL & PCU.NEXT & JMAP
      ;       ======================================
      ;
      ;               RX TYPE INSTRUCTIONS
      ;
      ;       ======================================
      ;
      ;       LOAD                            58      RX      CC: NONE
      ;       LD R1,X2(D)       R1 = [(X2) + D]
      ;
 000C LD:     ALU YBUS,ADD & DAB & CARRYCTL & OEY & WORD & CONTROL & RTB &
      /       DATAPATH ,,,,,YMAR,LDMAR,,,ENZ0,,, & MEM.CONT REQB,MREQ,,,MWORD &
      /       AM2904 & PCU.NOP & JSB FETCHOP
      ;
 000D         ALU REG,PASSR & DAB & CARRYCTL & OEY & WORD & CONTROL &
      /       DATAPATH ,,,,,,LDMAR,,ZII,ENZ0,,, & MEM.CONT REQB,MREQ,,,MWORD &
      /       AM2904 & PCU.NEXT & JMAP
      ;
      ;       STORE                           50      RX      CC: NONE
      ;       ST R1,X2(D)       (X2) + D = (R1)
      ;
 000E ST:     ALU YBUS,ADD & DAB & CARRYCTL & OEY & WORD & CONTROL & RTB &
      /       DATAPATH ,,,,,YMAR,LDMAR,,,ENZ0,,, & MEM.CONT REQB,MREQ,,,MWORD &
      /       AM2904 & PCU.NOP & CONT
      ;
 000F         ALU YBUS,PASS & AB & CARRYCTL & OEY & WORD & CONTROL &
      /       DATAPATH ZZI,,,,,,,LDD,,,,, & MEM.CONT REQB,,,,MWORD &
      /       AM2904 & PCU.NOP & CONT
      ;
 0010         ALU YBUS,PASS & AB & CARRYCTL & OEY & WORD & CONTROL &
      /       DATAPATH ,,,,,,LDMAR,,,,,, & MEM.CONT REQB,MREQ,,WRITE,MWORD &
      /       AM2904 & PCU.NEXT & JMP RNI
      ;
      ;       ADD                             5A      RX      CC: CSVZ
      ;       ADD R1,X2(D)      R1 = (R1) + [(X2) + D]
      ;
 0011 ADDX:   ALU YBUS,ADD & DAB & CARRYCTL & OEY & WORD & CONTROL & RTB &
      /       DATAPATH ,,,,,YMAR,LDMAR,,,ENZ0,,, & MEM.CONT REQB,MREQ,,,MWORD &
      /       AM2904 & PCU.NOP & JSB FETCHOP
      ;
 0012         ALU REG,ADD & DAB & CARRYCTL & OEY & WORD & CONTROL &
      /       DATAPATH ,,,,,,LDMAR,,ZII,ENZ0,,, & MEM.CONT REQB,MREQ,,,MWORD &
      /       AM2904 ,,EZ,EC,ES,EOVR,CEM, & PCU.NEXT & JMAP
      ;
      ;       SUBTRACT                        5B      RX      CC: CSVZ
      ;       SUB R1,X2(D)      R1 = (R1) - [(X2) + D]
      ;
 0013 SUBX:   ALU YBUS,ADD & DAB & CARRYCTL & OEY & WORD & CONTROL & RTB &
      /       DATAPATH ,,,,,YMAR,LDMAR,,,ENZ0,,, & MEM.CONT REQB,MREQ,,,MWORD &
      /       AM2904 & PCU.NOP & JSB FETCHOP
      ;
 0014         ALU REG,SUBR & DAB & CARRYCTL COEQ1 & OEY & WORD & CONTROL &
      /       DATAPATH ,,,,,,LDMAR,,ZII,ENZ0,,, & MEM.CONT REQB,MREQ,,,MWORD &
      /       AM2904 ,,EZ,EC,ES,EOVR,CEM, & PCU.NEXT & JMAP
      ;
      ;       AND                             54      RX      CC: CSVZ
      ;       N R1,X2(D)        R1 = (R1) AND [(X2) + D]
      ;
 0015 N:      ALU YBUS,ADD & DAB & CARRYCTL & OEY & WORD & CONTROL & RTB &
      /       DATAPATH ,,,,,YMAR,LDMAR,,,ENZ0,,, & MEM.CONT REQB,MREQ,,,MWORD &
      /       AM2904 & PCU.NOP & JSB FETCHOP
      ;
 0016         ALU REG,AND & DAB & CARRYCTL & OEY & WORD & CONTROL &
      /       DATAPATH ,,,,,,LDMAR,,ZII,ENZ0,,, & MEM.CONT REQB,MREQ,,,MWORD &
      /       AM2904 ,,EZ,EC,ES,EOVR,CEM, & PCU.NEXT & JMAP
      ;
      ;       OR                              56      RX      CC: CSVZ
      ;       O R1,X2(D)        R1 = (R1) OR [(X2) + D]
      ;
 0017 O:      ALU YBUS,ADD & DAB & CARRYCTL & OEY & WORD & CONTROL & RTB &
      /       DATAPATH ,,,,,YMAR,LDMAR,,,ENZ0,,, & MEM.CONT REQB,MREQ,,,MWORD &
      /       AM2904 & PCU.NOP & JSB FETCHOP
      ;
 0018         ALU REG,OR & DAB & CARRYCTL & OEY & WORD & CONTROL &
      /       DATAPATH ,,,,,,LDMAR,,ZII,ENZ0,,, & MEM.CONT REQB,MREQ,,,MWORD &
      /       AM2904 ,,EZ,EC,ES,EOVR,CEM, & PCU.NEXT & JMAP
      ;
      ;       COMPARE                         55      RX      CC: CSVZ
      ;       CMP R1,X2(D)      CC = RESULT OF (R1) - [(X2) + D]
      ;                         THE CONTENTS OF R1 AND (X2) + D ARE NOT AFFECTED
      ;
 0019 CMP:    ALU YBUS,ADD & DAB & CARRYCTL & OEY & WORD & CONTROL & RTB &
      /       DATAPATH ,,,,,YMAR,LDMAR,,,ENZ0,,, & MEM.CONT REQB,MREQ,,,MWORD &
      /       AM2904 & PCU.NOP & JSB FETCHOP
```

Figure 31. Microprogram for 16-Bit Computer.

```
AMDOS/29 AMDASM MICRO ASSEMBLER, V1.1
MICROPROGRAM FOR 16 BIT COMPUTER

          ;
 001A             ALU YBUS,SUBR & DAB & CARRYCTL COEQ1 & OEY & WORD & CONTROL &
          /       DATAPATH ,,,,,,LDMAR,,ZII,ENZ0,,, & MEM.CONT REQB,MREQ,,,MWORD &
          /       AM2904 ,,EZ,EC,ES,EOVR,CEM, & PCU.NEXT & JMAP
          ;
          ;       #########################################
          ;
          ;       SUBROUTINE TO FETCH OPERAND FROM MEMORY
          ;
          ;       #########################################
          ;
 001B FETCHOP:ALU YBUS,PASSR & DAB & CARRYCTL & OEY & WORD & CONTROL &
          /       DATAPATH ZZI,,,,,,LDMAR,,,,,, & MEM.CONT REQB,MREQ,,,MWORD &
          /       AM2904 & PCU.NEXT & RTN
          ;       ========================================
          ;
          ;             IMMEDIATE INSTRUCTIONS
          ;
          ;       ========================================
          ;
          ;       LOAD IMMEDIATE                  41      RSI     CC: NONE
          ;       LI R1,DI          R1 = DI
          ;
 001C LI:         ALU REG,PASSR & DAB & CARRYCTL & OEY & WORD & CONTROL &
          /       DATAPATH ,,,,,,LDMAR,,,ENZ0,,, & MEM.CONT REQB,MREQ,,,MWORD &
          /       AM2904 & PCU.NEXT & JMP START2
          ;
          ;       AND IMMEDIATE                   94      RSI     CC: CSVZ
          ;       NI R1,DI          R1 = R1 AND DI
          ;
 001D NI:         ALU REG,AND & DAB & CARRYCTL & OEY & WORD & CONTROL &
          /       DATAPATH ,,,,,,LDMAR,,,ENZ0,,, & MEM.CONT REQB,MREQ,,,MWORD &
          /       AM2904 ,,EZ,EC,ES,EOVR,CEM, & PCU.NEXT & JMP START2
          ;
          ;       OR IMMEDIATE                    96      RSI     CC: CSVZ
          ;       OI R1,DI          R1 = R1 OR DI
          ;
 001E OI:         ALU REG,OR & DAB & CARRYCTL & OEY & WORD & CONTROL &
          /       DATAPATH ,,,,,,LDMAR,,,ENZ0,,, & MEM.CONT REQB,MREQ,,,MWORD &
          /       AM2904 ,,EZ,EC,ES,EOVR,CEM, & PCU.NEXT & JMP START2
          ;
          ;       EXCLUSIVE OR IMMEDIATE          97      RSI     CC: CSVZ
          ;       XI R1,DI          R1 = R1 XOR DI
          ;
 001F XI:         ALU REG,EXOR & DAB & CARRYCTL & OEY & WORD & CONTROL &
          /       DATAPATH ,,,,,, LDMAR,,,ENZ0,,, & MEM.CONT REQB,MREQ,,,MWORD &
          /       AM2904 ,,EZ,EC,ES,EOVR,CEM, & PCU.NEXT & JMP START2
          ;
          ;       ADD IMMEDIATE                   9A      RSI     CC: CSVZ
          ;       AI R1,DI          R1 = R1 + DI
          ;
 0020 AI:         ALU REG,ADD & DAB & CARRYCTL & OEY & WORD & CONTROL &
          /       DATAPATH ,,,,,, LDMAR,,,ENZ0,,, & MEM.CONT REQB,MREQ,,,MWORD &
          /       AM2904 ,,EZ,EC,ES,EOVR,CEM, & PCU.NEXT & JMP START2
          ;
          ;       SUBTRACT IMMEDIATE              9B      RSI     CC: CSVZ
          ;       SI R1,DI          R1 = R1 - DI
          ;
 0021 SI:         ALU REG,SUBR & DAB & CARRYCTL COEQ1 & OEY & WORD & CONTROL &
          /       DATAPATH ,,,,,, LDMAR,,,ENZ0,,, & MEM.CONT REQB,MREQ,,,MWORD &
          /       AM2904 ,,EZ,EC,ES,EOVR,CEM, & PCU.NEXT & JMP START2
          ;
          ;       COMPARE IMMEDIATE               95      RSI     CC: CSVZ
          ;       CI R1,DI          CC = RESULT OF R1 - DI
          ;                         THE CONTENT OF R1 IS NOT AFFECTED
          ;
 0022 CI:         ALU YBUS,SUBR & DAB & CARRYCTL COEQ1 & OEY & WORD & CONTROL &
          /       DATAPATH ,,,,,, LDMAR,,,ENZ0,,, & MEM.CONT REQB,MREQ,,,MWORD &
          /       AM2904 ,,EZ,EC,ES,EOVR,CEM, & PCU.NEXT & JMP START2

          ;       ++++++++++++++++++++++++++++++++++++
          ;
          ;             BRANCH INSTRUCTIONS
          ;
          ;       ++++++++++++++++++++++++++++++++++++
          ;
          ;       BRANCH UNCONDITIONAL            74      RX      CC: NONE
          ;       B X2(D)           PC = (X2) + D
          ;
 0023 BX:         ALU YBUS,ADD & DAB & CARRYCTL & OEY & WORD & CONTROL & RTB &
          /       DATAPATH ,ENTREG,,,,,LDMAR,,,,,, &
          /       MEM.CONT REQB,MREQ,,,MWORD & AM2904 & PCU.TR2 & JMP START2
          ;
 0024 BX1:        ALU YBUS,PASS & AB & WORD & OEY & CONTROL &
          /       DATAPATH ,ENTREG,,,,,LDMAR,,,,,, & MEM.CONT REQB,MREQ,,,MWORD &
          /       AM2904 & PCU.TR2 & JMP START2
          ;
          ;       BRANCH ON CONDITION             47      RX      CC: NONE
          ;       BC C,X2(D)        IF CC = 1, PC = (X2) + D
          ;                         ELSE PC = (PC) + 2
          ;
 0025 BC:         ALU YBUS,ADD & DAB & CARRYCTL & OEY & WORD & CONTROL & RTB &
          /       DATAPATH ,,LDTREG,,,YMAR,LDMAR,,,ENZ0,,,BRIEN & TEST 57 &
          /       MEM.CONT REQB,MREQ,,,MWORD &
          /       AM2904 ,OECT,,,,,, & PCU.NOP & CJP BX1
          ;
          ;       BRANCH NOT NEEDED
          ;
 0026             ALU YBUS,PASS & AB & WORD & OEY & CONTROL &
          /       DATAPATH ZZI,,,,,,LDMAR,,,,,, & MEM.CONT REQB,,,,MWORD &
          /       AM2904 & PCU.NEXT & JMP RNI
          ;
          ;       BRANCH AND LINK                 45      RX      CC: NONE
          ;       BAL R1,X2(D)      R1 = PC + 2, PC = [(X2) + D]
          ;
 0027 BAL:        ALU YBUS,ADD & DAB & CARRYCTL & OEY & WORD & CONTROL & RTB &
          /       DATAPATH ,,LDTREG,,,YMAR,LDMAR,,,ENZ0,,, & MEM.CONT ,,,,MWORD &
          /       AM2904 & PCU.NOP & CONT
          ;
 0028 BAL1:       ALU REG,PASS & DAB & CARRYCTL & WORD & CONTROL &
          /       DATAPATH ,,,,,PCUY,,,,,,,, & MEM.CONT REQB,,,,MWORD &
          /       AM2904 & PCU.NOP & JMP BX1
          ;
          ;       BRANCH AND LINK REGISTER        05      RR      CC: NONE
          ;       BALR R1,R2        R1 = (PC), PC = (R2)
          ;
 0029 BALR:       ALU YBUS,PASSR & DAB & CARRYCTL & OEY & WORD & CONTROL &
          /       DATAPATH ,,LDTREG,,,YMAR,LDMAR,,,ENZ0,,, & MEM.CONT ,,,,MWORD &
          /       AM2904 & PCU.NOP & JMP BAL1
          ;

          ;       BRANCH REGISTER ALWAYS          08      RR      CC: NONE
          ;       BRA R1            PC = (R1)
          ;
 002A BR:         ALU YBUS,PASS & DAB & CARRYCTL & OEY & WORD & CONTROL &
          /       DATAPATH ,,LDTREG,,,YMAR,LDMAR,,,,, & MEM.CONT REQB,,,,MWORD &
          /       AM2904 & PCU.NOP & JMP BX1

          ;       ========================================
          ;
          ;             SHIFT INSTRUCTIONS
          ;
          ;       ========================================
          ;
          ;       SHIFT LEFT ARITHMETIC   8B      RSI     CC: CSVZ
          ;       SLA R1,CNT        R1 = SHIFT (R1) ARITHMETIC LEFT CNT PLACES
          ;
 002B SLA:        ALU YBUS,PASS & AB & WORD & OEY & CARRYCTL & CONTROL &
          /       DATAPATH ZZI,,,,,,,,,,,SHTCNTEN, & MEM.CONT ,,,,MWORD &
          /       AM2904 & PCU.NOP & LDCT
          ;
 002C             ALU AUR,PASS & AB & WORD & OEY & CARRYCTL & CONTROL & CNTLB H#F0 &
          /       DATAPATH & MEM.CONT ,,,,MWORD &
          /       AM2904 SHIFTEN,,EZ,EC,ES,EOVR,CEM, & PCU.NOP & RPCT $
          ;
 002D             ALU YBUS,PASS & AB & WORD & OEY & CARRYCTL & CONTROL &
          /       DATAPATH ,,,,,,LDMAR,,ZII,,,, & MEM.CONT REQB,MREQ,,,MWORD &
          /       AM2904 & PCU.NEXT & JMAP
          ;
          ;       SHIFT LEFT LOGICAL              89      RSI     CC: CSVZ
          ;       SLL R1,CNT        R1 = SHIFT (R1) LEFT LOGICAL CNT PLACES
          ;
 002E SLL:        ALU YBUS,PASS & AB & WORD & OEY & CARRYCTL & CONTROL &
          /       DATAPATH ZZI,,,,,,,,,,,SHTCNTEN, & MEM.CONT ,,,,MWORD &
          /       AM2904 & PCU.NOP & LDCT
          ;
 002F             ALU LUR,PASS & AB & WORD & OEY & CARRYCTL & CONTROL & CNTLB H#F0 &
          /       DATAPATH & MEM.CONT ,,,,MWORD &
          /       AM2904 SHIFTEN,,EZ,EC,ES,EOVR,CEM, & PCU.NOP & RPCT $
          ;
 0030             ALU YBUS,PASS & AB & WORD & OEY & CARRYCTL & CONTROL &
          /       DATAPATH ,,,,,,LDMAR,,ZII,,,, & MEM.CONT REQB,MREQ,,,MWORD &
          /       AM2904 & PCU.NEXT & JMAP
          ;
          ;       SHIFT RIGHT ARITHMETIC          8A      RSI     CC: CSVZ
          ;       SRA R1,CNT        R1 = SHIFT (R1) RIGHT ARITHMETIC CNT PLACES
          ;
 0031 SRA:        ALU YBUS,PASS & AB & WORD & OEY & CARRYCTL & CONTROL &
          /       DATAPATH ZZI,,,,,,,,,,,SHTCNTEN, & MEM.CONT ,,,,MWORD &
          /       AM2904 & PCU.NOP & LDCT
          ;
 0032             ALU ADR,PASS & AB & WORD & OEY & CARRYCTL & CONTROL & CNTLB H#E0 &
          /       DATAPATH & MEM.CONT ,,,,MWORD &
          /       AM2904 SHIFTEN,,EZ,EC,ES,EOVR,CEM, & PCU.NOP & RPCT $
          ;
 0033             ALU YBUS,PASS & AB & WORD & OEY & CARRYCTL & CONTROL &
          /       DATAPATH ,,,,,,LDMAR,,ZII,,,, & MEM.CONT REQB,MREQ,,,MWORD &
          /       AM2904 & PCU.NEXT & JMAP
          ;
          ;       SHIFT RIGHT LOGICAL             88      RSI     CC: CSVZ
          ;       SRL R1,CNT        R1 = SHIFT (R1) RIGHT LOGICAL CNT PLACES
          ;
 0034 SRL:        ALU YBUS,PASS & AB & WORD & OEY & CARRYCTL & CONTROL &
          /       DATAPATH ZZI,,,,,,,,,,,SHTCNTEN, & MEM.CONT ,,,,MWORD &
          /       AM2904 & PCU.NOP & LDCT
          ;
 0035             ALU LDR,PASS & AB & WORD & OEY & CARRYCTL & CONTROL & CNTLB H#E0 &
          /       DATAPATH & MEM.CONT ,,,,MWORD &
          /       AM2904 SHIFTEN,,EZ,EC,ES,EOVR,CEM, & PCU.NOP & RPCT $
          ;
 0036             ALU YBUS,PASS & AB & WORD & OEY & CARRYCTL & CONTROL &
          /       DATAPATH ,,,,,,LDMAR,,ZII,,,, & MEM.CONT REQB,MREQ,,,MWORD &
          /       AM2904 & PCU.NEXT & JMAP
          ;
          ;       ROTATE RIGHT            A8      RSI     CC: CSVZ
          ;       RR R1,CNT         R1 = ROTATE (R1) RIGHT CNT PLACES
          ;
 0037 RRL:        ALU YBUS,PASS & AB & WORD & OEY & CARRYCTL & CONTROL &
          /       DATAPATH ZZI,,,,,,,,,,,SHTCNTEN, & MEM.CONT ,,,,MWORD &
          /       AM2904 & PCU.NOP & LDCT
          ;
 0038             ALU LDR,PASS & AB & WORD & OEY & CARRYCTL & CONTROL & CNTLB H#FA &
          /       DATAPATH & MEM.CONT ,,,,MWORD &
          /       AM2904 SHIFTEN,,EZ,EC,ES,EOVR,CEM, & PCU.NOP & RPCT $
          ;
 0039             ALU YBUS,PASS & AB & WORD & OEY & CARRYCTL & CONTROL &
          /       DATAPATH ,,,,,,LDMAR,,ZII,,,, & MEM.CONT REQB,MREQ,,,MWORD &
          /       AM2904 & PCU.NEXT & JMAP
          ;
          ;       ROTATE LEFT             AA      RSI     CC: CSVZ
          ;       RL R1,CNT         R1 = ROTATE (R1) LEFT CNT PLACES
          ;
 003A RLL:        ALU YBUS,PASS & AB & WORD & OEY & CARRYCTL & CONTROL &
          /       DATAPATH ZZI,,,,,,,,,,,SHTCNTEN, & MEM.CONT ,,,,MWORD &
          /       AM2904 & PCU.NOP & LDCT
          ;
 003B             ALU LUR,PASS & AB & WORD & OEY & CARRYCTL & CONTROL & CNTLB H#FA &
          /       DATAPATH & MEM.CONT ,,,,MWORD &
          /       AM2904 SHIFTEN,,EZ,EC,ES,EOVR,CEM, & PCU.NOP & RPCT $
          ;
 003C             ALU YBUS,PASS & AB & WORD & OEY & CARRYCTL & CONTROL &
          /       DATAPATH ,,,,,,LDMAR,,ZII,,,, & MEM.CONT REQB,MREQ,,,MWORD &
          /       AM2904 & PCU.NEXT & JMAP
          ;
          ;       ROTATE RIGHT THROUGH CARRY      A9      RSI     CC: CSVZ
          ;       RRC R1,CNT
          ;
 003D RRC:        ALU YBUS,PASS & AB & WORD & OEY & CARRYCTL & CONTROL &
          /       DATAPATH ZZI,,,,,,,,,,,SHTCNTEN, & MEM.CONT ,,,,MWORD &
          /       AM2904 & PCU.NOP & LDCT
          ;
 003E             ALU LDR,PASS & AB & WORD & OEY & CARRYCTL & CONTROL & CNTLB H#E9 &
          /       DATAPATH & MEM.CONT ,,,,MWORD &
          /       AM2904 SHIFTEN,,EZ,EC,ES,EOVR,CEM, & PCU.NOP & RPCT $
          ;
 003F             ALU YBUS,PASS & AB & WORD & OEY & CARRYCTL & CONTROL &
          /       DATAPATH ,,,,,,LDMAR,,ZII,,,, & MEM.CONT REQB,MREQ,,,MWORD &
          /       AM2904 & PCU.NEXT & JMAP
          ;
          ;       ROTATE LEFT THROUGH CARRY       AB      RSI     CC: CSVZ
          ;       RLC R1,CNT        ROTATE (R1) CNT TIME LEFT THROUGH CARRY
          ;
 0040 RLC:        ALU YBUS,PASS & AB & WORD & OEY & CARRYCTL & CONTROL &
          /       DATAPATH ZZI,,,,,,,,,,,SHTCNTEN, & MEM.CONT ,,,,MWORD &
```

Figure 31. Microprogram for 16-Bit Computer (Cont.)

```
AMDOS/29 AMDASM MICRO ASSEMBLER, V1.1
MICROPROGRAM FOR 16 BIT COMPUTER

     /        AM2904 & PCU.NOP & LDCT
     ;
0041          ALU LUR,PASS & AB & WORD & OEY & CARRYCTL & CONTROL & CNTLB H#F9 &
     /        DATAPATH & MEM.CONT ,,,,MWORD &
     /        AM2904 SHIFTEN,,EZ,EC,ES,EOVR,CEM, & PCU.NOP & RPCT $
     ;
0042          ALU YBUS,PASS & AB & WORD & OEY & CARRYCTL & CONTROL &
     /        DATAPATH ,,,,,,LDMAR,,ZII,,,, & MEM.CONT REQB,MREQ,,,MWORD &
     /        AM2904 & PCU.NEXT & JMAP

     ;        ======================================
     ;
     ;                I/O INSTRUCTIONS
     ;
     ;        ======================================
     ;
     ;        INPUT                       A0      RX       CC: NONE
     ;        IN R1,X2(D)      R1 = PORT (X2) + D
     ;
0043 IN:      ALU YBUS,ADD & DAB & CARRYCTL & OEY & WORD & CONTROL & RTB &
     /        DATAPATH ,,,,,YMAR,LDMAR,,,ENZ0,,, & MEM.CONT REQB,,HREQ,,MWORD &
     /        AM2904 & PCU.NOP & LDCT H#001
     ;
0044          ALU & WORD & OEY & CONTROL ,IOEN & CNTLB H#FD &
     /        DATAPATH & MEM.CONT ,,HREQ,,MWORD &
     /        AM2904 & PCU.NOP & RPCT $
     ;
0045          ALU & WORD & OEY & CONTROL ,IOEN,, & CNTLB H#FF &
     /        DATAPATH & MEM.CONT ,,HREQ,,MWORD &
     /        AM2904 & PCU.NOP & CONT
     ;
0046          ALU REG,PASSR & DAB & WORD & OEY & CARRYCTL & CONTROL &
     /        DATAPATH ,,,,,,LDMAR,,,ENZ0,,, & MEM.CONT REQB,,,,MWORD &
     /        AM2904 & PCU.NOP & JMP START1
     ;
     ;        OUTPUT                      A2      RX       CC: NONE
     ;        OUT R1,X2(D)     PORT (X2) + D = (R1)
     ;
0047 CUT:     ALU YBUS,ADD & DAB & CARRYCTL & OEY & WORD & CONTROL & RTB &
     /        DATAPATH ,,,,,YMAR,LDMAR,,,ENZ0,,, & MEM.CONT REQB,,HREQ,,MWORD &
     /        AM2904 & PCU.NOP & CONT
     ;
0048          ALU YBUS,PASS & AB & CARRYCTL & OEY & WORD &
     /        CONTROL ,IOEN,, & CNTLB H#FB &
     /        DATAPATH ,,,,,,,,LDD,,,,, & MEM.CONT ,,HREQ,,MWORD &
     /        AM2904 & PCU.NOP & LDCT H#001
     ;
0049          ALU & WORD & CONTROL & OEY &
     /        DATAPATH & MEM.CONT ,,HREQ,,MWORD &
     /        AM2904 & PCU.NOP & RPCT $
     ;
004A          ALU & WORD & CONTROL ,IOEN,, & CNTLB H#FF & OEY &
     /        DATAPATH & MEM.CONT ,,HREQ,,MWORD &
     /        AM2904 & PCU.NOP & JMP START

     ;        ====================================
     ;
     ;              STACK OPERATIONS
     ;
     ;        ====================================
     ;
     ;        PUSH REGISTERS                  C0       RR       CC: NONE
     ;        PUSH R1,RN         (SP - 2) = R1
     ;                           (SP - 4) = R2
     ;                           (SP - 2*N) = RN
     ;                           SP = SP - 2*N
     ;
004B PUSH:    ALU YBUS,PASS & AB & CARRYCTL & OEY & WORD & CONTROL &
     /        DATAPATH ZZI,,,,,,,,,,,, & MEM.CONT REQB,MREQ,,,MWORD &
     /        AM2904 & PCU.NOP & CONT
     ;
004C          ALU YBUS,PASS & AB & CARRYCTL & OEY & WORD & CONTROL &
     /        DATAPATH ,,,,,,LDMAR,LDD,,,,, & MEM.CONT REQB,MREQ,,,MWORD &
     /        AM2904 & PCU.PUSH & CONT
     ;
004D          ALU YBUS,PASS & AB & CARRYCTL & OEY & WORD & CONTROL &
     /        DATAPATH ,,,ENCTR,INC,,,,,,,, & MEM.CONT REQB,MREQ,,WRITE,MWORD &
     /        TEST Q#70 & AM2904 & PCU.NOP & CJP PUSH+1
     ;
004E          ALU YBUS,PASS & AB & CARRYCTL & OEY & WORD & CONTROL &
     /        DATAPATH ,,,,,,LDMAR,,,,,, & MEM.CONT REQB,MREQ,,,MWORD &
     /        AM2904 & PCU.NOP & JMP RNI
     ;
     ;        POP REGISTERS                   C1       RR       CC: NONE
     ;        POP R2,R1          R2 = (SP)
     ;                           R1 = (SP + 2)
     ;                           RN = (SP + 2*N)
     ;                           SP = SP + 2*N
     ;
004F POP:     ALU YBUS,PASS & AB & CARRYCTL & OEY & WORD & CONTROL &
     /        DATAPATH ZZI,,,,,,,,,,,, & MEM.CONT REQB,MREQ,,,MWORD &
     /        AM2904 & PCU.NOP & CONT
     ;
0050          ALU REG,PASS & AB & CARRYCTL & OEY & WORD & CONTROL &
     /        DATAPATH ,,,,,,LDMAR,,,ENZ0,,, & MEM.CONT REQB,,,,MWORD &
     /        AM2904 & PCU.SP & CONT
     ;
0051          ALU YBUS,PASS & AB & CARRYCTL & OEY & WORD & CONTROL &
     /        DATAPATH ,,,ENCTR,,,,,,,,, & MEM.CONT REQB,MREQ,,,MWORD &
     /        TEST Q#70 & AM2904 & PCU.POP & CJP POP+1
     ;
0052          ALU YBUS,PASS & AB & CARRYCTL & OEY & WORD & CONTROL &
     /        DATAPATH ,,,,,,LDMAR,,,,,, & MEM.CONT REQB,MREQ,,,MWORD &
     /        AM2904 & PCU.NOP & JMP RNI
     ;
     ;        SUBROUTINE CALL          C2       RX       CC: NONE
     ;        CALL X1(D)         SP = SP - 2
     ;                           (SP - 2) = (PC)
     ;                           PC = [(X1) + D]
     ;
0053 CALL:    ALU YBUS,ADD & DAB & CARRYCTL & OEY & WORD & CONTROL & RTB &
     /        DATAPATH ,,LDTREG,,,,LDMAR,,,ENZ0,,, &
     /        MEM.CONT REQB,MREQ,,,MWORD & AM2904 & PCU.PUSH & CONT
     ;
0054          ALU YBUS,PASS & AB & CARRYCTL & WORD & CONTROL &
     /        DATAPATH ,,,,,PCUY,,LDD,,,,, & MEM.CONT REQB,MREQ,,,MWORD &
     /        AM2904 & PCU.NOP & CONT
     ;
0055          ALU YBUS,PASS & AB & CARRYCTL & OEY & WORD & CONTROL &
     /        DATAPATH ,ENTREG,,,,,LDMAR,,,,,, &
     /        MEM.CONT REQB,MREQ,,WRITE,MWORD & AM2904 & PCU.JUMP & JMP START1
     ;
     ;        RETURN FROM SUBROUTINE          C3                 CC: NONE
     ;        RET                PC = (SP)
     ;                           SP = SP + 2
     ;
0056 RETURN:  ALU YBUS,PASS & AB & CARRYCTL & OEY & WORD & CONTROL &
     /        DATAPATH ,,,,,,LDMAR,,,,,, & MEM.CONT REQB,,,,MWORD &
     /        AM2904 & PCU.SP & CONT
     ;
0057          ALU YBUS,PASS & AB & CARRYCTL & OEY & WORD & CONTROL &
     /        DATAPATH ,,,,,,LDMAR,,,,,, & MEM.CONT REQB,MREQ,,,MWORD &
     /        AM2904 & PCU.SP & CONT
     ;
0058          ALU YBUS,PASSR & DAB & CARRYCTL & OEY & WORD & CONTROL &
     /        DATAPATH ,,LDTREG,,,YMAR,LDMAR,,,ENZ0,,, &
     /        MEM.CONT REQB,MREQ,,,MWORD & AM2904 & PCU.POP & CONT
     ;
0059          ALU YBUS,PASS & AB & CARRYCTL & OEY & WORD & CONTROL &
     /        DATAPATH ,ENTREG,,,,,,,,,,, & MEM.CONT ,,,,MWORD &
     /        AM2904 & PCU.JUMP & JMP START1

     ;        ======================================
     ;
     ;             INTERRUPT INSTRUCTIONS
     ;
     ;        ======================================
     ;
     ;        LOAD INTERRUPT MASK             CA       RI       CC: NONE
     ;        LIM DI             LOAD LOWER BYTE OF DI INTO MASK REGISTER
     ;
005A LIM:     ALU YBUS,PASSR & DAB & CARRYCTL & OEY & WORD &
     /        CONTROL ,,,INTRIEN & CNTLB H#FE &
     /        DATAPATH ,,,,,,LDMAR,,,ENZ0,,, & MEM.CONT REQB,MREQ,,,MWORD &
     /        AM2904 & PCU.NEXT & JMP START2
     ;
     ;        ENABLE INTERRUPT                C8       CTL      CC: NONE
     ;        EI                 ENABLE INTERRUPT SYSTEM
     ;
005B EI:      ALU YBUS,PASS & AB & CARRYCTL & OEY & WORD &
     /        CONTROL ,,,INTRIEN & CNTLB H#FF &
     /        DATAPATH ZZI,,,,,,LDMAR,,ZII,,,, & MEM.CONT REQB,MREQ,,,MWORD &
     /        AM2904 & PCU.NEXT & JMAP
     ;
     ;        DISPABLE INTERRUPT              C9       CTL      CC:NONE
     ;        DI                 DISABLE INTERRUPT SYSTEM
     ;
005C DI:      ALU YBUS,PASS & AB & CARRYCTL & OEY & WORD &
     /        CONTROL ,,,INTRIEN & CNTLB H#FD &
     /        DATAPATH ZZI,,,,,,LDMAR,,ZII,,,, & MEM.CONT REQB,MREQ,,,MWORD &
     /        AM2904 & PCU.NEXT & JMAP
     ;
     ;        RETURN FROM INTERRUPT           CB       CTL      CC: (SP+2)
     ;        RTI                PC = (SP) ,PSW = (SP+2)
     ;                           SP = SP + 4, INTERRUPT ENABLED
     ;
005D RTI:     ALU YBUS,PASS & AB & CARRYCTL & OEY & WORD & CONTROL &
     /        DATAPATH ,,,,,,LDMAR,,,,,, & MEM.CONT REQB,,,,MWORD &
     /        AM2904 & PCU.SP & CONT
     ;
005E          ALU YBUS,PASSR & DAB & CARRYCTL & OEY & WORD & CONTROL &
     /        DATAPATH ,,LDTREG,,,,,,,ENZ0,,, & MEM.CONT REQB,MREQ,,,MWORD &
     /        AM2904 & PCU.POP & CONT
     ;
005F          ALU YBUS,PASS & AB & CARRYCTL & OEY & WORD & CONTROL &
     /        DATAPATH ,ENTREG,,,,,,,,,,, & MEM.CONT ,,,,MWORD &
     /        AM2904 & PCU.JUMP & CONT
     ;
0060          ALU YBUS,PASS & AB & CARRYCTL & OEY & WORD &
     /        CONTROL ,,,INTRIEN & CNTLB H#F9 &
     /        DATAPATH ,,,,,, LDMAR,,,,,, & MEM.CONT REQB,,,,MWORD &
     /        AM2904 & PCU.SP & CONT
     ;
0061          ALU YBUS,PASSR & DAB & CARRYCTL & OEY & WORD &
     /        CONTROL ,,,INTRIEN & CNTLB H#FF & TEST Q#00 &
     /        DATAPATH ,,,,,,,,,ENZ0,,, & MEM.CONT REQB,MREQ,,,MWORD &
     /        AM2904 ,,EZ,EC,ES,EOVR,CEM, & PCU.POP & JMP START


     ;        ++++++++++++++++++++++++++++++++++++
     ;
     ;             INITIALIZATION ROUTINES
     ;
     ;        ++++++++++++++++++++++++++++++++++++
     ;
0180          ORG H#180
     ;
0180 INIT:    ALU REG,PASSR & DAB & WORD & OEY & CARRYCTL &
     /        DATAPATH & MEM.CONT ,,HREQ,,MWORD & CONTROL ROM,,, & CNTLB 00 &
     /        IMMD H#0000 & CONT
     ;
     ;        INITIALIZE REGISTERS IN AM2901A
     ;        R0 = 0, R1 = 4000H, R4 = 2, AND R5 = 4
     ;
0181          ALU & WORD & CONTROL ,,,INTRIEN & CNTLB H#F0 &
     /        DATAPATH & MEM.CONT ,,HREQ,,MWORD &
     /        AM2904 & PCU ,,PCUDZ,A0,B0 & IMMD H#0000 & CONT
     ;
0182          ALU & WORD & CONTROL ,,,INTRIEN & CNTLB H#F8 &
     /        DATAPATH & MEM.CONT ,,HREQ,,MWORD &
     /        AM2904 & PCU ,,PCUDZ,A1,B1 & IMMD H#4000 & CONT
     ;
0183          ALU & WORD & PCU ,,PCUDZ,A4,B4 & CARRYCTL & DATAPATH &
     /        MEM.CONT ,,HREQ,,MWORD & IMMD H#0002 & CONT
     ;
0184          ALU & WORD & PCU ,,PCUDZ,A5,B5 & CARRYCTL & DATAPATH &
     /        MEM.CONT ,,HRFQ,,MWORD & IMMD H#0004 & CONT
     ;
0185          ALU & WORD & CONTROL ,IOEN,, & CNTLB H#FF & DATAPATH &
     /        MEM.CONT ,,HREQ,,MWORD & AM2904 & PCU.NOP & CONT
     ;
     ;        INITIALIZE CONSOLE AM9551
     ;
0186          ALU REG,PASSR & DAB & WORD & OEY & CARRYCTL &
     /        DATAPATH & MEM.CONT & CONTROL ROM,,, & CNTLB 10 &
     /        IMMD H#FFFB & CONT
     ;
0187          ALU REG,PASSR & DAB & WORD & OEY & CARRYCTL &
     /        DATAPATH & MEM.CONT & CONTROL ROM,,, & CNTLB 20 &
     /        IMMD H#00CE & CONT
     ;
0188          ALU & WORD & CONTROL & DATAPATH & MEM.CONT & JSB IOW
     ;
0189          ALU REG,PASSR & DAB & WORD & OEY & CARRYCTL &
     /        DATAPATH & MEM.CONT & CONTROL ROM,,, & CNTLB 20 &
     /        IMMD H#0035 & CONT
     ;
```

Figure 31. Microprogram for 16-Bit Computer (Cont.)

```
AMDOS/29 AMDASM MICRO ASSEMBLER, V1.1
MICROPROGRAM FOR 16 BIT COMPUTER

018A          ALU & WORD & CONTROL & DATAPATH & MEM.CONT & JSB IOW
      ;
018B          ALU & PCU.NOP & DATAPATH & MEM.CONT & JMP START

      ;       ##################################
      ;
      ;            I/O WRITE SUBROUTINE
      ;       THE ADDRESS OF I/O PORT IS IN R1
      ;       THE DATA TO BE WRITTEN IS IN R2
      ;
      ;       ##################################
      ;
018C IOW:     ALU YBUS,PASS & AB & CARRYCTL & OEY & WORD &
      /       CONTROL ROM,,, & CNTLB 10 &
      /       DATAPATH ,,,,,YMAR,LDMAR,,,,,, & MEM.CONT REQB,,HREQ,,MWORD &
      /       AM2904 & PCU.NOP & CONT
      ;
018D          ALU YBUS,PASS & AB & CARRYCTL & OEY & WORD &
      /       CONTROL ROM,,, & CNTLB 20 &
      /       DATAPATH ,,,,,,,LDD,,,,, & MEM.CONT REQB,,HREQ,,MWORD &
      /       AM2904 & PCU.NOP & CONT
      ;
018E          ALU & WORD & CONTROL ,IOEN,, & CNTLB H#FB & DATAPATH &
      /       MEM.CONT REQB,,HREQ,,MWORD & AM2904 & PCU.NOP & LDCT H#001
      ;
018F          ALU & WORD & CONTROL & DATAPATH &
      /       MEM.CONT ,,HREQ,,MWORD & AM2904 & PCU.NOP & RPCT $
      ;
0190          ALU & WORD & CONTROL ,IOEN,, & CNTLB H#FF & DATAPATH &
      /       MEM.CONT REQB,,HREQ,,MWORD & AM2904 & PCU.NOP & RTN

      ;       ++++++++++++++++++++++++++++++++++
      ;
      ;            VECTOR JUMP ENTRY POINTS
      ;
      ;       ++++++++++++++++++++++++++++++++++
      ;
01D0          ORG H#1D0
      ;
      ;       INTERRUPT 0, PC = 10H
      ;
01D0 INT0:    ALU & WORD & CONTROL ,IOEN,INTDIS, & CNTLB H#F7 &
      /       DATAPATH & MEM.CONT ,,,,MWORD &
      /       AM2904 & PCU ,,PCUDZ,A0,B0 & IMMD H#0010 & CONT
      ;
01D1          ALU & WORD & CONTROL ,,INTDIS,INTRIEN & CNTLB H#FD &
      /       DATAPATH & MEM.CONT & AM2904 & PCU.NOP & CONT
      ;
01D2          ALU & WORD & CONTROL ,IOEN,, & CNTLB H#FF &
      /       DATAPATH ,,,,,,LDMAR,,,,,, & MEM.CONT REQB,,,,MWORD &
      /       AM2904 & PCU.NOP & JMP START1
      ;
      ;       INTERRUPT 1, PC = 14H
      ;
01D3 INT1:    ALU & WORD & CONTROL ,,INTDIS,INTRIEN & CNTLB H#FD &
      /       DATAPATH & MEM.CONT ,,,,MWORD &
      /       AM2904 & PCU ,,PCUDZ,A0,B0 & IMMD H#0014 & CONT
      ;
01D4          ALU & WORD & CONTROL ,IOEN,, & CNTLB H#FF &
      /       DATAPATH ,,,,,,LDMAR,,,,,, & MEM.CONT REQB,,,,MWORD &
      /       AM2904 & PCU.NOP & JMP START1
      ;
      ;       INTERRUPT 2, PC = 18H
      ;
01D5 INT2:    ALU & WORD & CONTROL ,,INTDIS,INTRIEN & CNTLB H#FD &
      /       DATAPATH & MEM.CONT ,,,,MWORD &
      /       AM2904 & PCU ,,PCUDZ,A0,B0 & IMMD H#0018 & CONT
      ;
01D6          ALU & WORD & CONTROL ,IOEN,, & CNTLB H#FF &
      /       DATAPATH ,,,,,,LDMAR,,,,,, & MEM.CONT REQB,,,,MWORD &
      /       AM2904 & PCU.NOP & JMP START1
      ;
      ;       INTERRUPT 3, PC = 1CH
      ;
01D7 INT3:    ALU & WORD & CONTROL ,,INTDIS,INTRIEN & CNTLB H#FD &
      /       DATAPATH & MEM.CONT ,,,,MWORD &
      /       AM2904 & PCU ,,PCUDZ,A0,B0 & IMMD H#001C & CONT
      ;
```

```
01D8          ALU & WORD & CONTROL ,IOEN,, & CNTLB H#FF &
      /       DATAPATH ,,,,,,LDMAR,,,,,, & MEM.CONT REQB,,,,MWORD &
      /       AM2904 & PCU.NOP & JMP START1
      ;
      ;       INTERRUPT 4, PC = 20H
      ;
01D9 INT4:    ALU & WORD & CONTROL ,,INTDIS,INTRIEN & CNTLB H#FD &
      /       DATAPATH & MEM.CONT ,,,,MWORD &
      /       AM2904 & PCU ,,PCUDZ,A0,B0 & IMMD H#0020 & CONT
      ;
01DA          ALU & WORD & CONTROL ,IOEN,, & CNTLB H#FF &
      /       DATAPATH ,,,,,,LDMAR,,,,,, & MEM.CONT REQB,,,,MWORD &
      /       AM2904 & PCU.NOP & JMP START1
      ;
      ;       INTERRUPT 5, PC = 24H
      ;
01DB INT5:    ALU & WORD & CONTROL ,,INTDIS,INTRIEN & CNTLB H#FD &
      /       DATAPATH & MEM.CONT ,,,,MWORD &
      /       AM2904 & PCU ,,PCUDZ,A0,B0 & IMMD H#0024 & CONT
      ;
01DC          ALU & WORD & CONTROL ,IOEN,, & CNTLB H#FF &
      /       DATAPATH ,,,,,,LDMAR,,,,,, & MEM.CONT REQB,,,,MWORD &
      /       AM2904 & PCU.NOP & JMP START1
      ;
      ;       INTERRUPT 6, PC = 28H
      ;
01DD INT6:    ALU & WORD & CONTROL ,,INTDIS,INTRIEN & CNTLB H#FD &
      /       DATAPATH & MEM.CONT ,,,,MWORD &
      /       AM2904 & PCU ,,PCUDZ,A0,B0 & IMMD H#0028 & CONT
      ;
01DE          ALU & WORD & CONTROL ,IOEN,, & CNTLB H#FF &
      /       DATAPATH ,,,,,,LDMAR,,,,,, & MEM.CONT REQB,,,,MWORD &
      /       AM2904 & PCU.NOP & JMP START1
      ;
      ;       INTERRUPT 7, PC = 2CH
      ;
01DF INT7:    ALU & WORD & CONTROL ,,INTDIS,INTRIEN & CNTLB H#FD &
      /       DATAPATH & MEM.CONT ,,,,MWORD &
      /       AM2904 & PCU ,,PCUDZ,A0,B0 & IMMD H#002C & CONT
      ;
01E0          ALU & WORD & CONTROL ,IOEN,, & CNTLB H#FF &
      /       DATAPATH ,,,,,,LDMAR,,,,,, & MEM.CONT REQB,,,,MWORD &
      /       AM2904 & PCU.NOP & JMP START1

      ;       ==================================
      ;
      ;               INTERRUPT HANDLER
      ;
      ;       ==================================
      ;
01F0          ORG H#1F0
      ;
01F0 INTR:    ALU & WORD & CONTROL &
      /       DATAPATH & MEM.CONT REQB,MREQ,,WRITE,MWORD &
      /       AM2904 & PCU.DEC4 & CONT
      ;
01F1          ALU & WORD & CONTROL  &
      /       DATAPATH ,,,,,,LDMAR,,,,,, & MEM.CONT ,,,,MWORD &
      /       AM2904 & PCU.PUSH & CONT
      ;
01F2          ALU & WORD & CONTROL &
      /       DATAPATH ,,,,,PCUY,,LDD,,,,, & MEM.CONT REQB,,,,MWORD &
      /       AM2904 & PCU.NOP & CONT
      ;
01F3          ALU & WORD & CONTROL ,,,INTRIEN & CNTLB H#F5  &
      /       DATAPATH & MEM.CONT REQB,MREQ,,WRITE,MWORD &
      /       AM2904 & PCU.NOP & JMPV
      ;
      ;       ***********************************
      ;
      ;             INTERRUPT ENTRY POINT
      ;
      ;       ***********************************
      ;
01FF          ORG H#1FF
      ;
01FF          ALU & WORD & CONTROL &
      /       DATAPATH ,,,,,,LDMAR,LDD,,,PSW,, & MEM.CONT REQB,MREQ,,,MWORD &
      /       AM2904 & PCU.PUSH & JMP INTR
      ;
              END
```

Figure 31. Microprogram for 16-Bit Computer (Cont.)

MICROCODE TRANSLATION

It is often convenient for the microprogrammer to assign microword fields such that they occupy positions that differ from those in the actual hardware implementation. This is often the case when the microprogrammer, for convenience, allocates bits according to the functions to be performed and then needs to translate the object code produced by AMDASM® to be consistent with the hardware microprogram memory design.

There is another instance where the ability to shift bit assignment is important to the engineer. As a given product evolves, bits may be added or deleted from the original microword format. When this occurs, a mapping function is desired to minimize hardware changes.

The program in SYSTEM/29® that performs such a mapping function is called AMSCRM. The AMSCRM maps the output of AMDASM (logical bit pattern) into the bit pattern that is consistent with the 16-bit computer hardware. A table of the logical to physical mapping is shown in Table 3.

ENGINEERING MODEL AND MACROCODE

With the proper tools – designing, microprogramming, prototyping, and checking out a new computer design is not overly difficult. The major tools used for the high-speed 16-bit design described in this application note was System 29[(1)]. System 29 is a software driven hardware prototyping system which allows microprogramming, hardware design/checkout, and macroprogramming (programming in the language of the target machine) to occur simultaneously. At the point where the design is reasonably rigid, and the hardware is mostly fabricated, System 29 allows the engineer to create "instant" microprograms to check out the new computers' internal data paths. Microprogram software support features of System 29 also allow the engineer to single cycle, single instruction step, instruction trace, and trap on pre-specified events coming true. Simultaneously with this initial internal check-out, the microcode for some very simple machine instruction should be written (i.e., load register, add register, or register, etc.). The next step is to check out the main memory paths with load and store instructions. At this point, a reasonable

Table 3.

```
            ************************************

            BIT ASSIGNMENT FOR 16-BIT COMPUTER

            ************************************

BIT POSITION    MNEMONIC  *              DESCRIPTION
LOG     PHY

 95     95      RTB       *     REG. FIELD 2 TO B PORT OF AM2903
 94             SPARE
 93             SPARE

 92     54      ZZI             LOAD Z REG. INTO ZI REG.
 91     94      CCEN      *     AM2910 CONDITON CODE ENABLE

                AM2903 ALU CONTROL BITS

 90     93      WORD      *     WORD MODE = 0, BYTE MODE = 1
 89     92      EA        *     ENABEL A LATCH ON AM2903
 88     91      OEY       *     ENABLE Y OUTPUT ON AM2903
 87     90      OEB       *     ENABLE B LATCH ON AM2903
 86-78  89-81   I8-I0           INSTRUCTION LINES FOR AM2903

                DATAPATH BITS

 77     80      ENTREG    *     ENABLE TRANSFER REG
 76     79      LDTREG          LOAD TRANSFER REG.
 75     78      ENCTR     *     I-REG ENABLE COUNTER
 74     77      INC             I-REG INC=1/DEC=0
 73     76      PCUCD           PCU TRANSFER CHIP DISABLE
 72     75      PCUY            PCU TRANSFER TO Y-BUS
 71     74      LDMAR           LOAD MEMORY ADDRESS REGISTER
 70     73      LDD             LOAD D-REGISTER
 69     72      ZII             LOAD ZI INTO I REGISTER
 68     71      ENZ0      *     ENABLE Z0 REGISTER TO DA BUS
 67     70      PSW       *     ENABLE PSW REGISTER TO DA BUS
 66     69      SHTCNEN   *     SHIFT COUNT AM2910 ADDRESS
 65     68      BRIEN     *     BRANCH INSTRUCTION ENABLE

                AM2901A PROGRAM CONTROL UNIT

 64     67      PCUI7           F TO B-RAM = 1 (DEFAULT), F TO Q-REG = 0
 63     66      PCUI3           ADD = 1 (DEFAULT), SUB = 0
 62-60  65-63   PCUI2-0         PCU SOURCE CONTROL
 59-57  62-60   PCUA2-0         PCU A-RAM SELECT
 56-54  59-57   PCUB2-0         PCU B-RAM SELECT

                MEMORY CONTROL

 53     52      REQB            BUS REQUEST
 52     51      MREQ            MEMORY REQUEST
 51     50      HREQ      *     HOLD REQUEST
 50     49      WRITE           MEMORY READ = 0 (DEFAULT), MEMORY WRITE = 1
 49     48      MWORD           MEMORY BYTE OP = 0 (DEFAULT), MEMORY WORD OP = 1

                CONTROL BIT STROBES

 48     56      IMMD      *     ENABLE IMMEDIATE FIELD TO DA BUS
 47     47      ROM             I-REG ENABLE = 0 (DEFAULT), ROM ENABLE = 1
 46     46      IOEN      *     I/O CONTROL REGISTER ENABLE
 45     45      INTDIS    *     AM2914 INTERRUPTS DISABLE
 44     44      INTRIEN   *     AM2914 INSTRUCTION ENABLE
 43     43      SHFTEN    *     AM2904 SHIFT ENABLE

                GENERAL PURPOSE CONTROL BITS

 42-35  42-35   CNTLB7-0        BITS TO BE STROBED BY CONTROL STROBES

                AM2904 STATUS REGISTER CONTROL BITS

 34     34      OECT      *     OUTPUT ENABLE OF CONDTIONAL TEST
 33     33      EZ        *     ENABLE ZERO FLAG UPDATE
 32     32      EC        *     ENABLE CARRY FLAG UPDATE
 31     31      ES        *     ENABLE SIGN FLAG UPDATE
 30     30      EOVR      *     ENABLE OVERFLOW FLAG UPDATE
 29     29      CEM       *     ENABLE MACHINE STATUS REGISTER
 28     28      CEU       *     ENABLE MICROPROGARM STATUS REGISTER
 27     27      I12             AM2904 I12 CARRY OUT CONTROL
 26     26      I11             AM2904 CARRY OUT CONTROL

                TEST BITS

 25-23  25-23   TEST5-3         AM2904 TEST BITS
 22-20  22-20   TEST2-0         AM2904 & AM25LS251 TEST BITS

                AM2910 SEQUENCE CONTROL

 19-16  19-16   NAC3-0          AM2910 NEXT ADDRESS CONTROL

                NEXT MICRO ADDRESS OR IMMEDIATE FIELD

 15-0   15-0    M15-0           SHARED FIELD FOR NEXT ADDRESS OR IMMD

                END
```

instruction sub-set should be microprogrammed (a phase 1 instruction set) that will allow a simple monitor to be written in the target machines's language. This monitor should run on the target machine and provide commands for: memory display, memory store and jump to memory location. The phase 1 instruction set and simple monitor now provides the basic foundation for completing the full computer design.

The standard System 29 configuration provides automatically for microcode and hardware development. In order to efficiently develop and implement the target machine's software, a target machine assembler and a mechanism for loading the machine's main memory must be provided. System 29 uses an Am9080A microprocessor, dual floppy disks, and a full function disk operating system to support microprogrammed hardware and firmware development. The Am9080A microprocessor can address 64k bytes of memory. The disk operating system uses only the first 32k bytes and the remaining 32k is used to memory map (page) functions from the hardware development side. Through this mechanism, the designer has the ability to directly load and manipulate microprograms, monitor hardware functions, etc. There are extra enable lines from the page register which allow the System 29 user to map other functions into the support processor's upper 32k of memory.

The main memory of this 16-bit high-speed computer design was mapped into the support processors upper 32k via one of the unused page register enable lines. Besides the normal 16-bit interface, a simple 8-bit interface was added to the main memory thus making it a simple two port memory. When the 16-bit computer is halted (via a System 29 command) location 0 of 16-bit main memory would be addressed as location 8000 hex of System 29 support processor memory. Location 1 would be 8001, 2 would be 8002, etc. This affected a mechanical link between the 16-bit prototype design and System 29.

In order to efficiently write a reasonably complex piece of software (such as a simple monitor), an assembler for the target instruction set is needed. Since this 16-bit computer design is not exactly like any other 16-bit computer, ready to run software tools are not available. A macro assembler is available as an optional enhancement to the System 29 software base. Even though this macro assembler is for programming in Am9080A assembly language, there is a user installable patch which will disable all of the Am9080A operation codes (Figure 32). With this patch installed, the user may now write a macro library defining the target machine's instruction set. It is not necessary to code the entire instruction set, as the first level of programming for the new machine (simple monitor, etc.) will be using only the phase 1 instruction set. A complete macro library of the AMD high-speed 16-bit computer phase 1 instruction set is contained in Appendix B.

Now that the tools are in place, it is relatively simple to code and implement a simple monitor for the target machine. Appendix C contains the complete simple monitor listing for the AMD high-speed 16-bit computer. Only the phase 1 instruction set was used which does not include byte instruction, call and return instructions, stack instructions, any special instructions, etc. This simple monitor understands three commands: Display (D), Store (S), and Jump (J). Typing D followed by an address value will display 256 bytes of main memory beginning on the address given (rounded back to the nearest eight word boundary). Typing an S followed by an address, followed by data, will store the data consecutively, on a nibble basis beginning at the given address. Typing in J followed by an address will cause the processor to begin execution at the main memory location given by the address. Commands, addresses, and data must be separated by at least one delimiter (space, comma, or period).

The change file shown below can be integrated into MAC to produce a new program, which we will call MAC29. The MAC29 program will not recognize 8080 mnemonics, but will recognize all the MAC pseudo operators and arithmetic functions.

```
                ;
                ;       MACRO ASSEMBLER "MAC" CHANGES TO DISABLE 8080 OPCODES.
                ;
                ;
0019 =          RT      EQU     25      ;8080 REGISTER NAME
001A =          PT      EQU     26      ;PSEUDO OPCODE TYPE
2561 =          TAREA   EQU     2561H   ;FREE AREA IN TOKEN MODULE
                ;
2444                    ORG     2444H   ;OVERLAY INX H  MOV B,M  RET
2444 C36125             JMP     TAREA
                ;
2561                    ORG     TAREA
                ;       TYPE IS IN THE ACCUMULATOR
2561 FE19               CPI     RT      ;BELOW RT IF ARITH OP
2563 DA6925             JC      TYPEOK
2566 FE1A               CPI     PT      ;PSEUDO OP?
2568 C0                 RNZ             ;RETURN WITH NON-ZERO FLAG
                ;       OTHERWISE, PSEUDO OP OR ARITH OP
2569 23         TYPEOK:         INX     H
256A 46                 MOV     B,M
256B BF                 CMP     A       ;SET ZERO FLAG
256C C9                 RET
                ;
256D                    END
```

Figure 32. Macro Assembler Disable Opcode Patch.

After writing the monitor, and putting it onto floppy disks via the System 29 editor, it must be assembled using the modified macro assember (described earlier). The result of the assembly is a hex file which is suitable for loading into the 16-bit computer's main memory. This hex file is now loaded into support processor memory beginning at location 8000 hex. As discussed previously, this is mapped at location zero in the 16-bit computer's main memory. Assuming the microcode is loaded and a terminal is connected to the 16-bit computer, the monitor in 16-bit main memory may now be executed. The complete System 29 session from editing and assembling the monitor to loading and executing it is given in Appendix D.

SUMMARY

As can be seen throughout these application notes, designing a high performance Bipolar microprocessor system is a straightforward task. The Am2900 Family is ideally suited to provide building blocks for the various elements of the computer. These include the Computer Control Unit, the Central Processing Unit, the Program Control Unit, the Interrupt Structure and the various bus controls. Together, these elements allow the designer to build computers using the current state-of-the-art architecture with LSI building blocks.

As technology improves, Advanced Micro Devices has been able to redesign these building blocks to offer increased performance. Thus, the Am2901 has evolved through an Am2901A, then an Am2901B and now an Am2901C is in the planning. In addition, the Am2903 offers additional architectural advantages and soon an Am29103 will provide additional speed and performance features. Similarly, the microprogram sequencer area began with the Am2909 and Am2911; then was followed by the larger Am2910. Soon, the Am2909A and Am2911A will provide higher speed in the microprogram sequencer area and will be followed by an Am2910A.

Thus, the future for Bipolar LSI building blocks includes not only more advanced product designs offering higher levels of integration and new functions for new architectures, but also offers higher performance versions of the already existing products. Advanced Micro Devices is committed to providing high performance Bipolar LSI circuits utilizing proven technology designed to operate over the full military operating range as well as the commercial operating range. As always, these products continue to meet the performance requirements of MIL-STD-883.

APPENDIX A
Complete Description of Instructions

LOAD

RR, RS, SS

OP	R_1	R_2

RX, RSI

OP	R_1	X_2	d

The second operand is loaded into the general register specified by R_1.

STORE

RR, RS, SS

OP	R_1	R_2

RX, RSI

OP	R_1	X_2	d

The first operand specified by R_1 is stored at the location specified by the second operand.

ADD

RR, RS, SS

OP	R_1	R_2

RX, RSI

OP	R_1	X_2	d

The first operand is added to the second operand and replaces the first operand.

ADD WITH CARRY

RR

OP	R_1	R_2

RX

OP	R_1	X_2	d

The first operand (16 bits) with carry is added to the second operand and replaces the first operand.

SUBTRACT

RR, RS, SS

OP	R_1	R_2

RX, RSI

OP	R_1	X_2	d

The second operand is subtracted from the first operand and replaces the first operand.

SUBTRACT WITH CARRY

RR

OP	R_1	R_2

RX

OP	R_1	R_2	d

The second operand (16 bits) with carry is subtracted from the first operand and replaces the first operand.

AND

RR, RS, SS

OP	R_1	R_2

RX, RSI

OP	R_1	X_2	d

The AND of the first operand and the second operand replaces the first operand.

OR

RR, RS, SS

OP	R_1	R_2

RX, RSI

OP	R_1	X_2	d

The OR of the first operand and the second operand replaces the first operand.

XOR

RR, RS, SS

OP	R_1	R_2

RX, RSI

OP	R_1	X_2	d

The logical difference of the first operand and the second operand replaces the first operand.

TEST IMMEDIATE

RX, RSI

OP	R_1	X_2	d

The first operand and the second operand are logically ANDed. The contents of R_1 and X_2 are unchanged.

COMPARE

RR, RS, SS

OP	R_1	R_2

RX, RSI

OP	R_1	X_2	d

The first operand is algebraically compared with the second operand. The result is indicated by the condition code.

COMPARE LOGICAL

RR, RS, SS

OP	R_1	R_2

The first operand is compared logically to the second operand. The result is indicated by the condition code.

MULTIPLY

RR

OP	R_1	R_2

RX

OP	R_1	X_2	d

The first operand $(R_1 + 1)$ is multiplied by the second operand and the 32-bit product is contained in R_1 and $R_1 + 1$ registers. R_1 must be an even address. The sign of the product is determined by the rules of algebra.

MULTIPLY UNSIGNED

RR

OP	R_1	R_2

RX

OP	R_1	X_2	d

The first operand $(R_1 + 1)$ is multiplied by the second operand and the 32-bit product is contained in R_1 and $(R_1 + 1)$. R_1 must be even.

LOAD BYTE

RR

OP	R_1	R_2

RX, RXI

OP	R_1	X_2	d

The 8-bit byte stored in the low order byte of the second operand location is stored in the low order byte of R_1. The high order byte of the R_1 is set to zero.

INSERT CHARACTER

RR, RS

OP	R_1	R_2

RX, RSI

OP	R_1	X_2	d

The byte at the second operand location is loaded into the low order byte of R_1 without changing the contents of the high order byte of R_1.

STORE CHARACTER
STORE BYTE

RR, RS

OP	R_1	R_2

RX, RSI

OP	R_1	X_2	d

The least significant byte of the first operand is stored in the location specified by the second operand. The other byte of the second location is unchanged.

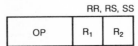

EXCHANGE BYTE

RR, RS

OP	R_1	R_2

RX

OP	R_1	X_2	d

The bytes specified by the first and second operands are exchanged. When the operand specifies a register (i.e. R_1, R_2) only the low order byte is exchanged.

BYTE SWAP

RR, RS

OP	R_1	R_2

RX

OP	R_1	R_2	d

The two bytes of the second operand are swapped and loaded into the register specified by the first operand.

COMPARE LOGICAL BYTE

RR, RS

OP	R_1	R_2

RX, RSI

OP	R_1	X_2	d

The low order byte of the first and second operands are compared. The result is indicated in the condition code.

AND BYTE

RR, RS

OP	R_1	R_2

RX, RSI

OP	R_1	X_2	d

The AND of the low order bytes specified by the first second operands replace the first operand low order byte. The high order byte of R_1 is set to zeros.

OR BYTE

RR, RS

OP	R_1	R_2

RX, RSI

OP	R_1	X_2	d

The OR of the low order bytes specified by the first and second operands replace the first operand low order byte. The high order byte of R_1 is set to zero.

XOR BYTE

RR, RX

OP	R_1	R_2

RX, RSI

OP	R_1	X_2	d

The XOR of the low order bytes specified by the first and second operands replace the first operand low order byte. The high order byte of R_1 is set to zero.

LOAD PROGRAM STATUS WORD

RX

	R_2	d

A 32-bit new PSW is loaded from the memory location specified by the second operand as the current PSW.

EXCHANGE PROGRAM STATUS

RR

	R_1	R_2

PSW (0:15) $\rightarrow$ (R_1)
R2 $\rightarrow$ PSW (0:15)

STORE PROGRAM STATUS WORD

RX

OP	R_2	d

The 32-bit PSW is stored at the location specified by the second operand.

SUPERVISOR CALL

RX

OP	R_1	X_2	d

OLD PSW → $[(X_2) + d]$
$[(X_2) + d] + 4$ → NEW PSW

SET, CLR, COMPLEMENT, TEST BIT PSW

OP	N

The condition flags in the current PSW are set, cleared, complemented, or tested. N defines the bit(s) to be affected or tested.

CALL

RX

OP	R_1	R_2	d

Jump to the memory location specified by the second operand and push PSW (16:31) onto stack.

RETURN

OP	X	X

POP STACK
STACK → PSW (16:31)

PUSH

OP	X	X

PSW, R_0-R_{15} } → STACK

POP

OP	X	X

STACK → { PSW, R_0-R_{15}

P/PUSH

RR

OP	R_1	R_2

R_1 THRU R_2 → STACK

P/POP

RR

OP	R_1	R_2

STACK → R_1 THRU R_2

LOAD STACK POINTER
LOAD STACK LIMIT LOWER
LOAD STACK LIMIT UPPER

RX

OP	R_2	d

STORE STACK POINTER
STORE STACK LIMIT LOWER
STORE STACK LIMIT UPPER

RX

OP	R_2	d

The stack point, stack limit lower or upper is read from or written into the address defined by the second operand.

TRANSLATE

RR

OP	R_1	R_2

R_1

LENGTH
ADDRESS

R_2

ADDRESS

The addresses specified by $R_1 + 1$ and R_2 define two tables, $R_1 + 1$ address is the top location of a table to be translated, R_2 address the first location of the translation table. The value (one byte) pointed to be the $R_1 + 1$ address is indexed by (added to) the address value of R_2 to find the translation code. This translation code replaces the value pointed to by the $R_1 + 1$ address. After one byte is translated, the length is decremented and the address of $R_1 + 1$ incremented and the instruction repeated, until the length equals zero. This instruction is interruptable. If this instruction is interrupted, the PC is left pointing to this instruction so that this instruction can be resumed after the interrupt service is complete.

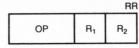

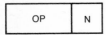

TRANSLATE AND TEST

RR

OP	R_1	R_2

R_1

LENGTH
ADDRESS

R_2

ADDRESS

This instruction proceeds like translate except that the bytes of the first operand (defined by R_1) are not changed in storage. When the bytes of the translate table (R_2) the instruction proceeds to the next byte of the first operand. If the byte of the translate table is not zero, the instruction is halted with the address pointed to last in the translate table held in register 1.

MOVE LONG

RR

OP	R_1	R_2

R_1

LENGTH
ADDRESS

R_2

ADDRESS

Moves bytes defined by R_1 to R_2. Both adresses incremented after each transfer. This instruction is interruptable.

COMPARE LONG

RR

OP	R_1	R_2

R_1

LENGTH
ADDRESS

R_2

ADDRESS

Compares the first operand against the second operand. The length is decremented and the address incremented after each compare. When length = zero of the bytes compared are not equal, the instruction is halted.

EXECUTE

RX

OP	R_1	X_2	d

The upper 16 bits of the instruction at the second operand is 'OR'ed with R_1 and executed.

DECIMAL ADD

OP	R_1	R_2

OP	R_1	X_2	d

Nibbles in operand 1 and operand 2 are added. The result is placed in operand one.

DECIMAL SUBTRACT

	R_1	R_2

	R_1	X_2	d

Nibbles in operand 2 are subtracted from nibbles in operand 1 and the result is placed in operand 1.

DECREMENT INDEXES

RR

OP	R_1	R_2

$R_1 - 1 \rightarrow R_1$

$R_2 - 1 \rightarrow R_2$

One is subtracted from R_1 and the result placed back into R_1. One is subtracted from R_2 and the result placed back into R_2. R_1 and R_2 may specify the same register with will effectively subtract two from that register.

SHIFT RIGHT ARITHMETIC

SHIFT RIGHT DOUBLE ARITHMETIC

RX, RSI

OP	R_1	R_2	d

The contents of R_1 for single shifts and R_1, $R_1 + 1$ for double shifts are shifted the number of places specified by the second operand. The sign bit is unchanged. Bits shifted in are set equal to the sign bit. Bits shifted out are shifted through the carry bit.

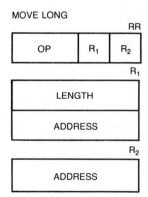

ROTATE RIGHT
ROTATE RIGHT DOUBLE

RX, RSI

OP	R_1	R_2	d

The contents of R_1 for single shifts and R_1, $R_1 + 1$ for double shifts are rotated right the number of places specified by the second operand.

SHIFT LEFT ARITHMETIC
SHIFT LEFT DOUBLE ARITHMETIC

RX, RSI

OP	R_1	R_2	d

The contents of R_1 for single shifts and $R_1 + 1$ for double shifts are shifted left the number of places specified by the second operand. The high order bit (sign bit) of the register a register pair is unaffected by the shift. Low order bits are filled with zeros. If a bit unlike the sign bit is shifted out of the position adjacent to the sign bit, the overflow flag is set.

ROTATE LEFT

RX, RSI

OP	R_1	N	d

The contents of R_1 for single shifts and R_1, $R_1 + 1$ for double shifts are rotated left, the number of places specified by the second operand.

SHIFT RIGHT LOGICAL
SHIFT RIGHT DOUBLE LOGICAL

RX, RSI

OP	R_1	R_2	d

The contents of R_1 for single shifts and $R_1 + 1$ for double shifts are shifted right the number of places specified by the second operand. High order bits shifted in are zeros, low order bits shifted out are shifted through the carry bit.

SHIFT LEFT LOGICAL
SHIFT LEFT DOUBLE LOGICAL

RX, RSI

OP	R_1	R_2	d

The contents of R_1 for single shifts and R_1, $R_1 + 1$ for double shifts are shifted left the number of positions specified by the second operand. High order bits shifted out are shifted through the carry bit. Zeros are shifted in. R_1 for double shifts must be even.

INPUT WORD

RR

OP	R_1	R_2

RX

OP	R_1	X_2	d

One 16-bit word of data is read into the first operand from the device which is addressed by the contents of the second operand.

INPUT BYTE

RR

OP	R_1	R_2

RX

OP	R_1	X_2	d

One byte of data is read into the low order 8 bits of the first operand from the device which is addressed by the contents of the second operand.

OUTPUT WORD

RR

OP	R_1	R_2

RX

OP	R_1	X_2	d

The 16 bits of R_1 is sent to the device which is addressed by the contents of the second operand.

OUTPUT BYTE

RR

OP	R_1	R_2

RX

OP	R_1	X_2	d

The low order 8 bits of R_1 is sent to the device which is addressed by the contents of the second operand.

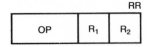

BRANCH

RS

OP		R_2

RX

OP		R_2	d

Unconditionally branch to the location specified by the second operand. The first operand is not used.

BRANCH AND LINK

BALR — RS

OP	R_1	X_2

BAL — RX

OP	R_1	X_2	d

The address of the next sequential instruction is saved in R_1, and an unconditional branch to the jump address is taken.

BRANCH ON CONDITION

RS

OP	CC	R_2

RX

OP	CC	R_2	d

Branch to the location specified by the second operand if the condition code specified in the first operand postion is equal to the current PSW status bits.

Condition codes are:

Carry	= B	(Sign=0)	
No Carry	= A	Minus	= F
Zero	= 5	(Sign=1)	
Not Zero	= 4	1's Comp>	= 9
2's Comp>	= 0	1's Comp<	= 8
2's Comp<	= 3	1's Comp>	= C
2's Comp>	= 2	1's Comp<	= D
2's Comp<	= 1	Overflow	= 7
Plus	= E	Not Overflow	= 6

BRANCH ON INDEX

BXH HIGH — RX

OP	R_1	X_2	d

BXLE LOW OR EQUAL — RX

OP	R_1	X_2	d

R_1 is incremented by the value in $R_1 + 1$, and logically compared to the index limit held in R_1+2.

INDEX HIGH

$(R_1) + (R_1 + 1) \rightarrow (R_1)$

$(R_1) : (R_1 + 2)$

IF $(R_1) > (R_1 + 2)$ THEN $d + (X_2) \rightarrow$ PSW (16:31)

IF $(R_1) \leq (R_1 + 2)$ THEN PSW (16:31) $+ 2 \rightarrow$ PSW (16:31)

INDEX LOW OR EQUAL

$(R_1) + (R_1 + 1) \rightarrow (R_1)$

$(R_1) : (R_1 + 2)$

$(R_1) \leq (R_1 + 2)$ THEN $d + (X_2) \rightarrow$ PSW (16:31)

IF $(R_1) > (R_1 + 2)$ THEN PSW (16:31) $+ 2 \rightarrow$ PSW (16:31)

APPENDIX B

```
;       **********************************
;
;        MACRO DEFINITIONS FOR MICRO/29
;
;       **********************************
;
;       DEFINITIONS FOR CPU REGISTERS
;
R0      SET 0
R1      SET 1
R2      SET 2
R3      SET 3
R4      SET 4
R5      SET 5
R6      SET 6
R7      SET 7
R8      SET 8
R9      SET 9
R10     SET 10
R11     SET 11
R12     SET 12
R13     SET 13
R14     SET 14
R15     SET 15
X0      SET 0
X1      SET 1
X2      SET 2
X3      SET 3
X4      SET 4
X5      SET 5
X6      SET 6
X7      SET 7
X8      SET 8
X9      SET 9
X10     SET 10
X11     SET 11
X12     SET 12
X13     SET 13
X14     SET 14
X15     SET 15
;
;       PRESET CONDITION CODES
;
CY?     SET 0BH         ;CARRY
NC?     SET 0AH         ;NO CARRY
Z?      SET 05H         ;ZERO
NZ?     SET 04H         ;NOT ZERO
GT?     SET 00H         ;2'S COMP GREATER THAN
LT?     SET 03H         ;2'S COMP. LESS THAN
GE?     SET 02H         ;2'S COMP. GREATER THAN OR EQUAL TO
LE?     SET 01H         ;2'S COMP. LESS THAN OR EQUAL TO
PL?     SET 0EH         ;PLUS, SIGN = 0
MI?     SET 0FH         ;MINUS, SIGN = 1
HI?     SET 09H         ;1'S COMP. HIGHER
LS?     SET 08H         ;1'S COMP. LOWER OR SAME
HS?     SET 0CH         ;1'S COMP. HIGHTER OR SAME
LO?     SET 0DH         ;1'S COMP. LOWER
OV?     SET 07H         ;OVERFLOW
NV?     SET 06H         ;NOT OVERFLOW
;
;       =================================
;
;             RR TYPE INSTRUCTIONS
;
;       =================================
;
;       LR      LOAD REGISTER                   18
;
LR      MACRO R1,R2
        DB 18H,R1*10H+R2
        ENDM
;
;       AR      ADD REGISTER                    1A
;
AR      MACRO R1,R2
        DB 1AH,R1*10H+R2
        ENDM
;
;       SR      SUBTRACT REGISTER               1B
;
SR      MACRO R1,R2
        DB 1BH,R1*10H+R2
        ENDM
;
;       NR      AND REGISTERS                   14
;
NR      MACRO R1,R2
        DB 14H,R1*10H+R2
        ENDM
;
;       ORR     OR REGISTERS                    16
;
ORR     MACRO R1,R2
        DB 16H,R1*10H+R2
        ENDM
;
;       CLR     COMPARE LOGICAL REGISTERS       15
;
CLR     MACRO R1,R2
        DB 15H,R1*10H+R2
        ENDM
;
;       XR      EXCLUSIVE OR REGISTERS          17
;
XR      MACRO R1,R2
        DB 17H,R1*10H+R2
        ENDM
;

;       =================================
;
;             RX TYPE INSTRUCTIONS
;
;       =================================
;
;       LD      LOAD MEMORY                     58
LD      MACRO R1,X2,DI
        DB 58H,R1*10H+X2,(DI) SHR 8,(DI) AND 0FFH
        ENDM
;
;       ST      STORE IN MEMORY                 50
;
ST      MACRO R1,X2,DI
        DB 50H,R1*10H+X2,(DI) SHR 8,(DI) AND 0FFH
        ENDM
;
;       ADD     ADD FROM MEMORY                 5A
;
ADD     MACRO R1,X2,DI
        DB 5AH,R1*10H+X2,(DI) SHR 8,(DI) AND 0FFH
        ENDM
;
;       SUB     SUBTRACT FROM MEMORY            5B
;
SUB     MACRO R1,X2,DI
        DB 5BH,R1*10H+X2,(DI) SHR 8,(DI) AND 0FFH
        ENDM
;
;       N       AND WITH MEMORY                 54
;
N       MACRO R1,X2,DI
        DB 54H,R1*10H+X2,(DI) SHR 8,(DI) AND 0FFH
        ENDM
;
;       O       OR WITH MEMORY                  56
;
O       MACRO R1,X2,DI
        DB 56H,R1*10H+X2,(DI) SHR 8,(DI) AND 0FFH
        ENDM
;
;       CMP     COMPARE WITH MEMORY             55
;
CMP     MACRO R1,X2,DI
        DB 55H,R1*10H+X2,(DI) SHR 8,(DI) AND 0FFH
        ENDM
;

;       ========================================
;
;             IMMEDIATE INSTRUCTIONS
;
;       ========================================
;
;       LI      LOAD IMMEDIATE                  41
;
LI      MACRO R1,I2
        DB 41H,R1*10H,(I2) SHR 8,(I2) AND 0FFH
        ENDM
;
;       NI      AND IMMEDIATE                   94
;
NI      MACRO R1,I2
        DB 94H,R1*10H,(I2) SHR 8,(I2) AND 0FFH
        ENDM
;
;       OI      OR IMMEDIATE                    96
;
OI      MACRO R1,I2
        DB 96H,R1*10H,(I2) SHR 8,(I2) AND 0FFH
        ENDM
;
;       XI      EXCLUSIVE OR IMMEDIATE          97
;
XI      MACRO R1,I2
        DB 97H,R1*10H,(I2) SHR 8,(I2) AND 0FFH
        ENDM
;
;       AI      ADD IMMEDIATE                   9A
;
AI      MACRO R1,I2
        DB 9AH,R1*10H,(I2) SHR 8,(I2) AND 0FFH
        ENDM
;
;       SI      SUBTRACT IMMEDIATE              9B
;
SI      MACRO R1,I2
        DB 9BH,R1*10H,(I2) SHR 8,(I2) AND 0FFH
        ENDM
```

```
;
;       CI      COMPARE IMMEDIATE                       95
;
CI      MACRO R1,I2
        DB 95H,R1*10H,(I2) SHR 8,(I2) AND 0FFH
        ENDM
;
;       ========================================
;
;       BRANCH AND CONITIONAL BRANCH INSTRUCTIONS
;
;       ========================================
;
;       BX      UNCONDITIONAL BRANCH                    74
;
BX      MACRO X1,DI
        DB 74H,X1*10H,(DI) SHR 8,(DI) AND 0FFH
        ENDM
;
;       BC      CONDTIONAL BRANCH                       47
;
BC      MACRO CC,X2,DI
        DB 47H,CC*10H+X2,(DI) SHR 8,(DI) AND 0FFH
        ENDM
;
;       BAL     BRANCH AND LINK                         45
;
BAL     MACRO R1,X2,DI
        DB 45H,R1*10H+X2,(DI) SHR 8,(DI) AND 0FFH
        ENDM
;
;
;       BALR    BRANCH AND LINK REGISTER                05
;
BALR    MACRO R1,R2
        DB 05H,R1*10H+R2
        ENDM
;
;       BR      BRANCH REGISTER UNCONDITONAL            04
;
BR      MACRO R1
        DB 04H,R1*10H
        ENDM
;
;       =====================================
;
;           SHIFT AND ROTATE INSTRUCTIONS
;
;       =====================================
;
;       SLA     SHIFT LEFT ARITHMETIC                   8B
;
SLA     MACRO R1,CT
        DB 8BH,R1*10H+(CT-1)
        ENDM
;
;       SRL     SHIFT RIGHT LOGICAL                     88
;
SRL     MACRO R1,CT
        DB 88H,R1*10H+(CT-1)
        ENDM
;
;       SLL     SHIFT LEFT LOGICAL                      89
;
SLL     MACRO R1,CT
        DB 89H,R1*10H+(CT-1)
        ENDM
;
;       SRA     SHIFT RIGHT ARITHMETIC                  8A
;
SRA     MACRO R1,CT
        DB 8AH,R1*10H+(CT-1)
        ENDM
;
;       RRL     ROTATE RIGHT                            A8
;
RRL     MACRO R1,CT
        DB 0A8H,R1*10H+(CT-1)
        ENDM
;
;       RLL     ROTATE LEFT                             AA
;
RLL     MACRO R1,CT
        DB 0AAH,R1*10H+(CT-1)
        ENDM
;
;       =================================
;
;               I/O INSTRUCTIONS
;
;       =================================
;
;       IN      INPUT                                   A0
;
IN      MACRO R1,X2,DI
        DB 0A0H,R1*10H+X2,(DI) SHR 8,(DI) AND 0FFH
        ENDM
;
;       OUT     OUTPUT                                  A2
;
OUT     MACRO R1,X2,DI
        DB 0A2H,R1*10H+X2,(DI) SHR 8,(DI) AND 0FFH
        ENDM
;
```

APPENDIX C

```
                $*MACRO
                ;
                ; SIMPLE MONITOR FOR THE AMD HIGH-SPEED 16-BIT COMPUTER
                ;
                ;       BY:     JIM BRICK
                ;
                ;
                        MACLIB  MICRO29
                ;
FFFA =          DATA:   EQU     0FFFAH  ;USART DATA PORT ADDRESS
FFFB =          STATUS: EQU     0FFFBH  ;USART CONTROL PORT ADDRESS
0A0D =          CRLF:   EQU     0A0DH   ;LINE-FEED, CARRIAGE RETURN
                ;
0000                    ORG     0
                ;
0000+1700       BEGIN:  XR      R0,R0           ;CLEAR R0
0002+45E00028           BAL     R14,R0,DOCRLF   ;NEW LINE ON CONSOLE
0006+45E00016   MONLP:  BAL     R14,R0,PROMPT   ;I/P PROMPT
000A+45E00040           BAL     R14,R0,GETIP    ;GET USERS I/P
000E+45E0008C           BAL     R14,R0,SCANER   ;DECODE & EXECUTE COMMAND
0012+74000006           BX      R0,MONLP        ;REPEAT LOOP FOREVER
                ;
0016+50E003EA   PROMPT: ST      R14,R0,@PROMPT  ;SAVE RET
001A+4120003E           LI      R2,'>'          ;PROMPT CHARACTER '>'
001E+45E003D8           BAL     R14,R0,CRTOUT   ;PROMPT TO CRT
0022+58E003EA           LD      R14,R0,@PROMPT  ;RESTORE RET
0026+04E0               BR      R14             ;
                ;
0028+50E003EC   DOCRLF: ST      R14,R0,@DOCRLF  ;SAVE RET
002C+41200A0D           LI      R2,CRLF         ;CR/LF CODES
0030+45E003D8           BAL     R14,R0,CRTOUT   ;O/P LF
0034+8827               SRL     R2,8            ;GET CR CODE
0036+45E003D6           BAL     R14,R0,CRTOUT   ;O/P CR
003A+58E003EC           LD      R14,R0,@DOCRLF  ;RESTORE RET
003E+04E0               BR      R14             ;
                ;
0040+50E003EE   GETIP:  ST      R14,R0,@GETIP   ;SAVE RET
0044+4130040E           LI      R3,BUFFER       ;A(I/P BUFFER)
0048+41400080           LI      R4,0080H        ;MAX I/P COUNT
004C+45E00398   IPLP:   BAL     R14,R0,GETCHR   ;GET NEXT I/P CHARACTER
0050+8917               SLL     R1,8            ;POSITION I/P CHAR TO HI BYTE
0052+1851               LR      R5,R1           ;SAVE HI BYTE
0054+16FF               ORR     R15,R15         ;TEST RET CODE
0056+47500082           BC      Z?,R0,DOEOF     ;TO EOF IF RC = ZERO
005A+45E00398           BAL     R14,R0,GETCHR   ;NEXT CHARACTER
005E+941000FF           NI      R1,00FFH        ;SAVE ONLY I/P CHARACTER IN LC
0062+1651               ORR     R5,R1           ;COMBINE TWO BYTES FOR ONE WORD
0064+16FF               ORR     R15,R15         ;TEST RET CODE
0066+47500082           BC      Z?,R0,DOEOF     ;TO EOF IF RC = ZERO
006A+50530000           ST      R5,R3,0         ;DATA TO I/P BUFFER
006E+9A300002           AI      R3,0002         ;TO NEXT BUFER SLOT
0072+9B400002           SI      R4,0002         ;COUNT-2
0076+4750007E           BC      Z?,R0,DOEOF2    ;STOP IF MAX I/P
007A+7400004C           BX      R0,IPLP         ;CONTINUE GETTING I/P
007E+41500D00   DOEOF2: LI      R5,0D00H        ;EOF AFTER MAX LINE
0082+50530000   DOEOF:  ST      R5,R3,0         ;DATA/EOF TO BUFFER
0086+58E003EE           LD      R14,R0,@GETIP   ;RESTORE RET
008A+04E0               BR      R14             ;
                ;
008C+50E003F0   SCANER: ST      R14,R0,@SCANER  ;SAVE RET
0090+4140040E           LI      R4,BUFFER       ;A(I/P BUFFER)
0094+58540000           LD      R5,R4,0         ;GET COMMAND (FIXED FORMAT)
0098+55500408           CMP     R5,R0,DMPCMD    ; D  FOR DUMP?
009C+475000C2           BC      Z?,R0,DUMP      ;GO IF TRUE
00A0+5550040A           CMP     R5,R0,STRCMD    ; S  FOR STORE?
00A4+475001B0           BC      Z?,R0,STORE     ;GO STORE IF TRUE
00A8+5550040C           CMP     R5,R0,JMPCMD    ; J  FOR JUMP?
00AC+475002F2           BC      Z?,R0,JUMP      ;GO JUMP IF TRUE
00B0+45E00028           BAL     R14,R0,DOCRLF   ;NEW LINE ON CRT
00B4+4120003F           LI      R2,'?'  ; ?
00B8+45E003D8           BAL     R14,R0,CRTOUT   ;UNKNOWN COMMAND
00BC+58E003F0           LD      R14,R0,@SCANER  ;RESTORE RET
                        BR      R14             ;
00C0+04E0
                ;
00C2+41400410   DUMP:   LI      R4,BUFOP1       ;A(ADDRESS PORTION OF BUFFER)
00C6+45E00304           BAL     R14,R0,CVADDR   ;ASCII ADDRESS TO BINARY IN R6
00CA+9460FFF0           NI      R6,0FFF0H       ;BEGIN ON EVEN WORD BOUNDRY
00CE+41C00010           LI      R12,16          ;O/P LINE COUNT
00D2+50600404   DMPLP:  ST      R6,R0,DMPAD     ;SAVE CURRENT O/P ADDRESS
00D6+45E00110           BAL     R14,R0,TYPAD    ;TYPE CURRENT CONTENTS OF R6
00DA+41200020           LI      R2,' '  ;SPACE
00DE+45E003D8           BAL     R14,R0,CRTOUT   ;TO CRT
00E2+45E003D8           BAL     R14,R0,CRTOUT   ;2 SPACES
00E6+45E00126           BAL     R14,R0,DMPOUT   ;PUT OUT ONE LINE OF DUMP DATA
00EA+41200020           LI      R2,' '  ;SPACE
00EE+45E003D8           BAL     R14,R0,CRTOUT   ;TO CRT
00F2+45E0015C           BAL     R14,R0,TYPLIT   ;O/P LITERAL DATA
00F6+45E00028           BAL     R14,R0,DOCRLF   ;NEW LINE ON CRT
00FA+58600404           LD      R6,R0,DMPAD     ;CURRENT DUMPOUT ADDRESS
00FE+9A600010           AI      R6,16           ;ADDRESS NEXT LINE
0102+9BC00001           SI      R12,1           ;LINE COUNT -1
0106+474000D2           BC      NZ?,R0,DMPLP    ;LOOP THRU O/P DATA
010A+58E003F0           LD      R14,R0,@SCANER  ;RESTORE RET
010E+04E0               BR      R14             ;
                ;
0110+50E003F2   TYPAD:  ST      R14,R0,@TYPAD   ;SAVE RET
0114+A867               RRL     R6,8            ;HI ADDRESS BYTE
0116+45E0035E           BAL     R14,R0,BINOUT   ;O/P
011A+8867               SRL     R6,8            ;LO ADDRESS BYTE
011C+45E0035E           BAL     R14,R0,BINOUT   ;O/P
0120+58E003F2           LD      R14,R0,@TYPAD   ;RSTORE RET
0124+04E0               BR      R14             ;
                ;
0126+50E003F4   DMPOUT: ST      R14,R0,@DMPOUT  ;SAVE RET
012A+58700404           LD      R7,R0,DMPAD     ;GET O/P DATA ADDRESS
012E+41D00008           LI      R13,8           ;O/P WORD COUNT
0132+58670000   DMPLPP: LD      R6,R7,0         ;GET NEXT WORD
0136+A867               RRL     R6,8            ;HI BYTE FIRST
0138+45E0035E           BAL     R14,R0,BINOUT   ;O/P
013C+8867               SRL     R6,8            ;LO BYTE
013E+45E0035E           BAL     R14,R0,BINOUT   ;O/P
0142+41200020           LI      R2,' '  ;SPACE
0146+45E003D8           BAL     R14,R0,CRTOUT   ;TO CRT
014A+9A700002           AI      R7,0002         ;BUMP I/P DATA ADDRESS
014E+9BD00001           SI      R13,0001        ;WORD COUNT -1
0152+47400132           BC      NZ?,R0,DMPLPP   ;LOOP THRU LINE
0156+58E003F4           LD      R14,R0,@DMPOUT  ;RESTORE RET
015A+04E0               BR      R14             ;
                ;
015C+50E003F6   TYPLIT: ST      R14,R0,@TYPLIT  ;SAVE RET
0160+56700404           LD      R7,R0,DMPAD     ;GET O/P DATA ADDRESS
0164+41D00006           LI      R13,8           ;WORD COUNT
0168+58670000   TYPLLP: LD      R6,R7,0         ;NEXT O/P WORD
016C+A867               RRL     R6,8            ;HI BYTE FIRST
016E+1826               LR      R2,R6           ;TO O/P REG
0170+45E00196           BAL     R14,R0,DOCIT    ;CHECK FOR PRINTABLE CHARACTER
0174+45E003D8           BAL     R14,R0,CRTOUT   ;TO CRT
0176+8867               SRL     R6,8            ;GET LO BYTE
017A+1826               LR      R2,R6           ;TO O/P REG
017C+45E00196           BAL     R14,R0,DOCIT    ;CHECK FOR PRINTABLE CHARACTER
0180+45E003D8           BAL     R14,R0,CRTOUT   ;TO CRT
0184+9A700002           AI      R7,0002         ;TO NEXT WORD
0188+9BD00001           SI      R13,1           ;WORD COUNT -1
018C+47400166           BC      NZ?,R0,TYPLLP   ;LOOP THRU O/P LINE
0190+58E003F6           LD      R14,R0,@TYPLIT  ;RESTORE RET
0194+04E0               BR      R14             ;
                ;
0196+942000FF   DOCIT:  NI      R2,00FFH        ;GET LOW BYTE
                        CI      R2,' '          ;BELOW BLANK?
```

```
019A+95200020
                BC      LT?,R0,SETPER   ;SET PERIOD IF TRUE
019E+473001AA
                CI      R2,007FH        ;BELOW DEL?
01A2+9520007F
                BC      LT?,R14,0       ;RET IF TRUE (CHAR PRINTABLE)
01A6+473E0000
        SETPER: LI      R2,'.'          ;SET PERIOD AS CHARACTER TO PRI
01AA+4120002E
                BR      R14             ;
01AE+04E0
        ;
        STORE:  LI      R4,BUFOP1       ;A(ADDRESS FIELD)
01B0+41400410
                BAL     R14,R0,CVADDR   ;ASCII ADDRESS TO BINARY (IN R6
01B4+45E00304
                LD      R4,R0,DATAD     ;GET CURRENT I/P DATA ADDRESS
01B6+58400406
                XR      R13,R13         ;CLEAR NIBBLE COUNT REG
01BC+17DD
        STLP:   BAL     R14,R0,UPSTOR   ;UPPER BYTE FIRST
01BE+45E001E6
                LD      R14,R0,@SCANER  ;GET RET
01C2+58E003F0
                CI      R5,000DH        ;END? (CR = END)
01C6+9550000D
                BC      Z?,R14,0        ;RET IF TRUE
01CA+475E0000
                BAL     R14,R0,LOSTOR   ;LOWER BYTE
01CE+45E001FA
                LD      R14,R0,@SCANER  ;GET RET
01D2+58E003F0
                CI      R5,000DH        ;END?
01D6+9550000D
                BC      Z?,R14,0        ;RET IF TRUE
01DA+475E0000
                AI      R4,0002         ;TO NEXT WORD
01DE+9A400002
                BX      R0,STLP         ;CONTINUE STORING DATA
01E2+740001BE
        ;
        UPSTOR: ST      R14,R0,@UPSTOR  ;SAVE RET
01E6+50E003FA
                LD      R5,R4,0         ;GET NEXT DATA
01EA+58540000
                SRL     R5,8            ;GET HI BYTE
01EE+8857
                BAL     R14,R0,STDATA   ;GO STORE BYTE
01F0+45E00210
                LD      R14,R0,@UPSTOR  ;RESTORE RET
01F4+58E003FA
                BR      R14             ;
01F8+04E0
        ;
        LOSTOR: ST      R14,R0,@UPSTOR  ;SAVE RET
01FA+50E003FA
                LD      R5,R4,0         ;GET DATA
01FE+58540000
                NI      R5,00FFH        ;KEEP LOW BYTE
0202+945000FF
                BAL     R14,R0,STDATA   ;GO STORE BYTE
0206+45E00210
                LD      R14,R0,@UPSTOR  ;RESTORE RET
020A+56E003FA
                BR      R14             ;
020E+04E0
        ;
        STDATA: ST      R14,R0,@STDATA  ;SAVE RET
0210+50E003FC
                BAL     R14,R0,CKDEL    ;CHECK FOR DELIMITER
0214+45E0023C
                LD      R14,R0,@STDATA  ;GET RET
0218+58E003FC
                BC      Z?,R14,0        ;RET IF RC = 0
021C+475E0000
                BAL     R14,R0,ASCHEX   ;ASCII BYTE TO HEX NIBBLE
0220+45E0025A
                BC      LT?,R0,SETND    ;.NZ. RC = END
0224+47300232
                BAL     R14,R0,NIBBLE   ;STORE THIS NIBBLE
0228+45E00290
                LD      R14,R0,@STDATA  ;RESTORE RET
022C+58E003FC
                BR      R14             ;
0230+04E0
        SETND:  LI      R5,000DH        ;FAKE EOF
0232+4150000D
                LD      R14,R0,@STDATA  ;RESTORE RET
0236+58E003FC
                BR      R14             ;
023A+04E0
        ;
        CKDEL:  CI      R5,' '          ;SPACE?
023C+95500020
                BC      Z?,R14,0        ;RET IF TRUE
0240+475E0000
                CI      R5,'.'          ;PERIOD?
0244+9550002E
                BC      Z?,R14,0        ;RET IF TRUE
0248+475E0000
                CI      R5,','          ;COMMA?
024C+9550002C
                BC      Z?,R14,0        ;RET IF TRUE
0250+475E0000
                CI      R5,000DH        ;CARRIAGE RET?
0254+9550000D
                BR      R14             ;LET CALLER DECIDE
0258+04E0
        ;
        ASCHEX: NI      R5,00FFH        ;LOW BYTE ONLY
025A+945000FF
                CI      R5,'0'          ;LOWER THAN '0' ?
025E+95500030
                BC      LT?,R14,0       ;RET IF TRUE
0262+473E0000
                CI      R5,':'          ;0-9 ?
0266+9550003A
                BC      LT?,R0,VNUM     ;NUMERICAL IF TRUE
026A+47300268
                CI      R5,'A'          ;LOWER THAN 'A' ?
026E+95500041
                BC      LT?,R14,0       ;RET IF TRUE
0272+473E0000
                CI      R5,0047H        ;HEX ALPHA?
0276+95500047
                BC      LT?,R0,VALPH    ;HEX ALPHA IF TRUE
027A+47300284
                CI      R5,0FFFFH       ;SET .LT. CC
027E+9550FFFF
                BR      R14             ;
0282+04E0
        VALPH:  SI      R5,0007H        ;ASCII ADJUST
0284+9B500007
        VNUM:   NI      R5,000FH        ;LOW NIBBLE ONLY
0288+9450000F
                CLR     R5,R5           ;RC = ZERO
028C+1555
                BR      R14             ;
028E+04E0
        ;
        NIBBLE: LD      R7,R6,0         ;GET OLD DATA
0290+58760000
                ORR     R13,R13         ;R13 = ZERO ?
0294+16DD
                BC      NZ?,R0,NXNIB1   ;TEST FOR ONE IF NOT TRUE
0296+474002AC
                AI      R13,0001        ;BUMP NIBBLE COUNTER
029A+9AD00001
                SLL     R5,12           ;POSITION THIS NIBBLE
029E+895B
                NI      R7,0FFFH        ;PREPARE OLD DATA FOR NEW NIBBL
02A0+94700FFF
                ORR     R7,R5           ;INSERT NEW NIBBLE
02A4+1675
                ST      R7,R6,0         ;DATA BACK TO MEMORY
02A6+50760000
                BR      R14             ;
02AA+04E0
        ;
        NXNIB1: CI      R13,0001        ;NEXT NIBBLE?
02AC+95D00001
                BC      NZ?,R0,NXNIB2   ;TO NEXT IF NOT THIS
02B0+474002C6
                AI      R13,0001        ;BUMP NIBBLE COUNTER
02B4+9AD00001
                SLL     R5,8            ;POSITION THIS NIBBLE
02B8+6957
                NI      R7,0F0FFH       ;PREPARE OLD DATA FOR NEW NIBBL
02BA+9470F0FF
                ORR     R7,R5           ;INSERT NEW NIBBLE
02BE+1675
                ST      R7,R6,0         ;DATA BACK TO MEMORY
02C0+50760000
                BR      14              ;
02C4+04E0
        ;
        NXNIB2: CI      R13,0002        ;NEXT NIBBLE?
02C6+95D00002
                BC      NZ?,R0,NXNIB3   ;TO NEXT IF NOT THIS
02CA+474002E0
                AI      R13,0001        ;BUMP NIBBLE COUNT
02CE+9AD00001
                SLL     R5,4            ;POSITION THIS NIBBLE
02D2+8953
                NI      R7,0FF0FH       ;PREPARE OLD DATA FOR NEW NIBBL
02D4+9470FF0F
                ORR     R7,R5           ;INSERT NEW NIBBLE
02D8+1675
                ST      R7,R6,0         ;DATA BACK TO MEMORY
02DA+50760000
                BR      R14             ;
02DE+04E0
        ;
        NXNIB3: XR      R13,R13         ;LAST NIBBLE (LSN)
02E0+17DD
                NI      R7,0FFF0H       ;PREPARE OLD DATA FOR NEW NIBBL
02E2+9470FFF0
                ORR     R7,R5           ;INSERT NEW NIBBLE
02E6+1675
                ST      R7,R6,0         ;DATA BACK TO MEMORY
02E8+50760000
                AI      R6,0002         ;BUMP MEM POINTER
02EC+9A600002
                BR      R14             ;
02F0+04E0
        ;
        JUMP:   LI      R4,BUFOP1       ;A(ADDRESS)
02F2+41400410
                BAL     R14,R0,CVADDR   ;ASCII ADDRESS TO BINARY ADDRES
02F6+45E00304
                LR      R15,R6          ;ADDRESS TO R15
02FA+18F6
                BAL     R14,R15,0       ;JUMP...
02FC+45EF0000
                BX      R0,BEGIN        ;BACK TO MONITOR IF CALLEE RETU
0300+74000000
        ;
        CVADDR: ST      R14,R0,@CVADDR  ;SAVE RET
0304+50E00402
                XR      R6,R6           ;CLEAR R6
0308+1766
                LD      R5,R4,0         ;GET TWO ADDRESS BYTES
030A+58540000
                SRL     R5,8            ;UPPER BYTE FIRST
030E+8857
                BAL     R14,R0,ASCHEX   ;ASCII BYTE TO HEX NIBBLE
0310+45E0025A
                BC      NZ?,R0,CVHOUT   ;STOP IF NOT HEX DATA
0314+47400350
                ORR     R6,R5           ;FIRST ADDRESS NIBBLE TO R6
0318+1665
                LD      R5,R4,0         ;GET ADDRESS BYTES AGAIN
031A+58540000
                BAL     R14,R0,ASCHEX   ;ASCII BYTE TO HEX NIBBLE
031E+45E0025A
                BC      NZ?,R0,CVHOUT   ;STOP IF NOT HEX DATA
0322+47400350
                SLL     R6,4            ;POSITION ADDRESS FOR NEXT NIBB
0326+8963
                ORR     R6,R5           ;INSERT NEXT ADDRESS NIBBLE
0328+1665
                AI      R4,0002         ;BUMP MEMORY PTR TO NEXT WORD
032A+9A400002
                LD      R5,R4,0         ;NEXT ASCII ADDRESS DATA
032E+58540000
                SRL     R5,8            ;HIGH BYTE FIRST
0332+8857
                BAL     R14,R0,ASCHEX   ;ASCII BYTE TO HEX NIBBLE
0334+45E0025A
                BC      NZ?,R0,CVHOT1   ;STOP IF NOT HEX DATA
0338+47400354
                SLL     R6,4            ;POSITION ADDRESS FOR NEXT NIBB
033C+8963
                ORR     R6,R5           ;INSERT NEXT NIBBLE
033E+1665
                LD      R5,R4,0         ;GET ADDRESS DATA AGAIN
0340+58540000
                BAL     R14,R0,ASCHEX   ;ASCII BYTE TO HEX NIBBLE
0344+45E0025A
                BC      NZ?,R0,CVHOUT   ;STOP IF NOT HEX DATA
0348+47400350
                SLL     R6,4            ;POSITION ADDRESS FOR NEXT NIBB
034C+8963
                ORR     R6,R5           ;INSERT NEXT NIBBLE
```

```
034E+1665
          CVHOUT: AI      R4,0002         ;TO NEXT MEMORY WORD
0350+9A400002
          CVHOT1: ST      R4,R0,DATAD     ;SAVE AS DATA ADDRESS
0354+50400406
                  LD      R14,R0,@CVADDR  ;RESTORE RET
0358+58E00402
                  BR      R14             ;
035C+04E0
          ;
          BINOUT: ST      R14,R0,@BINOUT  ;SAVE RET
035E+50E003FE
                  LR      R2,R6           ;O/P BYTE TO R2
0362+1826
                  SRL     R2,4            ;UPPER NIBBLE FIRST
0364+8823
                  NI      R2,000FH        ;KEEP ONLY GOOD DATA
0366+9420000F
                  BAL     R14,R0,HEXEX    ;BINARY NIBBLE TO ASCII BYTE
036A+45E00386
                  BAL     R14,R0,CRTOUT   ;NIBBLE (BYTE) OUT TO CRT
036E+45E003D8
                  LR      R2,R6           ;O/P DATA TO R2
0372+1826
                  NI      R2,000FH        ;KEEP ONLY LOW NIBBLE
0374+9420000F
                  BAL     R14,R0,HEXEX    ;BINARY NIBBLE TO ASCII BYTE
0378+45E00386
                  BAL     R14,R0,CRTOUT   ;AND OUT TO CRT
037C+45E003D8
                  LD      R14,R0,@BINOUT  ;RESTORE RET
0380+58E003FE
                  BR      R14             ;
0384+04E0
          ;
          HEXEX:  CI      R2,000AH        ;A-F ?
0386+9520000A
                  BC      MI?,R0,CON      ;BR IF NOT TRUE
038A+47F00392
                  AI      R2,0007H        ;ADJUST FOR A-F
038E+9A200007
          CON:    AI      R2,0030H        ;MAKE ASCII
0392+9A200030
                  BR      R14             ;
0396+04E0
          ;
          GETCHR: ST      R14,R0,@GETCHR  ;SAVE RET
0398+50E00400
          RDCHR:  IN      R1,R0,STATUS    ;STRIP PARITY
039C+A010FFFB
                  NI      R1,0002         ;I/P READY?
03A0+94100002
                  BC      Z?,R0,RDCHR     ;LOOP UNTIL CHARACTER READY
03A4+4750039C
                  IN      R1,R0,DATA      ;READ DATA
03A8+A010FFFA
                  NI      R1,007FH        ;KEEP ONLY DATA BYTE
03AC+9410007F
                  LR      R2,R1           ;DATA TO R2
03B0+1821
                  BAL     R14,R0,CRTOUT   ;ECHO I/P
03B2+45E003D8
                  LR      R1,R2           ;DATA BACK TO R1
03B6+1812
                  LD      R14,R0,@GETCHR  ;GET RET
03B8+58E00400
                  LI      R15,-1          ;SET R15 .NZ.
03BC+41F0FFFF
                  LI      R2,000AH        ;LF CODE IN CASE OF CR
03C0+4120000A
                  CI      R1,000DH        ;DATA = CR ?
03C4+9510000D
                  BC      NZ?,R14,0       ;RET IF NO
03C8+474E0000
                  BAL     R14,R0,CRTOUT   ;DO LF IF PREVOIUS WAS CR
03CC+45E003D8
                  XR      R15,R15         ;SET RC = ZERO FOR CR
03D0+17FF
                  LD      R14,R0,@GETCHR  ;RESTORE RETURN
03D2+58E00400
                  BR      R14             ;
03D6+04E0
          ;
          CRTOUT: IN      R1,R0,STATUS    ;GET STATUS BYTE
03D8+A010FFFB
                  NI      R1,0001         ;XMITTER EMPTY?
03DC+94100001
                  BC      Z?,R0,CRTOUT    ;WAIT FOR XMITTER TO EMPTY
03E0+475003D8
                  OUT     R2,R0,DATA      ;O/P DATA TO CRT
03E4+A220FFFA
                  BR      R14             ;
03E8+04E0
          ;
          ;
          ;
03EA      @PROMPT DS      2
03EC      @DOCRLF DS      2
03EE      @GETIP  DS      2
03F0      @SCANER DS      2
03F2      @TYPAD  DS      2
03F4      @DMPOUT DS      2
03F6      @TYPLIT DS      2
03F8      @STORE  DS      2
03FA      @UPSTOR DS      2
03FC      @STDATA DS      2
03FE      @BINOUT DS      2
0400      @GETCHR DS      2
0402      @CVADDR DS      2
          ;
0404      DMPAD:  DS      2
0406      DATAD:  DS      2
          ;
0408 4420 DMPCMD: DB      'D '
040A 5320 STRCMD: DB      'S '
040C 4A20 JMPCMD: DB      'J '
          ;
          ;
040E      BUFFER: DS      2
0410      BUFOP1: DS      128
          ;
          ;
          ;
0490              END

025A ASCHEX   0000 BEGIN    035E BINOUT   040E BUFFER   0410 BUFOP1
023C CKDEL    0392 CON      0A0D CRLF     03D8 CRTOUT   0304 CVADDR
0354 CVHOT1   0350 CVHOUT   FFFA DATA     0406 DATAD    0404 DMPAD
0408 DMPCMD   00D2 DMPLP    0132 DMPLPP   0126 DMPOUT   0196 DOCIT
0028 DOCRLF   0082 DOEOF    007E DOEOF2   00C2 DUMP     0398 GETCHR
0040 GETIP    0386 HEXEX    004C IPLP     040C JMPCMD   02F2 JUMP
01FA LOSTOR   0006 MONLP    0290 NIBBLE   02AC NXNIB1   02C6 NXNIB2
02E0 NXNIB3   0016 PROMPT   039C RDCHR    008C SCANER   0232 SETND
01AA SETPER   FFFB STATUS   0210 STDATA   01BE STLP     01B0 STORE
040A STRCMD   0110 TYPAD    015C TYPLIT   0168 TYPLLP   01E6 UPSTOR
0284 VALPH    0288 VNUM     03FE @BINOUT  0402 @CVADDR  03F4 @DMPOUT
03EC @DOCRLF  0400 @GETCHR  03EE @GETIP   03EA @PROMPT  03F0 @SCANER
03FC @STDATA  03F8 @STORE   03F2 @TYPAD   03F6 @TYPLIT  03FA @UPSTOR
```

APPENDIX D

The System 29 operating system manages two floppy disk drives, A and B. The system will prompt with a A> or B> depending upon which disk the operator selects as the default. Generally, most system programs (editors, debuggers, compilers, etc.) are on the A disk and most user generated programs (source programs, user libraries, special assemblers, etc.) are on the B disk. In the following session, lower case letters are what the user typed-in, upper case letters are what System 29 responded, and comments (added as a tutorial) are in curly brackets.

A>ed b: amd16bit.asm	{call the editor to edit AMD16BIT.ASM from the B disk}
*	{any program additions, changes, and/or deletions go here}
*e	{exit the editor and save the new AMD16BIT.ASM on the B disk}
A>b:	{switch to the B disk as default}
B>mac29 amd16bit $ab hb pb sb	{use the modified macro assembler (MAC29) to assemble AMD16BIT.ASM and put the HEX, PRINT and SYMBOL files back on to the B disk}
ASM29 VER. 1.0	
0490	
03BH USE FACTOR	
END OF ASSEMBLY	
B>a:	{switch back to the A disk}
A>ddt29 h e	{run DDT29, Halt the 16-bit computer's clock and Exit DDT29}
A>set pa 3d	{set the page register bit to enable the 16-bit computer main memory as 9080 upper 32k}
A>ddt	{load 9080 DDT}
DDT VERS 1.4	
#ib:amd16bit.hex	{reference the simple monitor's HEX file on the B disk}
#r8000	{read AMD16BIT.HEX into 9080 memory beginning at location 8000 HEX (upper 32k)}
NEXT PC END	
840E 0100 577F	
#↑C	{exit DDT via control-C}
A>lbpm m29 wcs cl ul dc 1	{load the 16-bit computer's microcode (phase-1 instruction set)}
LOADING: M29.OBJ	
TITLE: MICROPROGRAM FOR 16-BIT COMPUTER	
VERIFYING: M29.OBJ	
TITLE: MICROPROGRAM FOR 16-BIT COMPUTER	
VERIFY COMPLETE	
A>ddt29 ir 0 j r	{run DDT29, set the instruction address register to zero (IR 0), jam the address on to the microprogram address bus (J), and run the 16-bit computer's clock (R)}

At this point, the AMD 16-bit high speed computer is running phase 1 instruction set in microcode and the simple monitor in target machine language in 16-bit main memory. A CRT terminal set to 9600 baud and connected to console USART can now exercise the simple monitor.

APPENDIX E

Memory Board

The 16-Bit Computer Main Memory board was organized with 8k by 16-bit RAM section and a 2k by 16-bit ROM section. The RAM section occupies address 0-8k while the ROMs are assigned addresses 8k through 10k. The memory word consists of two bytes. The least significant address line specified whether high or low byte but is not used in the word mode. The address value from the computer is captured in a register at the beginning of the cycle; however, the most significant address lines are routed straight from the bus to the clock decode logic to make an early decision as to whether the memory board has been selected.

In the word mode, the read and write transfers are straight forward. For the byte read mode, data is output on bus bits BD_{0-7} while BD_{8-15} are forced to zero. During byte write mode bus bits BD_{0-7} are duplicated internally on lines D_{0-7} and lines D_{8-15}. The signals WRHIGH or WRLOW select which byte in the RAM memory is effected.

The control logic generates the bus control line sequencing required by the 16-Bit Computer. The memory read and write timing is shown in Figures E1 and E2. The bus controller function is simulated for the purposes of the prototype. Bus Request is clocked into a flip-flop and Bus Acknowledge is returned to the computer. The Memory Request signal from the computer initiates a memory cycle. Fifty nanoseconds later the memory board responds with Address Accept. The computer then follows this with Data Request. The memory board responds with Data Sync and 50 nanoseconds later the data read out of the memory is clocked into the output registers and output on the data bus. Looking at the memory read timing diagram, it is seen that a read cycle is initiated with Memory Request but the data is not sent back to the computer until the beginning of the next microcycle.

The write cycle is extended one oscillator cycle. This is necessary with the Am9124 RAMs because the data are not sent to the memory board until Data Request goes active (see Figure E2), which is 100 nanoseconds into the write cycle. With the clocked handshaked memory protocol of the 16-Bit Computer, this is easily done by delaying Data Sync one oscillator cycle. Since normally a computer performs many more read than writes, this impacts throughput only slightly.

Additional logic was appended to allow the memory to be accessed by the System 29 microprogramming development system. The Map Page (MAPP) of System 29 was used to specify the memory. The logic interfaces the control signals required by System 29 and the 16-Bit Computer Memory board. With this logic, the System 29 user can readily read or write into the memory.

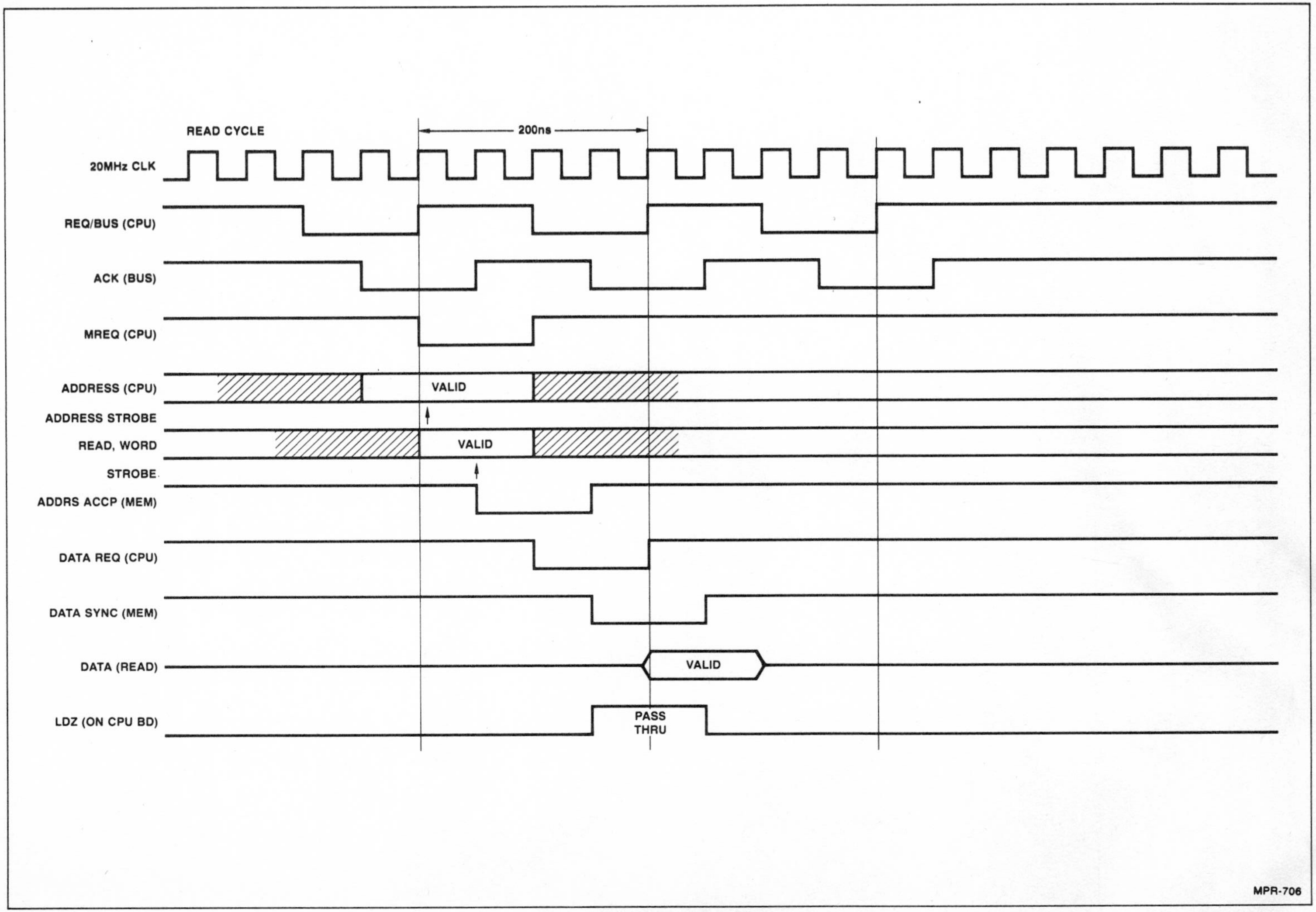

Figure E1. Memory Read Timing.

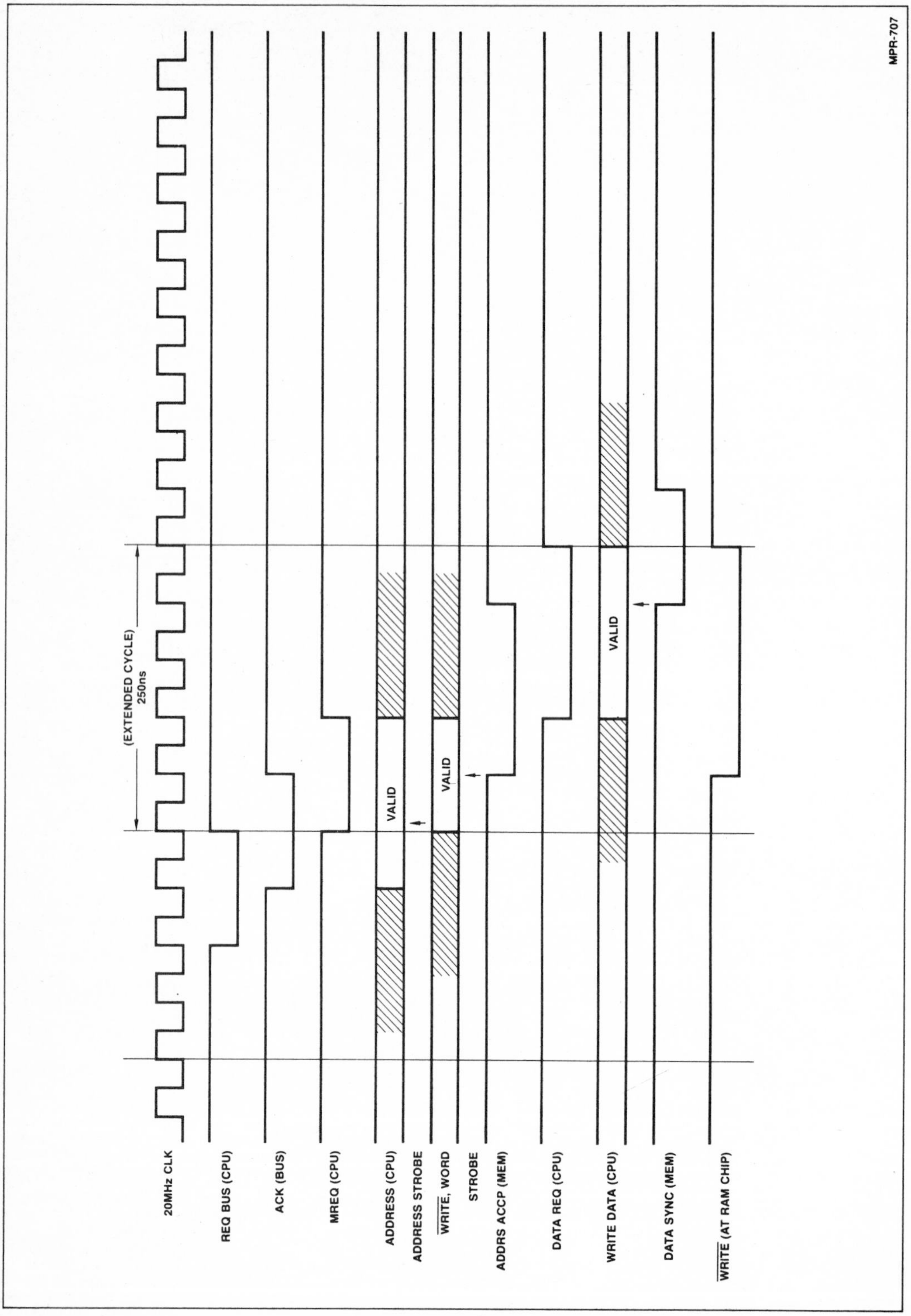

Figure E2. Memory Write Timing.

Block Diagram 16-Bit Computer.

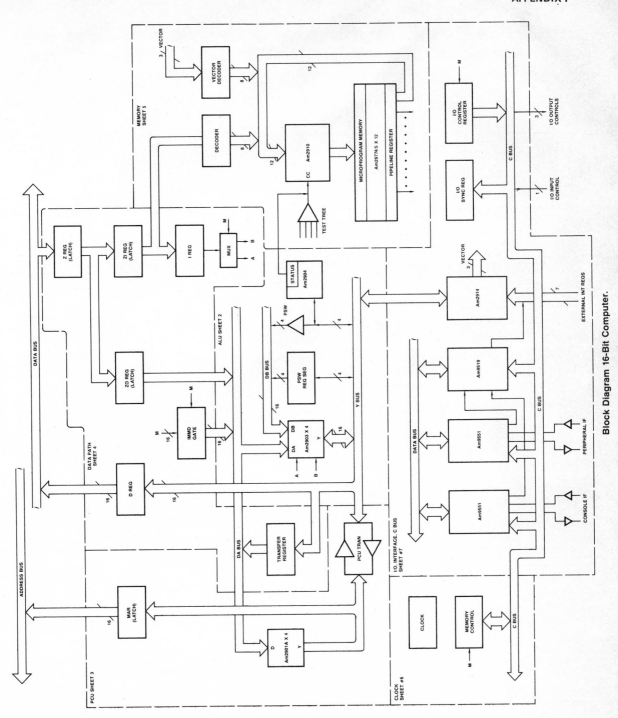

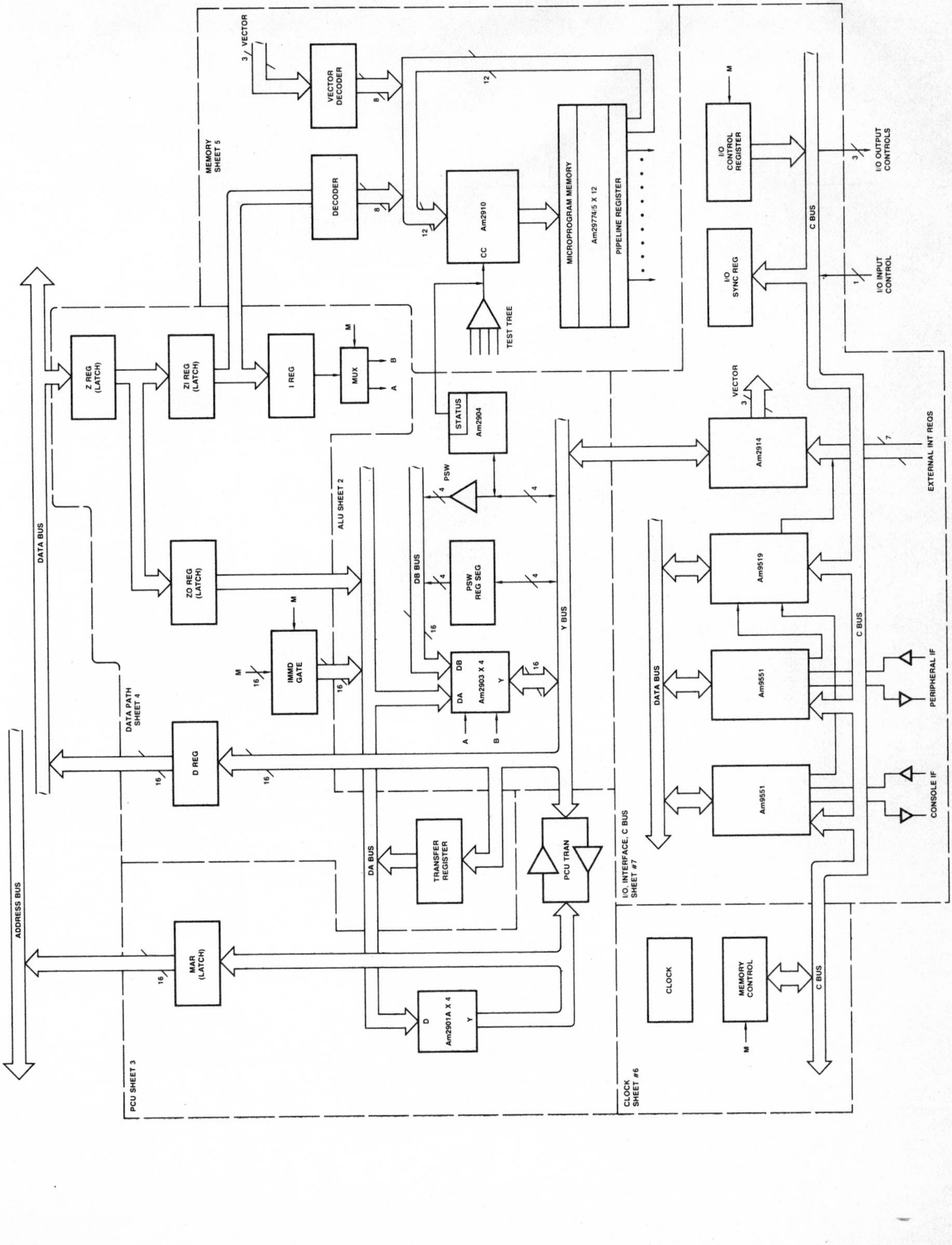

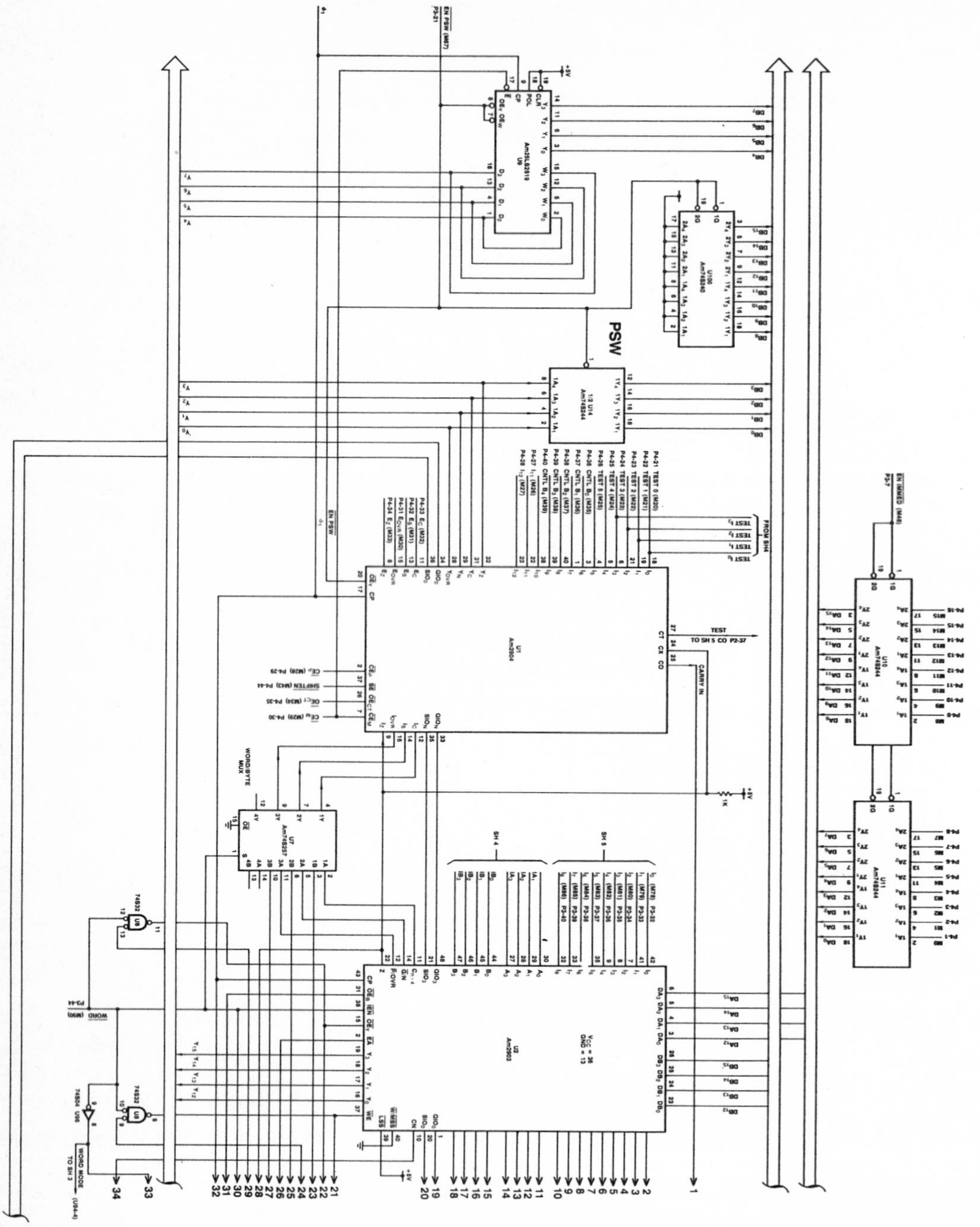

16-Bit Computer ALU.

PSW DEFINITION

INTERRUPT MASK – Am2914	RESERVED	STATUS Am2904	PC
8	4	4	16

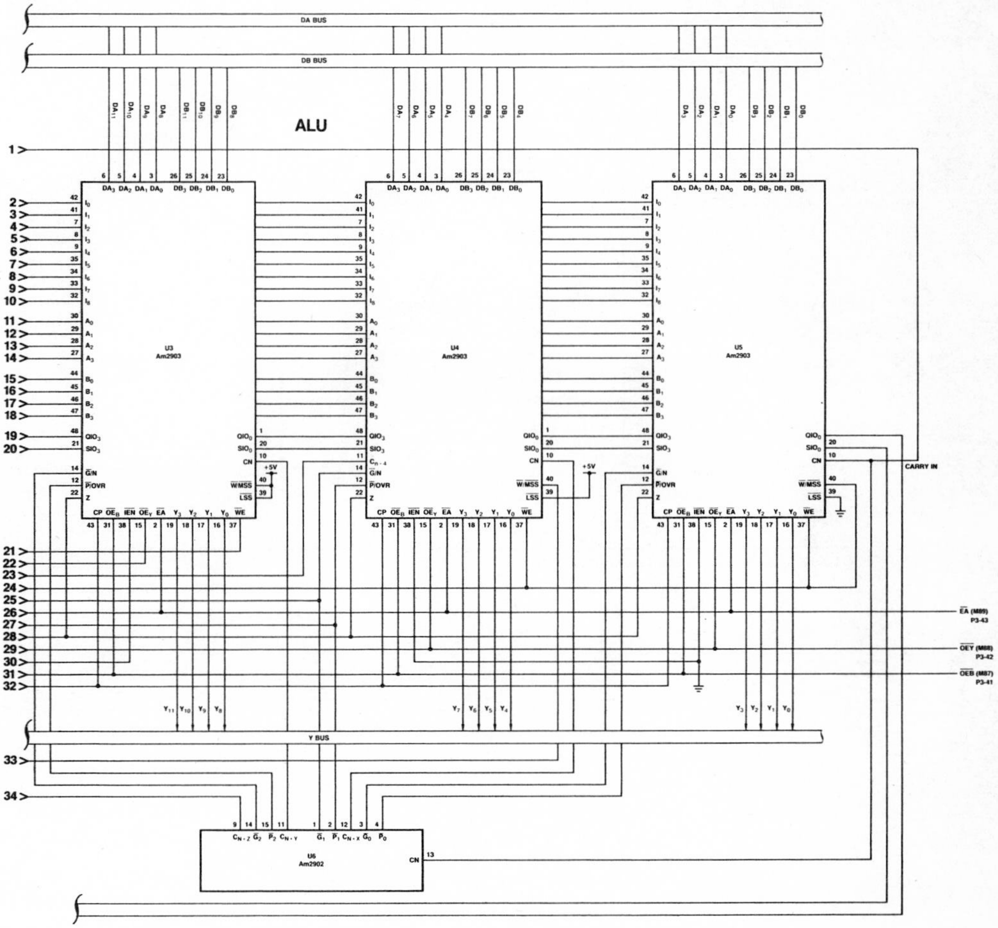

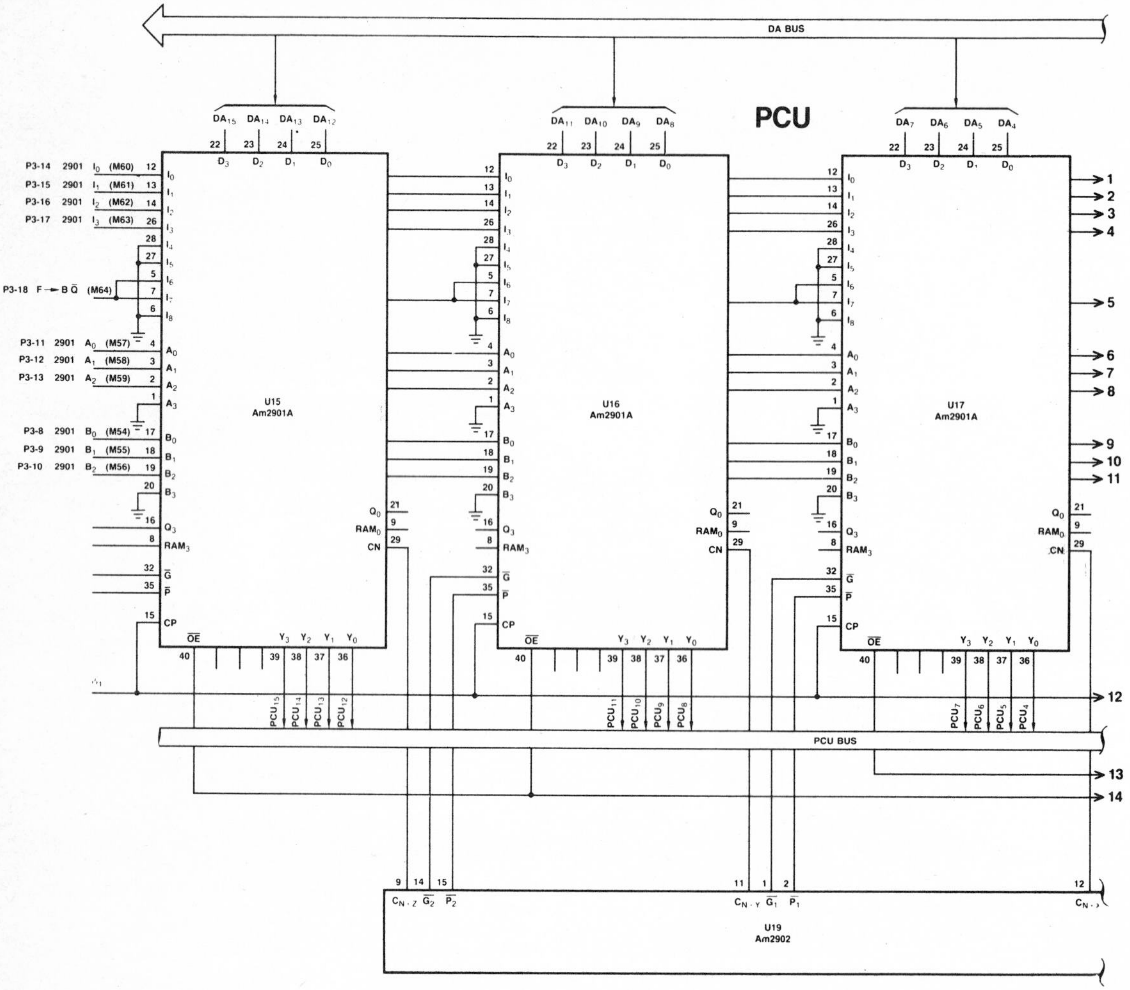

16-Bit Computer PCU Memory Address Register.

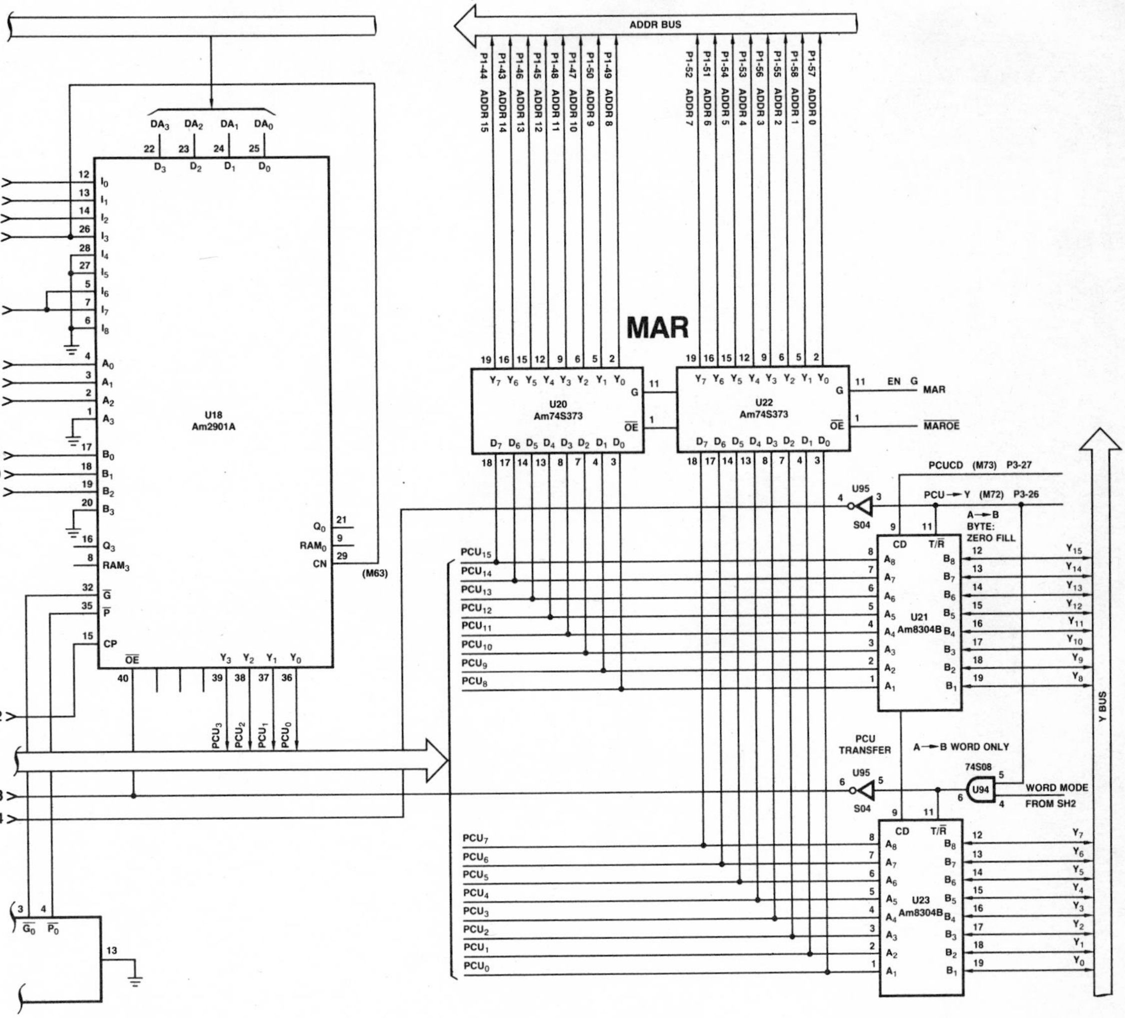
ADDR BUS
P1-44 ADDR 15
P1-43 ADDR 14
P1-46 ADDR 13
P1-45 ADDR 12
P1-48 ADDR 11
P1-47 ADDR 10
P1-50 ADDR 9
P1-49 ADDR 8
P1-52 ADDR 7
P1-51 ADDR 6
P1-54 ADDR 5
P1-53 ADDR 4
P1-56 ADDR 3
P1-55 ADDR 2
P1-58 ADDR 1
P1-57 ADDR 0
MAR
U20 Am74S373
U22 Am74S373
EN G MAR
MAROE
U18 Am2901A
(M63)
PCUCD (M73) P3-27
PCU→Y (M72) P3-26
U95 S04
A→B BYTE: ZERO FILL
U21 Am8304B
PCU TRANSFER
A→B WORD ONLY
74S08
U94
WORD MODE FROM SH2
U23 Am8304B
Y BUS

APPENDIX F

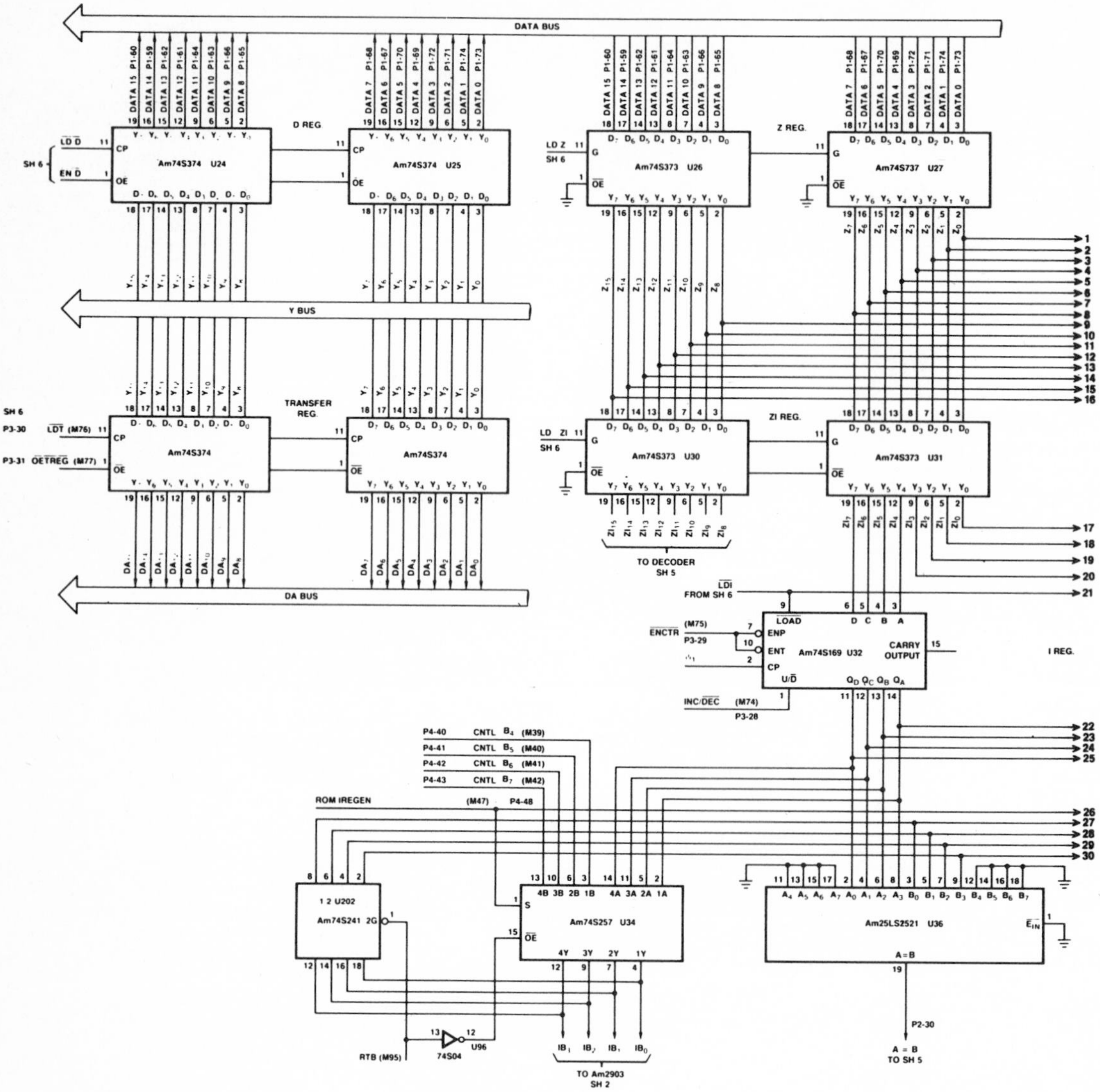

16-Bit Computer Data Path.

TYPICAL INSTRUCTION FORMATS

ADD
RR: (R1) + (R2) → (R1)

OP	R1	R2
15 8	7 4	3 0

M FIELD GENERATES Am2904 TEST I0-3 SIGNALS
TYPICALLY:
R1 FIELD → Am2903 – B INPUTS
R2 FIELD → Am2903 – A INPUTS

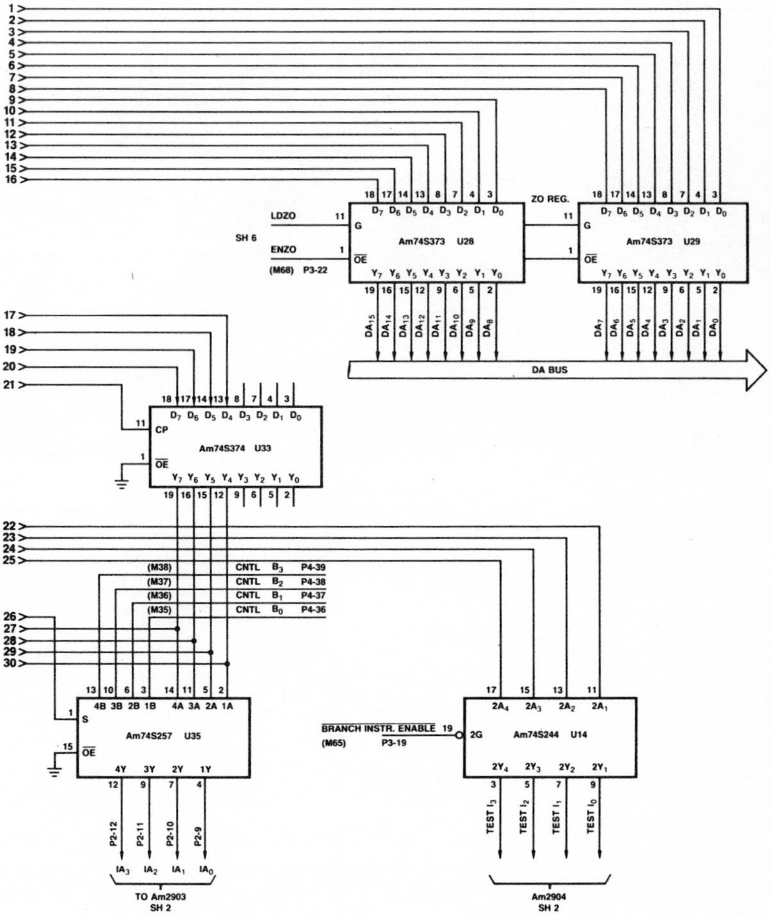

APPENDIX F

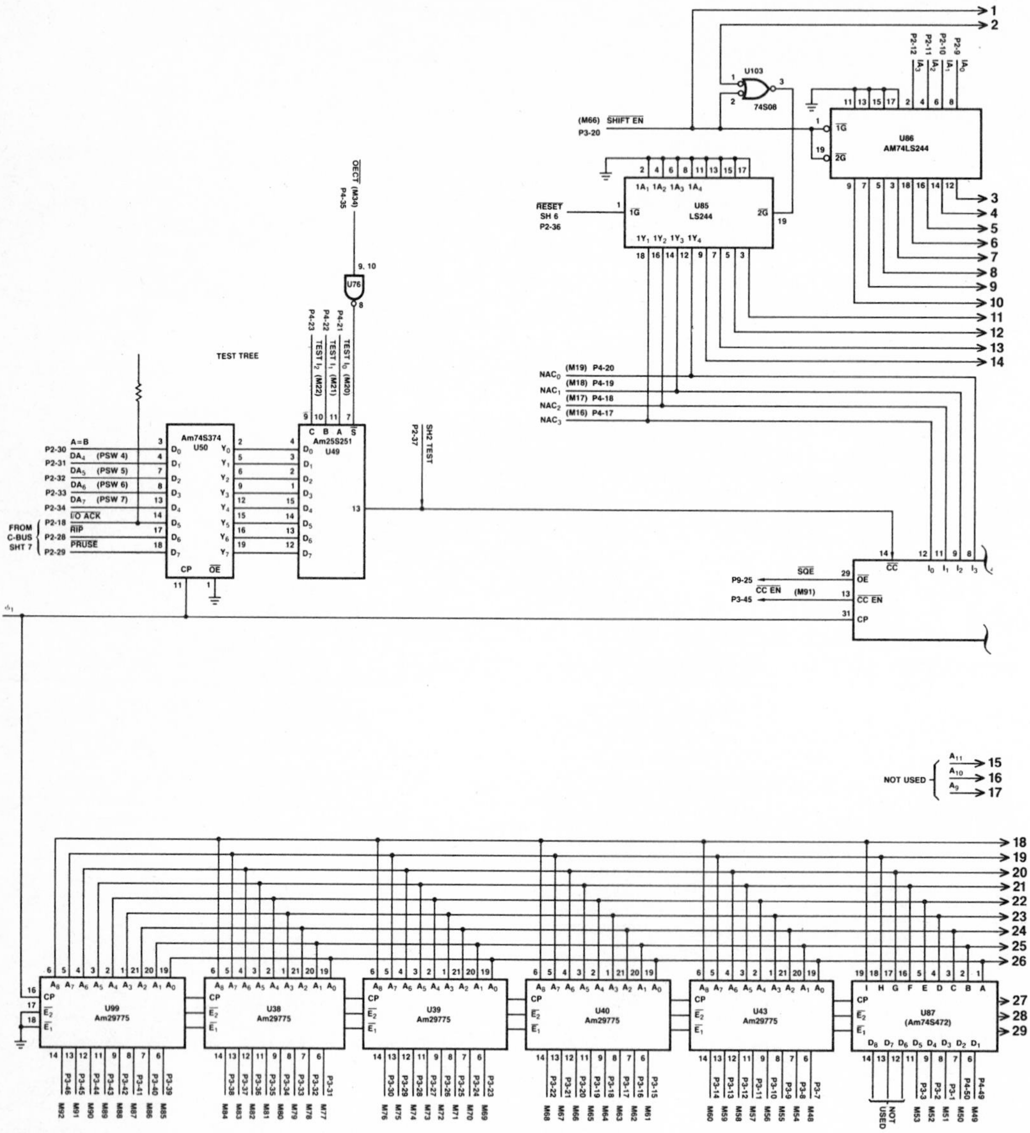

16-Bit Computer Microprogram Memory.

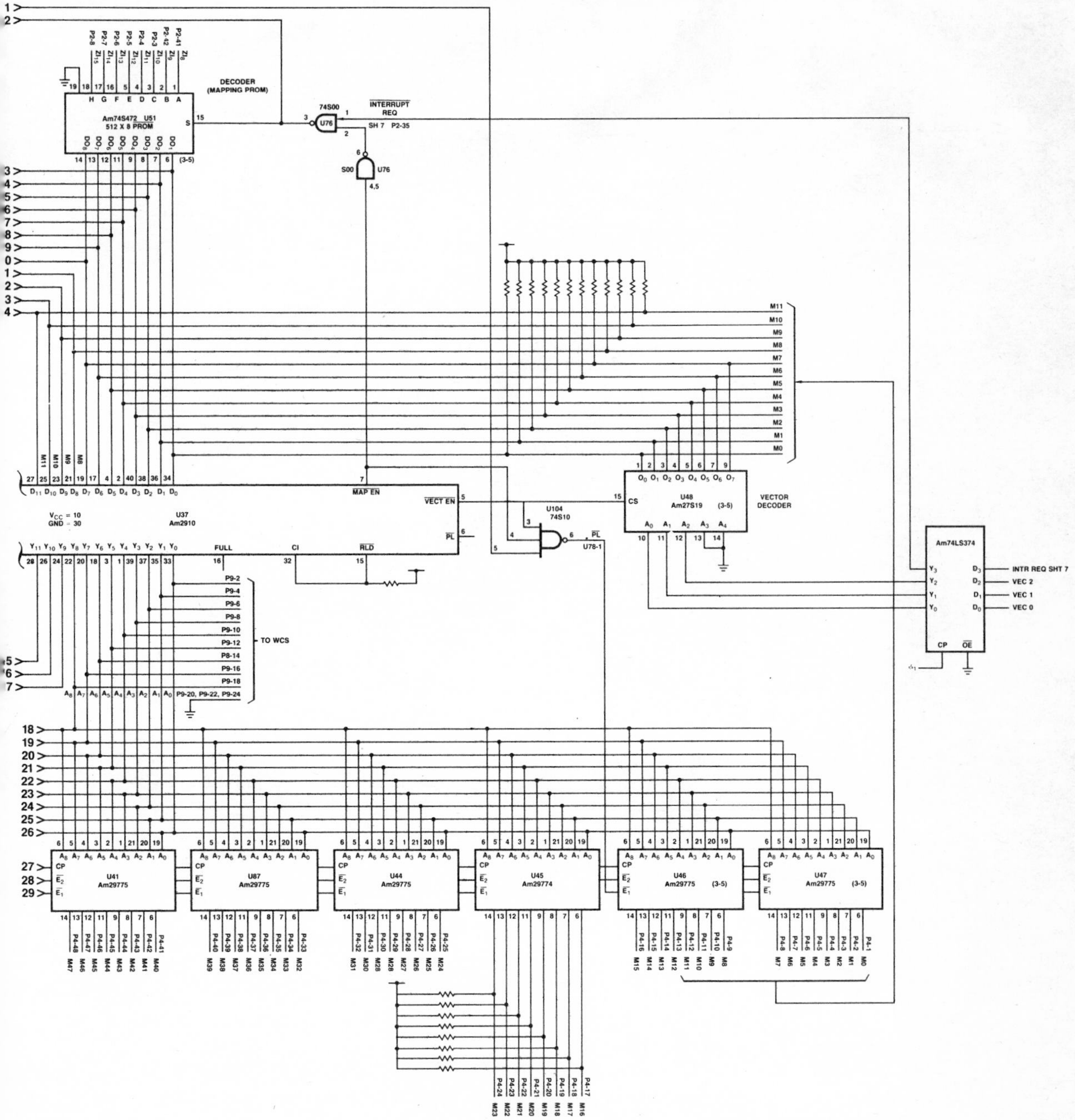
DECODER (MAPPING PROM)
Am74S472 U51
512 X 8 PROM
74S00
U76
INTERRUPT REQ
SH 7 P2-35
S00
MAP EN
VECT EN
U37
Am2910
V_{CC} = 10
GND = 30
FULL
CI
RLD
PL
U104
74S10
U78-1
U48
Am27S19
VECTOR DECODER
Am74LS374
INTR REQ SHT 7
VEC 2
VEC 1
VEC 0
TO WCS
U41
Am29775
U87
Am29775
U44
Am29775
U45
Am29774
U46
Am29775
U47
Am29775

APPENDIX F

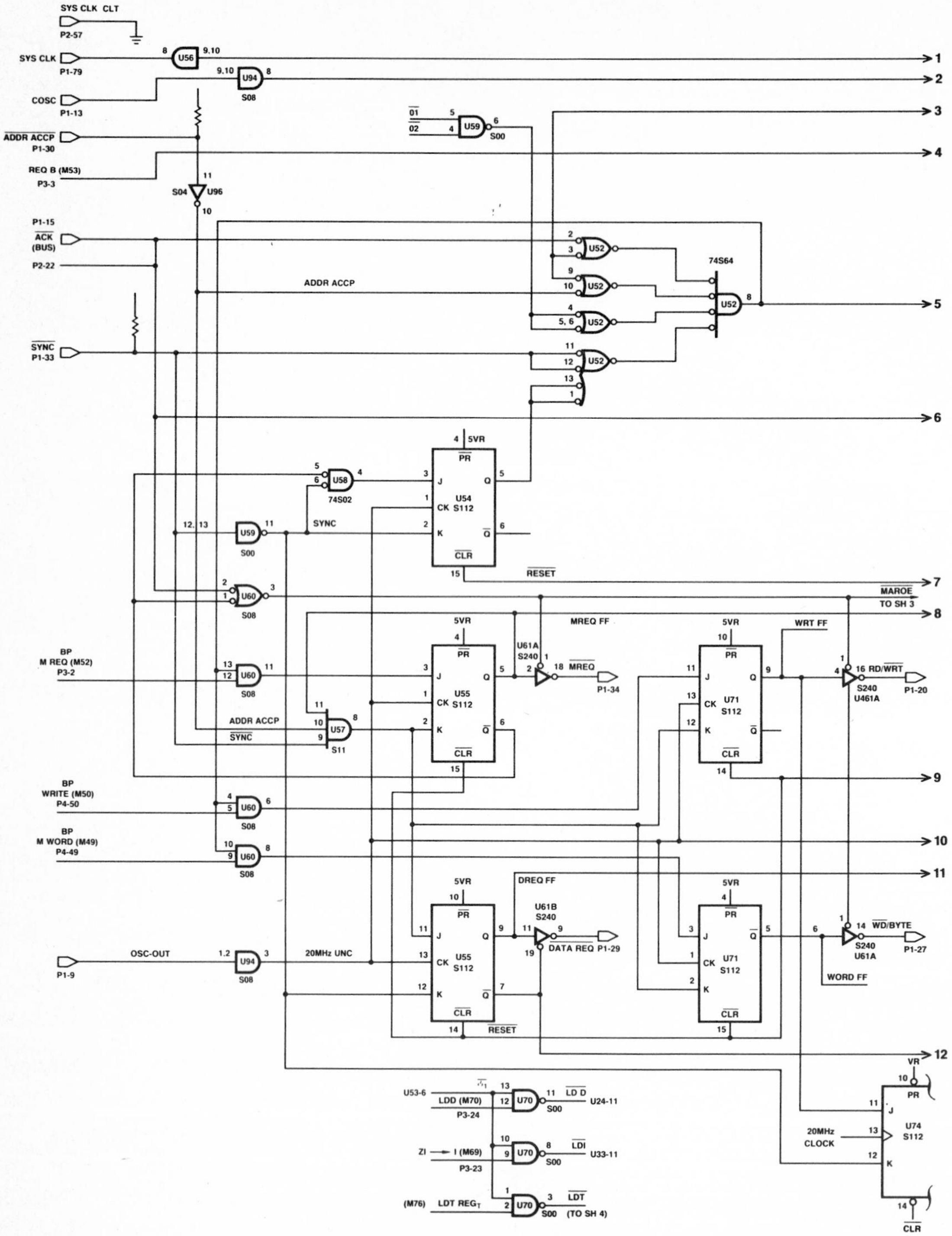

16-Bit Computer Memory and Clock Control.

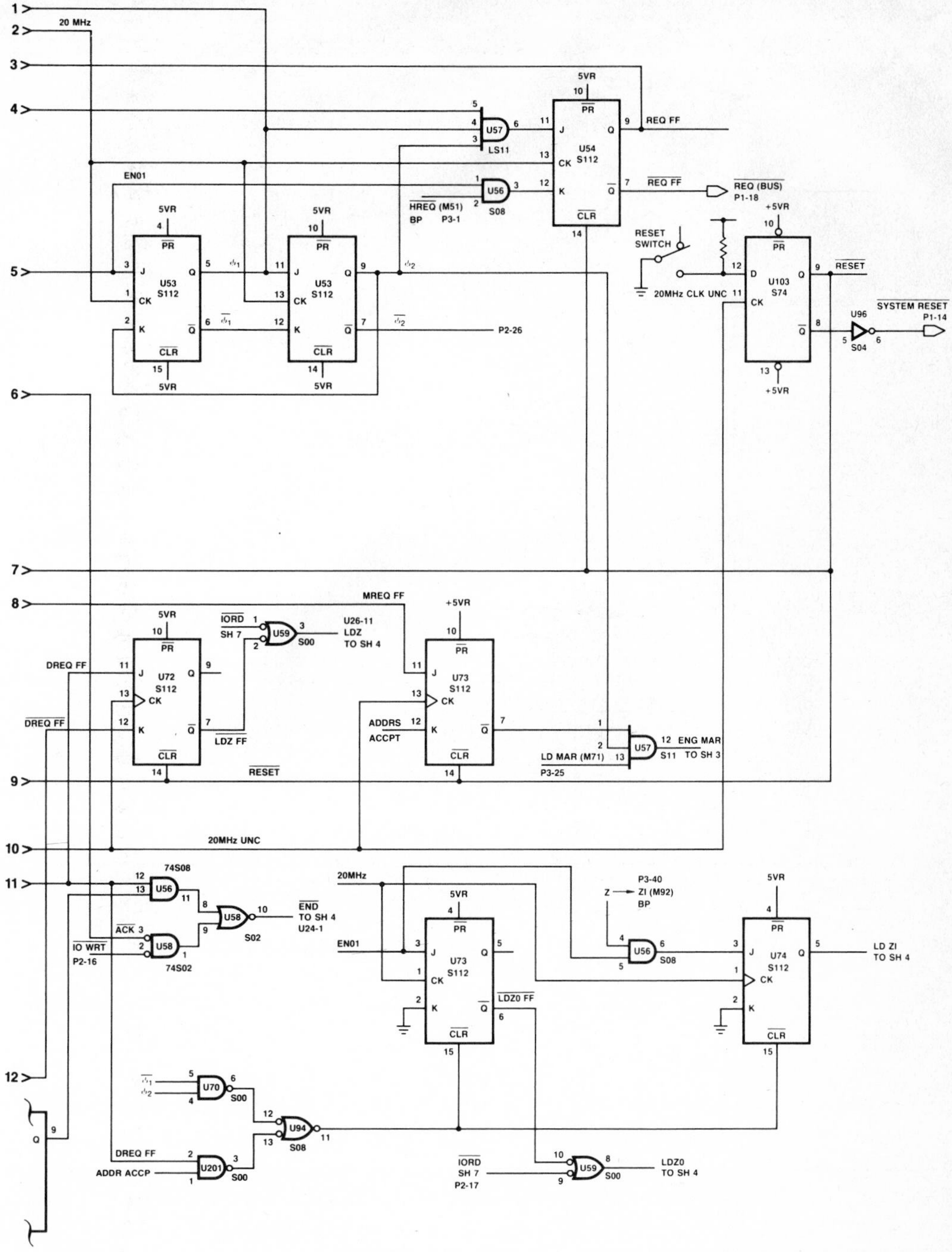
20 MHz
5VR
PR
U57
LS11
U54
S112
CK
REQ FF
EN01
U56
S08
HREQ (M51)
BP P3-1
REQ (BUS)
P1-18
+5VR
RESET
SWITCH
U53
S112
CLR
P2-26
U103
S74
20MHz CLK UNC
RESET
SYSTEM RESET
P1-14
U96
S04
MREQ FF
IORD
SH 7
U59
S00
U26-11
LDZ
TO SH 4
DREQ FF
U72
S112
LDZ FF
U73
S112
ADDRS
ACCPT
ENG MAR
TO SH 3
LD MAR (M71)
P3-25
20MHz UNC
74S08
U58
S02
END
TO SH 4
U24-1
ACK
IO WRT
P2-16
74S02
20MHz
P3-40
ZI (M92)
BP
LDZ0 FF
U74
LD ZI
TO SH 4
U70
U94
U201
ADDR ACCP
IORD
SH 7
P2-17
LDZ0
TO SH 4

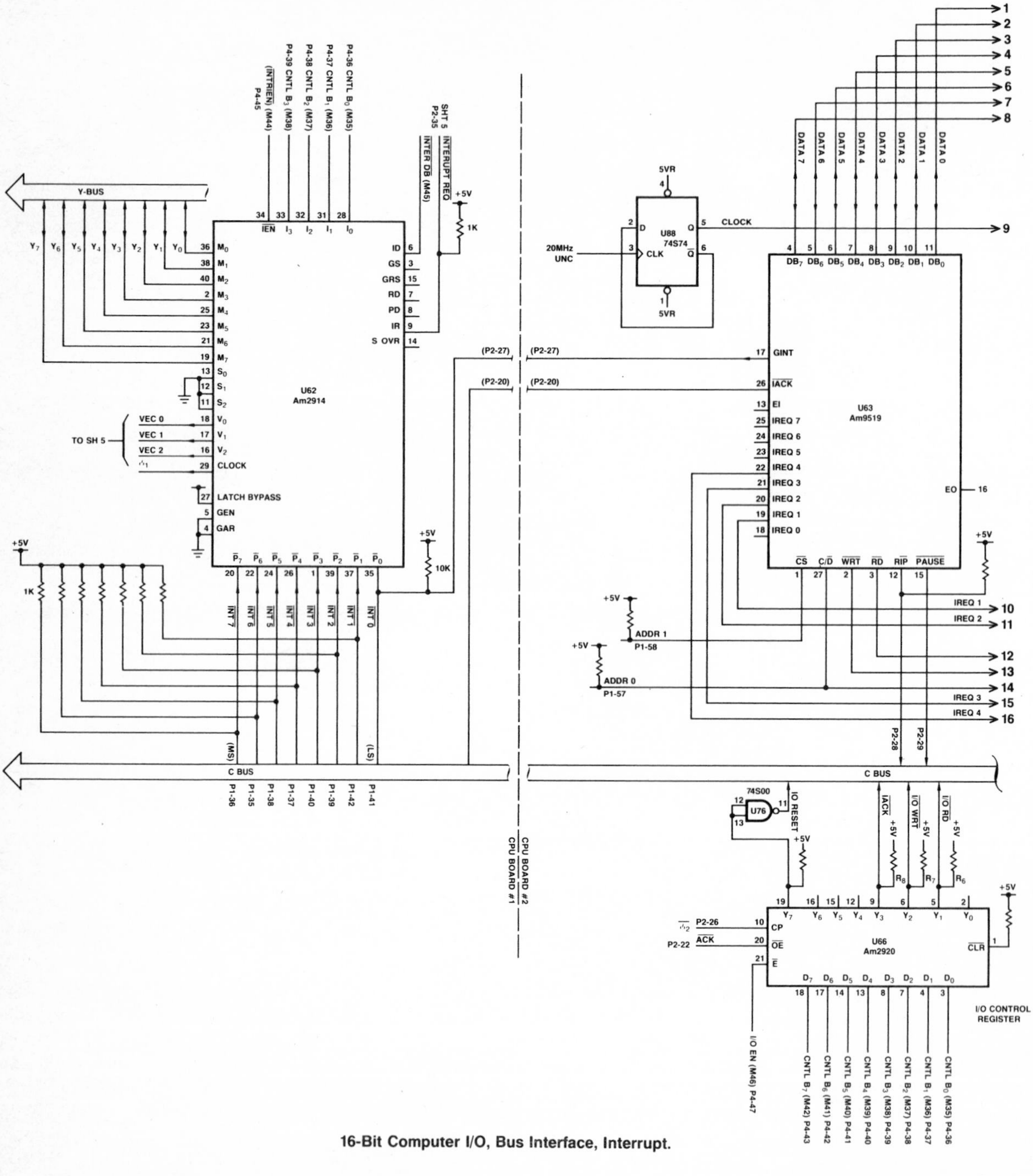

16-Bit Computer I/O, Bus Interface, Interrupt.

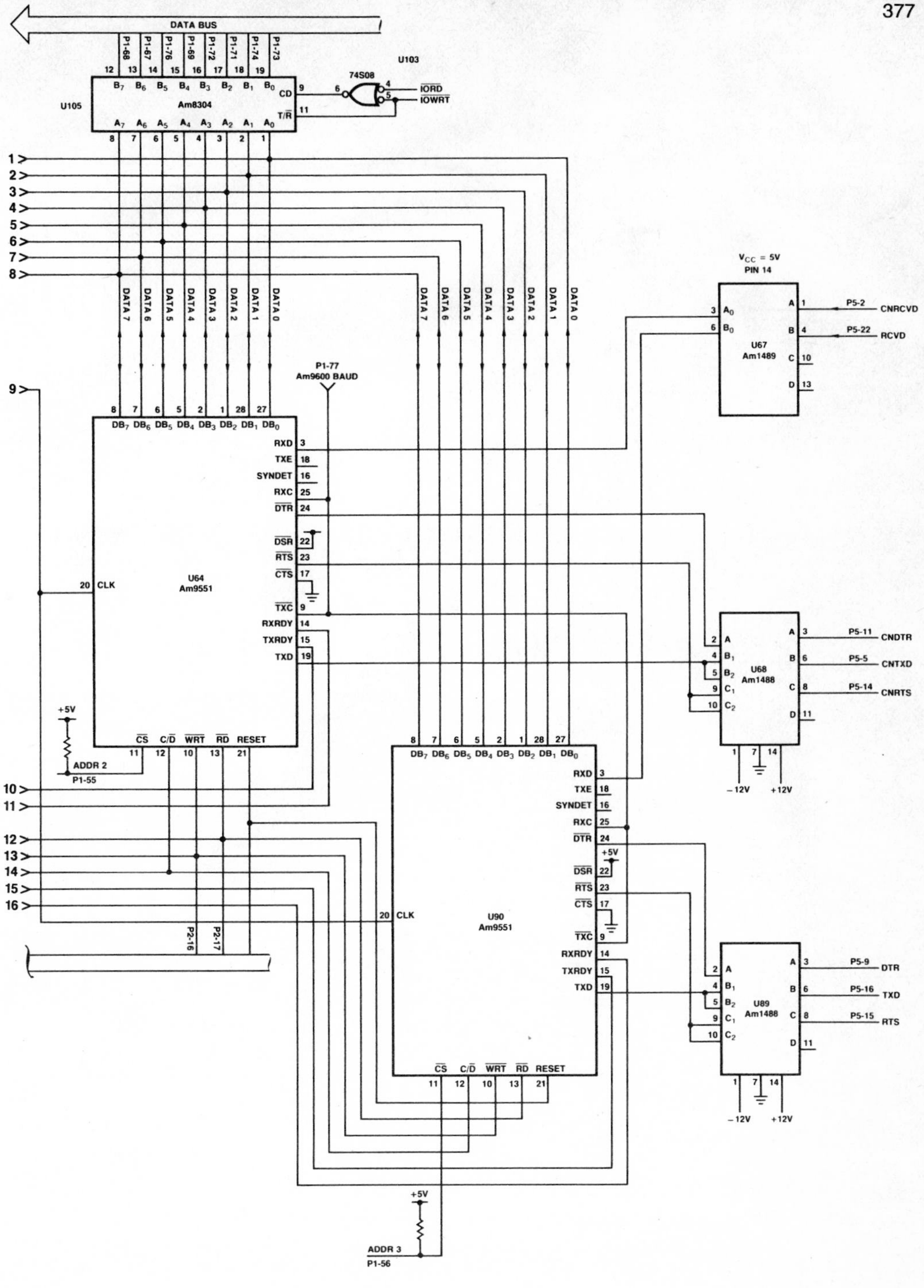
DATA BUS
P1-68 P1-67 P1-76 P1-69 P1-72 P1-71 P1-74 P1-73
U103
74S08
IORD
IOWRT
U105
Am8304
B7 B6 B5 B4 B3 B2 B1 B0
A7 A6 A5 A4 A3 A2 A1 A0
CD
T/R
DATA 7 DATA 6 DATA 5 DATA 4 DATA 3 DATA 2 DATA 1 DATA 0
P1-77
Am9600 BAUD
U64
Am9551
DB7 DB6 DB5 DB4 DB3 DB2 DB1 DB0
RXD TXE SYNDET RXC DTR DSR RTS CTS TXC RXRDY TXRDY TXD
CLK
CS C/D WRT RD RESET
+5V
ADDR 2
P1-55
P2-16
P2-17
U90
Am9551
ADDR 3
P1-56
VCC = 5V
PIN 14
U67
Am1489
P5-2 CNRCVD
P5-22 RCVD
U68
Am1488
P5-11 CNDTR
P5-5 CNTXD
P5-14 CNRTS
U89
Am1488
P5-9 DTR
P5-16 TXD
P5-15 RTS
−12V
+12V

APPENDIX F

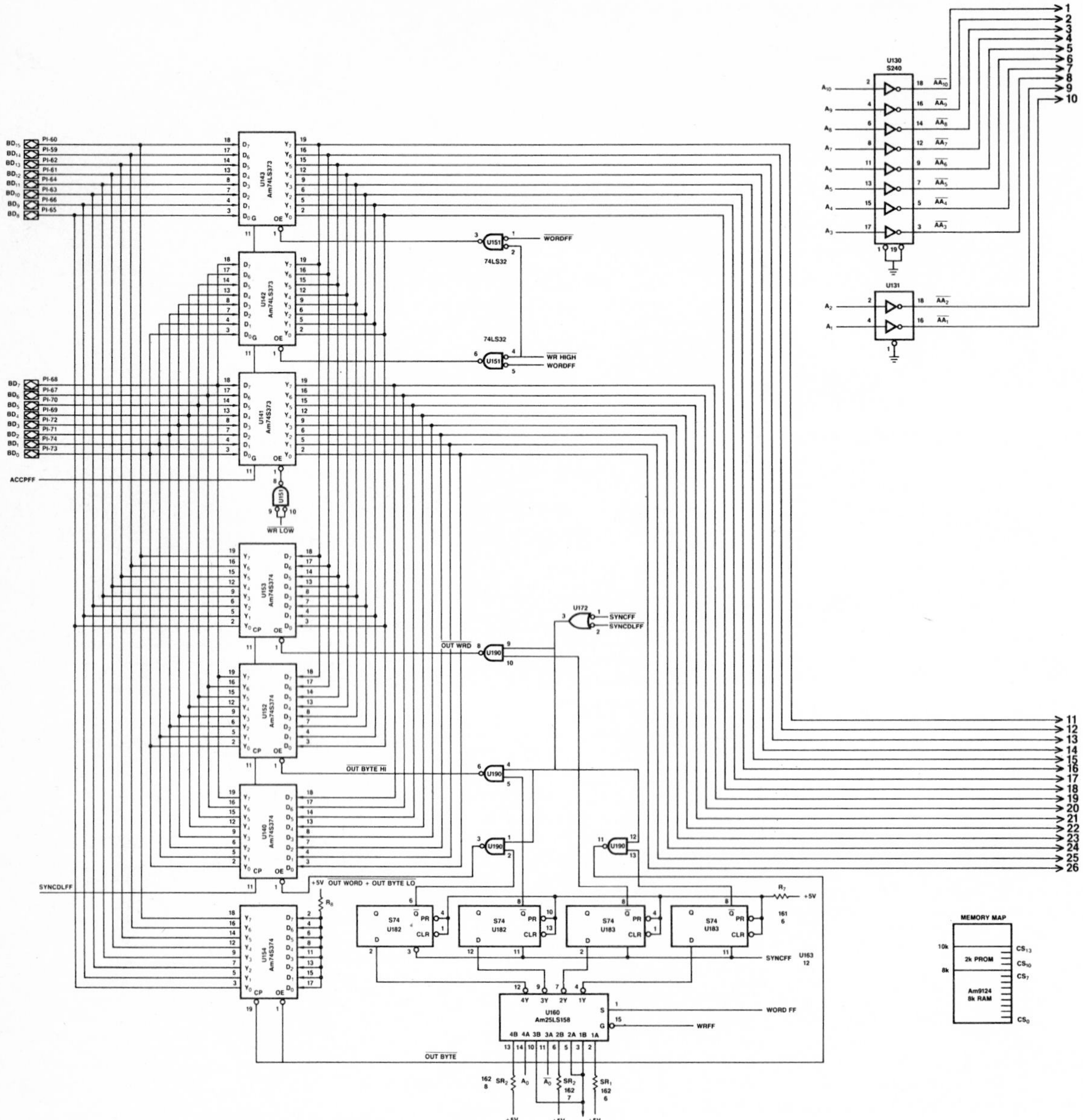

16-Bit Computer Memory Board.

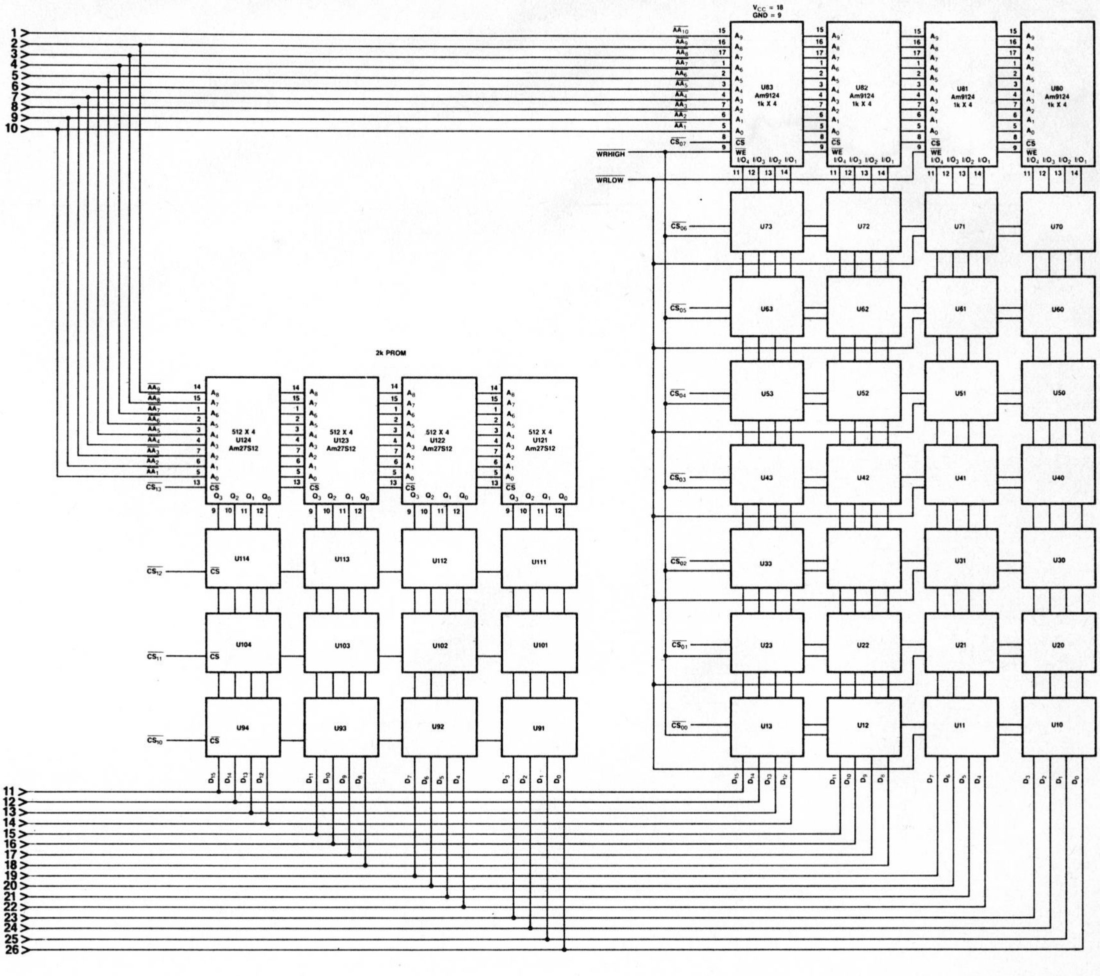

V_{CC} = 18
GND = 9
U83
Am9124
1k X 4
U82
Am9124
1k X 4
U81
Am9124
1k X 4
U80
Am9124
1k X 4
WRHIGH
WRLOW
U73
U72
U71
U70
U63
U62
U61
U60
U53
U52
U51
U50
U43
U42
U41
U40
U33
U31
U30
U23
U22
U21
U20
U13
U12
U11
U10
2k PROM
512 X 4
U124
Am27S12
512 X 4
U123
Am27S12
512 X 4
U122
Am27S12
512 X 4
U121
Am27S12
U114
U113
U112
U111
U104
U103
U102
U101
U94
U93
U92
U91

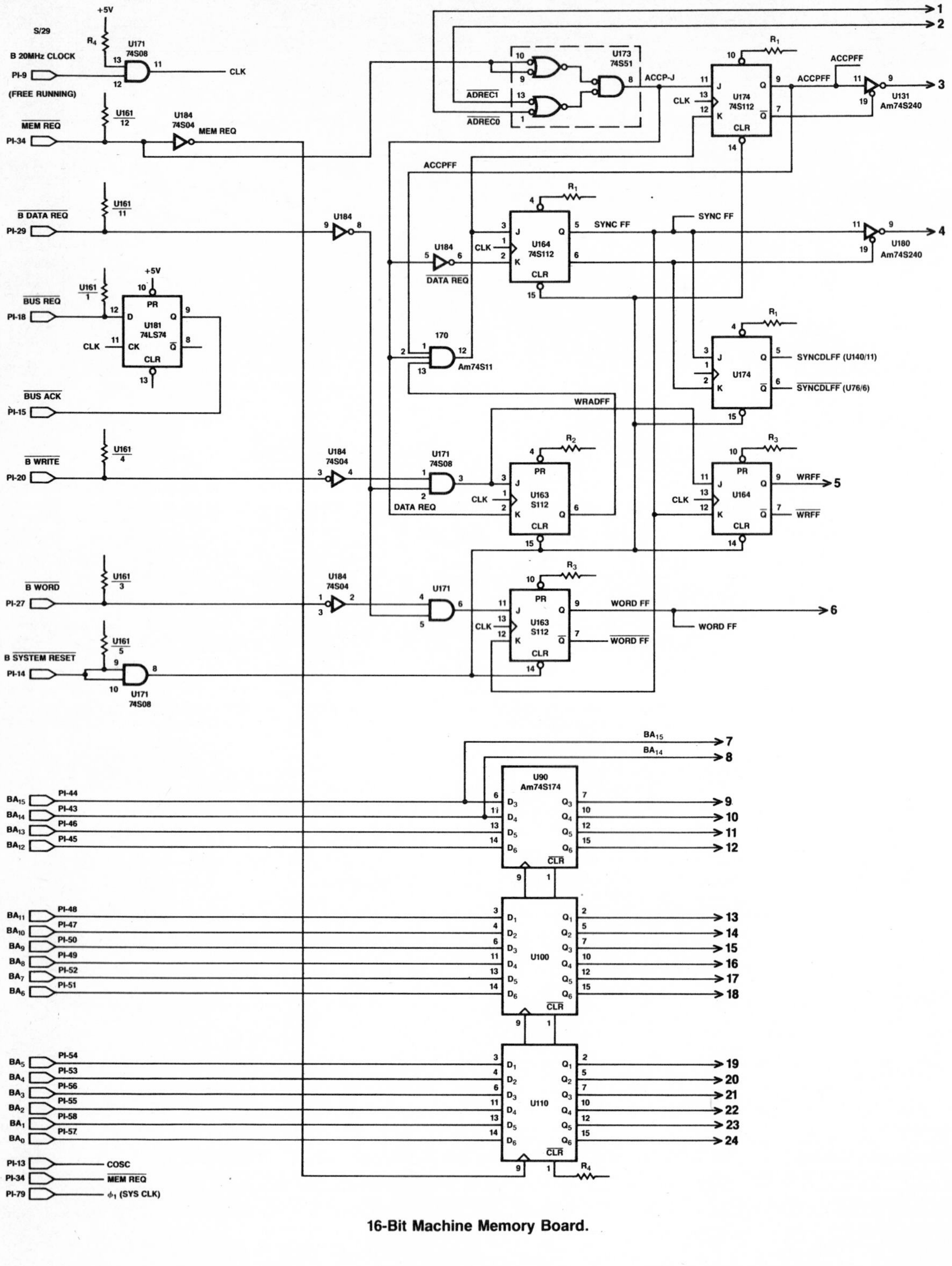

16-Bit Machine Memory Board.

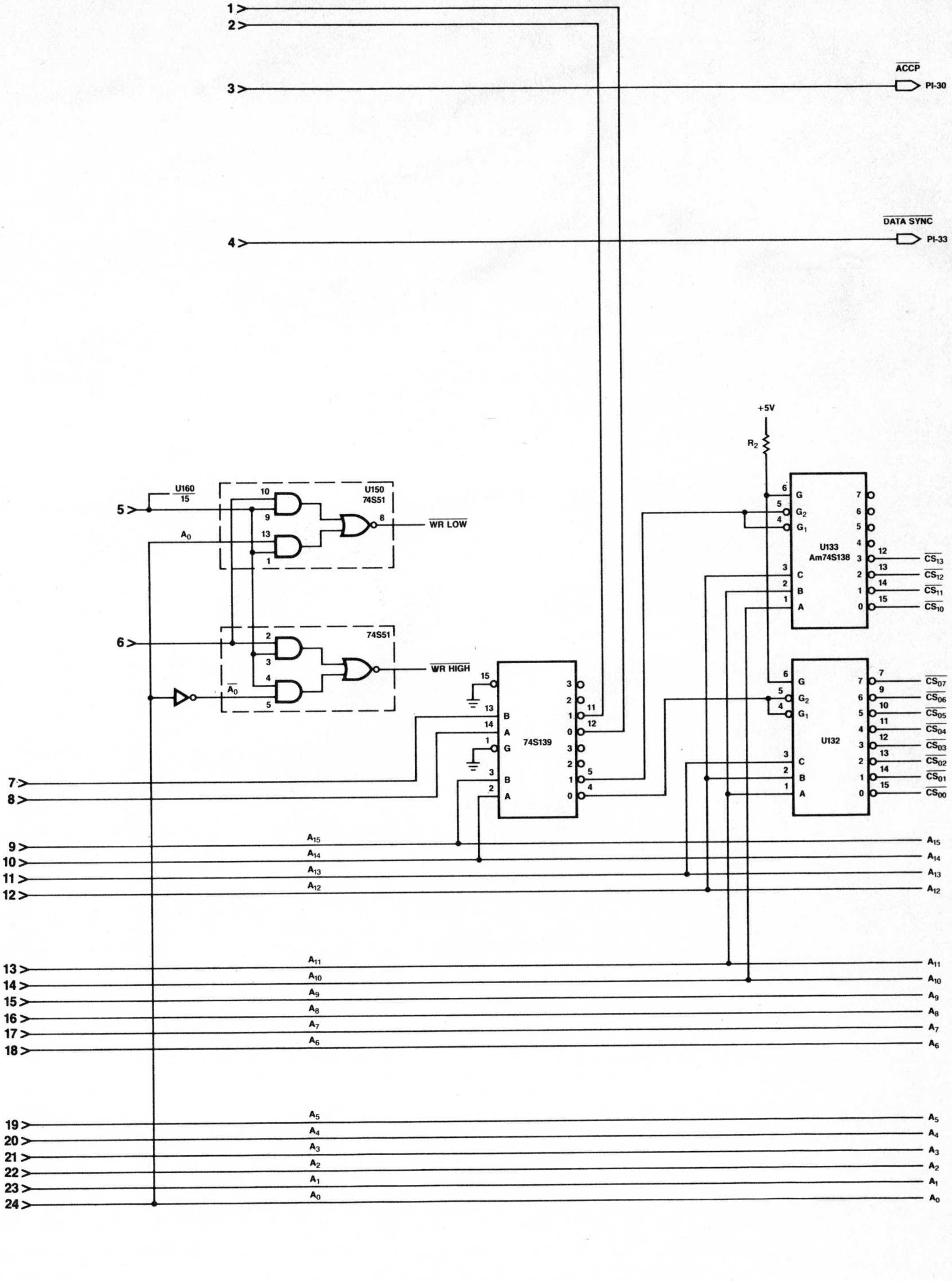
ACCP
PI-30
DATA SYNC
PI-33
+5V
R2
U160
15
U150
74S51
WR LOW
74S51
WR HIGH
A0
74S139
U133
Am74S138
U132
CS13
CS12
CS11
CS10
CS07
CS06
CS05
CS04
CS03
CS02
CS01
CS00
A15
A14
A13
A12
A11
A10
A9
A8
A7
A6
A5
A4
A3
A2
A1
A0

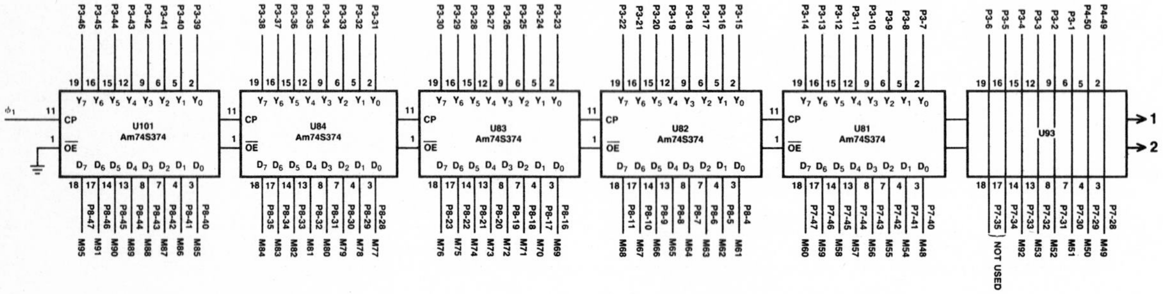

16-Bit Computer S/29 WCS Interface.

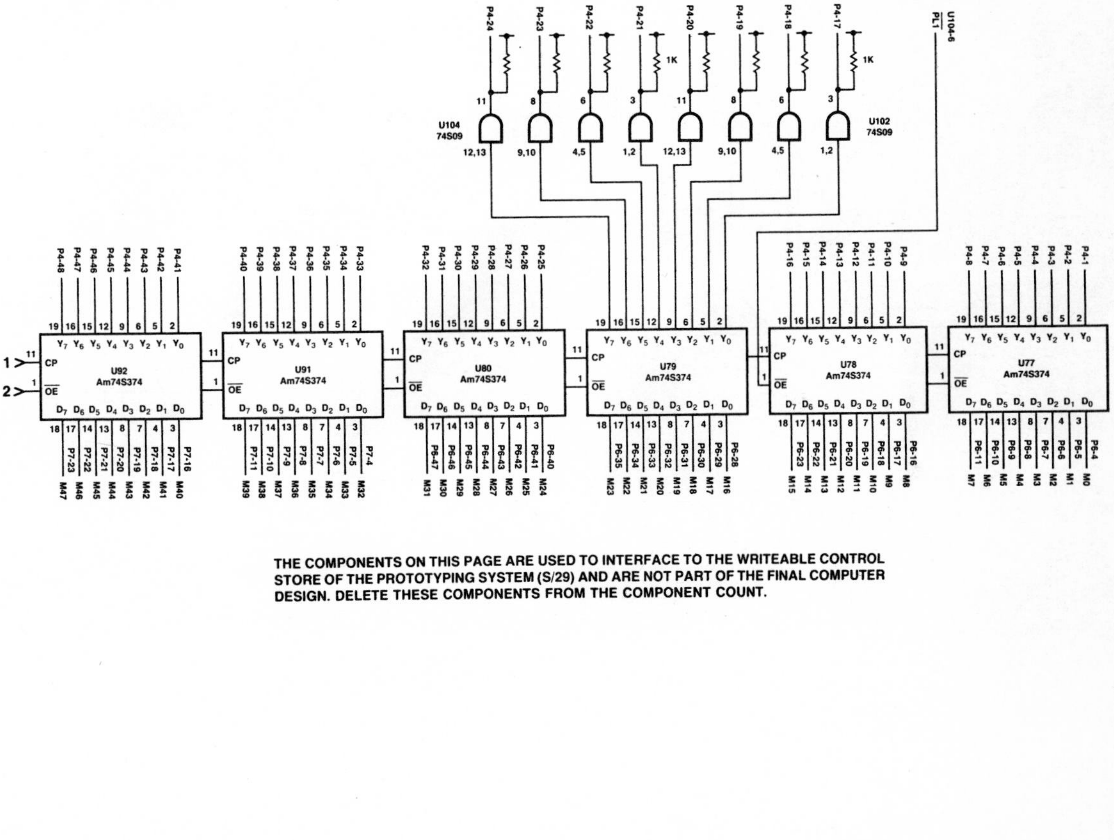

THE COMPONENTS ON THIS PAGE ARE USED TO INTERFACE TO THE WRITEABLE CONTROL STORE OF THE PROTOTYPING SYSTEM (S/29) AND ARE NOT PART OF THE FINAL COMPUTER DESIGN. DELETE THESE COMPONENTS FROM THE COMPONENT COUNT.

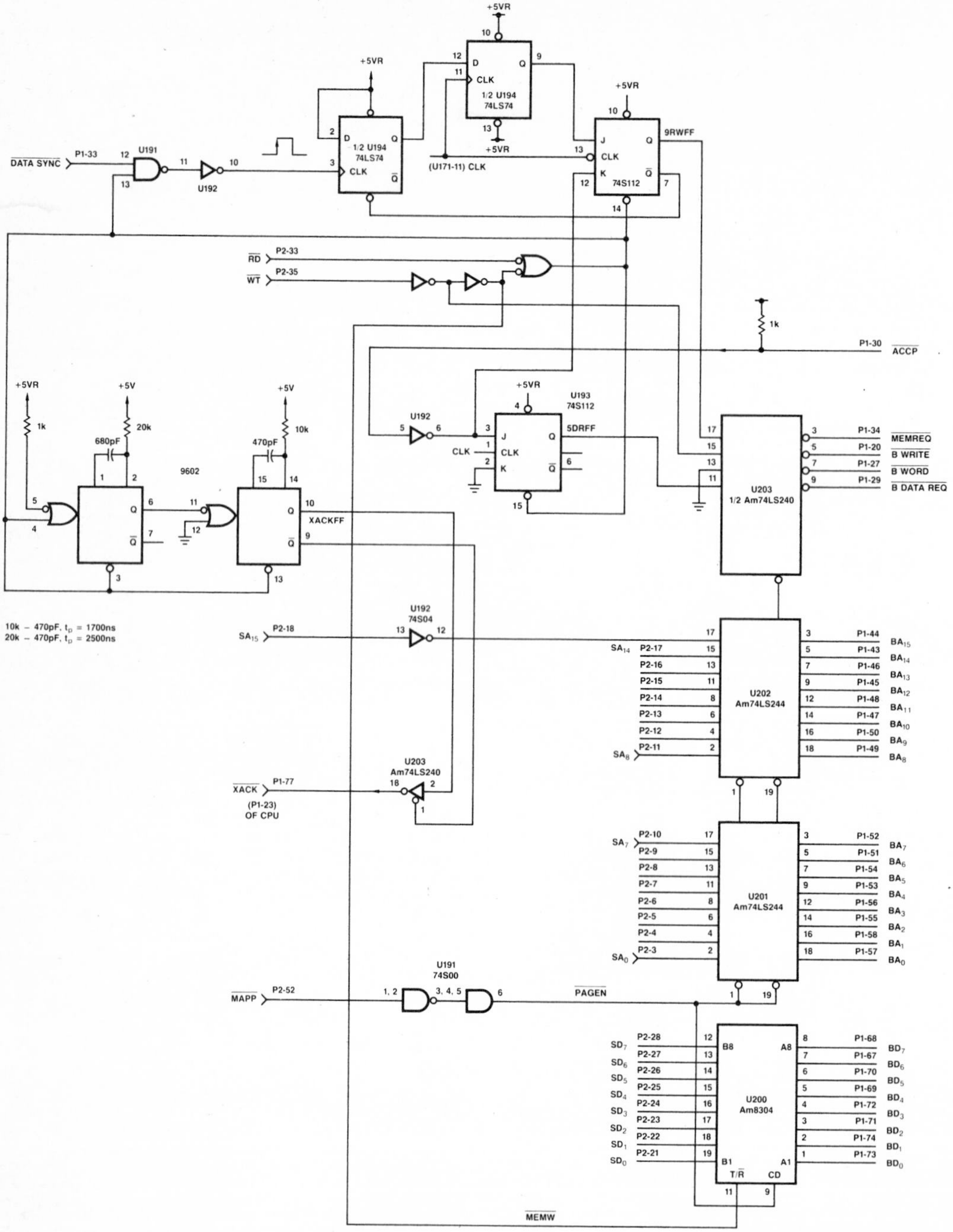

Memory
Sheet 2A

16-Bit Computer Memory Board (S/29 Interface).

MPR-718

INDEX

INDEX